THE INMAN DIARY

The Inman Diary

A PUBLIC AND PRIVATE CONFESSION

Edited by Daniel Aaron

VOLUME II

HARVARD UNIVERSITY PRESS

Cambridge, Massachusetts, and London, England

1985

Library of Congress Cataloging in Publication Data
Inman, Arthur Crew, 1895–
  The Inman diary.

  Includes index.
  1. Inman, Arthur Crew, 1895–   — Biography.
  2. Poets, American — 20th century — Biography.
  I. Aaron, Daniel, 1912–   . II. Title.
PS3517.N84Z466   1985   818'.5203 [B]   85-954
ISBN 0-674-45445-6

Contents

Illustrations

Arthur's Churning World: Domestic and Foreign

1937–1941

After an interval of relative tranquillity, Arthur experienced a sinking of morale that customarily accompanied the resurgence of old aches and pains. Falling stocks and money worries synchronized with collapsing ribs, depressed lungs, and stomach poisoning. He could not make money no matter how hard he tried, thanks largely, he believed, to the policies of "Roosie the Rat" and his Irish and Jewish henchmen. True, the New Deal had met with some salutary checks, but the unctuous president was still playing his nefarious game.

Arthur was ready to give up. His father refused to die, and Arthur had not the "fortitude" to kill himself. "What a bruised, spineless, squirming semblance of a thing I am," he wrote. "I exist in mortal terror of the known and the unknown behind a masquerade of dissembled interest, laughter, conversation." And to make matters worse, the extension of the Boston subway and the tearing up of St. Botolph Street by the lazy "W.P.A.'ers" filled his waking hours with noise and dust. In his desperate search for diversion, he tinkered with the idea of collecting old light-opera scores. More than ever he depended upon his sadly depleted corps of readers, especially Roderic and "Old Cesspool" or "Old Outhouse" (his private names for the salacious Mrs. Cash), and upon the reassurances of steady Edna, helpful Ella, adoring Janice, and strong Dottie Bottomley.

With the shifting of the world spotlight from Europe to Asia, Arthur excitedly watched the progress of the Japanese armies. America, he predicted, would eventually have to fight that energetic and admirable people. An alliance between Japan and Germany ("clever Hitler" was establishing his hegemony over Central Europe) would soon "cause England and France to do some head-scratching."

Meanwhile at Garrison Hall, Arthur was having trouble maintaining "hegemony" over his domestic "troops." Evelyn, at least in her uncompliant moods, still mulishly balked at his orders. Billy refused to divulge his private history. Mrs. Banks, Naomi, and Roderic required tactful handling. Those of his employees who read or copied the Diary resented the slurring references to themselves instead of accepting these occasional thrusts as expressions of momentary pique.

After two years of silence, Patricia Caffree sent the Inmans an enormous letter in which she spelled out her marital and extramarital adventures.

August 13 I might as well continue my diary. I like doing it, it passes the time, and what the hell. I'm going to write again. The urge to chronicle the fascinating panorama of today is stronger than my distaste for doing what may be a bungling job. I've had a rest — if existing through weeks of heat and humidity can be called a rest (anyway it has been a reprieve) — and now I'm raring to go.

Much of the credit — if there be credit in persuading a man to return to what may be a faulty job — lies with Naomi. She gave me a tongue-lashing for being a quitter. That made me think. She told me that I was doing something unique and unusual and would be a coward to give up just because I was discouraged at lack of approbation. Good Naomi — a person must love you a lot to call you down with all the vehemence at their command. And Evelyn, Mrs. Banks and Woodwork have chided me for my defection. So here I am back again, pushing the old pencil vehemently across the old paper and getting an occupational crick in my back.

August 14 Ella at present is engaged in making me some pajamas. She has searched the downtown stores by the hour to find the kind of cloth I want. There seems to be no trouble she will not take to please me. She tells me all her troubles, asks my advice, takes it. At present her husband, Robert, is embarked on a venture of selling Joe Louis favors to the colored population of New York, Brooklyn and Boston. "He's going to put in a hundred and fifty dollars," explains Ella. "Even if he loses every cent of it, I consider that the experience he will have with the business will well be worth the loss. He tends to live a restricted existence. It will be good for him to come in contact with people and to spread himself out. And the chances are at least even that he'll make a success of the scheme. If he does, think of the self-confidence it will give him."

If I didn't get female affection and education when I was a boy, well you can't say I'm not having it now. And do I like it! In a measure it compensates for the years when girls passed me by and when I was so wary of them that I crossed the street when I saw them coming. If they spoil me now, I'm not the one to complain. Not I.

August 15 Very low in my mind. When you get down to bedrock, I don't like expressing myself artistically. Fundamentally, I possess as much disdain for any art other than utilitarian art as does my Father. I write because I must do something, not because I admire the art of writing. I am Anglo-Saxon. What I really want is to do something useful, self-evident, of unquestionable merit. I would rather forge a sword or collect maple syrup or build a staunch boat or plow a straight furrow than compose the finest verses or predicate the deepest philosophy or write the most stirring novel. I disdain art for art's sake and the artists whose milieu is art; hence, basically, I disdain myself, for if I am not an artist, at least I am striving to be one.

August 19 East wind. Cooler. Enjoyed morning. Billy and I went to Bernard's Elm. Sat on ramp. Wind in leaves overhead. Jays calling to each other. Chipping sparrows. Showed Billy how vines grew clockwise, what sort of roots various trees have, the burrs on the chestnut tree, the seed-berries on the ivy, the feather of a bird and how it is constructed for lightness and wind resistance. New knowledge for him. He was interested. He is at last really commencing to like me ever since I told him how to manage Sadie when they experienced their first misunderstanding. Billy ate an apple and I ate a can of deviled ham and some crackers. The lawn is brown from lack of rain. The Place is weed-grown and needs grooming. Enjoyed every minute of my stay.

And now I am sitting in my room with the wind blowing on my back and no one about. Evelyn went with Billy in the Pierce to Brookline to buy whitefish for my lunch at the Jewish fish store. I like being alone. I can read the paper headlines about the war in China and the Rat's last sneering attack on the wealthy.

August 22 Roosevelt so frightened the Supreme Court Justices that not a decision of major importance went against the Administration and one Justice resigned. In the place of this Justice, Roosevelt has appointed and the Senate, after some acrimonious debate, has approved Senator [Hugo L.] Black of Alabama, a radical New Dealer, a former Ku Klux Klan man, a sneerer without brains or judicial experience, a pure and simple yes man. The Governor of the State of Alabama appointed to the Senate in his stead a woman, his own wife forsooth.

August 23 I asked Woodwork if, should anything ever happen to Evelyn, she would marry me. She replied that I couldn't mean that. I said that I did, for despite how angry she made me at times, she and her mind pleased me as no one else's did. Moreover, I was by now resigned to the conviction that I loved her in spite of myself. She thanked me for the compliment. "Nothing's going to happen to Evelyn," she said. "I hope not," I said, "but you never can tell. It may be God's next move. Who knows?" "Anyway," she pursued her reasoning, "I love Allan. When I love my man, I love him all over." "That's all right by me," I said. "You've plenty of strength and emotion for two men. Allan could take care of you sexually, and that would relieve me. I wouldn't be jealous. I could give you a name and freedom from office work, and no one ever said that life with me was dull or dragged." I believe that she was touched, at least temporarily. I have a theory that much of Woodwork's hardness would vanish were she to have a fixed position in society, a name, a husband, a home. I believe, too, that she would make a fine wife.

September 2 A new depression is brewing, of that we can be sure. Perhaps next year. Perhaps not for three years yet. When it hits, however, it should outdo the last. The country, chiefly due to New Deal meddling, is not as fit to meet it and cope with it as in 1929. We are as a patient who has been administered so many medicines that when another attack comes medicines will not do for us what they did.

September 3 Evelyn home. The dog she ordered from Alabama came. The first thing it did was to let go on Billy's floor. Billy looks tired. The heat is terrific. Evelyn has washed the dog, which is no more bloodhound than I am, albeit a nice creature, albeit with a menagerie of fleas. Evelyn takes the dog to Angel Memorial Hospital to have it de-flead and wormed. She intends to housebreak it. I am jealous but am saying nothing. Funny, to be jealous of a dog. She treats it as though she owns it. She takes off all her clothes when she washes it. The mind of the male is a queer mess where women are concerned.

September 6 Confused. Mrs. Cash told me of motion pictures of Shanghai at the Paramount Theatre on downtown Washington Street. I decided to go. I went. I have just returned, my eyes seeing double and my stomach sick and myself bewildered. Pictures nothing wonderful, not far advanced beyond the newsreels in 1916. They run them too fast, never give you more than a moment's glimpse at any one view from any one angle. The light and the sudden movements which my eyes wouldn't follow confused me. I was glad to leave. If I hadn't enough girls when I was young, if I wasn't permitted to do things other boys of my age were, at least I saw enough movies to last me the remainder of my life and to leave no regrets that I can't watch them now. I don't think I miss much anyway, from what I hear. As with the radio, the newspapers and the pulps, the movies studiedly take into account the inability of the American mind to concentrate beyond a certain limited time on anything. I think that the publishers and the producers are as much wrong as right, but perhaps they know best. They have to make money.

September 15 I have given up working. Evelyn reads to me every afternoon. We are now reading a fine biography, 'Ships and Women.' When I don't work, I can become more lost in what others have to say. We are also reading a tiny book called 'Mr. Bulkeley and the Pirates.'[1] It is a gentle and whimsical book, all about Mr. B. and the

[1] *Ships and Women* (1937), by Bertram M. Adams (Bill Adams, pseudonym), is not a biography but an account of the author's seafaring adventures before a severe illness forced him ashore to become a writer of sea stories. B. Dew Roberts's *Mr. Bulkeley and the Pirates* (1936) relates the life and times of an eighteenth-century Welsh squire and contains extensive extracts from his diary. The "pirate" of the title was Bulkeley's scapegrace son-in-law turned privateer, Captain Fortunatus Wright.

life he led as a squire on the Island of Anglesy off the Welsh coast in the 18th century. The author writes as though, when thoughts came to him, he gave up his pruning of roses for a small hour or so, stepped inside his French windows and put down a bit more toward his antiquarian book. So these volumes give me pleasure.

Sometimes, too, there are other happenings which distract me a while from the melancholy that is now so steadily with me. Janice last evening, for instance. No one else makes so much of me, seems so genuinely to enjoy touching me. She kisses me. She runs her hands over my body. She sings snatches of tunes in her husky singing voice. She ruffles my hair. She tweaks my nose. In a word, she makes herself master of my body to such a degree that I am solaced and persuaded to forget myself awhile. "I wonder," said she, "just how much of this you would stand if I were with you constantly?" Not much, probably, but as an interlude her apparent devotion is a healing unguent to my tired spirit.

September 18   Billy left this morning for his five-day vacation. He went in his car; Sadie and Sadie's mother ("Ma") were with him. He appears to like Ma about as well as Sadie. Mrs. Banks asserted that his penchant for older women is a sign of his undeveloped mind. Billy has common sense, tact and a pleasant nature, but there's no denying the limitations of his mentality. Imagine an ordinary male, not six months married, taking mother-in-law on a trip with himself and his wife and footing the bill to boot. "Billy," I said, "I'll bet there's not one man in a hundred would do it." "I bet you," he answered, "that there ain't one in a thousand." They have no idea whither they are bound. "We just go where our inclinations lead us."

October 6   Night before last the first work on the subway in this near vicinity began, digging up St. Botolph Street for a two-block, U-shaped deflection of the city water main from Huntington Avenue. No sleep all night. Pneumatic machines tearing up the pavement. Boards being thrown about or driven in the ground with huge mallets, men shouting, whistling, trucks coming and going. All in yesterday. The day spent finding out whether or not a curb could be put on the night activities of the workmen.

I fear I must admit defeat insofar as stopping the building of the subway is concerned. One or two courageous men willing to fight for the beliefs they expressed and with sufficient daring to buck the politicians, and one lawyer with ingenuity, and we could have halted this particular politicians' dream in its tracks. I am sure of it. But where in America are courageous businessmen, men not so afraid of losing what they have left that they stand inept and cringing on the possessions left them by the Jews and the Irish and the women and the educational funds and foundations? And where is a lawyer with real ingenuity and perseverance? I am disgusted with the American male. He is a gutless, timid, cautious shadow of what he was forty years ago, a straddler with one eye on the hold he still has on his possessions and the other on the politicians, his acknowledged lords and masters. He is a de-spurred baron who has climbed to his last fortress while the mercenaries of greed and avarice swarm the broad domains that once were his, unchallenged and unmolested. He does not intend to die fighting but to hold on to what he has left by caution, bribery, acquiescence, subterfuge and the camouflage of remaining unnoticed.

Yesterday the Rat cut loose in a speech at Chicago and renounced the American policy of isolation, calling for a "quarantine" for aggressor nations. Is it the first step toward a war with Japan? Roosevelt has been on a Western tour. Has he seen his power slipping and resorted to the subterfuge of those who will retain power at any price, war and the talk of war? Or is he being used as a cat's paw by the British, even as Woodrow Wilson was? It is a momentous right-about-face if he means it. The League of Nations, China and probably the English are jubilant.

October 13 Evelyn left this morning for Portland to see Father. She dreads the job. "Nobody else will talk to him. Somebody has to. It seems to be up to me. He depresses me beyond words." She plans to ask him for money and, if the outlook is propitious, to bring up the subject of the will again. Coca-Cola has dropped some but not at all when compared with other stocks, so that he should still be financially cheerful. What the outcome of the interview will be it is impossible to guess. I only hope that the sledding goes not too hard for Evelyn and that she makes a couple of good runs on the sandy soil that is my parent. I told her to let him know that I was better than a week ago and would love to see him if he wished to stop by Boston. I pray that he stays away. Poor Evelyn, it is a dog's job, thankless, that she is undertaking.

October 14 The door opens and Evelyn comes in. She throws a check for $250 on my writing board. "I'm sorry," she says, "but it was the best I could do. I had a hard time getting that. Your father left Portland this morning to take the Mohawk Trail. He was overjoyed not to have to see you." He told Evelyn that I was ruining him, etc. As a matter of fact, the dividends he gets from Coca-Cola alone, and that after paying income taxes, would support me. Evelyn thought it expedient not to push him to get more money nor to raise the question of the will.

October 27 On Sunday and Monday I inserted an ad in the 'Herald' for someone to read and sing to an author. Mrs. Banks has been telling me for a long time that, did I acknowledge I was a writer, I would obtain a better class of people. It seems as though she were right. Four excellent possibilities thus far—an old bird of energy and vehemence who can both play and read, an art student who cannot earn a living painting so is going to be a nursemaid, a girl, twenty-four, divorced from her husband, and someone else. We have had at least two hundred answers, seventy or more Irish and, consequently, for the wastebasket. Have interviewed people until dream about them nights. More of them today.

October 29 What pleases my Father is an admixture of flattery, apology, sentimentality, self-deprecation, blunt forthrightness and sinuous evasion. I didn't want Aunt Louise to blackball me when Father reached Atlanta, so I resolved to send him the sort of missive he would wish to receive. The following is what I composed, but for heaven's sake don't believe most of it — as though, assuming that you have read much that has come before in this record of mine, you would.

October 25, 1937

Dear Father: —

I was very sorry indeed that I felt so badly and you felt so badly that we didn't see each other. But probably I couldn't have been lively, and seeing me would only have worried you. I hope to be stronger in the spring so that you can have a nice visit. I assure you I don't like being down in health the way I have been for two years now.

It is nice that Evelyn had a good visit with you in Portland. She is a grand wife, and I appreciate her daily.

Evelyn tells me that you told her that "certain persons in Atlanta" had suggested to you that all I cared about you was for as much money as I could get out of you. While I suppose it must seem that way to "certain people in Atlanta," I want to assure you that it is not so. While I do worry about what sort of plans you have made about your money should anything happen to you, I do that because of my physical helplessness and not because I wish to value your money more than your devotion. If sometimes I have been unwise in my expenditures in the past, I have learned from my mistakes to be more careful and to put a high value upon your unusual wisdom as an investor. I can promise you, for instance, that my Stock Market days are over and behind. As you once told me, "It is too easy to be taken for a ride." I try harder every year to make my expenses come within the income you send me. If I weren't sick so much I could easily do so. I shall not cease to try. I seem, I am sorry to say, to run about two thousand dollars behind each year now, but I give you my word it is not because I want to. I appreciate your generosity with me too much to want to impose on it, and I want to say in plain words that I don't enjoy asking anyone, not even you, for money.

So will you please tell those "people in Atlanta" that they don't know what they're talking about. I have always been honest with you and will always be so, as I value honesty myself and know that you do. I shall probably have to continue to ask you for extra money as long as this present sick spell continues, but it isn't because I am trying to milk you. I ask only because I have been so ill and the doctors cost so much. It makes me annoyed to have people suggest things to you when they aren't so. I do the best I can. You'd think, I know, that with all the money you give Evelyn and me, we'd have a lot to spend on ourselves for clothes and trips and luxuries. But it is not so. Doctors and rent and people to care for me eat up the cash, as Evelyn has explained to you. And yet I honestly try to live not more expensively than will prevent me from suffering. Some of the burden of caring for me has to be taken off Evelyn's shoulders by other people, as she isn't as strong as she looks. She should be away from me some, as no one ought to be made to stay with me the year around; it is too confining.

But I think that undoubtedly you personally understand that I am doing the best I can and in no wise or any way wish to take advantage of your generosity, so I'll stop before you begin to fear that I want something or have some worry to burden you with.

I hope that you will be even more sure of how I feel now, for I have written my heart in this letter. While you and I don't always agree on small points, that in no wise stops me from loving you and admiring you and feeling the respect and devotion a son feels for his father.

Devotedly,
Arthur

That is what I wrote, had censored by Evelyn and Edna, sent by air mail to Charlotte. I always like to write Father at Charlotte, for Mr. Johnson, the man with whom he chums there, is a good influence on him. He answered air mail. His letter, as Evelyn puts it, is all I could wish for and should make me feel sheepish. Perhaps it does, a bit. If Father were as human as some of his letters, or at least if he acted as human as they sound, he and I would get along with less friction. He certainly can write a heartrending epistle.

Oct. 27, 1937.
My Dear Arthur:

Thank you very much for your nice letter, and am very glad you wrote it as it gives me a chance to get you straight on several things which I feel that you have been needlessly worrying over.

The first is that my advice to you is, so long as you feel that you are doing right not to worry too much about what other people think as it is as far as I can see a personal matter entirely between you and me and it is not the business of anyone else.

The second is that while I have always said that you were most secretive and that it seems almost impossible ever to get the whole or to the bottom of anything with you, and have often thought of you that at times you showed very poor judgement in getting the full value for your money and in some of the things that you put your money into, never for a moment have I doubted your absolute honesty and sincerity nor have I ever thought that you were willingly trying to hold me up for more money than you thought you actually needed.

It is with a heart full of gratitude and relief to my peace of mind to hear you say that your stock market days are over and behind. Some lessons are hard to learn, as I have found to my sorrow in my own case, but once learned they seem worth the experience as I feel certain that I would have nothing today if the stock market had gone my way when I was younger.

I also appreciate very much your efforts to try to live within your income and I think I understand and realize just what you are up against when you have your long sick spells and have always tried to impress on you that I did not want you to ever suffer for anything that would add in a reasonable way to your health, happiness, or comfort.

Remember my dear son that you are all I have and my whole effort in life is to try and see that you are taken care of both while I am alive and after I am gone, and for this reason I have had to play as nearly safe as my human judgement would allow me.

I hope and trust that this letter will relieve your mind, stop any worries that you may have had about my ever having doubted you, and give you in a measure some of the happiness and relief that your letter has given me, and with dearest love to both you and Evelyn, I am devotedly your father,

H. A. Inman

P.S. Your expressions of love for and trust in me go a long ways towards helping me struggle on.

You are too much like your old Dad to ever be dishonest about anything.

A couple of days ago margin requirements were lowered from 55% to 40%, and a margin requirement on short sales of 50% was instituted. The Market is answering favorably. Paid Dr. Pike another $500 last week, leaving a debt of $1,500. This morning I am sending a check for $500 to N.P. Putt & Company to be used on a commodity account. Mr. Putt has been making money for everyone who has given him cash on account. Bet I ruin his business.

November 2 I listened to a radio play. Radio actors and motion picture actors are on the whole more natural, less affected performers than were the stage folk of my youth. The men are better than the women. And why not? Most of the female motion picture stars look as if they had been raised from the gutter or suasioned out from behind the counters of second-rate eating joints to play down to the undiscriminating tastes of humanity in general.

November 4 Be it noted here before I stop writing for the day that James Curley failed to win the mayoralty election two days ago. He is out of luck for the first time and bitter about it. Some of the Irish have turned against him for killing policemen with his car, for running around with his friend's wife, for this and that. One of his partners in pilfering has been indicted. He has obtained no Federal sinecure from Roosevelt. And now he is at last out. He sounded both angry and amazed on the radio. Another young Irishman was elected Mayor in his stead. Wonder what Curley will do now. It cannot be possible that his gay days of political racketeering are over and done with. We passed his home this morning. I wondered if he were there and if so what were his thoughts.

November 7 Billy has many times promised to relate to me his life story. Today I was ready to hear it. "Come in and sit down, Billy," I said, "and tell me about yourself like you said you would." "I've decided not to tell you about myself." He wouldn't budge. And I am deeply disappointed in him. I have a disdain for persons who will not keep promises given in good faith to friends. And I have a disgust for people who feel that they are so important that information volunteered about themselves will weaken their individuality. The more a person divulges about himself, or so it seems to me, the more he grows, and if he talked for a full year he could not completely divulge himself. Each person is, in the final analysis, a mystery even to himself. Narration of the events of his life will in no wise expose this mystery to sight. Ten Broek would not tell about his past. Nor will my Father. A few old cranks who have answered my ads would not. Some Englishmen I have met would not. Otherwise I find people amenable to questions as soon as they are convinced I am not on mischief bent.

Here is as much of William Henry Minor's life as I know. I feel sure that he has either Indian or negro blood in him. He doesn't know about his ancestors except in a vague sort of way. He is the oldest of five brothers. The other kids in the neighborhood used to tease him for having to take the brothers out for an airing. He didn't resent it; he felt helping his mother with the children was part of his duty. He used to wash, dress and feed them. At an early age, Billy had a newspaper route. He hated school, was anxious to get through. He was candy boy on a train. He wanted to be a locomotive engineer. When he was six or seven, someone threw him into a swimming hole and told him to swim out. The most serious interest in his young life was being a boy scout. He worked his way up in the organization. He tried to do his good deed every day. What he was taught about truthfulness and loyalty and discretion and honesty made, he said, a deep impression on him. It has colored his attitude even to this day.

He wanted to become a Marine. He got his father's consent. Some slight occurrence changed his aspiration on the day he went to join, and he entered the Army instead. The rough soldiers made him miserable. He cried for his mother. Then he took up boxing, fought some of them, and they left him alone. He became the pet of one of the officers who took him under his wing. Billy was the best shot in the company. After three years in the Army, he came to Boston, "to be further away from my mother," and went into the washing department of the Colonial Laundry. He was there two or three years, when he went to the boss and told him he wanted an outside position. So he was put on a truck. He had become a Catholic and had met Sadie. The remainder you know.

Billy is secretive. He cannot hide how he feels but is an adept at making a secret of what he thinks. He believes that women are lower in the scale than men. "I never fully confide in any woman, not even in Sadie. It's best for everybody concerned that they don't know what's in your mind or everything you do and don't do." He purposely stays away from seeing his mother more than once or twice a year. "Mothers have a way of castin' a spell over you. I stay away, I don't write, and there's nothin' she can do." Billy can be very cold-blooded in a dispassionate sort of way when it comes to following out the conclusions he has arrived at. On the evenings he studies this winter, he does not see Sadie. "It'll do her good not to have me at her beck and call every night. That's part of my plan."

November 15 Evelyn and I have been married fourteen years. There should be more give and take in the contact between us. I should not be made to dread the consequence of making a direct statement, and she should accept a direct statement from me as something other than meat to pounce upon. I don't like to argue. I feel my hackles rise at thoughtless and unprovoked contradiction. I want to live peaceably with my wife, free to speak what is in my mind without having it torn to pieces before she hears it. I will not practice the sort of indirection which alone appeases her. As I tell her, I will fight her on this matter as long as we are together, and I will keep after her to be different in this respect as long as she sees fit to argue and to contradict without provocation and without end.

While we were in the midst of our set-to yesterday, Hassie and Johnny arrived. Johnny didn't stay. He said he wanted to have a Syrian supper and would be back to take Hassie home at nine.

We talked to Hassie all afternoon, Evelyn took her to the Ritz for dinner to please her, and after that we talked until nine.

Johnny weighs two hundred and fifty pounds. "Aren't you," inquired Evelyn, "worried about his being so large? He might die or something. It's dangerous to weigh that much." "Oh no," said Hassie, "I'm not worried. I've got him insured. There's enough to bury him, so that I won't be pinched as I was when Harry died and left me to foot the funeral expenses. If he dies, there are other men. I don't really believe I've ever been what you'd call in love in my life. Men displease me too easily. There're always more of them to be had, anyway. Oh, I don't mean to imply that I'm not fond of my big fat greaseball. I am. I'm used to his ways and he's used to mine. We team up pretty well. It's just that no man ever swept me off my feet. I'm too critical."

November 19 Woodwork had supper with Evelyn yesterday. Then she talked with me until ten-thirty. She enjoyed her trip to New York with Allan. She went to night clubs and theatres. She was telling me that Conrad Aiken has married the third time and gone to England. Before that, someone else told me, he was living off the W.P.A. writers' project. Woodwork says that she is afraid of him. She feels that he is cracked in the head. Woodwork has been having all sorts of hemorrhoid operations. Some quack doctor seems to be taking her for a ride. She avers that the operations don't hurt her. What is she made of, iron? She is full of stories about Peggy — riding her pig-a-back, reading fairy stories to her, scolding her, commanding her, punishing her, altogether admiring her and enjoying her and spoiling her.

This morning Edna and I drove to Bernard's Elm. It was cold and clear. Home again, I brought out a box of old pictures and with Evelyn's and Edna's assistance sorted them for possible ones to be used to illustrate this diary someday. The ones I choose I keep in Mr. Flood's little old-fashioned trunk that he so carefully fixed up for me. Have quite a comprehensive collection.

November 20 The Japanese continue the conquest of China. Since this time last year they have seized control of slices of territory as large as Italy proper. Their possessions in Asia, exclusive of Korea, are now triple the size of Japan proper.

I am reading a gripping book about the Russo-Japanese War, 'The Voyage of Forgotten Men.'[2] Even then the Japanese would not give up. Death was and is preferable to dishonor. They possessed and possess an ingenuity to achieve their goal that is disconcerting and a pertinacity that is unshakable. No one knows whether or not they can stand up under persistent defeat. A marvelous people. Unless we become involved in a war with them, when my patriotism would assert itself, I am all for them. They are more a credit to the human race at this juncture than are we.

November 22 I heard three ministers on three different radio programs inveighing against Roosevelt and the politicians yesterday. That is something new. One reverend closed with the equivalent of "May God save America in this hour of peril."

November 23 The technique employed by Japan, Italy, Germany of acting first and talking afterwards seems to bewilder the Democratic nations. Thus far the technique has worked to perfection. The aggressive nations are becoming slower and more dilatory with their apologies and excuses. They must feel a tremendous scorn for England, France and the United States, so full of words we are, so slow as to acting. For all I know this opinion of us may be correct although I suspect that we possess a final capacity to act which is grossly underestimated by Japan at least.

December 4 Alec Dark spent an evening with me. He told me that "the Street" is full of rumors of Roosevelt's insanity. A man high in the bituminous coal industry went to lay before the President the plight of the industry. In the middle of his recital, Roosevelt began to laugh. He laughed and laughed, spoke no reply to the man's plea, and was still laughing when Roosevelt's aides showed him out. Dark heard this from the personal friend of the man concerned.

December 10 Naomi was here yesterday. The unpalatable truth, I suspect, is that Naomi is tired of me. Do you suppose that there is any friendship in the world that endures? People claim that I demand too much of my friends. I do demand a great deal but likewise expect to give a great deal. Nor do I ever intend to let my friendships

---

[2] Arthur is misleading here. Frank Thiess's book (1937) is an account of the great sea battle Tsushima in 1905, in which the Russian fleet was destroyed by the Japanese navy under Admiral Togo. Thiess justifies and glorifies the Russian admiral Sinovij Petrovich Rozhestvensky, and attributes the debacle to czarist corruption and bureaucracy.

bog down from lack of effort to keep them alive. It is all poppycock to assert that friendships stay alive without effort. _ _ _

December 16   Whoever sets to work some centuries from now to study original sources in order to compile a history of these times will be sore put to it to winnow the grain from the chaff. There is enough source material to daunt the most courageous scholar. Thousands of newspapers. Scores of magazines. Thousands of pamphlets. Government documents by the ton. Hundreds of memoirs. When you consider with what labor historians arrive at conclusions concerning Rome or Greece, with only a comparatively few documents and inscriptions outstanding, think with sympathy of the task which awaits the future historians of our times. I suppose that the final directions and the manner of conclusion of trends will guide them as to what historical material is of concern and what is not. But even so, how can they discriminate? They, even with the advantages of distance and perspective, cannot be aught but bewildered by the mass of written, recorded, filmed material. No one man will be able to scan the available source matter concerning a single year — his life will be too brief.

When I, who am quite as interested in the contemporary scene as will be any historian of the future, look about me and seek to choose what to chronicle and what to pass by, I am in a quandary as to what will be important and what will not, when the tale of today is finally told.

A number of days ago Japanese planes sunk a United States gunboat on the Yangtze River. Scareheads were broken out in our newspapers. There was and still is discussion of the possibility of war. I would not record the incident did I not suspect that it will prove another cornerstone in the slowly growing misunderstanding and lack of sympathy between Japan and the United States. England appears to be using every conceivable trick and much pressure to line up the United States on its side in the Far East. The 'U.S.S. Panay' incident will not be overlooked by the British, you may be sure of that.

I don't believe that the Japanese can see well. The perspective in their works of art runs toward them, as it would with near-sighted persons, not away and to a point as with us. On this imperfection of eyesight may lay much of the future course of history. In all their battles they appear to have to make up in rapidity of fire what they lack in effective aim.

December 18   Our prestige in the East has declined. But are not the Japanese entirely underestimating our capacity to accept insults forever with only words in reply? You would think that they had enough to do conquering China without having us in their hair. I am a sincere admirer of the Japanese. Living in a world muddle-headed with meaningless talk, it pleases the Anglo-Saxon in me to see a nation act, any nation. But my feelings are not those of the average American. He detests "the dirty little yellow beasts." He nurses an unwarranted and erroneous contempt for them as fighters. He underestimates their courage and their power. He would like to see us "get into a brawl with the little fellows and show them what real Americans can do to them." It is a dangerous feeling of superiority that we harbor. Roosevelt could have us in a war before we knew it if he lost his head or was caught up in the mounting hysteria. Perhaps with the help of Great Britain, we might defeat the Japanese. But if Germany and Italy should side with Japan, English and French hands would be tied and we would have to bear the brunt of war alone, with possibly the dubious aid of Russia. Then the outcome would not be as certain as Americans like to think. The war would have to be fought in the Pacific. I doubt if we could invade Japan or if Japan could invade us, although of course there is that possibility.

December 21   When Ella was in New York working in the fur trade, she decided to study stenography. She was recommended to an accountant who was going blind.

"All my life I had yearned to have someone to whom I could tell what was in my mind. This man drew me out. He was a person of wide experience. He made me see things I'd never seen before. I soon discovered that I wasn't learning stenography, but I figured that perhaps I was learning something still more valuable. He wasn't happy. His wife was one of those animal-like females who want nothing more than a roof over their heads and enough to eat. Her children were like her, not like him. He was fifty-seven. He soon had me reading aloud to him. He would correct my pronunciation and explain anything I didn't understand. I liked it, that is, until one day he broke down and informed me that he loved me and couldn't live without me. He was in earnest, too. He offered to leave his wife. He suggested that we go to Canada. Of course, I replied that he was silly. I wanted, I said, to marry someone my own age. Anyway, he was losing his sight, and we couldn't live on dream-cake. But he wouldn't be stopped. I quit going to him. He phoned and phoned until my brother told him he would call the cops if he didn't stop. Then he took to meeting me outside the shop. He became a nuisance. I finally had to threaten him with a policeman to make him show some sense. At last, I met him one day in the park, and we thrashed the matter out. I got rid of him, although he swore he would always love me. Six months later he went stone blind. I've often wondered what happened to him. I feel I owe him a deep debt of gratitude. I'd like to get in touch with him when I'm in New York. But I haven't. If he has put me out of his mind, it would be sheer cruelty to remind him of me. Or his love might have turned to hate. Anyway, I've never looked him up. I can understand now how he felt about me. I couldn't then."

December 26   Evelyn kept cheerful yesterday until the afternoon. "Nobody likes us," she exclaimed. "Christmas day and not one person has called on us; not a person has even telephoned. People haven't any use for us." "When I was at college," I replied, "I came to the conclusion that having people come to see me was worse than not having them come. Don't forget how tired of people you become after a couple of days." "I know. I know all that. But you'd think—"

Evelyn has gone to Bernard's Elm this morning. The evening before Christmas, she had supper with Dr. Pike and Virginia. I wish I could make Christmas more cheerful for her, but I cannot overcome my boyhood hatred of the day and all it connotes. Any effort to act otherwise than I do would ring false.

December 27   Mrs. Cash is still reading aloud 'The Greatest Norman Conquest.' A magnificent book. She likes it as much as I do. She says: "They were buggers, those Normans, but I like them." For some time now I have been pursuing a sensible policy with Mrs. Cash. All it takes to keep her happy is a fairly continual flow of flattery. Under such treatment she purrs like Evelyn's kitten when rubbed along its spine.

Mrs. Cash has been a lifesaver to me. Since I have prevailed on her to keep most of her salacious stories to herself, I have been able to bear with her barbarianism much better. Last night she said, "I'd like to pull your hair, Mr. Inman." "Don't be childish," I said. "Now," she said, "you've hurt my feelings. How would you like it if I left you and went to Florida?" "I wouldn't like it. You've been a great help to me. Why Florida?" "The Hollinses want me to go there to manage the dining room at the new hotel they have just purchased. Mrs. Hollins was here pleading with me yesterday. They offered to pay me well, far better than I get at school. They want me to leave Wednesday." "You aren't going, are you? Florida's an awful place. You wouldn't be happy away from New England anyway." "Wouldn't you like to be rid of me and my annoying ways?" "Oh no. I'll even let you come in and pull my hair if you'll stay." "Well," she said, "isn't that just lovely of you. I mean it. Now I'll never want to pull your hair again. You are an expert psychologist, aren't you, Mr. Inman?" I felt like a damn fool holding a conversation with a playful nut. "I mean it," I said. "Well," she said, "I'll tell you. I don't intend going. There is more money in it, but I'm not going." "Fine," I said. "Now we can finish our 'Greatest Norman Conquest.'"

December 29 Snowed yesterday. In dark all day. Mrs. Cash read 'The Crowd' by Gustave LeBon. In afternoon Evelyn read 'China at Work' by Rudolf P. Hommel. In evening Mrs. Cash read 'Everybody's Autobiography' by Gertrude Stein and 'The Greatest Norman Conquest' by James Van Wick Osborne. 'The Crowd,' as its title indicates, is a study of crowds, their psychology and their mentality and moods and wherein they differ from those of men as individuals. I am fascinated by it. The essay was published in 1896, and I am reading the seventh edition. More about it later. The mind of the crowd, the author contends, is inferior to the mind of any intelligent individual, while the collective emotions are intensified, either towards heroism or villainy as the case may be. Query: What has happened to the French scholars, poets, painters of yesteryear?

1938

January 3 Evelyn and I listened to the radio—the New York Philharmonic Orchestra, John Barbarolli brilliantly conducting Tchaikovsky's 'Violin Concerto in D Major,' Mischa Elman as soloist. When they went into Beethoven, I quit and turned to hillbilly music. Beethoven and Bach give me a pain. Arithmetic is all right in its place, but the place of pure arithmetic is not in music. I want some melody, theatricality, emotional push, not just a specified number of short themes rolled over and over again with various trimmings until I become annoyed and impatient. Bach sounds to me like a finger exercise no matter who plays his stuff. In my maturity I am convinced, as was Victor Herbert, that the best music is that which is readily comprehended at first hearing by the common people. Lizst and Tschaikowsky have melody and emotional verve. Lizst and Debussy know how to build up vibrational effects which I like but which others do not, calling them ordered noise. I am now at the stage where I like what music I like no matter whose name is on it or what artist or conductor presents it, and the rest can go hang. I consider 'The Blue Danube' just about the greatest music ever written. Beethoven and his 'Ninth Symphony' would never be played again for all of me. I don't like most jazz (now called swing), but I do like some. Folk songs, when they haven't become hackneyed through repetition, are pleasant. What I don't understand is this—why don't orchestras play and artists sing some new music occasionally?

Ended the afternoon by listening to Pepsodent Tooth Paste's new program with Walt Disney, creator of the famous movie cartoon characters, Mickey and Minnie Mouse, Donald Duck and the rest, and a whimsical skit. Amusing. There is too much advertisement on the radio. It undoes the effect it sets out to create. I have an antipathy against buying what is dinned into my ears too vehemently.

January 4   This morning Edna is taking the Baby-Carriage to the Packard Company to be scraped and painted, to be upholstered and refurbished. At last I have made myself face the project. I am weary of being yelled at. The car is falling to pieces and rusting under my eyes. If it is to be preserved, it must be done over. It will cost nearly two hundred dollars. Edna takes her responsibility very seriously. She will stay with the job until it is finished.

Ella was here last night. She is worrying about what is happening to the profits from the lamps Robert has sold. He refuses to answer her questions. As I told her, she is not the first woman to goad her husband to be ambitious and then to find herself put aside for his new interest to succeed. It will be interesting to watch what will happen.

January 5   Edna has just phoned that my car "is as naked as a baby — no paint at all." She is the only one who is as concerned about the Baby-Carriage as am I. She said yesterday, "It looked positively pathetic going into the room where they burn off the paint. My heart fell when I saw its tail disappearing out of sight. Oh, Artie, I do hope that all goes well. I've done my best, of that I can assure you. I've had a separate struggle with about everyone at the Packard Company. I've told them what the car meant to you."

I am deeply grateful for Edna's concern, for I feel as though my pet child were undergoing a dangerous operation with the chances against a proper recovery. I certainly do love that car. It is an irreplaceable part of my limited life. I sometimes wonder if loving and being dependent on are not synonymous in me. By nature I am solitary, taciturn, independent — or would like to be.

Traffic has been routed down St. Botolph Street, and there is noise and grit over everything and in my eyes. All I can think about is the Baby-Carriage.

Last night, Roderic. Two weeks ago when he read abominably, he neglected to take his money. I thought for a couple of days that since I had stopped him and let him go an hour earlier, he had considered I hadn't had my money's worth and had left the envelope behind on purpose. Not he. He has asked me for it every time since. No matter how late or how poor the performance rendered, he wants all the money he can get. Last night he came half an hour late. He asked me for the back money. "Well," I said, a bit weary of his avarice, "you were good and late tonight. Suppose you take something out for that, and I'll pay you the rest." "Now look here, Arthur," he said, "I only come here to accommodate you, not because I want to. I'm tired toward evening. I'd much rather not come. Perhaps it would be a good plan if——"

I interrupted before he could put his thought into words. I knew I had spoken unwisely. I have for a long time been well aware that he continued to come either because he liked me or was grateful for past favors and for no other reason. I said, "I'm sorry I spoke hastily. I realize that your days are both full and hard and that you come with some trouble to yourself to help me out and only on that account. I want to take this opportunity to tell you how much I appreciate the reading. It helps me out more than you know. So forget the slip of my tongue, won't you?" Apology seems to be the open sesame to most men's hearts. I suppose it makes them feel big. Roderic was pleasant again. "Okay, he said, "let's forget it. What do we read tonight?"

For a person who is by nature honest and straightforward, I have been forced by circumstances to assume secretive and devious ways. It makes me feel crooked. I would have preferred to say, "Oh, don't be such a goddamn tightwad. When you read well, I like to pay you, but when you fail to, I don't. You're a good fellow to come, and I do appreciate that, but likewise you're hard as hell to get along with, snotty, snippy, even more clumsy with me than I am with you. If you don't want to read to me and are doing it only as a favor, let's quit for good. I don't want to be indebted to you or to anyone else." But no. I say what I think will please him. No doubt my nature is made the sweeter by having to exercise self-restraint and be tactful, but I'll tell you, I don't like it.

January 6   Am not reading the papers for a while. I become too carried away by the melodramatic superlatives in which the news is presented and must take a vacation to restore a proper historical perspective. I am reading the letters of Sidonius, the Roman official who lived during the middle half of the fifth century.[3] "Though the style is often tiresome . . ." writes the translator, "as a whole they should be read." I do not find them tiresome. Far from it. They delight my sense of style.

Sidonius witnessed, writes his editor, O.M. Dalton, "the last

---

[3] Caius Sollius Appolinaris Sidonia (c. 431 – c. 482), Latin poet and letter writer, was appointed bishop of Clermont-Ferrand on the eve of the Gothic invasions. Since Arthur was constantly drawing analogies between moribund Rome and deteriorating America, Sidonia's letters describing domestic life and manners in Gaul at the time of Rome's ebbing authority had more than an antiquarian interest.

sickness and death of the Roman Empire of the West." He saw the frontiers collapsing inward. As Walter Lippmann points out in one of his articles, we are not being threatened by the collapse of frontiers but by a revolution and uprising of the masses within the borders of the European and American States themselves.

January 9   The Baby-Carriage looks less shiny than I thought possible. The workmen at the Packard Company have done an excellent job — dull paint, new top cover, red wheels. But people still yell at me.

January 15   Heard a motion picture commentator last night describing the premier of 'In Old Chicago' in Hollywood. Galleries erected so that people might watch the movie stars drive up to the theatre and go in. Floodlights. A blimp overhead. The theatre burning with electric flares. All the stars brought to the microphone and persuaded to speak — Tyrone Power (America's most popular male star), Don Ameche, Alice Faye, Alice Brady, Douglas Fairbanks Jr., William Powell, Barbara Stanwyck, William Morris, Basil Rathbone, etc., etc. Most of the men are like exaggerated college sophomores, and the girls look and talk like quondam waitresses. Yet the impact they and their Jewish directors wield upon civilization is tremendous. About the motion picture stars of today hangs all the glamour that was the perquisite of the matinee idols and theatrical stars of pre-War years. But the stage folk of that era were never in possession of such undreamed-of power to sway the social mind and emotions. They could not reach as many people in a year as one movie star can now contact in a week. It seems to me that the morality of the nation could be changed for the better almost overnight by a stepping up of the tone of the movies. But perhaps not. If the people are not given a reflection of themselves, they are apt to desert even such a popular medium as motion pictures.

January 18   Mrs. Banks has been copying Volume 43 [1930]. Yesterday she delivered me a lecture. "What you write about the people who are close to you doesn't make pleasant reading. Whether you intend it or not, what you have to say about me, about Edna, about Mrs. Inman and Dr. Pike is caustic and bitter. There is a sneer to it. It is as though you harbored a deep contempt for us. And I want to take this opportunity to tell you that I believe that you make a decided mistake to show your diary to people you wish to keep as friends. They read what you have to say about me or Dr. Pike and immediately come to the conclusion, whether it is justified or not, that you really don't care a hang for anybody and that you treat them nicely only for what you can get out of them. Then you lose their friendship, for they become suspicious of you and no longer trust your motives. It happened with Millicent. It happened with Claire. No doubt it is one reason why Naomi doesn't come any more. People don't want themselves scourged in writing. When they see how you talk about your best and closest friends, they naturally assume that they won't receive any better literary treatment at your hands. It is a pity that you draw such unattractive pictures of your friends and intimates, and it is eminently unwise to let anyone you can help have the chance to read what you have written."

Mrs. Banks was in earnest. It was apparent that she had given the matter thorough thought. I always listen to her or to anyone for that matter who has advice to offer. I appreciate both the advice and the thought behind it. I didn't enjoy the taste of what she had to say, but if my writing made that impression on her, I thought it well for me to listen attentively. Such an impression wasn't the one I wanted to give, wasn't a thoroughly true one. Edna is convinced that the picture I make of her is inaccurate and causes her to appear as a "lumpish boor." Mrs. Banks doesn't believe that I have portrayed her accurately and in proportion. I recognize that I have not always been fair with Dr. Pike and Evelyn. The colors of anger, of pique, of temporary irritation, even of unrelieved honesty are starker colors than those of love and admiration and appreciation. I am grateful to Mrs. Banks for her criticism and advice.

January 23   Last night Betsy Simons brought a girl, Karen Kendall, five months married, to see me. What the twenties termed sex appeal crackled from her the moment she stepped inside the door. She talked lightly and facilely. I was enthralled. She works at the Barton Furniture Company for seventeen dollars a week. I hope she comes again. If she does, more about her. Betsy says that the men follow her about like so many puppies. I can well believe it. What is sex appeal? Does it originate in the body or in the mind? Does it come because a woman has her mind on the subject of sex and hence radiates appeal? Yet I have seen it stare out at me from paintings and photographs. Yet I did not lay eyes on the girl, Karen. Infectious, like a yawn — mysteriously infectious. Many things we humans don't know about ourselves. Savages sometimes know them, but we don't.

Have been listening to Francis Bacon's essays on the talking-book. A mind so profoundly clear that the English language sometimes refused him a pellucid medium of thought conveyance. Much meat in the nuts he presents to the reader, some mockery also. A savagely illuminated mind. I don't believe that he and Shakespeare were one. The latter is more human.

January 26 Hardly keep my eyes open, what with dust and lack of sleep. At midnight on the dot the W.P.A.'ers commence to toss eight-by-eights about and to bang on them with huge mallets. Instead of running the car tracks from the reservation to the sides of the street and then doing their digging, the engineer in charge is digging and trussing up the tracks as the excavating progresses, an endless job. You know, sometimes I can understand thoroughly how the Reds come to hate the Government in power and wish to upset it. Nothing I can imagine would give me more real delight than to put exterminating bombs under the entire New Deal and blow them to hell.

But enough of such fruitless ranting. Evelyn has gone downtown to see what can be done towards making the W.P.A.'ers commit this social folly at a less unearthly hour. Evelyn has many unpleasant duties to perform in order to sustain enough strength in me to work and live. From the bottom of my heart I pity her for being my wife. No buffer state was ever more used. While she may fuss a little at times (and who wouldn't), as a rule she is a soldier and a loyal wife, going forth to do my battles with determination and the will to succeed.

February 10 Dr. Pike certainly is a wonderful person. The average physician would have lost a live interest in me and my case years ago. But not Dr. Pike. And his friendship is something special and unusual. And how he has been about Evelyn has touched me deeply. He has come to help me when he was too sick to be out of bed, when other more pleasant avenues of spending his time were available, when it was deep night or storm and snow were swirling, without murmur or demur. I am ashamed that I have railed against him so many times. He has been an anchorage in a buffeting world.

Have been having a long talk with Edna. Because she reads my criticisms of certain phases of her character and activities in my diary as she copies it, she has been arriving at the conclusion that I don't like her. She holds that one person cannot be fond of another and at the same time be critical of his faults and acts. The two, she says, cannot exist conjointly. I contend that they can. Because I abhor the ugly dumpheaps of a city, certain buildings, the flaunting signboards, doesn't mean that I can't love that city. Faults and acts of which I disapprove in any person are incidentals not at all destructive of my wholehearted respect for that person.

I love Edna, admire her profoundly, count her as one of the finest people I ever met in the world. In my talk with her I have been trying to persuade her of my genuine regard for her. The power of the written word never ceases to amaze me. A couple of written pages containing criticism of a person may, when that person has read them, overbalance in his mind and emotions a year of spoken praise. It is my misfortune, a great one, that those intimate with me should have access to my private thoughts in written form.

February 11   Ella wants to write a book about her life. She had the idea of telling her story anonymously as though she were not colored. I persuaded her that if she could honestly put down her story, the story of a colored girl, it would constitute (provided it were well done) a social document of considerable merit. Probably she will never write it, but I figured it wouldn't hurt to encourage her. She wants to do something creative or constructive so earnestly that at times she falls sick wishing.

Ella's white great-great-grandfather came from England and settled on a plantation in northeastern Alabama. His name was Johnson. His son carried on the plantation. His son, Ella's grandfather, was a wild young man, worthless. He had an affair with the family cook, whose father was a pure-blooded Indian and whose mother was a pure-blooded negress. The resulting child, Ella's father, grew up on the plantation a free man, working for his grandfather. When he was seventeen, his father threw the child of a poor white over a fence because it was bothering him by crying, and accidentally killed it. He then fled the country. When Ella's father was twenty, he left his grandfather's plantation and went to work for an old man who owned a plantation and ran a cotton gin. He married. He saved. He ran the cotton gin for the old man. When he was thirty, he bought a farm of his own where he raised cotton and peanuts. He was respected by whites and negroes alike. His wife died. He married again, Ella's mother, who gave birth to Ella when Ella's father was sixty. Ella's mother's father, whose name was Coleman, had considerable white blood in him. His wife was colored and dark. Ella's father was both proud of and ashamed of his white blood — proud because it was white, ashamed because it came to him through his ne'er-do-well father.

February 18   "Roderic," I said, "you'll have to read louder. They're tearing up pavement outside my window." "Artie," he said, "you'd think, wouldn't you, that after all these years I'd be used to hearing you say 'have to' to me? I'm not, though. I know you don't mean a thing, but it rankles me to my foundations. I don't want anybody throwing 'have to's' at me. Mind you, I'm not sore tonight. I'm just remarking on a phenomenon of my nature. Queer, isn't it?" "I don't think so. If it bothers you, I want to change it, especially when you're so equable about it. You're as temperamental as a woman, very hard to keep cheerful, and I can assure you that I have no desire to say or do anything that will throw you off balance. My Mother used to say 'you've got to' to me until I cringed every time I heard it. So I recognize how you feel about 'have to.' What do you want me to say in its place?" "Well, Artie, you might say 'will you.' I know I'm temperamental. 'Have to' does bother me." "Very well," I said, "there's a mess of noise outside my window tonight, Roderic, and I would appreciate it very much if you'd read a bit louder." Roderic laughed. "Thanks," he said. "I'll do just that." "And," I added, "as you would phrase it, how's about an evening of reading next Thursday?" "Okay," he grinned, "as far as I know." "And it would please me very much if you could read Sunday. Do you think there's any chance?" He laughed again. "I don't know. I'll see. I'll give you a ring." "It's dangerous, Roderic," I concluded, "to tell me how to please you." "I see it is," he said.

February 20   Snow. Evelyn has been reading to me the following epistle from Patricia. I should hate to be caught in the toils of any institution, the Catholic Church or otherwise, as she has been. Institutions and organizations are blind and peremptory masters of a person's particular destiny, with which I want nothing to do. I have no faith in the authority exercised by sanctified bodies and would avoid being caught in the toils of such authority almost with my life. All of which is a disproportioned introduction to Patricia's letter, since it deals with only one phase of what has happened to her. Without more ado or further remarks on my part, here is the letter:

Dearest Arthur and Evelyn;

I've taken longer than I had expected to get this letter started, but I simply didn't have the heart to write all this in longhand, since I must tell you "all" it would have been far to much of a task. So I waited until I got this typewriter. I'm not much of a typist, but it isn't as tiring.

Since you haven't heard from me in so long I shall have to go back two years and tell you everything that happened up until now. It is going to be a task, so I will probably be days in writing this.

I believe that when I last wrote I had just left Ted, at his request, to live in a hotel. He wanted to be alone with Mike, to see if things would work out better that way. There was nothing for me to do but go, since they would have left if I had stayed; at least Ted would have, Mike was too self centered to care very much as long as he was being taken care of. So he took the line of least resistance.

Ted found the hotel for me, I hadn't the heart to look for

myself. I didn't care where I went. Strangely enough he found and hired a room right across the street from the Compton Arms Hotel where he was working. That gave me some comfort as I thought that he did care enough to have me near him.

The first few days were pretty awful, I was so heartsick that I was really ill, and it was torture for me to work. But I simply had to, I was only making eight dollars a week as I was on part time, so I needed every cent. I had a chance to get on full time if I stayed, and I did like the place so much, the girls were all so nice. It was a very high class restaurant in the best part of the city. Of course I only worked three hours a day, and that gave me far too much time to think. I had no money for movies so I just haunted the libraries and about read my eyes out. For two whole weeks I sat in that room waiting for some word from Ted, and not even a telephone call came.

After two full weeks I finally got a note saying that they were being put out of the apartment for nonpayment of rent and Ted would like me to come over to the apartment and sort out the things that belonged to me. Ted had a far greater salary than I and could easily have kept up the place. But he was used to my paying the rent and didn't bother to put away a little at a time. And of course all the money was going for liquor; they both drank like fish. Mike had to be amused all the time, and Ted was so blinded that he did everything to please him. That's the trouble with those affairs, all perspective is lost.

We were both very quiet when Ted came for me and drove me to the apartment, talking in ordinary tone about any and all subjects, as one will when under stress. Ted left me at the apartment for a couple of hours to pack, while he went back to work. In the meantime Mike was being his usual ingratiating self, helping me with the packing and being very sweet. It takes a great deal of resistance to withstand his charm, even then I didn't dislike him, I didn't really blame him for all that had happened, since he wasn't the cause. The trouble really lay in Ted's own brain, and Mike was only the instrument at that particular time, at any other time it would have been someone else as it has always been since his late teens.

Ted was especially nice to me on the way home, and said that he thought that things would work out my way eventually if I would only have patience, from which I gathered that things were not going so well between the two of them. So of course I was elated and happy for the first time in months. But the next day there was a note in my box saying that the payment on the car was due and he had no money to pay it. That was my cue to say that I'd raise the money for him. The car was a present to Ted from his parents and it was paid for, but he had borrowed money on it, he was forever doing that and not telling me about it. I borrowed ten dollars from one of the girls at work and gave it to Ted. He drove me to work that morning, but wasn't nearly as nice as he had been the night before. So down went my spirits again. He had moved into the Compton Arms again, he was entitled to a room there, but I don't know how he got away with Mike, he passed him off as a relative.

Four days later I drove to Hollywood with Ted and Mike on some errand, and while Ted was absent from the car for a few moments Mike told me he didn't think I had a chance. Which nearly floored me, as I was sure that Ted had told him to tell me that, and just after he had given me to understand that things would straighten out for me too.

For the next month Ted called me once or twice, and one evening he and Mike came over for a little while, but there was no change in Ted's attitude. On the day before the payment on the car was due again he came around to tell me that he had five dollars toward it, so I told him I would give him the other five each month, but I couldn't pay the whole thing. He came around in the morning, got the money and drove me to work, acting as if he were really glad to be with me, and he left me a manuscript to read.

During the month of Feb. I saw him one or two times, I invited him to have breakfast with me one Sunday morning, and he took me to a party one evening, Mike was there too, of course. In March I saw even less of Ted, about once every ten days, and I was rapidly becoming a fit case for an asylum. He turned up promptly on the day the car payment was due, but I didn't care why he came as long as he showed up.

Ted has a friend in San Francisco, a German teacher at one of the schools there, His name is Otto Holzwasser, he is a grand person and I am so fond of him, so when he got the chance to come down here on his Easter vacation I was delighted to see him. He read Ted the riot act for treating me the way that he did. He is one of the few persons who knows the whole story. He came to see me all the time he was in town and took me around, of course I gloried in the attention.

Just at this time I got on full hours at the Cafe, so had less time and more money to myself, I started to put a little aside each week for clothes which I badly needed. Nothing helps a female like having a new outfit. I had invited Ted to have breakfast with me on Easter morning, April 21. We went out to Hollywood, I, dressed in my best, wearing a corsage my boss had given me the night before, so I looked pretty grand. I had a new tie for Ted in his pet shade of blue. He had overslept that morning, so he had neglected to shave and didn't look so festive, I did so want to make it a gala occasion, but it can't be done with a bearded man. The breakfast wasn't too successful, Ted had a headache and I had the blues, so we didn't stay out very long, we were back in the hotel by noon.

I had no intention of having my entire day ruined, especially since I had a new outfit to show off. So I called one of my oldest friends, Karen Bidford, she was an English girl I had known for years. She was married to a Russian, Viktor Rosnikov, mad as a hatter. They had a lovely home in a canyon in Hollywood. She was all alone and told me to come right out to the house, so I gathered up a large bunch of flowers and took the bus right out there. When I got there Karen was in the bath, so I went in and sat on the toilet seat and visited with her. While she was still bathing I heard a strange male voice in the living room, so I went out to investigate, and found an enchanting Irishman roaming around, Karen introduced us through the bathroom door. He was Sean Michael Patrick O'Casey, I adored the name immediately. I had to entertain him while Karen dressed, we were friends instantly, you know how you are with some people. The O'Casey was tall, and slim, dark hair and blue eyes, a thin face, with the merriest twinkle. He had the most beautiful speaking voice I've ever heard. He was educated in Dublin, which accounts for that. And with one or two words a slight brouge. We had the grandest afternoon. Karen's husband had gone off for the day, leaving her without a penny, so we went to the grocery store and got fresh muffins, rare roast beef, salad, and dessert. We had a grand supper and had so much fun while eating it. We stayed until nearly nine o'clock Sean drove me home, I hated to get out of the car, it was a long time since I had liked anyone so much. He said he hoped he would see me again some time, but I really didn't put much faith in it, as it seemed too good to be true, and things didn't seem to be happening that way to me of late. But sure enough, the next Saturday night I had a call from him. He asked if he could call for me and take me visiting with some friends of his. I didn't care very much for the people we went to see, but I did enjoy being with Sean, he was so sweet to me, and I was falling rapidly, so was he, I could feel it. We got away from his friends early and went for a ride to the beach. It was beautiful at Santa Monica, a full moon and everything. He told me all about himself. He was born here, in Portland. His father was an Irishman, and had something to do with the Canadian Pacific Railways; Sean and his sister lived in Dublin from infancy, so he never felt like an American, in fact he is an Irish fanatic. He ran away and enlisted when he was a youngster, the war left him with T.B. of the throat, so for years he was in hospitals and nursing homes.

Just about the time that he was discharged as an arrested case the market crashed and his father was ruined. Sean had to live in a warmer climate and hadn't the money to do so, so his Mother sent him to an old friend of hers. Mrs. F.R. Heenan, the wife of the oil magnate. Mrs Heenan has an enormous estate, and she gave Sean a job as under gardener, at twentyfive dollars a week. There are forty gardeners on the place. Sean didn't have to work very hard, and he was out of doors all the time, so it was just the place for him. He enjoyed the work, and the money went a long way out here where things are cheaper. He bought himself a nice little car, and was doing quite well. While he was in Vancouver in a nursing home he became engaged to a widow, a nurse, who was very kind to him. He wasn't in love with her, but he was very fond of her and he felt obligated since he really didn't believe he would have lived without her care, so since she seemed to want him he proposed to her. He hadn't seen her for a year and a half, but expected to be married by September.

Time passed, as it has a habit of doing, and Mr. O'Casey and I were in each others company constantly. He was adorable to me, bringing me corsages and filling my room with flowers. I loved to drive and he took me everywhere. One night he drove me all night long. We talked of how wonderful it would be if I were not married and he not "promised". We are both Catholics, so there was simply no way out. I quite frankly wanted him as much as he wanted me, so we decided to take what few months we had and be happy for that little time anyway. It was a pretty hard thing for me to do, and I must admit that I put up a good deal of resistance. It was eight o'clock in the morning and we were on the race track at Santa Anita when I finally gave in. I've never been able to discover why we picked that particular spot. When I told him I wanted it to be as nice as possible and as if we were really married, he understood and drove me to his place where he packed a suit case and I went to sleep in the car while waiting for him. We drove out to Hollywood and to a little Hotel on Sunset, where we registered as Mr. and Mrs. O'Casey, I did like it because he gave his real name, it made me feel better. By then I was getting slightly cool feet. Sean had thought of everything, he brought a pair of his pajamas for me, I looked sort of cute in them they were so large. When the fatal moment came I got in a blue funk and shook like mad. Sean felt so sorry for me that he wasn't going to touch me, but I convinced him that I wanted to be persuaded. I must confess that I didn't enjoy it very much, the old morals got in the way, and I was so tense. Not being exactly used to the business. I hadn't much practice with Ted you know. Sean was a dear he was so gentle with me, I finally fell asleep from sheer exhaustion. We woke up in the late afternoon, and all my fears and compunctions had left me, I was quite as avid as my beloved, and it was grand when I finally let myself go. I had never realized that sexual intercourse could be such a glorious thing, but of course it takes two to make it what it should be. For the rest of the day we just stayed in and made love to each other. When he finally brought me home at night I was exhausted and fell into bed.

We continued to see each other constantly, spending each week-end in our dear little hotel, where we had become well known as the O'Caseys from Bakersfield. We had such fun. While Sean shaved I'd bathe, and he would always dry me off and carry me back to bed, we invented all sorts of games, I suppose all people in love do that, but it was new to me. He had such a dear way of calling me darlin' and sweetheart. I was in seventh heaven most of the time.

He had loads of friends, most of them were very nice, and they all liked me, so we used to go visiting every Sunday afternoon. They all knew we were terribly in love of course, a blind man would have known that. They all knew we were living together too, though Sean never gave the slightest hint and would have denied it to save me. I didn't care though, I was proud of it. One family we were unusually fond of. An actor, his wife and little five year old daughter, I was crazy about the little girl and she loved me. So we used to see them every week. Like all the Irish, Sean had a yen for the flowing cup, I drink very little myself, and hate drunks, so I kept an eagle eye on O'Casey and I'd stop him just one drink this side of to many. I could always tell the right time. He'd get a particular expression in his eyes. Then I'd whisper, "you've had enough for tonight sweet", and he'd answer, "very well my dear, if you say so", and he would quit, to the amazement of the assembled company. I was terribly proud of the power I had over him, that was only natural, but I tried not to show it too much. Drinking was bad for his throat anyway. His health had been perfect all the while he had been going with me. I would see him only over the week-end and on holidays when we were both off. He would go to bed early every week night.

A good start, but my friend who owned the typewriter had to have it back so I lost heart at the idea of writing all this in longhand. So for nearly a year it has been laid away

If ever it is to be finished it must be now, so if you will excuse the pencil, it is too fatiging to write with a pen, I will on with the tale. I only hope Evelyn can read it.

After a few weeks Sean prevailed upon me to move to Hollywood, to take a small apartment in the home of my English friend Karen. It was a dear place, Karen's home was built into a hillside. The garage and my place on the first floor. I had a small stone paved terrace & a tiny goldfish pond. My apt. consisted of one large room, two steps up from the entrance hall, a large wardrobe and a bath. No kitchen, but I had all my meals at work. The hall & living room even completely paneled in dark wood, and all the windows were casements opening outward. The place was unfurnished but my friends all contributed. Sean gave me a studio couch upholstered in soft green. A wicker chair I enameled in yellow with brown cushions. A slipper chair I upholstered in cotton, brown with white coin dots & bound in yellow, we painted the insides of the bookcases yellow, they were built in & ran to the ceiling. I bought a coffee table and lampshades, plain ivory burlap bound with green ball fringe. The curtains were brown & yellow glazed chintz hung on iron rods. Sean kept me supplied with flowers so it looked charming. I had a grand time with the bathroom — the walls were all white, so we painted the floor black and the woodwork Chinese red. And I used red & white towels, had curtains of white organdy with red polka dots & four white pots of geraniums in the window. Sean loved it too, because we didn't have to go to a hotel every Saturday night. He brought me all sorts of plants and put them around the little fountain, and was forever bringing me something he thought I could use, a clock, a vase, a cocktail shaker he adored, and books! Twice a week he'd bring me from two to three books, and you've never seen such an assortment. He'd get them in second hand book shops, anything that happened to interest him, but mostly Donn Byrne & Maurice Walsh. He loaned me his copies of Ancient Irish History, but it was to much of a dose — Irish history is terrifically complicated at its best, and this particular publication was not the best so I never did learn much about the old

Celts. We'd have heavy arguments because I'd stoutly maintain that Scotch history was more romantic — I guess the kilts got me, until I learned that the Irish wore them first —

All the summer we had a gorgeous time. S didn't particularly care for the beach, but I'd haul him there, every so often, the sun was good for him. He had originally planned to be married after Labor Day so as September approached I waited for the blow to fall. We intended to end it with a trip down the coast for a few days. So when we made plans for the Labor Day holiday I fully expected it to be our last time together. And I arrayed myself like the lamb for slaughter. S adored suits so I got one to please him. Everything new from top to toe, just like the bride I felt, and off we went. We had planned to go to La Jola, just below San Diego. I'd never driven south, and the country was all new to me.

It isn't very attractive at first so many oil wells all the way to Long Beach. But as soon as we had left L.B. it was lovely. We came to Emerald Bay and then Laguna, enchanting spots. Past Laguna, we came to a sign pointing to the San Juan Capistrano Mission — It was eight miles off our route, but I'd always wanted to see it, so on we went. Its a lovely mission, the prettiest of them all I think, we went through the whole place and by the time we got out it was getting dark. There is no twilight here you know. We debated on whether to go on or look for a place along the road. Since it was to dark to see there was no point in driving further, so we decided to return to Laguna, as I'd liked it so when we passed through. Back we went and found a charming Spanish inn, and procured a room looking out upon the ocean. The season was over so it was most inexpensive. My lover was most impatient, you would think it was his wedding night, but I insisted that he must wait, so we went to town and had a lovely dinner & walked about seeing all the art shops for which the colony is famous. By that time my new shoes were bothering me a bit so I was quite as anxious as my eager companion to return to the hotel. I did myself up in my very best satin nightie and my best blue negligee, it has a train, & sprayed toujours moi all over me. Sean kept me supplied with it as he loved it. Was I elegant. In my suit case I had a gift for Sean, a book "The Seven Pillars of Wisdom" by Lawrence of Arabia. Lawrence is one of Sean's heroes. I put it under the pillow, but since he made a dive for me instead of getting into bed I had to tell him to look under the pillow. He was delighted with the book but appalled that I should spend so much money. Five dollars meant a great deal to us, as we had to work a long while to earn it. We had a lovely night. We pretended that we were just married and had the nicest time, much nicer than if we had just been married, since I was a bit more adept.

The next day we had a late and leisurely breakfast and drove many miles more. Sean asked me if I'd like him to stay with me until my birthday that he could arrange it if I wished. Of course I was overjoyed at having him for two months more. The days slipped by too quickly and the end of October was upon us. My birthday fell in the middle of the week, and we planned to have a little party the following Saturday—but on my birthday night when I got home I found the house lighted and a radio playing. It was his gift to me to keep me from being lonely when he went away. I loved it. Its a small one, but very good, just the right size to move about easily. On the week-end all of our friends gave me a lovely party, and the little girl I love came in wheeling her doll carriage filled with gifts, and singing "happy birthday to you". among other things Sean gave me two dozen powder puffs, I was always losing mine.

About two weeks before Thanksgiving I became quite ill with intestinal flu, and Sean took such good care of me, and since Thanksgiving was so near of course, he'd postpone sending for Lenore until Christmas, by then I must confess that I was quite convinced that somehow or other things would work out so that we could be together always, how I didn't know, I just hoped.

After Thanksgiving Sean told me that the deadline was Christmas and he'd simply have to leave me then—I shed a few tears but really wasn't alarmed he'd cried wolf so many times. So I went headlong into Christmas plans. Sean had always wanted one of those quart seltzer bottles the kind you can charge yourself. So I got him one, and as many other things as I could ties tobacco etc. I knew he wouldn't have many gifts and I'd have many from the family. I had Christmas day off, so it was perfect. On Christmas Eve, we drove all over town and finished up by trimming a huge tree for little Christine Heflin, the child I am so fond of. On Christmas morning we took our gifts in on Karen & Viktor's bed and had a grand time opening them. Sean had given me what I'd asked for, a silver link bracelette with a little heart attached, the heart was engraved with 4-21-35 the day we met. I wanted something I could wear always—Something inconspicuous since I do not care for jewelry—He also gave me a large bottle of my pet perfume with a crystal bottle to put it in. For breakfast we drove out to Pasadena stopping on the way to buy me a corsage. S wanted me to have violets, but I held out for holly.

We went to visit a friend of his & took him driving—We had dinner in the late afternoon with the Heflins, a lovely dinner, it was a perfect Christmas day. Sean took the rest of the week off and stayed with me, meeting me when I got through work, I worked split shift 11–2 5–8<u>30</u>. That should have warned me, as it was a most unusual procedure—But I was too blissfully happy to see ahead.

On the 28th, a Sunday as he was driving me home he announced suddenly that Lenore had already left Toronto. She had become impatient at the continued delays and had left without saying anything until she was halfway to Los Angeles. I was completely numb and we drove for miles with Sean begging me to say something, anything, but I couldn't speak until he stopped the car and put his head down on the wheel sobbing. Then the ice in me cracked and I wept until I was completely exhausted. He finally took me home to Karen and they both put me to bed, in Sean's pajamas—clutching a hot water bottle. do you know it was months before I could go to sleep without that hot water bottle. I'd sleep with it in my arms.

Never do I want to go through a period like that time right after Sean left. I was nauseated all of the time I went around in a daze—and with that awful hard lump in my throat that I couldn't swallow. This went on for months until the Heflins, thinking that if I saw Lenore & Sean together it might snap me out of it arranged to have us meet at their place. But it was pretty awful. My stomach just turned to ice and the rest of me burned up. They stayed a short time mercifully—but drove me home. I couldn't refuse, but it nearly killed me to see Lenore sitting in my place in the car. I saw them twice again, once on Easter Sunday. Ted had taken me to the beach and stayed for a while when he brought me home.

Strangely enough, it was the first time they had ever met. I haven't seen Sean again. I couldn't it wouldn't have been fair, but now I'm not sure what to do the way things have turned out. Lenore has completely antagonized every one of Sean's friends. She didn't like any of them and ridiculed them to their faces. But worst of all she went through every penny he had. He'd had about a thousand dollars, she insisted on a new and larger car, though the other one had just been paid for—then she talked Sean into leaving Mrs. Heenan and going into a partnership raising rabbits. They took over some abandoned land by paying for the taxes. And put up tent to live in expecting Mrs. Heenan to build them a house, since she was so fond of Sean, but Mrs. Heenan didn't come through — she doesn't like Lenore's ways so just dropped them. The rabbit business fell in after a few months, and now they are completely down & out living in a room with some friends of hers in Alhambra. How they live I don't know. Sean is unhappy and has tried to find me, but I'd moved & wouldn't let him know where I'd gone since I couldn't hurt Lenore, but now that she has hurt him so much I don't care about her. What I'd planned to do is to drop them both a card and ask them to come over and see me if they'd like. I don't intend to start an affair, tho it might run into that, I realize. But Lenore is noted for not letting him stir without her. This seems to make Sean out to be an awful sap. He isn't really, just very gentle & easily influenced.

Perhaps if I got another look at him I'd get over it a bit. I still dream about him & think of him constantly. But I'm darned if I'm going to moon about and let it blight my life — far from it. I am now quite busy and having a very nice time nor wanting for male companionship. In fact I've had a constant swain for over a year. We have a grand companionship, of course we slip a bit now and then into something more intimate. But since Jerry is certainly not the man I'd choose to occupy the rest of my life I'm thinking of casting about. I'm getting tagged as Jerry Nortons girl & of course have no one else making eyes at me. I guess I want too much, decency, a home, children, love and companionship. I should have started hunting when I was eighteen, the eligible males all seem to be accounted for.

I suppose you want to know what Ted was doing all this while. He got a job in a hotel out here, and I'd see him now & then, he call for an hour or so every few weeks, but I wasn't awfully interested. I had plenty to occupy my time with Sean.

Along about April in '36 he came up one evening and wanted to know if I'd like to go to San Francisco with him & try it again. I didn't feel particularly enthusiastic, but I thought if we could make a go of it it would help erase my longing for Sean, so I said I was willing and would start saving for my share. Ted had set the date of his leaving along about the middle of May. He somehow had the idea that if he did not leave by a certain date he would never get away. And to give him credit, he really did want to get out of the life he was leading. Mike had become an obsession, and as long as they were together there was no hope for Ted. So the weeks went by, I put away every penny I had to spare, and as the departing date grew near I began to feel a bit squeamish about leaving, but since Ted really seemed to want me I squashed all my misgivings. Just a few days before we were supposed to go Ted called me and said he simply couldn't make it, he hadn't been able to save any money, knowing what it meant to him to get away I decided to let him have my share and stay here until I had enough or he sent me the fare. Off he went vowing to send for me the moment he got his first pay check. He was invited to stay with Otto until he found a job. Otto was so pleased because we were going back together again. In a week or so Ted got a job, at the Versailles Hotel as desk clerk, he didn't get much salary, but it did include his room & board. A week or two went by and little Ted began to enjoy his freedom and to rue the day he asked me to be with him. Each letter contained some reason for my not liking San Francisco. I just let things ride, as I didn't care really — I'd been let down so often that I'd anticipated it this time.

The first of June brought a friend of mine from home — Shiela Montgomery, she is the girl with whom I went to New Hampshire, and the one I was living with in New York. Shiela had become tired of New York and thought she'd see if she could find work here. Until September she lived with a friend, after that we took an apartment together and have been living here ever since. The restaurant at which I worked went out of business, and thru a neighbor I got a job right across the street at a place called the "Pign' Whistle". It's a lot like Schraffts. I got Shiela in there a few days later, and we've been very happy at work. It's a splendid place to work. The hours are good and so is the pay in the right season. We've made a great many friends among the girls and the customers and are quite content. We have a dear apartment. It is right off Hollywood Blvd, so we can walk to work. We have what is called a single — living room, kitchen & dinette, dressing room & bath. It is nicely furnished we get 24 hr switch board service, laundry & linen & weekly maid service, all for forty dollars a month. Divided by two it's almost indecently inexpensive. We are very proud of it, and constantly add things, colorful linens, pictures, lamp shades, small tables, and glass ware (5 & 10) — Last month we did over the bathroom in apricot & blue. Oiled silk shower curtains & window curtain to match. We got tired of the white one the house furnished. Shiela bought a desk too, one in knotty pine in a Monterey finish. We are always coming home with gadgets — I've a penchant for growing bulbs and have the window sills full of the objects. We give dinner parties almost every week on our day off. During the slow season (now) we have two days a week off and have grand times. Every Thursday morning we go horseback riding — I adore it, and am becoming quite an expert. The pictures I enclose were taken at the stables where we ride in San Fernando Valley, about fifteen minuets bus ride from the house. It's beautiful in the valley now — the acaca trees are in full bloom & smell heavenly. Shiela & I have acquired a reputation for good food & we have the best time getting up snacks for our visitors. All the girls at the store envy us because we get along so well together and have such a nice life. Many times one or another have asked to share an apt with us but I've definitely refused, for to add another would break the charm.

Last May Shiela & I went to San Francisco for a week. Ted was very nice to us and took us everywhere but I had no feeling for him, nor he for me as I could plainly see. Otto was grand to us — he hadn't been seeing Ted at all, he was so angry with him at the way I'd been treated. But he came right over to the hotel (not Ted's) as soon as he heard we were in town. I was so glad to get back to Hollywood. I'd never be happy in S.F. too noisy, & dirty and no trees. I'm spoiled for city life I guess, but its so beautiful here — you can't imagine it until you see it.

A month or two ago I got an infected foot and had quite a doctors bill to pay. I thought it about time Ted paid back the money I had loaned him & wrote to him suggesting he think about it, explaining about the doctor's bill. You should have seen the letter I got back. I certainly hit his vulnerable spot — his pocketbook. He proceeded to drag up every little thing that happened during our brief married life, constantly referring to the fact that I had failed him, & that if I had been more understanding things would have been different! I simply ignored it, which I found is the most maddening thing I can do to him — so I shall just let him sit and stew, wondering just what I do think, and trying to remember just what he had written, tho I don't put it past him to have kept a carbon copy. Last blow of all, he wrote to Mike & asked him to snoop about and find out if I had really been ill! Mike isn't at all bad at heart, & it burned him up, so he came over here a few days before Christmas to warn me that Ted was getting in a bit of dirty work. Also he brought me a gift — A bottle of very expensive perfume. He is working steadily now and it's amazing what it has done to change him — he gives now where he was always satisfied to be on the receiving end.

Ted has at last asked me for a divorce, but he wants me to help pay for it. I put my foot down at last and said he'd pay for all & furthermore give me written proof so I'd be able to get a Church anulment in case I want to marry again. At the time he agreed. It will undoubtedly iron itself all out in time. In the meantime I'm having a very full life and I'm not even anoying myself by thinking of him.

I think this covers all the most important ground for the past four years. It certainly has been hectic, one husband (slightly the worse for wear) and three lovers. No more complaints of monotony. And yet, you know, I don't feel a bit like a loose woman. The girls at the store call me the "Constant Nymph" because I've stuck to Jerry for two years, somehow it seems all right to me, I've got to have some outlet. Jerry knows all about Sean & that I'm still in love with him. Jerry has been married & divorced & has no intention of being caught again so we console each other in our trials and tribulations. He has a vile temper, being part Italian, but has never used it on me, since I'm to useful to break off with. I feed him when he's broke & pay his bills when he gets behind. He's in pictures and works one month & not the next. When he is working, I collect part of his salary & put it away for him. I do all his shopping, write to his family and generally keep his menage in order. In return he beaus me about whenever I feel I must have a male escort, and would do anything in his power to help me if I were in trouble. So it's a fifty-fifty proposition.

Since I've had one great love, I can't expect nor ask for more. Few people have in a lifetime what I had in eight months with Sean — so I'm content.

This is an awfully messy piece of literature. It's been written in spurts & starts for over a year. I'm dreadfully ashamed to have made you wait this long for it. I should have written more often & it wouldn't have been such a task. I don't dare read it over for fear of deleting the spiciest bits, which you enjoy the most, so I'll just leave it, with all the mistakes and only hope poor Evelyn can decipher the thing.

I've probably left out a great many things you want to know, so just let me know what questions you want answered and I'll attend to it.

With my love to you both and the hope that this will amuse you

Patricia

P.S. The family still
know nothing about
all this.

February 21   Hitler made one of his long and militant speeches yesterday. He announced his support of Japan and Italy. He demanded the return of the German colonies as a prerequisite to world peace. He reiterated his dislike for the League of Nations and for Bolshevism. He declared his good will toward every nation save Russia. He warned neighboring nations that unless persecution of German minorities within their borders ceased there would be a day of reckoning. He attacked Anthony Eden as being sympathetic to the Russian ideology.

The result of this speech was that Foreign Secretary Anthony Eden resigned from the English Cabinet before the day was over. It has been due in large measure to his insistent idealism that England and France are now on the defensive against Italy, Germany and Japan. He has been an almost fanatic advocate of the League of Nations and of the policies laid down by Woodrow Wilson. A handsome man, he has enjoyed the support of the British public. He has been anything but a realist. When Sir Samuel Hoare might have made a deal with Italy whereby England would have emerged with a substantial slice of Abyssinia and no lost prestige, it was Eden who acted the moralist and balloxed up the plan. There has been friction between idealist Eden and realist Prime Minister Neville Chamberlain for some time.

I breathe more easily for the peace of the world now that Eden is out of the picture, for I verily believe that the most vindictive villain can stir up the stream of history less violently than a confirmed idealist in power. It now remains to be seen whether or not Chamberlain can buy off or side with Italy and Germany in such manner as to assure peace and prestige for England. If he cannot, you may be sure that England will strive with might and main to entangle the United States as a militant ally, in which case woe is us.

Edna's announcement that she intended to quit Arthur's employment for a more "creative" job sent him into a tailspin. It could not have come at a worse time. Janice Oliphant was a possible substitute, but she did not know whether she really wanted to leave the shoe factory. Mr. Davis, her boss, had always been a kind and thoughtful employer. Besides, Arthur still regarded her "with critical eyes." The Hollister girl, a newcomer, seemed to be "breaking in nicely," but no one could ever fill Edna's shoes. Her departure made Arthur agonizingly aware of how much she had meant to him and to the others at Garrison Hall. And it was just his luck that Mrs. Banks — already sniping at Janice — should choose this moment to be particularly upsetting and that Billy should ask for a night off once a week.

Arthur knew he could not persuade Edna to stay. He was shortly to write her "history."

February 27 Overcast. Sunday. Streets without traffic have appearance of being wide. Columbus Avenue. Houses that once were fine look more squalid with neglect than houses which never were fine. Negroes living in the houses that once were fine, sauntering the streets with the air of being in their own African village, idling before poolrooms and drugstores. The mansion with the carved lion recumbent before it is now a colored undertaking establishment. Before that it was a religious meeting place. Before that it was empty. The building still beautiful, though soiled. A nurse in black, a child with golden curls, a man wearing a top hat, a woman in silks should be coming down those red sandstone stairs which turn so gracefully, and an equipage with jingling harness should be waiting at the curb. But that is fancy. Down the steps comes a small black negro with oiled hair.

March 2   Edna said: "I've something to tell you, Artie. I hope it won't upset you too much, and I hope you'll understand. I wanted to wait until Dr. Bottomley had finished treating you, as I thought perhaps this would be the most opportune time to tell you. I'm afraid I'm not going to be with you anymore. I have a new job." To myself I said, "Well, here it is, what you've been dreading. No use storming or cajoling. You can tell she means it." At that moment Evelyn came in. "Edna," I said to her, "says that she's got a new job." "Oh my goodness," exclaimed Evelyn.

"I don't want you people," continued Edna, as though reciting by rote a prepared speech, "to think that I'm leaving because I've any fault to find with you. No one could have been nicer to me or nicer to work for, and I can assure you that I'm fond of you both and want, if you will allow me, to stay friendly. It's simply a matter of money. I can't live on my present salary. My daughters are growing up and deserve more than I can at present give them. I must somehow make money. I feel that the capacity to do so is in me. I believe that this is my opportunity. I start my new position on what you are paying me, but the chances to better myself are without limit. I may in time even make ten or twelve thousand dollars a year. So I want to give two weeks' notice. And, believe me, I thank you folks from the bottom of my heart for all you've done for me, and I hope you understand."

I felt a segment of the wall which protects me from the outer world crumbling and knew from my knowledge of Edna that there was nothing I could do about it except accede to the inevitable gracefully. I imagine Evelyn felt the same. "Of course," I said, "we can't raise objections if you find that you can better yourself. To put it bluntly: I am too fond of you not to hope you succeed in making more money. In the second place, it wouldn't do any good for me to object. So I hope your new position will be a pleasant and profitable one." "We both hope it," said Evelyn. "What sort of job is it?" "I'd rather not tell. I know Arthur. He'd play on my emotions and find all sorts of arguments against it, and he has too much ingenuity and I'm too newly arrived at my conclusion, so I'd rather not say. I hope you understand." "I don't," I said, "for if you asked me not to dissuade you and I gave you my promise not to, I would not. But if it's what you want, that's all right." "I'm sorry, but I'd rather not say." "Will you be in Boston?" Evelyn asked. "Oh yes, right where I am. And if I can ever help you out in any way, don't hesitate to call on me. I still owe you some money. You'll get it back as soon as I'm able to repay it." "Don't worry about that, Edna. I only wish I had enough to persuade you to stay. But, since I lost my floating supply in the Market, I haven't. I certainly will miss you. The chief grudge I hold against you is that you've never believed how much you've meant to me and how devoted I've been to you." "Well," said Edna, still skeptical, "that's nice." "You're sure," asked Evelyn, "that you're being wise?" "As sure as anyone can be. Naturally, I'm filled with trepidation and quite scared. It isn't a trifling matter to decide to change from moderate, permanent security to a new position, no matter how secure it may look. I only decided last night. I haven't even told Manuel yet." "Well," I said, "luck to you — and I mean it from the bottom of my heart." "So do I," said Evelyn. "It has meant more to both of us having you than you will ever know."

So that was that. When Edna informed Mrs. Banks of her resolution, Mrs. Banks said, "Oh my God." I told Billy. Billy said, "I can't believe it possible. Why, Edna seemed like part of the furniture — here for good. How can we get along without her? Gosh, I don't like it." Evelyn is upset, but it takes her some time to realize the full implication of things. I am down and out, though. What is the use of being otherwise, smiling? Slept only three hours last night. Woke with Dr. Cass driving a car headlong down a steep spiral hill. He had gone insane. He had drawn a razor and was striving to slash my throat. Evelyn was in the back of the car. I was attempting to steer the car with one hand so that it would not plunge out into space while with the other I was trying futilely to fend off Dr. Cass and his razor.

Edna has meant more to me than she will ever know. She has been Mother Earth to me. Knowing her has altered my character radically. When I think on the rides we have had, will no longer have, I feel bereft. Edna correcting diary with me. Edna in the garden. Edna playing the piano. Edna encouraging me. Six years it has been, if I recollect rightly. It seems longer than that. Why do those you love have to pass out of your life, your intimate life, so abruptly?

Who to get to take Edna's place is going to be a problem. Evelyn says: "We can get along without anyone else; I will do some of the cooking; we could keep our bills paid." "No," I say, "not yet. Not until we have to, until there is no other way, until we can no longer get extra money from Father." First off, I am going to try to find a man. There are too many women around me. I would like a man. However, I doubt the probability of finding a real male for what I will pay—no more than twenty dollars a week, less if possible. If not a man, then whom? Janice Oliphant? If not Janice, perhaps Patricia Caffree? I must have someone who is pliable, willing to jump from one task to another on the instant without losing equanimity. It is too bad that Mrs. Banks dislikes cooking so deeply for then we might get along without a third person. But if she did cook, who would typewrite? I really need a third person both for my own sake and for Evelyn's. He or she must be able to drive well and not object to riding with the windshield open, must be willing to cook, must be able to typewrite and have at least a better than ordinary intelligence, must be willing and able to work in the garden, must be willing to run errands. If he or she can read to me and play the piano, so much the better. Going to be difficult to find someone with adjustable inclinations.

March 3 Snowing once more. Up early before the whiteness begins to cover roofs and yards and streets. Neck very painful again after yesterday's ride. Worrying about being without Edna hasn't helped it any. Saw one man yesterday. He was tall and thin, silent and dumb, bore a sour odor about with him. Another man coming this morning. Will have Edna interview him.

Janice due here tonight. Should I broach the subject to her now or wait until later? Will she want to come? Would her constant lack of physical composure give me the jitters? Would she be too much under the domination of her family? Would she be too moody? Would she be sufficiently accurate typing? One-half of whether anyone will please me or not is dependent upon whether they are devoted to me or not. Janice is. She doesn't mind jumping from one job to another. She has presence. She dresses well and is pleasant to look at.

As I feel now, I'm sure I'll never find anyone to take Edna's place. Evelyn says: "Don't forget how she has irritated you sometimes, how she has smelled, how she has refused to wear a hat to please you, how you have fussed about this and that concerning her." I don't. But I also remember what a psychological comfort she has been to me by and large. My Lord, but I will miss her. I hope that she will not pass out of my life for good and all, as people, once propinquity is broken, have a tendency to do.

March 4 Janice was here last evening. I informed her about Edna and the trouble I was having finding someone to take her place. "Have you got me in mind?" she queried. I proceeded to explain that I wanted a man if possible but thought the chances meager indeed, that I did have her in mind because of her fine qualities and because of her devotion to me. I set forth her good points, also her bad ones as I saw them, and explained what was required insofar as duties were concerned. "Well," she said, "I won't promise to come, for I shouldn't like to go back on my word. I would meet opposition at home. And, Arthur, I'd hate to leave the shoe factory. I've worked there now for five years, day in and day out, and I'm sentimental about the place and the people. On the other hand, I have always had the notion I'd like to work for one man. I know of no man in the world, darling, whom I'd rather work for than you."

Janice is a dear. I don't think I could find anyone better than she. She would be absolutely trustworthy, interested in me and in Evelyn, and would keep her mouth closed almost to the point of being secretive. "Mrs. Banks wouldn't like me, would she?" she inquired, as though expecting the answer her question postulated. "No," I replied, "I'm afraid she wouldn't. She distrusts all women. But she'd probably accept you in time." "I'd put my mind on making her like me." "She's really awfully nice." "I'm sure she must be, or you wouldn't have kept her ten years. I think we'd get along all right."

I think so but am not sure. Mrs. Banks's nature as regards other women is essentially feminine, and she looks with a leery eye at any woman encroaching on what she deems her bailiwick.

March 5   Yesterday afternoon I decided to find out how Mrs. Banks felt about several matters. I said: "Earlier this year you wrote applying for a job, went to see the man, and the job was offered to you. I was stirred up by the prospect of your leaving me. And that is not the first time you have toyed with the idea of another position. What I want to ascertain definitely is this: Do you intend staying on here for two or three more years, or have you any expectation of leaving me for another better job? If there is any such expectation in your mind, I wish you would let me know now, not later, as I would rather make a complete change at this point than half now, half later. If you have any idea of leaving me, I want to be informed of it."

"No, I haven't any hidden expectation of leaving you, if that's what's worrying you. As far as the other job you speak of was concerned, I just wanted to find out if I could write a letter that would bring in a position. I could. That encouraged me. As for taking the place you speak of, I never considered it seriously. Sixty-five dollars a week couldn't pay me to work for a Jew. So just put that worry out of your mind."

I continued: "And now as to someone new coming here. You act as though you were ready to oppose anyone I might choose. I want to ascertain your intentions on that score." "I propose being as agreeable as possible. You've had people before this I didn't like. I endured them, didn't I? Anyway, you probably have your mind made up as to whom you will have. I'm not so dumb that I don't know who it is. If Mrs. Inman can stand your leman, I guess I shouldn't kick." "You have an evil mind, haven't you, Mrs. Banks?" "Well, it's so, isn't it?" "No, it is not. I care more for Edna than for the person of whom you speak. It must make you miserable to have the attitude toward other women that you have." "I got along with Edna, didn't I? And if I don't like the person you get here, I can leave, can't I?" "Yes, you can, and if you decide on that course I only hope you'll do it quick. It's a pity you can't take a more constructive viewpoint. Anyway, I trust that you'll do the best that's in your nature to do. All this business of changing is difficult enough without your acting the prima donna." "I think it's a crime the way you grow to depend on people. And you invariably center on the wrong ones. Now that Edna is going, you expect all the rest of us to leave. Don't be so foolish. And anyway, nobody is so indispensible that they can't be replaced."

"Well," I said, "I couldn't stop being fond of people if I wanted to, and I don't want to. If I get hurt, what of that? At least I don't turn into an old frozen-face. Edna has been here six years, and six years isn't to be pushed aside as nothing." "Oh well," said Mrs. Banks, "you feel as you do, and nothing I can say will make you change. Perhaps there are advantages to your way. Anyway, it's your way."

March 7   Janice had lunch with Evelyn yesterday. I regarded her with critical eyes. She is too eager to be pleasing, the result being that she moves self-consciously, in nervous abrupt jerks. She seems to be always aware of her hands and feet as a growing child would be. She is, nevertheless, both stylish and pretty in a dark, Sicilian way. She has, whenever she is not careful, a strong body odor. Her teeth are white, her chin pointed, her eyes brown and alert, her hair very dark, her nostrils insensitive. "I'd call her," summarizes Evelyn, "pretty in any man's language. She's sweet, too, and stylish." Janice read the writing in this diary haltingly. I don't know about her. I think I shall interview some more people. I saw three yesterday afternoon. Two were impossible. The third, Pearl Hollister by name, nineteen, had a quiet personality. She read my handwriting quickly and fairly well. Hope other applicants come today.

Evelyn tells me that she phoned Mrs. Banks yesterday and asked her to be more careful about upsetting me. I don't believe that Mrs. Banks always realizes how bitter and gloomy she sounds. She has, as she says, no desire to injure me in any way. The rub comes when she doesn't realize how she sounds or how bothered I am — or so I want to think. Anyway, Mrs. Banks seems to be more amenable this morning.

Mrs. Banks just came in. We had a talk. I tried to make clear to her how she sounded, and she tried to reassure me that she had no intention of sounding that way and furthermore did not feel as I said she sounded. So now I believe that we are again on our usual friendly basis. She has a temper and I have a temper, and I swear I will not write about her again while angry, and again I have done it. But I suppose a percipient reader by this time knows all about how I feel toward her and she toward me. I am of the opinion that she cares more about me with her little finger than Edna cares about me with her whole self. I told Mrs. Banks that. She seemed pleased. Mrs. Banks nurses an erroneous conviction that I am a babe in arms where perceiving the faults of those I am unusually fond of is concerned. She misses the point, as I tried to explain to her. I perceive the faults but see no use in mulling them over to myself or in acknowledging them to others. The very fact that I am fond of a person endows that person in my eyes with a certain immunity. Does the deeply moved Catholic acknowledge to himself that the image of the Virgin has blotched paint on her cheeks? He may be cognizant of the fact, but does he admit it to himself? By such an admission he would lose all or part of his faith, and he does not want to lose his faith.

March 9   Edna and I had a fine ride on this cold clear day, the longest I have taken for many weeks. I know why I enjoy having her around. She is calming. She will say, "Now, Artie, what's the use of getting riled about that? Just rest easy. It will all work out." Or, "Don't get excited. I'll fix it for you. Worrying won't mend it any sooner." She reassures me. Billy is jerky, Evelyn is erratic, Mrs. Banks is temperamental, but Edna is calm, and she somehow transmits her calmness to me, as much as anyone can transmit calmness to me. I shall miss her sorely when she goes.

I have just been interviewing Pearl Hollister. "The blond duplicate," Evelyn says, "of Edna." A big girl, not very well educated but gentle and friendly. Edna likes her.

March 11   The Hollister girl is breaking in nicely. Each time I see her I like her better. She is taller than Edna, weighs a hundred and sixty pounds, dresses attractively. She has plucked eyebrows, hazel eyes, an aquiline nose. Her mouth and lips (a bit of toughness about them, lack of breeding) are her poorest features. She drove me this morning. A good driver. As we passed the Great Atlantic & Pacific Tea Company, she remarked, "My father works there. He's a whole-sale salesman." Her speech is deplorable, few "g's" on her "ing's" and many "no's" for "any's." However, that is of little conse-quence, and she is young enough to learn. Her smile and her ap-proach are agreeable. She woolgathers at times. Altogether, I like her and doubt if we could do better. She is to be paid fifteen dollars a week. She may never learn to be of the assistance Edna has been with my diaries, but they are fairly up-to-date and I can't expect every-thing for fifteen dollars. Anyway, says the pessimist in me, she may not wear well.

Edna: "I didn't like you at all when I first came. I thought you were terribly conceited and didn't realize that it was just your de-fense complex manifesting itself. Mrs. Inman seemed such a scared little rabbit that I didn't know whether I liked her or not. As soon as I began to comprehend that you had an inferiority feeling just like myself, I commenced to like you. But I was sore as hell because you cheated me about money, making me pay my carfare to bring greens in to you. I haven't forgotten that yet, as a matter of fact. I got to like Evelyn gradually. I've enjoyed it here, although it has been terrifi-cally trying at times. I don't think Evelyn likes me. I think you like me in a way, while in a way you don't. I like you. I don't love you. I can't weigh my feelings for people like so much flour on scales. I'll miss you. I imagine I'll marry Manuel when the two years the law makes him stay single after his divorce are over. I've lived a lot in my thirty-one years, Artie. Do you wonder I feel ancient and above petty disturbances at times?"

March 12 Pearl Hollister is a likeable girl. She seems to have taken a fancy to us. I enjoy having large people about me. She appears to be anxious to please. Edna and Mrs. Banks are working hard to establish a proper psychological attitude in her mind toward me and toward the job. Mrs. Banks is outdoing herself to be pleas-ant and to be encouraging. She's like me: Get her in a bad enough box and her best qualities shine. She said: "Artie, you and I scrap, you and Peters may scrap, but it is well to remember that sometimes your best friends are the ones with whom you fight the most." I'd never thought of it in just that way. As Eddie used to say: "There's more truth than friction in it."

Janice Oliphant was here last evening. I don't believe that she would do for this position. She is too anxious, not precisely to please, but rather to be pleasing. Her feelings would constantly be hurt and I would as constantly have to bolster her up.

Edna has told me about her prospective job. I didn't miss my guess by a centimeter. I told Evelyn that it would be advertising, that it would be with a Jew, and I even wondered if she would work with Henry Green. You remember that Henry went into business — before he reassumed his job at Summerfield's — with a Jewish girl. Her name was Bella Berg (naked name) and both Henry and Naomi considered her smart and up-and-coming. Well, it seems that Henry has sold out his interest in the free-lance advertising agency to Bella. Bella has been searching for an assistant. She went to the same art school that Edna did. She offered Edna the position for twenty dollars a week, with two raises promised. "I didn't feel," elucidated Edna, "that I could turn the proposition down. On that job I will have a chance to exercise my creative talent and advance myself financially at the same time." "What if there's a depression coming, a still bigger one?" I asked. "She probably couldn't weather it. Has she any capital?" "Oh, yes. She told me she had." "How much?" "She didn't tell me, naturally, but I guess it's enough." "And you're willing to take the chance of not knowing?" "Yes." "Do you like her?" "Very much. She's a worker."

I mused aloud, "Another Anglo-Saxon mortgaging his soul to a Jew." "They, the Jews, are the only people," asserted Edna, "who are getting along these days. They like us for fronts. Every Jew wants a Nordic for a front." I continued to muse: "And they become more and more cocky about it. And by and by they become too arrogant and too successful and step too hard on the necks of the people they have subjected. And then those people rise up and kill the Hebrews and dispossess them of what they have taken by hard work and artifice and lack of scruples. It has been history throughout the ages." "Well?" said Edna. "Oh, nothing," I said, "I was just thinking out loud. With the best side of me I hope you are successful and that you make your twelve thousand a year. With my other side I hope you get enough of Jews in short order and come back here to me." "Jews have always treated me well," stated Edna. So that was that. If business gets better, Edna should, under an energetic boss, do well. If times become worse, it wouldn't surprise me to see her back here. I'll bet Bella Berg works the pants off her. God, I'd hate to be under a Jew.

March 13 When Edna kissed me goodbye, her dark green eyes filled and blood rushed up into her cheeks. She was moved. So was I. I wanted to have a wailing wall to make a noise against. Instead, I suppose I wore my usual poker face.

Billy's long bout of flu and pneumonia and Mrs. Banks's ankle sprain deprived Arthur of their services and multiplied his anxieties as he exhausted himself interviewing candidates for Edna's position. And then when Billy came back to work, he again had the gall to demand vacation time and a night off every other week. As for "the Hollister girl"—young, ignorant, distracting ("she is just about the sweetest thing there ever was. I call her 'Honey'")—she clearly lacked the education to handle secretarial assignments. Moreover, she was an ill-bred country hoyden whose speech set his teeth on edge. But she was valuable in other ways. What to do?

Arthur vacillated about whether to keep Honey. Could he afford Honey and Janice? Could he persuade Janice to come aboard? Was she capable enough? Evelyn thought so but not Mrs. Banks. Her persistent innuendoes against Janice and her officiousness (who was hiring whom anyway?) led to what in effect was really a dismissal, although Arthur in the flush of his self-exoneration blamed the sad denoument on Mrs. Banks's refusal to ratify in words an agreement to be gracious to Janice. Billy objected to Arthur's oblique tactics and stood up for Mrs. Banks until Arthur overwhelmed him with arguments and blandishments. After rejecting a number of applicants, Arthur settled on Janice.

All through this trying period, he grew increasingly splenetic over the Boston subway construction—offensive to his ears and eyes—and the Roosevelt government bent upon sapping the "Nordic" foundations of the republic. He reserved his special abuse for the president's Jewish and Irish hirelings.

Arthur's anti-Semitic and anti-ethnic outbursts—directed mainly at "vicious Mediterranians," dark-skinned people, Jews, and Irish— rose and fell according to his state of mind. When unthreatened economically or politically, he could entertain cordial feelings toward individual members of these groups. When stocks were down, when he was reminded of the personal costs exacted by the welfare state, when he saw "shiftless" W.P.A. louts resting on their shovels, when the ethnics took on the airs of "white" Americans, his Diary crackled with hate.

Some time before, after conceding that he ought to revise his low opinion of Jews, he launched an especially virulent assault against all Jews— good and bad—with the possible exception of that "eminently sane Jew," the columnist George Sokolsky.[4] *"Hebraic traits," declared Arthur, contaminated "the very headwaters of our nature." Sorry for*

---

[4] George E. Sokolsky (1893–1962), author, lecturer, industrial consultant, and newspaper columnist, started out as an enthusiastic supporter of the "Soviet experiment," but his newspaper days in the U.S.S.R. and China turned him into an apologist for capitalism. From the outbreak of World War II until Pearl Harbor, he opposed American aid to England and Russia and called for friendly relations with Japan.

*themselves, the Jews "transmitted to our Anglo-Saxon minds a like
sentimental concern for downtrodden groups" and "induced into our
veins this poison of altruism toward, pity for, charity in the case of the
underdog," thereby blanching "our fortitude and ambition and our
certainty of superiority."*

*Arthur later repudiated these views, but in moments of crisis and
stress, his prejudices were likely to surface.*

March 13 [P.M.] Mrs. Cash read to me in the evening. "Have
you ever met Billy's Sadie?" I asked. "Why yes, Mr. Inman, I have
met her." "What is she like?" "You'd tell Billy if I gave you my
opinion." "No." A little persuasion and she opened up. I felt not
exactly as though I were being above the surface with Billy. "I'll tell
you, Mr. Inman," said Mrs. Cash with the air of a beldam at a church
social unfolding something choice. "Billy is such a nice boy that I
hate to have him tied up to Sadie. Sadie is a mama's girl. She once
informed me that she 'couldn't go anywhere without Mama.' I told
her that I had hated the very dirt my mother stepped upon and that I
had scratched her face and run away when I was fourteen and hadn't
even gone to her funeral when she died but went to a party instead.
That shocked her. It's my frank opinion that Sadie and her mama
pulled a fast one on Billy and hooked him in. Of course that is only
my opinion. Sadie isn't very bright in the head. She admits to being
thirty-six or -seven. If I know women at all—and God knows I've
had plenty to do with them—Sadie will never see forty again,
perhaps not forty-five. I feel sure that she has undergone her change
of life. She'll never give Billy any children. He'll tire of her soon, I
feel sure. I understand she throws tantrums. Billy will be looking
around before long—you mark my words—for another girl. And
if he wants me to help him find one, I will, and gladly. He's a
handsome boy, and he's beginning to grow up."

So held forth the Old Outhouse. I felt like washing my ears when
she was done, despised myself for listening. But nevertheless there
certainly is something dopey about this Billy, Sadie and Mama
business. Evelyn says, "Sadie is coarse to my way of thinking. But I
don't believe that she's over thirty-seven or so. Her mother is one of
those dumb but jolly and kindly people of the servant type." I am
curious to watch how the marriage will turn out. Billy is becoming
less strict in his Catholicism all the time.

March 14 Took a ride on this fine overcast day out along the
Charles River with Pearl. She certainly is a nice girl. She drives a car
better than either Billy or Edna. She is pretty. No one yelled at us,
perhaps because she is pretty. Except for her lack of education, I

wouldn't be at all surprised if we have a treasure. Edna met her father and liked him. Pearl spent the weekend on her grandfather's farm. She went in the woods and helped set traps. I hope that she likes us and stays. The first two days she was here, when she smiled she showed two undeveloped teeth, which took away from her looks somewhat. "My mother had teeth just like them. So had my grandmother." Saturday morning she arrived with caps the dentist had made for them. Now she has as fine a set of teeth as anyone could wish. What dentists can do approaches the incredible. As I have said and will probably say again, she is a pretty girl.

Manuel cooked my meals for me yesterday. He has taken on an older look than when I first knew him. He is thirty-one now, a bit younger than Edna. His skin is swarthy. He is short. His hair is parted in the middle and is crinkly curly. His teeth are self-evidently boughten ones. His eyes are dark brown and bright. He is forever smoking. He struts his chest slightly as so many small men do. He has a habit of studying people from the corners of his eyes. He could not be more considerate of me. Edna had coached him as to how to cook and what plates to use. He did very well. He is a confirmed Roosevelt admirer. "I don't think anyone couldda done better under the circumstances." He resigned last year from the National Guard. "Too many youngsters coming in." He studies tactics and weapons. A gangster by nature, held in check by Edna in practice, he is a lost person. In a war, he might be a hero.

Mrs. Cash read to me last evening. What a cesspool of a mind she has. I said: "I'm sort of tired tonight, Mrs. Cash; perhaps I'd best read my 'Astounding Stories.'" "Just as you wish, Mr. Inman," she said. "Just as you wish. They're nonsense to my way of thinking, but if you want them you shall have them." What a woman — peppermint and slop and red meat and saccharine and filth and a spiritual odor that stinks to high heaven.

Evelyn mothers Dr. Pike. He kicks like a steer against it and loves it. Theirs is a fine friendship. She wants to go to Harvard to visit him next summer. So why not? Dr. Pike is good to her in a fatherly, platonic way. He likes whimsy and she likes whimsy, and they enjoy each other. She goes to supper with him Wednesday.

March 16 In Europe the pot is boiling at a great rate. I strive to be impartial in my reporting of the news, but the fact is undeniable that I always favor the aggressor nations, believing wholeheartedly that those peoples and those nations who are aggressive are most admirable. I may be sympathetic with 'the underdogs,' but my cheers go out to those who whirl the most effective ax. This certainly is not my English ancestry speaking, certainly is not my Philadelphia sporting training. It must come to me direct from my Scotch clansmen forbears. Nor am I in the least ashamed of feeling as I do; it seems to me the only sane way to feel. I am all on the side of the Japanese, all for Hitler and Franco and Mussolini. That doesn't mean that I should fancy being a German or an Italian. Far from it. If I were a German I should in all probability detest Hitler, even as I despise Roosevelt. As long as the behavior of the 'top dogs' doesn't touch me, and only that long, do I admire them and their behavior.

March 19   Manuel said: "I study everything I can get my hands on about military matters. We'll have a war yet — you wait and see. When we do, I want to be so situated that they'll need me to teach and I won't have to go to the front." Manuel said: "I read a lot. I read anything I can get my hands on that I like. I never notice who the author is. I just read." Manuel said: "I been washing clothes all day, doing some cooking, sweeping up, minding the kids." There must be thousands upon thousands of men in Boston alone doing the cooking, minding the babies, taking care of the housework, while their wives and their women go out and earn the living for the family. Unnatural.

Pearl certainly is pretty. She may say "a" and "er" every three words, she may shy away from literature like a horse from white paper, she may use farm American, but she is thoroughly and undeniably pretty. Her hair is blonde and soft, gold-colored in certain lights. Her eyes are hazel, mild and merry. She has practically no eyebrows to speak of and pencils a pair on with a new curve each day. Her nose is properly aquiline. Her chin is firm. She uses no rouge. Her teeth are white and her tongue is very red. When she smiles, her too-full lips draw out into most alluring lines. She has a well-proportioned shape and dresses with considerable artistry and in well-chosen clothes. She is both clean and neat. As Evelyn says, it is almost worthwhile having her around just to look at. She is willing, cheerful, full of fun. When her face is composed, the features are heavy, even at times immature. However, she is rarely without a smile, and when she smiles she is something special to cast your eyes upon. She reminds me in some intangible way of Katinka, only that Katinka was never so playful. I hope that Billy doesn't fall for her too hard. She did some copying for me from the 'Haverford College Weekly' and did it well. "I love to eat," she says. "That's one of my failin's. But how I love it." I asked her if she liked the boys. Oh, I like some of 'em. I go out lots. If I don't like 'em, I tell 'em so. I say: 'I don't like your style, but if you still want to take me out, that's okay by me.' And usually they do. You can't talk that way to the boys you like, though. They just walk off. Anyway, you don't want to tell 'em you don't like 'em if you do, do you?"

I wanted to go to Bernard's Elm to calm down and be alone. When all is said, there's no company like my own. I renew my fortitude from inside, not from outside.

March 26   The Rat's latest idea is to allow "the oppressed minorities" of all nations refuge in the United States. Jews from Germany, from Austria, from Russia to be permitted asylum here. No matter that there is not enough work for the people already in the United States. Let more of the damned Semitics in to take more jobs away from white people. And that crazy Hull, whose one sane idea in a welter of idealism is that foreign trade should be restored, reinforces the Rat's noble gesture to the "downtrodden." I should think that every foreign nation in the world would be scornful of us. We butt into every nation's business, issue ultimatums everyone knows we will not reinforce by arms, talk and talk and talk, admonish and lecture and slap on the wrist, bungle our own affairs and continue to tell others how to handle theirs, accept the grossest insults to our property and prestige without demur. And now we will allow more Jews into our already Jew-ridden country, whereas it is Hebrew ways of thinking predominate to the confusion of all men of action and all native Anglo-Saxon virility.

I see by the paper that the Mexicans, having preempted our oil, will now sell to the Japanese who have hitherto been buying in California, so that we will suffer doubly by the Mexican expropriation, suffer in meek and acceptive silence. Ugh, has Roosevelt, have the Jews deprived us of all manhood, when even the greasers can put it over on us with impunity?

March 29   Yesterday died one of the evil geniuses of this nation, Colonel E.M. House, the power behind Woodrow Wilson. He was pro-English, being the son of an Englishman. He advised Wilson, and Wilson acted. He was the chief tool in America of England during the World War. He carried on secret negotiations with England prior to our entry into the World War. No doubt he had much to do with the abandonment of our policy of isolation and our entry into the War on the side of the Allies. He had much to do with the drawing up of that abortion, the Versailles Treaty and, if I remember rightly, with the formation of the League of Nations.

The longer I live, the more profoundly am I impressed by the power of one individual to sway history. Truths, lies, deceptions, semitruths — it makes no difference. A master-man utters them, and we hear them as clarion notes and follow. Lincoln said: "Shoot low, not high." Hitler says: "Repeat and repeat and repeat." It is like Americans listening to an opera in Italian or French, not understanding a word, swept away by the emotions engendered by how the words are sung. Utter simple words, repeat them over and over until they become either meaningless from repetition or are sunk into the subconscious mind of the thing, and the crowds will follow.

March 31   I am running into debt again. The man downstairs was $50 behind on his last rent, so we kicked him out. We are now searching for a new roomer. My doctors' bills, try as I may, don't diminish. Dividends are smaller than last year. It is incredible that expenditures can add up so swiftly — two bottles of vitamin pills, a new switch for the light, a new dish, a paper of needles, new pillow cases, always taxes and interest due, something always broken on the Pierce, gasoline, vegetables, bread, fish, cream, butter, shoes, pajamas, notebook paper, typewriters repaired, laundry, seeds and coal for Bernard's Elm, rugs and clothing cleaned, electric and gas bills, soap, brushes, pictures enlarged, books and fines from lending libraries, newspapers and magazines, glue, ink, ads in newspapers and so on, on and on.

April 1   I have a feeling that the crippled monomaniac who is apparently willing to tear down the complicated structure of America in order that he may rule has reached, unless he gets us into a war, the zenith of his power and prestige. Perhaps I have had that feeling before, and it did not materialize. Perhaps it is only wishful thinking. And yet what is there to make the downfall of President Roosevelt impossible? Down he may not come, but down he can come.

April 10   [From Patricia:]

I'm relieved to find that you dont regard me as a "fallen woman," I was a bit worried, as I didn't know how you would take my assorted male appendages. The last & present woman's home companion is about to celebrate his second year in my company, he still seems content to be around, no visible straining at the leash. And goodness knows what I'd do without him. I can't go about wearing crepe for Sean indefinitely. Tho I would if I thought it would get him back. So — since I can't have what I really want I shall try to be satisfied with "second best." We Caffrees have had to do that so often during our lives Molly started calling us "second besters."

Jerry Norton is the one I now lavish with my maternal affections. But I'm darned if I let him know I like to mother him — He is aggressively male, a strange object in this land of fairies. And as tactless as a five year old. Simply has no social graces, and is always putting his foot in it. But I rather like his downright honesty even if it does make my hair curl at times. He thinks I'm swell because I helped him over a few bad financial difficulties. But good Lord thats what money is for, and goodness knows it won't do us any good to hold on to the few dollars that would get someone out of a hole.

For the past few weeks we have been combing the San Fernando Valley for an acre of ground with a small house on it. And last week we found just the thing Jerry wanted. He craves to start a truck garden & raise rabbits. He used to do that in Florida. His home is in Tampa.

The place we found is twenty minutes from Hollywood. A corner acre with a five room house, more like a summer camp but it can be fixed up nicely. A one room studio shack, a garage, rabbit and chicken houses and four enormous pepper trees, also a barbecue pit. The whole place has been neglected so Jerry got it for twenty five dollars a month. He moved out two days ago and with furniture in the place it is very cosy. But colder than perdition at night. The house isnt too well built of course, and it has no heat since Jerry's heaters are gas and the house has just electricity. But he is going to a second hand shop and get one of those old fashioned pot-bellied wood stoves for the kitchen, it has an electric cooking range.

April 11   Mrs. Cash read 'The Hidden Lincoln' last night, and a book about fishes and a book by a Communist who went to Russia from the United States and became disillusioned. Later on, in the middle of the night when I couldn't sleep, I listened to [Lytton] Strachey's 'Elizabeth and Essex' on the talking-book.

'The Hidden Lincoln' is one of those volumes which influences me. I am fascinated by the way it is written, by the vigor of Herndon's abrupt style, by his flashes of percipience. I am so fundamentally repelled by Lincoln that I want to find out everything I can about him. He could be kind when it cost him nothing, but his ambition allowed him to be ruthlessly cold. He was, it seems to me, always cold underneath. He lived with ideas, not with flowers and bright skies. A fascinating figure, capable of writing beautiful flowing English one minute, of telling vulgar brothel stories the next. When a man asked him why he didn't write a book containing all his stories, Lincoln replied: "Such a book would stink like a thousand privies."

Six feet, four inches tall, strong as an ox, small gray eyes, heavy thatch of untidy hair, superstitious, shy, reticent, having a movement only once a week, walking with flat feet, believing himself a force impelled by nature, selfishly ambitious, approachable to a certain point and coldly unapproachable beyond that point, a politi-

cian of the first water, an irritating aloof husband, an overindulgent
parent, kindly when it interfered not at all with his career, so sure of
himself that he dared use his enemies when they were gifted, an ape
of a man with the face of a simian, a tragic figure from the Book of
Destiny, a vulgar clown, a hybrid molded of slime and granite, a sad
and appealing caricature of the genus homo sapiens. That this weird
and secret being, hardly human and more than human, should have
become the mythical apotheosis of ideal Americanism is nothing
short of incredible. Lincoln, shorn of his earthy faults, his earthy
virtues, polished and refined and made sacrosanct by men's unsuspicious and earnest minds, became the idol and the ideal of the
people, the great American.

April 13   One hour's sleep last night because of subway noises.
Evelyn has gone downtown to see Sullivan about the noise at night
and how it may be alleviated. The 'Herald' has refused to take my ad
for a secretary, and Evelyn is also seeing the man in control of that,
likewise an Irishman, Donovan by name. Some woman kicked
about the dark the last time I advertised. And so it goes. Evelyn is
very sweet about it all. She came upstairs and talked to me for an
hour last night when I couldn't sleep. Dr. Pike is to have supper with
her tonight. Last evening she saw Claudette Colbert and Gary Cooper in the movies. Tomorrow night she leaves for Washington. She
looks very well this spring. I love her greatly.

April 15   Pearl inquired whether I liked her or not. "I certainly
do," I said. "You are a sweet girl, as far as I know honest, industrious
save where it concerns your intellect, willing, pretty, clean, winning.
If only you were ambitious to learn, you would be a first-grade
person." "Oh my," she said. I am paying Mrs. Cash to give her some
lessons in grammar and literature. The man who gets Pearl for a wife
will be lucky indeed. I might wish she didn't smoke so much, but
that, I take it, in these days and times is no sin save that it causes an
unpleasant breath and nicotine fingers. I am fond of her as one
would be of an attractive child. "I feel paternal toward you," I said
to her. "What's 'paternal'—huh?" she asked.

April 16   Roosevelt sent a message to Congress on Thursday
demanding approximately five billion dollars with which to 'pump-
prime' the nation back to prosperity again. The same evening he
delivered a 'fireside chat' to the great American public. I listened.
Had you not heard a dozen previous speeches on the same subject in
the same convincing voice, you might have listened more gullibly.
As it was, you yawned and exclaimed "Yeah?" and went to sleep.
He's tried it all before, has Roosevelt, and look where we are now.
What sense trying it all over again? It cost some eighteen billions

before. God knows what it would cost again. 'Works Progress Administration,' 'Farm Security Administration,' 'National Youth Administration,' 'Civilian Conservation Corps,' 'Public Works Administration,' highway aid, flood control and reclamation, new Federal buildings, 'United States Housing Authority' and so on, down the long lists of spigots stuck in the body of thrift and diligence to suckle the avid mouths of the lazy and the worthless.

April 18 I was awake all night with the beams banging and rattling on Huntington Avenue. One foreman told Billy that Sullivan had given orders to put horses where they would deflect the traffic. The night foreman would not cooperate. The bastards aren't scared of losing their jobs. They obey nobody, do no work, are contemptuous of those who support them. I fume in my spirit when I think upon what four years of Hoover and five years of Roosevelt have brought to pass in this nation, the foundation of the ruination of the character of a people.

Saw the Cash woman as I came in from my ride with Billy this morning. Hair white. Reminds me of a ferret or of a strong-swimming fish. Could go insane under proper stimuli. Very short. Moves in jerks. Her walk is nearly a run. Strange sort of creature. Says nearly died of heart stopping the other night. Lives on one meal a day. Afraid of obesity. "I think Lincoln was a gorgeous man. I'd like to have swapped smutty stories with him." Mrs. Cash scorns imagination and whimsicality in any form. "I threw away twenty-five cents on that goddamn 'Snow White and the Seven Dwarfs.' What silliness." And again: "I never had any imagination, and I don't want any. You can't earn your living from thirteen on and retain imagination. That's for people of leisure — like yourself, Mr. Inman." Meet the word "ass" in a book and Mrs. Cash goes into convulsions of laughter. She is out of Chaucer's time. She is tutoring Pearl for me. She certainly is good to me.

April 20 A girl. One year out of Vassar. Face crooked. Had had operation on eyes to uncross them. Had dived into shallow pool and hurt neck. Had fallen off horse. Had had pneumonia. Had spent a summer in Heidelberg. Disgusted with colleges in general as being places for political discussion and country clubs rather than of learning. Jewish descent yet a Nazi sympathizer. Wants to write for a career. Talked abruptly. Pretty ankles. Temperament but no special brains, although she thought so. Wanted the job. Didn't want her. Her father a buyer in Raymond's (cut-rate) Store.

April 23 I told Pearl I was going to let her go and why. "Well now, Mr. Inman," she said, "you've had your say. I wanna have mine. I like you, I like Mrs. Inman, I like Billy and Mrs. Banks and I like my job. I don't want to leave. I'm sure I can please you. You haven't given me a chance to do any work for you lately. Isn't it fair for you to give me a chance to show you what I can do before you dismiss me? I'm readin' three nights a week now. I can learn to say 'com*ing*' and 'go*ing*'—I know I can. I want you to give me the chance to show you I can. Will you? It's only fair." And she smiled that wide pleasing smile of hers, and there was color in her cheeks, and I was put back on my haunches in spite of myself.

So what could I do? "You don't talk enough," I said. "I'll learn to talk," she stated. "I can please you — I know I can. Only give me the chance. You will — won't you?" "Gosh," I said, "you have my number. Sure I'll give you a chance. What else can I do when you put it that way? I like you. You please me. If you can stop saying 'was' for 'were' within three or four days, I'll believe that you mean what you say. If not — well —" "I'll show you," she said, and smiled again. Lord, but she is pretty at times. All this, be it noted, is against my better judgment. She is a distraction, and both herself and her looks take my attention from work. But what can I do? I'm really very easy to handle, and Pearl seems to know by nature how to handle me. I'm not so sure I like it either. Or perhaps it is that I like it but not the distraction from my chief ambition in life.

April 25   Was discouraged with Janice yesterday. Told Pearl that if I decided to keep her she must be classified as a chauffeur in order to avoid social insurance, not smoke while on the job, read a book a week. I said that I would add two dollars a week and she would put in two dollars to go for educational purposes as I saw fit. She agreed to everything save the book a week. She said that she would stay until she was married. She told Mrs. Banks Saturday that "I couldn't find a job ever anywhere that would suit me like this one does." We'll see how she drives while Billy is away on his vacation next week.

May 6   Roosevelt has gone fishing on the cruiser 'Philadelphia' off Puerto Rico, and a pretty item of expense that will be out of the taxpayers' pockets. He may yowl to the underprivileged about being the friend of the underprivileged, but boy, do he and his family use his exalted position to cut a swathe. A private yacht at the expense of the taxpayers, all servants and household expenses paid, a private train in which to make campaign tours, battleships to fish from, a private guard to watch over him, no income taxes, one son marrying a Du Pont and the other son working for Hearst, the Mrs. R. selling her books, her time on the radio, her speeches to clubs, articles to newspapers, and so on and so on. Son James becomes rich selling insurance to those who want to stand in well with the Government. Hey-ho. I suppose that if a man has had to sell his immortal soul to gain political office, the least he can do before he fries in hell (unless hell is myth and the efficiently unrighteous prosper, which latter tenet history at least seems to verify) is to make use of the perquisites and emoluments and grafts that go with office.

May 7   And now Evelyn has just come upstairs to say that Father, wearing cotton stockings to economize, has arrived. He wants to smoke a cigar before he comes up. He sent me some tuberose rhizomes. I feel better this year and don't dread him so much. I opened the letter from Beatrice Grim to him, as I wanted to ascertain what was afoot. I have no scruples regarding my parent. If he ever dies, I shall most certainly contest his will and attempt to gain control of the estate, though probably he will have it tied so tight that I can't touch it.

May 10   I want Janice on this job. Mrs. Banks is so sure that some sort of woe will befall me if I have her that it gives me to pause. She is perfectly calm about it at times, not rancorous nor belligerent. As she says, she is not infallible in her judgment, but one cannot help being impressed by the persistence and gloominess of that judgment. That Janice can assist me with my work I am sure. That she can drive I am fairly sure. That she can talk to me I know. That she bores me often I am aware.

I have always found her willing and anxious to perform personal services for me. She is neat and clean and has acceptable social manners. She is as discreet and as shut-mouthed as anyone could wish, so that my business will remain my business. She is loyal. She likes to work. There is nothing coarse about her. She is directly descended, if that means anything, from the Dukes of Marlborough. It is all a gamble. Well, there are times when I am a gambler.

May 13   Small ride this morning. Hay smells odorous in the sun and wind. Billy said: "I went to church last night. It was crowded and I had to sit down front, right under the priest's nose. I didn't pay no attention to what he said. I just watched him attentive-like, as if he was a man and not somebody sacred. You know, you've had a great influence on me, makin' me see both sides of this religion business. Two years ago I'd have swallowed everythin' whole. As I said, I scrutinized him close. He didn't seem to have no real interest in what he was sayin'. It was mechanical. I was disappointed. Do you s'pose I'm growin' up? I still like the ceremony, but I'm gettin' to realize that when all is said it's me what orders life, not a priest or the Catholic Church. I've you to thank for that." I warned Billy not to forget that any church has some good in it. The way he joined the church was very simple. One day he wandered into a service and liked the ceremonial aspect and joined up. "Nobody put no pressure on me."

May 15   I certainly do miss Edna. Reports come that she likes her new job and is working day and night. Will her interest lag soon? I notice that magazine advertising is on the decrease. Very soon, unless conditions improve, newspaper advertising should diminish in volume. I wish something would happen to put Edna back here. That is one reason I have delayed committing myself to Janice.

May 16   I have just finished an unusual book about Japan, 'Children of the Rising Sun' by Willard Price. The book makes you consider a number of matters. Here are we, the richest people in the world, retiring from our conquests, abandoning the Philippines, removing our troops from Haiti and Nicaragua, allowing Mexico to preempt our property unrebuked by force. And there are the Japanese, crusading, out to conquer the East and perhaps, in time, the world, recking nothing of paucity of numbers, of a land poor in natural resources, of the opposition of the world. Their star, it would seem, is rising; ours is declining. Yet we have infinitely more advantages and resources at our command, at least in a physical and financial sense, than has Japan. But we have lost our spirit, our sense of manifest destiny, the basic ethical force without which a civilization is doomed to retrogression. How anyone can put a halt to Japan at this juncture I cannot see. They are on the march, the Japanese, as surely as were the hosts of Genghis Khan, and with as much assurance that the world is theirs for the taking.

This week's 'Life' has pictures of the atrocities committed on the Chinese by the Japanese. And if so, what? It is part of the Asiatic method of warfare. And I sometimes wonder if our idealistic anger against atrocities is not unnatural. Maybe we are too effete to commit atrocities (in which case our tale is truly told), but I doubt it. Atrocities are not pleasant, to be sure, but they have always been an implicit accompaniment of inspired warfare. Each American values his separate life to an extent any Japanese would find difficult to comprehend. The less one values life, the easier to inflict death and atrocities on others, especially when those others are enemies. I do not excuse the Japanese, for I am American, but I do understand their actions.

I should like to be a Japanese at this juncture in history. I admire their ethical background, their efficiency, their world dream more than I do my own people, fat with luxury and laziness, with a dim and hypocritical code to reinforce them, with a wavering efficiency, with a vanishing dream.

May 20   Mrs. Banks and Billy don't like Janice, and it looks as though if I want to keep them I'll have to bow to their prejudices. We could save fifteen dollars a week by having nobody, I suppose, and Mrs. Banks and Billy could do more work. If they don't want

Janice, I know of no one else right now. I shall miss Pearl, but also I shall be relieved of a distraction that has taken my strength. I hate to be put in a box by Mrs. Banks and Billy. It makes me lose respect both for them and for myself.

May 23 The Old Outhouse finished Confucius' life last night. Another man who died with his dreams unfulfilled and with no realization of the fame the future had in store for him.

There has been considerable excitement in the papers over the possible war in Europe that might be brought on by German invasion of Czechoslovakia. The Czech Government, on news that the Germans were mobilizing soldiers on the frontier, called out their troops and manned the fortifications. This was accomplished, so experts state, with speed and efficiency. It now appears that the Germans were given pause, so that perhaps another European crisis is past. They do things now exactly as they did them in the Middle Kingdom twenty-four hundred years ago.

May 24 "Thought," writes Dos Passos somewhere, "is the acid that corrodes." Thought, in the Jewish form, is deadly to the Anglo-Saxon. I am sure of that. The Jews can stand up under thought. We disintegrate when we come to the place where we believe in our hearts that we must advance a reason for every action. It seems terrible when Hitler causes Semitic books to be burnt. And yet is it? When Germans think along patterns set forth by Hebrews, they become shorn of force. All luck to Hitler.

June 1 Have been talking with Billy all morning. I asked him directly what he would do should I have Janice and should Mrs. Banks put into effect her threats and leave. I told him that of course I didn't want Mrs. Banks to go, but that she had made all sorts of statements which she might live up to. I told him that I was paying Mrs. Banks and didn't intend being bossed by her against my best judgment and my inclinations. What would he do if she left? "Nothin'," he said. "After all, it wouldn't concern me directly. But I'm sure you'd miss Mrs. Banks." "Of course I would. I don't want her to go. But neither do I want to be bossed. I'd miss her like the devil. I don't think she'd go. In the first place, I'm fond of her and she's fond of me, and her bite isn't as bad as her bark, usually. In the second place, this job, while it doesn't pay excessively, just suits her temperament. But if she did go, that wouldn't concern you?" "No. I always try to be fair. I'm working for you." "Thank you, Billy, that's all I wanted to know. And please understand, it isn't that I have anything against Mrs. Banks or that I want her to go. I want her to stay. But from the way she talks she may go."

I verily believe that Mrs. Banks's catty attitude has made me want

Janice all the more. Mrs. Banks—and she didn't mean this part as being catty—warned me that Evelyn would be jealous of Janice. She advised me not to tell Evelyn. I thought that all foolishness. I laid the matter before Evelyn. Evelyn wants me to have Janice. So there at present the matter stands. Where it will end no one knows. You might think to hear Billy and Mrs. Banks talk that Janice was a deep-dyed villainess.

June 15   Bottom said: "You know young John Roosevelt, the one who's to marry, the President's son? Well, I have a patient who knows a woman who is the best friend of Anne Clark's chauffeur's wife. The other day the chauffeur was driving John and another boy somewhere. The boy asked John if there was anything to the rumors that his father was going to run for a third term. 'No, indeed he isn't,' John said. 'You may not know it, but my father's a very sick man, both mentally and physically.'"

June 16   If I were well and strong, I'd run away from this muddle the world is in and retire to the sea or to the deep woods, or I would gather together a secret society to terrorize the politicians, the Jews, the Irish and the renegade Americans. The fear of God and of the Anglo-Saxons should be put into them. I would be a reactionary revolutionary. I hate our rulers with a deep-rooted ire. All government is rascally, but ours is especially despicable. Tar and feather a couple of hundred of the politicos and they'd walk a more considerate way. And if a secret society in league against them turned rough and got out of hand, what of that? Meet fire with fire. Christ Almighty, I hate our overlords.

The whole New Deal is Hebraic in conception. Prosperity never comes from penalizing the rich to pander to the poor, the lazy, the indigent, the unsuccessful, nor does a stable civilization. Prosperity comes from the top down, not from the bottom up. The American businessman is confused and afraid and trembles in his boots. He will not get together and buy up the politicos. He retreats before them, seeking to retain the lessening hoard which is left to him from their repeated graspings and penalizings. I could shoot down the Frankfurters, the Roosevelts, the Farleys in cold blood and never feel a twinge of conscience or regret.

But enough of that. I become carried away by emotions of helplessness and dreams of vengeance.

Chamberlain is not succeeding in his policy of arbitration and conciliation with the dictator nations. They listen, vaguely promise, go on unconcernedly about their conquest. The time to arbitrate was long ago. The time to bluff with force was long ago. Nothing but force itself now can stop the march of the aggressor nations.

They may be poor, they may be without gold, without proper food, without adequate material, but by God they are motivated by a moral vision, which is more than England, France, America are at this present time. I don't see what will stop them (unless Britain is clever enough to sow dissension among them) except war. They are hardened to words, callous to any bombardment of moralistic or idealistic platitudes. They are hellbent on growing, and no commands, pleas, empty threats will stay them.

June 18   The gasoline motor has been going steadily since Sullivan promised Evelyn to see to it. She is attempting to get in touch with him. Yesterday he had the day off with all the other Irishmen to celebrate Bunker Hill Day and make speeches about their forefathers (probably then they were in Erin hovels) and how they fought at Bunker Hill and gave liberty to the world, etc., etc. Today he is interviewing Harry Hopkins and Jim Farley and the rest of the Roosevelt hierarchy who are here for the wedding of the Rat's son John to Anne Clark at Nahant. (And won't she be sorry before she's through?)

June 22   It was one o'clock. Billy and Pearl and I were laughing about something. I heard a small knocking at the door. Billy opened it. There was Abe Harris, the little round-faced tailor, his forehead beaded with perspiration. "Mrs. Bates," he said, "she's fell off the streetcar and hurt herself. She's in my shop. I carried her in. She's hurt bad." "Who?" I asked. "Mrs. Bates—your sec'etary." "He means Mrs. Banks," exclaimed Billy. "Oh my God," said Pearl. "Run quick," I told Billy. He was out of the door and away before an eye could be winked. I had visions of Mrs. Banks with her head smashed open. My stomach sank. "Poor Mrs. Banks," moaned Pearl. "She was such a lovely woman. And this was her day off, and she wanted Friday instead. Wouldn't you know it. If she'd taken today off, this wouldn't a' happened. Poor Mrs. Banks."

Billy was back in a few minutes. "She wrenched her back and sprained her ankle. She's a brave one. She didn't know whether to cry or to faint—you could see that, but she just said, 'Hello, Billy.' The sweat was standin' out on her forehead, and she was white as a sheet. Her ankle was twice its usual size. I'm goin' to get my car and take her home. I've already phoned the doctor to be there. It makes me feel awful."

It made me feel "awful" too. And I knew Evelyn would be upset. She was. It means more responsibility for her. "We've gotta be as thoughtful with Mrs. Inman as we can," announced Pearl, "and take care of her so she won't get tired out. I'll do everything in my power to help. You know I will."

Mrs. Banks is in bed this morning. Mr. Banks phones that she feels somewhat better. "She can still move her tongue and wiggle her jaw," he said to Evelyn. "It is fortunate everything wasn't hurt all at once." I had to smile. I could hear in my mind's ear Mrs. Banks propounding against the politicians who backed the subway and the W.P.A. workers who left the loose plank on which she fell. I hope she'll sue the damn bastards. I hate to think of her lying there suffering.

June 25 I have been trying to read Thoreau's 'Walden' but cannot stomach it. What a young boob he was in many ways, so cocksure, with so many trite, dogmatic aphorisms tumbling incoherently off the end of his pen. I rather liked his 'Maine Woods' but decidedly dislike his 'Walden.'

June 27 Last night I dreamed that Evelyn and I climbed out of a window at Grandfather Inman's house, walked down the road by the Merion Cricket Club at Haverford and sought to escape from civilization along a path by a black and turgid river, over sere and yellow hills, through damp and windless forests. We encountered various horrific adventures. I recall a crazy man who lived on a farm surrounded by pollarded willows. He would not give us water. I recall being pursued by dogs. I recall dark nights. And Evelyn died. And I kept on, hopeless and afraid.

The nightmare world into which I reluctantly venture each night possesses a certain disorderly order. I have to do with the same people much of the time, known and unknown. Most of the topography has come to be familiar and is as a torn map many of the pieces of which are missing, a torn map flexed unreasonably in its parts by a sardonic and melodramatic hand. I am forever feeling that there must be an entirety to the course and to the geography of my dreams but am never quite able to come upon it. It is as though I were a denizen of a realm I should be familiar with, a dweller in some continuum sporadically recognizable, personally intimate, yet altogether tramontane.

July 2 Billy said: "There's somethin' I gotta tell you. You won't like it, but you might as well hear it now because some other person'll be tellin' you. It's this: Your friend Pass is dead. He dropped dead this noon — just like that. It got me, and I know it's goin' to bother you. He was a good guy, Pass was, always willin', full of comic talk, a real worker. You're gonna miss him."

I am going to miss him. He was a real friend, always fixing this or that for me, always smiling, always talking of the weddings he attended and the girls he kissed there. I shall miss him because he was helpful to me and because I liked him for himself. No one ever made more effort to keep the noises in the water and heating systems at a minimum on my account. A fine death, to drop suddenly of heart trouble, but the catch is that, of all the people I know, few as thoroughly enjoyed living as did Pass. I wonder what the parasitical relatives who battened on his industry and generosity will do now? I want to send some flowers to his funeral, not for the sake of his wife but because he would have liked it.

Here he comes, Roosevelt. He is tall. His eyes are too close-set above an aggressive nose. His mouth is both bitter and weak. He leans on a cane. His personality is both winning and overbearing. He asks for the toilet. I lead him there. He leans heavily on my arm while he urinates. "Well," he says at length, "what do you want?" I think to myself that I should like to kill him. He stumps up the corridor to the sitting room. He looks at my poems. He pushes them to one side. "Show me your diary, my friend," he orders. I do as he demands against my will. He riffles the pages. "What," I ask myself, "will he do if he catches sight of the passages about himself. He stops where there are some political passages. "No sense to these," he snaps. "Just bunk. What do you know about statecraft? Nothing, I'll warrant." Then his eye lights on some nature passages and passages about people. "These," he asserts, and snaps the pages with his forefinger, "are fine. They should make you one of the three or four most illustrious writers of the age." He gets up. I think of a bull rising from the ground. He opens a door. "Here are my good friends waiting for me," he states. Men and women mill about him, flatter him, feed him with praise. He departs, leaving for me a toothy smile. I hate the floor he walks on. Yet he has told me I will be one of the illustrious writers of the age. How can I hate him? What personality he has. My diary seems flat and obscure, now that his eyes are removed from it. Yet I feel deeply that he is an evil personage. Did he say what he did to win me, an enemy, or did he mean it?

July 5 It has been three months now since Edna left. She phoned me on my birthday, and I saw her the one time I sent for her. Aside from that, I have not seen sign nor hair of her, though both Evelyn and Mrs. Banks have phoned her and given clothes to her children. While I expected to be dropped from her life, I hadn't thought the process would be either so expeditiously performed or so thorough. I did a great deal for Edna, and while she helped me, for which I shall always be grateful, I am convinced that I did more for her than she did for me. That she has, either through carelessness or willfully, seen fit to push me out of her life has been gradually getting under my skin. Aside from anything I owed her or she me, I loved her more than anyone except Evelyn. I doubt if I would take

Edna back here now if I could although I certainly do miss her. She was a grand person in many ways.

July 7 I drove the Baby-Carriage over the bridge with the green planks and on up the hill beyond the cove. When my errand was done, I drove the Baby-Carriage down the hill again. The tide was in, and the water lay in unruffled, milky green translucency, deep. There were men idling along the railing of the bridge. A wooden horse stood casually to one side and a large W.P.A. sign. I began to cross the bridge with the green planks. There were no planks, only green water the color of green planks. The Baby-Carriage went into the green water, stalled and lay there half submerged, supported dubiously by a beam or so someone had thrust by chance across the space where the planks had been. I sat still and surveyed the situation. A careless movement, a slip of one of the beams, and my automobile would plunge under the milky green surface of the cove to the deep bottom. I loved my car. Anger welled up from some hidden subcavern within me. I felt in a cold fury at the men along the bridge railing whose indifference had caused my predicament, who still idled indifferently there.

I stepped from my car and approached the group. "You fellows," I said, "where's your goddamn boss?" "Oh," replied one of the group listlessly, "he's gone to Washington." "Which one of you is in charge?" "Well, sometimes one of us, sometimes another; nobody at present." "Who's the lousy bastard who neglected to put a sign up warning about this bridge?" There was silence. One of the loungers spat without interest into the green water. I spoke to the man I thought to be in charge. "You lazy rat, you, get your men together and push that pile of planks under my car. If you shove enough of them under, my car will float until your no-good boss gets back. Come on, get a move on." No one stirred. I jerked the man I had addressed. "Are you going to do what I said?" He shook his head. "Well," I said, "I may not be able to make you push the planks under, but by God I can raise hell with you." I grabbed him. I thought of my poor car helpless in the water. I wanted to be re-venged on someone. The man with whom I was struggling personi-fied the Government, so indifferent to others like me; the lazy masses who served the Government; the boss who had gone to Washington; the careless foreman who had neglected to place a warning sign at the bridgehead.

I grabbed the fellow's head and commenced to pull. I was strong with resolute anger. The neck stretched. The face contorted. The tongue pushed forth from between the swollen lips. I loosed my hold long enough to snatch at the tongue and jerk it forth. "You'll never talk again," I thought. The neck stretched. It became the size of my upper arm, of my wrist, of my thumb. It was about to snap. And then I awoke, and the world of darkness about me and the noises of traffic coming through my window were unreal. And I was half in a continuum where I was wreaking vengeance on a man and through him a class I hated, and half in a realm of discoordinate sound and incomprehensible darkness. I was a nether being of no world and of two worlds. And there was Billy Minor at my door. And my mouth was so dry my tongue clove to the roof. And my limbs were in cramps. And I was wet with perspiration.

July 8 I had a nice ride this morning and am now waiting for Dr. Mac. My doctors' bill last month amounted to $375. That is preposterous. Were it not for doctors' bills, Evelyn and I could live the life of Riley quite within our income. Father sent the $1,000 we asked for. With that and with $350 from dividends and with $150 from this month's $1,000, we still have a debit balance of $630, which makes us owe $200 more than in January. It bothers me very little but depresses Evelyn. I owe Dr. Pike $1,300. Clarence owes me $600. The stocks I own outright, aside from those derived from Mother and Aunt Helen, are worth $1,900. My margin account could be cashed in for $1,500. In other words, my debits, exclusive of mortgages on the Jamaica Plain Place and on the St. Botolph Street house, amount to $1,930 and my credits to $4,000. So why worry? I have been in worse jams than this one.

July 12 I wish Mrs. Banks would get something done about her foot so as to be able to come back here. She is so afraid of osteopathy and so in fear of losing her insurance case that she obeys her doctor and does nothing and sees nobody. She may derive more damages by letting her ankle linger on, but I'm sure those damages won't be divided with me, and in the meanwhile I am paying salary and being deprived of her presence here at the same time. I miss her talking considerably.

July 14 Everything goes as smooth as silk with Billy, Honey and Janice. They are three unusually pleasant people with exceptionally winning personalities and with looks above the ordinary. I like the combination. If Janice stays, I hate to consider the possibility of Mrs. Banks returning with rancor in her heart toward Janice to break up the amicable setup. If Janice definitely decides to remain, I shall send Mrs. Banks a letter I have already written on the subject of her relationship to Janice. If she doesn't intend to treat her well and talk about her politely and cooperate with her, she ought to let me know now, not later, so that I can make other plans. I haven't liked Mrs. Banks's attitude toward Janice. I don't intend to be bossed again by anyone working for me, no matter how helpful their record or how fond of them I am or they are of me. It is too unpleasant.

July 18   Evelyn tells me that I should stop writing about Mrs. Banks. "Who," she queries, "do you think will stay interested this long about Mrs. Banks? After all, she is only a secretary." Yesterday Evelyn took her the flowers. This morning she took her some more work. I had her say, "Mrs. Banks, will you write Arthur a letter saying that you understand the matters about which we have been at variance if he sends you a list, and acquiesce to them as they are not unreasonable? He feels that if you and he can establish an under-standing on a new basis, things could go along fine." Evelyn says that Mrs. Banks declared she would write me no letters, that I didn't know my friends when I had them, that I had been a poor friend to her during her trouble and so on. All the old Eddie stuff. Evelyn says that she is wildly jealous of Janice. My common sense tells me that the time has come for Mrs. Banks and me to part company. She'd never come back and be reasonable now. Evelyn I know feels that I should make a break, the sooner the better. As soon as I find out definitely that Janice will come, I ought to make the split conclusive. I could stay friends with Mrs. Banks afterwards, but she couldn't. It will, I am sorry to say, be the end of our relationship.

July 20   By hook or by crook I'm going to put Mrs. Banks out of my life. Janice telephoned this morning and said that she had talked to Mr. Davis and would be in Monday-week. So now I have the assurance that she will be here and Billy's promise to stay come weal come woe, and I am ready to go against Mrs. Banks. Should Pearl leave, I shall lose no sleep. If I can't outwit Mrs. Banks, I'm a Dutchman. If I haven't more ingenuity and tenacity than she, I deserve to lose. My problem is to get her out of here without incensing Billy. First off I'll stop giving her work on the excuse that she is caught up to me. I'll put off seeing her as long as possible, then give her a letter to sign that will seem harmless to Billy and will make her so angry she won't sign. If she does sign, I'll keep her sitting in the other room without work until she tires of it. If that doesn't work, I can pick a scrap. I'm done with her. And I don't believe, after she has so carefully dripped acid into the minds of Billy and Pearl, that I will be sentimental whatever happens. She's dug her own grave; it's my business to push her into it. Then maybe I can have some peace around here. Billy will like Janice eventually, I'm sure.

Later   Here is a note from Mrs. Banks. It's only decent to give her side of the affair. Let her state what she thinks of me.

Dear Arthur—

What is the meaning of your latest effort in histrionics? Such play acting as your present scene, with me in the role of helpless victim, adds nothing to your prestige either as actor or man.

Please send no more conscription notices for me to make out; it's a wasted gesture.

I have given you long, loyal and helpful service. I have worked for your interest without any deceitful pretense or double dealing, and shielded you from the effects of your own prankish folly. You know and determine your own behavior pattern, and I have *not* tried to dictate, but always when the ice has gotten too thin for safety, you have found me cooperating to your rescue. In these years of association I have cooperated regardless, and have never refused—the record is its own witness—yet now and out of nothing you raise a bogey of noncooperation, and practice methods of liquidation worthy of an OGPU.

Are you losing all sense of proportion, Arthur? Come out of the fog and be honest with me. If you no longer want my services, why not tell me like a man, with or without your reasons, and be fair to me, and honorable to yourself? I have no wish to dictate your course, wherever it leads, but you are more than stupid to think I could enjoy working with you as just a proscribed human animal. You wouldnt want me long if I did.

Please let me know your wishes—by letter if you will.

Sincerely
Dorothy Banks

I only wish I could come out in the open and inform her I don't want her any more. She has given me, as she says, long, loyal and for the most part helpful service. It would, as she says, be fair to her for me to tell her like a man that I no longer want her services. But not now, with the way Billy and Pearl feel, not with the box she has gotten me into, not as I am at present minded. I want Evelyn to get the diary that is in Mrs. Banks's possession this afternoon, then let her sweat. Evelyn is going off to Woodwork's tonight or tomorrow morning. Time to settle with Mrs. Banks later, after she has waited awhile. I'm sorry for Mrs. Banks, yes, but now above and beyond that is a disgust at her puling attempts to control my actions about Janice and a desire to set her back on her heels and a wish to be forever rid of her.

July 23   Evelyn typed my letter to Mrs. Banks yesterday and sent it off. I am under the weather now from being sorry for her. What a sentimental critter I am. A few palliative sentences from her would melt me like molasses before a warm fire. I trust she doesn't utter them. The letter reads:

Dear Mrs. Banks:

I am writing you by letter, as you said you wished me to do in your letter. I see no use of your coming back on this job. I will not take you without a signed statement signifying your exact understanding and intentions, which you refuse to do, for to return without such an understanding would mean only continual friction between us. If a person has honorable intentions on any matter, that person should not hesitate to put his name to a statement of what his intentions are. Since you see it otherwise, we had best part. I am sorry for the delay but, until lately, I had hoped you would see things in a more friendly light. You think, however, judging from what you have said to other people and from the caustic tone of your letter to me, that I have been trying to pull a whizzer on you. It has been your mistake nearly always since you have been with me to put the worst interpretation on my acts and motives. It is too bad, for you have been wrong and it has been poor psychology as well.

I wish to thank you from the bottom of my heart for the many times you have stood by me, for the many hours you have talked to me, for the earnestness with which you have assisted me in my work. I only wish you had been more ready to compromise this time.

Of course you believe that I am taking advantage of your accident and your condition to press my wishes, and nothing I can say will alter that opinion, though I assure you that it is not so. You have taken much pains to impress upon me the ease with which you could find another, perhaps a better job. Until you are able to walk sufficiently to find such a position, it is my duty and my pleasure, in return for all you have done for me, to keep you going financially, so don't worry about that.

I have been and still feel devoted to you, whether you believe it or not. It is in my nature to be that way. I hope that you will stay friends with me, if that is not too much to ask. I am sorry things have turned out this way.

Affectionately,
Arthur

July 25   Evelyn returned after lunch yesterday with "Well, I saw Mrs. Banks. I brought the typewriter, the books you had lent her, the crutches home. She is walking around. She looked both bitter and sad. I tried to be nice to her. I told her that if ever we could do anything for her or she needed help to call on us. She replied that we couldn't do anything for her and that she wouldn't need any help. She said that she would take two weeks' wages and then she hoped never to see either one of us again. So that's that. It should be a perfect example to you of what trouble a loose tongue can get its possessor into. There are lots of things people don't want to hear, resent hearing. Mrs. Banks thought that she could say anything that entered her mind and get away with it. You do better than formerly, but remember her example. And now let's forget her. It is my opinion we will lead a more peaceful life without her."

All afternoon I felt very downcast. You can't live eleven years with a person and not have the sensation of having lost some part of yourself when they walk out of your life. I don't understand how people, women, Naomi, Edna, Millicent, Corn, can do such a thorough job of exorcising you from their lives when they decide to take the step. I can't do it.

July 26   The continued emotional stir has been too much for me. My mind is tired and I am snappy. It is difficult to work with adequate concentration. I have tried Holmes's 'Autocrat of the Breakfast Table' on the talking-book and found it even more conceitedly nonsensical than I thought it to be as a child. I am endeavoring to persist through 'Eugenie Grandet' though it is drowzily slow. At least Balzac is a man, not just an author who achieved fame because of the paucity of authors existing in his time. Longfellow's 'Tales of a Wayside Inn' bored me to sleep. Washington Irving is more manly than the rest of the early American authors who, by and large, were a pretty slender lot. Aside from Poe who certainly had something new and virile to offer, I find the writers of the early 19th century in America puny fish indeed. I like 'The Scarlet Letter' and 'Evangeline' but not Whittier, not most of Longfellow, not Emerson, not most of Thoreau, not Holmes. Prescott and Parkman and Motley and [George] Ticknor had something to say and a manly way of saying it when they came along, and there were many fine war narratives written during and directly after the Civil War. In the main though, American literature did not stand on its own feet until the 20th century was a decade under way.

I had a talk with Billy yesterday. There were some points that needed clearing up. I raised his wages to the maximum I promised him when he came, not waiting for next year. His mathematical mind responded slowly. He felt he was being gypped. When he realized the facts he said: "I'm satisfied." I said: "I don't want you to be satisfied, Billy; I want you to be grateful. I'm doing this because I've appreciated what you've done for me and the effort you've put into it. You'll be the senior person here now, and I'll expect even more of you." I raised Billy for two reasons. First, I thought it due him. Second, I figured that if he were raised, he couldn't afford to let any backkick from Mrs. Banks get under his skin.

I have no faith in human nature. It is a wolf-dog that must be watched each moment lest it turn on you and rend you. It takes unconscious advantages of your weaknesses and your generosities and your consideration and serves you only when it is afraid of you or feels it has something to gain or is bent upon hunting the same prey or loves you for a mystical adoration or a spiritual obedience which you inspire. Pascal says: "We never care about persons, but only about personal qualities." I believe him. If the personal qualities exercised fail, your best friend may desert you or turn on you or cause you ill.

July 30   Evelyn saw Mrs. Banks last night. She cannot walk well yet. She is going to have a specialist. It is a shame she was too stubborn to have Dr. Pike. Evelyn explained again why I didn't have her back. She told her that she had talked without control, then refused to compromise. She said that she thought I might be willing to have her back if she would put her understanding in writing. She informed her that she underestimated my affection for her.

Another volume ends. Janice, as has been said before, comes Monday. I hope to God she can read my handwriting, read it correctly and with speed. If she does, I can relinquish all idea of having Mrs. Banks back. If she doesn't, I will have to think about Mrs. Banks again.

Next week will tell. Here's luck!

With Edna and Mrs. Banks gone, Arthur convinced himself that his amiable team of Janice, Pearl ("Honey"), and Billy had brought a welcome harmony to Garrison Hall. He might complain in his Diary about Honey's bossiness or Janice's accent or Billy's "unfairness" (that is, his demanding more free time), but he was genuinely fond of all three and hoped to escape the agonies of having to replace them. The younger brother of Janice's old boss at the shoe factory had begun to court her ("it would be a lamentable pity for such a fine girl to marry an Irishman and a Catholic"), but her common sense, he thought, would prevent such a catastrophe. Ella and Roderic still read and talked to him (he doted on

Ella), and the adventures of a new talker, the lumpenproletarian *Anthony Abruzzo, introduced him to the noisome world of Bottom-Dog America. Dr. Lakian (who would be with Arthur until the end) joined the Garrison Hall medical corps as chief stomach pumper.*

As the European crisis deepened, Arthur accused the perfidious busy-body in the White House of planning to drag the United States into the coming war. His virulent attacks against international Jewry at this time coincided with the dismemberment of Czechoslovakia and the collapse of the Spanish Republic. Arthur wrote:

The weaker becomes the foundation of the New Deal, the more easily will the New Deal be made an instrument in the hands of the Jewish Brotherhood, an instrument to fulfill their vengeance against Germany, not, you may be sure, to better the condition of America or of any other nation which harbors them.

Wherever he looked, he detected evidence of Jewish machinations.

Meanwhile Arthur himself threatened and flattered and plotted to keep his own employees and (much to Evelyn's displeasure) his father in line. Unfortunately he was less successful in persuading editors to accept his poems. A clique of poets "intent upon artistic obscurity" blinded them to the merits of his clear and "virile" verse.

July 31   Joe has just finished cutting and washing my hair. Last winter he bought "the wife" a three hundred dollar stove. Then there was the automobile. "An' now guess what?" he queried. "I glass in the whole pilazza for her. She want it. I say, 'What de hell goddamn. You want; I get.' It cost six hundert, maybe more — but she want it. She is one grand, fine woman, my wife. Nobody like her. She's growin' older! Should anythin' happen to her — myself an' de kids go nuts, not know what to do. So give her what she want, make her live long. Right, eh what, Chappie? Never find another like her. Six hundert dollar — what de hell."

Joe brought a box of piecrust for me and a fresh-baked cupcake for Evelyn. "My birfday," he announced, "just passed. Me an' Henry Ford an' Mussolini same day — big bosses. Your mother too, you say. Funny, isn't it, how we all bosses?"

August 1   There are rumors in the papers this morning of fighting between the Japanese and the Russians on the Manchukuoan border.

Outside in the alley the garbage men are shouting to each other. The iceman cries, "I-i-i-ce." Children wearing sunsuits of various sorts, their backs and arms brown, ride red streamlined velocipedes up and down the asphalt. The ailanthus trees, small things of no beauty when first I came to Garrison Hall, now spread heads of gently waving green up and down the alley and are pleasant to look upon. Down on the roofs where a man raises pigeons, he opens the cote door and lets his flock free for their morning exercise. I can hear the whistle of their taut wings as they wheel the light-blue sky in ecstatic maneuvers, as geometrically ordered in movement as though a sergeant were parading them.

August 4 The Japanese-Russian fighting along the Manchu-kuoan border appears to be increasing. Large forces on both sides are engaged. Each time an incident such as this occurs, one asks oneself, "Is this the beginning of the next world war?" It may well be. Germany's fortifications to guard against France are nearly completed. England is frantically arming. Japan is meeting with less success than was expected in China. The clash between Russia and Japan would appear inevitable. The longer Japan waits, the stronger Russia grows. Should Japan strike at Russia now, and at the same time Germany strike at Czechoslovakia on the way to Russia, Germany and Japan would have less to lose than by waiting until England is rearmed. The Italian part of the Italo-German-Japanese alliance would be to keep England and France busy in the south of Europe. Unless the United States is propagandized into joining England, France and Russia, the aggressive states would stand more than a fair chance of dismembering Russia.

August 7 Janice declares that she "loves the job." She is quiet, a persistent and conscientious worker with less self-confidence than Pearl, a much finer character. She is gentle and willing and eminently trustworthy. Pearl is a much more emotional, a more primitive type. There may come a day when I will be sorry I ever took Pearl on, for I feel that in her are possibilities of emotional trouble. I note this now for the future reference. As it is, I like her, like her sense of fun, her walk, her body, her affectionate nature. But there is a part of me that always holds aloof in my dealings with her. I don't quite trust her. Sometimes she acts superior, and that arouses my ire. We may clash on that. I had enough of it with Ten Broek. However, by and large, she is a sweet and pleasant extrovert, as opposite from Mrs. Banks as any mortal could well be. She is plenty smart, though intellectually lazy.

August 10 I asked Evelyn to get in touch with Edna and find out if she would spend part of an evening with me. She replied that of course she would. She was here yesterday. I like her, and that's all there is to it. "Sure I've thought about you, Artie. You can't spend six years with a person and forget them as quick as this. Of course I think about you. I haven't come because I was so busy and because

you're so hard to see when you're busy or tired or talking to someone else. But I've thought of you often."

Edna enjoys her work. "I never did anything more fascinating.
You take a blank piece of paper, and on that paper you put what will
appeal to people and make them buy what you want them to buy.
What could be more creative? And people fall for it. I don't know
why, but they do. They accept what appears in an advertisement as
gospel truth. It's awfully queer." Edna works hard, long hours,
small pay. She enjoys meeting people. She feels that she is being both
useful and creative. She enjoys arguing with her boss, Bella Berg.
She always comes superficially to resemble those with whom she
associates, so now Edna talks a bit like a Jew. I had to smile. Manuel
works at an upholstering job Bella obtained for him — twelve dollars a week and the use of the truck Sundays. Edna's children are
growing. She is always in debt. She is as full of odd theories, backed
up by half-knowledge, as a tick is full of blood. A Jew, she assures
me, rules Boston — the Irish, business, the mortgage racket. There
will be no war in either Asia or Europe. And so on. But she was
always that way. She asked after neither Billy nor Mrs. Banks. She
would accept no payment for her visit, offered to come again. I
have in mind a possible time when I might be able to buy
a printing house, set Edna up in it, print my diary. I don't intend to
let her walk out of my life if I can help it. She's a grand person
whether she believes I like her or not. I miss her constantly.

August 11 Woodwork had supper on the Ritz roof with
Evelyn, then spent the evening and night here. "My gosh," she
exclaimed, "I'm a saphead. I let whole tribes of people I've no use for
impose on me. And I overdrew on my bank account. And I owe
money right and left. And my life's a mess. And Allan is never wild
like me. Do you suppose I'll ever go on a spree again? Allan is sweet
and all that, but he doesn't ever raise hell for the hell of it. Oh yes. And
my hair's getting gray. And I cough all night. And I'm miserable."

August 19 We Americans are enthusiastically for China as
against Japan. It will be a catastrophe for us should Japan be defeated. China in that case would become Communist, and Russia
and China would hold the balance of power in the world. I am
gloomy as to the outcome, one way or another, of the future of
Western civilization. Yet we may have a swing back to conservatism.
I am no prophet, though liking to play at being one. One hundred
thousand children to be clad at Government expense. And Art. Pay
worthless people to tootle in orchestras, to act in propaganda plays,
to paint blotches on canvas, to sing off-tune. Where will it end? It is
all against common sense, self-respect, progress.

August 20   Mrs. Cash has been somewhat nasty of late. She is jealous of Roderic. I decided to scotch her petty temper (I don't want it to grow into wrath; she would make a vile enemy), so I made her a present of the two volumes of 'Macready's Diaries' that I own. She likes the 18th century in England and knows considerable about it, especially the stage, so I calculated the 'Diaries' would please her. She went into effusive transports of appreciation. She has been good to me after her primitive fashion so that it pleases me to have pleased her.

Last night I listened to one of the finest plays I have heard on the radio. Here was the plot: A farmhand has worked over a period of forty years for a farmer, assisted him to build his house and barns, till his fields, gather his fruit, tend his cattle. The farmer dies and his son takes over. The son tells the farmhand he is no longer needed. The farmhand pleads that it is only common justice that he should be kept on. Has he not spent of his very life on the farm? The son is adamant. So the farmhand goes forth to seek justice from the courts. He meets a young tramp on the road who tells him that there exists no such thing as justice. He reaches the city. He goes to court. He is shouted at and insulted by the judge. He is told that the judge is concerned with the law, not with justice. He is locked up overnight with a criminal. The latter asserts that the only justice is that of revenge, that, were he to be just, he would kill the policemen who had maltreated him, the judges who had sentenced him when guiltless, would burn down the prisons and the courts. The farmhand next goes to the highest court in the land. Without money, he is impotent even to get a hearing from justice. So he wanders the land seeking somewhere to find justice. Children mock him. Dogs chase him. His spirit is broken. He comes to be convinced that the tramp and the criminal were right, that there is no justice. If there is any justice, it is the justice of revenge. He returns to the farm and sets fire to the house of the farmer's son. There is heard the exultant cry of the mob giving chase to seek revenge on him, justice. A strong play, human, imaginative, acted with feeling. It made me think.

August 24   Billy went to Brookline where Manuel is working to ask him if he would stay here nights while he was away on his vacation next month and one night every two weeks thereafter, to be paid as he has been before. Manuel refused to put himself out to that extent.

It is nothing more nor less than what I had expected. But the incident again brings to my attention my position in society. People have to do with me because I have money to dispense, because my personality somehow seems to cast an immediate, temporary spell on those I attract, and because I devote constant thought to the problem of keeping my friends interested. Money is not enough, at least in the limited quantities I have at my command, to buy the quality of service I receive. However, should the funds with which I am supplied by Father cease, I have no doubt that practically all my friends would slough off. I regard friendship as a short-term tenure only and enjoy it while it lasts.

August 27 Janice at the end of this month will have about a hundred-fifty pages compared with the two hundred a month Mrs. Banks did. Very good. Her work is ten times more presentable than was that of Mrs. Banks and I believe more accurate, surely less crowded with typographical errors. She declares she enjoys the copying.

September 2 [From Patricia:]

We have been quite busy at our store these past few months, the Hollywood Bowl season is on and that always brings us quite a bit of business. And too, we get a lot of the tourist trade. In September we will have the American Legion National Convention out here, and we are not looking forward to it at all. They are a rowdy bunch and extremely bad tippers, besides demanding all sorts of special service, and expecting us to be thrilled when they try to date us up.

Jerry's place is coming along well, he works so hard at it. Eighteen hours a day and he thinks nothing of it. One has to dig him out for meals or bed since he never comes up from the furrows until dragged. I spent two days out there one week and saw him for twenty minuets. So I gave it up as a bad job and came home and went to the movies. Imagine having a hoe for a rival! He has about an acre under cultivation, and more vegetables than he can possibly use, still he keeps on growing more, the man has a possitive mania for planting things. He has everything under the sun growing, even gourds. His luck with flowers has been excellent, and he has sold quite a lot of plants and done a bit of landscaping for some of the directors for whom he works. The rabbits are increasing by leaps and bounds as rabbits have a habit of doing. So far he hasn't sold any on a large scale, just a few here and there. But he is building up his stock and holding on to all of the does, just selling the bucks.

I finally got up my nerve, and getting his address in a round about way went calling on the O'Casey's a few months ago. They are living about four miles from Jerry's place. Sean took over a few acres of land for the back taxes. Its rather baren, not a tree on the place, and it's practically in the Los angeles River bed, which went on a rampage last winter and flooded them out. When I went to see them they were living in a little shack that Sean had built, but they were in the throes of building a real house, up on the land above the flood mark. Sean is doing it all himself, with the exception of the frame and the plumbing. They are living in it now, tho it is less than half finished. They are having ahuge living room, kitchen and bath. A bedroom and dining room to be added later. The outer walls of stucco are on but the inside is just tarpaper, and the rooms have no partitions as yet. But the living room has an immense fireplace that heats the whole place beautifully. It's going to be a terrific job since Lenore and Sean are doing it themselves, but they love the work, and have a grand time planning. I do envy them I'd like to be building a place of my own. Sean is very well, looks better than I've ever seen him. And he is terribly keen about the place. Lenore and he seem very happy together and I think she makes him a splendid wife. I can't see why all his friends are so against her. They just don't understand her type thats all. She is very conservative, and a bit dowdy. Like most of the British she simply hasn't the remotest idea of how to dress. But as she says, she never pretended to be a beauty, and can't understand why people should be disturbed about her clothes when Sean isn't annoyed, mybe some of them will be kinder to her when they see that we are friends, because a lot of the snubbing was done out of mistaken loyalty for me. I go out there now every week, and each time I go I get over a little bit more of my love for Sean. Because seeing him happy and content with Lenore makes it easier for me to get my own perspective again, and able to plan a life in which he has no active part. Something I hadn't been able to do until I saw him again, I kept on dreaming that perhaps some day some way we might be together again. And now I finally see that there is'nt to be that someday, and it's time to stop dreaming and get in a little ground work of my own. So I'm girding my loins and starting all over again from scratch. I guess I was born to be a second bester.

The first few times I went to see the O'Caseys I didn't mention Jerry it not seeming to be a particularly delicate subject to discuss before one's ex-love, but I started to think that someone might be mean enough to make some remark to Lenore if they heard that I was seeing them. So I told them about Jerry and his place and the fun we had getting things fixed on it. And it seems to me that Lenore has been a lot more intimate since then. I discribed Jerry's place, and Sean was very much interested since he plans to raise rabbits too. And lo and behold, last week Sean picked up Jerry who was hitchhiking home from the studio! Jerry told him where he lived and spoke about his place. Sean recognized it immeadiatly and asked him if he knew me. Don't I get mixed up in the darndest situations tho? Sean stopped for a bit at Jerrys, met the other boys, saw the rabbits and got an armload of vegetables. They liked each other immensely. Yesterday S got a new refrigerator and gave his old one to Jerry, and Jerry sent over a couple of rabbits to Sean. Real chummy I calls it. If they only don't compare notes.

September 6   Premier Daladier has called French reservists to the colors and is manning the great line of fortifications facing Germany, the Maginot Line. The English Fleet has set sail for war maneuvers in the North Sea. American Ambassador Bullitt has intimated to the French that the United States will stand behind England and France in case Germany makes a military move against the Czechs. Evidently the armament program in England has progressed far enough for Chamberlain to believe that he can safely sit in on the game of European bluff. French and English pressure has been brought against the Czechs in order to make them yield a greater measure of autonomy to the Germans of Czechoslovakia, so that a general war may be avoided.

It looks to me as though Hitler had delayed striking too long if he wished success. But perhaps he did not want to use active force. His territorial successes thus far have been won by a show of force rather than by force. A queer business, that of being a dictator. People often query: "What do you suppose goes on in Hitler's mind?" No doubt he wishes to be considered great. No doubt he wishes to leave an illustrious name behind him. No doubt he is exhilarated by the feeling of power possessed. And no doubt he is motivated by a desire to help the German people. Any man who could have led the Germans out of the slough of despair, international degeneration, discordance in which they were prior to his accession to power — and do it within the space of five years — must have considerable greatness in him, whether he be, as he looks, a homosexual puppy with megalomania gnawing his vitals and conceit whipping him or not. I do not, at this juncture, see how he is going to find his way out through the meshes of the net that is closing over and around him.

September 9   Honey is acting superior again. I get out of temper with her. She calls me "Mr. Inman" or "Artie" or "Arthur" at the end of every sentence. Such repetition bothers me and depletes the integrity of my name and makes it meaningless. I can't prevail upon her to stop that. She says "a" between words. I don't like her today.

And now she brings me a matchbook. "I saved it for your diary," she says. "Here. I copied out what's on it. You know all sorts of companies and businesses advertise with these matchbooks." This one reads:

Do you remember when you were a wee, wee tot
and they took you out of your warm, warm cot
and made you sit on a cold, cold pot
and made you wee-wee whether you could or not?

September 11 Some critics consider 'The Education of Henry Adams' to be one of the finest books in American literature. I have striven without success to read it. Adams is vain, acrid of wit, pessimistic. His pages are sequined with notable characters, yet few are notably drawn. His is a vainglorious mind, flashy, pompous, purposely inhuman. He certainly does deem Henry Adams a smart fellow. When I was a boy, in some of the packages from the grocery store came gelatin fish. These you could hold in the palm of your hand where they would contort to various purposeless shapes. Adams' mind reminds me of those bright and fruitless pieces of restless matter. Last evening Mrs. Cash and I tried to read his letters. A man with a reputation for wittiness and sapiency who feels he must sustain that reputation to the very end is by way of cutting a pitiful figure in most cases. If there was warmth in Adams, he hid it very well. I dislike the man, dislike his books and his letters.

September 12 I am reading an abridgement of the 'Storia do Mogor' written by Niccolao Manuccio about 1700.[5] The author is a man of discernment, courage, character, and what he has to say has in it none of the brittle decadence of Adams' writings. A comparison of the two authors, at least to my mind, leaves Adams a poor second. Both were intellectually alert, both met many illustrious figures, both lived close to the well-springs of important happenings, yet one stiffened as the other mellowed. An interesting dissimilarity.

[5] Manucci (1639?–1717), a runaway from Venice, spent most of his life in Asia Minor, Persia, and India serving a set of royal masters in a variety of capacities. The exciting story of his vicissitudes (which Arthur ridiculously contrasts with Henry Adams's) was translated in four massive volumes by William Irvine (1906–1908), *The "Storia Do Mogor" of Niccolau Manucci.* Arthur read an abridged version of this work by Irvine's daughter, *A Pepys of Mogul India, 1653–1708* (1913).

From my newspaper:

Lost Sisters Just Camping

South End Girls Spent Night Under Stars —
Found at Dawn in Brookline

After having spent the night under the stars in a wooded section
of Brookline, Gwendolyn Mercer, 12, and her sister, Bernardine, 8,
of 14 Dartmouth Place, South End, were found at sunrise yesterday
by their mother, Mrs. Edna Mercer, who with the aid of police had
been hunting for the two little girls all night.

Taking blankets to sleep on and their dog to guard them, the
children walked to Brookline Saturday afternoon, choosing for
their campsite a place off Goddard avenue where they had often
gone picnicking when they lived in Jamaica Plain.

Early yesterday morning, their mother remembered the picnic
spot and went there to look for them. None the worse for having
spent the cool night outdoors, the sisters were found, sound asleep
under the trees, with their dog lying beside them.

Evelyn telephoned Edna. The kids had drawn plans for erecting
huts. It was their intention to take to the road so as to avoid having
to go to school. They were planning to be away indefinitely. Noel
refused to accompany them. Said Edna: "I've been mobbed by
reporters all day long. I simply can't get rid of them." When asked
whether or not she would punish the children, she replied, "I've told
them I'd take the dog away if they did anything like that again."
Edna is an individualist in an aggregate world. She is bringing up
her daughters to be like her. I am curious to observe the outcome.

September 13   Janice has her fingernails enameled an oxblood
red, hideous. When I asked her why she did it, she replied, "Oh,
everybody else is doing it. So I did it too."

Listened to Hitler yesterday. Emotional push. Repeated the same
idea over and over again. German is an ugly, unimaginative language, cumbersome. Organized cheering for Hitler. There must
have been someone to give signals when and how to cheer much as is
done with the audiences at American radio performances. No wild
tumult as when Mussolini speaks. Hitler is now fomenting disturbances within German Czechoslovakia.

Roosevelt's candidate has been defeated in Maryland despite the
High One's speeches, despite the two new bridges. In seven cases
out of nine now his purge has failed.

September 17   There should be war before winter or capitulation
by the Czechs unless England restores the German colonies.

I was listening to a broadcast of German news last night. The

Germans must be sheep to believe such arrant propaganda, such twisted facts, such imprecations used for the obvious purpose of whipping up their emotions. Yet remember Americans before and during the World War. The longer I live, the less respect I have for the mentality of ordinary people. An exciting and picturesque leader is worth ten armies. 'Heil Hitler!'

September 19 The heads of the British and French Governments, after thirteen hours of almost continuous discussion in London, have concluded to surrender to Germany without a plebiscite all predominantly German areas in Czechoslovakia, preceded by an exchange of populations so as to protect both Czech and German minorities. What a bloodless victory for Hitler! What a betrayal of the Czechs by the French and by the British. The tiger has claws that are too sharp unsheathed, a growl that is too loud, mighty muscles that ripple — throw the young child to the tiger. Avoid conflict by so doing whether the act be honorable or not. Was it the Germans in 1914 who talked about a treaty being "a scrap of paper?" No doubt I should have done likewise had I been Chamberlain and Daladier.

And now what will Beneš and the Czechs do? If the British and French proposals are complied with, Hungary and Poland will demand for themselves slices of the partitioned nation. If the proposals are not met, it is to fight save for the problematic intervention of Russia. The termination, surely, of a free Czechoslovakia, should the French and British recommendations be complied with. A bare chance, otherwise, that Russia may furnish effective aid. If I were Beneš, I would choose, I think, to fight. His army, it is said, is the finest-equipped in Europe. What will he do? Woodrow Wilson certainly did make a mess of Europe with his insistence on the recognition of the theory of self-determination for nations and races and with his abortive effort to arrange Europe accordingly.

September 22 It wasn't a storm. It was a 99-mile-per-hour hurricane. All the Boston radio stations save two went dead. Electric current was off in the suburbs. Telephone and telegraph service was disrupted. I listened to the radio broadcasting the news. In addition to the terrifying gale, the whole of New England was ravaged by floods caused by the downpours of the last week. Bridges were swept away, roads and trainbeds flooded, dams burst, houses inundated. Ships and yachts and boats of all sorts were driven ashore and pounded to pieces. Signs and roofs were torn from their moorings and hurtled into other buildings or to the streets below. Trees were uprooted, plate-glass windows and neon signs smashed. People were killed by flying missiles or drowned. I could imagine the hundreds of thousands of helpless birds swept to death. Airplanes at the fields were torn from their storm-moorings and flung away like pieces of paper. Providence was flooded. New London was on fire. Governor Hurley had declared a state of emergency to exist in Massachusetts.

This morning the papers state the hurricane to have been the worst in the history of New England. The day is bright and clear with a gentle southwest wind blowing and the odor of crushed leaves scenting the air, a very dream of an Indian summer day. Evelyn left for Bernard's Elm at eight. She was back at nine, trembling and unstrung. Bernard's Elm, she said, was down, fallen the length of the ramp, pushing with it, as children push a row of cards, the Carolina poplars. All the butternuts were down. The largest Norway spruce was leaning to one side. The pear trees were down. The big ash was down. The small crab apples and spruces were pushed to one side. Evelyn looked pale and undone. She is taking this more to heart than am I, for I have never expected the Place to remain without some sort of catastrophe happening. It will cost us hundreds of dollars to clear up the debris if we cannot sell the timber to some portable sawmill company or at least give it to them for taking it away.

I drove through the Fenway. Trees stripped of branches. Trees broken in half. Trees blown to earth, their roots like helpless arms, stiff and still in the sunlight. I felt choked in the throat. I love trees. I had not minded so, I verily believe, had it been people. I wanted to weep. All the schoolchildren had been given a holiday. They were running up and down the prone trunks like joyous monkeys, yelling, laughing, grinning. Somehow, they made the whole business seem more pathetic than ever, as did the fleckless blue skies overhead. "Let's go home," I said to Billy. "I've got enough." "I guess I have too," he said. "I didn't think I'd mind, but I do. It sort of gets you."

September 25   I wouldn't want to be a soldier marching to war to protect any nation or the government of any nation. As a matter of fact, my studies in history have convinced me that the common man stands just as good a chance to live his own life, just as good a chance of getting somewhere, of collecting worldly wealth and happiness, just as ill a chance of being taxed and robbed and browbeaten under one set of rulers as under another. To be a soldier, unless what you like is being a soldier, is to be a dupe, with misery and deprivation and the chance of being killed or wounded more likely than not. If peace without decadence were possible for the human race, I'd be all for it, but history has shown that continued peace leads invariably to decadence and decadence to destruction.

I am certain of one thing, though: Were I well and strong and were I to be conscripted to go to war, I should dissent or cut off a toe or malinger or take any means fair or foul to avoid marching off to be mangled. If my country were invaded and my wife and property endangered and I felt convinced that it would boot me nothing to flee and might help protect my wife and property to fight, no doubt I would fight, and with might and main — but I would still count it an unfortuitous business.

As to the drama of wars in which I am not personally engaged, that is another matter. I am surely an appreciative spectator of war and wars, of the strategy and tactics of conflicts, of the characters of leaders, of the march of victory and the rout of defeat.

September 28 In my humble opinion, if Hitler is being the fool all Americans seem to think him in leading the nations of the world to the brink of war, the leaders of England and France are fools to prepare to take their peoples to war under the present circumstances. Let Hitler have his way in Central Europe and Southern Russia. That would strike me as the part of sense. He would have enough to do to build and consolidate an empire there to keep him busy for the remainder of his years, and perhaps the vast spaces of Russia would consume his growth as they did that of Napoleon and of the generals of Genghis Khan.

To me the leading of the French and English people into a war that Hitler would like, I am sure, to avoid seems as criminal as does Hitler's leading of the Germans into a war toward the east — in fact more so, for wars of conquest are historically more justifiable than are meddlesome wars. Hitler asserts that he wants no fight with England and that France's score (remembered for forty years by the French) was settled during the World War. I believe he means it; at least he does now. Perhaps the English and the French go in fear that what he means now he may not mean tomorrow, and there is that to consider. Nevertheless, I cannot perceive that the two nations, especially England, are any more warranted in going to war against Germany because of what has occurred to date, or what may occur should the Germans begin their march eastward, than was the United States warranted in going to war with Germany in 1917.

October 1 My Lord, but that Hitler man is astute. The next thing he will get is some colonies from England. I verily believe he will get some colonies back. He handles statesmanship precisely as I would like to were I in his place: same methods, same arms, same manner. I can't help, therefore, admiring him. He certainly is a living refutation to the thesis of the proponents of education that it takes learning to make a man fit to cope with life.

October 7 I have been wanting to find time to speak of the nut who has been here three or four times, one Mrs. Delia Lane, professedly thirty-five, actually close to fifty. Early in her life she commenced to see ghosts and have the power of divination. "I have The Power. I am one of the three people in the entire world to possess The Power. I have Knowledge. I am an initiate, even as Christ was, as St. Paul was. The world is to be saved by Me. I am 'of the Light and in the Light.' I know everythin'. Everythin'! I know why and how plants grow. I know all Hidden Things. I am the earthly Apotheosis of Wisdom. I have written twenty-eight books — they are in storage waitin' to be given to a thirsty people. I have the power of freein' myself from my body at will and journeyin' backwards or forwards in time. I am familiar with spirits and with bein's in other dimensions."

So she talked, on and on, swiftly, emotionally but with a certain facility for words and pictures. It always gives me the creeps to hear such persons hold forth. I can never determine what portion of their spoken attitude is real to them and what is charlatanism. While I am certain that thought reading and thought transference exist, that there are some rare individuals gifted with a capacity for prophecy, that many persons can read character and the trend of events from palms, stars, the shapes of heads, I am nevertheless dubious as to the verity of familiars, spirits, ultradimensional worlds, messages from beyond.

October 16 I have been reading the thousand-page 1936 edition of the famous 'Diary of Philip Hone, 1828 – 1851.' While the author's style is too stiffly self-conscious to intrigue me, much of the contents is extremely interesting. The chief fault I have to find, however, is with the editor, not with the author. A diary expurgated and deleted is a eunuch of a diary. I hope to God no one will ever castrate my diary.

I have also been reading the journals of John Muir, naturalist, 1867 – 1911. I am not enthralled by them. Journals are rewritten diaries, rewritten notes. The element of not knowing what will happen the next day, the next hour is invariably smoothed out of them. They lack the exciting uncertainty derived from not knowing what is ahead until it comes to pass. Also, they are toned down and made discreet.

I have likewise been perusing 'The Heart of Burroughs's Journals,' selections from diaries, notes, journals kept by the naturalist [John Burroughs] between 1854 and 1921. As far as I am able to judge, these selections are really diaries and notes, not journals in the true sense of the word. I like what I read. The author had imagination and style. I would wish that there were an edition of the full diaries, even including the "profuse observations of the weather" of which the editor speaks.

B. DewRoberts, referring to Bulkeley's diary, asserts: "Candour, indiscretion, and an unfailing zest for the detail of life — these are the chief ingredients of the perfect diary."

Dr. Francis McD.C. Turner
Magdalene College
Cambridge
England

c/o Pepys Library

Dear Dr. Turner: —

In recent issue of the American magazine, 'Time,' I noted an account of your research into Pepys' diaries. The small article stated that you had determined, after eight years of study, not to include in your new edition the indelicate passages which previous editors had seen fit to delete.

For twenty years I have been keeping a diary with in view the purpose of recording from day to day the pulse of America as exemplified in my own life, the lives of my friends, newspaper clippings, public events, songs, poems, letters. Into this work I have put my entire heart and energy. Certain critics, such as Walter Lippmann, have had the kindness to tell me that I am succeeding.

The point is this: Should whoever edits my diaries after my death see fit to expunge the indelicate passages (and there are such in the life of each person who lives life at all zestfully), I should, were I a ghost, regard the one who took it upon himself to delete at his judgment as one who had cheated me. Having read Mr. Pepys and come to know him in some sort, I seriously doubt whether his spirit (a mundane one surely) will be grateful to you for your reticence on what he would consider the 'spiciest' moments of his career, though of course not the most important.

It seems to me that in all literature there exists no livelier medium for the recording of the spirit of an age than the day-to-day diary. And it also seems to me that the very moment an editor, however friendly, commences to choose from any such diary what shall and shall not be published, that moment the diary commences to lose its authentic flavor. I feel very strongly upon this subject.

I trust that you will not consider my letter an imposition. I would value any assertion of why you see this matter oppositely from myself. I am always ready to be convinced of the other side of any debatable question.

With a sincere interest,
Arthur Inman

October 17   Anthony Abruzzo. He wrote two letters in answer to my advertisement. He wrote:

> Why don't I write my own stories? Because I can't write very well, as you can see by this letter. English is my greatest fault. I don't know about nouns, verbs, pronouns and all that.

He wrote:

> So far I have had no excuse for exsisting, for I am living for myself, for that I am a useless creature inso far as society is concerned. Now is the chance for me to do something worthwhile.
>
> But what, you may say, have I to offer. This is what I can tell you, that I have traveled for five years never spending more than a month in one place, I can tell you of life in the hobo jungles, of life on the Missisipi River, of dive's from the Bowery to the water front of New Orleans, of love in the south, of booms of the oil field towns of Texas, gambling and crime of New York, of the beauty of the picturequse Catskill Mountains, of the husle and busle of the avarge New Yorker, of the gold mines of Colerado, of the plains of Kansas, of farms in Missouri, ranchlife in Texas, cotton plantations and tobaco farms of the south, of the coal regions of Penn. and Ill. of bloody Harlem county in Ky. of race tracks.

"A funny-lookin' little chap," said Billy. "He's got the appearance of havin' been pushed around by the world. He must be all of thirty-one."

"I'll bet he has a way with women," said Evelyn.

He talked slowly, deliberately, couldn't be hastened. I had half a mind not to have him come.

This morning I was sitting in the car to get some air. A couple of dozen W.P.A. musicians were idling on the steps of the hall across the street. Weak faces, every last one of them. Directly in front of me one of those nondescript men who make a living polishing cars was busy dusting the slick spots and leaving the dirty ones alone. On him, too, a weak face. Men driving trucks passed. Weak faces. Some students walked by. Weak faces.

Any one of those men, I thought, might have been Anthony Abruzzo. Most of them bore a dark foreign stamp. Vanity and animalism and lack of sensitivity and lack of ambition and lack of an ethical code to live by writ large on their faces. Poor specimens all, existing neither as masculine fighting machines nor as gentle, purpose-sustained humans.

Abruzzo is twenty-four. His paternal grandparents came to the United States from Palermo. His maternal grandparents were of German extraction, and the grandfather fought in the Civil War on the side of the Confederacy. His father sold insurance in Hartford, Connecticut, made about forty dollars a week. His mother died when he was eleven, his father when he was fourteen. He is at present without employment, having lost, so he says, his savings betting on the horse races and at the dog tracks.

I hardly know how to chronicle his story. Most people speak as they speak and, unless they are under emotional stress, their mistakes of language remain fairly constant. Not so with Abruzzo. One minute he says "de" and "dis" for "the" and "this" and the next says "the" and "this." "Watcha" is interchangeable with "what do you," "an" and "n" with "and," "goin" and "gonna" with "going," "wich" with "which," and so on.

He was raised in a poor section of Hartford. "I hardly remember my mother. My father was a guy wid a strong temper. I recall once he trew me up against the ceiling; I hit my head, then fell to the floor. Ten minutes after, he was apologizin' to me an' givin' me ten cents. I thought nothing more about it. He was like that. It was his way. Another time he put a box of pictures of movin' picture actors and actresses I'd been collecting in the furnace because they was dirty 'n frayed at the edges. I couldda killed him then. But wat de hell?"

Abruzzo belonged to a gang. They would fight another gang with fists or stones for possession of the baseball field on the playground near the gasworks. When he was eight, his best friend drowned in front of his eyes. He used to steal eggs from his mother's refrigerator, sell them, buy food for himself. "I loved to eat. I couldn't get enough food inside my belly. Yet I never grew big." He wheedled nickles from his Italian grandmother and spent them at the movies. Of all his pleasures, he liked the movies best. He played the games that all small boys play. He enjoyed school but still more enjoyed playing hooky. His father was Catholic, his mother Episcopalian. She sent him to her church to Sunday School. He enjoyed that. The boys played such pranks as putting one of their number in a dumbwaiter and leaving him between floors. The teacher was a Yale student, son of a missionary to China. "He was a swell guy. He took us on walks in de woods an' showed us how nature woiked."

Of his mother's death, Abruzzo said, "I cried some, but, as I said, I was not very close to her." Of his father's death, "Dat was a different matter. It touched me so close I was unable to cry. I jus' felt like de world 'd dropped away."

Abruzzo had an uncle, his mother's brother, a baker by trade. The uncle had thriftily saved his money, purchased a bakery, become well-to-do. Someone left him some money. He lumped all his cash together and bought five sea planes with the idea in mind of starting a line between New London and New York. Two planes were destroyed by a storm. A third was wrecked. The fourth landed on top of a house, and the uncle had to pay for the repairs. The fifth plane he sold, as well as the garage, to meet deficits. Then someone else left him more money. He went to North Carolina to become a farmer. He failed at that. He went to work and himself earned another stake. With that he decided to run a truck farm in Georgia. He concluded to take his orphaned nephew, aged fourteen, with him.

"I liked Georgia well enough. Me 'n the uncle didn't get along none too good, but he wasn't hard on me. Workin' in the ground was fun. It was summer. We raised tomatoes and lettuce and stuff like that. I used to get a hoe and a rake and wander along the ditches and catch moccasins and kill dem — sometimes twelve or more in a day. Once I ran away. A bootlegger give me a ride. He said he was haulin' apples, but I knew there wasn't any apples in Georgia. A copper stopped him an' he shelled out, an' the copper let him go, so I was certain that he was a bootlegger. I lef' him an' came back to my uncle. We was in Georgia six months, at which time my uncle went broke again and we come north to New York. My uncle went to Brooklyn and set himself up in de roomin' house business. He kep' a clean house and did very well for himself at first."

Abruzzo betook himself to the Western Union offices and was hired immediately "because I had on high shoes and the other guys didn't." At first he was assigned to Herald Square. "I liked bein' a messenger fine. You met all sorts a' people. Once when I was deliverin' a message to the wholesale clothing district, a woman wanted to take me ridin' in a taxi. But I was young then an' didn't know what it was all about. I wisht since I'd gone wid her. I had a pal. Maybe you won't believe me, but he was a Postal Telegraph messenger. He used to put all the messages down de sewer. I told him he'd get caught someday. He was caught, too, an' lost his job. I pushed telegrams for a year or more. I got acquainted with all the speak-easies. I took to drinkin'. Boy, I was a guzzler. I was soused most a' the time. The uncle didn't like it, so I told him to go to hell and lef' home.

"I was makin' seventeen dollars a week. I hired a room. One day I decided to find out what women was all about. I knew where de red light district was, so I went there. I got myself a Southern girl. She showed me wat it was all about. I took to it like a fish to water. She was a country girl come to New York to make a success. She'd hit the bumps an' landed up as a prostitute. She was twenty-three. She'd tried woikin' for a boss but didn't like it none, so was on her own. She was a nice baby. She took dope an' wanted me to, but I told her no dice. She didn't make me pay. Three other prostitutes I had did, though. Then there was a stenographer. It wasn't a matter of sex with her — I just liked her. And oh yes, dere was a house maid in de Bronx. She didn't cost me nuttin'. As a matter of fact, I borrowed money from her and never paid it back.

"Women wasn't my whole education either. I took up with a waiter in a restaurant. Gees, dat guy could tickle the ivories. He and me used to have some swell drinkin' parties. Everybody made fun of him, but I was young and didn't suspect a thing till one day he got me in his room when I was drunk and did his doin's on me. I told him he ought to have his mouth sewed up and lef' him. It was about that time dat I meets de big boss of de slot machine racket in Harlem. I tought I was a pretty wise guy by then. He offers me five bucks for every machine I can get installed in the Bronx. You see, he wanted to muscle in there. I didn't have no success. I was too drunk, an' there was an honest district attorney in the Bronx, one what couldn't be fixed.

"I became more and more of an inebriate. One night a taxi hit me. Then I got to seein' things. I saw a streetcar runnin' off de tracks an' headin' straight for me. I guess I screamed. A cop grabbed me. I socked him. He socked me. Den he takes me to the psychopathic ward at Bellevue Hospital. What a place. I was there for two weeks. They gave me ether and alcohol to cure me. You never seen such a place as them two wards. Drunks sprawlin' on the floor on mattresses. Drunks tremblin' an' seein' things an' having d.t.'s and losin' up their guts. Guards beatin' up drunks. Insane men in strait jackets an' insane men out a' strait jackets. An' moanin' an' hollerin' an' shoutin'. Honestly, Mr. Inman, it was the first time in my life that I had ever given thought to my fellow creatures as individuals. Hitherto, I had just lived, done no thinking whatsoever. It was also the first time I had ever given thought to my future. Gees, I did some thinkin'. I was grateful to them guys at Bellevue. I decided that perhaps New York wasn't the place for me. I decided I'd leave the Big City."

October 19 "Your shabby little man is waiting," said Evelyn. "Show him in," I said. So she did.

Abruzzo may speak slowly, but once embarked upon a tale, it is rarely necessary to interject a word. His speech is self-perpetuating. "I think," he explains, "in mental pictures. I never know ahead what's comin' out. The right picture clicks in place after the one before, an' dat's all dere is to it.

"To continue," he said. "When I got out a' Bellevue, I went to my room and packed my clothes. I had about forty dollars in cash. I decided to go south. It was early spring. I took a bus to Philadelphia. I landed there late in de afternoon. I wanted a drink. I hunted up a speak-easy. I got a woman. Before you could say Jack Robinson, I was lit. De girl takes me to a room in the New York Hotel. I didn't know nothin' till I woke de nex' mornin'. I lef' Philadelphia dat afternoon. A railroad detective holds me up at the station. I knew he was the Law. I showed him my ticket. He let me pass. That was my first introduction to the railroad dicks, 'bulls' we calls dem on de road. I'd spent too much money drinkin' in Philadelphia, so I walked through Washington to save money. I crossed the bridge into Virginia. I met a bum there. I was gonna hitchhike my way to Richmond. He asked why I didn't ride the freights. I hadn't thought about it, I said. So I lef' him an' went to the railroad yards in Alexandria. A yard bull saw me and give me the chase. I went back to the road. A pair a' Jewish newlyweds rode me to Richmond in dere car. They was good people. They invited me to keep on. I said no, I wanted to look at the city. So I lef' dem. Dere wasn't much to look at. I saw the yards and decided to hop a train for Petersburg. I hid myself in a gondola. We was almost to Petersburg when a bull grabbed me. He handed me a line about trespassin' on railroad property. He wouldn't haul me up in Petersburg because he said the courts dere didn't have nothin' against hobos. He took me back to the county seat where Richmond is and to the courthouse there, a dump if ever dere was one. The judge give me ten days in stir. A man got up in court an' asked him if that wasn't a mighty stiff sentence to give a boy of my age. He offered to pay my fine. The judge ordered him to keep silence or he would put him up for contempt of court. So he shut up.

"Dey took me to the county jail. It wasn't a bad place, clean enough. The niggers was in one tier an' the other tier was for the whites. I was the only white. Dey fed me salt mackerel an' bread an' coffee for breakfast an' stew an' bread an' coffee for lunch. I couldn't eat the first two days, the fish was so salty, but then I did. I walked up and down, and swept and mopped the cellblock. At night the niggers would sing the blues, an' I liked that. After a while, they put another man in wid me. He was a carnival man, drunk. He told me about carnivals. When I got out, I went to the carnival grounds. I put some money on de cigarette wheel. The owner of the outfit thought I was his shill. I wins six cartons a' cigs. Den I beats it. I hides the cartons in the woods in the dark. The nex' mornin' I tries to find dem, but dey aren't dere. I met a nigger. He got me some corn whiskey. I drank till I passed out. The nex' thing I know I'm aboard a freight train bound for Charlottesville. I got off there. I go to a factory to get a job. There wasn't any for outside people. So I bummed a meal. The lady give me real baked ham. I loafed around all afternoon. Den I bummed another meal. I hung around in dat yard till a freight came by. I hopped it. I didn't have no idea where it was bound. There was seven or eight other bums in de boxcar. In the middle of the night we stopped at a one-horse town somewhere. A bull rounded us up and took us to the combination hotel, court and jail. The judge owned the hotel, was justice of the peace and sheriff. He said he didn't have jail room enough for such a crowd. He told de bull to take us to the town limits an' let us go. He did wat he was told. It was cold. We built a big fire in the gutter an' lay down on de road to sleep. In the mornin' I left de mob an' walked back to town.

"I was commencin' to like bein' a bum by that time. You see, when I was a boy I had read Jim Tully and Jack London and other authors who told about the open road and the delights of being a tramp. I was a bum, and I liked it. I was gettin on to de ropes, too. But to continue. I boarded the freight. It was on the Clinchfield, Carolina and Ohio, the C.C. and O., a jerkwater line that run over the mountains from Spartanburg to Elkhorn, Kentucky. The people was folks from Spartanburg goin' on an outin' to the nex' division point an' back — men, women and children. The scenery was swell. Pretty soon we was windin' up the mountains. It took two engines with sixteen drivin' wheels each to pull us, the grade was so steep. I struck up acquaintance wid a mountain boy from Morganton, N.C. He was about my age. Dat night we slep' in a boxcar. We woke up somewhere an' saw a freight car wid a whale on it an' heard a barker whippin' up the curiosity of the people. We didn't think that that was very interesting so we turned over and went back to sleep. The nex' morning we wakes up on sidetrack in a small minin' town somewhere, an' such a miserable place you never saw: tumbled-down houses sticking precariously to the steep slope of a hill. We bummed some bread and apple butter. We waited for another freight, hopped it and eventually wound up at Elkhorn."

I inquired of Abruzzo what he was doing here in Boston. He replied, "I have a sister here. I've been toying with thoughts of settling down. I've been to the Library every night checking up on details of my experiences to be sure they were correct. Also, I've been considering some new ideas. I'm doing research work on something I read somewhere—the theory that people can work better by music. If I can get all the figures from the Public Library, then perhaps I might interest certain manufacturers to install phonographs and amplifiers in their plants. In that case, I would get a rakeoff from the phonograph and amplifier people. But hell, maybe it's just a dream. I'd a' been out a' this here town las' week if it hadn't a' been for you an' your ad. Yesterday I got a job as assistant cook at de Golden Spoon down on Tremont Street. I peel potatoes, cut up squash, fix apples for bakin', an' like-a-that. I work six hours, that is, half a day, get seven dollars a week, eat three meals. I'll stay there till I get a stake. Then maybe I'll put my idea about music over."

October 27 Congressman [Martin] Dies, Democrat, chairman of the House committee investigating un-American activities, has attacked Murphy of Michigan as well as Secretary Frances Perkins. The Rat has seen fit to come to the aid of his Michigan minion, referring to him as "a profoundly religious, able and law-abiding governor." Dies answered by stating that Roosevelt could know nothing about it since he hadn't read the testimony. Last night the Rat gave a fireside chat in which he asserted that, while America was a peaceful nation, it must arm to meet armaments. He, whose main occupation has been baiting the successful businessmen, spoke against Jew-baiting.

October 28 Whenever I am tired in the evening, I have people read to me stories from 'Weird Tales,' 'Astounding Stories,' 'Amazing Stories.' Many of these stories are based upon scientific fact. Some of the authors are scientists writing under pseudonyms. The authors are permitted to adorn scientific facts with any sort of imagination which pleases them. The result is an exposition of free imagination and fanciful theory, sometimes nonsensical, at other times exhilarating. I enclose the following paragraph from an otherwise overdecorated story in this month's 'Weird Tales.' It was worth reading the story for.

We demand of science improvement, discovery, bigger and better toys to play with in order that we can more easily forget the briefness of our stay in the playground itself. The science we support is obvious, spectacular, dealing only with matter, dealing with our bodies very specially that they may be bigger, better bodies so that we may stay longer to play with our toys.

[From Patricia:]

Don't ask me what I thought of the Legion Convention, because it can't be printed. Here in Hollywood we were not disturbed fortunately. All the damage was done downtown in the business district of Los Angeles. It was simply awful from the accounts in the papers. I stayed right at home. I've no patience with such carryings on. If the Legion is a sample of our great American middle class I've not much hope for the country. I'm afraid of organizations of that type, they are dangerous, and they incite mob hysteria too easily. I'm afraid I'm pro-British in that I believe in aristocracy and the ruling classes. It's a good thing that I didn't live during the French Revolution. I'd have been the first one on the guilotine.

Jerry has finally discovered that he can make more money raising flowers than anything else, so he is going to specialize in them and just grow enough vegetables to feed himself and his friends. He will specialize in potted plants there is more profit because of the little waste.

Sunday is Jerry's birthday and I am giving him a dinner, luckily there were five weeks in this month, so I used the rent money for one week to buy him an electric clock and to pay for the dinner. I'm going to have roast chicken, I just can't bear the dressing that you get in restaurants, and I havent had a good old fashioned stuffed chicken since I left home. I asked for the day off so that I'd have plenty of time to cook. Jerry never had a birthday cake until I gave him one three years ago, now I give him a party every year, it embarrases him and he always asks me not to, but I know he likes it so I pay no attention and go right ahead. He just doesn't know how to take anything since he has been out on his own since he was fourteen. He ran away from home and worked on cattle ships, he has been to Spain, Portugal, Honduras and goodness knows where else. He loves a place of his own, and is determined to have a home. He has all his own furniture, that he has bought in the last two years, and now he has a dog whom he adores, so all he needs is to make a success of his gardening and buy the land he is on. Which he is planning to do.

I've become very friendly with Lenore O'Casey, Sean's wife, I go out there all the time. She and Jerry are always swapping plants and advice. One night Jerry and I went out there for dinner, and stayed for the evening, and lo and behold, I discovered that Sean bored me. He drank too much and was so very dull that I became quite irritated with him, as did Lenore, she said "thank God for a man who knows when to stop," referring to Jerry and Sean got quite huffy. He told long pointless stories and I could have screamed. So I guess I'm cured. I've felt a lot happier since.

October 29 "Have you checked on my stories?" queried Abruzzo. "Do you find them accurate?" I replied, "Either you're telling the truth or you're a doggone smart guy." "I'm telling the truth," he said. "Very well, then," I said, "let's go on."

"To continue," said Abruzzo in his voice so much softer than the average American's, a voice you would never associate with the rattle of boxcars, the din of carnivals, the loud talk in speak-easies. "To continue —

"I bought a ticket and rode to Shreveport, Louisiana. Say, dat's a wild town for you. For its size, I never seen a wilder. I started gettin' drunk immediately. I visited de red light district. I looked de town over. In one a' my sober moments, I decided to take precautions so I wouldn't get rolled in some clip joint. A young fellow bummed me on the street. He said he was a sharecropper. He said dat he an' his mother an' father an' brother was starvin'. I go to de grocery store and buys him some flour, some black-eyed beans, some sowbelly an' other things. I told him I'd give dem to him if his old man 'ud put me up. Dey lived in a filthy shack about two miles out a' de town. Their clothes was torn an filthy. Dey couldn't read or write. Dey crawled wid lice. Not even among de niggers had I ever seen people like dem. Dey was happy, but dey didn't know nothin'. Dey had no shame. I've seen de father an' den de two sons take turns layin' wid de old woman, an' dat right in front a' me. I bought an army cot an' set it up in an outhouse an' slep' dere. I got a job as clerk in a grocery store in Shreveport, but I got so soused they fired me after a week. I tried out the prostitutes. An' all de while I drank. I talked to everybody an' asked questions.

"I learned about de prison farm, where politicians sold prisoners to work an' where de boss beat the convicts wid bull whips to keep dem workin'. I made the acquaintance of a girl — let's see, what was her name? — Brown — 'Brownie' I called her. She was young an' pretty an' was secretary to a doctor. I fell for her. We was goin' to get married. She wasn't intelligent; she was dumb. But she gave the impression of being intelligent. What I mean is, you had to tell her everything a dozen times, sort of drum it into her, before she learned. She never picked things up for herself, which is what I call intelligence. Gees, but was she passionate. She liked to be petted. She'd lay on de bed, an' I'd fool wid her an' she'd moan an' bow herself up jus' like a cat. But I got tired of her. She lef' de dishes dirty. She'd pin up her skirt instead a' sewin' it. In a word, she was sloppy. I wasn't gonna get hitched up to no sloppy wife. So I lef' her. Just about den de Farleys, de sharecroppers I was stayin' wid, was evicted for stealin' dere own cotton. My money was spent; I'd been in Shreveport for a long time, so I decided to pull up stakes an go elsewhere."

October 30 Billy asked: "What'll I get Sadie for her birthday? She's got a good fur coat. I gave her a radio. I gave her a set of bedroom furniture. I've given her a silver toilet set, a camera, a wrist watch, a cameo, three rings and lots of odds and ends. I dunno what she wants she hasn't got." Yesterday Billy was showing me his new $850 automobile, bright and shiny, equipped with a push-button radio and all sorts of gadgets. Billy and Sadie together make about $3,000 a year. There is nothing within reason that they cannot have. Looking at it with detachment, what earthly use would it be for Billy to be ambitious, to slave his life away to make a fortune? The more he made, the more would go to the Government. A strange civilization, one that penalizes success — all save the most violent success — until it is not worthwhile for an ordinary person to climb financially beyond a certain point.

November 1 Abruzzo is always late. He doesn't apologize. He simply states that he was detained at the library or by the traffic or shaving. You feel as though you might as well tell water to stand upright as to admonish him to order his movements by the clock.

He is now working a full twelve-hour day at the Golden Spoon, twelve hours a day, twelve dollars a week.

He obtained a job working on derricks for drills at fifty cents an hour. The work was heavy, the ground ankle-deep in mud and oil, the labor disagreeable to him. When he came upon Ginger, the prostitute he had known in Colorado, "slinging hash" in a small restaurant, he threw up his job and went to live with her in the shack she rented to ply her trade. She had fallen in love with a man, he had taken her savings and decamped, and she was following him east. She was making money hand over fist — her salary as waitress, tips, five dollars a man. "Dat man wid whom Ginger was in love was a fool to take her money an' beat it. Boy, dat girl was a gold mine. She was a hustler. If I'd a' been dat man, I'd have realized I had a meal ticket for the rest of my life. He lacked a long-range viewpoint."

After a week with Ginger, he departed, with a stake of forty dollars given by her, for the even newer oil boom town of Kilgore.

His description of the town sounds like the description of Benton in the days of the Union Pacific I have been reading in one of Zane Grey's novels on the talking-book. Saloons wide open, gambling joints, a house of prostitution with "CAT HOUSE" in electric lights over the door, a branch railroad run straight through a graveyard, the stones thrown helter-skelter; tough men, tough women, laborers black and white, drill workers, engineers, civil engineers, lawyers, prostitutes, get-rich-quick storekeepers, pimps, gamblers, men with money anxious to buy up options on oil properties; truckdrivers, saloon keepers. Abruzzo obtained a job as a blackjack dealer in the back room of a saloon at ten dollars a week and forty percent of the winnings, plus all he wanted to drink. He made a hundred dollars the first week. Then he and two other fellows decided to start a joint for themselves. "The trouble was that we was small fry. No sooner was we set up than de Law descended on us for their rakeoff. Dey wanted more dan we could give dem, so dey closed us up an' took us before de judge. Dey made sure jus' how much money we had, then imposed fines on us for that exact amount. Den dey let us go."

November 6   Last night I had a wild dream. Someone moved my beds. I went berserk. I beat up Pearl. They told me Billy did it. I pushed him down the stairs. He beat me up. He said Evelyn had ordered the change in furniture to be made. I rang her on the phone. Then I woke. I was sweating with anger when I woke. I told Billy of my dream. "Why," I asked, "do you suppose I wanted to beat you and Pearl up? I've nothing against either of you. You've both been gentle and considerate with me." "Dreams," announced Billy, "don't take no account of who you hate and what you do. I murdered my mother in one once. Shoot, you didn't do nothin'."

November 8   Today is Election Day. Curley is running for Governor. We have a traitor in our midst. Janice voted for him, I suppose because all the Irish she goes with told her to. Curley is avowedly against those with wealth. He promises to tax them for the benefit of the underprivileged. Should he get in office, the more he taxes me, the less chance Janice will have for an increase in salary. It is as simple as that. Yet she voted for Curley. I almost lost my temper with her. She is a strange girl in many ways, meek and stubborn at the same time, smart when she is engaged in single-track work, very confused when suddenly shifted from one task to another or when a logical choice between courses is placed before her. As with Mrs. Banks, she is apt at any moment to retreat into some inner never-never land of her own where it is almost impossible to reach her. She is only sporadically alert. Yet her intentions are without alloy. She loves to work. She never watches the clock as Mrs. Banks and Edna did. She is generous and loyal and kindly. The work that Janice does on my diary is eminently satisfactory.

November 12   Three or four days ago I wrote a letter to be sent to Father over Evelyn's signature. Then I became conscience-stricken as to the painful worry it might cause him. So I thought about it for a while. I brought to mind the many things he had done to worry and hurt me. I downed my conscience. Even should the letter upset him, what of it? He has it coming to him. And if I can frighten him with the idea that it is possible for Evelyn to leave me perhaps he will come across more easily with more money. If I don't get it, Aunt Louise will, or Granny or the Community Chest or the Church or God knows who. Of course, there exists a chance that the letter will not draw the sort of reaction I want. But nothing risked, nothing gained. He has just received or will receive a nine or ten thousand dollar extra dividend on Coca-Cola. I might as well get my share. Here is the letter:

November 10, 1938

Dear Father:

I am awfully sorry, but I am going to have to ask you for financial assistance again. We are about the usual amount in the hole, some fourteen hundred dollars. If we could have a thousand dollars around the first of the year, I think I can make ends meet, provided some new serious illness does not happen to Arthur.

Arthur has been in bed a week with an attack of influenza. Although he is up now and out in his car a bit, I am very discouraged, not so much about this particular attack as about the whole situation. Arthur grows weaker, and he has less strength year by year. It is pitiful. I do the best I can to help him, but nothing seems to stop his slow but sure physical decline. And his bad luck never ends. As I said, I am discouraged. I almost feel as though I would like to run out on the whole job. I have tried my honest best to take care of him for you and for his mother, as well as because I wanted to. But I am discouraged. And this business of expenses preys on my mind. I would like to live within the generous income that you allow us, and so would Arthur, but what with one sickness after another we don't seem able to do it, and then I have to come to you for extra money, and I certainly hate that. I don't know what lies in the future. I'm discouraged. But I guess you are too. I don't know how Arthur keeps his spirits up as well as he does. It seems to me he has an indomitable courage. Do you suppose I'm losing mine? I don't want to. I try not to complain ever, for I don't believe in it, but you haven't any idea how weary I grow sometimes. It is a never-ending fight to keep Arthur's small amount of strength intact and to make both ends meet financially and to retain a sense of equilibrium myself.

We have had an exceedingly warm fall. There was a black-eyed susan blooming at the Place today, and the grass was green. I sat in the sun and tried to regain my composure. I am going on a little trip this weekend to visit some friends, and hope I will return in a more cheerful state of mind next week.

Lots of love, and I do hope you are feeling better.

Devotedly,
Evelyn

Evelyn came home. She looks as though she'd been through a fight and come out the wrong end. Her face sagged. All the spring was out of her. Tears were in her eyes. It was Hassie. Johnny had been away last evening. Hassie had gotten drunk. She had dragged an unwilling Evelyn downtown, had made eyes at the men she passed, given them sordid remarks, introduced Evelyn as "Mrs. Murphy," been on the loose generally. She had confided to Evelyn that she didn't love Johnny, had only married him to keep her house. "That woman," asserts Evelyn, "destroys my confidence. She makes life look vile. I'm not going there again. Maybe life is that way, but I don't have to stare it in the face, do I? Anyway, I'm not going to."

November 14   A letter from Father to Evelyn. He is leaving for Atlanta because Aunt Louise and Uncle Frank have given him no peace away from them. They are howling down his trail with the kill in sight. As a postscript, Father wrote:

Your letter came after the above was written. Please keep up hope and don't get too discouraged. Will see what can be done when I reach Atlanta and write you. I love you dearly.

Evidently touched the right chord. What money we don't get from him Aunt Louise will. It would be dour to be an old man and have people cater to you for your money. Yet on the other hand, it would be worse to be an old man without the money that makes people cater to you. Without money, no one would cater to me. Great stuff, money.

I am struck, while listening to Abruzzo's story, with the abundant kindness manifest by the ordinary Americans toward bums, tramps, hobos and the jobless. Abruzzo's tale is punctuated with the daily handouts he received from householders, merchants, wholesale houses, restaurant keepers, truckdrivers, those accosted on the streets and in the saloons.

November 15   Yesterday afternoon the following letter arrived, by air mail, from Father:

(Confidential)

hotel Charlotte
Charlotte, N.C
Nov. 13, 1938

My Dear Evelyn:

I had just written you when I got your letter of the 10th and as I do not want this letter to go through my office I think I had best write you from here.

Your letter was a complete knockout blow to me, not on account of the financial part of it but on account of your absolute feeling of discouragement.

The part that I do not understand is where you say, "I almost feel as though I would like to run out on the whole job."

I can absolutely understand your feeling but surely you do not mean that you are thinking of leaving Arthur at this time, this I think would be more than I could live through.

I have struggled on and worried over this situation for twenty-five years and your courage and strength has meant more to me in my old age, and has taken a greater burden off of me, than I can ever tell you.

Arthur has always been one who was unwilling to take advice from anyone and I think this has been the cause of a great deal of the sorrow and anxiety that he has caused his mother and me and if you should give up the job it seems there would be nothing left for me to do but to place him in some kind of an institution where he could be taken care of.

I hope I have misunderstood your letter, and I think have, but you have been the most wonderful person I have nearly ever known and I do hope and pray that you will find the courage and the strength to carry on until the end which I do not think lies so very far in the future.

Please, Please do not worry about the money part of it, that is my job, not yours, and I will try and see that it is taken care of.

Evelyn disapproves of most of the viewpoints and actions by which I govern my life. She didn't want me to engage in this present attack upon the fears of my Father. Indeed, she disapproved heartily. "It isn't," she said, "straightforward." Yet, after a certain amount of objection, she ratified my course by acquiescence, however unwillingly given. I am perfectly ready to admit that my plan to scare Father by presenting to him in veiled words the notion that Evelyn may lose her courage and leave me, thereby frightening him into a mood where he will be almost anxious the next time to surrender to her any money she asks for, that my plan is underhanded, dirty, at odds with all my convictions as to how friends should be dealt with. However, if the plan works I am more than willing to suffer my own scorn as well as Evelyn's. I know of no other way of dealing with a man who has so much of my future in his hands and with whom I am, at the best, on terms of armed neutrality. He has always disdained me as a human being and as an effective masculine person. While I have a conscience about what I am doing, I have no conscience about rationalizing the right and the wrong of it all until I am in a state of mind to go ahead with what my intelligence tells me is, unless I slip, an effective method of handling my parent.

I nor anyone else can contradict that I live beyond my means. As long as I can wangle extra money from Father, I intend to do so. It is both a satisfaction and a gesture of defiance in his direction. The only part of it that bothers me is concerned with the semiannual 'asking process.' So I set myself to solve the problem of how to get Father in the mood where he would be willing, even anxious, to finance my excess expenses. The letter to which Father's above letter is an answer constituted the result of my machinations. I have always wanted to be ruthless enough to prey upon his fears. This time I have done it, to what purpose, effective or otherwise, time will tell. Evelyn wished to telegraph Father immediately in order to allay his state of mind. So did the soft side of me. But we sent no telegram. I dictated the following air mail letter, which Evelyn sent over her name. The very fact that she will let me use her name, despite her indignant disapproval of the whole business, evidences a show of love for me that is reassuring. The letter reads:

November 14, 1938

Dearest Father:

Your two letters have just arrived. I do not think that you fully understood me, or perhaps I wrote as gloomily as at that moment I felt. I did not mean that at this point I was going to give up; I meant that at times I feel like giving up. At this time I have only the intention of sticking to my job. If I worried you too much, you will have to excuse me, as I didn't know it but I was coming down with influenza, and you know how discouraged that makes a person. I have stayed in the house and in bed and am better now and am not so depressed. You have always been very sweet to me; I love Arthur very much, and on both your account and his I will always do the best that is in me not to fail either one of you.

Am hurrying to get this off on the air mail. Thank you for the sweet tone of your letter. It reassures me.

Devotedly,
Evelyn

I am sorrier than you know that I worried you so much.

And now all I can do is to await developments and pray that they be favorable.

November 21 The press in Italy is attacking the United States as the chief foe of Germany. It is declared that America is the principal tool of Jewish influence and that Roosevelt is of Jewish stock and the Pope of world Jewry. Not having any information to the contrary and having heard again and again the assertion that Roosevelt is of Jewish descent, do you suppose that there is any truth to it? When Woodwork's Allan went to Washington on business, he was appalled by the numerical predominance of Jews in high places in the Government.

December 1 Janice and Mrs. Cash and, to a lesser extent, Honey have made me so conscious of the ugliness of the coastal New England accent that the beauty of English in general has come perversely to be in question. If I weren't concerned with language as an avocation, it wouldn't matter, but it does matter, and greatly. Right now I don't care if I don't hear Janice for a month.

December 3 Mrs. Cash and I are reading Hans Fallada's long novel about Germany during the post-War deflation. It makes clear why the people so joyously accepted Hitler. Mrs. Cash likes the dirt, and I like the character drawing. Mrs. Cash reads to me every weekend. I do not feel nearly as antipathetic towards her as once I did. I have gotten used to her foibles. She has tried to tone down her vulgarity. She makes a real effort to please me, and I am grateful. "If I possess one virtue, Mr. Inman, it is that of being loyal, come fat days, come lean days, to my friends."

December 10 Claire here yesterday afternoon and this morning. She gives lessons in pronunciation to Janice and Pearl once a week. She and Pearl have taken quite a fancy to each other.

I asked Claire if, should I pay all her bills, would she have a baby and give it to Evelyn. "Sure I would," she replied without hesitation. "Whom would you want to be its father? But I couldn't guarantee that it would be a girl." Claire meant just what she said. It is, as I told her, a real pleasure to come in contact with anyone as completely unconventional as herself.

December 17   Boys and kids yell at me when Honey is driving. Usually they yell, "Where'd you get that piece of junk?" The small boys double over in glee. The small girls exclaim, "Oh Mama, look." The cops all know us. The negroes, who have a weakness for big cars, ask, "What year is dat car?" Usually the greetings — if you'd call them that — are friendly, though the small children are invariably derisive. I don't mind as much as I did. Honey says, "Don't let 'em get your goat, Artie. They don't know no better." Honey has the time of her life driving. She laughs when we go fast. She waves at the fellows. She frowns at the kids. She exclaims, "Boy, aren't we havin' fun."

Father sent Evelyn and me, in case I haven't mentioned it, fifteen hundred dollars for our bills. Five hundred went to Dr. Pike and five hundred to Bottom. The rest will go so swiftly it will make the hair curl. Doctors, mostly. Without them, we could live the life of Riley. Never forget, though, that the amount of money I pay them doesn't pay for the interest they have in me that money can't buy.

December 20   Entire back has been collapsed for two days, so haven't done much work. Finished, however, my book of poems. Evelyn has an appointment with Greenslet at Houghton Mifflin at ten-thirty this morning. The book is good, much better than most volumes of poetry that are published. It is ninety-two pages in length, the majority of the pages fat with print. Janice has done a fine job of typewriting.

If Evelyn can catch Greenslet's attention by one subterfuge or another, I may have some chance of the book's being accepted, otherwise, none. As a man in charge of an armory gives to the warrior about to do battle a bow and arrows, a spear, lances, a sword, a mace, a dagger, advises him as to their probable merit in the coming encounter, blesses him and lets him go, so have I accoutered Evelyn with all sorts of possible methods of drawing Greenslet's attention and with advice about using them.

In Boston there may be a hundred persons so gifted with personality, guile, ingenuity that they could sell my book to Greenslet. Is Evelyn one? The book, it is sure, will not sell itself. Poor Evelyn, I do not envy her her task. She likens Greenslet to a bellicose old turtle who disconcerts her by sticking his head out and drawing it in, by being to all appearances uninterested and unapproachable. Yet his firm is honest, of impeccable standing, and the books printed are well done.

December 23   I have been reading 'The Rise of Silas Lapham' by William Dean Howells. Twenty years ago, this American classic would have bored me. Now to my surprise I find myself enjoying it immensely. It is a novel about life in Boston and the social adjustment between old bluebloods and rich new-bloods. Lately I have reread the remainder of 'The Oregon Trail' and all of 'Two Years Before the Mast.' Those old Bostonians certainly thought well of themselves. They were, in their own minds at least, the salt of the earth. In large measure the secure fortunes of the nation were centered in Boston. The elite of the city felt themselves to be the social and cultural arbiters of America. Behind them were Emerson and Thoreau, Holmes and Longfellow, Dana and Parkman and Ticknor and Prescott. They were snobs and proud of it. Bryce called the debates in their Bulfinch State House the finest in the world. The Bostonians of the last century must have been charming among themselves and in the presence of foreigners (whom they considered their equals or their superiors) but insufferable to others outside their circle — insufferable, condescending and boorish.

Have just been in Billy's room to get something. The place is littered with Christmas packages and paper and ribbons and cards. Pearl and Billy go as crazy over Christmas as any advertiser might wish. The entire business makes me gloomy beyond belief. Billy is worn out from many afternoons and evenings of shopping in crowded stores, and Pearl is almost frenzied, laughing shrilly one minute, her eyes burning with tears the next. It is like being in a madhouse, just as it was when I was a child. Janice somehow manages to keep her equanimity in the midst of it, and Evelyn is saner than other years. It is a mania. Mrs. Cash says she received 125 presents.

December 24   Ella said: "I went home from here the other night determined to give my man the very dickens. I found him feeling bad, so I modified my attack somewhat. 'Now you look here, Robert James,' I said. 'I'm not going to spend any more money on this house. I'm going to spend it on myself. I'm sick and tired of going around like a dowdy old housewife with one foot in the grave and the next about to follow. I'm not old yet, but I will be soon. I'm tired of sitting at home and gazing at street scenes through the curtains. I want to have my fling before it gets too late. I want to step out. And I want you to step out with me, and if you aren't willing to, I want you to hire me a gigolo to take me. And I mean it. Here you've gone on the night shift because you thought you could make more money, and I never see anything of you then, and you're gone off on your mysterious business every day. I want a change. I want you to go back to the day shift, even if you make four or five dollars a week less. What's four or five dollars a week in a lifetime. And I want to be taken out evenings. And I want to know what you're up to behind my back with our hard-earned money. I'm laying down the law. So you listen. If you don't listen, I'm going off to New York where I know people who treat me as though I were somebody special and who are willing and glad to step out.'

"Well sir, Arthur, he looked at me as if I'd lost my senses. He didn't say a word. He filled his pipe and walked around me scrutinizing me, I guess to determine whether or not I was real. 'Mama doesn't love Daddy any more?' was what finally came out. 'Mama does love Daddy,' I replied. 'But Mama wants some fun before she becomes an old woman. And Mama wants a husband, not absent treatment. And Mama wants an end to the great mystery that envelops Daddy's doings.' He knew or he thought he knew I meant what I was saying. He promised to change to the day shift when the Christmas rush was over. He said he'd take me out. Then he told me what he'd been up to all this time.

"You'd never guess in a thousand years, Arthur. He and two other chaps are making caskets. They've been at it for three months. They've already sold three. He said he wanted to make good before he told me what he was doing. Caskets! 'For heaven's sake, Robby,' I said, 'I didn't know you knew a saw from a hammer. And now you all of a sudden blossom out as a coffin maker. Will wonders never end?' So he proceeded to explain. There's a little old alley that branches off Dartmouth Street. The houses there are tumbled down. When the P.W.A. first started, a negro from Africa and his wife (she was educated at Portia Law School) tried to make the alley into a colored art center on Government funds. Later, he bought up the shacks there. Then P.W.A. dropped him. Robert and his two partners have rented one of those houses (without heat of any sort) for ten dollars a month. There they build the caskets. One of the largest negro undertakers (he buries five persons a week) has contracted to take the caskets, as Robert can turn them out cheaper than the National Casket Company. The boys hired a drunken Irish carpenter for a dollar a day to teach them carpentry and to install the saws and the lathe. Robert said that if there was money in it, he could learn anything, carpentry included. And I will say this for the boys, the jobs they turn out are as neat as you could wish. I wouldn't mind lying down in one of the caskets myself and taking a snooze, they look so comfortable, all padded and lined. 'If this don't succeed,' said Robert, 'all well and good. I'll try something else. But it may succeed. I've made up my mind to get somewhere yet, one way or another. I'm as good a man,' he said, 'as many who arrive, and better than most.' You know, Arthur, I admire the boy's spirit. He may succeed at that. I only wish he'd started ten years earlier. But anyway, now I'm the proud mama of a casket maker, believe it or not."

December 28   Roosevelt is advocating a huge rearmament plan.

The other day Secretary Ickes in a speech insulted the Germans. Germany demanded an apology. Sumner Welles, the conceited, supercilious Under-Secretary of Foreign Affairs, returned a blunt no, adding that he believed the average American thought as did Ickes. The Germans did not break diplomatic relations as it seems to me they had a perfect right to do.

Roosevelt has completed a plan by which twenty thousand college students will be taught to fly each year at Government expense. He looks forward to a hundred thousand reserve fliers and a fleet of thirteen thousand planes. He is certainly keen on armament, ostensibly for the purpose of causing other nations to leave us alone. Perhaps he wants a war before 1940 so that the American people will reelect him again to office. It wouldn't be beyond him nor, if the Jews have their way, an impossibility.

1939

January 4   Snow. Sitting up for half-hour in small spare room. Had answer from Houghton Mifflin. Didn't want book. Evelyn phoned and asked why not. Greenslet replied that he didn't want to hurt my feelings but that the book was mediocre. So that's that. Either my viewpoint or my artistic objective is cockeyed, or else the publishers of books and magazines are without imagination. After reading hundreds upon hundreds of modern and classical poems, I cannot believe that my poetry is as negligible as the sum of critical opinion would have me think. But whether the poems ever become popular or not, I do enjoy writing them.

January 5   Listened to President Roosevelt's message to Congress on the state of the nation yesterday. It was chiefly directed against the dictator nations (nations unnamed, of course) and for increasing armament and for using economic warfare against said dictator nations. If that bird, pushed on as he must be by the Jews and ambitious as he is to be top eagle at any cost, doesn't involve us in war or try to, I'm dead wrong. As I see it, if we'd leave Germany and Japan alone and mind our own business and quit talking so much, there would be absolutely no danger of any war. Both Germany and Japan have enough to do to carry on their own plans without bothering about us, save as their penetration of South America concerns us, and we could combat that sub rosa as well as they can carry it on sub rosa. As for Germany or Japan invading us, that is all poppycock — at least in the immediate future. It is more sensible to spend money on armaments than on W.P.A., that I admit, and less degrading to the American people, but on the other hand, it is the nature of an ambitious, egotistic man such as Roosevelt to want to use huge armaments once they are at hand.

One of the saddest sights in the world to me, sadder than a tumbled-down house, than an abandoned bridge, than an old plow in a field, is the sight of a library, of any large collection of books. So much work has gone into them, so much ambition, so much expectation, and most of them are sure to have passed into the ghostly limbo where disremembered books go, and all the work, the ambition, the expectation will have been in vain. What is the urge that causes men just emerging from the animal to scratch picto-graphs on the walls of caverns, men of today to endeavor to put down their thoughts and ideas in undying words? Is it merely an effort to escape the feeling of futility attendant upon the process of thinking?

January 14   Last night, lying awake, I was wondering just why I do fall so thoroughly for young girls. It is not only that I was thwarted in that direction when I was young myself. It is that life is before them and every hour is an excitement to them. It is that they haven't been frozen by responsibilities and experiences in more or less solid molds. It is that the little that is in their minds allows them to be receptive to suggestions and promptings. Young people, espe-cially young girls, are not suspicious. And when they put their attention on you, it is really there, not part there and part on business or part on the child at home or part God knows where else. And I like to tend their development.

January 23   Had my stomach pumped out two days ago. While I may not take to Dr. Lakian personally, no one could be more gentle or more receptive to suggestions. He changed the antiseptic at my request, the result being that I got through this time without a sore throat. It has been hard living with me these last two or three weeks. I have been as wild as a badgered fox.

Have finished 'The Sea Wolf.' It is a grand book up to the point where the heroine enters. American literature has traveled a long way since such an unbelievable 'female creature' as Maud Brewster was allowed to suffer an unreal existence in a best seller. The attitude in the United States towards women has certainly undergone a violent change in the last forty years, especially in novels.

January 24   Aphorisms of Evelyn, aimed my way:

1. There is no one more cynical than a disillusioned idealist, that is, than a synthetic cynic.
2. There is no one more dishonest than an honest man who has become convinced that dishonesty pays.

January 27   The Spanish Rightists have marched into Barcelona with bands playing and flags flying. Only a third of Catalonia now remains unconquered. There is rejoicing in Italy and in Germany, the jitters in England and France. Stocks dropped violently here and abroad. The Daladier Government announced that Italy must leave Spain after the war there is ended and that there is complete military solidarity between England and France. There are rumors that England will offer a huge loan to Franco in an attempt to buy him away from Italy and Germany. The world is awaiting with bated breath an address that Hitler is to deliver in the near future. France is buying planes in the United States.

Japan carries its war into inner China, not being wise enough to stop, not having been wise enough to have stopped long ago. What is the use of cutting up an enemy's body when you have a noose about his throat? You may lose your grip on his throat in the attempt, lose control, lose everything.

By February of 1939, Arthur had worked out to his satisfaction the dynamics of the approaching war and its probable contestants. From his headquarters in Garrison Hall, the armchair general devised a correct strategy for the anti-German coalition — in brief, to let Germany have her way in Eastern Europe, since in any event the French and the English had been outmaneuvered. However, he expected them to pressure the United States into a conflict that Hitler stood a good chance to win. Although he claimed to be a disinterested and uncommitted onlooker and a hater of war, Arthur could not stifle his admiration for Hitler's audacious tactics or his thrill at watching the spectacle of naked power. He even pondered the gains the United States might expect by collaborating with the Nazis and the Japanese — the seizure of Canada and northern Mexico — in return for granting them free rein in their spheres of interest. Should war come, Arthur declared, Chamberlain's England must bear the responsibility for trying to frustrate Germany's legitimate territorial ambitions.

He interspersed among these reflections an account of his own efforts to break out of obscurity. One publisher after another rejected his verse, but a crushed Arthur kept his faith in his talent. He experimented with new forms and analyzed the work of published poets. Still convinced that poetry had to be "sold" to ignorant editors, he enrolled Evelyn once again to market his wares in New York. She periodically irritated him by her intransigence and stubbornness, but he relied upon her to represent him not only to publishers but also to his father, whose money he feared he might be deprived of and whose death he devoutly wished.

The Garrison Hall retinue continued to perform well, and dozens of talkers, a cross section of Depression America with more than a sprinkling of cranks and liars, passed in and out of his dark sanctum. Former intimates resurfaced in the Diary. New revelations from old "charac-

*ters " like Woodwork, Ella, and Millicent (now married to "her Hal")
filled in the gaps of their private histories.*

*Lines of continuity wavered as the Diary expanded. Arthur fattened
it with long excerpts from books and articles; with political speeches; and
with letters from relatives, friends, and strangers. He tried but failed to
hold in place his disintegrating body. ("I ripped my rectum, then had
diarrhea for three days; the pelvis went out of place; Billy grabbed my
shoulder and gave me bursitis in it so I can hardly move; the spine and the
ribs have collapsed.") All this time, however, as he critically examined
other diaries, he was forming his aesthetic for diary keeping and was
sharpening his expository skills.*

*And with the announcement of the German-Soviet nonaggression
agreement and the outbreak of World War II, he had to decide whether
the Diary as public chronicle should supersede the private record.*

February 4 Ten years ago, Herbert Hoover was about to become President of the United States. There was to be an era ahead of
unparalleled prosperity. Stock prices were booming. Interest rates
were excessively high. Buoyant optimism was rampant. As for myself, I was lying in a state of semidelirium from having my mouth
burned by violet rays and was making, unbeknownst to myself,
sometimes as much as five thousand dollars a day on stocks. I
wanted to be a millionaire and saw no reason why not.

Ten years later, today, all is different. One-fourth of the world is at
war, and the threat of further conflict hangs heavy on people's
hearts. Trade and commerce carry on with difficulty. The national
debt has nearly tripled. Government control has been placed upon
many phases of private activity. The United States owns most of the
gold of the world. Taxes mount. In the White House is a megalomaniac advised by Jews and Irish and fanatics. Very few persons are
sanguine as to the future. At least a fifth of the citizens of this great
and rich land are receiving relief. Graft and dishonesty are rife, for
they pay. What tomorrow has in store for the world no one knows.
France has become a second-rate power, while Germany is preeminent in Europe. Hitler is the man of the hour.

Today is Evelyn's birthday. I had a cake made for her, bought her
some Tokay wine. Honey and Billy and Janice gave her some flame-
colored tulips. Her mother sent freesias and roses. Dr. Pike has
invited her to supper at the Statler tonight. What she liked best was
the cake with her name on it and the candles lit. I thought she would
cry when she saw it. "It's the first cake I ever had," she exclaimed,
and continued to regard it the rest of the morning.

February 5 After two days, the Rat issued a statement declaring that whoever had quoted him on France being the American frontier had lied, as had the newspapers. He declared that it was all only a political plot to discredit him. He issued a somewhat ambiguous declaration as to what his foreign policy was. He was riled. The German and Italian attacks must have gotten under his skin, attacks such as "Roosevelt is a man of catastrophe and ill chance, and he wants to bring the United States ill luck. His policies are explained by infantile paralysis. Not only his smile but his policies are those of a mental case." Plenty of Americans agree, but not hitherto has such plain speaking appeared in print for the Rat to read with his own eyes. An explanation of the attack has been demanded of the Italian Government. While I enjoy watching someone get under the Rat's skin, I regret that this has happened; it will serve to align the United States still more with France and England. Additional orders for planes are arriving daily from those two nations.

February 7 A large portion of the population of Catalonia — soldiers, citizens, women and children — with their cattle and their beasts of burden, with what possessions they are able to carry with them, are fleeing into France to seek asylum there. The soldiers are being disarmed at the frontier by French troops, and all Spaniards registered and inoculated before being placed in concentration camps. It must be a dramatic and harrowing scene, this flight from a conquered land. How many times in history has the same cyclorama of defeat and rout been enacted. Leftist gold was long ago sent into France for safekeeping. The Leftist Cabinet is in France. Leftist battleships, fishing boats, craft of all sorts have allowed themselves to be interned in French ports. A hundred war planes have landed on French soil to avoid capture. Artillery is being dragged over the border to save it from the hands of the victors. The Leftists are ravaging the countryside behind them, dynamiting, burning, destroying, so that the smoke of destruction rises into the sky.

There is always something sad about the final giving-in of a people, a particular type of civilization, the sharp termination of an era, whether the scene be enacted in Catalonia, the Confederate States of America, Imperial Russia, Austria.

February 11 I know how Edward VII felt waiting for Victoria to die. There is the Old Man with more than a million capital. Here am I, forty-three years of age. If I lived to be ninety-three, if I had that million, I could spend twenty thousand a year for fifty years and not even have any interest. With the interest included, life, financially, would be strawberries and cream. But no, the old bastard will leave the capital tied tighter than a criminal and all I will get, if that, will be the interest, and anyway he will live to be eighty or ninety. I wish to God he'd die. I wish to God I'd die. But if he'd die, maybe I wouldn't want to die so much. He has a psychological stranglehold on me. I ought to be strong enough to throw it off, but I'm not. All parents should be killed off at fifty unless their offspring wish otherwise.

February 12   It is said by everyone who comes to Boston that we have the dirtiest streets in America, and I can well believe it. Not a whitewing [streetsweeper], or what goes for one, from the first snowfall until the last. Not even the sewer vents are opened. Sand collects and rubbish and scum, ice and snow. A few snow-removal machines have lately been put into operation but none until recently except downtown. No rides for me until April or May, so it would seem. Eyes are gritty with fine-ground sand.

Mrs. Cash and I have finished 'Imperial Byzantium' by Bertha Diener. An interesting volume to read even though it is arranged out of chronological sequence and even though it lacks a proper bibliography. Not much was taught me at college concerning Byzantium nor much said of the historical importance, less in fact than of the Arabs. To know about this important cuff link between Europe and Asia, this guardian of Roman culture during the Middle Ages enables one to get a readier grasp on all history. Must read a history of the Arabs next. Have already read two biographies of Mohammed, a history of the Seljuks, a history of the Turks, several histories of the Mongols, a history of the Moguls, a history of Egypt, etc. Want to read another history of Byzantium as well, also a history of Venice.

February 14   Juliette was here last evening for the first time in many months. I've tried to get her, but she's always pleaded busy. She, coyly: "I'd thought maybe you'd outgrown me, Arthur, and didn't want to be bothered with my presence any more." She talked and talked and never stopped. Clarence, she said, has so much business that he can't handle it. He twitches in his sleep and is tired. He can't get enough capital to finance himself. Two men with money want to come into the firm. He is bidding on a sixty thousand dollar order for the New York World's Fair.

Juliette hasn't been working steadily. She has been having a mild affair with a Dr. Somebody Sillitoe, an eye and ear specialist. Sillitoe's wife is jealous of her and Clarence of him. Juliette doesn't intend to have a baby. "I've such a swell shape now, Arthur; I couldn't bear to lose it. Anyway, all women, especially Jewish women, think of after they have children is children. I don't want to be that way. Do you think I'm very selfish, Arthur?" Her tone changed from query for approval to smug satisfaction. She concluded with "Well, if I'm selfish, I'm going to keep right on being so."

Clarence and Juliette are bringing into this country a Jewish family from Germany. Clarence has to guarantee to provide for them until the man gets work. "It's such a cunning baby, Arthur. You should see his picture. Adorable. The family name is Mann. They wrote us to find out if we were related. The man said he'd kill himself if he couldn't get out of Germany. But I suppose you have no desire to hear about that, taking into account how you feel on the subject. But the baby is adorable."

February 18 Roosevelt is off on a two weeks' vacation. I hope the warship that carries him sinks. Sometimes I can view contemporary history as Tacitus would have wished, with judicial and impartial detachment, but most of the time it is more interesting to give free rein to my emotional partiality. In the end, I believe that such a course will best serve the purpose of such a chronicle as mine purports to be. Roosevelt once in a while may be studied without personal bias, but generally he strikes me as being a rat, The Rat, a subversive, conceited, ebullient personage of undeniable courage, little wisdom, much personality, a flattered and headstrong megalomaniac hellbent on ruining the country for self-respecting and self-supporting people.

February 19 The 'Haverford News' in this year of 1939 is full of political and social reporting. The students appear to be acutely interested in what is happening in Spain, in China, in Germany. They appear to be violently and emotionally anti-Nazi, anti-Fascist, anti-Japanese. They plead the cause of the Jews. What is happening in the world must be mightily important to them or they wouldn't write about it at such length and in such variety. I can only wonder if they aren't sacrificing a certain charming sort of suspended peace in return for a vicarious excitement of dubious value which will all too soon become real. Are they not relinquishing a period of mental and imaginative gestation that might be of more importance to them in their future lives than any amount of premature and somewhat artificially induced attention to world affairs?

I, for one, am thankful indeed that my days at Haverford were not made irritable with ideologies and causes. Few enough in a man's life are the isles of withdrawal, the sanctuaries where count may be taken of one's inner resources and strength to endure and to contend.

February 24 Charles Fulke Greville early in his career resolved to be among the world's greatest diarists. He kept an account of what he thought and was from 1814 to 1860. His notes concerned the

great and near great of England. He left what he had written to
a friend to be published after his death. The friend cut and pruned
and brought out a deleted edition. The Macmillan Company has
just published a limited edition of 600 copies of the complete and
unexpurgated Greville Memoirs in eight volumes, price $80.

I remarked to Mrs. Cash, who was reading me the review of the
diaries, "I wonder if I'll ever be that successful?" "No," she replied
promptly, "I feel sure you won't. Greville lived among successful
people and in exciting times. While I won't say what you do may not
be meritorious in its way, it can never touch Greville." Mrs. Cash
harbors a profound disdain for my diary, what she has seen of it. She
has rather a disdain for me, too. She has a number of friends and
ex-students, some of whom sound interesting. She will not let them
meet me. Very few persons will allow their friends to meet me. The
way I live is queer to them, and if it is queer to them, what will their
friends think?

To return to diaries. There must be hundreds of them that people
have kept during their lives that are tucked away and never will be
printed. I have been reading the 'Secret History' of Procopius. There
was he, spending many years of his life writing and issuing his
'Histories' and his 'Buildings,' receiving recognition, only to surrender at last to the inexplicable allurement that causes so many
men to write down their secret thoughts, ideas, knowledge, interests, what not, whether what they write ever sees the light or not.

February 26   Janice's poise has increased since she came here six
months ago. Bertram Davis has been giving her quite a rush, and I
suppose that that increases her self-confidence. She is dressing more
neatly. She takes better care of her person. Her hands are strong,
mobile, capable, really beautiful hands. Some day I hope to get some
decent-looking shoes on Janice's long, narrow feet. While she is
clumsy with her hands, is no cook at all, has a South Boston accent,
her good qualities so far outweigh the few that irritate me that I want
to make evident to her in a tangible way my appreciation. She is a
darling.

March 1   I got the first volume of the Greville diary from the
Harvard Library and have been reading in it here and there and
studying its setup. A well-edited edition. About two hundred thousand words to a volume and seven volumes of the diary proper,
roughly a million and a half words. From a very casual scrutiny of
the contents, I should judge them to be most interesting, the author
shrewd, whimsical, observant.

March 3   The old Pope has at last died, and a new one has been
elected by the College of the Cardinals, a man not sympathetic, it is

said, to the dictator nations. The Roman Catholic Church has made and unmade wars, crowned and uncrowned kings, swayed the course of history, remained through the ages powerful and rich and ready to adjust itself and its policies to circumstances, if needs must, in order to maintain its preeminence as an international state functioning within numberless states.

Cardinals from many sections of the earth gather to elect the new Holy Father when the old Pope dies. They meet in Rome. They are supposedly held incommunicado until the election is made. I suppose they are held thus so that Catholics all over the world will have no opportunity of becoming disillusioned by being witness to the politics taking place when the Pope is being chosen. Terrific pressure must be brought to bear from many directions when a Holy Father is to be elected. Chateaubriand, sent to Rome more than a hundred years ago to see to it that the Cardinal the French had in mind was elected, wrote as follows:

I have to bring influence to bear on an invisible body, locked within a prison to which all access is strictly guarded. I have neither money to bestow nor posts to promise. The senile passions of fifty or so old men give me no hold over them. I have to struggle against crass stupidity in some, ignorance of the world in others; fanaticism here, craft and duplicity there; ambition, self-interest and political enmities in nearly all, and I am shut out by walls and mysteries from the assembly in which so many elements of discord are fermenting.

Pius XII is the new Pontiff's churchly title, chosen by himself to signify he will carry on the policies of his predecessor.

March 4   Got weary of fooling around and this morning took nose and yanked and pulled it to the right. Could feel the cartilage slip in place with an audible click. Now we'll see.

For three years now, off and on, I have been toying with the idea that insulin injections might be of assistance in my case. Have just read Paul de Kruif's 'Men Against Death' on the talking-book, and my interest in insulin has been reawakened. I want Bottom's books in order to study up on the subject.

March 5   Reading Greville's diary. Becomes tiresome. Less a human document than a retailing of gossip that had to do almost solely with the English upper classes. The English upper classes sound very uninteresting, very much without the light and gallant touch, very self-serious and self-satisfied. The French nobility at least lightened their self-importance with wit.

Browsed through John Evelyn's diary. Much more readable. Evelyn had imagination and was something more than a purveyor of
secondhand gossip.

Tried Ticknor's journals. Quite vivid and amusing in places but
lacking, as journals always do, the moment-to-moment spontaneity
characteristic of diaries. A journal wears a unified aspect due to its
being written up afterwards, smoothed out, deleted and expurgated, polished and groomed to please prospective readers. That is
impossible for any self-respecting diary to attain to, thank God.
Better an out-and-out narrative than a journal.

March 6 My doctors are good to me. Arthur Garner asked:
"What do you do with your mornings? Do you work?" I replied: "I
get up about eight-thirty. I read the headlines in the papers. I ride
awhile. Then I write and work for a couple of hours." "And your
afternoons?" "I correct for two hours and a half, usually. In the
evenings I get read to or else talk to people to find material to write
about." "Every evening?" "Practically every evening. Then I listen
to the news on the radio and play my talking-book until twelve or
half past. Then I sleep on an average of four or five hours." "That
all? Do you nap during the day?" "About twenty minutes in all —
ten or fifteen after lunch, the rest before supper." "My Lord, man,
you do a day's work. How much do you write a day?" "Oh, on the
average of five hundred words, not including letters and poetry."
"Well, no one can rightly call you lazy. Do you ever walk at all?"
"Only to the car and back." "What happens when you do walk?" "I
get exhausted and usually have a migraine, or my bones go out of
position. I wish I had some strength. I wish I could walk." "Well,
don't you worry that you can't, Arthur. You do more work in a day
than I do. It's nice to be able to walk, but it's also nice to have a mind
and be able to use it as you do. It's just up to fellows like me to keep
you running. What you do in this world will probably be of more
account in the long run than what we do. So don't lose heart,
Arthur."

March 10 Honey came to me two days ago and announced that
she had been on the job a year. Wouldn't I give her a raise? Was she
pleasing me? I told her that, while I was extremely fond of her, it was
my honest opinion that she was receiving precisely what she was
worth. I praised her willingness, her manual dexterity, her readiness
to adjust her hours to mine. I pointed out, on the other hand, that
she couldn't read to me, that she hadn't put her heart into learning
bookish matters, that Edna had been able to do research for me, had
been more willing to work at the Place, had been able to play the

piano and write letters, etc. If, I said, she ever proved to me that she could consistently occupy an executive role in our household, I would be glad to pay her more.

March 11   Last evening a Mrs. Haviland came to talk to me. She lasted for not quite an hour. "She seemed like a sweet sort of person," objected Evelyn. "How can you know her in an hour or less?" "Well," I replied, "I asked her how old she was, how long she'd been married, whether she loved her husband, whether he loved her, whether she loved her son or her husband best, why she'd been to the hospital lately, if she used contraceptives, how much salary her husband made, who her ancestors were, how she budgeted her money, if she believed in God, how many friends she had, what did she look forward to in life, what sort of childhood she'd had, was she calm or emotional, did she read, like music, the movies, and so on. Most of her answers I believed, some I didn't. I could judge from the way she talked that her upbringing was a bit out of the ordinary, for both her accent and her use of words were resolutely correct. What else could I have learned if I had talked a week with her? Any originality of experience or of imagination would have been sure to crop out within the confines of an hour. She didn't interest me. Why should I have drawn out the interview? It isn't whether she's sweet or not, but what sort of material for my diary she is, what kind of material for a possible friendship." Evelyn sighed.

March 12   A large portion of the night I listened to the services in St. Peter's leading up to the coronation of the new Pope. Several points interested me. The chanting, for instance, seemed to vary in character and origin, some of it being as barbaric as that of an American Indian lament. And I could not help wondering what private thoughts were passing through the head of the chief attraction of the gorgeous ceremonial proceedings. When the subdeacon brought the Body of Christ on Its ceremonial platter of gold held high above his head to the Pontiff and the Pontiff partook of the Body of Christ and drank of the Blood of Christ (if the priest describing the Holy Communion looked upon it as symbolic, his words conveyed complete reality, as though he believed implicitly that it was in sooth the very Body and Blood of Christ the Pontiff was eating and drinking and swallowing), when, then, the Pontiff munched and sipped his gruesome snack, I felt a repulsion which I was at pains to analyze.

I bethought me of the barbarian custom of tearing out and eating the hearts of illustrious enemies. Christ was illustrious in the eyes of His followers. Eat His Body and drink His Blood, ingest His particular qualities of godhood. Unpleasant. And I thought of the thousands of people gathered in assembly there in St. Peter's and of how it was necessary, in accordance with the amenities of civilization, for them to restrain (many of them doubtless at the cost of considerable pain and discomfort over an unnaturally long period of time) the natural physical functions of the body. Then I pondered upon how much the acquisition of this artificial control over the excretory functions of the human body had had to do with the rise of civilization. And then I considered the fact that, as far as I was aware, among all the moving creatures of the earth the only one to share with man the ability of regulating and controlling the discharge of the waste products of the body was the dog. And by that time it was the hour of my breakfast, and I was glad to shut off the radio and shut off my mind and eat my cream of wheat and bacon.

March 14   Yesterday Allan Trow telephoned Evelyn and made an appointment to see her at suppertime to discuss Woodwork. Woodwork, it seems, is unable to get and keep help. Much of the winter, therefore, all the household work has devolved on her. Her health has failed. She has the constant jitters. She cries upon the slightest provocation. She is melancholic. She has asthma. Allan says that she is delirious at times. However, she tenaciously refuses to do anything about it. Allan has offered to finance a trip for her. Finally, in desperation, he located a doctor in Pawtucket whom he considered intelligent. Somehow or other, he prevailed upon Woodwork to let the doctor see her. What he wanted Evelyn to do was to go to Pawtucket and persuade the doctor to order Woodwork to take a vacation. Allan believes that there is something out of kilter in the functioning of the ductless glands. Woodwork has never undergone a thorough examination. "I would rather die," she has said to me, "than lie naked on a table with a lot of doctors pawing over me." So Evelyn is off to Pawtucket this noon to see what she can do.

Myself, I think that the ribs and the intestines are dropped from all the overhead painting Woodwork did and that an osteopath could help her immensely. However, it would be more to the point if someone touched that farm of hers off with a match. Allan must really be devoted to the green-eyed one. Evelyn likes Allan but with reservations. "He's too cold a proposition for me. He sees everything from the inside outwards. He never stands off and looks at himself humorously. What he does and what he thinks is of too much importance. Anyway, when we walk along the street he's not as tall as I am."

Evelyn and I have just read a short story in book form called 'Address Unknown' by Kressman Taylor. It is concerned with two partners in business in an art gallery in San Francisco, one a Jew, the other a Gentile, the letters they write back and forth to each other when the Gentile goes back to Germany to live, how they become estranged because of the rise of Nazism, the fate which befalls the Jewish partner's actress sister and the revenge the Jew takes upon the Gentile for that fate. It is a gripping piece of psychology, a small masterpiece, as fine in its way as 'Of Mice and Men.' It reminds one of de Maupassant.

March 15 Janice and I read the hundred and thirty or more additional letters in answer to the ad. Again and again those interviewed stated: "There is no room in the world for a man after he is fifty. There is little room for a man after he is forty." As one clever Jew expressed it: "I don't see why it wouldn't be the part of expediency for the Government to have all men killed off at the age of forty. What use," he exclaimed, "is a man over forty now? None. Candidly, Mr. Inman, none."

The people have gotten under my skin this time. Many of them are not just riffraff and tag ends. They are men who earnestly want work, who cannot find it, who are bewildered that all the training of a lifetime can be so worthless after forty. Pharmacist, headwaiter, laborers, a British Army captain, students and teachers, fortune-tellers and criminals — all are up against the great American prejudice against employing middle-aged and elderly men, up against the surplus of employees in the market.

March 19 Mrs. Cash has been seeing Mrs. Banks. Mrs. Banks is unable to find a job. Whether she won her case or not no one knows. Her well-to-do sister died a few months ago. She was to leave Mrs. Banks some money. Mrs. Cash says that she has tried several times to find a position for Mrs. Banks.

March 21 Ella was telling me a long story about how she had a twenty dollar bill and went with it to the ticket window at the Back Bay Station and asked to have it changed. The agent behind the grill abruptly refused to accommodate her. One of the redcaps saw what happened, took the money, got it changed for her. Ella reported to Robert how she had been treated. Robert marched up to the window and demanded an apology. "This is my wife," he said to the agent, "and I'm not going to stand by and see her insulted. Either you give her the apology you owe her, or I'll see you outside as soon as you leave station property, and then God help you." The man apologized grudgingly. Two weeks later, the Irish station manager heard of the matter, called Robert before him, dismissed him for having insulted the agent. He swore at Robert; Robert swore at him and promised him a thrashing. Then a committee of redcaps came to the station manager and threatened to report that he had fired a man for having taken his wife's part. The manager reinstated Robert immediately. "You see," explained Ella, "before the redcaps became unionized, the station manager might have let Robert go and no one could have said him nay. As it is now, the boys can put a stop to many of the petty annoyances and much of the unfair treatment to which they were subjected heretofore. Robert may not receive as much money, but he's treated more like a human being by the petty Irish officials over him."

Sometime ago I came across an article on diaries in a new magazine called 'Hobbies.' It was written by one Robert N. Smart. He was so enthusiastic about diaries that I wrote him complimenting him upon his article and telling him a little about my diary. When Evelyn went to New York, I had her take Volume 87 [1938 – 39] to Mr. Smart. He read it, then wrote me the following, the critical portion of which serves to validate the complimentary sections. I was quite pleased.

March 7, 1939

Dear Mr. Inman,

I enjoyed talking with your attractive wife very much, and thanks for sending the volume of your diary for me to read. As I told Mrs. Inman, I can think of no form in which such a diary could be published at the present time; though it is sure to be of tremendous interest, and even importance, in time to come. You appear to be doing a remarkable job. While reading your pages I was again impressed with the uncanny revelation of a person's character conveyed by this form of writing. It is inescapable! Someday your accounts of contemporary world events will have a significance now naturally lacking. The adventures of your various friends and correspondents will also in the future have even greater value than they do now, though I learned a great deal about U.S.A-1939 from the young hoboe's story which I did not know before. The stuff of contemporary literature is present in your diary, but of course it cannot be published now in diary form, because the personal angle would have to be left out. If I were the Sunday Editor of a Boston paper, however, I would certainly send a reporter around for a swell feature about your monumental journal. Had I known about it last year I should have mentioned it in the Hobbies piece, as a perfect example of writing for the future.

There is no way in which you could improve upon the technique you have adopted. You are courageous in your frankness and definitely a good reporter of the current scene as you see it. You will, I hope, pardon me if I say that I think you are sticking your neck out in regard to F.D.R. It is my opinion that history will disagree with your estimate of him and many other present day affairs, such as the virtues of fascism. The violence of your expressed views is undoubtedly characteristic of one group among us, but I fear posterity will place you in a historic spot somewhat akin to that occupied by the Black Republicans of the Reconstruction. In all the literature of partizan strife in the past, I have never found the President of the United States characterized as "the Rat". It is an odd-sounding phrase, and I would hesitate to embalm it as my judgement of even such men as Harding or Hoover.

You see, our politics diverge . . . but accept my congratulations on the diary, itself. I enjoyed it thoroughly. You are engaged upon a thankless task, but one — I firmly believe — that will keep you alive when the rest of us are forgotten.

March 22 Then a man, forty-five, one Norm Marks, Jewish, a sentimental romanticist who would, as Billy says, "talk the ear off a post." Kindly, generous, eager to express his views on anything and everything, a philosopher by avocation, a poet by preference, a cynic because of adverse circumstances. He was the only son of a Polish immigrant who through his own persistence came to be worth three-quarters of a million. He owned a movie house on Broadway. He became interested in being a producer, took a cast to Vienna, made a movie based on Jewish history, put it on the market just as talking pictures were making their appearance. He lost all his money. "I am not bitter against my daddy," stated Marks. "He done the best he could. He did it against my advice — but what of that? If there is a heaven, p'raps he sees the mistake he made. You never can tell about such things. So why foster a grudge?"

Marks went to a pharmaceutical school on Long Island. He ran a drugstore near Kenmore Square in Boston. He was unhappily married. He went to Reno and obtained a divorce, marrying another Jewess there. He worked as clerk in Liggett's Drug Store chain. He went to New York and worked there. He invested all his savings in Canadian oil stocks, lost them. He returned to Boston and started another drugstore in Cambridge. In order to send his son to college, he sacrificed the store. The son has now graduated from medical school and is interning at the Beth Israel Hospital in Brooklyn.

Marks is unable to find a job. He hates his wife "because she's got no soul." He has three other children besides the son. "Candidly,

just between you and me, Mr. Inman, I don't know, I can't say
what's going to happen to me in the end. There's no place in the
world now for a man past forty. To let you in on a secret, just
between you and me, I'm up against it. But I always say that as long
as a man can keep his courage, he's not licked. I got a wife without a
soul, I got no money—I got courage—and, Mr. Inman, I got
books. As long as a man's got books, he's not lost. You know that
yourself, Mr. Inman. My ancestors was all great Talmudic scholars.
I guess books are in my blood—Tennyson and Kant and Emerson
and Tolstoy and all the great ones."

At one time Marks was a practicing chiropractor in New York. He
wanted to be a doctor, but his wife discouraged him. He spent half
an hour telling me about what he had heard of the trials of the Jews
in Germany and Austria. He wasn't a bad sort, garrulous, pushing,
kindly, but I'd hate like hell to be his wife.

March 23   I trust that I am not boring you with the enumeration
and analysis of too many discouraged and downhearted men, but
I do believe that it is necessary to meet them to understand the
temper of the United States at this moment. While I wish that I
might give you the other side of the picture, portraits of the prosperous and the well-to-do, to counterbalance them, you will have to
remember that this diary is for the most part a chronicle having to do
with the middle and lower middle classes. I am in no position to be a
Greville, nor would I had I the opportunity. In my heart I find those
classes with whom I necessarily come in contact more genuine, less
bound by conventions, the most interesting.

March 24   Sometimes we Americans are apt to forget what vast
spaces of practically uninhabited country lie within our borders,
terrain without roads, houses, railways, towns. Wyoming is full of
such wild places. Listen to some of the names of some of the wild
places—Big Horn Mountains, Salt River Range, Oil Creek Mountains, Bad Land Hills, Snake River Range, Great Divide Basin, Wind
River, Granite Mountains, Antelope Hills, Greybull River, Stinking
Water Peak, Sunlight Creek, Adobe Hill, Sheep Mountains, Powder
River, Sierra Madre Range.

Twenty-six years ago, there was born to a respected rancher in
Powell, Wyoming, a young son named Earl Durand. As the boy
grew up, he became very proud of his woodsmanship. After one
year in high school, Durand left in order to devote himself to
ranging the wild country. He was a great hunter. He became famous
for his marksmanship. He could throw a baseball in the air and put
four rifle bullets in it before it fell. He let his hair grow long. He
reached a height of over six feet and weighed two hundred and fifty

pounds. He boasted he could live in the wilds alone with only a knife and gun to help him. He once traveled to Mexico on a saddle horse. He crossed the Mojave Desert clad only in trousers and shoes. He learned to eat raw meat. In fine, Durand was a throwback to pioneer days. To the people of the countryside he was something of a joke, but he had never been what the neighbors would call a "bad boy."

Then last week the game wardens arrested him for having killed a bull elk out of season. He was placed in the jail in Cody. When a deputy took Durand's supper to his cell, the huge man grabbed him, snatched his keys, found a rifle, forced the deputy to drive him to his father's ranch. Two law officers followed, and Durand dropped them dead in their tracks with three shots from his rifle. He then clubbed the deputy unconscious, made his father put up some provisions for him, headed for the snowy Beartooth Mountains. A posse of a hundred men was organized to follow him. The posse besieged him in a natural rocky fort in Clarks Fork Canyon. Durand shot and killed two of his attackers. A howitzer and a three-inch mortar were obtained in order to dislodge the fugitive from his fortress. A plane was engaged to drop gas bombs. All the preparation was in vain, however, for Durand, after having in the night climbed down the cliff and stolen the shoes and the gun of one of the men he had killed, was found to have escaped. The next installment of what reads like a dime-novel thriller is yet to happen.

I do not tell this story to emphasize the adventures of a single antisocial individualist who, because of the pressure of civilization, has run amuck, but to stress the fact that there still exist in many localities vast wilderness tracts where a man fleeing for his life may have a chance of eluding his fellow creatures who so zestfully take to his trail in the greatest of American sporting ventures, an organized manhunt.

March 27   Yesterday Evelyn told me that I made her feel as though I thought I had a fence around her and she couldn't get out. That is the last way I feel. My trouble is that I'm afraid she might run away if given a profusion of chances. Funny how diametrically oppositely two intimate people can look at the same factor in their lives.

March 29   Madrid has fallen. Soon the remainder of Leftist Spain will fall. Then Generalissimo Francisco Franco will be supreme commander of a million soldiers, disciplined, hardened, accustomed to fighting, and he will have no money in the treasury. England and France may fail to buy him to their side. If I were France, I should be more afraid of him and his million fighters than of Mussolini.

England is wooing Poland. Hitler is making gestures against Poland. I cannot believe that Hitler actually wishes to go to war with Poland. Probably what he is doing is preparing for an alliance with Poland in his shrewd, strategical way.

March 31   It is announced that England is about to pledge itself to defend Poland against invasion as one article of a tripartite agreement between France, England and Poland. Hitler is said to be massing troops on the Polish frontier. Hitler cannot afford to have Britain alienate Poland at least from a position of neutrality. If I were Hitler and any such tripartite agreement were signed, I should immediately take over Danzig and the Polish Corridor and march on Warsaw. What else can Hitler do unless he wishes to relinquish all ideas of expansion? If I were Poland, I would join the Germans immediately. An arrangement could be made between Germany and Poland by which Poland would relinquish the Corridor and take over instead one of the Baltic States and, in case of war with Russia, part of Russia. I can think of no more efficient way of bringing on a war than a tripartite agreement between England, France and Poland.

April 1   While I am waiting to hear the broadcast of Hitler's speech, it might be well to take a look at us Americans. The latest craze is goldfish-swallowing. College students vie with each other to see who can swallow the greatest number of live goldfish. The record now stands at 67 live goldfish swallowed in fourteen minutes. Crowds watch. People cheer. The Animal Rescue League promises prosecution if any more live fish are swallowed in Massachusetts.

This week there has been a Candy Fair at Mechanics Hall. There have been lotteries and various orchestra leaders and their orchestras offered as attractions. Paul Whiteman was billed. Billy and Sadie decided to go. From fifteen to twenty thousand persons thronged the Candy Fair to see Whiteman and hear his orchestra. Billy agrees with me that to no class of men in America, not even to the athletes, is offered the blind adulation rendered to orchestra leaders with the one exception — perhaps — of film stars. What sort of people are we to abase ourselves maudlinly before the low-grade morons that most orchestra leaders are?

Hardly had Hitler begun to speak before the address was abruptly cut off the air. No one knows why. No cables have come to newspapers. It is a mystery to date. What does it mean? Does it mean war?

April 2   Evelyn prophesied that Adolf Hitler would blow off steam, call the British names, do nothing. And that is precisely what he did. Nobody appears to know why the broadcast was suppressed.

April 3   Yesterday afternoon I had George Bricker, the boy from Tufts, come here to read through 'The Moon Drifter' in order to call my attention to repetitious words and phrases and grammatical mistakes. I was quite well aware that he would dislike the book. He did emphatically and in no uncertain terms. "It's pretty. It isn't specific enough in its imagery. You use cliches. You strive after a joy which is not conveyed. I hope you'll take this criticism in good part — I don't believe in pulling my punches."

I took it in good part. Indeed, I begin to like the long, slightly shabby, slightly dank, earnest, honest drink of milk. He has, as Evelyn says, quite a nice mind. His handwriting is that of a scholar. That we disagree utterly as to what poetry is in no wise blinds me to his good points. He is forever striving for a hidden meaning, a larger implication behind the obvious meaning in a poem. That which is obvious can hold no merit in his eyes. "Too pretty," he continually asserted, as though being pretty were in itself a crime against taste. I should hate to think poetry the complicated, double-edged, esoteric compound of surface effect and subterranean implication that he and most of the modern school of poets consider it to be. Anyway, a nice chap. Must see more of him sometime.

An announcement stating that Isolde Raleigh DeBray was married to Mr. Franklin Hart on the thirtieth of March. So Corn has married another Gentile. Would like to know the details. Of all the people I have ever known, Corn had the most spritely imagination. I miss her constantly. Probably will never see her again.

April 10   The other day Billy arrived with a telegram. I had no idea where it was from. I felt a momentary hope that Father had died. No such luck. It was from Uncle Frank saying that Father was in the hospital for a hernia operation and that the operation was a success. I'd like him to die, but I hate to see him suffer. A note from Aunt Louise this morning saying that he "is doing far better than anybody expected." The doctor has stopped him smoking and drinking. "You can well understand," continues Aunt Louise, "how these two things, suddenly ceasing, would make him nervous, but," she concludes piously, "every denial is done for his recovery."

April 11   Each night, awake in the dark hours, I wonder what will happen next in the world. Mussolini has a million men under arms. A British fleet is gathering in the Mediterranean. England has guaranteed Greece against attack. Holland is fortifying its borders against Germany. An Italian editorial states that the United States has undertaken 150 armed actions and eight invasions of Mexico within the last hundred years and that therefore the United States had no moral right to raise its voice against Italy.

It is time this ended. Let the United States stay in America. Let them look after their own many and complex problems. If they reject the advice this time, don't let them complain if European states chosen for their targets decide in self-defense to busy themselves in the same spirit with North American matters.

April 12 "Roderic," I said, "I want to ask you a question. Think carefully before answering, because I want a real answer. It's this. For years you've sworn up and down that wild mules couldn't drag you off to war. Mr. Roosevelt now hints that we may become involved in a general war. If so, how will you feel about joining up?" Roderic whistled under his breath, tunelessly. "Well," he said, then whistled some more. Finally, "To be honest with you, Artie, I'm weakening. Six months ago — definitely no. Now — I don't know. Six months from now — probably yes. They're working on me. And the most idiotic part of the whole business is that I know they're working on me and can't do anything about it. It's silly, but it's so. You know," he said, "I'm terribly afraid that one of these chappies one of these days soon is going to make a mistake and say something he can't retract. Then there'll be war for sure. Oh well," he concluded, "let's read."

April 13 Billy's mother-in-law has had an operation for varicose veins. He has been going around like a monkey whose tail has been chopped off and who doesn't know whether it is lost for good. He hasn't been able to sleep. Large black circles are under his eyes. I really believe that he cares more about "Mama" than he does about his wife. He said: "You know, I love Mama more than I do my own mother. She's the swellest person what ever lived." Billy intends to pay all the hospital expenses. When I mildly suggested that it would be only fair for Mama's two sons to chip in, Billy replied: "Oh, Mama wouldn't let them pay. She'd let me pay, but she wouldn't let them pay."

April 15 Roosie the Rat has several times opened his mouth and made noises which sounded to the population of the United States as though he were sure war was inevitable and that we would be involved. He has done everything possible short of forthrightness to incite a war hysteria and to insult Germany and Italy. Everyone here and abroad thinks that he wants a third term and is willing to ride into it on mangled corpses if necessary. It may be so. Or perhaps he is just a fool and 'knows not what he does.' Yesterday he opened his mouth and blapped some more. "Beyond question within a scant few years air fleets will cross the ocean as easily as today they cross the closed European seas." He declared that the United States is ready to defend the entire Western Hemisphere not only against armed aggression but also against economic pressure, whatever that means.

I have talked to fifteen or twenty men during these last weeks. Not a single one of them has wanted war. Not a single one of them desires to go to war. More than half of them believe that, if it weren't for the Jews and Roosevelt and English pressure, there would be no slightest need or occasion for America getting into any war. Most of them feel that with the cards stacked as they are, war is inevitable.

Personally, I am sick of the whole business. I wish the Rat would run down a hole and lose himself and leave the United States in peace. I am beginning to think there won't be any war now anyway. Perhaps a division of Yugoslavia, but no war.

I don't believe that any civilization ever achieved will be able to change man's nature, do away with war. But that doesn't mean I want war in my day or time. If I were omnipotent, I'd blow Hitler away with one breath, Mussolini with another, Roosevelt and Chamberlain and Stalin with other breaths, and arms and armaments with the most comprehensive gust of all. Or would I? Is a series of major wars with peace between any less desirable than hundreds of constantly occurring minor conflicts? It is one or the other, man being what he is. Anyway, I know I don't want war in my time.

April 16   Yesterday Roosevelt addressed a plea for peace to Hitler and Mussolini. I have read the note thoroughly. Portions of it are in a style apparently written by someone else than the President. The entire note takes for granted that Hitler and Mussolini are the villains of the world, and hence it will be no surprise to see them turn down the appeal peremptorily. That there is a plethora of common sense in the message, no one can deny.

April 28   Word from Macrae. He will publish 'None Now Are Quietly Wise' for $600. Have sent him the check. Evelyn will take up further details with him when she goes to the World's Fair about the twentieth of May.

May 1   [From Patricia:]

Just before Christmas Jerry left for Florida to see his mother, he hadn't been home in eight years so felt that he should go while he had the chance. While he was gone I had to keep an eye on the place, and it kept me running around in circles, working at my own job and dashing out each day to see if everything was alright. By the way Jerry hitch-hiked both ways, it took him seven days each time. The day that he started I drove him a hundred miles inland and left him at the place where he would be most likely to get a ride. He wore his very best clothes, and had his camel hair top coat cleaned, he didn't wear a hat, and in his pocket he carried his toothe brush, razor and all the other small essentials. He had sent his bag home by express. His dog had puppies two weeks after he left and of course I had to play mid-wife. She had seven pups, so I had to drown three of them, because Baby couldn't feed them all. I had to go out twice a day to see that Baby was fed, because the people who had the house were away from home all day. When the puppies got big enough I gave two of them away and kept a little female for myself. She is a darling, honey colored, with seal brown tail and ears and a white shirtfron. I call her "Kim" and board her with Sean and Lenore O'Casey for fifty cents a week.

When Jerry left here he had planned to get a partner from one of the dancing schools and pick up a bit of work at the hotels, as it was the season. He wasn't very enthusiastic about it but felt he could do with a bit of money. His letters were full of instructions for his place, of how often to water this and that and to see that certain plants were turned etc. Oh, yes, I built a trellis for the sweet peas, it may not have been a work of art, but the sweet peas seem to like it, I got a mashed thumb out of the darned thing. After the first month Jerry's letters were not so frequent and he was no longer concerned about his place, I was to do just as I pleased about everything, but that was too much responsibility for my liking and I wrote and told him so. He wrote back that after all the years of searching for the right partner he had finally found her and from then on was determined to dance and nothing was going to stop him, and he wasn't sure when he was coming back if at all. Which put me in a pretty spot, but I wrote and told him that he must do whatever made him the happiest, but that I had to be advised about the house and furniture, for which I paid, by the way. I thought that the best thing to do would be for him to put the furniture in storage until he decided just what he was going to do. I had no answer to the letter, but in a week had a post card that he had already started back. When he reached here he was awfully tired of course, but even that was no reason for his being so cold and uneasy with me. I knew that something was troubling him but felt that it was up to him to speak to me about it first. The first night back I asked him if he was returning soon to Florida and he said no, that his partner was coming on here, that she had relatives here. So of course I knew that it meant the finish of the intimacy between us, I waited for him to tell me that it was all over, but he didn't say a word, the first week he was back I saw him a few times, but never alone. Then when I'd call him he'd make excuses that he was tired or busy, so one night I just said to hell with it all and never called him again. It ended just like that. I've a very dear friend, a Hungarian jewess, I met her thru Jerry, and she told me what it was all about. It wasn't only the girl, as he has no other interest in her except the dancing, but he felt that I was too strong for him, that buy helping him out everytime he needed money and paying for theatre tickets and anything else that we did was bad for him. And he resented the fact that I was able to do it all the time he accepted it. Marie asked him why, if he felt that way did he continue to take everything that I offered and he answered that "it was easy". That one remark killed any feeling that I had for him and I stoped being a fool then and there. I didn't even have any regrets except for the time I'd wasted and I went right out and telephoned two boys that I know, one of them was Mike, you recall the famous Mike don't you? I hadn't seen him for over a year, when he had come around at Christmas time with a very expensive bottle of perfume for me. Mike was not in, nor was Donald, so I just got mad and went home and washed and ironed everything I could find.

That was on a Saturday night, on Monday morning when we were scarcely up Mike appeared at the door. Talk about telepathy, he didn't know about my call and just got the urge to see me. He wanted to know if he couldn't start taking me out, and I grabbed my hat and let him start by taking me out to breakfast, and from then on we've been having steady dates twice a week. He has been working for three years as an engineer at a large department store in L.A. where he makes an excellent salary, he has an apartment of his own in an excellent neighborhood. And oddest thing of all to one who knew the old Mike he has a most complete wardrobe. He used to be satisfied to go about in dungarees all the time. He used to drink all the time, but over two years ago he got arrested for drunk driving and had to spend seventy two days in the local bastille. He got a sentence of ninety days but got five days off for diving in a lake and recovering a gun for the police and the rest of the time off for good behavior and helping out at the sheriff's picnic. While interred he made himself useful about the place and got to see the awful peices of humanity that were dragged in each night. So he turned a new leaf with a vengeance, and now drinks only beer and very little of that.

I have a grand time with him, he takes me every where I want to go and pays the way of course, I'm not going to be a fool like that again. From now on it's thumbs down on the sturdy oak business, I'm out to be a clinging vine, I'm getting so feminine that it would slay you. Mike feels that he has to protect me and I just eat it up (with a tongue in my cheek). But here is the payoff, he wants to marry me! In fact he has decided that it is all settled and has begun to discuss the grandchildren already, quite indelicate I calls it. He wants a house and he told me last night that we are going to have the biggest airedale he can find, luckily I adore them. Since he has a passion for marksmanship he has informed me that I am going to have a gun and learn too, also that I'm going to have to go deep sea fishing, I hate fish, wont even eat them. For a lady who is still married to one husband I calls it fast work, don't you? But what a sop for the ego.

And speaking of husbands, Ted is still very much in the picture, he constantly writes to me extending an invatation to visit him and the Fair on my vacation.

He said that he couldn't offer me any money toward the trip, but that I could stay with him, and that later on when and *if* I got a divorce I need not mention the fact that I had stayed with him for a few weeks. Isn't he magnanimous? Sheer unadulterated nerve I'd call it. And to top it all off listen to the household I'm being invited to. He shares a large apartment with his boy friend and said boy friend's girl who is impartial with her favors; sounds a bit reminiscent to me. They all drink like fish and are constantly having to take cures for the d. t's. Swell environment for me. I'll have none of it, but I don't want to sound too abrupt, so I'm saying that my vacation falls at the time when his Mother is going to be in San Francisco. He promised he would send me the money for my divorce by January and here it is, almost May and not a sign nor mention of anything but how broke he is. I can get one for sixty dollars and if I had the money I'd pay for it myself, I've started saving but so far have only ten dollars, I could get a loan, but the interest charges are so outrageous. I can't ask Mike to pay for it naturally. It makes me so mad, Ted owes me over three hundred dollars and the least he can do would be to pay for a divorce. Out here it takes a year for a divorce to become final so I want to get started as soon as I can. Not that I'm sure that I will marry Mike when the time comes, but I'm just sick and tired of being attached to Ted in any capacity, even that of a wife in name only.

This is my day off and I've just been out to the San Fernando Valley to visit the O'Caseys, they are in a bad way financially, Sean got laid off three months ago and has not been able to get a job since, they are down to their last few dollars and I am worried about them. They work so hard on their little place it is just a shame that things have been so difficult for them.

I've seen Jerry once since we broke up, I ran into him at a friend's house, he was obviously very glad to see me, but also quite embarrased, which pleased me, as he certainly should be ashamed of himself. His partner was with him, she is nice enough in a silly way, but is she dumb! That is probably what he likes since it makes him feel superior, he always resented it because I was more intelligent than he, as if I could help the brains I was born with, tho I should have been more reticent about showing them. I feel a bit sorry for the poor girl, she is quite mad about him and he treats her dreadfully, not in front of people of course, but while he is dancing with her, Marie told me that the poor child is in tears every day, so he is probably having a wonderful time flaunting his ego. He was never rough nor rude with me but every one else complained of his manners, particularly the O'Caseys, they were quite upset about it and were glad when we broke up. So that is that. It is funny about Mike tho, looks like that old adage, "the first shall be the last", to misquote the New Testament.

This about carries me up to date, I'm waiting now for a call from Mike, he is taking me to dinner and to the theatre tonight, so I must needs go and make myself beautiful, I hope this makes up a bit for the months that I've neglected you.

May 11 Roderic and I have been reading 'Grapes of Wrath' by John Steinbeck, a very long novel, a 'best seller' and to my mind one of the grandest books I have read in many a moon. There can be no doubt about it; Steinbeck is the greatest novelist in the American or English language today. No one can portray with such moving simplicity and precision the thoughts and emotions of the lower classes of America. He possesses a fine sense of the dramatic, increasingly less melodramatic as he grows older and more experienced.

May 16 Roderic and I have finished 'Grapes of Wrath.' I didn't like the melodramatic ending, thought the tale prolonged some three score pages too far, but Roderic considered the termination in impeccable dramatic taste.

May 22 Billy stands and waits. Brown face. Brown eyes. Neat suit and tie. Shoes polished. Curly hair combed. Not a sharp face but one transformed pleasantly by a smile and white, strong teeth, two back ones missing. He regards me devotedly. My topcoat is in his two hands. He stands patiently.

June 2 Was riding nearly an hour. Sat under willows in Fenway.

East wind. Now back in my room ready to study more poetry. Some of 'John Brown's Body' wearies me — the parts about Melora in particular. Don't follow Benét in what he is maundering about. Portions of the book, too, seem more prose than poetry. I like Sandburg. The style in which he writes should result in prose but turns somehow to poetry. Then Robert Frost. His work looks like, sounds like poetry in the traditional style; and it is so simple in appearance that it is not until you copy down some of the poems and analyze them that you discover how fastidiously intricate they are. They are no jackhammer verse as Sandburg's, no short stories corseted and clothed to resemble verse as Jeffers'. I am enjoying my study of poetry.

June 3   Had Evelyn read to me from a diary written in the early twenties. Wanted to ascertain if that, too, was inadequate. Intense, vivid, but written as though from a submerged world. Not a healthy chronicle. But neither was I, am I, healthy. Neither are the times.

The diary is a conflicting tapestry of rebellion and bewilderment, arrogance and humility. A fox who has never met hounds before turns to fight the pack that some destiny beyond his conception has loosed on him. A curious chronicle, my diary, and though here and there it disgusts me or bores me or makes me ashamed that it was I who so meticulously turned himself inside out, in the main it carries itself. It possesses the untiring, rushing, nervous pulsation of a long rapids, and that I like. One wonders if calm water ever will be reached. Evelyn insists that I am in everyday existence more gentle, more whimsical, more loveable than the man who writes the diary. I do hope so. There must be another side to me, surely, or people wouldn't worry about me, slave for me, devote themselves and their energies beyond any recompense of mere money to my interests and welfare.

June 10   Listening to the excited reception of the King and Queen of England to New York and to the Fair. Never was a piece of propaganda more successful. America, if anything can do it, will be won to England by this royal visit. The Queen talking to the populace. The King conversing with politicos. The King and Queen visiting a small New Jersey town. The King and Queen going to Arlington. The King laying a wreath on the tomb of the Unknown Soldier (a gesture which may signify the sacrifice of hundreds of thousands more unknown American soldiers). I feel sorry for the King and Queen, so conscientiously doing their duty for England as they see it. No slaves ever were used more callously. But perhaps they haven't perceptions enough to realize it. If I were a king, I'll be damned if I'd act like a useful flag to be waved on every occasion a group of men decided it useful or needful or politic. But then I'm not a patient and benignant man, while George VI looks as though he were. He is a perfect person for his position, not as the 'late' Edward, a rebel with ideas of his own.

June 15   Letter from Father. What do you suppose will happen to his garden in Maine without his care? How long will he be in Atlanta?

Evelyn writes that you are still worrying over me. Will you please get this out of your mind? I am up and around the house everyday, I just don't seem to be able to get rid of the slight fever.

I have no appetite and am not gaining strength like I should.

Two things that are hindering my recovery are, the weak heart muscles and poor circulation.

The doctor assures me that although it is going to take some time that I will be well and strong again.

He thinks better than I was before. I am most comfortably fixed here and strange to say, am not suffering much with the intense heat.

Now please forget about me as much as you can and give your time and attention to getting well yourself.

June 16   I have often thought how queer and unusual the people I interview in the dark sometimes appear when in the ordinary routine of their existence they may not seem half so eccentric to their fellows, half so unusual. All of us more or less hide behind screens which we believe we have designed to cover those characteristics that tend to make us different from the majority. If we lose or discard this tendency to color ourselves protectively with an accepted social hue, we become outcast, freakish, even, in the minds of the majority, insane or demented. It is necessary that this should be so in order that the community and the race survive.

June 17   While rereading some of the political portions of my diary, it occurs to me that I give the impression, because I dislike the English and the French, of admiring all that goes with Germany and Nazism. Far from it. I would rather live in a wild country of sporadic organization such as the United States than in a regulated nation such as Germany. The actions taken against the Jews, the Austrian patriots, the Czechs would (were I there to see them) disgruntle my sense of fair play. I realize that the ruling Nazis must be a supercilious and overbearing class under whose control I should hate to be. While I admire Hitler historically and approve of conquest philosophically, as a close witness I should abhor him and it. I believe that

Hitler has done well. But I do not desire to be in Germany as a German.

June 18 The dapper little Sicilian who smells like a colored person and whose touch I dislike but who is the best barber I have found has cut my hair and gone. Evelyn has returned from her bird excursion with Dr. Pike and has departed for the Place. Billy is cleaning and cooking the first turnip greens from the Place and I am left alone with the 'New York Times' and my pencil.

June 22 Have analyzed the reading matter specified in the English courses of some thirty preparatory schools. In some schools the students are given nine English books to study for every single American one. At one girls' school there wasn't a single American book read during the four senior years. The lowest proportion is three English books for one American. It is preposterous that young Americans should be fed English literature almost to the exclusion of American literature. How can youngsters, many of whom read only what they are forced to read, come into an understanding of American life when their diet has been predominantly English?

And why English books anyway? The literature of England that students are given starts with Shakespeare and the Elizabethans at about 1600 A.D. The Americans started writing a literature of their own about 1770 A.D. So why should the proportion, if preponderance against American literature there must be, be so wide? It doesn't make sense. Crèvecoeur and Paine, Jefferson and Adams and Gallatin, Irving and Longfellow and Ticknor, Hawthorne and Prescott and Parkman and Emerson and Poe and Thoreau all come before 1860; and there is a really fine Civil War literature that has been sadly neglected. So why the emphasis on Scott and Dickens and Wordsworth and Cowper and Sheridan and the rest? And certainly, since 1914, we have written rings around the English. Nor are men like Bierce even touched upon. The whole business is screwy, to say the least. If I had strength to wave a cause, I should certainly shout aloud for American literature to be taught in American schools to American boys. There is nothing to be ashamed of in our literature.

June 27 Mrs. Cash has suddenly decided to go to England for the summer after all. The teacher friend with whom she first planned to go lost her nerve because of war scares and so Mrs. Cash, to her annoyance, found herself out of a trip. She planned instead to take doctorate courses at Tufts. Then the secretary of an elderly woman fell ill and Mrs. Cash received an offer to accompany the woman as secretary. The woman didn't want to pay enough. "I named her a price and told her it was immaterial to me whether she took me or not. She decided to take me. So now I'm off." She leaves tonight. She refuses to write me. She will spend most of her time at Oxford. I hate to have her go because of the reading. As for the rest, it will be a pleasure to be without her low talk and cesspool mind.

June 29   Billy says that he and his Sadie can't have children. The doctor claims that there is something wrong with her. "When Sadie quits work, she and me'll adopt a kid, probably a girl, one not more than a year old. When Sadie quits work, she'll go potty without somethin' to put her mind on. Anyway, I'd like a kid."

July 6   Woodwork loves liquor. The more she drinks, the more affable she becomes. Evelyn said: "I'll fix her for you. You just see if I don't." She did. For the whole evening Woodwork was amusing, sprightly, amicable. She related parts of her history hitherto concealed. I said: "Did Allan know you planned to have a baby?" She: "Why, of course. What kind of a fourflusher do you think I am? Of course he knew." Myself: "Doesn't he like his wife? What sort of a person is she?" "Oh, she's a mediocre woman, nice enough I guess — not very bright." "Does Allan love her?" "I really don't know. I wouldn't, if I were he. She's nice." "And their children?" "They're not as bright as Peggy — not by any means." "But Allan didn't know that Peggy would be bright?" "No." "So he just allowed you to have your way to please you, wasn't that it?" "I suppose you might put it that way. Anyway, it turned out well. Peggy's a witch, and I love her."

"Woodwork," I said, "where was Peggy born? Was she born in Connecticut?" "No, and she wasn't born in New Hampshire." "In Concord?" "Oh goodness no. I just told you those stories to put you off the track." "Then where was she born?" "She was born in Pawtucket, in a hospital there. Just after I became pregnant, Mr. Wight, the lawyer I had been working for, went off his head. That was a terrible mixup. Being out of a job, I decided to go somewhere in the country and be quiet and peaceful until Peggy was born. I saw an advertisement about a home in Rhode Island southeast of Pawtucket. I went there. It was for crazy people. Being half crazy myself, that didn't daunt me. All the people weren't crazy; some of them were just doddering. I stayed there two months. It was awful but it sort of fascinated me. I used to go berrying when my belly was so fat I could hardly see over it. In spite of that, I could climb the stone walls more spryly than the other idiots. They always expected me to fall down, but it was they who fell, not me. The people who ran the place thought, I'm sure, that I was a fallen woman. But my money was good and so, as much as it pained them to harbor sin, they stood for me."

I interrupted her. "Who was paying your expenses?" "Allan. I didn't have a cent." "And didn't you mind?" "Maybe I did. Maybe I didn't. I forget. Anyway, that's the way it was. One day I decided to go to Pawtucket and consult a lawyer on the proper way to bring an illegitimate child into the world. I wanted to be sure there weren't any pitfalls for me to avoid, or legal technicalities. That man persuaded me to use a false name, something I've regretted ever since. So now poor Peggy hasn't any birth certificate and can't get one, no matter how frantic the teachers at the public school become every year. I just tell them I've lost it. They calm down after a while." "Did you have any trouble giving birth to Peggy?" "It began to hurt so that I told the doctor I couldn't stand the pain and he shot me full of stuff to quiet me, and, doggone it, I passed out of the picture and missed practically the whole show. They kept slapping and pinching me to keep me awake, but that didn't bother me much — all I wanted to do was sleep. They had a terrible time making Peggy live. That scared me so it woke me up with a jolt. When I heard her first squeal, however, I knew she was all right and dropped off again. I was at the hospital until I moved to the rooms on Spencer Street. The next two months were a nightmare. It was right in the middle of the depression. I thought Allan had done enough for me. I didn't want to take his money any longer. I wanted to earn my own money. So I gave up nursing Peggy and started out to find a job. I haunted the employment offices in Pawtucket till they hated me. I interviewed dozens of people. I became increasingly discouraged. Then when I was just about to give up hope, I was taken on by Mr. Keene, who had lost his secretary. And there, God help me, I've been ever since, hating it, feeling hemmed in by morals, but not being able to leave because I have Peggy to consider and because it would be almost impossible to find another position that paid so bounteously."

"Why," I inquired, "didn't you tell us, Evelyn and me, the truth about yourself?" "Oh, I don't know. I think I was afraid that in some way it would redound against Allan. For myself, I'd have told anybody." "Does your mother know whether Peggy is your child or somebody else's?" "No, she doesn't know. And what's more, she'd best not ask. It's no business of hers. It's nobody's business except mine and Allan's. Nobody knows except you and Evelyn and perhaps Julie (my friend in New Jersey). And that doesn't mean that I'm not glad I had Peggy. I wouldn't have missed having her for anything in the world."

Woodwork has never given Peggy any information as to her parentage. "I'll tell her when she's old enough to understand. I don't know when that will be, and I don't know what I'll tell her."

Woodwork is feeling better. She has found a woman to take care of Peggy on the farm and a little girl, a sort of waif brought up by a charitable institution, to play with her. "And man, you don't know what a relief it is to have that settled and out of the way. I can breathe again." Peggy runs wild during the week, wears a sunsuit. "You should see her. She's really beautiful. She's honey-colored all over. One of the farmers came by the other day, looked at Peggy, remarked: 'God A'mighty, Mrs. Williams, that there youngun a' yours is sure pretty.' An hour later I found Peggy examining herself in front of a mirror."

I guess Woodwork really loves Allan a great deal. She said: "Last night I took a drink before we went to bed. I slept all night without waking. That made me mad. I like to wake up at odd hours and poke Allan in the back, tickle him or give him a kiss while he's asleep. I get a whopping kick out of that."

I was sorry when the evening was concluded. I said: "You've been swell tonight. We fight a lot off and on, but I certainly do appreciate you in between." She said: "Yes sir, you're a wild man. And I'm a wild woman. For a couple of wild ones, we do get along pretty well, don't we? I've had a swell evening myself."

July 13   A few words while waiting for the stomach-pump doctor. Evelyn is downtown at ex-Governor Curley's office seeing if she can, through him, get the Fenway cleaned, all other methods of attaining that end having failed and the sand still lying untouched in the gutters.

Am reading on the talking-book the old detective classic for want of better stuff—'The Moonstone.' Am certain I read it once before when I was a boy. Some scenes, such as pulling the box from the quicksand, etc., come back to me as though a negative had been laid over an old forgotten print and the two found to be identical.

Pearl went to the movies yesterday afternoon and slept through the entire performance. She goes there to cry, to rest, to sleep—not off alone somewhere but to the movies.

July 16   Ella's Robert has been planning to take a trip south to spend a week or ten days with his family in Virginia. He wanted Ella to accompany him. Said she, truculently: "If he thinks I'm going to take that trip with him, he's got another guess coming. Not on your tintype. Here I sweat and fume and make myself small before a measly Jew, scrimp here and save there and do without things that I want, lead the life of a wage slave, all to put a few dollars between us and the poorhouse—and what then? Robby Boy wants to go back to the old home town and scatter his quarters, strut his stuff, just so he can feel big. Well, I don't intend to be party to it. And furthermore—he'll pick up all the ungentlemanly ways pertaining to his family. He'll forget how to eat. He'll forget all I've so painstakingly taught him. He'll come back to me talking mush-mouthed. His family will make a fuss over him, yes, but do they care anything about him? No. They'll say: 'Cain I have five dollars, Robert?' and 'Len' me five bucks, ole fellah.' They'll milk him dry; they'll give him the gravy; they'll make a fuss over him — and he'll come back broke, every cent spent. And did they ever help him out when he was down? They did not. If he wants to go south and be sucker for a lot of backslappers, that's his business. Let him go. But I don't have to go, and I'm not going. Sit around and sew for the family. Eat too much and get loggy. Frizzle in the heat. Have to listen to a bunch of low-lived women bragging to each other about the sexual prowess of their husbands. Un-unh. Not Ella. I stay here."

July 20   [From Patricia:]

About Mike, I've decided not to see him any more, I can't quite trust him. Mike would never tell the truth if it were more agreeable to fib a bit and I caught him in a few unimportant ones. Too, I'd always be afraid that I'd get into the same sort of jam that I did with Ted.

I'm not at loss for male companionship tho thank goodness, even if nothing has turned up that I could get serious about. I'll probably never feel as I did about Sean ever again. But I do go about most of the time with a very nice boy, Paul, from Muncie Ind. He is here in pictures, I met him through his agent. He really ought to do something in pictures, he is definetly the type they want, he is six feet two and looks like Errol Flyn if that means anything to you. But he is much younger than I so of course that is out, as a rule I don't like such young men but Paul is so mature he had me fooled for a while. He likes me because he is a bit fed up on the glamour girls, seems that they don't wear well, and since he is essentially a simple person they got in his hair. We spend all of our spare time driving about over the mountain ranges and exploring new roads, we go to the beach at night and sit and eat hamburgers while listening to the surf. He manages to see me every day even if he has to come into the Pig'n Whistle and talk to me while I work, and I'm beginning to get a bit worried because I've detected that marriage gleam in his eye several times. And I firmly believe that six years is too much when a woman is the older, what do you think? Paul isn't ready for marriage yet anyway, he has to become adjusted to this particular way of earning his living, and he is just on the edge of good things, I don't know how success would wear with him. He is quite vain, but I've found that in a good many actors, it is what makes actors in some cases, and I suppose the boy can't help if he is proud of his grand body. He is terrifically masculine and I suppose that is what appeals to me, I've been featuring the clinging vine business lately, I'll admit it gets out of hand now and then and I assert my right to be an individual too, then he shakes his head and says he will never understand women.

I'm having a grand time tho, and am going to enjoy every bit of life that I can, and if I never do get married again as I really want too I'll still manage to have a full and happy time with whatever comes my way.

I haven't read "Grapes of Wrath", havent been able to get it at my lending library, too popular, the opinion out here seems to be divided, everyone agrees that the situation is acute but not nearly as lustful nor sordid as the book portrays, we hear very little of the dust bowl victims, whether the papers withhold it deliberately or not I don't know, but outside of one Movie star, Melvyn Douglas, no one seems to pay much attention, which is all wrong to my way of thinking. With all the sentiment being stirred up about the Spanish refugee children I think a little thought could be spared for those in our own back yard.

July 21 Tonight Evelyn goes to Fitchburg to visit Millicent Barnes and her Hal. These visits are Evelyn's ideas, not mine. As far as I am concerned, Naomi and Millicent are out of my life, they not having kept me in their hearts when circumstances became distracting, albeit I felt they owed me at least that for what I had done for them.

July 22 Evelyn enjoyed and did not enjoy her visit to Millicent and Hal. They live on the outskirts of Princeton, about fifteen miles beyond Concord. Hal bought a sleazy twelve-room house and eighteen acres of wilding countryside for $4,500 from the bank which had foreclosed an $8,000 mortgage made in the good predepression days when land values were higher. Hal goes into Fitchburg in his secondhand Packard (price $450) each day to his office and back again for supper. Millicent, in shorts and halter, stays on the place, gardens, cleans her sloppily kept house, cooks. Hal buys old furniture and reassembles it and puts it in order. They have two dogs. There is a brook on their property, partridge, woodcock. Now and again Hal hunts. They have guests to whom they give Bourbon whiskey bought by the gallon, "vile, raw stuff," according to Evelyn. They drink half a pint or more a day themselves.

Hal, so Millicent explained, obtained his divorce and they were legally married. They are in love with each other. Millicent has split with her family because they disapproved of her marriage. Evelyn says that it is obvious that she is blissfully happy. "Her shorts may be dirty, her hair graying, her skin red as a beet, but she is in seventh heaven, her dreams come true." Evelyn dislikes Hal, he being cocky and officious. Millicent's chatter bores her (Millicent talked until midnight, and Evelyn was an unwilling audience). But Evelyn is glad that she went and says she will probably go again in the autumn. "At least," she smiles, "going places makes me glad to be home."

Evelyn plans to visit Dr. Pike for a couple of days this week while Virginia is away and to leave for Maine Sunday.

July 25   Back collapsed yesterday. Had Armstrong, Pike, Bottomley. Then pelvis went out. Wanted Bottom this morning. Was off playing golf. Was away Saturday and Sunday. It seems to me that if a person decides to be a doctor, a certain obligation to be available to the ill goes with the decision, and it also seems to me that Bottom is failing to live up to such an obligation. Two months' straight vacation in one year is too much, not to mention being unavailable about two-thirds of the weekends. Her reason that she must "see the world" while she is young isn't valid. Wish I could find a doctor to take her place.

Tonight Evelyn starts for Southwest Harbor to attack my Father on the money and the inheritance questions.

I can only hope and pray that my Father will die before another ten years. Had he attempted to be more comprehending, less adamantly opposed to recognizing me as a person and a grownup, I could easily have been won over. But his disdain for me has never moderated, and I have rarely been able to approach him in any capacity save as an indigent son kowtowing before a wealthy father. I hate the ground the old devil walks on. I hate him for his disesteem of me, for his sanctimonious self-righteousness, for his talking poor mouth to me while giving thousands away to those who are better able than I to fawn and flatter, for his intolerance of my aspirations and hopes. I admire certain traits of his character (I am not so blind as to be unaware of his blunt virtues), but, by God, I wish he were out of this life even if he has to be gone without leaving me a red cent. I want to be rid of his presence, his disapproval, his condescension. I want to be able to stop rubbing my belly on the ground to impress him with my meekness and sensibleness. I want to be a man rid of a spring that dispenses bitter sustenance to one thirsty, even though I suffer from drought thereafter. I hate my Father. I resent him. I do not care if Evelyn causes him to suffer. It is a pity she cannot cause him to die.

August 1   Evelyn is constantly on my mind. She should be talking to my Father about now. Or maybe not until this afternoon. How much of our future hinges on her conversation? Or perhaps the man will refuse to yield an iota of the determination he has taken and chosen to maintain. Hope, at the least, he will not be antagonized and will surrender some definite information as to what he plans to do with his estate.

Abruzzo bet a third of the money he had made playing the horses on the dogs and lost it. Now he is playing the horses again. He has another job. He has been trying to get people to talk with me. "I know an old soak who used to be in de striptease racket," he observed. "She's a waitress and small-time night-club performer now. I tried to get her interested. It was no dice. She was suspicious-like. God knows why, because dere ain't nothin' she's not done. She gets so lit she changes her costumes in the kitchen — stark bald naked — an' all the help gather 'round an' tickle her. She don't give a damn. But she wouldn't come to see you. I shall keep trying. It's easy money sittin' here and shootin' off your face, and I'd think there'd be lots a' persons glad to draw in a dollar. But it's not that way. Most people is afraid of their shadows."

Must have written at least twenty letters to persons listed in various marriage bureau circulars. The majority of answers are uninteresting. I do not find that most of the women are bent upon the satisfaction of sex by hook or crook. They are in general interested either in marriage or in corresponding. A large proportion of applicants live in small rural communities in the Middle West and South, some on farms. I suppose that, as she grows older, when the supply of eligible men in a small town has been exhausted by marriage and the drift towards larger cities, a woman is really hard up for male companionship and for husband material. Most of the women who answer my letters are devoid of imagination, and their humor, such as it is, is heavy-footed. On the other hand, many of them give evidence of courage in the face of adversity. The applicants range all the way from women with college educations to young girls who have scarcely been off the farm.

August 3   Here is Evelyn's report, not very encouraging. What on earth makes the Old Man so secretive? It is hard to fathom. I suppose he expects me to take advantage of any information he might give. His silence must have something to do with his confirmed distrust of me and of my judgment.

Evelyn's letter (I had her send me a duplicate, registered, which I will leave unopened, hoping that someday it may be of use in breaking or contesting his will):

As for specific information gleaned from your father, it amounts to this — that you will be better off financially after his death than you are now. I asked him if that meant you were to receive the entire income from the amount held in trust for your benefit. He didn't answer that, but maybe I can get him to later. I asked him also about advancing any legacy to me now, instead of later, but he said no to that. However, after listening to my tale of woe, he said he couldn't see what he could do, but that he would send me a check for $100 a month for my personal use. He said further that I had certainly given him something to worry over, but that he hoped I could endure things, or become adjusted, because if I ever felt I had to quit it would kill him. He said of course he could see how I would become discouraged, and he didn't blame me, and I assured him I would do my best to show spartan endurance, but that I wasn't making any guarantees.

August 4 Evelyn home. Besides the $100 a month Father gave her for clothes, travel, etc., she obtained $1,500 with which to meet outstanding bills. He refused to tell her what he intended to do with his money on his death. He said that he would leave her some and Uncle Frank and Aunt Louise some, that my income would be larger than what he gives me now. "Arthur," he said, "would rather have the money and me dead. I never saw anyone in my life who thought as much about money." Evelyn assured him that I would rather be well and independent but, since I wasn't either, it was only natural that I was worried about how I would be provided for in the future, that he couldn't blame me for that. At one point in the proceedings he lost his temper — "It wouldn't have entered my mind to ask my father what he intended doing with his money. It was his money, not mine."

When Evelyn was discussing leaving me, Father began pointing out what he liked in me. He liked parts of my poetry. He thought I was honest. Evelyn handed him a line about how for some years I had thought of ending my life but now I felt that it was my duty to those who had been good to me to keep on as long and as courageously as I could. He swallowed that. "No Inman wife has ever left an Inman," (a misstatement) he reminded her. He thought her noble not to have laid her state of mind before her mother. Said Evelyn to me: "I lied and lied. My soul is thoroughly disturbed, for I don't like to lie. I don't know how long it will take to calm down."

I feel very cold-blooded about this whole business. I'm sorry if my attitude disturbs the reader. I feel that no matter what I can put over on my Father, it won't even the score.

August 9 Roderic has received a raise and is, he thinks, in line for another. I remember the time I helped him out with money and advice (money never repaid or repayment offered that I can recall), and I can remember when he came here and slept when I had the flu and Evelyn was worn out. Probably our debt to each other is equal, but I do wish he wouldn't be so petty about money and so nasty about what chances to displease him. I call him down at least twice a year, then flatter him. It isn't the money; it's the way he acts about it. I am heartily appreciative of his coming here when he is tired and the room is hot and he would prefer going home. But on the other hand, he usually arrives late and leaves early. Very fond of Roderic in a cautious sort of way.

August 10 Dr. Pike is as big a problem in his way as Roderic is in his. For a doctor, he is a genius sometimes without the judgment of a five year old child. He did a fine job on my rib yesterday, then, so quick I couldn't stop him, jammed at my intestines which were in no pain at all and messed them up so that I was awake all night from gas and am as big as a pregnant mother this morning. He has pulled this same stunt a dozen times during the last year in spite of every wile I could think of to stop him.

If there is a general war, it will be England's fault. Germany, allowed to expand into Russia, would have had its hands full. I believe that France without England would have permitted such expansion. Then France and England together could easily have handled Italy, and England would have been more fit to cope with Japan. There's a lot going on under the surface we ordinary people can no more than guess at. England and France are conjoined — we know that. Germany and Italy are together, and probably Hungary — we know that. It would be to Japan's interest to sign a military alliance with Germany and Italy — we know that. Not so sure of Poland's position or Spain's or of any of the other powers. Russia ought to join Germany now, and the two partition Poland. That would be sensible.

On the talking-book I have been reading 'Wuthering Heights.' It is refreshing to find an English classic that has no wish to be smart. There is plenty of emotional push in the story. A suppressed temperament seeking relief in the writing of a black fairy story. I know little or nothing about Emily Brontë, but certain it is she must have been a woman urged on by a natural confined wildness. The story is superbly constructed. The author is a genius, and I can accolade very few renowned English novelists with that commendation. I should have enjoyed knowing Emily. She writes as Woodwork lives, with a sort of unreal melodramatic surge that by its very intensity comes close to escaping or does escape (I am not sure which) the melodramatic to become dramatic. So much for 'Wuthering Heights' and Emily Brontë.

August 22   It was announced yesterday that while the representatives of France and England were soliciting a military alliance with Russia, the Germans had won from the Russians a nonaggression pact. That means or should mean that Russia will remain neutral in case of war and that English and French troops will not be allowed across Russia in case, which is almost sure, the Polish Corridor is forcibly closed. What a coup for the Nazis. England's only military access to Poland will be Rumania, and that access can easily be blocked by Hungarian and German forces. The poor Poles, scapegoats for England. There may be no major war now, as Poland surely cannot remain intact alone against Germany and Hungary. The way is opened to the Germans to exert pressure against Russia and Yugoslavia.

What will the English and French do now? What can they do except sit on their hunkers and moan? It does my heart good to see those two prideful nations get it in the neck, however the matter may recoil on the United States at some date near or distant. Had England minded its own business and allowed Hitler to expand into Russia and Rumania, Job's retribution would not be about to descend at this moment. England has been put deeply in debt to arm against a foe which would have been kept busy elsewhere had England kept its fingers out of the hot pie. What will Germany do next? How will Japan react? All of it more interesting than a high-powered drama.

August 24   The Russo-German nonaggression pact is signed and sealed. There is no abstract moral defense for Hitler's right-about-face, but I am becoming mature enough to realize retention of one policy by any leader in power when expediency warrants an abandonment of the policy means nothing short of ruin. The German course of action was mapped out — expansion into Russia and Rumania and the setting up of a Ukrainian State under German hegemony. England decided to interfere and to throw a ring of allies around Germany and Italy in order to put a stop to any such expansion. Poland was made one of these allies. Could Russia be successfully wooed into the British fold, Germany would be fairly well surrounded and the Russian military might be induced to do the dirty work. Faced by this strategy, Hitler changed his plans. The pact is the consequence.

I suppose, when you come right down to essentials, the leader who keeps in mind the eventual good of his own country, no matter how ambitious he is personally or how he lies and cheats to attain his ends, is the worthiest leader. Thus far Hitler qualifies as a great leader of his nation and his people.

August 28 The more I think it over, the more do I swing to the conviction that Hitler, in allying himself with the Soviets, made the major mistake of his brilliant career. To move people, a leader must prosper a cause. Many peoples followed Hitler because of his crusade against the Communists. The crusade, as crusades have always done, furnished a rallying point for otherwise naturally antagonistic races and cultures. His own action has now removed such a rallying point. It may be that, through this psychological error he has committed, he will altogether lose the support of nations such as Spain and Japan. Any immediate gain he may have achieved by alienating Russia from England will, I believe, be more than offset by the loss of the handle of one nutcracker, Japan, to be used against Russia, and the handle of the other nutcracker, Spain, to be used against France and England. Hitler will now be more or less at the mercy of the dubious constancy of Russia, and England will have lost an unnatural bedfellow and hence will be yet more able to play on our American sympathy. Of all dictators, Stalin possesses the shrewdest countenance. He is a brigand by nature and by training rather than a suppressed neurotic seeking self-justification. He may direct Hitler rather than Hitler direct him, now that his Eastern flank is safe and the Nipponese handle of the nutcracker has been broken. Hitler had the world under his thumb. Now I am not sure that he has.

September 1 "There's war," I said to Evelyn. "A man is coming at eleven to talk to me about reading your poems in public," she said.

"There's war," I said to Honey. "My God," she said, "I got a hole in my stocking."

"There's war," said Billy to Janice. "My shoe hurts," said Janice.

How am I to record events international and personal? Should I—the more dramatic course surely—scrap the personal save where it elides with the international. Or should I—the honest course, life progressing thus—mix the two? A perplexing quandary.

September 2 This is my diary. I am writing about America, Americans, myself, rather than primarily about what eventuates in Europe. The history books will tell that. So, except somewhat sketchily, except as I am interested, except as actions there concern or seem to concern America, I shall, I have decided, maintain in here my usual course.

With the Poles and Germans "already deep in the gore of the killing pen," Arthur's thoughts constantly turned to "what is going on across the Atlantic." His sympathies were with Germany, "but my partiality must go to what, unless a miracle occurs, will become 'our side.'" The diarist, of course, must dispassionately observe the conflict and not "rant and rave as a partisan of either side." Arthur contrasted two-faced Roosevelt, underminer of American neutrality provisions, with the noble and prophetic Lindbergh. He condemned the Churchill "clique" for spurning Hitler's peace offering. But he faulted Hitler too and threatened to give him up for good if he invaded the Netherlands. Arthur sorrowed for the gallant Poles (after justifying Germany's need to subdue them) and for the out-manned Finns (Russia seemed to be the real beneficiary of Hitler's fateful treaty with the Soviets), whose agonies he likened to those of the defeated Southern Confederacy.

He tried to keep the war out of his mind, at least out of the Diary, by quoting at great length the dizzy letters of Abruzzo (all about bumming, binges, sexual encounters) and letters from women he received after joining several correspondence clubs under pseudonyms. Some of the letter writers touchingly opened their hearts to the engaging "George Bricker"; some hinted of marriage or simply of carnal joys.

Writing verse was another way to keep the war from absorbing him, but painful rebuffs from publishers intensified his depression, and Evelyn once again bore the brunt of his displeasure. She had failed in her mission to win over the publishers; she was stubborn, cocky. ("Give me my head and I'll be amicable and grateful and responsive, but cross me when I feel that doing so is unjustifiable or is prompted by a lack of trust and I become cantankerous and resentful.") Only when she said she was leaving him did he pull in his horns and apologize. He was suffering horribly at this time as a result of Janice's "clumsiness" and of Dr. Pike's bullheaded treatments. Hence Arthur was doubly sensitive to real or fancied injuries, and although he was wonderfully successful in helping others (witness his comforting of Woodwork, now undergoing her own ordeal after her long affair with Allan appeared to be finished), he could not, even with his team of medicos, keep himself on an even keel.

Only the Diary, now twenty-one years in the making, refreshed his spirit. Excerpts from the corrected volumes had been turned down by a literary agent, but as he listened to the early parts being read aloud, he saw new possibilities for it. Cutting would make it more readable. For the moment, however, he preferred not to change it, because it showed growth of character and improvement in writing skills.

It is a strange and unconventional tale the diary sets forth, the story of an individual who is harassed by physical weakness and pain, who is an idealist faced by the necessity of having to build up within himself a philosophy of life to suit his case.

September 2 I wrote Lewis Gannett, the reviewer on the 'Herald Tribune,' asking why my books made no success. He replied briefly, dismissing my poetry by a polite but derisive shrug. "There isn't much poetry being written these days," he wrote, "which strikes fire with me, and I am always puzzled to explain the magic of that fire when I feel it. Perhaps you touched the heart of it yourself": and he quotes "Greatness" in full. That was all. And yet, if I touched the heart of a man's failure to write poetry, have I not written something worthwhile? The letter makes me feel worthless. I must strive to bear in mind my own convictions as to the merit of my work. And people seem to like this book. May it not be — and this is more definite than a mere suggestion — may it not be that critics, as so often before in history, can be deaf to a new sort of artistry, unrecommended, unvouched for, entering the poetic stadium by a postern gate without flare of trumpets or enthusiasm on the part of the promoters or the press box? I am nobody. I have few friends. I have no standing in the logrolling fraternity. No one finances my work with huge expenditures for advertising. I cannot travel the country and lecture in my own behalf. So why should 'None Now Are Quietly Wise' be a success? It shouldn't. Might as well resign myself to that. Dutton for the most part treats me literarily as an inferior artist who must be indulged to a point to be rid of his importunities, even as my Father treats me as a person.

Many evenings I listen to a broadcast of German music from the Hofbrau, a restaurant. The announcer has always been careful to emphasize that the restaurant is German, the orchestra Bavarian, the costumes of the waiters Bavarian. Last evening it was "an old-time restaurant," "an old-time band," Alpine costumes. The orchestra played "The Stars and Stripes Forever" and Victor Herbert and not a single German piece, and all spontaneity had vanished. Trim sails to American public opinion and, if possible, survive. Reminded me of the last war, with no German opera.

The Gallup poll has it that 76% of Americans expect us to be drawn into a general war. Only one man of the many I have talked with and of the many I have heard on the radio has expressed a willingness to fight England's fight. Yet they all say they will go if they have to. Are we sheep or men?

September 3 I have neglected to put down Mrs. Cash's conclusions concerning England. Bear in mind that a more violent Anglophile never went abroad. The vilest weather "on the face of God's wide earth." The most "abominable food." People with rotted teeth or false teeth. Jerry-built little houses. Stupid people. The rich wealthy, the poor poor. Underdeveloped men. Little use of electricity. Sanitation poor. Few modern conveniences. Cold and damp and raw. "Honestly, Mr. Inman, the people there are fifty years behind the times in every way. Live in England? God no, not while I can get back to the United States." However, she enjoyed her summer, went to London, Birmingham, the Lake Country, Glasgow, etc. Took two courses at Oxford. Visited the shrines of the various English authors. Someone congratulated her on Roosevelt. "Jesus Christ," she said, "you take him. Have him and welcome. We'd be glad to be rid of him. But I'll tell you this, mister, you wouldn't enjoy him once you had him."

September 8   Three columns of Nazi troops are converging on Warsaw. The French and English offensive against the Siegfried Line or West Wall, as it is sometimes called, appears to be about to commence. I feel like shouting "Hurry, Hitler! Hurry, Hitler!" to urge on the conquest of Poland in order that the war on the western front might become a stalemate with perhaps peace in the offing. I pity the poor Poles, but I hope they are quickly conquered. Their army does not seem in retreat so much as retiring. Only twenty-five thousand Polish soldiers have been captured, the Germans announce, and that seems remarkably few for such widespread and large operations. It must be a superbly executed retirement before superior forces and armaments.

The problem of selecting a prose volume of extracts from my diaries bids fair to be a difficult one. It seems to me neither politic nor honorable to use portions concerned with my friends without asking their permission, whether their names are changed or not, and if I show them what I have written about them, they will say, as people invariably do, that I haven't put down what they are or what they have spoken. After which they will hold a grudge against me. I showed Billy the piece about Mechanics Hall. Angrily he declared: "I don't talk that way. I don't drop my 'g's.' I don't say 'none.' It sounds like some nigger from the swamps. You can't use that that way. I don't intend to be mispresented." So you see. Perhaps I had best be cautious and leave out everything concerned with those with whom I come into regular contact. What will that leave? Approval of anything to do with Hitler or disapproval of Roosevelt or censure of the Jews or Irish will be sufficient to ban acceptance by most publishers.

September 9   And now President Roosevelt takes another step toward involving us in war sooner or later. He has put the United

States on a "limited national emergency" footing, whatever that may be. The National Association of Broadcasters is urging all radio stations to exercise restraint and caution in the method and manner of handling war news and to remain neutral.

The spoken word is probably far more inflammatory than the written word. The human voice is a more potent conveyor of emotion than is the printed page; it is less likely to appeal to reason; it is more capable of being misunderstood; from time immemorial it has been used to sway and control masses, and this possibility has been incalculably augmented by the radio and the power of reaching millions.

Within the last twenty-four hours, there has been a noticeable curtailment in war bulletins and war news. In particular the outflow of propaganda from England has been lessened.

Mosley, the British Fascist leader, has this to say — and forget that he is a Fascist for a moment and hear a small voice of sanity. "I am not offering to fight in the quarrel of Jewish finance, in a war from which Britain could withdraw at any moment she likes with her empire intact and her people safe."

September 13 Ella's Robert was hit by an automobile and knocked unconscious a week or so ago. Someone told her he was at the City Hospital. She rushed there. They treated her, she said, as coldly as though she were buying something in a store where they didn't want to sell. She could obtain no information as to whether Robert had been brought in or not. After an hour or so, she said: "I can understand your attitude, how indifferent you become after watching hundreds of persons brought in here dead and dying and after listening to thousands of inquiries about them, but I wish you'd take into consideration my account. I'm a wife. My husband's been injured. I am told he's here. I come here to get information about him, and everywhere I meet indifference. Suppose it was your wife or sister or mother and you wanted to find out about her. How would you like to be met with indifference? So I would appreciate it if you would try to show some heart." "After that," explained Ella to me, "I obtained some service, the best that was in them to give."

When Robert, who had been taken to his doctor, was being strapped and his shoulder put in place, he became conscious for a moment. "Was I hit?" he inquired. "Yes — not fatally, though," he was informed. "Well," he said, "that keeps me out of the war for a few weeks anyway." Then he fell into unconsciousness again. He is still in bed, smoking, entertaining visitors, talking about the war, reading 'Grapes of Wrath.'

September 14   Under 'Marriage Intentions' in the newspaper two days ago, this:

Manuel Pena, 14 Dartmouth place, upholstering; Edna C. Mercer, 14 Dartmouth place, advertising.

September 16   Lindbergh has been in this country for several months now making an official survey of the American Air Force, of landing fields, of production plants, of engineering equipment and design. His duty done, he spoke to the nation last night in the capacity of a citizen advising against the entry of America into the European imbroglio. What he had to say was simple and to the point, couched in no flowery language and delivered with no fireworks. I found myself thinking: "My God, if we only had a man like that for President."

September 20   Hitler made a speech at Danzig. Many true things he said, many false things. It is to be gathered that he is incensed against England. Again and again he repeats that he has no designs against France. Chamberlain replied in a speech. Hitler's speech was full of bellicose assertions in the German manner. Chamberlain's speech was full of bellicose assertions in the British manner. Of the two, I prefer the German manner. The British always remind me of a little plaster-cast model that was passed around from hand to hand when I was at school. A priest at his altar was unctuously delivering a sermon while under the altar, his robes girded up, he was raping a woman. I prefer blunt and exciting deception such as Hitler practices to bland and self-righteous deception such as the English indulge in. There is little doubt that in the average English mind Hitler, not the English leaders, is unequivocally responsible for the uneasy seat England now occupies.

September 22   On the whole, I have enjoyed my memberships in the various correspondence clubs. The letters — perhaps seventy in all — have thrown a light on the inner souls of many lonely people. The persons who write lack imagination. They are restless. In joining the correspondence clubs, it is as though they were fumbling for a way out of something or into something, a blindish effort toward change of some sort. The majority seem kindly. Some are suspicious. Some are blithely trustful. A few are curious merely. A drab lot, most of them, living monotonous lives in small country towns.

My correspondence pseudonym is A.C. Emmons or George Bricker (the latter accorded me permission to use his name). When I write members of the clubs, I write as I think will suit them, making up fabrications as I go along, shocking Evelyn. To each correspon-

dent I arrange myself as a different person and have a fine unham-
pered time doing it. I try to lead them on to divulge themselves.

Here let me introduce to you Mrs. Darlene Mack, from her
picture about as emotionally and sexually unrestrained as you could
wish, yet kindly and with a certain coarse flair for living boldly. The
second letter was sent air mail and special delivery on lavender
paper. Evelyn and I have striven to adhere faithfully to her misspell-
ings except when she haphazardly confuses the use of the vowels "a"
and "o," for instance writing "hove" for "have." Letters such as
these and the people who pen such letters are part of America, and I
feel that you should read what Darlene has to say. Anyway, the
letters should amuse you.

LA. Aug 16–39.

Dear Mr. A.C. Emmons
So you like girls with green eyes. My eys are green at times Some
say I have Cat eyes are Dreamy eyes. but Just Now they are Very
blue because I am lonely and Would like to Write you very much.
I belong to the Club. I am 30 years old 4 11— 1.39 Red hair
affectionate Natur. love to go places Dance Rid hike hunt fish. So
you have a home. I have a heart for a home but as Yet the Right
Man hasent come along Yet. True I have been Married Divorced
but I do So hate to live alone. I love to Cook & pepaur Nice Meals
& love a Nice home Coming husband. Some day my prince will
Come Soon I hope. I will Say no more I hope you will answer this
Short Note. Will Send you a SnapShot in Return letter.   Yours
Very Truly
A Friend
Darlene

blue Sunday. Sept.17—

Dear Arthur.
Your Very Sweet letter written Aug 24- but as We have been away
in the Mountains all Summer we Just arrived home the 10th or
Maybe I Should Say for a few weeks. but when We got back I
found Your Sweet letter. Yes I Still am Very blue You See I
Married when Just a we girl of 13— and Soon there Was a Baby
girl I Still have her She is my one happyness. We are Very Close to
each other. but then there is a place in my heart for the Love of a
good Strong man. I am to young and every one Says to Beautfull
to live alone. but out here Art— if I may Call You that, the Men
are Just well Maybe I Should Say they look like Men they Take
You out for a Dinner & a Dance. they think they own you Body &
Soul. Thats Why I am lonesome. I can cook my own Dinner. an as

far as a Dance goes I Can live with out it. I love a home I love
married life. I am a Very good cook and a Very good housekeeper
in every Way. I love to be loved and most of all I want a home to
Share with a good honest Man who When he Comes home &
Says he loves me I Can believe him. I have all of my own Furniture
and I have a Ford. I love to Drive Very much. but When evening
Comes theres no place like home. but you know & I know, home
is not a home With out a Wife or a husband now is it. Art I Want
very much to leave here and I am in about a week or so. I am
Coming east. as far as K.C. for thats how much money I have.
Work I Can Sew Dress making. I do it in my home but there is
None now and I am tired of Calif as a whole. but my friends Say
if I go east maybe I will find piece & happiness I am looking for.
You ask me about my friends I have a few ones Who are my
friends True blue. good Kind of people you are Not ashamed to
know. They are all married & happy. With homes of there own &
Children thats what I want but maybe I havent met the Right
Man Yet, and I Never will here. My Rent is up Oct. 10th. and I
have 70 Dollar left in the Bank. We are going to take that and
leave here. for the east. I have a Very good Lady friend and her
husband in K.C. I have Knowen them for 18 years Nearly all my
life I can Stay there for a while. I would like to come & make you a
Call if I could. if I ever Cooked You a Dinner I am afraid You
Would not let me go. here is a Snap Shot of me. now You Can
Stop Writing. or maybe You Would like for me to Cook that
Dinner theres no harm in a little lonely too having Dinner
toghter. No — hurry then & Write me S.D.A. So I will get it
Soon. as I need a little encourging to Start that long Drive along
with my little girl and our Dog. I think I will get half of my Rent
back and leave Soon about 10 days. or less. I could be Your
housekeeper you know. they do thoes things you know dont they
then we could be Very good friends at least We would never be
lonely I am Sure. me Art I like to do most any things thats because
I am Still Young. but Jitturbug Danceing is not for me I think it is
Very bad tasts. thats they way they Dance in Deep Dark Jungles.
but give me a fine Waltz Merry Widow Waltz, or Dark eyes. they
fill me With beauty of Soul. I Shall Stop now hope Your in the
City & get this Soon & answer if You dont answer by Wednesday
will its been nice in hearing that you would like to keep my Green
eyes from turning blue. I hope You can read between the lines, &
do Something about it. Your Very Truly Darlene

xx.

P.S. how much gas & oil from KC. to Boston. & if I Should Come
there I Could Work there Just as easey as here.,

I hope you have to Strong arms as I will Need them if I Come
there. and too good eyes to See me with too.
Oh the reason I Says
this. I got a letter from a
Man one arm gone poor Soul.
I need two armes See,
I hope I am not to late & You have found another girl With green
eyes.

September 23   Poland has been divided, two-thirds to Russia,
one-third to Germany, and the Germans are withdrawing from
conquered territory and turning it over to the Russians. Why? Of
course, regarded historically, it is the sensible course for Hitler to
pursue, for that much foreign population incorporated into the
Reich would only become a source of endless grief, would be better
left unincorporated. But who expects a conqueror to evince historical sense? However, it may be so, though more likely Russia has
squeezed the scissors-grip for all it was worth. I still think it will be a
sorry day for Hitler that he played footsie with Stalin.

September 29   A famous Japanese seer predicts that this war will
be over and done with before 1940, but that within a year another
war, to last five years, will visit the world. To put it mildly, this
certainly is a phony war, and nobody seems to want it except the
high British politicos.

October 2   Wrote poems yesterday. Henry Gross paid us a visit.
The same Henry, gentle, courteous, with only his hair graying and
receding farther from his high forehead to betoken the passage of
the years. Now and again he passes a hand over his hair to assure
himself that every strand is in place. A gentle person, Henry, with no
harm in his soul for anyone. He has been engaged in arranging
'Rhapsody in Blue' for youngsters, reducing chords to the size of
their hands. He has sold the arrangement to a music publisher who
wants more of the same.

October 7   Tried once more to read Thomas Wolfe, he that is so
violently lauded by American critics. Sometimes I know what he is
talking about, sometimes not. Words, some vivid, some tawdry,
many repetitious beyond patience, bold words and mean words and
meaningless words — harried and vehement outpourings of a sen-
sory system bearing an overload of impressions. I have seen a fire-
hose escape from control and thrash about as Wolfe's supercharged
attempt to unburden himself thrashes about. Gone slightly cuckoo
on the heady draught of America, somewhat maudlin, somewhat
incoherent. Flashes of brilliance but not enough flashes to warrant
my enduring his tedious, disorderly flow of words.

October 8   Not a single review of 'None Now Are Quietly Wise' save the one in the 'Haverford News,' and the book has been out two months. Another failure. 'One Who Dreamed,' 'Red Autumn,' 'Bubbles of Gold,' 'Of Castle Terror,' 'Shadows of Men,' 'American Silhouettes,' 'Frost Fire,' 'Silhouettes Against the Sun,' 'The Night Express,' 'Soldier of the South,' 'None Now Are Quietly Wise'— all failures. 'The Moon Drifter' will be a failure. 'Where Find Sanctuary'—if any publisher will take it—will be a failure. I expect nothing but failure until after my death and perhaps failure then. My entire life has been, is, will be failure. It seems predestined thus.

October 11   'The Atlantic Monthly' sent back my 'Where Find Sanctuary.' Nobody wants anything I do. I have been reading Louis Untermeyer's memoirs, just published. More than ever convinced success with poetry to be a matter of personal contact and pull. Poetry is an unhealthy art as the majority of its proponents practice it and regard it. If I attempt to bring some health into my attitude toward it, I am laying myself open to the charge of putting prose thoughts into verse, of using cliches, of using unusual and antique words, of lacking symbolism. I realize all this and wish to keep on, so I suppose I should accept nonrecognition gracefully. However, that's not my nature. Keep trying to break through. I am convinced that a poet should be a man first and a poet second and that poetry should have virility and push. Oh well.

October 15   My Father arrives tomorrow for two days. Bow and scrape and pull my forelock and be anything in the world except myself. Well, it has to be endured; I have escaped two visitations, and that is something. Evelyn is not anticipating his visit either. He usually succeeds in depressing her.

October 23   Tried to persuade Evelyn yesterday afternoon for two hours and a half to alter her attitude toward me, to trust my intentions and have faith in them so that this endless bickering and arguing might stop. If not, I said, I would close in on her—which I didn't want to do—and remove every privilege I could that she enjoyed until she came to her senses and treated me as a husband rather than as an enemy who wished her ill.

October 24   When I was having the talk with Evelyn the other afternoon about not arguing and contradicting, I asked if she would let me cut down on her time away, her visits. If that didn't work, would she let me give away her cat. She wouldn't consent that I hit her. I intended none of these but was striving to make an impression. I waxed vehement and, I suppose, said nasty things and true things. But I assumed after she had come upstairs to see me, that everything was all right and that she would try to control her answers. I had no intention at all of putting the pressure on, believing that I had gone far enough.

Yesterday afternoon we corrected in amity. This morning I asked her, innocently, if she had been thinking some more on our talk, thus, I thought, giving her a chance to tell me everything would be all right. She said: "I'm not going to consent to restrictions. I've seen Mr. Whitcomb and have everything planned out. I'll stay here, but I won't consent to any restrictions. That's final." You could have knocked me down. I felt hit in the solar plexus. I said things. Then I went riding.

I knew I had made a mistake. I wondered would Evelyn be home when I returned. The autumn leaves looked more beautiful than usual, the sky more blue. Home — and Evelyn gone. I had forgotten my other lessons and had pressed her too hard. When I press her too hard, she loses all perspective. If she has no character, naturally she can't stand up under a grilling. It had been my fault. She has no faith in my love nor any trust in my intentions. I sat and considered. I don't want a wife to take her place, merely want to exist without bickering. I love her, as I told her the other night, more than anyone in the world, though I do have a contempt for her failure to practice self-control. I believe that I might persuade Janice to marry me, but I want Evelyn. If she isn't on her way to Washington by this time, I'll knuckle under. I haven't the feet to follow when she runs away.

I have been answering every ring of the phone. Finally, Evelyn speaking to Janice. She didn't intend, she said, to come back. I persuaded. I promised. I told her that I loved her and that the fault had been mine. She wanted an end to long talks. She wanted more trips away. She thought that we might as well split up. I asked her to come here and talk with me. She asked if I would be gentle. I promised. After all, she is nothing but a child in many ways, and if I want to keep her I should bear that always in mind. She said grudgingly that she would come. A half-hour has gone by and she hasn't arrived. It would surprise me not at all if she didn't come. Once she has decided to take the bit in her teeth, there's no reckoning on what she will do. Sixteen years together, and this — my fault. Someone should kick me around the block. But I still insist that had Evelyn had more faith in my motives it would not have happened. However, the culmination is entirely my fault, not Evelyn's. I am to blame.

Later: Evelyn came. It isn't easy to write about her and myself without making one of us seem entirely in the wrong. If I have more insight into the handling of people, it is my fault entirely; let it go at that. I began by apologizing for my lack of common sense and for the ordeal I had put her through. She began by making demands on me as exigent as any I had made on her. I told her that I could promise to do what she demanded but would rather not. What she desired of me was that I should remember always to be more gentle, and what I desired of her was to have faith in me. Why not leave it at that, without demands or conditions on either side, and strive hard to be thoughtful of each other.

Her earnest bellicoseness gradually dwindled. It is a shame and a pity that she doesn't have faith in me. I talk too much. I try to be too minutely and undecoratedly honest. I suppose, as is the case with so many other persons, I am my own worst enemy. To inspire trust, discreet and well-judged words count more than proper actions, and I should always remember that the world at large prefers England to Germany in great measure merely because the English talk prettily and the Germans do not. I hope things here will go better now.

October 29 The Senate has passed upon a revision of the Neutrality Act. It was a Roosevelt victory with modifications. Arms and munitions may be sold to belligerents, though no credit will be allowed. American ships may not transport arms and munitions through waters deemed by the President to be dangerous. Americans, with few exceptions, may not travel on foreign ships.

Business indexes, corporation earnings, carloadings continue to improve. Earnings of many companies have risen precipitately. Prosperity, partly sound, partly based on the war in Europe, is returning with considerable vehemence. The front pages of newspapers have been more concerned for some months now with the war than with setting forth every word uttered by Roosevelt. This absence of Roosevelt from before the eyes of businessmen every morning at breakfast has had a salutary psychological effect on them, and they are regaining self-confidence, daring, vigor, initiative.

October 30 I am sitting in the library writing while a Miss Farmer plays musical comedy scores for me. She must be in the thirties, an old maid, a nice person. She wears a reddish knitted dress, a red hat that doesn't match, black shoes. She has on gold spectacles. Her hair is done in a large knot on the back of her head. Her hands are long and her fingers are long. Her voice is pleasant and accurate. This moment she is singing 'Allah's Holiday' from 'Katinka' by Friml.

I need music this morning. The axle on the Baby-Carriage is broken. Beecher cannot find another in Boston. Billy is out searching for a secondhand one at the junkyards. Perhaps it will be weeks before the Cadillac can be repaired, so difficult is it to obtain parts for an old car. Oh well.

November 1 Last evening Ella was telling of her latest activities.

She has enrolled for a series of sixteen lectures on the growth and significance of American Labor. She has joined a group fostering birth control. She is helping organize an entertainment to be given for the benefit of an ill redcap. She still sews for the small Jewish furrier in Brookline. "I don't receive any more money than I did, for I haven't asked for a raise. The poor devil is in the red up to his ears. His rich creditors don't pay him. He couldn't give me a raise if I asked for one. As it is, I'd rather work where I am for two, three, even five dollars less than I realize I'm actually worth, because, taking into account his many faults, my boss is a pretty decent fellow. He's as honest as a Jew can be. He's too kindly for his own good. He knows I'm worth more than I get and allows me the freedom to come and go, to be late or to stay away that not one boss in a hundred would grant. He doesn't make passes at me or talk filthy the way most Jewish small-time businessmen do. Taken all in all, I could be worse off." Ella's Robert is well again and back on his job. "I think his accident brought us closer together. It made us realize we needed each other." Ella chatted for two hours, hardly drawing breath. I enjoyed the evening.

November 3   The House of Representatives has sealed the doom of the arms embargo and declared itself in favor of the 'cash-and-carry' sale of arms to belligerent nations. Might as well have sent the Allies a hundred thousand troops. Money will pour into the United States for the purchase of weapons of warfare. It is said that the Allies are ready to spend a billion dollars in this country. There will be a boom in 'war babies.' We will experience prosperity, for a while at least, whether it be sound or not.

November 11   Hitler, as far as I can determine, is trapped and desperate. The Russian move ruined him. Germany, to put it baldly, is friendless, surrounded by enemies and half-friends who wish the Nazis ill. Much blood may be shed, but Hitler has already lost the struggle, or so it seems to me. Air bases seized in the Netherlands cannot win the war, nor can a flanking movement through Belgium on the Maginot Line. And as I said, if Hitler orders an invasion of Holland, I'm through with him.

November 23   Poor Woody. What a curious, jagged, intense, unfulfilled yet full life she has led—born out of wedlock, not wanted by her mother, called names by her schoolmates, beginning to earn her own living as a child, in love with a worthless boy, married, unhappy, divorced, working on her own here in Boston, an efficient secretary getting higher and higher pay with a food concern, afraid of men, Allan, Peggy, a job in Pawtucket, the farm, and now. And all the time a love of the beauty of nature, a craving for the exciting, a morbid interest in her own reactions, a wild and untamed personality. An interesting and a fascinating person, Hedda Williams. Existence has been less dull for having been acquainted with her and for having watched her story progress.

December 3 I have some pins and necklaces that belonged to Mother, Aunt Helen and Mother's mother. They have been stored away doing nobody any good. Evelyn won't use them, preferring for some strange reason ten-cent-store jewelry to the real thing. "I don't have to bother whether I lose it or not," she says. Tomorrow is Janice's birthday. I gave her the gold and garnet necklace (in style at this moment) which belonged to my Grandmother, Tillie Maffitt. It is an unusually pretty one, and she seemed pleased. "I'm awfully grateful, Arthur. Honestly I am. I'll treasure this always. You're a darling." And I told her the story about how Grandfather Crew had first caught sight of Tillie Maffitt when she was picking blue violets of a spring morning long ago, of how he had wooed and won her, of how the necklace had been one of his presents to her, of how his hair was red and hers was red-gold. Janice is as rank a sentimentalist as I am. "That," she said, "makes it twice as nice."

December 7 The Soviet invasion of Finland appears to have precipitated what amounts to a world-wide revulsion of attitude towards Communism and the Communists. England is rushing planes, high-test gasoline, munitions to Finland. Mass meetings are being held in Italy against Russia, and volunteers are attempting to enlist in the Finnish Army. German and Italian planes have been ordered by Finland. The South American nations desire the United States to join them in a New World protest against Russian aggression. President Roosevelt is considering rebating the interest on Finland's debt and placing the money to their credit and allowing them to buy supplies from one of the Administration's authorities at low prices.

December 8 The contract with the Oglethorpe Press is signed and sealed. 'The Moon Drifter' is to be published during the spring. I pay nothing and receive a ten percent royalty. Dr. Jacobs appears to be really interested in furthering my success. I suppose, regarded one way, it is a feather in his cap to have the name of an established, if unsuccessful, author on his lists. This is about the only good I ever got out of S.M. [Inman] since he died, for I don't flatter myself Dr. Jacobs is taking the book on its merit.

December 12 All the traffic is being routed down St. Botolph Street, and there is endless passing of cars and trucks. Don't know how Evelyn sleeps through it in the mornings. You can feel the vibrations of the trucks beneath your feet. Every time I turn my

mind on that damn subway and consider the noise, the inconvenience, the wakeless nights, the dust and sand, the new dirt-holding
pavements, the fruitless waste of money and the needlessness of it
all, I feel my ire boiling up within me. Those cautious people on
Huntington Avenue who refused to sign a petition against it have
had cause to regret their lack of foresight, and I, for one, hope they
have spent rueful times. Much of the subway is finished but much is
not. Right now they are working on an underpass below Massachusetts Avenue. Hardly any traffic moves up and down the crazy quilt
that is left of Huntington Avenue. And all over Boston and Brookline trolley tracks are being ripped up or covered over with pavement. No longer do the Huntington Avenue streetcars run to
Brookline Village and Harvard Avenue. Tracks on Huntington
Avenue could have been taken up, the street repaved, buses bought
and free service given for a hundred years, all for what this useless,
politically inspired subway is costing. It will take another year more
at least to finish it. I dread the racket of the traffic on Huntington
Avenue when the street has been paved and cars whir past with no
occasional rumble of streetcars to break the rush of it.

December 16 ". . . even apparently bad luck is rigorously
bound up with character."—from 'Discord in Scarlet,' a story in
'Astounding Science-Fiction.'

December 17 This morning Billy and I drove back streets
through the Armenian quarter and the Chinese quarter, past the
leather section, the South Station and the wool section to the Fish
Pier. Calm mist over calm water. A single trawler in. Sea gulls
everywhere, sitting, flying easily, silently. Black piles. The only
sound, planes overhead. Ferryboats, their walking-beams seesawing. An anchored dredge. A policeboat. Liners in their berths. The
sleeping bulk of the city. The one trawler rising and falling gently, as
though breathing, hawsers slack. Red mast and lifting-boom. Black
hawse-holes and black anchors and black ladders and black galley
pipe. Red bell. Neutral-colored nets and corks and lines coiled in
tubs. Red-faced seaman, smoking. Black davits. I should not, I
thought, want to be a fisherman. A hard and endurance-demanding
life. No softness of line or texture as in the old wooden and canvas
sailing ships. All iron, cold and unfriendly. But I suppose that those
with sufficient vigor to lead the arduous life do not pause to consider the contrasting degrees of friendliness between wood and
iron.

I signaled to Billy to move on. We came home through the
narrow downtown streets with stonework towering on either side of
us. The Italian barber who smells like a negro and who is cocky and

pushing and who wishes, calculatingly, to be pleasant has been here and gone. Now down in the alley members of the Salvation Army are playing dolorously on brasses depressing hymns and more depressing carols. They have been repeating the same pieces over and over again. Their women, with tambourines in their hands, bonnets on their heads, are walking around with faces peering up at windows, for all the world like so many scrawny chickens waiting to be fed from a porch. I suppose that they do good, but they give me the creeps. How can human beings immolate themselves to such a life? I'd rather be a crook or, as Abruzzo writes me he has been doing in St. Louis, pick dumpheaps for salable scraps.

December 19 The German captain blew up the 'Admiral Graf Spee.' British submarines claim to have sunk two cruisers on daring raids and to have shot down a dozen planes. During the first part of the war, German reports were more accurate than British. Now German reports are no longer trustworthy. The coups at sea came just in time to reestablish Winston Churchill's waning popularity. He is now crowing like a rooster.

The Finns have lost the far northern part of their land to the Russians, blowing up the nickel mine there before retreating. The Finnish strategy has been superior to the Russian. General Mannerheim is a fine figure of a man and appears to be considerable of a general. It is a pity that Finnish manpower is so limited. It is always thrilling when an inferior force, inspired by love of country and by superior leadership, withstands a larger and more powerful foe. It was so when the South withstood the North during the Civil War, when the Boers held off the might of Great Britain, when the Berbers delayed the Arab invasion. It is so now in the case of the Finns. This siege of the Mannerheim Line can prove to be one of the decisive battles of the centuries. Should the Finns continue to balk the Soviet invasion, smaller nations may be induced again to take heart, and the myth of the invincibility of mere size may be discredited.

"What," I asked Billy, "did you buy Sadie for Christmas?" "A fur jacket." "A fur jacket? What sort of fur?" Nonchalantly, "Oh, silver fox." "What did you pay for it?" "Oh, three hundred and ninety-five dollars." "You paid that much — for a jacket?" "Yes sir, I paid that much. Sadie likes fur." "But don't you think, Billy, that in relation to your station in life, you were pretty extravagant?" "Nothin' is too extravagant when it pleases my Sadie. And say, what do you mean by my 'station in life'?" "I mean this: that judged by your other normal expenses, this is a lot to spend. It's as if I bought Evelyn a five thousand dollar car." "Well, if she liked it, that'd be okay. And

Sadie'll like this. Boy, it's a beauty. I'm havin' it sent by special messenger — not by ordinary delivery — Saturday. Nothin's too good for my little girl." So Billy's Sadie will be clad in furs of a superior quality. She already has jewels, fine furniture, a Persian rug on her bedroom floor, a silver toilet set, fine sheets and blankets to sleep under.

More letters from Abruzzo, chapters in what he calls his "adventurious life." In St. Louis he is living in a shack with some other fellows. The shack, I gather, is on or near a dumpheap. They make enough money to buy food and drink by picking salable debris from the dumpheap, "scratching the junk" he calls it. The life he describes strikes me as being incredibly sordid and wearisomely aimless. They "scratch" a little, then sell their gleanings, purchase whiskey or alcohol, get drunk. They bicker together, endure discomforts, do not know when "the law" will get them. The longing to be footloose, independent of authority, unrestricted by responsibility goes sometimes to curious and rather debased lengths to fulfill itself. I do not include here most of Abruzzo's letters. They are generally filled with routes he has taken from town to town, city to city, names of railroads, encounters with "dicks," nights spent in the jungles, "hitting the main stem" for food, etc. — repetitional items once told covered sufficiently. The following is the letter I received yesterday and is, I believe, worth rendering.

In this letter I am only going to tell of sidelights that I forgot to tell in previous letters.

One thing all of us have noticed is the absence of real old-timers on the road. There used to be an old-timer that bummed in and around the vicinity of St Louis. He hasn't been around for quite a while. Some are shacking up, but the large majority have completely disappeared. Most shacks are on or near the railroad. Just why I dont know but when a bum retires it seems that he wants to be around something familiar. The shack in which I am staying is just off the railroad. Close by is a good section to bum in, but we dont go there often, so as to keep it for a cold or rainy day. Most of our food is from some kind grocer or butcher. What little we buy is esentials or tobaco. Ned, the original owner of the shack, has lived here about 5 years. He has a crystel radio set and we have quit a time hearing some of the better program as we only have two ear phones. A deck of cards and a checker board provide the rest of our relaxations. When one of us makes a luckey strike and gets a roll we spend it on wiskey and "ladies of the street." There is one in perticular that Ned and Nick go for, she is negress and is called Della. Ned also has a negro queer who drops down to see him. He is generaly good for a dollor. I have a queer who runs a fruit store. We all think this is funny, as we call queers fruit. This fruit is about two hundred and fifty pounds and looks very sloppy. But he is good to bum so we all make him. We have several neighbors, one is a negro family living right across the tracks. The rest are all fellows. We have a black dog called "nigar". He's sort of a mixed dog, but quite inteligent and is black in color with a very fine coat of hair. There are two things needed here at the shack, coal and water. We hike down to a factory for water. No one interferes, and we use an average of about twenty gallons per day. Coal is some times obtained from empty cars on the railroad, but mostly we get it at night from a coal yard. Of course they have a watchman, but so far we have been able to outwit him, but one of these days there will be no more coal, then we shall have to look up a new sorce of supply. Washing our clothes is curtail because of lack of water, we do manage to keep clean how ever, inspite of the handicaps. We use the bed roll to sleep on as there is only one bunk in the shack and it is too small to build any more. We spread the roll out on the floor every night and it makes a warm, if not too comfortable bed to sleep on. Cat also got a couple of blankets & all together we are not to bad off. Our diet is fairly consistant generaly stew or beans. We use about one pound of coffee per day which means we drink plenty during the day. Work is not eagerly swort but is not avoided either. None of us has realy worked since I came here. The police are tolerent except when some thing is commited in the vicinity then they come down and generaly work them over and hold them for a while. Ned was here once when a murder was done near here. They came down and arrested the hold bunch. Ned said even after being released he could not go back to the shack as the cops were hot. They finaly got the real murderer and they let the boys move in again. The one thing that impresses me is how they, the boys in the shack, talk about sex. That seems to be upmost in thier minds, and I think it is because of lack of any active. They talk of all sorts of sex and its various phases such as queers and prositutes and the diferent experences they go through. An other topic of our conversation is experences we have had on the bum.

Well I hope you enjoy this discriptive letter of the surroundings of which I am staying. Perhaps too you will better understand why we have so many drunken brawls and why we, more or less, act as we do.

December 25   My Christmas is as follows. Five days ago Janice carelessly hit me in the testicles, nearly making me faint. Since then I have suffered with them almost constantly until by now I am in mortal fear of having acquired another permanent handicap. I wish I were thoroughly and unalterably dead and out of this everlasting misery. I take every precaution not to be hurt that I can bear in mind at one time, but always God has an unforeseen trump card to flash, and I am tired of a losing game.

Mrs. Cash reads to me nearly every night and some afternoons. Though I speak of her seldom, she reads every weekend, does it well and is therefore a person of definite importance in my scheme of things. She reads my science fiction magazines by the hour, although I know she has no use for them. She even reads Will Durant's voluminous history about Greece backwards to me without comment, that being the way I want it, since an altered perspective causes me to get a new view of it.

December 29   While having the pelvis fixed, I rolled on a testicle and have been in torture ever since. Have waked the dead yowling three times in the last two days, the testicles and the bladder pained so intensely. Evelyn got Dr. Pike, and he worked to place the bladder in a normal position while the tears rolled out of my eyes and I couldn't stop. Will have to wear a suspensory for a while, it seems. God damn that Janice for starting all this and then sitting around smug and cheerful. I wish she had it for a while and she wouldn't be cheerful any more. Sometimes I wonder if there is any sympathy in her make-up. A great sentimentalism yes, but sympathy perhaps none. As she says, she's never herself hurt. So I suppose she's not to blame for remaining self-contained while I take the bumps. Right now, I hate her shadow.

1940

January 1   Billy said: "Sadie's been offered a job at Jordan Marsh for forty-five a week." That was all it took to start my imagination off on a train of thought which saw Billy becoming discontented because earning less than his wife, being offered a position himself with better pay, in the end, one way or another, leaving me. "Is that so?" I said. "Yeah. A man got it for her. She can be head saleslady in the curtain department. They like 'em dressed snappy, and that's Sadie. Tell me, what do you think about her shiftin' jobs? She's just been given a raise at the laundry and expects another soon. I'd like to hear what you think about such a move." "Do you really want to know?" "Of course I do. I wouldn't asked if I hadn't." "Well, Billy, I haven't had time to think a lot about it. I can tell you my general ideas on the subject, though of course they may be wrong." "I'd like to hear what you have to say." "Okay, then. Will Sadie be on the road?" "Yes, she will. She'll have a car at her disposal and a man to drive her. She'll be home four nights a week anyway." "Is Sadie happy now?" "Oh yes!" "Are you happy?" "Yes indeed." "Betsy Simons got a job selling surgical instruments on the road. Three months later she was applying for a divorce." "Sadie's not Betsy Simons," indignantly. "Of course not. But all women, good or bad, possess some traits in common. They are all of them factualists, that is, what is immediately in front of them comes to be of more importance than what has been in front of them. If you want to keep Sadie and want to keep conditions as they are (you say you are happy and she is happy), then you'll be taking chances to let her go into a different environment with people you don't know, away from you. You can't give a woman too much freedom if you want to keep her, Billy. I used to think you could, but I learned better, and you know how devoted Evelyn is to me."

"So you think I'd be takin' a chance — huh?" "I couldn't say for sure, of course. Sadie may be exceptional and stay constant away from you. But I do know that if I were you I'd hesitate a long time before allowing such a radical change in my routine to occur." "Well, I been considering a long time already." "You don't want to seem selfish, do you, Billy?" "No, I don't." "The question is, if you are happy and Sadie is happy, is it being selfish to maintain that happiness. I don't think so, myself. You know, Billy, you're one of the nicest fellows I ever met inside, but you always want to remember that there are dozens of men slicker-looking, better educated, with more money and poise than you ever had or will have, loose in this world and on the watch for an attractive girl like Sadie; and there's always the chance that she won't see through them and that maybe they'll look better to her than you do. There are a lot of wild and unscrupulous people, fast people in the buying and selling racket in these big department stores and commercial houses. And as I said, women always tend to be interested in what is directly in front of them, and I don't believe they can help it." "I guess I'll think some more," said Billy. "It's a thing that seems to require considerable thinkin'."

"I surely would think a lot if I were you, Billy. You don't want to lose either your happiness or Sadie just for fifteen dollars a week more. How old is Sadie now?" "About thirty-seven. Why?" "Well, in five or six years she'll be having a change of life. You don't want to lose sight of the fact that some women — not all — become pretty flighty then and lose all sense of perspective. You'd have to take that into account, too. Yes sir, if I were you, Billy, I'd give the matter a lot of consideration. Whatever way you regard it, there's possible dynamite in it for you. If I were you, I know what course I'd take — but of course, I'm not you." He thanked me for telling him what I thought. I meant most of what I said, only of course I didn't even mention the fact that it was the reaction on him which interested me in the situation. I hope to God I gave him pause. I don't want to lose him, and I sense danger ahead.

January 3   Billy said: "Well, it's all settled. Boy, am I glad to get that off my mind." "How did you settle it, Billy?" I inquired. "Sadie's not going to change jobs. I thought over what you'd said and I put it together with what I felt, and I said to Sadie, 'Dear, I've been giving the matter a lot of attention in my mind, and I've decided that you and I are happy the way things are and that it'd be foolish as well as unwise for us to make a change and maybe lose our happiness,' and — perhaps you won't credit this with the truth, but it's just that — she didn't object or anything. She said: 'What you decide is all right with me, dear.' I didn't even have to explain or go into details. So that's settled. Now I feel as if I'd lost a weight." I said: "I'm sure you did just right, Billy. I'm certain you won't regret it. I felt much stronger on the subject than I let you know." Billy relapsed into his usual dropping of 'g's,' a sign of relaxation with him. "I know you felt stronger than you made out. You thought you was foolin' me, but you wasn't. I was hep to the way you felt. It kind a' cleared things up in my mind because I wanted to be fair with Sadie at the same time that the idea didn't look good to me. Well sir, it's all settled now. Boy, am I on air." Again I congratulated him. It takes a load off my mind to have the matter turn out fortuitously.

January 4   Congress convened yesterday. Enter again the unsquelchable Franklin Delano Roosevelt, President of these United States, enjoying the last year, we hope, of his second four-year term in office. For the first time, he acknowledged in his address to Congress that "We have not yet found a way to employ the surplus of our labor which the efficiency of our industrial processes created." Many social and economic needs still to be met. Asked for "national unity" to safeguard "Democracy." Guard against demagogues. Watch out for "overstatement," "bitterness," "vituperation." Doesn't want to have to go to war. More money for "self-defense." More taxes to pay for more self-defense. Sentence after sentence burbling over with our duty to mankind and peace and Democracy and with snappy idealistic aphorisms. The same old tripe. Doesn't want war, so prepare for war. Wants to economize, so prepare to spend still more. It's sickening and, I imagine, doesn't catch as many suckers as once it did, although it may.

Between January and June of 1940, Old Man Mach died and Corn remarried. Bottom got herself engaged to a "persistant and pure man" she did not like at first, but when "he strained himself working and had to be operated on for double hernia, that was the end of Bottom." Abruzzo's paid letters kept Arthur up-to-date on jails, asylums, flophouses, and prostitution. Woodwork, in deep depression, described her feeling of loss and resentment and her attempts to put herself together since Allan's departure.

Arthur's own condition, bad eyes — brought on by the failure of Boston authorities to clean up the sandy streets — and sore testicles, often distracted him from the grand and terrible campaigns of Hitler. He had no heart, he protested, to keep up the historical chronicle at a time when he despaired of both the effectiveness of his doctors and his literary prospects. Yet for all his professed abhorrence of war, he was aroused by the audacious tactics of Hitler, the new Genghis Khan, victorious on land and sea. In lengthy entries he summarized vividly and succinctly the maneuvers of the Wermacht in Scandinavia, the Lowlands, and France and predicted Hitler's next moves. To halt America's growing commitment to the Allied powers, he called for a swift and decisive Axis victory. If Hitler stopped short of invading England, "we will be in the mess as sure as shooting and Roosevelt will be reelected. The single chance of being rid of the Rat is to have Hitler win. That's another reason why I want the Germans to make it short and snappy." Americans would not be "a whit worse off under German domination than under the present Irish-Jewish-radical combine."

January 9   Each year at this time the Democrats hold what they call a Jackson Day Dinner. The primary purpose is to fill the treasury of the Democratic Party. Those who attend the Jackson Day Dinner in Washington are charged $100 per plate. The big bugs shoot off their faces, and those who are not as big as the big bugs have the privilege of sitting and listening and of having camera shots taken of them by photographers and of being among the elite. Here is the menu:

> Diamondback terrapin soup with
>   amontillado.
> Hot butter crusts.
> Hearts of celery, olives, pecans.
> Graves rosechatel, 1933.
> Lobster, crabflakes and scallops
>   a la newburg, with madeira.
> Cucumber sandwiches.
> Margaux, 1933.

Heart of filet mignon, excelsior.
New string beans anglaise.
Potatoes macaire.
Hearts of romaine with melon,
    grapefruit and asparagus tips,
    vinaigrette.
Cheese wafers.
Real spumoni ice cream with
    spun sugar.
Anis madeleins.
Demi tasse.

I remember when I was a little boy, how I used to enjoy reading the large menus and wine cards at the hotels where we stopped. It was like stepping into another world, a realm where food was all-important, where indecipherable foreign names predominated. I couldn't make much of the names, but here and there a word I knew would stand out, and that would please me. I had certain favorite dishes. I would hold the program up as though its words were familiar to me, appear to study it while the attentive black-and-white-clad waiter, order pad in hand, would lean forward expectantly. Then as nonchalantly as possible and always with a secret thrill, I would make my decision. It was usually tomato puree, pullbread, filet mignon, creamed potatoes, artichokes with Hollandaise sauce, strawberry parfait. I could never become reconciled to the fact that a half-order was an order for one person.

Before I grew old enough to be self-conscious, I used to enjoy taking my meals in the dining room of the Waldorf, the Holland House, the Touraine. I liked the clean smell of the table linen, the jungle of the silver in the waiters' hands, the cubes of ice mysteriously inside the small-necked carafe, the flourish with which the waiter would remove a silver cover and hold the dish — a planked shad, brown and amber, lamb chops with paper frills and greenery, a tenderloin steak brown with mushrooms — for you to see and, in my case, to whiff before serving, the comings and goings of diners, the orchestra playing, in the evenings the ladies in their low-neck dresses. I was always watching for a waiter to drop a tray, and for the sight of one of those women on whose bare skins appeared delicate purple-blue veins, hardly discernable.

January 11 Arthur [Garner] has just been here about my shoulder. "Say," he stated, "I saw 'Gone with the Wind' the other day. I was disappointed. Those damn Jews always manage to lay things on too thick, to overdo. And they underestimate the intelligence of the people at the same time that they overestimate their endurance to a single sort of sensation."

January 13 The talking-book in a measure spoils me for ordinary reading; it is so impersonal, and you never have to talk to it. For one who talks as much as I do (I talk to keep awake during the day, to give directions, to ask questions, when I am bored, when there's nothing else to do), I have an innate distaste for using my vocal cords. I should by choice prefer to be taciturn. Yet all day long it seems to me I am chattering. Talking tenses me up and causes me to forget my pains and worries and fears to some extent, in particular when I am attempting to influence or restrain other people. But I don't relish talking of itself and always feel somewhat deflated after much of it.

January 18 Abruzzo continues to send me his thousand-word missives, for each of which I send him a dollar. Here is part of a letter written from St. Louis.

Christmas was spent in a happy manner partly due to the fact that we had a gallon of wine and some booze to top it. On the Sat. before Xmas we went out bumming and we also bought some stuff so we also had some good food and Nick prepared a most excellant meal. After dinner we continued to drink. We all decided to go visiting and we went over to see the life time mayor of Pease ful Valley, as that is what they call this place. The mayor is a retired fireman and after his wife tricked him out of most of his pension he came down here to live. What little of the pension he does get he spends on booze and when down to his last dollor he starts drinking derail (denatured alcohol). After recuperating from our Xmas hangover we started digging for money for New Years Eve. We all struggled in our own way to get our quoto. I made a play for the fruit fruiter and he paid off. He is a strange person of Italian parentage and conducts with his brother a very prospering fruit market. His brother goes for women the wrong way and he goes for young fellows the same way. Both look the same as they wiegh well over two hundred pounds. I then dropped over to Lamberet and made the druggest there. I then had more then my share towards our planned new year eve stampede. Sunday finally rolled around and all of us were clean having washed our clothes and bathe on Sat. We went down to one of the joints. It is a sort of night club and though they were only alurwing couples in, they let us in because they knew Nick and Cat and also because there were four of us. Once inside the waitress showed us to a table on the side of the floor, but we could with a little cramming, see the floor show. Soon we were roaming about the place talking with the diferant tables. There we encountered Mitch. A heavy sort of guy with the look of a pug on his mug (an intended pun) but on enquirey on my part I found that he worked in the nut house. He joined our party and tole us some grim and sorrid stories of the bughouse. One reason for his friendness is that while on duty there isnt any one that he can have a normal conversation with. He looked as if he himself were ready for the alcoholic ward, for he was quite soused. Later on he was fired because he was with us for several days and did not show up for work. Since we were out for a good time and we had some one with money we just kept on drinking and slept down town in a cheap hotel. We ended up at the shack, one by one, in the end. And because of the serverity of the weather we bought most of our food. The only bumming we did was for the most part bread and meat. Macaroni, beans and rice has been our diet for more then a week. I have prevaled Mitch to write some of his story for me and I am enclosing same which I hope you enjoy. Boy what a story he writes, it makes very interesting reading.

Dear Sir.

I chanced to meet your friend Anthony and he asked me to write you about some of the facts I related to him. I hope I can make you undertand these things as I am not much of a writer but will try my best. The first time I ran across this work, I happened to answer an ad for no apparrent reason other than I wanted work and didn't care what kind. I got an interview from a private doctors institution and told him I had never done this kind of work before. All he did was look me over and said he thought I would do, but to keep watchful as any thing might happen. He didn't need to tell me as I soon found this out in a hurry. First day I reported for work and another fellow showed me around. I saw many strange things. I saw an old man and a young kid in the same bed bundled up together and asked my partner how come. He just said well you know life, well the nuts get that way too and the doctor doesn't care as it keeps them quiet for a while anyway. I was told the best thing to do was not worry about what I saw and keep my mouth shut if I wanted to work. I found out that perversion, rape, torture, brutality and horror make a nut house. A normal person will dream of something big and keep it to himself but a nut just takes it for granted you know he's Napoleon waiting to mobolise an army and even will try to force you to join. Its queer, but pathetic for some. I've got so used to their ways I can tell by looking at one if he's getting ready to throw a fit, or if he just wants to give me the latest dope on Paul Revere. There is always a chance too, that some harm less looking nut will try to stick a knife in your back or anyone else near him. There are other kinds too, Guys that got railroaded in, others who bribe their way in so they can stay out of law trouble. Ive worked in society places where they only cater to the quality nuts too. Like the boys who drop in for a month or so to prolong a drunk in pleasant surroundings, so they can keep shy of their friends and not run afoul of the law, or a nice girl who gets tossed in by her family so they can break off a love affair with the chaufeur. There's the so called nymphomaniac who goes nuts and tears off her clothes every time she sees a man, and the nicey-nicey boy who wants you to handle him with care because he's a glass coffee percolator. There is all different kinds of doctors also. Quacks with a good line of gab and slick guys who could double for hotel managers. Some of them wouldnt think of going in a ward unarmed and others who handled homocidal maniacs with a whisper. My job was taking care of the old soaks on the third floor. Those guys were too far gone and didn't even pretend to want to sober up. One old guy started out by getting railroaded in and refusing to leave. It seems he was a selfmade millionaire and his wife and sons were trying to prime him up to keep up with the other society bugs as they were. Everything he did was always wrong to them and he was always getting bawled out so he stuck with his bottle as it didn't talk back. After one bad hangover the wife told him he needed a rest. He drank more and when he came to his lawyers told him the court judged him incompetent mentally. Well he came up there and he was plenty satisfied as he had a lot of soaks with him who agreed on his views. He told me all about it one day and told me by god I dont want to be sane as long as I can stay here. He was a great fellow and I made plenty of money off him. All I had to do was worry about not getting stiff my self. I soon got in a jam there though and had to leave. If you are satified with this letter I will tell you of the difference between state and private institutions in another. There is quite a contrast between the two.

Mitch

January 20 Senator Borah is dead. Roosevelt luck — that is, should he decide to mix us in the war. Borah was, I believe, that unusual anomaly, an honest politician.

January 23 I used to think it would be only fair and proper to include everything in my diaries. I can't think that after rereading them now. Nobody wants to read about bones and how they slipped out of position and how they were put into position again — not even myself. I remember that at the time I harbored some sort of idea of keeping an osteopathic case history as a matter of gratitude to the osteopaths for having helped me when other doctors could not. Hell, even an osteopath would become bored at the intricacy of my recording and complaining. I'll have to blue-pencil most of the stuff, as well as some few other pieces such as the one about women and dogs, which would only disgust readers and turn them away from me. If I want to obtain and hold readers, I mustn't repel them, bore them or arouse their disapproval before their sincere interest in me and in what I say is well-established. So I am of the opinion that considerable cutting and pruning is not only justified but called for as well.

January 29   Ella has become interested in organizations. She belongs to a colored group which proposes to form a purchasing cooperative. She attends meetings of the Civil Liberties League. She goes to New York and New Haven to be present at various meetings of the Redcaps Union and the Ladies Auxiliary. She is taking a night course in the history of the American labor movement. Her contention has it that in the United States exist many "social wrongs" and that, if she and people like her sit and do nothing to rectify abuses, the present state of affairs will never be improved. "We may fail, but at least we shall have tried." She enjoys meeting various kinds of people. She and Robert have become intimate with Bill Tappley, the colored man who has organized the redcaps into a union affiliated with neither the C.I.O. nor the A.F. of L. She was offered the presidency of the National Auxiliary when in New York but refused it. "What do I want with tearing around the country like a wild woman from meeting to meeting? I like my home too well. Besides, I'm not mentally equipped to understand fully the responsibilities of such a position. Until I am, I shall refuse it. There's plenty of time, anyway."

January 30   Aspirants for party nomination to run for the office of President in November are beginning to speak their separate pieces. Roosevelt has not as yet committed himself as to whether or not he intends to seek the Democratic nomination. The longer he delays, perhaps the happier will become the chances of the Republican nominee. The four Republican aspirants seemingly most likely to obtain the nomination are Senator Vandenberg, an old-style loudspeaker politician with a dishonest countenance, many words and problematical virtues; Thomas E. Dewey, young thirty-six year old opportunist, dynamic, with appeal for women, a platform restoring the leadership of the nation to business and business freedom from irksome restrictions, a man who might make an excellent leader; Senator Taft, son of President Taft, with the simpering face of a rectitudinal, not very intelligent reformer, a poor, even a vicious choice; and Representative Joseph W. Martin of Massachusetts, energetic, with many adherents.

February 3 This is one of those mornings when I could enlarge upon my troubles and my rebellions for four or five pages. Take note, reader, of the restraint I am evidencing.

Evelyn said: "Who, may I ask, was the little toughy you were talking with last night? It was amusing when you asked if she had read 'The Swiss Family Robinson' and she replied what was it, the latest 'piccha,' no she hadn't 'took it in yet.'" "The little toughy" was Esther Quenten—("My Gawd, I hate my name. They call me 'Essie' an' 'Estie,' an' I hate it. I took 'Dorothy' for my confirmation name, but now I haven't no use for it any more since goin' to high schooal an' findin' haf the kids there called 'Dorothy'"). Esther is seventeen, a junior in high school, taking a commercial course—("I'm sick a' learnin'. I jus' stay on 'cause I dunno wat else ta do"). Esther is the youngest of a family of eight—("An' there isn't one uv us married. I guess we're kind a' crazy to have our good times too well"). Her father and mother came to this country from Ireland when they were young. He worked on the Boston Elevated for thirty years, was retired two years ago because of ill health, three months back had a stroke, will not receive a pension until he is sixty-five, three years from now. They own their house, rent the lower floor. Two brothers and two sisters are working, assist the family budget by erratic contributions.

February 7 Billy and I sat by the New Haven tracks and watched the trains go by. A ruddy brakeman called to us; a porter grinned at us; a strange young man who walked the ties with a bag and a determined expression shouted, "What business is it of yours?" when I interestedly inquired his destination.

February 9 The Dies Committee has brought to light, among much inconsequential claptrap, the fact that alien-minded groups, some in direct contact with Soviet and Nazi authorities overseas, are engaged in efforts to sap and in some cases to overturn the American form of government. The chief of the Nazi movement is serving a jail sentence (of course, à la American, put there on another charge), and the head of the Communist movement is under sentence (albeit, while under sentence, he has been allowed to run for political office). It is well that subversive influences be publicly aired even if (as I suspect is the case at this particular moment) their importance be exaggerated. The American Youth Congress, which anyone knows is Pinkly inclined, is now under attack. It has been one of Mrs. Roosevelt's pets. Five prominent men, among them Gene Tunney, have accused the American Youth Congress of plotting "to lead American youth into unconscious alliance with the Communist United Front." While so much publicity may serve to draw certain restless elements toward the interdicted "fronts," more people are likely to be inoculated with the virus of suspicion and resentment against what they will consider unwarrantable alien penetration.

[From Abruzzo, Pittsburgh, February 7, 1940:]
It was a cool over cast day as I walked along 4th St on my last day in St Louis. Even now I can still picture most realistic the prositutes tapping and beckoning for me to stay, but I walk on. And sinse, walking along a wet and cold hi-way, I remember that day and wish I were back there in the sweet arms of some chubby girl instead.

One ride of about twenty miles got me to Highland after a long walk on my part. Along the road I had passed a series of mounds used by the Indians as a fort. Built in the flat plains they had the advantage of being about 15 or 20 ft higher. I also passed Fairmont Park racing track. Man o War and Minister Fox are two famous horses studded here at Creek Side Farm enjoining the track. The fellow who gave me the lift was a referee for the big ten (Schools) and was going to Highland to referee a wrestling match. He was quite generous giving me fifty cents for my super. That night I went to the jail for a nights lodging. The cop on duty was a pleasant fellow and after signing me up, showed me to my "room" (cell). Soon four others drifted in. Out of the bunch were a pair in direct contrast to each other traveling together. One was old and not to well informed, the other was young and well educated. In my usual way I started asking questions about world affairs the war, relief, and work. In our conversation he let slip that he had a collige degree. I would of liked to talk further with him but fate degree otherwise for the next day I lost him along the way. Rain and snow made the second day most miserable. Rides were short and the walking long. I stopped over night in the county jail. All you had to do was ask them and they were glad to have you. In the morning you had your choose of leaving between 6 to 10 a.m. I left about 7 and walked out the hiway. With luck I made Indianapolis, Ind the third day of my journey.

Weather was cold and clear. A mission there provided me with a plase to stay. In return I had to put in four hours work. That night they made all us fellow attended a temperence meeting. Was very dull. The next morning I noticed that Indianapolis, the capatol of the State, was as smokey as St Louis. Thick heavy clouds hung low making visablity to about 10 ft. The people here were lined up for two blocks waiting to see the picture "Gone With the Wind". The center of town has some splindid parks, monuments and public buildings. A large monument marks the center of town and is dedicated to the Civil War died. I again hit the road battling ice and snow and had to walk 10 miles for a lift. I got a lift in to Dayton and being wet and tired from walking I drop in the County Welfare. They gave me an order good for supper, bed, and breakfast. I dried out a bit and after supper started cleaning up. Vinny drifted in and tole me he had just got in. We washed and went out and panhandled a dime a piece and took in a show. We got to bed about eleven after picking up a couple of live wired gals. They were out for a good time but as we were broke we made a date for the next day. But as always tomorrow never comes, as we left town the next day without keeping our "date". Our luck was good and as we walked out toward the hi way a truck stopped for a red light. I ran over and asked the colored driver for a ride and soon Vinny and I were riding right into our destination of Columbas, Ohio. The driver was a very good talker esspecially things concerning his race. His one complain was lack of employment for his race and people. Well educated and trained, holding a degree from a colored colledge, he is forsed to drive a truck. We parted feeling like old friends in Columbas.

February 11   Now, down in the back alley, the Salvation Army plays mournful dirges upon brasses. I am studying, in a new book on Froissart, the reproduction of one of the medieval illuminations found in the Harley manuscripts. It is entitled "The Dance of the Wodehouses." It is fascinating. On a floor of blocked green, blue-green mummers with white feet and hands dance. Their brown wooden clubs are on the floor, and white dogs bark at them. In a green balcony beneath a ceiling the color of old wood groined with filigreed gold, musicians played lustily on long horns. In the background are two screens, one red and green and cream color of conventionalized flowers, the other blue and green and gold and white of conventionalized trees and hawks and stags. In the right foreground stand two important lords in long robes, one of ermine and pink, the other of golded blue. On the left on a brown dais with a canopy of royal red, blue and gold, sit the ladies and the ladies-in-waiting in garments of pink and blue, conical headdresses of black and caps of gold. Behind them stand their male attendants in black and brown and blue. The musicians play. The lordliest lord observes the scene as though gratified that the mummery is proceeding well. The ladies clap their hands. The male attendants discuss and criticize among themselves. On a sideboard in the rear stands a lavish display of goldware. All — the dance of the mummers, the dog barking, the discarded clubs, the puffed cheeks of the musicians, the commenting attitudes of the attendants, the enthusiasm of the ladies — is so real, so vital that I feel as though I had looked my way into the past.

February 14   We received a Christmas card from Corn. Being curious about her and her new husband, I requested Evelyn to call on them in Cambridge. Two or three weeks ago she did so. They live in an apartment near Mrs. Raleigh. Corn, Evelyn said, looked well and happy. Her husband, Franklin Hart, is a man of some six feet, not handsome but with an air of ease and a facile flow of conversation. He is twenty-eight, four and a half years younger than Corn. Evelyn invited them to dinner. Last night they came. Corn talked to me for more than an hour and a half. She seemed pleased to see me, hugged and kissed me. She more resembled her old self than she did two years ago.

"I was all upset then. You know, Miles's death. I'd never been face to face with death before. I was all at sixes and sevens. My painting went up the spout, and I didn't know what I wanted. But I'm not that way now. Maybe I didn't love Miles (I don't know), but I'm sure I love Frank. He has a gorgeous sense of humor. He likes to play, too. I didn't like him at first, but I did before long. I made up my mind to catch him. I used all my wiles. Then when he got good and hot, I sent him away for a couple of weeks to think about it. Then I took cold and went to bed. Then I sent for him. I had on my best bedjacket and my saddest expression. He squeezed me some orange juice, rubbed my chest, told me I needed somebody to take care of me. I winked to myself. Then he lay down on the other bed and talked to me. All of a sudden he said: 'I'll marry you in March.' 'How do you know I want to marry you?' I asked. 'Oh, I know,' he said. 'Well,' I said, 'I do.' So we were married in March in Cambridge Chapel. Frank teaches when he has to. At other times, he writes. He had a book published on Hart Crane. He does magazine articles and reviews. Sometimes he stays up very late at night writing. The cat just sits and watches him. He's a smart cat, very percipient. When Frank goes to bed, the cat sits in front of the typewriter

and keeps on where he left off. Sometimes, when he doesn't like what Frank has written, he tears it up and writes it over. He—"
"Are you happy, Corn?" I interrupted. "I certainly am. Feel how plump I am. Frank hates it. He calls me 'Plumpy-dumpling' and things like that. But you like it, don't you, Arthur? Here, I'll stand up and let you feel what a big sit-down I've got." I was busy slapping Corn's bottom when out in the hall sounded Evelyn and Hart. I was sure he must have heard me spanking her. I was a bit embarrassed, but not Corn. It was with entire composure that she greeted Evelyn and Frank. I have forgotten to mention that her voice has dropped in pitch. She is more like her old self than since she married Miles.

I talked to Frank—at least he talked to me—for close to an hour. A pleasant person with a deep voice, a voluminously pedantic way of speaking, somewhat dogmatic in his utterances, not, I should say, very brilliant, turned out, lock, stock and barrel, to be a teacher. He seems devoted to "Tessa," as he calls her. His conversation is filled with "damn's" and "God's" and "hell's." He is affable and not at all difficult to get along with. He is anxious for Corn to resume her painting and to do imaginative work rather than landscapes. I laid myself out to make him like me. Evelyn and I spent an enjoyable evening, and I think that Mr. and Mrs. Hart did so as well. I want to see Corn again soon. As I told her, she's one of the most fascinating persons I have ever known.

February 26 Roderic has announced that he is too tired to come any more for the present. Just as well, I suppose, as his reading has been abominable.

February 29 Snowed all yesterday. Downstairs in Evelyn's room now. Postcard from Abruzzo:

Dear Mr Inman:
  You won't hear from me for a few days as I am now in jail as guest of the rail road for 15 days. I will write a letter soon as I get out.

Best Regards
Anthony

This sent care Hearthstone County Jail, Queensville, Pa. What a man.

Juliette was here last night. She talked me to a standstill. This is not the Juliette of six months or a year ago, whenever it was I saw her last. While she still converses in the funny, affected voice, she is no longer, by any measure, a girl. Juliette spent a week in the hospital having her womb straightened and the opening to it enlarged with the hope of becoming able to have a baby. She has had no baby.

I enjoyed listening to her. She talks steadily and graphically. She constantly refers to "we of the Jewish race." Beneath her airs, her posturings before the mirror of self-approbation, she is a person whose feet are planted upon ground which usually slopes in the direction of her own advantage. Whether she harbors toward me any of the affection the many evenings we have spent together and the mutual experiences we have shared would warrant, I am unable to say. In fact, I have no idea as to the measure of my affection for her. A curious relationship.

March 2   At this stage in my career, I don't give a hoot in hell who wins what war in Europe as long as we don't get into the rotten mess. Those in power are just a lot of rats anyway. If Finland were in a position to pick on someone smaller instead of being small and being picked on, that would happen. No delusions left. Weary of wars. Hope the Chinese lick the greedy Japs, the cocky Japs, the overbearing Japs, and send them home from their strutting, their pillaging, their raping and their killing.

March 3   A small ride in the Baby-Carriage, the streets being less dusty than on weekdays. Waiting for Dr. Pike now. Evelyn has gone for a walk.

Just finished 'The Convent,' an autobiographical novel setting forth the life in a Swiss convent and the reaction of a novice thereto. I was reminded of a like tale I read some years ago, 'Female Convict,' which gave a sketch of life in a Midwestern penitentiary for women.[6] Existence in the convent and existence in the penal institute appear to be not widely dissimilar, save that one is entered upon voluntarily while the other is not. The convent may include religion and mysticism, but the penitentiary is less hard on the body and the mind. Work, routine, suppression of individuality fill the hours in both places. Hatred of the Law and worship of God are not, emotionally, so far apart as might at first thought appear.

March 4   I have been attempting to read O. Henry on the talking-book. When I was a boy, I used to consider O. Henry pretty awful. As a young man, I thought him even worse. Now, adjectives fail me. He and Mark Twain could, for all of me, be dumped in a boat and let go upon a sea of forgotten authors. Last night tried to read 'Soldiers of Fortune' by Richard Harding Davis. My God, what

---

[6] Alyse Simpson's *Convent* (1940) describes two years of convent life that the author, a novice, spent in the Swiss mountains and her discovery that she had been mistaken in her vocation. *Female Convict, As Told to Vincent Burns* (1934) is an exposé of barbarities in a women's prison by the author of the better-known *I am a Fugitive from a Chain Gang*. Both books strengthened Arthur's loathing for what he called "institutional authority: abbeys, prisons, hospitals, vast business organizations, armies."

tripe. That period of American literature between the Civil War and 1900, save for a few war memoirs, is for the most part a sterile place inhabited by a few intrinsically poor writers such as Bret Harte and Mark Twain and a plethora of petty pilferers with artificial hearts, water for blood, pens dipped in saccharine. Truly, modern literature owes an incalculable debt to Kipling, de Maupassant and Mencken. With the exception of Ambrose Bierce and Walt Whitman, who in American literature during the late Victorian era possessed virility? Herman Melville seems a flop to me. Must read more Howells and James and Crane.

March 9 I had an idea. Corn's husband was a fluent talker, had presence and self-confidence and conceit, was hard up. Why not pay him to take 'Where Find Sanctuary' to New York — fifty dollars as a starter and one hundred and fifty if he succeeded — and do the work of persuading a publisher to take it? Talked with him yesterday afternoon. He thought the idea fair but wished to look at the book first. He looked at it. His decision was that he couldn't afford to endanger what reputation he had by recommending a book that he honestly felt was not "important" to any publisher, and that furthermore he was not willing to lower his "integrity" by sponsoring work of which he had so little opinion. He spoke straightforwardly and without malice, though his disapproval of what he considered my puling and unavailing efforts was in his voice and words.

I thanked him for considering the project and said that naturally enough I disagreed with him. I inquired what poet he particularly admired. Yeats. That encouraged me; to my way of thinking Yeats' poems for the most part are rather puerile and ineffective. I showed Hart the diary. He thought that somewhat better. He is an excellent critic of the mechanics of writing and a nice chap, though a bit sure of himself. Corn, I imagine, will knock some of that out of him before long. We parted amicably, no doubt with emotions anent a wasted afternoon on his part, I am sure with disappointment on mine, for the idea was a good one. What then am I to do with 'Where Find Sanctuary?' It is at the Oxford Press now but will be back directly. The manuscript will wear out soon from so many unsuccessful goings and comings.

March 10 Spent yesterday afternoon reading Yeats, Hart Crane, Emerson — the poets Frank Hart admires. Yeats is even more watery than I remembered, lacks vigor, is as full of outworn cliches as a shad is full of bones, jingles. Crane is plain crazy. Emerson is a self-satisfied, platitudinous old stuffed shirt. Read a considerable number of Whitman's poems, for Hart also admires him. Spotty, with much straight prose, some excellent rhythmic sense. But the personality of the author is somehow lewd, just why I can't figure out. It is as though he were hiding something behind a mask of artificial virility. So much, and that summarily, for Hart's taste. If my poetry isn't more admirable than that of Yeats or Crane or Emerson, I'm a man of no detached judgment whatsoever. If there must be poetry, give me the virility of Sandburg or Amy Lowell or the perfection of Tennyson or Sara Teasdale.

A letter a week or so ago from Abruzzo, relating his jail experiences. Same country jail you read about, kangaroo court, liquor smuggled in, dice, poor food, homosexuals, some prisoners more or less demented. After his release, Abruzzo proceeded on his way. Yesterday, came an air mail from Scranton.

Every car that passed me splashed me and when I got to Wayland I was soaked. As there was no stop there I had to continue on. About a mile from town a car with Canadian plates passed me and stopped and then backed up. The car was crowded and I tole the driver that as I only had about 20 miles to go I could walk, but he insisted I ride so I got in. He and his wife and baby and his mother in law and sister inlaw were on thier way to Pittston, Pa. He asked if I wanted to ride all the way, so I went. We talked a while and he wanted to know where would I sleep when I got there, so I said the jail. I found out he was a Italian and they were going to visit his folks. Several times he skidded on the icey road and scared the women, but we finaly got to Pittston. There he refuse to let me go to jail to sleep. I was taken into his home and treated like an honored guest. A nice bed for the night made me feel like a million. I got up early about 6.30 and found Jame's father had sat up all night in the kitchen. I felt bad that he should give up his bed to me. After breakfast I got ready to leave but they kept me until after dinner. And when I went they gave me money and thier address. They asked me to write them and let them know how I made out. This is the second time in my life that strangers have taken me in like that. I picked up a ride into Scranton and walked around town. I bummed a resturant and the guy fed me and then asked if I was willing to work. I replied in the afirmative and was given the job of dishwasher. I still dont know what the pay is. The hours are 7 am to 7 P.M. I get plenty to eat and every night I get 25¢ for a bed. Maybe this is where I settle down but I doubt it. I think that the pay is going to be so small that I will quit when I get paid. After loafing all winter it feels strange to be working again. And the place is just a joint. They boys who hang around are ex pimps and carny's waiting for spring to go out on the shows. I am getting aquanted with them and might have some good material for my next letter.

March 14   Old Man Mach died today. Until a few days ago, he was fussing and fuming about whether he should allow us to have French windows to the balcony we want to put outside Billy's room. No more fussing and fuming now. I'd guess the Snake and the Adder are delighted. No longer will they have to lackey their successful father who once sold shoestrings at the Chicago World's Fair and since has been, now and again, a millionaire. Evelyn and I will have more difficulty dealing with the sons than we have had with the father. Or maybe the sons can grow up now. I sometimes think all parents should die at fifty.

March 15   Out of some 100 city and college libraries which have answered the questionnaire I have sent out to determine for myself the distribution of my books, only 25 have poetry books, only 10 have 'None Now Are Quietly Wise,' and 90% have 'Pickett's Letters.' Not very flattering to me. I think I'll send some 25 copies of my last book to college and university libraries, as I can imagine no more profitable method of advertising. Macrae will never pay royalties anyway, and I can make use of what he doesn't pay this way.

March 16   Reading and writing poetry. Reading Robert Frost. Poetry irregular. Use of imagery moderate. A quiet spirit to the man. Many times, when he writes of dramatic things, he waxes melodramatic. By and large, an admirable poet. Reading Conrad Aiken. Writes words as though they were musical notes, poetry as though it were symphonic. Beautiful sonority to lines. Mechanical repetition of themes becomes wearisome as in music. The dark legions of hell are loose in Aiken's soul. If poets are to be judged by the best they have written, this man is greatly underestimated. I know of no one who uses labials more resonantly. It is effective.

April 3   Waiting now for the stomach-pump doctor. Miserable from shoulder and from testicles. Written several long poems. Been studying poetry, American, 19th century. Only Bryant, Poe, Longfellow, Whitman, Dickinson, Stephen Crane worthwhile. Been reading more Conrad Aiken, too.

April 20   Am writing a series of poems on Hokusai's sketches and prints for a book to be called 'Hokusai Saw.' I enjoy doing it. Hokusai, I feel, is a kindred soul. I see things in great measure as he did. Enjoy his sense of the dramatic, the whimsical, the sly and am attempting to transfer those qualities to the poems. Writing them gives me a needed lesson in objectivity.

April 22   Back has been improving steadily under Bottom's treatment. Yesterday had Dr. Pike. He ruined the entire structure in a couple of jerks and pushes. What weakness ails me that I can't give over having him except in times of crisis? Must make a point of not having him so often, if for nothing else then for a matter of character.

Hard up for people evenings. Roderic informed Billy he had married. He may never come again. Miss him and miss Emily.

April 29   [From Abruzzo:]

Am continuing this letter after a day's interuption. I went out and walked along 3rd Ave up to 55 St from the Bowery and on the way I only could bum 5 cents. I walked back along Second Ave and I ran into a plain clothes man down Twelfth St and he gave me a lecture but I talked him out of arresting me so he tole me where I could obtain releif. As it was too late then, he gave me fifty cents so I was able to sleep in the Grum's Hotel for 25 ¢. I went in and took a shower and of all things I discovered that I was lousey. My first thought was how to rid myself of them vermin, but this morning on second thought (?) I decided to do a little investigating. I found in the Musium that they think the louse spreads the dreaded desease Typhus Fever. I talk with Dr. Ahearn, the head of the Entomology department and he refer me to several books. I soon found out that medical science is not sure, but only suspects the louse of spreading this disease. So noble little me is going to experiment, and find out for sure. It's time some one did some thing about it and if its true that it spread Typhus Fever then the city can do a little cleaning up. I looked up all the symthoms and as soon as I contact any thing I am going to the hospital. That it is dangerous does not matter because I have a fifty-fifty chance of beating it. Wish me luck and you can answer me at 3432 West 77 St Queens N.Y.C.

May 4   Most of my emotional objective excitement nowadays comes from the war. While I am no longer a Hitler enthusiast, I want mightily to see the British and the French licked and that quickly. The Norwegian commanding general states that he was left in the lurch by the Allies without consultation when they withdrew. News comes this morning that German planes have sunk a big British battleship. I hope so. I should guess that all the lies Chamberlain and Churchill can concoct will not prevent one or both from losing cabinet position. If England and Italy become entangled in the East, I have an idea Hitler will go into Holland or Belgium with no invasion of France in mind but the establishment of air bases close to England. Then perhaps later in the summer an invasion of

England. There would be no point in Hitler's invading France. England is the German enemy that must be conquered. Could German air power overwhelm British sea power, that would be the end of the preeminence of England, and a right excellent thing it might be for the health of the world. And if I'm rancorous against England, I'm sorry, but that's the way I feel and the way I like to feel and the way I believe I'm warranted in feeling.

May 8   Have written 45 poems for Hokusai book. I transmute the pictures through the medium of my imagination, striving to retain Hokusai's superbly unsentimental viewpoint, his sly and provocative humor, the sudden intentness of his impressions, the sketchy quality of his drawings, his catholic interest in a thousand attitudes of men and nature, his tempering of melodrama by whimsy. I feel myself to have been made to grow by studying closely the style and temper of the man. I think I like his black and gray sketches better than I do his colored prints.

May 10   Well, here we are. German troops have taken advantage of the political upsets in England and France to invade Holland, Belgium, Luxemburg. Parachute troops landed first; airports were bombed; tank barriers were destroyed. By now the German Army is some ten miles across borders. Again I feel ill at my stomach thinking about the poor neutrals. The goal is air bases on the coast nearer to England. Before blaming Hitler as the one ruthless Attila of the contemporary scene, it might be well to read in a neighboring headline that a British force has just landed in neutral Iceland. I can only hope that the Germans will be quickly successful in their most ambitious aspirations and that France and England will have to sue for peace in the near future, a possibility though, I fear, not a probability.

May 11   I was thinking to myself this morning, I'll bet I know one country that is snickering up its sleeve, and that is Ireland. No Irish troops being forced to fight this time. For hundreds of years the Irish used force, assassination, treachery, words, subornation — every weapon imagination and cunning could devise — to rid themselves and their country of their English masters. They are reaping apparent dividends at this moment.

[From Abruzzo:]

Plenty has happened since I last wrote to you. The experiment I started ended rather sadly for me, but it also gave me some thing of interest to write to you. The louse is supposed to spread Typhus Fever. When I looked it up, I could only obtain old medical books and naturely they (the doctor's) have found out a lot since. Being unaware of all this, I started for the hospital, with some idea that all was not right, to be examined. There the doctor sent me to Psychopathic Ward for observation fully isolated just in case my experiment did work. Being stuck in the observation ward was quite a surprise to me, but then it was to be expected.

May 14 Evelyn looks as though the wrath of God had descended on her. It was no pleasure jaunt to Portland. Here is what the Old Man wanted. The Groundhog [Mildred Inman, Arthur's step-grandmother], he said, has no income, the downtown property S.M. left her in lieu of money having become increasingly worthless each year. Neither have Uncle Frank and Aunt Louise much money. His idea is to leave me an income of $17,000 a year, with any income from the estate over and above that to be divided equally between myself, Aunt Louise and the Groundhog. He wished to tell me of the plan.

Of course I deem it unjust. Neither the Groundhog nor Aunt Louise are blood relatives of his. Uncle Frank has four stalwart sons and a rich son-in-law to support him. Why should I have to defer in any wise to them? I shouldn't. But what can I say? After all, it is the Old Man's cash, and I can't seem too money-minded, else I may come out worse than ever. He told Evelyn he was going to leave me some cash and was going to give me what stock he got from Mother's estate "when he got home," whatever that means. He'll probably fall dead and I won't get it. I'd rather have him dead.

May 17 President Roosevelt spoke yesterday, demanding $1,182,000,000 for defensive measures. He warned of America being invaded. It was a scarehead speech, calculated (the recent events of the war in Europe being preeminent in people's minds) to cause Congress to shell out the money. Roosevelt's steady stream of welfare money having lately become less than formerly, this new way of spending opens lusciously before him. However, if the New Deal must spend money, it is less baneful to morale to spend it on arms and armament than on indiscriminate welfare.

May 21 Dr. Pike is again on the rampage. He hasn't come to dinner with Evelyn for some while. She has been worrying about it, though I found out only two days ago. I asked him yesterday why not. He had, he said, felt an air of hostility lately and thought it best not to see Evelyn. He said he did the best he could for me always but that I seemed to feel he was purposely hurting me and that that made treating me a mental and nervous strain and that he was an old man and Evelyn was a young woman anyway. I was surprised. Of course, I told him that this time he was on the wrong highroad. I told him that his company was one of Evelyn's chief pleasures in life and that I didn't want him to cease seeing her, that it was never his intentions that I questioned but his being in a hurry. And so on. He was so tired he was trembling. I felt sorry for him. He certainly goes off half-cocked when he is as tired as now. I tried to reassure him but hardly think he heard. He tried to give back the key to the Place. I wouldn't accept it. Billy says that later in the afternoon he was out there resting. He goes there often, and I like to have him do it. It is a sanctuary for him. I felt much older than he yesterday.

May 28   Hitler's career helps my soul. A paperhanger, disdained by the world for his artistic proclivities, now one of the great artistic geniuses of all time, an artist in military science, in psychology, in government, in conquest. The ignored can sometimes rise to prominence. No one sneers at him now, no one ignores him. Better had they praised the pictures he painted. Better had they declared his work with brush and canvas magnificent and hung him in great galleries. At least, better for those who ignored him.

May 30   History is a queer bloke. Today is our Memorial Day. Abraham Lincoln is the hero. Yet it was that same Lincoln who fostered and furthered a war as cruel and as devastating in its way and time as the one Hitler is now fostering and furthering. It may be that he whose name is accursed now, should the war be won by him and the effects of the victory redound beneficially to Germany at large, will be in the future honored by a Memorial Day in which he will be the benignant patron saint.

June 1   A queer world. I can feel the spreading dread of Hitlerism. Hitler is now greater and more powerful than Napoleon. When he has finished with France and England, will he turn toward America? I think it is all nonsense, yet feel the pull of the dread. Everyone whistles in the dark and is sure the Allies will win in the end, but everyone by now wonders. No longer do people put aside the name and ambitions of Hitler as inconsequential. The Battle of Flanders has halted scoffers stockstill in their tracks. As to the fate of the trapped English and French. Luck as usual has come to the English in the shape of a heavy fog in which they have been able to remove a hundred thousand troops or more from Dunkirk. Lord Gort's retreat and withdrawal has been one of the masterpieces of military history. Even the Germans are filled with admiration for the feat. One cannot scoff at English bravery and steadiness under duress. Nevertheless, when the smoke clears, a part of the flower of the English and French forces will have been killed or taken prisoner, and the loss will be irreparable. Everyone wonders what Hitler will do next and how soon. It is harrowing but incredibly exciting.

June 6   Day by day public opinion in this country waxes in favor of the Allies. Dr. Pike advises me henceforward to keep my opinions to myself, a step I had already commenced to take. Billy tells me I should see the horror pictures in the movies. Practically every radio commentator is against the Germans emotionally. Politicians are riding the Nazi terror for all it is worth. The Jews, who own or direct most of the newspapers, the movies, the radio, Roosevelt, are doing an effective job, aided and abetted (though not as efficiently as prior to our entrance into the last war) by the English.

June 10   At one o'clock today Premier Mussolini in a speech from his palace balcony announced that Italy had declared war on Great Britain and France. He was so excited that his voice rose in that high falsetto habitual to Italians under stress. The cheering was multitudinous and stirring. I later listened to Premier Reynaud making (and what else could he make) an ineffectual reply in the much less dramatic and harsh-to-the-ear French tongue. Then I listened to Duff-Cooper promulgating, absolutely without fire, an ineffectual and rather pathetic (not intentionally so) answer. Roosevelt is scheduled to make an important address to the country tonight. It was rumored early in the day that he was going to warn Mussolini that, should Mussolini enter the war on the German side, the United States might be forced to enter on the side of the Allies. If this was true or in any part true, Mussolini, thank God, got the jump on Roosevelt. I can't say too often that I'm all for having France and England trounced before we are ready and able to join them.

If American leaders could see straight, they would take over English, French and Dutch possessions in the West Indies, Central and South America, Greenland, perhaps Newfoundland and any islands in the Pacific belonging to England or France and not out of our military sphere of influence. We would also tell Mexico the how and when of things. Should we take this course, an impression of our might, whether justifiable or not, would be made on the minds and emotions of the Japanese and the Germans. This is a ruthless world in which we live, and he who would survive must be ruthless. It is all poppycock to maunder on about defending Democracy.

My intelligence tells me that unless we suffer a naval defeat from the warships of Japan in the quixotic adventure to maintain the status quo of the Dutch East Indies, our land is in no possible danger of invasion.

June 16   Last night took bromide and two sleeping pills. Marvelous, what seven hours' sleep can do. Superb cool day, with east wind and bright cloudless sky and sun-glints stippling Jamaica Pond and heavy green foliage everywhere. To our Place with Billy in the Baby-Carriage. Enjoyed myself.

He is the cock and Janice and Honey the chickens. Mighty spoiled he is getting. But I always bear in mind how his treatments on my back have saved me hundreds of dollars and how willing he is to get up nights and how sympathetic he is. A good boy, conceited, untutored, getting too touchy but on the whole entirely satisfactory. I'm fond of him but not devoted to him for the basic reason that I don't trust his devotion. Have to remind him forcefully at times that Evelyn is my wife and that when it comes to choosing between his convenience and hers, I'm all for her. Honey has improved since last winter more than anyone. Despite my previous convictions on the subject, I feel I should raise her a dollar a week. I'd be lost without her, so it seems only sensible to give her a raise. Janice I really love and she loves me.

And so to the end of yet another diary. The five months covered by this volume have been most discouraging. Without the war to interest me, I should have found them even more flat. Following Hitler's career has given me self-confidence. No doubt following his career has given eighty million Germans self-confidence. The very fact that I have been able to foresee and predict the majority of Hitler's strategic moves has given me reassurance as to the worth of my imagination and mind. Heil Hitler! Heil Hitler — though in the end it is quite possible that because of him the United States may stand alone against an antagonistic and powerful world, because of him and of our own propensity for never minding our own business.

Discouraged by the crushing rejections of his early poems, Arthur had pretty well decided to give up verse writing. Then out of the blue, he declared himself "done with the keeping of the chronicle as the be-all and do-all of my life." He felt like a slacker for not putting down in detail "the daily pulse of humanity," but now poetry came first.

And why was that? Publishers kept sending back the volumes of verse he churned out. He still had to pay E. P. Dutton to print his poems. It was because Arthur believed deep down that the poetry favored by an influential coterie of wrong-headed critics — a poetry obscure, "contortionary," and allusive — would eventually yield to the kind of "virile," undemanding poetry he wrote. In the meantime he savored the few crumbs of praise occasionally tossed to him (like the friendly comments of the Amherst poet David Morton) and scanned the poetry of the masters for "pointers."

In Arthur's many discourses on the craft of poetry, T. S. Eliot was the chief target; in politics, his old enemy "the Rat," hellbent on dragging the country into catastrophe at home and abroad. Arthur held firm to his tough Realpolitik *(he agreed with Lindbergh that the United States might have to make terms with victorious Germany) until England's survival of the Blitz turned him abruptly into an advocate — a lukewarm one — of the Allied cause. This reversal of position did not mean any softening in his hatred of FDR, whose interventionist schemes and reelection campaign he continued bitterly to oppose.*

Throughout these stirring days, Arthur devoted a lot of space as usual to his multifarious woes: his problems with cocky Billy; ungrateful Pearl (holding out for more pay after her accident and long convalescence); hasty Dr. Pike, who had apparently lost his touch and was wrecking Arthur's lower and middle back; and blundering and (most irritating of all) uncontrite Evelyn and Janice. Yet if their "carelessness" and "lack of restraint" enraged him, he cherished them all the same. As he remarked about his father after the "Old Man" presented him with a hundred shares of Coca-Cola stock, "I talk hard all the time, but I have, alas, a heart like wax when the proper sort of heat is tactfully applied."

June 18   I have, I believe, told elsewhere in this diary how Hitler came to final power. Of his private life I know next to nothing. He is a mystic. He is capable of winning and keeping great devotion. He can be kindly or ruthless as suits his larger purpose. He rules his life, so I have heard, in great measure by astrology, nor — considering the many great generals and rulers in history who have almost slavishly depended upon astrological suggestions for every step towards success — is there reason for doubt. Hitler has the face of a homosexual. His final decisions, I have read, are reached, as are the decisions of all mystics, through himself — it may be in flat opposition to the advice of his counselors. His sense of historical timing is incredibly accurate. He seems to be a man of fairly simple personal habits, caring less for grandeur of personal setting than for the grandeur of his place in history. All of which leaves me practically without intimate knowledge of what sort of daily person this fabulous conqueror of nations is. I wish I might discover a book which would give me what we Americans call "the inside dope."

People who hate Hitler in this country, and most people do, hate him with a wholehearted personal vehemence that is akin to frenzy. They are willing to acknowledge no good in him. He is a monster breathing fire and corroding whatsoever his influence touches. But they no longer make fun of him. Your average pro-Ally American is emotionally convinced that it is only by accident Hitler stops short of eating babies. Not since the time of Tamerlane have so many diabolic qualities been accredited to one man by so many people. Hitler wants to win his war and naturally employs military ruthlessness. From all firsthand reports, it would seem that after occupation the German conquerors (aside from appropriating those material elements belonging to the conquered which are necessary for their continued military functioning and from exercising a strict yet not unreasonable political domination) are being neither unwarrantably cruel nor even unwarrantably severe with the conquered.

I by no means wish to convey the impression that I think Hitler is a stainless conqueror if ever was such a person. There is behind him a trail of false statements and broken promises as long as the one behind Roosevelt and even harsher to the unfortunate ones in the way of the juggernaut of glory. And yet, were I a German, I should feel a something in me expanding and growing proud that I lived in the time and under the sway of one of history's all-conquering figures. I can fear the man, I can abhor him for the suffering he causes, but I cannot but admire him and cannot convince myself that he is any more heinous than you or I, given a like nature and a like amount of luck, would be. I do not disdain the man as I disdain Roosevelt, for instance. He is no longer one to be disdained.

I hope I have made myself plain. It is most important that one reading these pages should bear in mind always how I regard the man who is perhaps the greatest political and military genius of our times. I flatter myself that I can perceive greatness where greatness is evinced. Should Roosevelt suddenly undergo a metamorphosis, I am sure I should be fair enough to perceive greatness in him, however much I still detested him. Should Hitler invade this country and threaten or destroy all that is needful to my existence, I should still count him a great man, though no doubt I would be glad and ready to finish him off on sight, opportunity permitting.

June 19 Roosevelt is drafting a plan for compulsory Government service for one year of all young American men and women as an aid to national defense. If Germany doesn't hurry with the conquest of England, we'll be in it abroad. When I listen to speeches on the radio, as many audiences cheer at the notion of entering the war as at the idea of staying out of it. A few more prods by Roosevelt and Churchill and we'll be hastening, weaponless as we are, to add ourselves to the list of victims caused by the Circe song of perfidious Albion — Czechoslovakia, Poland, Norway, Holland, Belgium, France. For the love of God, why don't we mind our own business? Arm, yes. Seize French and Dutch possessions, yes. But keep our face and our hands at home.

June 21 Roosevelt, after having denied emphatically that he had any intention of appointing Republicans to his cabinet, yesterday appointed Frank Knox, Landon's running mate in the last Presidential campaign and owner of the 'Chicago News,' as Secretary of the

Navy and Henry L. Stimson, Hoover's Secretary of State, as Secretary of War.

You who have read these pages in the past will remember Stimson and his talk, talk, talk against Japan until they hated us and his eternal fuddyduddy meddling in international affairs and his supreme lack of imagination and his idealistic tactlessness and his pro-British mania. I thought he was out of politics and put away and I'd never have to see pictures of his smug face again and read his schoolgirl diatribes. But no. Here he is again, bad cess to him.

June 22   It looks to me as though Wendell L. Willkie, president of Commonwealth and Southern Corp., one of the few industrialists who was not cowed by the New Deal when it was in its majority, will be the Republican nominee for President. Dewey is losing ground.

June 23   I sent telegrams to Senators Walsh and Lodge asking them to vote against appointments of Stimson and Knox and also to keep us out of European war. Billy got twenty names within hour. Had Billy send two wires, also Honey. Neither met anything but readiness to sign. The people are decisive about not wanting to get in a European war. Many have swung away from Roosevelt, though many Jews have swung back to him. Juliette reports that all the Jews want immediate war against Germany. Their international bankers are without doubt putting the pressure on Roosevelt, he being lousy with Jews anyway. Clarence is learning to fly so as to battle the Nazis. Juliette wants to be a Red Cross driver. To hear the Jews talk, Hitler is on his way here now.

The war with England should soon take on a sterner phase than nightly German bombings of England and nightly English bombings of Germany. I have been studying maps of Great Britain and Europe until I can shut my eyes and see Leeds and Plymouth and Aberdeen dancing a rigadoon. Where will Germany strike, and how will England protect?

June 24   The dirty British are now pulling another one of their perfidious whizzers on France. France having fought for nine months in effect to protect England and having succumbed practically without any wholehearted British assistance to a stronger, more brilliant and more heavily armed enemy, England now turns to viciously rend the body of the nation that has been its protection in this war and in the last war.[7] Even the excuse of acting primarily to

---

[7] Arthur is referring to British reaction to the French surrender. Churchill, in a radio appeal, urged the French people to reject the Nazi-dictated armistice, to repudiate the government of Marshal Pétain, and to continue the struggle against Hitler.

maintain England at any cost does not, it seems to me, warrant Churchill's bitter and unscrupulous attack upon a fallen confederate, an attack the success of which is problematical. It is a lower trick than even Italy played on France. I hope to God that the Germans invade England and castrate the English power forever from the face of the earth.

June 28   Listened to nominating convention in Philadelphia from 3:30 P.M. until 1:30 A.M. last night. Wendell L. Willkie was nominated on the sixth ballot. Dewey led at first, with Taft second. Towards the end Willkie led, with Dewey second. The galleries all the way through were vehemently for Willkie, and I don't think it was merely a claque. The Republican platform is rather nebulous. Willkie seems less opposed to war than other Republican applicants for the Presidency, so the best we can do is to hope on that score.

This Willkie, in appearance a bellicose fighter by nature apparently possessing under his thick dark thatch of hair much charm, fearless by look and by act, a born debater, quick-witted, ought to be precisely the type to oppose Roosevelt. He has, I am told, considerable appeal for women. A virile man with the looks of a polished-up lumberjack, strong, forceful, perhaps not brainy, yet with sufficient mind. More about him later. Hitler, underground rumors have had it, has been holding off his blitzkrieg on England until he ascertained who was nominated. I wonder what he thinks?

June 29   Am having another wild time with the old pirate, Mrs. Cash. She says so many thousands of mush-mouthed compliments that I wear down and believe that she likes me more than my money. Not at all. She is now threatening to stop coming unless she is guaranteed three specified nights a week. The Cash woman refuses to see me. Too bad, for it puts the brunt on Evelyn, though I am all set to go to town. She is down talking to her now, attempting to persuade her to come up. Degrading to have to kowtow to a money-mad barbarian whose services, alas, are of value to me. I wish it weren't so difficult to obtain and train new readers and that I could peremptorily dispense with her.

Later: The latest and I hope the final installment on Mrs. Cash. She wouldn't come to talk to me, called me vile names, shouted and swore until Evelyn had to threaten to leave her until she came to her senses. "She is," stated Evelyn to me, "a cesspool, and the lid came off. Most unpleasant." The arrangement for the summer which Evelyn is typing now to slip under her door (keeping a carbon) is for her to be paid $2.00 an evening from now on (she is worth it when in form) and $1.00 an afternoon and is to be guaranteed $4.00 of work a week. I hope to Harry this ends the matter. Hope she has had

her fury with me now, turns elsewhere for victims. Will never believe
her lying compliments again. If I mention her no further, the agreement may be assumed satisfactory.

July 4   Buying a library of poetry. Am studying the satires of
Alexander Pope. Very disjointed though eminently worth reading.
He may have been four feet tall and a hunchback, but at that he was
more masculine in what he wrote than a score of other poets with
straighter backs and larger limbs. And there is more than witty
virulence to his verse. His scansion is beautiful to observe. Taking
into account also the literary nadir in which he lived, he is that much
more to be commended.

July 14   Have been reading a recent book, "Directions in Modern Poetry" by Elizabeth Drew and John L. Sweeney. It is a critical
study of poetry—at least of that portion of verse the authors consider as poetry—during the 1920's and 1930's. After explaining
that poetry has gradually been slipping away from contact with the
people (that section is excellent) the authors explain trends, cite
poets and poems, elucidate poets and poems. The gist of the book is
that poetry is only poetry in the modern sense when a barrier of
some sort is raised by the poet which the reader, before understanding the poem, must needs sit down and study through. Any poem
that is simple enough to be understood at once cannot have merit.
Frost is classed as a secondary poet, and Sandburg and Benét are
ignored in that they are secondary poets. T.S. Eliot is next to God. In
his train are Yeats and Auden and anyone who is sufficiently ambiguous and involved. It is admitted that poets write for poets. Some of
the poems cited are completely incomprehensible, affected, mawkish, evidently compiled with all sorts of contortionary efforts. The
authors explain what the poems mean or affect to do so, and the
explanations are as involved and as daffy as the poems. I feel like a
sane man walking through a side show of freaks.

All very encouraging to me to see such madness put down explicitly in black and white, though the writers regurgitate a couple of
dictionaries to make themselves esoterically clear. It's not I who am
off the track in this poetry business; it's the elected poets and the
hashish-eating critics. The book has encouraged me no end. Reading this book and studying intensively current and classical poetry
has encouraged my faith in myself.

Watching Hitler perform has likewise given me one of the largest
lifts I ever received. I wonder if the result of an increased confidence
is apparent in what I write? It should be, for I feel less subdued, less
mouse-like, insofar as both myself and my work are concerned. If
people fail to discern my value as an exceptional person, that is their

misfortune. Not conceit yet but an assuredness I have never felt before.

July 19 The French representatives voting under Hitler's watchful eye to change France into a corporative state were not less obedient than the delegates to the Democratic Convention. Roosevelt was nominated. Roosevelt said: "I want Henry A. Wallace, Secretary of Agriculture, for Vice-President," and lo, it was as he said. Wallace is what Mrs. Cash calls "just another one of Roosevelt's ass-wipers." His face is that of a half-baked labor leader or of an unsuccessful farmer.

Roosevelt last night spoke to the members of the Convention by radio accepting the nomination. He had, he unctuously pointed out, wished to retire to private life, but due to the stress of the times and the public danger, his "conscience will not let me turn my back to a call to service." Noble rot. As if he was not bursting with joy to have received his mete. The odds on Wall Street are six to five that the Rat will be reelected. I still think not.

Have tried to read T.S. Eliot's lectures on poetry. Boring. Thinks too much of self. Is god of the symbolists. A poem, according to him, is not what it says but what it is. Yeah?

August 4 Evelyn just read to me an article in the 'Atlantic Monthly' by Conrad Aiken. Had ideas in it. That magazine publishes quite a few poems but never a one of mine. Well, to hell — and not as loudly to hell as formerly, for I feel much more sure of myself as a person and as a poet — to hell with the self-important critics.

August 5 A Chinese I was talking with tells me that we have not the slightest idea of the strength and numbers of the Japanese Fleet. Lindbergh spoke yesterday and warned that we would have to make terms with a victorious Hitler and advised against meddling in European affairs. Last evening General Pershing spoke and advised sending fifty outworn destroyers to aid Britain before it is too late and appealed for passage of a draft law. Much opposition to draft law. Myself, I think it should be passed. We support the idle anyway. Might as well enroll them in the Army where will be of real potential use as well as get a touch of discipline.

August 15 This is the day Hitler was supposed to be in London. This is the day that Jupiter and Saturn are in conjunction. Yet the Germans, despite their blasting air operations on English harbors, airdromes, munitions factories, are no more in England than they were when France capitulated, with the exception of the Channel Islands.

August 16 A thousand planes a day now bombing Great Britain. Italy picking a fight with Greece. Congress has passed the act enabling the President to use the National Guards (a presumption on states' rights that would have at periods of our history brought about threats of secession) anywhere in the Western Hemisphere. Much talk about the conscription bill. Considerable organized opposition to it. I have concluded it should be passed. It should state that all eligible W.P.A., P.W.A., C.C.C members should be conscripted or else forfeit their dole. But it won't, if it passes. I'm disgusted with Democracy. It is slow, inefficient, blundering, costly and takes away as many rights as it gives. It is a delusion.

August 18 Listened to Willkie's acceptance speech yesterday. Am not favorably impressed by the man, his looks, his voice, what he has to say. The usual amount of prefatory political hokum about Democracy. Roosevelt, he said, was attempting to put through his plans by stifling business; he would get the same results by encouraging business. He flayed Roosevelt for taunting the dictators without being able to back up his words. Whereupon he, Willkie, dared Hitler to attack us. He ended by challenging Roosevelt to a platform debate. Not a very inspiring address delivered in a voice which broke, as a boy's does, and with an inability to pronounce the 'i' syllables in long words. Bet that bozo will get us into war if Roosevelt doesn't. However, I'm still open to being persuaded to like him. He will, if elected, at least have a better gang around him than Roosevelt — I hope. It is annoying how abruptly politics can undermine an individual.

September 4 [From Abruzzo, Hudson Hospital, Queens, N.Y.C., August 26, 1942:]

Though it has been ages since I last wrote to you I never the less haven't forgotton you. Since I started working here I have, more or less, been leading a quiet life. Though I have been quiet pysically my thoughts and mind have been most active. One of the dietician here, with whom I do considerable talking, is most definately on the pinkish side (communist). Most of her ideas are quite logical. She is single and on the elderly side. Swell girl but too much brains. I find her most attrative though because I have more or less been rather erotic in my tastes. She (incedently her name is Miss Swartz) gave me a patition to sign being against consription. A pal of mine and I tried to get some of the boys to sign this bill but we ran into trouble with a thick headed mick (Irishman) who ripped into shreds after a brief trussle with us. On our second patition we couldn't get one employee to sign even though the union (C.I.O.) here is against conscription. I had to go out to get it filled. By the way my job goes on Civil Servise soon. Perhaps you think that Anthony has settled down to a drab and nonexciting live of an ordinary wage earner. Far from it, I seem to get the blues every so often. I still hope to see Mexico and South America, and perhaps I will ride the chushions instead of the rails. Mean while I shall endeavor to save.

P.S. Once you advised me to read "Manhatten Transfer". I recently bought it and find it most entertaining and also a bit melincolly.

September 9 I pity the poor people of London. God, but all this is foolish. You'd think that in five thousand years of history men would have learned to meet over the council table and settle their differences in a more adequate and less destructive manner. The political systems of nations are all wrong, it seems to me. A system in which kings married their half-sisters appears to have resulted in the best and longest rules in history, but perhaps that was accidental.

September 14 We have a new janitor here. He is a slouchy, reprobate, backcountry Yankee with treachery, temper, no cowardice writ large on his face. The moment I saw him two weeks ago, I caught sight of trouble. So did Billy. It is in my contract with Garrison Hall that I have the use of the back elevator. This morning when I wanted it, he got nasty and insulting to Evelyn. I used my tongue, but of what effect was that? I'm so red mad I shake. It is hell to be a man, hear someone insult your wife, have nothing but your tongue. A man without bodily strength is a worm indeed. Poetry, hell. I wanted good muscles to match my temper. He is strong and wiry, could manage me with one hand. I'll see Mach this morning. There's no end to trouble ahead with this janitor. I doubt whether Billy can lick him. Again I have to sit and take it.

September 16 Talked with Mach, Sid. Is more of a man since his father died. Don't feel so badly about janitor today. Odd how one can reason oneself back to normality of outlook. It is like a tight-rope walker regaining balance. He's just an ignorant, cocky thug, while I — well, let it pass. Put it that he's not in my line. Forget it if I can.

September 17 Pearl was hit by a truck in the garage this morning and thrown to the floor and up to now we don't know how badly injured. She is at the x-ray doctor's now. It is her left shoulder and her right elbow. Dr. Pike wants to find out if the ribs are broken. Poor Honey. It is a dark dismal day. If only I hadn't wanted to go riding in the rain or had gone earlier, had had Billy take me. This is from God just to show me he had slipped up about Billy and the draft.

September 20   Been reading Austin Dobson's poems. De Musset in English, dainty, wearied, without vigor or élan. Effete perhaps. Strange that the ruggedness of Kipling and the languor of Dobson could have run parallel. Service and Kipling from the colonies; Dobson and Dawson and Wilde and Noyes from the motherland — the old story, it may be, of the creative ability of a dying empire moving ever outward from its center. The sometimes brilliance of Auden and MacNeice doesn't alter the argument, and T.S. Eliot, such as he is, is an American, as is Ezra Pound.

September 24   I have come to the conclusion that Hitler has lost his opportunity to invade Britain successfully. He waited too long. The recent storm and the British bombers broke up the latest massing and, it is said, caused the death of fifty to sixty thousand German soldiers. The British now are actively on the offensive, and it is doubtful, very doubtful, whether Hitler will succeed if he attempts an invasion. This in spite of the fact that Hitler and Mussolini seem to have lined up Spain on their side.

Willkie's popularity is steadily declining. He has literally talked himself out of public favor. He talks, talks, talks and that not very well. Instead of making his own figure, he has wittingly or otherwise conformed himself to the shadow cast by Roosevelt.

September 28   Yesterday a diplomatic, economic and military alliance was announced by Germany, Italy, Japan, the agreement being that should any of the three powers concerned become involved in war with any country (the United States) not at war now, the other signatories join in. Roosevelt has declared an embargo on steel exports and scrap iron exports to Japan. This throws us straight into the company of Great Britain. We will not join Germany as we should and divvy up the loot, so with England we must join for better or for worse. It is just too bad for us that England was not invaded and overwhelmed at once. The English are putting up a superb fight. You can't help admiring them for it. I might as well reconcile myself to a right-about-face in my personal policy and from here on be all for England.

It is done. Out the window with the Axis nations. I hope, for the sake of our chances of not being invaded, that England wallops hell out of both Germany and Italy. I haven't liked the way Hitler has treated the conquered nations. If we can only cut through enough red tape and enough political chicanery to arm ourselves at a reasonable rate of speed, England and America and the English Colonies (don't count on South America) ought to stand a fair chance of weathering the gale. Pictures of whole apartment houses demolished by a single bomb look wicked to me. There is small chance that England will ever bomb us. There is a chance that Germany or Japan may sometime in the future if they continue to be successful. So go to it, England.

We should counter the alliance by sending planes and ships and every aid possible to England. It is the Second World War now, out in the open, with Roosevelt and Churchill vs. Hitler and Mussolini and France and the Japanese and possibly Stalin. I guess it was inevitable. And I guess it is inevitable for us to have a dictator. From what I have seen of Willkie, we might as well have Roosevelt, for the machinery and power of the latter are immediately organized, and speed is essential, perhaps more essential than the freedom of business or private property or individualism. If the Germans had ruled their conquered territories more reasonably, I might still have some doubts. But my doubts have vanished. I am for England and for the United States and for victory over the Axis powers from now on. Amen.

Who came to see me today but David Morton. I like him. He has more character than intellect, which in my estimation is always to the good. He has a gentlemanly and scholarly manner, with none of the blown-up frog-throat attitude of the average pedant. He sat in the dark with me for an hour and a half. He is very tall and very much at ease. "I want to tell you, Mr. Inman, that you have two very beautiful secretaries." He was quite taken with Janice and she with him. He said so many approving things about 'Hokusai Saw' that I am a little off-center, not being used to enthusiastic commendation of my poetical output. He approved of the use of antique words in 'Hokusai Saw,' of the few Japanese words I used, had nothing to say against inversion even. He said that what delighted him was my evident immersion in Japanese culture and in the Japanese viewpoint.

October 19 Wrote Pearl a letter saying would take her back for $20 if had to but would rather pay $19 and would trust to her generosity to concede a third when I had conceded two-thirds. It was a nice letter, not stark, as the above sounds. She was to come yesterday. Had Billy posted downstairs to talk to her about fairness, if that was necessary. It wasn't. She had decided to accept $19. And so my face is saved and much danger of dissatisfaction in the Billy and Janice direction averted, I hope.

Honey was very pleasant, asserted she would go out of her way to be agreeable and helpful.

October 25   [From Patricia:]

Here is a surprise for you, I filed papers for my divorce last week, I'm going to sue on grounds of disertion, but I'll tell the whole story if it isn't awarded on those grounds. I discovered that if Ted was drafted I couldn't divorce him so started proceedings right away. I don't see how we can possibly stay out of war, regardless of the man who is to be president, and I don't want to be tied to Ted any longer, now that my family knows about it. My Aunt came out here to visit me in July and told me she would lend me the money, I'm paying fifty dollars and court costs, which isn't so much. Out here a wife is resposible for her husband's debts if she is working, also he has the right to take every cent of my wages. I only held back on the divorce because I didn't want my family to know. But this past year they have had so much trouble that I knew my news would lose it's importance, so I told them.

I'm still going about with Paul, we've been together now every day since a year ago the first of July last. And that is quite a record. Particularly since he is such a handsome devil, I've got plenty of competition. The ex-follies girl who came to my house demanding that I give him up has evidently given up. At least she hasn't been showing up at the store lately, she used to come in and sit on my station, and I always refused to wait upon her, it's a good thing my boss likes me. She would call him up at my house and cry over the phone, saying that she was ill and must see him, and when he went over there was Gilda all decked out in her most revealing neglegee. That went on for about a month, then she took to calling the girl next door who works in pictures with her, to check on Paul and me. Like a fool Paul thought he could still keep on seeing Gilda as a friend, when will men learn that you never can be a woman's friend after you have been her lover. I don't think he sees her anymore, I don't ask him as it's none of my business, tho I keep him so well occupied that he hardly has time for anything else. We have a grand time together, he is a bit younger than I but looks the older, he has the stern type of face with a lot of character lines, in pictures he usually plays the villan. He has been working mostly in serials. Not much prestege, but steady work. He is awfully good for me. I'd let myself go too much and had put on a lot of unbecoming poundage and Paul has kept at me until I went on a diet and kept me on it too. I've lost a good bit but will take a few more months before I'm down to where he wants me. I have to take it slowly as I'm on my feet so much at the store. And I've a tendency to walk with stooped shoulders, but now I've straightened up. If I were left to myself I'd be content to go home every night and read my eyes out, but Paul says that contacts are important and he hauls me about to see the most interesting people. A director who has a Swiss cabin in the mountains, musicians, actors of all types, and artist or two, even a few of the electricians and carpenters at the studios. I've met a lot of grand people through him. He knows how I want a home of my own, and for a while he talked about meeting someone to whom I'd become attracted and fall in love and marry. But lately he has taken to remarking about how well suited we are to each other and how he thought that he was the type to fall in love at first sight but has come to the conclusion that the real love is the kind that grows. But let me sound one possessive note and he is off like a scared rabbit. He just hates to admit to himself that he has fallen in love with me, because it upsets all his plans. He is determined upon a career in pictures and the powers that be like their leading men free to take about their contract players for publicity for the studio. And I suppose he'd like to play around a bit for a few years, all men hate to think of being tied down for good and all I suppose. And to Paul marriage is a lasting thing. He has had a very happy home life, and wants to make his own marriage as happy. So of course he is scared to death for fear he might pick the wrong one. He certainly has piled up a lot of grief with the glamour girls he picked out so now he is gun shy. I'll probably wear him down yet. In the meantime it is certainly comforting to have him at my beck and call, not that he beckons too well. He is aggressively masculine, sometimes overpoweringly so. I've lived with women so long that it is hard to accustom myself to the male point of view. I'm always being irritated when he doesn't react the same way I do to certain things, when really it would be unnatural if he did. Then, too, I've lived alone for so long. It is hard for me to share my privacy with anyone. At night when I'm ready to go to bed I usually read for a few hours before I go to sleep. Paul stays so late that I have to turn out the light immediately if I want to get my full quota of sleep. I like to putter around at home, and I never talk very much then, so he thinks I'm being sulky, or, even more of a crime, I'm taking him for granted. I've a hobby I like to pursue for hours, but it's one that I can't share and that leaves him out. And I will say that I do not enjoy sharing my bath with anyone, especially someone six feet two. All the bath water swishes out when he gets in with me. And he is so gosh darned virile. Nighttimes are swell, and I love it, but I simply can't become passionate at nine in the morning when I've gone to bed at two. Do you think I'm frigid?

Otherwise we have so much in common, we both love the beach, and drives, and the out of doors, horseback riding, and Paul has as much desire for a home as I have, even more I believe. Because I can make my own little place quite comfortable, but he just has a room and to him it is only a place to sleep, while my room is my home. He is awfully good with children and dogs and cats adore him. Cats follow him wherever we are, and he is always bringing some kitten to me to adopt. I'd look like an animal refuge if he had his way.

October 26   Listened to the old buccaneer, John L. Lewis, speak for Willkie last evening. What a liar he sounds, not afraid of man or devil. A well-calculated address. Should swing hundreds of thousands of votes.

October 28   Just looked at a garden magazine and saw pictures of knee pads similar to the ones my Mother used to make me use until I was twelve or so to save stockings. Hadn't thought of them for years. Anger welled up in me. All the money they had, and I was made to save wear on tearing ribbed stockings. And how I used to hate those pads. They chafed behind my knees. They itched. Sam and Jennie didn't have to wear them except when very young. No children in Atlanta had to wear them. But I did. I remember crying and protesting in vain. The righteous young mother was adamant. I suppose she thought that once I had begun to wear the things, my soul would be ruined if I weren't made to continue wearing them.

October 30   I have been seeking to win Willkie converts. I haven't much use for the man personally and tell people so, but history has shown that the Republican Party is less wasteful than the Democratic Party, so I am for Willkie. I thought over this business about the Rat being better prepared in case of war. There's so much graft that maybe that wouldn't be so. Anyway, Willkie couldn't get us in so quickly. And also, what happens to a nation militarily is not so important as what happens financially, and Willkie couldn't do worse than Roosevelt. So I have been gathering Willkie adherents.

October 31   You know, for the first time in my life I have become as old as my years, do not longer feel younger than my age. It is a good feeling, and although these scanty entries may give little or no evidence of growth, I at last feel caught up with my years of life. The poems, I think, show it better than this diary does.

November 2   I was analyzing last night when I couldn't sleep just what influences have gone into making me feel my age lately. The most important is, I believe, Hitler's rise to power. A nobody, a man with dreams, rose through endurance of purpose to his present estate. If he could do it, why not I? His machinations for the most part have seemed reasonable and understandable to me, what I might have done with less sentiment in me under the same circumstances. Secondly, relief from constant bickering with Evelyn has given me a new lease on self-respect. Thirdly, studying poetry and gradually concluding my work is of value has removed creases. Cessation of writing in here has, strangely enough, helped — allowing my mind to be more imaginative and less reportorial. Fourthly, I have come to accept my imprisonment in Boston and to all intents in this building as unavoidable. Also, I am learning tact and patience, to keep my mouth shut sometimes and to wait.

November 4 Feel awful. No rides, as wind comes up every morning. Have so much dust in my eyes can't sleep and so much up nose am awakened by my own snoring and by tongue cloven to roof of mouth. Hate life. Seeing double. Dr. Pike twisted intestines carelessly four or five days ago. Can't sleep from gas and poison. He certainly does get return business from his mistakes. And probably Roosevelt will be reelected. He has to lose New York and three of the four states of California, Illinois, Ohio, Pennsylvania, and I don't believe he can lose that much. The one bright spot in a dour world is that the Greeks are doing a job on the Italians and even that may only last until Germany gets ready to smash toward Constantinople.

November 5 Election day. Disturbing that by the whims of a few million untutored minds entirely unacquainted with history, the fate of a nation, perhaps for a century to come, may be settled. God knows what's going to happen to this country if Roosevelt is reelected. Certain it is our way of life will suffer further debilitation.

Evelyn and Billy are out with their cars transporting voters to the polls.

November 6 Well, Roosevelt is in again and by a huge landslide. The epic conflict between businessmen and politicians has been decisively and perhaps permanently won by the politicians. We who are to be ruled may expect little mercy or consideration save in empty words. Kingship without the title or the inherited responsibilities. Dictatorship surely. The final evidenced failure of the Democratic system of Government in the United States, the final evidenced failure of the American educational system to warrant the claim that it really educates, the triumph of emotion over calm reason, the sign and signature of a disintegrating national character. The old order has passed. A crippled egotist rules us, and Wallace, with the face of a cunning, ignorant Southern mountaineer, will rule us if Roosevelt should die. Perhaps we will muddle through, but right now it is difficult to see how. Heil Roosevelt!

November 10   Married seventeen years and like it.

Pearl has a hardish face, the face of a weak person, the face of a resolute farm wife. Not any prettiness now. All gone, not with the accident but with the bloom of girlhood gone.

Janice is on a trip to New York. Pearl's return has disturbed her and made of her, temporarily at least, a futile person tangled in the caverns of herself.

November 11   Have been reading 'Whitman' by Edgar Lee Masters coincidentally with the poems of Whitman. A queer unformed or overformed man toward whom I feel an antagonism and a curious scorn. Egotist, vociferous speaker of too many dictionary words, a mind filled with indulged disorder, a big red apple with some sort of unpleasant worm at its core, a male who never managed to quite mature, a virile and solitary bush growing from twisted roots. Had Whitman not besprinkled his pages with sex and dung, he might have remained in literary obscurity insofar as his 'poetry' is concerned. A luxurious vine, his 'poetry,' growing without restraint or discipline. And I'm not at all sure that his 'poetry,' much of it, is poetry. Whitman's prose on the average is better than his 'poetry.' His opinions of authors are as a rule astute and percipient. A figure of a legend, Whitman, much more than primarily a poet.

November 15   When I do sleep, two hours is the utmost stretch of continued unconsciousness. Last night was unusually debilitating. Elevators dropped dozens of floors at a time, rammed through roofs; automobiles got into accidents; my glasses were broken in my eyes, and my Mother told me it was good for me; and so on and so on. A very distressing one concerned a fight with Walt Whitman. He had an edged tree saw. With it he slashed me again and again until my arms and torso were cut to bloody ribbons. When I awoke, I dared not move for fear of the lacerations I felt sure were on my body.

December 23   Roosevelt now has a scheme by which American ships will be sent to Irish ports convoyed by American warships and loaded with goods for England. That will be straight through the submarine area in which the Germans have produced the most havoc with English shipping. If there is any other hairbrained idea calculated to involve us in war which Roosevelt hasn't thought of, he'll think of it soon. Everyone expects us to be in the war inside of six weeks. People speak of this as "the last American Christmas."

December 29   I am reading a volume of poetical criticism by Richard Blackmur (remember him?), Corn's friend. He has certain definite ideas but uses too many large words and is many times obscure because he is making such a nervous effort not to state things in a commonplace manner.

Listening to MacLeish reading his poems on the talking-books. He doesn't read nearly as well as does Evelyn and his poems aren't as good as mine, but he has arrived.

Stop now and rest. Have written two poems this morning, or was it three? They pass the time by requiring intense concentration.

December 30   Listened to Roosevelt as planned. "There is danger ahead." The ocean will not save us if Britain falls. Britain is our outer line of fortifications. No one can trust Hitler, so no peace with him. Must make mighty effort to help Great Britain. No American expeditionary force. No strikes and no lockouts. More taxes. Less luxuries. It was as belligerent and as caustic and as insulting a speech as one country could well make to another and not be at war. Should Germany conquer England, our turn for having incensed Hitler may come next. Boston will be the first American city to be bombed by the Germans in case we ever become involved in a war with Germany.

What in heaven or in hell will 1941 bring?

1941

For years Arthur had convinced himself that posterity would eventually acknowledge him a better poet than the reigning favorites. Every rebuff checked his ardor, but the impulse to versify and his hunger for recognition drove him to plan new volumes in which he would deflate his countrymen's fraudulent illusions and indirectly chide contemporary poets for their "leftist" ideologies, their "incomprehensible private symbolisms," and their "defeatism" and "paucity of inspiration." Yet they were read and he was not. Perhaps the time had come again to pay full attention to the Diary. "Fed up with all poetry," he announced. "Artificial chicken food for artificial birds. Stuff mostly outside the vehement and pressing realities of existence. Fun to do. Prose more forceful as well as more plastic."

Arthur discovered more "poetry" in the "terrifying" beauty of Adolf Hitler's imagination than in all the current verse. The war itself was a grand poem. He charted and analyzed the "pseudopodic" movements of the rival forces, hoping without much confidence the Axis might win decisively before an unprepared United States joined England and prolonged the contest. In behalf of the isolationist cause and inspired by the speeches of Senator Burton K. Wheeler, he contributed an antiwar poem to the Boston Transcript *and described for future Diary readers the steps by which the "diabolically misleading" Roosevelt escorted the nation down the road to war.*

So be it. He knew that clear-eyed Lindbergh spoke, alas, for a minority, that Hitler's invasion of the U.S.S.R. lessened the chances for a quick end of the fighting. In fact the tenacity of the Russian defense prompted disturbing thoughts about the Soviet experiment. The question now was whether the United States was capable of mounting a defensive war, much less an offensive one, after being drained by the Allies. Ominous movements in the Far East (the result of deliberate Anglo-American provocations) augured new dangers. Behind the verbiage of the Four Freedoms he detected agreements "less unspecific, less harmless, less abstract" and envisioned an America standing finally alone, friendless and unequipped.

Still Arthur found life "much more interesting being a reporter for this diary than a would-be creator of poetry" and events at Garrison Hall no less absorbing than those abroad. Honey, whom he never had rated very highly, suddenly became indispensable, and her indecision whether to return as a full-time employee kept him hopping. So did Billy's hints of quitting to take a higher-paid job (obviously "his Sadie" was behind that nefarious maneuver) and the possibility that he might be drafted. Such uncertainties put Arthur on the lookout for new recruits. He had to spend a lot of time during the dog days interviewing applicants. Moments of contentment (a pleasant excursion to the railroad yards, gossiping with the Garrison Hall regulars) were more than offset by chronic ailments and by anxieties about his ability to carry on in a time of increasing material shortages and a dwindling servant supply.

January 7 When I first came to Garrison Hall in 1919, there was little or no traffic on St. Botolph Street — no dust, just a quiet slightly down-at-the-heels back street with pigeons strutting in it. Now cars rush past continuously, horns blow, the building shakes from heavy trucks, one school is opposite and another cater-cornered. We are emphatically in the city rush. The old hotel has been made into a fairly up-to-date apartment house for middle-class people. Old Man Mach, having worked himself up from peddling shoestrings at the Chicago World's Fair to ownership of this building and seven million dollars' worth of real estate and having been caught in 1929 and having descended to being dictated to by banks, has passed on. The Snake and the Adder, his sons, run the place in their and the bank's interest. We have five apartments, one of which we sublet and one of which (over me) is kept vacant so that people will not bother me. We pay exorbitantly for our apartments, more than anyone in the building but have the use, practically privately, of the side elevator.

I am forty-five and Evelyn will be forty next month, Billy Minor will be thirty and Pearl Hollister twenty-two. Janice Oliphant was twenty-seven in December. I ride little or none in my two cars, the 1929 Pierce-Arrow phaeton and the open 1919 Cadillac, being weak and being subject to dirt in my eyes. We are comfortably situated. Evelyn has a 1938 Ford. All of us have radios. I have a piano and many books. We have comparatively few friends, Evelyn not wanting them and I having to pay my way so much that I am not sure who are friends and who recipients of money. Neither Evelyn nor I have a religion. Evelyn belongs sporadically to the Wells College Club. Dr. Pike is her companion on trips and walks. We take three papers every day, the 'New York Herald Tribune,' the Boston 'Herald' and the Boston 'Transcript,' with 'The New York Times' on Sunday. I take 'Life' and a collection of fantastic, imaginative adventure magazines, and Evelyn takes 'The New Yorker' and 'The Saturday Evening Post' and 'Horticulture.' My last book of poetry, 'Where Find Sanctuary,' came out last month and was a fizzle. Mrs. Cash and Miss Brooks read to me each week, with Roderic Peters and Lorraine Foxx filling in odd evenings. Ella James and Juliette Stern talk to me about once a week. My Father and Evelyn's mother and father are in Florida.

We are on the verge of a war with Germany and Japan. Adolf Hitler, German conqueror, sits fairly well astride the world at this moment. The Japanese and the Chinese are still at war, and the Japanese occupy much of Northern and Eastern China. Our President, Franklin Delano Roosevelt, has just been sworn in for a third term and is preparing for the eventuality of a war with Germany which he expects to bring on by rendering excessive and boastful aid to England. The times are precarious. Taxes mount. Danger grows. Americans are still unwilling to give up luxuries. A mad world. We are in the midst of a war profits boom. The trend toward State Socialism seemingly has been halted at this writing but in reality is probably being speeded up.

January 11 Roosevelt now wants blanket powers to supply England or any other nation with arms for cash, for credit, as a gift and (note this well) to repair or refit the ships of any power in American dry docks. This last defies international law and treaties of all sorts and places us as close to an alliance with England as is possible without a declaration. Step by step the lord of all of us edges us into this catastrophic war. It is my belief that he has meant to do so since the beginning and would have done so last year but

pursue this step for months. This morning he has finally gone to see Mr. Barber, the boss. I do hope that some arrangement can be worked out and that it will help Billy evade the draft.

January 23 Yesterday morning Honey broke my cut-glass glass. I lost my temper, having warned her four days ago not to be careless with it. I recovered my temper and thought that troubles for the day were over. But no. Honey came in at suppertime shaking and crying. She had been to a doctor because breaking the glass had given her a headache and unnerved her. My anger hadn't helped, and the doctor had scared the wits out of her by telling her that if she didn't quit her job she would have a nervous breakdown. She announced that she was going to leave. That was a bolt out of the blue.

Honey fosters an obsession that her mother is a nervous woman and that accordingly she too is a nervous woman and that she is hence constantly liable to a nervous breakdown. The accident naturally was a bad shock to her and strengthened her obsession. She is strong as an ox physically, though indifferent as to endurance and stamina and flighty as a canary bird. Her temperament and her imagination eat her up. Right now she is both scared and sorry for herself. I soothed her down and pointed out this and that and used my throat up generally. She said that my talking helped her and that she wouldn't make any decision for three or four days. I don't want to lose her.

January 28 Billy and I have been worrying about the draft. He went to his old boss at the laundry and broached the idea of letting Sadie go for a while. The boss told him that Sadie's department was run more efficiently than any other and that he would pay her five dollars more a week rather than lose her. And he offered Billy a forty-two dollar a week job soliciting laundry orders at the military camps plus an immunity he claimed to be able to furnish him from the draft. Then I did what I should have done in the first place, called up the headquarters of the draft here in Boston and stated Billy's three year military service and asked what were the probabilities of his being called. The man said that he would be among the last to be called, was in the fourth and final class and that his case was a cut-and-dried one. I told Billy at suppertime. Now I shall worry for some time about that forty-two dollar job and hope to God he won't get it in his head to want it. I feel like a tightrope walker treading carefully above the foibles and weaknesses, the influences exerted upon my employees. I trust I shall get through without a tumble.

February 3 Billy said: "I wish to heck you hadn't sent me to see Barber." "Why?" I inquired, foreseeing the tenor of the answer. "Because ever since he hasn't given Sadie no peace and she's been on my tail every time I see her." I remained silent. He continued: "He tells her I'm wastin' my talents with you. He tells her I'm worth more than I'm bein' paid. He tells her he's willin' to give me a job for life. He says I'd be drawin' fifty within a matter of years. He talks to her every day. And she gives me no peace. It sure was a bad move to get in touch with the old fellow." "I see it was," I agreed.

I thought quickly. I was up against a problem. "Sadie," Billy went on, "feels that you don't appreciate me because you don't jack up my salary. She can't understand any other sort of appreciation, it seems, than money." "Maybe," I suggested, "that's because of the French in her. Mrs. Cash is that way. She can't comprehend that there's something deeper than money between people." "Yeah, I thought of that. Anyway, she don't give me no peace. She thinks I oughtta get more money." "Well, you mean a great deal to me, Billy. If I have to give you more money, I can do it. You understand my finances. I can stop having Pearl and pay you more. Only you don't realize, I think, how much more work that would put on you." "I'm not afraid of work." "Of course you aren't. But neither have you a full idea of how wearing the extra care of a hundred and one details would be." "Maybe not." "Billy," I continued contemplatively, "I'm in a situation where if I give you advice it may sound given for my benefit, although it's not. I gave you a dumb piece of advice on Barber. But by and large I've given you darn good council. Isn't that so?" "Yeah, that's so." "Well then, it looks to me that right now you're face to face with wife trouble. You've been lucky so far, but you're up against a crisis this time." "I know it." "If you let Sadie persuade you to give up this steady job for one which may pay more and which may stop when Barber dies (you say he's nearly sixty) and do it against your better judgment, she'll ride you for the rest of your mortal life, and you'll be like Uncle Joe was after Aunt Nellie stopped him from being a Senator, like thousands of other husbands who let their wives get the jump on them. I don't know why, but women with not more than one exception in a hundred always stand ready to take advantage of any weakness or even temperateness on the part of a husband. It's their nature, apparently, to want to dominate if they can. You've seen such things. You know that's so. And Sadie's no different from any other woman. This is your first run-in with her, that's all. If you let her get away with pushing you around, you'll be ridden, saddle, spurs, Spanish bit and all, by her from this day on. It's up to you to have your way or let her have hers."

"I think you're right," said Billy, and his fat face looked worried. I meant all I said, so it wasn't hard to adumbrate my thoughts. "By

God," he exclaimed, "I ain't gonna let her boss me. I'd be miserable from today on, wouldn't I?" "I'm afraid you would, Billy." "If he offers me sixty dollars, I won't leave you. There's other things in this world besides money." "I think you're right, Billy. And another thing: Sadie is older than you are. She probably feels that she's wiser and more capable of reasoning than you are. An older wife is more apt to be bossy than a young one. You have that to contend with too." "I know it," he replied, returning to his former gloominess. "But you leave it to me. I'll tend to it some way or other. I'm no namby-pamby, to be shoved around by a woman." And I can only hope he isn't. I did very well and can only wait now and keep my mouth shut and anticipate that Sadie will nag him until his Indian is aroused.

Yesterday afternoon Evelyn read "Final Moment" ('American Portrait') to me. Was disappointed. Then she read some old diary to me. Liked it. Tired of poetry. Decided then and there to return to diary with full energy. More alive than the poetry.

February 4   Mr. Serrill has been ill most of the winter. He had Mrs. Serrill write to ask for his photograph albums. I am taking a final look at them before phoning the express company. The pictures of the Pennsylvania countryside are like dreams of a softer past — the open valleys and wooded slopes, the gentle runs and creeks, the covered bridges, the stone farmhouses and Dutch barns, the magnificent trees, the flocks of turkeys, geese, chickens, the herds of cows grazing in lush meadow bottoms, the small shaded roads. Eastern Valley, Cobbs Crick, Mill Crick Valley, Darby Crick Valley, Gulph Crick Valley, the Valley of the Schuylkill — a gentle, lovely, pleasant land. Days passing gently — Pennsylvania days.

February 5   Janice and I have been spending the last hour and a half going over some of the books in my library. There are more books by a third than there are shelves and no adequate arrangement or listing. All I can do is to retain on the shelves the reference volumes I think I shall be most apt to use, put the others in storage to forget. The rough divisions in the library include Spanish America, Asia, American history, Civil War, diaries, novels, poetry, general reference works. It would be immensely interesting to possess the eyesight to browse all day among so many books. There are sufficient volumes on a range of subject matter so varied as to portray pretty accurately to a scholar the history of this world to date. Everything from Hakluyt's 'Voyages' to the most modern encyclopedia of history, from ancient Babylonian texts to 'The Moose Book.' Had a very fine library before dampness mildewed the books and the painter pilfered them when the books were in the country. As things, books mean little to me, as compendiums of knowledge and emotions, much.

February 6   Reading more of 'David Copperfield.' A very irregular performance, but the high spots compensate for the low ones. Repetition of theme words, "humble" and the like, wearisome. Some of the characterizations are indeed immortal. Altogether enjoying the book. One classic which lives up to all the touting, not windy and wearing like 'Vanity Fair.'

February 11   Ella said: "Well sir, I paid a visit to the Maternity Hospital yesterday. Arthur, you never laid eyes on the likes of it. Ward after ward, bed after bed of women pleased with themselves for having added another life to the world's population, each one dressed just like the next in the cotton shift they make them wear and the blue bedjacket. It was nice and clean and sunny, and the nurses were pleasant, but oh my. So many mothers doing their bit for Democracy."

I am scanning 'American Portrait' for final corrections. It improves upon reading. Dutton sent me the few reviews that were given 'Where Find Sanctuary'—"All of important stature. All the verse is clear and easy reading," says one paper; another says, "Verbose and affected poems, done in the manner of a college sophomore at a bull session. Crossword puzzle words abound"; and another, "There is poetry, good poetry, in the volume. Pity that one must fight his way through so much mumbo-jumbo of prose to find the jewelry of thought"; and again, "These are poems of beauty and understanding"; and still again, "The poet's personal sensitivity seems to have reacted to a point of callousness toward others. I like the quality of his lines and figures, the sound of his richly clever words; but I have a rash feeling here is a man condemning himself"; and finally, "Arthur Inman, whose softly spoken words of pity and memory salve our weary consciences, stands like a kindly philosopher looking into the mouth of Medusa. His descriptions are really beautiful to read, little bits of marble whiteness gleaming with shining liveliness from the all too few pages of his book." So there you are. Take your choice. Very few reviews and very little attention to me in any case, which speaks more distinctly, I suppose, than what any single reviewer says for or against.

February 12   Read further in 'David Copperfield.' In a way, the book fascinates me. Uneven of texture it may be, but it has the stuff of genius in it. Glad I was antagonized by 'Christmas Carol' and 'Oliver Twist,' so that did not encounter this volume until mature. It is making an impression on me. As I look back, I can discern what a deep impress it made on my Mother's character. I realize now that numerous quotations, expressions, lines of thought which she used originated in 'David Copperfield.'

February 13   Willkie is throwing his inept weight around. I grow more pleased each time he puts his foot in the mud that we didn't get him for President. He's stupid and quite as misled as Roosevelt without being anywhere near as clever. As I listened to his speech last night, I became more and more reconciled to Roosevelt.

February 14   Billy meanders around as dejectedly as a sick puppy and with the same look. He has been on a liquid diet recommended to him by an old doctor. He has been on the diet for two weeks and still weighs 210 pounds. He is persistently hungry. "Cripes," he said this morning, "I wisht everything wasn't coming at once." I could foresee what he was going to say, most of it, the part concerning me anyway. "I wish to God I'd never went to see that Barber. He gives Sadie no peace and she gives me no peace. He tells her I'm not bein' paid what I'm worth, and he's got her convinced. And she never lets up on me. And I'm in no mood to fight back what with this persistent gnawin' at my insides. Everything at once."

Instead of replying at length, I made him go drink some beef bouillon. Right now at my instigation he is out buying some lentils and a ham bone to boil himself some soup. It seems to me more important to keep his spirits up than his fat down. My private opinion of that Sadie is what it has always been. If he lets her boss him this time, his name will be henpecked from now on. I still feel that my wisest course is to let things drag in the hope that she will overnag him. If she does and he doesn't crack, the tug-of-war will be mine, or should be.

It certainly looks as if the fatal hour is approaching. Although it would seem that Hitler has sent too many troops to the Balkans to permit an early invasion of England, a million men are deployed in Belgium, Holland and North France. Perhaps the blows will fall simultaneously or perhaps in sequence. A blow at Salonika, another at Gibraltar, another by the Japanese at Singapore or against the Dutch Indies might be attempted either in order or timed together. And the blow at England may be held in abeyance. This business of history in the making is of unfailing interest to an inquisitive mind such as mine. These months ahead bid fair to be more dramatic than any pyrotechnics since the Spanish Conquest of the New World. I am right well pleased that there is a lull in my poetic endeavors at this juncture, so that adequate concentration may be applied to the recording of the next phase in the Germanic conquest of Europe.

February 17   A word as to finances. I am acting upon a conviction that no matter what sort of war boom intervenes, it will be followed by hard times, inflation, perhaps revolution. In the first place, before prices rise, I am stocking up on tires, sheets, blankets, clothes. I am retrenching to some extent by not spending on needless luxuries. Preparing for the harshest eventualities, I am doing what Evelyn disapproves of, saving quarters against the time when paper money may be like toilet paper. All of which may be foolishly cautious but not as foolish as it looks right now. I have listened to people's advice before. Not listening now. Have sixty dollars in quarters already. Want almost five hundred dollars in silver. Still have a hundred and twenty-five in gold.

March 2 Somewhat in a quandary as to what real names to change in 'The Maples Are Red' so as not to risk being sued by anybody. This because people seem to think I run a chance of trouble. Read life of Paul Verlaine last night. As fluid a character as water falling down the course of a brook. Career, before it arrived, reminds me of Abruzzo's. Abruzzo, in case I don't get around to telling more about him, has become a secretary in one of the Communist units in New York.

March 4 Honey called up and said she was in town and would drop in if I wanted to see her. She is tanned and while a bit thin in the face, doesn't look badly. I was very glad to see her. Have quite a fondness for her, I reckon. Honey says that no longer does she start awake at memory of the accident. Her doctor told her that he couldn't find anything specifically wrong with her but that she might be upset for a year and shouldn't work until she felt quiet again. So she is going to loaf. I saw no use in urging her to come back here, so I suggested that she rest and that when she feels better we can talk over her coming back. She thought that sensible. I asked her, though, to promise not to accept any other job before discussing this one. I miss her.

March 9 Finished reading 'Daily Life in Ancient Rome,' a fine instructive volume.[8] Reading a history of the Doukhobors, 'Drums along the Mohawk' (an overrated book), a life of Hawthorne, a life of Boss Hague of Jersey City.

The 'Aid to Britain' Bill passed the Senate yesterday by a two-to-one majority, and few restraining amendments were inserted. Our soldiers cannot be sent overseas nor our ships used to escort vessels

---

[8] Jérôme Carcopino's *Daily Life in Ancient Rome* (1940) is a vivid re-creation of Rome and its people "about the middle of the first century A.D.," when Rome was at the apogee of its power. It is packed with the kind of social and institutional detail that Arthur wanted to include in his own Diary, and he rightly calls it a "fine, instructive volume." Walter B. Edmunds is the author of the "overwritten book," and "the life of Boss Hague" is probably Dayton D. McKean's *The Boss: The Hague Machine in Action* (1940).

nor our arms given wholesale to England. English men-of-war may be repaired in our navy yards. We are now, to all intents, at war with the Axis powers.

March 11` I feel as despairful about life as 'the lost poet,' [T. H.] Chivers, whose poems I have been reading and whose concentration upon death was so morbid and unremitting, only I have sufficient sense of balance and reality to realize that even the most patient neighbors will move away from a leaking drain if it never pauses in its unpleasant dripping. I have to act cheerful at least. I have been reading Sidney Lanier's poems, too. Verbose, meandering, depressing. No particular merit in them, with the exception of 'Song of the Chattahoochee' and one or two others. Where on earth did he ever come into such a reputation? No wonder I hated 'The Marshes of Glynn,' etc., when I had to suffer through them as a boy. So many literary reputations are altogether unmerited, handed down from one generation to another like outworn modes of thought, threadbare observances, sterile figures of speech.

March 20   And still the troubles. Billy received a notice last night to appear before his local draft board. Why? He is there now. "I dreamed about war all night," he said. "I couldn't sleep. By God, I don't intend to go if there's any possible way of slidin' out of it. What do you s'pose they want with me? Sadie couldn't sleep all night for cryin'." I said: "Well, we can only hope. It's too bad Sadie didn't do some of her worrying last year. Perhaps it'll teach her there are other things in life more important than money. She could have kept you out of this if she'd been willing to give up her job." "Yeah," said Billy forlornly, "there's that to it. Maybe it'll teach her something — when it's too late."

As far as I can see, the board has no right to draft Billy, but what is legally right or legally wrong has little to do with this country when those in power wish to make exceptions. Have a mind very busy with notions about how to circumvent the Government if occasion arises. Hope better than my last catastrophic idea.

March 21   All our fears for naught, this time at least. The demand for Billy's presence had to do with a special offer to him to go to Fort Benning, Georgia, to train men. He would be given the rank of brevet sergeant, paid $150 a month, allowed to take his wife and be given a house. He was all grins that he didn't have to go to war. They told him they were powerless to do more than make him the special offer, couldn't exert pressure. Being in class 4-A, he will be among the last to be called unless we become involved in a great and continued struggle overseas. That won't be for a month or so, maybe longer. Thank goodness that is off my mind for a while.

April 2 Perhaps many times a day I say to myself: "Well, at least you aren't bedridden; at least you aren't malformed or disgusting in appearance; at least you weren't born into this world a monster kept private so that people will not see you." I start to wonder what it would be like to be born some sort of monster—without bones or hideously malconstructed or without eyes or with a head too large to lift or without legs or distorted of mind—and to live in shut-away horror of a life span. Then I don't feel so abused by my restricting circumstances.

April 4 In the midst of all my other troubles and efforts, I have been interviewing applicants for the secretarial job—huge-nosers, red-headers with pallid skins and tiny eyes, smellers loaded with perfume, women with keys locking their talking-apparatus, picked sparrows, one almost beautiful woman who couldn't talk, a fetid-smelling oafish girl who threw herself around and who had eyes the size of your thumbnail, an undershot jaw, uneven teeth, red arms and looked with her scraggly blonde elflocks as though she had stepped out of a nut house. Humans certainly can stink, either of themselves or of the powder or perfume they affect.

In this country the strikes are first-page news. It boils down to this: The C.I.O. is taking this occasion, undoubtedly urged on or subsidized by the Soviets and Nazis, to sabotage defense efforts. When they haven't enough majority to stop work in a plant, they establish picket cordons and keep men who wish to work from doing so. There have been bloodshed and deaths and riots. The situation is made more than usually bad because the National Guard is now in the Army and the states have only the police to maintain order. This puts the matter squarely up to Roosevelt whether he will use Federal troops or not. He has been mum so far. The C.I.O. leaders have flouted Federal orders to go back to work. Roosevelt is supposed to be going to open his great I-am mouth today and issue statements on the strikes. If he sends troops, he will antagonize his labor pals. If he fails to do so, he will antagonize people in general. No doubt he will take a middle course. God, I hate that man. I wish he'd die. I wish he'd been shot years ago when the attempt was made on his life in Florida. Roosevelt, Hitler, Stalin, Churchill, whoever is the big shot in Japan—put them all in a bag like unruly kittens, weight the bag and throw them in the deepest ocean.

April 6 And now the sun is out and Billy is still away. There are a few yellow and purple crocuses Evelyn brought me from the Place yesterday in the little black vase on the chest. The handsome Japanese elephant we bought a dozen years ago, when tens of dollars meant no more than dollars do today, is standing, trunk uplifted, on the ledger book in which I keep my as yet uncorrected poems. My caps and leather jacket and scarves and the little brown sweater, patched and mended, that I have had since college, are on the ship chest in front of me. An amber tumbler is full of retinispora sprigs which I occasionally burn in the sunbowl because of the pleasant odor. Notebooks and old newspapers and magazines and books are on the chests, on the couch, in chairs, on the floor. The 'Columbia Encyclopedia' stares me in the face. I see a tin box of Huntley & Palmers Biscuits and think that you can buy them no more now. The writing pasteboard rectangle under this diary, on which I support it, is chewed and worn and frayed. I have had it more than ten years and used it almost daily. It won't last much longer. I still use the yellow Eberhard Faber Mongol No. 2 pencils, and this is one of the last of my dwindled stock of National notebooks.

April 12 Poetry and war. Poetry and war. My life at present. I find a strange and mystical, a dynamic and terrifying beauty to the substantive unfolding of Adolf Hitler's imagination, his conception and execution of conquest. It is fascination to watch the fragments coalesce into expansive historical movements, to see the bits resolve into wholes, to forecast in one's mind the possibilities and potentialities of the imagination of a very great man.

I must have considerable imagination as well for much of the time I seem to be able to apprehend and understand, to foresee Hitler's moves, not, of course, in the detail he does but in their objectives and essence. In most moves I would have done what he did, always allowing for contingent developments altering plans.

April 17 Have interviewed a girl, rather attractive in a pert, knowing way, about this job. Listen to more war news on the radio in few minutes. Girl said: "Don't make me read war news to you. I don't read war news." Well, I do. I want to write a poem upon how strange, even appalling it is that a person, myself or you, who isn't at heart in the least bloodthirsty can find himself wishing with ardor that hundreds of thousands of men be defeated.

April 22 Yesterday afternoon Millicent Barnes Wright called up. Evelyn was in the country. Janice answered. Millicent said that Hal had died Friday unexpectedly. She was taking his body to Canada and would phone us on her return. I offered to do anything I could to help her. She said that I would know that this was just about like ending her life. Well, she had four or five years of married life and a home of her own and dogs and all she wanted to drink. But I can see how her props are knocked from under her. Hope she'll come back to Boston to live. It would be helpful to my life to have her read to me again. There will be some money from the estate, I suppose. She will have to sell the country house.

April 26   It is cool and cloudy, too dirty to ride. Sit in chair and feel twisted in spine from Dr. Pike's treatment and use misery to write three crazy poems to send to 'Poetry' under assumed foreign name. Want to see if make meanings obscure and put in dirt poems will be accepted. Will write that I am a refugee from Europe.

May 2   The 'Transcript' died Wednesday. Not enough people wanted quality to keep it going. A commentary upon our times and culture.

May 5   Am working so concentratedly on 'Selected Poems' that haven't energy or eyesight for much else. Mrs. Cash and I finished the 728-page biography of Amy Lowell. Liked it, especially the center portion. Had drive, that woman, vigor and virility and daring. Wonderful to friends. Caustic to enemies. Superb letter writer. Sane view of poetry. Debt American poetry owes her is incalculable. No sacrifice too great to make towards its furtherance. Mrs. Cash began by hating Amy Lowell and ended by sincerely admiring her. A noble woman in many senses of the word.

May 9   My Old Man, for a reason known only to himself, showed Evelyn a copy of his will. As much as she remembers of it, this is it, though he was careful to tell her that he might change it at any time. Forty thousand dollars to be left to me in cash or securities. Twenty-five thousand dollars in cash or securities to Evelyn. To four or five servants, five hundred dollars apiece; Horace [Fuller] to be paid ten dollars a month until his death or until a thousand dollars is used up. Certain stocks set aside to furnish a moderate income to various schools and colleges. A larger group of stocks set aside, the income from which, between two and five thousand dollars a year, to go to the Groundhog until her death. The remainder of the income from the estate to be paid to me after tax deductions and expenses of administration. Upon my death, one-fourth of the income of the estate to go to Evelyn until her death. The whole estate then to be divided between his nieces and nephews, who will have the pleasure of spending it.

In one way, it is fairer than I expected. In its treatment of me as a functioning individual, it is quite as unfair as I had thought it would be. Evelyn says that no mention was made of Uncle Frank or Aunt Louise. It is my belief that he has already made over sufficient capital to Aunt Louise to support them the rest of their lives. I am to have no voice whatsoever in the administration of the estate. I am going to write him, or Evelyn is, and tell him that I think I should at least have a veto voice, just in case the estate should fall into bad hands.

The Old Man expects the worst that can happen to the country to happen. I wish he would go on and die.

May 13, Jamaica Plain Cool east-wind day, dusty in Boston. When arrived here, sat outdoors for nearly an hour enjoying quiet and fresh dustless air. A bit cool in building today. Try out new bed. I wish to God I could stay out here all the time. Life is less worth living not being able to ride. Lilacs are in bloom, and some crab apple trees, and early iris, mostly cristata. Place looks sadly neglected, as truth it is. Chestnut tree dying. Let it die. Evelyn downtown. Billy and Janice here. Newspapers full of Deputy Fuehrer Hess's flight (for a reason not yet divulged to the commonalty, you and me) from Germany to Scotland in a plane and there landing by chute. Much mystery. No doubt we shall be informed of some of the truth before long. Yesterday saw Honey. She announced she isn't coming back on this job. That wasn't much of a surprise. She is enjoying herself too much, she says, to take any job. Is being spoiled to death, I suspect, and likes it, and why not?

May 18, Boston I am studying pictures of a Sunday at a training camp. Like old home week. Tables groaning with foods. Guests eating at the cost of the taxpayers. Guests being shown the newest military weapons. Smiles everywhere. A picnic. I have heard that the Government runs trains each weekend to take rookies to and fro to cities so that more visitors may be accommodated. France all over again. If there is as much danger as Roosevelt, the Jews, the newspaper editorialists and columnists, the college professors, the politicians, the movies, the writers of books and articles would have us believe, it is time we served cake without frosting.

May 29 Janice's affair with Bertram Davis drags on. You'd think he'd want to marry anyone so attractive, but he is evidently willing to let things drift. He has been notified by the Government that he must be ready at an instant's notice to be sent anywhere in the country to take charge of any plant or any department of any plant. He is in the act of turning his old car in for a new Cadillac. The shoe factory is doing well, so much business they can hardly handle it. "Are you happy, Janice?" I ask. She smiles at me. "Yes, I guess so. Yes. Well, yes. Only I wish I was married. I wish I was married to a man like you, a man with your qualities." Her eyes twinkle. "You didn't expect that answer, did you? Well, it's so."

I wonder if all this war talk gets tiresome? You of a hundred years from now, will this diary of military and political events bore you as diaries of the Revolution bore me? Will future wars of greater magnitude make this war seem as small as the Pequot War seems to me today? It is inexpressably exciting to be poised on the verge of you know not what. I only hope that I am able to transmit to these pages some of what I so acutely feel.

May 30   At the outbreak of the war, according to the Gallup poll, 46% of Americans thought the United States would go into the fight. In February, 1940, only 32% thought so. In May, 1940, 62%. Since then, never less than 59%. Now, 85%.

Nearly overlooked the following review in the 'Globe,' coming, thank goodness, quickly on the heels of the two bang-'em-boys reviews which cast me down yesterday:

THREE MOODS, by Arthur Inman. E. P. Dutton & Co., $2.50.
Those of you who lament living in these troubled times could do nothing better than read Arthur Inman's latest volume of poetry. Here is a poet who has an answer to all the defeatists who need courage. Here is a poet who will not flee from chaos into an ivory tower. Here is no whining voice, no cringing soul. Here is a poet who remembers a better day with joy, not with sadness. He recognizes the inevitable change and is proud to be alive now.
Arthur Inman is prolific; he writes from an inner necessity but knows that the printed page does not hold all the wisdom of life. His latest volume contains three books, "This I Know" in which he feels and reasons his way to a definite faith in the present, "Hokusai Saw" in which he sees the Japan of the artist, the best piece of art criticism this reviewer has read in many a day, and "The Maples Are Red" in which the poet looks back on his boyhood in Atlanta, Ga., and in Maine and finds pleasure in his memories.
Arthur Inman is not a dealer in obscurities, nor yet blatantly obvious. He writes not for a select few but for the common man, without writing down to him. He regards himself as a Boston poet and one Bostonian reading his verses has the feeling that he would be a good man to know.

June 7   I feel that an interest in the diary is reviving. Suppose the poetry in me has had enough exercise for the present. Things in the world are too goddamn exciting to continue to bend head over regulated lines on pages, with scansion and rhyme and piddling matter claiming attention.

June 10   Am reading 'Les Miserables' on the talking-book. Very boring in parts. Too full of morality for a modern. The psychoanalysis of souls is longwinded, though it must have been something new and exciting eighty years ago. I don't like novels in which the author has a private wire to the hidden thoughts, emotions, motives, reasonings of the characters. It is well enough for an author to surmise, and say so, what goes on inside characters but not well enough for him to be unnaturally prescient to an extent that contradicts ordinary life. I can only surmise what goes on behind faces and conversations and actions. I cannot state dogmatically that I do. So how can an author do so without seeming unrealistic? In my opinion he can't. "John took off his shoes and crept along the floor to Janet's door. John turned the knob and entered." Not what John, walking up the stairs, thought about Janet in her room. John, his mind in tumult, etc.

Stocking up on all needfuls which will later rise in price. Saving quarters — have $270 in silver now. Want to have at least $1,000. Putting in coal at Barn, buying shirts and suiting and sheets, stocking up on paper of various sorts, purchasing shoes. Getting ready, in fine, for the payoff, of whatever sort it proves to be.

June 12 Juliette. Has been devoting time and energy to work in the Boston Red Cross women's corps. Juliette said: "I never had a real interest in life before — you know? — a real interest. I eat and sleep Red Cross. I feel as though I were engaged in an activity that is useful to mankind. Do you see what I mean, Arthur? It makes me bigger than myself. It keeps me busy. It concentrates my energies. I'm the only Jewish girl in the entire corps, and everyone treats me with no condescension whatever, and that gives me — you know? — a lift. I'm busy all day, and Clarence is busy, and we only see each other in the evening, and we lie awake and talk till twelve or two. It's wonderful. Clothes and men and all that fall into their proper proportions, if you understand.

"Tonight," continued Juliette in a rapt voice, "I'm walking on air. Honestly I am, Arthur. You've heard of the Powers girls, rich, on all the social pages in the papers, pretty, talented, in society? Well, they've had sixty of us for luncheon at their home at Manchester-by-the-Sea. Arthur, it was like a dream. I never knew such luxury, such taste existed. The perfectly huge estate. The formal gardens. The sixteen-room house. The four swimming pools. The chinaware. The furniture. The tennis courts. The automobiles. The four butlers. The maids. The chauffeurs. The gardeners. The service. The food. My head's in a whirl. I couldn't eat my supper. I'm in a daze. Never, never as long as I live will I be the sort of person to have all that, no matter how rich Clarence becomes. You need to be born into it, don't you, Arthur? And to think that there are people and estates like that all over the country, and here am I, thirty, almost thirty-one, and this is my first contact with them. Gosh!"

June 15 Roosevelt has taken another war step: He has frozen the assets of Germany and Italy (which, since our assets in Germany and Italy have been tied up since the war began, is well enough), but he has seen fit to do so insultingly, blatantly. When you come right down to it, what brings on wars is as much what is said as what is done, perhaps more what is said. New York Harbor is being mined with live mines. We are to train seven thousand British air pilots in this country during the year. Practice blackouts with fake bombings are to be carried out along the eastern seaboard in the near future. We are to build a million and a quarter tons of shipping this year. Roosevelt is turning over two million tons to England now. It is announced that we are building planes at the rate of a thousand-plus a month. The draft age will be lowered or so it is planned. Too many Americans above twenty-seven are unfit, more than in last war.

June 18 A Government order has closed all the German consulates in the United States on the grounds of subversive activity. Another step towards war. Yesterday an order was issued to prevent the three hundred thousand German nationals from leaving the United States pending further instruction. All borders are closed to their exit. American property and money have been seized in Italy and Germany. Everything that can be thought of to incense the Germans is being tried. Daily now we are being pushed towards the brink.

June 19 The papers are full of rumors of a time ultimatum sent to Moscow by Berlin and of a possible war between Russia and Germany. The French in Syria continue to hold out. A British attempt to break the German lines in North Africa failed. Night after night the British bomb Western Germany, the Ruhr and the French 'invasion ports.'

June 22 Germany has invaded Soviet Russia, marched in at one o'clock this morning. Rumanian troops are also invading. Finland is armed and waiting. Hungarian and Slovak armies are mobilized. Leningrad, Kiev, Moscow, these must ultimately be taken or capitulate. That, together with a swing to the east around the Black Sea. Can Hitler do it? Sufficiently, I should say, to get what he wants, though the distances to be traversed are immense. This is not Napoleon laboriously marching northward toward inimical winter. This is Hitler advancing fifty, sixty, seventy miles a day against a foe whose weakest link is organization in an age and under conditions when the organization is perhaps as important as courage or fighting ability or capacity to accept punishment. As mechanics, too, the Russians are notoriously inefficient. What Hitler wants are the crops of the Ukraine, the eastern and Polish oil fields, the Baltic States. It is my guess that he will get them and quickly. His forces are on the outside of a circle of concentration, an advancing perimeter whose center is Moscow, whose flanks are the Caspian Sea oil fields and the Arctic Circle ports. News comes through slowly on this hot summer morning. Leningrad should be the first great objective, with columns converging upon it from Finland, Northern Norway, East Prussia through the Baltic States. There should be naval actions on various seas. There will be air bombardments of Soviet cities to cow the people.

This action of Hitler's has, I am frank to admit, taken me by surprise — not most people, but me. Yet all the signs were there to read: practical cessation of air attacks against England; failure to assist Iraq and Syria; the massing of troops along the Russian borders; conclusion of a nonaggression treaty with Turkey, thus securing the right German flank against danger; the mobilization of Finnish troops; the visit of the Rumanian Prime Minister to Berlin. The Russian Army is the largest mass army in the world. Roads and railways are in lamentable condition in most of Russia. The swiftly moving self-contained panzer units of the Germans may cut through resistance with expedition and dispatch. The goal of Hitler's move is oil and food. The excuse for the invasion that is given to the world is really of no importance, all excuses for active offensive military action being throughout history of little importance.

Today's war activity pales Roosevelt's bellicose note to Congress denouncing Hitler and Germany into temporary obscurity. What effect will Hitler's latest move have upon our President's war drive, if any effect? It may be that with threat of invasion removed for the time being from England, Roosevelt will go slower during the next weeks.

June 28 Last night Evelyn phoned Hassie. We have had no word since Evelyn grew disgusted at her — for drinking, for the callous way she talked about Johnny, for the manner in which she gave the glad eye to not very prepossessing strangers on the street — and refused to go near her again. She only phoned because I wanted it. Hassie sounded delighted to hear from us. She and Johnny are now running a night club, 'The Downtown Social Club,' no less — about four miles from Everett. Hassie works all day as head of the hat store; Johnny works all day selling cars. At night they run the Downtown Social Club (capacity when full three hundred), are not in bed until two or three in the morning. Up again after practically no sleep and to work. Hassie says that they aren't making money yet.

What a novel Hassie's life would make: small village in Nova Scotia, comes to big city, trains for being nurse, marries man and grows to scorn him. He dies, she works way up in hat store, marries Armenian because sees chance to better self and be secure, starts night club. In between has all sorts of adventures, operations, trips. I could hear her ask Evelyn to ask me if I "still loved my Jesus." I called back that I "still loved my Hassie." Riotous laughter exuding from telephone earpiece.

July 5   Have been telling Evelyn how bitter it made me to have Dr. Pike injure me, how bitter that he didn't seem to be regretful. She has been holding forth that it isn't the nature of men to apologize and that the best you can expect from them is a compensatory gesture.

Then she told me of a call Dr. Pike had made last week to the home of a woman he had known for years, a woman with a husband, two healthy children, greenhouses filled with orchids. For an hour she showed him through the greenhouses. Then she took him to a secret son he didn't know she possessed, a young man-creature who had had spastic paralysis all his life, whose knees were bent to his chest, whose helpless hands were like flippers, who couldn't talk, whose eyes were bright and intelligent. Dr. Pike was shocked. He chatted to the poor thing of baseball and other trivial matters and could see that he was understood. He couldn't mention the visit for a couple of days, he was so disturbed and touched. "There's no one I know," finished Evelyn, "who's more deeply concerned to relieve human suffering than Dr. Pike." "God," I said, "if there is a God, is a demon. Do you suppose there's more to come after death, more like the hundreds of thousands being maimed and wounded right now in Russia, more like the tens of thousands who pack the insane asylums, say, of this state alone?" "When we die," asserted Evelyn dogmatically, "we die. We become fertilizer, and that is all there is to it." "I wish," I said, "that I had your faith." My neck, my arms, my hands hurt less, or I felt that they did, after hearing about the man with spastic paralysis. Perhaps that is why Evelyn told me about him.

July 8   On the assumed premise that German activity in Europe menaces America, that the fate of England and America are inseparable, that the British Fleet is a first line of defense, that the economic system of America will be menaced by a German system in a united Europe, nearly all of Roosevelt's acts and actions are explicable. That his assumed premise may be violently miscalculated, detrimental to the interests of safety and growth in the United States, does not minimize the influence of the theory upon his acts and actions and upon the eventual fate of the American people, you and me and all the rest of us. We are, as I see it, progressively falling into the toils of Britain and into the morass of Europe where we have no business being. England began this war for the purpose pure and simple of maintaining a balance of power in Europe, that is, British control over Europe. England is now fighting for its life, and to keep that life American assistance, gotten by hook or crook, is necessary.

Draw your own conclusions as to the constant pressure being exerted upon our vain and susceptible President. Discount the reluctance of Americans to enter a shooting war. It can be only a matter of time unless some unforeseeable occurrence takes place to swing or reverse the general current before Roosevelt has us in this war.

July 13 We American nonbelligerents sit on the sidelines, and many of us with all our emotional vitality root for the destruction of the forces of the combatant we feel should not win. Myself, for instance. I wouldn't hurt a fly or a person unless sufficiently provoked or annoyed directly; yet I find that I wish intensely and with all my heart the discomfiture, for instance, of the English.

July 20 Tried 'Evelyn's Diary' last night and the night before. Not really a diary but a journal. Evelyn a man of the world. Was surprised at the level of culture described by him in Holland and Belgium in 1641. More money than Lowlanders could spend, so put it into art and improvements social and architectural.

July 22 The Russians have put up a better fight than I had deemed possible. However, at this point there are symptoms evident that the morale is commencing to have fissures in it. I had not dreamed that such solidarity of spirit existed in Russia. The younger generation must have been taught as much Nationalism as Communism. It is disturbing to wonder if an experiment such as the Soviet one might not, had it been permitted a century of development, have reached some sort of splendid conclusion between the idealistic and the practical.

July 25 Millicent Barnes had supper with Evelyn last night. Talked to me for an hour or so. Making a fetish of her grief for Hal. "Not in all my life, Arthur, have I taken so much liquor as during the last three months. I want to forget, but I might as well drink water for all the good it does. My life is done."

Millicent has been visiting in Ohio for two months. She didn't like the men. She didn't like the climate. She stayed with a huge girl of twenty-six who had gland trouble and was having a change of life, was desperate because no man looked at her and because doctors said she would become more mannish each year. Millicent has an idea that she would like to be a nurse in England where there would be a chance of her being bombed.

Am reading the life of Santa Rosa of Lima. It seems to me that she was a demented creature. But not even understanding the first need for a religion, how can I comprehend the ecstasy derived from the degradation of the body? To scourge oneself with iron chains, to thrust one's feet into live coals, to wear nettles and hairshirt, to bind one's body with heavy chains that eat into the flesh, to administer self-scourgings, to recline upon a bed of sharp fragments of pottery and when the urge for sleep becomes too irresistible to suspend oneself by one's hair to a nail tiptoe high in the wall, to wear a heavy crown with ninety-nine needle-sharp points pressing into the head, to have against one's breast a spiked crucifix — the way of the Bride of Christ appears to be an insane way.

July 26   Hot today despite east wind. Janice and I in railroad yards. Talked with long-necked yard brakeman who was shutting freight-car doors with pinchbar. Had been in yards for thirty-five years. Told us all about cars had driven — Model T Ford, Metz, Essex. Getting old. Too tired of wheels in yards all day to sit behind one in automobile. Moved as slowly as though the world beyond the yards moved slowly too.

Home now, with both fans going, trying to write with pencil, getting tired, putting down quickly in the next few lines that the United States and Great Britain have frozen all Japanese assets, that all Japanese vessels are hastening to leave our ports, that further economic reprisals against Nippon for the occupation of Southern Indo-China are threatened by England and America. The Netherlands Indies will no doubt join any action taken by England and America. This is supposed to end the appeasement of Japan policy.

July 28   Honey came to be with me until two-thirty this afternoon. Had a long talk with her. Told her I would pay her twenty dollars a week, more or less adjust time so that she would have majority of afternoons free, let her take time off without pay whenever she was tired or found she had to drive her father. "Gosh," she exclaimed, "you could talk anybody into committing murder."

I gave her the blue enamel locket Aunt Helen used to wear so much. "Is this a bribe, Artie?" she asked. "Why, naturally," I replied. "But it's not all bribe. I want to give it to you whether you come back or don't come back. I guess I want to give it to you because I love you. I don't know why I love you, because you make me all sorts of trouble, but I do."

July 30   Juliette asked dramatically: "Arthur, do you like me?" "Of course," I replied. "One person can't have known another as long and as intimately as I have you without more than liking the other. Of course I like you." "You know," she continued, as though listening to my answer had to her been a matter of form only, "I've never lied to you, Arthur — at least not very often — and you usually ended by finding it out. Well, I lied to you about Dr.

Sillitoe." "I know you did," I said. "I know you slept with him."
"Well, I did. You know I'm not indiscriminate, Arthur, don't you?
You know my story. You know I must have liked the man a great
deal."

She went on to explain how it had all begun when he operated on
her. "I had never felt more drawn to a man in a sex way. I didn't love
him; I just felt drawn to him." Within six months she was sleeping
with him. "My sex life with Clarence was so miserable. Night after
night he, oh you know, tried to make a success of our marriage but
couldn't. I was wild. Do you have any notion, Arthur, what that
meant to one of my nature? Probably you don't. But it made me
eager for John Sillitoe. Then my conscience told me to stop, and I
did. He had a wife and children. His wife is most unattractive. He
hates her. She was rich when he married her. He doesn't know why
he ever married her. I tried to cause them to become reconciled.
Every day he'd meet me in his car and we'd eat together and then sit
by the river and talk. He was a fascinating talker. One day I met his
wife. She asked Clarence and me to have dinner with them."

For two years or more Clarence and Juliette went around with Dr.
Sillitoe and his wife. The wife became jealous, accused her husband
of not ever taking his eyes from Juliette. The two couples went to
the World's Fair together and on other trips. "Didn't Clarence get
wise?" I asked. "Oh no, he didn't suspect a thing." Then Juliette
commenced to go to bed with the doctor again. "Oh, Arthur, it was
wonderful." That, I gather, lasted some six or eight months. He
tried to persuade her to leave Clarence. He told her that what had
been passion at first was "deep love." Juliette couldn't make up her
mind whether to leave Clarence and run off with him or not. Dr.
Sillitoe and his wife quarreled with increasing tartness on both sides.
He was working with considerable ambition at his practice, fighting
with his wife and carrying on a clandestine affair with Juliette.

One day he came to Juliette, broke down, cried, told her he had
become impotent. "I'd never had a man grovel to me before, Arthur. It was terrible. He had been to some of the biggest specialists
in the city, and they had told him that the trouble was purely mental.
He was afraid of losing me. Nothing I could say reassured him. He
said that next to his work he was more proud of his virility than of
anything in the world and that without it he was 'a worm.'" Juliette,
who, when it is dramatic to do so, has a soft heart, and who seemed
to be really fond of Dr. Sillitoe not only because of his relationship
with her but also because of his many kindnesses toward her family,
continued to see him in order to solace him. "Do you know, Arthur,
that from the day John went impotent, I began to get along — you

know how—with Clarence. By now we are in perfect union. I love Clarence as never before. I'd be willing—and perhaps you won't believe this, but it's true—to go along now without another man in my life except him—oh, for ten years anyway (one can't tell any further ahead than that).

"I sort of wanted to break off with John, not because he was impotent you understand, but just because of Clarence. But John wouldn't let me go. He became wildly jealous. He wouldn't even let me ride with one of Clarence's salesmen to New York when I wanted to go on a visit there. He went into a tailspin because I went to the dentist for a month. One day when we were stopped in traffic and a man looked at me, John jumped out of the car, went over to him, yelled: 'You can't look at my wife that way.' It frightened me. But he wasn't jealous of Clarence. He said that if anybody had to have his arms around me, he was glad it was Clarence. Several months ago I decided I wanted to have a baby. I asked John to recommend me to a specialist. He gave me three names. I went to a Dr. Chandler. He is a gentlemanly sort of man about fifty. Clarence approves of him. He looked me over thoroughly and couldn't find a thing wrong. He's giving me thyroid extract and injections. Every time it's hot now, I faint. Well, John began to get jealous of Dr. Chandler. I told him he was crazy. How could I fall for a man who looked up my vagina with a nurse properly in attendance. He wouldn't listen. I began to get really frightened, he was so jealous. A week ago I went to him and told him that I thought it was time for him to stop telephoning me and telegraphing me and writing me and seeing me, and that I would always be on hand if he needed me. He told me that if he ever caught me going with another man he'd kill me. He ordered me to stop visiting Dr. Chandler.

"Arthur, this morning my mother brought me two letters. I opened them without looking at the address on front. On a piece of paper in one of them was a note, printed, unsigned, to Clarence. It said: 'Dr. Chandler means more to me than your brassiereless, perfumed, overdressed slut of a wife, whose name is trouble.' I was ashamed to have opened Clarence's letter (I never open other people's letters). I knew no one else but John could have written the letter. Since I'd opened the letter, I felt in honor bound to tell Clarence, so I phoned him. Arthur, do you think I'm a slut?" I pondered the question. "Well," I said, "you're self-indulgent. If being self-indulgent is being a slut, then you're one. If being self-indulgent isn't being a slut, then you're not one." "If Clarence ever finds out, he'll walk out on me." "I know he will. It's the risk you take when you're self-indulgent." "I'm afraid Dr. Sillitoe is almost out of his mind with jealousy." "It looks that way. I'm glad I'm not you." "What can I do, Arthur?" "Oh, you could do quite a few things, only I'm sure you won't. By the way, what will you do?" "I'll wait."

I told Evelyn the long story. She was shocked. "Jews!" "Well," I said, "to be quite fair, not entirely Jews. It's more sex than Jews." "Oh dear," she said, "I guess I don't understand." "Honey," I say, "have you enjoyed writing down this yarn?" She, bent over the writing-board, blonde hair falling towards the white page, heels under rung of chair, red combs in hair to please me, replies: "I don't know what to say."

August 2   The United States Government has done the one thing that the Japanese claimed would bring about war with us, that is, cut off the supply of airplane gas and oil. The Japanese press now asserts that a single untoward incident will bring about conflict. Must gall them to see us shipping airplane gas and oil to Russia, depleting our own army supplies to do so. An order has been issued by the Priorities Administrator forbidding the use of the raw silk in the United States except to manufacture parachutes and powder bags unless a special license is obtained. The movement from silk to rayon and nylon will gather momentum.

Listened to fine speech by Senator [Gerald P.] Nye last night. Blames much of war fever on movies. Says twenty propaganda movies in last year played at twenty thousand movie houses. Gave names, all Jewish, of heads of eight largest motion picture concerns. Army and Navy representatives sent by Roosevelt to direct filming of propaganda. Hollywood filled with English actors. Called it "British Army of Occupation" in America. Says American and English Governments lend ships and troops free to movies. Says dividends of American motion picture companies dependent on English markets. Much of what he said must be true, not because he said it but judging from relevant bits of information gleaned here and there.

August 3   For the first time Germany is losing great quantities of trained men. Russia has held out longer against Germany than anyone had believed possible: A fanatic faith, a dominating religion if you will, has at last butted headlong into its counterpart. Russian manpower doesn't think; it acts. It is like German manpower. Should Russia be able by its policy of scorched earth and of purposely leaving in the rear of Hitler's advance islands of resistance armed and provisioned for siege and equipped for harrying, to delay the German occupation of Eastern Russia until autumn, or should the contest continue so fierce as to deplete German soldiery and

German equipment beyond German expectations, only then is it probable that the German dream may have received an irreparable setback. To date, the Germans are winning this world war. There is no final signature as yet to write finis to their dream, but there may be an uneasy hand holding a waiting pen.

August 4   [From Patricia:]

I don't think I told you that I got my divorce last December. I had rather a time serving the papers on Ted, he got coy at the last moment and did a disappearing act. He said he was duck hunting! So we finally had to contact him thro mail. I wanted to get the divorce on desertion, but in this state you have to have a third person who can swear that in their presence the absconding party has said that he is leaving and never coming back. I had proof enough that he had gone, but none that he had said he was going. So my lawyer advised me to sue on mental cruelty, and tell the real reason why our marriage went bust. I hated to do it, and when I got to court and saw the crowded courtroom I knew I'd never make it. My lawyer, being a kindly soul, had my case transferred to another court and also had a private hearing for me. It wasn't as bad as I thought, because I didn't have to tell the judge the actual happenings, Ted did it himself, in his letters to me. It rather looked as if I had kept the letters to trap him, but as it happened, in each one of them was a reference to the money that he owed me. And I had kept them to refresh his conveniently faulty memory. Ted loved to let himself go on paper, and he certainly couldn't be accused of reticence. In fact the letters were so damning that my lawyer says that the church will give me an annulment on the evidence. I could have gotten the annulment first if the draft law hadn't been passed. No one in the army can be sued for the duration of his service, and I had to work quick. It was a good thing. For Ted was drafted. He tried to join the navy, but was over age, then he tried to get in the army, but they wouldn't accept him because his divorce wasn't final. A bit ironic, because the draft army took him anyway. He is now in air squadron training school, he is in the radio repair shop, something he has never done before, but he seems to like it. He writes to me regularly, I don't know why. He wouldn't if he knew he was listed as a Homosexual in the City Hall. I'm still wondering how he ever got in the army, they certainly don't know what they've got. Wait till he starts breaking loose. As he will eventually.

Paul is in the army too, I certainly am a daughter of the regiment these days. Paul enlisted in the National Guard last March.

He didn't want to wait around for the draft. Things were pretty bad in the picture game. And he knew he'd have to go soon anyway, so he hied himself to the Armory, and enlisted. It proved to be the wisest thing too, for the draft army is sent thither and yon, while so far, the Guard has been kept in California. He is a Corporal now and is getting fifty six dollars a month, to the draftee's twenty-one. They wanted to send him to officer's training school in the East, but he said he didn't like the army that well, and as he'd be made a 2nd Lt, and they get all the grief, he'd rather stay where he is and study for a Seargency.

And things do happen so fast and furious to me that I never get caught up. I rather like my life, it's not dull, and I can always live in my other world where I've attained my heart's desires. That's a bad habit I grew into years ago, and it's such a delightful world I hate to give it up. I have all manner of lives, and shhh, all manner of husbands, and even families! I just choose which one I feel most like being each night, and that's the way I go to sleep. In one life I've four of the nicest children, two of my own and two of my husbands by a dead wife, I like the two oldest, Kevin and Pamela the best. Babies seem to pop up in all my other lives, but thats the nicest way to have them, no bother. I tried having a Boston husband and family, but just couldn't see them. I've one Irish husband, & one with whom I commute between here and New York, he's the masterful one, and I go about dripping in chiffon. Then there is always Paul, but with Paul I never seen to get beyond the honeymoon. Yet we seem to have the nicest house together. It's yellow, and I have a four posted canopy bed in my bedroom. It's such a happy house, always cool and clean and full of flowers. Once in a while I'm a glamour girl and dash about being very elegant and Lady Bountifulish. And never, never, do I have to worry about expenses, we always have a nice income, except the masterful one who is filthy rich; but I've arranged to have him lose most of his money, and just have enough so that we can have a nice fieldstone house. I suppose everyone has their dreams, but perhaps not so detailed as mine. Of course I've put in a lot of work on mine. Somtimes I get so involved I can't get to sleep.

August 6   The phone rang. Janice answered. "But I don't understand," she said. "You mean you can't come in today. What? You mean you won't come today. Not ever come? But I don't understand." To me: "It's Pearl. She says she won't come today. She says she's never coming again." To the phone: "But Pearl, you can't treat people you love that way. You just can't. You're serious? But you can't be serious. Is it your family?" To me: "She says it isn't her family." I took the phone. "What is it?" I asked. "I just called you up to tell you I'm not coming to see you anymore." "I don't understand." "I'm not coming anymore. I'm going on a trip. I'll come back. Then I'll go on another trip. I'm going to spend my life doing just what I want. I can't see you again." "Is it your family?" "No, it's not my family. It's me." "But I don't understand. A person can't simply walk out of the life of a person who loves her that way." "I can. I'm going to. And my family don't know anything about it." "What's happened to you since I saw you Monday?" "Nothing. I just made up my mind." "But you can't leave a person who loves you that way. You just can't. It isn't human or reasonable. You'd hate yourself always." "I know it. But it's what I'm going to do. I'm sorry." "Are you all right in your mind, Pearl?" "No. I was hit on the head."

Her voice was neither bellicose nor angry. It was toneless, like a bell with a hand on it, the way demented women sometimes talk. She didn't seem in any hurry to end the conversation. "Don't you think you ought to see a doctor?" I suggested. "People who love other people just don't treat them this way." "I know I ought to see a doctor. I'm crazy. I'll get crazier the older I grow. I'm no good. I'll never be any good. But I'm not going to see a doctor. I'm crazy, I tell you. Don't you understand—I'm crazy." "How long have you felt this way about me? Did you feel this way yesterday?" "Yes." "The day before?" "No." "What has happened in between?" "Nothing. Absolutely nothing. I just decided to call you up and tell you I'd never see you again. That's all there is to it." "Well," I said, "I don't understand. If you are this way all of a sudden, perhaps you'll change back again just as quick. I'll call you up again in a couple of days." "Do as you wish. It won't do you any good. I've made up my mind."

Janice says that she can understand how I've pulled Honey one way, her family the other, and she wants to be herself between, so that she's made up her mind emotionally to walk out of my life. Maybe, though I can't understand that myself, as I didn't press her much last week. Maybe she was hit on the head. Maybe she is losing a grip on herself. I don't know. She certainly sounded strange. Should I tell her parents? No, they wouldn't understand. What should I do? I don't know. Even if I lose her, I don't like to think of her going along without psychological attention if she needs it. All rather shocking. I feel upset. So does Janice. I always expect everyone to throw me over sooner or later but not exactly in this queer way. Poor

Pearl. Wonder how on earth she will end up, so kindly, so sprightly, so capable in many ways, so out of balance, so emotional, so suddenly headstrong, so self-sacrificing and so self-indulgent.

Juliette has been in touch with Dr. Sillitoe a couple of times since last week. She's sorry for him. Clarence didn't do anything about the letter. He merely observed that people had to expect those kinds of things and that you couldn't go hunting perpetrators of slurs you didn't know. "Arthur," Juliette concluded, "Clarence is wonderful. Do you know what he said to me the other night? He said that seven years ago he hadn't had any money or any business or me and that now he had a good salary and all the credit he wanted and a business employing seventy men and the most beautiful wife in the world and that he thought he was very fortunate indeed. When he says things like that, Arthur, I think I ought to be a better wife or go jump off a cliff. He's wonderful."

August 9   Hot and breathless. Janice and I sat in shade of red freight cars and watched negro crew pulling crab grass from between ties. Big, evil-faced bucks, those negroes.

August 12   [From Patricia:]

Paul is difficult to describe, because his appearance is a bit overwhelming. He is immensely good looking. Six foot two. Very straight. A gorgeous voice, it was that which attracted me first, voices impress me so. I can't stand shrill thin ones. I met him first in the dark, and liked his voice before I ever saw him. We were both on our way to visit a mutual friend and got lost looking for the house. My first attraction was purely physical, Paul was all that I had always wanted in a man, in appearance. Like you I am most sensitive to beauty. Paul makes a very fine first impression on people, but to most proves disapointing later. His mentality doesn't measure up to his looks. He was always overanxious to make a good impression and of course overdid it. With women he had one line, flattery, but laid on with a trowel, and naturally they all saw through him. Men have always resented him, he has never had an easy way with them. He used to look at them with a superior smirk, and always gave them what he called "a mans hand-shake", it was really just showing off his strength. Paul has a good slice of vanity. He has always had things too easy at home. The most popular boy in High School, football at the University, enough money behind him, and the German logic that he was the chosen of God. Why on earth I put up with him I don't know, he was extremely rude to me. And he had the awful habit of trying to reform everyone, he still is learning to let well enough alone. He can't seem to realize that people are what they want to be and they don't like to be reminded of their shortcomings. So he made some enemies. He has a strange liking for old people, and will sit for hours letting them ramble on about their lives, old ladies and men adore him. We battled like mad for months, Paul would pick a fight deliberately, just to stir up things. But month by month we grew on each other. For one thing, we can talk to one another, I've never been able to do it with anyone but you, I mean about personal things. If we didn't like something we said so. I'd got in a dump and let myself go and got far too heavy from inertia. He is alergic to fat women, yet he kept coming back, and kept at me until I went on a diet and paid some attention to my appearance. That was vanity on my part too, expecting to have a love life and not looking the part. Paul's passion for making people over came into full play with me, and it worked, since he wasn't at me to change my ideas. I don't know what kept us together, I wasn't what Paul wanted in appearance and he wasn't what I wanted in character. So we agreed that he help make me over and then find a husband for me. Since I certainly had no designs on him.

Physically we are idealy mated, Paul says I "give," and that's what he loves about me, and he certainly co-operates. Our sexual life was the only thing that held us together at first. Then at Christmas time his young brother came out to visit Paul. He is twenty one, and the dearest, finest boy that I've ever known. He has always adored Paul, and he didn't like some of the things he saw, and he did like me. We hit it off beautifully, he said I was the only sort of person to keep Paul's feet on the ground, and Paul felt ashamed that Richard could see the clay feet of his idol. When the boy went back home Paul started to grow up, he became more sincere, and stopped trying to make an impression, particularly when I told him that I felt that it showed lack of poise. The poor lamb, he did so pride himself on his poise. My friends started to like him for himself instead of putting up with him for my sake. All but Sean, he dislikes Paul intensely, but that's normal, it pleased Sean's vanity to have me go on carrying the torch.

Now that we have become serious about our feelings for one another I couldn't want for a more attentive lover. He is gentle and charming to me, brings me gardenias (which I hate) all sorts of little trinkets and leaves me notes to find when he has gone. I even get telegrams saying, "darling, I love you," when he thinks my letters are becoming too cool.

He sleeps with his arms around me all night, where before he couldn't bear to be touched, and nicest of all, he has twice come down to see me when he knew that Mother Nature had a previous date, so that I wouldn't think that it was just "sex" that he wanted from me. He has sworn that he has been faithful, and I believe him, with a population of nine thousand in San Luis Obispo, he's pretty safe.

Paul's family is full blooded German, and the name is Allmendinger! About which something drastic will have to be done. He always uses his stage name of Bowe, which his agent christened him. He is from Muncie Ind. and the background is good, I checked with one of my cousins who married a Muncie boy. The father is in real estate, and the family were pioneers, the grandfather was a contractor and built most of the town. One uncle is President of the best bank in town. His mother is lovely, and his dad writes him the finest letters. He is the oldest of four boys, and the family is a bit pinched getting the youngest through college, real estate business not being what it was. If Paul wishes he can go home and work in his Uncle's bank, which he tried and hated. What he will do when he gets out of the army I don't know, picture work is so precarious, and Paul feel fed up with it.

I wrote Pearl last Thursday telling her that I had at last gotten it through my head that she didn't want to come here to work for me and that I wouldn't press her to do so anymore if that was what was bothering her but to please come to see me once or twice a week at her convenience. No answer. This morning Evelyn phoned her. Evelyn said: "She's not crazy. She's not sick. She insists she thinks just as much of you as she ever did. But she's not coming to see you. I think I have the answer. I think I have it. It's in my mind that she's afraid you're falling in love with her." "Me? In love with her? I love her, but I'm not in love with her. I love Janice ten times more than I do Pearl." "Oh yes, I know and you know, but I'm not sure she knows. She's pretty darn conceited in certain ways. You realize what a fuss you make over her. Why shouldn't she take it for being in love? And your loathfulness to let her go out of your life. It all adds up." I considered. "Well, maybe," I said.

"And this," continued Evelyn, warming to her subject, "I'll bet she's in love with you. Maybe you don't believe it, but you're something out of a storybook to an imaginative girl like Pearl. You're pretty special. You're handsome when compared to most men. You have enormous fascination. You make each person think he or she is filling your gaze. Pearl doesn't like young boys her own age. You know that she likes you. It all falls into place. I'll bet she's in love with you. And it tears her up to be near you and feel you're unattainable." "I think you've got the answer. I'm sure you have. And it never even entered the back of my consciousness. It would account for the way she looks at me. It would, as you say, account for the way she's acting now. It's Katinka all over again, almost in duplicate. I'm bound to think you've put your finger on the key to the puzzle."

August 13 Perhaps the above diagnosis of the Pearl rebus is without foundation. It looks rather silly to me today. Why should an attractive young girl of twenty-two have to sever relations with an employer of forty-six so abruptly as a defense against infatuation? To believe that without violent doubt requires more conceit than I possess. There's probably another reason, quite simple if I knew it. And yet, somehow, Evelyn's thesis holds water when judged by the symptoms manifest by Pearl.

The entire front end of the Baby-Carriage — pump, gears, timing chain, shaft, bearings — is wearing out. Can't buy new parts. Billy telephoned to West Lebanon, New Hampshire, to a parts man where we have had good service before and asked what they could supply. They have several old V-59 motors. Billy is hiring a U-Drive-It truck and is going to go to West Lebanon about 170 miles from here to pick and choose and bargain and bring home. Best get all the parts I can while I can. Have a large stock on hand already — rear end, valves, crankshaft, radiator, chains, etc. This will set me back another pretty penny.

Great God, what next? Evelyn comes in. "These are pictures of my house in Camden," she says. I glance casually at an ordinary New England farmhouse, white, with a big shingled barn, not unusually attractive. "That's what you took pictures of when you went there in June to play at looking for a house?" "It is my house. I bought it. I own it. Isn't it nice? You can see the Camden hills." "You say you own the house?" "Yes. It's mine." "My God!" I say. "Uncle Charlie and my father helped buy it. I own it all myself." I sit, unspeaking. I think: "She knew I'd oppose getting a white elephant like that at the end of the world. She did it behind my back. Trouble ahead. She'll tire of it but trouble ahead. Why on earth . . . ?" She says: "I can go there. Perhaps I can rent it. Isn't it pretty?"

I think: "What an infant. What a foolish step to take. But I've taken steps just as crazy. Can't object to it on that grounds and be fair. What makes it cause me to feel so sick at the pit of my stomach then? I know that she'll be tired of it after just so long. What, then?" "When you went to Camden in June," I say, "you told me seriously that you had no intention of buying a place." "I didn't. I bought it in July, when I was at Southwest." "Then you did what you told me you had no intention of doing. You did it without consulting me, for you knew I wouldn't approve. You wanted to do it anyway, so you did." "I wanted it." "It isn't," I explain, "the tangible fact that you've purchased a piece of property at a place as inconvenient as you could well have chosen, though you can guess what I think of that. It's that you did it sub rosa. I don't regard marriage or, more important, love between two persons as being something to be circumvented when the desire of one person goes contrary to the desire or judgment of the other, by completing a transaction on the quiet and then announcing it. You knew I wouldn't approve. But you wanted to fulfill a whim more than to listen to me. And you feared that if you brought the matter up before you had your way you'd be argued or persuaded out of it. It seems to me that your love for me has holes in it." "I didn't want to hurt you. I just wanted a farm." "Well, you have it. You'll tire of it, probably. My point is that your love has holes in it. You have an affection for me, yes. You have a great sense of duty. You're sorry for me. But you don't trust me. You never have. I can't say why, whether it's the unhappy years we spent at first, whether you're too cold by nature, whether you just plain lack the perception to realize that as men and as husbands go you've got someone better than most women have. I don't know whether it's because I lack physical mobility or social mobility or what. Whatever it is, you underestimate the husband you have, and you fail to treat him with confident love. I'm not angry. I'm sad. And I'm a bit frightened at what can go on secretly in your mind, just like in Pearl's mind, and then come out."

Evelyn tells me that she loves me, admires me, doesn't want to hurt me. She's forty. She's wonderful to me, and I am fully aware of it, but I do not have faith in the wholeness of her love. Query: Does anyone love wholly? I don't know. I'm very downcast. Don't mean to sound melodramatic. Don't feel melodramatic. Feel, rather, the insubstantiality of human relationship, even the closest. Hope Janice doesn't end by sliding out of reach. She's about my last handhold on faith in humankind.

With the war entering its second year and after Hitler's Drang nach Osten, Arthur, in his Garrison Hall bunker, surveyed the international scene. Here was the United States siding with one eager gangster against another. Stalin's enormities outdistanced Hitler's. Communism was more to be feared than nazism, for it clashed less discordantly with America's national priorities. Duplicitous England, of course, played the tune Americans danced to. Churchill's rhetoric was persuasive; Lindbergh's honest but dull warnings were not. Was Arthur pro-Nazi, as

Juliette charged? Not really. He wanted Hitler to win because Arthur identified himself with all ruthless conquerors in history, because the thrilling spectacle of a nobody's rise to power encouraged his hopes that he too might someday dazzle his astonished enemies, and because he wanted to see England trounced before Churchill and the Jews pulled the United States into the fracas. But America was already enmeshed. Hitler, if he won, would surely make the United States his next target. The fortunes of the country — as well as those of Arthur — demanded that Hitler be defeated.

Yet Arthur strenuously condemned what he took to be Roosevelt's plan to instigate Japanese retaliation as a way of propelling the United States into a shooting war, and he angrily reported the administration's efforts to whip up anti-Axis sentiment. In anticipation of America's entrance, which he now believed was imminent, he began to hoard canned goods. His idea of collecting quarters for emergencies backfired when someone broke into his apartment and stole $200 of the cache stored in his bathroom. (Luckily an additional $100 worth concealed under sheets of toilet paper escaped the thief's notice.)

Arthur's premonitions of financial debacle and bombed cities affected his disposition and, indirectly, the lives of the Garrison Hall "characters." Satisfactory "talkers" became scarce. Billy grew touchier and asked for more time off. Rising household expenses necessitated dunning letters to the "Old Man." Evelyn, in his eyes as stubborn and blundering as ever, was insufficiently contrite and refused to curb her erratic disposition.

Among the many candidate talkers Arthur interviewed at this time, one man in particular appeared promising — the fat and loquacious "fixer" George Dicey, soon to figure prominently in the Diary as paid agent for Arthur's undercover activities. Dr. Lakian ("Fred") also became a frequent caller. Fred was Arthur's chief stomach pumper, supervising an operation sometimes described in nauseating detail.

Arthur tried to soft-pedal his complaints, but by November he could no longer hold back. Added to the indignities of eye strain and coccyx pains were the horrid noises of Huntington Avenue traffic. The cacophony intensified in spite of Billy's and Evelyn's urging the politicians to slow down the rush of cars with signs and traffic lights. Unable to sleep and driven frantic by noise, he dosed himself with pills and was out for forty hours. Arthur's attempt to kill himself cost the Garrison Hall family a good deal of time and trouble but left the would-be suicide spiritually refreshed. Not long after, bombs fell on Pearl Harbor.

August 16   It may be that we are in a secret alliance with Soviet Russia, for all we know. In any case, no one can deny that the

Administration has obligated us to a moral alliance with Soviet Russia and with Joseph Stalin. It is an alliance with an autocrat and a scoundrel beside whose deeds the aggressiveness of Hitler, however much woe and desperation it may have caused, assumes a pallid hue. And this alliance in spirit and in action gives evidence, if such evidence were needed by now, that our rulers (they are our rulers) contend against Hitler primarily not as a force of evil, not as a nation expanding ruthlessly at the expense of small nations (these qualifications fit Soviet Russia more justly than they do the German Reich), but because the British rulers and the internationally frightened Jews have wished us patently and skillfully into our present attitude.

None of the Eastern states have heeded the pleas for a reduction in gasoline consumption save New England. The amount of gas sold to retailers is now to be cut by ten percent. Billy says: "God, I hate that Ickes. They can shove me around any other way they want, but I get hot when they touch my car. My car's the most important thing in my life. I could shoot Ickes. I could go to Washington and bump off that damn Roosevelt, and it wouldn't take much to persuade me either — I'm that sort of guy. Gasoline to England. And now gasoline to Russia. I tell you, it's not right."

August 18   It is a mystery why Janice likes Bertram Davis so much, save that every Yankee girl of her walk in life feels that she has lost face if she hasn't a 'steady boy friend.' I haven't known a single person who has met him to have a complimentary word to say about him.

He doesn't sound like the man for her, not to mention being an ardent Catholic and having a large Catholic family and being Irish to boot. Janice will read this when it comes time to typewrite it a couple of months or more from now and will wish I hadn't written what may disturb her. It won't harm her, I hope, to read in print what I'm sure she senses I feel, and I am honest about what I say. I love her and don't want to lose her, and I don't think Bertram Davis is the man to be her husband.

August 20   Evelyn left this morning. As always, I feel as though my light had gone out when she departs. Am in love, there's no doubt of it. Wish had five wives as long as I didn't have to keep them sexually satisfied. Ought to be easy to choose wives not highly sexed. I should say that not more than one-third of the women of the United States cares particularly about sex of itself. Another third is indifferent. The last third is antipathetic.

August 21   In the north, Leningrad is being more closely invested daily. It doesn't look too good for the Russians. No British, no Americans have been allowed by the Soviets at their front. While

Stalin has consented to a convention of Americans, English, Russians at Moscow, he seems to be in no hurry to have the caucus take place. His shrewd peasant mind, it is abundantly evident, still doesn't trust the English. And why should it? Hasn't he seen with his own eyes what has happened to practically all British allies? The English and the Americans are planning on a long resistance by Stalin. Why does that have to be? He is a realist and an Oriental realist to boot. If things go too badly against him, would he not have more to lose by continuing an adverse war that might eventually cost him his throne than he would by giving Hitler what he wants in return for peace and for the retention of his throne? We shall see.

August 23   One of the magazines — perhaps it was the 'New Yorker' — remarked that the heads of our Government never appeared in photographs without smiles. That would be reassuring if they didn't smile so much. Government attitude does seem wrong. When Senator Byrd seriously and sincerely challenges the progress of the American war effort, Roosevelt is off-handed, inaccurate, flippant in his response as though replying to a naughty child. The Administration's contempt for the public is every day apparent. We are the cows to be driven, stalled, milked at pleasure, and no one of us is as wise as our masters.

The failure of Germany to 'blitz' Russia into subjection has given heart to many rebels among the subject peoples. There are riots and sabotage in nearly all countries under German rule, and strong measures are being taken to combat the unrest. There are no ruthless and efficient mass killings such as were indulged in by Tamerlane, to leave depopulation and ruin, and hence acquiescence, behind. Only the subjection of England will secure to Hitler his conquests.

August 25   Churchill has made another of his speeches. He is what the English would call "deucedly clever" with his words in the unremitting way in which he includes the United States with England. In the event of the United States having trouble with Japan "we shall of course range ourselves unhesitatingly on the side of the United States," which means that, if there is trouble in the East we shall expect the United States to do its part. In his sly way Churchill is continually telling us what to do, formulating our policies. Another campaign to get us into the war is being launched. If Russia falls, says Churchill, attempting to save us, Britain may not be able to hold out, in which case Hitler "will settle his account — and it is already a long one — with the people of the United States and generally with the Western Hemisphere."

September 1   The Second World War is two years old today. It feels to me as though it had been going on forever. Unless Germany subdues Russia before the ice and snow, Germany's chances of winning will be so diminished as not to be worth betting on. The key mistake made by Germany was made, I think, when the fall of France was not immediately followed up by an invasion of England.

Two evenings ago had a long talk with Evelyn about being more affectionate and responsive with me. Told her that even if she didn't love me, acting affectionate would repay the effort. Said she did love me. Replied that if she did, which I knew with my head, what harm to evidence it by not constantly being aloof or withdrawn? Said that she thought maybe she had intrinsically a jealous nature and that perhaps what I called her coldness was merely her attempt not to mind how much fuss I made over other women. Told her I liked her more than other women and wished she would believe me, that some of the reason I sought affection from them was because she withheld it. Cited the Bert girl and how she had been the straw that broke the camel's back. Told her that Bert had been a mere passing incident. Said was no incident to her. Well, we talked and talked. Yesterday she was perfect. Made little gestures of affection, didn't draw away when a whim touched her or through lack of tact. Could fall headily in love with her if she would continue to use primary rules of how woman should be with man to get her own way. Practically anyone who is attractive can captivate me, and certainly Evelyn should be able to lay me low with a minimum of effort.

September 4   Ella endured an unpleasant vacation. It was unusually hot in Virginia. All the fat relations insisted on kissing her. She went to the orphanage party and got sore feet standing up for hours. She pulled corn and developed a rash from the silk. She stayed at Robert's mother's house and refused to go to the filthy, uncared-for outhouse and was constipated until she fell ill. The flies on the food disgusted her so that she couldn't eat. Five of Robert's relations were in an automobile accident and two were killed. A sister fell ill to death and Ella had to run back and forth sixty miles to nurse her. And no one would leave her alone.

Have just finished an unusual novel, 'The Black Fox Walks' by a writer of whom I have never heard, Edwin Sarsfield. It is about Ireland and the Irish and the Irish Republican Army and the Black and Tans. Never read a book setting forth more neatly, and I think truly, the character of the 'wild Irish,' their droll whimsicality, their reckless physical bravery, their cruelty, their unreliability, their moral lechery, their almost fanatical resentment against overlord-ship and control, their disorder and their lack of stability. To read this book is to understand much in American political life that might otherwise seem reasonless.

September 11 I do hope that the Germans, if they are to meet with eventual defeat, will give a final coup-de-grace to the Russians and to the Communist dream before that happens. If not it would have been far better for us in America had Hitler won.

The nature of the American people, or so I feel, can withstand the infiltration of the Nazi ideology far more efficiently than that of the Communist ideology. The tenets of Christianity prepare us for an easy acceptance of the doctrines of brotherhood of the Communists, as does our long inurement to the promissory lies of our politicians. There is a natural antagonism in most of us to the Nazi out-and-out manifesto of force that is not present against the talk-one-way-act-another course of the Communists. We Americans are fundamentally antagonized when a spade is called a spade. Better a million homicides with the crime disclaimed than a hundred homicides with the crime admitted without proffered excuse or reason. We do not seem to have any basic objections to the criminal acts of states or individuals so long as a tenable gloss surrounds the acts or the persons who commit them or why they are done. The unmitigated starkness of crimes, rather than the crimes themselves, disturbs us. We crave, therefore, palatable reasons why, acceptable vindications.

In all respects the Communist dogmas seem less foreign to our natures than the Nazi conventicles. Which makes them the more dangerous to our system of life. Wherefore I am convinced that a complete Russian victory would, in the end, threaten our well-being in America more than a complete German victory. We will come out of this orgy of spending, this dislocation of our economic and social coordination, at the least weakened, when we will be as a tired man, open to attack by infection, in this case the virus of Communism.

September 13 Dr. Pike came to fix the cartilage in my gullet that one of the many applicants for the job had dislocated when attempting to give me a neck treatment. He said: "Have you anything to eat? I'm out on my feet." Janice fed him cheese and crackers. He puts everything into his cavernous mouth that it will hold. "Love cheese," he said. "What's the trouble, Arthur?" When he was done, I thanked him for the vegetables he sent me the other day and for having been so nice to Evelyn during the summer. "It's a real pleasure to have Evelyn," he said. "She enjoys the country. She's fun to watch, too. Just like a little girl in lots of ways. Get a great kick seein' what she'll do next. Fine sense of humor."

September 21   When I feel as hopelessly sunk as I do today, then is when I miss Honey most. She would pat me on the head, make the pillow comfortable behind my back, see that I had water to drink in my bottle, not ask a thousand and one inane questions, not get rattled if I was short-worded or brusque. "You sit right there and rest, Artie, and Honey'll do everything. See, she'll fold up your coat nicely, get your radio for you, make sure that nobody disturbs you. It's just too darn bad Honey's Artie has to feel this way, and all he has to do is to relax and know that Honey will take care of everything. That's the boy — take a big breath and relax. That's what Honey's here for, to see that you get taken care of. Never mind telling me what you want for lunch. I know pretty well. And I know you don't want any melon today; you're too tired. I'll just leave you alone awhile. I'll be back in fifteen minutes. If you want anything then, just say so. If you don't, keep quiet and I'll understand. Honey's sorry her Artie feels so badly. Really she is." Then she would deliver a moist kiss of sympathy on my forehead or my hand and go out the door so softly you couldn't hear it close. And I would feel taken care of. And this isn't an imaginative concoction based on sentimentality; it is word-for-word what took place.

There is, I am thinking, a finality to the memories of those who have died or to those who have passed for good and all out of your further cognizance that is as reassuring in its own way as what has happened in the pages of a book when you have shut the covers. The plot has been enacted. The character or characters have done what they have done, said what they have said, and no epilogue can by its unexpectedness put into altered perspective a close sequence. Reflecting upon Jennie, for instance, gives me a particular satisfaction in that the story has been told, finished, ended. In my mind is a completed drama. I know what I know, and only my imagination can add light or shadow to what I know. The character of the heroine cannot suddenly assume new guise, be deflected this way or that by contemporary currents. It is finished, and what I recall is intensely private to my mind alone, an etching on which none can modify lines.

September 25   Enjoyed Woody. "Yes sir," I said, "you're my particular and unique wild woman. There's nobody in my repertoire exactly like you. I'm awfully glad I met you. When was it I met you?" "Oh, go on with you. I think it was in 1928 — or was it 1927? A long time, anyway." "Think of all the traveling you've done since then. How old are you now?" "Thirty-nine. I'll be forty next March, forty and married (if I don't change my mind) and fat. Feel my ring." "Not very big." "Say, of course it's big. You don't want me to wear a walnut, do you, Arthur? Everybody at the office asks me about it, and I tell nobody; they're dying to know." "So you're really going to get married at last? When?" "I don't know that either. It just seems the next step." "Do you know yet whether you love Allan?" "No. How can I be sure? I suppose I do." "Do you intend giving up your job?" "No." "Why not?" "Because (why do you insist on probing me?) — because, my tireless inquisitor, because I don't know whether the marriage will be a success or not. How can I know, when I don't even know whether I love the man? I'd be foolish to give up my job, wouldn't I? Now wouldn't I?" "Why should you marry at all if you're unsure?" "Because I'm a cold and calculating woman. It always comes right back to giving Peggy a name. I had such a horrible time not having a father when I was growing up — and it's hung over me like a shadow ever since — that I don't want Peggy to endure the same thing. Not if I can help it by taking a chance. You see, I fixed everything for Peggy except a birth certificate, but I didn't fix that. The least I can do for the scamp is to get a name for her. Each time I grow angry with Allan (and I get plenty angry many times), I restrain myself just before arriving at the point where he'd walk out with a 'To hell with you.' I'll go through with the marriage and I'll hope it will work out, but I'm not at all certain it will. And that, Arthur, is why I'm hanging on to my job."

September 27 Evelyn took me riding in the yards. Her interest in what she sees is catholic and unfailing. She sees as much as, possibly more than I do. She becomes so carried away with a pile of lumber, a stack of tiles, a pigeon flying, how a man is washing car windows that she forgets she is driving and the car commences to yaw. "Watch where you're going," I yell. It is an experience to drive with Evelyn when we go slowly (she does better when moving faster), and I sometimes expect to come back in a bag after having hit something. It constitutes a variety of excitement I don't yearn for.

September 30 [From Patricia:]

I had a very nice letter from Ted, I thought I should tell him about my marrying again. And he was very sweet about it. But insisted that if things had been a bit different we could have made a success of our marriage, and I suppose in a way we could have, but it was his own fault that I left, he asked me to, and I was willing to go back to him until he changed his mind again. I hadn't the knowledge to handle Ted, tho I did have the patience. I think my life has been much better the way it is. I know how to handle Paul, I stand no nonsense from him and it pays. Once they get the upper hand you are sunk, not that I intend to be a shrew, but I demand respect and politeness and consideration and by golly I get it. I didn't demand enough from Ted, I just gave, but I've learned my lesson now. Paul has to do his share, and I'm not going to try to make things easy for him. I want him to have to struggle, then he will appreciate every thing he earns.

I know Paul must be in love, he thinks I'm beautiful! And you know that by no stretch of the imagination can I be called that. And he is spending his hard earned money on long distance telephone calls. He called me last night to tell me that he loved me and missed me and how much did I love him? You'd think we were a couple of high school youngsters to hear us, and I love it. I love the flowers and the telegrams and the ridiculous gifts he keeps sending me, and the planning and the quarrels, oh, yes, we still have them. We got along beautifully for three days and then twenty minutes before his bus left we started. Because I disagreed with him! He was so amazed, he thought that because I said I'd marry him I'd agree on every thing he said, and does he know better now! I told him that just because I was a wife didn't mean that I ceased to be a person, and that I'd fight to the last drop of the hat if I felt that I was right. Paul has a habit of calling people who see things in a different light than he does "narrow minded", and I took him up on it. The poor lamb thinks that married life is going to be all sweetness and light, and that we are going to set an example for all marriages to come. And is he in for an awakening! But I'm glad he is taking it seriously, tho for a man in his thirtys Paul is singularly naive. I don't want to rub the bloom off him too quickly, but he'll come too in time. He is a few years younger than I, as you doubtless suspected, but it doesn't make any difference to him and it doesn't bother me a bit. Since I was never a glamour girl I don't have to worry about losing my looks, and since I've used so little makeup all my life I'm not a shock with my face "as is". In fact I look rather nice all scrubbed up and ready for bed.

Arthur, I loved your new book, I was so delighted with it that I wanted to announce to all the world that I knew you. I haven't read it all yet, because I couldn't resist lending it to a few kindred spirits, and I just got it back. It's too much to digest in a few hours, I want to wallow in it. Thank you so much and thanks too for the inscription.

October 6   Fred visited for a while before and after pumping the goo from my stomach. He went, he said, to the University of Kansas and then to the Osteopathic College in Topeka. No one could be more gentle with me than he is. He and Billy, while I am being pumped, discuss interestedly what is coming out through the tube. "Lumps, Arthur," says Fred. "Isn't that so, Billy?" "Yes it is. And green. Say, I've never seen it worse." "That's the migraine," explains Fred. "Yeah," says Billy, "but now it's a bit better in color, don't you think?" "I should say so," agrees Fred. "It just takes time. Are you comfortable, Arthur?" "Sure," I murmur. "Then we can do a good job," says Fred. I do believe that the pair enjoy the business. I am sure that they enjoy doing it well.

When I read 'Buddenbrooks' and note that Mann was no older when he wrote it than I was when I wrote Volume 11 [1922] and compare his maturity of viewpoint and style with my immaturity, I feel resentfully dissatisfied that I remained youthfully undeveloped for so long and envious of his early stature. It takes a deal of self-control not to delete those passages which exhibit me in my most unprepossessing private aspect, and I have to hold hard to the conviction that one of the principal virtues of a diary lies in its unedited honesty, no matter how unpalatable that honesty is in retrospect. I am not a brilliant person, though I am an earnest one, and I have undergone severe growing pains in reaching maturity. It may be that those growing pains will be of as much interest should this work ever achieve publication as the more level and substantial portions of my existence. I shall proceed on that assumption anyway and resist the temptation to annul and expurgate.

October 7   Father arrived, a little more bent in the upper part of his back but otherwise looking well. He told me ten or fifteen of his traveling salesman jokes. He said he thought Roosevelt honest. He told Evelyn and me of how he and Mother had met Mr. and Mrs. Howard at Saratoga on their wedding trips and how Laura Howard and Mother had started a contest to see who could drink the most water from the Congress Spring. "That," concluded Father, "wasn't any water to have a contest on. George and I stopped them quick, I can tell you." Then he laughed until he shook. He makes very little noise when he laughs.

He calls me "Frank" more often than he does "Arthur," said he had no idea how old I was. I try to bear in mind that he's only an aging old man with a diamond stickpin and small unimaginative eyes and a whitening moustache and that he's more that than he is my Father. He told me of having a long conversation with T. Roosevelt in the Yosemite and of his dynamic personality, and of another conversation with Harding in Florida.

October 9   Another new man, a character in his own right, came to talk with me after Millicent left. His name is George R. Dicey. He is not working at present, being under care of a clinic in order to remove weight. He has lost eighty pounds and now weighs only two hundred and sixty. He is thirty-two years of age with a voice younger than that and words which flow from him as though by the very impetus of mental and emotional ebullience. "My make-up," he writes in his letter of application, "is such that I really like to have people know of things about which the most of them never would come to know. The ability to relate my experiences in such a manner as to be of interest to my listener is I feel sure one of my strong points." He says that he has "an inquiring mind," and to listen to him certainly verifies his statement. Everything interests him. He has ideas on everything. He owns a regular system of come-on chatter by which he draws people out. I should say that the chances are in favor of his amounting to something out of the ordinary someday. He has had an interest in a small company making college jewelry. He has studied law and engineering. He has been an assistant executive director of adult education. He has done some writing and some public speaking. Right now he is interested in the politics of New England and is considering how he can use what he knows in some sort of writing. He is convinced that old Cardinal O'Connell practically rules Boston and the seaboard of New England.[9] More about Dicey later, I am sure.

October 16   Dicey talked with me again last evening. He dabbles in politics with all the zest of a small boy watching the snakes at the zoo wriggle and squirm, only he is not at all persuaded of their reptilian aspect. His eager chatter of graft, double-dealing, internal conflict over public plunder, lying and cheating and deceit and mendacity in political circles is the more appalling for the cheery way he mulls the aspects of his subject in his complacent mind. Oh yes, he is willing to admit that an aggregation of honest men could govern any community in a manner to benefit the people to the point of perfection, that there is really no need for graft and war and inordinate taxation except that men are dishonest in practice. But the concept that men will ever be different never enters his head. He is an interested realist with a "terrific" (his favorite word, used once

---

[9] Whether or not Cardinal William Henry O'Connell (1859–1944) actually "ruled" Boston and the New England seaboard in 1941, he was considered dean of the Roman Catholic hierarchy in the United States and a powerful social and political force. Elevated to the cardinalate in 1911 with a well-deserved reputation as an organizer, he steadfastly opposed theological modernism, new scientific theories, and "radical" economic and political programs of all sorts.

or twice in each sentence) curiosity and an eye cocked toward some opportunistic door or other that will eventually open to permit him to use the low-downs he has aptly gathered. Meanwhile, he refers to all "the boys" by their first names and to himself and a problematical group to which he is allied as "we." There are many things Dicey may or may not be, but he enjoys himself and his existence intensely.

October 18 I have been trying to read Montaigne on the talking-book. Find it on the whole thoroughly uninteresting. I wonder if the contents of an inquiring and replete mind of today will seem to an inquiring and replete mind of four hundred years from now as much of a hodgepodge as Montaigne's mind seems to me? Not necessarily, I am sure, for the minds of Caesar or Tu Fu, to choose at random, are not the cluttered attic that Montaigne's mind was. A dog emerging from the waters of Medievalism is the intellect of Montaigne, and his thoughts the drops thrown off by the energetic efforts of the dank creature to shake itself free of clinging constraint.

October 20 Some while ago, I had a volume of pictures of Roman faces from the library. High wide foreheads, ears set lower than our ears are set and usually not large. Aggressive Roman noses. A tendency toward weak chins, at least toward recessive chins, and full petulant lips. Men of a stubborn, active force. Men pleasuring in having their own way. Men born to bend circumstances as often through injured pride as because of conceived dream.

Somewhat idealized is the profile of Augustus on the sardonyx cameo in the British Museum but by and large truer to the impression of him that emerges from the events of his life than are some of the more sensitive or more florid heads elsewhere. High wide forehead. Sensitive yet commanding nose. Full magnetic eyes, low-set ears. Compressed full lips. Not a dominant chin but one set back, giving, as is often the case, a certain self-indulgent weakness to the physiognomy but indicative conversely of an additional stiffening of the will to endure. It is, withal, an imperial countenance.

October 21 Sometimes when I am correcting diary and being transported in thought to another stratum of time with its attendant phenomena, I am profoundly moved by the miracle of myself in 1941 engrossed in one existence, being able to so lose myself in 1922 that the present diminishes about me as though lights were being turned off and I am another man in another year, and what closely concerns me are the appointments and happenings, the persons and reactions of then. It is as if one had devoured one layer of cake and yet was able, while consuming another layer, to re-eat the eaten layer, savoring flavor and essence so reliably that only a narrow iota of insubstantiality remains to warn the same mind that what has been cannot in facsimile be again.

October 22   In Nantes, in occupied France, a German Lieuten-ant Colonel has been assassinated. Fifty 'hostages' have been shot by the Germans as retribution. Unless the assailants are turned over to the French or German authorities by the end of the week, fifty additional hostages will be shot. A reward equivalent to three hundred thousand dollars has been offered to persons who contrib-ute to the discovery of the assailants.

I know of no one who would more resent being highhandedly treated as a chattel of conquest than myself, and the manner in which the Germans have treated peoples their cultural equals if not their equals in might has incensed me against them more than much others have taken exception to. Yet how govern a conquered people to their satisfaction and not to your detriment?

October 24   "Clarence," announced Juliette, "has been making all kinds of money. His latest venture was buying six hundred sets of bowling pins at six dollars a set and holding them till the price rose to eighteen dollars a set."

Here is the conclusion of Juliette's affair with Dr. John Sillitoe. Her Uncle Samuel fell ill. They sent him to the hospital. Her mother couldn't find out what was the matter with him. Pauline [Juliette's sister] works at the hospital. Dr. Sillitoe saw her one day, stopped to talk with her. She told him about her uncle. He volunteered to ascertain his trouble. He did so and telephoned Mrs. Stern. When he had finished speaking with her, he asked for Juliette. It was the first time he had bothered her since he had made a promise to leave her alone. He told her he loved her and missed her and wanted to warn her that his wife, Gail, had threatened to "get her." She made him promise not to call her again. It so happened that while he was calling her, his wife called him at the hospital and was told by the operator, upon request, the number he was calling. He telephoned Juliette later in the afternoon and explained what had happened and that his wife had given him hell and had sworn to kill Juliette and to telephone Clarence, that she was all but mad.

That afternoon Clarence did receive a call. A woman's voice said: "Keep your goddamn wife out of doctors' offices." That was all. When Clarence saw Juliette next, he told her, saying that he recog-nized Gail Sillitoe immediately. Juliette explained what the doctor had told her about his wife. The next day Gail called Clarence and apologized for the anonymous invective. She then told him that her husband was in love with Juliette, that they went out together, and so on. She named dates. The dates happened to be times when Clarence was with Juliette himself. He told her that he would be happier and she would be happier if they fostered no such foolish suspicions. He ordered her to cease interfering with his family affairs. He promised Juliette would never again see her husband. She threatened to kill herself and Juliette. Later in the afternoon, the doctor telephoned Clarence and denied whatever allegations his wife might have made. He swore to Clarence that Juliette, with whom he admitted he was in love, was innocent. "I guess he was afraid of Clarence," commented Juliette. "He crawled abjectly on the phone."

Clarence took Juliette in the car to a secluded spot and talked with her. "I know," he said, "that some people have been thinking me very dumb. I know that John Sillitoe loves you. He told me so. I have my own thoughts as to whether or not you may have been indiscreet with him. I love you and have built my life around you. I consider whether or not you have been indiscreet to be of less importance than to keep you as my wife. I don't want to know whether or not you've been indiscreet. It's one of those things a man is better not to know of his wife. The affair is ended. I don't want to hear your side of it. I don't want to know anything more. You are to stay away from John Sillitoe, and there the matter ends as far as I am concerned."

"Arthur," Juliette said to me, "I was ashamed of myself. It was a new sensation. I wanted to tell Clarence all. I told him so. He said: 'I warn you that if you tell me what I don't want to hear, as much as it may hurt me I'll leave you and never come back.' So I didn't tell him. Isn't he wonderful, Arthur? Oh, he's so perfect in all ways except sexually. Why can't he be perfect that way as well? Sex is about the most important part of my life. I'm miserable if it isn't fulfilled. And he can't fulfill it. He handles sex as if he were filling an order in his factory. That isn't the way sex should be expressed. It isn't what I want. And whether you believe me or not, Arthur, I haven't any desire to cheat on Clarence. He's too fine. But I must be satisfied. And he can't do it. I'd rather have just one man. You know I don't want to go with more than one man if one man can satisfy me, don't you? But I can't guarantee, whatever my intentions are now, that there won't come a time when I'll cheat again. It's something bigger than me. It's something irresistible. I don't want to be this way, but I am. Sex is the most important thing in life."

October 26 Unless a miracle happens, it would seem that Russia's days as a dangerous opponent of Nazi expansion are numbered. With the production facilities of the Ukraine and the Donetz Basin in German hands, with the production output of the Leningrad area segregated, with the production capacity of the Moscow area threatened and, at least in part, disorganized, and with the only large production still in operation east of the Ural Mountains, it would appear inevitable that the loss in mechanized armaments and in ammunition will be irreplaceable in quantity, thus necessarily depleting the fighting strength of whatever Soviet forces will be left in the field when and if the Germans are done for the winter.

As for receiving matériel from England and America. In the first place, if, as is claimed by the English Government, the British are too weak in equipment to invade the continent, of what valid assistance will the little they can spare to Russia be to that hard-pressed country? Not much, I suspect. Archangel is icebound during much of the winter. Vladivostok is so far from the scene of operations that goods shipped through it must, of necessity, be comparatively few and slow of delivery. Seizure of the Donetz Basin severs all direct rail communications for supplies routed through Persia and the Caucasus to Moscow. Russia has announced a cessation of the delivery of matériel to China. The most capable Soviet general has been shifted from Moscow to the South, denoting that Stalin expects the chief theatre of war to be there.

October 29   [From Patricia:]

This business of trying to marry a service man is getting me down. First he is going to be discharged at the end of his year. Then he is going to be discharged on December 10th. Then he is going to be discharged on November 15th, and I'm going wacky trying to wrestle a trouseau together and do a bit of wrangling for time off. Now he isn't going to be discharged at all, subject to change, and damn the Germans and the Japs and the Russians, what do they mean by upsetting my private life. But come hell or high water I'm going to get married. I've had a hundred Christmas cards ordered for Mr and Mrs Paul Bowe and I will not have such tricks played with my budget. So if you get a Christmas card along about February think nothing of it, thems my announcements.

Paul and I had planned to take a little apartment when he was released, and I still think I'll go ahead with those plans. He will need some place to come on his leaves. And tho he is most welcome here it isn't quite the same as being in a place of our own. Paul will be down the first day of November, he is going to get me a set of tires for a birthday gift, and he wants to buy them himself, I always get gyped on tires. Everytime that Paul comes down I go about in a daze and come to about Tuesday, when I've had a chance to catch up on lost sleep. It's lovely, but slightly wearing when you have to sandwich your sex life between split shifts at the Pig n' Whistle.

The last time Paul was down we spent five hours looking at model homes and had the grandest time. Time was when Paul dreamed about setting the world on fire, now all he wants is a good matress and box spring. Those army cots aren't exactly luxurious. The army life has certainly taken my young man down a peg, he has come to be not only content, but to long for an ordinary life. I don't want to be married to a man who wants to make a lot of money. I'd rather cook and sew and clean and garden and be thought a wonderful manager than to have servants and a big house. I want five rooms, a fireplace in my living room, a barbeque pit in the back yard, a badminton court in the driveway, a lot of trees, and ruffled curtains. I want to hook my own rugs and re-paint the furniture when I'm in the mood, and have mid-night snacks and buffet suppers on Sunday nights. I want gobs of sheets in the linen closet and a shoe box for my shoes. Smelly soap and bath salts for the bathroom and big fat towels. Why on earth do people want to be rich? Perhaps they've never discovered what fun it is to do things for one's self.

Arthur, you don't know what you miss by not being able to go shopping in the five and ten. I just go hog wild, they have the darndest things, you can equip a kitchen in one of them. I'm even going to buy some dishes there as the ones you get in furnished places are so unimaginative. I'm going to get plain white pottery service plates, and use colored accessories. I love a riot of color for informal meals. I like color in everything but sheets, there I'm all for pure white ones. When I get a place for Paul and me you are going to be bored to death with descriptions of each and every gadget, but you asked for it.

October 30 Dicey is a walking encyclopedia of the misdemeanors and delinquencies of men. He is convinced that ingenuity and pull get people places, not necessarily their particular gifts or merits. "Touch the right button and you can reach any man or make any man or ruin any man." I asked him if he would be interested in trying to place a book for me. He said that he would. He knows the owner of Houghton Mifflin, admires the salesmanship of Random House, feels that I ought to approach Mrs. Lars Anderson, backer of so many arts and artists. I loaned him a book to read. "I can't do anything till after the election." He's a persuasive talker, and I happen to interest him. "By gosh," he says, "you certainly have ideas of your own, and sometimes there's something back of them. It's terrific. You make me think. I've remembered you every day I've been away." All of which may or may not be blarny. As an entrepreneur he should be "terrific."

October 31   Evelyn and Dr. Pike bagged no birds, enjoying, however, the walk through the autumn woods. Evelyn was invited to his house for dinner. He was in a reminiscent mood and told her of his African trip and of how he had casually pushed a chief's son to one side in his hurry to go to where he had been told there was game and of how the chief's son and his party had trailed the safari for days, shaking spears and ejaculating invectives, before, by a show of rifles ready to shoot and some bluffing, he had finally shaken them. He told Evelyn that he had been afraid then. The trip across Africa must furnish him with many memories to call on when he needs them. A man, to have successfully completed such a jaunt at the time when Dr. Pike did it, might feel himself justified as a competent male animal capable of caring for himself when on his own and in another environment, a most satisfying self-assurance, one which must have been like a shadow of encouragement walking in step with him from then on.

November 2   I have been enjoying myself, despite a night thronged with spectral murders and phantom fights and blazing arson. Yesterday afternoon I listened to the Army-Notre Dame game, and that was exciting. Last evening I read Baker's 'Tiberius,' and that was more exciting.[10]

November 4   Am nearing the end of Volume 12 [1922] and thank God it is so, for the close perusal of what I wrote hasn't added to my self-esteem. I have no objection to confessions artistically set down, but I find myself ashamedly rejecting inartistic thoughts and events inartistically expressed. I have, in this volume, taken the liberty of deleting perhaps a page worth of stuff on the grounds that it is so ill-expressed or so needlessly raw or so defiantly violent that it tends to blur the picture and repel the reader to an extent where a hundred 'good's' will not offset the few 'bad's.'

November 5   Evelyn said: "I've been putting my mind on various problems. There's Woody, for instance. I'm perfectly sure she shouldn't marry that Allan. He may look boyish, but when you come right down to it, he's as old as you are and he's not boyish; he's a typical businessman with a leaning towards comfort and drinks and girl shows and smoking and lack of imagination. He's no more fitted to cope with Woody than my cat is. And that's why she's constantly annoyed with him. The more subtle elements of being alive don't even touch him. Anyway, I don't believe she really wants to marry him; it is simply a means to acquire a birth certificate for

---

[10] George Philip Baker's *Tiberius Caesar* (1928), a readable biography of a complex and controversial figure by one of Arthur's favorite historians.

Peggy. Not that one person in a hundred would ask for Peggy's birth certificate or think about it or care if it wasn't available. She had a bad experience growing up without a father, and she doesn't want Peggy to be at a like disadvantage. Now this is my latest idea. Why don't you tell your new friend Dicey about the situation and ask him if, say for a hundred dollars, he could pull strings and obtain a birth certificate for the daughter of a close friend of yours? There's no reason it mightn't be done. You try it, will you please? I don't want Woody getting into a situation which is pretty sure to end up a mess. I'm going to see her tomorrow and tell her what I think."

November 6   Dicey. I asked if he could obtain a birth certificate for the child of a friend of mine. "Provided it isn't for any purpose which will tangle up with the F.B.I. I have a respect for those boys. If it's a 'green-light case,' certainly I can get the certificate. It's not as difficult as obtaining a permit for a man to carry a gat. It'll cost between a century and a century and a half—no more. There won't be any kickback when it's done, either. I never double on a customer. If everything runs off as usual, I could have it in ten days after setting the wheels going."

This Dicey is a character. His business, besides being an entrepreneur, is what he calls "legitimate grafting." "No bones about it. I study human nature and its weaknesses and profit thereby to the extent of my shrewdness. I'm not honest, if you will. I'd just as soon raise my hand and say 'So help me God' and then lie as eat a meal, and think no more of it. I'm not a criminal—get this distinction—I'm a legitimate grafter. There's money in it and power and excitement and very little danger of having to pay the piper. That's all poppycock; people like me seldom get caught."

One night when Dicey was twenty-one, he was sitting in the municipal court listening to Judge Adlow[11] trying a young fellow for adultery. The sentence was two and a half years. Dicey was sitting in a chair later thinking about the case when the Judge came by. "Listen, you," said Dicey, "what business did you have giving that chap two and a half years? Why didn't you commute his sentence and place him on probation? Or why didn't you give him three months and let it go at that? Why you goddamn sanctimonious

---

[11] Elijah Adlow (1896–1982), Boston legislator, jurist, and author, retired in 1973 as chief justice of the Boston Municipal Court after forty-five years on the bench. During his tenure he was praised for his humane interference with the letter of the law and damned by his many critics for bringing the judiciary "into public disrepute." Adlow's unconventional outbursts against coddling criminals, decisions of the superior courts, and city politics entertained spectators ("back benchers," he called them) and made lively copy for reporters.

hypocrite, I know all about you and your housekeeper mistress and how many years you've practiced adultery on her. What about that?" "Well," explained the unruffled Judge, "it's this way. Nobody can get me. My robes protect me. And anyway, a warrant can't be sworn out against me unless I okay it, and you know what chance there is of that. As to that young fellow I sentenced for two years, it was his bad luck that he was caught. Don't you know that I don't pass judgment on people because they're guilty or not guilty but because they're caught. Remember that and everything will look clearer to you." Dicey says that that was the turning point of his life. If other people could practice to their advantage behind immunity of one sort or another, why shouldn't he? He decided that he would order his life so that he could.

From then on Dicey has painstakingly collected all material — clippings, documents, ascertained facts, verified rumors — in a large filing system arranged in a double rotating flexible code. He spends, so he says, some four hours a day mulling over in his mind what he has learned the day before and bringing his file up to date.

Dicey has no morals, no conventions, no scruples save where his friends are concerned. "I'll say this for myself: I've never let a friend or a customer down. I'm proud of that. As for the people who aren't my friends, that's another story."

He has three ambitions. He wants the power to make any group or anyone accept him perforce, whether they wish to or not, because of respect for his potential capacities. He wants to be able to lay hands on a moderate amount of money or its equivalent whenever he pleases without too much effort. He wants to have a myriad friends in all walks of life so that he will never have to remain in one circle.

Last week he and his friends threw a party at a hotel. It cost seventy dollars. When he asked that he be allowed ninety days to pay the bill and the owner refused, he reminded him of the unwarranted carelessness in conditions which had permitted a robbery to take place in one of the rooms last summer. In the end his party was "on the house."

Dicey came at nine, was due to leave at ten-thirty. He stayed until twelve. I enjoy him and to a limited extent feel in him a kindred spirit. I recognize the power that comes to one at times who has no respect for the keeping of conventions when they can be advantageously broken. Precisely what species of rogue he is I shall doubtless discover in time.

November 7 Stalin, in a speech, again urges the establishment of another front by Great Britain and the United States. Roosevelt has announced that he has arranged to give Russia a billion dollars under the Lend-Lease Act. It is being donated under such liberal terms that the United States will have practically no chance of ever recovering a penny.

Shades of war against Finland, the overwhelming of Latvia, Estonia, Lithuania, the filching of Bessarabia, the conquest of Mongolia, the killing off of White Russians, the starving of the Ukrainians into subjection, the decimation of those landowners who loved their land, the enslavement by the O.G.P.U. of millions of citizens to perish of cold hewing timber in the northern forests, in concentration camps, to die of malaria and fever digging canals. Is this Roosevelt a moron without historical perspective of any sort? Add up all Hitler's killings on the field of war and off it, and I doubt if they will equal the killings of Stalin off the field of war. I cannot understand Roosevelt and his accomplices. Have they no perspective whatever? Have they no patriotism? Are they so frenzied by the fear the Jews feel that their heads are lost?

November 10   Married eighteen years today. Sent my wife roses and have a box of big chrysanthemums coming later in the day. I love her deeply. I have seen in all these years no girl or woman I would rather have as wife than she. I recognize her faults and short-comings and accept them as parts of the final definition of her character rather than as insurmountable obstacles to fulfillment. I feel that I was most fortunate to marry Evelyn.

November 16   Mrs. Cash is helpful. I was able to halt noticeably her flow of obscenity and profanity by the counterirritant of sacrilegiousness (though why that should bother her I don't know) and a mutual agreement to cease what annoyed each other. I went to some pains to let her know in so many words what a help she had been, how I realized she shifted other dates in order to give me precedence, how grateful I was, how she made life easier for me by her reading, how good it was to have someone in this callous world of luxury on whose word you could count, and that when she soft-pedaled her dirt and her temper, how much I liked her.

November 19   Billy nailed a rug across the window side of the room last evening. I guess I was frantic, to put it mildly, more at the speed of the noise than at the noise. I thought a lot about death. I tried strangling myself to find out how it felt until I hurt my gullet and stopped. I rehid my pistol so that no one would abscond with it. More master of normal human emotions today.

When I become exceptionally aware of noises, my mind is as open to all aural impact and is as helpless to withstand it as the unclothed body stripped to sleet and snow and violent wind and with no house

wherein to retire from impinging forces. It is an unpleasant sensation. I suppose there are people who feel in their spirits the same
consuming human emotions and their inability to cope with them.
Each one of us, it seems, must exist within a cocoon of adjusted
habit, wrappings for the assailable individual consciousness, delicately and tremblingly fragile at best.

November 21   Nearly went wild yesterday. This morning the
Huntington Avenue traffic is heavier than it has ever been. As more
and more drivers find out about the underpass, the traffic will
steadily increase. I can't sleep with the roar of it after seven and the
whiz past of separate cars and trucks before that. My intelligence
tells me that living here, with my sensitivity to noise, will become
increasingly impossible. In simplest terms, the matter resolves to a
choice between two decisions — either kill myself and get out of all
the woe that is ahead for me in life, or to move to the Hemenway if
conditions there are as good relative to noises as Evelyn and Billy
seem to think they are.

As to killing myself, I'm still debating that. I don't think I could
bear to shoot myself in the head; it would have to be the heart. If I
took sleeping pills, they wouldn't work. A pistol, the only way. Still
dread a miscarriage of the act, resulting in injury. Still dread the
superstition that consciousness may endure after death, though
know that is silly. "When you die," says Mrs. Cash, "you simply rot,
and that's all there is to it. I'd like to believe otherwise, but I can't.
Any person who thinks is unable to believe in life after death. When
you die, you cease to exist."

I should not be afraid of killing myself. It is, I suppose, the crucial
pulling of the trigger that disturbs every natural instinct to remain
alive and functioning as much as the fear of the possibility of a
continued conscious existence. No it isn't. I know it isn't. What's
the pulling of a trigger? A final gesture requiring a certain nugatory
bravery of the kind I know I possess. When you look at it calmly,
there's no reason why I can't aim calmly and properly and pull the
trigger firmly. I'm tired of evading life like a panicked rabbit.

November 27   I have almost finished 'Broad and Alien Is the
World,' the novel about the Andean Indian community and their
collective and individual vicissitudes. It is, unless the ending collapses, an impressive volume somewhat on the order of 'Grapes of
Wrath,' a convincing portrayal of avarice and corruption and cruelty personified in the preying upon one class by another. The
author is Ciro Algeria, born in Peru, now living in Chile. He is only
thirty-two. Will this success spoil him?

November 29   So much has transpired during this last seven days that I scarcely know where or how to begin. That my handwriting has not changed in accordance with a great deal that is fundamental in my nature astonishes me. The currents of character must indeed run strongly that the handwriting, the features, the lines in the palm alter so negligibly. In a way it is reassuring; in a way it is not.

I think I finally made up my mind last Saturday at about 8:45 in the evening, told Mrs. Cash I didn't want to read longer, kissed Evelyn good night. At 9:45 I commenced taking sleeping pills. I can remember swallowing with water at five minute intervals seven 3-grain nembutol tablets and three 5-grain Veronal tablets. The schedule called for at least two more of the latter, but whether I took them or not I am unable to determine. Billy found me the next morning with an undissolved tablet in my mouth. I was out for forty hours. I regained consciousness (and a realization, vague but certain, that my efforts at self-destruction had failed) in a walled bed in what I was aware was a hospital. The first contact with the life I had striven to leave was Billy's moist hand which, I do not know how, I recognized.

At this moment I am in my sitting room at Garrison Hall and the script in front of me is shifting back and forth. There is a sharp constriction at my heart and not much strength in my legs, but in me is a composure and a cognition of myself as a valid person and a feeling of being a unified somebody such as never in all my years have I known before. With every thought and emotion I am glad that what happened transpired. I had rather died, but if I must live I am very nearly exultant that I made the thorough attempt to die. And why I have reacted in this I shall try to explain tomorrow or the next day or whenever I regain the strength adequate for clear expression of myself.

November 30   However melodramatically I may have experienced the process of matriculation toward my present mental and emotional stand, the conclusions, once reached, are flatly unmelodramatic. They are, in order of significance to myself:

1. I have had the courage (and make no mistake about it, it is courage) to step, in a manner from which I knew no reason at the time to expect otherwise, into the potentially pregnant mystery of death. I consider myself a finer, more worthy man for having evidenced such courage. Other trials of courage diminish in importance and measure accordingly.

2. I have ascertained at last, and in a degree calculated to satisfy me now and forever, that I hold a deep place in the hearts of more persons than I had dreamed and that this thing that is me is of

more importance to them than the money I command. The stigma attached to suicide is real in the United States, and dubious friends do not cleave to one who has attempted it. My friends did not run from me, did not even astringently criticize me, stayed by me. More than that, they expressed their feelings for me in moving words and acts. I must, I conclude, be not the paltry person my diffidence and the treatment of me by my parents and those at school had led me to feel.

All in all, I have come out of this experience with a new respect for myself as a man and as a person.

December 1   As to the reverse aspect of the picture. I naturally was aware when I entered into the venture in destruction what a shock it would be to at least some of those about me. Now that the attempt has been made and has failed, I as naturally regret the bootless concern and worry the attempt inflicted. The three persons closest to me in point of association and devotion, hence under the hardest strain, were Evelyn, Janice, Billy.

As to Evelyn. She has done herself proudly. Long ago she must have decided that I was in earnest as to my longing to go into oblivion and that when the time came, she would stand aside as much as possible and interfere to the minimum to block results. In this emergency, therefore, she acted with consistency and with a daring in my behalf that has impressed me as much in life has not. She left me without medical aid as long as possible, longer, Dr. Pike and Billy feared, than was judicious. She argued with the doctors the point that I wished to die and had little to live for, so why bring me back if leaving me alone would permit me to go. Then when advice against her course and the laws against letting anyone die had overruled her, she evinced judgment and tact in steering her way to clearer water again. She used her head. I was so touched and so proud and so pleased with her that a right-about-face in my attitude occurred. I am, as I have told her, without reserve or compunction and with all my heart, hers. I am grateful to my very boots. I see her as a newer, more complete person, diademed with a corona of admiration and respect and love. Not once did she berate me for my selfishness. Not once did she cry in front of me. Paramount for her was my interest, and not only my interest but the interest she felt I would want. She was magnificent. She arranged details. She contested this and that, fought for that and this. She answered telephones from Aunt Louise and wires from Granny and Father. She held herself intact against duress. And she did not cease to persist in my behalf because of self-pity or weariness or rebellion.

As to Janice. She, too, has surpassed herself. I can imagine that this thing jolted her perhaps more than it did Evelyn, for in some ways Janice is more dependent on me than Evelyn. Also, her conventionalities are more deeply based and fundamental. Hour after hour she sat in the dark with me exercising, I am sure consciously, the power she possesses to soothe and heal my spirit and to make me drop off into resting sleep. It was good to have her there, and as she says, she was stronger than she had any idea she could be. Last Friday and Saturday she was as wilted as a deflated bag.

I have a feeling that other complications at which I can only fumble are entering the scene now. Those complications have to do with Billy. He, too, has done well. He sat with me all Monday night at the hospital when I was coming to and fought with the nurse who was Catholic and therefore had a contempt for me. He stopped the Jewish doctor from pummeling me too hard in his attempt to bring me to. He encouraged me. He passed up voluntarily the two days' hunting trip. I don't know what I would have done without him. He made the rooms ready at the Hemenway, moved me back here. Commencing Friday, he began to wilt.

Of course, the shock to him was not pleasant, but I feel that more than that is involved. I sent some flowers to Sadie and a note of thanks for her generosity in doing without Billy, as I wanted to forestall a storm in that direction. It was, I fear, the wrong approach. The French one, and probably the Catholic Church, are at this moment doubtless digging the spurs into poor Billy, who is in so many ways a defenseless child. I don't doubt but that Sadie, who cried all day over me when they thought I would die, will end by getting Billy away from me. In that case I could doubtless find someone at long last to wait on me more efficiently than he does, but probably no one to fix my back and few persons with my interest more at heart.

And now I had best stop writing for the day. All the while I have been away, the United States and Japan have been coming closer to open warfare. The German and Russian tides sweep back and forth. The battle in Libya is still being waged and is still an unsure conflict. The world, I still conclude, is mad. It is in the toils of the great created octopus of machinery, and what will happen is dubious at best, horrible at worst. Oblivion would have been welcome to me, I think.

December 2 When Billy brought my breakfast Sunday morning, he couldn't wake me. He says: "I knew in an instant you'd taken the pills." He waited until 7:30 when he phoned Fred, who recommended a caffeine enema which Billy didn't give. I was lying there motionless, inert in the bed. At nine, Billy told Evelyn. She waited until eleven or so when she phoned Dr. Pike. He was away hunting but would be back within a few hours because it was raining. I had planned on Sunday because so few doctors are available. He returned about one. He told Evelyn that she would be held accountable if I didn't have medical assistance. He recommended a Dr. Blake. Dr. Blake came. He thumped me and hauled me, but I wouldn't waken. He called in a Dr. Isaacs. They said I would have to go to a hospital. Evelyn protested. They said that if she didn't consent, they would have to report to the Medical Examiner, and that then steps would be taken to make me go to a hospital. So Evelyn had me sent to the Phillips House, a branch of the Massachusetts General Hospital. In the meanwhile, the doctors had injected coromine, had pushed me for reactions, had moved me about to avoid pneumonia. In the hospital, a private room, they ran 2,000 c.c.'s of glucose into my ankles and arms. I showed no signs of stirring until Monday.

Dr. Pike stopped by a moment to say: "Don't let them try to sanitarium you, Arthur. There's no law can let them take you there against your will, and I'm behind you." Billy drew me a vivid word-picture of how Evelyn had endeavored to persuade the doctors to let me alone so that I could die as I wished. I felt a great tenderness mounting in me toward her. I did a large quantity of thinking while I was flat on my back or creeping around the big room in the dark to regain strength. I slept little. I could hear at night the heavy traffic whirling past, the exhaust pipe of the hospital power plant, the cries of newborn babies on the floor above me, the rattling of dishes in the serving room across the corridor, the whir of the electric refrigerator in the corridor, the words of people passing, the clipping of flower stems by scissors as nurses rearranged them outside my door, the drawing and emptying of water, the tooting of a boat at long intervals for the entrance to the basin to be opened. I was very afraid of what would happen to me at first, gained strength of purpose quickly.

December 3 I don't wonder I tried to bump myself off. This noise is almost unendurable to me. Less than three hours sleep last night. Am inside out with wildness this morning. Preparing another hegira to the Hemenway. There's much I don't like there, and it feels to me like a regular breeder of colds, so damp and drafty it is, but almost anything at this juncture, even being immured in the dark because of no way to combat snowlight, seems preferable to being kept awake from two to eight in the mornings, thus becoming conscious of a daytime noise I otherwise might forget. I'd rather be ill than be confined with unavoidable noise.

Later: At the Hemenway. The floor is drafty. There is air down on the shoulders. The light is abominable, hard, so that my eyes want to cringe away. I don't know. I don't know. I wish the doctors had let me die. There's nothing to life or living that equals the woe of carrying on. Those forty hours in which I was unconscious were bare of all the furniture of awareness, as dark and motionless to me as night without light and substance without form. It would be good to vanish from all consciousness forever. I wish I were dead. After taking the first two pills, the rest was easy, the will to live drowsy and the heart gradually lessening its staccato of fear. The whole affair, save for the hospital part, was no worse than a bad illness. I shouldn't be afraid to try again one day, should I?

December 4 Back at Garrison Hall. While the noise at the Hemenway at night is far less than here, the daytime rush along Hemenway Street is ten times more. It is an amazing spring day, blue sky, sea gulls whishing over the railroad yards, soft wind, mild warm sunshine. I am frightened of the future and of my increasing inability to contest noise. Evelyn is being wonderful. So is Janice. So is Billy. Billy volunteered that if I want to move to California, he would stay by me. I should think that by now they would all be pretty weary of my songs about noise. I am.

Millicent spent a couple of hours last night with me. She told me of how she had been attempting to catch pneumonia by getting hot, then standing without clothes in front of the open window. Life, she says, isn't worth living without Hal. She wants to die. I told her of the noise and pain. We became maudlinly sorry for ourselves and each other and exchanged tears for all of an hour. That should have calmed me but hasn't. Need sleep.

Millicent said that she would take my weakness, my hurtings, my sensitiveness to irritants and endure them cheerfully if thereby she could regain Hal. What, she asked, do physical sufferings amount to anyway? I said that I would be deprived of everyone I loved and like, of all my money, of any position I have held in the world, for surcease from physical debility. What, I asked, did mental suffering amount to anyway? So there you are. Her peace and happiness are to be formed in the merging of herself in someone else. Mine are to be found only in the withdrawal of myself to the secret fastnesses of the cave of myself. She wants to expand. I want to contract. When Hal died, she had her pointer killed. "Sandy," she said, "I'm sending you to your father to take him a special message from your mother. Find him for me, boy, and if there's any way for me to join him come back to me and guide me to him. You're so much wiser than we poor humans are, and you aren't afraid of death or any of the things we are. So find Hal for me, boy. Oh, find him for me." She sobbed. "But he never came back. I know he understood. But he never came back. He couldn't come back, I guess. Oh, Arthur, I'm so lonely, so dreadfully, emptily lonely."

December 7   A psychologist, a Dr. Brainard, is coming today to interview me. No faith in them as a class and many bitter memories but a conviction that should I ever be fortunate enough to locate a man smarter or more percipient than myself, I could be considerably assisted, though I doubt if anyone can effect a cure on an habitual nervous disorganization based upon inheritance, an unhappy youth and a basic inability to absorb the elements needed from foods. I dreamed last night that this new doctor turned up with a prescription made out before he had seen me (which he refused to explain) and a supercilious contempt for my ideas and assumptions.

Later: The Dr. Brainard has been here, asked me questions, is gone. It dispirits me, this being queried about my unprofitable past. Brainard seems to be a kindly young fellow. He says he doesn't know whether he can help me or not. Wants to talk with me once more. Why not? Nothing to lose, have I, save dollars? I told him I wished I didn't hurt so much, could sleep more with fewer nightmares, was not so weak.

Afternoon: Japanese dive bombers have today, suddenly and without warning, attacked the naval bases at Pearl Harbor, Hawaii, and at Manila. War has come to America. President Roosevelt's final appeal to Japan made to the Emperor direct, a really stately document, has been without avail. Our policy of economic blockade has borne one of the two fruits possible: capitulation or armed defiance. No more could a sovereign Japan yield to our demands to "get out of" China and forfeit voluntarily all the territorial gains accomplished through years of battle and sacrifice than would a sovereign United States have been willing to "get out of" its newly won Spanish territorial possessions in 1899 at the demand of, say, England.

I think that the whole procedure, or most of it, has been bungled, that is unless the underlying purpose of our policy was to force Japan into a war which, of course, it may well have been. Japan has been encircled and is in the process of being strangled. While war may not prove to be a way out of Japanese difficulties, it at least is a prideful expedient to take, one consistent with Japanese nature. If the British Commonwealth of Nations, the Netherlands Indies, China, the Russians in Siberia conjoin with the United States against Japan and retain a solid front, I cannot perceive, no matter to what heights of fury the war rises, how Japan can be victorious. The odds are too heavy; the Japanese nation is too tired. Another war and this time closer home.

Arthur's War and the Postbomb Years

1941–1951

*A*fter *Pearl Harbor, the speed with which events tumbled into the news had Arthur begging for a respite —"two or three days off at least for undisturbed reflection." Unlike most of his countrymen, he had never shortchanged the Japanese, but the celerity and power of their military machine surprised even him. Every rumor appeared to back up his unshakable belief in English perfidy and the American government's incompetence; confidently ("You may be certain . . ."; "I feel more sure than ever . . ."; "You can't tell me that . . .") he predicted further Axis gains. How well the United States did in the Pacific, he announced, depended on whether or not the Russians, who were doing better than he expected, could stop and then defeat a still powerful Germany. It was time to make General Douglas MacArthur, a giant among pygmies, supreme Pacific commander; time to stop "sitting on our hunkers and waiting for the assembly lines to roll out an incredible superiority before we attack"; time to divert flow of planes, tanks, and guns from greedy, do-nothing England to the Pacific theater.*

Arthur railed against the waste at home and the coddling of organized labor ("Labor should be made to suffer proportionately with other civilian groups"), and called for the obliteration of the forty-hour week. He had no compunction, however, about squirreling away canned goods, butter, bacon, sugar, tires, gasoline, and typewriter paper instead of buying defense bonds. Conceding an apparent inconsistency in his admiration of the Bataan heroes and his diligent hoarding, he attributed his "contradictory double standard" to the "selfish grafters" who made him and many others reluctant "to obey the laws." Every example of alleged corruption provided by George Dicey, that fount of misinformation, gave him reasons to justify his admittedly unpatriotic behavior.

The cheerful Dicey had become a Garrison Hall familiar. Arthur paid him to "tell off" the Machs and to extricate Billy from the draft, but he also relished, without quite believing, Dicey's wild stories of Boston and Bay State venalities. Arthur felt that he needed protection. Pressed for money and wondering whether he would be able to afford his current living standard, he suspected everyone of overcharging him, including the doctors at the hospital (whose "ill-gotten levies" he self-righteously scaled down before paying) and even the "loyal" Billy. Billy had demanded a raise, his resources taxed after his father was injured, and Arthur had to wheedle, play poor, and threaten suicide before he could come to an agreement with his man-of-all-services: "Rather a simple person, with not much intelligence and not much character, yet sufficiently on the job for me not to want to let him go."

Hardly less troubling to Arthur were Evelyn's bad judgment in not loving him enough and the impending marriage of Janice Oliphant to Mr. Davis, a match Arthur thoroughly disapproved of for various reasons but chiefly because he wanted Janice for himself. Yet all in all, he had survived the winter pretty well and now awaited "adverse contingencies" with whatever "courage" and "ingenuity" he could muster.

1941

December 9   I am convinced that the Japanese attack on Pearl Harbor was more disastrous than we have been given to understand, than we will be permitted to know. It well may have been a blow that will cripple our Pacific Fleet for many months. The loss of a battleship, a destroyer and a number of planes is admitted by our Government, but the 3,000 casualties also admitted bespeak another story. Everyone is asking how (all the plans for a war with Japan presupposing a sudden air attack by the Japanese on Pearl Harbor) aircraft were allowed to approach and bomb the naval base just as though there were no scouts watching or crews on guard or interceptors ready.

December 10   Americans by and large harbor in their hearts a profound disparagement of the Japanese. They are suddenly losing some of it. The Japanese ships are newer, and at least one of them is among the largest afloat. In fine, we by now are either at a disadvantage or close to it, probably at a disadvantage. That is to say, the Japanese Grand Fleet should be more ready to meet our Pacific Fleet than we to meet them. Should the Japanese Grand Fleet seek out a battle, what should we do? A defeat would leave the Pacific Coast open to raids and attack.

This morning comes word from Japan, acknowledged by London, that the two great British battleships recently arrived at Singapore have been sunk by the Japanese, which surprise success will reduce the menace to the Japanese of the English 'fleet in being.' Thus far the Japanese have manifest superiority on sea and in the air. They seem to have used the tactics of synchronizing air and naval effort which came into being with the great British air and naval attack on the Italian Navy in the Mediterranean.

December 11   Germany and Italy have declared war on the United States of America. Shortly after noon Congress will admit a state of war as existing. So here we are, with every prospect of the lavish spending of life, limb, money, time, industry, ingenuity toward the rather vague purpose of contesting an idea and a threat of conquest which had we strictly minded our own business might never have implicated us.

We are in it now for good or bad, and there is no more purpose to be served railing at the Jews for their part in our predicament or at the English for using us to their advantage or even at the misguided President of the United States. Our interest from now on, mine and yours, our nation's interest, runs coadjacent to the interests of the Jews, of the English, of Roosevelt. I do utter a hope though that some heads in power will sooner or later decide to supply our own fighting forces rather than England's, if that is not too much to hope.

December 13 Last evening Dr. Brainard talked with me. He's a gentle person without much push or particular intelligence. He asked me all sorts of puerile questions. He has a medicine he wants me to take. He says he charges twenty-five dollars a visit. What a racket. No more of him. This doctor racket is certainly a fine one for the doctors. How they lay it on when they think you can take it. Oh, I don't mean most of the osteopaths — they give you more for your money — but the medicos and their ilk. Blake, $220; Isaacs, $150. And for four or five hours. A gyp. And they tried to work the sanitarium racket on me, those two, when I was at the hospital. The Jew with the semiastute face and the dirty fingernails took the floor and talked at me while Blake examined the ceiling. I said yes, it sounded sensible; I'd think about it; there was probably something to it. But all the while I was holding on to Dr. Pike's words: "Those buzzards can't do a thing to you, Arthur, or put you away if you don't want it, and furthermore, I wouldn't stand by and see anything like that happen. It's a game. They get you in a sanitarium and then split fees." It looked fishy to me too, not that they weren't interested in my case and probably trying to be kind.

December 15 I have been reading the will I drew up some weeks ago and didn't get around to signing. It gives everything to Evelyn and makes her the executrix. It requests her to give something to Janice and take care of her in case of need: At least that is what I have explained to Evelyn. It requests that she leave her estate in case I die to some such institution as the Massachusetts Historical Society to publish my diary and introduction. I figure that Evelyn, should I die, will have enough to live on except in calamitous times. She will have the Jamaica Plain Place, the income from 43 St. Botolph Street and an income from stocks averaging at least $1,800. If her mother continues to give her or leaves her $600 a year, she should be comfortably off even should my Father fail to leave her anything.

December 17 When I was 'out' at the hospital, Father offered to come north. He was very worried. He suspected a suicide attempt. It must have shocked the poor old fellow to his foundations, not only because he is a sincere and unquestioning believer in the tenets of the Presbyterian Church but also because of the social onus he would feel in having a son death-minded. He asked Evelyn outright whether or not I had taken the pills with suicide in mind. I had her answer him — indeed, I dictated most of the letter — vaguely stating that I was so upset from want of sleep that I probably didn't know whether I took them on purpose or not, and that she didn't feel it was the proper time to query me.

Later on we wrote asking if he could help us with the medical doctors' bills, the hospital bill, a new furnace and hot-water boiler and three heaters at the Place. I thought of telling him how dangerous a spot this was should Boston be bombed. He wrote the following letter, and it made me feel almost ashamed at my duplicity, though I know I shouldn't be; he has always preferred sugary deceptiveness to forthright honesty. The poor old fellow, he hasn't had much pleasure of me, has he? The letter:

My Dear Evelyn:

I was just, when I got your letter, thinking of writing you about the probable danger of living immediately in Boston for a while, as we must expect German planes to make some attacks on Boston and New York.

I understand that you will be obliged to have some additional money and I am writing Mr. Matthews today to send Arthur a check for $1500.

My suggestion would be an oil furnace as mine has been such a wonderful comfort to me and as it is controlled by a thermostat and can be used for a short time only if you want it. I find it very much cheaper than my coal furnace was and I do not have to have a man to attend to it or ashes to be removed.

In getting an oil furnace be sure and get one that is so constructed that it will not explode.

Am afraid that you and Arthur will have to take this check as your Xmas present and I can assure you that lots of love and best wishes for a Happy Xmas go with it.

I have not yet recovered from my last two awful shocks but am getting better.

With dearest love to you both, I am

Devotedly yours,
H.A. Inman

December 20 Yesterday morning Evelyn startled me when she woke me. As I have said before, I have little or no control when peremptorily awakened from a sound sleep. I wanted to know why she couldn't exercise enough self-discipline not to startle me once out of four times she waked me. I asked why she didn't either impose some sort of penalty on herself to cause her to remember not to forget or let me suggest such an expedient. She said no. I said I didn't understand why not. She said it would undermine our relationship. I remarked that she took care not to frighten her animals and that I thought I merited as much care; how about letting me scare her dog? No. I said that she had no trust in me, no confidence in me else she would be glad to try some means of making her remember. It was, I said, a physiological weakness of mine to tend to wake up startled, and all I desired was to develop some scheme which would prevent her continued thoughtlessness or ineptitude or whatever it was that caused her to do it wrong. We bickered. Evelyn reminded me that I had promised once never again to discuss punishing her. I said that I felt I was right. I said that I thought she was wonderful and that I loved her more than ever I had before and that all I wanted was to make our life together even more smooth. Evelyn said no. I began to feel she wasn't being fair. We talked some more in the afternoon. I requested that she not work with me but think about what I had said instead.

Later on, she came upstairs to read me the paper. "I've had three straight whiskeys," she announced. "I'm slightly tight. I'm discouraged. Maybe this'll make me feel better." Claire had been due to phone at four. She hadn't phoned by six. I asked Evelyn to promise not to cross streets in a hurry if she went out. I was worried. Mrs. Cash and I read about the girls in a state reform school, very abnormal. Claire came upstairs a moment. "Oh," she said, after she had hugged and kissed me warmly, "Evelyn's soused. She was ripe when I came, but she's insisted on having another drink. She says that you are angry with her. You should hear her talk. She's lost her lunch three times. She loses her lunch, the dog yips and yips, and I've a hell of a toothache. A quiet evening with the Inmans."

December 21   The Germans—there is no doubt of it now— failed crucially in the Russian campaign, so crucially indeed that from this autumn history may date the beginning of the downfall of the German dream of European domination. The casualties in Russia must have amounted to at least one-fourth of the potential German Army. Should the Germans be unable to establish and hold a strong line against the Russian advance during the forthcoming winter, the results may be catastrophic to eventual German hopes in the Soviet direction.

Douglas MacArthur, Commanding General of all the United States Armed Forces in the Far East. This is an honor applicable temporarily to Chiefs of Staff but which has been accorded during the officer's life only to Washington, Grant, Sherman, Sheridan, Pershing. I like MacArthur as much as I dislike General Marshall, Chief of Staff. He has an ambitious, forceful, intelligent, arrogant face, a masculine bearing, a presence suited to command. He knows how to make use of that high-flown rhetoric which so often can inspire soldiers, as well as of the clipped phrase which spurs them on.

December 22 My opinion of Dicey's ingenuity is high. He possesses the sort of intelligence which is able to cut through masses of details to reach the nub of the question under consideration. I am convinced that he is a man to tie to. He likes me and has respect for my capacity to think and plan. I wanted to discuss Billy and the draft with him last week, but he had the flu and wasn't available.

Last evening when Dicey came to talk to me, I placed the problem of Billy before him. "I hate to be a pessimist, Mr. Inman," he said, "but if you have Billy another month you'll be lucky. There isn't a class 4-A any more. He'll automatically be shifted to 1-A. An ex-serviceman, a noncom, a crack shot, a fine record — terrific. He'll be snapped up like coffee on a cold day. I was flat on my back when the war broke, so I'm in a position to compare the temper of the people before and after. I tell you it's amazing. Everybody's one hundred percent for war. There's no longer any indecision, any division of purpose. It's all patriotism and when do we get at 'em and let's go. Enlistments at the Navy Yard at an office being kept open twenty-four hours a day. Terrific. And whereas you could buy your way with the boys, not now, not until the shine wears off their patriotism and they aren't so timid about Army control. They just sit tight and talk about the flag. And if you and Billy and I don't want to go to war, who are we? A minority who has to keep its mouth shut or else. So it looks as though you'd have to lose Billy."

I should be willing without a quaver to pay two or three hundred dollars to keep Billy out. Let someone else die for Roosevelt. It gives me a horrible feeling to imagine Billy in Malaya or Siberia or North Africa shot and left to die, perhaps mutilated by shrapnel or machine-gun fire.

Dicey is certain that before thirty days are up an attack will be made on this part of New England by German planes. "Think of it, the Watertown Arsenal where the big guns are made, the Navy Yard, the Springfield Arsenal, the Fore River Plant, the Portsmouth Navy Yard. Cripple these, in particular the Arsenals, and you'll have put a crimp in the American effort to arm itself that'll be worth any amount of planes and pilots lost. Say, Hitler can't afford not to do it. And are we prepared to contest such an attack? We are not. No antiaircraft guns to speak of. No organization. No psychology of taking it on the chin developed. Hell, Hitler would be a sap to overlook such a chance." I disagreed with him, placing the first attack next spring. Billy bet him a meal, drinks and the theatre that there wouldn't be an attack within thirty days.

I realize that what I am writing and thinking could be, in its mild way, construed as treason to my country. If it is, it is. I don't mean it precisely that way. I simply and selfishly would rather have someone else as cannon-fodder than Billy.

December 25 Churchill is my enemy because he has hoodwinked and made use of and misguided my country. But I can't find him culpable as an Englishman for having done what he has to us, in fact, rather admire him for his shrewdness and success in making dupes of us. Roosevelt I hate and despise because of what he has done to my country, deeming it to have been needless by and large to pander to his own vanity; hate and despise him for what he is, for what he stands for. I could be won personally by Churchill, not in a thousand years by Roosevelt, so fundamental is my distrust of and antagonism toward him.

December 26 Christmas is over, hurrah, hurrah. Billy must have spent $300 on it, giving Sadie alone $200. Janice splurged, too. Her boy friend gave her a wristwatch. Mrs. Cash has a cartload of presents from her children and her friends. We received many cards. I gave Evelyn the radio she bought some weeks ago. The Groundhog sent us a package; Miriam and Dr. Pike each an azalea. It was a bad day for me but it's past now.

December 27 Evelyn saw Woody and Allan married at the Courthouse. She liked the marble corridors in the building. They gave Evelyn an early lunch and she came home before they had thoroughly settled down to an afternoon of drinking. Wonder if Woody will stop writing me letters now. Never can it be foreseen what influence marriage will have.

December 28 As to the bombing of Manila by the Japanese after it had been made an open city with troops and defense guns withdrawn: Certain it is that bombs fell on the old walled-city section of Manila killing people and damaging buildings. No action could have been taken to more effectively weld the American people together and to imbue them with a fervor for war. A needless, a brutal, a very foolish action. For it the Japanese will deserve retribution, only that retribution will fall as it usually does in modern war on the people who did not order the raids, the workers and citizens of Tokyo and Kobe and Yokahama. Well, here we go with throttle wide and sirens screaming and fire in our entrails.

Billy and Sadie were downtown yesterday watching the news being posted on the 'Globe' bulletin board. "The crowd was so angry and the men were swearing so at the Japs that I had to take Sadie away." Janice went to a movie yesterday. "A few bars of 'The Star Spangled Banner' were played. Everyone in the audience rose without a sound. It was unutterably impressive. It gripped me. I felt the tears rolling down my face."

December 29   Billy has gone out to look for secondhand tires for his car and Evelyn's and Janice's. It is almost impossible already to obtain seconds. I feel very sanctimonious, what with my eight or nine tires for each car stored at the Stable. I have been buying hot-water bags ahead, and rubber tubing for my enema can. Have ordered two dozen of these notebooks. Will buy more canned goods soon. It is all right to say that there won't be any food shortage here, but it won't do any harm to be prepared. I'd be no one to thrive on lack of proper food. And if it isn't patriotic to stock up ahead on things, why I suppose I'm not patriotic. I feel more as if I'm a citizen impressed against my will to serve in a marauding band led by very dumb freebooters or worse by very dumb idealists if you wish it that way; and to that extent I'm not patriotic.

My wide knowledge of history makes me impervious (because of the many comparisons between now and the past filed away in my head) to the spirit of militarism that is sweeping people off their feet.

1942

January 1   Never heard such a wild night of yelling and horns blowing and traffic zooming as last night. Hoodlums in the alley had target practice with stones at the lamps. Across St. Botolph Street, the dance went until four. There was some sort of celebration at Mechanics Hall. Usually, I can sleep through New Year's Eve — but not this one. Billy, who did the popular spots from the Copley Plaza Merry-Go-Round to Lindy's, tells me that never before did he witness such an outpouring of money. The driving, they say, was wild. The paper calls it a night of record drinking although Billy saw few drunks. It was, he says, as though everyone was attempting to enjoy to the utmost what they felt might be their last real celebration for some time.

January 3   Roderic reads to me once or twice a week now, nor does he doze while reading as often as formerly. Last night we were reading 'Pattern of Conquest,' a fine coherent book about the Germans.[1] "Roddy," I said, "how are you fixed for tires?" "Well, Artie,

---

[1] A collection of the dispatches reporter Joseph C. Harsch sent from Berlin to the *Christian Science Monitor*. Although he was unqualifiedly anti-Nazi, Harsch dispassionately viewed the National Socialist German state on the eve of the invasion of Russia. He described a people who feared the war their leaders planned and who, while not true believers in the Nazi philosophy, welcomed the tangible benefits of Nazi conquests.

I'll tell you. It's like this. By the time my tires wear out, we won't have gasoline. By the time we have no gasoline, I for one will have no job. So why should I worry?" "I've already thought of how many motor car agents and tire dealers will be forced out of business. You think the insurance companies will be affected adversely?" "No doubt about it, Arthur. Not the slightest doubt. As cars for one reason and another are withdrawn from the road, the larger part of the business of companies such as I represent will dwindle. Then all employees save a skeleton force will be shaken goodbye by the hand and let go. I may or may not be one of the skeleton force retained." "And if you aren't?" "Well, I'm just not, that's all. There's nothing I can do about it. And I won't be alone in my misfortune. Boy, you haven't seen anything yet. This is a real war. If we keep our shirts, we'll be lucky. Not that I mind, you understand. I want to do my part, whatever that part is. If it consists in giving up luxuries and even necessities, why I won't complain." "How about storing up food and other things? I hear that some people are doing it." "No. In the first place, that's what makes for scarcity. In the second place, I don't consider it patriotic. In the third place, they'd probably requisition whatever you saved anyway." "Do you dread the future, Roderic?" "Oh no. What comes will come. I'll have company. Why dread it? That won't do any good, to dread the future. Just do the best I can and hope that Herr Hitler and the little yellow men will soon be booted off the map and then hold on. Maybe they'll take me to fight — who knows?"

January 10 Snowed all night and most of morning. Evelyn and I have been correcting Volume 13 [1922–23] with only fourteen pages to go now. It is my opinion that poor Katinka was treated rather shabbily — not that I intended at the time to be despicable, rather that I was hurt and took it too much to heart being young, and that I purposed to impel her by any means at hand to become a more adequate actress. She deserved better from me, for she was a tolerant and loving friend. I had no idea, strange as it may seem, that she was in love with me. I took her love for what it evidently was not, sisterly. Too bad, the entire muddle.

January 11 Billy left Friday for his home in Springfield. He returned late last night. "Was the snow very bad, Billy?" "No, it wasn't bad." "Was it very cold?" "Twenty below. Sadie and I nearly froze." "Did you have a good time?" "Awful." "What was the matter?" "Oh — everything." "You always run into something when you go there. What was it on this occasion?" "My father got run over and had both his legs broke. He's in the hospital. They say he won't ever walk again." "Lord, Billy, that's terrible." "The day before we got there he did it. Two drunken boys driving a car run into him. The bones above his knees are crushed so bad they can't put them together. Ma's all to pieces." "I'm awfully sorry, Billy." "I wouldn't have come back, but I couldn't stand any more of it. Sadie cried all day. And I cried. I couldn't eat. I haven't eaten for twenty-four hours. I'm sort of numb-like—you know?" "I certainly do, Billy. When I was twelve and they brought my Mother in, four of them carrying her, with her hip torn where the carriage had turned over on her, I was put to bed for a month with the shock of it, and a week, two weeks maybe, of the time I was in bed I don't remember, just a blank space." "Yeah, that's it. It gets you. But I can't give in to it. I gotta keep up." "That's right, Billy. You can't give way. When you're a boy and something like this hurts you, you aren't prepared, haven't any defenses to use, and it bowls you over. When you're a man you're more fitted to contest the effect on your nerves." "Yeah. But that wasn't all. Teddy—he's the youngest—got his hand caught under a stamping machine at the plastics plant where he works and had it crushed to a pulp. That was this morning. He won't have the use of it for weeks and maybe not much then, and they'll have to cut off one finger anyway. He said he was thinking of Pa. I couldn't stand it all. I came home."

January 12   Dicey said: "If we can put this Mayor Tobin on the hot seat, why, Mr. Inman, I can do anything for you you want. I think we've got him on the run, too. All of us are busy night and day finding and collating evidence." "Who are 'us'?" I asked. "Oh, Curley and Coakley et al.,[2] the boys." "I thought Coakley and Curley were enemies?" "Oh Lord, no. They got together years ago. They're only hostile in the papers. They flay each other alive before the public, but that's all camouflage. They're really buddies with coinciding aims. They play ball." "And you work for Coakley?" "That's right. Swell guy, too. One of the best." "In spite of all the chicanery he's practiced during his long career?" "Oh sure. That's

---

[2] Daniel Coakley (1864–1952), James M. Curley (1875–1958), and Maurice Tobin (1901–1953) all figured prominently in the Massachusetts merry-go-round. Curley dominated the Bay State political scene as mayor, United States representative, and governor for over thirty years. In 1937 he lost the mayoralty to Tobin, his former protégé, and again in 1940. Tobin was still mayor when Dicey told Arthur about the Curley-Coakley plot to unseat him, and Dicey's boss, lawyer-politico Coakley, still wheeled and dealed from his Parker House suite despite his having been disbarred in 1921 and forced to resign from the Massachusetts Executive Council in 1941. Four years later, Curley was elected mayor for his fourth and last time even though he had been indicted for mail fraud. He spent five months in jail before President Truman commuted his sentence. At this time Tobin was serving as Truman's Secretary of Labor. Dicey, the inside-dopester, seems to have been close enough to the political Boston scene to be a plausible observer, but his facts are invariably tinctured with lies and inventions.

all part of the game. Anyway, he isn't half so bad as he's painted, not by a couple of miles. He's square with his friends." "His headquarters are at the Parker House, where you hang out?" "That's it. He has — let's see — three rooms on one floor, three on another, three on another. He pays three thousand for each set. He has his own private bellhop, paid by him. He fees the telephone girl. He has his own cop in the guise of a hotel dick. He has special phones and special locks on all the rooms. Oh, it's a sweet setup, just what I'd like myself, but it runs into big money, believe you me. Myself, I hole out there sometimes, and sometimes I'm in my own place in Bulfinch Street. I live with an old Irishman there. I've done him favors with his children, who are in institutions, and he's grateful. I pay no rent so I haven't a legal residence there. In that way no warrant can be sworn out against me. Everything's double-locked. I wish I had another hideout in addition to the one on Bulfinch Street. I'll get one some of these days. Just give me time. If we can drive Tobin out, I can have anything I want."

January 14   Roderic, being asked whether he was not more happy now than with his first wife, responded: "Why, there's no comparison. No comparison whatever. Doris is a jewel. And the baby she's given us has altered my entire viewpoint as I had never believed anything could. I'm happier than I ever was in my life. And she's a wonderful manager. Twenty-five cents goes where before it would take fifty, and all with no fuss or disturbance, as though it were the easiest thing in the world to balance checks, pay bills, watch expenditures, keep smiling. It's the nuts, Artie. Yes sir. Of course there are certain disadvantages implicit in living with the family, but if my dad can hold on until next summer, things may be better. His old-age payments begin then, and that with his Spanish War pension will amount to a hundred dollars a month, so that Doris and I will be relieved of responsibilities in that direction. We hope to move into a house of our own. And if I have to go to war, I have to go. And if I lose this job, I lose it. I'll get along. We'll get along. A fellow's bound to get along, with such a wife as Doris."

January 16   An alert round man, three or four inches shorter than myself. Large blue-gray eyes, bright, darting, missing nothing, impersonally curious rather than friendly or inimical. Hair brushed neatly back from a fairly high, intelligently wide forehead. Somewhat heavy eyebrows dipping to a point above a rather straight nose. Jowls, but not too pronounced. A firm but mobile mouth. Here, you feel, is a clever person who misses few tricks and those because his versatility permits him too easily to spread his interests profusely. It is a face somewhat after the pattern of Jim Farley's face. It is such a face as Wolfe, the detective creation in the fiction of Rex Stout, should possess. It is an interesting physiognomy to study. A great rotundity of stomach. A neat, clean, starched white shirt and a neat black tie. Blue-jewel cuff buttons. Pants, very tight-fitting, with innumerable buttons to the fly. Serviceable shoes, socks held up on fat legs by visible white garters.

He was closeted with the Machs for upwards of two hours. "They were harder nuts to crack than I had expected. The Sid one is rather shrewd. And boy, do they hate to see dollars vanishing." To shorten Dicey's word-for-word report, he told them a cock-and-bull story about how he represented my Father in a drive for a general economy in my affairs due to the stress of war conditions. They filled him full of rank lies, and whether he returned as good as they gave remains to be seen. It was, I gather, a combat in twisting the truth. Dicey was at a disadvantage in that I had instructed him not to bluff to a point where I might be taken up and the bluff called. So a matter that might have been settled by two white men one way or the other during a few amicable minutes dragged on, as I have said, for upwards of two hours, with no decision reached. Dicey is to come for the verdict today.

A telephone call from a voluble Pearl last night. After various adventures which she promises to relate to me, she has taken a job as superintendent, hours seven-thirty to five, pay twenty-seven-fifty, pay and a half for overtime, inspecting primers for big British shells. The plant is in South Boston. "It's the kind of money I always thought I ought to make."

January 17   Dicey ran into a stone wall with the Machs. Evidently my Father at one time or another in the past wrote them some sort of 'take care of my son' letter, interfering, as he used to do, with my good in mind but without my knowledge, and that letter they have been treasuring for years, so they told Dicey, in their safe. They even offered to show it to him. Finally, they challenged his right to represent my Father and requested proof.

When there's a movement against the Jews, I hope that I can do my part in it. And it's as much how they do what they do as what they do. But I might as well close my mouth on this subject. Everyone directly around me knows precisely how I feel about it, and I run the sure danger of becoming boring if I continue to ride it. Millions disagree with me, and other millions are indifferent, and still other millions are afraid to voice their feelings and thoughts. But there are also millions who agree with me.

January 18   "Jesus, what a week," exploded Mrs. Cash. "This war is driving me out of my mind. All the rich people in Goshen have literally taken it to their bosoms. They're having the time of their lives. Well, they and their uniforms and meetings and knittings and first-aid classes and air-warden courses and civilian-defense preparations would be all right if only they would leave the school alone. But they don't, damn them. It's one air-raid drill after another — march downstairs, line up, lie down — do it all over again. Hell, I could scream with the futility of it. And making the children listen to pompous rich people who haven't a thing to say. And issuing orders and counterorders. My God, kids nowadays learn little enough, and what they do learn is hard enough to pound into their unattentive heads, without all this. And who in the name of heaven wants to bomb Goshen anyway?"

January 20   Dicey, with my Father's telegram to back him, talked to the Adder and the Snake for close to two hours, got nowhere again. With one trivial argument after another they put him off. "As soon as I punctured one set of nonsense, they'd have another ready and waiting. I hadn't thought, to be absolutely honest with you, Mr. Inman, that they'd be such hard nuts to crack. They're terrific. I could handle Arnold alone, but Sid's a story out of another book. He's born clever, and his mind has some arrangement in it which Arnold's mind has not, decidedly. I'll be back for more battle tomorrow. I really can't tell you, though, how far I'll get in the end. They're tough."

The Prime Minister of Canada was elected on a pledge not to send drafted men overseas. Instead of ignoring or turncoating his promise as any Roosevelt or Churchill would do, Mackenzie King plans to have a general national referendum to determine whether or not the country wishes him to change or maintain his stand. Are there occasionally honest politicians, or does this move just look honest to me because I'm not in the know?

January 22   Dicey carried on a two-hour monologue with a sore-throated myself. I listened to the ins and outs of city politics and knew not whether to be more disgusted than amused.

The Curley-Coakley outfit is at this juncture straining every effort to build up a case against the present mayor that will cause him either to resign or to be ousted under the 'corrupt practices' act. While engaged in proceeding towards this goal, they are careful to keep their own hands temporarily as clean as may be. "When the deed's done, then the gravy," pronounced Dicey. "Meanwhile, my good sir, I would have it known to you and to all the people that we engaged upon this tack are your humble and untiring and thoroughly highminded and unselfish servants acting with only your good in mind and offering our efforts without hopes of remuneration or reward other than that of doing what is right, no more and no less." The various contractors and others who wish to back the Curley-Coakley group with funds in order that they will be in line of favor should the maneuvers succeed in getting rid of Tobin and supplementing him by Curley are being told to wait until the ouster hearings are over. Meanwhile, the group digs for evidence of corruption in office and during elections. Tobin, on his part, so Dicey says, makes trips to Washington to sue for Administration help.

Should Curley win, Dicey wants as his part of the loot to become one of Curley's secretaries and to be granted the charter for a detective agency. He is only thirty-two, doesn't seem to know exactly what he does want. He sloshes back and forth in his purposes and desires rather than flows steadily in any one direction. His girl wants him to finish the detective story he began, 'Murder at the Pops,' for Houghton Mifflin. He says, "Oh, I don't know; I'm terrifically busy."

Last evening he was asking me how to judge character by voice and physiognomy. I told him a few details. He was concentratedly interested. "So you really believe that it is possible to sum people up by just looking at them or listening to them? I have to become engaged in conversation with anyone before I come to a correct conclusion; otherwise I'm liable to be wrong. I'll think over what you've said about the color of the eyes and the shape of the nose, but I don't suppose I could ever reach your state of—shall we call it intuition?—for the simple reason that I'm not in the unfortunate position where everything depends on my immediate and correct analysis of character, as you are."

Pearl called up and made an engagement to spend half an evening with me. There seems to be never a dull moment in her life. Pearl is as full of gathered rumors about how the Government plans to "crack down on people" as a flea is full of blood. The Atlantic & Pacific, she tells me, can't obtain toilet paper to sell. "Why, Artie, do you realize that the Government has bought up enough toilet paper for one year so that every soldier will have three hundred sheets a day to wipe himself with? That's what Pa says, and he knows." She sounded tired. "The men where I work," she said, "all like me, but I don't truck with them." The waste, she said, at the water meter factory that is manufacturing the primers is "terrible. You'd be surprised how much of the work isn't good and has to be thrown out."

I persuaded Billy to take Sadie and go to a performance of the Russian Ballet last night in order to get something new to think about before he went to bed to try to sleep. "I liked it pretty well," he admits. "There was a fairy story called 'Swan Lake' about a prince and some enchanted swans and the queen of the swans. That wasn't bad. Then there was the piece called 'Russian Soldier.' In it a wounded soldier gets delirious and thinks about his past, the wheat fields, his parties, his weddin' and all that. I didn't care so much for that. The last ballet was the best. You know the story of Bluebeard and his wives. Well, it was about that. It was swell. I liked one girl in it. She was pretty. Sadie enjoyed herself. It wasn't over till late. I slept better. Didn't you just hear me whistlin'?"

January 28   When Roderic arrived to read last evening, he was in a pleased mood. "Well, Arthur, I've just done my good deed for my country. I've donated a pint of blood. They need it—I give it. I feel expansive with patriotism and self-satisfaction. But seriously, I believe it is the least I can do. And somehow—God knows how—I've scraped together a hundred dollars and bought defense bonds. That, too, is the least I can do." I told him about how Pearl had declared that she intended to bury her money. "Those people," he expounded, biting off the words in his pleasant, flexible voice, "those people in my estimation are despicable, as are the persons who hoard sugar and otherwise attempt to circumvent what but for them and their lack of patriotism would probably not develop into shortages and emergencies." I mildly suggested that perhaps the Government was bringing on shortages and emergencies synthetically, solely for propaganda purposes. "Nonsense," he countered. "Those fellows in Washington must know their business. I think they're doing a darn good job of it. If we'd listened to the isolationists, just imagine where we'd be today. As long as we can keep the war away from our country, no sacrifice is too great. And make no mistake, Hitler and the Japs long ago planned to invade the United States. So I'm all for Roosevelt and the boys in Washington. He's doing a swell job."

February 3   Billy is downtown in the 'Globe' office calling for the very few answers to my ad for talkers. There are only about twenty this time compared with one, two, three hundred other years. They are few enough to convince me how difficult it would be to replace Billy and how wise it is to keep him with me at any sacrifice. These are lush and busy times for men of any character and ability whatever, and the free supply of them due to the military and industrial demand grows constantly smaller, and even women are harder to get.

February 8   I have been thinking of Janice. It may be a month or perhaps two months before she arrives at this point in my three hundred-page diary, so I have decided to put down what has been bothering me. It is that I'm afraid she is seriously considering marrying Bertram Davis and in the not too far future. Grant at once that I don't want to lose Janice and that I wouldn't know what in the world to do without her; that is still far from all that is on my mind. I don't believe that he's the man for her, and I don't think, furthermore, that she's in love with him so much as she's in love with love. Yet I can't come right out and make a stand against her choice and her problematical marriage, however strong my impression of its unwisdom may be. That would only crystallize what may still be in the nebulous stage in her emotions.

I have a very accurate faculty for sizing people up through the descriptions of those who know them, and my idea of Davis is anything but favorable. I don't, as Janice once suggested, dislike him. In fact, I can only feel rather warmed toward him for having in some ways been so good to Janice. He is certainly fond of her, a pleasant conversationalist, loyal to those he likes. And yet — and yet — I see him as weak, not overly attractive, lacking a something — I can't precisely name it — that would be necessary for Janice's happiness.

February 10   I was talking with Ella last evening. She heard me out on the subject of Jews. "This country," she asserted, "is rancorous with racial hatred. It is in the air. It is everywhere. So you feel that way about Jews. So I feel that way about white people. So the whites feel that way about negroes. So the Californians feel that way about the Japs and the Chinese. So the Texans feel that way about the Mexicans. So what? Democracy. There's no such thing, Arthur. Why, when I contemplate the long record of the indignities my race has had to suffer at the hands of the whites — the lynchings, the race riots such as have been taking place at the military camps, the Jim Crow laws, the contempt we have to bear just because our skins are black — I have to hold tight not to go mad, stark crazy mad, with the lust to kill. And if I had to die for it, what then? It's only because I was brought up to respect self-control that I don't go berserk. I hate white people from the very pit of my stomach up. And I reckon most colored people feel the same. You'd be surprised, Arthur, how many of the best members of our race have turned toward Communism. They feel that things can't be worse and they might be better. By God, we've nothing to lose. I have an awful hunch, Arthur, that before all that is going on in the world now has run its course, we're due to see terrible things happen. There's a lot of social unrest in this country right now. If we win the war, the Russians will flood the nation with their propaganda, and there's likely to be bloody revolution. If we negroes are weak on organization, there are plenty of disgruntled Jews to organize us and plenty of disgruntled whites we can use to lead us. And we're only one of the suppressed minorities."

February 15 Billy took me riding in the yards, and I feel better for the air and the shaking up. He is a good boy. The other evening when we were commenting upon the headlong course of the world toward apparent self-destruction, I asked the hypothetical question as to what would happen to me if things became very bad in this country, not being able to walk, helpless without money. "I don't know, Arthur," he said, "but I hope I'll always be with you to take care of you." And he said it so earnestly that I was touched. He is doing his best to spend as little as possible for me and for himself. He seems to have appreciated my effort to meet him halfway, and that is helpful. I know that I did wisely.

Juliette spent an evening here for the first time since November. She has had a Fallopian tube pregnancy and a four-hour-and-a-half operation and weeks of illness when she wanted to die. The story was long. It began late in November when the ambulance unit went to practice in the country and she was buried under leaves as a wounded soldier and told to stay there until the stretcher bearers found her. So well buried was she that it took them three hours to discover her whereabouts, and by that time she was numb with cold. "But I couldn't move, Arthur. You have no idea how earnestly we take this." She came down with a bad cold. Next week, she was sent to Charlestown to take some undernourished children to the hospital. There were six children in the family and another was on the way. Each child had something wrong with it — one blind, another an idiot, another with crooked legs, another deformed. The father was an Irish truckdriver with only sporadic work, and the mother made eight dollars a week washing dishes, and the children were underfed. "It was disgusting, Arthur. And they stank — pardon the expression — they positively stank. It turned my stomach to have anything to do with them. When I had delivered them at the hospital, I took my car to a garage and had it scrubbed inside. Then I went home and to bed."

Clarence, she says, is doing a big business making large leather chairs for officers' clubs and the furniture for warships. He was offered quite an important position with the Government but turned it down.

I said to her: "You've been so mad to get us into this war, and here we are. Why don't you send Clarence to fight?" "He can go to war if he wants; I wouldn't hold him back. Or he can go if he's called. But he's certainly not going to volunteer. He's too valuable elsewhere."

"Making luxury chairs for officers' clubs and captains' quarters?" "Well, someone has to make them. Why not Clarence?" She continued: "I was lying awake the other night thinking of you, Arthur. I was supposing you were a fifth columnist. I had informed on you. Then I had grown sorry I had. I'm a loyal person—in my way. So I took a gun and went to your rooms and shot you. I did that rather than have you fall into the hands of the F.B.I. and be shot by them. Do you think I did right, Arthur?"

February 16 I should not like to fall into the hands of the Japanese. Word of their cruelty continually seeps through, and I have no doubt, having become acquainted with Japanese character through books and pictures and carvings, as to their nature. They are an Asiatic people, not restrained by humanitarian morals such as often motivates us, nor by any so-called sense of sportsmanship. I can imagine that the grimace of torture is sweet to their eyes. What happened in Nanking and in the Chinese cities and villages bears out the worst you can think of their cruelty. They are taught neither to value life too highly in themselves nor in a foe. Honor should be of more worth than one's life, and if one's own life is of such dubious value except to the State, then surely the life of an enemy is worthless. Whether he be made to suffer or not is a matter of relative unimportance.

February 18 Practice blackout in Boston last night. Billy, as a member of the auxiliary police, was on duty with truncheon and flashlight, patrolling Huntington Avenue between Dartmouth and Exeter Streets. I looked out of my window at ten o'clock when the sirens first sounded, and by three minutes past ten, with the exception of one window across the back alley, the city was pitch-dark. It gave one an eerie feeling. You could see the stars twinkling, the rays from searchlights fanning the sky, hear planes droning overhead. The thorough compliance of the populace to orders from above is either very encouraging or very discouraging, according to the way you regard it. Boston is the first great American city to attempt a total blackout. "Extraordinary beyond all reasonable expectations," declared Mayor La Guardia of New York, who had flown here to observe the demonstration. "What happened might become a reality at any moment." In addition to the entire police force and the auxiliary police, there are twelve thousand air wardens. Few infractions of regulations took place and no robberies.

February 19 It must occur to the one reading these pages that I surround myself with clippings, observations, people critical of Roosevelt, the Administration, our conduct of the war, the Allied strategy. In a degree this is so, for as I have explained, I feel it important to constitute myself of the party of the opposition, not only because I am conservatively inclined, but because the party in control has things all their own way and history will be crowded with their actions and beliefs. Yet I have no inclination to be one-sided when those in power act in a way I or others consider competent or wise. I had liefer, to tell the truth, relate that the newest battleship, the 'Alabama,' has been launched nine months ahead of schedule than have to note that Congress becomes less and less important in our managerial system of Government, where boards and commissions and administrations have taken over the vested authority in great measure, in particular the judicial and executive aspects.

February 22   The destruction of our tankers day after day brings gasoline rationing nearer. Billy and I have bought two 58-gallon drums, one for him, one for me, at double the normal price and glad to pay it. If I were anyone else than myself, I should fill them with high-test gas and store them in the inner room at the Place, and there they would be safe and hidden. But if I did that, they'd be certain to blow up or to be hit by a bomb and burn the building to ashes with no insurance recoverable. So we plan to dig a big hole and bury them two feet down.

Am continuing to stock up on food. If they make you tell how much you have, I'll lie, or get Evelyn to, and have the food by that time hidden at the Place. The cards we are going to have to fill out for sugar rationing amount to nothing short of a military census of heads. I am buying more bacon in glass jars. I have laid in ten pounds of dried lima beans and ten pounds of split peas, and these Billy will put into sealed jars.

The American attitude strangely and alarmingly resembles the attitude of France before it fell — no faith in leaders, no enthusiasm to fight, no basic hatred for the foe, at least not enough. I am not altogether untypical in my attitude to hundreds of thousands of others, only I know in my heart that no matter how we came into this conflict, unless every effort is made by me as well as by everyone else, if not defeat, then at the best stalemate and ignominious peace may happen.

Know this or not, I yet feel protected by oceans; I still feel reluctant to lend myself to a mass effort at war conducted by a second-rate, Jewish-inspired bevy of misfits and one unbalanced megalomaniac ordering actions from Washington in what seems to me to be an unimaginative and fumbling manner and on a course taking into account foreign nations before ourselves and our interests and needs. If war is to be successfully waged at this juncture in history, it must be waged in an all-out, totalitarian, make-the-individual-a-cog, take-away-his-rights manner, and I know that and I am reluctant to comply, and others who do not realize it are reluctant to comply.

February 24   [From Patricia:]

For the first few days after the war was declared this part of the state was in a turmoil, you never saw such rushing about and donning of uniforms (female). I still don't think the woman lives, outside of Madeline Carroll, who can look anything but ridiculous in a uniform. They all bulge in the wrong spots. The night of our only blackout, an overwhelming failure, by the way, all the old gals were out on the Blvd. being very officious about ordering the rank and file off the streets. The rank and file paid no attention whatsoever, if there was anything to be seen by golly they weren't going to be cheated. Many of the large business places and banks were closed when the warning for the blackout came over the radio in the late afternoon, consequently their time lights were left on. Crowds of young hoodlums went careening about in old jalopies, throwing rocks at the lighted signs. The accident toll from traffic acidents was terrific. People simply insisted on driving even without lights. I actually wished for a bomb to scare some sense into the morons. San Francisco has had numerous blackouts and has become most proficient, while here are we, with the whole town teeming with plane factories, and nary a practice alert. Why do we have to wake up when it is to late? About the only thing that is actually making people realize the fact of war is the dearth of tires. They just can't be had out here. I'm going to have to get rid of my little car as I can't replace the tires. It's a small sacrifice to make, and as long as I've the public library and the movies for entertainment I'll be content.

Paul was released from the army on November 27th and we had planned to be married on the 17th of December when along came Dec 7. We expected that Paul would be called up immeadiately, as the reserves in the navy were being recalled by radio. So instead of waiting we left the next morning for Las Vegas, since we could be married there without the five day wait that the California law demands. I had my suit ready, but had not bought my hat, so while Paul was at the bank I dashed into the first hat shop and got just what I wanted, and vastly becoming too.

Paul is much more in love with me than I am with him, which I think is the best way for me. It isn't as exciting, but I've had one exciting marital life and am in no mood for another. We still have terrific fights, but it doesn't mean a darned thing. It's the way Paul blows off steam, and I've gotten over the days when I'd sit down and feel injured, I just scrap right back and have a swell time. I don't take from nothin'. If I'd started that way with Ted I'd perhaps be still married to him. But I thought I'd be the understanding forbearing wife. I don't think men want those kind of wives. I know that if I didn't fight with Paul he'd think I was taking him for granted. I demand certain attentions and beleive me I get them. But the only thing that's getting me down is my love life. I don't think I'm cold, but I get so everlastingly sick of finding myself on my back. I suppose it's because Paul hasn't anything else to occupy his mind right now, and when I'm through work I'm tired and certainly not in the mood for strenuous love excercises. In the mornings I have to sneak out of bed and get dressed and ready for work before Paul wakes up, else I'd be snagged into a little eye opener. I don't understand why men have to be passionate before nine in the morning, but all the ones I've known are that way. I feel like wearing a sign, "all passion spent". Maybe I was meant to be an old maid, or I may be just tired. One thing I'm sure of, I'll always have twin beds. If it weren't for the ones we have I'd undoubtly be up and down all night. This sounds as if I weren't happy, but I really am, Paul and I are well suited to one another, besides being good for each other. We have a swell time together and if only this war ends before I have a long grey beard we'll have a successful marriage. Right now it's hard to settle down to anything with this world upheaval around us. Paul is bitter about having his life pulled right out from under him just as he was getting established and was ready to settle down to a home. I find most of the boys feel that way. It was stupid bungling that left us unprepared and now thousands of young men have to pay for it with their lives and hopes.

February 26 I am grown very modest in setting a term and boundary to Japanese successes, so beyond any territorial or temporal limits projected in my imagination has the conquest run. I feel about the Nipponese — and this is a natural human quality — as I did about the Germans before the Russians turned them back, that they are by way of being extraordinarily invincible. Yet what has happened in Russia should have taught the rest of the Allies a lesson, and that lesson is that only by violent aggressiveness of attack can a modern armed motion be halted, never by consistent defensive tactics. We should bend every effort towards arranging a slashing attack on the body of the octopus, Japan itself, and it would be well if we could persuade Britain to attack something, anything on the Continent of Europe.

Dicey has been to Portland for a week. A wife is attempting to pin enough on her husband not only to obtain a divorce but a very large alimony as well. He was framed by a woman, a friend of his wife. It was Dicey's task to find out about the woman, to make her testimony invalid. He ascertained that she had stayed at the Eastland Hotel for four days with a man, in that time had spent four hundred dollars on gambling, liquor, etc. He obtained photostatic copies of her signature and picture, countersigned by the hotel clerk that she was the woman of the signature. The husband paid Dicey and his companion two hundred and fifty dollars plus expenses for their effort. He will also have to pay a sum to a police inspector in Portland to maintain his silence.

Dicey enjoys these little adventures immensely. He carries a thirty-two automatic with a thirty-eight stick slung under his arm. He has been shot twice, stabbed once. "It's a matter of judging your man correctly and of timing. I learn from each failure. If you feel yourself not as good a man as your opponent or if you're sure he'll have the draw on you, fade out as neatly as possible before the trouble comes to a head. Otherwise, if you can't control things by talking, which you usually can after you've let him blow off steam, get the drop on your man and hit hard and quick, not ever half-heartedly or halfway. You can tell by a man's tensing up and by his voice rising when he's about ready to make a move; then you move first. Unless a man's a dead shot and you know it, in which case stand still, no ordinary man, unless his pistol is in your back or your stomach, is good enough with a gun to kill you if you move sufficiently fast. He may wing you, but the chances are against his killing you. I've taken plenty of chances, but I'm still here. I'm very careful, though, about having a covering man when I think I may be going into danger."

Sometimes it has been Dicey's job to fill a position in an office or with a rival political gang while searching for evidence or attempting to frame someone. Once he became fond of the man he was framing. "When he proved so shrewd we couldn't uncover anything on him, I had to turn him over to the boys for a physical work over. I didn't want to but I did it. It was too bad, I figured, and he'd been swell entertaining me in his house for two weeks and personally I liked him; but business was business, and my first loyalty always belongs to the fellow I'm working for. So I let the boys loose. Only I didn't stay to watch, though usually I do and get a terrific kick out of it. I never let an employer down. And I never sell out an employer. I've got my code, Mr. Inman, although it probably resembles not at all your code."

Dicey claims that the only person in the world he would deliberately die for is his mother, not his girl, not Coakley. "The girl, if I died for her, would simply get another fellow. Coakley's old; I'm young." But I'm not sure I believe Dicey.

February 27 Talked with Janice yesterday about not getting married to Bertram Davis, a delicately difficult expedient. I can sense that her mind is either struggling with some sort of decision or has arrived at one, so I have to proceed as though on eggshells. I do not believe that this match would be a proper one or a happy one.

I should be desolate beyond measure should I lose Janice. I not only love her deeply; I am in love with her. She is a part of me. No one occupies or can probably ever in my life again occupy a position of intimacy analogous to hers. She is my Janice. And it makes me somewhat bitter to be living under laws and customs which do not permit that I have her as wife myself. I am convinced, and that with no unwarrantable conceit, that I am a stronger, a finer, a more interesting, a more loveable man than Davis. Yet because of the laws and the customs under which we live, he can have her and I can't. I don't want to lose her, and I don't want to have her take a step she is likely to regret. I have written Janice a letter setting forth how deeply I love her and begging for, at the least, a postponement of any contemplated decision. I meant every word I wrote.

March 1 Talked with Evelyn. Says she is getting more confidence in me and in my motives. Says she doesn't know how to love me the way I want her to. I observed that if she didn't react after the letters I wrote her, I might as well give up wanting what I wanted and enjoy as much love for me as she felt capable of feeling. She felt sad, she said, that she was unable to be as I wanted her to be, perhaps didn't know how, would like to please me if she could.

So we compromised that she dissemble being in love with me. Am I queer to wish my wife to have all the ardor for me, the illusions—delusions if you will—about me that she harbored when she first gave me her affection? Perhaps I want a sunrise back. Doubtless I should be amply satisfied with the already bounteous solicitation she bestows upon me. One thing is clear, however: Did I not feel so deeply for her, I should long ago have accepted relative conditions as they were and let it go at that. My wife has a fateful and unremitting fascination for me.

The Groundhog told her that I should get down on my knees every day and thank God for having such a wife. Perhaps I do, in my own unsanctimonious way.

Here, before I leave off writing, is a letter from Dr. Jacobs. I'm afraid I'm less impressed than Billy is or Mrs. Cash will be when I tell her but am, of course, pleased. The conferring of honorary degrees by the colleges and universities of the country is in some of its aspects a racket designed for publicity, but on the other hand men must be chosen whom the authorities deem will have a sufficiently high standing in their accepted fields to possess publicity value.

> Oglethorpe University
> February 26, 1942.

My dear Mr. Inman:

I am writing in behalf of the Board of Directors of Oglethorpe University to request the privilege of conferring upon you on the occasion of our approaching commencement, May 16th and 17th, the degree of Doctor of Letters in recognition of your outstanding achievements in your chosen field. All of us here in Atlanta have watched your steady growth in popularity, ability and reputation with pride and satisfaction and we desire to have the privilege of honoring ourselves by honoring you in this way.

Should you graciously accept this invitation, the degree will be conferred with a suitable ceremony of investiture during our commencement season, followed by a short response on the part of the recipient.

You may be interested in knowing that among your predecessors in receiving this and similar honors at our hands are President Franklin D. Roosevelt, President Woodrow Wilson, Bernard M. Baruch, Walter Lippmann, Harlow Shapley, director of the Harvard University Astronomical Observatory, Thomas J. Watson, President of the American Business Machine Co., Edward W. Kemmerer of Princeton, Chancellor John G. Bowman of the University of Pittsburgh and others of similar quality.

We are going to lay the cornerstone of Faith Hall on this occasion and we are hoping that your cousin, Rev. Sam Inman of Richmond, will be present with us.

Looking forward to your acceptance, I am

> Heartily yours,
> Thornwell Jacobs, President[3]

---

[3] Of course Arthur could not attend the ceremonies — a requirement for receiving the degree. "I am afraid he is privately greatly disappointed," Evelyn wrote to Dr. Jacobs, "because he thought you must know that he has been unable to travel for years, and planned to confer the honorary degree in absentia, as other colleges often do. It is most unlikely that he will ever be able to go to Atlanta again, much as he would like to do so" (March 23, 1942).

March 7 I seem to be particularly interested in the reactions of the fighting men to fighting. My own physical experience of life was terminated at such a premature age that I find myself very curious as to how those who engage in combat actually feel. To me, physical combat is something to be avoided at almost any cost, albeit I am aware that a like attitude in a man not hampered by physical ineptitude would be out of the normal. The Japanese slinking alone along unfamiliar forest trails in an alien land, danger on every side, how do they feel? The besieged men on Bataan, how do they feel? Is killing a joyful act zestfully undertaken or does it constitute an act of duty reluctantly discharged? In the large, I know the answer: that the reaction differs among individuals. Nevertheless, my interest remains intense. And I have a persuasion that engagement in battle and the occupation of killing are simple masculine prerogatives, not mysterious at all, rather matter-of-fact.

I don't like Evelyn's dog. It's too restless and too unreceptive to orders. The other day she persuaded me to follow her into Billy's room and observe how it had improved. The very first thing it did was to make a big puddle on the floor. Evelyn's face was a study. I'd whip the animal until it obeyed or it chewed me up, if it were my dog. A dog is a pest anyway, and one which will not obey is worthless. Perhaps Evelyn isn't very good with animals. I've seen other dogs obey. Well, she enjoys it, though how and why is a mystery to me.

Now Evelyn has gone for a walk with her dog, Billy is vacuum-cleaning the library, and I am alone with my writing-board on my knees, my good notebook before me, writing in it with a green pencil. I am reflecting how far I rode on this my first real trip of the spring as compared with last year. Something yet may knock the props from under me, but physically speaking, I have come through the winter rather well. My back being less twisted, I feel stronger. I have been sleeping better, both because the noise of traffic has diminished noticeably and because I have learned how to pass the nights with less air, that is, with the windows almost closed in order to exclude the noise. Lack of fuel oil has made the Boston & Albany give up the diesel engines in the yards that made such a racket, and the old steam ones are back. More sleep causes me to be less discouraged. I am working very hard, and that I am able to do so encourages me and permits me to forget or minimize my physical troubles. Having been able to use the yards and the open car this winter has made me not subject to so many colds. I have broken in a brand new pair of shoes, always a process painful to my spine, and that is a cheerful thought.

What happened to me in November alone has made a new man of me, for I am practically convinced that death is death, which conviction removes from my spirit dread of living forever. The world scene is enthralling and demands my closest attention. I am engaged in keeping one jump ahead of impending deprivations and dangers to my way of life, and that has its excitements. Billy may have to leave me at any time, Janice may feel bound to get married, Father's income may be taxed so heavily that he will feel justified in reducing what he gives me, wherever we live may be bombed, so that, all in all, I feel that I have to be alert. I feel as though I am existing in a time and under circumstances where only my own courage and my own ingenuity and my foresightedness may stand between me and God knows what adverse contingencies, and I find the situation stimulating.

The war seemed at once remote and uncomfortably close. Reports from the Russian and Pacific fronts indicated that the Axis drive had slowed down if not petered out, and Arthur found it hard —given the claims and counterclaims — to get a real picture of what was happening. At the same time he was readier than ever to credit the wildest rumors about the loss of convoys, a Russian-German peace settlement, undisclosed shortages of food and fuel, and the sinking of American capital ships. Fires, explosions, and manhunts figured in his nightmares. The likelihood of Boston being bombed and the East Coast invaded spurred him to deposit microfilms of the Diary in distant libraries. He had "labored too hard and too long" on the Diary to see it go up in smoke.

Alternately reassured and depressed by the news, he continued to rail at a flabby Congress, greedy labor leaders, an unawakened public — and to hoard tires and gasoline and other scarce items. Citizen Arthur called for totalitarian measures and an immediate second front. Arthur the hoarder trembled lest the government seize his automobiles and deprive him of his life-preserving rides. He proposed grand strategies to win the war while drawing the direst consequences from Rommel's desert victories and Russian reverses and a German threat to plug the flow of munitions to the U.S.S.R. For all the thrills and chills the war provided, Arthur usually saw it from a Garrison Hall perspective, that is, as primarily a personal inconvenience.

What would happen if Billy were drafted? High wages in factories and offices tempted the loyalties of his women. Arthur needed someone who could pull strings and deal with crooked favor-granting officials. George Dicey, the self-described right-hand man of the Boston politician Daniel H. Coakley, seemed to fit the bill. To a fascinated Arthur he explained at length the ins and outs of racketeering and spun out tales of *corruption that involved not only Coakley and Curley but also such eminences as David I. Walsh, John McCormack, Leverett Saltonstall, and Maurice Tobin. Indeed the White House itself did not escape Dicey's muckrake. Arthur could not decide what was fact or fiction in Dicey's plausible yet cock-and-bull stories. And he became more uncertain after Dicey had extracted $200 from him to get some diamonds out of hock on the promise of selling them for a big profit. Dicey could not pay up and Arthur was sore, but he still believed in his entertaining, windy inside-dopester. Only George, he thought, had the brains and influence to intimidate a delinquent tenant, check up on Janice Oliphant's unreliable suitor, and keep Billy out of the draft.*

Billy professed undying loyalty and love, but Arthur worried about his restlessness, his mentioning of higher-paying jobs. To Arthur's relief, Billy turned down an offer to work at a higher salary in a fish market, but not even Dicey could prevent the army from grabbing Arthur's irreplaceable cook, driver, osteopath, stomach-pumping assistant, and hanger of curtains. Eleanor Bachand Oates was an invaluable copyist, but her respect for Arthur chilled after she read the Diary. Besides, her soldier-husband took precedence over Arthur. Darling Janice might marry the unworthy Bertram Davis in spite of Arthur's efforts to dissuade her.

Other Garrison Hall regulars — Roderic, Ella, Mrs. Cash, Claire, Woodwork — served as buffers and confidants. Periodically Patricia filled out the breathless chapters of her life in pages and pages of letters. Abruzzo occasionally surfaced. And finally there was the precious yet incorrigible Evelyn, who after interludes of sweetness and submissiveness would flare up in unlovely independence and repel him with her coldness and bluntness. "A few guiles and a few wiles and a bit more gentleness," and he would have been "putty in her hands."

March 11 Roderic tonight. Hear more about what villains hoarders are. Keep my mouth tight, wonder at the adolescent credulity of Roderic and his real and unquestioning faith in Democracy. Then 'Quo Vadis' until after midnight, when to sleep.

Juliette and Clarence are still searching for a house. She was telling Evelyn and me of their tribulations. "The most desirable neighborhoods they won't let us in because we're Jewish. They just won't sell to us in those neighborhoods. And sometimes, Evelyn, they're rude beyond what you'd believe possible. It makes me feel badly. I can't help being a Jewess, even though I'm proud of it." Evelyn uttered soothing platitudes such as how salesmen probably weren't used to Jewish people wanting houses in the country districts when they'd always lived in cities. When Evelyn had left,

Juliette said: "Now I don't know how you'll take this, Arthur, but one of these days when I'm rich I want to buy a piece of property in a 'select' district like Weston, right in the middle of the Gentiles, and there erect a huge base for immigrants. That'd make them tear their hair."

March 17 While Billy went down some steps and into a place where ranks of cut jonquils were in the window, I sat and regarded the passing scene. A boy in a loud black and red checked shirt, fat, whistling. A man mounting steps to a tiny restaurant where "delicious pastromi" was advertised. Then two little girls, one regarding the other with admiration. The admired child was about twelve, as conscious of being female as any native lady of leisure could be. She wore high red rainboots nearly to her knees, a very short flaring red skirt, a red jacket, a red Montenegran bonnet showing her abundant brown hair. Her bare legs were white and developed. Her mouth was large and generous, her eyes cold. She walked with the strut of a drum majorette. A strumpet at twelve if ever I saw one, a brazen hussy and conscious of it. She made a picture some lush medieval painter would have enjoyed transferring to canvas, and I shall recall her when all the other drab characters of this morning on Tremont Street will be forgotten.

March 19 Evelyn and Eleanor are downtown for the second morning having my typewritten diaries microfilmed. Am having two series of films made to assure dissemination and safety in case of bombings. The work costs ten dollars a thousand pages. Having all Diary Introduction work microfilmed as well. I've labored too hard and too long on my diary to be willing to run any risk of having it destroyed. If everything breaks exactly for the Axis, there is the remote chance that America can be invaded and Americans forced backwards into the Mississippi Valley plains. So I take no chance.

March 25 Corn is due to have lunch with Evelyn. Wonder has she changed? Sixteen or seventeen years since first she answered an ad and came to talk to me in her thin excited voice. I always think of her sitting on the rooftree in the middle of the night, naked, enjoying a thunderstorm, the rain pelting, the thunder rolling, the lightning flashing. She was an experience in my life, a rather exciting one, an elf in human form peering out at the world of man through large green eyes. Like Nero, she has been moved by the dramatic and the beautiful, each as she happened to value them, not by pity, fear, justice, anger, sympathy. I wonder will her hair be soft still, like an halo. I am very curious. Perhaps she is really very commonplace and I have endowed her with those extranatural qualities I wished to find in someone.

Later: Have been talking with Corn. Same voice. Same excited manner. Hair browner and cut raggedly like a tramp's. Green eyes darker. She very plump, weighing 160 pounds. Dress unbecoming. Hat unbecoming. Shoes unbecoming. Lips inartistically rouged. Cheeks whitened with powder. A mess, if ever one was seen, yet carrying with her animation, vitality, a strong emanation of being solely and unchangeably herself. Seemed pleased to be with me again. Said how well — and younger — I looked. Commenced talking a mile a minute. Showed me her fat legs and her fat "rear," remarked, "How disgusting they are." Said: "Frank is going to Washington Thursday. He wants to enlist in the Navy but can't find out anything here. He doesn't intend being stuck behind a desk. He says he's tired of the academic life. He's going to leave me in New York for a week. Hmm. Says if he goes in the Navy he'll leave me with child, so I will behave myself. I tell him I'll never have just one child and how will he like it when he comes home and finds somebody else's child in the house with his child. Says he'll get leave. I wonder, does he expect me to behave while he's in Australia or Egypt. I say: 'Do you expect to behave?' He says: 'Well, that's different.' I say: 'That's what you think. That's not what I think.'

"I get along very well with him, all in all. I manage him with a series of emotional subterfuges. You'd think he'd get on to them but he doesn't, and they work over and over again. If I get bored with him, I take all my clothes off and wave my fat fanny at him around a door. Or if he's immersed in a book, I lean over and kiss him on the glasses and spoil his vision. Or if nothing else works, I strike a match and set fire to his newspaper. I keep him livened up one way or the other. We fight something awful sometimes."

Corn's mother is still living by herself, still erratic. "She hasn't been in our house for a year. She's peeved at me and angry at Frank." Elizabeth is still in Cleveland. Her Jewish husband appears to be turning into a brain surgeon of some prominence. At thirty-five, he is making, according to Corn, ten thousand a year. They are buying their own house. Elizabeth has false teeth and is doing war work. "Myself," concludes Corn, "I can't get het up over the war. It hasn't touched me close enough personally as yet. What interests me in life has to touch me. Otherwise, it's outside my periphery, like something unreal or in Mars."

Corn promises to visit here again. She may. I hope that she does.

March 30 Ella's Robert went to school at Turner College, colored, in Missouri. There he met a boy named Les Smith. Robert came to Boston as a redcap, and Les Smith went to New York, the Grand Central Station, in a like capacity. Les Smith studied the violin evenings. He was best man at Ella's wedding. Then Robert and Les Smith lost touch with each other. Robert heard that he had left redcapping and had gone into a swing orchestra. At one time he was with Duke Ellington. On Friday a man knocked on Ella's door. She didn't recognize him at first. It was Les Smith, grown fat and prosperous. He was in New England with an orchestra engaged by the United Service Organizations to play at the recreation centers of various service camps. He had, he explained, done very well for himself. He had married a "hoofer" who had been with a colored revue, later been hostess at the famous colored Savoy Ballroom in Harlem, now owned and managed a grill and tap room in Harlem. His wife appeared later in the afternoon. The Jameses invited the Smiths to spend the weekend with them, surrendering their bedroom to the guests.

Lena Smith was, according to Ella, beautiful, dressed stylishly, owner of two large dimples, a sweet expression and "a tongue hung in the middle." When Les Smith returned from his work, late because the boat he had been on had run afoul of the net at the harbor mouth, he brought with him a pint of gin, a pint of rye, a dozen cans of beer. Lena had already been out reviewing old acquaintances at night clubs with a friend of Robert, at each place drinking. "But then she and Les settled down to drinking in earnest. Arthur, I hadn't believed people could take that much and stay sober. But they did, and next morning after a pick-me-up of beer, Lena was fresh as a daisy. That was Friday night. The next evening Artie Shaw took her out again and spent seven dollars and seventy cents on drinks alone. After which, about eleven, she and Les began again, six cans of beer and a quart of Scotch. Evidently, it's the sort of life they lead, though how they can stand it I don't understand. Even Robby regarded them with his eyes popping. Arthur, when I told them I'd never even been to a night club, they were shocked, positively shocked. I've had a hundred chances to go but never wanted to. I always preferred a show or a museum or Radio City—something I could think about pleasantly afterwards, that would improve my mind. Well, Les and Lena are gone now, and I'm a dead dog with both feet in the air. I can't take it, Arthur. And I'm not as old as Lena. Well, it takes all sorts of people to make a world."

April 2 I spent several hours probing Dicey, endeavoring to ascertain why Coakley likes him, why he likes Coakley, what their relationship is.

Coakley is an old man, well along in the seventies. He has built up what Dicey calls "the organization" during a lifetime of political adventure. The organization is a sort of inner growth taking its life from and giving direction to the Democratic State Committee. The organization is divided into two parts, one of which metes out contracts to the politically worthy and to those who are to be remunerated for services of various sorts; the other has to do with elections, who is to be elected, who is to be put to one side, etc.

"In a way," continued Dicey, "the Boss is sad, and naturally so, that there's no one in his family to carry on. Even his grandsons aren't politically inclined. That is one reason, undoubtedly, that he has his eyes on me. Some of the boys have been with him as long as thirty years, but that makes them too old for what he wants. The ones who are the right age aren't the most capable. That leaves me. If I do say it myself, none of the boys ever came along faster than I have. D.H. likes me because I remind him, he says, of his dead brother, Tim, who was the apple of his eye. He likes me because I take orders. When he gives orders, he wants them obeyed to the letter and no questions asked. He doesn't want any objections or reasons why not or any assertions of impossibility or any hesitation; he wants obedience. If his orders go wrong, he blames himself, not the one who carries them out. He's almost a fanatic on this business of orders and rightly so, I think. And he likes me because I report back to him minutely and in detail, word for word, what happened and what was said, and I don't mix in what I thought or think until he asks me; and boy, I'm a whiz when it comes to remembering details. And he likes me because I learn fast and because I never have to be told a thing twice. He doesn't like to waste time repeating. And he likes me because I'm loyal and he knows I'm loyal. As long as I work for him, his interests come first, and he knows it."

Coakley wishes Dicey to give up all other activities for two years, study government for a year at Harvard and for another year in New York. After two years direct training under Coakley, he will be put in command of the organization. Dicey is making up his mind as to whether he would be willing to accept such a lifetime responsibility or not. He is inclined to think that he would. He doesn't seem to doubt his capacity. What worries him is the prospect of entering a field which, once definitely engaged in, does not permit withdrawal.

April 11   It was most amusing to observe what a dislike Mrs. Cash and Dicey took to each other. "That man," she yodeled. "I don't like him. I wouldn't trust him. Of course if he's your friend, that's all right; I won't say anything. But I can't see him for dust." And he: "My Lord, man, where did you pick up that addition to your staff? What a woman. If you like her, that's your business, but personally—well, let it pass." I admonished each to be as polite as possible to the other for my sake and to keep peace around here. I told each that the other had been good to me and that that, I thought, was all that concerned me.

April 13 Mrs. Cash called my attention to a very long editorial in yesterday's 'Globe' by the famous 'Uncle Dudley.' It concerned the value of diaries. He concludes with:

> Forty years ago when our imaginary diarist, as a schoolboy, began his unintentionally authoritative secret chronicle, the rules of the game of life were, in general, agreed upon. Since 1914 everything, rules included, is molten metal in a white-hot flood seeking new molds which are probably even now in the making. . . . Who knows? and when the sounding literary reputations are dust and ashes, dead and done with, your quiet chronicle may walk coolly off with the honors as the supreme spokesman of your age, and for the simplest of reasons, because it is true.

I wrote 'Uncle Dudley' and told him of my diary and asked if he would like to see a volume. I am still searching, rather in vain, for an enthusiastic 'angel.'

April 17 Alma sent me a woman named Gwendolen Hamilton. Violently perfumed. Used to have made and sold expensive ties. Was well off. Played stocks. Lost. Business went up the spout. Now people will not buy fifteen dollar, five dollar or even three dollar silk ties. She makes barely enough for a living. A queer woman, frightened at something. Asked her what. Pains in her "female parts," she explained. A Christian Scientist. Thirty-nine. Afraid of men socially, she said, though I have my doubts of her frankness. Mother died when young. Brother brought her up. Told her if she kissed a man would have a baby. She believed him. Though she studied art and thought nothing of going about naked—this is her story—she allowed no familiarity. Men, she said, disgust her. When I asked her was she cold with the windows open, she replied: "My goodness no. I'm a fresh-air citizen. I don't wear a girdle. I wear very little. As soon as it warms up, I wear only a dress. I go about the house naked—let my body breathe. My friends are critical, but I tell them it's my body, not theirs." A queer, queer woman, somewhat touched in the head, with much left untold about herself and much awry from the truth.

April 18 Was too tired to take a long ride this morning and also thought it unwise as Janice has one of her apathetically dumb spells on, when you have to direct her every next act as if she were a robot. In that condition she makes me uneasy. I can never tell whether she will run into a car, strip the gears, step on my heels when walking, lock us out of the apartment. "Now don't get upset with poor Janice," admonishes Evelyn. "You love her and her sun rises and sets in you. She's just a little tired, that's all. She's the same Janice, and you're the same you, even if you did have nightmares and aren't all back from them yet."

April 19   Mrs. Cash boards in Goshen with a Mr. and Mrs. Clapp. He is sixty-four, has, states Mrs. Cash (who has helped him with the income tax he hates to pay and should know), a hundred thousand dollars in the banks, owns and rents seven houses, works as janitor at a private school for eighty dollars a month, transports public schoolboys and girls to and from school in his bus for four thousand, five hundred a year. His wife, Sylvia, is fifty-four. She is, according to Mrs. Cash, "a hot number," looks twenty-six, has a lover, an "affinity," two other men and isn't sexually satisfied even then, deceives her husband, rents two rooms and boards Mrs. Cash and uses the money for clothes and a car, works out as an accommodator for fifty cents an hour forty and fifty hours a week, gets to bed at one, rises at six, day after day. Mrs. Cash admires the husband but considers him dumb. She enjoys Sylvia and helps her out of scrapes but doesn't trust her.

Mrs. Cash has always had a hankering to run a "fast house." Once or twice a month she gets drunk. The other night she came home to Mr. Clapp and said: "Say, Papa, how about you and me making some real money? Suppose we set up a cat house. There's lots of money in it." He went to his wife and explained that Mrs. Cash thought she could make money maintaining a house for old cats, but that he couldn't himself see any money in it. He told Sylvia she ought to tell Mrs. Cash what "cat house" really meant. Mrs. Cash related this anecdote, then laughed and laughed and laughed. "Somebody," she exclaimed, "ought to enlighten Papa about me."

April 20   "The hoofer we were nice to," continued Ella, "was so grateful to us for having helped her that she sent Robby and Les Smith tickets to the midnight show. It was a burlesque, a white show and a colored show in combination, playing at the Globe. It hadn't struck two before Robby was home. He was disgusted, he said. He'd never heard nor seen anything so raw. The white show was first. All they wore to begin with was a fig leaf, and very soon they were wearing nothing. Robby said he got tired of wiggling rumps and shaking tits and flocks of indecent women strutting around raw-naked. So he didn't wait for the colored part. Colored people, he explained, always try to go white people one better. But Les Smith, who stayed on, assured us the colored part wasn't nearly so lewd.

"Les Smith was with us for a week. The boys call him 'Tom Cat,' he's so hot after women. But he didn't make a single pass at me. He was a perfect gentleman. We used to talk late at night when he came in. I'd wake up and cook him some food and he'd relay the latest gossip of the nightspots. He was as clean as a hound's tooth, always picked up after himself, helped dry the dishes, was considerate and polite generally. When he went, he offered Robert some money for the bother he'd been to us. Robert naturally turned him down. Then he approached me but got nowhere. When he left, he pinned a ten dollar bill under his pillow with a nice note telling me how much he'd appreciated our hospitality and to buy myself something personal. I was touched, Arthur."

April 24   Dr. Pike is gifted with a droll manner of relating anecdotes. He was telling Billy and me how a friend had put wool in his pipe underneath the tobacco and how he had finished his smoke unaware of any unusual odor. He showed Billy how to treat his own back in order to avoid getting fatter. "Really works, William. I show the fat ladies, they use it, it helps them. They think I'm tops." Then he proceeded to explain to Billy at my instigation how to skin squabs. Tonight he leaves for North Dakota as his brother is dying. "It's a hell of a country. It's killed him. You have to be plenty tough to live there. Damnedest country you ever saw, rich, but the damnedest." I inquired if the small Minnesota towns were as drab and uninspiring as Gopher Prairie in 'Main Street.' "No doubt about it, Arthur. Just as bad. I ought to know. I grew up there and I've read the book. True to life. A place to get away from. Good to grow crops and hunt ducks but for nothing else."

April 29   Roosevelt, in his mellifluent and smug and doubtless to many reassuring voice, last night in a 'fireside chat' explained to 'the people' in words and thoughts arranged for their easy comprehension his message to Congress. The talk, delivered without sneers but with the usual emotional build-up, was masterly. I was filled with admiration for the savory concoction served to the millions of listeners.

May 6   Corregidor and the other Manila fortresses have fallen. So now the naval port of Manila will be available to the Japanese, and their gunners will man Corregidor and the other fortresses. First Spain. Then the United States. Now Japan.

If it takes courage to defend a fortress such as Corregidor, it seems to me that it takes more courage, if less long-term endurance, to storm it. No one can breathe a word against the quality of Japanese intrepidity as exemplified in this war. They have been brave individually as well as collectively, never quailing nor faltering before peril or hazard. The troops appear to be a groomed, oiled and tested machine. I think of the anecdote told by an American officer who some time ago was observing their training. For three days and nights with only a snatch of sleep here and there, the officers had been putting the troops through severe field maneuvers in rain, at night, on short rations, unremittingly. There was a lull at last. The American suggested to the Japanese officer in command that the troops were tired and he should think the lull would give them an opportunity to sleep. The officer, who had just ordered some apparently needless work done by the men, replied: "They already know how to sleep. What we teach them is how to stay awake."

May 10 Tomorrow I shall be forty-seven. Tonight I read 'Rogue Male' and 'Lanterns on the Levee' on the talking-book, listen to 'One Man's Family,'[4] hear Ella tell me stories, listen to an operetta program, hear the war news. Tomorrow I shall be forty-seven. They have been long years.

May 11 Yesterday Churchill made a speech, an unworthy, vituperative, lowlife, flaunting speech evidently aimed at the lower elements of English society, a speech patterned after Roosevelt's worst. There won't be any holding the British down if the Russians and ourselves win this war for them. Churchill announced baldly that if the Germans use poison gas on the Russians, the English will use it on the Germans. Mighty cocky now, Churchill is, obnoxiously so.

May 14 (Note — for what it is worth: I can scan a newspaper in ten minutes and get as much out of it as an average person would require an hour to secure, and it is not as with Edison or Macauley that I have left in my brain any picture of the page or paragraph — it is simply that ingredients of the printed whole leap out at me as it were, in quick answer to my general curiosity, to my general interest, if you wish.)

May 15 [From Patricia:]

Yes, Paul has left again for the army, he left two weeks ago today. At present he is at Ft. MacArthur, that is the clearing house. The men stay there for a week or so until they get assigned. He came home over both week ends, because the Fort is in San Pedro and he can get home in less than two hours on the street

---

[4] Geoffrey Household's *Rogue Male* (1939), an absorbing adventure novel about a big-game hunter's private war with the Gestapo, evoked no comment from Arthur, but he responded more positively to William Alexander Percy's memoir of the Mississippi delta country (1941), in which the author, according to Arthur, mingled "sentimental and factual astute observations indiscriminately" and sighed "over the decline of the old Southern culture." For the interminable (1932–1959) radio drama *One Man's Family,* an American saga of a middle-class San Francisco family through three generations, he had a special affection. The slow unfolding of the lives of believable people paralleled the chronicle Arthur was spinning.

car. Last week he looked very red and raw, but this week it had all turned to a nice tan. He is supervising the ditch diggers, and by the grace of one stripe he is on top of the ditch instead of in it. The men are making bomb shelters, as the Fort is most vunerable, being right in the middle of the fleet. There isn't a blade of grass nor a tree on the reservation and of course it's pretty hot work. Paul has it pretty easy. He has a private room in the barracks, which pleases him mightily, as they are mixing the whites and the negros temporarily, and from what I can gather the negros are a bit odiferous. Later of course the negros will go to their own regiments, but right now there are not enough of them to be segregated. Paul expects to be shipped this week, he hasn't the slightest idea of where it will be. As long as it is in this country I won't mind, but I worry about him being sent abroad.

Our business is absolutely screwy, we are swamped over the week-end and have nothing to do the rest of the time. It was perfectly awful yesterday, Mother's day. We had to turn people away. I still average about twenty five dollars a week with my salary and tips, have two days a week off and my meals, so I think I'm darned lucky. I really like my job, Paul hates having me a waitress, but I've not that kind of pride. He doesn't mind my being at the Pig n' Whistle because it's tops in it's class. We are patterned after Schraffts. But he does hate to have me waiting on the morons. We have a large Jewish clientle, and Paul despises the Jews, so I have to be careful not to mention when anything goes wrong at the store, or he will go up in wrath. I don't give a hoot, the meaner they are the nicer I try to be, and it works a lot better than snapping back at them. It usually makes them ashamed. Paul thinks I let people walk on me when I'm polite to the rude ones, but I'm really just conserving energy. I don't let things get under my skin unless I really care a lot. I can be firm when I want to, which Paul very well knows. Particularly about money. I refuse to live up to my income. I always try to leave a margin for safety, and, of course, since I make my money in change I know the value of every dime. While Paul, manlike, isn't interested in anything but folding money.

May 20 A woman in Brooklyn hoarded canned foods. She almost filled a basement room with assorted tinned goods. One day while she was away, a water pipe burst and flooded the cellar. Practically all the labels had soaked off the tins and were floating around the room when she returned. Now she is unable to tell a can of hash from a can of cranberry sauce, for she had piled them helter-skelter as she acquired them. She isn't very happy about it.

May 24   Last night, a fifteen year old girl, Helen Trianos, and her mother, came to talk to me. A veritable slice of America, the pair. Mr. Trianos, I was informed, is Greek and a foreman in the Brigg's Machine Shop in Waltham, in charge of making the hard rubber parts for submarine batteries. Mrs. Trianos' parents and grandparents were German, pioneer settlers in Ohio and Indiana. Both Mr. and Mrs. are Catholic.

Mrs. Trianos opened her mouth and never shut it. Her conversation was like one of those hasty and earnest wound-up toys which hurry across the floor, collide with something, change direction, hurry across the floor, collide with something, change direction, hurry across the floor, till they run down — only Mrs. Trianos never ran down. When my interruptions changed her direction, she would hasten just as diligently along the new route of thought. A good woman but what a conversationalist. I'd want to choke her before half a day was up. No reservations. She told me everything except how often she cohabited with her husband, and with time I'm sure that would have come out.

May 31   Evelyn said: "You don't think by any chance you're getting too chummy with Dicey? I know you like him, and I like him, but how do you know for certain he won't use his familiarity with your affairs to his advantage or Coakley's" (he's been mixed up in blackmail before) "or somebody's? Probably you've given this thought. If you haven't, you ought to."

"Certainly I've given it thought," I replied. "Of course there's always a chance of anyone's doing you dirt, but I don't believe that Dicey has a malicious idea as far as I am concerned. A steam-engine person such as he is wouldn't be giving up one or two nights a week over a matter of half a year to be with me if he had any scheme against me in his mind; he wouldn't have the patience, and the scheme would have come to a head long since. Neither would he do the little kindnesses he performs for me. Nor are you dealing with an Irishman or an Italian or the like. No, Evelyn, I'm sure he means well towards me. Besides, I have too much to teach him, and he's astute enough to realize it for him to jettison me. Thank you for worrying, but I'm sure you can put your mind at rest." "Well then, I'll stop worrying. You're more apt to be correct in your estimates of people than wrong."

Dicey was telling me how he'd begun to analyze and dissect his actions and his plans ahead relative to how they fitted into larger theories and practices. He notices, he said, that the process has helped him considerably, and he thanked me for having taught him the virtue of it. He has also arranged, in response to my criticism of his slips in language and pronunciation, to take two ten-week courses in speech correction. "You see," he said, "I listen to what you say. Why not? I've found there's usually something to it." While the words had the sound effect of flattery, the tone of the voice in which they were presented did not. I'm sure he was sincere.

So much for Dicey. He is one of the most interesting characters I ever met.

June 1   Melinda (Lindy) Le Jeune is from Belmont. She is graduating from high school this year. She has, she says, blue-green eyes, blonde hair, ordinary features, is five feet, six and weighs about a hundred and thirty. Her mother and father are divorced. Her mother is Scotch from Nova Scotia with (she insisted on coming here to find out if I was all right) an attractive voice. Melinda lives with her mother, her grandmother and a dog on top of a hill in a house they rent. "The dog is the only man in the family." Her mother teaches.

June 12   Melinda Le Jeune I like. She possesses emotional vitality, imagination, ease of manner, charm, a fluent tongue. It is my hope that she can be eased into becoming a permanent friend.

June 18   As to Dicey: We spent the evening talking of the draft and picking to pieces my answers to Billy's questionnaire. Billy is to be a personal valet and attendant nurse, preparing meals for an invalid, regulating his diet, administering medicine, operating a stomach pump monthly, specializing in massage, checking temperature twice nightly and the pulse, driving car, collecting rents. Dicey's idea was to give as many details as possible so that it would sound convincing. Billy is to say that he is best fitted for his present job and after that for buying, selling, arranging vegetables, which occupation he was in for a year and a half once — the period he lengthens on the questionnaire. He doesn't mention his five years in the laundry, for I understand that there is a crying need for laundry-men and that some have even been sent to Australia.

Dicey was inquiring about Janice's boy friend. "What sort of bloke is he anyway, to trail around with a girl like Janice and not cop her off?" I was uncommunicative, not deeming it the part of loyalty to discuss Bertram with Dicey. "All right," he said, "keep mum. I'll find out. I'll spend a couple or three days doing a little private investigating on my own." "Why do you want to find out?" I asked. "Oh, I've got my reasons," was his vague reply. The truth of the matter is that he's becoming interested in Janice. You can sense that he thinks about her. And there is another worry on my mind. To foster or to oppose. "You know," remarked Janice, "George's sort of nice."

June 20   The other day Evelyn was very disheartened at Dr. Pike.

She has constituted herself special custodian to prevent him from drinking too much. Evelyn is always very earnest in his behalf. I wonder if he loves her? Except when on a temperamental jag, he treats her in a most considerate and fatherly fashion.

June 21 Just before Evelyn and I stopped correcting yesterday afternoon, the phone rang. Claire's voice: "I've left home." You could tell that she flavored the melodrama of the statement. Evelyn invited her to dinner. When she showed up late as usual, she proved to have a fever of 101°. Sam, it appeared, had gone to Nashua to collect some money owed him. He didn't return the first night. He didn't return the next day. It was evening before he put in an appearance, a bun on, a raw leg of mutton and an English sailor. He staggered into the house and within a few minutes had passed out on the floor. The English sailor, in the meanwhile, apparently with no self-consciousness, had made himself at home on the couch with the afternoon paper.

Claire slammed out of the house and down the street to some friends. She was, naturally enough, incensed at Sam's behavior. She sent the friend back to find out how the children were getting along. The English sailor was reading 'Alice in Wonderland' to the children whom he had awakened. Sam was still out on the floor. Claire spent the night with her friends. The next morning, yesterday, the girl walked down the street to the house to find out if Sam and the children were all right and to spirit away some underwear and a dress for Claire, who by then had resolved to have a vacation for herself. I don't know what she did all day, but by the time she arrived here she was a wreck. Mrs. Cash, with her usual lack of tact, accosted Claire with: "Well, Mrs. Mercer, how many more children this time? Is it three or thirty-three? My, but you keep busy." I don't think poor Claire minded particularly, she being what she refers to as "blotto."

Evelyn has persuaded her to remain in bed this morning. Sam called her. Evelyn told him how sick she was and that she didn't know whether she could speak to him on the phone. He had the grace to sound worried. It must be discouraging to be bound for life because of three children to a moral weakling and a sporadic souse. It's just a good thing for her that her nature isn't as sensitized as her rather cultured English voice would indicate. Sam has left both his jobs and is doing from fifty to one hundred dollars' worth of wood turning a week.

June 22 Claire, before she left, said: "I really do love Sam. While I know he has his faults, still I want to remain with him. He has his good points, too." She had been spending the afternoon with a woman, a confessed blind drunkard for the seven years before she stopped herself. "Tell me, Arthur, what am I to do about Sam? I hate drunkenness so." When I inquired whether she nagged him each time he took a drink, she replied that she did. I advised her to quit nagging on lesser occasions and to buy some beer and light wine and keep them in the house and to drink some of it herself with Sam and to try to keep him away from hard liquor on the grounds of how much it cost rather than on moral grounds. She stated that not once since their marriage has she ever admitted herself in the wrong to Sam or apologized to him. I opined that it was no wonder he drank. I advised her to get busy and find herself in the wrong and to think up some apologies. I said that it was lucky he hadn't either bopped her or left her. Then I told her that she ought to go to a doctor and have herself examined, for it wasn't fair to Sam not to. I think that she listened, in part at least. She hasn't much native intelligence, I'm afraid.

I lay awake last night attempting to perceive World War II with detachment. I think that this war might be won expeditiously or at least more expeditiously under certain conditions.

Here would be my plan, for what it is worth and because it will not be used and because it is unconventional; it is nevertheless, I am convinced, a feasible plan. I should attempt to buy Minorca from the Spanish if I had to pay one, two, three billion dollars for it. But we do not make use of our great riches to 'buy' our victories as did the Byzantines and the Venetians, so forget the purchase of Minorca. Send (these are rough figures and rough plans) one, two thousand troops from England to Gibraltar. Then send a huge convoy with the hundred thousand soldiers and equipment that experts declare such a convoy is capable of transporting to seize the island of Sardinia, supporting the seizure by immense fleets of bombers sent across France directly from England. Establish on Sardinia a great military base. Let it be known that an attack on Italy is contemplated. Gather another great fleet in English harbors to transport an invading force to the occupied French coast. Now, under prearranged timing invade Unoccupied France at Toulon and Marseilles, screening invading operations by the dropping of large quantities of parachute troops from transport planes sent directly from England to points between the invaders and the German and Italian frontier troops. At the proper moment, unloose an invasion of Occupied France at a designated point on the Atlantic coast, bombing railroads and highways with an all-out air fleet.

I believe that some such plan as this might be of inestimable assistance to the Russians, alleviate pressure on the Middle East, establish a firm foothold on French soil. If the Marseilles-Toulon invasion were successful, additional forces could be transshipped from Gibraltar and Sardinia. I think that some such large strategic movement is immediately necessary to our cause, the more so with a Japanese attack on the Russian flank in Siberia imminent.

June 27 Last night I was in an elevator with an attractive elevator girl. She slammed the door and up we started. She switched off the light. She rubbed against me suggestively. She went further. I was enjoying myself until we passed the twenty-fourth floor. Her back was to the controls. The floors whizzed past. I ceased to enjoy myself.

June 29 Lindy pleases me. When she smiles, she looks young and cheerful and beguiling. When her face is in repose, she looks tired and strained. Her mother shouldn't be letting her work as hard and play as strenuously as she does. Somebody should slow her down. I said: "You're the sort of person I get all excited over. Most people bore me, as they have neither imagination nor drive. Can you and I stay friends for years, Lindy?" She put out a hard-palmed, long-fingered, dagger-nailed hand. "Shake," she said.

Janice is back. She has her hair piled pompadour-wise, and do I have an aversion for pompadours. I have to get used to her over again, she has been away so long.

July 1 Let me tell of Ruby, the woman who used to clean for Evelyn. We saw her as we were returning from my small ride in the yards, standing by the garage. I drew up, and she clambered in the car to talk with me. A more homely little woman never existed — scraggly sandy hair, eyes brown like a small dog's, crumpled nose, lips too flexible (they curl up to expose teeth browning at the edges), arms blotched with freckles, bare legs blotchy with freckles, a too loose cotton dress, slightly soiled Panama hat and dark tortoise-rim glasses. Yet she has to her a certain gusty warmth of spirit, social insouciance, physical vitality, kindliness which cause you to feel drawn towards her in spite of yourself. She sat in Billy's seat. She smelled slightly of sweat. She told me of her son in the financial department of the task force at New Caledonia. After being flown in a bomber to Australia to be examined for his fitness, he was made a lieutenant. She bubbled with pride. Her husband was, she said, in the Armory that moment, enlisting. He had had a varicose vein operation in order to fit himself for service. In reply to my "why," Ruby answered, flaying her hands about expressively, "Oh, to have excitement. Might as well have excitement before you're too old.

Better to do things than sit around and rot. Too bad they don't take females. Bang—bang—bang—give me a gun. Bloodthirsty, we women—huh?"

July 7 How can I tell, without sounding silly, about this new individual who appears to have entered my life? I am a man approaching fifty; she is a girl just past sixteen. And yet I feel as excited about having found her as though I were her own age and generation. There are, it seems (and so people have repeatedly told me) qualities in my nature, emotional and mental attitudes if you will, that are more or less timeless. I readily adjust myself to whomever I happen to be with, especially if I like him or her. I don't feel Lindy's elder by double and more when I'm with her, and she, being also in some measure without age, does not, I am certain, feel seriously my junior, though of course the element of years cannot help entering into the picture from a social angle. I am an intense and an imaginative person, and so is she; and we are mutually drawn toward each other. I feel excited at her proximity and pleased with her presence.

July 11 Lindy left a Liberty Mutual booklet called 'Our Office Customs' which had been given her to study.

> Some expressions to avoid are: Yeah or Yup, Nope, *Hell*-o, You know, OK or Okey doke, You bet, Fix you up, Bye-Bye, Goodbye now.

More admonitions:

> Do not run in the aisles. Open doors slowly. Pick up foreign objects on the floor. Receive visitors courteously. Discourtesy to a visitor or to a fellow employee is never warranted under any circumstance. Startling styles, vivid colors and sportswear are out of place in a business office, also the overuse of cosmetics.

July 12 Edith Sole was telling me of herself and of her recent trip by train and bus to Florida, New Orleans, St. Louis. She noted landscapes, conditions of riding, single men and girls with whom she came in contact, the drinks she had. The husband of a friend of hers is in training at Tampa. The friend wrote Bill, the husband, that Edith would be coming through. He looked Edith up. Within an hour he had her on her back in bed, where they remained all night. The next morning she left for New Orleans. A Jewish salesman of children's dresses whom she had met on the train sought her out in New Orleans and, after some persuasion and a few drinks, also had Edith on her back for the night. The next day he disappeared, and she never saw him again. She took the bus ride to Mobile and back as she desired to have a look at the Gulf shore. She went through Pass

Christian without even knowing that before the Civil War it had been the famous resort of the rich Mississippi planters. She became acquainted with a soldier. He propositioned her. "But I wasn't interested. I'd had enough for a while. He was a nice boy, though." In a little town in Indiana, I think she said, she was again propositioned by an old friend of hers, a Baptist minister. "I didn't regard him that way. It rather shocked me."

She was gone two weeks. "I came back rejuvenated and with some newer memories. There seems to be no hope of my ever catching a husband — that's plain even to me — so I've decided to take my pleasure where and when I find it, as long as it harms no one else and it's not commercial. I've given up the Y and church gatherings as unfruitful. My doctor takes care of me when I get in too bad a way emotionally, and I've a man or two besides I can call on, so I might be worse off. I've a swell job. And I just met the grandest man. Boy, what technique. He says I have something, too. Well, I'm not passive — there's that to be said in my favor. Altogether, I lead a not unpleasant life. I study radio three nights a week. My friend Dot — you know, the hairdresser who came to talk to you several times — studies radio and has been accepted by the Government and sent to Bayonne, New Jersey. She always detested hairdressing. She left her boat captain boy friend to me. I can use him occasionally. And so the days pass. I feel that I'm more acceptive of conditions and more ready to make the best of them than I used to be."

Edith figures that she must have had sexual connections with at least a hundred men. "I don't know what Janice would think of me if she knew. I tell you because you don't look down on me for something I really can't help and would like otherwise, and because you don't tell people what you know. I have my fun, but I don't mean anyone harm." Edith is too unimaginative to concoct narrations for my benefit.

I haven't any notion what has happened to Dicey. Janice received a post card from him dated July 4, Milford, New Hampshire, saying that he would be in Boston Friday. But he failed to show up. The telephone at his office has been "temporarily disconnected," New England Telephonese for "bill not paid." One day Billy stopped by the office. It was closed. We are told by Coakley's office that they haven't seen Dicey for weeks. My curiosity is piqued. It sounds as though the collection agency has gone up the flue. Or perhaps the ill-assorted members are taking a vacation. Or maybe Dicey had to "take it on the lam," as the expression has it. Or it may be that he is simply steering clear of me, though there would seem more to it than that. I miss him. I am deciding that the diamond story was a concoction from beginning to end, myself the chap who was sold a gold brick. Well, that is profit and loss, and I hope Dicey will turn up again soon and relate more tall tales, true or false, either or both indicative of his outlook on existence.

July 15   Roderic will not discuss the war with me because, so he says, my picture of what is happening is colored by my detestation for the English. Of course it is, for it was the English who got us into this — the English and the Jews — and it is the English for whom we send our men to battle and for whom we chance eventual bankruptcy. They are the core and the nemesis of this war, as far as we are concerned, and the war cannot be considered without considering them, but because I abhor them as a people and as an influence in no wise signifies, as Roderic thinks it does, that I cannot discuss the war detachedly and with a fairly unbiased perspective. I hope that whatever action the British leaders decide to take or not to take will be not only for their good but for ours as well, and that it will not be disastrous to us or too late to win the war. I hope that they will have proved themselves right, in which case I shall be one of the first to reverse my opinion of them. They are in many ways a wonderful people and I only wish we had a government analogous to theirs, more interested in our country than in theirs.

July 16   Two weeks ago, Daniel H. Coakley announced that he intended to run for the United States Senate in November. He is seventy-six. "As usual," he announced, "I will be my own campaign manager." Since his impeachment as an executive councillor last autumn for "maladministration and misconduct" in connection with the pardoning of Massachusetts criminals, he has been barred forever from holding State office. Coakley announced that he had decided to run for Senator in order to give 'the people' an opportunity to show by their votes whether they approved of his impeachment or not. When a reporter congratulated him on his healthy appearance, he replied: "It's because I have a clear and good conscience."

Dicey has not showed up. Coakley's office doesn't know where he is. His own office is closed tight. I can see no use waiting for him to return from wherever he has gone to keep an eye on the matter for which I paid him — not the diamonds — that money is down the drain. After considerable thought, I decided to have Billy consult Coakley. He was rather loath to do so, but I could see nothing to be lost, as probably Dicey has already informed Coakley about what he was doing in Billy's behalf, and there might be something to gain.

Before Dicey disappeared, one of the last services he performed for me was to locate the name and address of Anthony Abruzzo's sister. I wrote her, inquiring if she could put me in touch with her brother. I have missed the sometimes unique letters of the fawn-like creature straying among the manifestations of mechanized civilization. This morning came this letter from New York, which I shall hasten to answer:

> Just heard from my sister & she wrote that you were inquiring of my where abouts. This may be a suprise to you but I am still in N.Y.C. & am still a active "Red" To you I am most grateful for indroducing me to Maxim Gorky & indirectly to my present activities, the class strugle of the worker.
>
> Much water has passed, (to used a phrase used much to often in the wrong sence) since you last heard from me. A complete transformation has come over the old Anthony you knew, a lad who was out to get the most out life at the least possible price. Perhaps a subconcious rebelion against life, but always alone and with no direction or thought as to how best to carry this rebelion to its successful conclusion. Now I have found what I have been seeking for so long. A way of life that is organized and with a clear perspective for the future, a goal to work and fight for to the end. To say that I am now happy would be wrong, but I hardly know what else to call it. I am completely tied up in this fight. Engulfed over my head in strugles with others at my side to share victory and defeat. A history to study and read that burns its message deep inside you to remember to your dying day. A history and tradition that was born of strugle, to look to for guidance and comfort in times of stress. A history and its "scarlet banner" to carry on in mids't of battle.
>
> These are the things that have changed me from a life of useless dodging and running away from into a life of strugles and fights and to say that I plan to carry on with banner held high and the refrains of the Internationale coming from my lips, is just an confirmation of this complete change.
>
> Shall close with sincere hopes that you are feeling better and that this bit of franical raving did not bore you. With best regards

July 17   "You know," said Billy, "I sort of took to that Coakley. He's quite a guy. He musta' taken to me, too, for he talked to me for two full hours. I'm glad I went now. We discussed you, and we discussed George. I felt him out, like, and then told him about what Dicey had been doin' for us and how we couldn't locate him high or low. I got him to say he'd help us if we was unable to locate George. He did some phonin', and ascertained that George had been in town the night before. Then he told me about himself for the rest of the time. He calls you 'the old man.' He doesn't look his age. He said if ever he could do anything for us, not to hesitate to let him know. Yes sir, I think the visit paid. I went against my judgment, but I'm glad I went."

Billy tried to locate Dicey and tried again this morning. No success. I not only want him for what's on our minds, but I want him because this traffic is going wild nights again and I can't sleep, and I would like to know if conditions of routing have altered. Anyway, I miss him, for I both enjoyed his company and learned from it. I wish two things: that I'd never lent him two hundred dollars and that I'd been less outspoken about being gypped.

Dicey just called up. He said that he saw a note at Coakley's office that we had called him there. Which means, doubtless, that Coakley admonished him to get in touch with us. I had Janice say that we had all missed him, and that life had been less exciting without him. I intend to save his face for him from here on. Probably this lesson will be worth two hundred dollars to me at some time in the future. Very pleased, however it happened, that he got in touch with us.

In spite of no sleep from the traffic last night, I feel like a new person today. I think — I hardly dare think — I think with my fingers crossed — that last night the lumbar spine went into position. This has been a terrible siege.

Eleanor has been correcting Volume 18 [1923–24]. "You wanted to be a bigamist," she says, flirting her skirts and looking out the window. "It fills me with distaste." She has no understanding, intrinsically, of my nature. She is a self-satisfied person, smug, cold, filled with a feeling of superiority as far as *all* of us here and our unconventional actions are concerned. It is impossible to become wholeheartedly attached to her. She would, I feel sure, leave me at the drop of the hat. While I admire some of her qualities, and while she is proving to be very helpful with the diary, I cannot but experience a certain contempt for her lack of perspicacity and warmth.

July 18 I don't want to be unfair to Eleanor. She is, I am sure, a much more admirable person than many people are. We have been working together amicably this morning for all of two hours, and it is a pleasure to work with her. She has an exceptionally pleasant voice. Her interest in my diaries is genuine. She will read a difficult passage for me ten times over without impatience.

July 25 It would squeeze the juice out of an orange, this staying awake all night. Three hours and a half sleep last night. I tried to figure out how to repair the piece of rubber on the bottom of the windshield in the Pierce. Janice, when I asked her yesterday to push it in line (the rubber being old) to keep the rain and the streak of sun out, dumbly jabbed and broke a fingernail file, and instead of stopping at the first break kept on breaking. You can't buy new ones. You can't buy old ones. I was out of my wits to ask Janice to fix anything like that, she having neither manual dexterity nor horse sense. So I began by considering the problem of what to do and of how to order my judgment not to be so stupid again and ended by remaining awake from three-thirty on.

And it was a hectic day yesterday in other ways. Billy was run into in his car. Evelyn and Eleanor spent all morning at the microfilm place, only to have the negatives come out blank. Billy left the beans on the stove to burn. Eleanor had a crying spell after being nasty. Mrs. Cash, because I wanted her for only half the evening yesterday, is on the rampage, she having become accustomed to making two dollars rather than one on Fridays. She is a bitch when her expectations of money are thwarted, whether for a dime or a dollar. She will be morose and snappish for weeks. Well, her anger causes her to read better and not to talk so much, which decidedly helps. I'm grateful to her, but I don't actually like her. She keeps every bit of loose change pinned securely in a wallet under her girdle. I'd hate to worship money that way. She and Dicey are, whatever words you use to describe it, misers pure and simple.

Billy at last saw Dicey. He had, he said, been tailing a man recently released from jail who had vowed to get him and Coakley. He had, Billy said, a gun under a towel in his room and was jittery. The man had almost bumped him off once before. Two days ago he phoned and announced that the man had been put in jail, would I like to see him Saturday evening. I had Billy tell him that I guessed so. I have little enthusiasm left for the man. He has not only lied to me; he has not only taken my money for good. He has been thoroughly stupid throughout insofar as I am concerned. At the least, I was a prospective income. Dicey carries, he told Billy, three annuity policies to mature when he is forty-five. On one of them he pays sixty-five dollars a month. He further informed Billy that he would go without anything to meet the payments. He had, he said, lost good friends meeting the payments. That, thinks Billy, is where my money went. Perhaps the tailing story is merely just another cock-and-bull fabrication but perhaps not. I still don't comprehend why he failed to get in touch with me. He received, he told Billy, all my notes. Billy says: "You may think you understand how his mind works but you don't, because you don't live his sort of life and have his sort of standards. You couldn't look yourself in the face if you did."

Last night I tapped on Billy's door where Evelyn was sleeping. She woke and let me in. I lay on the bed and told her stories. She was part asleep. I had been looking forward to a midnight visit with her for months. "Do you like my being with you?" I queried. "It's all right," she replied. I left and returned to my own room. She didn't hug me; she didn't say she was glad to have me with her. It was "all right." There isn't much tact about Evelyn where I am concerned. She nearly always manages to say the unpleasant truth when discretion or guile or self-interest would prompt a pleasant prevarication. She has nothing to lose by a bit of flattery and some blandishments and much to gain. She can successfully take the wind out of me in the wink of an eye. There's no use chiding her, and I try to restrain my temper at what seems to me mere self-indulgent stupidity, but I do wish she were somewhat more skillful in handling me. And it wasn't just last night; it is almost every time when there is a choice between a deflating truth and a beguiling falsehood. It seems to me that I'd be a pushover for the first smart woman who took a modicum of trouble to manage my comparatively uncomplicated nature.

July 30   Mrs. Cash is toying with the idea of enlisting in whatever the women's naval auxiliary is called. Her forbears, she says, followed the sea, and perhaps that is where she belongs. Anyway, she is discontented with the school situation in Goshen where she has been placed in entire charge of junior high with no title and no additional salary. I hope that she is merely talking.

She has been endeavoring to find Mrs. Banks a position, for Mrs. Banks has had no work since she left here. However, Mrs. Banks will do this, won't do that, so that Mrs. Cash is dubious that she can help her.

Edna, I hear, is making very good money in her partnership with Henry Green. Manuel has some petty job, is not in the army.

August 6   "God damn the war," exclaimed Dicey, as he light-footedly made his way through the darkness to the chair beside my bed. "God damn the war. I'm afraid it's got me. It was putting down on my questionnaire that I once worked with direction finders. It seems that what they need now and can't find are radio technicians. I've had to appear before the Boston Procurement Board of the War Production Board twice now. The first time I told them that naturally I wanted to serve my country, but that I was sure I'd just about forgotten what little I ever knew. They sent me to the Lawley Shipyard to a man named Dennis. Dennis gave me three simple questions, worth not more than twenty minutes each. I did them the long way and the cumbersome way, returned the paper at the end of four hours with one right answer and two wrong ones. He sent word to the Board that I was rusty but could be trained. The

Board called me again. I made the same plea as before. They didn't listen. I said why not put me to work as a carpenter or something, anything for my country; but they wouldn't want me to bungle the fields and perhaps cause disaster to a ship, would they? They suggested sending me to Wentworth Institute for a three months' course and then to an apprentice school for eight weeks. Every excuse or reason I could think up, they were right there with a counter answer. They appealed to my patriotism. There were seven on the Board, six businessmen and a Government man. There wasn't any bribing or fixing them. They weren't pols. They were honest and they meant business. They wanted me to go to Portland to help rig up radio direction finders on submarines, and they felt I was inherently capable, and God damn it, that was all there was to it; I ought to be glad to serve my country. And after listening to them awhile, by Christ, I did feel my patriotism stirring. I'm to call them Friday for their decision.

"The Old Man thinks I ought to go to Portland for a week and act so dumb they'll want to get rid of me. I don't see it that way. In the first place, if I was inaccurate, those fellows in the sub might lose their lives for it. Avoiding service and having that happen are two decidedly different matters. And more than that if I'm to make politics my life's work and if I had a bad record behind me when the war's over and the American Legion (they already have a plan for a permanent A.L., with this crop of war veterans to join their organization) is powerful, where would I be with a sloucher? Coakley's lawyer says I ought to go to Portland for five or six months — it won't kill me and will give me a clean record for service — and then bribe a foreman to fire me or something. I went to the personnel director of A.S. Glenn Machine Company — he's a friend of mine — and he concurred with the lawyer. He said he'd give me a job there if I thought best, then fire me later, but in his opinion it was dangerous. I suppose I'll have to go to Portland and do the sick act there — you know, out three or four days a week till they fire me. I won't fumble on the actual work, though — it's too damned important. That is, I'll have to go unless I can think up a way out before Friday, or unless the Board gives me a reprieve."

Before Dicey left, I suggested a way out that on quick thought looked foolproof. If I make myself valuable to him, he'll stick around. He says that if he goes to Portland, he'll be sure to fix matters up about Billy before he leaves.

He has not mentioned money and neither have I. He accepted without demur the dollar I gave him for the evening. But he stayed until twelve. He comes again Saturday evening.

August 11 [From Abruzzo:]

It was rather hard to start the first letter as I had to rack my brain to remember some of the details even though I remember the incident itself. And so with the Army induction, my memory needed a bit of prodding to bring out some of the routine I went through. I had recieved my notice so I quit my job and just loafed around for a week. On the eventful morning I got up about five and rode up to my draft board which is located way up in the Bronx. I got there about six and soon more fellows drifted in until all were accounted for about seven. We then started out by taking the subway to South Ferry, which is a five minute ride from where I live. I could have saved three hours sleep if I could have reported down town. There we waited for over an hour as more and more drafters showed up from all over town. They finally took us aboard a boat to Fort Jay. There was about two hundred fellows in all — and what a mixed crowd. Some elated and others indifferent and still others really sore. I walked around a bit & talked to some. Most of them seemed very untalkative. When we arrived at Govornor's Island we were herded over into a cornor until a fleet of trucks could pick us up. Each draft board was allotted a truck so some were almost empty while others like mine was filled beyond capacity. We had a ten minute ride to the induction center and not a comfortable ride either. That Army truck jolted and bounced us about so that it was a relief to get out. All of us were lined up single file and each of us recieved a tag with a number and the mass production line was on its merry way. They must have taken a few of Fords ideas of an assembly line. We kept moving we knew not where as there was about four cornors to turn along side a building with two wings. An hours moving at a snail pace brought us within sight of the door. Most of the guys were quite exited and much speculation of what we were to go through. When I got in I found myself at a desk where they wanted a few facts such as if I had ever been in jail and why. Then followed a finger printing. Then into a large recreation hall. There was no one at the door so many of us went out for some air. There I got to talking again. This guy talked my language and sure enough it turned out he belonged to the Party. He was in the student movement and a leader of some youth organazation working in Washington, D.C. All this time a Sargent was calling our numbers and one by one they went. Luckly I was one of the last so as it was way past noon they took the remaining bunch and marched us to mess hall for an Army meal. The food was good.

Plenty of it too. It was served cafeteria style and as we were all hungry there wasn't much left when we got through. The line was then started again. We went first into a check room where we undress and then out and line up quite nude. I caught a nice cold standing there for half an hour. Then into another building where xray, blood test and urine spicimen were taken then on with the line. The ear doctor took but a second then on to eyes and throat and chest. Then came my down fall, the pyciatrists. They started to ask me all about the jails I had been in and the reasons behind it. One thing lead on to another and the first thing I knew they were asking my views on religion and politics. Also what sort of lititure did I read. I mentioned some unimportant works but I also stuck in Maxim Gorky. They jumped on this. Well they passed me on to the other doctors and I completed my physical. When I got out they sent up to a reception room where there was a bunch of fellows and the queerest lot you ever saw. Whacks and queers and a few fairies. So I knew what was coming and after a short wait I got an offical statement that I was unfit for the Army for obvious reasons. By the time I caught the boat back to New York it was almost six p.m. So I spent an entire day just to find my self rejected for Army duty. I put in an appel and waited and what a wait. Almost 8 months and I have just heard from the local draft board. They had me interviewed by a social servise worker and I convinced her that what I wanted was a chance to fight for victory. She was impressed enough to send in a favorable recommandation so that they still might take me I hope. Mean while I continued my party work. One night to advertise a meeting we were giving out leaflets. I was on one cornor and a girl was across the street. All of a sudden I noticed a crowd and rushed over to find that some guy had been stabbed. The guy who had stabbed him got away. It all started by this guy starting to molest the girl and this seamen came to her aid. Well he was rushed to the hospital where it was found he had a puntured lung. A blood transfusion and a robust body pulled him through. We gave him what aid we could. He was a very un-informed youth for he had never met any Communist before. We still had the task of tracking the thug down and all of us went to work. We got several leads and finaly found the guy. He was one of Joe Burn's muscle guys and we had some job to get a conviction. He got two years. Joe Burn has his gang on us, as he hates our trying to organize the longshoremen. Some of his boys have already got me twice. They generaly surround you and just start slugging without any words being said. One of the girls I run around with (nothing serious, just comradely friendship) has been slugged three times and always down in the same niegherhood. Last week one of our boys who sells our paper was attacked, and not long ago another of our paper guys was slugged and robbed as well as all the papers being destroyed. So you see there is a bit of danger. One of my exflames was giving out leaflets one night. A bunch of guys came over and each took as many as posible. When they had enough they built a fire all around her. The only reason she wasn't slugged was that the police station was just a short distance away and there generaly are a couple of radio cars around. The fire attrected people but they all laughed. So the girl gave it up and reported back.

Shall close now with best wishes.

Salud

August 13   Dicey and I talked of odds and ends. He described the joints for sailors springing up everywhere in Boston and the young girls who service them. We discussed graft in general in this country and I expressed my trepidation at the amount of it and wondered whether or not we could win the war with the nation as pitted with petty grafters and major grafters, crooked lawyers, unscrupulous politicians, acquisitive officials, grasping businessmen, etc., etc. as it is. Germany and Japan, I continued, no doubt had their unscrupulous and piratic upper oligarchy, but there was, I felt sure, nothing in those nations, our fighting enemies right now, to compare with the general state of corruption existing in this country. He saw what I meant, he said, and I might be right; but he had noticed lately a spirit of patriotism creeping into some very hardened sinners and with it a more rectitudinous attitude.

August 14   Evelyn and Eleanor are at the microfilm place. All my women are pretty today — Evelyn in her red dirndl dress and red shoes, Eleanor in a pastel-pink woolen suit she made herself and new high-heeled brown shoes, Janice in a candy-stripe jumper with a pink waist. Billy and I rode around Brookline. Then Janice and I took some pajamas to Ella to fix. She had been out shopping, and we caught her on the way home. She looks much older than she did ten years ago and not so pretty. A drunken colored man shuffled up the sidewalk, his large feet dragging with a sound like sandpaper on stone. Two disreputable Mediterranean-type men cut pieces of meat at the back of a peddler's cart, and flies buzzed and crawled. A gray cat convulsively spasmed up its meal and lost it nonchalantly on the pavement where it lay like a hot cake dropped in a pan.

August 15   One of the bewildering aspects of this war to an observer with an analytical mind and an historical sense of proportion is that it is fairly impossible to disengage truth from propaganda. Rumors of all sorts postulate sinkings on a scale larger than we have any idea of. Billy, for instance, was talking to a friend of his last night who has been in the Coast Guard for eight months and on duty in Long Island Sound. He said that two heavily loaded munition ships were recently blown up by German submarines almost within sight of New York City. He reckons that seventy-five percent of what is being sent abroad fails to arrive. He feels that the shipping situation is so frightening that it is well that the American public is kept in ignorance of it. Nor do I believe all that either. But what to believe?

The English announce that they have shot down a new type of German bomber which is capable of crossing the Atlantic, disposing of a thousand-pound bomber, flying home. This may or may not be English propaganda to spur our efforts. An article in the 'Globe' today purports to be a warning from Germans escaped from Germany that Hitler is building a great bomber fleet with which to attack American cities and industries, and that all that is needed to make it effective is Russian oil. You can believe that or not.

August 16 Claire had supper with Evelyn. I saw her for a moment afterwards before she hurried off to Cambridge to the small playhouse there to see Paul Robeson, the negro actor who made his reputation in 'Show Boat,' playing in 'Othello.' She arrived home at twelve-thirty and stayed with me until one-thirty or thereabouts. Every seat had been sold out. She and a Jewish girl she struck up an acquaintance with moseyed around the theatre until they chanced on a door which let them in behind the stage. They appealed to a stagehand with the story that they had come all the way from New Hampshire just to see Robeson, could he not get them in? He allowed them to stand in the wings. "It was thrilling," exclaimed Claire. "We were so close we could see the spittle flying from his mouth when he was vehement. I loved every minute of it. And the girl who played the part of Desdemona was simply stunning — blonde hair and long white arms." "Did Robeson embrace her and kiss her?" I inquired. "Oh yes. Three times." "Did it disgust you to watch a colored man fondling a white woman?" "Oh no. Why should it?" "Did the audience object?" "Of course not. Don't be silly." "Fifteen years ago something like this wouldn't have been permitted on the boards." "Well, it is now, and what's more, it will probably open in New York this autumn. I loved it."

Claire has gained some weight, also some energy. "It's the housewifely life, Arthur." She lay on the bed with me and I teased her by pretending to want to seduce her, and she amused me by turning very proper at once and acting disconcerted so that I laughed until the tears came from my eyes. Claire is dear to me, and I guess I'm very fond of her, no matter what she looks like.

August 18   Lindy rocked me on my heels last night by calling me "Father." "Well," she said, "that's the way I feel about you. I've never known any older person I could talk to as a father and be listened to and be understood. Why, you solve most of my problems for me before I've expressed them." Myself, I'm not anxious for the parent role. And here comes an unusually attractive girl who seems ready and anxious to endow me with parental attributes. "Do you know why I like Ben so much?" she asked, and answered: "I like him because he reminds me of you, a younger edition of you."

I thought about the matter much of the night. Lindy's attitude towards me is certainly more normal and sensible than mine towards her. And maybe most of my attitude towards her has in it fatherly implications. I can't maintain a posture of not being my age indefinitely, thinking or hoping that a girl Lindy's age can regard me otherwise than as a middle-aged man, which I am. And this I know: that those people who refuse to grow mature with their years usually turn unpalatably conspicuous. It is as much of an art to grow older gracefully as any art in life. The time has arrived, self-evidently, for me to assume the expected habiliments of my years and not to be rebellious at doing so. And I couldn't well have a more attractive daughter.

I inquired of Evelyn what she thought. "I think," she replied, "that you should accept the role Lindy wishes to assign to you and be pleased with it. It's a natural role and the only one permanently possible between two people as far apart in age as you and Lindy are. You certainly can't compete except very temporarily with her various boy friends. And you do want to keep her affection over a matter of years, for that's what you like. I'm certain that Lindy, who seems to have intense emotions, will only become confused if you treat her as someone with whom you fall in love, and then you'd only lose her—while the relationship of father and daughter is a sane and understandable one from her point of view and will give you a unique and an unchallenged place in her affections. Anyway, I think it's nice."

I thanked Evelyn for having expressed herself so aptly. She is, I am sure, correct in her assumptions and conclusions. I am, from today on, a newly born parent. I wouldn't be surprised were I to be very pleased with the idea when I become fully accustomed to it.

August 20   [From Patricia:]

When I last wrote you Paul was in an induction camp, waiting to be shipped to a more permanent post. He stayed at Fort McArthur for two weeks, during which time he came home five times and we did one of those "goodby forever" acts at the station each time. He had more farewell performances than Bernhart. And then after our anguished farewells he was sent to Van Nuys, a suburban town, eight miles from here! It was a new outfit for him. The 110th Quartermaster Battalion, General Lear's famous "Yoo Hoo" outfit. They were a bunch of Nebraska farmers, and had all been friends for years. Paul being the only foreigner and an actor to boot was loudly resented as he was put into headquarters with the commanding officers. He raised cain trying to get his promotion in rank, which was due him for length of service, but it was no go, as all the Nebraskans had first choice. So Paul asked for a transfer when he found the regiment was going to be moved anyway. Now he is back at San Luis Obispo, where he spent nine months before, but he is with a new outfit, The Intelligence division of the Military Police. It's the first outfit of its kind, a training school for the police. They are all over six feet, so must be quite a spectacle. Paul is in charge of Personnel and Pay Roll. He does the investigation of the men's records. There are but twenty three men at headquarters and they camp four to a tent, all are N.C.Os. so it is much more pleasant than the former barracks at Van Nuys, forty men to a room. The men were given the privilege of picking their own roomates, so Paul is very happy. Unfortunately he expects to be transfered in September, somewhere in the middle west he thinks, but there is no knowing in this war.

August 26   I have received another letter from Abruzzo. How on earth is one to discriminate between the fictitious and the straightforward? It has always more or less been my policy to let my characters say their say and only when I am convinced of the truth or falsity of stories or statements to tender my opinion. There are very few people who will purposely tell you stories or anecdotes they are sure you will disbelieve, which attitude tends to hold them, even when they are lying, to such semblance of the truth as they are pretty sure you will believe. So that what people say is usually (even if it errs from the strict truth) a truthful indicator of American character and incident. In this last epistle of his, Abruzzo tells of working in a rubber plant and of stirring up strikes among the workers, of being financed by his brother in a candy store venture which failed, of playing the horses and making money and living with a "couple of dames," of gambling and drinking and losing his money. For some reason, while all the incidents are possible, they ring absolutely untrue. So whether wisely or not, I am refraining from appending the letter.

August 27 Billy and I had a long talk while sitting by Beech Park. It was mild there with a mowing machine cutting grass, birds twittering, sunlight slanting through leaves, a low pearl-like sky. "By God, Arthur," said Billy, "when I think of havin' to leave you I could break down and cry. After so many years of bein' intimate, to have to be separated — and you like this, with nothin' to say about it." "And it makes me feel that way too, Billy. I hate to lose you, and I hate to think of you going into a war which doesn't give a hoot about you as an individual."

What sort of future will I have? Billy's leaving me will make a great breach in my self-confidence. And I will as well be lost osteopathically without him. The hours of misery and pain his treatments have saved me are uncounted, and in many complications of bone and muscle no osteopath can do what he does. And what will happen to the capital structure which gives me support? And will Evelyn get sick now that she is older, if too large a portion of caring for me devolves on her? And will Bottom be overcome by the urge to serve her country which is sweeping the nation? Will we be bombed or taxed into poverty or what? Will the United States of America — it is not absolutely impossible — be defeated? And even if we win, what will happen to our present culture?

Calls from Washington for sacrifice left Arthur cold. True enough, the United States was funneling its wealth into three continents, but he refused to believe the claims of serious shortages concocted by FDR (a "tyrant" no better than Hitler or Tojo) and his minions, and chose to regard rationing as a personal affront. Defiantly, he justified his hoarding. Why should Americans like himself be regimented and overtaxed "chiefly to help nations that hate us fundamentally keep their heritage of empire intact?" As for the British, whom he both admired and detested, he wished "like so many Americans" that "it were they we were fighting instead of the Germans, though I hold no brief by now, God knows, for the Germans."

The government threatened to deprive him of tires and gasoline. Worse, it exacerbated the servant crisis. Despite the shady efforts of Dicey and Coakley to keep Billy from being drafted, it looked bad for him unless the eighteen- and nineteen-year-olds were called up first. Billy did not cooperate very well. He spoke of joining the Volunteer Officer's Corps and spurned Arthur and Dicey's advice to pressure Sadie into quitting her job in the laundry and thereby get himself reclassified. In short, Billy was "bullheaded" (that must have been the "Indian" in him), and he further angered Arthur by his demands for more times off.

Who would take Billy's place? Pearl, possibly, if she could be persuaded to leave her well-paid position as superintendent in an arms factory. She and Arthur had patched up their differences, but she only toyed with the possibility of returning to Garrison Hall (her mother, she said, opposed the idea) and agreed only after some hard bargaining. Arthur was on the spot, with Eleanor about to leave and Billy's departure in the offing. Evelyn seemed incapable of providing him with the care and adulation he craved. And now his adorable Janice, whom he had counted upon to see him through the war, tremulously informed him of her engagement to Bertram Davis.

He brooded over her unfairness, her ingratitude, and was not comforted by her assurances that she would never desert him. She knew how he felt about Davis, yet she had accepted Davis's belated offer of marriage. A detective Arthur hired to check on Janice's lover turned up nothing. The year 1942 petered out with Arthur querulous, disgruntled, "and filled with trepidation concerning the future."

August 29 I am living at Garrison Hall, a seven-story apartment house on the corner of Garrison Street and St. Botolph Street, one block off Huntington Avenue, where I have been fairly continually in residence since 1919. The building was renovated in 1935. The tenants are middle-class white-collar workers, mostly non-Jewish, although the landlords are Jewish. The people are orderly and well behaved. Everything is a bit second-rate, the employee service and the attitude of the landlords in particular. However, the location is as quiet as can be found within the city. My wife, Evelyn, and I rent five apartments: three for ourselves and two — the ones directly above and below me — which we sublet at almost the price we pay for them, to insure quiet for me. Evelyn occupies the three-room apartment on the fourth floor, fronting on St. Botolph Street. I have the corner apartment at the back of the house, the sixth floor; and Billy, my man, has the apartment next mine. My apartment has four rooms — my bedroom, a sitting room facing east-southeast, the library, and the kitchen, which we use for a spare storage room. We have limited personal use of the back elevator.

I am forty-seven. Evelyn is forty-one. Billy Minor is thirty-one. Janice Oliphant is twenty-eight. My other secretary, Eleanor Oates, is twenty-nine. Billy has been with me going on six years, Janice for four years, Eleanor one year. I am, on the whole, very satisfied with my staff. Billy is about six feet tall, weighs two hundred and twenty-four or so, has a stomach, double chins, a dark round face with dark eyebrows, white teeth, curly hair and an infectious smile. He is part Indian, Sioux. Janice is darker than he is with a face like a Mayan princess, eyes as brown as Billy's but clearer, a straight nose, very white teeth, beautiful long-fingered hands. She weighs one hundred and thirty-three, is five feet, five or six inches tall. She is quiet and gentle. Eleanor is shorter and slighter, a blonde with very blue eyes and a tasteful way of dressing, an unusually pleasant voice but not the warm person Janice and Billy are. Evelyn weighs what Janice does, as do I. Her hair is brown, parted in the middle with bangs. Her forehead is wide, her eyebrows heavy and far apart, her eyes brown, her teeth strong and white, her nose wide but pointed at the end as in the old Dutch paintings. In front, her face resembles the faces in those pictures more than it does the oval American face or the long American face or the hatchet-shaped American face.

Evelyn has a fairly new Ford coupe. I have a 1919 Cadillac phaeton and a 1930 Pierce-Arrow phaeton. I have three radios and Evelyn has two. We live, while not in style, at least in comfort.

I own between sixty and eighty thousand dollars' worth of stocks. We own a three-quarters acre piece of property at Jamaica Plain with a partly renovated stable on it as well as a house at 43 St. Botolph Street which we hold as a place to move to in case Garrison Hall blows up and which in the meanwhile we rent for seventy-five dollars a month.

It costs us about $1,200 a month to live, most of which my Father supplies by monthly check. He is having to dip into his capital, the income taxes now being levied commandeering three-fourths of his income. He is seventy-three. His money will not be left us, though if we are fortunate, we will draw an income from the estate. Evelyn's father and mother are seventy-seven or seventy-eight. Mrs. Yates gives Evelyn an allowance of fifty dollars a month, and my Father gives her a hundred dollars a month.

I ride and work mornings, correct what I have written afternoons, talk to people or am read to by someone evenings. Mrs. Cash, who is fifty or fifty-one and was the mistress of my former man and is a schoolteacher at Goshen, reads to me at least twice a week and does extra work. She is short and energetic and foulmouthed, with large blue eyes, white bobbed hair, overpainted cheeks. Roderic Peters reads at least once a week. He has been coming for some fourteen years now. He is short, has a vile disposition, is an insurance adjuster, has a second wife and a baby girl. Ella James, thirty-six, colored, married to a redcap, comes usually once a week. She talks to me. I have known her for eight years. Millicent Barnes Wright, her husband dead a year, comes. She is short, blue-eyed, blonde, full of energy, about fifty. I have known her for fourteen years. Juliette Stern, Jewish, is thirty-one. I have known her for seven or eight years. George Dicey, thirty-three or thirty-four, very fat, dynamically energetic, talks. He is unmarried, a politician and racketeer. I have known him not quite a year.

My doctors are Dr. Pike, tall and forceful, nearing seventy; Dr. MacIntosh, tall and stooped and strong, white hair and blue eyes, not quite as old as Dr. Pike; Dr. Dorothy Bottomley, thirty-six; Dr. Fred Lakian, Armenian, about thirty-two; Dr. Pusey, about thirty-five; Dr. Woodbine, over seventy. My doctors seem unusually devoted to me and to my service, willing to put themselves out to be of assistance at any time.

We lead a life that is run more or less on schedule. It revolves mainly around me. The mainspring of my existence is the keeping of this diary. I am very weak physically and am troubled by bones and cartilages which do not for longer than a matter of hours stay put or in order. My eyes are weak but stronger than formerly. I cannot walk any distance. I sleep little. I spend from sixteen to seventeen hours of the full day in bed.

August 30 Billy is cleaning my rooms and bathroom. He talks of being tutored in algebra, geometry, trigonometry, English, preparatory to being mustered into the Army. He signed up yesterday. As a Volunteer Officer Candidate, he receives no warning of when he will be called, gets no two weeks to settle up his affairs, which is going to be a disadvantage to me, since I won't know when to engage someone new. He thinks that he has done the right thing. I am dubious. Dicey disagrees with the course taken. Evelyn and Mrs. Cash approve.

Evelyn and I were discussing Sadie. There's something more than meets the eye there. Why is she so loath to quit the Colonial Laundry where she has been for — is it eighteen years? Where does she get her closetsful of clothes — five hundred dollar fur jackets and coats, so many dresses she gives them away? It could be that some man at the laundry is interested in her. Billy says: "This sex stuff doesn't set me crazy like it does so many men. There's other things more worthwhile." And night after night, when Evelyn is out and Billy is staying in, Sadie will refuse to take the trip over to keep him company. And she is always going out evenings "with the girls." It is a strange relationship. That he is devoted to her I am sure. That she is devoted to him is open to considerable doubt.

September 1 Three years of war today with more than a million square miles of Europe conquered and some one hundred and seventy million people made subject, with more than a million and a half square miles of Asia conquered and some one hundred and forty million people made subject. Not for us a very comforting record, and the conquerers still roll on. That they are at the moment rolling more slowly may be in the nature of a pause, may be the retardation at the end of the pendulum's swing; we, watching, have no means of interpreting which. The news from abroad this morning states that despite the desperate resistance of the Soviets before Stalingrad, despite the counterattack successfully launched against the Germans northwest of Moscow, a new wedge has been driven into Russian positions southwest of Stalingrad. Rommel's forces are thought to be on the move again.

September 2 Evelyn and I thought of Pearl for Billy's job if he goes. Evelyn wrote her. Pearl replied by telephone that she was chief inspector of gun sights, received thirty-five a week, wasn't interested. Evelyn says that she was superior, condescending, self-satisfied. Too bad. She had good material for a nice human being. She probably won't be worth shooting before she is much older. "You might as well cross her off your books," remarked Evelyn. "She's gone to crab grass."

September 3 I certainly am a strange person insofar as my conscience goes. Here am I, because I love Janice and because she is so good to me, exerting my influence with Dicey to have Bertram Davis' deferment extended in January, when it probably wouldn't be if I let it alone. He helps fill up Janice's life and gives her pleasure, and therefore I want to keep him out of the war for her if it is possible.

September 5 Mrs. Cash says: "Everyone I know is going to war. There's not a man teacher who was there last year left at Goshen High. I tell you, Mr. Inman, there may come a day and not too far away when you'll be so damn glad to see this old bitch walking in the door that it will surprise you." "I tell you, Mrs. Cash," I replied, "I'm already glad to hear the old bitch stamping bump-bump-bump down the hall and keeping time by exclaiming 'shit-shit-shit,' and I don't even mind when she hits a chair and ejaculates 'whale shit.' So you can't tell how dirty I may let you get and still be pleased to see you." She laughed just like Namma used to do, until she bent double and the tears streamed from her eyes. Such a needlessly salacious woman never was; she loves you when you "dole out a little dirt." I should think more of her services did she restrain her purile enjoyment of filthy words and filthy thoughts, but such restraint is more than I shall ever obtain, save sporadically.

September 6   Listening to a Bach concerto on the radio. Turn it off and find something else quickly. Finger exercises. Church services on one station after another. Yiddish light music. I rather like it.

September 13   Not having Ella again in the mornings. Our relationship in the evenings has been so different that I feel uncomfortable ordering her around, and I suspect that she feels uncomfortable being ordered around. She's a very spoiled person with a large bump of self-esteem and doesn't, I'm sure, take easily to being directed by anyone. Nor is she very efficient. All in all, therefore, I have decided it is best not to risk a misunderstanding that might impair our pleasant evenings together. She isn't as pretty to look at as she used to be, and her taste in clothes is frightful.

I have finished 'The Queen's Doctor,' it being, so the subtitle informs the reader, 'the Strange Story of the Rise and Fall of STRUENSEE, Dictator, Lover, and Doctor of Medicine.' The scene is laid in Denmark in the 1770's and has to do with the mad King, his English child Queen and the doctor who rose to be Premier. A note in someone's handwriting in the back of the book announces: "Maybe you'll think I'm nuts. *This book is messy.*" I have, on the contrary, enjoyed it tremendously. However, the note set me to analyzing just why I had enjoyed it so much. I like period pieces. I am partial to books which leave something to the imagination, which is probably just why the writer of the scornful note did not fancy the story or the style. 'The Queen's Doctor' is by Robert Neumann and is a translation from the German, I think, and a very excellent translation indeed.

September 14   Oh yes, the war. The Germans have captured one Black Sea naval base. Their drive on the oil fields of the Caucasus has come to a stop, undoubtedly in order to wait for the fall of Stalingrad. Stalingrad is now closely invested by a huge German army enclosing the city in a semicircle extending from Volga bank to Volga bank. It is said that the Russian defenders have destroyed all bridges behind them and all boats, as Cortez did, and are resolved to make of Stalingrad another Sevastopol. The punishment that a collection of resolved humans can endure appears to be almost limitless. Or is it that the rain of explosives has hiatuses which men grown accustomed to the noise and demolition around them are able to take advantage of with ingenuity, tirelessness, courage?

September 15   Millicent has agreed to interview and sort applicants answering my next ad for a secretary. I pay her and she winnows out the chaff. She seems to possess an adequate idea of what I want. Having the selecting done at her apartment and only the few approved persons brought here will reprieve Evelyn and Janice from considerable drudgery.

September 16 Fred fixed my stomach and then my ribs. I felt better than for many weeks. Then Evelyn startled me again waking me, and the heart muscles jammed and that pulled the ribs out of place, and now I'm miserable and angry with her for having to be given directions so many dozens of times over and over again. The Pierce battery is dead and my car isn't adjusted to run well.

September 17 The fall of Stalingrad appears to be imminent. There is street fighting taking place in the city. From the Russian Embassy in London, new urgent pleas for the opening of a second front are forthcoming.

From Moscow by shortwave yesterday came the following revelatory anecdote, which Soviet censors assuredly would not have passed were Russia not more than mildly out of patience with the British. God looked down and noted that the world was engaged in battle, nation against nation. On inquiry, a counselor suggested that Russia was probably to blame and that God would do well to talk with Stalin. So God asked Stalin if he were to blame for what was happening. He was not, Stalin answered. Hitler had attacked Russia. God should talk to Hitler. So to Hitler God went. No, said Hitler, it was not his fault. God should talk to Churchill who was culpable for the war. How about it? God asked Churchill. Utter foolishness, replied Churchill to God. Why, he said, how could God be short-sighted enough to blame the English for what was happening. God had only to look to see Germans and Russians fighting fiercely. But God, no matter where he looked, could not discern a single Englishman engaged in battle.

September 21 Billy got back last night. Was away too long and I suffered too much while he was gone for me to be exceptionally glad to have him back.

September 29 Billy's Sadie's sister's boy friend is being drafted. Billy asked permission to stay out late for the farewell party. I needed him to fix my covers, because it had turned cold but told him to go ahead. "I always want to please you," I said, "when I can." He told me that he would be back at twelve. At twelve, no Billy. At twelve-thirty, no Billy. At one, no Billy. At one-thirty, no Billy. I teetered between worry and anger. At quarter of two, I wakened Evelyn and she called Sadie's house. Billy, she was informed, had just left. He arrived after two-thirty. I was ready to jump him. I told him that I considered his getting home at that time a goddamn dirty trick.

September 30 Billy took his car, found a country road, slept, so he said, for three hours. When he returned at suppertime, he was a lamb falling over himself to please. I certainly gave him an emotional licking, and I'm pleased he reacted as I had hoped he would but had feared he would not. It was high time for me to take him to task if we are to live cooperatively together until he goes to war. I hope nothing else crosses us up for a while.

October 2 A little after six, Claire appeared. She sat down, took my hand, sighed. "We depart tonight, this very night, for Florida," she announced melodramatically. "Oh, Arthur, it's so exciting. I've been stuck in abominable little one-horse towns for so long — and now I'm uprooting myself and my family, going to a new place to start over. I didn't get to sleep till three-thirty last night. I've been rushing like mad all day. I can't eat. I stopped at a bar and had a whiskey. Do you think I'm doing right? I think I'm doing right. There'll be no oil-scarcity troubles in Florida. I hate the winter and it will be warm there. My children won't have to associate with toughies. We have a house engaged overlooking a lake — fifty dollars a month. I'm scared, but I'm sure I'm doing right. What's to hold me here? Sam will be in the Navy (he'd have volunteered in Boston only he was told that they needed men like him so badly he'd be snapped up and not even given ten days — he'll enlist in Florida). A few friends like you and Evelyn are all that hold me here, and I'd be foolish to stay just for that, don't you think? Do you feel I'm being wise, Arthur?"

The flow of words ceased. She squeezed my hand. I weighed my words. "For myself, Claire," I said, "I feel as if something bright were going out of my life. I may not have always seen much of you, but I always knew you were there. I wish you weren't going. That's for myself. As for you, the move sounds eminently sensible, and I'm sure you're doing right." "Oh," she sighed, and added: "How about Sam's going in the Navy? What do you think of that?" "Absolutely dumb." I replied. "He could get work and as much pay in a navy yard somewhere and not risk the life of the father of three children." "Oh," she said.

I asked her if she had enjoyed her life to date — she is thirty-four. "I most certainly have." Did she love her children? "Yes." Did she love Sam, despite his faults? "Yes." Would she change her life if she had it to do over? "No." Was life exciting to her, worth living? "Yes. Yes. Oh yes."

Claire expects to be gone "for the duration." It makes me feel queer to realize that I may never see her again. I have known her for fourteen or fifteen years, since she went to Baldwin College. I remember how hard I used to work on her to alienate her from the female influence of her school friends. I recall how much I liked her hair, how she used to sing to me, how she would lie in bed with me and fit nicely, how she met Sam and married him against my advice, her stay in Nashua, her trip to England, her jobs, her children. Most of the advice I gave her she never took, and I didn't mind that. Advice is something you advance in the hope it may help someone you want to assist or some part of it may help. "Some of it did," she assured me. "And I've loved you through all of it and through your various disapprovals, and I always shall love you, Arthur, and never forget you and Evelyn. Some day—who can tell?—I may come back to Boston, although to be honest, I have a decided hunch I never shall." We kissed each other goodbye, and I felt miserable. She refused to accept any supper, being too nervous to eat, I suspect. She telephoned Evelyn at Dr. Pike's and bade her goodbye. "I detest goodbyes," she said.

And there goes Claire. I feel that I have lost Woody to some extent since she married. Eleanor, her help in the diary correcting, is gone. Roderic may go. Billy, sooner or later, surely will go. Hassie, busy with her hat shop, I never see now. The world encroaches on me through the breaches in the stockade of friends I have chosen and built, and new protection I cannot erect as fast as the old falls.

October 3   I told Dicey some of Millicent's off-color jokes the other night, and he squeaked the chair laughing. He told Coakley the jokes, and Coakley has passed them on to his associates, and everyone—so queer is the nature of men—now thinks more of me than formerly. "All these months I've known you," ejaculated Dicey, "and I had no idea you were keeping treasures like this back on me." He credits me with having ideas on everything. An evening with him I always consider well and profitably spent.

October 5   Ella is resolved to take a job in the drafting department of the Somerville Arsenal doing the copying and tracing she studied this summer. It pays around twenty-eight a week. Robert has received reclassification papers and has been told by a major he knows that he cannot hope to remain out of the Army beyond the first of the year. He declares that he has too much temper to become an ordinary soldier and be "shoved around." His plan, then, is to enlist within a week or two in the State Guard and try for a noncom position, he having pull. Having such a noncom rating in the State Guard, he reasons, will let him get a comparable one in the Army. Ella, as soon as he enlists, will go to work. He has saved a thousand dollars for her, and it is in the bank. If he gets killed, he says, she will at least not be left penniless.

I told Ella that bearing her volatile and easily bored nature in mind, I should consider taking such a job as she had in mind a foolish step indeed. Already men can't leave the Arsenal without Government permission, and that is difficult to obtain. Within eight or ten months, the women working there may be frozen to their jobs. Then what would she do? She would become an old tired-out woman in no time, for there never was a position yet she didn't want to leave after just so long. She could, I further reasoned, obtain a twenty-five dollar job easily now with labor as short as it is. Was three dollars or five dollars or even ten dollars a week worth ruining herself and her disposition for?

I hope she listened. I'm very fond of Ella and I'd like to save her from a false step. She rubbed my head last evening and talked to me in her soft restrained voice, and I dozed off and rested. She is balm to my spirit when I am tired and discouraged.

October 7   Tamara Arken yesterday afternoon. She is still taking educational courses at Harvard, is "bored to death with them." She has resigned herself to a career of teaching. Being Jewish, she says, bars her from obtaining a good post with a good publisher.

With her usual wish to cheer operating in conjunction with her customary devotion to truth at any cost, she related the following: "Well, I gave you a push yesterday. I'm taking a course under Professor [F. O.] Matthiessen in American poetry. He asked us to name our favorite poets. When it came my turn, as bold as brass I named Arthur Inman. 'And who,' he asked, 'is Arthur Inman?' 'Oh,' I replied, 'he's a poet living here in Boston. If you don't know his work, you should.' 'Is that so?' he said. 'One of those thin volumes, I suppose?' 'The thin volumes,' I said, 'are often the best — if overlooked.' 'Well,' he said, 'I'll look into this Arthur Inman.' 'Thank you,' I said. I had nothing to lose, I felt, and he had something to gain. And I really admire your poetry as a whole, however vile some of it is. I'll be interested to watch reactions."

Tamara read Volume 90 [1939–40] to me, I having in mind using her to correct Volume 20 [1924] and on. She was satisfactorily enthusiastic. "It's really marvelous," she said. "It makes me want to read on and on to find out what happens to the various characters. I like the way you 'stagger' your subject matter. It prevents the reader from becoming bored."

Roderic: "I decided to wait until I was called and forego for Doris' and the baby's sake my impulse to be of some quick service to my country. And there was this to consider. I'm a middle-aged softy with a paunch. The men who are being inducted now are younger men with an edge on me in strength, in endurance, in celerity of reaction, in everything in fact. The training that makes them fit would finish me. If I wait until the young men have gone into service, then they'll have to use different methods of training with the less fit remainder, of which I am one. And if I let the draft take its course, I'll have that much longer with my wife and child."

October 8   I'm funny about Ireland and the Irish. Disliking the Irish as I do, I yet admire their literature, their humor, their imagination, their physical fearlessness. What I dislike, I think, is their inability to stick to the truth, their arrogance in office, their slackness generally, their religious cant. And yet I know of no place in the world where I have a greater longing, perhaps misplaced, to go and to abide the remainder of my days.

October 9   What a day. Have a headache, sciatica, and my hands won't work they hurt so violently. The Old Man arrived yesterday. He talked to me for over an hour this morning. I hate his guts. It isn't particularly what he says or how he is, it is because he is what he is and reminds me of the past.

October 10   Thought of Old Man and attempted to bring calm into my emotions by stressing the fact that he was merely a lonely old fellow of limited understanding and no imagination. Very poor success.

October 11   Father relating the time he had the barber use mange cure for dandruff, then went to tea with the Groundhog, who apologized to her guests for the antiseptic someone had been using in the house.

I asked him outright why he didn't take up residence in Maine or Florida and save ten or fifteen thousand dollars in taxes. He fixed his cold eyes on me. He said: "I could probably save more than that. But people don't think much of fellows who give up their citizenship in the state that has given them what they have. I don't want to give up my citizenship. I'm proud of it. And money isn't everything in life by any means. I could have been a rich man many times over if I'd wanted to buckle down and devote myself to getting rich. I wouldn't care a rap about money if I hadn't wanted to support you and your mother as I felt you ought to be supported. All I wanted was enough money to help people out and give to charities. And if this taxation business keeps up, it kind of looks as though I wouldn't be able to do that, that and support you."

October 13   Hitler set his heart on taking Stalingrad and Stalingrad has not been taken, nor Grozny oil fields. Nor has the Black Sea littoral been overrun. Unless further amazing advances are accomplished in the face of a nearing winter, the Germans again will not only have failed to subdue the Russians, but they will have likewise failed to cut off the Caucasus and to make its vast supplies of metals and oils and cereals their own. Unless Stalingrad be taken, the length and cost in men and equipment of the siege may prove to be historically a major turning point in the war, a high-water mark from which the tide will recede.

Churchill, in a speech at Edinburgh, sounded a jubilant note. We are building merchant ships, he said, faster than they are being sunk. We are dropping the greatest tonnage of bombs on the Germans. Submarine sinkings have diminished. Air superiority is increasing. He touched upon the growth of fear in the Axis. He stressed his view that each victory for the Axis now leads to ruin. And Roosevelt, in paler words, last night echoed the sentiments of his lord and master, though to hear him stress his personal pronouns, you could not escape the conclusion that he felt himself a superior sovereign talking down to his moronic subjects.

October 15 Abundance of material to write about this morning.

When I woke up from my after-lunch nap yesterday, Janice said: "We have a surprise visitor. It's Pearl, of all people. She looks very well. Do you want to see her?" "Sure," I replied. "Tell her to come on in." "I just couldn't stay away any longer, Arthur," said Pearl, as Janice left and she entered the room. "Are you angry with me?" "No. I'm glad to see you." "Just a little put out, though?" "Well, would you blame me? It's been a long time." "I know it has, Artie, and I'm sorry." She sat down. "My feelings were hurt. But they aren't any more. And here I am. I was sent on an errand by the boss. I said to myself: 'By golly, I'll stop and see Arthur.' Oh, Artie, I've got such a swell job now. I'm superintendent and timekeeper and sort of bookkeeper all rolled into one — and there's not a female in the department — only men — and I'm the queen bee. Honey, with nothing but men, and thirty-five dollars a week, and every day I think: 'Well, this is all due to Arthur. If he hadn't taught you everything, you wouldn't be what you are; you wouldn't be called the most tactful girl in the factory.' And then I feel very grateful to you. And I really mean this. It isn't just hokum. I'm deeply grateful. Nobody ever did as much for me as you have, Arthur."

By that time I could feel myself becoming putty. "What a push-over I am," I thought, "for a little flattery and some soft soap. And by George, I like it whether I know it's real or whether I doubt its honesty or not. And I don't mind in the least that I'm this way. I like it, in fact." "Why did you stay away so long, Pearl?" I asked. "Oh, because." "Because what?" "Because you said something about me and it got back to me." "What?" "I'd rather not say. It's all gone now." "What?" "Well, if you must have it — when you called me last, that is, when Mrs. Inman did, I heard you say, 'Well, if she won't come, to hell with her. I don't care if I never see her again.' That hurt me to the quick." "By God, I did say that, didn't I? And I meant it, too, just as you'd have said it and meant it if you'd wanted to see me and I'd put you off six times. I'll have to talk softer next time, won't I? Gosh, I thought you'd really heard something I didn't say. Sure I said that. Sure you'd have said the same thing. Why didn't you come to me and raise hell instead of sulking. And by the way, you've no business answering Evelyn high-hat when she calls you for me." "I didn't mean to be high-hat." "Well, don't be, next time. And there's something else I'd like to know, Pearl. What was the matter with you that summer when you called me up and told me you wouldn't ever see me again?" "I don't remember doing it." "Oh yes you do. Why did you do it?" "Well, you wanted me to come back to you, and my mother was dead set against it, and I couldn't leave her, could I? I wasn't feeling good. Oh, I don't know. But I'm not that way now. Here I am, in the flesh. Just feel how fat I've gotten. I weigh a hundred and sixty. Like to feel, huh? Oh, Artie —" and here she began to kiss me —"I'm so awful glad to see you! So awful glad."

By then I was thoroughly melted. "The girl," I thought, "has personality-plus. And emotional push. And cleverness. And a complete knowledge of men when she wishes to use it." Pearl scarcely dropped a 'g' while she was with me, a sure sign that she is striving to please.

And that was Pearl. Evelyn and I corrected some. Suddenly, she asked: "Do you consider me abnormal in my relations with you? I'm to go to that psychologist [Dr. Arvin] tomorrow, and I feel it's important to know just what you really think."

The query out of a clear sky took me aback. I replied negatively. Then in thinking it over, I changed my mind and told her how I felt. "I feel," I said, "that anyone who can be around me for twenty years and remain in many aspects comparatively uninfluenced by miles of advice, argument, pointing out, suggestion couched in every manner my active ingenuity can suggest, and reinforced by a battery of multirayed emotions, must be abnormal insofar as I am concerned anyway. Anyone who took seventeen years to consent to cease contradicting by rote, when it would all along have been to her advantage to stop, must be abnormal. I get along with other people, and they listen to me in great measure. But I feel utterly thwarted in making you impressed by reasons so simple as to seem to me childish. It is as though you understood the words of the language I spoke, but the meaning of it quite escaped you, which is not a normal state."

"You don't respect me, then?"

"Well," I replied cautiously, "I respect what you are — your loyalty, your promptness, your long-term patience — but I do not respect how you act — your lack of tact and self-control. I love you, but I do not respect your failure to do more with your natural gifts."

She asked other questions. She had never before appeared so interested in what I thought of her. All the answers have been given in these pages time on time, so that there is nothing to be gained by restating them. They did not please her. She cried.

I was, I found, shocked by the violence of my feelings conjured out of a calm in which fitted no anger or impatience. I wished I had not answered her questions. If I know anything in this world, I know it does not pay to be honest with a woman one loves.

October 17 In the Solomon Islands, the Japanese, after having landed additional forces on Guadalcanal Island (about one-third the size of Massachusetts, mostly mountains higher than Mt. Washington), are attacking by land, sea and air the American foothold (about the size of Boston, including the seized Japanese airfield). I cannot perceive how our marines and soldiers can hold out if the Japanese effort is relentlessly pressed; the foothold has not been, by all indications, sufficiently garrisoned since we took it, and bombings of the airfield are fairly sure to make its use precarious at best. It may be the old story of failing to bring all our energies to a focal point. This scattering of men and machines across the face of the earth, a handful here, a handful there, is not even, to my way of thinking, good defensive strategy. Unless the American Pacific Fleet is moved in to support the garrison at Guadalcanal, the action there may prove to be merely another Bataan.

We need a generalissimo of Allied forces and need him badly. If winning the war is more important than preventing infiltration of Sovietism or than keeping the British Empire intact, then Marshal Timeshenko, the ablest Allied general to have arisen from the ruck of generals thus far, should be made generalissimo.

October 20 On her way back to Boston, Evelyn stopped at the hat shop to say hello to Hassie. "Hassie's hair is getting gray and she looks older. Her little shop is just as neat and efficient as you could wish. 'Hassie,' I said, 'you seem gloomy. What's the trouble?' 'Oh,' she said, 'I'm getting divorced from Johnny today at two o'clock.' 'Whatever is the matter?' I asked. 'Oh,' she replied, 'everything. He didn't do right by Hassie.' 'No,' I said, 'why not? What did he do?' 'What did he do?' she said. 'Why, he cheated, he gambled, he wouldn't work, he practiced adultery, he courted women, and all the rest.' 'Where is he now?' I asked. 'I don't know,' she said, 'and I don't care. I kicked him out of my house. He does the night club still. But he don't work and he goes with all the waitresses. He's no good.' Hassie says that she is to have a married couple live with her — rent them rooms I suppose — so that she will be able to come to visit us some weekend. What a woman.''

October 25   "You know," said Evelyn, "I should think you'd get tired of being so interested in women — you know — find them all alike under the skin or become bored with them, anyway lose interest." "It's partly assumed, my interest," I replied. "It's like a hobby, something to keep me from being bored. But it's not entirely that. I really like women." "Do you keep hoping to find the ideal specimen?" "Yes, and no. I learned so much about boys — 'the boy is father to the man' — when I was in school and college that I haven't much curiosity about them left. I'm still curious about women. And I have years of affection to make up. Anyway, they're fun to have affairs with. I've never found one I liked more than I do you, so you should not object." "Oh," she said, "I don't object, I just wonder."

November 1   A dark and dismal day, with rain falling insistently. It is some minutes past nine. Evelyn has not come upstairs yet. We had a miserable day yesterday. She is afraid that she is pregnant and Bottom believes that she has entered the menopause, and whichever it is she is downcast and sorry for herself. She can, she says, do nothing to please me. If I'd let her alone, she'd be all right. She's no good anyway. The old story. And she makes blunder after blunder, looks stricken. In the afternoon, she proceeded to get drunk again. No amount of gentle talking impresses her, so I yelled. I don't know whether that impressed her. She is a defeatist by nature. She must be dumb or she'd have managed me and herself differently by now. I get very tired of attempting to make the portion of her that concerns me into anything. You simply cannot put any permanent stiffening into her character. I guess I don't think she's much good in many ways, however much I love her, although that I do love her I have now long since ceased to doubt. I don't understand her, and she doesn't understand me, and that is that.

November 2   I am considering seriously writing a novel. The stage of war has been sufficiently set, the drift toward totalitarianism sufficiently designated for an overdwelling upon them easily to become prolix. The direction of my adjustment to the new order, too, has been sufficiently presented. I'd like to lose myself in another time, other personalities, a different sort of work. And more than that, I'd like to find out if I can do anything in the novel line, though I'm not at all sure. In each such attempt hitherto the endurance has been insufficient to sustain the effort necessary. It would have to be a short novel. I have Byzantium in mind—one of its emperors—I forget his name but recall noting in a chronicle what an interesting plot his life drew.

November 4 I loaned Evelyn's car (with her permission) to Coakley yesterday. Billy drove it. He had Dicey call up and announce to Janice that he wouldn't be back for supper. High-handed. His head swells continually. He has less and less consideration for other people. My patience is stretching. And he knows and he knows I know that he could walk out of here and get seventy or eighty dollars a week. That is bound to affect his opinion of himself and lessen the size of his job. I didn't say a word last night. What was the use? Well, I suppose it's better that I should become gradually incensed against him than that I should lose him suddenly while not incensed.

Evelyn has lectured me several times lately on the danger of having Dicey and Coakley know too much about me. She considers them dangerous, if not now then perhaps at some indefinite time in the future. I listen to her but doubt if I shall comply.

In the first place, I am on my guard. And in the second place, Dicey says more complimentary things about me in one week than Evelyn or Janice do in a week, and it builds me up even though I accept it as pure opportunistic flattery, which for the most part I do. I've come to the stage in my life when I want to hear buttressing statements about myself, and I don't give a hurrah where they come or who says them. There's a heap of disparagement to make up for. If those close to me fail to butter me up with vehemence, why I'll go somewhere else—just about anywhere—to get it. So I'm all for Dicey and all for Pearl, and whether they mean what they utter or not doesn't matter—it sounds good to me.

November 29 I heard sirens but paid only casual attention to them, supposing that it was some sort of practice. When Billy returned at eleven-fifteen, he was goggle-eyed with excitement. "Say, I'd like to know what's going on. I saw at least fifteen ambulances drawing up to City Hospital. What's happened, do you think?" I was tired and paid not too much attention. The ambulances whizzed by until I fell asleep at two. I don't understand why I failed to turn on the radio. This morning the papers are filled with descriptions and features of the great fire at the Cocoanut Grove, a popular night club.[5] Somewhere between seven hundred and one

---

[5] The death toll in what was called "the nation's worst fire disaster in four decades" came to 491.

thousand guests were there, and in the neighborhood of four hundred were killed and numberless people burned and trampled.

December 1 I have been thinking of the boy who accidentally lit the fire that burned the Cocoanut Grove and killed nearly five hundred persons and burned a hundred or two more. What would it feel to have done that, however accidentally? Will it ruin the rest of his life? Will he blame his lack of care on someone else? Will he be unaffected save superficially?

The fire and police authorities make smug statements as to their lack of culpability. The burden of their exculpation is that legally they were vested with no powers to require the Cocoanut Grove management to take more safety measures than were taken. The management naturally asserts that they took all safety measures required by law and by the inspectors. That almost double the guests permitted to be there were squeezed in on the night of the fire will be glazed over by both the management and the authorities. And all sorts of new inspection and safety laws for night clubs will be passed and, for a while, strictly enforced.

Stanley Tomaszewski worked at the 'Grove' two nights a week, $2.50 a night. At first a bus boy, then carried drinks to guests at the tables. On the night of the fire, a bulb went out in the Melody Lounge. He was ordered to fix it. He couldn't see, so he struck a match. The artificial decorations flamed up though they were supposed to be fireproof. And there was the fire.

Stanley led guests out as long as he could see through the smoke, then went to the kitchen, conducted other guests to safety. Yesterday he gave himself up to the police who now have him in custody, with four men guarding him. There was a hearing yesterday afternoon. The boy (he is only sixteen) testified clearly and to the point.

Stanley lives in Roxbury. His parents are poor. His mother is ill. He was working two nights a week to help out. Over and over again she repeats, "Stanley is a good boy." His brother is in the Army, a second lieutenant. He's a nice-looking boy, Stanley, and on his face is a stricken expression. Half of the money he earned he put into defense stamps. His teachers and friends have all rallied to his support. He was sickly when young. He attended the Sarah Greenwood Common School and the Oliver Wendell Holmes Junior High School in Dorchester before entering the Roxbury Memorial High School for Boys. He has been preparing for college. According to his biology teacher, he "went out for football hoping that, through athletic prowess, his chances of getting a scholarship would be better." He was first-string tackle on the team. He was captain of one of the twenty-three companies which make up the Roxbury

Memorial High School Regiment. "I consider," states Captain Kelley, military drill instructor, "his prospects excellent for the highest honor, that of being named Colonel of the Roxbury Memorial High Regiment. Stanley would, in my opinion, have been an ideal candidate for West Point." Stanley's father was formerly a janitor at Temple Beth El.

December 2   Marie, Janice told me, witnessed the fire. I drove to her apartment this morning; Evelyn went in and took care of the baby; she came out and sat in the car with me and told me of her experience. Her eyes were as large as saucers, and dark rings were under them. She and the members of her family had had supper at the Alpine near the Cocoanut Grove. They were opposite the Cocoanut Grove when the fire broke.

"The screams were terrible. It made you cringe to hear them. We weren't fifty feet away — no farther than that car right in front of us there. Then the people commenced jumping from the windows. For some reason, one is slow to grasp the real extent of such a calamity — at least we were. It was more like a dream than an actuality. The fire engines arrived and ambulances. My brother had presence of mind enough to send my aunts home. They began bringing the bodies out. I felt bound to see if I could help, so Bobby and I went to the police and told them I was a nurse and we were passed on to the door. All the people were lying there in every sort of attitude, and firemen were coming out with more all the time. 'These people are negroes,' I said to myself, and it was several minutes before I realized that they were white and had been burned that color. That unmanned me. Bobby began to cry. Some of the women were stark-naked, and some had only pants or only shoes or only a bra, and some of the men were like they were in rags. Most were dead. I tried to help one man with half his face burnt off — he was asking for his wife. The doctor gave him morphine. It was terrible, Arthur. I had to take Bobby back to the car, he was so emotionally upset. We sat there and watched for an hour and a half, and I wish to heaven I'd never seen it all. I went back to help again, as I felt I had to; but there was really nothing I could do, especially with Bobby insisting he stay with me and in no condition to do it. It is a night I'll never forget — all the faces with terror in them, the hands like claws, the skin completely burnt off some bodies. And the smell. It was terrible. Finally, we decided there was little we could do. My brother, who used to be a taxidriver, somehow maneuvered us out of the jam — I don't know how he did it — and we came home. Neither Bobby nor I could sleep that night although we both took sedatives. I have to take Luminal every night now. But it doesn't exclude the scene from my mind. I'd have given anything in the world not to have witnessed what happened. We were there an hour and a half, and it was only just before we left that the police roped off the area to keep out people and traffic. And I saw firemen in their own district hunting around like strangers for the hydrants they should know by heart. The whole business was handled most remissly. Someone ought to have to pay for the remissness, but I suppose no one will. I wish to heavens I'd been anywhere else — anywhere."

December 5 Janice came in. She was wearing the sky-blue jumper I had given her. She looked very pretty. "Well," I said, "your boy friend gave you the party last night, didn't he, just as I predicted he would?" She nodded. I was sitting in the chair. She leaned over and held my hand. "Oh, Arthur, I love you," she exclaimed. "Gee," I answered, "that's great. But why, today?" "I wish everyone knew you as well as I do, so they'd realize how wonderful you are." She pushed out her hand. She dropped to her knees. "It's my engagement ring," she said. Her eyes filled with tears. "I've waited so long, Arthur. And I really love him so much." I answered nothing.

I was taken aback. "It was all very lovely," she said, the tears falling. "And all the time I was thinking about you. It doesn't mean I'll leave you, Arthur. I love you so." I was at a loss what to say. I felt numb, as though an arm were being removed under anesthesia. "I'm glad you're happy," I said, lively enough, "but sorry you're engaged to Bertram. I still don't believe he's the right man. I hope, for your sake, he is." "I think he is, Arthur. It's been two years. He takes good care of me, just as you do. He doesn't even press me to go to his church." "Why hasn't he asked you before?" "Oh, because there was so much on his mind — his father, his brother, the business. I don't think he wanted to marry me at first. But now it's all settled." "Will you stay with me until after the war?" "Oh yes. Just because I marry doesn't mean I'll leave you. I love you so."

I wish to God I could stop this development but see no way to do it without hurting her, even if that accomplished the result I wished, which it probably wouldn't. I am deeply loath to go behind her back, delve into Bertram's life, unearth what I sense may be there. I must find out some facts from Dicey if he has any and judge for myself whether I would feel warranted in laying them before her, should I be convinced she should know them, albeit the whole procedure goes against the grain. I should, I know, consider her welfare before my own feelings. How on earth can she know about him otherwise? I'm strained a dozen ways.

Evelyn tells me that my standard of loyalty is quixotic. If I love

Janice as I say I do, I should make it my business to find out what is the story with Bertram Davis. Should I? Evelyn is certain that Janice is making a dire mistake. It is her observation that a man who can afford a Cadillac car could have afforded to buy Janice a less cheap-looking engagement ring.

December 6 The further waxed the day, the more sharply I realized the potentials of Janice's engagement. I'll think it over some more. I sound melodramatic, but Janice is so innocent and so romantic that I feel overwhelmingly a desire to protect her. No one, not even Evelyn, has ever been as unquestioningly devoted and admiring, and that, for me, has been a gift for which virtually any return will not be enough. I must be guardian and sentinel for her.

December 7 This morning I am feeling resentful against Janice for not having told Davis definitely that marriage would have to await the end of the war, since she was determined to take care of me until then, what with conditions as they are. She promised some time ago to stay with me until the war was over. And now at the drop of that Irishman's hat she is willing to leave her promise unaffirmed. And, as far as can be found out, he made her no proposal of marriage, just presented her with the cheap engagement and marriage ring set. Nor did they mention a wedding date. It's very queer. And I think he's no good and she'd be throwing her life away to no purpose. And what I feel today is paramount in what I think. I'm tired of trying to be worthy and idealistic with her or with anyone else; it gets me nowhere.

I have written a letter to Dicey, care of Coakley's office, to be forwarded, asking him to run down from Springfield and tell me all he knows, promising that I will pay expenses and for his time. Evelyn has gone downtown to find out about engaging a private detective agency (very expensive) to check on Davis, as I will not necessarily trust Dicey's story without proof or corroborating evidence. (This is me writing on a separate piece of paper: Janice will never copy it.) I want to spike that Davis if possible. I would be lost without Janice. It is a risky marriage. And, as I said above, I'm resentful that she didn't arbitrarily put off the wedding until after the war. Billy will go; she will go. Then where will Evelyn and I be?

Billy, who has been probing Janice, was told that she is attempting to persuade Bertram to leave and find something else. This new executive order (he is thirty-eight) exempts him from the draft. That shows that Janice is seriously considering marriage and — in case he takes a position somewhere else or she has a baby — leaving me. I have been too good to her for her to look at things that way. I wish I had talked Davis down consistently. If he were not Irish and if he had treated Janice in another manner all this time, I wouldn't feel it my right to stand in her way. As it is, unless I have a change of heart, off with his head if I can get it off without turning her against me. It will be a ticklish proposition if I am given irrefutable evidence against him, and practically an impossible proposition if there is no adverse record. I hope it is or has been another woman. Mrs. Cash, Ella, Evelyn, Billy, each says that it sounds as though there is or has been.

Marriage and children are 'musts' in Janice's mind, and evidently in her mother's mind. When a woman broods on that long enough, almost any suitor looks good to her. And this is enough for now. It may not present me as a knight in shining armor, but it is a true statement of how I feel — think today.

December 8 Mr. Whitcomb recommended a private detective in Brookline, recommended him highly. Evelyn consulted with him. He is an elderly man; his fee $15 a day plus expenses. He thought that he would be able to get the information for us within two days, three at the most. He has been on numberless cases, when fathers wished to have knowledge of prospective sons-in-law. He believes that all parents should have their daughters' men investigated. He thinks it only reasonable. In fact, I gather that he has strong convictions on the subject.

It is doubtful if I hear from Dicey before this afternoon.

I was miserable yesterday, am miserable today. I hate this going behind Janice's back. It is always my impulse to meet problems head-on, in the open. I decided to write Janice a letter.

This morning when she came in my room, she said, "Arthur, dear, I don't want you to be worried the way you were yesterday. We'll work things out. I've always been able to work things out to help everybody. I will this time. So don't you worry." I thanked her monosyllabically. In front of her I have been leaving my face unmasked and saying as few words as possible just as gloomily as I felt them in my heart. She wants to relieve my worry, and that is good of her. While we were riding, she talked of what she would wear to keep warm when she drove me this winter. That was to tell me that she would be with me during the winter. It helps some but not enough. And I burn up when I reflect upon her going to Davis. The cheap ring. The absence of any proposal of marriage. The hundreds of hours he has kept Janice waiting for him when he was late. The fact that he would see her only on certain evenings. The cheap locket he gave her and she has so zealously worn day after day. Small things perhaps, but who can say for sure they are not indicative things?

Here is the letter I wrote Janice but have not yet given to her, being engaged in 'thinking it over' so as not to act solely by impulse. I mean every bit of it.

Janice —
    Several months ago you told me that you would stay with me until the end of the war. Now you say that you will 'take care of me' *provided* some crisis does not arise. That is not what you promised. You have the privilege, naturally, of directing your life as you wish, regardless of what I may think of the wisdom of the course. But I have loved you and cherished you and had your good and your attractiveness and your well being close to my heart all these years, and I do not feel that you have the right to cancel your promise to me for whatever reason. Should you desert me when Billy has gone to war and when conditions are as bad as they are in the world and I am as helpless as you know I am, I shall never have faith in the word or the intentions of another human being. My faith and my soul are in your hands. I have never trusted anyone in the world as I have trusted you.

Arthur

December 9   "I read your letter," said Janice. "Well?" "Well, I've stopped worrying. I'll do the best I can to please everybody. It seems to me my life has always been spent pleasing somebody or other. I'll do the best I can." "Is that all?" "Yes." "Well," said I, "let's go riding."
    Went riding. Janice drove the Cadillac, as Billy still has the remnants of a cold. I think of the war as lasting two more years. Janice thinks of it as lasting five. I told her that two years would be all I could personally ask. She did not come right out and say yes, two years would be possible, but neither did she say no. I explained that I did not wish to press her as then her acquiescence would be worthless insofar as retaining my faith in her was concerned. I did permit myself to remark that Bertram had kept her waiting for years; she surely could keep him waiting for two years. I am, to put it boldly, disappointed in Janice and the measure of her devotion to me. I feel myself a man much more worthy of devotion than Davis and (allowing for her expressed and felt yearning to marry and have children) one deserving what had been promised to me. I hope she hurries and makes up her mind before I become hurt into antagonism and go after what I want with a bludgeon. The poor girl is doubtless so torn apart that it takes time for her to know her own mind. I'm sure she desires to be fair.
    Dicey showed up yesterday. I asked about Davis. "We really found out very little about him," said he. "He gets a very good

salary, forty-five a week and an interest in profits amounting annually to two hundred and fifty a month more or less, but in spite of
that he is always in debt. He does quite a lot of petty gambling. His
brother has gotten him out of trouble several times. He's behind in
payments for his car. If he has a steady girl, we couldn't find one.
And that was all. Really not much, nothing to shout about."

I told George I wanted to give him some money for coming down
and for the train fare. "Oh, think nothing of it, Arthur. I'd do this
and a lot more for you. Don't you know that by now?"

When Billy came home at quarter of six, I asked him questions.
Yes, he'd been to the V.O.C. After all, it was he that was going to
war, not Coakley. He wanted to be an officer. Maybe he would be
put in the Navy. He didn't want that. Sadie wants him to go in the
Army at once. I don't know what he'll do. On top of the Janice
problems, it is too much and rather futile to contend with. The
service will get him eventually anyway. I'm just fighting the wind.
He wouldn't have been drafted by this time if I'd sat still and done
nothing. Maybe I'll sit still now.

December 10   The detective was here last night after two days on
the case. A dumb man, with nothing to add to my fund of information. He ate lunch next to Bertram in the drugstore where he is in the
habit of going. Bertram had a paper. He read about the draft and
perused the racing page. The detective said that he had a weak chin.
And that cost me $45. The last of him. I'll use Dicey. I wish I knew
whether Bertram has an interest in the shoe factory or gets a percentage of the profits. He sounds like a haphazard provider.

This morning while Janice and I were sitting at the Place, I asked
her what conclusion she had arrived at. Bertram, she said, had been
sick with a cold last evening so that she hadn't been able to talk with
him. "After all," I said, "it's up to you, Janice, not to Bertram.
You've the final decision. He'll do what you decide, and you know
that he will." She leaned over and put her arm across my shoulders.
"I think you're safe in counting on me, Arthur," she said. "You
know very well I couldn't leave you in an emergency."

How she remains apparently calm and fresh during all this I can't
understand. I inquired. "Perhaps," she explained, "it's because everything in my life has always worked out for the best. When complications prove too much for me to find my way through, I just sort
of sit back and wait. Everything usually clears up if I do that, and
usually better than I could have expected or hoped for. It's always
been that way. Perhaps I trust my good luck just as you believe in
your bad luck. I sort of stand aside, try to remain composed, and
wait." We had a beautiful ride together. Calm, still, quiet air, cold
enough to be exhilarating, not too sharp.

December 11 I asked Pearl to stop by after work yesterday. I inquired of her if, when Billy went to war, she would like this job. "The salary and as much as possible the arrangement of time will be what you want — forty dollars, forty-five. I'd rather pay you more than someone in whom I didn't have so much confidence. I'd feel absolutely secure with you." "Well," she said, "I think I'd like it. But there's my family. I'll tell you what, Arthur; I'll ask them. But don't get your hopes too high. I can't hurt them by going against them. I'm sure I could take care of you." "If," I added, "you know now there's no chance, tell me." "Oh, I would. But I'm not dead certain. If I had only myself to consider, I'd take it. I enjoyed working for you before, and I'd like it even more with more responsibility." She was very sweet. She said that she had worried about me all day. She will let me know when she finds an appropriate time to ask her parents but doesn't want to be hasty for fear of choosing the wrong moment.

(Billy to go into the V.O.C. January 20th. Has placed name on active list.)

December 12 Evelyn, when she came upstairs to fix my windows for the night, was tight on beer. She turned over a chair. I jerked and put my pelvis out of place. I lost my temper. Mrs. Cash insisted on making inapropos jokes about how Billy would people the South Sea Islands with offspring. Altogether a miserable evening. Sadie cried some, Billy told me when he came in at midnight, but had "taken it better" than he had expected. This morning I feel washed up. Evelyn has promised to forego alcohol of any sort, and I hope she keeps it.

An order by Governor Saltonstall requesting people to abstain from Sunday driving unless they are workers or unless they have no other way of getting to church. I suppose that that will mean an end to my best driving day. Well, without Billy it wouldn't be feasible anyway.

December 18 Leon Henderson, the functionary in charge of the Office of Price Administration (rationing), has resigned because of congressional antipathy. I have no use for him because I have no use for any Jew who is in authority over me, and also because he has been bombastic and arrogant. But in all fairness to him he has done just about as well with a disagreeable and unpopular job as a man could do, and I believe that by and large his intentions have been honest. His successor is not likely to have a better time or an easier role no matter what his qualifications.

Have bought more foods. Washington may not cease to bungle all sorts of matters. The Army and the armed forces are being gorged with food. How do I know how long the food supply may last? This year's meat supply is gone, and for the rest of the year we are to be given meat from next year's supply.

December 21   I gave Janice the sapphire and pearl cross which came to me from Mother via Aunt Helen, and a pearl and platinum chain Evelyn volunteered "because she's been so good to you and I like her." Janice observed that she didn't want me to give her anything that would make her feel obligated to me. I replied that she needn't feel obligated. I wanted to make her the present before she continued to disappoint me and eventually decamp or something. Anyway, I said, it seemed to me that there were many abstract things I had given her that made her much more obligated to me than a material present. Someday, I said, I might remind her of them but not of the cross and chain. But if she didn't want to take it I could sell it and pay my debts. It is really a beautiful bauble and necklace, unusually beautiful. She took it. "I don't know what to say," she stated. "I don't know how to thank you and Evelyn, Arthur." I instructed her not to wear it in front of Bertram if it would make him uncomfortable. I hope she liked it.

[From Patricia:]

Paul left last night for Battle Creek, Mich. He is going to Camp Custer to Officer's Training School. On his way there he is going to stop off at Muncie Ind. and see his family for the first time in eight years. He is going to the school for Military Police, it's something new, as there have never been any official M.P.s before, just non-commissioned men who were appointed M.P. for punishment duty, consequently they were given a bad name, and this new outfit has a lot to overcome. They are trained for occupation of captured territories, guard vital plants, arrange transportation of supplies, and like the commandos, are trained for hand to hand fighting, they carry shot guns instead of side arms, their insignia is crossed pistols and I am already wearing mine. One of Paul's officers gave them to me when I visited Camp in September. Paul never wanted to be an officer, he just wanted to make Staff Sergeant, because with his base pay and my allowance and all his uniforms furnished we would have more money and he wouldn't have so much grief as a 2nd Lt. who gets all the troubles of the regiment piled on him. But his superior officers thought that he was excellent officer material and insisted that I urge him to do it, because the M.P. unit has every chance of staying in this country until after the war when they will be the army of occupation, and all the men in the outfit were told that they could look forward to at least five years service after the duration. The only way that I could go with him to occupied countries would be as an officer's wife, so he finally made up his mind. He had to go before a board and take preliminary examinations to see if he had a chance to pass the very stiff course at school, they give them the vital courses of two years of War College in three months, which means constant cramming.

December 22 Pearl was here last night long enough to talk to me. She made Billy come get her. This hold-up racket is her scheme as well as her mother's. "My mother wants," she said, "every Saturday and Sunday, two five-day holidays, every Wednesday afternoon, forty-five dollars, two dollars a week for my garage bill, five dollars for my food. I've just had a raise to forty-five dollars a week." I didn't believe the raise was real. "I guess I'd best put an ad in the Sunday paper for a man," I replied. "Okay, Arthur. You won't hurt my feelings." She got up and went to the door. "I tell you," she said, "you might try this. Write an agreement between us; we'll both sign it. I'll show it to my mother. You can put down that one week I have both days and the next I have either Saturday or Sunday. You'd better put in all details — pay, hours, everything. Maybe she'll listen then. I won't promise."

I told Mrs. Cash. "Mr. Inman," she shouted, "you should be ashamed of yourself if you let her get away with that. Haven't you any pride, to let a couple of two-timing females shit on you like that? My God, I'd hootin-tootin send them walking. Let them wait. They'll come to you. I wouldn't kowtow to them if they were the last people in a servantless world. I'm ashamed of you for even thinking of it. To let yourself be shit on like that. It's not decent."

I dictated the agreement. I can't afford the sort of pride that an independent, foot-loose woman like Mrs. Cash recommends, however much I'd like to have it. Pearl is taking advantage of me lock, stock and barrel. I have no more love for her left and only a puny amount of affection. She's a calculating squeezer, and I don't believe her mother is solely back of this by any means.

Evelyn is at employment agencies now finding out what chance there is of getting a man, and how much we would have to pay if we got one. I think that Pearl will come on the above terms. It rather took her aback when I announced that I would advertise in the paper. She calls for the agreement tonight and is to let me know definitely one way or the other by Christmas. I've lost my enthusiasm to have her.

December 23 Everyone says if can get good girl, do so immediately. Pearl took typed agreement to mother yesterday. What answer will be have no idea. Rather offer her more money than have her have two days off at end of each week. Man here about job this morning. Large. I should guess a chronic drinker, a liar. Wanted forty a week. A man with only a ghost of a man inside, like Uncle Joe. Think not. Wait and hear from Pearl, then bargain with her.

December 24 Billy and I sat in the yards and talked about the war and whether he would come back to me or not after it is over. I stressed how outside forces worked like yeast on the firmest of intentions to pry people apart when propinquity was absent. He looked glum. "I'll tell you this, though," he said. "If I get seriously maimed, I'll not come back. I'll shoot myself. I can do it, too. I'm not goin' to return and have to be taken care of. I'm like my dad. It's killin' him right now. But I think I'm comin' home. If only I can become an instructor. That's my aim."

The sky was gray. The straddle-legged electric crane in front of where we were parked cut a rectangle of black against the gray. Sea gulls flew by overhead. A pigeon sat on a beam, huddled and silent. Trains, long and dark, rolled by on the right of way, and people sat at windows like figurines in a mobile receptacle with ventricles of glass. "I'll think about it here," Billy observed, "when I'm marchin' or doin' guard duty. Just like you, I like it."

December 25 I have been reading various Christmas messages. So much God stuff, Holy Day claptrap. There must be a lot of religious people left in the world for it to pay to use the jargon so generally. I do not seem to be able to get it through my thick head that men can be villains and still, with another side of their nature, mean the Jesus Christ bunkum they utter. And I cannot seem to comprehend the ready duplicity which permits public figures so facilely to expound what they do not believe in because it is utilitarian to do so.

Russia. Now there's a phenomenon just as strange to my understanding as is all this bowing and scraping before the memory of a nineteen-century dead Jewish fanatic and reformer. How can men so wholeheartedly — it must be wholeheartedly, else they could not have done what they have done in this war — fight for a regime and a nation which has kept them for twenty-five years in a virtual condition of slavery? There is, I suppose, a religious fervor, a fervor analogous to that of the Mohammedans in the seventh and eighth centuries. Men in the aggregate do not seem to object to slavery so long as it is called by another name. And they will readily die for the system which sustains that slavery provided that they have faith that the condition they are in promises future reward.

December 27 I have been reading 'Escape' by Ethel Vance, a novel, very well done, concerning some characters in Germany directly before the outbreak of the war; 'The Green Stone Door,' a New Zealand classic; 'There Go the Ships,' a tale of transport ships to Russia; 'Marie Antoinette' by Stefan Zweig, superbly translated and most interesting, 'The Norns Are Spinning,' a novel of adventure translated from the Norse; some Schopenhauer; and 'I Came Out of the Eighteenth Century,' autobiographical essays by John Andrew Rice, preacher's son in South Carolina, Rhodes scholar, for thirty years a teacher, one of the inaugurators of the Black Mountain College experiment.[6]

The last is a bitter book. Rice is a bitter man, a thwarted idealist, hence a troublemaker and rebel. The essays are filled with mordant aphorisms. He is devoured by a venomous acerbity toward the South, for what it pretends to be and is not. His acrid descriptions of his father's poor white relatives and of their life is so bitter as almost to crackle. There is a vitriolic rendition of his father, keen evaluation of the English and of Oxford. I wouldn't like the man, yet he has the courage to say what he thinks. I am surprised that any publisher would have the temerity to launch such a fulminating, corrosive volume with any hope that it might be a success. Still, Americans love to be pummeled. It flatters their vanity, and they are dead sure usually that there's nothing to it.

Billy just telephoned Pearl. She is coming. (I should put an exclamation mark did I have faith in it before I see her here.) Two days and one night off every other week, either Saturday or Sunday every alternate week, Wednesday afternoons, two five-day vacations, fifty-two dollars a week. Everyone except Mrs. Cash believes that I am doing right to take her at any price. She will, I am sure, watch out for my cars and for my interests. How long she will last is another question. Billy and Evelyn seem very pleased. So am I, if a bit reluctantly so. Thank God the bickering for position, the waiting, the uncertainty, is over. She has given notice at the plant where she works.

December 28 This theory of penalizing those with money and foresight who attempted to be provident against an uncertain future for the benefit of the thoughtless and the improvident galls me. I

---

[6] A good example of Arthur's hit-or-miss reading: an adventure novel (1939) by Ethel Vance (pseudonym) about bad Nazis and the escape of their secretly tried victim; an ambitious historical novel (Arthur mistitled it) about Anglo-Maori relations in the 1830s (1914) by the New Zealand writer William Satchell; a tale of revenge and blood in the days of the Vikings (1928) by the Norwegian novelist Andreas E. D. Haukland; an ex-newspaperman's report (1942) of the hazards of shipping arms to the Russians (fog, ice, submarines, bomb attacks); and the tart autobiography (1942) of a South Carolina educator and writer.

have no conscience as to my actions depriving others of food, losing the war, aiding the enemy, being unpatriotic. And if I had loved ones fighting, I still would feel no different. What use would it be to feel different? How I feel does not matter.

I realize full well that this viewpoint will be considered unmoral or immoral or just definitely bad. That does not concern me. I have myself and those I love to take care of. If I really believed my actions would halt an impending invasion that would threaten those I love, that would be another matter. But we are not being invaded, and it doesn't look as though we would be now. What I do or don't do will in the end comfort no one but our overlords. That men by the millions are fighting (so the politicos say) in my behalf and "for the good over evil" and for "freedom" in all sorts of odd ends of the world leaves me unenthusiastic. I'm a pawn without voice, and by God, I take care of me and mine first.

And why should I testify or exonerate myself to some dubious future reader? Millions of men are no better than I am, and millions are worse. If it is merely that the others keep their council and fail to spill over on paper that saves them in the eyes of their neighbors and contemporaries, why should any reader disdain me for following my resolve to be honest in this diary at any cost? I hoard. I break laws. I bribe. I cheat. I lie. I steal. I am, until I am caught, thoroughly unashamed and impertinent. It is just lucky for me I don't dwell in a small community. I should then, I fear, be found out and impugned or ostracized, in which case I should become more of an outward conformer and dealer in cant. Query: Is all of this just big talk?

December 31 I am discouraged about everything. Janice and Billy and I are repacking canned goods so as to get them out of sight. It is very tedious work, hard and laborious. Have been piling up old books to sell to get rid of them in order to make room for canned goods. That is difficult, too. Wish we could get more than a few nickels each for them. The nearer war comes to him, the gloomier Billy becomes. Sadie weeps on him all the time. Evelyn has a bad cold and you might think from the face she makes that she had pneumonia. I envision nothing much to live for, foresee no satisfying goal ahead, thank God that I escape the violent and vicious slaughter that constitutes mechanized warfare in this year of 1942.

Field Marshal Inman closely watched the movements on the Russian and Pacific fronts. The Japanese held on to New Guinea and Guadalcanal with "suicidal tenacity" as American forces nibbled "upon the hem of their acquired empire." Soviet victories under Stalin and the brilliant Zhukov suggested to Arthur the abhorrent thought that the

Russian social system "appears to have in it the proper fertilizer for greatness." And what was Hitler, "one of the world's great conquerors," thinking after Stalingrad? Churchill and Roosevelt, "the two playboys of our destiny," undoubtedly talked about a second front. It was about time the Allies acquired a toehold on the continent. The Russian victory was almost too decisive.

Arthur's uneasiness about the U.S.S.R. and his disgust with the management of the domestic economy mingled with his concern for his own care and comfort. He anticipated further shortages and more rationing. Possibly, Janice might be drafted for war work. As usual at such moments when he felt threatened, Arthur resumed his tirades against the Jews, whom he charged with controlling the government, the press, and all propaganda outlets and preaching a deadly idealism. He wrote: "I hate the Jews, the English, Roosevelt, life, myself."

1943

January 1 Billy went downtown last night. "You never saw such a wild New Year's Eve. Whether everybody was havin' a good time or was just attemptin' to forget I couldn't make out. They was spendin' money like water. There was three women to every man. There was any number of stag women—as bold as brass—accostin' you. Most of 'em was drunk. I never saw more drinkin'. And in front of movie houses people lined up so thick they musta' stood for three hours before gettin' a seat. We had a snack and a couple of drinks at the Bancroft. We came home early."

January 2 When I lie awake nights and think of Billy's pending departure, I feel dolorous. He has his petty faults—his grasping attitude towards time, his readiness to fib to avoid trouble, his occasional outright prevarications, his readiness to "let the girls do it," his wasting of time—but by and large we have gotten along with very little friction for two people so consistently together. It has taken us years to arrive at a workable mutual understanding, and it seems regrettable that an outside face should now come along and jerk us apart, as though long partnership counted for less than naught. God knows how he will return, if he returns. And I dread what will happen to my bones and my pocketbook without him. I do hope that Janice will stick, but she will not commit herself in direct words, and I obviously can't keep after her to obtain what would be worthless if secured by coercion.

January 10 Evelyn lost her cat and had a harrowing hour or so until she found it in the cellar. She did everything wrong all day. Then Mrs. Cash announced that she thought she wouldn't be coming into Boston weekends soon, conditions of transportation being unstable and tutoring jobs diminishing, and the college where she has been teaching Saturdays giving every evidence of folding up in the near future. Conditions at last are getting under her skin. Liberal arts education, her thesis runs, is going rapidly to pot. Less and less is required of students. Senior high-school students will graduate in February and with or without credits be allowed to enter colleges and universities with hitherto high standards, there to finish in three or two years with little or no real education. Standards are being lowered in all educational institutions. A revolution in liberal arts education is taking place. Restaurant prices are advancing to such a point, also, that it hardly pays her to come into Boston. Her entire attitude toward me alters abruptly when she is contemplating making a change which will remove me as a source of financial profit. I'll miss her. She has been of assistance in many ways.

January 11 Billy did all the talking with Pearl yesterday. He is convinced that she wishes to put her heart into doing her best for me. "I told her she's just gotta take my place and stand between you and the world." She has, he says, forgotten remarkably little. He is convinced that she will catch on quickly. He is afraid that Janice may resent Pearl if she grows too bossy and that she may feel put out anyway about how much money Pearl will be getting. He says he wants to talk to her. "It's up to Jan to stay with you, and I intend tellin' her so in no uncertain terms."

Billy's Sadie suggested that she go in the Waves. He has, he says, quashed that. He is earnestly endeavoring to anticipate everyone's good before he leaves. I have never known him to show to more advantage. I unreservedly admire his attitude. Great guns but I shall miss him. Three women, at times, will be more than I can accept with equanimity. I wish George were back in Boston. A note from him arrived yesterday. He seems to cross the continent and back periodically. No hint of what he is doing. His discretion on paper is tantalizing.

I am making a wash sale of my Pierce-Arrow to Millicent to avoid any step the Government may take to confiscate all cars or tires on cars over and above one car to a family. The subterfuge may be fruitless, but again it may not be.

January 12 The ambitions of men such as Roosevelt and the havoc they may wreak on individuals and on the nation permitting such men to gain and hold sway are, have always been beyond the conception of ordinary people, who with astonishing celerity seem to become habituated to the gyrations of dictatorship. He's very astute in a low and cunning sort of way. I hope I shall see the day when Franklin Delano Roosevelt gets his comeuppance.

Probably, when I rail at him, you are led to discount my estimation of him. You may be correct. He may go down in history as a second Lincoln. His motives may be evalued highly by posterity and his deeds lauded. Yet I think not. I only hope that my fulminations against him have not pushed you to his side completely nor have blinded you to the virtues of loyalty to friends, courage, ingenuity, fearlessness which he seems to possess. No man, to be trite, is all villain. Roosevelt, for all I know, may be merely a conceited tool in the hands of another or others more long-minded than himself. One of the most baffling aspects of contemporary history to the historically minded is that you can be sure of nothing except that you can't be sure of anything, so much is secret, hidden, unapproachable to inquiry or mere stage-setting.

January 13   Roderic has said that he will read to me twice a week if Mrs. Cash doesn't come to Boston weekends. He's much happier with this wife, adores his little daughter, so is less grumpy than formerly, although he still has spells of being sleepy evenings when the reading fails to go well. He works fairly energetically at his job, and by the time night comes he is, as he puts it, sometimes "all pooped out." I'll need all the men around me I can find when Billy goes — to offset so many women.

Billy is afraid that he will catch some of the diseases prevalent in the camps: syphilis, gonorrhea, athlete's foot, etc. He has heard that in some camps seventy-five percent of the men have athlete's foot. Then I suppose there are various skin diseases and trench mouth. I don't blame him for worrying. He promises to write me and not to forget me. "How could I forget you, Artie? You're part of my life." I counsel him not to come to one of his sudden temperamental decisions and on the spur of the moment give up his determination to remain in this country if possible. "If I get a quick impulse to do anything else, Arthur, I'll tell you what I'll do: I'll write you. You've got a level head, and I'll listen to what you say when I won't to what most people say. I think, with what I know about the Army already from the three years I spent in it and not bein' in awe of my superiors, yet respectful-like, you know, I'll get along. If I'm put under a superior officer I can't do anything with, I'll apply for a transfer. Believe me, I intend makin' a study of all possibilities. I don't want to be sent overseas."

Pearl is unpacking in Billy's room, wiping off shelves, arranging, putting in order, all with the utmost vigor, a torrent of conversation issuing forth meanwhile. "See this necklace, it . . ." "See this dress, you remember it . . ." "This brush needs washing. A brush makes my hair greasy; I prefer a comb." "My goodness, why isn't there more room?" "Are you going to buy me a new rug, Artie?" "This picture — it came out in the Canton paper. Look nifty in a swimsuit, don't I?" Her sleeves are up, her stockings rolled, her hair flying. Energy. Ella regards her with a slight distaste, probably not obvious to anyone but me. Janice looks on amusedly. I find myself wishing to God Billy weren't going.

January 14 Neither Pearl nor I obtained any sleep last night. The pelvis kept me awake and her clocks went off prematurely. I'm going to have a problem restraining her from getting discouraged until we get accustomed to each other.

I'm completely cured of her, much to my pleasure. She's what Ella says she is, a two-timing gold digger with her hands out for all she can secure. She's sensitive and high-strung and has a dominating personality and I fascinate her in addition to my money fascinating her, but she now leaves me cold. Ten of her isn't worth Janice's smile. I will say one thing for Pearl. Now that she is here she is trying with all her energies to please, trying too hard it may be.

Poor Billy is downcast. He and Sadie and the double bed had a tough night of it. Billy swears that if he returns from war he and Sadie will have single beds. I think it dispirits Billy each time he sees Pearl making use of his room, his bureau, his closet. I hope that our last ride together tomorrow morning will be as good as today's.

January 15 This is Billy's last day here. It is balmy, the sun warm on the face, water dripping from the eaves, an unflecked sky overhead. We drove in the railroad yards and there sat awhile behind Mechanics Building. They have been a godsend, the railroad yards. Billy told our friends, the engineer and fireman, goodbye — said he was going in the Army, and they laughed and didn't believe him.

Last evening Ella told Billy goodbye. "Well," she sobbed, when he had gone to bed, "I didn't cry in front of him, anyway. Of all the people I hate to see go to war, Billy is foremost. He's so cheerful and friendly always and so full of life. And he doesn't want to go. Oh God, what will the war do to him? I feel that he won't come back the same. He's one of those people who take on the coloring of the people they are with. He's bitter at having to go. He'll be more bitter when he gets back. He'll probably be so changed he'll never fit in with you again." And she sobbed again.

I feel fairly certain that barring some unforeseen concentration of circumstances favorable to me, I have probably seen the last of Billy as an aide-de-camp. And there's little or nothing I can do about it. I gave him a case with razor and brush, etc. in it, so that he will think of me.

January 16 Billy had said: "Can I borrow Mrs. Inman's car to go get Sadie?" I didn't like it as the snow was falling in whirls but could think of no way of saying no. About eleven, Billy called up and told Evelyn he had had an accident and the front of the car was smashed. I groaned. More money, probably. Anyway, a new batch of details for Evelyn to worry about. Billy returned later. He was so apologetic and abject that I couldn't show my irritation. This is the third or fourth accident he has had going to Springfield. He always hates to go and going probably upsets him.

January 18   The details in Zweig's 'Marie Antoinette' fascinated me, the small recorded minutiae of existence. The book is a historical study in the finest sense, scholarly, imaginative, judicially impartial. I can almost forgive the Jews when I become enthralled in some creation of art one of them has produced. I enjoyed every iota of the volume with the exception of the last paragraphs, which after the beheading were anticlimactic.

January 19   Poor Evelyn is very downcast, and I must make as much requisition upon Billy as I can. She has been very proud of this car, has nursed it like a baby. How many of the shining parts will be replaceable remains to be seen. Evelyn is talking with her insurance agent now.

January 20   I told Billy the simple preventatives for athlete's foot and trench mouth Bottom had prescribed. I suggested that he ought to leave with Evelyn the lawyers' fees ($12.50) which the insurance robbers say that they would have to charge in case the man who bumped into Billy contested the claim. "Do you think I ought to, Artie? If you think I ought to, I'll do it. I feel sick about what happened. I won't have any use for money in the Army anyway. I gave Ma the fifty dollars you gave me. They needed it bad." We talked a little more, then bade each other good night. I felt like crying. I thought he would cry. It's wearing on the emotions to bid someone goodbye whom you've seen day in, day out for seven years and are devoted to.

January 23   Pearl has done very well this week. She is set wholeheartedly upon pleasing me. "Billy," remarks Janice, "never remembered as many details in his life." She has surpassed my expectations. She is already learning to some extent to help me with my back. She has slept afternoons to avoid becoming overwrought. What bothered her most was eating alone Wednesday evening when she was here. "I can't eat alone, Arthur. I'm used to eatin' with people. I get miserable when I have a meal by myself. I'd rather not eat." Yesterday she made me a present of a chicken pie. Already she is looking less and less coarse as she loses the coloring assumed at the plant. When she puts a head kerchief around her fat cheeks and blonde hair, she resembles a peasant girl from Sweden. She has a way with people, too.

January 24   Ella continues to apply for jobs. Agents continue to turn her down. The need for labor, no matter what the papers say to the contrary, isn't yet stringent enough to open the average industrial plant to colored people. Ella comes here four or five days a week and one or two evenings. She keeps house and shops and reads four or five newspapers to keep herself informed — rarely a book. She enjoys sitting up late, rising late. She has become much more reconciled to her husband. Robert is making better money and has a fairly high place in the Redcap Union, of which he is an active member. He has saved a thousand dollars since last year. It is possible that Ella has gathered a respect for him (which she never had before) since he won a recognized place in the union. He refuses to accept a higher office. Ella likes the leaders of the union with whom Robert deals. While she feels that her life has been thwarted because of her color, she is now resolved to make the best of it and to quell her instinctive rebellion as much as she is able. She believes that she has never been allowed, due to social prejudices, to fulfill herself and realize her ambitions.

Ella, since she became more rested, looks younger. At times she is almost beautiful, her face quiet, her skin smooth, and when she is feeling well, light, her eyebrows heavy, her mouth wide, her hair, when freshly washed, a strange shading between brown and blue, soft, with less curl than Evelyn's. She invariably speaks softly, and her words come easily forth, robbing an oftentimes caustic humor of bitterness by its gentleness. She has the capacity of her people to withdraw herself utterly when she so wishes. I am convinced that, in her racial way which denies complete confidence in any human, she loves me. There is nothing she will not tell me. Of my antisocial conceptions she disapproves heartily. She is very emotional, very proud, very individualistic. Within her there is often a sharp conflict between her white traits and her colored tendencies. I should say that her white traits urge her toward individualism and ambition and her colored tendencies pull her toward acceptiveness. She is a most interesting study. "I am what I am," she will say. "If you like what I am, you like me. If you don't like what I am, I'm poison to you. I'm one or the other to nearly everybody, no matter how indifferent I am to most of them."

In many expressions of her nature, Ella is more akin to me than anyone I know. Rebellion in great measure rules her and pride and the recognized need of dissembling her rebellion and disguising her pride. Her innate arrogance hides behind expedient humility but never is quelled, will burn to the last if it does not one day consume her, which is unlikely, she being as tough as a yew bow however quietly biding when unstrung.

January 26   I want to make my feelings clear at this point on the Russian situation. I still feel that ultimately our culture will be more menaced by the Soviets than it ever would have been by Nazi Germany. But it will be the Russians who will beat Hitler. The faster they turn him upside down now the better, if it has to be that way. I do not, therefore, begrudge the sending of all the guns and armament and planes and food to Russia we can get there. They are doing their part in the winning of the war and more than their part. We might send them margarine instead of butter, to be sure, but that is a trivial detail. If you grant the premise that this war was inevitable and our part in it was inevitable and that Russia had to be our ally—why then nothing we can give Russia to assist them is too great.

England, doing incredibly less than its part, is another matter entirely. If I were Roosevelt, I'd say "no fight, no food," and mean it. That the Royal Air Force and the Royal Navy are active in no wise excuses the inactivity of the British soldiery. I resent every dollar spent for England, every man sent to fight for it, every pound of food donated.

January 27   Sadie, of all people, telephoned yesterday afternoon. She spoke to Evelyn. Billy, she said, had called her Saturday and again Sunday and had asked her to call us, but she had lost her voice and couldn't do it. Evelyn asked questions. No, Sadie did not believe that Billy was in a Volunteer Officer school. He had simply used that as a means of getting into the Air Corps. Yes, he had wanted to fly for a long time. He had had it on his mind to become a machine gunner in the Air Corps. He had given up all idea at present of becoming an officer. Billy, she volunteered, was good-hearted and big-hearted, a little quick sometimes, but there was nobody with a bigger heart. She had often been, she said, jealous of me and wanted to apologize to Evelyn for having been jealous. It was the way Billy loved me that made her jealous. He would have been in the Army long ago, she said, if it had not been that he wanted to stay with me. When he left, he told her that what he minded most was leaving me. That, she concluded, made her very jealous. She was sorry she had been jealous.

Sadie's reasons for expressing herself were very mixed, no doubt. I do not believe that she was disturbing my peace of mind intentionally. Probably she was doing the unwelcome job of breaking the news about Billy for him, he not having had the fortitude to tell me himself.

February 1 [From Abruzzo:]

It's been some time since I last wrote to you and as usual much has happened. I was working in the garment district as a "delivery boy", one of those guys who handles a hand truck scooting in and out of traffic all day. Worked in the union on the side and was quite active in politic's generaly. Was also running after a swell girl twas love with me. But what a climax! I began to wither along the edges. On the night of Jan 11th I proposed to "her" and got turned down. The next day I folded up on the job and had to go to the doctor. He gave me strict runnings orders and as a "dead head" I have got to take all the sidings to let the "red balls" through. Meaning that I got to take it easy and on a Strict diet, with no smokes or stimulents. Drinking is taboo and so you can imagine how the tranquility and peace (?) has effected me after the hectic life I have led. After two weeks of rest I went out job hunting and have finaly landed a war job in a radio factory. But factory work is hardly the thing for a guy of my temperment, particularly *hard work*. And so I am forced to quit my new job before I was able to do any agitational work. Most of the workers are very indifferent to the fact that we are at war and that our work is playing a vital role in winning. That has been my self appointed task to explain to these worker's just what the score was and why we must not shirk on the job. If it wasn't for my rent being due I'd quit now, but as it stands I have to continue for a week. This is the time that Tony took an evaluation and sort of settle down to something easy and tried to save some money. Particularly since I still love the girl and still desire matrimony and a stable foundation is needed. That she said no doesn't fase me, for I am determined to change her mind. I repeat, I need an easy job to achive my goal and such a job I have lined up at almost double my present pay (50¢ an hour). This job is easy and I can learn a trade. So these are my plans for the coming year, and I am hoping that all runs smoothly. Mean while I am seeing the doctor on Thursday and find out just what is wrong, because though he has been treating me, he did not explain what was wrong.

February 5 Dr. Pike took Evelyn to lunch yesterday and she spent the night at his house. She's a discreet one sometimes. She let slip the other day when talking on the phone to him that she calls Dr.

Pike "Cy." She's never let on to me, not that I care. It simply indicates a phase of her character.

February 9 The most important news is that yesterday a national war service act designed to conscript men and women for labor was introduced jointly in both houses of Congress. It will, in all probability, pass. We are well launched upon semienslavement to the State. I do believe from the bottom of my heart that what we are wanting to do in Europe and Asia could be done without the Government's acting as omnipotent overseer, wasting time, meddling with allotted jobs, padding and duplicating bureaus, spending money madly, giving and rescinding orders like the crazy institution it is, destroying private initiative and putting out of adjustment the capitalistic system.

February 11 Evelyn is doing well. Every time she talks to Dr. Arvin she comes home with another edge off. It's exciting. I'm very pleased. And she becomes discouraged now when she fails to do better or has a relapse, which is the most encouraging indication of all. Boy, that man can have my shirt if he keeps this up. I don't ask Evelyn what he tells her. That would be poor policy psychologically, but from stray bits here and there I can gather fairly accurately that he is saying to her in his words almost exactly what I have been saying in my words for twenty years. That can't help but impress even her. It does make me somewhat melancholy, however, to have her pay attention to him when she wouldn't to me.

Am waiting for Fred to pump my stomach. Need it. Just talking to Janice and Pearl. Pearl says she ate too much yesterday. Idly interested, I inquired what. This is what she lists, and she swears it is the truth: two cups of coffee, two coffee rolls, two glasses of milk for breakfast; then two oranges, two pieces of candy, two crackers with peanut butter, two glasses of milk during the morning; for lunch, roast lamb with gravy and mint jelly, mashed potatoes, peas, two rolls, coffee; when she got home, two glasses of milk; for dinner, baked American chop suey, tea, parsnips, apple salad, three pieces of bread and butter, blueberry pie; at her brother Charles' later in the evening, French pastry cookies and chocolate candy, a glass of milk, a quarter of a pound of potato chips, ginger ale; before she went to bed, two glasses of milk. I laugh and laugh.

February 17 "Kharkov has fallen," said I to Roderic. "Has it?" said he. "Swell." "Does it worry you, Roderic, to observe the successes of the Communists?" "Worry me? Not at all. If they come out on top, fine. If they can sell Communism to us, well and good. In the meanwhile, any man who can bump off a Hun or a Jap is my friend — my very excellent friend." "How soon do you expect you will be called up, Roderic?" "Oh, in a matter of months. I'll tell you this, Arthur, I'm not going to slink into a war job to avoid it. I don't believe in that."

I shall miss him if he has to go into the Army. With reservations, I am fond of him. I have known him for fifteen or sixteen years and we have spent innumerable evenings together. As a rule, we read science fiction stories. One in ten is good and occasionally one is excellent. In the best of the magazines, the standard of writing is workmanlike and readable. 'Astounding Science Fiction' is the best magazine, and one of their authors, A.E. van Vogt, writes with power, imagination and vigor. Mrs. Cash dislikes what she calls my "slop," so that if Roderic goes I shall have no one to read the magazine.

February 26   Feel quite a little better today. I lost my caution and poked ribs down in front with fingers. Was a gamble but helped. Dr. Pike has been splendid. When I am in a bad enough jam, he often comes through with a sharpened interest. Adversity and a difficult problem only whet the knife of his aggressive nature. And that, I take it, is a grand quality in any person, one which should cause anyone to overlook small foibles.

Evelyn and he are winning when together. She says: "How about coming downstairs after you get through with Arthur and having something to eat?" She regards him tentatively, as though he were her little boy and a temperamental child and she didn't know which way he'd spin. "Oh, I don't know, dear," he replies, as though to a small child. "I have a one-thirty appointment. Anyway, I'm not hungry. Anyway, it'd be too much trouble." "No trouble at all," she reassures him. "I love to have you." "I don't know," he says. "I'd love to have you," she repeats. "Well," he concedes, and you can tell he'd like it very much though he tries not to let on to the fact, "well, perhaps a half a cup of soup, if it isn't too much trouble." She smiles benignly. He looks stern. The boyplay is done. They've both enjoyed it. I grin to myself. I do not doubt that each of them is aware that I am amused. It is so like a boy, and so like a mother. They are, in the main, very sweet with each other. She does his petty shopping for him. He feeds her often. "I like to see her stoke up. She's got an appetite, Arthur." They keep their financial dealings exact to the last penny. He likes that.

March 2   Not being allowed to ride gives me more time mornings to catch up in here on odds and ends. Mrs. Cash is busy in the other room recopying Volume 20 [1924]. She has lost weight and looks better.

[From Patricia:]

Paul left the thirteenth of December for Camp Custer in Battle Creek Micigan for Officer's Candidate School of the Provost Marshal General, which in plain civilian talk means the Military Police. Then came Christmas and the usual mad holiday business, even worse this year due to the added populace of defense workers and service men on leave, all looking for movie stars, I think that every man stationed in California heads for Hollywood when he gets leave. On the weekends our place used to look like the U.S.O.

Paul is supposed to rate a ten day leave after graduation, whether he gets it or not depends on further orders. A certain percentage of men are shipped overseas at once, and we may only have a day or two, but whatever it is to be I can take it in my stride. I've never met Paul's parents and we thought this a good time for me to come east, meet him, and then if he is to be stationed in this country go on with him to my new home, which is what I'm praying for naturally, if it isn't to be that way I'll stay with Paul's people for a bit, then go on to Boston for a while and return to California in the summer and go to work with Ruth at Vega. I won't go back to the Pig N' Whistle anyway, I simply can't take the tension and the amount of work we have to do now, if I've got to work so hard I'd rather it be physical labor and something connected with the defense work.

March 7 Evelyn and I have finished correcting Volume 20 [1924]. Mrs. Cash has been busy all vacation week recopying it. If I could do as much work at my best as she can do at her worst I should be in seventh heaven and would doubtless be as uninteresting as she is and perhaps with as little imagination. She is always one woman with one viewpoint — her own.

Yet she occupies, somewhat against my desire, a fairly important buttress position in the structure of my existence. I see much of her. Her iterated assertions — that without money man is at an insuperable disadvantage while with money he is in a place of undeniable advantage — have influenced me. She is a fine fast reader. Her knowledge of rhetoric and grammar have assisted in filling out the little I learned at school on the subject. She has given me a wider comprehension of the values of English literature. She has caused me to feel more certain of the desirability of having imagination and perceptions. I am in a measure ashamed not to like her more. She represents much against which I am antagonistic. I sincerely admire the vigor with which she works and cannot say enough for her determination to give full service for value received.

My back yells for Billy. No word from him except through Sadie, who has called up a couple of times. I miss his ministrations on my spine more than I miss him. I do not miss him nearly as much as I missed Mr. Flood or as I missed Edna.

Pearl is doing her best. She informed me the other day that she was aware I didn't like her as much as I used to but that she intended making me like her at least as much as I did Billy. I protested her assumption, though not too violently. Not much misses her. I have an idea — I hope not a wrong one — that some indifference, not too blatant, piques her and causes her to try harder to please.

March 11 Roosevelt yesterday transmitted to Congress two documents, a 640-page social security report prepared by the National Resources Planning Board and an 18-page general recommendation for postwar security activities.

Jobs would be guaranteed by the State, and "freedom from fear" and "freedom from want." It is all very utopian and very idealistic and very calculated to give the State and those in control of the State (assumedly not 'the people') dictatorial sway over how people exist, what they do, what they may not do, their activities and aspirations and ambitions. Congress is even warned that plans such as the social dreamers (or schemers) outline are necessary of adoption now in order to prevent a back-to-'normalcy' movement after the war.

Does Roosevelt wish to be Stalin? Do his followers wish to profit by his becoming Stalin? Is it all a grandiloquent plan? Or is it merely American idealism and sentimentality gone amuck? It cannot be, I conclude, a long-term plan deliberately conceived and carefully executed, what with the caliber of men now in control at Washington. And yet, and yet, there is the barest chance it may be, for the convolutions and machinations of men screaming for power, so history shows, may progress with infinite patience and unbelievable duplicity and unexpected perspicacity toward a chosen goal. The culmination of the ambition does not (again history shows) always have to be promulgated and concluded within the bounds of a single life or set of lives.

March 17 I was listening to the Governors of a number of Midwestern states discussing food the other night. They predicted everything from starvation to less food than Americans had ever had unless the Government did something. Lack of expert farmhands and the Government's policy of not allowing new farm machinery to be built and sold shared the blame for what is happening.

March 21 I am looking at 'Life.' In it are sample photographs from one of the manuals issued by the Army to teach men the art of expert killing. The photographs are startlingly alive and vivid. "Be

Quiet," "Be Alert," "Be Quick," "Be a Killer." A black cat against a black background enacts these titles, and next to it a man enacts them in duplicate. Then there is a series entitled "Three methods of Killing." Stark photographs of killing "with a knife," "with a piano wire," "with a hatchet." You can shut your eyes and have these photographs still before you, so gruesome and convincing they are.

March 23 Ella is working for the Jewish doctor and the Jewish dentist around the block on Huntington Avenue. Dr. Pearl was the doctor who cured Robert's jaw when he was suffering from some obscure ailment that even the Massachusetts General doctors were unable to diagnose. He has taken care of Robert and Ella ever since. "Yes sir," exclaimed Ella, "the old fellow has seen me inside and out, stretched on a table with my legs up and wide, under the covers with the influenza, every problem, every scratch and every operation that comes into his office he worries and frets over just as though one of his own had it. He's kind. They say he's rich. But he gives generously to charities of all sorts. He pinches pennies as Jews do, but no one in trouble ever appeals to him without result. He's old and ugly and small and has a son he's giving the best of education and a sloppy Jewish mommala. He treats social diseases, although I didn't know that until he tipped over his card index one day.

"He likes me. He says I'm beautiful. All I'd have to do would be to give him a little sympathy and a little mothering and he'd be a ripe plum for the picking. You know he must like me, for he actually gave me a raise. He gives me no peace as to staying on the job. I don't want his old job with bellyaching people and sour-faced people and the tag ends and bobtails of the sidewalks coming into his office in a steady and depressing stream. No sir. 'The first thing you know,' I told him, 'would be if I stayed here, that one day I'd say just what I thought of all the misfits who come to you; and then I'd put on my hat in a huff and go home; and you wouldn't like it worth a nickel. You think you know me and that I'm all sweetness and light, but, man, you've no idea know how wrong you are.' That made him keep quiet for a day or two, but he really didn't believe me and that I meant it. I'm just about ready to say I'll stay for a five dollar raise. That will slay him. I can just see the expression he'll wear. I receive more as it is than anyone who ever worked for him. But I don't want the old job, Arthur. It depresses me even if the hours are good and both doctors are considerate. I'm getting tired of being there. They'll see the last of my tail swishing out the door one of these fine days."

March 25 Millicent is, I should say, fairly contented with the life she is leading. Some weeks ago Millicent was introduced to a man about her own age in the afternoon. By night she was in bed with him. "What a man. Inexhaustible. Nothing like him has come my way since Hal. And it's my first deviation from the straight and narrow since Hal died. We were at it all night. I loved him." He came again a couple of weeks ago and gave Millicent a repeat performance. He travels for a company. "If he weren't married, I'd marry him in a minute. He has charm and savoir-faire and is altogether a man of the world. He's handsome, too."

March 26   It seems to me that the best time of all to have been born into this world—if you had to be born at all—would have been about 1850. You might have grown up then in an era of rank and unashamed individualism. If you wanted walls around your estate fifteen feet high, there were no laws against it. There were no income taxes to rob you of the fruit of your labors. After you were grown, there were no great wars to earthquake your life and habits. And the music was melodious. And there were private cars on trains. And the countryside was not just next door to some city. If you lacked many modern comforts and didn't know that you lacked them, you didn't miss them. And one bath a week is really enough to keep a person healthily clean. And a person should have died before 1914.

If I were well, I'd pull anchor and go to the most hidden place that could be found, there wait for the end of it all. If I were God, I'd march down and smash every machine and tear up the patterns for them and erase from men's minds the memory of them.

Damn those droning, those ceaseless, jitter-producing planes. I wish I might sleep. It is the hour to go and try.

March 29   The war, today, seems unreal to me, I having my own troubles. The more intense personal troubles are, as a rule, the further outer matters recede from both interest and reflection. I simply record what is happening so as not to lose the thread of the larger story. Men dying, bombs falling, flames leaping, wounded screaming. My pelvis is dislocated. I crave sleep and a silence such as used to be at Southwest Harbor on a still night among the second-growth spruces.

March 30   Read that a well person enjoys noise, a sick person does not; sure diagnosis between well and sick. May be. Thinking back now to noises. Not at first very conscious of them one way or the other. Recall tootling on toy trumpets and whistles. Recall using one of those tin things with a hole in it which boys put in mouths and blow shrilly through. Recall Fourth of July at Southwest and spending most of day setting off small firecrackers in tin cans. Recall wondering why my parents complained of church bells ringing the

Fourth in at midnight. Recall marveling that a cock crowing could bother Mother. Recall fire engines racing down Belgian blocks of Spring Street and myself getting up at night when didn't sleep through it and going to window to hear wheels on stones and watch sparks on hoofs. Recall when a bit older, how I liked wheels clicking on joints of rails when traveling, the sounds of small stones rolling down mountain trails. Noises at night did not ever bother me then. When I went to Haverford School, the first year I was there English sparrows nested in the eaves of the Junior House outside my window, and traffic passed along Lancaster Pike, and trains puffed upgrade out the Maine Line. I was not bothered. I do not recollect being kept awake by any noises while I was at school.

The two noises that I remember bothered me during that period of my life were the blinds slatting and slamming in the wind at Southwest and the mosquitoes humming in my room at night. I gradually became more conscious of minor sounds — waves lapping, trees soughing, hammerers on wood, saws sawing, birds calling, foghorns blowing, bells ringing, brooks gurgling, leaves rustling underfoot, motors running, children calling, locusts chirring, sea gulls screaming, boats blowing, wheels trundling along dirt roads, locomotives whistling, sleet tapping on windows. I recall the steampipes waking me early in the morning at college with their banging. Records played too often began to annoy me. A motor out of kilter would bother me. I couldn't sleep if the blinds banged too hard. But in the main noises were no problem in my life, and I didn't object to loudness. The starlings in the ivy of the Marlborough-Blenheim at Atlantic City in 1916 was the first objectionable dissonance to really get under my skin.

It is my inability to get up and leave that adds almost a horror-like quality to sounds to which I am antipathetic. I want to escape them at any cost. I want silence. And each year, as I become weaker physically, the noises bother me more. And that is the story. If how much one minds noises is a measure of being sick, then I'm an ill person indeed. With the possible exception of a dislocated pelvis, I am cognizant of nothing worse in life.

April 2 Must stop now and rest a bit in preparation for talking with Arvin. Hope he's not the dope most psychiatrists are — book knowledge, conceit, a vast condescension.

April 3 I liked Arvin. A chunky man with keen blue eyes, parted upstanding iron-gray hair, slightly brownish teeth, a kindly and humorous mouth, an unimpressive nose, fingers slightly swollen and blunt like my Father's. A very genial smile and an exceedingly shrewd and roundabout manner of suggesting ideas.

"Now don't you think that perhaps it might be that . . . ?" Intelligent. I can imagine that he assists many tangled and puzzled people. "What's life worth if you can't give a hand?" Agrees, I suspect, a bit too readily with patients when he may have contrary notions. I liked him and he liked me. Said that my grasp of my own problem was so thorough, didn't feel he could help me. Said was sure he could help Evelyn. Called her intelligent. Remarked that he was certain of her intention to be all I wanted her to be, but that she became confused. Rather enjoyed his visit. He told Evelyn that I was remarkably honest about myself, which, he added, most people weren't. Told her that he was struck by what a sweet nature I had in the face of the troubles and pains that beset me.

It discourages me to have to retain many of my impatient dictums about Evelyn, which only proves, does it not, how my feelings toward her have altered. It is the lack of taste I sometimes evince rather than the significance of what I say that rankles. It takes courage not to delete certain crass and youthful observations and attitudes. I cut and prune only enough to make the book readable and hope that the not inconsiderable task has been adequately done in such manner as not to alter the viewpoints and impressions I then indulged in.

April 5 How can I manage to read enough thought-provoking matter to keep my mind in new and exciting food, so that my mental processes and observations won't stale and harden? It is a real problem. The other afternoon I worked diligently correcting the diary and in addition read and tried to absorb Chinese philosophy and military strategy. Yesterday I was exhausted. Should I indulge in cycles of hard work followed by exhaustion or does a minimum amount of work each day achieve more? I have never been able to decide. I must conserve sufficient strength to listen to the radio and the talking-book for an hour and a half each evening from eleven to twelve-thirty. Then there is the writing—done fairly slowly—in here. While it may not strike someone with the energy of a Mrs. Cash as a demanding schedule, it is a stiff one for me since it goes on day after day, year after year, with only the interruptions made obligatory by periodic exhaustion or sickness. I love to work and can imagine little else other than perfect health that would give me more pleasure than to be able to labor sixteen hours a day. I resent each hour of rest I am forced to take.

April 9 Sun Tzu's treatise on the art of war[7] is a competent and

---

[7] Arthur read this Chinese classic (c. 500 B.C.) in a collection of military works edited by Major Thomas R. Phillips, *Roots of Strategy* (1940). His references to Marshal de Saxe, Frederick the Great, and Napoleon come from the same text.

urbane book dispersing basic ideas on martial matters with little or no condescension and with a minimum of repetition. It is an instructive and thought-provoking study of strategy and tactics, most of the wisdom and observation in it as applicable today as when it was written some twenty-four centuries ago. It is designed for the instruction and illumination of leaders and of those men ambitious to be leaders. "The general is skillful in attack whose opponent does not know what to defend; and he is skillful in defense whose opponent does not know what to attack." Quotable aphorisms dot the book.

> There are five dangerous faults which may affect a general: (1) recklessness, which leads to destruction; (2) cowardice, which leads to capture; (3) a hasty temper that can be provoked by insults; (4) a delicacy of honor that is sensitive to same; (5) over-solicitude for his men, which exposes him to worry and trouble. These are the five besetting sins of a general, ruinous to the conduct of war.

What Sun Tzu has to say concerning the waging of war might, I think, be applied to the governing of one's own life with general profit; the conclusions of the astute Chinese man are based primarily upon human nature, its weaknesses and its strengths.

April 10   The electric wiring fused yesterday directly in front of my eyes, and today I can focus with difficulty and bear light only with some pain. I was in the dark when it happened. It was a sudden, violent, instantaneous leaping forth of latent force, too quickly done to cause fright. I was most interested in my reactions. Last night I dreamed again and again of corruscating lights and lewd people. I was imprisoned in a sort of freak show with bawdy, disgusting, horrible, fearful, loathsome, creature people in rooms and stalls without end, soliciting, threatening, mouthing, mumbling, weeping, balefully inert, insanely active. Bedlam was in the place and strange cohabitings and gruesome struggles and inept combats. And there was no way out.

April 13   And now Pearl is in a huff. She eats and eats on my time. I said: "This is the time of day for you to take care of me. I wish you would." I can scarcely whisper and that not for long. Pearl, whether she knows it or not, resents not being soft-soaped as I ordinarily do all day. Janice and Evelyn prefer me this way. It must be a relief to them to have me shut up, with no words tumbling forth impetuously. I must have considerable temperament in me to cause people to hate or love me as they do and to alter so suddenly. There is quiet in me only when I am alone and occupied; otherwise there is tumult that is more easily expressed than withheld. It is only with constant conscious effort that I get along with people over any period of contact with them.

"As our life is ours," writes the ancient Chinese philosopher, Yang Zhu,[8] "we must bear it, yet scorn it; get what pleasures we can out of it and wait until we die. When death draws near, we must bear it, yet scorn it; look where it is leading and go on until the end. Scorn everything, bear everything." And, I might add for myself, dissimulate, dissemble, recognize that except insofar as your exterior can make and hold friends, you are as alone and unwanted in this world as the shadow of a dark star.

April 14   I have finished Marshal Saxe and enjoyed his book tremendously.[9] He's the sort of man I'd like to be, vital, with a sly wit, arrogant, with an eye for every detail, a person you would hate or love with all your heart, an Eddie in the large, a Hokusai in reverse. Frederick the Great's instructions to his generals I have also read, dull for the most part, in certain aspects brilliant. The writings of men are like photographs of them, sometimes exact, usually unflattering, sometimes overflattering, always when unsupported by other evidences not to be assumed to be exact by the student of character. I tried a volume written about Saxe by an Englishman but gave it up as dull and without percipience. Read Napoleon's martial epigrams, observations, aphorisms next. Nasty business, war, for the unfortunate common soldier but (if the general be fortunate and intelligent) chess with live pawns, knights, castles: an enthralling preoccupation.

April 15   The more I read of war as it was waged in the past and is waged now, the more it is brought home to me that the leitmotif of it all is "destroy! destroy! destroy!" and he who destroys the most the quickest is victor. What a subversive basis for human aggregate action. But why can I not be realistic, acknowledge wholeheartedly and without reservations that man enjoys destruction, will never be able to avoid it and still carry on the race with health and vigor. I have known as much for a score of years and more. The most that can be hoped for are covenants and accepted customs which will modify the horrors of war, such as the code of chivalry and the

---

[8] A Chinese philosopher (Yang Zhu) is believed to have lived in the fourth century B.C. Yang advised his disciples to live for the day. Death is the end of all men; the wise and foolish, saint and sinner end up a pile of rotten bones, so why yearn for a reputation that will outlive you and pass up the joys of life without ever knowing that you have missed them? Care neither for fame nor for death.

[9] Arthur is referring to *My Reveries Upon the Art of War*, posthumously published in 1757, the work of a brilliant military mind far ahead of its time in its tactical and technical conceptions.

Geneva rules for warfare. Of course nations will not adhere to these restrictions, but there can be no doubt that sometimes they do minify destruction and ferocity.

April 18   I am in contact with fewer and fewer people this winter. I don't seem to miss them. Evelyn, Janice, Pearl; in the evenings, Mrs. Cash, Roderic, Ella, Millicent, then Dr. Pike, Fred, Bottom. That, with occasional exceptions, is the roster. I depend increasingly upon the talking-book. I have plenty to think about in my own head and find myself readier to continue writing up the lives of familiar characters than to essay explorations into new ones. If I weren't so debilitated by the pelvis, it would be a passable existence.

I have been enjoying books of late. Finished 'Roots of Strategy,' found Napoleon's utterances on war dull. Am still reading about the Chinese philosophers. Have a couple of novels going. Reading the Congressional Record. In the midst of a long English novel on the talking-book called 'The Water Gipsies.' It is a satire and suffers from the usual British complaint—a yearning to be witty in print at any cost. Amusing, nevertheless, in spots. I have almost finished 'Black Elk Speaks,' the life story of a holy man of the Ogalala Sioux as taken down by the poet, John G. Neihardt. It is a deeply moving document, a very great book, perhaps the finest exposition of a native Indian soul that exists.[10]

April 21   I had lost Joe [Cooper]. I inquired his whereabouts of passers-by on the crowded, squalid street. They directed me indifferently. It appeared that Joe had lost his mind, was in the care of a woman. I found him playing on some steep stairs. He failed to recognize me. He tossed his ball to me. I tossed it back. He lived, he said, across the street. I went there. I was sad about Joe.

A plump woman with dowdy clothes, serene face, greeted me. She led me to a small room. We sat together. I explained that I was Joe's cousin, how melancholy it made me to see him as he was now. She was impersonally sympathetic. She took my hand. I found her physical presence oddly exciting. I had thoughts about her. An automobile drew up before the entryway. Five men with expressionless, weak, cruel faces were in it. One of them left the driver's seat and came into the room. He was short, swart, like gray iron, and his face was immobile save for very black eyes. He regarded me. The

---

[10] For *Roots of Strategy* (1940), see note 7. A. P. Herbert is the author of *The Water Gipsies* (1930), a Dickensian novel about the Thames barge people and "their grotesque pagan world." *Black Elk Speaks* (1932) is the life story of an Ogalala Sioux warrior, hunter, and holy man as related to (in later editions "through") the Nebraska poet John G. Neihardt.

woman explained that this was her husband. He continued to regard me malevolently. He accused me in a flat voice of seducing his wife. He stated that he and his friends were about to put an end to me; had I anything to say? I knew myself innocent of the charge he made. Yet I knew just as certainly it would serve no purpose to say so. He bade me wait. He conferred with the men in the car. The woman informed me that if her husband said he would kill anyone, he would do it. I thought of escape. I thought of walking to the car and explaining the truth of the matter to the other men. I wondered was I afraid of death. The woman continued to hold my hand. A small girl with red hair appeared at a side door and beckoned to me. I was aware that she intended to guide me to safety. I sat where I was. I found myself to be more afraid of not facing the man and attempting to outface him than I was of the chances of death. I waited.

I waked then. And I have been pondering ever since what I would do in an identical everyday circumstance. I believe that waking, sleeping I should take a like course. But I do not know. The substrata layers of one's own nature are, very strangely indeed, oftentimes more hidden to us than are the fundamentals of another's nature as manifested in physiognomy or expression or action. I wonder why. Perhaps it is the very fixity of our judgments of ourselves which confuses us.

I am reading the Congressional Record word by word. I find it rather interesting. I am surprised that as many of the politicians sound as intelligent as they do and possess as large a command of language. There seems to be a notable gap between the intelligence with which they express themselves and with which they vote. One, I suppose, is intelligence of the mind, the other the intelligence of opportunism.

I find the extraneous matter—letters, reports, clippings, etc.—included in the Record and its appendix to be in many instances exceptionally illuminating. The volume of complaints and protests pouring in to Congress against bureaucracy is interesting. And many Congressmen protest themselves. But they do little or nothing against it. They seem as cowed as do the small businessmen cited, who are afraid to express themselves honestly when summoned to Washington for hearings for fear of reprisals from the bureaucrats.

April 22 It cannot be a very utilitarian mind which at one and the same time counts any wholesale rubbing out of Jews in Europe as beneficial to the human race as a whole and imaginatively suffers with the Jews who are under the German yoke.

Last night I was a Jewish child of about two years. New York had been occupied by the Germans. All Jewish children were to be killed. I was smuggled uptown in a truck, carried in a basket through back alleys, hidden in a wheelbarrow load of wallpaper and thus taken into a huge apartment house where the help were Jews and the tenants Aryans. The mystic and binding brotherhood of the Hebrew race protected me and caused a quiet to my fears. It was as reassuring as stars in dark night. It had always been there. It would always be there. It was there for me and for each individual of my race. The women whispered expressively of the pogrom that was in prospect. I was he who had inherited tradition and solidarity. I was the inestimable scion of Judah. I was escaping from the edict of Herod. There was in my hitherto undeveloped spirit a deep quiet and a reassurance in race and bourn that made me feel a pride beyond measure.

I often wonder about the harried races of men now upon the earth: the Chinese existing upon roots and grasses and selling or eating their children; the French brought low; the Poles laboring in Germany on starvation rations; all the others; the Germans in Russian prison camps. Yet I cannot be in any degree sure that the cases of these peoples are as they are represented to us Americans. Perhaps they are worse off. Perhaps it may be that they are not nearly so badly off. And besides, it is difficult, almost impossible indeed, for an individual to assume to himself the travail of a people, the more so if the people be not his own.

April 25   Evelyn had lunch at Corn's house, a little toybox affair. Corn's husband will not let her talk of what he does. Everybody in Washington, Evelyn says, is afraid of the F.B.I. They are, many of them, deadly serious about their work, feeling that they are saving the nation. Frank makes five thousand a year, quite a step up from being a sporadic schoolteacher and writer at Tufts. After ten percent for bonds and what the income tax and other taxes demand, about four thousand is left. Corn, Evelyn says, is much more proper outwardly than she was in Cambridge. Frank tells her that she was spoiled there and felt she had to have her own way and that Washington is good for her. Corn doesn't like it too well. They entertain in a small way and go out some. Mrs. Raleigh came to visit them for a couple of weeks. She behaved herself except when she claimed there wasn't enough humidity in the house and threw boiling water on the floors to make it, thus spoiling the finish so that they had to be done over when she left.

Evelyn at my instigation saw Fulton Lewis, the radio commentator,[11] who was in her class at school. He possesses a considerable following as commentators go and a ponderable influence. He is imbued with the crusading spirit. He received a national award last year for his research work on food. He travels up and down the country at a great rate. Evelyn writes of him as follows:

April 23, 1943
On train from Washington to Boston
A perfect early spring day, this, with soft blue haze over the treetops of Rock Creek Park, and a mockingbird singing all morning high in a sycamore. I had made an appointment to see Fulton Lewis at eleven, but arrived early at the building where he has his office, the WOL building. Fulton hadn't come yet, so I sat listening to the staff talking, and the newsticker tapping, while I waited. It was like a newspaper office, with a touch of theatre colloquialism thrown in. Two or three men shuffled papers desultorily; two girls typed a little, talked more and smoked constantly. Everyone called everyone 'darling' and one of the girls kept pawing through papers, hunting for a certain manila envelope, and saying "Christ, what will we do if we can't find that woman's script!" in a conversational tone of voice.

When Fulton appeared, about ten minutes late, he walked past me into the main office, greeting all the staff jovially and holding up for their admiration a broad brimmed light grey hat—"I got that in Texas, isn't it a beauty?" After a few more remarks, he went toward his private office, motioning for me to come too. I could see that he did not place me. I told him who I was, & he fairly bubbled with enthusiastic welcome. "Good gracious, Evelyn honey, why didn't you tell me. I'm so glad to see you. Sit down & tell me all about yourself." But I asked him what you wanted to know about the Jews instead. And here is what he said.

"Of course, no one can say what is in men's minds, but I don't think there really is any concerted objective among those people. It is certainly a fact that many of the key positions of our government have fallen into the hands of men who simply are not American. That has taken place because they are emotional aggressive people. But their ideologies are utterly foreign to us. The men themselves, many of them, have practically never been off the Island of Manhattan. Their ideologies are a slopover from

---

[11] Fulton Lewis, Jr. (1903–1966), a journalist and radio commentator for the Mutual Broadcasting Company, was a clever and articulate right-winger whose "Top of the News" program suited Arthur to a T. An inveterate anti-New Dealer, he later attacked the president's Fair Deal and strongly backed Arthur's hero Senator Joseph McCarthy.

Europe, entirely so. When one of them is put at the head of a bureau, he wants to carry out his ideas as quickly as possible, so naturally he brings as many of his own people with him as he can, to fan out into the organization, and so accomplish results more quickly. But I don't think it's any plot. I don't think they purposely create confusion in order to gain control. I don't even think the situation is dangerous. We've got Roosevelt now, but we won't have him long. The South isn't *going* to revolt. It already has. They feel that the Democratic Party has been swept out from under their feet, just as I could pull this rug out from under the furniture in this room. So we won't have the present administration much longer, or I miss my guess." Fulton thereupon made a face, to indicate his distaste for it.

April 28   And this is the end of Volume 100. It has been a long and disturbing winter, and I'm pleased it is on the way to being over and done with. The pelvis has given me no peace. I have been unable to accomplish as much work as usual on account of lacking a voice. Billy left. Pearl came. I put $500 into a business venture and am on the route to losing it all. Have fared better in the Stock Market. My circle of immediate friends has narrowed. The war in Europe has, on the whole, progressed not unfavorably for the United Nations, and the time approaches when further important movements should occur. In the East, Japan has unwisely been given time and opportunity, due to the American concept of dealing with Germany first, to consolidate and fortify its conquests. On the home front the food situation has claimed the most attention. Machineries of war are being produced so fast by us that there is not shipping enough to transport them overseas, and many plants and factories are having to slow down. The submarine war against our shipping appears to have been doing more damage than we are permitted to know.

Here is how Arthur saw the war in "its larger aspect" between the spring and fall of 1943. Thanks to American supplies, Germany had been stopped. Now was the time for the United States to focus on the Pacific theater and to launch a full-scale invasion of Japan before the Japanese consolidated their conquered provinces. Yet the swiftness and power of the rejuvenated Soviet Union disquieted him. Ultimately Russian successes might prove far more menacing to the West than those of the Nazis. He discounted Eddie Rickenbacker's prediction that Russia might "come out of the war the greatest democracy in the world" and, citing Max Eastman's articles in Reader's Digest, *called it a brutal corporation directed by a shrewd and ruthless leader. Stalin's dissolution of the Communist International meant nothing. Churchill would be well advised to switch sides before the Soviets became irresistible.*

At home "a group of planners and dreamers," most of them Jewish, were driving the nation to serfdom. The "tall man with the shriveled leg, the close-set eyes, the weakly petulant mouth, the lush voice," together with his wife and the "intuitive panderer" Harry Hopkins, fronted for the "parasites" who, through the Office of Price Administration (O.P.A.), were liquidating the American "kulaks." Arthur relied on the good authority of the right-wing columnists (Upton Close; Fulton Lewis, Jr.; Bill Cunningham) to wrap up his case against the Washington "totalitarians." He gave credence to every charge and rumor he read or heard to convince future readers of the Diary that he was not talking through his hat; and he screened the news for any hint of a decline in Roosevelt's popularity or weakening political strength: a recalcitrant Congress, say, or a showdown between the administration and John L. Lewis's miners.

As for the Garrison Hall family, Arthur blew hot and cold. He alternately praised and cursed volatile Pearl, depending upon whether she pampered him or behaved like a horse with its ears laid back. Darling Janice moved closer to marriage. When she and her undeserving lover began to dicker for a house, Arthur felt a stab in his heart. Evelyn continued to "disappoint" him by her stubbornness and by her unwifely refusal to merge herself in his larger purpose.

May 1   I seem to be filled with hates and resentments these days. They are innocuous, most of them, and are caused in large part by the feeling of helplessness and unprotectedness that seizes me when I lose the weapon I depend on for every situation, my voice. I'll pull out of this depression sooner or later. Much of it is also caused by the unstable pelvis. I'm not riding this morning, for I'm cold and the wind is shrilling in cornices and cracks, beating smoke from chimneys flat. What would it be like to live in a land where violent winds were absent? I liked them when I was a boy. I hate them now. I remember no winds like this in Atlanta and fewer winds than this in Philadelphia.

May 2   Stefan Zweig's 'The World of Yesterday' lacks the meticulous finish of 'Marie Antoinette.' The author writes it a year before he commits suicide. He has been harried from pillar to post. He has lived, he concludes, in many homes, in many lives. The first portion of the volume is concerned with life in Vienna before 1914. It was a world of security and gentility, of solid men and solid thoughts. It is Zweig's contention that the greatness of Vienna as a cultural center in the 19th century was due primarily to the taking over and rejuvenation by the Jews of an otherwise fading Germanic era of brilliance. From what I have read elsewhere, I should say that he is nine parts correct in such an assumption. It is his implication that without the enthusiasm and backing of the Jews, we might have had no Strauss, no Brahms, no Kalmann. In which case the world owes a debt to the Austrian Jews. It is a tenable motif.

But in the very process of proving to the world that Jews love their countries, he makes evident the irradicable Hebrew internationalism, being at heart a boundaryless and pervasive people abiding awhile among other peoples. And the nationalistic mind of today, which expects all comers to a geographically bounded land that is under a single government to merge racially and patriotically into the body of the population, abandoning past loyalties and past adherences, and to take on one ordained coloration, is as always secretly incensed that the sons of Israel do not forget their semi-oriental past, submerge themselves wholeheartedly by dominating interest, by marriage, by choice into the common scene and tradition of the land of their residence. The Jews, of course, claim that this is just what they want to do but are not, because of their race, permitted to do. We know by historic precedents and by present actions that this is only a claim.

May 4   It might be that this day-to-day chronicle of myself and of what surrounds me would be more worthwhile could I be sure of my form and course. However, the best I can do is to be honest and truthful; the rest depends on the discernment and percipience of him who reads. I am in a sense shapeless or, more precisely, whatever shape is imposed upon me, not having within myself a sure form, albeit a sort of fluctuating yet stubborn core of durability. And while I may not like the way I am, it seems to be out of my power to change in that I am unable to define myself. I write in here, and why I write, although in the past I have thought I knew, I do not know. Yet I write. And I attempt persistently to be honest. And I am enchantingly puzzled by myself.

May 6   I came across this bit, written by a reporter of the 'Denver Post' after he had made an investigation of a concentration camp (we refer to them as "relocation camps") for some ten thousand Japanese (one thousand of them admittedly disloyal to the United States) set up and financed by the Federal Government at Cody, Wyoming, at a preposterous expense to the taxpayers (five cents less per meal per man than it costs to feed a soldier—little or no labor demanded of the internees). The War Relocation Board is responsible for the Japanese. Either they are raking in the graft by the cartload or are lavish with public funds beyond vindication.

May 7   Actually fairly warm today. Sat in railroad yards in sunlight and let it soak into me. Felt healing. Pearl came home from the ration board yesterday as proud as a peacock. In response to a note I'd had Bottom sign stating that Mrs. Inman had anemia and needed additional meat, she has wangled 96 extra points a month. "Boy," she exclaimed, "do I love to put somethin' over on the bureaucrats." This morning she has gone to a couple of gas stations to attempt to arrange to get couponless gas. The cop who slows the traffic on Huntington Avenue, when Pearl had made friends with him, took her one day last week to a certain gas station and informed the man there that she was his friend and to "treat her nice."

Ah, we Americans. How well we will be fixed if either that gas man or the Sun Oil man where I get my gas will give us black-market gas. We now have Evelyn's coupons, all the heavy cream I want, and other things the opposite of restraints. If only I could feel better I'd be doing well.

May 9 I've been doing some tall thinking lately, commenced upon it before I began to make money — well almost before I did anyway. It's about what will happen after the war. History — and I seem to set considerable store by what it teaches — has proven time and time again that the nation which wins a war that is not exhaustively prolonged nearly always comes out of the conflict with prestige, profits and opportunities bettered. We are so rich and so filled with productive energy, our ingenuity and inventiveness is so fertile that neither this war nor the wastefulness of this regime can quell our industrial, scientific, economical advance.

It is well to keep this in mind. Run over the scientific possibilities ahead of us: the flowering of electronics, the development of manifold plastics, the designing of glass for new uses, the bringing to being of undreamed-of medicines, the perfection of rail equipment, the redesigning of automobiles, the marketing of the airplane to the public, the utilizing of the helicopter principle for safety in the air, the industrialization of television, the perfection of three-dimensional motion pictures, the inauguration of travel and express by immense airliners, the making general the use of new, lighter and more desirable metals, the invention and utilization of all sorts of chemicals, experimentation in the breaking up of the atom, the manufacture of superoctane gasoline, the invention of more utilitarian storage batteries, air conditioning and filtering, the conquest of viruses, the designing and construction of superhighways, the use of ultraviolet sterilization, and an immense backlog of housing needs to be satisfied.

May 10 Ella was here last evening, the first time for several weeks. She is still working for the Jewish gynecologist and the Jewish dentist, permanently it seems, twenty-five dollars a week. The Jewish doctor, Pearl, has a grown son and a family. He calls Ella "sweetheart" and "dear" and tells her she's the most beautiful woman he ever knew. Her duties are light, and he spoils her. Two weeks ago Ella came down with German measles. He took care of her without charge. He was afraid she might have caught syphilis from touching some of his tools and then not washing her hands with antiseptic soap. He gave her a Wasserman test under the guise of a blood count. "Arthur, he's wonderful to me. A little too wonderful, I'm afraid. I just hold tight and wait. He thinks I'm a madonna, no less. I say to myself: 'Joseph, you may know all about one end of me, but by golly you sure don't know the other end.'"

May 12 It was announced late yesterday that Churchill is in Washington with a full military staff. Whenever he and Roosevelt get together, it means more men and supplies wanted of us and more taxes to be levied. Roosevelt, in the photographs of himself and Churchill, always wears an expression he evinces with no other companion, a cat-that-swallowed-the-canary look. It is easy to perceive that Churchill is one man who has him in hand. It will probably be decided for sure where the next move will take place against Germany and Italy. Roosevelt announced yesterday that we Americans are now turning out more planes than the entire rest of the world.

May 13 The Tunisian campaign is at an end. Some one hundred and fifty thousand men, uncounted supplies and military matériel, twelve generals, transport planes have been taken. The reporters at the front have been unanimous in their astonishment at the wholesale surrender, the willing surrender, the surrender without sullenness of the Germans and the joyous surrender of the Italians.

These Germans have borne with military authority for years, because it was a machine they could not escape separately and dared not organize to escape. And now comes, all at once, a chance to get out from under. Hitler was miles away across separating waters, unable to impose punishment upon them. So they quit. And who can blame them? I'd quit were I beaten in battle and did I perceive an opportunity to be captured by sentimentally generous enemies and to sit peacefully on the sidelines out of the tough scrimmage for the remainder of the game.

Am reading 'Uncle Tom's Cabin' on the talking-book — about one-fourth through it. Been figuring why so popular for ninety years, it being inaccurate as to dialect, social scenery, filled with preachments, fulsome and melodramatic. I should say, however, that its reputation is deserved. Only two other novel classics I can think of offhand in the English language possess what it does, a mythical intensity: 'For the Term of His Natural Life' [12] and 'Wuthering Heights.' All three appear to have sprung irresistibly from an undeniable emotional and mystical will which drove the authors inexorably to write what they wrote.

May 18   Dr. Mac for pelvis. My Father coming.

May 19   Would have been sustaining to have had a comradely father. A man is not a complete man without a comprehending father and without a son with whom to be comprehending.

Listening to Churchill addressing Congress. A man, Churchill, head and shoulders above Roosevelt. Of course much that he is saying is pure hokum, but hokum being spoken by a man can be inspiring when hokum coming from a lesser human being can be merely irritating. Queer, the pull exerted by a leader, the aura of authority with which he is vested by the wielding of great power. I wish we had Churchill and England had Roosevelt.

May 22   One was a deaf-mute. She sat on the curb in front of the shabby house and played with two dice, fumbling them from one hand to the other. The other was demented. She tore her hair and picked at her dress. Neither was aware of the other. I turned away from them and walked up the hill. An old Chinaman with parchment-like face and small sharp eyes fell into step with me. We discussed the making of pies and how best to correct the faulty trajectory of rifles. He invited me into his house. No one spoke to me there. He was, he said, wealthy. People came and went. He removed a carbine from the wall and prepared for a state of siege. The entire city could be seen from the rear window of the room. I left him. The road became red and muddy. On a high balcony there was an orchestra. Girls and boys danced wildly to its ululating rhythms. "They're hepcats," a red-headed girl explained. Suddenly they leaped down over the railings and executed formations on the red street. They wore costumes of violet and purple. The negroes laughed at them. I faded into a gray wall.

June 4   I don't know what sort of natural sinner I am. I still would like to own slaves—not necessarily as they did in the Old South, though that would be preferable to no slaves, but by choice as they did in Rome, when in many cases the slaves became honored

[12] A favorite book of Arthur's by the Australian writer Marcus Clarke (1846–1881). *His Natural Life* (1874)—which subsequently and for some unknown reason was reissued as *For the Term of His Natural Life*—is an intensely realistic story of the convict system revealed in all its horrors. The horrendous scenes in Clarke's documentary novel resemble Arthur's nightmares.

and regarded members of the household: teachers, seneschals, craftsmen, scholars, companions, entertainers. It would be wonderful to take two thousand dollars and go downtown to the mart and buy someone whose character and face were pleasing, to have and to hold by less tenuous bonds than friendship or employment. A lifelong associate contracted to your interest, your interest being in the last analysis his interest. What an unregenerate throwback I am.

The miners, even after Roosevelt's order that they return to work, say that they will obey Lewis. It is interesting to watch the combat between Roosevelt and Lewis. Lewis seems to hate the President above all other people. If Lewis gets back into the A.F. of L., maybe he will control a block of anti-Roosevelt votes that will topple the New Deal. He's an unreliable man, however, and may turn about-face again before the elections. Personally, I hope that he remains Roosevelt's enemy. It does my heart good to see one man with the guts to trade him dirty blow for dirty blow. And again, as with slavery, I suppose I am unregenerate, not to think as I do but to express how I think in bold, uncurtained words.

June 8   Woody had supper with Evelyn. I didn't see her — first because she leaves so early and has so little time here and Evelyn amuses her more than I do so that I felt she ought to have all the time, and second because I'd rather not see a friend at all than be limited to a hurried passage of words. Evelyn drank too much and was befuddled. I was both disheartened and angry. This morning she said: "Now before you say a word, I want to tell you how ashamed I am of myself. To impress myself, I broke the decanter I love so much. It's against my theory on the subject, but I know you believe a person ought to impress oneself by some such penance, so I did it. I'm very sorry for last night. Indeed I am." So I said nothing, will say no more.

Pearl spent most of yesterday pushing and prodding Haggerty to work on the Baby-Carriage's bearings. He's slack as so many Irishmen are and in addition has more repair work to do than he can handle and no one to help him. It's lucky he fancies Pearl. He took her to lunch yesterday. I've seen his face and know I couldn't handle him. As we returned home in the Pierce-Arrow just now, Haggerty was starting out somewhere in his Pierce-Arrow and Pearl was behind him in another car. She runs errands for him, encourages him, acts the part of plumber's helper. She's a very good girl in numberless ways.

Ella brought a picture of herself and Robert the other morning. She was pretty and he was handsome and they looked very spiffy together. "Only," she commented, "I'm not really that pretty." "You're really much prettier when you are pretty and not in one of your old-lady spells," I assured her. "Oh, go on with you," she said. "Well," I said, "I think so." "So does Dr. Pearl," she said. "He says he never cast his eyes on anyone sweeter. Arthur, that old fellow is head-over-heels in love with me. He's always before been absolutely circumspect, but the other morning he said something that angered me and right afterwards offered me some tickets to 'The Merry Widow.' I told him he couldn't say things to me and then buy me with tickets, I wasn't that sort. What he did then frightened me. He looked berserk. He seized me in his arms and bit my lip till it bled and then bit my cheek. 'I love you,' he said. 'You've no right to hurt me.' I was shocked as well as angry. I was too upset to express myself. He had to wipe the blood off my lip. Then he stuck out his tongue and put it on the blood. I drew away in disgust. 'Don't be disgusted,' he said. 'It's your blood.'

"The next morning I gave him a long talking-to about how foolish it was for him to care for me and that I had my husband whom I loved to consider and he had his practice and that I liked the job and if he wanted me to stay he'd have to restrain himself. 'Oh,' he exclaimed, 'only to have you in my arms. You're beautiful and gentle and good.' Arthur, I get myself into the queerest messes. The dentist is having me taught x-ray and laboratory work, and that will give me something for the future when the worst comes to the country. And I don't want Dr. Pearl's attitude towards me to interfere with my training. I like him. I admire him. He is a slave to his profession and no labor is too arduous and no hours too long for him if it helps anyone who needs him, and he's very good to me, but I don't love him. How could I? He's an old codger with his best days behind him. And anyway, he certainly has got a wrong view of Ella James as a madonna of sweetness and light. But I think I've straightened him out for the time being at least. We'll see. I hope so, anyway. In the meanwhile, I'll learn everything that's to be learned.

"And Robby is saving up money for a future he thinks is going to be bad. They've a new stationmaster now. The old one and he had gotten to be fast friends after he'd reached for a pistol one time to get Robby and Robby had drawn a knife and told him not to reach for the gun if he wanted to keep his hand on his arm. Robby was able to hold out fifty-five dollars last week over and above what he was supposed to turn in. 'I stole for you, Mama,' he said. 'Go buy yourself a wedding ring with diamonds all 'round it.' So I've picked it out. I'm real excited, too. It's worth about a hundred and twenty-five dollars without the discount Robby gets through a friend. He's been spreading himself to please me lately. I reckon he likes me better since I recovered my looks from all the candy and iron and vitamin pills the doctor has insisted I take. Life, Arthur, is getting exciting again. I'm buying new clothes, too."

June 12 Janice and I are at sixes and sevens. No matter what she forgets to do or what mistakes she makes, she only rarely sounds sorry or put out with herself. She replies, "Well, I thought . . ." or, "Oh well, it doesn't matter, does it?" or some such unruffled or defensive reply and lets it go at that. I can't put in writing how condescending and uninterested the drawled "well" sounds. It's getting so bad I dream about it.

Last night we were in the Baby-Carriage at the top of a cliff; between us and space was only a wooden fence. She got out. She had left the hand brake off. The car rolled forward and banged the fence. The fence rocked and bulged; the car almost went through. "Well," she remarked indifferently, "it didn't go through, did it?" Then she bought ten gallons of gasoline, poured two into the tank, the remainder wastefully on the ground. "Oh well," she said, "what difference does it make?" That was what I dreamed.

Sometimes, if I don't do most of the talking, she will remain silent and taciturn for many minutes at a time. "I wasn't thinking of anything," she will reply to my query. "I just wasn't talking." The other day I deliberately set out to make her angry in order to find out if possible what was the matter. I talked of Jesus and his red beard and the lice in it and of Mary being unfaithful to Joseph and sneaking off with God. I could feel the repulsion gathering. "Why," she finally burst out, "do you have to talk that way?" I asked her if she really believed in God and Jesus. "Yes I do. It's something you've got to take on faith and not think about. Why do you have to destroy all my ideals? You've made me look at everything and everybody different, and I don't like it. I just want my little world, and I just want to see people as I see them. I've lost so many ideals I used to take for granted. Why do you have to make fun of God and Jesus and sacred things?" That was instructive.

Perhaps the world is touching her too directly and she lacks the emotional dynamics to withstand its aggression. Perhaps she resents me as the agent which has caused her to become conscious of impending realities. Or perhaps she doesn't love me any more. She comes in the door, tossing a large melon she has bought for me from one hand to the other. "Do you love me?" I ask. "Of course," she replies. "Why do you ask?" "Because," I rejoin, "I wasn't sure." "Well," she says, "I do. And if I receive any more cross-examining or analysis, I'll jump through a hoop."

June 13 At the Personal Book Shop, the lending library where I get most of my new books, there is a woman, a Mrs. Barber, in charge. She was born in upper Virginia, affects a Tidewater accent, is middle-aged, deafish, interested in people, somewhat pretty in a passé sort of way. She has an Austrian husband, no children, her thirteenth dachshund. She has always been very interested in us, draws historical and technical books from stock to let me have them. Yesterday she remarked to Evelyn: "Mr. Inman is absolutely the most eclectic reader I have ever known." "Oh," replied Evelyn, "you don't know the half of it. You should see the stacks of pulps and financial magazines."

I do have a catholic taste, I suppose. I am at present reading the story of a Russian fighting for France and taken prisoner by the Germans and what happened to him and wondering if it is not a fabrication, there being various slips in statements; 'Lavengro,' finding it bearable only because of certain lively portions; Anthony Trollope's autobiography with considerable labor and very little remuneration; 'Green Fields,' a pleasant narrative of Irish country life; 'The Journal of John Stevens, 1689–1691,' and liking it; 'Our Enemy the State,' rereading; 'Tawny' by Donald Henderson Clarke, a sex tale; 'The Wind that Swept Mexico,' about the Revolution there; 'The Book of Bays' by Beebe; 'The Fire and the Wood,' an English novel;[13] and so on, and so on, not forgetting the Congressional Record, the 'Reader's Digest,' 'Life,' 'Time,' 'Collier's,' 'The New York Times,' the 'Globe,' the 'Herald,' the 'Wall Street Journal' and many issues of 'Astounding,' 'Startling,' 'Amazing,' 'Planet,' etc.

June 14 I wrote Abruzzo some while ago and inquired how it was that a person with as much imagination as he possessed could be befuddled by the Communist patter. I recommended he read sev-

---

[13] *Lavengro* (1851) is George Borrow's picaresque tale about gypsies in the British Isles. *Green Fields* (1946) compresses into a year's cycle a ten-year diary kept by an Irish sheep-raiser, Stephen Rynne. John Stevens was a Jacobite soldier and ardent Roman Catholic. His journal (1912) records the campaigns and battles, replete with moral commentary, of the Jacobite war in Ireland. Albert Jay Nock's *Our Enemy, the State* (1935) is the "seductive anarchist's" quintessential attack against socialism, planning, and the welfare state. D. H. Clarke's "sex tale" (1936) is one of a series of Clarke's "realistic," sensational novels with a tough New York City setting. The heroine, Tawny, has affairs with a gangster, a lesbian, and a drug addict. Anita Brenner's brief and sardonic text on the betrayers of the Mexican revolution (1943) complements 184 historical photographs. William Beebe's book (1942) is an extended account of a marine expedition along the Mexican coast to Colombia. *The Fire and the Wood* (1940), by Ray C. Hutchinson, an English novelist, takes place in Germany during Hitler's ascension and tells of the moral awakening of a young German doctor who discovers belatedly the claims of humanity over science.

eral realistic books on Russia. While I was aware that I was risking the igniting of a fuse, I had no idea of the response I would get. The paper fairly crackled with revolutionary righteousness and anger at me for having dared question his earnestness in "The Cause." As I saw nothing to be gained by not backing water, I uttered platitudes to the effect that every man must have an interest larger than himself and who was I to challenge his interest. He returned a curt reply stating that he accepted my apology and we were friends again, but that he couldn't understand how I had thought he might not be in earnest and that he hadn't liked my method of finding out.

And George Dicey. One day about a month ago Janice ran into him on the street. He was, she said, wearing all new clothes. He told her that he had been in Detroit on a job for "the Boss," would be back in Boston again someday when he'd be sure to look me up. Right then he was so pleased to be in Boston that he and his friend were "doing" the bars and taverns. Coakley told Evelyn that Dicey had a job with the American Optical Company in Southbridge and was making good. You can take your choice. He may turn up here one of these days, or I may never see him again. He doesn't write.

Claire writes a short note and also sends me a long letter written to her by Edna. Edna still calls on Mrs. Banks. When Mrs. Cash visits Mrs. Banks, she hears about Edna. Edna left Henry Green's business. She went into another advertising office. She quit that or was let go. Then what happened is not quite clear. The second half of her letter to Claire takes up the story:

> Starvation got the better of me. I still believe I had a good opportunity to get a business of my own ready made, but I just couldn't stick it out when I saw the bills mounting and mounting. So I have now quit the advertising business entirely. I spent a futile two or three weeks traveling about from one defense plant to another, talking to smooth faced "personnel managers" and getting nowhere except for a couple of promises to be called in two or three more weeks. Then Jack Hooper (you remember . . . Russian War Relief) asked me why I didn't go to work for him. So I did. Started last Monday. Yup, I'm a wood worker. Imagine me bringing home the sawdust in my shoes! Surprised! Well I am. He has built himself quite a shop in his cellar, his garage, and his brother's cellar. Has Sam's lathe, a planer, mortiser, circular saw, etc. and a drill press. That's where I come in. I run the drill press. And I'm pretty good, too, if I do say so myself. I drill as many as a thousand holes an hour. Next week we are getting a multiple drill that will drill six holes at a time.

Then I should be doing six thousand holes an hour. How does that sound, eh! Well, I'm getting a decent wage, have no traveling expenses . . . I get picked up at my door at 8 A.M. and deposited back there at 5 P.M. I save two hours traveling time besides the expense. And, since I carry my lunch, I save money there. A sandwich, a cup of coffee and a piece of pie now cost 50 cents in town. Jack has three men working for him besides myself and we are turning out chicken crates at a good rate. May, his wife, often asks after you. She liked you, too.

Well, I guess I got that job just about in the nick of time. Now when I get a few bills paid up I'll feel like a human being again. And I really like working with my hands after sitting behind a desk for ten years.

June 16   Michel Chevalier, political economist, when he visited America early in the last century, characterized the American people as having "the morale of an army on the march."[14] The more I cogitate upon the observation, the truer I find it. We have little or no long-term philosophy as a people. We have convictions, but they are emotionally subject to violent shifts. We believe in our luck and our power in war and our potential greatness, but these are concepts of the heart rather than of the intellect. We are untutored historically, creatures of the moment, as Nock says. Our conduct is motivated by the immediate end rather than by any long or continuous objective. We foster the adolescent complex of an army on the march, a confident army usually, a discouraged army sometimes, an army emotionalized by rumors and drum thumpings and bugles and whisperings of the enemy's successes or failures and flags flying and defeats or victories in skirmishes however unimportant and hero worship and excitement at any cost and God knows what tomorrow will bring and who cares if it be exciting and we'll probably bungle through somehow and huzzah for our side.

June 17   Glass broke. Cord on lamp broke. Telephone broke. Pearl upset about car. Gasket blown on left block. Haggerty says ordered gaskets and new bearings four or five days ago. Cadillac Company says no order put in yet. Irishman probably lying. Easier for them to lie than tell truth. No Cadillac to drive in, whatever transpires, until parts come from Detroit, a matter of from five to

---

[14] Michel Chevalier spent the years 1833 to 1835 in the United States observing American canal and railroad construction for his government. The record of that sojourn, *Society, Manners, and Politics in the United States: Letters on North America* (1839), translated from an earlier French edition, is less memorable than Alexis de Tocqueville's *Democracy in America* but contains perceptive comments on American character and institutions.

ten days. No help to eyes riding in Pierce steadily. Drops bladder and intestines. Tried riding this morning. Windshields flashed in eyes, bewildering me. I feel as wild and balked as does Pearl. And Fred is due any minute to give me a stomach-pumping. Hope won't have too bad a time with it, as nervous as I am, but probably will.

June 18 There are days when an unmitigated diet of women gives me emotional indigestion. If I had been pleased to have Tony here Monday to cut my hair and talk of "the wife" and "the child" and show me pictures of both and to have Dr. Pike treat me, I was even more pleased to see Fred yesterday, with his round smiling face, his cheerful words, his gazelle-like eyes, his slow-moving hands, and in the evening, Roderic, telling me of being an airplane spotter one evening a week at Bedford. Yes sir, I was pleased to be in touch with men and wish I knew more of them at present. The sound of men's voices on the radio and the talking-book helps. Strange that one may obtain reassurance from canned sound.

June 19 It may be that Roosevelt's political future is at stake unless, as is so often the case, consultations and decisions are occurring of which John Q. Public knows nothing. We really know very little about what is taking place except what we are permitted to know. We are given a facade and allowed to criticize it to our hearts' content. It is really a more logical and workable method of subjection than the Nazi 'keep quiet or else' one, for it is human nature to accept meekly almost any penance or restriction after having been given leave to sound off about it until spontaneous opposition is talked out. It is like giving plenty of line to the hooked fish until he uses up his normal store of rebellion and can be netted or gaffed with ease and dispatch.

June 22 Twenty-three persons have been killed and some seven hundred injured in race riots at Detroit. Fighting between whites and blacks eddied wildly up and down the negro district with windows smashed, brickbats hurled, cars overturned, fires set, razors and clubs used, shops sacked for hour after hour. The metropolitan police evidently were unable to cope with the outbreak though they shot and killed a number of negroes. The state militia was placed in readiness. Then the Regular Army, after the Governor of Michigan had declared martial law in three counties, was called in. The streets are being patrolled by armed cars. The President issued an order calling for the mobsters to "disperse and retire peaceably to their respective abodes."

I have been anticipating some such outbreak for several months. It bids fair not to be the last by any means. The negroes, urged on by their outspoken press, are getting cocky and rambunctious. They are needed in plants as workers, and some unions have lowered restrictive bars against them. They are being taken into the Navy for the first time. Roosevelt and in particular Mrs. Roosevelt have seen fit to pander to them.

Now while I feel exceptionally grateful to the negro race personally, I cannot be blind to the fact that they are a different race from my own and in my estimation an inferior race. They are an emotional folk by nature, incapable of leadership though more capable than we are of governing under a tribal system. While I may consider a negro as a more efficient lover of life than myself or my white confreres, I do not consider him to be my equal in the peculiar genius the times and mechanized civilization demand. And I am certain that no amount of rioting will put them where they wish to be. They are not only in a minority but are as well not capable of long-range mental application as the Jews are, for instance. Riots such as the one in Detroit, whether whites or blacks are accountable for them and regardless of who wins temporarily, can only do the negro race harm. The dormant instinctive prejudice against them is very strong in the United States whosoever may claim the contrary. We Americans — I am not one of us in this case — despise the negro because he is a negro, because we deem him our inferior, because we are made uncomfortable by his proximity.

Ella was here yesterday evening. I was asking her about the riots. She sketched the outbreak at Beaumont, Texas, the one at Mobile, the one at a training camp when colored soldiers obtained ammunition for their guns and killed many whites. "I tell you, Arthur, this business is bound to become worse and worse. You have no idea of the feeling rife among the members of my race. Soldiers come home and tell Robby of how they hate their white officers when they set out to 'keep them in their places' and how they've taken some of them out on maneuvers and they just haven't come back (one of them they literally tore to pieces and buried the parts — they figure they're going to be sent overseas to die anyway and might as well be put in jail in mass for something they want to do as be shot somewhere abroad later), and how they'll be ready for any sort of bloodshed when they come home from the war. I tell you, Arthur, hell's going to pop. We're weary with being suppressed and borne down and imposed upon and held in prejudiced subjection just because our skins are black. We won't stand for it much longer. Really, I marvel at myself that I don't spit upon every white man I pass. I feel — I can't tell you how deeply I feel — that we are the victims of racial discrimination and injustice. I used to think in my uninformed days that time would heal all wounds. But now I know otherwise. Hate is abroad in the world. Unless we resort to physical violence, we'll continue to be held down. And we won't be held down forever. We shall rise up and the streets will run red with blood, and it won't all be negro blood either, and I shall be in there with the most violent of them when the time comes trampling down the white oppressors. And I mean this with every drop of my negro blood. I am aware of the limitations to my physical and nervous energy, and I shall stand by and wait until the proper moment comes, and then I shall help lead, if it is only for a week, a day, my people out of bondage. I'm not afraid to die, and I possess — I know I possess — the power of words and of leadership. When the time comes, I shall use my gifts and use them well. And I shall spare no person who gets in my way, and if you are in my way, I'll shoot you down like a dog and feel no more compunction than if you were a ravening dog. And that all this is so I swear to God."

I shivered. I had forgotten everything but Ella and the bitter words tumbling forcefully forth. Rather lamely, I said: "You wouldn't have the heart to kill someone like me who has always been your friend." "Don't you believe I wouldn't," she ejaculated. "My sense of race is so much stronger than my sense of friendship that you would be just another oppressor. And I could stand by and watch you killed or do it myself. And that's the trouble with you Anglo-Saxons. You let sentiment get in your way. You don't know how to be ruthless when you should be ruthless. You're soft. But I'm not soft. I'm weary of being held down, weary of watching you whites enjoy the fat of the land while we live in poverty." "And it would make no slightest difference, our relationship during these years?" "None." "If we were at war with the colored race, Ella, and I came face to face with you as an opponent, I couldn't kill you. I simply couldn't. I couldn't even kill a Jew friend or give him up even if we were in a death struggle with them. I don't know why it's that way, but it is, and I know it is. Personal relationships mean so much more to me than racial or class relationships. I've read too much history, too. Yes, you'd be spared and let escape, Ella." "Well," she snapped, "you wouldn't."

It is always difficult to discriminate between words spoken with emotional conviction and the deeds that may really follow them as there is generally a long hiatus between the two. However, I think that Ella meant every word she said and would, under certain conditions, hew exactly in deed to the line charted by her words. There's enough Indian in her to cause me to believe her.

June 23 I have all but finished [George] Borrow's 'Lavengro.' It is a queer book, with high points and low points. The hero is a callow individual of more learning than a boy of his age has any right to possess. The book sets forth a series of incidents and short stories and vignettes in a fairly loose and unrelated sequence. But the writer dares think his own thoughts, nurse his own convictions, and that is something. I have enjoyed the volume less than I have been bored by it. The author must have been a person and a personality in his own right, if nothing else, the narrative supposedly being in large part autobiographical. He holds a premise which is close to my own heart, namely, that though a man be endowed with all the virtues save pertinacity, he might as well be endowed with none, for it is pertinacity that will take a man further than aught else.

July 5   Through curtains of falling rain to the Fish Pier. In the railroad yards nearby, hundreds of trucks, khaki-brown, standing in unloaded rows. Soldiers and sailors strolling along wet streets. Dozens of small restaurants and beer joints and fish food places.

A minesweeper out in the harbor. Odor of sea. Odor of fish. Sound of a huge loudspeaker sending forth music. Tall ships' masts to the right behind the new dry dock, scarce visible in the rain, and a wharf with tall iron mines in rows and a loading machine ready.

Against Commonwealth Pier, two brand-new destroyers tied up. Things of arrogant lines and superb beauty with sheer bows, pointing guns, curved turrets, enclosed bridges, masts with crow's nests and grid antennae and slowly turning wind-speed indicators, hooded searchlights everywhere, long torpedo tubes amidships, davited dinghies and lashed life rafts, rows of depth bombs in racks, smokestacks flared back at the tops, steel guards on the hulls to protect them against sideswiping and innumerable gadgets and appurtenances of which I knew not the meaning. Sailors patrolling with rifles on shoulders. Doors. Portholes. Superb, compact, explicit for destruction, painted an ocean blue. Next to the destroyers a tender, also with guns and searchlights but with many fewer of each. One large stack only. Lacked life rafts. A sort of high forecastle equipped with a gun. Appended to her blue side, a semiflexible oilpipe.

July 15   Janice and Bertram came across a house in Auburndale, not far from the one we were looking at atop the hill years ago. Janice tactfully broached the subject. "The house is just what we've been looking for. If we can buy it, we want to. They're asking seven thousand, two hundred for it. It's Dutch Colonial and was built eighteen years ago. The agent tells us that lots of people are looking at it. If I put in my money and Bertram puts in his money, we'll have almost a thousand dollars. We've offered seven thousand for it. If we get it, we want to get married in a couple of weeks. I think it's an opportunity to realize my dreams and to present Bertram with a perfectly legitimate and understandable reason (paying for the house) for continuing to stay with you. Of course he doesn't want me to work when we get married. To be honest, I guess he's always been a little jealous of you. He naturally looks on this as just a job while to me it's not a job, it's being with you and pleasing you. Oh, it's made me so miserable this winter trying to find a way to realize my dreams and stay with you and make both you and Bertram contented at the same time."

My heart sank. Janice knows how I feel about her marrying a Catholic and a man who does not sound like a particularly strong character so there was nothing to be served by going all over that at length with her. As I told her, I can only hope that she will be as happy as she expects to be. I offered — an offer which she turned down — to lend her enough cash to be sure to meet the down payment on the house, provided she would rent it until the war was over and postpone her marriage until then. I then brought up sundry considerations. I tried to explain how desolate I would be did she leave me and how, no matter what men promised before they married in order to get their girl, they were apt, most of them, to renege on their promises after the marriage was consummated and that with no awareness or feeling of double-dealing. I brought up whether she would become a Catholic or not and whether their children would become Catholic. I brought up the matter of the use of contraceptives, it being against the tenets of the Church, whether Bertram would consent or not. I pointed out that if she had children, she wouldn't be able to remain with me full-time.

This morning she said: "Bertram and I had a fine talk last night. I want to tell you that everything is all right so you won't worry any more. He said that he absolutely would not try to prevent my coming here and being with you. He will use the preventatives Dottie Bottomley says are so good. He wanted to bring the matter up before but was too embarrassed about it. So you won't have to worry about anything now." "Thank you very much, Janice," I said. "But men are funny. If he does change his mind when you get married and does try to prevent you from coming here, what will you do then?" Without hesitation, she replied: "I'll continue to come. I'm sure I can handle the situation. I've always felt timid and hesitant about many of the realities of life, but now I don't feel that way for some reason any more. I feel fully capable of handling any situation that may arise. So will you please stop worrying."

I think that Janice is an exceptionally fine woman, almost uncannily understanding of my nature, how and why it reacts to stresses.

She is the only person who ever gave me full credit for the many beneficent inclinations which I know constitute a large portion of my emotional make-up. Should I ever lose Janice, I would be bereft beyond measure. She and Evelyn are the only people I am convinced I love.

July 18 The weather bureau, as I understand it, is atop a high building. From three to five degrees must be added to the bureau's readings to determine what the temperature actually is. Do this, and you have the longest spell between 90° and 98° that I have ever experienced in Boston. I am as wilted as a person may well be, yet keep going. I lose strength daily. I do no work. I can scarcely whisper. I have sciatica. My strained eye prevents me from writing and looking at pictures.

Listening to Arabic music on the radio. It sounds as I feel.

July 24 Last night about ten o'clock, Mrs. Cash, who was typing for me, rushed in with: "Guess who's here. Sadie. Billy's Sadie. My, but doesn't she look sweet. Do you want to see her? She says she has some letters from Billy for you." A damp hand extended to me, small. A very small yet penetrating voice. "I brought you some of Billy's letters. You know, he's been wonderful about writing me. I thot he'd not write, but I get a letter 'most every day. So I brought you some. But I gotta know you won't smile or make fun of them, 'cause I'd pin your ears back if I thot that. It's just because Billy's so fond of you that I let you see them. I wounna let everybody read them — you understand that, Arthur."

There was real exultation in her voice, more than a little smugness that she had received letters when I hadn't. I assured her of my appreciation. "He's such a good boy, Billy is," she exclaimed. "He's kind and considerate, and he never lies." "That's right," I agreed blandly, remembering the hundred and one lies Billy had foisted on Sadie and me, "that's perfectly right, Sadie. He always told the truth." "Hell," I adjured myself, "what's the use of telling the truth to this little vixen, this little two-timing bitch? She sounds worse than I'd expected. There's not a straightforward or uncalculating bone in her body. She's shrewd and sly and bold. She hides behind a fake screen of naïvety just like Juliette does, but her mind is always busy toting up her chances. What a woman. How could Billy stand for her? He must indeed be credulous to be taken in by her. And she is in her way very clever. And she's as hard as nails." "Yes," she said. "Ma is sick. She had a stroke. I come home to take care of her. She can walk to the porch now, but she's scared of the nights. She won't sleep without a light." I told her that my Mother had lived for years after having had a first stroke. "My God," she exclaimed, as though suddenly appearing from behind a screen. "My God, don't tell me that." Then she quickly switched the subject to the laundry.

July 26   Late yesterday the news was flashed that Premier Benito Mussolini had "resigned" and that the King had assumed command of Italian forces and had appointed Marshal Pietro Badoglio, former Chief of Staff, as Prime Minister.

There was a time, I can recall, when I looked upon Mussolini as perhaps the greatest man in the world, a leader bent upon resolving the muddled complications of present-day culture by new readjustments and rearrangements of the balance between governed and governors. He did, for many years, put on a convincing show. He might, had he been a more moderate and less conceited man and had under him a more amenable and less individualistic people, have indeed given to the world a successful example of a new and vital polity. As it is, he failed. Government by syndicalism may have received a black mark it intrinsically as a theory and a practice did not entirely deserve. The world, indeed, may have lost through martial failure, a precedent for government which seemed not at all illogical in its conception.

August 1   When Pearl came home to fix supper yesterday, she cried and stormed and announced the job was too much for her and that she was losing her health and couldn't keep on and there was too much for her to do and she was at her end and so on. She meant it, too. So, miserable and sick as I was, I had perforce to pull the pieces together and start thinking and planning. I tried to calm her down.

Mrs. Cash and I talked it over. She doesn't expect Pearl to last. Pearl, she said, was featherbrained — with no idea of the value of money — homesick, spoiled, emotional, sweet but not steady. She told me not to worry. She would see to it that I was taken care of somehow. She was a trump. She explained how sacred she herself held the obligations of a job. There was the time a rush was on at the Devonshire Hotel and she received a wire announcing her father's death, and she stayed where she was to do her duty, to the astonishment of the owner. "Call the people you're working for bastards and shits if you want to under your breath, but serve them well and faithfully while you're taking their money." The servant problem, she held forth, will become still worse.

August 2   After I have had a migraine, the ciliary muscles or nerves run independently wild. By day I am unable to assimilate and handle light. By night before my eyes is a veritable shimmering, shaking, shivering kaleidoscope of colors, lights, scenes, shifting, changing, glistering, shining, until I am amazed and delighted and a thought in awe at the apparently inexhaustible repertoire. Geometric patterns quiver into other geometric patterns, and color replaces color, and the scene before me trembles with the restless vitality of northern lights, and sunlit walls with a million clear and distinct bricks solid a moment before a thousand young blades of green corn appear in ranks as clearcut as though incised with godlike intricacy, each leaf clearly and emeraldly waving in its separate movement to a pushing wind; and again, as by swift alchemy, shape will fall apart and squirm into a myriad jiggling worms of vivid hues and incredible design. Hour after hour this show will continue, and I will be content to lie in my bed, my eyes closed, watching. There can be no other beauty, I reflect, like these living, transitory blobs of pure color which palpitate before me. This amoeba-like, irregular circle of primal yellow, for instance, with the motes of rose and the tubes of violet trembling astrally across it: Could there be a clearer, cleaner loveliness? And these tumbling hexagons of orange, spilled from utter emptiness into the expectant fingers of my vision? And these queer, intricate, involved, gyrating spinners of electric blue and clotted vermilion? And these gaping emerald circles, like indifferent crystalline vortices? A migraine, I think, is a trifling price to pay for so much beauty.

And then I will commence to muse upon the million bricks, the million solid yellow bricks, so precisely pointed, and I wonder what untapped cerebral power permits the creating before my eyes, with no volition for or against on my part, of such an exactly intricate semblance of man's labor, and I marvel and I pass to the idea that perhaps neither the insubstantial wall nor the wall I saw on the street a day ago, in no wise like it, is real. I become confused as to what is reality and what is not.

August 10   Was pleased to have Ella back last evening. Because of the curfew laws being enforced in Harlem since the riots there, she didn't stop in New York. Was sick on the train south, because it was so crowded. "I tell you, Arthur, that South is an awful place. There's no class envy there. If your neighbor's got more than you have, why that's his luck. If you've got more than he has, why he considers that your luck. There's so little discontent. People wear such placid faces. And they seem to have no intellectual or cultural curiosity. Go down on the main street of Talapoosa Saturday night and what do you see? You see people, white and colored, idling along, smoking, drinking pop, cracking peanuts, eating cheese and crackers, and apparently quite content doing only that. Their faces look empty to me and their wiry bodies pulled out and then bent. And they still have the red mud on their shoes. And heat hangs over the scene like a pall. And nothing exciting ever happens. It's like being in a backwash. Say, you can have the South and all it is and implies for all of me, and let it stay shut up tight forever in its steam cooker, in its sealed jelly jar, in the cage the hot sky makes. I don't care if never I see it again." Ella added that when she found herself once more in Boston and in her own little apartment, she felt like "dancing a jig" and crying "Glory Hallelujah."

"I missed you, Ella," I said. "There's nobody like Arthur," she said. "If I hugged you as much as I love you, I'd squeeze you into small pieces, and then where would you be? There's nobody like Arthur."

August 11   One of the authors in 'Astounding Science Fiction Magazine' I like best is named Alfred van Vogt.[15] He writes with imaginative understanding of the reactions of outworld animals transported to the environment of earth. He writes of a great, enduring secret society, the strength of which is based upon the invention, manufacture and sale to chosen clients through its own shops of superweapons obtainable nowhere else, and the aim of which is to balance and hold in check a powerful and corrupt empire by means of constant vigilance and counteraction. He writes of a man who has discovered the secret of immortality and returns to rulership periodically holding in his hands throughout centuries the course of history. His stories make me think. They leave gaps for the imagination to fill in. Several months ago, I began writing van Vogt. He is a Canadian.

August 14   I don't understand Evelyn. She must love me, but at times, so subject am I to uttered words, I am given to doubting it. If having her own way when the inclination strikes her means more to her than does the fulfilling of the finest realization of character that a living woman may enjoy, to wit, serving a husband who serves an idea, why we'll never be simpatico and she'll never be either happy or contented. And if she were married to Roosevelt or Legs Diamond, the crook, what I contend would still hold good.

August 17   I hope — no, I pray — that Janice never leaves my life. Without her, Evelyn and I would be desolate. If Janice reads this as she types it, this is to let her know that I mean every word. I think that she is wonderful. Please let her keep her life in step with mine down the years. She could never find another man who more loved and admired her and wished her well.

---

[15] Alfred Elton van Vogt (1912–), eminent Canadian science fiction writer, author of dozens of "basically, superhuman fantasies about super-intelligences, mind-readers, minds in multiple bodies, etc." Van Vogt's letter (July 30, 1943) in reply to Arthur's dealt largely with war matters. The West's hopes, he asserted, depended on the degree to which the United States managed to impose and spread its basic morality.

August 19 Evelyn read what I wrote about her the other day, evidently was impressed. Has been sweet and patient since. She makes a fine comrade when at her best. This afternoon she and Dr. Pike will be at our Place. Next week they go by car to her farm for three days.

August 29 What worries me about Janice, insofar as I am concerned, is that, when she marries, she will straightway have a baby. She says that she has talked it over with Bertram and tells me not to worry. But I do worry. She is very uninformed about the Catholic Church, having practically no knowledge of the long and purposeful history of that superbly organized worldly body.

Any and all means of circumventing pregnancy are frowned upon or outlawed. The more pregnancy, the more children; the more children, the more Catholics; the more Catholics, the more power for the Church. It is Hitler's theory dressed up in churchly habiliments. How do I know, how does Janice know, that when she and Bertram are once joined in wedlock, the priests will not find some means of persuading her not to use preventatives that will sound sensible to her? Years of careful training in how to present arguments in a manner to make them sound rational and convincing has gone into the education of every excellent priest. Janice, I fear, underestimates their tenacity, their guile, their devotion to the hierarchical intent of the order they serve.

And it is not that I have a thing against the Catholic Church. They have never done me any harm. Were I inclined toward religiosity and Christianity, I should rather be a Catholic than a Protestant. While the Church exacts from the individual the fundamental price of the surrender of his personal conscience, exacts unreasoning obedience, exacts all the wealth and service it can, it, in turn, enfolds a member in good standing in a cloak of spiritual and mundane protection, relieves him of the pain of moral decision, promises heavenly consolation for all earthly trials and heavenly rewards for all earthly virtues.

September 5 The French author, Gustave LeBon, in his book, 'The Crowd,' has this to say:

. . . nothing is more fatal to a people than the mania for great reforms, how excellent these reforms may appear, theoretically. They would only be useful were it possible to change instantaneously the genius of nations. This power, however, is possessed only by time.

September 6 Anthony Trollope asserts: "That I, or any man, should tell everything of himself, I hold to be impossible." I wonder if he is right. Are there certain deep shames, certain violent antisocial thoughts, certain ugly inconsistencies, certain inexcusable humors, certain egregious fulminations against God and mankind that one, however honest and forthright, withholds despite himself, restrains from uttering? I am not sure that Trollope is correct. Neither am I sure that he is incorrect. It may be that a man can tell everything of himself, manifest restraint only in that he is aware that a full and prolonged divulgence of the offside of his nature will paint him as worse than he is—readers being prone to shy from melancholia, horror, acerbity—whatever miasmas lie in the valleys of man's secret soul—and to congregate toward the pleasant, the amusing, the reassuring.

I endeavor to tell everything. But I do strive to hold to some sort of artistic moderation the nether aspects of the rebellions, the hatreds, the disdains, the fears that constitute my nature. And I seek to tone down for artistic purposes my tendency to view some things melodramatically. I am frank to admit that I desire to have what I am writing perpetuated, and I am convinced that what a man writes, just as how a man lives, is intolerable without a reasonable demonstration of self-restraint before his fellow beings. A man cannot relinquish himself unreservedly to his emotions and be accepted by other men. Neither can a man write without restraint and be read with sympathy by other men. Insofar as the restraint he exercises causes it to be impossible to tell everything of himself, just that far is Trollope's assertion true and valid and no further. That no man exactly comprehends himself does not of itself lend verification to Trollope's statement. I know this: If any man ever strove to be absolutely honest and to do it within the bounds of social palatability and artistic acceptability, that man has been myself. It is for him who reads to adjudge how well I have succeeded or how lamentably failed.

The approaching invasion of the continent, German retreats on the eastern front, and the new Allied beachhead in Sicily reminded Arthur of comparable moments in history when states and nations launched wars of conquest. He weighed reports of atrocities perpetrated by the Japanese (probably true; he "knew" the Japanese) and by the Germans (possibly true—but the Russians were just as bad); he had his own slant on the much reported General Patton "slapping" incident (perhaps Patton's rough therapy for the shell-shocked soldier had something to be said for it); and he kept harping on the government's stupid policy of dispatching precious resources to its swindling allies.

Events at home, however, bulked larger in his consciousness than the distant allies or apprehensions about the bamboozled republic. The "Baby-Carriage" continually broke down despite Mike Haggerty's efforts to repair it, and parts were hard to come by. Living costs soared. To make matters worse, Evelyn seemed as incapable as ever of meeting Arthur's simplest requirements (he kept admonishing her for her "petty lapses from tact and her native irascible contrariness"), and Pearl, who had slipped so easily into Billy Minor's niche, now periodically disgusted him by sulking and getting drunk. The possibility of a pregnant Janice kept him on pins and needles.

Yet Arthur was not doing too badly. He could still count on Mrs. Cash to type and read to him and tell him stories. Ella had her moods, but she, too, kept coming. The doctors — Pike, Bottom, Fred Lakian, along with some new faces — responded to his calls. Roderic would shortly be swept up in the draft, but until then he continued his reading sessions. Arthur passed Inmanesque judgments on dozens of books, mostly nonfiction but also including War and Peace *(good in spots but overrated),* Dead Souls *(Gogol was superior to Tolstoy), and* The Red and the Black *(started well but fizzled at the end).*

The Diary and diary keeping preoccupied his thoughts. If his work turned out to lack "distinctive merit," then his autocratic treatment of Evelyn and the Garrison Hall "family"—justifiable only on the grounds that the Diary transcended all personal relations — could not be condoned. As he read over the early volumes, he came face to face with his former selves and did not always relish the encounters. The Diary, he announced in the spring of 1944, "would be either one of the great works of literature or land on the dumpheap."

September 8 Interruption — The air raid loudspeakers play the 'Star Spangled Banner,' announce the unconditional surrender of all Italian armed forces to General Eisenhower. The European war now enters another phase. Unconditional surrender will permit the Allies to make use of Italian airfields so that sections of Germany hitherto somewhat safe from bombing will be open to air attack. And the impact upon German satellite nations — Hungary, Rumania, Bulgaria, Finland — should be sizeable. The announcer is very excited. So, I suspect, am I.

September 9 Either the novels of John Dos Passos have steadily declined in merit since 'Manhattan Transfer' so strangely excited me with what seemed then its vivid power or my taste has altered or matured.

September 10 My Mother will have been dead ten years this autumn. I should not have deemed it possible that an individual with so much vigor of purpose, so large an influence upon those around her, could have left behind her so little remembrance. It is almost as if her dominance over other, lesser persons has been resented silently, as if her death had permitted them to disburden themselves of her magnetism, her purposefulness, forget her utterly. I have felt since her death as though freed of a wrongly adjusted directional compass. I have not missed her. I have not mourned her. I have felt less confused of purpose.

September 11 To be the object of American popular adulation, should you be a successful general, a famous statesman, a great financier, a notable athlete, a culture-altering scientist? No, none of these. You should be dance orchestra leader, a Harry James with a hook nose, curly Hebraic hair, a glib tongue and a band that is 'hot.' Then will Americans cheer you to the rafters, mob the theatres where you appear, hound you for your autograph, go into swoons of rapture at your nod. You will rate headlines and special magazine articles and newsreel shorts, and what you say, eat, wear, do and the girl you like and the tie you sport will be national news. And if you cannot make an orchestra sound like a blatant percussive concatenation of ear-screaming sounds gone haywire, what then? Why, be a movie star of course. What else? Be a cheap, antic-acting Mickey Rooney. Truckdrivers will laud you and married women will risk trampling to get a glimpse of you, and no one will perceive the slightest oddity that you should rate the adulation and laudation of a prince of the realm.

September 12 A few pages more of 'The Journal & Letters of Philip Vickers Fithian, 1773–1774' and I shall have finished a diary that is more tantalizing for what it almost achieves than satisfactory for the not inconsiderable it does achieve. Fithian was a small-town young man from New Jersey, a Presbyterian graduate of the College of New Jersey (Princeton), tutor for one year at the Carter estate of Nomini Hall in Tidewater, Virginia, for the Colonel's daughters and sons. The Colonel was one of Virginia's first gentlemen, related by blood to most of the colony's important families. He owned in Virginia and Maryland some 60,000 acres of property, many plantations, slaves, mills, business ventures. On the Nomini Hall plantation there were some 600 slaves. Through Fithian's eyes we see a colonial feudal existence at its zenith, a close-knit family life, a patriarchal system, a leisurely culture at once artificial and relaxed. The 'great house' of Nomini Hall would seem to have been, to us at least, a barn-like affair, lacking in conveniences though not in elegance perhaps, cold in winter (it took four cords of wood a day to heat the 'great house' and the lesser satellite houses grouped around it), and with relatively few rooms. There were, of course, no bathrooms, no toilets, no running water, no this and no that. But there was good talk, good wine, music, a good library, dancing. And there was church on Sundays, and boat rides or horseback rides and shooting and much dining of guests. The cuisine was bountiful. The country was beautiful. The children were spirited.

Fithian seems to have had to try fairly hard not to like the life even more than he did and to need to call too often on his Presbyterian Puritanism. Slavery he did not like. It can be readily understood how some of the practices and punishments inflicted upon recalcitrant or obdurate negroes revolted him. It would have revolted me — if stories the overseer told him were true, and not just pulling his ear — to know that sullen darkies were stripped and rubbed down with a currycomb, then with handfuls of hay, after which salt was applied, when thereafter the negro was warranted no longer to be sullen. But that was the reverse side of the picture. In the main, such aspects did not obtrude. The colored population seems not to have been as a whole any more unhappy than we find it to be eighty or so years later. A pound of meat, a little salt, a peck of corn does not seem much to Fithian to live on for a week, but he also notes the plots of land on which the slaves raise most of their own foods according to the industry of each family.

As for Fithian himself, he is not unloveable, with his serious attempt to be polished and worldly, naïve devotion to a girl in New Jersey, his stilted letters, his small annoyances at this and that, his earnestness, the feeling somehow implied in his written words that he is close to his mortal end. Yet, as I have said, it is tantalizing that he did not do more with a unique opportunity for portraying an important Tidewater family. The will to do so was there, but the chronicler's skill was absent. Even so, I am glad to have read the diary and do honestly feel myself a little closer in understanding to a vanished age and people.

Dr. Pike, here to adjust a dislocated pelvis, sat on the end of the treating-table, one foot swinging, and expatiated with some vehemence upon the Russians. He feels that they are to be watched. He wished that "someone of those dopes in Washington would have the guts to be less afraid of hurting Russian feelings and demand something as well as give it." Evelyn and he have gone for a walk. Evelyn bought him a six pound roast of beef yesterday, and his cook prepared it, and they shared. I thanked him again this morning for the many times he is good to Evelyn.

September 14 It seems patent to me by now that the Germans have lost their great attempt to conquer Europe. They are not fools. It must seem patent to them, also. Then why do they continue to fight, to sacrifice lives, to bankrupt for no purpose their nation's wealth and energies? Why did the Confederate States continue to fight after Gettysburg and Vicksburg? That there is always a hope that the Allies may bungle military matters is not of itself sufficient reason for the continued stupendous expenditure of effort. Nor is the vague Nazi hope that they can in time drive a propaganda wedge between us and the Russians large enough to split us apart.

September 16 Millicent said: "Say, Arthur, guess who I saw in the store the other day? Someone spoke to me. I turned around. 'That flaming red hair, that flaming artificial red hair,' I said to myself, then: 'There's only one person on earth that wears such hair.' Yes sir, it was Dorothy Banks in person. She seemed glad to see me. You know, she looks ten years — oh, more than that — older. She limps. She wears the same too-long skirts. She has the same deadpan theatrical powder on her face. She looked like a worn-out old prostitute with a hard life behind her, someone you wouldn't dare to be seen on the street with. I was almost shocked speechless, and you know that's not easy to accomplish with me. She looked eighty if a day, and I don't mean maybe."

Mrs. Cash has attempted to no purpose to interest Mrs. Banks in a job. She won't take one. She spends her winters with Mr. Banks in an apartment in the same building on Gainsborough Street up by the Museum and her summers at her sister's cottage in the country. She constantly goes to the hospital clinics to determine why she is losing weight, why she has sore gums, why she has a rash. She tries to write, no longer with any hope of doing anything with it. She must lead a boring and miserable life, poor woman, though I'm sure half of it is still passed in the early years at the turn of the century in New York.

September 18 Evelyn went to see a doctor, a Russian woman who specializes in advising women about contraceptives, to make an appointment for Janice. The doctor, Evelyn said, was very understanding and assured her that she would be gentle with Janice. It is that Janice might have a child at once due to ignorance of physiological matters that gives me apprehension. She does not wish for children at once and neither does Bertram. It is the antiromantic aspect of prevention which bothers her, I think. I tried to tell her that it was one of science's greatest boons to women that they may now have for a small amount of foresight and care a year or two of happiness in which to learn to know their husbands, whereas in the past the immediate bearing of children all too often disrupted love, tolerance, contentment, romance.

Janice and Bertram saw the priest last evening. They are to be married on the tenth of October. "No," smiled Janice, "I'm not in the least worried or frightened. Everything has been going well. Everything will go well. Why should I be worried or frightened?"

The one thing that bothers her, she says, is that those she loves most are not enthusiastic about her marriage. I wish that I could be more enthusiastic. But I can't. It is not only that I am apprehensive of the forthcoming change; it is that I want Janice to be happy. But she probably will be. She has the home she has longed for. Bertram, I am sure, will be kind and generous with her. Why shouldn't she be happy? Bertram, for instance, tells her that he doesn't want her to stay home and slave over Sunday dinners; they will eat out. Not many men would be that thoughtful. Probably my worries about her happiness are all in my own mind, and she will be as contented as she deserves to be.

September 22   Pearl telephoned a girl she knew. To me she said: "I've spent all day down at that damn rationin' board arguin' for a 'B' book for you. Then I went to the movies to get rested. Did I get calmed? I did not. A fellow comes in and sits beside me and tries to feel me up. It was excitin' but it made me jittery. I don't mind those things if somebody else's with me, but I get scart alone. When he got nowhere, he got up and left. It wasn't hard to know what he wanted. I saw him out in the lobby later waitin' for another prospect. So here I am—wild—with no boy friend. So me and this girl'll go out and dance and drink and pick up a couple of fellows and maybe have some excitement for ourselves. What's life anyway without excitement? I'll be back at twelve—maybe earlier. I've been a good girl lately. I have to cut loose, don't I, once in a while? Sure I do. And if I pick up a guy, he'll be a good one; you can bet on that."

A few minutes after midnight in she came. "Oh, Arthur, he was wonderful." She hit a pile of books. "Bang. I guess I upset a book, didn't I? One book—two books—three books—my, what a careless girl. What a plastered girl. But what a wonderful man. Not a sailor. Not a soldier. A marine—no less. Oh boy. And did he kiss me good night. His name? Hell, I don't know his name—John something. He was gorgeous. And I'm plastered. And I'm happy. And now I'll go to bed."

When she came in my room early in the morning to put my curtains down, it was: "What a head. I believe that stuff musta poisoned me. I been losin' my insides all night. One hour's sleep. Oh. But—" more brightly—"it was worth it, Arthur. What a guy."

She wakened me for breakfast before it was time. "It's early," I said. "Yeah," she replied, "so it is." "What's the trouble?" "Trouble? No trouble." Vaguely—"He left some of his clothes with me to mend. I gotta get up early to mend 'em." "Clothes?" "Yeah." "What clothes?" "A coat. Yeah, a coat. I gotta mend it."

Fifteen minutes later, she was wide awake. "I came in here in a dream, I guess," she said.

Now she is as dead as an old piece of chalk in the corner and as pale. I wonder, do they grow specimens like her in other parts of the world—dynamic, weak, self-indulgent, smart and one way or the other always vital? I doubt not there are hundreds of Janices in other countries—earnest, kindly, diligent, reliable, worthy, the salt of the earth—but are there Pearls anywhere except in the U.S.A.?

September 26   The further I progress into 'The Education of Henry Adams,' the more I dislike it. It is a stupid book. The author's bland self-conceit is boring. The author must have been an empty portfolio of a man with only the crest and record of his family to give him the appearance of prestige. I find myself for the second time unable to finish the book. What Yeats said of Shakespeare, that he is "only a mass of magnificent fragments" is true in reverse of Adams: He is only a mass of wearisome fragments.

September 29   Recently finished 'Pitcairn's Island' by Nordhoff and Hall. Thoroughly enjoyed it. Tells what happened to the mutineers of 'H.M.S. Bounty' and the South Sea natives who accompanied them when they settled the lonely, rocky islet and there carried on existence in complete isolation from the rest of the world. It is a bloody and dour story, well told. Would like to know what happened to the children of the men who killed each other after they grew up. Did incest and intermarriage ruin their Eden? Did men from outside come there, spread disease and discontent? Must attempt to find a book that will continue the story. Being insulated against the encroachments of the world always intrigues my fancy. Were I well, I should surely find myself an island, probably off the Maine coast, there establish for myself a peopleless place to which to retire when pressed by the multitudes of mankind, their watching eyes, their foolish actions, the sounds and sights of their machine age.

October 1   I placed an ad in the 'Herald' for readers and talkers. There was a time when two to three hundred persons answered such an ad. I received a single tardy and lukewarm reply not worth consideration.

Millicent tells me that nearly all desk jobs in Boston start at $25. "But," she adds, "I could move to Detroit or Pittsburgh and receive forty dollars at once. Why, people no longer ask about your record, what you can or can't do. They take you. It's come to such a pass that if anyone leaves the store, they follow him up to get him back if possible. And if anyone takes a week off, if he returns he can reassume his old job and nothing's said. Oh, I tell you, it's fearful and wonderful, the employment situation. Rich women who come to do their own shopping now tell me that they can't hire cooks for love or money and that they're in their own kitchens for the first time in their lives, learning to cook. If I were ten or fifteen years younger, Arthur, I could walk into the kind of job I wanted and at the salary I wanted and be set for the rest of my life. There's still a feeling against older girls, and don't let anyone tell you there's not. I stay where I am for two reasons. First, we have considerable latitude as to what we do and when we do it, and I like that. Second, if I took a war job and the war ended, where'd I be? But one of these days I may up and make a move. You can't tell. I don't know, really, how I manage on twenty-five a week. I get a discount on my food; there's no car fare to pay; my men friends feed me. I just bought a new coat on the installment plan. I get along."

October 7 Dreamed all night of Haverford School. It is as though I were looking out upon the morning through an impalpable yet persisting screen of what happened to me last night. It would be reassuring to know that never again would I dream of Haverford School and the most unhappy years of my life.

Have to all intents finished correcting Volume 22 [1924] and am started on Volume 23 [1924 – 25]. Ten Broek is mentioned seldom. In that the diary is out of proportion. His presence irritated me. His supercilious and condescending answers offended my dignity. The manner in which I was forced to treat him in self-defense made me scorn myself. He was a small-spirited man on whom I found myself dependent, and I hated him accordingly.

While I think I did wisely to suppress mention of him in my diaries as persistently as I did (to have done otherwise would have been to clutter the pages with rebellion against a valueless and uninteresting character), I at the same time failed to draw a picture in inclusive proportions. This note is by way of being a rectification in retrospect. I write it with detachment. It is the harm Ten Broek did to me that alone keeps his memory alive. Otherwise, he was too insignificant a person to harbor hatred against. He is out of my ken, not a force like my Father toward whom I shall to my dying hour feel actively and all-inclusively bitter to the point of revengefulness.

October 8 [From Patricia:]

Paul and I have been here in the deep south for three months and as far as we are concerned the damned place can secede any time it wants to. When we left Michigan I knew what we were getting in to as I trouped down here. But Paul had no idea. We had a nice trip and enjoyed the drive until we got to the cotton country and then it became very monotonous and terribly hot.

Our last touch of civilization was Alexandria, about sixty miles from here. From there we went through swamp lands and poor white villages, and all along the roadway we had to dodge pigs and sheep and cattle. Paul got lower and lower and vowed he'd send me back by the first train. And when we finally got to Leesville it was all that we had feared, perhaps you saw some of it in the Sept 7th copy of Look. For Paul it's a terrible place, not a spot to go for recreation.

Leesville's former population was thirty five hundred, before the advent of Camp Polk, so you can imagine what happened when forty thousand men hit the town. It has three theatres, two being out of bounds because of sanitary conditions, two cafes, one out of bounds, twenty five beer joints, and two penny arcades. Not even a five and ten, and they looked at me in amazement when I asked for a book store, no library either. The one main street is jamed to the gills with the most god awful traffic, farmers in town, shoppers and the army constantly going through on maneuvers, this is a permanent maneuver area, and there is never a day when the air isn't yellow from the dust sent up by the passage of the big General Grant tanks. Boombers whiz over your roof and you are apt to wake up any morning and find a camoflaged machine gun nest under your clothes line, to say nothing of the wandering herd of cows who roam around eating up the vines. I don't find it dull.

Paul is at the prisoner of war camp, I don't know how much I'm able to write about it, nothing really I suppose, but it's terribly interesting and I'd love to tell you the things I know, but I'm afraid I'll get caught at it. Our camp is for Germans, enlisted men and non commissioned officers. I imagine there are about five thousand now. The first ones we got were from the Africa campaign, they were very young and arrogant and extremely healthy looking, brown as could be. But the last bunch we got in were not so cocky, and considerably underfed. I watched them unload last week. It was the first time that I'd seen a load come in and I only got in on that because I was driving to meet Paul and since his company was on guard the corporal knew me and let me drive near enough to see the men get off the train.

At present some of the men are working in the laundry and the shoe shop, also around camp at various odd jobs, if they work they get eighty cents a day, otherwise ten. But from the ones I've seen goldbricking they aren't worth much. They'd much rather play soccer, they play until it's too dark to see, and they are plenty rough. Almost every compound has built it's own theatre, and they make costumes of burlap, and put on excellent shows about every two weeks, no women allowed in the compounds of course. But we can hear the singing, also they sing on their way to work and every time they march. They have magnificent voices, I wish that you could hear them. They usually sing German marching songs, all mention of Hitler not allowed.

The prisoners do not believe a thing in our newspapers about the outcome of the battle, tho now that we are getting some men from Sicily they may change, they simply cannot comprehend the Russian situation and flatly say that it is propaganda, tho they have an undying hatred for the Russians, Paul says it's because the Russians seldom bother to take prisoners, they are more interested in killing. I don't believe they have much respect for us, they think we are too soft. At that I don't think they are far from wrong, most of our battles are won by sheer force of numbers, but I don't think that any country founded as ours was on the idea of peace and happiness breeds the warrior type.

October 9 We are more than apt to emerge from this war with our pants lost and our allies jeering at us for the fact and considering us, because the pocketbook was in the pants and we must retrench, as the Shylock of all Shylocks. Our only hope, as I see it, is that Secretary Hull when he goes to Moscow to confer with Eden and Molotov will become incensed at the grab-grab policies of the Allies. He is a stupid Wilsonian idealist motivated by intense and burning antagonisms on occasion. Should he perceive himself as getting a shabby deal, his Tennessee mountaineer blood might boil and his temper overcome his idealism. He's a silly old fuddy-duddy, stubborn as all get-out, a mountain man by nature despite his genteel appearance. He has rid himself of Russian-inclined Sumner Welles at last and is now in command of his own bailiwick. He seems to enjoy considerable prestige with the President and his kitchen cabinet.

[Averell] Harriman, one of the country's richest men, Chairman of the Union Pacific, son of the great Harriman, a man apparently of moderate abilities, has been named Ambassador to Russia to take the place of Admiral Stanley, who had the cheek to call Stalin to task once, maybe several times, and is after a decent time being called home. It would be interesting to be cognizant of the inner workings of changes and shifts in governmental setup. Harry Hopkins seems rightly or wrongly to be behind many of them. His favorites prosper. I should say that he is perhaps the second most powerful man in the United States, perhaps, for the influence he wields, the most powerful man. A true story of his life would read like a fairy tale.

October 10 Well, Janice gets married today at three. It is a clear cold day with a lusty wind blowing. The ceremony is to take place at a Catholic church.

October 11 Pearl went to Janice's wedding. "Say, Artie, she looked perfectly gorgeous. She wore a gown with a long trail and a sweetheart neckline — that's always becomin' to her. Her hair was fixed just right, and she had on a long white veil. She wore enough rouge and lipstick — you know, like we like her to — to make her eyes sparkle. She was lovely. She was so highstrung you could see her hands tight-like. But probably nobody knew it but me, because I'm acquainted with her every mood. It was a pretty weddin'. The best man was sort of funny-lookin' — he had a moustache and a German haircut, if you know what I mean — and Bertram still has his paunch; but the priest might have been Janice's cousin, he looked that like her. I think Bertram's a lucky man, and I hope he knows it. The reception was so crowded I only stayed to say hello to Janice. I think she was pleased to see me."

October 15 If the production of art in its divinest forms furnishes, as many claim it does, man's most unquestionable reason for being alive, then my disregard for the Jews is an inexcusable, even a reprehensible attitude for which I should be condemned. Myself, however much I may enjoy perusing art, am unconvinced that art is the proper criterion by which to measure man's validity. There is nearly always a certain unhealthiness to productions of pure art, intangible as the effluvia may be, which repels me and accounts, probably, for the uneasiness many uninstructed persons experience in the presence of art.

October 22 Janice begins to recuperate from the strain of getting married. She and Bertram are ensconced in their new house and as Janice observes very happy. "I feel," she says, "as though all my problems were resolved for me. Everything has turned out just perfectly." It is somewhat difficult for her to choose and serve food that will satisfy both of them, but she expects to learn soon. She's a fairly hearty eater, enjoying her meals. Bertram has a nervous stomach and eats lightly. He doesn't take enough all day to make one meal — coffee for breakfast, coffee and a sandwich for lunch, not much for supper. He lost thirty pounds before they were married, still weighs 180 pounds.

Night before last he and Janice went to a play. It was about "fairies" and very outspoken, and Janice missed the points until

Bertram explained them. They said "God damn" and "bastard" and "son of a bitch" and words which, in my day, would have landed someone in court. Janice still looks thin. Yesterday she had circles under her eyes. "Feel bad?" I asked. She pointed to herself. "Really?" I ejaculated. She nodded. I raised my hands to the ceiling as if in thankful prayer. She blushed. "You," she said. "You're incorrigible. What's a person to do with you?" "I'm awfully pleased," I said. I feel as though I'd been given an exceptionally fine present or a reprieve.

My car is still in the shop. Pearl goes there each morning about nine and remains until four or five. "But," I protest, "you should lay off about two and rest during the afternoons." "Now you know very well, Artie, that if I did that you'd never get your car. It's only because I help Mike and run his errands that he puts your car ahead of the many, many others he has to fix — that and because he likes havin' me around. The poor devil's simply swamped with work. He's there between eight or nine in the mornin' and isn't through till nine or ten at night. He can't hire a helper anywhere. Sometimes his son helps him after school, but his son's quite spoiled. Honest, Arthur, I'm sorry as hell for that poor man. He's got demandin' children, a housekeeper who don't let him mislay a shoe and put a chair in the wrong position without hoppin' him, and a married woman's wooin' his children's affections away from him for some reason of her own — and he's so gosh darn helpless. He's a good man, Artie, a really good man. He trusts people. And if anyone comes into his shop and starts cussin', Mike will say: 'Hey, none of that here. If you want to swear, go somewheres else.' And he means it. And he thinks I'm the berries. And he pours out all his troubles to me and I pat him on the back and tell him he's a good boy. And every day he takes me to lunch. And he works so hard to please customers that he's growin' old before your eyes."

Pearl, I discover by a process of probing, is doing much of the work herself, with her hands over her head, taking out cotter pins, removing nuts, fitting, testing. "I like it, Artie, but it sure gets you sore. And you should see the men stare when they get wise to the fact I'm a girl. They kid the pants off Mike about his 'female assistant.'" Pearl has been a veritable darling lately. I find myself again becoming devoted to her. She is cheerful, thoughtful, diligent, playful, filled with vitality and amusing tangents. I guess I'll have to admit to myself that like Evelyn she exercises a fascination over me which outrides what qualities in her I regard with disfavor or disesteem.

October 24   Evelyn met my Father at the train from Maine. "The train was late. It was dark. The redcaps used flashlights because of the dimout. Smoke rolled along the platform. People passed. I walked ahead. The crowd thinned. There, the last one to put in an appearance, was your Old Man. He looked pitiful. He walked as if he couldn't see well, it was so dark. His hands trembled. He sounded frightened. He said he'd been throwing up all day, hadn't eaten anything, was dreadfully nauseated. He was worried about his bags. He said the porter had grabbed them and he didn't know where they were. Well, the bags were there. The redcap put them in my car. We started for home. The traffic, he said, was so heavy it made him jittery. He sat on the edge of the seat. He made me stop and buy him some liquor. Now he won't eat anything. He just drinks, loses it in the bathroom, drinks some more. There's no sense to it, but that's what he does. He drinks to kill the nausea; the liquor makes him throw up; he drinks to calm his stomach; and so on, I gather, day after day, night after night."

My Father talked with me not longer than ten minutes. He's very fat, bloated almost. He walks with a creep. He's very frank about drinking too much. I asked him why he did it. "It was so damp this summer. I had to keep warm. I couldn't stay out of doors and keep warm without drinking. So I drank. It's a dog's life I lead, anyway," he added, more as though restating a conclusion than objecting.

October 25 Tell my Father goodbye. He's frightened over the trip to Charlotte. He's all drawn in upon himself, like a trepidatious creature at the back of a cavern. And over and over again he speaks of the trip from Bangor here, how ill he was, how fast the trains go, how dark the platform was.

His face is so puffy that it makes his mouth small. The lips have never moved noticeably when he talked and now they scarcely seem to move at all. He cut himself when shaving. A drop of blood wells slowly up on his lip. His hair, still dark but gray on the edges and streaked with gray, is brushed neatly. His tie, with the sapphire stickpin he likes, is neatly centered in the collar of his gray shirt. His vest has the edging of white fashionable a generation and more ago. His shoes are neatly polished. The large gold chain of his large gold watch hangs from right-hand vest pocket to left-hand vest pocket. No matter how badly he feels, his person is kept scrupulously neat. His teeth, being uncomfortable, are not in place. His moustache is shorter than formerly, like mine, red and white. His breath smells like a varnish factory and his blue suit is redolent of cigar smoke. Evelyn tries to give him some food to take with him as he is convinced he will eat nothing until he reaches Charlotte. All he will take are two cracker and cheese sandwiches which he places carefully in his overcoat pocket. His gray felt hat rim is bent down in front just as it used to be when I was a boy to shade his eyes from the sun. He is saying that no matter how nauseated he gets, he never has a headache. He reads detective stories at night. His eyes formerly were not so strong. He has had split pea soup for breakfast. I ask him to stop drinking. He smiles — he has a winning smile; he pats me on the arm; he says, "I'll stop directly. I always do."

He continually looks at his watch. He expects to be at the station at the very least twenty minutes before the train leaves. I can hear in my mind his impatient voice chiding: "You, Bert, do you want us to miss the train. Why don't you get a hurry on?" There are scores of fine frown wrinkles in his forehead, very white above an otherwise somewhat florid face and a very florid nose. His square fingertips drum impatiently on the chair arm. He clears his throat, and I think of the time he went off somewhere in the Jersey City station and left me alone and how glad I, a very small boy, was to hear that clearing of the throat again even before I caught sight of the glasses and the hat with the bent-down rim among the crowds rushing to the ferryboats.

Whatever I may think of this hunched-over man, sitting so miserable in the red chair with the high back and wing arms, I feel unaccountably drawn to him by the deep ties of blood I suppose and by the natural inclination of a son's heart, and for some reason I hate to have him go. My Father will be seventy-five in February. He has always been a person in his own inimitable right. It is not to be expected surely that he will survive the winter. I feel cheated of what might have so easily been otherwise. And I feel loath to have him go away from me into an uncertain future. I want to cry. He says: "Take care of yourself, old sport." He pats me on the arm. Then he shuffles slowly from the hall back into the apartment and closes the door. I hear him clear his throat. Well, that is that.

October 29 Juliette was here last evening for the first time since I have forgotten how long. Clarence has three plants now. He was offered, so Juliette said, sixty thousand for the one in Vermont several weeks ago. He has more Government business than he can handle. He gives thousand dollar checks to the Red Cross. He won three thousand dollars on an essay he wrote for a prize contest. Juliette drives for Tech officers every afternoon. When boatloads of wounded arrive in Boston, she transports them to hospitals in the ambulance she drives. It is usually after midnight, I suppose so that people won't see them. She figures she has helped move at least three hundred and has seen at least three thousand in all. She goes home and cries afterwards. She has bitten her nails to the quick out of sympathy. She is becoming convinced that "the Communists have something." She is too busy to "have a sex life." She goes with Clarence to Vermont and there rides horseback. She buys woolens in Canada and smuggles them home. She has been taking care of a refugee child. She is tired all the time. She feels younger than thirty-three while at the same time, "if you know what I mean, Arthur, more mature than my age, as if I had lived a more vital life than most people." She plays the Stock Market, choosing cheap stocks. She "isn't discontented."

October 30 I hold no brief for the Nazi theory of Empire since I am not a Nazi, though to be absolutely frank, were the Nazi ideology to be called, say, "manifest destiny" and were it the creed of those in power in America, I might (I am not as sure of this as once I was) approve of it at least in theory, at least until it made serfs of us citizens for the performance of the toil and fighting necessary for acquiring and maintaining empire. But I cannot for the life of me perceive that it is any more contrary to the American principles, any more to be feared than the Communist theory of Empire. The latter appears to be functioning at this point more efficiently than the former, that is all; and I still, with all its drawbacks, its despotisms, its regimentations, would rather be a German in Germany than a Soviet comrade in Soviet Russia.

November 3 The day we told Haggerty to stop working on the Cadillac, he ignored what we said. Monday night late he telephoned Pearl that the car was downstairs. Yesterday Pearl had it on the road working the motor in. Today I rode in it, and gorrah, it goes.

November 4 Pearl was late with my lunch two days ago, in fact, got me no lunch. Evelyn was put out and called her to account. Pearl was nasty with me. "It simply burns me up to be talked to by Mrs. Inman the way she does, as though I was the scum of the earth. It isn't what she says; it's how she says it. And it's not like I didn't have your interest to heart and bust a gut trying to please you. I don't care what you say to me, but by God, I burn up when she turns loose on me. I don't believe she can know how she sounds. It's just because I know what a fix you'd be in if I left you that I didn't leave. If I stay with you till after the war, I'll feel I've done my duty towards you, and it's only because you're good to me and I love you that I can endure being tied down this way. I like to move around, meet new people, go new places, raise hell and be independent and tell anyone who crosses me to go to hell. That's my nature, and I can't change it."

November 10 Married twenty years today. That is a long time.

November 15 As to Ella. It is probable that I have seen the last of her for a very long time, if not for good. She has been less and less amicable toward me for some time. The Jews where she works flatter her and make a pother over her so unremittingly that she has become spoiled. When she ceases to put herself out to please me by being sprightly, I become bored. Then we argue about world politics and ideals, and she becomes personally incensed at me for not believing in the brotherhood of men and the like. I think that due mostly to the enunciations of Roosevelt and Wallace which she imbibes whole, she has come to hate me socially, the more so that I am antipathetic to such impossible dreams. When I suggested to her that we were getting fed up with each other and that it might be a sensible plan to see each other less often, she no doubt, judging by her actions, sensed an opportunity to break with me, just as she has with all her friends and relatives in the past. She was rude and uninterested when I offered her some butter. The world is thronged with people — and Ella, I have always known, was one of them — who are sufferable only when fortune is not favoring them.

November 19 Like a spring day, yet odorous with damp leaves and pungent from drifting woodfire smoke. Squirrels running along split-hickory fences pause and pose, tails twisted up and over tiny rodent heads, the large orbs of which reflect sunbeams. Crows are purple-black in the top pine branches. In the small lily lake in the Sargent estate, a large heron stands on one leg. Ducks by the hundreds make black dots along the wide path to the low sun as it slants across Jamaica Pond, and squalls ruffle the green and blue waves. Intertwined birch branches form intricate patterns against the sky. Crisped leaves scud on their points, like so many diminutive iceboats, along the slick surface of the road's pavement. In a stucco house with green trimmings and pointed green roof that sits as though born there out of fitting timelessness, windows are open and white curtains flutter and clean panes shine. A road is blocked off. Workmen are gathered about a huge new mobile crane, its long, red-painted, structural steel arm pointed skyward, cables dangling from the tip into a large ditch below, tethers for a great mechanical 'Dinoceras.' Through the dusty glass of a large window in a small shop, a shoemaker looks out at us, his eyes pivoting down to his work, up to us, jerkily, his fat face expressionless. A doctor with a small bag hurries out of one hospital door and into another. American flags fly by filling stations. Traffic ebbs and flows. My car knocks louder and louder; we go more and more slowly. I am tiring. Colors assume additional brightness. The highlights on automobiles sparkle. An aluminum-painted police prowl car passes slowly, its antennae erect overhead. A small girl throws a blue ball to another small girl. In a window are rows of vegetables, green, taupe, scarlet. The blocks prolong themselves. One turn. Another turn. Another turn. Home at last. It was, though, a beautiful morning.

November 21   One of these days the malady I am suffering from may seem as plain to physicians as a bad tooth is now and as direct to remove or cure. I am not altogether ready to assert dogmatically that what ails me does not, cannot spring from the mind. It may, but the cause, it seems to my best judgment, lies deeper than that — in some inherited weakness, probably, which my unhappy psychological life at school together with the overuse of a not too rugged nervous system brought to depletion and disorganization. I frankly perceive no cure or relief ahead, only a steady diminution of physical capacity and an increasing subjectivity to the ill of the body and of the mind. It is not a pleasant prospect, but it is what I have to face.

November 22   Many of Mrs. Cash's former pupils are at various fighting fronts, most of them in the South Pacific. A Goshen boy sent his diary home to his untutored Catholic mother. She let Mrs. Cash read it. "I tell you, Mr. Inman, it was a document you would enjoy. It lets you right in on what really is taking place among the boys. He uses plain, unvarnished four-letter words and makes no bones about anything. He tells how the men pewk and shit in their pants when they go into battle for the first time. When they felt one fellow was holding out and not doing his share of work, they dragged him through the latrine ditch, and 'my God did he stink.' He tells about how a native woman came up to him and lifted her skirts and pointed to herself. 'I laid her right there,' he writes, 'and when I got done she wanted more, and I laid her again.' He tells about how the boys masturbate and use fruit to do it. He tells about a buddy with his guts shot out and dragging. He tells what fun it is to shoot the Nips when they're mad, and how they slashed a cross on one Japanese soldier's belly. It's a bawdy story, Mr. Inman, and it doesn't make war look any too good."

I heard a story on the radio last night which seemed to me to be illustrative of American character in various of its aspects. The commentator would not have dared release it without verification. It was this. Lieut. General Patton has not been heard of for some time. The publicity about the pearl-handled revolver, blood-and-guts general subsided suddenly. And why? Because one day Patton was inspecting a hospital in Tunis. He observed an apparently unimpaired soldier lying in bed. He was informed that he was a fatigue (shell-shock) patient. He scoffed at the verdict. He told the man off. He pulled him out of bed and hit him for a malingerer. The doctor interfered. He told Patton that while he might be in command of the war effort, he, the doctor, was boss in his hospital, and he wished

Patton to go. Patton started to draw his revolver. He was seized and disarmed and put out of the building. Eisenhower reprimanded him severely and relieved him of command. He is to suffer a "shift of responsibility." The story rings true. Dr. Pike says that along the North Shore he is hated for his overriding manners.

November 28 Mrs. Cash ejaculates: "The goddamn sons of bitches — I'm glad they're getting it. I hope every man and woman in Berlin is killed. It's what they deserve. They started it." I shiver. I feel in my heart a terrible pity for the bombed citizens of Germany. When a population has been or is being reduced to a condition of terrified suffering, then that population no longer wears the semblance of my enemy, and compassion bends my spirit toward the unfortunates who have been overtaken by a visitation I myself should have cringed to endure. I do not believe that I am maudlin or sentimental in this matter; it is simply that I am capable of historical detachment and that the quality of revenge in me has never been awakened to transcend mere words. I can feel that for the Jews to be scythed to the earth like greedy grasses overrunning lush fields might be propitious; but, did the power to order their destruction devolve on me, the order would never be fulfilled. I feel for the Berliners a sympathetic horror and an encompassing pity. Had the Germans wrecked my city with their bombs and killed my loved ones and brought ruin and grief to me, it might be otherwise, but they have not. So I pity them from the bottom of my heart.

December 3 Pearl stands in front of the mirror. She is examining her teeth. She runs a finger around them. The nail is enameled red, the identical color of the mirror frame. Her blonde hair is pulled back from her forehead, tucked behind her ears, leaving them exposed. She stares into her smallish green eyes. Her nose is aquiline and well formed. Her lips are full. Her chin retreats slightly. She wrinkles her forehead. She is intent upon her reflection. When she is spoken to, she does not hear. She doubles up her hands and rubs her eyes vigorously with the knuckles, as a child might do. She turns around. She takes note of us. She grins. She gives a hitch to her slacks. Her hips are very wide. "Well," she remarks, "I gotta be off. I gotta help Mike clean the carburetor and wipe out the inside of the new Caddie. I'll be seein' you." She grabs her coat, her headscarf, her purse. "So long, boys and girls," she tosses in our direction, and with another grin swings out of the door and down the hall. Her feet make the quick, springy sound of a young girl-child hurrying.

December 4 Ella so blew the horn of praise for her Dr. Pearl that I decided to let him have a go at me. This morning he came. I didn't like him at first, liked him better later. Short. Knuckleless fingers. Body curved forward from pelvis, so that slightly protuberant eyes peer at you through tops of spectacle lenses. Reddish complexion with burnt or scarred flesh by right eye. Yellow teeth. High-laced shoes. Earnest, it is soon evident, in his work and certain he can help. Asked me not too pertinent questions. Examined my body intelligently.

"Too quick reactions. Not getting enough from your food. I fix you. First, you walk. Second, you take aninoids from hog's stomach and D vitamins of high unit value. I fix you. I was born in Russia without the proper diet just like you had, and my mother she die of not enough proper food, just like your grandmother she died. But you must walk. And how is it you regulate your life? That is important."

I replied that I regulated my life just about in a fashion to drive any doctor crazy and, in my own estimation, so far as getting better was concerned, not wisely at all. But so far as enabling me to put as much strength as possible upon working, I did very well and had no intention of changing my habits. If he were a smart doctor, I said, he could help me no matter what my habits were, and if he helped me my habits would spontaneously change. And as for walking, I had no intention of doing that either. Did he provide me with strength, why I'd walk naturally as there was nothing I'd rather do. However, I agreed with him about the vitamins, that I should be taking as many units as possible, had told other doctors just that. He moderated somewhat his urgent demands that I walk.

December 5 People are like houses. You pass the outsides of them and wonder and make suppositions as to what is inside. The more suppositions you make and the more inner arrangements you have a chance to examine, the more accurate, as a rule, your diagnoses of the interior become. I rarely tire of analyzing the parade of human exteriors which pass me by. And the opportunity that comes in moments of stress or through long association of checking first impressions with gleaned knowledge always constitutes an exciting experience. I like to be correct in my analyses, of course, but verification or error is stimulating, the one to self-esteem, the other to education. But all this, I suppose, is apparent from my writings, superfluous to state.

December 13 In 'Weird Tales' (subtitled 'A Magazine of the Bizarre and Unusual,' now so poor I no longer read it, but once containing stories by such imaginative writers as Moore, Ashton Smith, Lovecroft) there appeared during the decade between 1928 and 1938 stories by one Robert E. Howard. Perhaps he and Ashton Smith were one author under two names but perhaps not.[16] Roderic and I enjoyed particularly the stories by Howard. They generally had to do with the adventures of two characters, first Kull the Atlantian, then later on, Conan the barbarian. These two men of almost superhuman strength, product of the outlands of the semi-mythical world in which they moved from one hazard to another, fought their way to kingship over the more cultured empires then upon the earth. They were fearless, tireless, often overtrustful, temporarily distracted by lovely women, now and again sentimental, but always alert, watchful, buoyantly alive, unbreakable in their intrepidity. Few obstacles blocked their assiduity of purpose, balked their strength of arm. They exemplified in their persons, their intuitions and their actions raw prowess impinging upon cultures becoming decadent. Their course through adversity to success was a swashbuckling one, their spirits being uplifted by an unquenchable brashness.

Pure action exerts on a stay-at-home such as myself, in constant rebellion against the limitations which confront him, a vicarious stimulation and a tremendous satisfaction. In the stories of Robert E. Howard I discovered such satisfaction. Not only was there pure action, but behind the action as well functioned always a varied and vital imagination. Though the style of his stories (Roderic and I are rereading some of them) is florid and flamboyant on the whole, at times turgid, the shortcomings of composition do not in the least matter. And many of the tales are shrewdly allegorical. They possess color, motion, variety of pattern. Had Howard been writing in a more baroque age, he might well have attained the stature of Poe. As it is, no one of any literary prestige has ever heard of him or his stories; the magazines in which what he wrote appeared are already, being of very cheap paper, crumbling. There will be no copies of 'Weird Tales' in libraries (they not keeping 'pulps'), the naked women on the covers sufficient of themselves to act as bar sinister. So it is not at all unlikely that within fifty, a hundred years Howard's tales will have vanished as completely from the archives of earth as have most of the old Roman writings, and his name will be no more than an obscure mention somewhere in an old book. It seems to me

---

[16] Arthur's hunch was wrong. Clark Ashton Smith (1893–1961) and Robert H. Howard (1906–1936) were not the same authors. The Moore he refers to may be Catherine L. Moore, prolific author of "swashbuckling, male-oriented space opera." Howard Phillips Lovecraft (1890–1937) was one of the great pioneers of the "weird" fiction Arthur so delighted in.

regrettable, but barring some providential accident, that is the way it will be.

December 14   Janice is in the doldrums. Her poor mind is snarled. She desires to please me and she desires to please Bertram, and Bertram, just as I knew he would, is beginning to put the pressure on about this job. I had a long talk with Janice yesterday. I wish she were more informed as to the masculine mind. It would be fairly easy for an experienced girl to twist Bertram around her finger, and I hope Janice can do it, but I'm not too sure. He will not, of course, adhere to the promises he made her before marriage unless she makes him. She was so very certain she could handle him after they were married. She told me not to worry. Well, it may be that she can handle him. She is always coming out with surprising latent resources.

December 15   I like American women as they are. Probably if I had an obedient or subservient Chinese or Malayan wife I should be bored into leaving her. Nevertheless, there lies in the back of my head a persistent suspicion that the Oriental attitude toward women is correct and ours may be wrong, and that the interrelationship between husbands and wives, males and females, is an element of our social structure which causes us Americans to be unsure of ourselves culturally and to remain immature internationally.

December 19   I have been reflecting what historical person I had rather be of all others. The answer comes readily. I had rather be Franz Liszt. Child prodigy. Tremendous personal success. Composer. Individualist. Lover. The admired and feted one of Europe. No soul-shaking setbacks. Greatness. Prestige. A long and adulated old age. A legacy of fame. He was what I should like to be: a smiled-upon one, a man capable of magnificent gestures, an irrefutable personage. Contemporary of Paganini, Lamartine, Strauss, Verlaine, Chopin, Hugo, Dumas, Tchaikovsky, Tolstoy, Rodin, Dickens, Sand, Goya, Guizot, Macaulay, Gounod, Verdi; father-in-law of Wagner and von Bulow—Liszt.

December 21   Piled timber in the sunlight makes splendid patterns—the ruddiness of the Douglas fir, the yellowness of the Southern pine, the clear whiteness of the white pine, and all the diminishing and ascending shades between—and the arrangements of the butts, square, rectangular, wide, thin—and the grains of the woods, close, loose, curved, jagged, straight—and the lengths of the planks, the beams, the joists, the strips. The softwoods are piled outside to weather, and almost any morning men can be seen unloading the sawn stuff from red freight cars or handling it into open trucks. In the long warehouse made of gray-painted corrugated iron, the hardwoods are stored—the beech, the oak, the maple, the birch. When the large doors are slid back, piles of divers hardwoods are discernible in innumerable prepared shapes and sizes. I should, I think, enjoy wandering through that warehouse, reveling in the odors and the touch of dressed woods. Such woods have always appealed to me as being among nature's materials most satisfactorily fabricated by man.

1944

January 1   I should propound that the four most important trends during 1943 in the United States were: 1. The passing from the military defensive to the military offensive; 2. The rejuvenation of the Congress as a responsible legislative body; 3. Moderation of the philosophy of reform within our borders; 4. The lowering of all standards of private expectation and the adjustment downward of the morality of the individual to fit him (or so he weakly feels) to cope with the dishonest interference of Government with his personal and group affairs.

January 2   Some several weeks ago Dottie Bottom remarked casually: "Well, I've been thinking it over and I've decided maybe I'll have a baby." "Why?" I queried. "Oh, I don't know. Maybe it would be nice." "I think you're crazy." "Maybe, but that's the way I feel." "My God, Bottom, you've got everything you want—a loving husband, money, a house, health. You don't want to risk everything by having a baby, do you?" "Sure," she replied complacently. "Why not?" "Why not? It's silly, crazy, daffy, nutty, senseless." "Well," she said equably, "I've decided." "What if you can't get one?" "Why I don't get one, that's all. If I get one, I get one. If I don't, I don't. I'll be contented either way."

Yesterday she announced: "Well, I'm pregnant, Artie. I did it by the book, and it worked the first time." I said: "I think you're daft." "It'll be fun," she said. "I should have it next August. I don't care whether it's a boy or a girl. I'm sure it will be a fine baby, anyway. Andy's pleased, too. I won't be able to treat you for six weeks or a month, but that's no longer than I was abroad. Aren't you pleased?" "No," I exclaimed.

January 6   Pearl wished Haggerty to come here to examine our collection of parts for the Cadillac. "I don't wanna take 'em up to his place. Besides, my car's there, and I can get a ride back with him." So she called him on the phone. "Hi, Mike," she said, slumping down in the chair and blowing cigarette smoke at the ceiling with evident satisfaction. "How's about comin' down here and drivin' me back with you? Why should you come?" She giggled. "I wanna show you my gears. Why, Mike, how could you think such things of me. Janice's here. You needn't be frightened—you poor big man. But seriously, will you come? Sure. Sure. I'll be waitin'. You're a honey boy." She turned to us with a grin. "It's all in knowin' how," she remarked.

As I was about to lie down for my noon rest, a large figure in tan coveralls came down the narrow hallway. It was Haggerty. I thanked him for his trouble on my behalf, sat on Pearl's bed and watched and listened while he went over the parts. A face a sculptor would delight in, such heavy creases in it, so blocklike and massive, almost a stupid face. He could scarce remove his eyes from the bridling, teasing Pearl. He regarded her with the calm devotion of a mature dog for its mistress. Also, with the tolerance of a father dog for its mettlesome puppy. He would, you knew, marry her in an instant if he thought it proper and she were willing. A simple soul if ever I saw one.

I am very nearly finished reading the biography of Henry Grady, the man who, Grandfather Inman told my Mother, influenced him more than any other. It is a well-documented biography, written by a Georgian—on the whole a fair portrait of the young journalist who edited the 'Constitution' and played such a provocative part in recreating the New South out of ante-bellum components. Grady died when he was thirty-nine, a few years before I was born. Now and again his phraseology rings nobly or powerfully, but usually it drips with cloying sentimentality. Grady's artistic admirations are puerile. His gifts are energy, personality, vision rather than mental capacity. He must have been an engaging person. He worked himself to death.

He was open-handed, almost lavish, in his disregard for accrued wealth. He must have influenced my Grandfather in his course of donating to charity, to education, to the needy. It is probably due to the slants of thought Grady induced in him that his wealth was passed on to Agnes Scott, etc. rather than to his family. I should curse Grady, I suppose, and the day he imposed his ideas on S.M. Inman. But there is always the chance that S.M. imposed his ideas on Grady. So let it stand. The 'Herald Tribune,' in a review of the biography, refers to Grady as "a minor journalist." I have read the Atlanta 'Constitution' of the nineties. Grady largely made it what it was. It was a better paper than the Boston 'Herald' is now, better than most American papers are today. So I should not call him a minor journalist. It would have been exciting had S.M. passed on his one-eighth interest in the 'Constitution' and had Father inherited it and handed it on to me.

January 9 I should say that more than one of ten Americans believe in the atrocities as a coincidental of war, but nine out of ten reject the prevalence and sizeableness of the atrocities as propaganda. As to Jews being murdered in mass, many Americans just don't give a damn about that. And anyway, why should we dwell upon such unpleasantnesses as atrocities? They're far away, and they don't in the main occur to our soldiers, and we'd go nuts, wouldn't we, keeping our minds on such subjects? And anyway, aren't we spending our money, our lives, our efforts to put a stop to all such atrocities, whether there are many of them or few of them? So why fret ourselves sick? If we fretted too much, we wouldn't be able to do our part toward winning the war, would we?

January 11 [From Abruzzo:]

I have completely settled myself here in N.Y. and am now shop steward for my union in the place where I work. I was elected unanimosly by the entire shop and naturaly I feel quite proud of it. You will notice my new address, and this bears out my statement of being settled. I have my own apartment and my own furniture and I must say that nothing gives one such a sence of security and well being than his own home.

My union and my political work keep my spare hours at a minnimin and so I havent too much time to write as I still enjoy running about. I shall try how ever to write a lenthy and discriptive letter of some events and I have had a few too since I last wrote you.

It might interest you to know I belong to the Newspaper Guild, the same that was organized by Heywood Broun,[17] and that there are many internal fights between Local & National officers. I naturaly run into lots of my left wing pals, even though I don't work for a red paper, and hear the tales they have to tell.

January 12 Joe [Cooper] arrived in Boston this morning. He is to spend the day discussing city planning with professors at Harvard and Tech, have dinner with Evelyn, talk to me during the evening. How glad I shall be to reestablish contact with him I do not know. Joseph Walter Cooper, Jr. is now forty-five, married to a woman of independent means, father of two boys and a girl. He carries on the architect's office he and Sam have had for some fifteen years, with

---

[17] Heywood Broun (1888–1939), at the time of the founding of the American Newspaper Guild (1933), was one of the most widely read and highly paid columnists in the country. Broun was active in the Sacco and Vanzetti defense effort, and in the 1930s his humorous and genial column, "It Seems to Me," became increasingly devoted to economic and political matters.

what business success in these times I cannot say, probably not with much. Whether Joe will be the stodgy bore Sam proved to be and as lacking in imagination or will be lighter-footed remains in doubt.

January 15 Joe and I talked from eight to eleven-thirty, covering twenty years. The first thing I noted was the change in his voice. His accent was Georgian, scarcely a trace of the Philadelphia "r's" left. Not a tone, not an intonation, remained as it used to be. I could not have recognized him had my life depended upon doing so. He began by telling me about the architectural mission he was on.

"I feel that architects have done very little, really, to improve the world. Most of them have no imagination and the engineers none at all. I feel that something could be done in the way of postwar planning to make architects useful and popular. I don't mean just plans. There are thousands of blueprints which will remain blueprints. I mean zoning and through highways but not that exactly. The problem has to do with people, businessmen and above all, architects, more than it does with architects' plans. I know in a way what I mean, but find it difficult to express. It's what [Robert] Moses (and say, there's a dynamic man for you, a Jew with a glittering mind, so full of ideas they jump out at you) told me in New York. It's working from the specific to the general, not from the general to the specific. Moses says do the job directly in front of you and do it well. That's the best you can do. It'll all be obsolete in twenty years anyway. Just bear in mind always the interest of your city and try to keep the theorists and parlor Pinks from Washington out of the picture and spend half your energy salving the politicians and getting them on your side, for without them you're helpless. A great man, that Moses, Arthur. He says he spends much of his time simply driving around the streets of New York in the four cars he uses practically continually. He says that most city planners don't even know their city or the people who live in it. He spends hours talking to the men and women he meets casually, asking what they want and don't want. The time I spent in Washington was virtually wasted. They are a bunch of dreamers, jealous of each other, buried in storerooms full of reports and statistics and anxious to dispense money on all sorts of silly things and to add you to their payroll."

January 16 To continue with Joe. He was with me for an hour the next day before he caught his train for New York. He's at least six feet, three inches tall. He weighs above two hundred pounds. He stoops forward slightly as so many tall men do. He still wears button-down soft collars and a watch chain across his vest, manners of dress which date him and, I suppose, indicate qualities of conservatism. He brushes his hair straight back just as he used to do. His hands, when you shake them, are soft and pudgy. He resembles Roosevelt startlingly, the same narrow forehead, the same protruding nose, the same close-set eyes, the same small mouth (to a physiognomist weak and self- indulgent), the same heavy porcine jowls. He has no gray hairs, no lines. Both body and features change position slowly as did Uncle Joe's. One eye is gray-blue and the other, the injured one, is brown-green with a white cast to it. As men go, he is not unprepossessing in appearance. His very bulk carries with it a certain weight.

The aftertaste of Joe is not as agreeable as the taste. He is too didactic, too coarse of fiber, too slow, too repetitious to long intrigue me. A good man as men go but boring in too large doses I'm sure. It was interesting to meet again a person whom formerly I knew about as thoroughly as I did anyone on earth and to analyze the intervening growth in him and in myself.

January 17   Ella said: "The Chinese won't keep appointments. Nothing can make them. They wander in when it pleases them. They say, 'I wait,' and they wait hours, but they never keep appointments. On Saturday, just after the new dentist had taken over, the Chinese laundryman from around the corner wandered in with his wife and big fat baby, the wife carrying the baby. He wanted his wife's teeth cleaned. As it happened, the new dentist was only pottering and chattering. So we put the woman in the chair. The man took the baby and stood in front of the woman staring down her throat, just exactly in the way. I tried to persuade him to sit down. 'No,' he said, 'I stand.' And stand he did. I wondered if he wanted to see his wife's tonsils. He said not a word. He just stood. When the wife was tended to, he handed her the baby and got in the chair himself. She wouldn't sit. She just wandered around and looked out the window and into the corners. Then the baby began to cry in Chinese. The baby cried; the dentist machine buzzed; the new dentist talked and talked. I beat it to Joseph. 'My God, Joseph,' I cried, 'what next? He stands and looks down her mouth. The baby cries in Chinese. The old codger talks and talks. The woman wanders around like a lost soul.' 'Well, baby,' he said, 'just be calm. They're queer, these Chinese. They're an oppressed people just like your race and mine, so you must be tolerant. At least,' he said, 'you don't have the man standing at your shoulder, like I do, looking up their wife's insides while I'm examining them.' 'Yes,' I replied, 'that is something.' So I went back comforted, and saw it through. It was like a scene from some crazy farce, Arthur."

January 27   Reading Gogol has been a delightful and unexpectedly stimulating experience. If 'War and Peace' is a worthy work, which after reading most of it I am willing to concede (though not surely the greatest novel ever written), then 'Chichikov's Journey,' or 'Dead Souls' as it is usually known, is a work of extraordinary genius, one of the finest novels it has been my lot ever to read. I feel now as if I had myself visited the dozen or so estates described in the volume, talked with the landed gentry of Russia, been amused, disgusted, delighted by their attributes of character. The estate on the hill with the fields below and the quiet willow-lined river mirroring back the chapel with its seven golden crosses aroused in me a desire to own it. The successful agronomist's description of the contentment to be had by working with land, seasons, crops might serve as a veritable credo for farmers the world over. The characters live for the reader, are seldom all good or all bad, or as with Tolstoy's characters, formalized and turned into proper types. Chichikov is a not unloveable rascal, a sort of idealistic materialist, weak, vain, affected, acquisitive, lively withal and possessed of a certain winning aplomb. Like de Maupassant, Gogol limns a character in a few strokes, makes him come suddenly alive. Whatever reputation Gogol enjoys, he eminently deserves it.

I am now embarked upon Turgenev's 'Fathers and Sons' and find it thus far very dull reading indeed. These talking-books have introduced me to classics I should never have opened otherwise. Whether liking them all or not, my education must have been considerably broadened. And all the junk among the classics has been compensated for by such works as 'Chichikov's Journey,' 'Uncle Tom's Cabin,' 'Wuthering Heights,' 'Buddenbrooks,' 'Tono Bungay,' 'Candide' and 'The Castle of Otranto,' 'The Red and the Black' and Hans Andersen's 'Stories.'

February 1 "What's the matter, Evelyn?" I asked. "Are you worried about having the wens cut off your head tomorrow? I think Fred's brother will do a good job for you." "Oh, it isn't all that. It's when I do the proofreading of those awful old diaries with Mrs. Cash Saturday mornings it takes me four days to recuperate. The present, it seems to me, is bad enough without constantly having to recall the past. I simply hate it." "What would you have me do? I try to bear in mind you don't like to do the work. I give you as little of it as possible, much less than I'd like to give you. I give you much less work of all sorts than I'd like to. You spend about five hours a day at the most with me, and that isn't much." "Oh, I don't know. It's just everything. And the atrocity stories. And that I have no more faith in mankind. And that Pearl and Janice have me tied down tighter than a roped steer. And that at my age I haven't any friends I can go on trips with — not that that bothers me fifty-one weeks out of the year;

I'm too independent — but it does now. And those awful diaries. They simply bring it home to me how little I please you." "You please me in many ways." "Oh, I know. But it's very saddening to think that the one person in the world you want to please the most has as little opinion of you as you have of me." "I have a large opinion of many sides of your nature." "Yes, that may be. But not of me as a person. Not of me as a person who helps you as you want to be helped. Not of me as a worthy individual. Oh, I know. Because I try to look at the rosy side of things doesn't mean I don't know. And you look down upon my little subterfuges and escapes as childish. And why you want me around I don't know. Probably merely because I'm of service to you. And don't answer me, because whatever you'll say will be wrong."

February 3   [From Patricia:]

I am completely content. I'd rather have a bored husband than a dead one. But it keeps me hopping to keep Paul amused. He is an out & out extrovert & is never happy when idle. He needs a great deal of physical exercise to keep him from feeling pent up. Yet amusingly enough he has sold himself on the idea that he is a deep thinker. Poor lamb — his profoundest utterances are time worn clichets (?). He does have a good grasp of things tho and if he'd spend more time in reading it would help him. But he has no real love of literature, and the introspective things that interest me would utterly bore him. He is well read on current events because I provide them within arm distance, & he is really interested in today — while I love yesterday, at least in book form — yet we are admirably suited. I get a great deal of pleasure from his beauty. He has a magnificent body, and his features belie his character. For he seems the complete sophistocate — indeed, regards himself as such. Yet he is childishly sentimental, particularly about his family & wife. He never forgets the little things. Notices everything I wear & notices far too much for comfort, such as bad posture — frowning, & all the little physical frailities one is prone to come the thirties. Its good for me as I need a prodder. Also Paul is a superb lover. Never have I experienced the extasy that we acheive with any one else, and my first lover, tho I didnt appreciate it at the time was quite superior (that was Mike, remember?). Paul takes this department very seriously, almost academically. Isnt it amazing how many ways it can be done! We do disagree on my lack of aggression, being completely female I prefer the male approach, but sometimes he wants me to start it & if he is too insistent I get embarrased. Once in a while tho I up & surprise him, & even invented one position he hadnt tried. He was so tickled you'd think I was an Edison. Paul wants no levity & at first I was apt to wax conversational in intimate moments. It would incense him, so now I've learned to approach the climax with much heaving of bosoms etc even if I'm not actually in the mood. And I still get just as thrilled when he kisses me as I did from years ago.

We have elegant fights — when Paul comes home dead tired — aching for a brawl I let him have it, he blows off steam & neither of us hold a grudge. The silent martyr type would never do for Baby, it would just enrage him. Since quarelling is foreign to my nature I'm often surprised myself. But these arent quarells — they are regular knock down & drag outs, & how they clear the air. Up & at 'em Caffree — thats me.

February 15   Norman Leuko is thirty-one. He has been in the Navy for two years. His home was Bradford in this state. Pearl let herself be picked up by him one evening, since when he has been her shadow.

Norm was in active service off North Africa and Sicily for seven months. He speaks vividly and with animation, is a man of some sensitivity and considerable imagination. That he uses "was" for "were" and says "not nothin'" intensifies these latter qualities for some reason (probably because he is by instinct a gentle person), so I shall disregard the errors of grammar in my reporting of what he said as being errors of custom rather than errors of mentality. "In all that time," he says, "I had only twelve afternoons off. When they tell you a sailor sees the world, why that's a laugh. He sees his ship, and he sees it week in and week out. Not that it hasn't got to be that way probably, just that it is that way. We were," he continues, "under fire off and on all that time. I was on a fleet escort minesweeper, only we spent most of our days laying eggs and fighting off enemy aircraft. I was attached to a twenty millimenter antiaircraft gun. I tell you, Mr. Inman, I saw a lot of things I'll never forget during those seven months. I saw divebombers rushing straight at me. I saw the air thick with falling bombs and pieces of blown-up planes. I saw planes go up in a dazzle of explosion when they were hit that was brighter than the magnesium flares they dropped. I saw ships lift right out of the water and fall apart. I saw men overboard and drowning. I saw terrible wounds killing men in agony. I saw my friends go insane in front of me. I saw corpses swelled up and floating on the sea and was sent out to get their tags, found them sometimes to be dead men I'd known; and when we got the tags we had to shoot holes in the bodies so as they'd sink, and the stench was beyond description. I've seen the night skies crisscrossed by tracer bullets, and I've heard more noise than I had ever believed possible in the world and been in the midst of it until I was stunned. I've heard men scream. I've felt explosions that were too big to hear. I've sat in the seat of the a.a. gun and felt the recoil hit me steadily until I was numb. I've lived through more than I thought any one man could live through, and I'm still alive when most of my shipmates are dead."

A big bomb dropped alongside the minesweeper when she was lying in harbor in Sicily and blew a great hole in her side. "The concussion lifted me from my gun amidships and put me down by the minelayers on the stern. I didn't even hear the explosion. But I couldn't think. And I couldn't feel. And it was days before my hands and feet got over being numb. There were three minor holes in my back. I was no more use to the ship. I jumped at every noise." They seem to have gotten him to the hospital very slowly, for he remembers how they used the oil to list the ship so she wouldn't sink and how they mended her. He was a shell-shock patient. His best friend, in a hospital in North Africa with him, went insane and jumped off the roof and killed himself.

February 17   A week or so ago, Roderic and I finished reading 'The Black Book of Polish Jewry,' in which are recounted the horrors and persecutions committed on the Jews of Poland by the Germans. I found myself, as did Roderic, emerging from the long chronicle of misdeeds with doubt in my heart, doubt that any conquerer would so slowly and painstakingly consummate destruction upon a people so despised, doubt that the facts were being presented accurately. I found myself, as did Roderic, strangely untouched by what was in the book. If it is real — and I do not doubt that some of it is — then it is too large to touch me intimately. Roderic and I agreed that, however much we despised any people, we could not slowly and by rote, as it were, inflict a comparable torture upon them. And yet, had we been raised from infancy on the milk of hate and the practice of cruelty, how would we have felt? Hate can be instilled. And cruelty appears to be a human quality that generally is enlarged by use.

I thought of several things as we read the book. I thought of how safe and swaddled in well-being we are here in America, of how Tamerlane had leveled cities and built of the citizens' craniums pyramids of skulls, of how no groups of Anglo-Saxons would dig graves like the Jews in Poland for each other progressively as they were executed down a long line but would exclaim, "Hell, if we're going to be killed for sure anyway, you can do your own digging and be damned to you." It was not a pleasant book to read, and the thoughts it engendered were not pleasant, but I felt it my obligation to regard the other side of the picture.

February 21 The first of the month Billy wrote me a small note from Salt Lake City where he had been taking a gunnery course. He said that he had spent five hours looking for a Cadillac motor for me but did not have time to write. He is now, Sadie tells us, at radio school in Illinois, not far from St. Louis. I wrote him there, asking how I could telephone him on his birthday. No answer. I have a notion that Billy is keeping himself insulated from home emotions as far as possible.

February 26 On Thursday morning, a special delivery arrived from Billy saying to telephone him at six prompt. Pearl called him for me. The call went through in six minutes flat. It was good to hear his voice, though it made me for some reason sad. He said: "This is your little boy." He wanted to hear about Pearl, Janice, Evelyn, the Baby-Carriage. He expects to be at Scott Field some twenty weeks longer. After that, he will join the crew of the bomber to which he will be assigned for final training. Pearl was so excited she shook. I said to her when we had hung up: "Eighteen months of intensive training to turn out a gunner-radio man — then, in one flight, he can be killed or captured or maimed for life."

March 6 Pearl says: "Where do you get your blood tested, Artie?" "Why?" I inquire. "Oh, just because." She grins. "Say because I might marry Norm." "The poor guy," I say. "You should see your expression, Artie. You don't know whether I've been a bad girl or not. Gosh it's a scream." "I was simply," I explain, "thinking of poor Norm if he married you, so soft emotionally and you so hard. What a life he'd lead." "Oh, I'd be very gentle. You said yourself I'm doin' better. I'd make him a good wife. Not," she smirked, "that I'm necessarily goin' to marry him. Oh, Artie, he's so cute. And you must admit he's good for me."

March 15 Fred has just been here to fix my ribs. He sat down and talked for a long time. I like him. I'm grooming him to take Dr. Pike's place if anything ever happens to him. He seems to enjoy me. He asked about stocks. We discussed contrariness in women. "They're just highstrung, Arthur. They go on their nerve. And the longer they go on their nerve, the more contrary they get. And if they know anything at all, they think they know everything." He sheepishly pulled out of his pocket an ad for a magazine about model trains and how to build them. "I like trains," he said. "I'm going to send for this."

March 26 To many American men, perhaps to most American men, and certainly to men of other races and nations less inclined to give to women a romantic build-up, women are like shadows. When any part of a man's nature needs a woman, he takes her out of his belongings as he does a cigarette from his case or a shot of whiskey from his bottle, uses her, puts her back to keep for the next time. He does not evaluate her in the same category with men. He may sing songs to her, may write verses about her, may fight for her favor, may erect palaces and tombs in her honor, but in a man of ordinary stature there remains from birth to death a portion of his nature never touched by woman.

March 31 Juliette still drives the Red Cross ambulance to incoming hospital ships and takes wounded men to hospitals. "I've gotten hardened at last; now I can sleep nights." She does volunteer work in a Catholic orphanage. She would like to adopt a child there, but she being a Jew, they will not let her have it. She says that because of the antipathy toward Jews, she is most unhappy.

I said: "Well, what do you think of your Churchill and your beloved English now? When Roosevelt suggests that Jewish people be allowed to go to Palestine, he says no. He says in very clear words that he is there to maintain the British Empire, and the British Empire is in great part founded upon keeping subject peoples in subjection, and no matter what the straits of the Jewish people, he will not have them entering Palestine if it will antagonize the Arabs. They are his peons just like the Indians. I hope you're beginning to realize it." For once, she listened. "I'll end up a Communist yet," she said.

"If your people would intermarry with other Americans," I said, "and merge with them in bulk, you could rid yourselves of hatred and suspicion. But you won't do it. You remain international in the midst of us and expect to be regarded as we regard ourselves. It can't be done. I don't know where it will end up, either."

She made a sound of pushing the idea aside as foolish, a typical Jewish sound. "It's not our fault," she said. "And you know it's not our fault, Arthur. We're broad-minded. It's you who are narrow-minded. It seems almost unbelievable to me that people could be as wrong as you and others like you are."

April 4 This is supposed to be a veracious record. And so it is. Yet I not seldom am overtaken by a realization of just how wide of downright verity it must be. The private thoughts and emotions of a man of intensity and unconventional mind are often outlaw even to his impious self and surely to written exposition. My hatreds, my fears—some of the violent daydreams of revenge with which I while away sleepless hours — must be censored or omitted else who would ever read the crooked pages.

April 8 Pearl stood before the mirror primping for thirty-five minutes by my watch. Finally, Norm arrived. Evelyn had said: "He's really handsome in a delicate sort of way." And that describes him accurately. He's shorter than I am, dark eyes, with dark hair parted on the side, a dark, very short moustache. He looked newly scrubbed, and his clothes were scrupulously neat, from polished shoes to blue pea jacket. His face twitched and showed that he had been hurt emotionally but only to close scrutiny. His chin is weak, and there is not in him, I should say, much resilient steel although considerable pride and stubbornness which might pass for strength. A likeable fellow, not looking his age, a man more liable to be hurt than to hurt others.

April 9 "Yes," said Mrs. Cash, "I've had a glorious day. Three drunks I waited on. The life of a headwaitress is never dull, Mr. Inman. May I never grow too old to wait on table. The first two were just the usual run-of-the-mill drunks. The third was the prize. I noticed an old fellow sitting alone at a table in a booth. I said to myself: 'I know that old shit-heel. He used to go around with my father. What's he doing here in Boston? He never was any good. I guess I'll keep out of sight.' But he saw me. He called me to him. 'Wilma,' he said, 'what the hell are you doing here?' 'Earning my living,' I said. 'A headwaitress,' he said. 'Yes,' I said, 'a headwaitress. If you were as honorably employed as I am, it would be better off for you.' He laughed. 'You always were an old penny pincher, an old money grabber, Wilma,' he said. 'That was what was always wrong with you. You weren't like your father. You loved money.' 'Yes,' I said, 'I loved money. And, by God, I still do. It's a pity you never did.' 'Me,' he said, 'I love women. I love a good bed party. I love a nice piece. I love tail.' 'You're drunk,' I said.

"And just then the boss came up. I've told you, Mr. Inman, that he was one of my first students years ago. He's about forty now. The old man — his name is Park — recognized the boss at once. 'Well,' he said, 'how are you? And how is your mother? She was a great girl with her tail, your mother was. She was a great Edwiny. Yes sir, and I'll bet she's still right there with the old tail action. She could put her shoes under my bed any time she wanted to. She could put them there right now. They've been there many a time before, I can tell you. Nobody I ever laid could wiggle her behind like your mother. Yes sir. She was a wonder. And how is Edwiny now? A great old girl. Yes sir, a great old girl.'

"He showed no signs of stopping, so I signaled the boss to beat it.

There wasn't a thing he could say, because Edwina had been just like Park said she was, a gay old bird, and he knew it. Everybody in my section of Maine knows it. And I've heard it rumored that my boss is Park's son, though whose son he is is anybody's guess. Finally, I got the boss away and Park a little quieter. I loved it. I wanted to sit down on the floor and rock with laughter. It was awfully funny, Mr. Inman, honestly. Only I was afraid the old fellow would start on my father. But he didn't. He kept calling me a money grabber. The old reprobate. I'll bet he didn't have another cent in his pocket besides the three dollars his food and drink cost him. There's never a dull moment in the restaurant business, I can tell you — and all the dirt wasn't in de Maupassant's time, either — thank God."

April 10   Listened attentively last night to Secretary of State Hull outlining his international policies. It is no wonder, if he guides us in large measure, that we are Snow White lost in the woods. He lives in a Wilsonian world of impractical idealisms. He thinks in outworn Victorian clichés. He constantly refers to "Bwitain," to "fweedom," to "Democwacy." It is all but pitiful. The "dweams" of nonage in the carapace of dotage.

April 11   The problem of what to do with my diaries eventually weighs on my mind. How to interest anybody in them? I hate to contemplate their lying unread and unnoticed in some depository for centuries or being thrown away by some unheeding hand or suffering conflagration in a future war. I am of the opinion that in them is considerable that is worthwhile. I expect that one of these days I shall have to pay for printing them. I am nearly fifty, and there should be a start made with them. I cannot make contacts with influential people — I do not know how. The diaries are too unorthodox, too heterodox perhaps, to interest most orthodox people. I am puzzled concerning them, their possibilities and their fate.

April 12   Most men are dishonest in matters large enough and profitable enough to cause them to compromise with their morals. American businessmen, if they are dishonest, which I believe they are in general when it is to their advantage, at least give some portions of the public some remuneration for their money, which is not only something but a lot. It is only an adolescent who believes that men are honest or dishonest by the line. The most honest man under stress is capable of conniving with his conscience in some respect, and the most dishonest man possesses certain streaks of honesty. It is the harm or the weal to one's fellow creatures that makes dishonesty and honesty reprehensible or commendable, not being dishonest or being honest; and what is more, whether the moralists like to face it or not, how a man is regarded by other men as honest or as dishonest is as often as otherwise merely a matter of whether dishonesty is uncovered or is not. The American business-man has benefited the world more than he has harmed it. By that and by that chiefly he should be judged.

April 14 A fellow, the assistant manager of a 'proven pictures' movie house downtown, has been calling every day to rent the room. He was in the Army, he told Janice (I didn't see him) but was discharged for medical reasons. He was on the stage until he lost his voice. He likes his present job, because it enables him to meet theatre people. One of his chief responsibilities is to bounce sexual perverts from the theatre. There are evidently many of them. "You get tired of turning them over to the police. Yet you can't beat them up where there are witnesses. So I take them out in the back alley and do the trick. Sometimes they lay for me and beat me up. But I've never been hurt badly. Once you give them the works, they never come to your theatre again."

April 19 I said: "Well, Roderic, it's been nice knowing you all these years." He said: "It's been good knowing you, Arthur."

We read 'Astounding Stories,' a copy which had just arrived. We read of the decline and disappearance of the city as a live organism in the scheme of American culture, what with helicopters taking peo-ple to country estates of their own, hydroponics supplying food and making land cheap by displacing farmers, the housing facilities of cities being abandoned, city government an anachronism. We read of transcendental education by pictures and gradually more diffi-cult and fascinating problems until education became a passion and those engaged in it became over a length of time intelligences capable of assuming aerial bodies and of sustaining those bodies through the absorption of cosmic forces.

I don't know how Roderic felt. I felt despondent. We exchanged the latest jokes on Mrs. Roosevelt which so mysteriously go the rounds. We acted cheerful.

"When you get settled," I said, "let me know what you need and I'll make you a present of it." "Why thanks, Arthur," he said, "that's super of you. I'll bear it in mind, and honestly I'll let you know. I leave with a razor and a toothbrush."

Garrison Hall doings began to bulk larger in the Diary than did the war and the economy. Arthur took for granted that Roosevelt "the limper" would beat Dewey "the twirp" for the presidency. Nor did the crunching campaigns in Europe and in the Pacific provide any surprises. Russian armies had broken the back of the Nazis, and their implacable leader — the Man of Steel — was top dog. Arthur reported almost cas-

ually the Allied invasion of the continent. He did not think it would slow down the coming hegemony of the Soviets, America's future enemy. Since the United States apparently had no intention of grabbing territories, it ought to abandon Europe to its squabbles and retain a large and well-equipped military force for future emergencies.

But these matters concerned him only intermittently. The breakdown of his ancient Cadillac (only after months of tinkering and rummaging for old parts in junkyards did Mike Haggerty manage to put it back on the road) and the influx of a new crop of women took precedence over the war. In spite of all Arthur's efforts to get Pearl to postpone her marriage, Norm Leuko practically ordered her to the altar (a most inauspicious union, Arthur thought). Arthur interviewed and tested a number of putative replacements for her jobs. The most suitable were Patsy Boland, red-haired, intelligent, and independent (at first immune to Arthur's "charm" and "whimsy" but soon to be adored); and Rose Trench, eventually the chatelaine of Garrison Hall and a key "character" in the "novel."

Arthur continued to agonize over Evelyn's exasperating behavior, her contentiousness, her proclivity to err, and followed his criticisms of her myriad failings with apologies to the reader ("the Anglo-Saxon in me is ashamed") for abusing the woman he professed to love most. Still there was less need to placate her than the paid help to whom he dared not expose his anger lest they leave him in the lurch. Some of them lingered at Garrison Hall for extended periods and temporarily supplanted the old reliables in his thoughts. Generally the new girls went off pretty quickly, however, and Janice, Mrs. Cash, Ella, Claire, Millicent, and Patricia reinstated themselves. So many women sometimes brought on bouts of "womanitis." Then Arthur would yearn for Billy (who wrote only sporadically) and for Roderic (who sent him detailed descriptions of navy life).

Arthur wrote confidently about the "average American" and "ejaculated" after "considerable thought" his views on the imminent peace talks, English perfidy, the baleful character of FDR, Communist infiltration, and the postwar economy. He found life tolerable even though he confessed to be "jittery" about what lay ahead.

April 24   The rain is dribbling against the windowpanes. It is a day to be inside. I sit and wish Roderic had not been forced to go away, that *they* had not taken him. The evenings bid fair to be long and monotonous without him. I put an ad for a reader in yesterday's paper but to date not a single reply. Although I raised the price to seventy-five cents an hour, I have a notion I shall get no answers — will not even if I raise the emolument to a dollar an hour. So probably I shall have to do with what I have.

April 28   Cardinal O'Connell died recently, and Church officials from all over America have come to Boston to be present at the last services in honor of the astute, dynamic, obscene-faced Prince of the Catholic Church. The services were broadcast from the Cathedral. Crowds lined up along the route the hearse took and bowed their heads in respect. A man with such a face and the innumerable stories that have been current about his shrewdness, his power, his immorality, must indeed have led a venal life, to put it mildly. To be a high official in the world's greatest organization carries with it prestige, glamour and a certain freedom of action that must be most attractive to possess. One of the right-hand emissaries of God on earth, the Cardinal, no doubt a rich-living old profligate, though in the purblind eyes of the people of his faith a figure of sanctity seen through a mist of reverence.

"Yes," said Pearl, "when I reached the Rationing Board office, everyone was listening with fixed faces to the service comin' out of the radio. They scowled at me when I said what I wanted. I got waited on quick, for once. Then I was hungry and went into a drugstore to get somethin' to eat. There was a little old lady sittin' at the counter. 'What do you want?' the woman behind the counter asked her. She said she wanted a bacon sandwich. You shouldda seen the woman behind the counter scowl. 'Huh,' she snapped. 'Huh. A bacon sandwich on Friday. Huh.' And she looked mad enough to eat rocks. The little old lady's face fell, and she looked as if she wanted to cry. I was sorry for her. I patted her on the back. I said: 'Never you mind. There's a few of us Protestants left in Boston yet.'"

Janice's face as she listened was amusing to watch. Pearl's story, made lively by gestures and postures of the face, was funny. Janice's inclination was to laugh. Yet, being now a Catholic, she wasn't sure she should. "No offense to you," repeated Pearl. "No offense, Janice." Presently, Janice laughed wholeheartedly. Her conversion, I should say, sits fairly lightly on her thus far.

May 4   Dottie Bottom is getting larger. "Where have you been today?" I inquired. "Oh," she returned, unemotionally, "I've been to the hospital to watch a Caesarean. She was in a bad way. It was a bloody operation. Fred's brother performed it. I don't think I ever saw so much blood. It would pour out of her as fast as they'd put it in. Maybe she'll live. The baby only weighed five pounds. They had trouble making it breathe. This was the woman's third Caesarean. They tied her ovarian tubes so she won't have any more babies." I interrupted: "With yourself about to have a baby, didn't you mind watching the woman scattering blood around?" "Oh no," she replied with supreme calmness. "Oh no. She isn't me."

May 9 Ella is going to Chicago with Robert next week. He is to attend some sort of C.I.O. convention. He climbs slowly upward in the union the redcaps belong to—I forget its long name. He is chairman of this and that. He has just become a member of the Masons. "It's making a man out of him," says Ella. "He has to watch the way he talks, and he can't be bellicose as he used to be. The men respect him. I think he's found his niche." Ella at this juncture is a firm believer in unions. I asked what she thought of the Communist influence in the C.I.O. "If it helps the unions, I'm for it. I'm for anything that helps them. If it doesn't, I'm not for it. Personally I think Joe Stalin has very little to say about what the American Communists do or don't do. God knows he's left them holding the bag enough times."

May 13 Decided that the moment had come to take what money I had in hoarding out of hoarding and buy stocks. The chances are that we will win the European war—not because of any inherent strength of our untested troops, but because the Russians, with a huge and successful force, will be in on the kill. Without Russia, I wouldn't give a dime for our immediate chances of defeating Germany. With Russia, the chances look more than good.

May 15 A dizzy night with no sleep. An ear specialist this morning, a gentle person who thought me a fool for protecting my eyes against the electric bulb he used and more of a fool because I didn't want my ear "blown out" but had the grace to keep his feelings to himself which is more than can be said of most doctors. He diagnosed that the infection from my throat had gone into the middle ear. The dizziness might last three days or two weeks but wasn't, he reassured me, anything to be worried about. It is no worse today than it was yesterday morning. He told me to move slowly and not to go riding, otherwise to do what I wanted. He seemed to know his business. I feel less uneasy.

May 20 Perhaps see a spot of light ahead. No one could help me. Dr. Pike said: "I tell you, Arthur, the only way to approach this thing is through osteopathy. You can't get at it directly. You gotta get at it indirectly. When you've made up your mind, we'll go to town. I'm sure I can help you." There's no doubt to it, Dr. Pike, compared with most other doctors, has a bearing that is imposing, that inspires confidence. He is in anybody's language a somebody.

May 22 Yesterday afternoon the blood began returning to my head in response to the correction Dr. Pike had made the day before. It was as though my head had been sitting on a fence until it was asleep and then on getting off the blood returned. The dizziness and vertigo diminished. As I told him yesterday, it must be a feather in his cap to have succeeded where others were at a loss. This makes still another time he has saved me from God knows what. I am on deck again.

May 23 Pearl returned at suppertime blanked-out. "I just couldn't help it, Artie, I was so pleased over your recovery. I knew you'd understand. I'm so pleased and so tired I got tight. It was as simple as that. You don't mind, do you?" She giggled. She laughed. "Norm's in the other room. You had oughtta see his face. Norm's shocked. To hell with him. He can shock right outta my life and never come back—and see if I care. Him and his jealousy. It gets boring. If you hadn't told me how wonderful Norm was, he'dda been out on his ear long ago. I been too good to him because I was sorry for him, and now he thinks he's my boss."

When Evelyn came up at nine, she, too, had been drinking. "Golly," she said, "you can't mind. The tension of last week was too strenuous. Anyway, I didn't drink too much. And if Janice doesn't get tight too you can consider yourself lucky." And I felt there was justice to what she said and held my tongue.

June 4 A small ride, with the air as bright and shining and crystal cool as on a day in Maine. Not so tired as yesterday. Been talking to the girl, Patricia Boland, tall, auburn hair, greenish eyes, color in cheeks, white teeth, not pretty but a thought handsome, seventeen, precocious, from a town in southern Connecticut, a Freshman at Boston University. Wishes to become a doctor eventually. Evelyn gone for walk. As soon as I eat, shall go to bed, there listen to a roundup described from somewhere in the West.

June 6 Well, the invasion of the European Continent began early today, frankly to my surprise, I having become accustomed to procrastination on that score. Americans, Canadians and British (?), preceded by landings of parachute troopers, made a couple of beachheads at or near Le Havre and Cherbourg. Opposition in the air and from antiaircraft fire was almost negligible. A great armada, preponderantly British, but not so much so as might have been expected, ferried invasion forces and supplies from the south of England. Small submarines preceded the sea forces and marked channels for invasion. News now is fairly thin. Fighting at first should be slight in volume. There are the beachheads to be consolidated. Perhaps another beachhead near Dieppe will be attempted, so as to control the terminals of three main lines to Paris. The real test is ahead. General Montgomery, he with the face and coloration so startlingly resembling Eddie Simms, leads the assault.

June 7 Sanctimoniously, unctuously and mellifluously, the prayer in the voice of Franklin D. Roosevelt issued from the radio, and my reaction amused me. I could not believe that a full-grown man in the maturity of what mind he possesses could himself be credulous of such claptrap, nor feel that the words were sincere, and I was repelled by the nonsense of them. I wished wholeheartedly to turn off the switch and have done with such double-talk, yet was restrained by a curiosity to solve the problem of how a man who had sent the people he ruled forth to war and death and suffering could yet so wholly absolve himself of culpability as to invoke the help of God in the movement he had fostered.

June 12 Patricia Boland here to help us yesterday morning. Were she anything else but Irish, I'd like her wholeheartedly. She is pleasant, easy to talk with and to look at, adaptable. As it is, I wait to see which way the Killarney cat will jump. Her hair is beautiful, long, over her shoulders, and auburn with glints of gold and red alternating, a cascade to please the eyes. Reminds me of Jennie's hair but not so ruddy or so long, not so fine. She reading diligently a large volume of 'Anna Karenina.' A diligent reader. Gets all 'A's' in studies. She is coming to spend the evening with me. Evelyn thinks her fascinating. Janice considers that she "puts on airs."

June 13 Patricia Boland spent the evening with me reading and talking. Her father was publicity man for a number of motion picture actors and actresses. He died when she was four. Her mother put her in a boarding kindergarten and went to work. Within two years, her mother had met and married a civil engineer of German descent. Patricia's mother is of English descent and a Protestant. She has had three children by her second husband. Patricia takes care of them when at home. The family has lived at various places on Long Island and in Connecticut and now has a small house in Reading, a town of about two thousand population. There Patricia attended high school. Her stepfather works at New England Telephone in Bridgeport. He has stomach trouble. And that is Patricia's background. She was on the rifle team at school. Being in the sun causes her to feel dizzy. Snow reflection bothers her. She does not tan. She reads endlessly, not by plan as much as by preference though with an eye always on the classics. She enjoys studying mathematics. She does her studying from six o'clock on in the morning. She plans on seven hours sleep a night. The color in her cheeks is her own. She weighs 145 pounds, does not look it. She endeavors with eagerness to please me. She pronounces words correctly. I foresee someone I can teach, develop, make into an even more attractive person. She is shy despite her outward poise.

June 15 Norm spent most of the day with Pearl, having persuaded those in charge of his case at the Chelsea Naval Hospital to permit him to be an ambulatory patient. He's an affable fellow to meet. He talks readily and sometimes interestingly. He knows exceptionally little about women. He's jealous of Pearl to the point of losing his head at times. Jealousy catches him and pushes him around just as hate and desire for revenge do me, save that he hasn't the control or the wish to master himself. He issues ultimatums to Pearl. One of these days he will issue one too many and find himself out on his ear.

June 16   General Charles de Gaulle has by sheer stubbornness of purpose, political maneuvering, arrogance — a few people say by charm — become the actual head of the French Government. It is evident that he feels himself endowed with a mission, a male Jeanne d'Arc. His nature disdains compromise. It is said that he is outspoken with his betters, Churchill and Roosevelt, neither catering to them nor flattering them, dealing with them rather as an equal and the representative of the French people. As a result, they shunt him to one side whenever possible.

It is my guess that de Gaulle will have to be given table room at least, and it may be (if the French adhere to him) Churchill and Roosevelt will in the end have to recognize him as someone of political potence and treat him with honor and equality. In the meanwhile the stand of England and the United States against de Gaulle cannot endear us to the French.

June 27   The Republican Convention is on in Chicago. It seems like Dewey, hands down. Governor Warren of California is favored for Vice-President. Should he turn it down and should Governor Bricker refuse it, there is talk about Senator Harry Byrd. For my money, Byrd would be wonderful, the one truly honest Senator I know. Dewey is the only chance to defeat Roosevelt really, for he is the sole candidate with a vigorous radio presence. Nationwide polls gave the Republicans an even chance of defeating Roosevelt. My opinion on the matter — which I'm sure is worthless — is that no one can defeat Roosevelt. Anyway, Churchill said that a reelected Roosevelt and a Republican Congress, which latter seems fairly sure, would be the worse thing possible for Britain so that I might be reconciled to Roosevelt if such is really the case.

June 28   I dreamed last night, this. I was in a huge basement shower room. Scores of naked men were walking about. Steam was curdling the air. Water fell from the showers. Along the aisles between the showers walked the two Machs, notebooks in hands. Into each shower cubby they peered. Dictatorially, they announced: "You, you can have no more soap. You're using it up." "You, turn off the water. You're washed. It's being wasted."

Sometimes they were obeyed. Sometimes they were ignored. Usually they were obeyed. I followed them upon their trip of inspection. Presently, alternate showers were occupied by women. They looked strange to me for some reason. I asked: "Why do you let the women bathe right with the men? So many naked men. So many naked women. Aren't you afraid of the consequences?" "Of course not," they explained with condescension. "The women, if you will observe, are sealed off where it is important." I observed as bid, and sure enough the private parts of every female were like the private parts of the marble statuary in any Victorian art gallery. "You see," they said, "it's cheaper this way. We have to keep only one shower room. If we had a shower room for men and another for women, why, we'd lose money or make less. So we seal the women off. It's simple. It's effective. It's profitable."

July 3 Pearl talked of "when I marry Norm." That, I told her, was her business. Personally, I'd be bored with him to the point of murder. And I wouldn't endure his jealousy. When Norm was a boy, his pony kicked him in the testicles. He now has only one and doesn't know whether he can have children. His divorced wife is angling for him. He told his mother he wouldn't marry her again and, moreover, when he came to live at home, wanted one floor to himself. Pearl spurred him on to do that.

July 4 Pearl said: "You might as well know it. I intend to get married in December. I know he's jealous. But so'm I. If we fight too much, we can leave each other." It sounds like a mighty questionable basis for marriage.

July 5 [From Patricia:]

You really should have been around for my operation. I thought every one in Camp Polk was going to be in on it. The operating room looked like the Grand Central Station. I had four doctors. One to operate, one to assist, one for the anesthesia & the fourth just kibitzed. I never did find out what he was supposed to do. Then there were 3 nurses, a stenographer, various errand boys & the boy who took my stretcher to surgery & hold my hand. It was quite a levee. And outside of a bad ten minutes with nausea I had a swell time.

They took out the uterus, one tube, the appendix & the womb — besides a tumor as big as a large grape fruit & one the size of a lemon. I saw the operative report & it was listed on 3 operations. They let me see the tumor & it looked like pink & white coral. Not at all repulsive, I was glad to see it as it set my mind at ease about cancer. Cancer is a soft gray mass, you couldnt miss it. I felt wonderfully coming back & grinned like a Cheshire cat at all the G.Is in the corridor. They were terribly intrigued because I was a woman patient. I sent for Paul right away as I wanted him to see me before the spinal had worn away & the morphine had taken effect, as I knew if he saw me so lively it would mean much more than a verbal report. He just couldn't get over it & went around muttering about the miracles of modern surgery. My doctor says that the main reason for my quick recovery was my attitude, since I knew exactly what had to be done and went to it without misgiving. I never did feel frightened not even in the surgery, so that helped a lot, I've had no post operative pains at all, just the plumbing dismantled.

I was afraid that my sexual life would be harmed, but the doctor says that to the contrary I'll be more avid than ever—aint that somepthin. I do regret tho not being able to have a baby. I did want a little girl, but Paul says I can adopt one after the war. Army people can't get them now, too much of a risk.

July 16 This morning dictated to a slightly supercilious Patricia Boland, she feeling evidently that what I was writing was trivial or foolish or contrary to her views, as the case was. Her sense of whimsy is sparse, and what there is of it I shall attempt to cultivate. I enjoy looking at her. Her eyes, though I didn't think so at first, are really beautiful. She's neat, clean, efficient in many ways. No one makes my lunches look so attractive. She keeps the kitchen as clean as a whistle. Whether she likes me or not, I have no idea, save that she wears clothes to please me, which with a female is usually the signal that you have made first base anyway. She reads me her boy friends' letters. Such large words the youngsters of nowadays use.

Dictating to Evelyn now, after she has looked out the window at what never ceases to interest her, the weather, and pronounced: "It's clouding over. It's the hurricane from off the North Carolina capes, messing around and switching its tail at us."

August 8 The city of Florence is being fought for by the Allies with the Germans defending it, despite their declaration that it was an "open city." Neither one side nor the other is usually willing to make strategic military concessions to artistic and cultural monuments which happen to be in the way. Each side blames the other for the fate that befalls these monuments. Not the loss of a million Americans could ever injure and set back the spirit of mankind as much as, say, the irreparable destruction of Florence. And if this sounds cold-blooded, it is so nevertheless. Destroy men's lives, and you do not necessarily destroy the level of their culture. Destroy their cultural monuments, and you deplete the aesthetic reserves of their civilization.

August 11 I was talking with Patricia. Evelyn came in and joined us. "I had a wonderful swim," she enthused. "The waves were high. They curled. Dr. Pike dived through, but I didn't. Back in Boston, I took him to the Esplanade Concert. I said to him: 'I want you to see this phase of the American character. You wouldn't believe that so many thousands of people could be so well-behaved and polite.' I said to him: 'It's something you ought to see.' So we paid ten cents a chair and sat down to listen. The wind was blowing too hard to hear the music from where we were. The people were orderly and nicely dressed. It was twilight and the big orchestra shell was lit. The sky was light and high and colored faintly in the west. Shroud lights were on the little sailboats in the basin, and they bobbed and pivoted as they scudded along. Overhead, wild ducks passed to light on the water. That excited Dr. Pike. He forgot everything else. 'Bang!' he'd whisper. 'Bang. Those fellows there— you'd shoot just under them. And those there—twenty feet ahead. I'll bet they came from Dorchester Bay. I bet they flew over here just to tantalize me.'"

August 13 If I were twenty-two, I could become infatuated with Patricia. Her shyness is wearing away, and she is being more talkative and less restrained. I gave her a green ribbon for her hair and some green beads Evelyn used to have. With her hair parted in the middle and the green ribbon around it, she's really pretty. I like to sit and look at her.

We spent some time in the less hot library. She is fascinated by books. She came across an old one I hadn't seen since the twenties. It was something about the practice of male and female circumcision, and it was I, not she, who felt ill at ease. "My," she teased, "what strange books you have." Like her more than anyone I have met for a long time. I gave her a 'Three Moods.' Always I feel shy when giving anyone one of my books. She probably won't like it, for she is of the Hemingway school which favors short utilitarian works.

August 27 It's rather easy to understand why foreigners of a certain type get along so well in the United States, aside from the fact that they are willing to outwork the average American. I guess they deserve what they get if you look at it one way, but I'd rather not have what they get if I had to travel the road they do to get it. Which is why they will own us presently until we finally smash them to earth, our long-suffering tolerance gone. It is to be hoped that we do not wait too long.

August 30 An article to 'The New York Times' from William

Lawrence dated Lublin, Poland, describes the mass killings of Jews and Poles which took place in the concentration camp of Maidenek nearby when the Germans were in power. A million and a half prisoners, Lawrence states, were put to torture and death at Maidenek by asphyxiation, by shooting, by other methods. Some of the bodies were burned to ashes in great furnaces. There were collective burials of others. "This is," writes Lawrence, "a place that must be seen to be believed . . . never have I been confronted with such complete evidence clearly establishing every allegation made of German crimes." And I, an American, still find it in my heart difficult to credit such assertions of evidence, preferring to regard them as at the least exaggerations.

I think that we in America must by now admit at least the quasi-reality of the German cruelty; and its quasi-reality is sufficient to justify our abhorrence of Nazi culture, if not our crusade overseas in aid of a nation, Russia, which has practiced cruelties alongside of which the German cruelties are as child's play. It is no wonder that fighting against a cruel and ruthless enemy at the side of a still more cruel and ruthless ally, we are ethically and morally confused, wish above all else to be out of war and home again.

September 4 I become, due to Evelyn's reminders that a man of my age has no business to become too fond of girls of Patsy's age, exceedingly self-conscious not only about liking them but also about writing down my reactions concerning them. Does it seem trivial to devote pages to them? Do I sound silly becoming, at my age, intent upon them? I don't feel my age in that direction.

So for good or bad, I continue, as did Shadrach Inman, my interest in attractive females until I am too old to win them or too sterile to consider them which will be, as Shadrach put it, when I die. To hell with criticisms. Self-consciousness can be ignored. And readers of these pages are just as likely to be intrigued by peccadillos of a trivial nature as by weighty considerations of mighty matters. There's not too much in my existence that gives me pleasure and reassurance, and the companionship, enduring if possible, of attractive youngsters is one of them. I have, I suspect, a fairly large paternal side to my nature which they satisfy. And they are acolytes to inculcate with new conceptions of how to meet life effectively. And I remember well how greatly I should have been aided by someone evincing a constructive interest in my affair. So for better or worse, bring on the girls and make them attractive and make them devoted to me. Anyway, this is woman's era in the United States, so that it is not improper that their activities and selves be given prominence.

September 5   I am forty-nine. There is no hope in my heart that I shall ever recover from a state of limited semi-invalidism.

My day is divided somewhat as follows. The curtains in my bedroom are dropped some fifty minutes before sunrise to keep the room dark so that I may avoid headaches. Breakfast is at 6:30 A.M., after which I wash and go back to bed until 8:10 A.M., when I get up. I ride at nine or ten for varying amounts, after having scanned the newspapers, listened to the news and waltzes on the radio, perhaps written in here without using my glasses, though I use them when driving. On returning home, I eat something, work, dictate, write in here. Lunch comes shortly after noon. I nap in my darkened room for a few minutes around one o'clock. Then Janice massages the soft tissue in my neck. With myself still in the dark and Evelyn or Janice on the other side of a curtain where the light is, I correct from three until shortly before six. Then I play the talking-book and the radio until 7:15 P.M., when Fulton Lewis' talk ends, when I eat supper. Thereafter, I listen to the radio, the talking-book or am read to or talked to for the evening, which extends until midnight or twelve-thirty.

My principal pleasure consists of writing in here, correcting, studying. I cannot work a tithe of the time I would wish to. I have no faith in God, the reality of progress, the predominance of good. I feel myself born under an unlucky star. I value my friends. I place more value upon money than formerly. I fear many things up to a certain point — always anticipating trouble and usually getting it. People, by and large, are very good to me, and I strive to return as I am able their affection and their efforts in my behalf. I am bitter and disillusioned with existence and wait for it to end but until it does attempt to achieve some measure of normality, to be cheerful and equable.

September 9   Have been talking with Pearl about this holiday she demands. It is a principle of mine that when you are cornered and there appears to be no means of evasion or channel of escape, you might as well not only yield to the inevitable but yield gracefully and with apparent generosity. The principle has been adhered to in this case. Who can foresee when or how I may need her help after she has left, and she might as well leave fond of me. "You still," I queried, "intend to marry Norm?" She replied that she did. They have ten thousand dollars in cash, his mother's garage at a minimum rent, a promise of the Chevrolet agency after the war. Maybe they can make a go of it together. I hope so, though surprised I shall be if they do.

September 17   Repeatedly it occurs to me that this world would be a less obnoxious place to live in with fewer inhabitants crowding the productive areas. Let cities be bombed to rubble as long as it is not my city that is under attack. Let earthquakes destroy, plagues ravish, civil conflicts decimate, as long as they do not directly affect me. The more men destroyed, the better. And although I still regret the various sufferings of humanity, I am less troubled by them than formerly. Take a swab; be God; wipe away a third, a half, two-thirds of us, of all human beings, like a boy erasing chalk marks from a blackboard. If I am annulled with the others, what matter, really? A roomier world will be available for those remaining. And while at it, break all scientific achievement, expurgate all scientific knowledge. Be ruthless. Turn the clocks back. We are, I greatly fear, upon the wrong highroad.

September 18   I wish I would refrain from exposing myself as I did yesterday. I have no wish to antagonize possible readers, and after all, it could have been said (I was tired and out of sorts) with more moderation. It's myself, though, to feel intensely.

September 22   Mrs. Trench has been here helping us for a couple of mornings. No one seems to care much for her. They say she's too slow and unsure of herself. I rather like her. She's gentle; she cooks well; and she apparently has taken a fancy to me. The other day she fumbled in her voluminous shopping bag, pulled out a wilted zinnia and handed it to me with: "A flower for you." She is divorced. One daughter is married. The other works at Station W.E.E.I. daytimes and teaches dancing at the Arthur Murray Studios evenings. This afternoon Mrs. Trench is to do shopping downtown for us.

September 28   The war must be mentioned, I suppose. The great German defense zone, the Siegfried Line, appears to be holding. No longer can it be suspected that the Germans may of their own will permit the Americans to invade Germany and take over in order to avoid invasion by the Communists of Russia. Gone are the weak troops who manned the outer fortifications of the Siegfried Line, and now our soldiers are face to face with premier quality fighters. This all means that tremendous supplies and probably considerable reinforcements will have to be brought up to support any major attempt of the Allies to break through into Germany. The volatile American public now foresees the end of the war a long way off. Not necessarily so, I still think.

September 30   Evelyn has turned over a new leaf, as the old expression has it, since she drank too much last time. As far as I know, she hasn't touched a drop. "I like it," she says. "It makes me feel better. I assure you I'm not proud of myself when something like that happens. I'm going to be a new person. You just wait." And she has been in general less contentious and argumentative. Often she asserts, "I'll try," but usually that's as far as it goes. This time she's indisputably been putting her mind to being sweet. It certainly pays insofar as I am concerned. Right now she is upset by the responsibility of getting answers to the lists of questions I have prepared for her to put to various persons in Atlanta, but that is, I hope, temporary.

October 1   Sat in the railroad yards by the lumber piles in my iron chair. It was quiet, save for the puffing of engines, and private. The east wind blew. The sun shone, went under clouds, shone again. The new lumber gave off its acrid odor. Dry weeds rustled. In the warm space between the ties of the siding where I was sitting, crickets chirped. Evelyn walked back and forth, peering at the structure of the red freight cars, poking the lumber, squatting to study the crickets making their stridulations. A lovely day on which to be alive were one more of what a man should be. I felt inordinately sad.

It is when Evelyn prepares to leave me for some length of time that I realize in full how much she means to me. I am very little by myself. Without friends, without money, I should be as helpless as a scarecrow waving in a frosty wind.

October 5   Roosevelt speaks again tonight and Dewey at the end of the week. Dewey, I fear, is more or less of a flop, with betting odds two to one against him. My idea of him is that he is an energetic twirp with a reasonable if nebulous home policy and a foreign policy synonymous with Roosevelt's.

The impending problem of finding someone to take Pearl's place keeps me jittery and gives me nightmares. If only I could take long rides in the Baby-Carriage. It is depressing to dwell in a city and never leave it, less depressing than to dwell in the country and never leave it — but depressing.

October 6   I walked into a room where Pearl had been spending the night with Stella, her cousin. They were both stark-naked. "Give him a kiss," Pearl suggested. Stella came over to me and put her arms around my neck. "How about all the young men in the other room?" I remarked. "I'm an old fellow." "You look good to me," she smirked, and I knew she was lying. She kissed me with her open mouth. I felt excited, was disgusted. Pearl sat on the bed without clothes and laughed and laughed.

When she finally awakened me from my night of four hours' sleep, I told her the dream, and she laughed what seemed just as heartily and said: "I gotta leave you now and put my girdle on. I guess you dreamed that because you walked in on me in the bathroom yesterday." "Yes," I said, "it was impressive, your sitting plump on the toilet. And Norm's expression when I came out was

Franklin Delano Roosevelt (Roosie the Rat) with Mayor James Michael Curley (right) and unidentified man, 1934

"Ready for Impeachment Proceedings — Daniel H. Coakley, member of the Governor's Council, as he went before the state Senate today as defendant in the state's first impeachment trial in 120 years." Boston *Traveler*, August 5, 1941

Arthur at 44, in the summer of 1939

Arthur and Evelyn in the Baby-Carriage, 1940. Fearful that reflecting light would damage his sensitive eyes, Arthur had his 1919 Cadillac painted a dull black.

Arthur at 45, 1940

The diarist in the 1950s

Arthur's Boston, c. 1960, on the eve of the great demolition and the erection of the Prudential Center. 1. Garrison Hall. 2. Railroad yard, site of future Prudential development. 3. Christian Science church. 4. Mechanics Hall. 5. Huntington Avenue. 6. Convention Hall. 7. Copley Square. 8. Boston Public Library.

"Never is the worry and dread of the Prudential Center and the proposed six-lane, toll-road expressway off my mind." *Diary,* December 8, 1960

"Lewdly, the high control crane, its heavy ball dependent, sways, comes purposefully, bangs into concrete reinforced by steel. Dust arises. Windows no one cared to save splintered." *Diary,* September 19, 1962

William F. Callahan at work, c. 1960. "Killing's too good for the likes of him as the saying aptly puts it." *Diary,* January 18, 1963

A page from the handwritten Diary, August 20, 1942. Compared to the virtually illegible handwriting of the later Diary volumes, this page is not hard to decipher.

not the homelovers they might be had they less education.

We Americans are a migratory people. We do not love land for land's sake, the invariable basis for the foundation of an enduring nation. If women loved their homes more, as homes, would not their sons also do likewise; come to tender an enduring affection to the place of their birth? Wherefore should not woman give over grasping after stars she may never attain; pay moot attention to that which is her natural consignment on earth; be more mother, chatelaine, hostess, social ambassador, mistress; less a self-conscious reasoner of transitory reasons which never eventuate?

Afternoon- A little after noon the wind came up strongly east. The temperature dropped 40° inside of an hour. We went out riding, since it had clouded, to South Boston again. The beaches were virtually deserted. The streetcars were being mobbed by crowds as eager to return home as they had been in the hot morning to start out. Always an interesting sight, to witness the precipitate emptying of a beach. Wished I might have gone out on the bay in a motorboat. So many tall ships in the harbor! So many white-capped waves! So many seagulls crying the joy of riding the east wind!

I came home and packed for Maine.

June 8-Boston- Downtown to inquire about gasoline pumps, generators, electric pumps, etc. I can install a water system complete for around four hundred. A combined water and electric system would cost around a thousand. Undoubtedly the latter costs more than I can afford, but it certainly would be convenient.

Downtown Boston still interests me as it did when as a child I used to tramp all day its queer ins and outs. I like the noise, the hurry, the bustle. I like the smell of burnt coffee, leather, fish, tarred rope. I like the rickety old elevated curving above Atlantic Avenue, tesselating the cobblestones of the street with white sunshine and black shadow. I like the odd little buildings of wood so unexpectedly interjected between the substantial stone and concrete edifices of today. I like the hurry, the bustle, the apparent confusion in reality so nicely composed of intricate order. I like to look into the different windows of the different shops, marine hardware, electric motors, wholesale china, stationery, leather goods, twine and rope, coffee and tea, paints. I like to catch, now and again, a glimpse, past old wooden wharves, of Boston Harbor with, say, the Charlestown Navy Yard in the distance, tall steel masts against a cloudy sky.

Within a circumference surrounding Faneuil Hall, the traffic jams into long compacted lines of impatient vehicles. In one of these rush-hour congestions we were caught, held, impotent to move. Motors chugged, throbbed, idled. Horses dropped restless steel hoofs upon resounding stone cobbles. Men shouted, or sat quiet in resigned impatience. Now and again one of them, more unquiet than the rest, would commence upon his klaxon a cacophany against inactivity. His

A page from the typed Diary, June 8, 1925. Arthur was in the habit of correcting the handwritten volume — that is, changing a word here and there and fiddling with the punctuation — before having it typed by one of his secretaries.

Evelyn and Lolo, 1953

priceless." "I told him," she laughed, "how embarrassed you were. You—embarrassed. But what else could I tell him?" We both laughed. I thought how pleasant she could be, and the night miasmas began to lift.

October 7 Claire has arrived. She is as skinny as a rail. The top of her spine has a large bend in it. Her arms and legs are toothpicks. Her face is long. There are dark circles under her eyes from riding on the bus all night. She coughs continually. Her front teeth are commencing to discolor. The dress she wears is sleeveless and simply God awful, perhaps all right for Florida beaches but not for Boston certainly. Her hair is pretty, her manner pert, her self-confidence apparent. She has shaved under one arm but forgotten to shave under the other. She resembles a consumptive. I am pleased to see her but aghast at her looks and impressed again within my own mind at how much looks mean to me. To be baldly blunt, I'd be several times more glad to see Claire were she several times more attractive to look at. Which means, I suppose, that I am a rank materialist or a pushover for looks. Perhaps I should be ashamed of feeling as I do but decidedly am not.

Mrs. Trench comes in. Evelyn declares that her hair is dyed. The bridgework on her teeth shows when she smiles, and the plastic supporting it fails to match her gums. Nevertheless, I consider her on certain days rather attractive. Her hair arranges itself. She rouges her white skin artistically. Her eyes, when not sad, are merry. She has a soft and pleasant voice and a weakness for me. A very proper lady intent upon remaining proper is Mrs. Trench. "What's your first name?" I ask. "My first name?" I can sense her reluctance to tell me, a stranger. "Yes," I say, and repeat: "What is it?" "Rose," she says, and blushes. Knowing beforehand what the response will be, I inquire: "Then may I call you Rose?" Her feet assume attitudes of embarrassment. "I'm afraid not," she says. "Why not?" I ask. "Because I guess I'm old-fashioned about a lot of things." Her eyes twinkle. "I wear more underthings than most people do. Once my daughter got me into a light evening dress and out of some of my underclothes. Everyone complimented me on my figure and a man kissed me, and after that I returned to my regular underthings. It's the way I am, I suppose."

Dr. Pike tossed his hat on the chair, directed me to lie face up on the treatment-table. He felt my insides. "Boggy," he stated. Then with his long, supple fingers he molded the intestines to the conformation in which they should be, restoring the circulation and slowing the peristaltic action. That done, he placed me on my face, stimulated the spinal nerves controlling the intestines by gentle, firm pressure. "That," he concluded, "should help, Arthur. There's a lot of this intestinal flu going the rounds — makes you miserable, a slight fever. You keep going, it hangs on."

October 8   Claire likes Florida. She has asthma seriously and has had to move houses four times, but other than that is satisfied. She enjoys the people. She evidently is enjoying for the first time a certain social status. Sam is away, and "To be truthful — thank God I can always be honest with you, Arthur — while I occasionally miss him (the call of the flesh, probably), in the main it's just as though a burden were off my shoulders. I had so many horrible experiences with him, and however other women feel about that sort of thing, I can't ever quite forget them. I never have to worry now about his stumbling in drunk. I never have to gird up my loins to give him the dickens or prepare my mind to baby him. I've been at fault, I know, not to have dissembled more, not to have been more motherly so to say, not to have jollied and scolded at the proper moments. But, Arthur, whether you understand it or not, I wanted a responsible father, not a fourth child and an irresponsible one into the bargain. So I'm just as contented that he's away and — as terrible as it may sound — don't care how long he stays. He sends me loving letters and money, and that is as it should be. Perhaps I like him better where and how he is. And by the way, he's been in Western Australia with my brother, Bruce. He says that Bruce is a wonderful chap. As for life in the Merchant Marine, Sam is completely fed up in it."

It is virtually impossible to put down on paper the steps by which a man of my age views the affections of a girl of Patsy's age without sounding like Casanova or like a satyr, neither of which I am. So perhaps I'd best leave the matter mostly to the imagination of the reader and let him guess correctly or wrongly.

October 10   Willkie died a few days ago, and I, for one, felt relieved. He was, it is said, about ready to support Roosevelt's campaign for a fourth term by throwing to him his not inconsiderable following of idealists and dreamers. It is better for the nation that he is dead. He wasn't very bright, though perhaps honest in a woolgathering sort of way. He was impractical and out-Rooseveltd Roosevelt in his ideals. And here again let me state unequivocally that no ruler, no character in high places can do more harm to a people than the wide-eyed idealist; and the more impractical he is the more harm he can do.

It is my feeling, borne out by photographs as well as by certain undercover rumors, that something has happened to Roosevelt's buoyant health. Some sickness visited him last spring. We were told it was a severe cold infection. Perhaps it was. Perhaps, though, it was a stroke, for he has that look in his photographs. It would be the repetitive hand of Fate striking were he to vanish from the scene à la Wilson. He is, to me, still a horrible man, 'the limper,' as vicious to civilization in his way as was Timur the Lame in his, an overlord who has depleted by his preachments and reforms, his philosophies and doles, his unstable tamperings with the foundations of our social and economic structure, the moral balance of the American people and thrown them needlessly into a great and exhausting war, subsequently signing us over without thought of recompense to do the major portion of the sustaining of a struggle not justifiably ours. He has caused to be wasted and given away to foreign peoples who mock at us a considerable portion of our heritage and wealth and natural resources.

October 11   Much of my life has been cast with people born in the astrological month of February or in the environs of that month — my Father, Sam, Evelyn, Pearl, Billy and others. Patsy was born on the 13th. Persons with their births in that month appear to have in common a certain defensive stubbornness, a certain spontaneous resistance against pressure, and is some cases a certain negativity of outlook. Think I'll get some horoscope books from the library and read up on February people. Might learn something.

Mrs. Carson (who used to work at Homer Dark's, who is cheap, whose husband went into training and was let out because of his physical condition) complained to Pearl about Mrs. Kelly. Her story was that Mrs. Kelly came in late every night and with a different man, and that she and the man took baths together in the bathroom which is directly behind her bedroom wall, and aside from any moral significance they were noisy and kept her awake. Would I, she inquired, do something? I left a note for Mrs. Kelly. She came in last evening while I was talking with Patsy. She was very drunk. She's cheap anyway, almost as cheap as Mrs. Carson, but more genuine. I was tactful. "Oh," she said thickly, "that's my husband." Whether her husband or a chain of men, I appeared to believe her utterly.

Her story. John, her husband, had become interested in another woman. They had separated. But she still loved him. A woman couldn't help loving the man she loved, could she? He had been away in the Merchant Marine for months. Now he was back and living with her. She wanted to make him happy while he was ashore. She had persuaded him to take a month's course. He was doing that now, a cram course. He would be gone soon. Until he did, they were enjoying themselves. She would be extra quiet from now on. That woman (Mrs. Carson) played the piano awful anyway. But she didn't want to make any trouble for me with the Jews who managed the apartment house; they hated my guts. She held my hand and patted it affectionately. She had trouble finding her way out. I guided her plump self to the door. I rather like her, odd-looking as she is, drunken, liar, rapscallion but friendly, genuine, good-hearted. Patsy and Pearl laughed heartily at my tale of what had happened.

October 12 I was lying full length on the treatment-table in the long hallway chatting inconsequentially with Pearl when she returned at suppertime. She had been in high spirits all day. We were laughing. "Is Norm in the other room?" I asked. She replied that he was. That morning he had showed me the Purple Heart decoration he had received for having been wounded in battle. "You know," I whispered, "that guy's handsome enough to stand a lot from."

Bang — the door flew open. "Come on, Pearly." An almost maniacal Norm screamed (he had obviously been listening at the keyhole): "I ain't going to stand no more of this crap. You get your clothes together. We're going to get the hell out of here. And I don't want no back talk." "What's the matter with you?" Pearl asked. He grabbed her roughly by the arm. "You come with me. Another minute and I'll knock shit out of that goddamn bastard there. I've had enough of this crap. Come on now."

And she went. And I lay there half expecting to be beat up, resolved, since I had no strength anyway, to be supine if it occurred. To get my gun and shoot the half-mad fellow would only land me in jail. I waited. My heart thumped.

In ten or fifteen minutes, Pearl returned. "He says I've got to get out of here. He says either I get out of here or he'll leave me for good. What am I to do, Arthur? I can't leave you this way. Yet I can't refuse to go and wreck the rest of my life. What should I do?" She was sincere, stripped of pose and pretensions. "Go back and talk to him again," I suggested, "he must have some sense somewhere." "You don't know him," she said. "He can't control himself. He told me if I wasn't back within three minutes he'd be after me, and he meant it."

She went to talk to him again, only to return defeated. "I can't do a thing with him, Arthur. He says I've got to leave. What shall I do?" "Well," I said, "do what your conscience tells you, I suppose. I'll get along. If it's the life you want, I can't ruin it for you." "Then I'll go. Will you call up Janice?" "And have her husband at my heels? No. Anyway, she's tired. Let her rest. Call up Millicent for me." "He won't let me. I've got to pack and get out." "You mean to say he won't even let you see that I'm in other hands?" "No. Arthur," she said, "it makes me sick all over to leave you this way. I hadn't planned it. What will you do?" "I don't know," I said, "but I'll get along somehow. It breaks my heart to cut short Evelyn's trip. Yes, it's all too bad. But I want to thank you for taking care of me since Billy left. I don't know what I'd have done without you." "Gee," she said, "you're so sweet about it all." "Well," I concluded, "it's the way I feel about you, I guess." And she left with: "God knows when I'll see you again." I pitied her from the bottom of my heart, being acquiescent to that cheap little fellow.

I telephoned Millicent. Yes, she would be over as soon as possible. Yes, she would spend the night here. She wouldn't let me down. What were friends for? She arrived in time to keep me from starving, I being ravenous from emotional upset. She talked to me. She telephoned Washington for me. It was very difficult for me to tell Evelyn that I needed her and couldn't see how she could take the trip to Maine. She all but cried. She couldn't come until the next day, she said, as no night accommodations were available. But she would be here then, unless I wished her to sit up all night, which she would do. I said no emphatically to that.

I spent a fiendish night. I couldn't get to sleep because of the emotional upset, and when finally I dropped off, it was to wake and stay awake so I wouldn't sleep into the light and get a headache and not be able to handle things during the day. Millicent slept right through two big alarm clocks and my bell jangling. She got my breakfast — finally. I slept half an hour afterwards, no more, for my hands and sciatica ached from overstrain. Total sleep, two hours.

Evelyn returned shortly after ten, jittery, naturally. I attempted to reassure her. Another change of plans and a continuance of her trip wasn't to her liking. "I've got my mind all set this way now." She was pleased that I had things arranged somewhat. "You're just like a cat," she said to me. "If you fall far enough you almost invariably fall on your feet. It's only when you fall a short distance that you get tangled."

Evelyn chattered about Atlanta. She dislikes the people there. "They're liars, practically every one of them. They all say 'yes.' They don't seem genuine. And they all fairly worship Roosevelt. It's like Joe said, they live on the surface. They're pleasant, and I don't believe the Southern women are as pressed and jumpy as many Northern women are. But I don't like them, generally speaking. I became so weary of saying 'yes' to everything that I wanted to poke them. And at that I didn't say 'yes' as much as I should have. I don't think I'm cut out for Southern life. 'The Inmans in Atlanta,' Aunt Louise asserted, 'belong to a past generation. All that remains are their good name and their credit.' She could, she said, get a check cashed because her name was Inman any place from New York to the tip of Florida."

October 16 It makes me laugh that I should like Patsy so much. She is, in many ways, a young duplicate of Evelyn, stubborn, perverse, reluctant to say complimentary things, chary in expressing emotion, yet fascinating nevertheless and doing for me a hundredfold more than her words would ever lead me to suspect. An astrological book says that February people are so firm within themselves that they never realize how other people are strengthened and cheered by expressions of affection. Patsy took dictation, typed letters, cooked lunch, searched for some lost items in my jackdaws' nest of a library, washed my hair, treated my neck, told me stories, kissed me goodbye as coolly as though she were putting a pot on the stove to cook. She wasn't pretty yesterday. I forget how immature she is sometimes, so carefully she sits. No boy, she told me, ever attempted to touch her legs, her breasts. "I was too fat and healthy. Do you think I missed something, Arthur?" When, in a romantic moment, I asked her if she'd like me to send her some roses, she made precisely the reply Evelyn had earlier in the day—"I'd rather have a potted plant. It lasts longer."

October 21 It is always difficult to extract from Evelyn stories of what she did while away. If you can sit her down immediately she returns and let her talk for three hours, you can find out something. But when time passes and you attempt to wheedle her into further conversation, it comes reluctantly and not very vividly, even with contradictions. This morning I have been pumping her on Aunt Louise, with only moderate results I fear.

Aunt Louise has been in innumerable automobile accidents with most of the bones in her body broken at one time or another. But, as she puts it, "God has saved me for his own purpose here on earth."

She told Evelyn the following story: "You know, Evelyn, I had a revelation. I woke up in the middle of the night and I knew that I must sell my house. I realized it for what it was, a revelation. So I woke Frank and said to him: 'Frank I've had a revelation. I'm going to sell the house.' The next morning I went to a real estate man I knew. I said to him: 'I want to sell my house. I've had a revelation. You'll get a good price for it.' It was just two months before Pearl Harbor, and I knew that when we got into a war it would be hard to find servants for such a big house. The real estate man found a buyer at once. He said to me: 'Mrs. Inman, what will you do when the house has been sold? Where will you live?' 'I don't know,' I said, 'but God will provide. God will not leave me roofless. God has always put out a hand to care for me, and He won't abandon me now.' We got a fancy price for the house. Then I told the real estate man what sort of house I wanted to buy—all the specifications—just what I wanted. 'Mrs. Inman,' he said, 'there isn't a house like that in Atlanta.' I said to him: 'You go look. You'll find it. God will let you find it for me.' So the very next day when he was selling a house he heard of another house for sale, and when he looked at it, it was just what I wanted, just exactly what I wanted. The woman who owned it asked too much for it. 'You go back to her,' I said to the real estate man, 'I've had another revelation. She'll come down on her price.' And she did, three thousand dollars. And we bought it. And we love it. And I made a handsome profit because I did just what God told me to do. You know, Evelyn," she concluded, "God does watch over me. Perhaps it's His will to keep me alive through accident and adversity in order to take care of my two grown-up children, Frank and Henry."

October 24   Do not miss Pearl, merely what she did for me. My existence is much gentler without her. I have a hunch I'll see her again one of these days. She won't be able to live with that oaf unless she can swallow her self-respect or subdue him, either of which is possible.

October 26   It is as a detached historian that I feel free to make the observation that it might be better for our nation in the end were we less wasteful of wealth and materials and more daring with the chances we took with the lives of our young men. Men, it seems to me—still in my historical cap and gown—are probably more expendable in warfare than economic wealth and certainly more expendable than material resources.

Ella gathered momentum. She was whipping up her favorite steed, class hatred. I was to her the personification of what she flays as "you self-satisfied, money-bloated, flint-hearted, coin-biting cutter-of-coupons living off the fat of the land, unheedful of the crawling, miserable, helpless worms others are to you." Her voice lashed with intensity like a quirt rising and falling. "I hate all of you. I would stop in the streets and spit in your goddamn smug faces. You should be made to suffer as we suffer. You should know grinding poverty and fear of poverty snapping at your heels. You should be made to pay through the nose for the misery you have caused others. And I only hope that I shall live to see you and those like you and your theory of Nordic supremacy and your stolen bank accounts and your foolish pride and your silly conceit laid low, with excrement tossed at you. And if you needle me again, I'm in the mood to push you out this window. It's you and your kind who make life not worth living for me and my kind. I loathe you all."

No red-headed radical ever spoke with more upwelling intensity than Ella. It is a delight to hear her. It is like Liszt in his stormy moods. As long as there is no fear of physical injury involved, no threat of the deprivation of further service — temper, hatred, violence (expressed vocally) stimulate my imagination, do not make me uncomfortable even when addressed in my direction. It may be that the parents I had and their autocratic, faultfinding and somewhat violent attitude toward me inured me against manifestations of passion which cause most people acute discomfort.

Ella cannot be reasoned with logically. "What do I care about logic? What do I care about your silly historical examples? I'm black and suppressed and you scorn my color and my class. Let it stand at that. There'll be a day of reckoning though, and I'll be on the winning side and you won't. And if it doesn't come in my time, you may be as sure as death and taxes it will come eventually. It must and will come."

Ella, in her way, is as much an individualist as I am, perhaps more, and a member of the colored upper class and proud of it, and "beholden to no one." I thought to myself: "This personification of an entire class in me must be stopped or I won't have Ella as a friend much longer." So I went to work on her. Logic I cast aside. I admitted pridefully to being an individualist. But I was, I said, not particularly class-conscious, having my friends from every class, mostly not from the class she so unfairly despised. Would I be appealing to her to stop making me the whipping boy of a class if I regarded her as representing her class? For me, classes could be damned; it was individuals I cared about. I was devoted to her and didn't wish her to cast me off unfairly for something I was not and didn't really epitomize.

Her reply was that no matter how I might feel toward her personally, there was still that stark racial and class barrier between us which neither of us could pass. I answered that no two individuals could really pass that barrier whether of the same race and class or otherwise. She began to calm down. She softened. "I'll do my best, Arthur, not to regard you as representing your class. I promise that much. Whether I'll succeed or not, I don't know. It will be terribly difficult. And you must not needle me if you don't want what you got tonight. How I feel is very close to the surface." I replied that I had needled her purposely to exhaust her in order to be able to make her listen to a little common sense. We parted amicably, on a better footing, I think, than for a long time. I don't wish to lose a single friend at this stage of my life, in particular not such a charming and vehement friend as Ella James.

October 29 Rose has been a real help to all of us. Without her it is difficult to perceive how we could have gotten along. I told her to call me by my first name. She said to Evelyn in her very soft voice: "Mr. Inman said to call him 'Arthur.' I wanted to ask you if it was all right with you before I did it." "Goodness," Evelyn laughed, "you don't know my husband. Of course it is." She's been divorced only a couple of years. Her husband took the method of staying out nights without warning as a means of exemplifying his freedom.

Rose at times is very pretty. Unless you regard her closely, she doesn't look her age, which is approximately my own. Her skin is white. Her eyes are brown. She's gentle. She talks fluently and at length if you wish it, keeps silent otherwise. She has had a major operation for a tumor. She has artificial teeth. She has had varicose veins. Despite all of which she's quite attractive. I like her and she likes me. She belongs to the Eastern Star and to a Unitarian association. She can ask more questions to the square inch than anyone I ever met save a child. "I find I haven't the memory I used to have before my operation. So I want to get things exactly in my mind to avoid mistakes."

October 30 I have given much thought to the Asiatic problem. While there is a bare chance that our altruistic policy toward the peoples of Asia might return a compensating yield on our investment there, I rather doubt it. Japan will be defeated. I anticipate a Soviet-dominated Asia, consolidated under the ideology of Communism and the empiry of Moscow. It should be our principal concern to oppose such an eventuality at any cost, put off the evil day when West and East will glare at each other across the narrowing moat of the Pacific Ocean.

November 4 Mrs. Cash says: "I don't pay much attention to the books I read you as a rule. I just try to please you in the way I read. My mind is full of other matters." Between school duties and head-waitress duties, it is a wonder she has sense for anything else.

"The other day," she said, "I realized for the first time how much Sylvia resented me. I just take her for granted. She feeds me well, gives me enough heat, supplies me with clean sheets. Once in a while I get her out of trouble. I've pulled her out of trouble and hidden her boy friends under my bed and slipped them out of the way numberless times. She's no kick coming. Why, I've had clean sheets for three weeks running. You know what that means? It means she's had her tail in my bed every night for three weeks. That's okay by me just as long as I have clean sheets. The other night I was using the rectal dilator when I heard a noise under my bed. It was a man. 'Excuse me,' he said, 'but I coughed to let you know I was here. Could you get me out? I didn't want to see what you were doing, but I couldn't help it, and it embarrassed me. Could you get me out?' 'Sure I can get you out,' I said, 'but in the meanwhile you needn't be embarrassed. I'm not. I was only doing what millions of other Americans do, and I guess you've seen plenty of assholes before.' Then I whisked him down the dark stairs. He still looked embarrassed. He was just another one of Sylvia's twirps."

Mrs. Cash looks up from the typewriter. There is a braided red bandeau (she fancies red) wound incongruously about her short white hair. She wears glasses. She says: "If you want to know what I think (of course it's none of my business) this diary portrays your Grandfather Crew as a penny-pinching old stinker. Any man who was as tight with his womenfolk as he was must have been little short of a tyrant. If he'd come into a hotel where I was waiting table and hadn't tipped me, I'd have dumped a pot of hot soup down his neck. So help me God, I would."

I spring automatically to the defense of Grandfather Crew. "He was," I say, "an exceptionally charming man. Aunt Helen always irritated him. And I never saw that side of him, because Father paid so much rent nothing was too good for us. And maybe Aunt Helen saw him with a jaundiced eye. And she was always astonishingly extravagant needlessly. As I recall my Grandfather, he was an exceptionally winning person and had both dignity and whimsicality. Everyone, servants, employees, family, business acquaintances, fell under his spell and stayed there." "I don't care," Mrs. Cash replies, "I think he was an old tightwad and bully. If you don't want your readers to think so too, you'd best change the context." "I can't do that, Mrs. Cash," I reply. "After all I was simply recording what Aunt Helen said." "Okay, okay," she concludes, "it's your diary. No hard feelings."

November 5 I feel myself a member of a racial group whose supremacy in this country is undergoing challenge. Those who challenge it I hate, not primarily the negroes, although I realize how easily that might be possible, but other racial groups. And as I feel, others by the hundreds of thousands must feel. Will all these interracial antagonisms simmer down gradually or will they flame up after the war into a condition still more ugly? There was the Ku Klux Klan in the twenties. It is rumored that the Klan leaders are preparing to organize on an extensive scale once more.

November 8 President Franklin Delano Roosevelt has been overwhelmingly reelected to office. Not only has he been reelected, but the Senate remains Democratic and the House of Representatives has added to its hitherto precarious Democratic majority. We who had wished a change of Government must now resentfully bear with another four years of waste and moral turpitude at home and fatuous idealism internationally. It is discouraging, to put it mildly. Practically every large urban district in the nation voted for Roosevelt.

Devoutly do I hope for the further illness and possible death of Roosevelt. Truman would, I believe, be less the tool of foreign and subversive elements than is Roosevelt, more subject to conservative influences.

November 10   I really miss Billy today. He was a good fellow in numberless ways, weak in some doubtless but with a genuine affection for me. "He never had a red cent left over from losing on the horses," Pearl commented. "He loved the girls too much," Mrs. Cash commented. "But he had a weakness for me," I replied to each. And he had. "The night," Mrs. Cash said, "that we thought you'd killed yourself, we sat down in my room and cried together." That, I am musing, was three years ago to the month. It was the most courageous step I ever took, one that has given me continuous solace since for having taken it.

November 11   The papers and the radio have been filled with details of the new rocket bombs being launched on England by the Germans. Their trajectory is supposed to reach a zenith of seventy miles, and the rockets are said to descend faster than light so that they make no sound before striking. Those with imagination foresee in the not too distant future intercontinental wars fought with showers of high-explosive missiles hurled across space. One wonders now and again, will the human race survive the ultimate accomplishments of the scientific mind? Or will there always be evolved defensive methods to counteract offensive weapons?

November 25   Evelyn, by and large, has handled herself with judgment and moderation since Pearl left. It is difficult at any time for her to keep herself under control, and it must have been doubly so what with putting me to bed at night and getting me up in the morning, interviewing and instructing people. She has tried to rest some during the day as well as go to bed very early in order to have a long sleep. I have striven to be gentle with her and to prevent her from throwing in her energies to the four winds with abandon. She hasn't been drinking, and that, too, has helped. We have managed, we both agree, with a minimum of friction. She has walked, shopped, had meals with Dr. Pike. She is never at a loss how to entertain herself. The other night she telephoned Washington and chatted with all the members of her family. She listens to the radio while dressing, while eating, while cleaning. She reads some, books chosen, alas, for their stories, because they are popular, rather than for style or merit. She enjoys, she says, her housework. The blue-eyed Siamese cat, Cookie, is a source of unfailing pleasure to her. She likes to sleep with it curled up on her stomach. She has taught it to retrieve paper wads. She studies its mental and physiological processes and habits with intense interest.

When her back hurts her, she takes a vigorous walk, usually downtown or around Jamaica Pond with Dr. Pike or she shines her maroon Ford from stem to stern with jerky and concentrated ardor. There is nothing contained or moderate about the way she cleans. She nearly always feels better for having made use of her body in physical exercise.

November 27 That doddering old sawbones, that fumbling, bumbling utterer of endless impractical ideals, Cordell Hull, probably one of the most revered and respected cabinet officers to preside over the Department of State in the history of the United States, has resigned, and I feel as though we had lost a very earnest and very misguided, hence a very dangerous director of our destinies and am accordingly relieved. The bad advice that Hull gave Roosevelt or took from Roosevelt must have been endless. Thank God he is out. Next to Roosevelt, no single person in the New Deal has probably caused us more ill unless it be Frankfurter or Hopkins.

December 2 I've been reflecting upon military customs and conventions. They aren't at all rational, really. It is much more rational and much more conducive to the quick termination of a war for prisoners to be shot. Then they wouldn't have to be fed, hospitalized if wounded, guarded, housed. The height of absurdity is reached, it seems to me, when the lives of captured airmen who have been hurling bombs upon women, children and precious architectural structures are by mutual pact between the martial contenders spared. Common impulse would call for the immediate execution of any of those hurlers of bombs who could be captured. Yet when the Japanese threaten to kill the airmen who have brought ruin and death to the citizens of Tokyo, Americans raise their hands in horror. While I suppose that these mutual military agreements conceded ostensibly for the purpose of making war less horrible are tenable, I cannot avoid wondering if they do not permit wars to be extended and prolonged beyond their natural terms.

December 9 I don't blame the English for grabbing every reward of victory—territorial, political, economic—they can lay their grasping hands on. It's the proper action for Churchill to take, viewed historically and viewed from an English standpoint. If we don't want anything out of our victory save the overturning of

Nazi rule in Germany and the freeing of subject nations, we ought (as soon as the latter are freed and the former overwhelmed) to get out completely bag and baggage and turn over what happens next to England and Russia. In that way we can at least escape making enemies of everyone by our carping and by our misrule — or would we even then escape some variety of odiums? We are — again and again and again I conclude it — the world's most naïve, most impractical fools internationally. If we want none of the perquisites of victory, let us shut up and let us permit our partners in war to enjoy them.

If we had any judgment historically and internationally we'd be feathering our own nest instead of griping at other nations for feathering theirs. They'd respect us the more, too, for doing it. We'd be a fellow bandit instead of an incomprehensible goody-goody.

December 13   Rose's mind interests me. She wishes to evade responsibility for the reason that she desires to avoid all risk of incurring censure. To evade responsibility, to avoid the censure that might fall upon her did she make a mistake of choice or determination, she will ask a hundred questions logical and puerile. If I want her to buy sweet potatoes, do I wish yams or sweet potatoes? Should they be large, small, mixed, medium-sized? How many pounds? Should they be boiled or baked? Shall she use slow heat or fast heat? What shall she do with the ones I don't eat at once? When I do eat them, shall she warm them up or let them stay cold? And so on. No five-year-old ever fired as many questions at his grandma. And because she has asked them one day in no wise prevents her from asking them the next day with additions and emendations. When Janice or I get cross, she will turn sorry for herself and say in her gentle, placid voice: "It's merely that I wanted to make sure so I could please you. I don't want to make mistakes. I assure you I have only your interest at heart. I'm sorry if I bothered you." And her good intentions are so obvious you can't remain put out. You think: "My God, what would you do if you were married to such a question box? Her husband had something on his side when he stayed out nights. Yet," you chide yourself, "she's so good and so earnest." Then Evelyn remarks: "Wasn't God mean when he gave Rose such a pretty face with such a Victorian disposition?" She's the kind of woman, really, who drives men to drink.

She can absorb flattery like a blotter ink. Yet "when people aren't good to me, I get through with them, and I stay through. You think I'm soft, but I'm not, at least not past a certain point."

And this is the end of still another volume of my diary. My car is running again. I have Evelyn and Janice. All around us heavy snow has fallen but not in Eastern Massachusetts. While I have made no money to speak of, neither am I in the red. My finances despite heavy outlays are in an improved condition. My doctors are very good to me. There are many blessings to be thankful for, plenty of food, heat, clothes, Mrs. Cash, books to read, my radio and my talking-book, my cars, no one dear to me killed or maimed overseas. In the two wars, our troops are winning. Inflation has not overwhelmed the nation. A great and prosperous country, one decides as one rides about this fragment of it, the people vigorous, vital, curious about everything, more busy than happy perhaps but not desperately discontented about anything, even the war, lulled to thoughtlessness by too much wealth, too many machines, a superfluity of gadgets.

Arthur dutifully chronicled the collapse of the Axis after the last and final German counterthrust. As the Allies pulverized the remnants of the Wehrmacht and American bombs ignited Japanese cities, he sorrowed over the destruction of irreplaceable cultural monuments (more precious than their destroyers, he decided), speculated darkly on the Yalta "sellout," grew apprehensive over the impending flood of returning servicemen. And how long, he asked, could the United States pour its resources into the insatiable European war?

Even more alarming to nervous Arthur was the crumbling of his little empire at Garrison Hall. His attempts to replace Pearl had only partially succeeded. The applicants, most of them headstrong and spoiled or insufficiently attentive, came and left with disheartening regularity. Overworked Evelyn had to pick up the pieces. Janice appeared less frequently after her engagement, and her announcement that she was pregnant sent him into a tailspin. Patsy Boland at first seemed the answer to his dreams. She was intelligent and handsome — but independent (rather too much like Evelyn in temperament to suit him). Arthur savored her beauty and tried by charm and gifts to make her respond to his greedy affections. Defiantly he defended his pursuit of young women. Red-haired Patsy softened a little but to his chagrin resisted his blandishments and (citing the objections of her alcoholic mother) turned down his offer to stay with him during the summer. Nor did another Garrison Hall recruit, the fat, emotional, and silly Annabelle Collier, pan out. There was no telling what this good-hearted but "spineless, confused, self-indulgent slob" would do when her Texas husband, Ted, returned from the wars. In the meantime she alternately enraged him by her messy habits and touched him by her bursts of solicitude.

Mrs. Cash rose higher in Arthur's esteem. He might deplore her filthy tongue, uncertain temper, and manifold crudities — but, by God, she *was loyal. And so was proper Rose Trench, adoring and compliant if a bit touchy. Visits from Ella and Juliette bucked him up. Patricia's revelatory letters flowed on. Only one event, however, momentarily lifted his depression: the death of his enemy, Franklin Delano Roosevelt.*

December 15 In a war, the faculty for organization is a tremendous asset. We plan and construct training camps from scratch. We build and man the world's largest merchant marine. No obstacle is too large for us to surmount. That we throw money around, overplan and overproduce are elements of our national character, and we discount them. Our psychology and our actions are impulsive, flamboyant yet organized efficiently for near-term success. Build airfields in days; fling pipelines across mountains; toss new locomotives on old tracks; bridge rivers by prefabricated bridges; teach pilots to fly in delicate mechanical ground machines simulating air flying conditions; design nylon hammocks that are bugproof; originate new medicines to deal with new diseases; construct mechanical ears to hear across scores of miles; develop a glue to stick skin on wounds — no limit to our dreams and achievements for success. "A rocket to the moon," says one. "Why not?" says another. "I'll pilot it," says a third. "How quickly will it be perfected?" says another.

December 19 You know, whatever is to be said against the Germans, they are a wonderful people. Every week or so as many tons of bombs are dropped on them as were dropped on England during months of bombing. Most of the military power of the world is arrayed against them, backed by the vast industrial resources of the United States and England. The natural resources of Germany are limited; the manpower is limited; the plant facilities have been bombed time and again. Yet notwithstanding the power against them and the difficulties within, they fight on with strength and resolution in the face of what seems to us to be inevitable disaster.

Of course, being an American, I want them defeated and as soon as may be. But deep in my secret heart I cannot but admire them and have (what would in all probability not endure upon contact with the genuine actuality) an academic sympathy for the ideology of the Herrenvolk and the master race and world conquest. No one, I'm sure, would more quickly wish to join the opposition than myself were I subject to the thousand and one rules, regulations, demands, obligations, restrictions, duties, sacrifices attendant upon being a citizen of a totalitarian state mobilized primarily for carrying on war. Yet the idea of belonging to a superior race, a privileged nation, administrating conquered nations and peoples, appeals to an element in my nature. I could, I think, love my own country even more were we frankly and avowedly committed to the doctrines of manifest destiny. How I feel is not a thing I can tell to other Americans. It is a hidden thing.

December 25 This has been a bearable Christmas morning. I resolved to metamorphose my attitude and be a pleasure to people during this holiday rather than a gloom fest. It snowed last night so that we have had no ride, but the roofs are clean and it is raining now. I am in the library. It is past noon. I read that we are counterattacking the Germans, long columns of tanks rumbling to the front, the G.I. Joes wearing holly sprigs in their helmets and waving at the Belgian girls as they pass. I read that rationing of food recommences on a large scale tomorrow. I can hear water dripping from the roofs.

Evelyn and I, earlier, opened a big stocking crammed with neatly wrapped packages left by Rose. The care with which she had selected the gifts was evident—two cans of Mor (a pork product without the usual heavy spicing), a packet of balsam needle cones to burn, some cheap envelopes to use for money for readers evenings, a candle made like a snow man, some potato chips in a box, an issue of 'Astounding Stories,' a red, green, yellow and purple baby toy. "Wasn't she sweet," Evelyn repeated. She gave Evelyn some cookies.

Dr. Pike came to work on my symphysis. I slipped several days ago on the salt Janice spilled by carrying the cellar upside down. He was in an affable frame of mind. He gave Evelyn a fine dark-brown leather purse. We talked of Civil War books (he enjoys that period) and I loaned him a life of Mosby as well as Cook's 'Stonewall Jackson,' accurate but colorful.[18] He took some of the coffee Evelyn was brewing for me. He made me lie down.

Janice will be having dinner soon. I hope she has an agreeable day. Evelyn gave her a red leather purse, and I gave her a purple sweater and a green fascinator. She seemed to like her presents. She gave Evelyn a large copper-pink glass for flowers. She gave me a dozen typewriter ribbons Bertram had gotten from the Raytheon, some carbon paper from the same place and a poppy dish, just what I wanted. Evelyn gave me a thermometer, a little partridgeberry plant in a sealed glass container, a map. Granny Groundhog sent me some books I didn't want. Mrs. Cash gave Janice a satin clothes hanger. I gave Mrs. Cash a bright red fascinator. Janice sat at her desk and

---

[18] John Singleton Mosby (1833–1916) commanded a company of Confederate rangers and was celebrated North and South for his daring exploits. Arthur's "Mosby" was probably J. J. Williamson's *Mosby's Rangers* (1896). John Esten Cooke (1830–1886) once enjoyed a considerable reputation as a Virginia novelist and historian. His *Life of Stonewall Jackson* (1863) is based on his firsthand knowledge of the general.

laughed until the tears came while Mrs. Cash chased me about the room to kiss me. When she finally cornered me, she cried. "I can't help it. It's just what I wanted. And you're so sweet." Evelyn and I gave Rose a pin. Evelyn received flowers from her mother. I gave her what she wanted: a bathmat and some slippers as well as a very pretty wool headscarf and a cleaning-powder container. Woody sent her some plum-colored slippers which she has been wearing all morning because she likes them. Father sent each of us twenty-five dollars, and Evelyn's father sent her fifty dollars.

1945

January 3   Been interviewing applicants for position until dizzy. Last night in my dreams they passed me by in endless parade, women old and older, short and tall, lanky and fat, lantern-jawed and hairy-chinned. A nice old red-faced battle-ax from Maine this morning, a sweet-faced gray-haired woman with a surprisingly loud voice, and another woman, and another girl.

January 5   My world pauses like a missing heartbeat. Janice announces that she is pregnant, will have to leave about the first of March. With her here, I could face almost any contingency. With her gone, I shall be vulnerable. There will be no one to calm me, no one to drive with me, no one to encourage me, no one to treat me, no one to love in the unique way I love her. The future looks frightening for both Evelyn and me. Janice has been our bulwark and our comfort. My heart is too perturbed to write more today. I had so hoped that Janice might not become pregnant before at least the European war was over and done with. She will love being a mother and her life should be fuller whereas mine will be bereft of one of the treasures it holds most dear.

January 6   The accepted code of American behavior has it that tears from masculine eyes are apt to evidence lack of courage, fortitude, self-restraint and should therefore be suppressed if possible, though there are a few instances when male tears can be overlooked or disregarded. Perhaps the sentiment angle will excuse me for the tears I shed yesterday about Janice and last night again. It has been a long time since I was quite unable not to weep. Evelyn reminds me that I wept when she was preparing to leave for Detroit just before we were married. It was this way when Eddie left me. If I should by American standards be ashamed, I am not.

January 10   I selected a woman, Madison, fifty-two, to do copying from diary, at least temporarily.

January 15   It was a long day. Evelyn was tired. Snow fell steadily. We corrected a little. Evelyn phoned Miss Madison to find out if she were coming to work for me. She was not. Undoubtedly, Volume 29 [1926] frightened her off. It's a honey, what with Corn and Ten Broek holding the spotlight. Mrs. Cash says: "You'd better not let any more youngsters correct diaries with you if you wish them to stay. They put the wrong interpretation on them." And so, I might add, do most people. After I'm dead, it won't matter; the percipient ones will have the patience or the interest to bear with me, if they don't like what I do or say or feel, because of the rest of the subject matter, and a few may even like me. If no one does, I really don't greatly care as long as my work is admired and respected. After all, I'm merely an instrument attempting to interpret my times, a faulty instrument if an earnest one.

January 18   Rose is coming every evening and cooking supper and doing the shopping twice a week. She's a real help. She's a good cook. She airs out well. Some of her stories and anecdotes are not uninteresting. "When I was a girl," she said, "I used to dream over and over again about a great wave that hovered over me and was ready to break. I woke up frightened every time. I dreamed the same dream over and over again."

January 21   Not an hour of my waking existence goes by without my thinking, "What are you going to do when Janice leaves? How will you get along? Who will love you as she does? Who will give you such devoted and loyal care? Who will work with you? Who will make your difficult hours less difficult?" I find no reply and am melancholy accordingly. "Janice," I say, "I wish, oh I wish to God, you'd been more careful with your precautions. I wish you had delayed until after the war in Europe is over." She sighs: "I'm sorry for your sake, Arthur, that it's happened this way. I hadn't intended it. But after all, I must begin to have a family soon. If I don't, who would there be to care for me when I'm old? If anything happened to Bertram, I'd be all alone. You say you'll always love me and watch over me, but you can die. I don't want to grow old and be alone." It is not the first time Janice has given voice to the dread of a solitary old age. It seems to be a lively horror to her. When one reflects upon it, she cannot be blamed.

January 23   Ex-Vice President Wallace has a very large and almost fanatically enthusiastic following. All the Pinks of the country adhere to him. He has the blessing of the C.I.O., of the Communists, of the radical farm groups. He is the standard-bearer of all those within the Government who feel themselves advanced thinkers. He is international-minded. He has theories about everything from astrology to how to please the Latin Americans. It is said that he possesses singular personal charm. His physiognomy signifies no particular intelligence. His father left him a large and flourishing newspaper which under his management failed. He was penniless when he came to Washington to become one of Roosevelt's braintrusters. He is the man who plowed under the corn and killed off the little pigs and advocated a philosophy of scarcity. He has incurred the enmity of the South Americans by his obvious attempts to buy their friendship through a lavish and impractical expenditure of American dollars. It is his pronounced belief that the federal Government should set up and run vast business and manufacturing projects in competition with American business for the purpose of furthering employment and keeping prices down. Very few projects, if any, to which Wallace has devoted his attention have ended to the advantage of anybody.

Roosevelt cannot but be aware of the enthusiasm for Wallace rife in the United States. He can ill afford to ignore him. He must keep him pacified and friendly. Wallace is, by present indications, the only feasible heir apparent to the Roosevelt throne should Roosevelt see fit to abandon it in 1948.

January 26 We're trying out a girl, twenty-five, named Annabelle Collier. She was preparing to take a position with a family who had a little girl, but we offered her two dollars more a week so she's trying out here. She has a pleasant and kindly face, brown eyes and brown hair, many back teeth missing. Her legs are huge almost to the point of deformity. She's had eighteen months' training to be a practical nurse, has taken care of children. Her husband, whom she married six weeks before he went overseas, is now in Germany.

January 27 For some time I have been asking Janice if she would do some copying at home when she leaves me. She is filled with reasons why not. Bertram wouldn't like it. What if he happened to read some of it? Where would she find time? She'd be too busy. How could she take care of her baby and do copying too? She has a feeling it would get her in wrong with Bertram.

Yesterday, no progress having been made, I brought up the subject again. She produced some arguments against the project. "I don't want to discuss it," she said. "I simply feel that it would be a wrong move. I can't risk making my life unpleasant by doing it. I wish you'd drop it. If I get an opportunity to bring up the matter with Bertram, I will. That's all I can say. I don't want to make any promises I won't keep." And she retracted within herself as a spider curls himself into a ball when too closely approached.

I felt somewhat angered. "You mean to tell me," I said, "that if you take work home and earn extra money, Bertram would mind?" "He wouldn't like it." "What gives him the privilege of preventing you from earning extra money?" No answer. "If I get you a cabinet with a key, would he open it?" "Of course not." "Then how could he know what you were writing?" "You don't know his attitude. He wouldn't like it." "In my estimation," I said, "it's none of his business. If it's private, that's between you and me. If he's suspicious of you, he's a queer sort of husband." "I simply know he wouldn't want me to do it. Anyway, where would I find the time?" "Of course you could find the time if you wanted to. Mothers all over the country find the time and the energy to raise chickens, can fruits, sew for extra money. If your baby has infantile paralysis or webbed feet, that's another matter. But you're a normal healthy woman, and you can certainly make time if you want to. Look at Dottie and all the treatments she gives. And she does the cooking and cleans the house and does the shopping. Probably you don't want to do it." There was no answer.

I gathered vehemence. "I doubt," I said, "if Bertram loves you as much as I do or understands you as well or is as perceptive. I've been very good to you. The sort of love I have for you deserves a yes to the request about my diary. I feel a deep duty to take care of you financially if you need it ever. If Bertram objects to your helping me, he ought to be put in his place. I've known you as long as he has and been just as good to you, and it wasn't my fault I couldn't marry you. And it isn't as if you wouldn't be paid for doing the copying. You would be, and you would well use the money. It's none of Bertram's business to object. And you should be ashamed not to want to help me. Are you listening to what I'm saying? I mean every word of it. You shouldn't let a baby consume your life entirely. Whether or not it would be good for him, it wouldn't be good for you. Are you listening?"

She sighed. She said: "I can't very well not listen. But I wish you'd talk about something else. I'll do the best I can, but I don't intend to make my relationship with Bertram miserable. After all, I have to live with him."

"Well," I said, "I'll stop. But if you don't do something in my behalf within a week or two, I'll start again."

February 3 Janice is explaining to Mrs. Cash my system of bookkeeping by which I juggle accounts so as to deceive myself into thinking there is less money than there actually is, thus putting a brake to my spending proclivities.

February 5 Stalin, Churchill and Roosevelt are meeting somewhere along the Black Sea, probably at Constanza in Rumania. Stalin causes his confreres to travel across half a world to meet with him while he merely stirs a couple of inches beyond the borders of

Russia as an empty gesture. The greatest rogue, criminal, murderer and blackguard in the history of the world crooks his little finger, and the proud overlords of Britain and America come running posthaste. You can regard it as you please. I have my own thoughts upon the subject.

February 12   Mrs. Cash and I have been reading, here a place and there a place, the 'Journals of Dorothy Wordsworth,' part journals and part diaries. I think of her, Dorothy Wordsworth, as a little woman, possibly stoutish, with a compressed mouth and big feet which transported her for miles each busy day, a transcendentalist by profession. Her devotion for her brother annexed her to him somewhat after the fashion of a horse collar to a horse. They must have made, Dorothy, William and Coleridge, an egocentric and slightly daft trio, roaming the hills and moors, the glens and tarns in search of BEAUTY with the concentration of monkeys searching for fleas. In a way, they were pathetic figurines representing in carica-ture the romanticism of the early nineteenth century. Such people would be impossible today, save on what is called "the lunatic fringe." Yet in their own day, they—at least Wordsworth and Coleridge—were esteemed, nay reverenced.

February 13   The question is: Can a valid picture of America be drawn when the range of firsthand observation is so constricted? The characters which occupy the foreground are not, it seems to me, sufficiently diverse. The background resembles the far-off castles, trees, towns in the Italian primitives. Yet do not those paintings give to the eye of another century an adequate representation of the culture, the imagination, the life, of the times? If I present those persons having to do with my daily life and present them truly and in detail, perhaps I am as apt to portray America. I suppose that a microcosm can be illuminatory of an age as a macrocosm, provided it be well and honestly limned. My effort is honest, that I can guarantee; whether my chronicling is well done I am too close to it to know. I in no respect hold with those who assert that honesty of effort necessarily results in artistic achievement.

Well, no matter what theory I hold or how I should prefer cir-cumstances to be, things are as they are; the characters for the diary are relatively few at a time, their stations in life and their activities relatively circumscribed. It is my responsibility to use the material at hand with proficiency and hope for the best artistically and histori-cally.

February 20   "What can you expect of a day that begins with getting up in the morning?" says a quip in a newspaper. For my part truer word was never said. I am too tired to wish to live. Annabelle, who has been prompter since Sunday, announces in her kittenish way: "A little bird whispered to me that you were planning to bumpsie-wumpsie me out of here presently. Is it so?" I groan inwardly. "As long," I say, "as you are on time, you can tell birdikins to stop whispering. The last thing I wish is to hunt for someone new. In the meanwhile, you would be more comfortable to listen to fewer tales and concoct fewer lies yourself." "Okay," she says, "I just wanted to know." A very boring girl, usually filled with good will but not always, and a mistress of sly innuendo. Wakes me very well and does my curtains when airing out not at all badly. As for the rest, if she will continue prompt, I shall be satisfied.

This Annabelle, I suspect, reads my letters and probably this diary and harkens to those unfriendly to me, of whom there are not a few in this building and elsewhere. Thank fortune for Patsy, Rose and Mrs. Cash. Shall miss Patsy while she is home.

February 21   Yesterday morning Annabelle sulked. Not until after I had had my stomach pumped was the reason revealed. During the moment Mrs. Trench had left her typewriter, Annabelle had read my letter to Billy. She quoted it exactly: "She doesn't know what self-discipline is, and a clock to her is something to be looked at occasionally and not very seriously. And she has hot pants." I don't know what Annabelle expected me to do, deny or apologize or sermonize probably, but it struck me as very funny. I laughed and laughed. "You're a devil," she exclaimed. "I thought I knew you completely. Then you make snap judgments like this. I had you on a pedestal. Believe me, mister, I came within an inch of packing my bag last night and getting out. Hot pants. Me. Never was I so insulted."

"Well," I replied, "women with husbands don't keep a chain of men on the leash unless they have hot pants. What else was I to think? What else would your husband think if he knew about your daily dates? I should have said 'I think she has hot pants.' I admit that much. As for the rest, you make me laugh. And I'm very glad you read the letter. If you have anything to you, it may do you good. But do you read all letters?" "No I don't. I was simply curious. If you were curious and in my place, wouldn't you have read the letter?" "Yes I would," I acknowledged, "but not when I became fond of anyone. Will you read all my letters and diaries if you get a chance? Are you that much of a snooper?" "Certainly not. But I'm glad I read this one." "How can I know you won't read the others?" "Because I say I won't." "Is that worth anything?" "Of course it is. When I give my word, I keep it." "Or so you say. Will you promise not to read any more of my writings on the sly?" "Yes I will. But I don't know why I didn't leave. No one ever thought such awful things of me before." "How do you know they didn't, Annabelle? Maybe they have simply been too polite or too indifferent to say them. The way you carry on, you lay yourself wide open to any sort of criticism." "You're a devil." "Perhaps. Or perhaps I'm blunter than most people to determine if those I'm learning to know have the guts to take it and the insight to realize that I'm an unusually nice person even so. If they can take it for six months or so without running away or hating my shadow, they usually conclude I'm worth being fond of. As to what I think of you, it's entirely up to you to make me think one way or the other. One of my commendable virtues is that I'm always open to being proved wrong and then changing my opinion. What you do away from here is none of my business, however I may think about it, so long as you're on time and do your work. You can bed with a man every night or not just as you wish."

Today, for how long it lasts, Annabelle cannot be of sufficient service to me, is cheerful and attentive. Last evening she gave the sack (or so she claimed) to two men. We shall see. We shall see.

February 22   For two hours have been sorting and cataloging diaries. A tedious task in which a single slip can lead to the misplacing of a volume. The list in the key book must coincide with where each volume — original, typewritten, carbon, first and second microfilm — is. Information, full and precise, must be put in the key book. Microfilm bits must be checked. Notes on what is to be done without errors and corrections must be made. Old correction sheets must be torn up. And so on. It would be a tense job perhaps did I possess strong eyesight, but with my wavering and unreliable vision it is a wearing task. I tore up, through a mistake in reading what was written, one very important piece of work, about twenty hours' worth. It is surprising that I have made so few blunders of that sort during twenty-six years. Given a modicum of strength, my tendency is to be systematic. Worn out now, as I said.

February 23   It has been intensely interesting to me to observe the Japanese character manifest itself under war conditions. A reporter on the radio talks of how in a Philippine concentration camp a guard beat a prisoner nearly to death for a slight infraction of discipline, then gave him a cigarette, brought water and was generally solicitous. When the American recovered sufficiently to berate him, the Japanese guard burst into tears. The Japanese people, despite their former strict ethical culture, are a primitive folk, jumpy, given to sudden alterations of attention and emotional viewpoint, without tenderness (at least among the men) as we know it, jittery in small things, immensely persevering in large matters, thinking emotionally rather than logically. They are not, fundamentally, without kindness. They have as high a regard for courage as do we. They're the most literate people on the face of the globe. They are kind to their children, cleanly, industrious, frugal, provident. Yet they are small craft whose only keel is the culture in which they live. With the culture altered (the keel designed solely for one brand of weather), no ethical standards to guide the daily intricacies of behavior, they have become lost and bewildered, and as with most primitives when lost and bewildered, they turn cruel, kind, stern, lax, violent, futile in irrational sequence.

February 27   Evelyn and I drove through the dirty streets of the South End. Uncollected garbage everywhere spilling obscenely out on dirty snow. Fragments of unprepossessing humanity. Depressing. Home after forty-five minutes to find Annabelle still standing before the mirror "getting ready to go." Discouraging. In my room by myself now and with a notion to lock the door and keep company with myself. No sleep all night. If naps came to me, they were concluded horrifically by nightmares calculated to squelch a stronger spirit than mine is at night. I thought of the terror the Berliners must feel when the two thousand aircraft fly in a two hundred mile stream over the city and loose upon it explosive and incendiary bombs by the thousands of tons. Nor did that train of thought benefit my lost equanimity. So I reflected upon the draft riots occurring in the French districts of Canada and upon how (would all ordinary citizens of all countries, bidden by their overlords to answer the call to arms stage draft riots, refuse to participate in military matters) the overlords would be left glaring and futile, and there could be no large-scale war. All of which, of course, took me to no valid conclusion save that people in the aggregate and separately are inordinately weak-willed to let themselves be bitted and ridden by scoundrels.

Rose is loath to talk about herself. Information has to be extracted by bits and particles. "I don't want to talk about myself, Arthur. I've never talked about myself. When I was deciding to get a divorce from my husband, nobody knew about it. You know how many women discuss their troubles? Well, the first thing my friends knew about our estrangement was when I called them up to inform them. I never discuss my private affairs nor air my troubles. Nobody but you, Arthur, is interested in them anyway, and I wish," she smiled lovingly at me, "you weren't interested. I can assure you, you won't find out much, not if I know it. You're almost uncannily clever, and you remember every little detail and put them together, but there are things no one will ever find out about me."

Her sense of privacy seems to be a governing one, her sense of social propriety, her modesty among the most important influences in her life.

"No one was ever so modest as I, Arthur. I wouldn't think of allowing my daughters to see me disrobed. When I was being operated on for the tumor, the worst thing about it was the lack of privacy. Anyone and everyone was continually popping in and out my door, whether I was being washed or on the bedpan. 'Will you please shut that door?' I would tell the dumb nurse over and over. She thought me daft, I suppose. But it did something to me not to have my modesty respected." Reluctantly she replied to a query: "No, as long as we were together, my husband never saw me in the nude. I would undress in the closet." And when she was to have her first baby, she would permit no doctor to examine her. "I'd rather have had the baby wrong than have to suffer the indignity of letting a man look at me." Childhood experiences appear to have influenced Rose to an immoderate degree. "When I was five or six, perhaps eight, I used to wear lacy drawers, you know, like girls wore then. The man next door never tired of exclaiming, 'See Rose's drawers.' It gave me a complex, I guess. It made me want to be modest. One time, to tease me, he sent me a cunning pair of silk drawers into which he had sewn with what must have been considerable trouble lots of little pockets containing dimes. I'll never forget him and how he teased me. It made me unduly modest."

Rose would provide a fiesta for a psychiatrist. Here are the fragments of her story I have been able to glean. Her father's father owned a business of some sort somewhere, a small shop or something. Her father sold stocks in Vermont and perhaps bonds. Her parents were of Dutch stock predominantly (she will not divulge their names). Rose was an only child. The first incident she will tell me of happened in Andover. Later, the family moved to Vermont, where they lived in various towns. Rose was ill much of the time. "I caught everything that was to be caught. I was so frail—or they thought I was—that they wouldn't let me jump rope, play hopscotch, run like other children. It made me feel out of things. I was in bed much of the time."

When she was seven or eight, her mother moved with her to a farm north of Rutland. She walked two miles each morning to a little red schoolhouse, so cold that she would be crying. On the whole, though, she enjoyed the life. She was made to go without shoes and stockings in the summer by doctor's orders, for her feet were weak. She felt it immodest and hated it. One day the boys and girls took her on a long walk, ran off and left her in the woods. She found her way home later, to be greeted by her mother with scolding words, which she thought very unfair. She played with the other children in the hay. One day they were present when a calf was slaughtered, and Rose cried and was sick and couldn't sleep without nightmares for many nights. They gathered berries and fruits. The little girls played with dolls. She had her own little garden. She seems to recall the experience pleasantly.

The family moved to Hyde Park. Rose attended school and high school there. Boys didn't pay much attention to her. She read and reread such books as the Elsie Dinsmore series, the Alger books, etc. Elsie Dinsmore impressed Rose profoundly as did Alger's 'up from the depths' convictions. "I must have read a score of times the part where Elsie refused to play the piano for the guest on Sunday because God wouldn't have wanted it and sat there on the piano seat at her father's command until she fainted. I thought she was wonderful. It wasn't that I was particularly religious; it was that Elsie, by being constant to her convictions, was being a heroine."

In her last or next to last year of high school, she fell ill again, so ill that it cost her father two thousand dollars. She studied very diligently upon her recovery in order to graduate with her class. She became so depleted that her father took her abroad the summer of the outbreak of the war. Few men, even though she was considered to be pretty, paid her attention. "I was too proper, Arthur. I'll never forget the man who took me to dinner and the theatre afterwards. When he left me at the front door, he wanted to kiss me. 'Nothing doing,' I exclaimed. 'But,' he protested, 'I always kiss the girls I take out good night.' 'Well,' I said very smugly, 'here's the first girl you won't kiss good night.' And I went in the door. I never saw him again. I'd rather be proper than have men, I guess."

She took a business course. She went to work for a man twelve or more years older than herself. They were married within a matter of months. "I simply will not tell you anything about my husband or my marriage, Arthur. You haven't any right to ask. And, anyway, it makes me so miserable I can't sleep when I remember how things were. So don't ask me."

Of course I did ask her. As I told her, I'm no respecter of privacy. She was, she says, happy enough at first. They lived in a house, later in an apartment. They had a combination maid, nurse and cook. Rose did some of the cooking. She had an allowance for household expenses. For the rest, she charged things. Mr. Trench does not seem to have been stingy. She liked him because he was "of a studious nature." She felt no passion for him. "When my girls were good, they were my girls in my mind. When they were bad, they were his girls. I feel now that I may have brought them up too strictly. I loved to dress them well and have them pretty. But I wasn't as strict with them as their father was. He'd get mad and order them not to see any boys. He wouldn't believe they were back when they were. I shall never forget the time he ordered the milk deliveries stopped when one of the children was ill. And another time he refused to let me have a doctor for them. I never forgave him for that. But let's talk of other things. It disturbs me to resurrect these remembrances."

Her husband was violently jealous of Rose. He staged scenes when she so much as spoke to a man. "Oh, I put up with a lot, Arthur. No one will ever know how much I put up with. I felt I owed it to the children to stay with him till they were grown and able to care for themselves. Finally, when he refused to come home nights or to let me know where he was, and when he began to call up the girls' bosses and attempt to make them lose their jobs, I decided I had had enough. So I left him."

I have, I suspect, been a revelation and an education to Rose. "Nobody," she asserts, with her funny laugh and her cheeks coloring, "ever got so far with me in six or seven months as you have. I never know what you'll be persuading me into doing next. You and Mrs. Cash have certainly pepped up the old lady and rocked her foundations a bit as well. It probably has been good for me. You're a wonderful person, Arthur, and you know so much without being stuffy or didactic, if you know what I mean. And the very Devil himself is in you." Rose is a Unitarian as is Mrs. Cash. They admire and respect each other. "If you overlook the crudities in Mrs. Cash's speech, which are merely incidentals, every one of us having her own faults, she's a very fine and staunch woman, Arthur, and you're lucky to have her behind you. She thinks the very world and all of you and Evelyn. She can never say enough about how generous and loyal you are. There must be something to you when you can get so much commendation out of a woman as worldly and as busy as Mrs. Cash is. Frankly, I like her a lot."

February 28 Janice's last week. There's an old fountain pen on her desk, rickety and mended but serviceable. Going to take it home, she is. "Some day," I said to her, "you're going to be generous with something you own, and then you'll split wide open." "You're not generous with your own things," she replied. Which is a misstatement as no one should know better than she. I may not want to be generous with my things, but watching her, so sweet and good and generous with her time and services has brought me up sharp in many instances and caused me to act generous with that which I want to keep for myself. I gave her a hundred dollar leaving present the other day and a promise of fifty more. What she has given me in the way of presents since she has been here could be counted on the fingers on one and a half hands: some carbon ribbons, some slices of her mother's turkey, a glass bowl with mosses in it, aside from small Christmas and birthday presents. This isn't being written because I am sour on Janice about her parsimony but rather to show that it is her single unworthy trait of character and thereby to put into bolder light her admirable worthiness as a person. I shall probably never in my life meet her peer again.

March 2 I listened late last night to a rebroadcast of President Roosevelt's talk to Congress concerning his meeting with Stalin and Churchill and what he expected and hoped would come out of it. It was the best speech in my estimation that he ever made, noticeably free from sneers and slaps, delivered in a voice filled with personality and earnestness.

He stressed the unity reached by the Allies, the terms of surrender for the Nazis, aid to the liberated nations, why and how the Polish plan was necessary, but most of all he discussed plans toward the furtherance of a permanent peace. I do not know, being neither British nor Russian, how close to the hearts of those two peoples is the longing for a lasting state of world peace. I do know that in the American heart it is a very real longing, not violent perhaps, but steady and not peculiar to any one class or group. And I feel, furthermore, that Roosevelt is not merely toying with words when he stresses his desire for lasting peace among the nations of earth. If ever he is sincere, he is sincere on this point.

Janice and I on an overcast day took what may be our last ride together in the railroad yards, at least our last ride for no one knows how long. All our friends spoke to us with exceptional amiability just as if they were aware it might be our last ride — the gnome-like man who piles lumber all day, the Jew who runs the lumber yard, the boys who unload the automobiles, men making firm a load of Army truck bodies on a gondola with strips of steel, the men who load the 'Christian Science Monitor' newsprint on trucks, etc. I was very sad inside and I suppose Janice was too, but we smiled and ate crackers and watched the pigeons flying. It was a pleasant morning on which to terminate many other pleasant mornings.

March 3 Annabelle was late again yesterday at suppertime. I would, I decided, give her the works, not caring whether she went or stayed if she remained in her present psychological condition, and thereby determine what the stuffing within her carcass contained. It is my theory that people rarely reveal themselves as unrestrainedly as when thoroughly angry. I am, if I do say it myself, an artist in making people angry. It has served me well. I know by intuition precisely what rankles and goads. So I set to work on Annabelle. Was she a jellyfish that she couldn't order her time? What sort of lack-brain was she that she couldn't keep a few figures? She didn't possess much character, did she? And, by the way, I didn't like people working for me to charge items about which I knew nothing at the stores; it made me feel untrustful. And would she keep her room clean. Did she quit having ideas and tend to the small things, it might improve her. And so on.

She answered back without restraint. I was spoiled. I had no right to talk to her that way. What did I think I was, God? She'd walked out from other jobs for less. I must admit, she has a crackling temper. "Gee, I'm mad," she exclaimed. "I'd love to bop you, you and your psychology. Who do you think you are, anyway?" "Oh," I remarked with feigned disinterest, "stop being so sorry for yourself." I knew that that would cap the baiting. It did. "Sorry for myself? Great guns, I'm not sorry for myself; I'm tearing, tack-clawing, violently angry." "Oh?" I inquired politely. And, forthwith, her stuffing rolled out to be regarded. It wasn't very reassuring, gunk and sludge mostly as disorderly and liquatious as I suspected it would be, without stiffening. Not very much to work on in her. I backed water then, had her laughing before she left me. "There was a minute," she said, "when one more word from you and I'd have left." "I knew it," I said. And I did. But she didn't leave, and that's to her credit. If I didn't make an impression on her, nothing will. Today I'm being as charming to her as I know how, though I'm worn out and so is she.

March 4 It was a difficult day in more ways than one. Janice and I have been finishing up all sorts of tag ends. Each time I looked at her and thought of her imminent departure and that this was her last day, I felt desolated. We attempted to correct in the afternoon but stopped soon. Before she left, she came into the dark room where I was sitting, stood behind me, cupped my cheeks in her two hands. "Oh, Arthur," she said, and I could feel her tears falling. She leaned over and kissed me tenderly. "Gosh," I said, "I don't know what to say. All my glibness has deserted me." "Me too," she sobbed. "You've been wonderful to me," I said. "You've been wonderful to me, Arthur. I don't know what I'll do without you. It's going to be hard." "Well —" I said. "Well —" she said. "Let's don't say good-bye," she said. "We'll say good night," I said. "Good night, darling," she said. "Good night, sweetheart," I said. And upon such an exchange of inept phrases we parted. I felt as though part of me were going with her.

March 6 Patsy speaks of her menstruation unconcernedly as though it were a subject not at all taboo and whether she wears Tampax or Kotex. "They tell me that Tampax is the thing, but somehow I can't persuade myself to try it. I wouldn't know how to get it in despite all those awful pictures explaining how it should be done. And I always think of the string dangling and wonder wouldn't it be untouchable. So I stick to Kotex. I've felt badly this time. If I exercise too much, it hurts. I shouldn't take gym while I'm this way, but you could never persuade anyone that you'd be better off without it so I don't mention it. I suppose it's nothing, anyway, only I get out of sorts when I have cramps. If I don't overexercise, I scarcely notice my condition save for the nuisance it is."

Patsy, as is evident, interests me as a study. That is why I present such details as the above. She exercises the same sort of fascination over me that Evelyn does. I shall one day suddenly recognize why she fascinates me and hence why Evelyn does. If not, the reader of these chronicles may be more percipient than I and hence be able to solve what puzzles me to his satisfaction. I know one thing: There are many duller characters that cross these pages than Evelyn and Patsy.

March 8 Corn — Mrs. Therese Isolde Raleigh DeBray Hart — was due between ten and eleven. She arrived on the dot of ten, with "didn't expect your old friend to be prompt, did you? Well, I fooled you." We kissed each other. Much older-looking than when I saw her last. Svelte figure. Stylish black suit. Gun-metal-colored stockings. Large dark circles under large green eyes flecked with black. Face thinner than I have ever seen it, so that the planes have altered and what used to be convex is now apt to be concave. Face less attractive with dissipated look, the nose more pronounced. Very wide mouth with strong even teeth. Flexible mouth, very wide. Unattractive hat, quickly jerked off and thrown carelessly on chest. Hair not so fine of texture as formerly and much darker brown. "Well," she laughed — the same uptilting series of bird-like sounds — "take a good look." She struck the pose of a clothes model, one hip up, and slowly pivoted. "Yes, much reduced. Yes, slim almost. Yes, not a young girl any more. But trim and a very shadow of her former plumpness. Not bad. On the whole (aside from having had too much to drink last night) not bad at all."

She giggled. "Really, though, Arthur, what do you think of the old lady, the grass widow, your old pal from Cambridge?" "Sure and it is a fine figure you have gotten for yourself since last I laid eyes on you. A girdle, I'll warrant." "Certainly that. And black lace panties. See. And still something left up here that isn't all chest expansion. But the face, Arthur? The face?" "The face," I replied, "looks to me as though the owner had experienced malaise of the spirit as she advanced through life. How about it?" "Actually, I've been very well provided for, and my life has flowed smoothly enough. But inwardly not so smoothly. Great struggles to adjust myself. All right for a while, then all wrong. I read Jung. I read Freud. I am helped. I gradually emerge into daylight. At this point, I am myself." "It seems to me," I remarked, "that you are more like your old self than I've known you to be for many years. Is it Frank's being in France? What's he doing there anyway? Have you had any lovers?"

"When you saw me last, I was in awe of Frank. Now he's in awe of me. Ever since I turned the salad plate upside down on his head when he made me mad and then threw a glass of milk in his face and I stood there watching the oil and milk, the green vegetables drip down over him and he looking bewildered and surprised, all his dignity lost, I've had no awe of him. It was time, I thought to myself then, that he be given a lesson. So I stamped my feet and made my eyes flash and swore violent swears and marched away to the car, throwing over my shoulder: 'I don't know whether I'll come back or not.' I drove the car around the curve and stopped to laugh; he had looked so lugubrious. Then I drove on into Ellsworth to the nursery there and bought out the place. I stayed away all afternoon. When I got home, he came out to the car and said, just as meek as a mouse: 'I see you've bought some plants, Pussy. Isn't that nice. Supper is ready for you.' Since then, I've had very little trouble with him. He's very remiss about writing. When he gets too bad, I go out and buy things and send him huge bills. Or I write obscene letters. Or I tell him about men, lovely, masculine figments of my imagination. I get him worried one way or another, so he'll write."

Evelyn was in and out of the room. She enjoys Corn. She told us of being in a store the other day. She was trying on earrings. The salesgirl said: "Do you know, madam, that you have big bottoms to your ears?" Evelyn, without thinking, replied: "That's not the only place I have a big bottom." The salesgirl, she told us gaily, was shocked.

"Oh," Corn asserted, gesturing with her hands, "that's nothing. I was in a store in Washington several weeks ago ordering a new hat with a whole flower garden on it. The salesgirl said to me: 'Are you a bride?' I answered: 'Hell, no. I've been married twice. This is for something special.' Her eyes all but rolled out of her head."

March 9   Corn brought me up-to-date on Elizabeth. She is married to a Dr. David Tobias. He is a Jewish surgeon in Cleveland,

Corn says, of increasing prominence, on the staff of several hospitals. Corn admires him, enjoys his sense of humor. They have a home of their own, two children, one an adopted boy and the other a baby girl of fourteen months. Elizabeth goes out socially somewhat, is still interested in music. She has to take insulin injections but is, Corn assures me, as beautiful as she was when young before she fell ill to diabetes.

Here is more about Annabelle, despite my wish to avoid the subject. One tine of my pet fork was bent at an angle. "Did you do this?" I queried. Indifferently: "Probably. I have a habit of opening cans with forks. I didn't notice." It was at breakfast. Shortly thereafter, she leaned her head on the telephone button and woke Evelyn downstairs. She was without remorse. She left the electric stove turned on until the grease from the bacon burst into flame and there was near to being a fire. She prepared one batch of beans — let it burn; prepared another — let it burn. She buys plants, permits them to shrivel for lack of water. She spills vitamin pills on the floor and doesn't notice. I got fed up yesterday morning, made some mordant remarks.

At suppertime last night, I could sense she had something on her mind. I probed. She couldn't, she said, stand the job any longer. It wore her out. It made her feel stupid. She had run away from everything all her life-long, and she was going to run away from this. She was accustomed to being appreciated. She was no longer optimistic as to her capabilities. I decided it was time to pick her up, pat her on the back, put her together. I said that her lack of optimism was the most encouraging sign yet. I thanked her for being frank with me. I assured her that she did the work at night very excellently. Had she thought that that was the most important phase of her job, one it took other people months to master? She should, I said, be encouraged rather than discouraged. Her trouble was that she was too impatient to achieve perfect results. It was my trouble too. I had blasted her purposely the evening she was late, I explained, to gain her attention, not simply to annoy her. She had been giving me her attention better since then, hadn't she? I should be encouraged if I were she, not discouraged.

I think it did the trick if anything can. I talked for an hour and a half without intermission. She'll still burn the beans and spill the vitamin pills and blithely disconnect light fixtures she's unable to reconnect, but her attitude will be different and she will probably eat tacks for me if I wish it.

March 10 Three hundred Super-Fortresses yesterday dropped a thousand tons of incendiary bombs upon ten square miles of Tokyo. The city is said to be "an inferno of flames." "This was much the most successful attack we have put on to date," remarked one brigadier general. Said another: "If fleets of one thousand of the B-29's are required to finish off Tokyo, we will produce them, and more." I suppose that as an American citizen, I should be highly pleased at the destruction of Tokyo. I cannot, however, seal off the processes of imagination which allow me to dwell upon the horror it must be to be one of the helpless citizens of a great bombed city, terror dropping from the skies, no sure place of refuge at hand.

The Japanese people didn't ask for this war or make it. People as such rarely if ever make a war, the incitement, the guidance, the very wish for war emanating from those in authority, whether greedy civilians in power, army officials bred to war or avaricious or fanatic churchmen. Even more than the horror brought to helpless people in this war do I deplore the artistic and architectural ravages. When you kill people, you destroy separate bodies and souls. When you demolish art and architecture, you destroy the collective soul of a nation.

March 19 I spent the morning explaining about the Diary Introduction on which I plan to work does Patsy come and showing her pictures of the characters from the collection in the little trunk. She seemed to be interested. I said: "If you come here, I'll want you to do Evelyn's work — no specified hours, no specified duties. Just take care of me, love me, treat me, read to me, drive me (if you can learn to drive), talk to me evenings, oh anything that comes up. It's only fair to you to say that sometimes I may be waked up wrong and will be grumpy for a while. And one of your chief duties would be to take care of the little things — putting my razor away, closing doors when it's time to close them, changing talking-book records, mending my clothes, telephoning for me, and so forth, and so forth. If you were stupid, I'd not like it, for I feel that you don't have to be stupid. Sometimes you forget details now, coming only Sunday mornings, but that's understandable. However, if you were here all the time, I'd demand that you remember them. How about that?"

She smiled sweetly at me. "I think I can do everything. I've heard your opinion of stupid service so often that I have no desire to be stupid. I won't mind your being grumpy. I don't want to see you mad, but you say you lose your temper only two or three times a year, and if it comes I suppose I can weather it if I have to. Only don't get mad if you can avoid it. I love to be with you and work with you. One of the things I enjoy most in life is doing physical things for people who are appreciative. I don't think I do them just to get appreciation, but maybe I do. I hope not. It would be fun being with you, Arthur, and I'll try to work it so that I can come."

Annabelle comes in with bundles of fixings for her room every day. The arrangement is that I pay for what I like, not wanting the room too dressed up anyway, and that what I don't feel necessary she pays for. I wish she'd leave off. It gives me a feeling of instability. "I want to make it into a regular fairy palace of a room, Arthur. Oh, it's going to be so beautiful everyone will love it. I'll just sit and knit and never go out. I must have beauty about me. When I do, I become so happy I could sing and dance." "Can a pig dance?" I murmer to myself, and: "You'll fix it up, perhaps, if I don't have the writhing heebee-jeebees first." Aloud I reply: "Yes?"

March 22   Do you suppose my heart is a shallow instrument — to be in love with three women at one time? Or is it larger than the ordinary heart? I am in love with three women simultaneously. And I am so thorough about it that I care little what is thought of me by those who perceive how it is with me or what readers of these pages may think at some future time. Janice says: "When people grow up, they usually change their attitudes. They love quietly and consider themselves lucky to love one person and have one person love them. They leave the way you feel behind them. They don't wish their lives complicated." Well, I do. And as long as I have any spirit left, I'll be falling in love, I suspect. Nor does the knowledge that the sort of affection I give Patsy and Janice — even to Evelyn — is not returned in kind suppress me. More than perhaps any ordinary man of fifty, I possess a something that must use itself up in devotion, else I am miserable. It isn't sex. It is an emotional tenderness strangely coupled with a need for excitement and the calm that comes from being loved. It is as much or more giving than taking. Is this volatile creature needing affection, demanding to give it the same person who as a child fled with disgust from affection?

March 25   The other night I found myself drawing up a set of rules, the observance of which should enable any ordinary American woman possessing tact and self-control to handle, manage within home limits and keep pacified and perhaps contented any average self-respecting American man more than ordinarily fond of her, whether her husband or not, always excluding the mischance occurring outside her range of control.

1. Be neat in person, in personal habits, in household affairs — quietly and without too much talk about it.
2. Conform socially to your man's inclinations at first and ex-

pand or contract social activities gradually and tactfully, very rarely precipitately.

3. Never, never say or do anything that will cause your man, any man, to lose face before the world or his own respect for himself.

4. Men can absorb an appalling amount of flattery. It seems as needful to most men as is their food or their sleep. A woman should no more neglect to flatter her man than she should neglect to keep in order her appearance, her clothes, her home, her mind.

5. A woman should pat a man lovingly, if not physically then emotionally, with looks, gestures or words, upon the small-boy shoulder that is, however stern his countenance and mien may appear.

6. A woman should accept favors and gifts within reason, of course, when and as they are offered and be enthusiastic and appreciative, not protest them as so many women do. It touches a man's self-esteem to be able to give acceptable presents to the woman on whom his attention is centered, and her gracious acceptance of them endears her to him.

7. Do not nag. Do not gossip inordinately. Do not jam female friends for whom your man feels disdain or distaste down his throat. Do not talk his ears off. Do not contradict without impeccable grounds and thinking twice, for it is more profitable to permit the male to keep his self-respect and swagger than it is, usually, to counter his misstatements and misassertions.

8. Meet your man's sexual moods and needs as nearly as it potentially lies within you to do, and always dissemble emotional reluctance, for the matter concerns masculine self-respect.

9. On no account through negligence or laziness permit your man to become bored with you or with your home. Interest him, cajole him, flirt with him, allure him, anger him if you have to — but on no account permit him to become bored.

10. Woman stands midway between man and his illusions. It is her proper function to reconcile the one with the other.

Note: Of rules for how men should be with women, I know none that would apply generally. It is what a man is, not how a man acts, that concerns a woman chiefly. Perhaps what impresses a woman in a man as much as anything is an attitude of very polite supercilious indifference, but even that without correlated charm or looks or sexual attractiveness or position may amount to nothing in and of itself. There are no rules for men relative to women.

March 27 When I grow gloomy because Janice isn't here, because Annabelle is inept, because I can find no suitable secretary and my diary languishes uncopied, I turn my attention to what the United States may be like when fighting ceases, feel more gloomy about that than about my present difficulties. As I am affected personally, I'd rather have the war go on than end. Since to any honest person what matters most in life is what concerns himself (however it may be denied or rationalized), I'd rather have the war continue and enough men killed off so that when those who remain return, our pattern of existence here at home will not be altered by an unassimilable surplus of unemployed.

There are many things I'd like to state baldly concerning my desires and predilections, such as the above, but do not dare to for fear of alienating or offending possible readers. My ways of regarding all sorts of things are heterodox and unconventional. They wouldn't look well on paper. Yet they are a part of me, and how can I be fully known unless I express them? One of these days, when I'm exceptionally bored or filled with derring-do, it may be that I'll set down what I cautiously hide from other eyes and ears.

I was expounding a few of my secret thoughts to Evelyn this morning. "You wouldn't," she said, "execute them even if you were able." "But I would," I assured her, "provided I could be guaranteed against social quarantine and scorn." The price I should have to pay, were I made to suffer under social obloquy, would make worthless any satisfaction I might obtain from realizing my wishes to the full since I am unusually subject to disapproval.

I have the untrammeled desires of an Asiatic potentate with none of his imperviousness to criticism. I wish, sometimes, that I might have been born into an era and nation when poets were highly regarded — Ireland, Persia, China — with, because they were poets, no rank or honor short of kingship denied them. I'd have liked best of all to have been the prime councilor of a powerful monarch, the 'man behind the throne,' in danger from conspiracy, perhaps, but all but removed from popular disesteem so long as I held the favor of the monarch.

It is strange to be possessed of one's own thoughts and to know many of them to be so antisocial that they are wiser left unexpressed — even to one's diary. It isn't, either, that I am ashamed of my thoughts. It is in the case of the diary that I have no wish to incense possible readers needlessly. If you are a reader and I say earnestly that I should have loved to have had an attractive incestuous sister, for it seems to me that no relationship if mutually enjoyed could be closer or more desirable, you are fairly certain to be outraged. I have no inclination, be it understood, to be a libertine; I hold a disgust for those who overindulge in any fashion. I am — or would like to be — arrogant and dictatorial, untrammeled and above social pressure, subject strongly to my own individualistic moral code, a code for friends and loved ones, not for those multitudes of men and women who pass their aggregate existences beyond my immediate ken and interest.

[From Patricia:]

Tho we are living in New Iberia, Paul is stationed in St. Martinville, about ten miles away. St. M. is a tiny place, smaller than Leesville, with no army to liven it up. We'd had enough of that life, and since Paul is on duty every other night he wanted me to be where I would have a little recreation. New Iberia has about 14,000, and is a very well to do little city. It has salt mines and oil, gas, sugar and rice. Besides being right on the Bayou Teche, the loveliest bayou in Louisiana. I'd become interested in this part of the country through reading Hartnet Kane's book, The Bayous of Louisiana. And have been crazy to get down here and explore, I didn't expect to be stationed here, that was too much to hope for, but we were in luck. Paul had asked for a sub-station as he was so fed up with Polk, but other officers wanted it too, they all like to get away from Polk. The colonel likes me because I am the only wife who did any Red Cross work in our unit, so he let Paul have St. Martinville when he heard I wanted to come down here. We don't know how long our stay will be. Some of these branch camps are just seasonal, and are open for three months, we are hoping this one will be a permanent camp.

Paul is trying to hire an outboard motor to take me for a ride up and down the bayou, I'm dying to live on one of the house boats and park it under a tree on hot days. Paul is also trying to get me a bycycle. He has to use the car all the time and it's too hard to go sight-seeing on foot in this climate. I hope he can get one. One of his Cajun chums will probably promote it. They are silly about him. He represents glamour to them. And especially the sub-debs, who are ready for marriage at fourteen here. Word has gotten about that there is an ex movie actor at the P.W. camp, and the town gals all line up along the fences as Paul goes by on his details. He eats it up the lug. We all like our bit of glory, and a wife is apt to know too much about one to furnish much of a cheering section. I'm glad he gets along so well with the natives, some of the men don't. It's hard to handle prison labor, some of the planters want them to work like the negros and Paul has to be very tactful with them, yet discourage griping. It's making quite a diplomat of him and I'm glad. As his usual attitude is if you don't like some one tell him so. He's learning a lot in this job, and if he expects to go in for occupational government it is a good school. He may have to go over as soon as Germany falls, as the Military Police which is his branch will take over then, yet he may stay here, as he manages the prisoner labor so well, and it will be a long time before they will be sent back to Germany. Naturally a well trained body of ex-fighting men can't be set loose in a war torn country, they'd cause no end of trouble and sabotage.

April 1 It's no dice; I can't regard Annabelle impersonally. She's too close geographically. She's an amorphous person, gelatinous mostly, save when she wants something badly enough, not unprepossessing from the waist up (she's neat, even pretty at times) but piano-legged and barrel-bottomed. That she means no ill to me I am sure. Does she ever pry into this diary and read about herself, my goose will be cooked.

I keep the diary under several newspapers, relying on her purblindness not to notice it rather than on her ethical training not to open and read it. In brief words, she's a slob, and whatever capacities, whatever looks (above the waist), whatever good will she may possess do not alter the fact to my eyes, to Mrs. Cash's eyes, to Evelyn's eyes. She's gained over thirty pounds since coming here, yet will not diet. "I'll diet when and if I want to." If she goes to church today, undoubtedly she will be wondering how many people are gazing at and admiring her. Well, a vacation from her until eleven tonight. She fascinates me as a specimen. "Don't think for a moment," Mrs. Cash asserts, "that she is unusual or unique. The country, my dear Mr. Inman, is lousy with her sort. God help them when the carnival stops."

April 2 "My but she's sweet with you," Evelyn commented yesterday. "She couldn't be much nicer. I don't think she really objects to your taking liberties with her; it's merely that her sense of what is improper rises up and gets in her way. Even then, she doesn't lose patience with you. In my opinion, you have a treasure." In mine, also.

"Patsy," I say, "I like this place. It's the softest place on you." "My goodness," she exclaims, her voice tilting upward, "you ought to know, certainly. You've tried everywhere, haven't you. Now how about stopping for a while until I recover my composure? I've been very good, now haven't I?" "Yes," I reply, "I'll stop — immediately. Yes, you have been good. Have you learned to like being touched yet?" "The truth is what you want?" "Yes, this time." "Then no." "Then I don't want the truth. Why don't you like being touched?" "It isn't the thing a young girl should like. And with most people I don't like being touched anyway. You can put your hand on my back and shoulders if you want. Anybody can. I've worn them bare all the summers of my life. But other places I'm not used to being touched. Can't you understand, Arthur? But I'm trying to learn for you, though it nearly slays me sometimes." "How about being hugged?" "Oh, I like that. That's different." "And being kissed?" "If it doesn't occur too often, so I become used to it."

April 3 Evelyn and I paid a call on Juliette yesterday morning. She's been so busy with the baby she and Clarence have adopted that I've seen nothing of her for a long time. The baby isn't Jewish. Juliette seemed delighted to see us. She's a pleasant hostess. She'd just gotten up. Her hair was streaming over her shoulders, a gray thread in it here and there. Her face is heavier and her body is plumper. She looks considerably older, not pretty at all now in her exotic Latin American way. She pulled her robe around her. "You've caught me without make-up on. I look simply terrible." "It's you I want to see, not your make-up," I said, and meant it. Nothing would do but she trot out the baby. From then on he yelled, she not bothered by it. "Oh, he'll stop when he's ready. Besides, he never does this."

When I put my arm around her, she was as plump as a partridge under the thin negligee. A piquant person in many ways, Juliette, not half so volatile as she would have herself appear. I have many pleasant and some exciting memories concerning her. I'll tell of the place she and Clarence have purchased on the North Shore another time, the news in the papers claiming my attention before it grows stale and out of date.

April 10 I am often inclined to view my experiences with young girls as having been unduly unfortunate. Taken in the large, I wonder if that is so. It is Evelyn's sage observation that I become so intense in my affection for youngsters that people look at me with suspicion. That, I feel sure, is partly correct. I have never been indifferent enough to females of any sort, in particular to the attractive ones.

April 11 Evelyn has been deeply distressed by Patsy's acquiescence to her parents' will; she had expected that at the worst some sort of compromise could be reached whereby she could get off on a deserved vacation. She was upset yesterday to the point of worrying me but this morning seems to have recovered somewhat. I wish Patsy would rebel against her mother. If I were a boy again and had my life to relive, I should walk out on my parents did I not get my way, migraines or no migraines, and either stay away or bring them to their senses.

April 13 Roosevelt is dead. Thank God! Thank God! Thank God! Grant him personal courage and pertinacity. Grant him — if history be kind (and I perceive no reason why it should not be) — fame and greatness. Grant him as many other virtues as you will. Still thank God or Fate or Providence or whatever it was struck him down with cerebral hemorrhage, that he is dead. It is as though a pall, a blight had been removed.

He has belittled those stable virtues which have always gone to make any people strong, self-reliant, prideful: the virtues of thrift, honesty, individual independence, reliability, pride, initiative. He took us into a great war that was not intrinsically or geographically our war and thereby prevented us from winning in shorter order a war that is our war. The souls of the dead and the bitterness of the maimed and incapacitated are his burden, and if there be a just God as so often he proclaimed, I should not like to stand in his shoes before the divine bar.

All yesterday evening lauding voices, emotional, mellifluous, sanctimonious, held forth on the radio upon the noble Franklin Delano Roosevelt, and no utterance was too sentimental, too maudlin, too unreal to command the audience. The canonization of a man had begun before hardly was the body cold. One would assume, to listen to the radio and read the papers, that no men inimical to Roosevelt still existed in the United States, although I doubt not paeans of relief and thanksgiving that he is no more rise, if secretly, from innumerable hearts and minds. Roosevelt is dead. It is well for the nation and probably for his fame that he is.

Harry S Truman looked pretty good to Arthur. His inauguration signaled the exchange of "Roosevelt's palace guard of Jews and Anglo-Saxon misfits and dreamers" for "a coterie of hard-headed, practical, self-seeking political adventurers" less capable "of blooding a nation so deeply, so wastefully, with such lasting consequences" than FDR's "muddle-headed idealists." But the picture was not rosy. The United States still had no foreign policy, still deferred to Stalin, still played "the part of a loyal colonial dominion" to England, still tightened its belt while the beaten Germans basked in the sun and ate steak.

Arthur's continuing depression fostered such cranky thoughts. Untidy Annabelle talked about leaving for Texas, the home of her in-laws, to wait for her soldier husband. Ungrateful and stingy Janice, having produced a large baby, seemed about ready to ditch Arthur (she did not even remember his fiftieth birthday). Patsy Boland, recipient of his many gifts—including a secondhand Ford—did not rebel against her parents as Arthur urged her to do, and she devoted inordinate amounts of time to her studies. He fumed as his love for her intensified. His staff depleted, Arthur advertised for "secretaries" and tried out a series of applicants, most of whom lasted only a short while. All the male job-seekers turned out to be flops. Cheerful letters from Billy Minor (now a radio man on a B-29) made Arthur yearn for his trusty manservant.

Old Garrison Hall friends occasionally surfaced. Claire had fallen in love with a married man. Would Arthur testify that Sam Mercer was a drunk? Ella seemed dispirited as she passed into middle age. Dr. Pike, as always the faithful attendant, worried over his delinquent son and his unmarried daughter. The years were catching up with this iron man too.

The future hung heavy over Arthur. What lay in store for him after the death of Hitler and the certain defeat of Japan? He admired the resolution of "these little yellow men," potential allies against America's future foe, Joe Stalin, and paid tribute to their heroic defense of Okinawa. The dropping of the Hiroshima bomb finished them off, but a terrible genie had been let out of the bottle. Arthur brooded on the sickening question: given the likelihood of world incineration, what was the point of continuing his diary keeping?

April 14 The demonstration that is being put on about Roosevelt's death seems to me, rank sentimentalist though I am, sickeningly mawkish. The papers are bad enough, but the radio is worse. All regular programs on the latter have been cancelled with the exception of commentators. Eulogistic speeches, reports, descriptions, sermons pour forth hour upon hour, interlarded between the sappiest music that can be selected. The words "shocked" and "stunned" recur with unimaginative frequency. The volatile American people are wallowing in an emotional orgasm.

They were honestly shocked by his death. They sincerely regret his passing as signifying the loss of their great friend in high places. In a way, they are wrong on no counts; it is simply that they are incapable of realizing that many of the reforms inaugurated are mileposts along a road that can lead directly to the totalitarianism they abhor. It is always lamentable that so many people of good will are out of touch with reality and ignorant of consequences; they feel rather than think. Well, Roosevelt is to be buried tomorrow morning at his estate at Hyde Park by the Hudson River, and I, for one, shall be glad to have him underground.

It is to be hoped that Truman will also prune away at least some of the bureaucratic deadwood. The bureaucracy that Roosevelt has encouraged to come into being is not among the least delinquencies to be charged against him. It may have helped reelect and keep him in office, but it is gross by now, cumbersome, at cross-purposes within itself, position-proud, filled with incompetents. It should certainly be shrunk and seeded though I doubt we shall ever be able to get rid of it any more than the citizens of the Roman Empire could unloose the grip of the officials who in time became parasites feeding upon the people. A hierarchy of bureaucrats appears to be so self-perpetuating that nothing short of revolution can oust them.

April 17 Truman made his first Presidential address, nothing brilliant but sincere, humble, appealing. Full of good stuff. Interested, apparently, in government by law rather than by personalities. Spoke of plans for world peace. "The responsibility of the great states is to serve and not dominate the peoples of the world." "Let me assure the forward-looking people of America that there will be no relaxation in our efforts to improve the lot of the common people." Carry on Roosevelt's doctrines. "Increased production, increased employment, and better standards of living throughout the world." "I ask only to be a good and faithful servant of my Lord and my people." How much is hooey and how much meant? Can't tell. So much icing on cakes of all politicians that impossible to know until cake is cut into what is like inside. I cast a leery eye at all this fanfare about the common people and God and our Lord and being good shepherd to all the world. Probably the politicians deem it necessary to let such sap flow. Not many, like Churchill, promise blood, sweat and tears or whatever it was. Too afraid of displeasing the people. Probably I eye anything political too suspiciously. Good in the men who hold office, sometimes. Must be. But when and where only time will tell and a straining out of the guff and blarney.

April 18 I have been lying on the bed in Annabelle's room talking with Rose and watching her while she shells peas. Her feet are too large and toe in and her teeth are discolored where they join the gums, but those two blemishes ignored or disregarded, she is a pretty woman in anyone's language. When she wears a thin face-veil on her hat, she is almost irresistibly pretty. Her clothes are always scrupulously clean and impeccably neat. She affects a slip which rustles.

I can watch her for hours and be pleased doing it. Hen-headed she may be, but I grow increasingly fond of her. She enjoys being teased and hugged and made a fuss over as long as she feels I don't regard her as a body. She keeps her bills pinned to her girdle. When I make them rustle or flip the elastic to her panties, she blushes. "Aren't you a devil," she will say. "You know right well no one ever did that to me. What about my dignity?" Without Rose's assistance, I don't know what we should have done to get along since Janice and Pearl left.

April 21   Evelyn said: "I took Corn to lunch. I was asking her about Roosevelt's death and how she felt about it. She'd been at home by herself all evening and hadn't heard the news on the radio. Elizabeth called her from Cleveland about something else. She asked Corn what she was doing. Corn replied that she was listening to a symphony. Elizabeth said wasn't it awful about the President. Corn said wasn't what awful. Then Elizabeth told her. When Corn went to bed, she couldn't sleep. So about midnight she decided to get up, dress and go out. She took a streetcar. The tears, she said, were rolling down her cheeks. She kept dabbing her eyes with her handkerchief. A Marine sitting behind her asked her what was the matter. She replied that nothing was the matter. She continued to cry. The Marine moved up beside her. He persuaded her to get off and walk. She then told him she was grieving for Roosevelt. 'Oh,' he said, 'is that all? This country,' he said, 'is a democracy. One man's death — any man's death — won't stop it. It will go on. You're foolish,' he said, 'to regard Roosevelt as irreplaceable.' When he found out he couldn't date Corn, he left her. I said to her: 'Did you really feel that way about Roosevelt? Why did you feel that way?' She replied that he stood for everything in the world she believed in. I remarked that he had tried to do the impossible, to arrange for the millennium, that no man in his lifetime could achieve the millennium. She asserted that Roosevelt could if he had lived and been left alone."

April 23   War news has by now become such an habitual matter that seldom does it stir me. That our troops continue to advance, that the Russians are fighting within the streets of ravaged Berlin, once the fifth city in the world, that we have taken Bologna at last and the entire Italian line appears to be in headlong retirement to the mountains — these items are but punctuation marks to what is now a foregone conclusion.

The American reaction to the horror tales emanating from Germany interests me somewhat. The meat shortage and the utter mismanagement of food distribution within the United States gives me thought and — as it concerns my eating — emotions, though minor ones to be sure. The conference in San Francisco this week (had not my idealism as to international sincerity long ago been shattered) might claim more of my attention than it does. I merely wonder to what degree Russia and England will use honeyed words to get their ways and use us; and I hope, not too trustfully, that Truman will give away less than I am sure Roosevelt would have. Truman did succeed in getting Stalin to send Molotov to the conference, a concession Roosevelt failed to attain. I have a hunch that Truman is not going to be the easy nut to crack that Roosevelt was. Perhaps now we will retain most of the Pacific islands we have won.

Woody arrived at eleven, expects to leave at two. Looks very well. Has on a fur neckpiece and a new perky pink straw hat with a stand-up black ribbon, a veil over her face. Her dilated green eyes, when she is feeling well, are really handsome. Her hair is becoming altogether gray. She has it parted up the back and brushed off her ears. Although not at all pretty, with each year that goes by she chooses her clothes with improved judgment, so that the impression she gives is one of considerable attractiveness. A long ways she has come from the scroozed-up stenographer I first knew — was it eighteen years ago? How she looks is quite dependent upon how animated she is, and today she fairly sparkles. The words tumble out of her mouth one upon another, and what she says is like a small and very bright rivulet flashing in the sun.

April 24 Woody is collecting old clothes for the drive to reclothe the Europeans. "It's been lots of fun. You'd never guess how many old ladies of means live in secluded retirement upon memories of the past within Victorian houses. They want to tell you the history of every article of habiliment they decide to donate. Some of them are awfully sweet. I'd like to know the history of the old-fashioned split drawers with the delicate lacework that one old lady donated the other day, a veritable museum piece — but of course I was told nothing about them. I sometimes speculate to myself that the needy in Europe will be the drollest-clad humans on the face of the globe — if they wear what we send them. Of course much of it is excellent and up-to-date."

April 25 Yesterday morning Annabelle went to Evelyn and told her that she had decided to leave. Her husband's family in Texas had invited her to come to stay with them, sending her the train fare. She would not, she said, leave at once. I had sensed when Annabelle went off for two days that she was in the throes of a decision and should not have been too surprised had she not come back at all. So Evelyn and I held a council, the upshot of which was that she should tell Annabelle I knew nothing and that she, Evelyn, didn't see how she could get along without her, the winter had been such an ordeal. Could she, Annabelle, at the least stay until next fall? Did she realize what a jolt it would be to her unconventional nature to live with relatives in a small Southern town, bigoted, watchful, alert for mistakes on her part, comparable with prison discipline, and hot, very, very hot? What I have sought to teach Evelyn for years is that with the majority of Americans when you wish to impress them, you must establish an emotional background before proceeding with logic or argumentation. I don't know how she succeeded with Annabelle, for I have not talked with her since.

April 26   Am reading 'The Road to Serfdom,' a book analyzing the steps by which the total state is impressed upon a nation,[19] a book on India and the Indian problem, and on the talking-book, Arnold Bennett's 'The Old Wives' Tale,' which I am enjoying greatly. 'The Autobiography of Benvenuto Cellini' I find much in the tone of Casanova's 'Memoirs,' bombastic, self-assertive, in paragraphs pithy, in sections rather dull, yet altogether illuminating as to the age. Read less than formerly since Mrs. Cash copies the diaries and there is no Roderic. Without the talking-books, I should be readerless most of the evenings.

Lilacs in a vase give off their perfume. The east wind is tangy with salt. I hear sea gulls. I think of Mount Desert.

April 27   Annabelle felt badly all night with her period. I let her stay in bed late this morning. She looks like the wrath of God. Getting her off shopping mornings is downright work. She's like a dog on the street with his nose and what it smells more important than any destination he had in mind when he started. Everything she sees distracts her. Like the dog, she leaves a trail of signposts behind her — an unwashed cup of cold coffee, half a cracker, notes, towels not hung up, open drawers, half-written letters, scrawled telephone numbers, cigarettes one-fifth smoked, pocketbooks, magazines, quarters and dimes.

April 30   Evelyn had warned me not to keep at Patsy too long until she tired nervously. So we went into the library to look at and try on the new dresses I'd been collecting all week. I'd rather spend my money on buying dresses for the women I like than on anything else I know. It gives me downright pleasure. I like female clothes, too, always have, from the days when Sam and I used to act as a board of choice for Jennie's clothes and she would kiss us when we admired her selection and sometimes weep when we didn't. There

[19] This influential book by the respected economist and social historian Friedrich August von Hayek (1899–) was an early popular warning against the totalitarian state. Hayek believed that the slightest listing toward a system of economic controls and the weakening of free competition would start an irreversible slide to tyranny. Some conservative magazines and big corporations cited Hayek in their campaigns against any sort of social planning.

were summer clothes, most with bare backs and one with a bare stomach. I sat in the judge's chair. Patsy stepped out into the hall. "I must preserve my modesty," she said, "for it's proper to do so. If I had more up above, perhaps I wouldn't be modest. I think women are that way, modest in proportion to what they think they have or have not. Don't you?"

Some of the dresses were good, some not. The green one with the naked stomach — price, thirty dollars — was most fetching on her. She liked it, too. Her sorrel hair, her green eyes, her very white stomach, the grass green of the dress made a pleasant picture. It's too bad she has a number of dark freckles on her otherwise very white back. I feel sure, so revealing are these sunsuit dresses, that American women, were it the fashion, would as leave go naked as not. And why not, when you come to think of it? It is only my Victorian background that influences me to find anything astonishing about it.

May 2   Hitler is supposed to have been killed in Berlin by enemy fire. Perhaps it is so. Perhaps he was murdered. Most likely, he has vanished into some long-prepared secret hideout. A meteoric rise, his, and his name will be scrawled largely across the pages of history and may in time accrue to itself the glamor of the name of Napoleon. He should certainly become a German myth. The admiral who has assumed the government announces that Germany will continue to fight to the last.

As I study the rise and fall of powerful historical figures, it is usually only those who do not overexpand too quickly who last. Their dreams of adding to their stature usually terminate in disaster. A nation like a person can be only so greedy, however good the digestion, without courting malady or ruin.

I wonder will not Mr. Stalin end by being too greedy? Molotov dominates the San Francisco setup. We come out the short end of the horn as usual. The details, insofar as this diary is concerned, are too Machiavellian to record. Suffice it that Russia is doing best, ourselves worst. End, not improbably, by letting ourselves be talked out of our rightful preeminence, surrendering our present might, financing those who mock at us, good-naturedly permitting ourselves to be shoved around. Idealistic numbskulls, we.

I hesitate to speculate upon what will happen does Annabelle leave and Patsy not come. Evelyn is upset enough as it is. She says: "I have to work upon myself constantly not to be resentful." I opened by chance her bill from the liquor store this morning. She's been drinking steadily again despite her promise not to, despite her assurances whenever I ask her that she isn't. It hurts me that she sees fit to break her promises and to lie. It worries me, for she never feels as well when drinking constantly, no matter what temporary pleasure she may derive from imbibing. And when she gets drunk I'm always frightened she will fall down the stairs and damage herself. Then what will become of me?

My diary isn't being copied. I have slowed down on the correcting of the old diaries. I have Evelyn around less afternoons to compensate for the extra time she gives me mornings. I spend increasing periods by myself. But my curtains must be shut down mornings if I am not to have such headaches that I lose all sense and perspective, and my fingers are too weak to do it myself as once I did. I must eat. There are telephone calls to be made. My room has to be aired out every so often when the curtains are down if I am not to stifle. People have to be hired and fired. Some letters at least must be written. Clocks have to be wound, dishes washed, laundry sent out and checked in. I am a pretty puling plant, when all is said, and it takes a lot of attention to keep me from wilting. It is not what the plant wants; it is the condition of the plant

May 3 I sometimes reflect that this diary is one of the strangest documents of autobiography ever written by anyone. In its pages is an agglomeration of subject matter only a catholic taste will wish to absorb — or so it seems to me. There is virtually no physical motion to sustain interest through shifts of environment. An unwilling celibate pens it. Philosophy and pages of history walk side by side with emotional outbursts and sentimental encounters. There is some beauty now and again, a facility of expression, a vehement earnestness but likewise not a little crassness here and there, much awkwardness of concept, as much juvenility as sapiency. I would give much to chance upon a similar chronicle despite its manifold faults, for in it I could lose myself. If it possesses that virtue for a handful of readers in the future, I shall be satisfied. Hate living I may, disdain people I may, long for oblivion I may; nonetheless I find existence exciting, people stimulating, oblivion not near. If I pass on to a small section of posterity the excitement, the tension, the bewilderment, the suspense, the confusion of these years, I shall be satisfied. The people in the chronicle are not great people, save certain of those in the historical background; the events close to me are not startling events; my days are passed, as it were, behind plate glass. Yet it may be that in this strange document I will have succeeded in perpetuating the beating pulse of an era.

May 4 In recapitulating the failure of the German dream to be realized, what were the cardinal mistakes in strategy that led to total defeat rather than to final success? First: The victorious Germans should have, close on the heels of Dunkirk, crossed the Channel in whatever craft they had on hand and rushed the conquest of England, thereafter rested militarily on their laurels, satisfied with Czechoslovakia, Poland, France, etc. Second: It was ill-advised to attack Russia with England still functioning diplomatically. Third: Italy should have been kept neutral. Fourth: With Crete won and British naval power in the Mediterranean cracked, at whatever cost the Germans should have taken Cyprus and from there gone into Syria, thus assuring themselves oil and threatening Russia from the south. Fifth: Stalingrad should have been by-passed. In my opinion, a secret treaty must have existed between Berlin and Tokyo whereby when the German advance reached a certain point, the Japanese would attack the Russians in Siberia. Perhaps that point was the capture of Stalingrad. Whatever the point, had the Japanese lived up to their portion of the agreement, it is not inconceivable that Russia might have succumbed. It was an error of Japanese judgment which may have been as costly for them as for the Germans.

The long months of air bombing of Germany and German-controlled nations appears now to have been eminently worthwhile, though not altogether in ways that had been expected. The most important results of bombing — if the destruction of housing and monuments of art and the adverse influence of that upon future culture and civilization in Germany and elsewhere be placed in another category — were twofold: to reduce the supply of oil and gasoline until the dearth of it crippled effective military action, and to hamstring transportation so thoroughly that troops could not be moved to points of stress with celerity, and supplies and munitions became scarce. These results seem to have been far more important to our military success than the bombing of ordinary plants manufacturing steel, tanks, chemicals, planes, etc.

Nor did indiscriminate bombing of cities and the killing of civilians appear to have done much toward ultimate victory, the populace having in time become either numb or inured to disaster from the skies. It has been one of the most astounding phenomena of this war that civilian morale has seldom been cracked irreparably by bombing. Some of the captured German generals claim that air attack upon artillery was a manifestation of bombing that did much to nullify the potency of their military machine.

May 7 Patsy has been coming Sundays and an hour Monday afternoons. She will not come any evening. "If you hadn't taught me how to interest boys, I'd still be coming evenings twice or three times a week. I won't give up the few nights I have left on which to study and sleep. Call me selfish. I have an argument with myself each time I refuse you, but I always win out. I feel deeply indebted to you, and I dislike being indebted to anyone. Perhaps that's one thing that stands between us." When I replied that I didn't want her to come because she was indebted to me but because she wished to, her answer was to the effect that she didn't wish to. I inquired did she wish more remuneration. No, she didn't, I was very generous.

Well, that's that. As I have said before, she's stubborn, willful, contrary, selfish — a packet of potential grief, in short. As I told her, every bit of common sense in me yelled at me to stay out of her way, the only difficulty being that she fascinated me and I couldn't. And she does. And I can't.

May 9 My Father is in excellent physical condition. He has lost weight. The hearing apparatus he uses this year is so good I scarcely need to raise my voice. "I haven't had a drink," he brags, "since February. I can walk right up to a barroom and spit in its face." We chatted with apparent amiability for forty-five minutes, Evelyn eyeing us watchfully. I should think he'd resent me as I do him. His final remark was: "Are these your books in this room? For goodness' sake, what can you do with so many books? Those books up in Maine, I don't know what on earth to do with them, there's so many." "Half the books in Maine are mine," I said. "Are they?" he said, and added: "I don't know what to do with them, there's so many." I could hear him mulling over in his mind whom to give them to. I hated his unjust guts. "He's a nice-looking man," says Rose in her mild way.

May 11 Fifty years old today. May there be very few more years to add to the fifty that are past. It has been an unwanted life.

Evelyn gave me four tumblers to make up for my favorite one that Annabelle broke, very pretty and expensive. I appreciated them. She also made me a present of a tricornered vase to put on the chest for flowers from the country. Patsy sent a card with a naked little girl imp blowing bubbles — symbolic, I suppose, of the dresses I've tried on her — and signed "All my love." Father presented me with a half-dozen handkerchiefs he had picked out himself, tasteful. Rose brought a lighted cake her daughter Wendy had made. Then there was a box from both of them. I opened it. The first object I caught sight of was the closed-eyed head of a chicken reposing on white tissue paper, very incongruous. I removed another piece of paper, and there lay a broiler on its back, wearing a tissue skirt and a paper hat, holding in one plucked wing five sticks of chewing gum. I bust out laughing. We all laughed, even the Old Man. It was remarkably comical. A fine gift, too, in these days of no chickens. Rose thought it up.

So that has been my birthday to now. Perhaps the succeeding mail will bring other cards, but thus far I've had neither word nor card from Janice. I feel hurt. Though I may have to eat these words later, if she fails to remember me I shall count her as ungrateful as Edna, who, at any rate, wasn't stingy. I've given Janice a truckload of presents in my time, and if she passes me by I'll certainly think less of her. She has been out and around for a number of days now, and there's no excuse possible for her forgetting at least a card. I think she's one of the stingiest persons I ever knew. Patsy should have sent me something after all the presents I've given, but she's young and may be waiting for a photograph to give me and anyway did send a card.

When the Old Man asked Evelyn what I wanted, because she told him it was my birthday (he never remembers of himself), and she inquired of me, I suggested that he tell me about my ancestors. He didn't say no. He has been with me for an hour, left so angry he was chewing his false teeth.

I began on Shadrach Walker Inman. He had little to volunteer there save that Grampa was a spry old man at eighty, offered to run him a race. He kept stale cookies in a drawer for the children. He never read books.

Of his mother he had a bit more to say. "She was just about the sweetest woman who ever lived. She didn't go out much with your grandfather. She concerned herself with home affairs. She was extremely particular about her house, was noted for her table, wouldn't permit a speck of dust to be in the corners. She had dark hair and was a little like your Aunt Nellie in looks, your Aunt Nellie when she was younger and different. She was much interested in church affairs. I never saw her in anything but black—she had so many children and they died so fast. I was crazy about her. When she and my father and Nell were in New York about to sail for Europe and she died, I was in Atlanta and had to prepare for the arrival of the body—they brought her home by train—and it was one of the saddest experiences of my life. I live in the present and have always had all I can do to make a living and tend to my own affairs—so how it can interest you what your grandmother died of in New York I can't imagine. She died of a hemorrhage. Too many children, I suppose, too quick one after another. Who told you it was tuberculosis? Maybe it was. I couldn't say."

His mother, save for having children, was not, according to him, ever sick. His father was never sick a day in his life after the war, though was frail before it or so he told Father. All the Inmans had thin legs. And that was all he would commit himself to on the subject of my forbears.

He was a bit more outspoken as to his college days at Princeton. He entered at eighteen. He took special courses, because he had been taught no Greek, and Greek was required. He liked Latin. Father passed the Latin examination at the end of the year, because he overheard one professor discussing with another what passages of Caesar to ask, and Father memorized those passages. In his Sophomore year, he decided he was tired of Latin and had himself transferred to a course in international law which he enjoyed. Mother used to tell me that his eyes were so bad he had to listen to most of his courses and learn by ear, but he has apparently entirely forgotten that. When I inquired why he left Princeton at the end of the second year and did he mind, he replied: "I left because I'd gotten all I wanted out of college. Of course I didn't mind leaving. I wanted to support myself." There is, as far as I can determine, no sentiment attached to the memory of his college days.

I asked if Mother had been pretty when he married her. "She was said to be," he replied, narrowing the pupils of his eyes and glowering at me. Did he recall proposing to her? Of course he did, but that was personal and no business of mine. He began to chew his teeth. He pulled out his heavy gold watch and looked at it. "We've got to go, Evelyn, if we're to see Rivers." Had he, I persisted, proposed to anyone else before he proposed to Mother? His ire mounted. "That's a personal question and none of your business. It's an impertinent question. You don't expect an answer, do you? If you do, you won't get one. How would you like to have me ask you why you didn't have children?" I was angry. "If you can't ask your own father personal questions, who in the world can you ask? I didn't have children because I didn't want them to suffer as I have. And it's a question you have a perfect right to ask. And that is the answer." He looked as if he could wring my neck. "Children," he pronounced, rising, "are overrated. All they want of parents is more and more. When they're grown, they leave you. But they never stop wanting things. Come on, Evelyn," he commanded, "let's be going." Before he went out the door, his innate conservatism came to his side and made him say: "I hope you'll have many more birthdays."

I thanked him, hated him, watched him progress down the hallway to Annabelle's door, heard him put on his manner-to-strangers and pass very gracious and winning remarks to Annabelle and Mrs. Trench, felt in my heart a tide of resentment against a parent who was about as approachable as a lizard the eyes of which were like his eyes, went into Annabelle's room when he had disappeared and tickled Annabelle to work off my spleen and because it always puts her in a good humor. Now I am by myself and about to sign checks to pay bills with the money he gives me because he not only feels in duty bound but probably loves me in a gnarled sort of way. He goes tomorrow morning and may his days be numbered, though I'm sure they won't be. He seems genuinely to admire Evelyn. He admires her, I know, because she can endure me. "Anybody," he says to me, "that can live with you has got to be wonderful."

May 13 I feel not only badly but put out as well that Janice failed to remember my birthday. It was my impulse to write her a note, but I didn't. I have given her at least a couple of dozen dresses, sweaters, scarfs, headscarfs, the sapphire and pearl cross and chain, my grandmother's garnet necklace, an automobile, gas coupons galore (oh yes, she did give me three of her mother's coupons once — when I asked), flowers time and again, the big mirror in her house, an electric clock, money for trips, $200 when she left, food and canned goods day after day, candy, bread, cakes, I forget what not. I have literally lavished presents on her.

It is probably better to write it like this than speak it to her, for voicing my disapproval has never accomplished results with her on these two subjects. Although I telephoned her every day or two when she was sick recently, she has not telephoned me once to say she was better or to wish me well. Which is enough steam blown off about Janice. Dottie pronounced, when I had said my mind to her: "It's my opinion that once she has had her baby you won't see Janice again. I think I'm correct. You might as well resign yourself to it."

May 16 This is what I think of President Truman. He isn't a show-off. He is conscientiously intent upon the duties of his incumbency. He goes slowly and has made few mistakes thus far. If he differs with anyone, he speaks his mind but does so neither sarcastically nor belittlingly as Roosevelt was apt to do. He evidently believes that others besides himself have the right of opinion. Although my judgment may prove erroneous, I am convinced that Stalin and Churchill will not find the new President the pushover for their wily schemes that Roosevelt was. If Truman is altruistic-minded, feels we should feed Europe, so would be most Americans in his position. I do not think that he will be the wild-eyed inaugurator of new theories and reforms that Roosevelt was. His conscience, I suspect, is of more importance to him than the plaudits and approval of the public and his intimates. The job's the thing, not what history will write about him. I'm exceedingly pleased thus far. It is as though a season of violent and unpredictable weather had passed.

May 23 Could a Japanese be at my window this moment and observe the almost continuous parade of air might across the blue cloud-brown sky from east to west, would he not lose confidence?

May 25   Annabelle heard from her husband for the first time in a month and a half. It was in incoherent V-mail note directing her to expect him any time, not stating whether he would be mustered out or only in the United States for thirty days' leave on his way to the Pacific. She is excited. If I find a couple of secretaries, I really don't care whether she goes for good or stays.

May 30   I wrote Billy a letter yesterday, asking him if, were men over thirty-five mustered out of the Army, would he be returning to me. I wrote a sentimental letter. I wrote a longer letter to Patsy thanking her for having been so good to me and telling her how much she meant to me. Janice telephoned yesterday. I wish she had been sterile, had never had this baby. Evelyn looks like the wrath of God. It is (the woman doctor to whom she went told her) the menopause. She's tired, too. I'm letting her have most afternoons off as much as I'd like to work. Nothing I've written is being corrected. She's going to the movies today, later with Dr. Pike to the Bird Sanctuary.

June 3   Annabelle yesterday heard definitely—so she says—that her husband's outfit is in transit on the way home, albeit she hasn't received direct word from him. "I'm so scared, Arthur, I could get under the bed." She's to go to Texas with him to a small town southeast of San Antonio where his father owns a cattle ranch. They have three barns, and there is a lake on the property. "And that," says Annabelle, "is about all I know about it. Ted has a horse, an old car and a motorcycle. They have a hired man and his wife and two or three other people to help. Mr. Collier is fairly well off."

I am teasing Annabelle about the heat, the wide flatness, the redbugs and chiggers, the strictness of small-town conventions. She takes it well but really in her heart expects her marriage "to be a complete flop." So do I.

June 8   Annabelle has gone, and Evelyn, Rose and I are left to carry on. What will happen next is anybody's guess. Evelyn looks harassed. I feel harassed.

June 11   The San Francisco Conference is by way of being a farce. Nothing emanating from it will prevent any big nation from making war. Congress and Truman apparently are committing themselves to the very foolish policy of lending money, giving it to every nation that wants it upon the assumption that only thus is world prosperity to be reestablished and peace maintained. Far better to put that money, billions upon billions, into armament, for it would serve our eventual safety better so. Stalin is calling up youths of fifteen for military training. Like it or no, we should have such training for our young men do we wish to persist as a nation. If money is to be loaned abroad, let individuals with the soundness of the ventures in mind do it, and companies and corporations — not the United States Government, where impractical idealism holds sway and no one is punishably responsible.

June 13 Woody with us for four hours, fretting about whether almost 15 year old Peggy could prepare a meal for Allan. Evelyn and she went out to supper at a restaurant. Woody held forth upon Allan's three children by his first wife making her house a home. She doesn't like it but says nothing.

She and I had a pleasant conversation, though I shocked her when I said that I wished Allan would die and she'd come back to Boston. I amused and shocked Woody by my description of how I was in love with Patsy, of how I had been in love with Evelyn, Janice and Patsy all at once. It was good to see her.

June 14 Dreamed last night was taking Patsy to a play. We sat in a box. The box was overcrowded. People pressed in on us. The show was cheap. The people were sordid. We agreed to leave. We walked to the end of the street to the side of a canal about as wide as a room, brown and dirty. Patsy fell in. The mud was too thick to swim. I jumped in to rescue her. I slogged my way across to where she was struggling feebly. I strove to rescue her. People lined the bank not eight feet above, looked on, offered no assistance. Their faces were blank. Patsy settled in the mud. Her auburn hair lay outspread on the brown fluid. I pushed back to the other side of the canal. A man had a barrow filled with empty boxes. I explained Patsy's plight, asked for some boxes. He refused. I knocked him down, took the boxes, recrossed the canal, raised Patsy to the boxes, somehow lifted her to safety. We were wet and muddy. I was exhausted. We commenced walking home. A young man appeared. Patsy walked with him. I could not keep up. I fell behind. Without further glance at me, Patsy and the young man disappeared in the distance. I was overcome with my own weariness and her ingratitude.

June 15 Have just conversed with the daughter of Raymond Gram Swing, the pro-English, pro-Russian radio commentator, relative to the position. She just graduated from Smith College, hotbed of young female radicals. She wished to determine my political views. "I had wished," she said, "you had been a left-winger. I couldn't work for anyone who didn't admire Roosevelt and think the English are wonderful. I really couldn't, you know." Which suited me. Another applicant down. I'm too difficult to please, undoubtedly. Probably I'll continue to find no one. I'd rather have a simple person than a would-be intelligentsia any day. I basically rate brains and education far below charm and warmth and character and personality.

June 18 Ella was here during the evening. We talked of her husband. He has been awarded a Greenwald Foundation scholarship to study labor and labor relations for a year at Tufts. The New York, New Haven, & Hartford Railroad has granted him leave of absence, with permission to work Sundays, Saturdays and holidays. The scholarship: $2,000.

"I watched Robby bringing all sorts of people to our house, turning it into a sort of combined office and beer parlor. I watched him helping all sorts of people get jobs and sinecures. He's sort of easygoing, as you know, and modest. He'd push others rather than himself. I kept on watching. I said to myself, 'Uhn-unh, Ella, if you let him alone he'll always be the helper, not the helped. There's no reason he should always be missing the gravy train.' So I wrote Bill Tappley and asked him if he couldn't look around and find out if there weren't some way in which Robby could learn more of the theory of labor, so he could get higher — at present he knew only the practice. Well, Bill looked around and came through with this Greenwald Foundation idea. I said it sounded good to me but to breathe no word of it to Robert until it was all set. So that's what happened. The C.I.O. officials from Phil Murray down got behind the project. Then we told Robby. He went to New York and talked to the secretary of the Foundation. She was favorably impressed. Robert is the first man to be awarded a scholarship to study labor and labor relations from New England. Most of the papers gave him a big send-off. He starts to Tufts this fall. I'm immensely pleased, Arthur. Bill says, 'What a wife. What a wife.' I don't know about that. But I am very ambitious for Robert. He's in earnest. He has the manners. He's a good mixer. He has the movement at heart. There's no reason he shouldn't shake apples from the top of the tree as well as other people."

June 24 Dr. Pike has been here. I have some sort of fungus infection around my anus and private parts, probably caught from Annabelle who insisted on cleaning my toilet with the tools she used on hers. It has itched for three weeks. Dr. Pike says to consult a skin doctor.

June 29 The Japanese defense of Okinawa has been of epic character if it be regarded with historical detachment. Up to the days of the final attack only some two thousand Japanese regular soldiers had been captured or had capitulated and not more than three thousand by now — in effect the entire body of troops fighting through rains of bombs, constant naval shelling, land mortars, flamethrowers, grenades, thirst, God knows what else, against superior attacking forces implemented by superior armaments to the long and bitter end. The Alamo was child's play to such desperate defense. The defense of Britain was on a far less self-sacrificing and heroic scale. If we rate our own courage as highly as we do, it seems to me we would do well to give due credit to the courage of a valiant foe however disdainful we may be of his less worthy qualities.

July 2 'Black Boy' by Richard Wright, the colored novelist. It is supposed to be autobiographical, nonfictional but bears every appearance of having been fictionalized, if not as to facts then at least as to psychological values. It is written with skill and emotional intensity. Wright draws a picture of the conflict in interests and wills between the Southern whites and negroes that becomes often luridly melodramatic. In small towns in South Carolina and Mississippi, for all I know, the picture may be accurate, even occasionally as starkly black and white as he draws it; but I seriously doubt if the friction he emphasizes is true across the length and breadth of the South, though truer, I doubt not, now than when I was a boy there before Roosevelt, Mrs. Roosevelt and the present war.

Once when I was about sixteen, I was eating lunch in the dining car of the 'Vestibule' on my way from school to Atlanta. Across the aisle at a table by himself sat a sour-faced man of the politician-Kentucky colonel type. He was having some difficulty with his order. The black waiter was scurrying to and fro to wait on him. Suddenly, the face of the man at the table became choleric. "You goddamn, black-faced, son-of-a-bitch nigger, you bring me what I want and do it quick, or I'll . . . !" I was thoroughly shocked. I had never during fairly close association with colored people heard any white man address any negro that way, even the bosses of the chain gangs I used to watch working on the roads. It seemed to me—and I am sure that the Philadelphia influence I had been subjected to for some years had nothing to do with how I felt—altogether unwarrantable and disgusting that a white man in a public place should so comport himself. And that is the single memory I have of a negro being badly insulted by a white man. In Atlanta, Decatur and other places with which I was familiar, it was so rare as to be obtrusive. The white men I knew felt so deeply superior to the negroes, yet at the same time so in sympathy with them as irresponsibles that they rarely broke their code of behavior to engage in violent action or upbraiding. Call it an armed truce with tolerance on both sides if you wish, an attempt to get along, habitual hypocrisy, but whatever it was that permitted two different races to live together at least in surface amity, it was very real and functioned adequately enough to assure a fairly peaceful if socially inequable structure of existence.

July 6 Morganthau, the very dumb but cocky Jew who has been

Secretary of the Treasury since I have forgotten when, is to step out at last. Slowly but surely Truman is breaking with those elements of the American social scene who supported and benefited from the New Deal. Every day or two when I feel discouraged, I look around me and recollect that Roosevelt is dead, feel better about everything.

July 17 Sent off letter to Patsy telling her either to write me more often or quit, in gentle language approved by both Rose and Evelyn. She's not much good, Patsy, in most ways, a chip on her shoulder too often, no mellowness, little genuine tenderness, fairly dumb. I wish I didn't love her so much, could ditch her. But I can't.

July 19 We must have received at the minimum fifty telephone calls in answer to our advertisement for a man. The labor market must have broken wide open. I wish we had put the salary lower than $40. Of course the majority of applicants were Irish, closely followed by Italians (no Jews for this sort of work), but a sufficient sprinkling were of acceptable descent. Quite a few were veterans. I have, I think, no notion of taking an ex-serviceman. Their psychology is out of balance. They resent civilians.

July 21 Another young fellow, Paul Temple, has just arrived from New York to interview us. He's a would-be writer and advertised for a job in the 'Saturday Review of Literature.' Do I end up with choice between three possibilities, I'll blow a gasket. As Evelyn says, "Bad luck, yes, we can take it, but good luck, we don't know what to do with it — it slays us." So more later, probably less optimistic. Gee, I'd like to get a man.

Later: First, about Paul Temple. "Wait," exclaimed Evelyn, "until you lay eyes on him." In spite of which, I recoiled involuntarily. He was like a bleached insect emerging from under a damp piece of wood, all save his hair which was auburn. A thin little fellow, his skin white, his hands thin, his clothes ill-fitting and baggy, his back somewhat stooped, steel-rimmed spectacles on his frail-appearing eyes, his front teeth discolored, his chin meager, the hair on his face resembling that of a young boy premeditating his second or third shave. Evelyn told him straightforwardly that we had chosen someone else. Fortunately, she had instructed him to wire collect when he was coming, which detail he had neglected. His face puckered as though he were about to cry. Evelyn offered him five dollars above the ten we had supplied for the bus fare. "I have a pretty hard time of it making both ends meet. I had hoped this job would put things in shape. No, I won't stay in Boston. I'll go right back. I need my girl's shoulder to weep on."

We talked at some length. He proved to be an intelligent little fellow with a sense of humor, a pleasant voice, an eager manner that made you forget how curious he looked and that he would be no front man for me. "I work at a job until I lay up enough money to write awhile. Then I write until the money is gone. Then I find another job. I live hand-to-mouth. I've had some success with the pulps, but what I really want to do is a novel. It's in me, all about myself, and I've got to put it on paper." He didn't seem particularly sorry for himself but rather regarded himself wryly. I soon liked him as well as felt sorry for him. He is engaged to a struggling young artist. He originally came from South Philadelphia. He now lives in Greenwich Village. "I've always lived in the slums, one place and another."

We fell to talking about science fiction. He is acquainted with many of the writers. Indeed, he has collaborated with another author on several printed stories. "There are no fans," he vouchsafed, "as fanatic as science fiction fans." I really hated to see him go out the door. If he lived in Boston, we'd be friends. Maybe I'll write him.

July 24   Marshal Petain, eighty-nine, is on trial for his life in France. I believe that this man, regarded by so many critics the world over as a traitor of the first water, did all he could to the best of his judgment to spare France as much travail as lay within his powers. It may be that history will deem his judgment faulty, but I for one do not misdoubt his purpose. A man of his age had nothing personal to gain from acting one way or the other.

July 25   We are being solicited by certain of the bureaus in Washington to cut down on soap so that the poor people in Europe can take more baths. It is also being borne in upon the American public that the poor Europeans, due to strikes in Belgium, indifference as to planning for the future, will not have enough coal for the winter to keep them from shivering and shaking and therefore coal will have to be sent them, so we'd best prepare to be short on fuel ourselves. Bill Cunningham says that the Germans under our control swim and talk and play and depend upon us to provide for them, while in the Russian zone German factories and homes are systematically plundered of machinery, supplies, plumbing fixtures, automobiles, etc. which are shipped away to Sovietland. We give. The Russians take. We are probably suffered. They are feared and respected. It causes my hackles to rise that we permit ourselves to be such gulls. If I were President for a while, I'd put American interests first if it cost me my life. It is criminal that our leaders lavish our heritage upon an unappreciating world.

July 27   The Conservative Party in Great Britain suffered a violent and unexpected defeat with the Labor Party winning its most decisive victory. So Winston Churchill is out and the socialist-minded Laborites, under the lead of the communist-inclined secretary of the Party, the Jewish Harold Laski, professor and author, are in. A program analogous to that carried out in New Zealand, with state ownership of railroads, coal mines, utilities, etc., may be tried out. There will probably be less friction with Russia. It must be borne in mind, however, that in England things rarely change as swiftly and as drastically as it seems they will or as they do here in the United States. For instance, whereas stocks have tumbled as much as three or more points on the news of Churchill's defeat, in London they declined only a point.

July 29 Yesterday an Army bomber, evidently confused by a low ceiling, became lost over New York City and crashed head-on into the seventy-ninth story of the Empire State Building. It plummeted through the wall of the tower. Flames from the gasoline it carried enveloped the upper portion of the giant structure. The building swayed in a two foot arc. Elevators dropped eighty stories.

It seemed to me, lying awake last night reflecting upon the incident, that perhaps it is symbolic of the age in which we live: man driving headlong into the great edifice he has in his pride pointed to the sky.

August 1 I think that it would be very instructive for any student of why Germany so easily demolished France in 1940 to read in as full details as possible the proceedings of the trial of Petain. The entire political hierarchy of prewar France has testified against him. The French, it seems to me, are a graceless, fickle, amoral people undeniably gifted but a low and disgusting set of grabbers and rogues in the eyes of any self-respecting American. It is a foregone conclusion, judging by their long past, that the French will rise again from their present debasement. Their very existence is symbolized by rotting, rebirth, flowering, rotting, rebirth, and the present state of the French spirit is no worse than it has been at other times.

August 4 I read word for word the Potsdam declaration. The thing can be found in any old newspaper or full source book. It imposes a harsh peace on Germany, from which Russia gains most. Germany will be stripped of all the paraphernalia of war and of all the machinery designed to make weapons.

Considering the whip hand psychologically that Stalin seems to hold — because we wish to conciliate him and keep him peaceful while he establishes himself firmly over more territory than Hitler except at his zenith — we might have done worse. Had Roosevelt been at Potsdam, I'm sure we would have. Truman no doubt had to undo much abasement before Stalin by his predecessor. Truman announces that no secret agreements were entered into, which is not to say that secret agreements entered into by Roosevelt may not still stand. If I were Truman, I'd get the hell out of Europe and stop Russian expansion short in Asia even if we had to fight to do it. I'd not demand such a demeaning peace of Japan. And by propaganda I'd frighten China about Russia. Russia has shown no indication of not wishing to hog as much of the world as possible. It is to our interest to stop the eastward expansion somewhere. And I'd keep every island in the Pacific I could get and be bold about announcing it. We have the air power and the fleet now to stop Russia; we may not have them fifteen years from now.

August 7 Sextus Julius Fortinus, famous Roman engineer and military authority, concluded some 1900 years ago that "The invention of engines of war has long since reached its limit."

President Truman announced yesterday the perfection and use of a new atomic bomb one-tenth the size of an ordinary two ton bomb, yet with two thousand times the blast power of the world's largest eleven ton bomb, possessing more power indeed than twenty thousand tons of T.N.T. The invention is the result of the combined labor of American, British and Canadian scientists financed by the United States and carried on mostly in this country. A German Jewess, expulsed from Germany, has been of great assistance in perfecting the invention which has to do with the breaking up of uranium atoms to release their explosive energy. It is called the first practical use to be made of the Einstein Theory and of certain of his equations. The invention was in large measure made possible by previous experimentation with the cyclotron in California and elsewhere. The Germans were striving to make use of atomic energy also but had not succeeded.

This releasing of atomic energy has been a goal in the minds of scientists for years. The science fiction stories I read are filled with the potential possibilities of such an invention. And now the President tells us it is here. Two billion dollars have been spent upon experimentation, an entire city the size of Atlanta when I was a child set up on Government land near Knoxville to work upon the perfection of the process and two other centers of experimentation as well, using at one time the efforts of a hundred and twenty-five thousand people, all but a few of whom were kept unaware of the purpose of their work. The achievement in making practical pure theory is a great monument to the brotherhood of science and to the dogged pertinacity of man and to the foresight of those who possessed the vision to imagine success and to Churchill and Roosevelt who approved the investigation.

On the other hand, it is a success to cause an imaginative man to shiver for the future of his race. Whatever blessings may stem from this invention, it is not beyond reason that the seeds of the destruction of the human race may be in it. The first experiment with the actual bomb vaporized the steel tower in which it was hung, toppled men five miles away to the earth, was felt a hundred and fifty miles away. A single bomb has been dropped on a Japanese war center, and it is to be determined what will be the result when aerial photographs are possible.

Truman says that Japan had best accept the terms of surrender offered before industrial Japan is demolished. Were I one of those in control of Japan and if, as is likely, these new weapons are all they are said to be, I should be inclined to advise capitulation, for it is doubtful that the Japanese scientists have invented any comparable weapon. Experiments in the United States have been carried on under the War Department. It is to be sincerely hoped that the secret of the new weapon will not be released to the rest of the world. Its invention will necessitate the invention of new weapons to combat it, probably rays that will explode what must be extremely volatile charges while still in the air. A new industrial era may be inaugurated by the perfecting of atomic power, but more likely, the process will be as slowly put to use as television, there probably being hundreds of problems to meet and overcome.

It may be that this single invention will top in importance to man's future the entire remainder of World War II. Could it be kept in the hands of the Anglo-Saxon nations and not allowed elsewhere, we might have on the earth a period of major peace comparable to that when the British Navy was supreme. It could be, were it not that usually processes are invented in pairs or the idea once proved feasible, reinvented, and were it not that we are likely to give the process to the world, a more forceful instrument for peace than a dozen Leagues of Nations and United Nations organizations.

August 8 The more I read and hear of the atomic bomb, the more dire seem the implications of the new weapon. Four square miles of the 300,000-population city of Hiroshima was destroyed by a single bomb weighing, apparently, not more than 400 pounds, the active principle within which could, it is said, be carried conveniently under one arm. The atomic explosion vaporizes all metals and makes all matter radioactive. The scientists have no sure idea whether this radioactivity will endure a matter of days, weeks or years. Until it subsides, no human being will be able to reestablish residence within its destroyed area. Those not directly killed by the explosion, which lights up the night sky as though it were daylight, must suffer from horrible radioactive burns. It is suggested that wholesale use of such bombs in a major war might exhaust or turn radioactive the atmosphere of earth.

Authorities appear agreed that it is only a matter of time before other scientists in other nations perfect analogous weapons. Do we wish to persist awhile longer on the face of the globe as a nation, we should, no matter the outcome of the present war, thereafter make sure we have the largest and most up-to-date air force, the finest navy, the latest weapons, the most mobile and best equipped army on earth, and be certain that no dreams of peace and safety lull our guard or lower our standards. If we are thus armed and armored, our chances of escaping attack will be best. The trouble is that we are by nature an optimistic people, historically uninformed—a folk not martial by preference, hence easily gulled and misled by talk of peace. Ten years from now, we shall in all probability be off-guard, with precautions for our safety muddled in red tape and politics and our attention upon the immediate present. The future looks ominous for the world and for us.

I feel — What's the use of writing in here? It will all be destroyed shortly, what I write, the civilizations I live in, unless I mistake matters and trends.

The end of the war brought no peace to Arthur, as he contemplated a murky and menacing future for his country and himself. Strong nations managed to "endure a Nero, a Caligula, a Roosevelt," but it was beyond the capacity of "the quiet, unassuming, unafraid, middle-of-the-roader" Truman to mend the fault "put in the framework of our civilization" by his infamous predecessor. In fact the good Truman turned out to be a flash in the pan. To Arthur's disappointment, he failed to check the augmenting power of the U.S.S.R. (it was only a matter of time before the Soviets would have the Bomb), and he advocated the suicidal policy of rebuilding Europe instead of tidying up affairs at home. The wave of strikes following the Japanese surrender; the debate over America's China position (Arthur swallowed Patrick C. Hurley's charge of a Communist-ridden State Department); the Pearl Harbor investigation (clearly the "dunderheads in Washington," including the president, had much to answer for); and the collision between the supporters and enemies of General MacArthur, now the most revered and most hated man in the nation — all augured ill for the nation. Arthur's reading of the Roman historians who had survived worse times encouraged him to press on with his own chronicle; he, too, would bequeath to mankind a true record of his tumultuous era.

But who would take care of him while he completed his historic task? Evelyn could not manage alone. Janice was gone (Arthur had his dutiful

wife invite the Davises for dinner — a vain attempt to lessen Bertram's
animosity toward him). Rose Trench was as volatile as a jar of nitrogly-
cerine. Invaluable Mrs. Cash reserved only a part of her life for Arthur.
Ella "floated up to celestial regions inhabited by colored people with
swelled heads." Patsy Boland, whom he obsessively loved but could not
dominate, began to show signs of her "mick" origins. Arthur furiously
resented her ingratitude and waywardness, but he had come to depend
upon her healing hands, and he feigned indifference to her slights in
order to keep her. Patsy warmed up a bit, yet he sensed her disapproval
(those green-eyed, February-born females always caused trouble) and
sought consolation in other people and pastimes.

The rising stock market offered one promising diversion. Another was
a month's experiment — a most awkward one, as it turned out — to
write the Diary in the third person, "no new shine or interest having been
imparted to the writing" for a long time. He was still operating at sixes
and sevens, full of self-revulsion and despair, when Roderic Peters and
Billy Minor reentered civilian life. Roderic resumed his reading sessions.
Billy was plainly skittish about resuming his old job. To lure him back to
Garrison Hall would require the most delicate handling.

August 9   Yesterday Russia broke its treaty and declared war on
Japan. It is too bad, really, for now Russia will snatch all the pie.
Another atom bomb has been dropped on Nagasaki, destroying it.
And in the meanwhile regular raids are dropping larger bomb ton-
nage on Japan daily than was dropped on Germany. Our warships
shell shore cities and installations.

August 10   A report has come from Tokyo that Japan will accept
the Potsdam ultimatum terms of surrender provided the Emperor
can remain in his semidivine position. No one appears to know
definitely whether or not an authoritative offer of surrender has
been made. Perhaps we will know later in the day. The Russians have
already broken through some of the strongest Japanese defense lines
in Manchuria. There should be more about all this later in the day. It
is just ten o'clock now.

August 12   I wrote Janice a letter this morning telling her how
much I love her and miss her and how unhappy I am without her. As
I told her, it is about like being cursed to love people as much as I do
her and Evelyn. She may not enjoy getting the letter, she being one
who doesn't always wish emotion put into words, but it is how I
feel. I've tried very hard to exorcize her from my life to no purpose. I
miss her endlessly and unremittingly. It is my present unhappiness
and disconsolation. I begged her to come to see me as soon as she
felt she might and explained that I understood why she didn't come

last week. My existence will take on permanently a darker shade without Janice.

August 13 No peace yet. We are told that the Japanese hit one of our warships with a suicide bomb so that we are now bombing Japanese cities with all we have save the atomic bombs. It is hinted that—do the Japanese fail quickly to surrender—the atomic bombs will again be used, bigger and more powerful ones.

August 14 It appears as though Japan had accepted the surrender terms.

August 15 Surrender was announced last evening at seven o'clock. So that damn war is over. No more Americans were killed in World War II than were killed on either side in the Civil War. It was more an outpouring of men, money, production, energy, natural resources than it was a concentrated business of getting killed.

Last night was a wild one. People yelled. Automobile horns blew. Toy horns screeched. Firecrackers popped. Planes zoomed. Fire engines screamed. Kids in the alleys upset garbage cans and broke bottles. And always automobile horns blew frantically. It was very hot and very humid. Four o'clock found me wide awake. I rang for Rose and shut out all sounds and sweltered in comparative silence. Two hours and a half of broken sleep. Rose very nice and understanding about it all. Not too much sleep herself. The room lunges back and forth. No ice for two days. No Evelyn or Pearl to get it when there isn't any.

While I lay awake, I whipped up resentment against Patsy for her thoughtlessness and against myself for being fond of such a basically self-centered, stingy, tactless chit of a girl. It is amazing when you are exhausted what a swivet you can whip up merely by thinking.

The telephone rang. It was Janice with her lilting voice. "I got your letter, Arthur. It was very sweet." "It said what I felt. I love you, darling." "I love you, Arthur." And we talked about this and that triviality. I felt restored in spirit. I should think she'd like me more than her husband, and perhaps—who knows?—she does. I may not be as attractive as many men are, but I'm certainly more attractive by all accounts and judging by her telephone voice than Bertram Davis ever was or ever will be.

And the damn war is over. And gasoline rationing is at an end. And thank fortune Roosevelt is dead and we will not swing too far to the left.

August 16 President Truman has, to this point, won the confidence and respect of most Americans. It is his avowed purpose to restore the production and distribution of goods and services to the American people. His actions have immediately proved that what he says in words he means to transmute into action. Gasoline off rationing and fuel oil and canned vegetables. Raw materials placed on the open market with the sole reservation that small business gets its share. Limits removed from production. You may be sure that under Roosevelt the left-wingers in the various branches of administration would not have so expeditiously let loose their grasp through rationing and restrictions upon the jugular vein of the nation.

August 18   Have started Pliny's 'Letters.' Think will like. Enjoying Will Durant's 'Caesar and Christ.' He makes the just point that we should never forget that the Rome of Tacitus and Martial was not the entire Rome, probably not ever the majority Rome, that there must have been many good, peaceful, industrious persons of character, anonymous because they were law-abiding and self-respecting. If I in this diary give the impression that we Americans are a people of lawbreakers, wild, dishonest, never forget that I am the party of the opposition and that for every violent character there must be three or four inconspicuously commendable persons. As the man on the radio observed last night, since one out of every six Americans was no good before the war, in all probability one out of every six veterans will be no good; regrettably they will give the rest of the veterans a bad name.

August 20   The Russians have swept across Manchuria to Harbin, Mukden and other key centers, cutting through Japan's finest armies as though they were cheese. The Japanese claim — and probably rightly — that when they wished to surrender the Russians kept right on rolling. It would seem to an onlooker that Stalin wished to make sure of his domination of Manchuria, Sakhalin, Korea before accepting the surrender of the Japanese.

And the Chinese Communists' armies have been attacking the Japanese in North China as well as flouting the Nationalist Government. Perhaps the Chinese Communists will join up with the Russian Communists and there will be a civil war in China.

August 27   I have enjoyed the major portion of 'Caesar and Christ,' finding it instructive as well as stimulating to the mind. As soon as it came to the subject of Christ, however, I found myself becoming not only bored but very antagonistic as well. I have heard enough of that Christ stuff to last me the remainder of my existence. It has made a sort of scar tissue on my spirit. Even when someone like Durant cautiously propounds ideas analogous to my own I find myself withdrawn from the subject resentfully. I have in me no demanding need for religion. I would not pick out a Jewish fakir as the subject of adoration, neither him nor his questionable teachings. I finally felt compelled to skip Christ, the teachings of Peter and Paul, the function of the Church. It was like tearing off scratchy clothes.

August 31 We are told of how the Japanese beat, tortured, starved, insulted our men. Undoubtedly it is true. But, oppositely, we are told how many prisoners were well-treated. It is deplorable that our men should be maltreated as prisoners, but that does not characterize the entire Japanese character as phenomenally below our own. The present record of our country jails and jailors is enough to make the hair rise in horror. From records received to date of Japanese treatment of prisoners, they seem all in all to have fared better than did German prisoners, and God of the hidden face alone knows what has happened to Russian prisoners. So I find no valid reason to modify my admiration for the little yellow men. However, keep it to myself I shall until tempers cool.

September 2 The duplicate documents by which the Japanese made official the surrender of their nation were signed yesterday aboard the great 'S.S. Missouri' in Tokyo Bay. The proceedings were very formal. General MacArthur managed them with dignity and panoply. There were some four hundred American and British warships in Tokyo Bay and covering planes overhead. Long, silent guns were canted skyward. MacArthur's voice was that of a trained actor and an intense man. I feel sure that he will perform excellently the task of governing the Japanese, who will appreciate his penchant for formality, his flare for showmanship, qualities which must at moments have irritated such dry and unemotional leaders as Admiral Nimitz. There is, I think, somewhat of the arrogant mystic in MacArthur as well as of the melodramatic poet.

The country at large appears to respect our new President as only a bit more than half of the people did Roosevelt and to have faith that he means what he says and is no reformer for reform's sake. The same energy that developed the United States into the arsenal for the world now seeks other outlets. We should thank our luck for Mr. Harry S Truman, the Trajan of our times.

September 6 [From Patricia:]

> When the Jap war ended we didn't know how it would affect us, but so far we are still fighting the war down here, with no change in Paul's status. Of course, being Military Police, concerned with prisoner of war work may be the reason. But we expect to be here until March or April, as the prisoners are needed for the crops until then. The farm hands are not returning to work, tho the factories have closed down here; they probably

won't until they have used up their savings. There is going to be a huge sugar crop, and it certainly will be needed, as the shortage is felt even down here. Then comes the rice. If we have to stay in the army I'd just as soon stay here for the winter, as it is beautiful country, and I am well settled. I've a horror of going back to Leesville. One would have to live there to realize the hatred we all have for the place.

Paul is hoping that he will not have to go with the army of occupation, he fully expects to put in another year in uniform, but the overseas duty will take at least three years, and Paul feels that it is about time he is about his business. He has already been in the army for five years, and for an actor, his best acting years. If he stays away any longer he will lose his ambition. And worst of all, we may have to stay in the army. Something we both hate. I don't mind it here, as I am the only army wife in town. But I hate living on a Post. The social obligations irk me. I like my friends regardless of the husband's rank, but no can do in the army. And besides, I want to put down roots, and in California. We want our own house, and our own sort of life, and I hope we get it before I'm ancient.

September 16 Evelyn and I drove to Jamaica Plain in the Pierce. Northeast wind. Blue sky. Leaves waving. Asters under the hedge. A lovely, lovely place. We sat in the big sitting room awhile. We walked into the big carriage room and sat there. I looked at the automobiles, the chairs, the bookcases neatly stored under a layer of thin dust. We poked into piles of miscellaneous discarded stuff— the 220-volt stove Ten Broek cooked on, the bed tray I ate on at the Ericson, the old weapons I collected, the heavily carved chair which used to stand in the big hallway at 552 Peachtree Street when I was a boy, an old ironing board from Maine. And the books. A set of 'The Rover Boys.' [Edward "Lord"] Dunsany's 'Charwoman's Shadow.' A tiny autograph book, 'Bertie Crew, Atlanta, Oct 22, 1879' with "Dear Bertie, Think of me when first you awake and send me a piece of your wedding cake, Hattie Inman."

And a segment of the past, forgotten quite, clicking as suddenly into my memory as a ball into a socket; a very old scrapbook, green, battered, with irises on the cover, and inside, on pages of browning paper, cutouts pasted, most of them instantaneously remembered with the emotion I experienced when as a child I was intrigued by shapes and color. "GIRRAFFF," tall, brown and tan. "BECHUANA WOMAN" with a baby on her back and a pot balanced on her head. Bright birds and bright butterflies. Child angels with white wings on another page, and sprays of forget-me-nots. A British tar and ships of the Royal Navy, 'Alexandria,' 9,400 tons, 12 guns. An English huntsman in red coat and top hat, and hounds and hares and deer and squirrels and birds. Young Rollo, his pony and his pets. Little girl and little boy enjoying a day at the country, seesawing, raking, feeding chicks, etc.— very Victorian. Then a page of passion-flowers, asters, butterflies. Then a jungle page with animals and plantation darky faces staring. More flowers and exotic fruits. A single simpering angel. Odds and ends of flowers and birds and one fish. And the book ends.

September 22 We've been trying out people for the job. One used to air conditioning and too uppity. Another abased because husband beat her for years, hence spiritless. Another, proclaimed a divorcee, telephoned by violent Irish husband five minutes after arrived. Another made nervous by working in the dark. Now a little woman of twenty-six with unfilled teeth, dirty-looking knees, honest hazel eyes, a soft voice, a willing manner. Very wearing to try these people. Tried a man to drive me by the hour, yesterday. Huge. Not bad. May get him to help later.

Evelyn has been telephoning Janice about what to feed Bertram tomorrow. He won't eat unless the fat is removed from his food before it appears on table. He is very finical about his food. I talked to Janice. I charged her not to look at me as devotedly as she used to do with Bertram around. I don't know what to say to or how to act with that bozo tomorrow. Be lumpishly pleasant, I suppose. It would be a laugh if I liked him. More to the point, I hope he likes me.

September 24 I should like to say what is in my mind in such manner that it will seem judicially considered, though I fear that will be impossible due to past assertions and commitments of preference. At any rate, I shall endeavor to record my observations accurately and with at least an effort toward impartiality.

Janice I found quite as lovely, quite as attractive, altogether as superior a person as I had remembered her to be, with her dark skin, her white teeth and eyeballs, her very dark eyebrows and hair, her long hands, the straight line of forehead and nose, the lilt to her voice, the sweetness of her expression, the composure of her spirit. I had liked to sit and look at her and forget her husband, her baby, my resolve to be as inconspicuous as possible in the face of her husband. The baby, in passing, was a pale, frail thing of inconceivably small fingers, feet in air, silence, a miniature in eyes and mouth of his father.

As to Bertram Davis. I found him far worse than any preconception had pictured him, a very unpalatable man. He is shorter than I am. His clothes were neat. He crossed the left leg over the right and held to the right ankle with both hands, rocking the leg slightly and continually while turning his somewhat bald head from one person to another with unceasing motion, talked facilely and easily. His face in its upper part faintly resembles a Pekinese in expression. His nose is inconspicuous and his eyes are muddy blue and unsmiling. His throat is fat and as though blown out by air so that I thought of an iguana. His beard is heavy, blue-black, and smudges his cheeks. His mouth is nothing short of lecherous in appearance, a series of unsymmetrical curves, a most unpleasant mouth, in combination with the queer throat, the cold eyes, giving to the man an unprepossessing face and an unsavory expression. Yet he was polite and apparently not ill at ease.

While it was very easy to size up what sort of man Davis was, it was quite impossible to guess or feel what he was thinking. My first thought on him was: How on earth can Janice bear to sleep with him in the same bed? Then: For God's sake, why did she ever marry such an unprepossessing guy? He's not in her class. She's an attractive woman in anybody's eyes while he's emphatically not an attractive man. I should say he'd be excellent at his factory job, not dumb, a hard worker. But there's no love for her in his eyes as he regards her. There's love for the baby, yes, but none for her. And how can she love him? She cannot find him a sustaining husband. He talks to her entertainingly, she says. Well, he's a talker by nature and would talk to the moon, other audience failing. He is a petty tyrant or I miss my guess. He is probably, from the looks of him, weak where he should be strong, demanding where he should be lenient. And there's something hidden about his past, something Janice would not like to know. I am sure of it.

I felt thoroughly sorry for Janice, as well as repelled by her lack of fastidiousness in the choice of a man. We talked for an hour or so about the baby, about Truman, about the implications of the atom bomb, I being careful to stay away from dangerous generalities which might offend the husband of Janice. Then I left and Evelyn gave them dinner. Later, about three, Janice ran upstairs to see me for a few minutes. I hugged her and kissed her and held her tight. "You're so pretty," I exclaimed, "and sweet and desirable. I love you to death. I like to sit and look at you." "Oh, Arthur," she said wistfully, "nobody has said things like that to me since I left you." "Well," I said, "in my opinion no one loves you and admires you as much as I do, and probably not even your son will ever think as much of you as I do." She had, she said, been very tired since having the baby. She would try to get in to see me when she could, and I would have to be patient. Was I, she asked, jealous of her son? No, I replied, I didn't think so, for my mind was adjusted to him by now. Then I told her to run along as I didn't want Bertram jealous.

Evelyn and I were exhausted by the time the Davises left. We discussed them later. Evelyn and I are of the same opinion separately arrived at that it is not unlikely that Bertram could have been earlier in his life a homosexual. I realize that by advancing such an assumption I lay myself open to the suspicion of being unwarrantably prejudiced in his disfavor. It is not that. I am by instinct a just person unless under the impulsion of a feeling of injustice committed on me, and Bertram has never done anything to me save be jealous of me. It is his lecherous mouth. I think that Evelyn and I are correct or at any rate not far from the nub of the matter.

September 30   I am writing out of habit and for something to do. The heart has gone out of it since the atomic bomb. If mankind is to destroy itself and its culture, what is the point of laboring with might and main to put into words a chronicle that may either be incinerated in an instant or else be useless to what is left of mankind and culture? Why should I work myself to the point of sickness to put together a picture that may be of service to no one? It seems bootless to keep on if my conviction has any merit. So why write? It would be more serviceable to devote my energy to making money or trying to. I find myself no longer being driven from within to labor the rest of my days to create a memorium of these our times.

October 6   Riding in Baby-Carriage with Mike. He was telling me of Pearl. He sees her every couple of months. She comes to his shop with "that fellow." Mike doesn't like "that fellow." "No man ought to be so overweanin' with his wife. She says to me, 'Mike, for my sake go easy with what you say to me.' She acted subdued-like, if you know what I mean. She used to be so free an' full of fun. Not no more. Of course I got only my feelin's to go by, but I'd say that guy was tight-fisted an' jealous as well as bossy. Personally, I don't know how she swallows him. Maybe she won't, too long. She always had so much spirits. Maybe she'll take him just so long, then throw over the traces."

I told Mike the tale of how Pearl left me. "That guy!" he exclaimed. "If I hadda been her I'd have told him to stick himself you know where an' thought myself well rid of him. That's no way to start off a married life. Did you ever hear of such carryin'-ons? An' she was such a good gal. Well, well, well." I enjoy Mike and his garrulity.

October 18   The atomic bomb is here to stay. It is so monstrous a weapon of destruction that it will be the nation, as with the gunmen of the old Wild West, who draws and shoots first who will do the killing and perhaps the defeating. What is most terrible is that at any instant in the future a sneak attack may be launched against us, and we will be destroyed before we are forewarned or prepared. There exists only one way to secure peace and safety to the American nation and the American people, and that way we are too soft to take. We might while we solely have the weapon destroy half of Russia, for instance, or any other nation we suspected of possible duplicity. We are the world's richest nation. It can be only a matter of time, if we do not, before some other nation casts eyes of envy and hatred at us and proceeds to make use of atomic weapons.

October 22 What the book said engaged my attention. I found it very real. Part of me entered the pages and took the street that circled the base of the hill. The part that was left behind dwindled in importance. I passed many commonplace houses, dwellings I had met within the book. I crossed the street to a large brick gate. I expected it to be locked. It was not. I pushed it open and stepped behind the black iron grillwork. I became a unified person. A man was standing there, tall, leaning on a cane. "Hello," I said. "Hello," he said. "Shut the gate," he said, and I found his smile and his voice both commanding and appealing to my sense of fitness. I closed the gate. I recognized the man. It was Franklin Roosevelt.

"I thought you were dead," I said. "That's what is supposed to be thought," he said. "As a matter of fact, my friend, I'm only in seclusion. I was very ill. I am recovering my health." "Well," I said. "Shall I show you my estate?" he inquired. I nodded. A long, cool, cloistered walk led on before us, diversified by vines clambering overhead, sudden vistas of the city outspread below us, seats in nooks, grapes in purple clusters, arbors, and not a person to be seen or heard anywhere though some sense informed me that hidden guards were on watch at various vantage points. "It's like a dream of quiet," I said. Then as we strolled along, the tall man spoke to me of what had been, of the aspirations he had had, of wherein he had failed and wherein succeeded, and I was, despite a deep-seated antipathy toward him and his history, drawn to him by his warm and friendly personality; and I marveled at myself. "It is," he said, "profoundly interesting and not a little discouraging to be one dead-alive, so to say, and observe the currents set in motion by my imagination seeking new riverbeds and watering new fields of human activity and dammed and turned aside, at least temporarily, by the greediness and avarice of men I attempted to make use of constructively. I do not think," he said, "that I shall ever enter the world again, although I may if I am sufficiently needed." So I walked with him, and I forgot the passage of the hours, and in due time we circled the hill and came to the gate by which I had entered. I left him.

I walked along the sidewalk of the commonplace street that was the street in the book I had been reading, and most of me ebbed back into the book and through the book to my usual self so that what I had experienced and what I had read lost reality and left me as a man who had crossed a spit to the mainland when the tide was out and stood with the tide full, wondering if there had been a spit and if he had crossed it, yet sure he had. And I woke. And more real than my trip to Harrison Avenue this morning and more real than the woman I interviewed remains the dream.

October 27

HOME FOR AGED MEN
M.A. Drummond, Secretary
Department of Outside Aid
260 West Amherst Street
Boston 18, Mass.
Oct. 5, 1945

Dear Sir:

Mr. Otto Ten Broek of 75 Hamilton St. Roxbury, Mass. has made application for admittance to the Home for Aged Men and he gives your name as a reference, advising he worked for you as a Literary Secretary from 1919 to 1929.

Will you kindly advise us what you know of this gentleman and any other information you think we might be interested in.

Thanking you, we are

Yours very truly,
M. A. Drummond, Secretary
Committee on Beneficiaries

I replied that Ten Broek had indeed worked for me, but that I hadn't realized what a troublemaker he had been until he and I parted. Then I fretted for a couple of nights because I had been vengeful to an oldish dunderhead. Evelyn said: "There's nothing either of us could do to that creature that would ever compensate for what he did to us. Your letter was very restrained under the circumstances."

October 28 Were I President, I should announce boldly that plans were under consideration to outfit planes to be kept prepared always and to equip and arm automatic rockets with atomic bomb warheads (aimed at all the possibly hostile nations of earth, their great cities and manufacturing centers) to be sent hurtling through the atmosphere to bring disaster the moment we suffered attack. Furthermore, whether warranted by future warfare or not, I should keep the largest and most efficient air force and navy in the world. I should take the fifty to a hundred billion dollars of money unexpended as yet, and when it was recaptured for the treasury I should set up a revolving fund to be loaned out at interest, the interest to be used exclusively upon scientific experimentation for warfare, with the proviso that upon attack by anyone the principal would become immediately available for the war in hand. And this too I should boldly announce.

October 30   No wonder Napoleon felt impelled to conquer Europe. Given the itch and the energy, there would be no halting me either. I can't sit still. I can't lie still. I wear myself out moving about. I have been to four skin specialists. All have told me solemnly that I had no fungus. It acted like a fungus of some sort, I contended. They smiled, gave my behind a single cursory look, took out their pads, prescribed something with a wise look. I still felt I might have a fungus infection. No, they didn't have time to make a microscopic analysis. They had seen hundreds of cases, indeed thousands, and knew whereof they talked.

November 1   I have bought new ties, shirts, etc. so as to keep up my appearance and a swanky new topcoat, the one I have been using all these years having been bought in 1913 or 1914 at Reed's in Philadelphia and still wearable for riding. That, I believe, cost $15. The new one cost $85. The one is no better intrinsically than the other. I try to heed Evelyn's contention that the older you get the more careful you should be as to your clothes. I have taken to bow ties again — I used to wear them all the time at college — they look better on me. New clothes of any sort are very difficult to obtain, returning veterans having bought out the stocks and new clothes evidently not yet being available in quantity sufficient for demand.

November 2   Jews are rioting in Palestine against the British decision to limit immigration into Palestine. The Jews cannot be blamed for wishing a freer homeland. Nor can the Arabs be blamed for standing out against such a postern gate into their bailiwick.

November 3   I was listening to Harry Bridges on the radio last evening.[20] He is a very clever man. He declared frankly that the

---

[20] At the time of this entry, Australian-born Harry Bridges, head of the International Longshoremen's and Warehousemen's Union, was again facing deportation for his alleged Communist party affiliations. Shortly afterward the Supreme Court ruled the order illegal.

unions were bent upon using political influence. If they weren't political-minded, he said, they would have no power. He controls the longshoremen of the West Coast. His union is now interested through threatened strikes in controlling the policy of the Government in bringing home quickly the soldiers from overseas. His men will refuse to unload ships taken out of transport service and put into the carrying trade. Also, he may order a strike against loading ships with munitions and weapons for the Dutch and British to put down revolts like the one in Java, thus exercising an influence upon the American foreign policy. They are very arrogant and very presumptuous, these big labor leaders, and their aims are often coercive. The fact that Government agencies have acted as mediators between labor and management during the war has caused a lull in direct bargaining between Labor and Capital, that is, in what is called collective bargaining. At present there are all sorts of labor difficulties the length and breadth of the nation.

November 11 On this Armistice Day with World War I twenty-seven years in the past and World War II supposedly concluded, some considerable portion of earth is still under the spell of war, and all the volubilities the do-gooders, the politicians, the idealists may speak can only seem like whispers against prevailing winds.

Our past words must indeed resound emptily to the vast Asiatic peoples. Great we are with tongue-noises but passing meek in backing them up. It takes not a rational conscience nor an ordinary leader but a sanctimonious demagogue like Lincoln, like Wilson, like Roosevelt to put fists behind words.

November 14 I'm seriously considering replacing the first person in this chronicle by the third person. For many months now, in particular since the advent of the atomic bomb, I have been dissatisfied with the end product of my efforts as well as with the efforts themselves. My problem is how to circumvent a wavering purpose and spotty effort. I can no more abandon the keeping of the chronicle whether it eventually be scorched to ash or not than I can cease to breathe at will. That recognized, the question resolves itself into one of deciding what subterfuge to select that will give renewed energy to what I write, in the process renew my interest and intensify my application. I want to continue writing. If I continue writing, I want to write well. To write well, my heart must be in it.

Writing in the third person should bring into play new words, new methods of expression, new approaches to thinking. It should be like swapping street corners as an onlooker at the passing parade.

Mrs. Trench isn't with him today. Yesterday she lost her temper, and he is having a relief from her today. It was: "You say I don't keep the sink in the kitchen clean. I say I looked at that bed last night and for the first time really saw the mattress. It is filthy. It has spots on it. As poor as I am compared to you, I wouldn't have that mattress in my house. God alone knows what germs are in it. I couldn't sleep for thinking of it. I . . ." And so on, on and on. In vain were his protestations that he had thought the mattress all right, that he would get another for her or a cover or anything. Her words tumbled forth. Not often did her ire seize control of her and he was bent upon bowing his head to the storm, but it was early in the morning and he was but half awake. He handed her over to his wife. His wife lost her temper at what she considered "utter foolishness" on Mrs. Trench's part. Later, he went himself to look at the mattress on which Mrs. Trench had been sleeping in equanimity for months. He found it neither very stained nor very dirty. He was put out by such pretensions. He was piqued. It has always seemed to him that pique against a friend could best be allayed by regarding that friend impersonally, as though he represented the human race, whereafter interest in what is under abstract scrutiny takes command and ire is subverted or repressed.

So he sat and contemplated Rose. Her lips were set. Her brown eyes sparkled. Temper, he thought, made her pretty. He decided that laughing at her, she being vain, would distract her. So he laughed at her. She kissed him before she left. He was glad to see her go, however, for he wasn't as eager for an emotional fracas as formerly. He felt no anger. The pretty woman who dresses in black and is fond of him had stood by him steadfastly. She was privileged to throw a spasm unjustifiably if she wished. He had his quirks with which she was expected to be patient. He would buy a cover for the mattress, put it on, say nothing to her about it. She was, he concluded, a dear person.

November 25 Roderic Peters telephoned that he would enjoy coming to spend an evening. He had been, he said, in the Naval Hospital at Chelsea. "Well," he said as he entered, "this indeed seems like old times. How are you, Arthur?" As Inman greeted him, he thought what a pleasant voice he had. "It almost seems," he said to Roderic, "as if you hadn't been away, you sound so natural." Roderic sat down in the chair beside his bed, and they chatted. Roderic told him of the nineteen months at Sampson. He was now, he said, a second-class storekeeper, would have taken examinations for first class but that suddenly three months of sea duty had been made requisite. "So I decided to stay second-class. I consider when I regard other fellows that I have nothing to kick about. I haven't been sent overseas. I have all parts of my body still. I've been able to see my family fairly often. In the light of the capacities I feel myself to possess, however, I feel that my services have been wasted; nothing has been demanded of me that thousands of other young chaps wouldn't have readily fulfilled. So I've been bored."

Roderic is figuring on returning to his old job. They have it waiting for him. He hopes that within a year or so they will move him to another city where there will be more chance of advancement. It was good to see and hear him, Inman thought. They read the last half of the evening a tale about beings from a different solar system, how the creatures progressed by sheer reaction through trial and error and no reasoning, and hence how men were able to trade with them to their own advantage by cutting corners reasoning made open.

It is odd, Inman muses as he writes this, that seventeen or eighteen years of association with a man you would never have voluntarily chosen as a friend can have made you so fond of him.

December 7 He is aware that he is apt to edge in his statements away from true exactitude at times. It is not his intention so to do; he would prefer to be exact. If he can extract and convey the emotional gist of events, whoever wishes to may go to the history books for precise facts — and even there they will not, he feels sure, find them. No two historians perceive the present or the past alike; no two reporters report the present with a single eye. So he is not altogether unhappy that he falls to port or starboard of recorded facts, considers it much more important to draw a mood, convey an emotion, etch an impression.

December 9 Patsy showed up yesterday an hour late with some lie or other. She said she was worn out. She'd been up late night after night. "It's my new boy friend, Phil. I'm crazy about him. He was in a German prison camp. He is engaged to be married, has two mistresses, is big and handsome, wants to sleep with me. And when I say he wants to sleep with me, I mean it. He's given me no peace for three weeks. He fights me to get what he wants. And he's strong. He bought a big automobile, and he takes me out and parks and struggles with me. My legs are black and blue keeping them together. It isn't that I would have moral scruples against sleeping with him; it's that I don't think it would make him like me any better. He claims he's teaching me how to love. Darn it, I think he is. He sure treats me rough. And, Arthur, I'm afraid I'm weakening. Tell me not to."

"Why not weaken, Patsy? Maybe you'd like it. Maybe it would take some of the cockiness out of you. Maybe it's just what you need. Maybe he'd lay you and leave you, which would make me laugh."

"Gee, do you s'pose I should? Hey, you shouldn't be taking his side. You've got me all hot and bothered just thinking about it and him.

And do you know what he does? He goes off every Saturday and Sunday and leaves me flat. And another thing, don't you publish your diary till I'm dead. Gosh, I'm mixed up."

December 23 Very cold still. Evelyn is in bed with a headache. Dr. Pike comes to treat her. He is very gentle with her.

December 25 The one who keeps what has become a thoroughly unsatisfactory series of serrated notes, myself having experimented with the third-person method, is now giving it up and returning to the first person, no new shine or interest having been imparted to the writing and it sounding artificial in places.

I dare to think what I think, which is something in the favor of my thoughts. I possess a catholic curiosity. I am often able to see through flimflam and camouflage to the nub of a problem. Not having faith in reason save as a means of buttressing conclusions, my thoughts are often emotional in texture, grasping the true outline of moods more accurately than of facts. Nearly all theories, wrong ones as well as right ones, hold for me some aspects of possible truth, and nearly all theories are easily comprehended. Sentimentality and wishful thinking, intolerance and emotional vehemence often lacquer my thoughts. Half-truths and half-conclusions, as with most Americans, often satisfy me. In the storehouse of my memory is a veritable chandler's collection of factual odds and ends. I know a great deal more than ever I use in my writings.

December 27 Jack Kirkpatrick paid me a visit last night. He is Helen's, Eddie Simms' wife's, brother, the one I used to know, he of the artificial leg and ailing wife. Jack told me much about Eddie I didn't know. He watched him put together his bus line "on personality, lies, hopes and a shoestring." Jack never discovered how he financed the project or persuaded the bus manufacturers to give him credit. He borrowed a thousand dollars, Jack knows, from a dining-car lunch man, a year later expansively threw down on his counter seventeen hundred dollars with a wide gesture. He always paid back more than was necessary. He splashed around the money he made for the show-off it gave, didn't put it back into the company. "It was a pity, for he had a nice business, good buses, good drivers, steady customers between here and New York. But his men cheated him and, as I said, he saved nothing. Money burned a hole in his pocket until it was spent. He'd buy his boys a hundred bucks' worth of toys and think nothing of it. He loved to make handouts. He got me to help him with the cash evenings. He had a complicated system of hiding the money, putting it in the safe, banking it next morning. He paid me twenty-five dollars a week, which was far more than what I was doing was worth. I saw all sorts of things going on right under Eddie's nose that shouldn't be happening, but when I tried to point them out to him he blew up and threw one of his tantrums. He wanted me to understand he was running the business and he knew what was and wasn't going on. Well, I saw more and more leaks and holes where the money was disappearing, but after a while I learned to keep my mouth shut. He hired a man named Heaney. To my mind, Heaney was as crooked as a dog's hind leg. I told Eddie if he kept him he'd be sorry. He told me to mind my own business. I took my hat and left. Heaney collected all the cash he could lay his hands on not two weeks later and absconded with at least four thousand dollars. Well, it wasn't six months before the company was on the rocks and Eddie was dead. It broke his heart. He had a lot of good in him, Eddie did, but he had a lot that wasn't so good, too. He lived to show off. He couldn't manage his temper. He concocted so many stories that he didn't know where the truth ended or began, and when he'd repeated them enough he believed them, no matter how fantastic they sounded. He lived a full life. He was, all in all, the most interesting character I ever met. He sure thought a lot of you, Arthur."

December 30 Having struggle with Mrs. Cash assembling income tax material. Hard to teach an old dog new tricks, she will say. Hard to teach her anything. She resents it. "I am pretty well satisfied with myself, Mr. Inman, in fact, entirely so." She's good to me. "My crossness with you, Mr. Inman, is only skin-deep. You wouldn't love me if I were mushy-mouthed. Now would you?" It's amusing to watch her esteem for me go up and down as I make money.

1946

January 1 Had odd dream last night. In great hotel. Girl picked me out against everyone's will. Went to room with me and we slept together. Loved her. Professor came in room, sent her out, lectured me for being antisocial. Walked out on him. Came upon wounded hawk. Made friends with it. Put it under coat and attempted to find way back to girl by long corridors. Woman accused me of stealing hawk. It grew small in the head and big in the belly and began to rot. Felt must do something with it. Lost in corridors. Took elevator. Wire broke and car dropped. Uninjured. Another floor of hotel like other floor. A thousand doors. Myself growing weaker. Hawk growing weaker. No longer hope of finding girl. Lost.

Dream so strong is with me yet, permeating sunshine, more real than Rose or Evelyn or cat lying in sun. Often been lost in that hotel before. Part of furniture of nightmares. Endless hotel, without beginning or limitation. Always dreaming of girls who approve of me wholeheartedly, then vanish or are removed. Portion of dream I recall only fourth or fifth of whole dream. Turgid plot without connecting sequence, illogical by daylight.

What sort of being am I to be possessed literally by such nightmares? That nightmare only one of seven or eight during night. Slight marvel I rise from my bed exhausted mornings. I feel a citizen (rather, to be exact, a partial citizen) of two worlds — the day one and the night one — and it is very confusing to keep my balance in either.

January 3   Rose is on the rampage again. The workings of her brain interest me. I said: "Couldn't you once in a while throw some of that rotten food out of the refrigerator?" She said, icily: "That I consider your wife's job." She's surpassingly vain. She will spend a week of afternoons shopping for exactly the right hat or dress. She is even less conscious of things around her than was Janice when she first came here. She will let flowers die rather than water them as she doesn't like them, hasn't since her daughter brought some into the house with ants on them. She never more than partially cleans the kitchen. She doesn't know how to make a bed and sleeps in one with wrinkled blankets and rumpled and creased sheets. She never glances out the window at the weather. The things that impinge upon her attention and consciousness are unbelievably limited. She is unreligious. Foul language and blasphemy pass her by. She never reads a book. World problems interest her not at all. Her hands are rough constantly but fail to bother her. She has the hands of a carpenter. Her skin is so white and thin that it bruises when touched. The blue veins show underneath it. She will work herself to exhaustion to please me but is likely always to conclude I have little or no gratitude. She's afraid of growing old. She won't tell how old she is.

January 9   American troops as distantly separated as Guam, the Philippines and Paris as well as troops awaiting demobilization at camps here in the United States have staged protest rallies that border upon insubordination, demanding in no uncertain terms that they be sent home and demobilized. The civilian soldier considers his war won, his duty done, and wants to get out of harness. The abstract notion that his presence overseas can be a force behind diplomatic bargaining interests him not at all. He sees ships carrying home munitions, even sailing empty, and he is resentful. He no longer credits the truth of varying reasons compounded by the War Department for his ears. He is willing, if loath, to govern Germany and Japan but not the rest. One can hardly blame him, the soldier, even if one can understand the overall use of his remaining under arms.

February 5 Evelyn has just gone out the door Bangor-bound to see my Old Man. She isn't very gleeful about the trip. I hate to have her go. We both feel it is necessary from various angles. I wish she could kick the Old Man off the edge of the world and out of my subconscious. He will be seventy-seven Friday. Evelyn was forty-five yesterday.

February 9 Yesterday just after two o'clock, the telephone rang, and it was Billy Minor. I talked with him for fifteen or twenty minutes until I had no voice left. He sounded just the same but even more sure of himself. He was in Boston, he said, because Sadie's mother and brother had died within the week. He had gotten special emergency leave for forty-eight hours, and he "just couldn't go without phoning" me—he would be leaving in thirty minutes. That he was pleased to be talking with me was indubitable, but that he was telling the truth in other respects was questionable.

He expects, he said, to be out of the service in two or three months; he's getting bored with so much flying. He asked after Mrs. Cash, Evelyn, Janice, Pearl, Roderic. I adjured him not to forget I'd like to have him back with me. I was not, I said, putting any sort of pressure on him, for I was well aware that that would do no good, but I was asking him not to forget me. He made a noncommittal answer to the effect that we could talk that over Sunday if he were with me. He inquired after the Pierce and the Baby-Carriage. By that time my voice was gone and I had to stop. It was nice to hear from him.

February 13 When Truman came to office, he stated that the speed with which the swingover from wartime to peacetime economy was accomplished was "of the essence." Now, while strikes flow back and forth across collective industry like restless tides the lapping waves of which are halted by no dykes, Truman sits in the White House and argues with his henchmen, and the days and weeks slip by, and industry does not even know for sure whether the left-wingers or the right-wingers yelling into the opposite ears of the President will gain his attention. An executive head of the State, still imbued with tremendous war powers, he could peremptorily dismiss the dissenters against the established American way, the Pink riffraff he inherited from Roosevelt, all those officeholders who stand in the light of the nation's getting back to work; and he could clamp down on the presumptive power and singular immunity from punishment of the inciting labor leaders or fortify Congress to do so. But he merely sits.

February 16 "Patsy," I said, "you didn't send me a valentine."
"I know it. By the way, thank you for yours. I didn't send any
valentines to anyone." "You know what I think?" I said. "I think,
next to Janice, you're the most goddamn stingy person I ever saw.
I've known you close to two years, and you've never given me a
thing, not a stick of gum, except that measly picture. You said you
wanted me to tell you things once in a while. I'm telling you this.
Stinginess is a low trait. I detest it." "I don't think I'm stingy."
"Well, if you're not stingy with other people and you're stingy with
me who has given you enough presents for five people, that's all the
worse. It's incredible that anyone as pretty and as attractive as you
are can be such a tightwad. And if you blame it on thoughtlessness,
that's just as bad and doesn't alter the effect of stinginess. I bought a
little leatherbound diary with a lock for your birthday. If you continue stingy, it's the last present I'll give you." "That's fair enough,"
she said, "and thank you, Arthur. Now can I tell you about my
week?"

February 18 A spy ring in Canada has been uncovered, with
Canadian officials selling radar and (it may be) atomic-bomb plans
to Soviet espionage and then permitting the agents to leave the
country with their booty. It is not improbable that through one
means and another the Communists already have a pretty fair idea
of how atomic bombs are to be made. What remains is the setting
up of plant facilities for manufacturing them.

February 22 James Michael Curley two years ago was elected
United States Congressman from the 11th Massachusetts District.
He soon became engaged in his usual nefarious practices, those of a
political scoundrel living by his wits. He was hailed before a court by
a grand jury on various charges, among them that of defrauding by
mail. I have lost track of how many times Curley has been convicted
on what counts. Perhaps he was convicted previously for mail fraud
and appealed. Perhaps the conviction handed down several days ago
by a Federal Court was the first on this particular indictment. In any
case, he was convicted and sentenced to a term of six to eighteen
months in a Federal penitentiary. Naturally, Curley has appealed to
a higher court. While serving as Congressman, he ran for and was
elected by a very large majority Mayor of Boston. The graft connected with Congress was not, I imagine, as bountiful as that he
derived from being Mayor of Boston. It is customary, I believe, for a
Congressman who wins a state or city election to surrender his seat
in Congress. Not so Curley. He holds both offices now.

Yesterday afternoon he arrived at South Station on the crack
train, 'The Bostonian.' When he stepped from the Pullman with the

second Mrs. Curley clad in a mink coat, his daughter dressed to kill and his two sons, he was met by a triumphant delegation of Irish friends and politicos with a brass band. An estimated ten thousand commuters and holiday-bound travelers in one of the nation's busiest stations were entangled in the welcome to Curley for half an hour, despite the efforts (probably half-hearted) of twenty-two sergeants, patrolmen and detectives. The band played 'Hail the Conquering Hero Comes' and 'Isle of Capri,' the latter sentimental ditty Curley's favorite.

Curley is 71 years old. He said: "It is extremely gratifying to find that people still have faith in me." His case, he went on, had been appealed and would not come up until April of next year. "I'll have ample time to conduct the duties of both positions (Congressman and Mayor) without interference."

February 25 If what I am about to put down transgresses good taste or augurs a sophomoric interest at a senior age in sex, I am sorry; but—and it is a large 'but'—the portraiture of Patsy demands it, even without taking into account that it fills in the black and white of the contemporary scene. And I am not uninterested in sex.

Patsy misses Phil. "Can I," I asked, "put some questions to you about him?" "Well, I guess so." "You say he tried hard to force you to have relations with him?" "That's correct." "Did he try to force you against your will?" "Yes he did." "Did you mind?" "No, I didn't. I rather liked it." "Was he ever what you might call brutal with you?" "Most decidedly." "And you liked that?" "Yes. It was just lucky for me I was strong." "Did he expose himself, as the books put it?" "Yes." "Were you shocked?" "No. Dick did the same thing, and I was rather taken aback then. But you get used to it." "Did he get you to touch him?" "Oh yes." "Did you mind?" "No. Why should I?" "Did you like it?" "I didn't mind." "There are few words in our language for such things, Patsy, save Anglo-Saxon ones and technical ones. When he became excited did he 'come off'?" "Why naturally." "Did it get on you?" "Sometimes." "Did you mind?" "Of course not. It's all perfectly natural." "Then you had to take your clothes to the cleaners?" "Yes, sometimes." "Did the idea of what they might conclude embarrass you?" "Certainly not. I never thought of it." "Did Phil touch you the same way?" "Naturally. He couldn't find any indications that I was a virgin. So he wouldn't believe me for a long time. So he felt justified in making me accede to him if he could. He finally believed me." "Didn't any of the routine shock you?" "Why no. It wasn't new to me. Why do you think I read certain books? And, believe it or not, there was Carl.

Maybe you thought he was without sex, but take it from me he wasn't. He had his own furnace inside him."

March 5 I playfully called Mrs. Trench "Grandma" yesterday. She sulked. She held forth. She gave me an ultimatum to the effect that I must call her "Mrs. Trench" or "Rose" or she would leave. She further implied that she had helped me out not for money but from the goodness of her heart (which is far from true, she having held me up at one time for the pay she wanted — or else) and I possessed no gratitude. I replied agreeably that I was in a pass where what she wished was law, but that she could get what she wished much more easily by tact and a gentle request. That brought forth further recriminations after the style of my Mother. She would not give over. I lost my temper — lock, stock and barrel. I wanted to tell her where and how to get off. I didn't. But I got no sleep. Early this morning I dissembled as I knew she would like. It makes me hate both her and myself. As with Pearl, I am by degrees losing respect and affection for her. She will not control herself and is always, it would seem, anxious to fly off the handle at trifles just when I'm off-guard. I suggested two days off. It would, she informed me, do no good since everything was my fault.

March 8 Mrs. Trench is within an ace of walking out, and Mrs. Cash is the only person I know who might tell her straight out what a silly fool she's being. I hate so much stirration about such essentially trivial matters as a few ineptly exchanged words. I'll call Mrs. Trench "Mrs. Trench" from now on, and while remembering to be grateful for the last year, not be so fond of her. Not being so fond of her, I can dissemble better. When a man gets fond of a woman, almost any woman, he becomes at a disadvantage in dealing with her; when he feels her power over him, sooner or later she begins to ride him with saddle and bridle if possible.

We had best fight Russia now than later when it will be a matter not of fighting perhaps but of several hundred atomic bombs planted to destroy us between sunset and sunrise. We are in a parlous position. Perhaps we should unite entirely with the British Empire in a close federation. They have the brains and we have the money and the men. We would be governed from London or by London but we might survive, for we would be, if poorer in wealth, richer in leadership and diplomacy. This is a great recession from my former stand but one warranted by conditions I feel.

One of my outstanding virtues is that I am subject to a change of mind when persuaded of the wisdom of an altered viewpoint, and always I am open to persuasion. I am all but ready to declare for a world-wide federation against Russia, including as allies Germany and Japan and China if we can win them at this late date. I would permit Japan and the parts of Germany we control to rearm and propagandize both nations against Russia. The world is now, in interests at least, dividing into two camps. We should take measures to unite and make efficient our camp, else we be in the near future destroyed or disassembled part by part. I cannot be more serious in what I am saying. The future of modern man is precarious at best, and we should leave off talking and get together with the like-minded peoples and take what steps we must to save ourselves from eventual annihilation. It is time to subdue words and take to deeds.

March 9   To have been less melodramatic in writing the last section of yesterday's entry would have been in better taste I suspect, but my feelings run deep and are, when I loose them, melodramatic.

March 10   No one can ever again rowel the flanks of my spirit as Janice has done. Never again will I lay myself so unreservedly open to loving a woman. I consider that she has been callous and unfeeling beyond the bounds of any reason or excuse. It must have been done deliberately. I wish her husband would die, her baby would perish, her house would burn down. The part of my nature that is Scottish clansman harbors a violent resentment. One that was loved as I loved her and was aware that she was loved has no right before God, if she believes in God, or before her own conscience, if she has one, to neglect and slight the one who loved her. May she pay for it one day.

I asked Evelyn to speak to Mrs. Cash to explain about Mrs. Trench, so that if Mrs. Trench approached her with complaints, she, Mrs. Cash, would be forewarned. Evelyn did so, and Mrs. Cash said that she "would go to bat" for us, "straighten Mrs. Trench out." Mrs. Trench did lament to her. "I told her straight from the shoulder," Mrs. Cash said, "just what was what. I told her what fine, honorable people you and Mrs. Inman are, how you'd stood by me during my various troubles. I told her that she had a good job, one which gave her a great deal of freedom and (a thing she couldn't get anywhere else) she was paid in such a way she didn't have to bother with income taxes. I reminded her how good you and Mrs. Inman had been to her. I want to give you a piece of advice, Mr. Inman. I don't want you to kick me in the ass for it—the risk people run when they proffer advice—for it is well-meant. It's this. If Mrs. Trench wishes to be called Mrs. Crap, call her Mrs. Crap. Call her what she wants. You and I may think she's silly and making a lot of fuss over a trifle (I do think it), but you must bear in mind that she's honest and reliable and in her own way fond of you and that the help situation seems little if any better than it was during the war. So I'd smooth her fur and forget her tantrums and that she didn't thank you for your note and anything else about her that annoys you and nurse her along. That's my advice. You ought to know by now that I have your interest at heart. And if you mention to her that I said anything, I'll never go to bat for you again. That's straight. I'm an old woman and I like to help my friends, but I'm probably a goddamn fool for sticking my nose into other people's business."

I thanked her. I was and am grateful. I call Mrs. Trench "Mrs. Trench" from here on. She told both Evelyn and Mrs. Cash that if I made a single slip with her name, she would walk out, which on the face of it is grotesque. I'll not tease her in any way. And she will doubtless think me wonderful. It's all been absurd, and I resent the emotion spent on it, the thought, the words said and written which might have been used to better purpose.

March 12 [From Patricia:]

As you see, we are still here in Louisiana, tho Paul and I are not together. His camp in St. Martinville closed on January the fourteenth, and Paul went back to Camp Polk for a short stay. He was busy shunting prisoners to and from Arkansas. Then went to the Lake Charles Air Base for a month. While there he managed to get home every week-end. Now he is at a branch camp in Donaldsonville, La. Not far from here as the crow flies, but due to the swamp lands between he has to take a long round-a-bout trip to get home. And he will only be able to get in on every second week end. How long Paul will be there we don't know. He seems to think another month. We had expected that he would be on his way overseas by now. But he is still waiting for his orders. He has picked Japan, China or Hawaii, in that order as his preference. Now that a new ruling has come in and familys can join the men, we are very anxious for him to get started. He will go first, and then send for me. As wives will not be allowed in some areas. I do think it's most philanthropic of the government to let me do a bit of sightseeing at their expense. They were really forced to do something to get the men to volunteer for overseas duty. As the re-enlistments were falling off terribly. Paul has signed up for eighteen months, which will take us up to June, 1947. By then we hope that things will be a bit more settled in civilian life. Particularly in our field. Paul wants to go in for television, and of course that is in it's infancy right now.

March 15 I'm losing money at a great rate. Prices of all my stocks with the exception of liquors, motion pictures and sugars fade out beneath my sell prices as I seek to jettison most of the cats and dogs on which I was doing so well. Grateful that I have $16,000 in the savings banks and may put more there if I do not buy more liquors and motion pictures. We shall see. My life would be much drabber without the Stock Market. Dealing in stocks also, as I have said before, causes what is happening in the world to take on sharper outlines.

March 20   Yesterday William Henry Minor returned from three years of service, "three years absolutely wasted, Arthur." In his uniform he was, with stripes and ribbons of action and buttons and wings. He seemed pleased to see me, and I was glad to see him, a gladness modified by lack of any notion as to his intentions regarding his former job. He was so anxious, apparently, to hear about everything that had happened during his absence that I talked rather than he, talked myself into a sore throat all night and today. He remembered all sorts of details about when he was here that I had forgotten and expected him to have forgotten. It was touching. He could not have recalled such minor trivia had he not returned to them often in his thoughts during these three years — what radios I had, where the tacks to pin the curtain were kept, small alterations and misplacements in the arrangements of furniture and things, what people had thought or said.

Kind brown eyes in a tanned face, Indian in cast, with pouches under the eyes and a smile for me each time I smiled. A neat man, with much of the boyishness oddly vanished and, I doubt not, a capacity for sternness latent, a trait often become a part of men given to teaching and leading in times of crisis. I told him that I wanted him back but had no intention of pressing him. He replied that we would talk of it later. He was contemplating, he said, a chicken farm. The less I say to Billy, I have a notion, and the more I see him, the better my chance of getting him back.

Billy insisted upon putting down my curtains (it being past one o'clock) and seeing that I got to bed. He has a winning way with him, gentle with me. I'm not sure but that the quality of gentleness, as I grow older, appeals to me as much or more than any other quality of nature. Billy thinks that Evelyn looks much older than when he left, and she thinks that he looks older. She does look older. It has been no silver-spoon-and-pink-doily tea party for her since Janice and Pearl left. Billy promised to come to talk to me some evening and, if he could manage it (Sadie, that phrase means), take me driving Sunday morning.

Arthur played it cool and finally managed to snag Billy Minor. It took some adroit bargaining and psychological arm twisting. Billy was still under "poor Sadie's" thumb, and Mrs. Trench's interests had to be safeguarded (she was now the linchpin in the Garrison Hall operations); but Arthur's efforts paid off, and Billy, his buffer against the world, returned. When Billy, a few months later, spoke of taking a higher-paying job in Houston (that Sadie never stopped prodding him about), Arthur told him it was about time he, not Sadie, wore the pants in the family, and Billy promised to take control.

Patsy Boland alternately annoyed and delighted Arthur. He devoted pages of the Diary to her quarrels with her mother and stepfather, her agitated love life, her intermittent visits, and the osteopathic treatments she gave him. Although he applauded her decision to apply to medical school, he dreaded the possibility of her leaving Boston. To keep her available, he gave her expensive presents and even promised to provide her with a room and to pay for her tuition. Much to his consternation and rage, she began to consider a move to New York after being accepted by the Cornell University Medical School.

Meanwhile mercurial Evelyn, "the bane and the treasure" of his life, kept him on tenterhooks. He simply could not adjust to her vacillating behavior. Yes, he loved her, could not praise enough her willingness to placate the "Old Man," whose periodic visits depressed him unspeakably, but she was lukewarm to his "innate aspirations," his "sensitivity," and his "desire to improve people." She seemed to him "incredibly stupid in numberless ways," unable to follow his simplest instructions. Arthur suspected that she stuck with him more out of a sense of duty than from love. Having renounced his hopes to be a successful writer and poet, however, and having accepted himself as an ordinary person, he could no longer excuse his "thoughtlessness," "ruthlessness," and "cruelty" on the grounds that he was "accomplishing unique things." Nor did he feel he could "get away with the sort of highhandedness and arrogance people pardon in younger invalids." Resignedly he determined to adjust his "elastic" nature to her unadjustable and inelastic one.

March 22 Patsy arrived at seven-thirty to treat me and spend part of the evening. She was in a nasty mood. "I'm in love again," she began. "With whom this time?" "Oh, with Milton Koretz, the man in the play the other night, not the drinker." "I suppose he's Jewish," I said, "since his name is Milton. Most Jews seem to love the name Milton." She suddenly grew rigid with temper. "What right have you," she snapped, "to be intolerant of the Jews? They're just as good as you are. I don't care whether a person is black or green, red or brown, if I like them. I like Milton. I don't think he's a Jew. If he is, I don't care. No, don't touch me. I don't want to be touched by you. You have no right to be so intolerant." "Go on and get nasty if you want," I said. "You make me sick with your racial abstractions. It's all right for you to laugh at individuals as you do, but when it's a matter of race, you get righteous. If you want to fight, I'm your partner." She gradually calmed down, and so did I. I didn't enjoy her much for the evening, as I consider it none of her affair whether I like or dislike the Jews, at least none of her emotional affair. She's very immature intellectually and not too bright. Her capacity to concentrate is taken by strangers as mentality, which it is not — merely a happy gift.

March 23   Billy talked to me, and I asked questions until I became tired. He talks more fluently and at length than formerly. He still makes use of phrases such as "half-hazard" for "haphazard." He spoke softly and not without vividness. In some cases it is difficult to tell whether he is twisting his report in a fashion he feels will coincide with some theory or observation of mine he remembers or is relaying his impressions. Accuracy, I am sure, seems to the kindly fellow with an affection for me of infinitely less importance than saying what will please, interest or reinforce my theories of life.

Billy is living alone with Sadie in Allston in the house, apartment, half-house, whatever it is, that used to be so filled with Sadie's family. He constantly refers to her as "poor Sadie." "Poor Sadie is desolated since her mother and favorite brother died." He pays $38 a month for where they live. "Poor Sadie" has four closets filled with clothes. "She loves clothes. It's something, Artie, I can't deny her." I gather that Sadie or Billy or both have saved money. They have sufficient money, I also gather, to enter the chicken business, though I cannot imagine the high-tension, emotional, clothes-loving Sadie on a farm. I am arriving at the conclusion that at present Billy has no intention of returning to me. Did I attempt to hurry or high-pressure him, of this I am sure, there would be no chance of getting him back. Again and again he refers to how "fed up" he is with "being ordered around." He's a particularly nice man, as men go.

I asked him if he had made any real friends during his period of service and what he thought of American men after having had contact with so many. "Well, I'll tell you, Artie, it's this way. I tried to study the men I met with your eyes, that is, like you taught me to. It was great fun. I must admit I was *very* disappointed in American men. Of course, I saw them under what was probably the worst conditions, when they were in service and not engaged in actual fighting. Just between you and me — and I know you want me to say just what I think — I found most American men lacking character, you know, like shells with no stuffing inside, empty-like. All most of them could think about was women and liquor and gambling. I've heard enough filthy talk about women to disgust a saint."

Billy's picture of the Pacific theatre after the war was a drab one — many island bases which "When you fly toward them you think are like Paradise, they're so beautiful, but when you land, they're squalid and filthy and hot and they stink"; landing fields untended and full of holes, men dissatisfied and disgruntled, gambling and whoring, inefficient officers, thousands of tons of equipment allowed to mildew and rot, tractors and jeeps and huge bulldozers and cranes pushed into the sea, buildings falling to ruin; in Shanghai, Chinese prostitutes permitted in the barracks, black-market operations in all sorts of Army equipment and supplies, gambling in the fluctuating yen; no morale anywhere save in Japan under the direct supervision of MacArthur.

"Another reason I wanted to get out was that the ground crews simply didn't give a hang how they serviced the ships. They didn't even take the trouble to balance the gas tanks. The motors weren't kept clean and tuned up. The crew had to go over everything twice and double-check it before every flight to make sure something wasn't wrong. It made flying dangerous. I didn't mind the danger when we were in it (once we were given a poor navigator who calculated wrong, wouldn't admit it so that we landed with only five minutes left in L.A. when we were bound for Frisco), but when we weren't in it and you thought about it, it wasn't pleasant. So I decided to get out."

Billy rather liked the Japanese, that is, the Japanese women. The Japanese men were "conceited little punks." He feels that it was all but incredible that they ever had the idea they could go to war with the United States and win. He was impressed by their squalor, their poverty, the unproductivity of their land. He feels that only by sheer courage and unadulterated gall did they ever get as far against us as they did. "Artie, you simply wouldn't believe how poor their land is."

March 24   I have been riding in the yards in the Baby-Carriage with Billy. Last evening he was here for a couple of hours. I told him again that while I didn't intend high-pressuring him I wanted him to know I wished he were back with me, that I would feel safer and more cared for were he here. If, I said, I had been for three years in the war, I'd want to take my time making any decision. He then surprised me. He'd been doing some reflecting himself, he said. Whatever he thought of me, Sadie came first. She was all alone in the six rooms where they live. He couldn't leave her alone nights. She

change the will insofar as he was concerned. I only did those kinds of things with people I felt had treated me unfairly or ungently or unjustly. If he didn't know by now he could trust me, he'd never know it. If he looked for more security, he'd never find it. If the country went Communist, he'd be better fitted to survive than me, and I couldn't do anything about that. If the atomic bomb hit us, security wouldn't be available to anyone. If he was so dumb as to doubt my sincerity, why he'd best go on about his business and I'd find someone else. I couldn't go through these constant upsets due to his unstable emotions week after week and not fall ill.

He will, he said, decide by tomorrow, one way or the other. He had, he said, witnessed so much double-dealing, knavery, dirty work in the service that he found himself doubting everyone. He appreciated my offers of safety, and he was drawn to come back with me, but his head was a whirl inside. He wanted to go out to the Place, paint the kitchen and think things over, because he wished this decision to be the final one, once and for all. He was sorry I got so upset and he hated to make me that way, but all this was in his mind and he had to tell me. He has gone now, and I have made as many concessions and promises as I intend to make. More would do no good.

May 11 During the night I dreamed that I was a small boy. I and another small boy were at two very long candy counters with glass tops, stretching outdoors up a hill. A pleasant young woman was waiting on us. It appeared I had unlimited credit at my command. I studied the shelves and chose the candies the young woman handed over to me — yellow and green and red gumdrops, little lavender pieces tasting of violet, yellow toffee, green sugar squares filled with liquid, bonbons white and pink and coffee-colored, chocolate peppermints, varicolored nougats, candied pineapple, sugared rose leaves, big chocolate creams. It was an intensive process and took a long time, and the bags in my hands and under my arms increased in number. There was a street to be crossed. Something hit me. I came to with my Father lying on the ground, his head in my lap. His head was that of a tiger, mangled, clotted with blood, the eyes closed. And all over the pavement, to the feet of the gathering crowd, the candies lay scattered and smeared with dirt.

May 12 Mrs. Cash talked with Billy for about two hours. She stressed what a good offer I had made and how unfitted he was by age and training for making money in the world. He, always determined to get all the traffic will bear, inquired if she thought I might give him a bonus of five hundred dollars a year. She replied that she most emphatically did not, that I had offered all I intended offering.

She told me that she thought she had gotten nowhere with him. Shortly thereafter, he came in the room, sat down beside me. He opened the subject. Mrs. Cash, he said, had been too blunt with him. What did I think? I replied that I thought the same as ever. I had said my entire say. If he liked what I had offered him, he would come. If he didn't, he might as well go on and do what else he wanted. When the next depression came and he was on the rocks, he could come to me — and I hoped he would — and, if I had no one else, I felt sure we could get together then. He wondered would I buy him an annuity? I would not. I felt I was being generous in the extreme. If he wanted an annuity, he could go buy one with his own money. If he didn't like my terms, Mrs. Trench would take care of me and I'd get a secretary who could drive. He needn't worry about me. I'd get along. Better than he would, probably.

May 16 Every day I miss Janice. Never before have I missed anyone gone out of my life as insistently as I miss her. For weeks I have been considering writing her a letter of the kill-or-cure variety. This morning I did write her. It was from the heart. If she doesn't respond, I hope God or Providence or circumstances will hurt her in some wise as she has hurt me, bitterly and deeply and lastingly. The letter:

Dear Janice —

I doubt if you have any conception of what your apparently utter abandonment of me has meant to me. I do not mean your not coming to see me. I mean your complete failure to telephone me, to write me a word, to show the slightest interest in whether I lived or died. I telephoned you and wrote you all last summer and fall until finally I gave up the one-sided appeal. You should not have given a casual friend the cold shoulder you have me.

There is nothing left but for me to conclude that you have — for whatever reason — seen fit to isolate yourself from me. You could not have been more cruel to me had you set out to be so — and maybe that is what you have done. I shall never have the faith I placed in you in another human being, for I do not wish to lay myself open to being so soul-destroyingly hurt ever again.

You have claimed to believe in God and the ethics of Christianity. If there are such things, for what you have done to my spirit these last months there will be marks against you that no conceivable reason you may have given yourself for abandoning me will alleviate.

I am certain that not your husband, not your son, probably no one else but your mother ever loved you more admiringly and more reverently. And you have — or so it seems to me — casually flipped my devotion out the window, careless where it landed or what happened to it. How could you have been so cruel or so cowardly or so heedless? I could wail against a wall.

Arthur

May 17 Twenty-five spoonsful of bromide last night to try to get myself relaxed. No use. The car, Evelyn driving, broke down in a little back street because Billy, after having been asked and reminded, had not as usual put in gasoline. While Evelyn went to a station some two blocks away, I sat. Laborers were digging a ditch. They banged the floor of a truck with shovels to remove the residue of concrete until the narrow way exploded with sound. Sound of that sort is like pain to me. I need to call on nervous reserves to withstand it.

May 19 Have ad in 'Post' for Protestant secretary. No one has answered. Probably conclude I am religiously intolerant, which is not so, merely that I don't want Irish or Jews. It's less than nothing to me what faith a man harbors.

May 23 This is Evelyn writing. Arthur has been sick in bed since Monday with a high temperature. Night before last Dr. Pike came, found Arthur's temperature 103° and his pulse 130, said he had never seen Arthur so sick. He and I were seriously alarmed, far more so than was Arthur. Dr. Pike felt the infection might easily develop into pneumonia.

Arthur asked me to write this entry because there is now a nationwide railroad strike, effective at four o'clock this afternoon. Also, the soft-coal miners are due out on strike Saturday. Arthur hopes that these two developments will make people feel the pinch to an extent where the Senate may at last feel the pressure and take action.

Arthur said: "If we have got to have everything regulated (which I don't like) we might as well have labor unions regulated."

Arthur wants to record also that someone let slip inadvertently in Congress the fact that the United States is now in possession of a weapon of offense infinitely more deadly than the atomic bomb.

June 3 Myself writing again. Have undergone a long and miserable bout with influenza, temperature lasting two weeks and weakness still at my heart. Must have caught because of upset emotional condition due to Billy and being chilled the one day we rode to the Place. Clothes on for first time today. Heart muscles ache. Much to tell and observe but no adequate strength to use writing. It is a superb, clear cool day. The room rocks back and forth. I'm disheartened. This was the severest flu since the attack early in the thirties which robbed me of strength never to be recovered. Time will tell what this has done to me.

June 5   About organized labor unions situation. The railroad strike took place. All rail traffic stopped. Truman spoke on the radio, threatening to take action, placing the blame for the strike squarely upon two leaders of the railroad brotherhoods. The two leaders called off the strike. Truman spoke to Congress recommending the passage of a drastic short-term measure calculated to prevent unions from carrying on strikes after the Government had seized the strike-bound companies and facilities. He was angry. He went so far as to recommend drafting into the armed forces those who refused to work for the Government in its capacity as manager of seized plants. The House passed the Truman Bill by a huge majority, but the cooler heads in the Senate took cognizance of the totalitarian slant of the draft citizens aspect of the measure and refused to pass it in the form Truman advised.

This Truman is a very weak man, all that will arouse him being personal anger, as with the two railroad brotherhood leaders. Our country must surely be losing in international prestige because of our confusion on the so-called home front.

June 13   Truman has proved himself an almost pathetic figure of a man, thank goodness with none of Roosevelt's charm and guile, an impotent person too small for his responsibilities. And an internal fight among Roosevelt appointees to the Supreme Court will do the Democrats no good. The faces of the justices, all but one or two of them, are the faces of scoundrels. Truman's latest appointee, Vinson, is dishonest, if faces are any indication whatsoever of inward character. One member of the Court has gone so far from his duties and dignity as to speak at a C.I.O. rally. Those who govern us have rarely been of lower caliber.

June 30   This afternoon, barring a sudden change in weather conditions, will take place at Bikini Atoll in the Marshall Islands the first of three separate atomic-bomb tests ordered by the United States Joint Chiefs of Staff, General Eisenhower, Admiral Leahy, Admiral Nimitz and General Spaatz to determine the effectiveness of the bomb against modern armor.

The men on board the nontarget ships, a radio commentator sets forth, are keyed up and nervous, though in good spirits; no one knows for sure what will happen. The knowledge of the tremendous devastation and death wrought at Hiroshima and Nagasaki cannot be ignored by any reasonable mind. The pilot of the atom plane has a wiffle haircut and a round head, and his picture is on the front page of 'The New York Times Magazine.' The plane bears the name of

'Devil's Dream.' The atomic bomb has been christened 'Gilda' by the scientist and engineers who have it under their direction, and on it has been painted "a revealing likeness" of the film actress Rita Hayworth wearing a low-necked black evening gown. The cost of the experiment, less than $100,000,000, not as much cash as we would blithely toss away on food for our past and potential future enemies, has been contested from various quarters.

In true American fashion, all authorities insist upon pronouncing the experiment—which should be and is an offensive one—as defensive only, so that no nation will be antagonized, as though the one nation in question, Russia, would heed our double-talk terminology. I am wondering idly if atomic radioactive impulses generated by the great explosion may not, so little do people know about them, travel across the world (with some sort of damaging effect) on radio waves.

July 11 It's my idea that I'm maturing emotionally. I'm learning—I hope—not to become so all but a part of the people I grow fond of. I am successfully expurgating my heart of Janice. Patsy I have become indifferent to long ago. I keep a reserve between myself and Billy, Mrs. Trench. To Evelyn alone am I bound emotionally.

July 15 Patricia arrived Friday. Her husband, Paul, is in New Jersey waiting to be sent overseas with America's final batch of returned German prisoners. She's a nice person, thirty-eight, brown eyes, plump in the middle, fairly short, with a tongue given to talking at high speed. Her nature is sunny. She finds interest in every little thing. Her eyes rove to see what she can see. Her thoughts are not profound. She enjoys every aspect of living, the good and the bad in stride, yet is not a masochist as Woody is. Evelyn says she makes an easy guest. She seems older than Evelyn both in looks and drive. I find a little of her goes a long way, for she bores me at the same time that I like her. Yesterday morning she had been chatting with Evelyn and me for an hour, and I was becoming uneasy, as a person gets who wishes to move from a stuffy room.

I dislike the way Patricia talks about her husband just as if he were her prize poodle, enumerating his virtues and vices with zest. Half her mind dwells upon sex in its primitive conception. Her direct calling of spades is not as whimsically done as when written in her letters. She's kindly, forthright, honest, emotionally energetic, tireless, affectionate, religious. "I told Paul once—and I think I meant it—that if I had to give up either him or books, it would be him. I simply love to read. I love to read, and I like houses. I like people, too. And I wear my foolish self out observing details of all sorts. I find immense fun living." She possesses a fleet of Irish relatives in and around Boston and is bent upon visiting all of them. "I really don't admire the Irish. They're too maudlin, yet not at all kindly really. But they're a lot of fun."

The first night she was here, Patricia leaned over my bed and banged me in the nose with her head and broke the cartilage loose. I was fairly stunned for forty-eight hours. When she sits in a chair, she hugs her legs. She possesses little modesty. "The human body is the human body, and I think nothing of it." She showed me the scar on her stomach and the sort of bras she wears. "I've gained all this plumpness in the breastworks since my operation. Paul loves it this way. If he likes it, that's okay with me. But he doesn't want me fat around the middle. He raises Ned with me about that."

July 16 Evelyn leaves for her farm with Dr. Pike tomorrow. She's enjoying Patricia more than I am. Mrs. Trench leaves for the Great Lakes cruise on the 4th of August. Mrs. Trench has been an angel lately. Billy seems, by all outward indications, to be enjoying himself. He's pleasant and more cooperative than before the war. I had Fred dig the wax out of his ears, so that he can hear me. I enjoy his solicitous company. We're still clearing up the library and the little spare room, throwing things out, rearranging. I think to myself, "You paid Eddie Simms as much, almost, as you do Billy, and Eddie doubled his salary, at least doubled it, by having you over-charged everywhere and pocketing the difference and by wangling you. He was infinitely less adaptable than Billy and not as earnest about your interests, so do not begrudge what you are paying Billy. He's worth it to you. You should be pleased to pay it." Then I feel better, for it is so. I only hope Billy stays and in his present frame of mind. He's stopped looking for a car and for a business. He seems less afraid and less bewildered. As men go, he's a grand fellow.

July 20 The Machs have sent us notice that we will be, when our lease expires next month, tenants at will. That is, they can raise our rents whenever it is legal to do so. The very contemplation of another joust with the Jewish bastards makes me lie awake nights. They'll be sure to raise our rent away and above anyone else's. I wouldn't mind if we were to be treated as are all other tenants. That Arnold, the Adder, is too dumb and troublemaking to be allowed to live. He's been attempting for years to deprive us of the use of the back elevator. I hope that Congress passes a rent control bill. Prices, otherwise, are this quickly beginning to recede from post-O.P.A. prices. Many of them should be below O.P.A. ceilings within two or three months.

July 22 Another four hour sleep night. Cousin Nellie walked in a door, a larger, older, bloatedly magnified edition of herself, with redder hair, eyes pale-green flecked with yellow, and teeth as large as almond nuts. She had not, she asserted, enough to do to fulfill her energy. She had made these dozen boxes of candy. She had made these dozen children. But that was nothing. All the children had red hair. They were husky counterparts of their mother. A man was present, and he was so strong I could not bend his arm. "This little girl," Cousin Nellie said, "is as well as the others, but—" here she pulled up an eyelid and ran a finger carelessly around inside an empty socket (the child smirked at the attention)—"but she was born blind." It was, by virtue of the circus of strength, very depressing to me. All of them scorned me.

July 25   The second atomic-bomb test took place at Bikini yesterday; this time the bomb fired under water. It would seem to me, an uninformed onlooker, that there is something hidden either about the power of the bomb used or about the information released. One would conclude that an atomic bomb the size of the ones used in Japan should have done more damage to the anchored fleet and to the island itself than those two bombs appear to have accomplished. Perhaps the Navy, to retain its importance or to fool the rest of the world, has diminished the power of the two bombs used. It would be smart to lull the rest of the nations into believing the power of the atomic blast had been overrated — too smart for us Americans in all probability, though maybe not.

Roderic and I read a vivid and violent story in 'Astounding' last evening of the final warfare of mankind after bombs on the surface of the earth had made living there untenable, warfare of giant earth-boring, mole-like warships seeking each other far within the dark underworld of rock. I have a horror of dying by radioactive destruction of my body tissue, though the Japanese say it is not a too-painful death.

July 27   There are far fewer unemployed than had been precalculated. Plants are busy the length and breadth of the nation. In certain vicinities there is a labor shortage. Earnings of many companies are at all-time highs. New small businesses, despite governmental interference and labor union handicaps, are everywhere. Yet a considerable discouragement lies on the land. While there are more people working than ever before, they turn out less per man-hour. Stocks have gone down steadily, more of them than have gone up since February. The shadow of Russia falls across everyone's concept of what the future will be, a cherished shadow by some, a dreaded shadow by most. The potentials of the atomic bomb and the end of culture, if not of mankind, dwells unwanted in every thinking man's mind. Those who do not dread inflation dread deflation. Crime, according to statistics, mounts. Most women do not worry widely, that not being their nature, and many men go heedlessly along; but enough persons are touched with apprehensiveness of what lies ahead to advance warily and with maimed confidence.

July 29   I spoke to Mrs. Trench in a roundabout manner concerning the kitchen, having previously given her more money for her vacation than she had expected. I was, I said, making a campaign, as she could see, to keep things neater and cleaner. I was thinking about the kitchen. Could we throw away that old dishmop? Whose old milk bottles were those on the floor? Would she like a container for the soap flakes? She got the point and was as sweet as pie about it all. I didn't always, she said, give her enough time in the morning. "Well," I said, "when I don't give you enough time, just come in my room and shake your finger at me and say, 'I want more time,' and I'll give it to you." It was easier than I had expected. She doesn't get as offended as she used to before Mrs. Cash took supervisory charge of her.

I have just sold most of my collection of poetry books. Received nine dollars for the lot. They will be resold by the secondhand-bookstore man for thirty or so dollars. To hell with poetry.

August 6   The scientists, ordinarily not public speakers, have taken to platforms, forums, the radio to warn that only effective outlawing of atomic weapons will save the world. When the bomb was perfected, many scientists banded together and signed a letter begging the President not to use it on Japan. The very fact, they argued, that we would use it on large enemy cities without warning would cause the world never to believe we would forbear to use it in the future, and that would likely cause other nations to make and keep their own atomic bombs. No attention was paid the pleas. I personally feel it would have been better to have lost a million men and taken another year to make the conquest of Japan than to have loosed such a calamitous weapon upon the world. I cannot feel that the years before we reap the destroying whirlwind induced by our avaricious scientific prying into the aloof secrets of nature are many.

August 8   I can't win over the weather. It doesn't pay me to ride when the sun is bright. I stay in; the sun hides behind clouds; I might well have ridden in comfort. It is cloudy. I go out. The sun, once I am out, shines glaringly. It is cloudy. I go out. It rains. I come home; it stops raining. For two hours now there has been no sunshine. When I went out, there was none. The moment I was out, the sun shone. It's got me buffaloed. I'm a good weather forecaster, better indeed than the weather bureau by far. If I went riding now after two hours of clouds, the sun would come out and dazzle my eyes. As with everything large and small, I feel that the cards are stacked against me before I start and only wariness and ingenuity are sufficient to protect me momentarily from the eye of God or Fate or individual bad luck—whichever it is. Had I a faith in my own good luck, life wouldn't be half so vitiating.

August 9 Of some 15 million veterans who can take advantage of Government-financed education, vocational and college, some four hundred thousand are registered at colleges and universities and another quarter-million have not been able to get into the crowded institutions. Buildings are not large enough, professors are not sufficient. Teenagers are being kept out of college, there being not enough room for them. It is the greatest experiment in mass higher education in the history of the world, and no one can estimate in advance what effect upon our culture the experiment will have.

Be the result of the ex-service students what it may, one thing is sure: The old cloistered college days are gone for a decade, perhaps forever, and that is too bad. It was a rather lovely world in microcosm. As to the vocational aspect of the Government-financed educational scheme, that bids fair to be a graft on a wholesale scale, employees and employers alike cadging on Government munificence in more ways than can be counted.

August 10 God knows when Billy will get a car. I had persuaded him yesterday to go ahead and start his leave of absence this month. He told Sadie, and evidently she wept on him, said she wouldn't go anywhere without a car. She wants to be driven to Texas and California. She has Billy thoroughly sorry for her because of her mother's and brother's deaths. All she has to do is to act emotional and she gets what she wants. Which leaves me high and dry with no plans to count on. I'm interested in having them go to Maine to fish and hunt. If they go traipsing all over the country Billy is likely to get new ideas in his head about moving elsewhere or starting a new business or something. The smallest seed, unwatched, can grow to a sequoia in his emotions in short order.

August 12 Patricia had supper with Evelyn last night and afterwards came upstairs to see me. She has been to Maine to visit the nuns at the convent where she spent her girlhood. She now is with her seventy-six year old aunt in Roslindale, an "old maid" living on the $200-a-month insurance paid her since her husband's death.

September 1 This diary has made me captive for years. It is good to talk and hear talk without sifting what is being said and has been said to glean material for these pages. It is good to forget myself as a point of reference between the present world and history. It is good to say to myself that I am disinclined to write one day and not feel bound by conscientiousness to write. And most of all it is good to have more energy for other matters. Of course the destruction of the compass, the loss of sailing orders have their disadvantages, but to my surprise, a slowing down of log-readings is not one of them. Time passes less slowly.

September 4   I commenced a psychological novel the other day, wrote the first chapter. I am no writer for this era. I am a romantic by nature, and the purple patches will come in no matter what I do to avoid or delete them. I am discouraged. To attempt to write at this stage discourages me more than does leaving the business alone. I'll scribble in here, probably leave it uncorrected, let it go at that. I do enjoy writing as I am writing now—giving the turmoil of my thoughts partial ordered vent on paper.

September 11   These are reasons why I feel that a depression impends. The continued shipment of money and goods overseas for no recompense cannot but weaken the situation at home; we are being bled drastically. Lopsided production due to the Office of Price Administration's blunders and restrictions plus strikes are not beneficial. Borrowing by individuals on a large scale is commencing, and companies and corporations are seeking bank loans on an increasing scale. Salaries and wages are too high for continued profits. The market for new issues will have been discouraged by the Stock Market decline, as will private spending by wealthy people. Real estate values are too high. Farm production is inflated to a point where, when normal crops are reaped by the rest of the world, prices at home will drop and there will be a farm excess. The veterans are sucking the money of the nation with avidity. Automobile business appears grounded.

All in all, the situation looks to me not too promising, and even if the Republicans do win, that will only postpone a depression. Everything is a mess.

September 15   [From Patricia:]

It is at least fifteen years since I have been back to the Mount, but things have changed surprisingly little. All the change was in me. Nuns with their throats and hair covered never seem to age, and life there is so serene it seemed as tho I could go back to being fifteen again. The gloomy old parlors with their lurid chromos of saints and martyrs smelled of the same old wax and furniture polish. Only now the gloom didn't seem so awesome, and I didn't tiptoe about.

Sister Hildegarde was given a holiday as long as I was there because I had come so far to see her, so we had a grand time sitting in the garden gabbing like mad, and we never did get bored. I asked about loads of things I'd never dared to before. How they ever got into those habits, for instance. Whereupon she and Sister Justin started hauling them off and showing me just how things went together. If there was a pin shortage they'd have an awful time, not a button on the things, just tapes or pins, the top overdress of black pleated serge, is made like a jumper and it has five yards of material in it. The underskirt is equally full, but not so heavy, they wear undershirts with long sleeves! And over this a tight black sleeve to the wrist made usually of silk or rayon, and then over that they hook on wide winglike sleeves that cover their hands completely. I won't attempt to describe the head dress, I don't know the terms, but it is made of ridgidly starched linen, with a light veiling topping all that, the veil takes nine yards. All this is worn winter or summer, in winter a shawl is added when they go out. That regalia alone would keep me out of a convent, I who like to go about raw in the summer.

Unless you have the temperment for it one never could be a nun. The submission alone would drive most people crazy. I brought candy and a plant to Sister, and she had to take them to Mother Superior and ask for permission to keep them. She broke her glasses and couldn't have them fixed until Mother got back from a trip and gave her the necessary permission. It would drive me mad, but they seem to be very happy. Of course they are so busy they don't have time to brood. Up at five thirty, Mass and their office to say before breakfast, off to school at eight and the evening filled with lessons and evening services and to bed at nine. It's a good healthy life, the graveyard has few occupants, but I'll take me healt' another way.

It takes seven years before the final vows are taken and even then if they are not content the Bishop will release them from their vows. Very few go the seven years and then leave, I think there have been but two in the seventy five years. But I'd not like to live with that many women, just think of fifty women going through the change of life at the same time. No wonder Sr Hildegarde says that she doesn't want to be Head.

September 24 Naomi Green showed up Saturday afternoon. Not changed much. Homely. Tremendous emotional vigor, dynamic personality, deep voice. Evelyn likes her. Sense of fun. Says not in love with Henry but could have done worse. "He's a nice little man but no whirlwind and no great money maker." Naomi, I noted, was manlike in her directness. "I antagonize some people. Others like me. Much to my amazement I find, as I grow up, that more people like me than dislike me. Perhaps I don't care as much as I did. I've been only half a person for years artistically; now that I go to New York once a month for piano lessons, I feel a full person." I wish Naomi could come to see me once in a while. "Two growing boys," she said, "give me very little time for anything."

Sunday evening Patricia spent with me. Wish she didn't bore me so, for she's a fine person. At one point she leaned over and kissed me. "I love you, Arthur," she exclaimed. "I think you're swell." Incorrigible me, while pleased, inquired "Why?" "Because," she said, "I can tell you anything. I can't tell anyone else in the world absolutely everything. And I love your voice. I've heard all sorts of voices trained and untrained but never one I like to listen to as I do yours. Oh, I don't know, I guess I've a weakness for you." Patricia is tired of Boston. "It's just another city by now. I've an awful habit of making myself at home wherever I am. I don't seem to have roots so that each new city is just another place. That's why I'm so anxious to go overseas. Maybe that will be different."

October 9 I'm certain I'm easier to get along with than before the atomic bomb fell on my ambition. I'll never write poetry again. One can't pole upstream endlessly without getting anywhere. For now at least—maybe for good—the shine is off writing in here. I'm just an ordinary citizen, neither better nor worse, with an ordinary citizen's equipment of good and bad qualities. I no longer have the excuse that I'm accomplishing unique things, that the final achievement relieves me of certain moral and ethical responsibilities. Nor can I get away with the sort of highhandedness and arrogance people pardon in younger invalids. Nor is the world at large as patient with people like me as once it was. In a word, the criteria by which I order my behavior have altered radically. I am a different person, one much more acceptive, forbearing and modest.

October 12 Much against my inclination, my whole attitude has changed toward [Evelyn] since the episode of the will. It was this. I had spent the morning making out a new will. I had wanted to make sure she'd get everything except the ten thousand to Billy if he were still with me and the three thousand to Mrs. Cash I felt I owed her for her loyalty. I asked: "If your parents die and leave you money, what are you going to do about that?" She said: "I'll leave you what your father has given me. The other should go to my nieces and nephew."

I was shocked. "Well," I said, "of course you'll give me the use of the income during my life. I might need it." No, she would not. Nor would she leave me any way to use any of the capital in case I lost my money and was in dire need. I tried to explain. She was sorry, but she was firm in her resolve. I was shocked to the roots that she could be so adamant about such a matter. Her nieces won't even visit her, yet to them the money was to go, all of it, and the income. I tried frantically to explain what such a course would do to my conception of her. She remained immovable. Finally, after hours of talking, she wanted the right to think it over. In the morning she hadn't changed. I talked some more. Later, she conceded leaving me the income and the use of some capital if I were in trouble. By that time the damage to my spirit and our relationship had been done.

It is, I fear, irreparable. That one who had lived with me for twenty-three years, one who was aware how my Mother had acted, one who often reiterated that money meant nothing to her, one who should, as a loving wife, have of herself wished to make my future safer in case she died, had been incomprehensibly callous. That she was "sorry" had nothing helpful in it. That hours of talking and pleading had finally and reluctantly brought her around didn't heal the lack of comprehension of her first stand. It was better for me that finally she changed, for my welfare that is, though not for the bruising done to my spirit. It was like the times she stole my pistol, bought the farm in Maine, ran away, chose Dr. Pike, etc., only infinitely worse.

So I regard her now with unsentimental eyes, a self-willed, unsensitized, rather dumb, altogether unwarrantably nasty woman with not much will power, composure or grace. That I love her I know, but that I love her as deeply as I do isn't too smart. Doubtless time will make things better, but right now I'm both hurt and estranged.

At this point Mrs. Cash bustles in to get some expense money for the envelope under the elephant. "You know," she volunteers, "there's no better boss than you, and that's not bullshit either."

October 17   If the Truman Committee won renown for its reports, someone else than Truman must have drawn them up and been behind the spadework. He is stupid, not as Roosevelt was, but annoyingly and blatantly stupid, made the worse because of a sort of coined stubbornness. A South Carolina editorial calls him the poorest President since Washington, and that probably isn't far from wrong. Of course, the poor little fellow inherited Roosevelt's crops, sowed with incantations and fanfare, producing in large measure weeds; but even so, he might have done better. At any rate, he is (being ineffectual) preferable to Roosevelt.

October 19   Have been most of the morning keeping accounts with Mrs. Cash. Now that I no longer am centered on writing, I find making my finances run smoothly lots of fun. I have a natural bent for it when my attention is directed that way. Probably I was cut out to be a businessman anyway, not a slinger of words. I have some $19,000 in the savings banks now, $3,000 in cash at Dark's, 4% rather than a 5% basis, am about to pay off $500 on the $2,000 St. Botolph Street mortgage and put the remainder on 4% instead of 5% basis. I owe no loan either to Dr. Pike or to the bank. The moment employment begins to decline — if it does — I'll be sure a depression is ahead. I've sold short on some General Motors. I'm as solvent now as ever I've been. I'm preparing to make over in trust to Evelyn $30,000 worth of securities secured to me by a trust fund, so that theoretically she will receive the income. Then I'll draw up separate income tax returns, she receiving the rent from the two houses, and thereby save about $500 a year on the Federal income tax. It's impossible to avoid paying the State income tax by any finagling I can conceive.

October 20 My Father arrived. I have seen him. He weighs less but seems fitter than two years ago, for he isn't drinking. We talked about his garden, his ear-device, impersonal subjects. He's not dead yet; having met Patsy on the way into my room, he wanted to see her again on the way out.

October 22 Old Man is about to leave — thank God, thank Providence. Some of the last times he was here he was so sodden and nauseated with liquor that he felt not up to hopping on me and was therefore bearable, the more so that I was sorry for him. This time he has been in form, gathering momentum by the hour. It is no wonder that he cast a pall over my boyhood and since.

He sits and watches me as though waiting for me to "do some fool thing or other" so that he can pounce. It is like walking under a loose and lowering cliff. I consider each word I am about to say. He can twist any meaning askew and apparently delights in doing so. He would depress an ox.

October 23 Several front-page Americans, among them Edgar Hoover of the F.B.I., have lately warned Americans in no mincing terms of the growth and strength of communistic influence and the Communists in the United States. Members or sympathizers, we are told, have infiltrated into the various Federal bureaus and the State Department, even into the Army and Navy.

November 6 Republicans won control of Senate, House and also of Massachusetts. Thank God!

November 9 Tomorrow Evelyn and I will have been married twenty-three years. I have a copper Swiss alarm clock for her, some silk stockings, a gardenia. She has consented at long last to stop smoking, to humor my dislike of it, a matter that has been irking me for years since she smoked not because she liked it in particular but because she felt doing so asserted her independence and lessened my influence over her. She's been breaking her neck to please me lately. I guess the result of the will question on me woke her up on several counts.

Women, I sometimes conclude, are at their best only when slapped down or when they sense that they are losing or have lost some of their sway over their men. They seem to have no answering equivalent emotion for consistent male gentleness and sweetness, thoughtfulness and consideration. They bask in male adulation for a moderate period, then attempt to dominate their men or to act toward them with unconscious contempt. Whereupon they must be jolted to earth. And this applies to the best and to the worst of them, the periodicity alone varying. I hate it that this is so but take it into account.

November 11   I should say that at this point in my life my hobby has to do with young girls. I enjoy them, like them, feel competent to understand and, as a gardener with those special shrubs he likes, prune and cultivate the special virtues of each. There could be worse hobbies. While I may have doubts about my powers as a poet, as a financier, as a keeper of diaries, I have no doubts whatever about my capacities to tutor and develop those young girls I select to help and improve.

November 21   Patricia is very sweet. She's more rested, livelier than when she stayed with us. She was telling me of her "show" life in the twenties, when she was in 'Hit the Deck,' 'Rose Marie' and 'No, No, Nanette.' She had three specialty dances in the last musical comedy. Her forte was high kicking. She was never ambitious to get to the top, enjoyed "show business" for itself and being "on the road" more than "on the big stem." "I was pretty darn good in my line, if I do say it myself."

November 25   If I write about trivia in my diary, why not? The life of any average citizen is compounded of trivia. If I am an interesting person, my book will be interesting. If not, it will not be interesting. And whatever the subject matter chosen, however it is treated, nothing can alter that truism. I may not be an interesting person. The chances would favor my not being one. I possess charm. I have emotional vigor. Now and again I evince imagination. I am not intellectual or, on paper at least, witty. If I were not loveable and did not possess charm, I'd have been deserted for my bad qualities long ago. But none of the qualities I possess necessarily make me an interesting person. Fame, when all is said, is no more everlasting than the long shadow one casts of a still afternoon.

December 7   Re: circumcision — I wouldn't circumcise my child if I had one. I was circumcised, and I don't believe in it. It keeps you clean, yes, but likewise makes you sex-conscious and jittery. Dottie, after inquiry and thought, decided not to circumcise her Angus and "leave him without the protection nature meant him to have and the sensitivity when in action nature also planned for."

December 11   I am a nailed-down person, unable to circulate, hence unable to find new friends. The friends I make I feel must be kept at any effort. They are to be studied, amused, interested, their natures directed if possible, their loyalties assured as nearly as is feasible with such unstable stuff, watch kept that their attention does not meander carelessly or deliberately. That most of the friends I own are women follows upon my sedentary state. Men, if they are worth having as friends, as a rule are not ready to sit and talk by the hour. So women it is, whether or not I prefer them, and lucky for me that at this juncture I do prefer them or have so worked upon myself that I am convinced I prefer them. And if I prefer young women to elderly women, which I do, that is well with me. Older women tend to become frozen, fixed shadows.

All of which elucidates why so many females, and young females at that, move across these pages, constitute important integrals of my life.

December 14   Tried to get Fred last evening. Said he was too rushed to come. Has just been here. "Arthur, I'm so damn rushed these days I can't call my life my own. I've made a new rule for myself: not to go out on calls to new patients. That helps some. Fewer doctors, more patients. I try to get to bed nights by nine o'clock. Sometimes I'm in bed asleep by eight. I couldn't keep going if I didn't." After which, we discussed secretaries. He said: "I might have worse girls. If you get them dumb but pleasant, you have to do most of the work in the end. If you get them smart, they'll end by bossing you if they can do it. You know how women are, Arthur, once in the saddle they ride you. It's how they're built, I guess. But I'd rather have them pleasant and dumb than efficient and bossy. Wouldn't you? Of course you would. So I get along with what I have and bide my time. Next year secretaries will probably be a dime a dozen, and I can take my pick at reduced prices. Don't you think I'm right, Arthur? Sure you do. In the meanwhile I'm working myself groggy. What can I do for you, Arthur?"

December 15   Mrs. Cash and I sat down to wrestle with income taxes. I can't see sitting facing the light; she can't see unless she faces the light. So like two stubborn monkeys we sat each his own way. I couldn't glance at her figures. It was necessary for Evelyn to interpret and to pass papers back and forth. Mrs. Cash was bellicose. I was nervous, not at the work in hand but because she makes such a personal and emotional affair over what should be set about with detachment. Her back is up at the most harmless suggestion. The energy and violence the primitive woman is capable of expelling from herself, like angry bullets random-shot from a machine gun, are past believing when described on paper.

December 17   Just finished 'Swing Low' on the talking-book, a novel by Edwin A. Peeples of negro life in Atlanta in the vicinity of where Grandfather Inman used to live on Peters Street and where my Father still owns property. It is a realistic book spoiled by a motion picture happy ending. But the elucidation of the negro nature is skillfully and perceptively accomplished. Though I came in contact with very little of the tragic aspect of negro life when I was a boy or was not aware of it at any rate, the nature of the negroes I knew would exactly fit into the setting depicted by Peeples. It is a strange, apart subexistence the negroes in the book spend, keeping out of the way of the law or acquiescing to its penalties meekly. They have found the law to be for whites, not for themselves, and whenever justice conflicts with white supremacy, justice is avoided or sidestepped or ignored.

December 25   Sun shines. Snow falls. It is a day partly gotten through, always a day that puts the stamp of the past on me, makes me frantic. Evelyn has gone for a walk and wisely so. Billy is stringing yellow beans in the other room, humming to himself, busy in order to get to special mass with Sadie at twelve-fifteen. We have opened Mrs. Trench's stocking for me. A lady bountiful of a woman, Mrs. Trench. I did well keeping up my crest until our presents were distributed yesterday morning and opened. Everyone had nice presents.

December 31   Last evening Patricia came to bid us farewell. Her "brides' boat" leaves for foreign parts on the third. Am ashamed to be pleased that she's leaving. She's been so good to me that I feel constrained to be sweet to her, but the truth is she bores me to fatigue. Sex, Paul, the Catholic religion, her relatives constitute her subjects of conversation, and in what she says is to be found none of the whimsicality evident in her letters. Doubtless she's a worthy woman. If anyone who bored me less were one-half as demonstrative and as vocal with affection as is Patricia, I should be enchanted. She believes that she is youthful and that the years have left her elastic emotionally. The years have not, save superficially. Her pattern is more set than that, say, of Mrs. Trench. Once know her well, there's not a surprise to be had from her. I hope that Germany will be as much fun for her as she expects.

1947

January 5   Dottie gave me her last regular treatment yesterday. She's fun to feel with her very smooth body skin. The surface available to the hands has stretched, naturally. I never knew anyone save Corn who so thoroughly enjoyed being caressed. I lectured her on taking care of her looks after this baby, buying and wearing better clothes, spending more time on her face and hair. She's negligent of her looks, and no longer has youthfulness to carry her along. Soon she'll resemble an eccentric oldish woman if she doesn't watch out. She listened but paid little attention I fear. "My Andy loves me. Why should I bother?" "You keep the appearance of your house in order," I argued, "and are proud of it. Why don't you spend some time and money on your own appearance? If Andy doesn't see you could do better for yourself, he's blind. I love you and feel you should be advised. I hope you'll listen." "I may," she said, "though I won't guarantee anything. I'll think it over." "It makes you mad," I said, "to be chided, doesn't it?" "Yes it does — at first. No one likes it, I suspect." "I do, if I'm sure the person loves me and has my interest at heart. It takes energy to scold anyone, and it isn't done by a friend unless he loves you." "Well," she concluded, "there's that aspect to it. I'll reflect upon what you've said. Maybe I'll do something about it." She added: "I doubt it, however."

January 8   It occurs to me that I haven't mentioned that Granny Mildred died of cancer some two weeks ago. Father sent us a wire. "Doesn't it disturb you at all?" Evelyn asked. "Not in the least," I replied. "It's just one more of the older generation out of the way. I feel that life, my life, is well rid of the whole kit and caboodle save Miriam and Uncle Ben Lee. Granny wasn't fair to me when I was a trusting little boy, preferred my cousins to me always, gave them better presents, had them stay with her at Palm Springs and took them on automobile trips when I was just as available. To hell with all of them. Whatever Granny did for me didn't repay me for what she didn't do." "Do you feel that way about Aunt Nellie?" "No I don't. She was always good to me."

Granny — Mrs. Samuel Martin Inman — was 79. She came from a well-known Virginia family, Leftwich. In her full name occurs Murphy. I'd never known that. I thought she was Scotch mostly. I wonder how much Irish she had? She used the only perfume I ever liked, a fragrance of fresh violets so aereal that you had to wonder if it was really there. She always had a personal maid, Lucy, during her prosperous years, a white colored woman with a sad face and loyal heart. She served dinners in color schemes. She rode horseback well.

She seemed to me a stuffed shirt. She was ridden by a never resting sense of duty. She called Grandfather Inman "Mr. Inman" invariably. She was combined hostess and housekeeper and nurse to that undemonstrative man. She bore no children. Doubtless it was in the marriage arrangement that she should not, Grandfather's first wife having given birth to three or four grave-occupying children and Aunt Nellie being violently antagonistic to her father's remarriage. He demanded that his new wife sit up with him evenings as late as he wished, he being a light sleeper, a sitter-up-late and an early riser. She did well by him. She was possessed of considerable style and poise, not too much brains or imagination, much executive ability, according to Evelyn a withheld temper (I myself never saw it in action). She was considered to be handsome. I never thought her handsome. She used lorgnettes. She invariably, as I recall her, dressed in black.

January 19 It was a distressful Friday, one calling upon all the residual vitality this guy possesses. To begin with, as Billy and I were peacefully driving in the yards, he said: "Artie, there's something I feel I must talk over with you." I knew the tone. He was striving to break bad news, probably of a financial nature, to me. It transpired that Sadie was on his tail again. Her brother Lyman is some sort of boss in a manufacturing company at Houston, Texas. He had written Billy offering him a traveling position at $75 a week to start, a $5 raise every three months. Sadie wanted Billy to leave me and for them to go to Houston to live.

I said — and I think this went home — "How would you like it if a man came along and offered to do everything you're doing and more for forty dollars a week and I said, 'Well, Billy, I'm sorry but it's too good an offer. I must let you go'? You'd be shaken to the roots, wouldn't you? I wouldn't do such a morally reprehensible thing, naturally, but it's exactly what you're contemplating in reverse." We got nowhere apparently.

Then I talked to Billy for two hours straight. Very warily I went to the root of the matter, Sadie. She, I said, was the one who influenced him each time we had trouble. I said that he underestimated how clever she was. She was French, I said, and all French people loved money. If he would reflect a moment, he would see that all the contests between him and me had been inaugurated by Sadie for money. Then I took a shot in the dark — well, in the twilight — and went on for five minutes pretending I was Sadie urging him to better himself: He had more in him than he was using; he was a fool to waste himself on this job; if he'd go with Lyman he would be well off. He wanted to get her things, didn't he? As for herself, she didn't care; it was only he, Billy, she was thinking of. "Didn't she say all those things?" I asked. He admitted she had. I inquired who was boss in his family, his wife or himself? His wife, I replied. He let her have her own way in the big things and got his way in the small ones, which was exactly as it shouldn't be. A woman, any woman, respected a husband she couldn't push around in the big matters. If he crossed her, naturally she'd fuss, probably cry, but that would soon be over. Hadn't she written him during the war that if only he returned she would be completely happy? Well, here he was back and here was she after him to shift his life. I knew women. She was ten years older than he, and therefore in no position to cross him ever, save as he let her get away with it. I wasn't blaming Sadie for trying to get away with it. All women do. But they respect the man all the more when they can't. I didn't mean to imply she was evil or anything like that. She was merely clever while he was innocent.

He listened attentively. I had skirted the question of money, which was bound to come up. He couldn't have been more attentive. I could hear the new thoughts about Sadie plumping into his mind. He wanted to stay with me, he said. He knew I would offer him as much as Lyman. What would I offer? I couldn't offer anything, I said, because I was getting older and felt I must save something. If I weren't honest, I said, I would offer him things and wait for a depression and then cut him and he couldn't then find another job. I wish, I said, I were dishonest. Since I wasn't, all I could think of would be to send Evelyn to talk to my Father and ask him for, say, five thousand, $500 a year bonus to be paid to him from the five thousand held in escrow by a trust. That should, I said, impress Sadie.

Did I really think it was a matter of money with her, he asked? I did, I replied. The proposition sounded okay to him, he said. He would stay. How, I asked, could I know that Sadie wouldn't again be down his neck and he after me for more money — this was the fourth or fifth time? He was willing, he said, to sign papers. A written statement, I replied, hadn't meant anything before. Would he write Lyman and tell him to lay off with him innuendos and offers? He would. And I didn't want Evelyn to make such a long and hard trip only to find Sadie had worked on him again. He promised, for what the promise was worth.

Perhaps I'm a sucker. But what is money for? Billy, when Sadie leaves him alone, has never been more agreeable and adjustable. He has, he says, never been so happy. Sadie fortunately came down with the flu Friday night. "Well," I asked, "do you have to wait for her to get better before making a final decision or are you man enough in your own right to make your own decision? It's time you were a man in your own right. She'll play on your devotion and your sympathy always if you don't. She knows very well how kindly you are and how you don't wish to cross her." "I'll make my own decision this time, Artie. I'm going to stay. I never thought of lots of things as you've presented them to me. You're 'most always right—ninety-five percent of the time—you've never advised me wrong. I'll write Lyman tonight and tell him to lay off; if he doesn't he may cause trouble between Sadie and I. And I'll tell him if we're to visit him in Texas, he's gotta lay off Sadie there. I'll be direct." He has written Lyman, he tells me this morning. Evelyn has just left for Charlotte. She's wonderful in a crisis. If the Old Man doesn't shell out, I'll have to do it myself. Billy's worth a hundred a week to me in reassurance. I shouldn't resent the fact that he's a pushover for females and a breaker of large promises. Many men are both and most men are the latter.

January 20 Spent much of yesterday discussing with Patsy the relative virtues of New York and Boston. Attempting to inculcate in her mind methods of approaching people in authority to get what she has in mind from them. The older I grow, the more grateful do I become to Eddie Simms for what he taught me of unorthodox means and methods. No person ever instructed me so functionally in approaches unrecognized or unacknowledged as workable by most Americans. It is not that Americans fail to practice the methods and means (as I explained to Patsy) advocated by Eddie. It is that such methods and means are never taught the young save by scoundrels. Yet they are fairly dependable methods and means, overplayed often by Eddie in his unquenchable faith in them but in the main and when practiced with reasonable discretion and some ethical restraint, serviceable to the user. How often, for instance, has "Knock 'em down, pick 'em up, dust 'em off and pat 'em on the back, kid" been useful to me, and "Every knock's a boost, if you look at it that way" and "Get 'em mad and by God you've got their attention, and that's half the battle."

After years of imbibing my Mother's jaundiced and idealistic tutoring, Eddie's teaching came to me as a strong, fresh gale dispelling mists. Each time I pass on what he taught me to young people I like, I feel grateful to him and indignant at my Mother and Father and the American educational system for the impracticable pap that was fed me. It strikes me that most Americans, even now, have to spend years and undergo unnecessary tribulations ridding themselves of the clutter of idealistic nonsense taught them in their younger days.

January 21   Billy said this morning, his Indianlike face with the combed-down, dark curly hair parted on the side framing it, his brown eyes earnest: "You know, Artie, I learned a lot from your conversation with me the other day. There was a lot of truth in what you said. I've been too easy with my wife. After all, I should be the boss. How can a woman respect a man if she can push him 'round. I think I see different from what I did, and I want to thank you for enlightening me."

January 22   The hours pushed slowly by last night. Evelyn cut off a man's head, thought the crime undiscovered. To us next morning were served baked beans, and one of the beans was the man's head perfectly diminished. I decided it was less harrowing to remain awake.

January 27   I love people in direct proportion to how sweetly and how quickly they give me my way. When they instantaneously, unfairly or prolongedly cross me, no matter how deeply I love them, for the time being I hate their guts. I like to get my own way. To compensate for this arrogant trait of character, no one, when tactfully made aware of it, is more ready to admit to having been wrong. I never mind having been wrong, for so often am I right that to be wrong makes me esteem the person who has been right; I learn something to avoid in the future. Nor do I mind being crossed when a contrary notion is fairly and judiciously presented. Prolonged, stubborn opposition makes a fiend of me when it seems founded upon nothing solid, but never do I act as fiendish as I feel, which is a little to my credit, I suppose.

January 29   Patsy was all but welcomed to Cornell Medical with open arms. She has now decided, despite previous statements contrariwise, to go to New York to study. I beg her to enter her name at Harvard with a note explaining she had been accepted at Columbia and Cornell but would rather get into Harvard. She will not do it.

I'm rather sorry for her. Going into training to be a doctor is not unlike entering a prison where work is the order of the day. Even Patsy is not dead sure she wants to go through the grind. I'm more or less sitting back and waiting. I won't see her again until Saturday.

January 30   Mr. Whitcomb and an assistant, Mr. High, came to explain to me what can and cannot be done with the income Father may leave me from a trust fund so that I won't be eaten up by taxes. My Father told Evelyn that his Federal tax this year amounted to twenty-eight thousand. High says that that means his income must be in the neighborhood of sixty thousand a year. He has just inherited more property from Granny, which will add to his income. Mr.

Whitcomb feels that there would be a strong chance of breaking Father's will, in particular since he has drunk so much and is as old as he is.

Whitcomb is an interesting man. I'm sure he's dishonest in a shrewd and well-judged fashion. I wouldn't trust him. Evelyn refers to him as "an old goat." He's been ready to branch out in her direction for years. I'd like to know his secret history; it would be not only interesting but illuminating as to our times.

February 1 Every morning, bar say two a week, when I have just gotten up, in comes Evelyn flashing white papers in front of my eyes, wriggling like one with the itch or letting her voice become louder and louder. I blow up. I scold, rail, get excited, spoil my morning and maybe my day. She might as well deliberately do what lights a flame under my wildness. And probably ten thousand speakings to her have made no impression on her. I'd rather not see her in the morning, but there are certain arrangements that have to be made and I can't tell her the night before for she wouldn't remember even if notes were made. Baldly speaking, she's one of the world's stupidest people. And when I blow up in front of people, which she must be aware I'll do at that time in the morning, she snarls at me and looks hate. And there's never a "yes" out of her— always "no." She'd drive a saint to distraction. She possesses no more self-control than a fly buzzing and butting against a window. I'm not certain she's any good. She riles me to the boiling point, seems as dumb as a calf. Why I love her I don't always know. She's the bane and the treasure of my life. She's fascination and repellation with the speed of alternating current. She doesn't make good sense emotionally or intellectually. She's my succubus and my closest dear.

Bored and listless much of the time, Arthur lost his zest for diary keeping, a "sterile occupation." He continued to comment passingly and passionately on his antipathies: rapacious Russia (the "Eastern sultanate"), greedy and ungrateful Europe, President Truman, the Marshall Plan, Communist infiltrators, and the architects of the coming economic depression. But uppermost in his thoughts were the "blows" that kept his life in feverish disequilibrium.

Patsy's indecision about where she would study medicine and her breezy indifference to his moods contributed to his uneasiness. So did the periodic visits from the "Old Man." They revived Arthur's unquenchable hatred for the hostile father who soiled and withered his spirit. The worst "blow" of all was Evelyn's breast cancer and subsequent operation.

Evelyn survived it, but shortly after the traumatic event, Arthur

resumed his by now familiar criticisms of his gifted and fallible wife —
her drinking, her ugly outbursts of independence, above all her under-
valuing of himself and her want of wifely solicitude. Hoping to make her
more manageable, he even consulted Dr. Arvin, the psychiatrist to whom
Evelyn had gone for occasional counseling. Arthur professed to love
Evelyn above all other women and marveled at his inordinate affection,
but he clove to her for practical reasons as well. Fickle secretaries came
and went. Friends were ephemeral. Mrs. Trench had to be handled with
kid gloves. Roderic, stuck in Bridgeport, Connecticut, no longer read to
him. Batty Mrs. Cash, fractious and foul-mouthed, made life hard for
the staff, especially Billy, so Arthur was not too unhappy when she took
another job. But Evelyn, his shield and buckler, stood ready to deal with
the crises at Garrison Hall. Although she refused to interrupt her Maine
vacation with Dr. Pike when Arthur summoned her home to deal with
the terrible bright lights installed in the hallways, it was she who bearded
the arrogant Machs on her return and who scouted for attractive girls.

They came to be interviewed and tested, and only a few met his
exacting standards. He wanted them to be pretty, to speak softly and
lovingly, to be at once demure and unconventional, to be entertaining
and motherly, to be his "daughters." And as the dream of writing an
immortal chronicle of his times began to fade, Arthur concluded that
perhaps his genius lay in the study of young girls.

February 9 A cold, clear Sunday morning. Evelyn is at her farm
in Lincolnville, Maine, with Dr. Pike. Billy and I went window-
shopping in the Pierce-Arrow up and down Boylston and Newbury
Streets in search of clothes for Evelyn and myself. Now I have had a
cup of coffee, looked through the Boston 'Herald' and 'New York
Herald Tribune,' and while Billy cleans my bedroom and hall with
vigorous strokes of the vacuum cleaner, I commence this volume of
my diary. The vicious whir of the motor in the cleaner might be
taken as symbolic of the machine age — useful and nerve-racking,
promising worse. As we drove down the shop-lined streets this
morning, I reflected upon how easily they could be made forever
rubbish by the next, the atomic war. Already are we informed that
bombs of six hundred times the power of the Japanese bombs have
been perfected, one bomb calculated to destroy the entire state of
Maryland. The futility of depleting my limited supply of energy
upon this diary is apparent.

I have no idea what lies ahead of the world, us, myself as an
American citizen. Unless Russia joins conscientiously with England
and ourselves in a plan to outlaw war, there will be another war. You
would think that Stalin and the governing Council of Russia would

see that. Maybe they do but don't care. Maybe they're only bluffing and will eventually join us. I doubt either contingency, however, for recent revelations outline clearly the Soviet policy of considering the United States as the major enemy against its plan for a world-encompassing Communistic State.

February 11   Billy has bought a car. So now he leaves about the 19th. I dread Billy's going for fear someone will get hooks into him or Sadie. He promises to stay only a short time in Houston where Lyman is, but I have not too much faith in his promises. His intentions, yes; his promises, no. He makes my life less hard to bear. I feel, Patsy away, that really she isn't much good as a person. That she exercises a charm for me doesn't alter my opinion of her basic character. Still, I may be wrong. I am determined never again to love anyone as I did Janice.

Note: The Baby-Carriage has broken. I'm sick about it. My pelvis is out of position.

February 15   Evelyn seemed distracted when she returned from Providence yesterday. She being so often wild, I thought nothing of it. She came home about five. She had, she said, noticed a lump in her right breast while at Providence. She had gone straightway to Dr. Pike on her return. He had taken her to a surgeon, a Dr. Robert Ball, for examination. The doctor and his assistant examined her. It was not, they ascertained, a cyst. They would have to cut the growth out, examine it under the microscope to find if it were benign or malignant, then, if the latter, cut off the breast. Needless to say, I was stunned. I started to shake. The very implications of cancer in these days and times are appalling. "Poor Arthur," Evelyn said. "Poor Evelyn," I said. "I'll cancel my trip to Detroit," she continued. "They'll take me as soon as I can have a room. I'm going to the Phillips House where you were if I can. I figure I might as well do this up in style if it has to be done. Dr. Pike is taking me to dinner now, so I'll have to hurry off. I think he's sorry for me."

I have been having a nightmarish time with the fifth lumbar. Fred may have gotten it in yesterday morning. As soon as I calmed down from what Evelyn had told me, I telephoned Dottie. I wanted to get the worst from the horse's mouth, so to say. What Dottie tells me I believe. She was encouraging. How big was the growth? About the size of an olive. New? Recent, anyway. Could it be moved about by the fingers? Yes. Then, she said, the chances were against its being malignant. And, I inquired, if it is malignant, what then? Still the chances were in favor of Evelyn even if the breast had to be removed. Operation plus x-ray treatments, unless the condition was too far advanced, usually effected a cure.

When Evelyn returned from dinner, I told her what Dottie had said. "Oh, I'm not too worried," she stated. "Either I'm too optimistic or too stupid to worry. I'm going to bed and get some sleep." And while I lay awake thinking, she slept. My worry makes me realize how much I think of her despite our friction. It also gives me a taste of how she must have felt when I tried to kill myself, in a way at least.

Much editorial furor as to Truman's appointment of David Lilienthal as head of Atomic Energy Commission. He was head of Tennessee Valley Authority, has Pinkish leanings, is supported by all the Communist newspapers and groups. Common sense should have it that no questionable American gets this post, not improbably the most important post in America next to that of Secretary of State, insofar as our future is concerned, and certainly no Pink. And, I would add, certainly no international-minded, basically unassimilable Jew.

It is difficult to perceive how the world will eventually escape going communistic. In this country the best course of combatting their infiltration and influence would not be to ban them but to engage in unscrupulous and unremitting propaganda against them. But how is that to be accomplished when steadily they infiltrate themselves to advise and alter? The bureaus in Washington are so overswollen that it is all but impossible for those at the head to know their staffs. The Secretary of War has one thousand civilian workers in his office alone. In the Army and Navy there are over a million civilian employees, as many men as there are in the entire Army, and many of them must be idle hands ripe for the communistic suggestion or Communists and Communist sympathizers busy sapping a system their avowed aspiration is to overturn. It is perilous, not to mention extravagant, to have Government overloaded with superfluous bureaucrats. Yet not a bureau, not the Army, not the Navy is willing save under duress to relinquish a single employee. Even when Congress orders the bureaus to cut down their staffs, little attention is paid. There are more civilian employees in the Army alone than there were in all Government before the war.

February 18 Dr. Pike inquired of Evelyn: "Did you sleep last night?" "Why yes," Evelyn replied. "Well," he commented, "you're just about the only one who did." She laughed. "Arthur," she said, "tells me I'm very stupid or very brave, one of the two." "Humph," he said, "I'm inclined to the former viewpoint." Whichever it is, she's surely bearing up well, far better than I am. She's being what you'd call "a damn good sport."

Her operation is to be at eleven next Monday, she to go to the hospital at four Sunday. I was worrying about who would be with her. I offered to drive to the Phillips House, get a wheelchair, be with her some. Betsy Congress offered, however, to be with her all day the first day after her operation and Woody offered to be with her the second day, so it would, I suppose, be foolish for me to chance the reaction to my bones that might ensue, especially now that my pelvis is in such foul shape. Dr. Pike will take her to the hospital and be with her some Sunday. The suspense of waiting is nothing to relish. I have tonsilitis. The pelvis being out so long has started up my hemorrhoids. The world seems inimical today.

February 23 Have been snow, worry, pelvis trouble, tonsilitis, relatively little sleep. I worry while Evelyn sleeps. I shut my jerky eyes at a few minutes before five this morning. As in most other matters, I understand Evelyn very little in this one. "Believe me," she says, "this state of mind isn't achieved without some effort on my part." That it can be achieved is what baffles me. Not being her, I'm not achieving composure although God knows I'm still struggling to. She believes in her luck. I believe in my bad luck. She hasn't been hurt as often and as basically as I have. And she possesses the rational empiric philosophy most women can order out to meet crises. "Just isn't it lucky," she inquires, "that I'm this way? It would be awful if there were two of us like you." And it would be. She looks spry and cheerful in the orange wool skirt I selected when window-shopping and the light-blue blouse that matches the color band in the skirt.

February 24 Eyes giving out. The cat has me climbing nervous trees. It's a much better cat than the last one, strong and handsome and fearless and not at all nervous or jittery, just energetic. Nonetheless, as far from any need in me for religion is any need for stupid animals around me, and they are all, as weighed against human intelligence, stupid, even the brightest. My ego isn't pandered to in the slightest by their blandishments. They are nuisances one and all. Evelyn's need for creatures is just another point wherein we differ. And also do Patsy and I differ about it even more radically. Nor is it that cats and dogs and horses dislike me. They all but invariably like me.

Later: Dr. Pike telephoned. They had to remove her breast. Poor Evelyn. Poor, poor Evelyn. I'm tough. I can take anything that happens. But aside from me, nothing awful has ever happened to her. My heart is wrung. Billy tries to comfort me. It will be five years before she'll know whether the cancer will be loose in her or not. The poor baby. She's so childlike in many ways. I cry and cry. I'm sorry for her, not me. I love her so.

February 26 All night long I worked myself up to going to the hospital only to gather a headache. Am unsure of my footing because of pelvis. Abandoned the project as liable in the end to cause Evelyn more worry than pleasure, for the sunlight would dazzle me and I'd likely fall apart. The object would be to help her, not to worry her. Billy saw her yesterday. He and Dr. Pike are both impressed with how well she came through the operation. She has a big room filled with flowers. "I was very pleased, Artie," Billy exclaimed. "She's much better than I'd dared hope. I gave her a great big kiss, and that pleased her. While of course she'd love to see you, she wants you to understand that she doesn't want you to come if it'll hurt you in any way. She's aware how much of a trip it'd be for you. She says she's getting everything she wants and needs, and she'd rather not have a private nurse just sittin' there takin' everything in, like, you know?"

February 28 I telephoned Evelyn three times yesterday. I'm not proficient at talking on the instrument but thought it might help her. Perhaps it did. Perhaps it constitutes simply another burden to be borne. I don't know. I have no notion most of my days how to please her. She rarely leans on me for anything, service or advice or affection. There's nothing I'd rather do right now than help her— but how? I'm not even certain that if I made the effort and went to visit her, the worry I would cause would not offset any pleasure my presence might give. Other people are bolstered by my affection, my advice, the services I can proffer. But Evelyn appears to be more or less independent of them and has never seen fit to dissemble otherwise. She's not only independent by nature but has never forgotten the first few unhappy years of our marriage when I hoped I might arouse her to being more of a person in her own right, less someone who must needs be guided and pushed.

And undoubtedly the many years when she has had to assume responsibilities large and small rightfully in the male province have given her a confidence and an habitual delegation to herself of choices and courses. Save in keeping her sweet and skimming off the constantly rising cream of arrogance from the milk of her nature (intangible benefits more often resented than appreciated), I am of not too much use to her. I am a habit and a duty and a responsibility. So in general I am left undone when it comes to helping her. She is secretive where she should be outspoken and outspoken where she should be reticent. I am a dweller in a house where many rooms are locked to me and the furniture, much of it, hard and unreceptive. This entire affair was arranged, for instance, without consulting me. Even if it was so done to save me worry, it was done, and Evelyn felt no compunction in so doing it.

March 1   Evelyn called up, so excited she sounded like a bird chirping. Dr. Church, Dr. Ball's assistant, reported to her this morning that insofar as this growth is concerned she need have no worry from it. It has been categorically eradicated. If there is ever a new growth, it will not come from this one, the operation having been thoroughly successful and all tests of the glands negative. I feel sick at the pit of my stomach with relief yet do not dare quite let go all doubt until Dr. Pike receives the written report today or Monday, so ingrained is my pessimism.

March 3   Evelyn arrived. I had intended to go downstairs, but she came early and to Billy's room where I was. She looks very pale and thin, and there was a wanness to her face which vanished after she had had some whiskey and lain down (she didn't want to) on the bed. She wore a black dress, one of the old-lady type she runs to when I don't watch, and not having seen her in a black dress for years, that made her look different. The right shoulder was carried up and stiffly, and she moved slowly but otherwise was filled with talk. "You look as if you were glad to see me," she remarked. "You don't know the half of it," I replied. "I could just about eat you up." And I am glad. It's like having someone you love return from a Siberia where the exiled never return. I'm going now downstairs to look at my wife some more before lying down for the day. Dr. Pike has just been here to work on my pelvis.

March 6   Evelyn wants to go to Bert's and try on dresses. I had Billy stop her. What a female. I swear this operation of hers and its implications threw me for a further loss than it did her. I wonder, does she lack imagination? Or is it sensitivity she lacks? She should have been a gun moll. Whatever else she is or isn't, she's tough. Ten days in the hospital is usual for a breast removal. It's ten days today, and she hankers to go shopping.

What I can't understand is how any goddamn fool on earth can be as impervious to her own interests as Evelyn is to hers in my case. Each time I soften, she kicks me in the teeth. She has as much tact as a hand grenade. At this writing, I hate her hard, uncaringly independent self. When I have built up my walls against her, the feeling no doubt will pass. I had hoped that what she underwent might soften her. But no. But no, no, no! She's arrogant about what she could undergo, how hardy she was. She wants no sympathy, no thoughtfulness, no consideration, no affection, apparently no love if love implies these humane qualities. The world will probably never hurt her sufficiently to make her yield a centimeter of her perversity and her arrogance. All that ever hurt her was myself when we were first married, and what that did was to make her never forget and forgive, not make her less perverse, less arrogant, less swaggeringly indifferent to consideration for her.

March 8 If we take Great Britain's place as the chief antagonist of Russia, we will have only begun a world-wide commitment against Russia that can but point definitely to World War III and the possible annihilation or submergence of human culture, whoever wins the war. In a word, we are to become the number one defender of what is left of the free enterprise world either way. That being the case, which course should we pursue?

It could be that if we let Russia spread widely enough, greediness will sap its vitality. Yet who knows that for sure. The British Empire gives every indication of breaking up fast. India has been promised its freedom by June of next year, which probably means a civil war, with Russia reaping hegemony. The Palestine question is to be put before the United Nations, British soldiers no longer being able to maintain order there. Great Britain is pulling out of Egypt and Burma. Great Britain at home appears to be in some straits. Our loan has been spent to hasten socialization, and socialization seems to be a failure. People out of work under socialization are so amply compensated that there is no fear left of unemployment, hence no incentive to labor hard during employment. A democratic socialistic state possesses of itself too little power to be a dictatorship, hence too little power to make socialism successful.

March 12 Another bang in the teeth. Roderic announced last evening that he may be moving to Bridgeport, Connecticut. He sounded sad. We have known each other for twenty years, good times and bad. His salary now is $4,000 a year. "And at that I'm getting more than any other adjuster in the company. I like being an adjuster. But it's as high as I can climb here in Boston unless the man ahead of me happens to die. In Bridgeport I'd have my own office and a raise of five hundred, and it would be one step up, as I understand it. I simply can't raise three children suitably on four thousand a year. I don't want to leave Boston, but if I must I must. I'm sorry, Artie, for your sake as well as my own, for I enjoy our evenings together. They mean a lot to me. Some people are large successes, some are not. I belong to the latter class, whatever you may think of my natural gifts."

March 13 President Truman yesterday made an address to Congress perhaps as epoch-making as the formulating of the Monroe Doctrine. We are bid to abandon fully our isolationism and to enter permanently the arena of world power politics as the established antagonist and leader against totalitarianism as practiced by Russia, unnamed by him but pointed at directly. I personally have no convictions as to the wisdom or the folly of such a course. It predicates the relinquishment of faith in the United Nations as a vital body. In that I concur. With Russia able to veto anything, the body is but a talking shadow, and there seems no likelihood that Russia will abandon that prerogative. Nor will Russia agree to any workable scheme to outlaw the atomic bomb. Perhaps boldness is our best course. I should prefer boldness without words defining it, but it has always been our habit to talk more than to act or to talk before acting. I believe that we should do what Truman advises and say nothing about it. We should have a firm policy in our dealings with other nations and stick to it.

March 14   Billy must have left by now on the first leg of his ten to twelve thousand mile trip. I am naturally filled with anticipations of possible accidents, jobs offered him, etc., though I did the best I could to condition his psychology to the idea of how much I need him and to returning. Whether the conditioning will be retained through eight weeks and ten thousand miles who can say. I shall miss him greatly. They will drink Poland water, just as Grandfather Inman used to do, everywhere they go, in Mexico particularly. I gave Billy two dozen postcards addressed to me here. He has promised to wire when safely beyond Houston and his brother-in-law. So there's nothing further I can do in that direction save pray for his return to me in his present frame of mind and wait. I'll be heartbroken should events transpire on his trip so that he will regard me and mine differently.

Occasionally Evelyn says something that jolts me. Yesterday we were discussing the beer she drinks. Each time I see her after ten or eleven o'clock in the morning, she is holding and sipping slowly a glass of the amber liquid. She goes through a case of 24 small bottles in four to six days. I haven't said a word against it; if it helps her to drink beer, drink beer she shall. I said as much. "Well," she said, "if I'm to live only two years, I figure I might as well drink all I want." I had no idea she thought that way. I anticipate the worst but didn't know she did, what with her optimism. This morning she allowed me to rub her back with alcohol and then powder it to moderate the itching. She's walking a bit more each day. I have my walls up and she's striving not to resist or oppose ideas and suggestions and services so that we're getting along better. Besides, I'm very sorry for her.

Ella James hasn't been near me for many months. She's upstage. I saw her on the street the other day. She no longer has prettiness, resembles a thin, harassed, tired middle-aged woman.

Very soon now I'll have to advertise for people to talk to me evenings. Evenings by myself are long and stultifying. If Roderic goes to Bridgeport, I'll have to start over, with no old guard left but Mrs. Cash. Evelyn will need to be stronger before we can embark upon the wearing project.

March 17 Am waiting to ask Dr. Arvin about getting along better with Evelyn, about how she could disguise her paramount sense of independence, say fewer things that deflate me. I dread the interview. What I wish to have occur is an alteration in Evelyn through a shift of viewpoint or dissemblement, either or both, so that my weak points are not constantly abrased. I don't understand her. Maybe he does. If he does, perhaps he can effect in her that alteration which would enable us to get along with less friction.

March 18 Arvin is a man of shrewdness and poise. I related my problems with a certain lightness. I recounted my difficulties with my independent wife, my February wife. If he wished me to change in any way, I'd be perfectly willing to act any part he advised.

Then he talked. The persistency, he said, with which certain traits occurred in people born in certain months could not be ignored as a factor. It might indeed, he said, be as I suggested, a factor more to do with the time of the year than with the influence of the planets, related, as I suggested, to the seasonal flight of birds, etc. February people, he said, had an independence of other people, a self-sustainment that amounted to narcissism. They weren't particularly interested in understanding other people. They couldn't place themselves inside other people. Therefore they were apt to be more or less uninfluenced by how their acts and words appeared to other people.

Be it noted that this shrewd man, Arvin, made use of my semibelief in the astrological theory rather than dismissed it as poppycock, neither denying nor affirming his own belief in it. With independent people such as my wife, he pursued his theme, he had discovered that the best way to overcome their indifference to others was to be attained by interesting them in handling others as if they were difficult problems to which artistry of solution should be applied. That removed each problem in human relationship from the emotional and placed it upon the intellectual plane, in which case they were less loath to make use of artistry in meeting it. I was Mrs. Inman's problem. He thought she could meet it best in this way. I agreed with him.

I don't know whether anything will come of all this or not. If anybody can bench Evelyn, he should be able to. I admire his common sense and have faith in his ingenuity. Dr. Pike says that he's tops in Boston, will take only cases which interest him. He's what a psychiatrist and a psychologist dealing with people and not with theories should be. He approaches people with shrewdness and earthy wisdom, not with hard and fast theories culled from sterile books.

March 25   Paid for Evelyn's operation, $500. Not much to pay for a wife — if it works.

March 30   Evelyn said: "Going to the hospital and not knowing whether or not I would die was nothing — nothing — compared with trying to please you. It was a straight matter of dying or not. I even felt that there were compensations to being in the predicament I was, because at least it was clear-cut. I've tried to please you always. I don't know how to do any better. I can't be kept after any longer. I won't be kept after. I may only have two years to live. All the assurance of ruggedness on which I counted no matter what else happened has been shattered. I won't be kept after, and I intend doing some of the things I want to do before I die. I'll give you five hundred dollars of my money each year and you can hire people to take my place. Money seems to mean so much to you, and it means nothing to me. I don't mean I'll leave you, but I simply won't be under pressure any longer. You say I've made a failure with you. If that is so, what's the use of struggling further? I'm forty-six. I'll never be different. And I'd like to spend the next two years in ways agreeable to me. I don't often say what I feel, but this is how I feel. You can like it or not. I would rather face death and the chances of death than strive fruitlessly to please you."

A moment has arrived when either I lose Evelyn for good or else alter drastically the pattern of our relationship. It is her contention borne out by twenty-five years that she cannot change. I can change. What is beneath the surface with me in no wise alters my capacity to change on the surface. I can even change under the surface. It is, it would seem, up to me to change. I cannot change her. The commonsense alternative is to change myself, to recognize fully and without reservation the defeat I have suffered in face of her adamant nature.

I thought about it all night. She might be a violent alcoholic. She might run up bills to a ruinous extent. She might sleep with men and bring syphilis home. She might be disloyal. There might be a dozen courses she might take by which my life and standing could be ruined. Instead, what is it to which I object? Merely that she fails to handle her words and the tones of her words felicitously. Merely that she argues, contradicts, takes the negative view. Had she been otherwise, our life, it is true, could have gone more pleasantly. But less pleasantly than I would wish or not, I have never seen another woman I would rather have. And, save that I might wish she were more executive, I have found little criticism of her acts. She has, as she says, striven to be a good wife. All in all, it is up to me to withdraw my hopes and aspirations, to face what is, to readjust my viewpoint and my actions since she either cannot or will not.

I talked to her this morning. I explained, in brief, that I was giving up. I would cease to scold and adjure and point out. If she could not change, I could. I was acknowledging utter defeat insofar as she was concerned. I loved her so much that contemplation of life without her was impossible. If I acknowledged defeat, I would stop attempting to persuade her to mold herself to my weaknesses. I would from here on take her at the value of her actions, not at the value of her words. To judge a person by his words, I had read the night before, was as foolish as to judge a man by the painting of him. On the practical side, if I started to lecture or scold her, would she, if we were in the light, wag a finger at me. I could and would stop. In the dark, would she put a hand over my mouth. If she, on the other hand, began to argue or contradict, I would wag a forefinger at her and in the dark poke her. If it got too much for me, could I leave the room? I would be what she wanted me to be. I loved her, as the Yankees say, "come hell or high water." I could change myself. I would change myself.

Whatever she is, I love her. Whatever I am, I want her near me. If she is inflexible, I am not. If concession is weak, I am weak. If it is strong, I am strong. I want my wife. I love her. I am without the ordinary masculine shame that attends conceding defeat to a woman. I admire women, American women. They are as good, perhaps better, than American men. I will take what measures are necessary to bind Evelyn to me.

April 7   Last evening Evelyn drank too much. She's not only inept with her body, hitting things and staggering, but snotty and nasty as well. Three-fourths of the time when she is with Dr. Pike she overdrinks on hard liquor. Rarely is she to be seen without a glass of beer in her hand. The hard liquor is what I object to most. She can't hold it like a lady. She was filled with beer yesterday morning when we all but had an accident. I thought all night how to speak to Dr. Pike so as not to offend or alienate him, he being touchy. I've decided to say that Evelyn has had one automobile accident and almost had another—can he help me modify her drinking propensities? It would be too bad to save her life by an operation and then have her die in an accident.

I must be tactful, for he gives Evelyn the normal part of existence I am unable to supply, and he and Woody are the only two people in this neck of the woods of whom she is fond. It would scare me to have only two friends, and both of them as temperamental as wild colts, but it bothers her not at all. She's as independent of other people as a lone mesa, independent of affection, of company, of love, of approval, of everything save the small birds and animals her four-year-old nature delights in. She's more independent than it is decent for any woman to be, the more so in that she little troubles to hide it. It is lucky for me, I suppose, that independent people usually possess a large and even commanding sense of duty which passes in their minds as love and that they are seldom disloyal — that being 'beneath them.'

April 8 Spoke to Dr. Pike. He was, unless he thinks it over afterwards and peers into badger holes, ready to be of assistance.

April 9 Dr. John A. MacIntosh died last week of high blood pressure, angina pectoris and softening of the brain. He was only 67. He was born in Alpena, Michigan. He graduated from the American School of Osteopathy, Kirksville, Missouri, in 1904, and began practicing in Boston that year in an office with Dr. Ada M. Frome. He had led a fairly adventurous life before that, the details of which I have forgotten. He worked on a steamboat one summer loading and unloading freight. At one time he was president of the American Osteopathic Association. He served with the First Corps of Cadets, whatever that was, during World War I.

He was a person of many talents, little orderliness and an almost bull-like energy. Fred, who worked with him a year or so, held forth about him: "I never knew a man who wasted so much energy. The amount he talked of itself would exhaust an ordinary man. He said: 'Fred, I'd like to take you in with me, but you know I can't get along with people.' He couldn't. The good secretary, Miss Hedge, who was the only person ever to bring any semblance of order into his life, couldn't stand it and had to leave. He drank more than any human should — sometimes as much as a quart of hard liquor a day. He'd take a swig, cram his mouth full of cough drops to hide the scent, tell his patients he had a sore throat. I guess he was a remarkable man, but he wasted enough energy to ruin a couple of remarkable men. He was a good lesson to me. I have no intention of ever burning myself up as he did."

Doccie all but worshipped Dr. Mac. He first came to me at her instigation in the fall of 1916 when we were at the Copley Plaza and I was slowly dying. I didn't like the treatments he gave me on my back; they were too slow and too painful. He saved my life by giving me high salt enemas for a month. "Maybe they'll kill you," he said. "Maybe they'll help. Do you want to go ahead with them or not?" Later, Dr. Pike took my spine, and I didn't see Dr. Mac again until the spring of 1919 when Dr. Pike was at a loss to fix the pelvis. Dr. Mac made a success with it. For years I have counted on him to put me together in the lumbar region when I fell apart. I was fond of him. I found his wildness both aggravating and amusing. He was never on time. Now he's dead and out of reach of ever helping me.

April 25   The preponderant majority of people who answer ads are worthless or unattractive or curiosity seekers or mere flotsam. To interview the applicant is wearisome and disheartening, and to have them agree to come and then not turn up is maddening. Right now I'd like a pretty girl, youngish, affectionate, garrulous. I'm unlikely to find such a person. Pretty girls are relatively few. Young girls are regarded by their parents with watchfulness, and my setup here doesn't inspire parental confidence. Affection isn't quickly given to me, an older man, by youngsters for various reasons that make sense and that have to be dispelled or overcome by dint of laborious circumlocution. And the few people who talk as fast and as untiringly as I like usually aren't imaginative or whimsical. Fishing without catching fish has always seemed to me a most discouraging occupation, a fatuous preoccupation. Thank fortune for the talking-books.

April 26   Mike took me riding, the sun going in the moment we had come upstairs. He apologized for not having brought me pickerel. Interviewed ad applicants much of morning, two young girls and a high-school boy. Liked all three for a change. Have four people from this ad, at least two of whom should be okay. Liked a tall girl, sixteen, Eva Karlsdorf, especially. Sweet smile. Reads well. Drives car. Gentle. Brown eyes. Dimple. It would encourage me greatly to find new people. Boy read well.

April 28   Dottie came to treat me this morning. This is the first time since the baby arrived a month ago. She told me about how easy the second birth had been. She looked very well. She's pulled out most of the hairs on her face, a detail she's usually slack to perform, and that improves her looks. It's a shame she insists upon wearing her hair in the 'windblown' short bob that became outmoded fifteen years ago and no longer suits her age. I was delighted to see her again. She regards me as though very fond of me.

A girl last evening named Ursula Lander, half Scotch, half Polish. Has wide, high cheekbones and ringed eyes. Met her mother, a peasant-type woman, intense, small beside her large daughter. Ursula's father died before she was born. Her mother peremptorily refuses to tell her about him. She recalls nothing at all of her life before she was six and very little of what happened thereafter. Her brother was given to his Polish grandmother to raise, and she was boarded out with various families while her mother worked in a woolen mill in Lawrence winters and cooked for camps, restaurants, etc. summers. Ursula was on a farm with another girl and the four sons of the family for six years, or four years. She fed the chickens, milked one cow, went to school, lived the free life. Then her mother "made a home" for her and her brother. They resented their mother's strictness and disobeyed in every way they could think of. She hated the inside cleaning work. She was becoming such a tomboy that her mother sent her off to a convent school near Buffalo, New York. She was there until she was sixteen. She liked the order of the life. Since then she has worked at various jobs. Now she is with a bonding company, earns thirty dollars a week. She has earned forty dollars a week working in a mill. She left her mother, since they quarreled over clothes, and now lives in Watertown by herself. She goes with the boys "until they become too familiar, or try to," when she leaves them.

"I wanna become a nun. People tell me I'm foolish to go with men if I wanna be a nun. I don't see it that way. I gotta learn about men to find out for sure if I wanna be a nun. I love clothes. I like baseball. I know all the averages by heart. I like my job. I never mind workin' overtime. They like me because I do, an' I get favors the others don't. I can't go into orders till I'm twenty. I'm not happy. I'll be happy when I join. I love order an' to be good to people." Ursula is a simple, energetic, dynamic person, strong, smart, I should imagine unusually capable. She reminded me somewhat of Pearl. Must keep in touch with her in case Mrs. Trench ever folds up. She could do her work well.

April 29   Evelyn and I drove to the Place in the Pierce, brought home jonquils and hyacinths. Evelyn is much more at ease with me since I changed myself. I sometimes wonder if I am a changeling, a weakling, a chameleon to so facilely change myself. I not only can change the outside; I change the inwardness that is secret to each person. I am another person, seeing the same scene from as different a viewpoint as if I had shifted from one room to another, one window to another to gaze upon the same landscape. I'm sure Evelyn enjoys me in my new guise, and I know that I enjoy her less on the defensive. Perhaps I'm smart to reconstitute myself, but perhaps I have been stupid not to have affected a transformation of myself long ago. At any rate, we had a good ride.

I often liken this diary in my mind to a transcontinental train. People get on and off. Some ride for long stretches, some for short.

May 1   Evelyn and I had a ride in the Pierce. Traffic conditions grow worse by the week, more cars, crowded parking places, too few garages, overcrowded highways. Tunnels, several highways, great underground garages are needed for the city not to strangle itself in due time. The wonderful harbor is all but deserted, relatively speaking. Many steamship lines, lacking up-to-date facilities and exorbitant longshoremen's wages, have removed themselves from Boston. The airport is bustling, but whether or not it will become an international center I couldn't say. Helicopter service from the Motor Mart Garage off Park Square to the airport has been recently inaugurated. The tunnel to East Boston is overcrowded, and a new one is needed. Taxes on Boston real estate continue to rise but— because of political wastage and knavery—will not suffice even with Federal assistance to inaugurate all the improvements needed to keep commercial Boston growing.

May 5 Fred came to paint my throat. He held forth to Patsy on the inadvisability of her going to medical school. It's only the second time since knowing him that I've seen him in earnest. "If I had a daughter, by God I'd stop her from even thinking about becoming a doctor. It's no career for a woman. They get married, most of them, half way through school. It's hard, grinding work if you want to become a good doctor. Then when you have your degree, these group medical insurance plans cut into your business more and more." He talked on and on, Patsy in the chair looking young and uncomfortable, her shoulders rising higher and higher from nervousness. When he had gone, I asked her if what he had said discouraged her. "Not at all. I've heard it before. But there's another side to it."

May 9 Billy is back looking fit, his mind apparently upon the job. We had a good ride. There are dozens of things for him to do. Here's fervently hoping there's no secret thing of which I know nothing in his mind. Time only will tell that. On the surface he seems contented, solicitous, pleased, making out lists, asking questions about future plans. I feel as if he had been gone a dozen years. If he is peaceful and contented, life will be much easier for both Evelyn and me. I thanked Mrs. Trench for being good to me while Billy was away and begged her not to get it in her mind I wouldn't need her as far ahead as could be forecast. I kissed her on the cheek; she blushed, said, "Thank you, dear." She's looking better.

Evelyn, all in all, did well while Billy was away. Subsequent to our second near-accident, she paid more attention to her driving. She has been more amiable about buying new clothes this year, and that puts me in a better humor. The new attitude on my part helps her morale, she says. She is very pretty at times. Dr. Pike has been west and is somewhat rested. I asked her if she loved him. "I don't know," she said. "After all he's done for you and with you, you don't know?" "No, I don't know." "Humph," I said, "if you don't love him, I guess you don't love me." "I never sat down and thought about it." A day later, she said: "I guess I must love him, Arthur." "Did you kiss him when he came back from the West?" "Yes." "A real kiss?" "Well," she smiled, "a kiss. If I'd given him a real kiss, he'd be running yet, wouldn't he?" "Yes," I agreed, "I reckon he would. He's what Southerners would call 'right easily scart.'" "And usually very conventional." "And usually very conventional."

May 17 Under the capitalistic system it might be possible for an absolutely honest and impartial government to ease a nation through recurrent depressions, but with governments (which are after all but ordinary men magnified) being neither honest nor impartial, it is impossible to avoid depressions. Indeed, the corrective acts of governments are much more apt to intensify depressions through disorganizing the free functioning of supply and demand than to ease conditions. Booms and busts are, I take it, unavoidable under Capitalism, and the price to be paid in subservience and restraint of action by the individual under a despotic socialized state is not worth the freedom from depressions it is said to bring. Liberty is a somewhat meaningless word, and the state of liberty a relative one, contingent upon the discontent within the individual. Freedom of action — freedom to come and go at will, to make a fortune or lose one, to speak the mind without duress, to take a job or leave one — is much more to the point. Depressions are inevitable and unavoidable, being essentially the unconscious pulsebeat of freedom of action.

May 18 It's no satisfaction to write on current phases of American life and probabilities as yesterday. I am not the possessor of an orderly mind. I know very little, am sure of very little other than what I like and do not like, want and do not want.

May 19 My Old Man arrives this afternoon, God help us. I have sold nearly all my loose stocks in the belief that the depression is gathering momentum. Dreamed last night I was caught in an American revolution, home rifled, friends killed, no idea whom to trust, crowds surging the streets in bloody abandon, myself chased, nowhere to find sanctuary, and all the rest.

May 20 I have myself set to be indifferent about Patsy. She comes, she acts sweet, I melt. No woman ever possessed a more caressable skin. To run your hand over her bare shoulders, her small soft breasts, her smooth stomach is as luxurious as touching a ripe grape or fine silk. I can forgive her much for the mere possession of such a surface to her body. And not only does it feel good to the touch; it is charged with animal magnetism — whatever you wish to call it. "It may feel all right," she replies in answer to my compliment, "but it doesn't look too good save by moonlight. It's inclined to look red." "Well," I reply, "when you fall in love, let him touch you. I'll guarantee it will work." "Oh," she smiled, "it does work. I've tried it." I'll miss her treatments and her skin and her beauty.

The Old Man arrived. His watch is on standard time and he refuses to change it and demands Evelyn feed him on standard time. She is provoked. Mrs. Trench had a tooth pulled and was too sick to show up for supper or the night. So Evelyn had me on her hands as well. Then the Polish girl didn't come as arranged. Then I suggested to Evelyn when she was fixing the window, wouldn't the light turned on help her, and the fat was in the fire.

She'd been struggling (and I mean struggling) with the cross-grained Old Man, she was tired caring for me, she felt frustrated. She stood (no she wouldn't sit!) for fifteen minutes by my watch telling me in a louder and louder voice what she thought of me. I was cared for, wasn't I? I had shelter and food and heat and money. That was enough for anybody. And yet I kicked because I wasn't spoken to with love and a modulated voice. Who did I think I was? I had no right to demand that people speak to me in any particular way. When she wasn't tired, she was willing to humor me, but that was what it amounted to, humoring me. (This is a condensation.) Over and over like thoughts were repeated. She was in a frenzy, screaming. I put my head under the covers and my hand over my uppermost ear and waited for her to run down. She said: "And you needn't think you can make me feel I'm bullying you by saying nothing." Finally, she stopped. It had all been caused by my attempting to be thoughtful and then suggesting, gently, that she needn't be so angry. I felt angry at what I considered her injustice and pitied her for her lack of self-control.

Then there was the Old Man to face. He's lost weight, looks well and must be feeling better, for he started right in on me. He was telling of Aunt Nellie's persecution complex just before she died. "It was like Arthur," he remarked to Evelyn, "that summer in Maine when he was insane and felt we were all against him and wasn't happy till we shipped him over to Dr. Frome. Many insane people are that way." I hated his guts and said nothing, recalling the trouble Mother had had getting me to go to Bar Harbor. I thought of the time the old devil had wished to "put Arthur away" and only Eddie yelling at him for four hours with probably more truths than he'd ever listened to in his lifetime persuaded him to desist. There was more of the same, his contempt for me evident, interspersed with off-color jokes not very witty. When Evelyn told him of her operation, he was, according to her, "quite unimpressed." The best part of his visit was his departure.

As Evelyn says, sex is always on his mind. He has a phobia about it. Also a phobia about insane people. Evelyn says that his knowledge of sex is rudimentary, his interest insatiable. A woman who isn't a virgin at marriage, according to him, can't be a "good woman." Divorce is for men who aren't satisfied sexually and reasonable on no other grounds. He went to see a motion picture about childbirth in Charlotte, I'm sure because there were "almost nude" women in it. "If," he said, "I'd known giving birth to a child was like that, I'd never have married." Evelyn says he doesn't even know the processes of conception and pregnancy.

May 22 The Old Man is now gone. He told Evelyn of the occasion when he and his three friends were abroad in Paris. They hired a guide and went to a whorehouse (a "cat ranch" he calls it). He remembers to this day that it was called "Madam Alexander's." There were seven nude girls and hundreds of mirrors. "It was too many naked women even for me. So we got out. I felt I was abroad to learn things, and that was just a part of learning. No good man uses those places."

Eva Karlsdorf was here last evening. I like her very much. She talks easily, wittily, amusingly, has an affectionate and unsuspicious nature, considerable charm. She's someone I want for a friend. Her family don't seem to mind. She goes to Y.W.C.A. camp this summer to act as counselor. She's a somebody.

May 27 This business of not sleeping would drive a porker frantic. The mind that cannot rest is a hypochondriacal instrument, brooding upon past wrongs or past mistakes or foreboding the future. Seven hours sleep a night and my entire outlook would change. But might as well wish for the strength to walk, cessation of pain, eyes that would see functionally and exclude light normally. Most of the world's greatest men have been meager sleepers. While others slept, they reflected and projected ideas. It is strange that very often the capacity to sleep little is accompanied by an overplus of nervous, mental and emotional energy. I don't know how Napoleon and Edison and Pliny and the rest felt about getting so little sleep — maybe a strong constitution makes of insomnia a blessing to the ambitious — but as for myself sleeplessness is a curse laid upon me for which no success could compensate.

May 28 No sleep. Riots and seeking for stolen goods through slums and horrible sights and fearful emotions and murder and frustration.

Evelyn tells me I should speak about food more, the food I eat. Today I had a pork chop, half a glass of goat's milk, three servings of buckwheat cakes and a small pitcher of gravy I concocted of the pork fat and juice in the frying pan, milk, water, juice from the boiled mushrooms, raw buckwheat flour — thoroughly delicious. On the stove cooking for later meals are mushrooms cut fine and flavored with salt, small beets, wild mustard tops with a small piece of bacon to give them flavor. During the morning I ate a couple of racines of wisteria (it would make delicious salad), the first small cantaloupe of the season, two cups of coffee. I have mackerel roe and milt each night for supper, broiled in bacon fat — delicious — a vegetable and half a glass of goat's milk. I can't eat too harsh or stringy foods for they raise havoc with my insides. While my diet is limited, the food is the best that can be bought. I eat well and try to eat in moderation. When I am in pain, I am inclined to eat constantly — a nervous habit like a chain smoker's.

June 8 Eva's father stopped by to pay a call, stayed an hour. Tall, gray, Prussian haircut and steep slant to back of head, gray-green eyes behind glasses, large nose, short gray moustache, hands that gestured to his words like birds tied to cords. Anxious to tell all about himself humorously. Loves to talk. Family used to have 19,000 acres, he said, in East Prussia, Pomerania. Is an agricultural chemist by profession. I should say an exceptionally smart man, perhaps a brilliant one, unconventional, which was doubtless why he didn't stay put in his class and country. Took a tremendous shine to my pretty Evelyn. Would guarantee Eva had heard every one of his stories a score or more of times. Sat, she did, with the sort of madonna smile women wear when their menfolk hold forth in reiterative fashion to a new audience. Put his arm around me (he probably about fifty-eight) in paternal fashion before he left, said: "You and I have got to be great friends."

June 16 That Eva is a love of a child. She's going to learn to treat me with some facility. Pleasant, willing, witty, intelligent, gentle, with character and some charm. She is to come again today to treat me and Wednesday evening. Perhaps not as colorful as Patsy but more reliable and honest. Her family seem to like both Evelyn and myself, which is to the good.

June 23 Woman came about reading, for past ad, a Mrs. Powers, pleasant face, iron-gray hair, brown eyes, a very love of a twelve year old daughter.

June 24 This morning being overcast, I went out in both cars. It was pure hell for me. The sky was silvery. On every new bumper it reflected. From my eyes to the back of my head is a path of cringing pain. It will be getting worse steadily as more cars are given to the public. Every street in the city that is at all central has parking lines, sometimes double, up and down every curb. There should be a huge public garage under the Commons, three or four express traffic tunnels under the city to it, parking meters along the curbs as in Western cities. Pretty soon the city will strangle itself. My riding days are over. I should thank God for the railroad yards (where there are a few spots left uncrowded still) and for rainy days. I suppose I can live with a minimum of air and sunshine. Saturdays are less crowded than formerly, and Sundays in the yards are deserted, so I can count on two days a week out.

June 26   Billy wrote the ad and I polished it off. It has black borders and is headed, in black capitals, "JUST GRADUATED?" It says:

> No general routine to this position. Just a pleasing personality and the intelligence to make yourself adaptable in the home of a Protestant writer. Drive car, read aloud, shop, etc. Permanent. $28. Ken 9087.

It seems to me that it's a transgression upon common liberty not to be permitted to advertise in a public utility organ, which is what a newspaper is, for a Protestant if you want a Protestant. I wonder if you would be allowed to advertise for a Jew or a Catholic? Well, that's aside from the point. The point is that the ad has had endless answers. There are still a dozen people to interview. I'm fagging out.

July 7   In yesterday's 'Herald Tribune' financial section was an article headed "Franklin Simon Plans Modern Store in Atlanta," accompanied by a drawing of the architecturally ultramodern building, with: "The store will be on the site of the old family residence of the late Samuel B. Inman, one of the pioneers of Atlanta."

There is always to one as sentimentally inclined as myself something sad about the submergence of a human landmark under another human landmark, perhaps the downhill of oneself. The symbolism is almost violent. I recall the mansion (it was that) my Grandfather built for his wife: granite, slate roofs, tall chimneys, broad lawns, elm trees, ivy on lower walls, curving walks, curving driveway on which hoofs rang out. All now a matter of the past, vanished as a worn-out life.

Rumors a monstrous new atomic bomb just tested in New Mexico that blasts a hole 112 feet deep and destroyed a facsimile city eleven miles in diameter. Rumors that an atomic bomb has been sent to Greece "just in case." Rumors of discs flying at incredible speeds across night skies. The world is atomic-bomb jittery.

July 11   This interviewing people is a chore. Right now am in a mental and emotional quandary. The best girl is Jewish. Tried her yesterday and today am trying her again. She's very nice. Everyone is laughing at me, aware as they are of my racial intolerance. I think it's funny, too. The problem isn't solved. Having been absolutely aboveboard with her, perhaps I have bollixed my own case in her mind. She says she'll come back Tuesday and try further. Maybe she will and maybe she won't.

July 15   Jewish girl, Judith Levy, here. Like her increasingly. Has all virtues save is lazy and inalert. But has had chance to finish senior year at University of Indiana and thinks going there.

July 18   Another torrid, humid day. Judy is to stay with me either until she leaves for college in the fall or until I find someone in case she still has her heart on college. She's not too tall, twenty, pleasant of face, with out-pushed chin, brown eyes and curly brown hair, her body on the plump side. Her face wears a sweet expression and she possesses composure. Her father was a cantor. She has a sister and a younger brother. She evidently likes all of us. Evelyn insists that I keep her and give us a rest from searching.

July 19   Judy, having been on a vegetable and coffee diet all week against my advice, got dizzy yesterday and went home. Jews can endure very little physical upset manfully. I felt her pulse, and it was steady as a hydraulic pump. Maybe she'll vanish.

July 24   Had this queer letter from Edna (remember Edna — big, green eyes, sloppy, did much for my self-confidence, cold woman, though, when through with me?):

Brockton 22, Mass.
July 15, 1947

Dear Arthur: —

Just a friendly tip because I know you desire to be famous. A certain school in Boston, in existence for two years, is changing its program and will this year offer a one year course, something new and revolutionary in education. They are willing to name the school for anyone who donates $33,000. They are planning next year to expand the course into two years and go after academic recognition. I know about this because they are trying to get me to teach in the school.

As ever,
Edna

July 26   Hot again, after a surcease. Woody arrived from Star Island brown as a mulatto. We gave her beer and chicken. She held forth in her best style for an hour to Evelyn, Rose, Billy and me, keeping us laughing. Two years ago, I'd have written it all down. A brief résumé might suffice now.

"Women," she exclaimed. "I've lived with them, listened to them, smelled them. Ugh! I sat on the grand rocks in the sun and watched the boats go by. I preferred the rocks to the women. And I found me a man where there weren't any. I sneaked out last night from the women and went walking down by an old dock. A fisherman was there. He was thirty-four and handsome! Two pretty girls were making goo-goo eyes at him, but he preferred me. He'd been all over the world during the war. He asked me if I wanted some fresh-cooked lobster. I said sure I did. So we got in his boat and he fed me shorts. They were delicious. Then he rowed me out to look at the waves careening on some shoals at Smutty Nose. The moon was gorgeous. It was incredibly beautiful. When I got home, they were just about to send a search party for me. Wouldn't that have been something. I had a lovely vacation."

July 28 Mrs. Trench is frightened that if I fire Mrs. Cash one of these days she'll try to get even by telling about how I cut income tax corners and don't make her, Mrs. Trench, pay a withholding tax. I tell her Mrs. Cash has cut too many corners herself to blab about me. That I believe, even though she probably would attempt to get even. She might write my Father or the Machs. But what the heck — I've been subject to attacks before this, and neither Mrs. Trench nor Billy would be touched by what she said. If she didn't read so well, I'd incense her into leaving. As it is, I'll hold on.

I figure it won't be long now before Mrs. Cash leaves for some reason or other. She's been a great help, but I've helped her. She doubtless figures she doesn't need me any longer. To me she's been almost too pleasant not to wonder what's in her head. She hasn't even used vile language. She may be planning to leave, for all I know.

August 12 I wish I could stay filled with beer. My pains are erased for the time being so that I can be myself. Myself seems to be outspoken, attractive, playful, bubbling over with conversation — at least the reaction of those around me gives me that deduction. Did I not hurt so all the hours of my life, I should enjoy living. I suspect I'd like to be arrogant, combative, imaginative, daring. Did I have a stalwart body, I'd love fighting and brawling and wenching. It's no credit to me that I'm not a cocky playboy.

Evelyn said: "Maybe I'm growing older or maybe I'm simply maturing. Whatever it is, the world looks in an awful mess to me. You used to say it looked in a mess to you, but it didn't look that way to me. Now it does. And when I think of all the things I'd like to have done, the places I'd like to have gone, I feel mopish. Then, I suppose, I drink."

This morning she's cheerful and busy, a swim with Dr. Pike this afternoon in prospect, a glass of ginger ale in her hand. Sleek back, green and pink dress, bangs, strong white teeth, nose up and sharp at the very end, nervous gestures, much dignity at moments, much childlikeness at many times, voice that ups and downs the scale according to her mood, prettier than ever hitherto, certain bony structure in face giving it old Flemish lines. Evelyn, treasure and bane of my years, more treasure than bane, a sense of observation and a sense of humor alike binding us closely, and the hardness of each piquing the other.

August 23   Mrs. Cash isn't uttering a filthy word. Mach's offer of $250 for information leading to the apprehension of "the fiend" (his words) who has been defacing the elevator has, according to Evelyn, scared her. Evelyn thinks she acts uncomfortable. Harris the tailor gossips that it has been a woman doing the defacing. Mrs. Cash is all right with me personally now. I never exchange pleasantries with her. Billy baits her by putting on a big smile and a "Why Mrs. Cash, how are you today!" It makes her slam doors. I egg him on.

August 28   Evelyn is to contact some of the secretarial schools this morning. Very few Americans want nonroutine jobs, really want them. Routine seems to spell a simplification of living to them. Our trouble is to contact someone enjoying variety, a Protestant with charm and looks, and someone neither too conservative (in which case they regard me as a freak) nor yet too bohemian (when they are apt to be without moral fiber). It's a problem. Thank God Billy's vacation is over and Mrs. Trench's will be over when and if she returns unhooked by some man. I'll certainly rest easier if I hear she is still a confirmed single woman. It's that she's so sure she'll not remarry makes me wary. We'll see. Maybe, as she says, I'll have been fretting to no purpose.

August 30   "Well, Mr. Inman," Mrs. Cash speaking, "I have gorgeous news. I have a teaching position with a college here in Boston with a superfine salary. I'll be leaving you. If you treat me right and I don't have to have any truck with that Billy, I'll show Mrs. Trench how to keep your books before I leave. That's if you treat me right." "Why," I inquired mildly, "should I not treat you right?" She didn't answer that one. She continued: "Furthermore, if you send me off in the proper fashion, I'll tell you what I'll do — I'll unsnarl Mrs. Trench if she gets hung up on anything. That's fair enough, isn't it? But I don't want any truck with that Billy. I have no use for people who aren't honest. I have more money, what with raises at Goshen, annuities, interest and dividends, to keep me the remainder of my life as I wish to be kept. I don't have to do anything I don't wish to do from here on out. You can find someone to take my place, I'm sure. No one is irreplaceable. I'll be around here less and less. I'll take trips, perhaps go to England, see more of my intimates. I've pretty well weeded out the worthless people, and I want to devote myself to the worthwhile ones. I think I have it coming to me. I've worked pretty hard to get where I am. I'm very pleased with myself. From here on I'll cut my cloth to the pattern I like."

I saw nothing to be served by being either solicitous that she stay on or yet disagreeable. She has been a godsend in bad years. Her era of usefulness is self-evidently at an end. To part with her agreeably is common sense. So I said: "Yes, you have worked hard. Yes, you deserve to enjoy yourself. I'll hate to have you go, but I can see your point." "So that's that," she said.

I shall miss the old buccaneer's reading, but I'll be more than glad to get rid of her lewd, half-insane, always-ready-to-be-offended presence in the other room Saturday mornings. Since she took such a spite to Billy and found she is richer than ever "I had hoped to be," she's insufferable. She's made me acknowledge the value of keeping money. I admire her zest for giving full measure in work for money received. I've been fond of her at moments but never believed her assertions of loyalty and faithfulness and devotion. I have always felt an all but violent distaste for her vulgarity, her gleeful cruelty to the unsuccessful, her miserly totting up of dollars and cents, her utter lack of sensitivity, the cheapness of her looks. I'll have to reorganize my entire system of living without her, for she will leave a gap behind her undeniably, but to be rid of her will be a relief. I could never have picked a person more my antipode.

She supported Mr. Flood for a number of years. That he was no good as a man — a drinking, unstable, childlike fellow — in no wise repelled her. She wrote me the letter in his name that obtained him this position. She kept him on the job when he swore he would leave. She couldn't prevent his drinking. At the last he was drinking, so she says, a quart of hard liquor a day. His death broke her up. The rest is in these diaries. It has been only with considerable forbearance that we have stood each other during the ten years. Now that she doesn't feel she needs me, she's done with me, the camouflage of her many protestations abandoned. And I still think her a small step away from being insane, demented at any rate. You should see the face she makes when angry, mouth down in one corner, teeth showing, color taking over the blobs of heavy rouge, blue eyes rolling up and sidewise in her face until the whites show, the expression of a mean boy taking over her countenance. A horrible woman, really, repellent when tough. "I've had to be tough in my life. If you handle waitresses and kitchen crews, you have to be tough."

I've been asking Mrs. Cash questions about where things are and how bookkeeping items are arrived at. That done, she said: "Now, Mr. Inman, you haven't me down on your income tax anywhere. I want you to promise me you won't put me down." "I hear you," I said. "For if you put me down"—her face assuming its tough look—"I'll get you if it's the last thing I do. I'll tear you apart limb from limb." "I hear you," I said. "So what about it?" she demanded. "It all depends on you, Mrs. Cash. If you leave me and don't try any of the tricks you've told me you'd done on other people, I'll not put you on the income tax. But if you do, I will. And there's plenty other stuff I have on you if you get nasty, too." I thought she'd have a stroke then and there. "You stay off me and I'll stay off you," I said, "and that's what I promise and all I promise."

September 4 A busy morning yesterday. Interviewed people. The dentist failed to appear. Fred arrived for once early, brown from his summer at the Cape. "Snap it up," he said. "I'm on the yellow line. What's everybody so slow for?" And he grinned his infectious grin. The pumping went well. He and Billy are a pair. Billy squats over the pan in which the refuse from my stomach is pumped. "See that, Billy," Fred exclaims. "Isn't that a buster." "Yeah," agrees Billy, "pretty gooey. I never saw it worse. Look at that." "Say, Arthur," Fred comments, "you sure needed this one."

September 20 Mrs. Cash is finishing her instructions to Mrs. Trench about taxes and bookkeeping. This is Mrs. Cash's last weekend, and in a way I am very pleased. Often she has been a damper on Saturday mornings to spontaneous teasing between the rest of us. She's leaving pleasantly and without any decisive cleavage of relations.

September 21 Mrs. Cash finished with the last evening, reading 'The Conscript' by Erckman-Chatrian.[21] I liked it. I liked it better, even though short, than 'War and Peace.' The French usually have a quality I like.

September 22 A grand ride yesterday. Then Evelyn spied on the first page of the paper an article about a ten-thousand-car garage over the tracks of the Boston and Albany in the railroad yards, with a helicopter landing stage for fifty helicopters, and I felt as if I wished

---

[21] The joint pen name of Émile Erckmann (1822–1899) and Alexandre Chatrian (1826–1890), a famous literary partnership. They collaborated on stories and novels, many with a military theme. *The Conscript (Histoire d'un conscrit de 1813)* (1864) went into many English editions.

to disgorge my lunch. I recalled how much noise the one helicopter operating from the Motor Mart roof had made and how complaints had caused it to go out of business. Even if there are only some forty commercial helicopters in use now in the United States, any day they may be perfected. An old American of 83, once very rich, was promoting the company. It was intimated that he had already obtained permission from the Boston and Albany. I was downcast. Evelyn was disheartened. We both realized she would have to get on the job to do her best to stop the plan. We discussed procedures. I became so emotional that this morning I'm a dead owl. So is she.

She has left now to find out first from the Statler how they stopped the Motor Mart helicopter and then to ask the Boston and Albany officials if they really have made any arrangements with the old man. I advised her to do what is a dirty trick: talk the old man down as having been responsible once but now an impractical dreamer in his dotage — which Dr. Pike who treats him says is really the case. When I recall how many years Mrs. Banks delayed the Huntington Avenue subway with her one-woman campaign in my behalf, I feel some hope, probably unfounded. You never can tell either, how much or how little truth is in a newspaper article.

Evelyn telephoned that the Boston and Albany people had never heard of the project and have no intention of allowing any such thing. Relief.

September 23 Last evening interviewed the blonde who had come in the morning. Older people and her boy friend had been whispering in her ear, and she was suspicious of us. The boy friend came upstairs with her. It made both Evelyn and me angry. Their parents, yes. Their boy friends, no. Nice girl, however. May consider her. This ad is for $30 instead of $32. More answers than on last one and more Protestants. Some eight applicants to interview this morning, if they show up. Am tired at the very thought.

Later: The best girl lisped when she read. She was a honey. Then there was a girl from Florida, easy-running but about whom we are all leery — as of all Floridians, they being neither fish nor fowl.

September 24 I'm wondering if perhaps there isn't some mean between the consuming concentration I formerly directed to the keeping of the entries and the comparative laxness of attention I have devoted to the diary since the atomic bomb fell upon history. I have often thought about cooks. They plan; they work. In a trice the result of their efforts vanishes down the red lane, and if a remembrance of their culinary art remains in the mind of the one who has eaten, that is generally the apogee of reward any cook can expect. Cooks come and go, and people eat on, and very seldom in history

does a name or a reputation survive. Yet often the most inconspicuous and unappreciated cooks take real pleasure in their unremuner-
ative labor.

So it should be, perhaps, with the keeping of a diary. If the long
record of private thoughts, emotions, experiences, observations
ends by being annihilated, the mind should not dwell upon that
probability but permit itself, as a traveler journeying to no destination yet enjoying the act of traveling, to enjoy the simple daily
exercise.

September 25   Could I quite surrender the idea that some historical and psychological value attaches itself to my efforts and believe
accordingly that they were absolutely vain and trifling, I could at
least be more at peace with myself, consider each entry a pleasurable
venture in idle scribbling only. But I can't, and for the simple reason
that, when I come across a record such as this, I'm enraptured by it.
'The New York Times' Book Section of week before last carries a
front-page review of the journals of André Gide. I must read them.
"My mind is becoming voluptuously impious and pagan. I must
stress this tendency." Did famous persons march across my pages,
their merit might be differently weighed. Well, they don't. Only
nonillustrious persons of no consequence artistically or historically.
Myself, I detest reading about the famous in memoirs and journals.
Is that sour grapes?

September 30   When Evelyn is away, I feel stripped of the chief
portion of my protective armor. Life without her would be worthless, and by no means merely because she protects me. It is as if she
were part of me, a trite figure of speech, nonetheless a true one. We
may fight. She may shock my sense of what ought to be to the roots
and doubtless I may try her forbearance to the breaking point, but
we have something fundamental in common evidently, else long
ago we would have parted. So the moment she is gone, sometimes
before she is gone, I desire her back. It is all very curious to me. Sigrid
Undset's theory of love and how it welds antithetic spirits together
despite circumstance and friction accounts for the bond.

October 3   [From Patricia:]

We went to Berchesgaten, but were billeted fifteen miles from
there, at Bad Richenhall. We stayed at the Berg Hotel. A little inn,
perched on top of Predigsstuhl Alp. The only way up there is by a
cable car. The view was fantastic. We were in the middle of the
Tyrol and could see Salsburg, only seven miles away. We stayed
up there for three days, before coming down to go sightseeing. I
was perfectly happy just to sit. The Inn was a small one, only

about thirty five rooms. It has one of the most famous ski runs in Europe, and I'd like to go in the winter to watch them ski. I being a spectator sportswoman. We went up the mountain in Hitler's famous mountain top house. It really was something to see. The drive itself, seven miles around and around the mountain, must have cost millions. Tunnels were dug out of the rock at intervals. And all had iron bars that could be let down to block the road. Only jeeps or trucks can go to the top. It is too steep for private cars. At the foot of the last cliff, we entered a long tunnel by great bronze doors. And went in to his nibs private elevator. It was lined in copper, with leather seats, and airconditioned. It came out in the hallway of the house, five hundred feet up the rock. The blamed thing gave me claustrophobia. I hate being shut up in the ground. The house is not large. But has an immense living room, with five sided walls. And the windows are set in great recesses. The place is built like a fortress. The walls must be four or five feet thick. The view is something out of this world. I don't see how any one could stay there, and think up the things that devil did. Perhaps that is why he didn't go often.

October 8   I have been perusing 'André Gide's Journals.' I always find such intensive concentration upon ART more than a little repellent to the Anglo-Saxon and Georgia inheritance in me. It seems a bit put on, quite a bit unhealthy. His inward examinations likewise bore me, as even my own self-analysis bores me upon rereading. Too many artists and authors pass through the pages as mediums to express Gide's witticism and aphorisms rather than as solid figures in whose progress through life he is authentically interested. Yet — there are his good points — he can make you see a person in a turned sentence. He portrays an artistic era doubtless. When he describes scenery or vignettes of nature, he is exquisite, as in the entry of October, 1894, at Neuchâtel, that begins with "Even here autumn has its charm." I shall not read the 'Journals' in full. As with Thomas Wolfe, the price you have to pay to find the fine spots isn't worth the paying.

October 11   Listened to ex-Governor Earle being quizzed on a radio broadcast by four members of the press about his anti-Soviet views.[22] All he said about Germany having been ready to capitulate

---

[22] George H. Earle, former governor of Pennsylvania (1935–1939) and early FDR supporter, had acquired his violent antipathy for Russian communism while representing the United States in Bulgaria and Turkey. In the postwar years (he joined the Republican party in 1949) Earle pressed his attacks against the U.S.S.R. and urged that the atomic bomb be dropped on any nation refusing international inspection of atomic facilities.

earlier didn't sound plausible, but to me at least every jot and tittle he said concerning Russia did. His views are my views, or, if you will, my views are his views. Russia is our mortal enemy, that is, the Russian Government is. If they had the atomic bomb, they would bomb us with no scruples. We should bomb Moscow, therefore, and destroy the Russian Government rather than wait to be bombed when they do have the atomic bomb.

To me, it was all but terrifying to discern with what incredulity, not to mention levity, as if he were a child with a naughty idea, the four reporters and the amused audience regarded the very serious Earle. One sarcastic reporter asked him why, if he felt about the peril of the atomic bomb as earnestly as he did, he did not travel across the country campaigning for his belief and spend his energy and wealth in furthering it. Earle replied with considerable acerbity that that was just what he was doing. The audience laughed.

There will come a day perhaps when the survivors of holocaust will regret not having lent a listening ear to a man with the courage, the foolhardiness if you prefer, to stand boldly forth for convictions politically unorthodox and contrary to the altruistic and simple-minded thinking of the moment. There was a man named Mitchell.[23] There have been in history many ignored prophets of preparedness, urgers of action while there was time. Neither the reporters nor the amused audience appeared to be possessed of any realistic notion of the actual state of affairs in Russia, nor of the most casual appreciation of the vital pertinent lessons of history. They seemed to regard Russia with utopian astigmatism. They were so little acquainted with the setup in Russia that they could not grasp the simple idea that to destroy Moscow, the seat and heart of Government and the governmental bureaucracy, would be tantamount to dealing a fatal blow to the Soviet setup as a whole.

'Carthaginem esse delendam!'

October 13 Evelyn and I had a good ride in the yards. A big-gauge Allis Chalmers roadscraper was standing there, to me very beautiful in its stalwart functional simplicity of design. The life insurance building continues upward toward the sky, in the haze the geometric skeleton black and delicate. I find much in this mechanical civilization, from the great silver diesel locomotive in the yards to the lovely simple bottle in which ink comes, beautiful to look

---

[23] Arthur saw Colonel William "Billy" Mitchell (1879–1936) as a farsighted martyr crucified by the pigheaded bureaucracy. Mitchell's advocacy of a separate air arm and his predictions of the crucial role of air power in the next war, Arthur pointedly observed, were borne out in 1939 and after; but Mitchell, courtmartialed in 1925 for "conduct prejudicial to the Military Service," died before his vindication.

upon. Evelyn, which is unusual with a woman, enjoys the creations of this age as much as do I. Of all that is beautiful in the functional way in our civilization, I think what is most beautiful is the glassware of various sorts, bottles in particular.

Mrs. Trench, who had lunch at the Ritz yesterday, brought me a menu. While of course I cannot remember exactly, it seems to me that foods at such a first-class hostelry cost at least double, in some cases triple, what they did prior to World War I, and the choice of foods (of this I'm sure) has decreased by a half to three-quarters. Here are a few prices: sirloin steak for two, $6.50 (note — in the old days a single order was sufficient always for two — not now); sirloin steak for one, $3.50; peas or string beans or summer squash, $.45; new potatoes, $.30; chicken salad, $1.75; cheese (only four sorts), $.40; ice cream (five sorts), $.50; tea or coffee, $.35; bread and butter (used to be free), $.20 a person; and special entrees (means body of lunch, more reasonable) — roast native turkey, sage dressing, cranberry sauce, Brussels sprouts, sweet potatoes, $1.75; broiled saddle of spring lamb, tomato, string beans, chateau potatoes, $2.00. It is in the meats that prices are most high. As I recall it, vegetables aren't very much higher than prior to World War I, though of course the helpings are probably for one now rather than two, which would really double or triple the price. Mrs. Trench (whose judgment in these matters I shouldn't trust too greatly) was impressed with the excellent service and the tastiness of the foods. How I used to enjoy the long menus at the hotels in New York, Boston and Philadelphia when I was a boy. It was fun to pick something new now and again from the large grab bag of foods.

October 19 "Eva, are you interested in sex?" "Me? Sex? I don't think so. Why?" "Most girls your age are. Why aren't you?" "Perhaps because I'm so interested in my church. I concentrate on that. Sex is immoral. My religion keeps me moral. It gives me an interest and keeps me moral. People need religion to keep them moral. Don't you find it that way, Arthur?" "Not I. I'm a heathen." "But you must believe. It isn't logical not to," she protested, and I was sucked into a religious discussion, always an unprofitable occupation. Soon she was more intent than I'd ever known her to be, words tumbling forth, she attempting with the surety of youth to proselytize me. Everything occurred, therefore it must be planned, therefore there must be God. As simple as that. She *knew*. That I felt I couldn't possibly know from any evidence at hand where I came from, whither I was bound, why, or that there was any deity behind it all seemed like folly to her. She likewise confused morality and ethics with superstition which, I take it, constitutes the essence and backbone of religion.

October 21

> Flowers flipped the pages of Atlanta's history from 1847 to 1947 at the auditorium annex Wednesday but the book mark rested on 1864 and a "Gone With the Wind" arrangement.
>
> Recalling the Sherman burning of the city, the GWTW display took top honors for the best arrangement of the show, "Atlanta Through the Years," presented by the Atlanta Junior Flower Show Assn.
>
> A white-columned fire-browned remnant, reminiscent of Tara, formed the background for a tree trunk glazed by fire, red flowers flowing like blood, magnolia branches tipped by fire and drifting with the wind, brown leaves curling upward, a lone cannon, one broken wagon wheel. . . .
>
> Pomegranates attractively arranged with red leaves told the story of Arthur Crew Inman's "Red Autumn" well enough to take second place in the book title class.
>
> —'Atlanta Journal'

October 22 The advisability of outlawing the Communist Party as a political organization in the United States, as has been done in Canada, is being debated. I have been thinking about it for months. I should say yes, did we have the backbone, along with such a move, to send out of the nation as revolutionaries all Communists apprehended and convicted either for activities that transgress loyalty or for being established members of the Communist Party past or present. Since the latter course is beyond our leniency, I should not outlaw the Communist Party as a political organization. I should allow no proved Communist to occupy any post in the Federal Government, nor any Communist sympathizer perhaps, and should at once purge (their word) the State Department and all military departments of Communists and their sympathizers. The states should exact of all teachers rigid tests to determine their loyalty and the color of their teachings, and should disbar Communists and those who teach alien sympathies and doctrines. All civil servants should be given annual tests to determine their loyalty and lack of loyalty and preference in jobs given to non-Communist sympathizers. A Secretary of Propaganda should be in the Cabinet at Washington (the nation should be deluged with anti-Communist propaganda), and that Cabinet officer should be removable by Congress at will. Feeling in the nation against the undermining Communists should be built up and maintained by newspapers and the movies and the radio, and the Government should post names of newspapers in line with Communist newspapers.

October 29 I have been listening to excerpts of the Sub-Committee of the Committee on Un-American Activities' hearing of some nineteen writers of the Screen Writers Guild to determine whether or not they are Communists engaged in Communist activities seeking to undermine the American Government. It is abundantly evident, from the queries the writers will not answer directly — such simple direct questions as "Are you, or have you ever been, a member of the Screen Writers Guild?" and "Are you, or have you ever been, a member of the Communist Party?"—that they are either members of the Communist Party or are in sympathy with it.

October 30 Raining at last, from the east, dark, colder. It is reassuring to hark the rain tapping at the windows. It is nine-thirty. Billy has gone shopping. I think of Evelyn and Dr. Pike and that they are having weather for their trip not to their taste. In a moment I'll turn on the daily waltz program. While Strauss and Waldteufel and Lehar make lovely music, I shall cut my stiff fingernails with a razor blade, a process which seems to give people the shivers but gets the matter through more swiftly than shaving my stiff beard, which I usually perform around midnight in the dark without cuts, using the old Gillette safety razor I obtained on Chestnut Street years ago with coupons given Father with the razors he bought. Though I've tried every make and type of razor since, none is as good. I should have to shave twice a day were I 'in society,' but as it is every other day or every third day suffices.

November 2 Billy found a house and land in South Weymouth he wanted to buy for a home. Fifty minutes' drive. It sounded like the dynamite that would eventually part us. I summoned all my wits and ingenuity and argued him out of it. Later I told him that if he would find a nice little summer camp within twenty miles of Boston that didn't cost more than a thousand dollars, I'd buy it for him as a present, and then he could wait until a depression to buy a house nearby Boston, saving meanwhile for it. He seemed enthusiastic about the idea. It would be, I think, money well invested. Fifty minutes of driving summer and winter would be calculated to sever any relationship at the other end eventually. With a summer camp, he could live on where he is, ten minutes away. He's very reasonable. I didn't offer the camp until he had told me he would give up the South Weymouth project.

It's a beautiful day, were I not so exhausted. All night I dreamed of Machs and noises.

November 10 Married twenty-four years today, and a strange ambivalent marriage of antipodes it has been, held together despite contrary natures, interests and circumstances, by an elastic and resilient binder, mutual attraction. Perhaps Evelyn would have been happier with children, though I'm not sure. I do know she would have liked a home, preferably in the country. I don't believe she would have liked a social life. Travel she has missed I'm sure, and mutual walking, riding, climbing, boating, though of these interests she has enjoyed a modicum in other company. Myself, I have longed for demonstrativeness, for executive capacity, for a quick under-standing of my points of view and an adaptability to them. How-ever, here we are with twenty-five years of close association behind us and more years, if one must live, before us. "The first twenty-four years," Evelyn comments brightly, "are the hardest."

It isn't normal, my Anglo-Saxon heritage chides me, to possess such an interest in and need for young girls. A man should be primarily interested in men and men's affairs, with women as an occasional indulgence of secondary importance and of physical and sometimes emotional need, not for mental companionship. To hell with my Anglo-Saxon thermostats. I'm fifty-two and a half. I la-bored and sacrificed toward a literary success that was never achieved. I enjoy young girls. For the years ahead, I shall have as many of them about me and fond of me as possible. There's not real call to be ashamed of my liking them. I like them. I write about them. I think about them. I follow their reactions to life with unfail-ing interest. Living for me is made more bearable. Who approves or disapproves, save as he can abet or abridge my avocation, is of no more concern to me than sea gulls crying, the fish too far below the surface for them to reach.

The year 1947 had been a bad one, and nothing ahead seemed likely to end Arthur's despondency. He wrote his daily stint in the Diary out of habit, but listlessly. The passing show of the world no longer diverted him.

With Evelyn drinking (he simply could not cope with her when she got drunk), with Patsy absorbed in her medical studies and pretty much out of the picture, he had to depend now on the loving solicitude of "highly sexed" girls like Sandra ("Twinkle") Booth and Trudy Daring or the unselfish ministrations of matronly Eva. Jane Powers, the thirteen-year-old daughter of an amiable but lackluster widow, charmed him momentarily (he toyed with the possibility of adopting her should any-thing "happen" to her mother). Trudy went to bed with him, and her ardor partially made up for the coldness of Evelyn. Evelyn, far from being disturbed, virtually encouraged these sexual flings. He may have enjoyed his flattering, hugging, kissing handmaidens, but he preferred, he kept insisting, his rebellious wife even as he ferociously denounced her and proposed marriage to Eva.

At the year's end, Arthur was as depressed as ever. Trudy swore fidelity to her husband, home from the sea; the Baby-Carriage broke down again; and Evelyn was still recalcitrant. He gloomily reflected on his sorry state.

November 16 Congress meets this week in special session to consider the interim grant of money and commodities to France, Italy and Austria recommended by Marshall, and then to take up the enormous sums recommended by Marshall for those nations of Europe not under Russian domination. I have no faith whatever in Marshall. I never liked the cut of his jib and never shall. As with so many American bureaucrats, he's much too ready to give away United States vitality in the form of generous and endless transfusions to an ailing, pockmarked and unappreciating Europe, asking nothing in return that is tangible. I have no idea and I don't believe anyone else has whether such transfusions will do good insofar as retaining Western Europe in our orbit or be futile efforts terminating only in making us weak and exhausted. The latter, to put it mildly, is more apt to follow than the former. We are dealing with ingrates and with opportunists who are without genuine appreciation of our efforts in their behalf.

November 22 I had a long talk with Billy. I told him I had decided to change my will again. I had appreciated, I said, how good he'd been about time and how generous about giving up the house he'd chosen. I had decided to leave him twenty thousand if he was still with me when I died instead of ten thousand. He would also, if he took care of me nights if emergencies arose, have the house. I had, I said, tried to show my appreciation in other ways but was showing it in this way so that if I died, he'd have plenty of money to get along on. I had talked it over with Evelyn. The one aspect that worried me was if any great crisis happened and my money were all lost save enough to keep Evelyn, would he relinquish claim to the twenty thousand. I knew he would from his very nature and was trusting him to do so. He promised me very solemnly that he would by no means take the money if it were Evelyn's only means of livelihood. He thanked me again. I think he was touched. He should be.

When Mrs. Trench came in, I told her virtually the same thing, leaving her ten instead of five thousand. She couldn't understand the details and the specifications until I repeated them four times. Then she thanked me with the remark that she wouldn't, she was sure, outlive me and didn't want me to die. She added that she liked her work but couldn't help getting upset when I talked a lot, for instance, about clean plates. Her husband had given her a complex about being picked on in little, unimportant matters. However, she promised not to lose her perspective. I was wonderful always in large matters. She had nothing to kick about, really. She doubted my motives at first but no longer did. I asked her please never to talk about me to people, as I was in a vulnerable position, and to blow off steam to Evelyn or Billy if it got too bad for her. Of course she replied that she never talked to anyone about me. I let that pass. I think that she was appreciative, more of the gesture than the act. Anyway, I'll feel better about showing my gratitude.

December 3   Too upset about noises and other matters to write in here. Also, spent a couple of afternoons going over with Evelyn the idea of compiling a selected poems volume. Gave it up. By nature I possess a contempt for all art that isn't utilitarian. Even if I enjoy specimens of art occasionally, for art as a whole I harbor no respect. I don't include architecture, for that is utilitarian. I don't care very much by now what happens to my poetry, even if some of it is better than much accepted American poetry.

I'm getting to the stage, also, where I don't care as much what happens to this diary. A normal human has no concern with keeping a diary. You have to be suppressed, vain beyond measure, or tied in some sort of unhealthy knot to go to the trouble and concentration of putting down thousands and millions of thought-out or emotional words on clean white paper. I am, I know, a warped, unnormal human. Of what value, then, this subjective chronicle? None, strictly speaking, none to healthy humans. But always, inescapable, the inkling that perhaps of some use to other warped and baffled humans.

December 9   [From Patricia:]

Boblingen, Germany.
      While Paul has been gone, I have been having a bout with prowlers. The D.P.s. watch our houses all the time, and know when our husbands are gone. In two weeks I had four attempted break ins. So I was issued a gun from the Kaserne. A forty five; whatever that is. It is a huge thing. And I'm scared to death of it. If my aim is good, I think a more lethal weapon would be a pair of Paul's Constabulary boots, size thirteen! Heidi has been a simply wonderful watch dog. There may not be much of her, eleven pounds. But what there is is dynamite. The first time we had the prowlers I very foolishly rushed out into the garden, and chased them. Heidi bit them both. Not that she could do much harm. I

was warned to stay in the house the next time. As they work in pairs, and one could bop me while the other held me. They are no respectors of rank. General McGruder was hit over the head, and his wife bitten, by one of the Polish guards robbing their house.

We get wild at the D.Ps. They are protected by M.G. and Paul can't touch them. He can't pull a raid on their camps. Even though he knows that the place is full of black market and stolen stuff, whiskey, deserters etc. Here we are, taking care of them, food, clothing and a roof over their heads, no work. And yet they are the ones who have been doing most of the robbing. But since they are "persecuted people", they must be protected.

A lot of serious incidences are expected this winter. There seems to be a campaign among the Germans to see how far they can push us without retaliation. We are already meeting surliness and grumbling in the streets, while a few are bold enough to start shoving us on the sidewalk. We just don't know how to occupy a country. We seem to want to return it to the people as soon as possible, and wash our hands of the whole affair. And it can't be done with the German people. They haven't changed in the least, and if Hitler were to come back, they would all be thronging around him. I don't trust any of them. Even the few I like. I don't mind the women so much. They are so brow beaten. But the men get my ire up, they are so darned arrogant. And the women fawn over them. This certainly is a man's country. Most of them need a good kick in the teeth. My Else just loves it when I give Paul a raking over. She says that no German woman would ever dare talk back to a man. And she thinks that America must be a wonderful place for a woman.

December 14   Very occasionally a cherished and long-prayed-for wish is fulfilled. Yesterday Arnold Mach, the Adder, died in his bed at about my age. His death, the death of a part owner of old Irving Mach's estate, will place the management squarely in the Snake's, Sid Mach's, hands, with no more buck-passing and crossruffing. It may make things easier for Evelyn. At any rate, the supercilious, stupid Adder will be out of the way with only the smart, temperish Snake to deal with. God, but I'm glad the red-headed bastard died not six months after buying his swanky new Cadillac car.

1948

January 1   Well, the goddamn lousy 1947 is over and done at any rate, and (except in dreams or memories) a thousand yowling devils are impotent to drag it back. It was a dumpling. Here's praying the next won't follow in its footsteps.

January 4   I gave Mrs. Trench an adding machine, and the "I don't want" on her face was comical. By now she has become used to it and says it will help her. She and Billy are good to me, and why not, with a hundred extra for Xmas and ten dollars each extra each week? My dividends amounted to some twenty-two thousand last year, three thousand of which I keep off "as a mistake in bookkeeping," while with the other dividends I am as accurate as I know how. I lost some eleven thousand dollars last year, of which only one thousand can be deducted against dividends. Boy, you sure work for the greedy Government. My taxes will be about $3,500 and Evelyn's another $700, and it is in large part to be wasted to pay interest on past wastage, to give to veterans to keep them quiet and to throw at Europe for the altruistic fun of it, with about as much effect as if we all lined up on the European shore and tossed silver dollars out over the gulping Atlantic. I'm disgusted. When we get the delayed depression, we should have a wow.

January 16   Patsy didn't even thank Evelyn for the present Evelyn sent her. Breaks her promises to me. I'm fairly well cured. Won't write her now. Hell with her, no-good but attractive February mick.

January 20   I see more of both Billy and Mrs. Trench than I do of Evelyn and am not having constantly to contend with them on needless and ill-advised grounds. Life without her, save where she stands between me and the world, me and the Machs mostly, is simpler and gentler and less demanding of my emotional and nervous reserves. Only Ten Broek and my Father have been more bullheaded, less open to comprehension of my nature.

January 22   The gods probably were alert to pay me off for writing my hidden thoughts about Evelyn. Another snowstorm. On the way to the garage to park his car to keep it from being buried, Billy slipped on the ice, fell down, hurt himself so badly he could hardly crawl upstairs. It was his pelvis. Dr. Pike came. He advised x-rays to determine whether Billy had broken his spine or pelvis. Billy lay on the bed and looked pale. I was in a funk as well as exhausted caring for him. I finally persuaded him to call for Sadie. She was (cold-bloodedly it seemed to me) busy, couldn't arrive until three. Mrs. Trench was good about everything, what my Mother used to call a "tower of strength." She even offered to empty the urinal for him, which in a way astounded me.

January 27   Billy back. Doesn't look bad at all. Smiling. Help to have him. Evelyn better. Better enough to be cross. Mrs. Trench has been a grand help.

January 29   When Dr. Pike dies, I'll have to rely on Fred and Dottie. Dottie says she loves me among the eight or so people she loves most, and I believe her. I wish I could have her more often. Her common sense and lack of bickering are reassuring. She talks a streak where, when I first knew her, she was silent and uncommunicative.

I still like Evelyn more than anyone in the world, make no mistake about it, however I may fuss about her shortcomings.

January 30 Gandhi has been shot and killed. Recently he went on another fast for the purpose of bringing about some sort of parley or reconciliation between the large Mohammedan and Hindu states into which India was divided upon British withdrawal last summer and between which an unofficial war has been raging, with deaths reaching, some say, as high as half a million and great exoduses of populations taking place. Gandhi had again won his point, some hope of peace in sight. God knows what his death will loose upon the world, unless it causes sudden peace in India, which is more likely than that Lincoln's death should at once have healed the breach between North and South and prevented the violent Reconstruction days. Unless the unlikely happens, war may break with sanguine results. Indeed, Gandhi's death may set World War III on its way.

January 31 Nightmares about Evelyn returning, starting an argument, walking out on me. Very disagreeable. Wrote her a seven-page letter pleading with her to stop being so contentious, so supercilious, so cross. May not send the letter, for the same reason I didn't send the one to Patsy. If she hasn't imagination enough by this time to understand me, what good will a letter do? In many ways Evelyn has been a torturer to me.

February 2 The snow was only a long flurry ("fleurrey," Eddie used to call it) and had stopped when Dr. Pike arrived. He'd walked in from Brookline. There's a professional reassurance to his manner and, when you're ill enough to claim his entire attention, a masculine tenderness. As far as his practice goes, he possesses two faults. One: "I'm an old dog and don't learn new tricks easily." In fact, he evinces a distaste for new methods and techniques, so that he's not only behind the times often but does his treatments the old-fashioned hard way, that is, hard on himself. The other: He treats without giving the problem in hand adequate consideration.

I have thirty-six thousand dollars in savings banks by now and right glad I am to have it there. Neither the Democrats, in office, nor the Republicans, hopeful of office, will get down to economic fundamentals and tackle the problem of inflation at its base. I shudder to contemplate the next large depression — national debt 260 billions, budget 40 billions a year, overplanted fields, too many producing manufacturing plants, borrowing increasing and time payments increasing, money so tied up by taxes that new financing has become a gamble, consumer resistance and overproduction in fields like radio already becoming manifest, no decrease in the tremendous bureaucracy, Federal, state, county, municipal.

February 4 Well, Evelyn has lived a year after her cancer operation, which to be honest is more than I had expected the forces that push lives about to have allowed. I'm thankful for that. And I'm thankful last winter's woe and this winter's weather didn't come packed together. And what if both had appeared the winter Janice and Pearl left and only a suspicious Mrs. Trench were here?

I rely on Mrs. Trench now in numberless ways. She's slow. My celerity often confuses her. I see more of her than I do of Evelyn. I tell her she has all the advantages of marriage save a bedfellow and yet isn't tied to me legally. We often listen to the radio or talking-book evenings until she retires to soak in her bath and wash her underclothes and stockings. I enjoy her company. She's interested in my affairs. She no longer is as gullible about people as she used to be. She puts her money in Government bonds and savings banks and keeps a large sum of cash in her deposit box.

February 5 Brita, homely face, talkative, very pleasant, is vacuum-cleaning in Evelyn's bedroom. She's to have an operation on her breast in a week or so. "No," she replies, "I'm not the least scart. If I die, I die. If I get well, I get well. I don't think I mind the pain. It all is yust in a lifetime." She takes the vacuum cleaner arm with the brush on it and playfully runs it down my coat. She likes me. She and Evelyn talk along at a great rate. Brita is forty-one. She came over from Sweden when she was twenty-one. She did general housework. "I had good places. I'll have to say that. I stopped when I got married." She married six or seven years ago. Her husband was a mechanic and repaired barber supply equipment. "I didn't leave him; he left me. He was a good musician. He got to playing in barrooms. That was the end. He got to drinking, you know. Well, that's life. He never comes to see Earnie or me, so I s'pose he's through with us." He pays Brita alimony. Brita is philosophical about what happens to her. She shines silver and talks. She has a large wart on her neck. Her teeth are as small as a child's. She wears glasses and her eyes are pale. She has on the same dress always when she cleans, and it smells of sweat. She's stocky, and her breasts hang down. She moves quickly and purposely. She smiles easily and is always pleasant. I find her helpful to have around. She cleans Evelyn's apartment and does our washing. I hope she's a fixture.

February 10 Evelyn is being nicer to me since her return from Pawtucket. She said she read my long letter and considered it. She's now fixing lunch for Dr. Pike in her kitchen. This afternoon she drives to Winchester to the high school there to interview two prospects. Girls, it seems, want jobs with big insurance companies, only $26 to begin but a regular scheduled rise in pay and only five days a week. The companies arrange parties, dances, ski trips for them, and they, being gregarious or trained by modern education to think being gregarious the proper attitude, like it. It is the thing to do when you graduate from high school if you don't go to college, secretarial or some sort of art or music school, if you are a girl and seventeen or eighteen. Few wish to depart the routine therefore and are not interested in a job like mine.

February 24   Finished 'Mutiny on the Bounty' last night. The second reading. Should be a classic. Fifty times the book the mushy 'Lorna Doone' is. 'Mutiny' is a fine example of unostentatious style and of the style fitting perfectly the subject. I did not enjoy the book as much the first time as the second. To one who writes in a nervous, jerky, often ornate, not seldom colloquial, irregular, haphazardly constructed as to syntax, self-conscious style, the smooth flow of language achieved by Nordhoff and Hall is very appealing.

Henry Wallace, the Communist sympathizer and unconscious stooge for Moscow, the sort of half-finished man (always appealing to Americans, a half-finished man), has his own party now, a running mate, has won a seat in Congress in a recent surprise election, is gathering votes and prestige daily. His campaign for the Presidency threatens to split the Democratic Party wide open. His appeal to Pinkos, the intelligentsia, the minority races, the half-baked and the emotional in general appears to be widespread and general. Truman, straining to appeal to the leftists, has come out strongly for so-called civil rights, mostly to win the negro and Jewish votes. Southerners from eleven states are in open revolt, which may lose Truman more votes unless he retracts his stand or glosses it over, which he is perhaps too stubborn to do. At this point, it would seem impossible for Truman to win in November. Or Wallace either, unless the Republicans become so sure that they break a deadlock in the convention by nominating a third-rate candidate.

February 27   Evelyn says that I am her work, yet she takes no joy in it. Nor does she give me her wholehearted attention, her moods, thoughts, views — resentments being more important to her than either aim or execution. She's egocentric. I warned her she was gradually losing my love and turning into a cross old woman. She saw Arvin. He evidently gave her the works, for she's better temporarily. In the everyday matters Mrs. Trench, Billy and Eva are all nicer to me than Evelyn. I also warned her without fanfare that I didn't want to speak to Dr. Pike but that if she continued to put me in second place and devote her energy and time mostly to him, I'd do so, and that he'd drop her—and she knew it—in short order.

February 29 In small spare room again. A twenty-four hour snow bringing the snowfall to an amount surpassing the 1919–20 snowfall, the year when I stayed in the dark, the heaviest snowfall in this century and the coldest winter since 1878. I have all but become reconciled to its going on forever.

March 1 Russia has taken over Czechoslovakia lock, stock and barrel and is now about to take over Finland. A Communist Government has been organized in northern Korea. Russian imperialistic expansion owes much to Roosevelt and to his dumb crony, Morgenthau, and since owes much to Truman and Marshall. After a year of throwing American money away in Greece, we seem no further advanced there. Instead of buoying up the Greek officials and taking over the army and running things, we compromise with realism and expect idealism to be able to meet stark facts. Gradually the foolhardiness and the dumbness and the generosity with American resources of Roosevelt come to light and are even worse than I had expected they would be. The man's ego, his vanity, his faith in his powers are simply amazing. The monstrous shape of the world is mostly due to his folly, and we haven't heard all yet. To his folly and our unwillingness to prepare realistically for what history indicates is ahead for us.

March 3 Told Evelyn off calmly yesterday saying that I had worked harder on her than on my poetry and considered I had made a dire and complete failure of putting myself over, for I had expected a noncontentious wife who wouldn't forever have sleeping, eating, shopping, another man on her mind to a degree that there would be only the tag ends of time left for me, and these doled out parsimoniously. While I loved her and she charmed me, I hate one side of her with a heartfelt hatred. By God, I think she heard all or part of what I said for once. She cried. She was sweet all the remainder of the day. She said she would give me more time. She suggested we find an interest in common. I replied that I was interested in stocks, in having a garden at the country, in finding a secretary, but she had never been ready to evidence any real genuine interest in any of these projects. She would, she said, do so. I'm probably a fool to hope that any lasting impression was made. I can teach Eva more in an hour than Evelyn in a year.

Trudy Daring spent evening with me. Was very bored, so made passes at her. A fairly homely girl of about twenty whose sailor husband is in the Pacific. Very emotional and very sexy. Love to hear her talk. Beautiful breasts and starved for affection. A warm evening. Said her grandfather tried to rape her when she was eleven, and it had made her chary of men all during high school. "Now I can't fight men off." Says she likes to be caressed because makes her feel like tortoise without shell, vulnerable, which is exquisite pleasure. I like her. Reminds me of Woody. So much emotionality rare. No wonder it attracts men, however plain her looks. Lovely breasts fitting the fingers softly yet resiliently. Had I been well and imbued with my present lack of conscience, I'd have had innumerable affairs with women. They're at their best when their attention is entirely upon a love affair. The only trouble with highly sexed girls like this Trudy is that they shut up entirely when you're caressing them, so thoroughly do they enjoy the process.

March 6   Sandra Booth is here, prompt. She's five feet five, slim, seventeen, birthday July 30. She has dark brown hair, green eyes, white uneven teeth, not too good a complexion, a youthfully enthusiastic air. She the youngest of five children, has a niece of nineteen. Her brothers have, she says, spoiled her. She feels that going to college is a waste of time for a girl. She gets very high marks. She has just been nominated for National Honor Society. She has been at high school a member of Symphony Guild, Girls' Glee Club, special member, editorial staff of 'The Chronicle,' voted the best school magazine in this section of Massachusetts. She goes out with the Tufts boys. "They seem to like me." She has no hobbies. She likes to listen to classical music. Her youngest brother went to Princeton. She likes clothes.

March 8   Sandra ("Twinkle" I call her), unless she vanishes or something untoward happens, is a find, a darling. Even if there are certain things she proves unable to do, her personality constitutes a treasure worth having. She sparkles. She told her family about the dark. They have, she says, objected to nothing. She's a dream realized of what I want, pleasant, attractive, I'm practically certain honest, loyal, straightforward, yet tactful. When Evelyn was cooking my pork chops for lunch and we were watching, I put my arm around the girl. What did she do then? With no embarrassment she put her arm around me. I was won in an instant. She wasn't afraid of the dark yesterday. She said: "If you think I'm full of fun and a tease, you haven't known me yet." She has three months more of school. Her marks, she says, are quite high — or did I note that before?

I'm bowled over by her. She's the sort of daughter I'd have liked to have. No intellectual but smart enough and with charm and intelligence enough to get by. She isn't afraid of Evelyn, which is unusual. She's to come next Saturday. When she was going home on the bus last night (she lives near Tufts), a drunken man attempted to feel a woman's breasts and another man knocked him off the bus. She was interested, though not afraid.

Trudy yesterday evening with me again. She certainly reminds me of Woody. I enjoy her. She's almost wantonly affectionate. She commenced sleeping with her husband three years before marrying him. "No one had a suspicion that that little, obedient, convent Trudy would do such a thing. It took Sammy, bless him, a long time to break my conscience down, and then quite a while to make me square with my conscience that I enjoyed it. But it happened. And now I'm lost without Sammy and without it. I look at men—two men at least—and wonder would I like to take them on. But one is too animal-like and the other is so fragile I'm sure he'd break. So I remain true to Sammy. My mother put into my mind a fear and contempt for masturbation. The psychologist tells me it's normal, and so do you. Sometimes it helps me and sometimes it doesn't. Riding on buses—so sexed am I—excites me by their shaking, and that makes me ashamed. I'm an awful problem to myself." Trudy is no beauty, but her yellow-red hair is sleek to the touch and her hands are nice. She meets a need in my affectionate nature, and I'm sure I meet a need in her affectionate nature.

March 14 I keep wondering if I have not been making a tall mistake not to have concentrated upon Eva. She is a wonderful girl. I admire her and love her and always feel better for her presence. I've persuaded her to use rouge, to laugh less in the middle of her stories, to take more pains with her hair, to cease saying "yeah," and a dozen like details with the result that she grows out of being a big school-girl into an increasingly presentable young woman. She could scarcely be more affectionate with me than she is, calling me "dear" and "darling" and "sweet," and touching me and regarding me as if I were her prize pig, and advising me what to do and not to do when I ask her, and going to sleep when I do, sitting in the chair by my bed and letting me caress her at option. Yet when it comes to the men and boys she meets elsewhere, she holds them at well-behaved arm's length where liberties with her person are concerned, feeling that course to be both wise and proper.

March 16 This United Nations, which has been nothing but the facade behind which the hornets and the termites of Communism have operated without opposition, should be immediately scrapped or Russia somehow outlawed from it. We should learn from Franco how to control Communists, use Franco's methods of putting the fear of hell into them. It is to be a world run upon slavery if Moscow succeeds. If we don't wish that, no measures should be too drastic to use.

March 21 Evelyn talked with me. We fought, mildly this time, on the subject of her always having to go to the bathroom, answer the telephone, get the mail, turn over the roast, see the stew the moment I begin to caress her instead of acting as if she enjoyed it and loved me. I wasn't, I said, repulsive to other women. If it wasn't for the other women, I said, I would be having a bad complex about myself in that direction. I'd rather make love to her than any of the others, but she wouldn't let me. How could I keep my face — man's most valued possession — when my wife, the very one who should take the most care not to, deflated or rebuffed me. She argued. Then she pointed out, to which I agreed, that she'd been doing better. Then she cried. Then she was sweet and protested that she did love me and didn't mean to hurt me.

But I was deflated, and later in the evening before she departed for New York, she and I again bickered, this time over clothes, she asserting that she wanted to wear a particularly commonplace dress and I observing that it added ten years to her looks and she saying she wished she did look ten years older so people wouldn't always be exclaiming how young she was and I saying that if she behaved older it would be better than looking older. This morning she sent me the following telegram, and I am no longer bitter: "Good morning, darling Arthur. Evelyn arrived safely and loves you." And that is the way to disarm me. I would be putty in her hands if she were more vocal about loving me, wouldn't argue and were acquiescent outwardly to my suggestions in her behalf.

March 22   Eva talks of school, of church activities or Jeffrey. She's joining the Old South Church. She has Jeffrey dated ahead for weeks. She's been accepted by Lesley College. She forms plans in her mind for transferring to a Western college after two years here. "Don't you do it," I object. "Why not?" "Because I think you're wonderful and want to be sure to have you around. Because you help me and I don't know how I'd get along without you." "I mean that much to you?" "Yes you do. And by the way, Eva, cram in just as much of this church activity as you can, so you'll get tired of it. If anything ever happens to Evelyn, I'm going to marry you." "You are?" "Yes, I am. You believe me, don't you?" "Yes, I do. You sound just like you mean it." "Of course I hope nothing happens to Evelyn. But you never can foresee these things. I'm getting somewhat old for a wild lot of sex, but I don't think you'd mind that." "Golly," she smiled, patting my head, "you think of everything."

March 23   Trudy is a strange little being. All she has to do to get me excited is to touch me. I could sleep with her if I wished but do not wish, first because that doesn't interest me as once it did, second because I have not too much faith in her discretion and do not wish her husband down my neck. She's not only passionate, she's what might be called violently affectionate. I was designed to be a philanderer. When Evelyn returns from New York and could have had an affair with Bill Jones, I feel she should have done it. Probably I'm as wanton in my way as Patsy in hers. New females are much more tempting to me than accustomed ones. As a mind, Trudy bores me, save for her pert remarks. As a body, she interests and amuses me. You wouldn't expect such a small body to have such luxurious breasts. She feels nicely. I like to have her touch me. When in bed with me without clothes, she presses into my body as if to become a part of it. She's vastly exciting. Yet, aside from the sexual side of her, I wouldn't care too greatly did I never see her again. I had three roses for her. She brought me a carnation. She describes in detail her sex life with her husband, his reactions, hers, and that interests me. She tells me I'm "inimitable" and "sweet" and "sort of exciting yourself."

When she came to bed with me, she said: "Now be good to me, Arthur, and don't make me regret trusting you. You know what I mean?" Perhaps I'm a sentimental dope and what she asked me to abstain from was just what she wanted, but it pleases me to be trusted and not to transgress that trust. Caressing the body and being caressed is perhaps more fun than the act of copulation itself, at any rate all save the final moment of it. I'd enjoy having a new woman a month to explore. Trudy remarked that I was much more gentle with her than her husband and that she liked it much more. "You have a way with you in bed," she added pertly. "Touch my nipples again. I love it, the way you do it. Oh dear, I'm afraid I'm a something-or-other—a sinner, a wanton, a strumpet—anyway something not quite admirable according to ordinary standards. What's the difference, can you tell me, between morals and ethics? Gee, it's nice here with you. Remind me to put my stockings on before I go. I left the house with them on. I ought to come back with them on if I wish to preserve my reputation as a very proper and somewhat inconspicuous girl." As I said, Trudy is a strange little being.

March 29 Trudy came soon after we arrived home. Her looks are mouse-like—light brown hair (not yellow), no rouge, beige suit, glasses. Her teeth stick forward slightly, and there are darkish hairs on her upper lip and heavy off-color rouge on her lips emphasizing teeth and hair. She has nice legs. Her looks grow on you. Her complexion is excellent. I took off her glasses. She has yellow eyes, yellow slightly tinged with green, predominantly yellow, really beautiful eyes, exceptional, such eyes as I've never seen before. Her eyebrows are dark. She could be, if fixed up, a unique person. Put her hair in a diluted yellow wash so it would match her eyes, darken her eyebrows. Put rouge on her cheeks and hardly any rouge on her lips. Remove the hair from her upper lips. Put the right colored dress on her and high heels. Accentuate her eyes and minimize her mouth. I told her what I'd do. "Oh," she replied, "why? I've got my man already." Evelyn came in about then. I repeated the above. "And emphasize her breasts. She has something there," Evelyn added.

Trudy blushed. She hasn't much brains, Trudy, but a touch such as Cleopatra must have had. She said: "I ran my fingers down a boy's arm last night. Do you know what he said? He said: 'My God, Trudy, don't do that. I'm not married to you, you know.' That's what he said. And before I married I was just plain Trudy and never excited anyone and didn't even know I could excite anyone." Trudy is what she refers to as "shameless" in the pleasure she derives from feeling and being felt. She will put my hand on her breast and rub herself back and forth, exclaiming: "Umm, I love it. I simply love it. More, please." And she will fool with me by the hour, telling me, meanwhile, how Sammy, whose instrument of sex is oversize, goes to sleep with it in her and wakes her up using it. "My oh my, if only my family was aware of what a passionate husband I have and how I love it. I wish, though, he were as affectionate as you are."

Trudy gave up Easter services and singing in the choir to come here. It was amazing to watch her fixing a can of soup for herself. "How do you open it, Artie? You're sure it's that way? Will the contents fit in this saucepan? How can I pour it without spilling it? Where'll I heat it? How do I turn on the gas? How do I turn it off? Anyway, I know how to wash dishes." Evelyn likes Trudy. I wonder, if she were aware of how Trudy and I affect each other, would she still like Trudy? I don't know. At any rate, I've learned to keep my big mouth shut.

April 4 Evelyn is putting herself out to be sweet to me and to give me her company, not as much as I'd like it but more than for years. Instead of acting as if I were the tag end of her duties on which she was loath to expend more time than a necessary modicum of attention, she is using an amount of energy and forethought at least equivalent to that she uses on Dr. Pike, and I am at least more important-seeming than the next meal, the next sleep, the next telephone call, the next bowel movement. I trust, but fear to hope, that this turn for the better will endure.

In the meanwhile, here are a few more observations concerning Sandra Booth. She dresses nicely. Her face, though, is a mess, bumps and blackheads when you are close to it. She's one of those children who are on the border between being pretty and being homely. I spoke to her about her complexion and Evelyn gave her advice. She took it well. She's only one matter on her mind now, her boy friend. She's a highly sexed girl, and evidently so is the boy friend. She wanted me to tell her whether she should sleep with him or not. I told her, at some length, that she was too young and to save that until later, in the meanwhile enjoy his ardent caresses and let it go at that. Did she want a baby?

When I touch her, she reacts as a sexual harp string. I told her flatly that I liked her and would probably touch her often but that if she became excited on each occasion she'd be miserable and so would I — to think it over. "I'll probably get used to it," she replied. "It's just new to me, you know?" I'd rather have undersexed Eva. Sex is fun as a pastime but not as a steady diet.

April 5 Jane Powers and Mrs. Powers arrived first. Mrs. Powers looked and smelled just the same, a sweet, worried, gray-haired woman on the stout side, the planes of her face somewhat flat, her clothes plain, a smile that comes and goes as if with effort both ways. She's either silent or, once started, sticks to a subject until used up. I like her and in some ways respect her, but her head really doesn't have many brains in it.

Jane has grown fourteen pounds since last summer, she stated proudly. She's nearly five feet four. She was dressed neatly and carries herself well save when embarrassed, when she cocks her head to one side like a sparrow and winks her eyes rapidly. She's a most attractive child, with twinkling brown eyes, teeth uneven but not unattractive, a fetching curve to her lips, no rouge, no lipstick, a complexion as smooth as one could wish, brown hair parted in the middle and the ends neatly turned under not to show, bare legs. Her fingernails weren't clean, but everything else was, and she was without odor. Her voice is soft. She talks sufficiently and with imagination. She is affectionate and playful. I was captivated. She receives the highest marks in her class, likes to write themes for English, reads my poems, has been in Girl Scouts, rides a bicycle, has a boy friend, dreams at night, reads novels and girls' books. She's thirteen and — it would happen this way — was born in February, the tenth to be exact. She didn't fancy the darkness in my room but said: "I don't think I'll mind it if I hold your hand." We listened to 'One Man's Family.' She sat beside my bed and put her hand out to me. I held it on my chest. She reached out the other hand, raised my hand, made a nest of it and slid hers under, then relaxed. She slept through the program. Earlier I said to her: "Golly, I like you." She exclaimed at once: "I like you too," and squeezed my hand. I was a gone goose.

I asked her mother if I could have her in to visit us during her April vacation. I told her I thought her daughter was wonderful and complimented her upon the excellent bringing-up she had given her. She said nothing, save: "I guess I'm a dyed-in-the-wool Yankee. Compliments embarrass me. I suppose Jane is all right. She gets out of hand sometimes, but that's probably to be expected. All in all, she's a good child." She said that I could invite her to visit us. I did. "Your mother said I could ask you, Jane." "Did you, Mummy? Oh did you?" On being reassured by her mother, she replied that she'd love to come. Evelyn showed Mrs. Powers the room upstairs and after her, Jane. They were both very pleased. Jane liked the desk and the view, Mrs. Powers the sunlight. We are to call up later and make plans. I'm excited. She's just such a daughter as I'd like to have, and the right age. "She's really lovely," Evelyn exclaims. "I'd love to have her for you. You have my hearty approval in this instance."

All night I dreamed of being on a long train traveling through a coal miners' strike district. Starved or half-starved miners and their women were lying dead everywhere or brawling brutally with each other or copulating or hurling rocks at the train. The tracks, we were informed by the conductor, a detached-looking man, had been torn up. The only way left for the train to get into the city was to haul it over trolley tracks. The trolley tracks climbed steeply up a long, high hill. Cables were attached to the train and slowly, foot by foot, the ascent began. The back door to the last car, in which we were, flew open and could not be shut. Luggage spilled. Strikers yelled and threw stones. We had been warned the cables might part, in which case short shrift to the last car and to us could be contemplated. Inside the car, scenes of raw passion, jealousy, fright, abandon took place. No nightmare could have conjoined more ingredients of emotional desperation.

April 8 Evelyn got tight the other night for no reason at all save that she loves to drink. Things were going along so well I said little. Yesterday afternoon our relationship collapsed again, and today I'm miserable. I was petting her. She drew away, as so often she does. I pointed out that if she loved me, which she said she did, and my touch wasn't repellent to her, as she said it wasn't, why did she continually draw away and make me feel badly and sad. I gave her several reasons why she'd get more response from my nature if she didn't. She replied that she didn't intend to draw away; she simply forgot herself and did so. She hadn't liked her mother to touch her; perhaps that was the reason she drew away. I gave her several similes about how it made me feel. I suggested that she wouldn't enjoy a flower whose leaves she had to pluck off to see the bloom, so tightly was it curled, as much as she would a flower which opened up to her gaze voluntarily. She flew into a rage. She wasn't going to be talked at, on and on. She didn't have to stand it and she wouldn't. She'd left me before and would do it again. That, as usual, was the push button which set me off. We exchanged unpleasant words. I dislike and disrespect her from the bottom of my heart.

Sometimes I think she feels I am the unfair turnkey who puts locks on her independence with malign intentions. Again I am a man who charms her because unsubduable to her. Then I am still again someone to be mothered and protected. Whether she loves me as I feel love I cannot say. I am caring less as to that each month now.

April 9   Common sense indicates that the shipwrecked sailor on Circe's island must, perforce, make the best of his lot. If I were well and strong, I'd walk out on Evelyn today. The country is full of potential wives. My knowledge of women is tenfold what it was when I married her. When alert, I look ten years, five at least, under my real age. Though I may be wrong of course, it nevertheless seems to me that I could somewhere find a wife to my taste. I'm all for wives. Maybe I'd marry several women in several vicinities. I'd like that. I'm lawless, unprincipled save where my established friends are concerned, daring by nature, held back when young by lack of size and an unfortunate concatenation of circumstances and a concept that my elders and established institutions were to be heeded and obeyed, and held back since by lack of strength and by illness and hence reliance upon people. Given size and given strength, I'd be off and away with a life analogous to that of my ancestor, Abednego Inman.

That man first appeared on the records as living in the county of Georgia renowned for its poorness of soil even then, the 'Tobacco Road' country. At or before he reached his majority, he trekked across South Carolina and began taking up a series of homesteads in North Carolina. He was tried for treason, that is, loyalty to King George, and acquitted. He and his two brothers determined to join Daniel Boone, a neighbor of theirs in North Carolina, in his projects in the then wilderness of Kentuck. They set out, were ambushed in Cumberland Gap by the Indians and Meshach killed. Abednego and Shadrach lay in a hollow log for days, hiding. Then they retraced their steps and settled in what became the independent State of Franklin. Abednego became a justice of the peace. He was a major in the Battle of Kings Mountain. He moved to Dandridge where he took up the allotment of land due veterans. He enlarged his holdings. He was Justice of the Peace. He bought slaves until he had twenty-five. He refused Andrew Jackson his daughter in marriage. When he was no longer a justice of the peace, at least on one occasion he "shot up the town." He led a wild, free, often lawless life, and one gets a picture of an arrogant, shrewd, reckless-within-bounds man "taking nothing from nobody." [24]

And the Maffitt side of my ancestry was as daring and lawless and charming, even if at times worthless, as you could wish. I come by my character by rights. One element in my existence that has made me feel inferior has been not being able to hit when angered by injustice or rankled by temperament I dislike. I know I am not taking account of the gentler side, the tendency as soon as I am cooled off to let what had been ill-advisedly done to me pass into limbo. I would today like to clear out and leave my wife. Tomorrow, maybe not. I know, were I well and strong, I would do it.

April 11 And now I've rationalized Circe back into acceptability. The convolutions of my adjusting mind are most amusing to watch as it seeks to make palatable what it doesn't like and to emphasize what it does like so that what it sees will become for the nonce the surface of what it doesn't see. Circe, it points out, is very pretty often. She is loyal. She possesses attractiveness. She is patient with delinquencies and shortcomings other women might give short shrift. She isn't jealous. Morality seldom makes her stuffy or hampers her services. She isn't religious. Her dumbness at moments is amusing, and no one can foresee at what moment she may appear smart or level-headed or even wise. He knew this years ago. Why has he been so stupid as to forget it? So let her get drunk. Let her say awful things — maybe, as she says, she doesn't mean them two minutes after. Let her be unaffectionate — there are other women who will give him that.

Evelyn has gone to the country to walk and garden. Billy and I have been for an east-wind ride in the railroad yards, many new piles of bricks of varied colors piled there in the bright sun. Trudy is upstairs, her breakfast not eaten after what must have been nine hours of sleep (she left me at midnight). No one could have been more delightful, more amusing, more affectionate and companionable than she was during a long evening. "By golly, Artie, I was bound I was going to please you or die in the attempt." It is rewarding indeed to have untied, sort out and put in running order the tangled elements of a confused and infelt nature. There's something creative to such a success. I tried to make her seem desirable in her own eyes as a woman with certain special gifts and attributes. I gave

---

[24] I have found no evidence of his family story in any biography of Andrew Jackson.

her affection for which she was yearning. I instructed her what to do and how and when to do it. I generalized her specific fears and complexes to take the personal bite from them. I took her confidences seriously. As so often happens with men of my type, I have come to love the object of my successful efforts.

In all my years I have never had anyone make such satisfactory and satisfying love to me. My nature uncurls under her manifestations of affection — her head tucked under my chin and her breath warm on my neck, her eyelashes fluttering against my cheek, her passionate kisses, her hands where only loving hands should be, my hands pressed firmly to her breasts. I feel more at peace, more renewed by the sweet wiles and close proximity of one who understands affection as I understand it, passion as I understand it, and the satisfaction derived from an evening such as we spent together. I hadn't hoped before old age caught up with me to have this sustaining experience.

April 20   John Lewis has been fined and his soft-coal union fined for contempt of court as a finale to this last strike. Someone should bump him off, if patriotism is a worthy ethical quality, about which I am by no means certain.

April 21   A small ride. Been playing with Jane. A born coquette she is. When a waltz or ballet is on the radio, she does an impromptu dance most gracefully. She pretends to draw pictures in ink on the back of my jacket. She runs the automatic elevator up and down with zest and glee. She makes compliments to Billy and Mrs. Trench, who grin with pleasure. She's a charmer and a darling. I'm somewhat frizzled out, she's so active.

[From Patricia:]

This Russian situation in Berlin has some of the dependents scared to death. Two families are going home. I may be wrong. But I doubt very much if Russia wants, or can afford, to have a war with us at this time. Anyway, I'm sticking on until the first shot is fired. Or the Government orders us home. Might as well stay and see the fireworks.

Another thing making the women nervous at this time, the men are leaving for six weeks in the field, next week. And so we will have to barricade our houses, as the populace will be out in full force, intent on robbery. They are giving us German police for pretection, but they are worse than none. I wouldn't dare trust them. So we will all be sleeping beside our thirty eights, forty fives, and carbines.

The people hate us here, it was always an active Nazi stronghold. It is the first time we have met real resentment among the children. Of course, they have been coached by the parents. They line up in the road, arms outstretched. Daring us to hit them. Paul has stopped that on our street. He chases them up on the sidewalk, into the yards, and practically into the kitchen. Our tiny Fiat, being able to go most anywhere. Then he hauls out the mother, and delivers a lecture. We get a lot of minor vandalisim. Last night our name plate was torn off the gate. Automobiles can't carry spare tires, and of course we don't ever leave anything in a parked car. The doors must always be left unlocked. As a locked car is always jimmied. Our house servants are ostracized, and told they will never be able to get jobs with the Germans when we leave. All of which we take in our stride. We didn't come over here to be popular. And you cannot expect to live in a destitute country and not have thieving. I do get tired of going around bolting and locking things every night tho.

I am again enjoying writing in here. Experts give us about five years more before Russia perfects the atomic bomb and warfare perhaps destroys our country and our culture, though some other experts give us not a year of peace ahead. What's happening in Palestine between the Jews and the Arabs, mounting warfare that is, or an incident in Berlin or Vienna, may, they say, precipitate a war. Myself, I'd give us some five years more of grace before holocaust. Meanwhile, I write on, too sure of the probability of disaster ahead to bother with correcting manuscript but often enjoying hugely snapshotting people and recording thoughts about events. For all I know, maybe in this postscript to my serious diary, I may be giving a truer picture of the times and myself than formerly when I was more meticulous and attempted to cover a wider field of recording.

April 28 Twinkle spent the evening with me. She's what I was certain she was, a highly sexed youngster. There may be what she calls "growing-up bumps" on her face, but there are none on her body, and, like Trudy, she takes to being caressed as a flying squirrel to the air. Like Trudy too, she admits she enjoys being touched. "I'm just not quite used to what it does to me yet. But I like it." As for myself, I know of few ways of passing an evening more speedily and delightfully than making ardent love to such a really attractive young person as Sandra Booth is. Many troubles are forgotten; time isn't long enough; I make a new friend. "Don't kiss me," Twinkle protested, "'cause I forgot my lipstick." The body odor she had came mostly from impregnation with bath salts and is no longer offensive. She is always tastefully dressed. I said, to remove any sting coincident to my not keeping her as a secretary: "You sure have sex, Twinkle. You can readily understand now, can't you, why having you as a secretary would keep me disturbed constantly?" "Yes," she agreed, "I can. And me too." "I've had a lovely evening," I said. "So have I," she said.

Her legs are round and firm and hairy. I like hairy legs or exceptionally smooth legs. Her body isn't hairy and is warm. She cuddles nicely. By God, I do right well for myself at almost fifty-three. It sets me up in my own self-esteem no end, equivalent to making money fast and consistently on stocks. I'm feeling a different person and, as silly as it may be, a better person. My capacity for absorbing affection is apparently limitless. Twinkle asked: "Isn't your wife affectionate?" I thought a moment before deciding how to answer, whether a straight answer would be disloyal. "No," I replied, "she isn't." "Gosh," she said, "what do you do, as affectionate as you are?" "Make love to you," I replied. "And to other women and girls, I bet?" "Well," I hedged, "seldom does someone as delightfully sexed as you come my way. My answer is—not very often in this fashion. You're awfully sweet and dear to me, and I appreciate it." "I like you lots—Arthur." She's coming again Sunday evening—I hope.

She asked about contraceptives and other matters appertaining to sex. I explained as fully as I could, for anyone as emotional as she should be informed. She's gained weight. "Both my father and I have gained since Mother's been away, about six pounds each. She had her insides all cut out and has never been the same since. She bickers at the dinner table until neither my father nor I can eat well. My mother isn't young any more. I was born when she was forty-five."

Evelyn looks very pretty this morning in the Czechoslovakian silk dress with the intricate embroidery I bought her years and years ago and which is now back in style as to length. Her cold is better. She's fascinating to me with looks and charm and a devil-may-care air. As long as I can find plenty of affection elsewhere, I regard her with more approval. She knows it. I told her about Sandra asking about how affectionate she, Evelyn, was, and my reply. "Is that all right with you?" "Perfectly all right," she replied, "for I can see what a difference your little girls' affection means to you." "Thank you lots," I said. "I still would rather have you for a wife than any of the others."

April 30   It is my contention that no one will indefinitely bear with a chronic invalid who forgets to smile, to be pleasant, to think of others, and I make it a point, whatever my feelings are, to be whimsical or affectionate or thoughtful or appealing or responsive to their troubles with those about me. No one loves a sourpuss, as the saying has it. Evelyn says that these diaries do not give an adequate picture of how full of fun, how fanciful and whimsical, how replete with guile and charm, how thoughtful of others I am.

May 2 What a day, yesterday. Fred came to paint my throat. Couldn't use hands. Sunlight was like searchlights dazzling me. My jaw cracked. My shoulder was dislocated. Dr. Pike came. By then I was in a daze from pain and nervousness. He was at his best. He said the hyoid bone was awry. All the treatments were painful. During the morning I had snapped at Billy, Evelyn and Mrs. Trench successively. I told Evelyn I'd bop her if she didn't quit qualifying each statement I made.

About five o'clock she commenced drinking ("Only Coca-Cola, that's all") and by six was drunk, with the usual banging into furniture, nasty answers, "I haven't touched a drop since morning. It's all in your mind. Don't be so suspicious." She could hardly get supper. Dishes dropped and banged. I felt like a man riding in an automobile with the steering gear broken. I think I got some water down her but don't know for she lies so. I asked why she had drunk the sherry (she finally admitted it was that). "I didn't have any time off. I felt pressed. I wanted to forget." She usually recollects nothing afterwards, being "out like a light." I loathe drunkenness. I hate her when she drinks. That she lacks moral fiber I am aware. It's expression in acts gives me the creeping willies.

Believe me I was pleased to see Trudy. I bawled and bawled from built-up pressures within me. "There, darling, there," she repeated, and couldn't have been more understanding. The evening ended with my sleeping with her. The saying, "All's fair in love and war," is, I believe, an exact one. I regret to say I think I broke (by gentle stages nonetheless reprehensible in my eyes for being gentle) several promises not to press her to sleep with me if she didn't want it enough to suggest it herself. I'm ashamed of that, yet (if I don't catch anything and her conscience doesn't wrack her — she declared it would not) pleased about the evening. I felt even with Evelyn for the afternoon in a thoroughly childish fashion.

Trudy couldn't have been sweeter. We fitted like clockwork. Her husband, Sammy, is due home on leave the eleventh; then Trudy goes to Honolulu with him for three months. Trudy said she loved it and me but not to repeat if we could help it, for she must adjust her New England conscience before his arrival. It's reassuring and heartening to be intimately inside someone you are fond of and to be so nakedly and unashamedly close. No one ever gave me such affection along with passion, and I loved it. I hope I haven't given Trudy a complex of some sort. I think not. I'm sure I'm the only person other than her husband she has "had relations with." I love her twice as much as before. The only trouble is I'd like it again.

May 3 Had a long discussion with Evelyn in the afternoon and almost think she heard what I said. I repeated how I believed that independence in a woman is not of itself a harmful possession but was harmful to its possessor and obnoxious to others only when not hidden, disguised, kept submerged—save only very rare occasions when it could be used with effect. Part of her propensity for drinking and virtually all of her propensity for smoking were, I was convinced, manifestations of her indulgence in independence.

Eva lost her temper with me yesterday for the first time. I thought she was teasing when in her mind was a tragedy of youth she wished to divulge "to the one person in the world who knows me best and whose advice I value most." Of all people, I would wish least to offend her. I apologized all over the place. She wept. The trouble, it appeared, is that she's being faced with the urgency of sex in the male animal and doesn't like it. She's been idealizing Jeffrey. She has forbidden him, on pain of having to leave her for good, to make passes at her. The poor fellow has done very well so far but is a normal man impelled by normal ardor no doubt. She's disappointed in him and her ideal is broken.

I tried delicately to explain the ordinary sex urgency in men. They are not, I said, Sir Galahads in passion-proof armor riding restrainedly through a world of virgin women. She expected too much restraint of males. It didn't mean necessarily that because they wished to pet her they felt less respect for her. It might mean that but not necessarily. She'd be much more contented if she could take sex as a normal quality of masculinity and learn to discern gradually its degrees and connotations in individuals, not be repelled by all sex, all passes at her, all passionate thoughts of her. Poor Eva, she's about as sexy as a chair arm. She'll put up with sex to have children. I hope she listened to me, for what I said, if accepted, will save a good and sweet person much grief.

May 8 Dear Trudy, with her lovely breasts, her feeling hands, her high-tension emotions, her lack of genuine intellect—I'm glad you wandered into my life, but I'm a trifle unresponsive already— ingrate that I am—to your unquestionable charms, to your unreserved affection. It was that way with Katinka. Poor Trudy—I shall have to make a special effort not to hurt you. You and your unselfishness are surely worth a dozen of me and my egocentric amorality. I hope that your husband—and an ordinary guy he sounds as you describe him — will please you and love you and reward you as you deserve; and that I can keep my boredom to myself and never let you know or suspicion it. You are a grand person, Trudy, and I'm not worth your devotion. May you prosper and flourish and have the many little Sammys and Trudys you wish. You are the salt of the earth, and I am but dung, with only the quality of making, sometimes, the beautiful grow. I prefer Evelyn, hard and fearless and at moments stupid and at moments brilliant, but a person who does not bore me by her goodness, her unselfishness, her meekness. You are the medicine I need to appreciate my wife the more, and that is in a way tragic, but true. The pair of us are probably not worth the one of you. May prosperity and devotion and an admiring family bless you, Trudy. You are a wonderful person, in that your capacity to give to others is limitless, in that you have no adamant core, in that you are selfless without common sense.

And this is sufficient and much more for today. It is written upon a basis of the best English Scotch whiskey, wherefore honest, wherefore cognizant of the best qualities of the people I love or admire.

May 10   I dread the corporealization of my Father as if a visitation of the plague were in the offing. Well, his semiannual visits are inescapable and must borne with what fortitude I can muster. He means no harm, I'm sure, has been generous with both Evelyn and myself far beyond any conventional obligation on his part. Both of us wish to make his visits, if they must occur, palatable. He's an old man, and regardless of how I hate him and wish he were dead, I have no desire to hurt him or cause him misery while with me, for what would that accomplish? Certainly not the vengefulness I feel. Certainly nothing that would by its pettiness do aught but bother my conscience.

May 15   The British now having withdrawn from the Palestine mandate, the Jews promptly announced the formation of the State of Israel. Armed forces from five neighboring or bordering Arab states are apparently waiting to consolidate to attack. The United States immediately recognized the de facto government of the new state. Within the last weeks Jewish forces have seized all cities and towns within Israel. At a glance, it would appear that the Arab states with a preponderance of population should easily wipe out the tiny Hebrew state. On second thought, however, maybe the shoe is on the other foot. The Jews are backed by the enormous international wealth of Jewry. Many of the Jewish men have either seen war or are the tough survivors of European holocaust. It is claimed that the Jewish forces are highly organized and mobile, equipped with the latest weapons and advised by American officers. While some Arab contingents are trained and organized, many are not. Five states cannot but be jealous of one another. The Arabs, though advised by British officers and equipped with British weapons, have been close to neither modern warfare nor to holocaust, hence are unproven.

It may be that Jews will now flock into Israel to supply new manpower. It should, this Holy Land situation, be interesting to watch. Should matters not be settled quickly between Jews and Arabs, Russia may interfere either directly or by infiltration and propaganda. Personally, I hope the Jews win, for then Jews from all over the world might immigrate to Palestine. But maybe they wouldn't, and the pressure against our huge oil holdings in the Near East would be imperiled. Those oil reserves must tempt Russian imperialism almost beyond self-containment, so near, so rich, so thinly defended by powerless Arab states.

May 18   Evelyn was tight again last evening, not reeling drunk as the time before but tight. I suggested that seemingly the only way to cure her was to leave off drinking at all. She would do so, she said. We plan to fill her kitchen with Coca-Cola, root beer, etc. If this doesn't work, I'll buy her liqueurs, the sweetness of which should sicken her before befuddling her head. She was bitchy yesterday evening but exceedingly sweet this morning. She has just been standing with her heel on my ribs and bouncing up and down on them. I'm out of my mind with the damn things. Dr. Pike tried earnestly three times to fix them to no avail. My jaw is again dislocated. I'm a wreck.

May 25   I informed Evelyn that if she ran over a month away from me, save in case of sickness, tiredness, etc., I'd leave her. Last evening I talked to her gently and explained what effect on me her controversial nature, her drinking, her leaving me at every opportunity every day and for days had on me. I appealed to her fairness, her love (if she has it), her generosity to reassure me she would stay within the generous limits of time I felt forced to name. It was to no purpose.

"I'm tired of trying to please people, you especially. It never got me anywhere. I never pleased anybody. If you want to leave me, do so. I assure you I'll get along. But I will not tie myself down to any definite time limit, and you might as well know it and go on from there. I'll help you all I can, but I won't have my personal freedom curtailed. After the operation I had, how do I know how long I have to live? I intend enjoying whatever of life is left to me and I won't let you limit me in any way. And you can think of me just what you please, and I know it's not flattering in the least. Perhaps I am shallow and egocentric and want my own way. Well, that's the way I am, and you can take it or leave it, as you please. I have no intention of being otherwise, since all my attempts to please have failed."

I can only thank fortune for the warmth and devotion tendered me elsewhere. Evelyn isn't worth my efforts nor my mourning. I wish I had another wife. She's a hard, cold, self-satisfied, unresponsive, callous person, not worthy of even such a failure as I am. She defies the bountiful springs of my nature.

May 26 I am at the verge of having enough of Evelyn's coldness and indifference. I've pulled over in my mind for months what a lovely wife Eva would make. I said to Billy while we were riding yesterday: "Do you like Eva?" "I'll say I do. She's a grand gal." "How about asking her if she'd like to marry me?" "I think it would be a fine idea, Artie. She'd make you a swell wife. You can't go on the way you are indefinitely being slapped down by Evelyn. It upsets you too much as well as sapping your confidence and pride. How do you think Eva would feel about it?" "I don't know. I really don't know. All I can do is to have a try. I think I'll have a try."

So when Eva arrived after lunch, I told her I had something important to me to say; would she listen attentively? She would. She did. I outlined my troubles with Evelyn at some length. I told her how much I thought of her. I asked her if, should I get a divorce, would she consider marrying me. She replied without hesitation that she would. I stressed my faults and my limitations and set against them my virtues and advantages. I called attention to my age. I noted that I was no longer of much continuous merit to a woman sexually. I said that I felt I had no right to hand down my ills and aches to children. I would not, I said, expect her to give me a definite answer for two years, for how could she know whom she would meet and how some younger man would stack up against me. She should, I felt, have her youth without strings. Nothing would hold her to me at this age unless she felt I possessed more charm, personality, worth, interest than the boys and men she would meet. When she was twenty, we could be more definite. Was she still interested? She was, she said. I was a darling, and my plan for her was fair and just, and she imagined I would continue to be held by her in preference.

So that is that. Maybe something will come of it. Maybe not. Her family will, of course, be opposed. She asked me what I was going to do about Evelyn, leave her, tell her, what? I replied that I'd keep on the way I was with her, loving her less though still loving her, swallowing the job she did on my pride, saying nothing about Eva. I felt that was best.

May 27 I said: "No more word from Trudy." "Do you know

what she said to me last time," Evelyn inquired, "said to me right out of a clear sky? She said: 'You know, I took Sammy to the psychologist.' 'You did?' I said. 'Why?' 'Because,' she said, 'he asked me to bring him. You know what he said to Sammy? He said, "Well, young man, how have your sexual relations been since your return? Are they satisfactory?" Sammy said: "Boy, you said something."'" Now why," Evelyn continued, "do you suppose she told me that? It sounded to me as if she were attempting to distract my attention. If you ask me, Sammy has you to thank, not the psychologist." And she laughed heartily at me. "It could be," I said, not discomfited, amused at her wily way of announcing she was aware what was what. I wish I'd hear from Trudy again. She doesn't keep her writing and telephoning promises.

If I discuss Evelyn with other people, I consider myself warrantably driven to it. I don't try to harm her in others' estimation, merely to ascertain if possibly I'm at fault. By treating me otherwise than she does, she could put a stop to my discussing her with others in exceptionally short order, for I am ashamed of talking behind the back of any friend, which reticence doesn't apply to what I write in here.

May 31   Yesterday, I said: "Can I sleep with you this afternoon?" "No," she said, "you can't. I've decided not to do that any more. You ask me as if you were asking for a drink of beer. You really don't want to sleep with me, just to relieve yourself physically. So I won't do it any more. You go weeks without it, and then it unsettles me and makes me rebellious."

I considered what she said. I replied: "You're exactly correct, Evelyn. That's my attitude. If I'm just to you and wish you were to me, I'll say okay. So I do say okay. Not, be it noted, that it's not one-half your fault for never appearing to enjoy intercourse, never wanting it, acting repelled by it. With very little trouble you could have had me wanting you before anyone else. But you didn't trouble. So in part I've been compelled by your indifference into the affection of other women (not that I don't enjoy it) in large part to fortify my self-esteem and my need for being loved against your palpable indifference. And don't think I like this latest ultimatum on your part. But it's just."

I asked Evelyn why the devil she stayed married to me. She replied: "I started a job and I want to finish it." It seems to me folly to stick with a job you refuse to accomplish in the easiest and most productive manner possible, refuse to a point where you become more apt to fail than to succeed.

Mrs. Powers came to talk with me last evening. She lapses into long silences as if she were very weary, and those silences discomfort me. During the day she had taken Jane to church, prepared a dinner for guests, entertained the guests. I wished to broach a proposition to her whereby I, or Evelyn and I, would, if she and Jane thought well of it, become, should Mrs. Powers die, Jane's legal guardian or guardians. I was at a loss how to approach her. I related some stories about my childhood, my family, my ancestors, dug the earth as it were before planting the cutting. She listened. She thanked me. I said for her not to answer at once, of course, but to talk it over with Jane.

I'm sure Mrs. Powers likes me, approves of Evelyn and me, but just how much of either I'm not sure. She said: "I don't know whether I should tell you this, Mr. Inman; it's so intimate. However, I guess you'll understand. I've always bought the best girdles. As I grew older, I felt I owed it to myself to keep myself neat. The other day I thought of you. I was at Slattery's choosing a girdle. My choice narrowed down to two girdles, one more expensive than the other but doing more for me. My natural Yankee impulse was to buy the cheaper girdle. Then I said to myself, 'Mr. and Mrs. Inman were thoughtful enough to fit Jane out with shoes, so that I won't have that expense, so why shouldn't I have the best girdle?' So I purchased it. And I thought of you. So you can see how you've woven yourself into the substance of our lives, Jane's and mine?"

June 3 I had another small talk with Dr. Pike: "Don't," I said, "let Evelyn get her feelings hurt. We've been wrangling about how much time she has off. I feel that a month away from home is plenty during a year. She doesn't. She's very greedy, and the nicer to her I am the greedier she gets. I feel she should stay at home more." "She never says a word to me about your differences, Arthur. She isn't as strong as she seems or she wouldn't get these colds." "She's plenty of strength, as you yourself told me once, to get her own way, to stand out for it. I feel she should stay at home more." "Well," he said, "that's your business, Arthur." "I know it," I said, "but don't let her get discouraged, for I think she's being unjust and I intend keeping at the matter until she moderates her greediness. I want to be fair, but after all she's supposed to be my wife. I feel she should stay at home more, not make so many or so long trips. You can see my point, that I feel she should stay at home more, can't you, Dr. Pike?" To which I received an ambiguous remark. But I'm sure he got the point. My idea is that if I can't control her, I can cause him to help me indirectly, he being a more sensitized person than Evelyn and far more ready to avoid psychological trouble or unpleasantness.

June 10   Planned a long ride on a cool, overcast day. Cadillac broke on overpass over Huntington Avenue. I sat while Billy telephoned Mike. Mike arrived in fifteen minutes. More trouble with timing gears, cam shaft or broken chain. We have no other cam shaft. Probably can get one now, war being over. I hardly dare contemplate what may be wrong with my car. There's never a moment of straight sailing in my life, without veering winds, tacking against wind and currents, sudden storms, unforeseen stretches of becalmed sea.

June 13   Saturday morning I told Jane I wished to talk to her like a grownup. I told her about how I'd asked her mother if she'd like to have Evelyn and me made legal guardians in case anything should happen to her mother, and how her mother had said it was all right for me to speak to her about it. I said how sweet we thought she was, how I had enough money to take care of her. What, I asked, did she think of the idea. Her eyes twinkled. She clapped her hands. She exclaimed: "I'd love it, Arthur. I'd love it to death." "Would it help you? I don't think anything will happen to your mother, but just the same such an arrangement ought to make you feel more secure. Would it help you?" "Oh yes, it would." She leaned forward and took my hand and kissed it. "I like the idea very much indeed," she repeated twice, very primly.

It is my intention not to love her too much and then get hurt, as with Evelyn, Eddie, Patsy, Sam as a boy — all February people. They seem to fascinate me. The guile that works on all other sorts of people often doesn't work on them. And they are dynamic with charm sporadically. And they seem to have a weakness for me when not reacting violently to elude the demands I make upon those who love me. The June people and the September people, I have found by now, are the ones I get along with best. If a seed comes up on a given date each year, a plant blooms on schedule, birds fly north almost within the hour annually, why is it foolish to think that the reverse is possible, that people born at a certain season of the year are apt to possess certain specifiable attributes of character?

June 14   Eva working on greens and mushrooms. She is painfully slow, unobservant, uncoordinated in her movements toward completing a given task. I fear I make her nervous. She would, I can tell by these relatively few days, be unable to bear up long under my rushing jobs to completion (the only way a limited allowance of strength permits me to function), my sudden shifts from one job to another to rest myself, the drive I put into what I am doing. She can't rush. Her change of pace takes place slowly. My drive destroys her composure. She'd be a wreck inside a month. She ran into a police telephone box on the way to get Jane Saturday, knocked it over, ruined the right fender. Out the door at once with any idea of ever marrying Eva. She couldn't take the emotional bundle I represent. She's a darling and a help to me three or four times a week. Let that suffice. Anyway, I could never love her as I do my wife with all her faults. To tell Eva at once, or not to?

In the evening, Juliette came. I kissed her. I didn't know I'd be so pleased to have her with me again, sitting beside me, talking away at a great rate. She seemed as pleased as myself. She told me about her trip to Europe last year, about how she and Clarence, as Jews, have been ostracized at Beverly, about the adopted son, David, about their new convertible Cadillac, about Clarence's flourishing businesses, about the gem of a colored maid they have and pay forty a week to, about the importing-from-China trade Clarence was in for a while, etc., etc.

When she was leaving, she said: "Arthur, I want you to know that even if we don't see each other often, I love you. I always will, and I'll never forget you." I was touched. "And I love you. I'll never forget how exciting it was to sleep with you. We must see more of each other. You're swell, and Clarence is swell. By the way, how is your sex life now?" "Clarence *is* wonderful, Arthur. And my sex life is all right. Maybe not as exciting as it was with you, but satisfactory. Just why, I don't know. Maybe the child has linked us together in a common interest. He's a darling. Clarence is mad about him, simply worships him. Everything is fine. And we really must see more of each other, Arthur. I love you very much." And I kissed her and she kissed me. It was a reassuring meeting.

June 17   Roderic and I read Beard's new study about Roosevelt and getting us into war. So far, America's most prominent historian goes along with my ideas stated in this diary at the time. He states chapter and verse along the road to war.

Evelyn is helping me. What a fascination she possesses for me. All other women are dull in comparison. When she stands above me on the bed and pushes my recalcitrant ribs with her heel and I look up her bare legs to her bare bottom, I have desires, as what man of parts would not. Then I feel bitter for the continence she imposes on me. Then I feel she has right on her side. Then I fall into a reasoning to and fro that debilitates me emotionally. Evelyn didn't go to Washington. Her father's operation was successful and someone in Washington, probably her brother, doesn't want her. I said to her yesterday: "Nobody wants you but me, and you haven't the brains to know that and to credit me with being special accordingly." She fell into a temper, but it's mostly true. She's too cold for other people.

June 22 Last evening, girl named May Rollins. Liked her. Twenty-one next week, not tall, dark hair and dark eyes, talkative. Small ride with Evelyn. Sat in rain in alley in negro section. Old woman leaned on fence and lauded dogs and belittled men while I listened to leaves on huge old poplar tree and Evelyn counted cats.

June 24 And this is the termination of another parenthesis in time, Volume 114 of my diary, four months' record in brief of the actions, thoughts, fears and aspirations, pains and pleasures of a single unimportant person of restricted activity and infinite rebellion against the involuntary process of being alive. The greater proportion of what has been recorded, I am painfully but helplessly aware, possesses little merit, much triviality and probably no general interest to anyone. But the keeping of the chronicle has abridged the futility of living to some degree. There will be other Books of Job to follow, unmeritorious as they may be. Man must work at something or fall sterile. Better to pile and repile the same bricks than sit unmoving while the bricks remain unmoved. The one action is at the worst less futile than the other lack of action. If the bird ceases to beat its wings while in flight, the body drops.

Vibrations from cars and trucks on Huntington Avenue having maddened Arthur to the point where he was ready to shoot himself, the Garrison Hall retinue under his direction mobilized to reduce the intolerable noise or escape it. Evelyn's mission was to persuade the Boston politicians — bribe them if necessary (what was money for?) — to have the streets dug up and repaved with softer surface. Billy tipped a man in the traffic commissioner's office to paint "SLOW" in big white letters on the street.

Meanwhile, on a frantic impulse Arthur bought a house on Cumberland Street and signed an agreement to buy what he hoped might become a noise-free home in Brookline. To pay for these properties, he planned to sell both the house he owned on St. Botolph Street and the "Place" in Jamaica Plain he had once called "Bernard's Elm." His dream of retiring to a quiet retreat did not pan out. The tenants in the Boston house refused to get out, and the Brookline house proved on closer inspection to be a dud. Garrison Hall, for all its disadvantages, was still the safest refuge. He reneged on the Brookline "white elephant" and resorted to sleeping pills, bromides, beer, and whiskey to tide him through the siege.

Other misfortunes complemented the plague of noise. Trudy Daring's husband ordered his sexy wife to stop coming to Garrison Hall and threatened to take "drastic measures" if she disobeyed. (Arthur thanked him for his "manly and straightforward letter" and promised that he would neither write nor see Trudy again.) Arthur's teeth, ears, eyes, and bones played hell with his disposition, but wife troubles eclipsed even these disasters. A bomb had been sputtering for months. Evelyn was beginning to put her foot down.

June 25   Thomas E. Dewey, age 46, was nominated at Philadelphia yesterday on the third ballot of the Republican Party Convention for President of the United States of America. He should become our next ruler unless (which is unlikely) the Democratic Convention nominates General Eisenhower instead of Truman. Dewey is small as American men go, only five feet eight inches, but solid, seemingly tireless, evidently a shrewd politician and a good mixer. He was born in Michigan, came to New York, rose to renown as a public prosecutor of racketeers. He was elected Governor of New York despite Roosevelt and is still Governor of New York.

I should surmise that Dewey is absolutely fearless. He has the cocky look of a young and successful man who will resist pushing around and flattery of the sort that made a sucker of Roosevelt. While subject to political pressure (witness the silly antirace discrimination laws in New York), on the whole his record as an administrator is, from my limited knowledge of it, commendable. New York has, I believe, a surplus rather than a deficit. Income taxes have been lowered at least twice since the war by methods so simple and straightforward as to seem obscure and unnatural to the usual devious and bureaucratic-minded politician. He doesn't believe in outlawing the Communist Party. He says he believes in putting the best men available into Government. He says he has American interests at heart but was not for economies in giving money to Europe. He believes we have neglected China.

He may make a good President. He may not. I'm at the point where I disbelieve every one of the bastards who rule until their actions speak otherwise. Honest rulers are as scarce as hen's teeth and happen to people anywhere very seldom and with wide interstices of graft, selfishness, corruption, overtaxation, waste, war, domination between. We at the bottom of the pile may only hope that our contemporary overlord—whether dictator, king, president, emperor, upstart military leader—may be one of those rare fellows, a beneficent and impersonally honest man with the genuine welfare of his country at heart. How many all but criminal rulers there are in history speaks badly indeed for the human race.

I am reading two excellent volumes on the Civil War, with stress upon the political and diplomatic aspects, the one, 'A Diplomat in Carpet Slippers,' about Lincoln and the North, and the other, 'Experiment in Rebellion,' about Davis and the South.[25] Whether the North would have won the war without Lincoln or not is debatable, but one is all but forced to conclude that the North might not have won the war without Davis. I still find few periods of history more intriguing than the American Civil War: violent clash of cultures in what amounted to the overthrow of the aristocratic rural culture in favor of the mechanical urban culture, final overthrow of the chivalric interpretation of warfare (whatever its reality), action made the more dramatic by the opposing parties speaking like language and springing from like ancestry.

July 8   Billy said: "Trudy sent me this. Did you ever read such a bunch of crap as that Sammy guy writes. It must be simply awful to be so insanely jealous."

July 6, 1948

Dear Arthur,

I have sent a letter in care of Billy so Twinkle wouldn't have to read it. It clinches the deal with Sammy. Dreams influence the dreamer strongly.

I can't come back! I'm sorry, Artie. He's my husband and I *love* him.

Always
Trudy

30 June 1948
Manila

My Darling Wife,

Hi "baby". I love you "darling". Here it is another month gone and a few days closer to my being with you again. Gosh "baby" but I love you so — so — much. Haven't heard from you for a couple of days. Had an awful night last night again. Killed Inman in my sleep and was being hunted by the law. Boy I woke up this morning and was all tired out from running so much I guess. "Honey" I don't know why I dream like I do but everything seems to be going against us. You were at Inmans and I came to get you and he was fondling your breasts and playing with Play-

---

[25] Jay Monaghan's *Diplomat in Carpet Slippers* (1945) is a readable history of Lincoln's diplomatic maneuvering with the European powers throughout the Civil War and his success in playing off one nation against another. Clifford Dowdey's *Experiment in Rebellion* (1946) covers the history of the Confederacy between the period just before secession until the fall of Richmond, with special emphasis on Jefferson Davis and the men around him.

mate and you had his penis in your hand and thats about all I could take "darling" I just blew my top. I'm so afraid for you "darling". I hate that guy. He gives me the creeps. Please write and tell me that all will be all right "darling" and that he hasn't and won't lay a hand on your beautiful body. I'm sorry that I have to write such a horrid letter "darling" but I dreamt that and it was so real like that I just had to tell you about it. "Darling baby" I want to come to you, to be with you, to tell you I love you and need you and that you're the most wonderful beautifulest wife in the whole world. Didn't have my wet dream yet maybe we'll get together tonight and no one will interfere and we can have the . . . you "baby" every single ounce of you. Be good my beautiful wife and in June we can really get together again. I love you "sweets". Real I do. I love you.

> All my love forever
> Your Sammy

I reckon that that's the last of Trudy. Thank God I'm not jealous. I've only been jealous once, of Sam Cooper, and that was no pleasure. Jealousy seems to take the cat by the tail and swing him around, clawing and screeching and spitting, and whether there's a real basis of inspiration for it or not appears not to matter. I'll give Sammy a couple of years of absolute control before she rebels or cheats. It was fun knowing her. She must have talked indiscreetly of me at one time or another. Feel sorry for her. It was fun knowing Trudy.

July 13 It's tragic to have to spend as much emotional energy as I do merely attempting to keep Evelyn sufficiently civilized and pleasant so that I can live with her. After a long and violent morning, she says very sweetly: "Don't you worry. I'll do better from now on." I reply bitterly: "Well, make it a few days at least. You have no idea how to get along with anyone save truckdrivers, Jews and artists, and you won't listen to me. Why, oh why can't you quit defending and arguing and listen—just plain listen? I'm a high-pressure boiler, and over and over again you turn the wrong controls and never learn better." "I'll do better from now on." "Well, as I said, see if you can quit turning the wrong controls for a few days. You want me to get off guard with you. How can I, when you don't heed your emotions and words?"

July 16 I think, if I survive what has me in terror right now, I'll go much more cautiously with other men's wives and sweethearts. I don't really understand violent jealousy, which lack of understanding should in no wise blind me to the potential headaches to be derived either from indiscreet words or deeds, the results of which I, an aging semi-invalid, cannot outface when they catch up with me, as once in a while they are bound to do. As Billy observes, I'm situated so that anyone can make a pile of trouble for me if they feel they want to.

To come to my worst woe, the one that's scaring the pants off me. Huntington Avenue has had to be repaved. The job is done. On the two sides of the Avenue is the best quality slick pavement. All night long automobiles at two or three minute intervals tore past at what must have been forty to sixty miles an hour. The vibration of the motors and the sound of the tires on the new pavement was so loud and so unremitting that I couldn't even get to sleep. It is worse than in 1941 when I tried to kill myself.

July 19 Saturday afternoon there was a trap for speeders on Huntington Avenue. Sunday wasn't bad. Last night I had a sleeping pill.

A very hot day. The situation in Berlin is causing the Stock Market to decline drastically. It looks as if we might have war at any moment. The Americans have announced that they will conduct aerial military maneuvers across the corridor by which our transport planes are flying with food for Berlin. There is discussion of running an armed train into Berlin to see what the Russians will do. Some overeager Russian can start a war in a moment, or so it would appear. We have just sent a fleet of sixty B-29 bombers to England and jet fighters to Germany. It is said that Russia is lining up 140 divisions ready for action. We have about two divisions in Europe, the French have five, and the British probably one. The Russians could sweep to the Pyrenees in a matter of hours and days, it would seem, with nothing to halt them save atomic bombs. It is rumored that the British Battle Fleet and the Turkish Army are under stand-ready orders. If I were a Russian and as hellbent on world conquest as they seem, I'd start a war now. They may or may not have the atomic bomb. If they have, it is sure to be inferior to ours and there won't be as many available.

July 22 No energy after striving to live through the Huntington Avenue traffic noise somehow to write in here. Evelyn and Billy are constantly on the go to carry out my frantic ideas. Billy was out in the middle of the night studying the traffic. I have no conception of where all this will end up. I'd rather be dead than anything in the world, certainly than be half-demented from noise I can't escape.

July 25 The clock strikes twelve. What a long, long, long day. Since the street was paved and I began to be wild, time has run out more and more slowly, and nothing serves to hasten it. I took both my pistols out the other day and made sure they were in firing order. At the least, I won't be afraid this time of life after death, what haunted me before. A pistol shot in the temple cannot be abrogated by medical skill as were sleeping pills. If I put the pistol butt in between radiator pipes and hold the barrel end with one hand, how can I miss?

July 28 Hardly had Evelyn gotten out of the state before the time bomb she had calculated to dynamite my self-respect and get her way began to splutter. Whitcomb called up. He requested an appointment to see me. Why? Mrs. Inman wished him to lay before me a demand that she be granted more liberty in going away when and how long she wished and a change of attitude on the subject. I told him I'd talk to him Thursday morning. I wasn't angry as much as shocked at her seeing fit to resort to a lawyer, "a clever old goat," as she terms him.

I'd been appealing to her not to go away so often to be sure but had long ago dropped as untenable the thirty-day ultimatum I made in the spring, untenable because unenforceable. If Evelyn wanted her own way badly enough, I reasoned, to take her case to a lawyer, she might want it badly enough to leave me if she didn't get her own way. Since I still loved her despite her constant forays against my masculine self-esteem, and since I knew of no one I liked better, I'd have to give in to her eventually. That being so, I'd hate her more for having to expose my defeat and myself to Whitcomb than I would if I surrendered to her. If I surrendered, I might as well do it gracefully and wholeheartedly; it's a wise man who takes defeat with grace and charm.

So when she telephoned, I talked with her at some length. "Don't you know," I said, "that I love you so much you can always get your way? Going through Whitcomb is quite unnecessary. I can't refuse you anything your heart is set on. You ought to know that. So have your way and call off Whitcomb as he is superfluous." "Get off the line. Get off the line," her harsh voice broke in. She added: "Someone's listening in." I was glad. I didn't care who heard. I hoped they all listened. She said: "Thank you for being so reasonable. I must have my trips away." "Well, you can have them. I don't like them, but I'll shut up about them. All I ask is that you'll be as generous as possible." I added to myself: "— you damned self-willed bitch." "I will," she replied, and "I said get off the line. Get off, will you." She wanted me to telephone her Thursday if she could stay Friday. I agreed. I told her to have a good time. I added a sentimental touch. "Bring me back some spruce branches, please?" I'm really not angry.

She's not worth being angry at. I hate her. I disesteem her. She's not much good. But I don't yet want to lose her, for I know of no one better. I'm going to change my will and leave Billy and Mrs. Trench more and Evelyn less and not tell her. They're both nicer to me and to my lame ego than she is, and such a change will make me feel better.

Later: What a morning. Whitcomb just called up. Evelyn, despite what she said on the telephone, wants him to talk with me. God damn her anyway. I wish I were in condition to be shed of her forever and ever.

Whitcomb will be here at eleven. Got to talk to him. Wonder exactly what Evelyn wants. Some sort of ultimatum doubtless. And I'll have to swallow it. Christ, I hate her. I wish I were a well man and could quit her. There's no end to what she demands.

July 30 The lawyer Evelyn sent up to interview me about what I didn't know—more time away it turned out—has been here and gone. I like him. He's seventy-four, dapper, intelligent, worldly, urbane, imaginative. I talked steadily. Unless I miss my guess, his visit will do me more good than it will Evelyn. If she can't comprehend me, he, Mr. Whitcomb, can. I suspect she has punctured her own case with him. I'm a compromiser by nature, being an Anglo-Saxon. She, being Dutch, isn't. I told him she could have anything she wanted provided he would guarantee to speak to her sternly were she, as usual, to turn compromise into greediness. This is the best morning's work I've put in for months. When men like me, they'll apparently jump through hoops for me.

I took Mr. Whitcomb into the library, shut the door so that the work on the air conditioner wouldn't bother us, began by asking him whether he was here in the guise of Evelyn's lawyer or as a mediator. "By Jove," he said, "I don't know myself. Say I'm here to have a talk with you. I'm fond of you and I'm fond of your wife, and maybe I can assist both of you." He then explained about how Evelyn has seen and written him about wanting more time. "She works very hard for you, Mr. Inman, as doubtless you know, and it would seem a wider latitude in time away wouldn't be amiss."

I asked if I could explain my side of the picture. I did, I think with fairness and fluency. I told him about the sex ultimatum, about how I had gotten Dr. Pike to be friends with her and she had fallen in love with him and how I had talked to him and what Evelyn's attitude had been, about how she had bought the farm in Maine in direct unobservance of a solemn promise, about her drinking, about her willfulness, about her income of $5,000 dollars, her own apartment, her own car, about how little I really saw her. He ejaculated surprise periodically. "I didn't know that." "That I'd never have guessed." I praised her good points, her charm, her self-sacrifice often. I stressed her unwillingness to compromise. He's easy for me to talk with for he's not only worldly and imaginative but is, I'm sure, unscrupulous in a safe-for-him fashion.

He asked if I were willing to try letting Evelyn have more time away and not to make it an emotional effort for her to get away each time. I replied that I was always willing to compromise. I warned him that she would become greedy and demand of me more and more time away. "I'll do it," I said, "if you will promise me to step in yourself and prevent her from overdoing the matter. She wants you to help her, Mr. Whitcomb. As a matter of fact, I'm the one you really can help. I can't talk with her and come to any compromise ever. And neither can I rely on her given word. Perhaps you can get her confidence, influence her to some moderation. Perhaps you're in a position to help smooth my life more than anyone has been for years. I want to be fair. I want to be just. When she wants her own way, Evelyn considers neither justice nor fairness. Maybe, if you'd gain her confidence, she'd heed you. You're intelligent and imaginative and worldly. I trust you'll do your best to assist me with my wife." "I'll do my best, you may be sure of that. I think I understand better your problems as well as your wife's. Maybe I can help you." "And I wouldn't repeat my arguments to her. She's heard them all before. Simply give your conclusions and your judgment and your advice." "You're absolutely right," he said, "and I'll do that, and we'll see what happens. Just be sweet to her and don't contest her when she wants to go away, and if she overdraws on your generosity I'll speak to her." I like him very much, and, unless I'm wrong, he likes and respects me and has revamped the impression made by my eccentric will and his pity for the 'poor little attractive wife.'

I related my conversation to Billy and later to Mrs. Trench. I told them that in the future I would be counting on them emotionally more and on Evelyn less. They're mainstays. I just gave Mrs. Trench a hundred dollars toward her vacation. She cried.

July 31 My jaw was out of place, and I called for Dr. Pike. I wanted to talk to him about Evelyn. I did so at length and, I think, successfully. I said I was having as much trouble with Evelyn about being away from home and travel as he had had with his wife about church and church doings. He remarked that he wished he had her back but still felt resentful. I said that he was an imaginative person and so was I and neither of our wives were and so we'd undergone somewhat the same baffling treatment. I told him I'd wanted Evelyn to have someone outside to go around with and had felt and still felt that it helped her and helped him at the same time. He replied that it did. I then assured him that Evelyn would pay more attention to him, not mistrusting his motives as she did mine, than to me. If he would nip in the bud some of Evelyn's travel ideas I'd be eternally grateful to him. "I stopped her from drinking," he said, as proud as a boy who'd shot a crow. "I know you did," I said, "and I'm deeply indebted to you. I couldn't do it alone, and I can't do this alone, and you can help me. It's very deflating to my self-esteem to have her want to be away so much, not to have her want to be at home. You can understand that. You can help me, I'm sure. Will you?" "You bet I will, Arthur. Only I have to walk cautiously. You and Evelyn are fine people, and you know I'm extra fond of you both. I'll do my best. We'll see what happens. Keep your crest up, old fellow."

It was a good talk, entered upon after days of thought and with a full realization that any bungling might have unpleasant consequences. Existing in a world of emotional women, I had for the nonce forgotten how reasonable and helpful men can be approached in apparent candor or with real candor.

August 3   I seem to have one thing and one thing only on my mind. At suppertime Evelyn informed Mrs. Trench that she would be leaving Wednesday and returning Monday — five days away — with Dr. Pike, because (to save face) she knew I didn't like her to make the long trip alone. Either Dr. Pike must have held down the length of the trip or Mr. Whitcomb must have spoken to her, for I find it impossible to give her the credit.

I have made an appointment with Dr. Pike for a treatment this morning, although I don't need one, and expect, if he is in a receptive humor, to approach him further on the subject of not taking trips with Evelyn. God knows he's told me enough times he'd "pull out" if his being with Evelyn bothered me. Nevertheless, he forgets what he has said and is a touchy, independent, arrogant person. So I'll be tampering with high explosive. I hope my tongue will spin the correct words and my face register appropriate expressions. I'm in deadly earnest, and he'll feel that, being as sensitive to emotions as a well-bred filly. Will thank him for not letting Evelyn be away too long, ask his help, remind him of what he has said, put it to him squarely that I'd like him not to take so many trips with Evelyn. We'll see. I'm nervous as a chihuahua dog when it's cold. I may be about to bring the structure of things down about my head. If he's harried or cross, I mustn't approach him. I must remember to look very, very doleful, for he watches expressions like a hawk a field he is quartering.

I have a schedule of things to do that will keep Evelyn busy today. No more afternoons and evenings off for her if I need her. My coldness doesn't bother her at all. I've started lying to her and only hope it doesn't catch up on me.

Mrs. Trench and Billy are on my side. They feel that Evelyn is both avaricious and unappreciative of my past generosities, not to say unfair. It's been amusing to watch Eva's emotions concerning me shift hot and cold, teeter between disapproval and approval. She feels also that Evelyn has been unjust and unappreciative of my essential goodness.

August 4   Well, maybe I've brought my world down around my head. I talked to Dr. Pike at length about helping me prevent Evelyn from being away so much. I asked him not to go on any long trips after this one for two or three months. He was not only complaisant, he was profoundly sad.

To be brief, Dr. Pike said that he understood me, said that he was only a third wheel anyway and was grateful for having let Evelyn go with him in the past, said that he was an old man and tired of his work and was thinking of retiring anyway and going to live on a farm and maybe this would decide him, said that Evelyn and trips with her were his only summer pleasure. He had me weeping inside by the time he was done. I told him how grateful I was for all he had done for me and that I had thought about speaking to him for several months before doing it. I told him it was a serious crisis in my life. Evelyn, I told him, had already been to a lawyer. Would he please understand it wasn't he I was in trouble about but Evelyn's greediness. He had given money to Virginia and since then she had been inconsiderate of him. My Father had given money to Evelyn, and since then she wished to be less and less at home. She wouldn't listen to any plea I advanced. My only method of approaching the problem was through the back door, so to speak, he being the back door. I only wished him to discourage her trips for three months at the most, not to ask him to stop having lunch and going out with her here in Boston.

He'd have to tell her if she asked him, he said, why he was stopping. "You do," I said, "and she'll walk out and leave me. You never hesitate to think of misleading excuses for everything else; you certainly can think of reasons not to take trips with her." He looked pained. "If you want to crack up my married life," I continued, "just tell her about my talk with you. I can't believe you wish to do that." He resumed to leaving his practice and going on a farm. I told him that at his age if he did that he'd fall apart emotionally and not to forget it. Hadn't he seen his men patients fall apart from giving up their chosen work? He admitted he had. He started to go. "And don't, please, please don't, brood on this, enlarge it, come to think of me as some sort of villain. I'm not. I'm simply on the spot and coming to you for help."

Evelyn was outside in Billy's room. I exclaimed to her that Dr. Pike was talking about retiring to a farm and that he made me sad. "Oh, he's been toying with that idea for months. He's been fifty years in practice. I'm trying to dissuade him."

Evelyn and he leave this morning for her goddamn farm. Maybe he'll tell her. Maybe he won't. Maybe he'll give up his practice. Maybe he won't. Hell with it all. If he feels this dependent upon Evelyn, time I put some sand in the gearbox. Might as well collapse everything around my head at one swoop. I'd feel rotten inside if I didn't attempt to take steps to counter Evelyn's injustice. Any man who accepts injustice quiescently is either a coward or indigent emotionally.

I can't help wondering, however, in what state of mind Evelyn and Dr. Pike will return next Monday, and what will avalanche on my emotions then. Oh well, save physically I'm a tough bastard underneath, and doubtless I can take it or turn it to some account.

August 5 Much consideration leads me to feel that I did the right thing to talk with Dr. Pike. He won't want to explode my marriage in my face. He should keep quiet. I'll be worrying, naturally, but that with my nature can't be avoided.

Mr. Whitcomb just called up. He said that Evelyn has been in touch with him and had wanted to be sure that I knew she was in earnest "about this business" and would get what she wanted or else leave me. This, when Fred is due any moment to pump my stomach. I wish I had another wife or felt prepared to drop this one.

August 6 I thought over Whitcomb's offer to come to talk to me. I had Eva telephone him this morning. He will be here to see me at eleven. I don't know what legal ethics are, if they exist even, but I consider that, after years of being my lawyer and taking my payments, it's wrong that he should turn around and act for her against me. I'm going to tell him so. If that doesn't get anywhere, I think I'll tell him she calls him "an old goat." That should shake him.

I've also written my fifth unsent letter to my Father begging him to give or will no more money to Evelyn. I'll send Billy to Maine with the letter, if it has to be sent, and with a second letter in his pocket (in case Father pays no attention and sides with Evelyn) telling him I have his letters to Mother while she was abroad, his pleading letters, and how she used to brag to me about her ultimatum to him that she'd travel or leave him. He didn't like that so he should understand my case now and side with me. That should blow the works one way or the other.

I opened a letter to Evelyn by mistake just now from the Bibb Manufacturing Company referring to a request made by her several days ago to change her address and send checks to Evelyn Inman, the First National Bank of Boston and to mail other communications to a different address, I don't know what address as the letter failed to specify. She's making sure she has her money removed from me. I'll respond by opening new savings bank accounts in my name only.

As for Billy and Mrs. Trench, they couldn't be sweeter or stand by me more heartily. They worry large circles under their eyes. Even Dottie, usually dispassionate, feels Evelyn in the wrong. They all take into account the shock of finding herself with cancer a year and a half ago and the operation she underwent and the feeling she must have that no one can assure her the cancer will not return somewhere, so that perhaps her days are numbered and she must therefore have more liberty and freedom than formerly.

I take that into account too and am willing to be generous. But this threat that she will leave me if her way is not had shames me in conceding to it. I'll make matters as hard for her, if I must concede, as I am able, directly and indirectly. She's my enemy. She showed no decency going to Whitcomb. I'll show none. Her Dutch blood has aroused my Scotch Highland blood. Evidently — and this is good — Dr. Pike hasn't spoken to her about my talk with him. If he refrains and still heeds my wishes, I can hamstring her activities. I'll talk with Woody this afternoon. She can be secretive. It's a nasty sort of married life, but I'd have no respect for myself unless I used every guile and wile and measure to circumvent and circumscribe Evelyn. Lord, she could have come to me sweetly and gently and said: "Arthur dear, I'm frightened about my future. I don't know whether I'll live or die. I'd love you even more devotedly if you'd be even more unselfish and let me go on more trips. I'd love you for it and make up to you for your generosity in every way. Please."

August 7 Woody's visit was by way of being a revelation. I had no idea she limned Evelyn so clearly and so correctly. "Sure I'll do something for you, provided it doesn't entail being disloyal to Evelyn. I'm very fond of her, as you know, and not even for you would I be disloyal or hurt her." I told her about Evelyn and the time-off question and Whitcomb and the money and Dr. Pike. She could assist me, I said, by not going on trips with Evelyn until November or inviting her to Pawtucket. She replied that certainly she could and would do that if I felt it would help. There was, I said, no other way of attacking the problem than via the back doors, she being, if I might be pardoned, one of the back doors.

She remarked that it was too bad about Evelyn and me, that she had been feeling something was askew between us. "But you can't change her, Arthur, and don't fool yourself you can. She absolutely refuses to look at anything realistically. And it's a reprehensible folly on your part that you ever inaugurated, even fostered and encouraged, the relationship with Dr. Pike. I know, and I know that you know, she's been good to you, always with reservations to be sure, for many long years. It's too bad this is happening. If you have a contempt for her, why don't you leave her? That's what I can't understand. You'll never change her."

August 11   Upon the assumption that Evelyn was amenable to my financial plan, I made so bold as to rest my mind, taking beer, sleeping a bit while Eva rubbed my head. Evelyn, after saying she wouldn't discuss the matter with Whitcomb, telephoned him. He begins to hang like a nightmare over my shoulder. Of course he advised her to say no. I'm going to tell that well-meaning old busybody where to get off and soon. He wants the business, I'm certain, of breaking my Father's will, and I'll tell him to edge out of my affairs insofar as Evelyn is concerned or he won't get that plum.

She brought me a beautiful box with many drawers. I said: "Thank you, but when you're being tough and inconsiderate I'd like it much better if you didn't bring me presents. I don't appreciate them then."

August 12   "Have you changed your mind?" I asked Evelyn. "No." "And won't?" "No." "And the months I struggled with Billy and Mrs. Trench to give you your nights, all of them, free from caring for me; your own assertion some months ago that I had helped you more than anyone in the world and that you owed whatever charm and sense you possessed to me; and how generous and good my Father has been to you all these years; and the idea that if I gave in to you on something you wanted, you might aid my security by giving in to me on something else — none of these affect you?" "No. I would be resentful if I gave in. So I won't give in." "Yet I give in to you." "You're probably a finer, better person than I am." "So it's no use talking further, no way I can breach your resolve?" "No use at all." "Tell me, do you wish to leave me?" "No, now that you've told me you'll be more tolerant about my trips." "You're sure?" "Quite sure. I want to help you." "You have been successful in your ultimatum. You have resisted any and all appeals I've made to you about my Father's money. Will you give in on one point or will you give in on no points?" "Certainly I will. What is it?" "That Whitcomb wrote me again this morning. If you don't want to leave me, you'd best call him off. He gave me his promise not again to represent you against me. And here comes another letter this morning. If he keeps it up, he'll drive me away from you; he makes me nervous with his endless telephone calls and letters. I like him well enough, but his tactlessness annoys me to exasperation. He's an old busybody. Would you write him a letter and call him off? Maybe you were correct when you called him an 'old goat.' I don't want to be driven to do something because of him that I'll regret." "Yes I will. And he is an old goat. And I'm dissatisfied with his handling of this business." "And will you show me the written letter?" "Yes I will." "Will you write it now?"

She wrote it and it was quite tart and to the point. I had hidden his letter to her, the duplicate of his to me, and will leave it hidden. I hope that's the end of him for a good long while. As for Evelyn, there's nothing to be served by being unpleasant to her. I told her not to blame me for what Billy said to Father, for I had left it up to Billy; and not to hate Billy for whatever happened, for it was a dirty job I had set him, and his only object was to gain what I wanted. She said that she wouldn't.

August 13   Billy left loaded with instructions. I have no conception of what success he will have. He is a comparative stranger to my Father. Here is the letter Billy took with him:

Dear Father,

This is a letter and a request — a plea, to be more exact — that I don't like to write. But I can't think of any other course. I'm sending it by Billy, so that he can explain if you don't understand or feel that I'm making a mountain of a condition that doesn't merit the stress I put on it.

I haven't been too happy with Evelyn these last months. Ever since you gave her the stocks and made her independent, she has been going away from home more and more and more. It has come to a point, with her lawyer delivering ultimatums to me she doesn't do herself, where I feel I must speak to you. I have put it off for a year, hoping Evelyn's attitude would change and wishing not to disturb you. While I am loath to upset you, I feel it only fair to you to let you know how things are, before they culminate through some future gesture of generosity on your part toward Evelyn in what would be little short of catastrophe to me — her leaving me.

It was the financial independence given her by the Bibb Mfg. present that overturned the balance against me. I do not mean to minimize her loyalty up to now, how good she has been to me, what a charming person she can be. It is, simply, that the possession of a private income has gone to her head. I don't want to lose her. I am not hysterical, I assure you, though worried naturally.

If you want Evelyn to stay with me on any sort of terms, I ask of you — I beg of you — do not give her or will her any more money. I realize fully that for anyone so generous as you are, this is a difficult plea to grant. I suspect that perhaps you are unaware of another side of Evelyn she has kept from you. Please, please help me. I cannot overstress the importance of what I ask, and as I said, I am not asking you in a hysterical way but after at least a year's consideration and in the light of what is happening at the moment with Evelyn's lawyer. My fault in the matter, I think, is that I have loved Evelyn too much and tried to be overgenerous to a person who, however wonderful otherwise, is apparently not fitted to keep her sense of proportion in the face of generosity.

If you write Evelyn or tell her about this letter, not believing my dispassionate summation of conditions, she will in all probability leave me at once. I am therefore trusting you implicitly to keep this between you and me, whether you decide to believe me or not.

I hope that Evelyn's and my opposite ways of regarding the same matter can be adjusted, and soon. I'm willing to compromise with her always on her demands, and this time is no exception. She is rarely ready to compromise with me, however. So adjustment of otherwise simple problems such as all married people have are usually made into a matter of my yielding. I think — I hope — she will stay with me, provided she gets no more money to turn her head and emphasize her independence.

Again I beg of you, concede me what I ask. The present trouble came about only after she felt, because of your last present to her, quite independent.

I owe you more than I can ever tell you, and I earnestly trust that you will abet me in this latest heartfelt request, which I am convinced is a wise request and one on the granting of which my future in great degree rests.

I'm sorry to feel impelled to write this, for the last thing I want in the world is to disturb you. But I don't know what else to do.

Devotedly, your son
Arthur

My Father believes that Evelyn is incomparable. He will, I'm sure, take her part against me. I instructed Billy how to appeal to his sense of justice, his desire to have me cared for, his religion, the fact that my Mother did to him exactly what Evelyn did to me, both as regards to sex and travel, his sentimentality. I instructed him to suggest that if he didn't want to leave me the money he had planned to leave Evelyn, to do with it as he wished.

I further instructed Billy to try untrammeled emotional attack such as Eddie used, for instance on the afternoon (or was it the morning) when he talked virtually for four hours to prevent my Father from putting me in a mental sanitarium. If reason fails, Billy is to give in gracefully, there being no other recourse, as I see it. He is to get my Father to promise not to discuss the matter with either Evelyn or myself when he is here this fall and of course not to mention it to the Yateses. I feel that if anyone can succeed for me, it is Billy. He functions as I do: The greater the emotional crisis, the better his brains work. It's a nasty task he has. May the fates smile on his efforts in my behalf.

August 14 Yesterday Billy telephoned in midafternoon to inform me in a woebegone voice that he'd gotten nowhere. He'll be in soon now, it being nearly nine o'clock.

Later: Billy looks worn out. He talked steadily, he says, for five hours. Father feels so grateful to Evelyn for "putting up with" me for twenty-five years that he will not change his will. He feels she is noble, wonderful, good to put up with me so long. He has, judging by what he told Billy, quite forgotten how he felt when Mother refused him further sex relationship when he was forty-eight. He has also quite forgotten (his own letters to Mother to the contrary) how he felt when she treated him as Evelyn has done me. So he sides with Evelyn against me as he has always done.

It is very difficult to convince a man who has forgotten most of what he didn't want to remember and absolutely forgotten, who has a mass of convictions, prejudices that are virtually unassailable, who feels he has always done the best he could and hence is righteous and bound for Heaven when he dies. As I said, Billy got nowhere.

I told Evelyn I would have to rely on her promise to turn over to me any money my Father gave or left her. I told her again that I was a loser and hoped I'd be a good one, that she could be sure I'd not be cross or nasty because of losing, that in fact I'd try to be nicer, that if I get to fussing at her too much she should write me sweetly and ask me not to in a note and that if she were away too much I'd write her a note and we'd try to be more civilized in our give and take. She replied that she appreciated my sentiments and would do her best not to be greedy or cross or demanding.

August 15 I guess I enjoyed Patsy. She's a cold girl. She couldn't have been nicer to me. My mind was elsewhere, I suppose. She wore the very backless green checked dress I had designed for Evelyn. She looks simply beautiful in it. "Artie," she exclaimed over and over again, "I love it. You missed your calling. You should have been a dress designer." She seems now to like to be petted. She lets me watch her bathe and dress. She tells me everything in her mind. She listens to me as if I were the Oracle of Delphi speaking—very flattering. I didn't tell her all about Evelyn, only that we were having a hell of a time. She says that she can't imagine what Evelyn does with so much free time. She says that if Evelyn ever left me she'd be a very lonely woman. She volunteered she was coming again in September and pay her own way. She borrowed Evelyn's car and drove to Tufts, where she was offered a teaching job.

I don't think I'll ever again fall under her spell. It's merely flattering to have someone so young and pretty appear to be so fond of me, and I'm fond of her. I tell her what I think and make no bones about it, and she seems to enjoy it. She's so vain she pleases herself artistically and likes to be analyzed, wherein she differs from Evelyn.

August 22 This diary constitutes the portrait of a frightened man going to pieces—and trying not to—with whining motors the dropping gouts of water in the Chinese torture. I feel as if I can't endure it another hour, another day, another week. But I do.

Yesterday, as if my troubles weren't enough, Dottie, whose fingers were on my neck where she'd been treating it, with complete carelessness leaned on it to push herself to her feet. A neck cartilage gave. All afternoon the pain grew worse. At eight I asked if Dr. Pike could come. He came. He put the cartilage in place but in doing so pulled the bottom neck vertebrae and top back vertebrae apart. I'm still suffering from that. There was all sorts of noise last night. I had nightmares and sweats and finally stayed awake. It's either somehow get the road paved or kill myself. I know of nowhere to move to.

August 26 [From Patricia:]

You probably know as much about the Russian situation as we do. We don't know what to think, if the Russians do not want war they certainly are going in a peculiar fashion to prevent it. I don't see how they can fight us if they do not have the atom bomb, and if they have, this place is as safe as any. It is too big a thing to be scared about. They were so incensed about the change in marks, as they are determined to keep Germany from recovering. They do such darned childish things, almost like little boys fighting, yet they are dangerous children. They have the largest air force in the world, and the biggest army, with no scruples about losing a hundred thousand men in a battle. If Russia really wanted to take Germany there is nothing to stop her, the small army we have here would be wiped out in three days. So we can only think that they do not want to fight us, but to get all they can without a battle. I think they were surprised at the unpopular reaction among the Germans over the Berlin blockade. The Germans will go with whoever gives them the most, and at the moment we are in the saddle. But if they feel that Russia can offer more, they will be off to the other side. Whichever way it goes, the Germans won't be the ones to lose.

I most certainly am not bored, and I've always been a happy cuss anyway. Being able to amuse myself is the secret. Paul is always restless, he always will be, he wouldn't know happiness when he found it. As he is always looking for perfection. He has the damnedest idea of women, wants them always to be on a pedestal. He hates to think of them as anything but ethereal. And it annoys him to think that women are obliged to perform their functional daily habits. It is really funny, I feel sorry for him. He seems to need constant conformation that he is desirable, handsome and irresistable. The poor lamb, but he is getting more domesticated, he is down to one mistress now, a record for him. The poor things always think that I'm the one who keeps him from marrying them. While actually, I'm the only woman he has been able to stand for more than six months. And if I suggest leaving him so that he can concentrate on the current girl friend, he goes crazy. I think he depends on me to keep him on an even keel. Besides that, he needs me socially. He makes friends quickly, but tires of them just as quickly. While I hang on to my friends to the grim end. Which doesn't make Paul sound like a very nice character. And he probably isn't, as morals go. But he is fun to live with, and he thinks I'm wonderful, which is probably the real reason I stick around. There are times when I could throw up the whole thing. Then I weigh what I have against what I would not have if I were by myself, and I stay on. He is most quick to make up, and can take any amount of criticism, and has very endearing ways. He notices every thing and never hesitates to give a compliment, and of course, he is superb in bed. Only I wish he wouldn't get his urges at seven a.m. every morning. I simply cannot be romantic at that hour. All I feel like is "all passion spent". I'm not aggressive enough to satisfy him. He loves his women to pant and groan and to go into ecstasies over his body. While he will never forgive me for saying, that, while his particular organ was most useful, it certainly wouldn't take a beauty prize. He was so hurt I was flabergasted. I never dreamed that you men were so vain about the creatures. To me they look just like an old turkey gobbler's wattles. So we have our ups and downs, and it makes life more interesting. I'd never be able to stand one of those nine to five men. I'd die of boredom. Tho at times I'd be happy to turn in my glamour boy for a nice reliable plumber.

September 4 Cadillac motor broke, with no warning, into crunching and banging silence. It was just opposite Sadie's door. Billy phoned Evelyn. She came for me. He phoned Mike. Mike away for long Labor Day weekend. So that's the catastrophe for today. Maybe the motor is broken for good this time. What an awful summer.

September 9 You wouldn't think that a single semi-invalid person like myself could keep so many people hustling, perturbed, when I do everything in the world to moderate my demands and muffle my ideas. I feel intensely, and undoubtedly my feelings permeate my ideas and wear those who would please me down. Things that seem so simple to me often seem woefully complicated to others. My energy eats me up. Why should it not devour others interested in me? I suppose my mental and nervous energy reacts on others the same way their physical vitality reacts on me — wears me down.

Evelyn is very pretty this morning. She should have been a pioneer woman with chores, dangers, hardships, children to keep her mind off herself and her body and interests entirely involved in the problem of existence, not a spoiled and somewhat affluent motherless woman in an era of gadgets and travel, with too much time on her hands. Just the same, she's mighty attractive, certainly more attractive than she would have been as a work-hardened pioneer woman.

Our State Department still appears to be filled with Communists and infiltrators sympathetic to Moscow. There are Pinkos in the Army and Navy and God knows where else, in the atomic plants no doubt. Truman refuses to give information. So closely are Communists and Labor linked in many instances that to inform on Communists would mean — or so Truman or his fellow traveler advisors figure — loss of Labor votes, and Truman is by his actions far more concerned with Truman's future than with the country's future. Let us pray that Dewey when he gets in will not be overrun by Pink advisors. Let us hope he does not appoint Dulles as Secretary of State. We can only hope.

September 19 Fred tried to pump my stomach. I burst into tears and gulped up the tube. I couldn't do it. I apologized, said I couldn't help it, asked why? "You're on the way to a nervous breakdown," he replied, "if you don't get the hell out of here, and quick. You can't help it, you know, crying. Don't be ashamed. Here, take this half of a sleeping tablet. And some whiskey. Get out to the country as fast as you can." He was most understanding. The afternoon was quiet, and I rested, even went to sleep under Dottie's treatment. She concurred in what Fred said.

Billy and Evelyn and Eva are being wonderful. Mrs. Trench is being a hellion, the same uncompromising, nasty, pettish female as several years ago. I'm not used to purely feminine women who under pressure revert solely back to themselves and how they are being annoyed or put out or worried. I guess she's been without the usual dose of endless flattery I dole out to her and she succumbs. I told Billy I'd turn her over to him — I can do nothing with her. "I'll take care of her, Artie, don't you worry. She has a small soul, but you'd be lost without her. Just you keep quiet and explain nothing and try not to get excited around her. Do that with Evelyn and me, who understand it's your condition and not you."

October 1 Wild again. A heavy truck parked on Garrison Street for forty minutes. Someone gunned the motor up and down steadily. You could feel the vibrations in the floor and through the wall as well as hear them.

The more Southerners I meet in my life, the less I fancy them. They emote in place of thinking. They are intolerant of all viewpoints save their own. They are intensely superficial. Grant them their charm, their bravery, their fearlessness, their emotional drive, their executive capacity. Still I do not fancy them. I do not fancy the undeniably Southern traits that impel me. Come to think of it, Southerners have absorbed many of the negro's worst qualities over the centuries. I don't think I'll ever employ another Southerner.

October 8 A cloudy day so far. I feel awful, no sleep. Fred isn't showing up to fix ribs, but by cracky it's cloudy. Maybe a long ride. Maybe get out of my prison. I wouldn't live in a sunny climate for all Solomon's gold.

Had a nice ride. Bought vegetables. Evelyn and Billy both look worn out. Mrs. Trench is flourishing. I don't think there'd be a quieter hotel or apartment house in Boston than this one. Am working hard to be cheerful and reconciled. I just wrote a dog thank-you letter for Evelyn to the person from whom she bought the pooch. The dog, by the way, dislikes both Billy and me, which suits me as there's no licking and petting.

October 20 Have felt no inclination to write in here. Columbus

Avenue was paved Friday. This morning the noise on Huntington Avenue has me frantic again, however. I'm trying out a new secretary but don't care too much for her.

Billy is worried about money. He's satisfied with only the best for his house so isn't clearing expenses. I'd rather give him money from time to time than raise his salary. I said: "I told you not to go into debt with an electric stove, a huge refrigerator, a washing machine, an electric garbage disposer and so on. My Lord, Billy, you have everything electric except the toilet, and you'd have had that if it was on the market. I warned you." "Yeah, I know you did. But I wouldn't listen. You know how you and me love to spend money. I shouldda listened, but I didn't. It's just too bad you and I haven't a million between us. My golly but couldn't we have a time spending it."

October 26 Yesterday, a sound-preventive expert from Johns Mansville came about making a soundproof room-within-a-room in the library, a Mr. Kittredge. He thinks such a room could be made of a floor floated on the coiled springs and walled and ceilinged with concrete or tile blocks and ventilated by pipes that would be nine-tenths soundproof, at the cost of about $1,200. He sounded intelligent, but he liked me and when people like me they are always apt to be carried away by their desire to please so that their answers are no longer given with detachment.

October 27 Dr. Peters, the ear specialist Fred recommended, arrived yesterday at 11:30 and remained until 1:00. "I'll tell you," the doctor said, in his thick, somewhat Australian accent, "how it is. You have [he used a long technical name I can't recall]. It's very, very rare. Some ear specialists go through their entire practice without a case of it coming to their attention." "I thought," I interrupted, "that it was psychological mostly, perhaps altogether?" "Not a bit of it. The entire basis for your trouble is physical: in the ear itself, in your oral condition, in your nervous sensitivity. It is only psychological insofar as the trouble causes the superacute hearing. If I were you, I wouldn't soundproof my room until the treatments have been tried. It's not a psychological problem but one of a physical nature, and I know from my experience with the other patients likewise affected what a time you must be having."

October 28 I'm waiting this moment for my Father to come upstairs to talk to me. He wishes to talk to me alone, and God knows what he wants. May I have the wits and the self-control to say and act as pleases him. My nature seems to demand that I tell people forth-rightly and to their faces what I think and feel about them, constructively if possible to be sure, but tell them anyway no matter what eventuates therefrom. Here comes the Old Man now. I must smile and bob and act affectionate. The price for what I get, it can be argued, is low. Well, here goes.

Later: By heck, I got some things off my mind and into listened-to words that never before have I dared express. He opened our private conversation by telling me how I had shocked him by not wishing him to leave money to Evelyn or give her any. He could, he said, not give her money, but if he didn't leave her money what would people say? I replied that he would be dead, so what difference did it make what they said? I affirmed that I knew I had disturbed him and was regretful but that I had thought about it a year and had found no other course but to disturb him. Then he dwelled upon Evelyn's virtues. I agreed with him that she possessed them, but, I added, he had known only one side of her, and I had virtues of my own whether he recognized them or not. If he genuinely wished to have us stay together, he'd leave her no money. He would, he said, leave her money if and when I died. That, I replied, was fine. She had, I informed him, stated categorically that any money she received from her parents' money would be left to her nieces and nephews, not to me; did he think that was fair? He did not. He would consider leaving her money contingent on my death. That, I said, was perfectly satisfactory, and I would be very grateful.

He brought up the subject of her not sleeping with me, tendering the change-of-life period as a valid excuse. I replied that it was not the absence of sexual relationship as much as the manner of my dismissal that irked me. He said: "Your mother wasn't a very well woman. I kept away from her as part of my duty." "That," I said, "is not what she said. She bragged to me over and over again that she stopped you. It was in 1907. If you have forgotten it, you have forgotten it to save your face. You didn't like it then. You were very resentful. And you never profited by it, judging by how nervous and jittery you were later. She shouldn't have stopped you. And of all people you should sympathize with me." Well, that wasn't what he recalled. "It's what she said," I insisted, "and what Mrs. Serrill remembered."

He switched to Evelyn's being away so much. He remarked that anyone taking care of me should be away a lot more than someone living a normal life. He wasn't nasty about it as on other occasions. I replied that I knew that as well as anyone, that I had tried to be more than generous, the trouble being that Evelyn was greedy — the more I gave the more she took. Also, she gave me ultimatums that scored my self-respect. I told him about the time she had fallen in love with the man at Sea Island Beach. I told him, without names, of the time she had fallen in love with Dr. Pike and wouldn't be sidetracked until I had had to speak to the man and tell him to lay off. "If," I concluded, "you feel that our relationship has been all one-sided, you're slightly wrong. I simply haven't told you these things because I didn't want to upset you and because you've never before been prepared to listen. Evelyn is wonderful and I love her, but she's no angel and without me she'd have been as worthless as her mother."

He brought up, as a hundred times before, how when Evelyn had been in Atlanta years ago she had had things to do for me. I tried to explain that that had been part of my plan to give her poise, not pure selfishness. It was amazing. He listened to me. He was this time with me as with strangers and servants. I went on to discourse on how too bad it had been that my Mother had set him and me against each other. Yes, he said, it was. Then I told him about the advice he had sent me to school with and how it had ruined my life. He stuck to the rightness of such advice. I stuck to its being wrong. He would have, he said, changed my school if he had had any inkling of how it was affecting me. I had, I said, written my Mother and she had failed to enlighten him. I knew, I said, that he hadn't wanted me to go north to school and that it was her plan.

Just the same he should have recognized it. I added that if he had taken me hunting with him probably our entire relationship would have been different. I had always wanted to go with him and had resented his not taking me. He would, he said, have taken me if he hadn't been afraid I'd have gotten hurt. He had no business, I said, putting his fears above what anyone would have assured him were my interests, his interests and a bond that would have bound us together.

I told him things I had never hoped to tell him. He on his side for once listened without sneering, really listened. I thanked him for listening and observed that it was a shame and regrettable for both of us that he hadn't been ready to listen years ago. I feel that I actually made an impression on him. If he lives to be a hundred and ten, doubtless we'll be friends. I gave him a new view of Evelyn and a new evaluation of myself. I don't think he'll leave money to Evelyn before I die. I don't think he'll disdain me from here on. I still hate him, but all my filial inclinations, very strong, pull me toward moderating somehow my violent feelings. I told him what a liar Evelyn had always been. That shocked him, really shocked him. I strove, for every criticism, to give her credit in another direction, as she deserves.

November 3   This is the day on which Americans have a choice at the polls between two political scoundrels, scoundrels because in our system of government seldom can a man get himself up without chicanery, trimming, double-dealing, lying, dishonest opportunism. I should say that our country carries on more despite than due to those who govern. The virtue of our system is that it allows for peaceful revolution periodically. There no longer exists a wide spread between the two parties of the two-party system. The difference lies chiefly in the somewhat conservative coloration of the Republican Party: The rogues are less apt to be Irish and Jewish than is the case with the Democratic Party. Also, I think the Republicans are less socialistically inclined.

Dewey, all sources are agreed, will be elected, and Warren. Dewey strikes me as being a dynamic and self-satisfied little squirt, not too honest or too brainy but with a good enough record behind him as Governor of New York and certainly the interest of the country at heart more than Roosevelt or Truman. Warren I like and admire. I feel him to be sincere, forthright, a patriot with common sense. The House of Representatives will have a Republican majority. No one knows whether the Senate will have a Republican or a Democratic majority.

November 4 I feel gloomy. At this point, the Democrats have done what nobody except Truman expected they could or would do, gained a majority in the House of Representatives. It looks as though they have won a majority in the Senate also. Furthermore, it would appear that Truman may have won, though that isn't certain even yet. Truman was given up as a hopeless candidate by his own party. His popularity was low. He waged a one-man campaign. He traveled back and forth across the nation, probably at public expense, in a private train. He spoke in large cities, at tank towns from the rear platform, over the radio. He was tireless. He campaigned not against Dewey so much as against the last Congress. He slandered Congress and members of Congress and Republican candidates. He told lies by the packful. He attacked reputations. He out-Wallaced Wallace in pandering to Labor. He misstated plain facts to the farmers. He twisted and distorted. He ranted and raged and used invectives. His cockiness apparently never wavered.

Dewey and Warren on their side attempted to wage a clean campaign and forebore to rant and slander and use personalities without scruple. And the American people swallowed Truman's words at face value. It looks as if, unless Dewey squeaks by, we will have to live under increasing expenditure and waste, under higher taxation, under controls, under the influence of Labor on Government, under further inroads by Communists, under what will in all probability amount to a social labor control. So I am gloomy. More later as to who will be the next President.

Noon: With the betting odds 15 – 1 against Truman, he has been reelected, Dewey having conceded the victory. The election is likewise a great compliment to Roosevelt and his gang, how thoroughly they trained Americans in leftist precepts. One cannot but have a sneaking admiration for the self-confidence and vigor Truman put into his campaign. I fear, however, that he has slid a long way to the left. He has no intellect and many times no intelligence. He is always ready to sacrifice the country to his own interests. He will be under constant pressure from Moscow-inspired leftists. He has already evidenced a stubborn reluctance to act against proved Communists, forbidding any branch of the executive setup to release documents to any investigating committee. He loves to spend money. Opposition incenses him.

November 8 Aunt Helen used to say: "You have no idea how charming Evelyn can be. She's at her worst with you, very unfortunately." On Saturday she made spry remarks, witty remarks, was pleasant all day, made a real effort to be pleasant and amusing in the evening. She was charming. But I can count those days almost on my two hands in a year. Her spry time is morning when I'm sunk. My spry time is evening when bed is her first thought. I wish she would make more effort to be charming and pleasant. Too many trifles annoy her or arouse her contempt. Perhaps I'm not attractive enough to warrant the exertion of her best qualities. And she underestimates and undervalues the traits I do possess that others find lovable and commendable.

As much as it irks me to admit it, the dog appears to have benefited her nature. The animal sits and looks at her raptly and scarcely is aware of the existence of others. It likes only women. I tell Evelyn it is a Lesbian. Some man must have beaten it or kicked it. The very movement of a foot causes it to growl. Her name is "Lady Mike." I call her "Lady Stinko," because she smells so highly. It's a gentle dog in the house and full of energy outdoors. It is smart as animals go, not handsome like the other English bull terrier Evelyn had but much more knowing and bidable. I don't believe I could object to a dog less.

November 10 Trudy called up last evening. She spoke to Mrs. Trench. She wanted to know if she could come see me evenings and make some money. I replied through Mrs. Trench that I was afraid not, for I had written her husband I wouldn't see her. If she got his written permission, I'd love to see her. And I would. It would help a lot. The very thought of her sets me sexually tingling. No one ever had so much attraction for me that way. But I've got to show sense and restraint and abstain. I wish no run-in with her sex-ridden husband. It takes all my will power not to take a chance and have Trudy here. She's a match to my fuse, that yellow-eyed piece of heat.

November 12 I'm sitting up waiting to find out just how badly my glass frames are bent. I asked Billy to change a plug. I was merely discussing it. The damn fool takes an open knife and slashes across the live wire at which I was looking. I threw my hands up to protect my eyes, my lids shutting slowly, and broke the lens and bent the frames I have so excruciatingly guarded all these years. When I could see again in half an hour or so, I tried to unbend the frames. I have no notion whether or not I succeeded or how well. Judging by past results from short-circuit flashes, I'll have one or two migraines. I could stick a knife in Billy's gizzard at the moment. He did exactly this before. I'm glad his long weekend comes tomorrow. He's abjectly sorry, but that doesn't cure the mess I may be in from bent frames and migraines.

November 16 I don't want to see Billy. I'm filled with resentment in his direction. I'll try to be nice, but I don't feel nice. I always temporarily hate those who carelessly hurt me, and no amount of rationalizing will stop how I feel.

November 18 What a year. What a year. Billy's back. The long winter of confinement indoors. Evelyn's ultimatums. Migraines. The noise. The trips to Jamaica Plain. Evelyn's trips away. My teeth. And other troubles such as car breaking and elevator breaking and stocks dropping and chair breaking and shoes wearing out. And bones always. And now this awful and overwhelming matter of the glasses. Where will this end? And what next? Evelyn leaves for Maine Saturday for three days.

November 21 I'm thoroughly disheartened. It's been nine days now since Billy cut the live wire. Pain and lights in the dark still are unremitting. Nights are worse than days. On the theory that I might be better off if distracted, yesterday I went to look at Billy's house. Sadie was so surprised she didn't recognize me. I saw only the first floor which they have fixed up with some considerable charm in a sort of pseudo-Victorian arranged clutter. So many vases and dishes and pots and knickknacks you never laid eyes on. The stairs are really beautiful. The kitchen is friendly. To be sure there are spots in bad taste here and there, but on the whole I approved.

On the way home, I told Billy that do what I might I couldn't avoid being resentful against him for how much I am being hurt. He replied that it was something, he supposed, bigger than me which I couldn't help. That, I said, was right, and it didn't mean I wasn't just as fond of him as ever.

December 2 Radio, unless you enjoy symphonic music or jazz, isn't much to listen to. There are lots of comical programs with the same old burlesque jokes and props used as when I was a boy. There are lots of quiz programs with hepped up masters of ceremony asking dumb audience members dumb questions and helping them answer. And a number of murder, police and horror stories virtually all ending on the moral tone that 'crime doesn't pay' though bloody enough for the old Romans, and dozens of soap operas with the characters all sounding alike. 'One Man's Family' is the only continued play written with thoughtfulness and intelligence. There are several long plays a week, but they are carefully broken up at intervals by music, so the feebleminded audience won't tire from steady concentration. Announcers sound like hawkers and side-show come-on men filled with artificial emotion and pep. Advertisements crowd the air before, during, after everything you listen to. I wish, almost, that there was at least one nonadvertising Government radio station on the air.

December 11 Billy returned from two days in Vermont searching for Cadillac V-59 parts without success. "It looks bad for us, Artie. They broke up all the old cars for junk during the war. We better advertise out West."

Evelyn's dog got in a fight with a small old dog who was unwise enough to charge it. She had great difficulty getting Lady Stinko to release its jaws. She was upset. "Maybe," she exclaimed, "I should get rid of her." "By no means do that," I said. "I believe that she's been a genuine help to you. I'd keep her at any cost. You never expected," I added, "to hear me persuading you to keep a dog, did you?" The dog does seem to help her. It is one-mindedly devoted to her. The other day she left it in the room for me to feed it some turkey I had left over. The dog sat and stood, nose to the crack of the closed door, and no word I said, no lure of turkey, sufficed to distract its attention. It bears with me now but dislikes Billy.

December 29 Evelyn has been shouting at me and talking contemptuous and blurring my directions by contrary suggestions. The dog's getting into a dogfight and her putting it to board at Dedham made her into a terror. I tell her she wouldn't treat her dog as she treats me if she wanted to gain its confidence. She's just left to get the dog. Having to take it out to answer nature's call, as the Victorians phrased it, supplies the only obligation in her life she can't edge out of, the only discipline in her spoiled life she can't avoid, and therefore I'm all for Lady Stinko. Any distaste I may have for dogs in general is offset by that one factor in this dog. Cats, being of her nature, made Evelyn wild. This dog doesn't.

December 31 Query: Can 1949 be worse for me than 1948? No doubt. Possibly. Probably. I am, whatever happens, grateful for my blessings and thankful 1948 wasn't worse. It easily might have been without as much health as I possess, without finances, without the love of Evelyn and Billy, Rose Trench and Eva, Dottie and Dr. Pike, Roderic and without the help of Trudy and Patsy and Mike and Fred and the rest. It could be a worse setup for me by far. Grateful I am, too, for the charm I possess, the initiative, the ingenuity, the perception where people are concerned, the ready mind, the emotional drive—those attributes which enable me to be a somebody despite spiritual scar tissue and physical debility.

Goodbye, 1948. You were a bastard.

The death of Dr. Pike in May, after a short illness, removed the man who had snatched Arthur from the pit in 1917. Although for years he had noted with varying degrees of asperity the flaws of his idol—spoiled, touchy, vain, stubborn—he had come to depend upon his surrogate father, always understanding and consoling, ready at any time to restore him with his healing hands. Yet Pike had been a kind of rival as well as superosteopath. Perhaps Evelyn, deprived of her old friend's company, would now begin to pay attention to her neglected husband.

It was not to be. Her immoderate grief, Arthur complained, made her oblivious to his own. Plainly she loved Pike in a different way than she loved him and took Arthur's affections (as he reminded her several times) more casually than she did Pike's. The doctor's sickness and death widened the rift between them. Angry Arthur held forth on Evelyn's deficiencies (while protesting he still loved her) to his Garrison Hall confidants, to visitors and correspondents.

It was just Arthur's bad luck at this miserable juncture to suffer an avalanche of pains—eyes, testicles, throat, neck, collarbone, shoulder—that turned his working and sleeping hours into a nightmare. He experimented with new doctors and regularly summoned his stomach pumper Fred Lakian, Dottie Bottomley, and others from his team of osteopaths. None could replace Pike, whom he yearned for "without end." Thanks to devoted Billy and darling Eva, he survived the weeks of unbearable sunlight and killing heat ("a horrible, horrible summer"), but he was still in the dumps when September arrived, still unhappy about Evelyn, and ready to give up on the Diary. "A worthless, unfruitful business, this writing," he noted, "like knitting off-size socks for children without feet."

1949

January 2 An unexpected bonus, an overcast Sunday morning with only a sprinkling of white snow, fine for riding. Billy and I went 'round and 'round the Fenway and Pilgrim Road. No one with me today but Evelyn, calmer at last, and of that I'm glad, for little attention have I left beyond my cutting lower ribs, my aching tooth and, most of all, my eye. I'm alone in my sitting room, beginning the entries for this year. I've looked at the newspapers. Cabbage is cooking. There's nothing to do but sit and concentrate upon relaxing and upon slowing down my mind.

Evelyn read a biography of [George] Catlin to me last evening and will read this afternoon. While the drawings in his illustrated diaries are doubtless invaluable as aboriginal source material and while some of the social activity groupings are somewhat compelling, I have this fault to find with them: The figures and faces of the portraitures are stiff and inexpressive and the faces more often than not those of white physiognomies rather than of Indian. Compared with the drawings and portraitures, for instance, by J. Wells Champney in 'The Southern States of North America,' 1875, Catlin's sketches are lifeless and amateurish, though doubtless it is unfair to compare the art of realistic drawing at its apogee with that of the mostly self-taught art of Catlin. I have never seen Catlin's finished oils. Judging by some of the examples in the book Evelyn and I are reading, they would seem inferior to none, the 'Buffalo Chase in Snowdrift,' as an example, seeming superb to me. I wonder if Frederic Remington studied Catlin's work. Probably yes.[26]

If I were well, I doubt if ever again I'd read a book. They are lame substitutes for action. Mrs. Trench never reads nor does Billy nor did F.D. Roosevelt, save detective stories. Books are more apt than not to confuse the simple mind and befog the outlook. Besides, if one is busy, what use are they? Aside from functional art, I'm really not taken with art of any sort, I fear. Roderic and I are reading a really urbane book, Thornton Wilder's 'Ides of March,' letters from various Romans in the time of Caesar to other Romans in the style of Pliny. If you would take the trouble to read Clodia's opinion of poetry, you'd have my opinion of poetry, which probably accounts in part or as a whole for why no one has ever paid my poetry any attention, the emotional content perhaps not ringing true.

January 5 I've read a couple of books on Hitler and a couple on Roosevelt. What constitutes the secret inner wellsprings of great

---

[26] George Catlin (1796–1872), painter, ethnologist, and author, spent a lifetime studying and painting American Indians. Both his paintings and written accounts of his experiences constitute a valuable record of Indian culture and domestic life. James Wells Champney (1843–1903), French-trained painter and illustrator, accompanied journalist Edward King on a 20,000-mile tour of the Southern states after the war for *Scribner's Monthly* and contributed 500 sketches. The *Scribner's* articles subsequently appeared in book form.

men—in this case both great men if measured by their influence upon history, though failures historically—never ceases to intrigue my curiosity. What rodents both men were. Yet of the two I'd rather have followed Hitler.

I've just finished a long book on postwar Japan. The author contends that the State Department's intention of democratizing an entire people has in three years given way to the purpose of fostering the conservative elements, keeping and using Japan as a base against Asia, China being considered lost to the Communists by the State Department. I hope so. Who the hell are we to will other nations to accept our form of government?

January 6   Many people state that Roosevelt was an incomprehensible person, very complicated. To me he seemed not in the least incomprehensible or involved. There was about Roosevelt none of the primordial mysteriousness of Lincoln or Lincoln's growth with office and responsibility. He was a lesser man than Lincoln became, a lesser character than Wilson, though perhaps a greater man for good or ill than either, because of his influence upon the character and ideals of the American people. Weak himself, he emphasized the qualities of weakness latent in all peoples, in his own people even, as he well understood, as Hitler, too, understood of the German people.

January 7   I enjoy my scheduled weekly visits from Dottie. Yesterday she wore slacks and a shirt, perhaps panties. Clothes are nothing to her. She loves to have me feel her large, smooth body, not a bump or a flaw on it anywhere, and I like it. She tells me stories of her family, her children, her patients. Did she pay attention to her clothes, were she ambitious, perhaps there's nowhere she wouldn't get to. Few if any people I've known have had so much common sense combined with luck. She's a crack diagnostician. Her treatments are too rough often, even for me. She tells me I'm one of the persons she loves most in the world, and if she says so, she means it.

In the evening, Annabelle came, seemed pleased to see me. With a Southern accent (she now lives in "Mis'sippi") she drawls: "I tell you, Arthur, I never enjoyed any job in my life as much as workin' for you. I tell you I've missed bein' with you. I've thought about you often—I honestly have." Annabelle has a pleasant voice, a pleasant manner. Of what she told me, I can vouch for little as she's probably still one of God's most apt liars.

"When I left you and went to Texas, Ted's mother and father met us at Belmont. They were very commonplace people. I was shocked with them. They drove us out across that flat country till we approached a vile smell. 'What's that smell?' I asked. 'That's our home,' Ted replied. 'God,' I thought. It was the oil wells stinkin'. I was dreadfully disappointed in their home. No effort had been made to keep it up. Ted's mother was dowdy and without ambition. It was hot. I hated everything. Then Ted came down with tonsilitis and had to be operated on. You remember, Arthur, Ted had promised to return to Boston and get a job here. When he was mendin', I reminded him of his promise. He told me he wasn't fit yet to go into a long discussion. I made bitchy remarks about his mother, the country, his friends. When he was better, he took me out one evenin' to a roadhouse. I'd never been to that sort of crummy joint before. Ted said it was where he and his buddies hung out before the war. I hated it and said so. I acted my bitchiest self. He drank a quart. He put me in the car and drove off eighty miles an hour. He turned up a side road and stopped the car. He jerked me out. 'You've been ratin' for this for a month,' he said. Then he beat me up thoroughly. I yelled and screamed. He paid no attention. He gave me a couple of black eyes. He worked me over from top to toe. Nothin' like that had ever happened to me before. Then he ordered me into the car again and drove us home. He went to sleep pronto. I lay awake and thought that if he was this sort of a guy, maybe I'd better stay with him. In the mornin' I worked the sob stuff just to see. Wasn't he sorry he'd beaten me? All he was sorry for, he said, was that he'd marked me up so much. He's a real man, Arthur. I'm perfectly happy with him. He's gentle and kind and thoughtful and madly in love with me. No, he's never beaten me again. Once he threatened to if I didn't lower my voice and be a lady. That was enough. He's a wonderful man. Since the baby came, I've been content. He must have somethin' I tell you for me to live in a little five hundred population Mississippi River town and be content. He makes two hundred and thirty-five dollars a month, just about what I made when I was with you, Arthur, and you know how I used to be about money. I behave myself, sew and cook and am happy. I don't ever have new clothes to wear. I never wanted to be a wild and bitchy girl, Arthur, but my mother drove me to it. It's been heaven without her. I love my son. He's very smart and very demandin'. We want three more children. I had an awful time givin' birth to this one."

January 12 Dr. Pike looked haggard and tired, very old. He has never recovered from the influenza he had last year. He insists upon walking to Boston and sometimes back to Brookline "just to find out if there's any steam left in the old man." There have been few occasions indeed in his long life when his body wouldn't respond to any need or objective his temperamental nature thought up for it. His psychology is as much governed by an ingrained determination not to be a "sissy" as by zest for his work. When he was a boy, as when I was a boy, it was a heinous crime to be charged with being sissy. So, by God, he'll show himself and the world he's no sissy, whatever it takes to do it, trekking across Africa, knocking the ice off a surly iceman's back, walking to Boston. Evelyn pleads and argues with him, but he's willful, pays no attention. It galls him to surrender to the letting-up process proper to his years. So he continues to exhaust himself unnecessarily. Sometimes he'll listen to me when he won't to anyone. I think I'll give him a lecture.

He worked very hard on my ribs yesterday. I don't know yet whether they're better or not, so sore they are. "Why are you so gloomy?" I asked. "It's my patients. They push me around." That was leveled at me. "You know," I said, "I think you're wonderful, sometimes stubborn, but wonderful. If you die, I don't see how I'll get along." He was pleased. "Be better off without me," he ejaculated. "I think," I said, "that if anything happens to you, I'll follow you into the coffin so you can keep me fixed up. I mean it." He finally smiled. But I'm worried about him, as Evelyn is.

January 13   The Jews in Palestine, using in the main arms and weapons from Czechoslovakia, have trounced all the Arab states surrounding them and have pushed outward their borders until they now include rich oil lands. They have shot down a number of British scouting planes, overcocky no doubt as Jews get with success, and now the British are landing troops to the south of them. The Arabs have lost face. It is to be hoped they will not now be open to the blandishments of the Communists.

January 15   It does something to an Anglo-Saxon American like myself to realize and admit that life is as Balzac pictures it: men and women driven by boredom, ambitions, petty spites, pure maliciousnesses, avarices, greedinesses, jealousies — in fine, a writhing nest of fratricidal, lust-driven, fear-reduced grubs, comedy to the gods, appalling in and of themselves. Perhaps it would be as well if these bitter diaries went down the drain. They are an outlet, a sluiceway into the cesspool of my utter misery and no more.

January 16   Poor Dr. Pike is still in bed. He's having bad bladder trouble, painful, with a fever. Evelyn and I are worried sick. He thinks it may be prostate gland. If he has that, he will never, he declares, practice again. Dr. Blake, the man he had for me when I tried to kill myself, is on the case. I hope it is an infection of the bladder only, but probably it's glands. Dr. Pike must be about 75. Selfishly speaking, God knows what will happen to me and to Evelyn if he dies or is incapacitated. Evelyn looks stricken.

January 24   Dr. Pike is better, provided he doesn't start out too fast. Eddie used to say that every man would be a wiser man were he ill, flat on his back for several months. Dr. Pike, Evelyn says, is filled with resolutions. I wonder, will they endure once he is on his feet again?

January 29 Dr. Pike was moved in the afternoon to Phillips House, new doctors feeling he should be under observation for a probable prostate gland operation. His bladder is now being drained. I worry greatly about him.

Myself am fatigued by the unremitting violent pain of the lower ribs jammed together and cutting into me. The ribs are so mobile there en masse that no one can move them specifically to obtain a separation. They make me wild and give me a headache. My mouth is filled with large cankers and my teeth ache. Fred comes to pump stomach.

February 1 Lenin once prophesied that the United States would spend itself into bankruptcy or something to that effect. It is still as it was with Roosevelt, spend, spend, spend — tax, tax, tax. Even allowing for the dollar's purchasing power being half or less what it was pre-Roosevelt, the budget is enormous. Rich as we may be, this cannot go on forever without culminating in something disastrous. The upper classes in the United States are being taxed dry and more and more ordinary people seek charity from the Government, relying on it for sustenance rather than sustain themselves.

Oh hell, who cares? Atomic bomb or throwing to the winds our patrimony. Rocks ahead, bitter way. Morning's paper announces perfecting and increased stockpiling of A-bombs. Will do us no good, for we will not attack Russia first, and to the surprise attacker belongs victory.

February 10 First of all, before telling the beads of my own woes, let me say that Dr. Pike was operated upon Wednesday a week ago and has come along so well that he was due to go home this morning. There was no malignancy, just a plain, straight operation on the prostate. He has been busy during the enforced idleness reorganizing the remainder of his life. Evelyn has been to see him at the hospital every single day.

February 12 Twinkle telephoned me once last fall but never came to see me. She works at the Shawmut Bank around the corner from Billy's house. I had him stop by one day to ask why she never came to see, would she? No, she replied, she never would. She had a job that paid her well for very little work so that she no longer needed my money. She had new friends so that she didn't need me that way. Anyway, she'd thought me over and decided she hadn't liked my attitude toward her last summer. So I might as well forget her. "There was nothing more to say," Billy concluded. "I left. I was surprised, to put it gently. I guess she's no good, another case of what you say about green eyes." I'll never see her again, which is too bad. I enjoyed her visits in the evening.

February 15   Evelyn sent me a sweet valentine. I think Dr. Pike's illness has shocked her into paying more attention to me, subconsciously that is. He's better, by the way. She goes to see him every single day.

February 24   Juliette spent the evening with me. Her stories are told with fluency and dramatic relish, and many of the interjections such as "you know?", "you understand" have been removed from her manner of speaking by the years. She's thirty-seven, most attractive, wilder than Evelyn because less conventional and with more imagination and more prodigal desires. She spends Clarence's money like water. I should think she'd drive him off-balance.

Juliette's stories sound like fiction but are, I'm dead certain, fact. Clarence is sure there's going to be a depression, has been losing money on his furniture business, can't find someone to buy it, is preparing to liquidate it. They are, I gather, worth nearly a million. They sold their house on the North Shore because the exclusive Gentiles there ostracized them. Juliette is looking for another house. She wants to go to Paris to have an affair with a doctor she met there. She couldn't be sweeter to me. She builds up my ego.

She asked if there were anything at all she could do for me. I said yes, sleep with me. She brought up the objection of Evelyn. I explained that Evelyn has put a sexual barrier between us and that she had told me she didn't care whom I slept with. Juliette said she would consider the project. She felt that as long as she loved Clarence more than anyone else, it could do no harm (as long as he didn't know about it) for her to have an occasional adventure. I vouchsafed that that was the way I felt, too. I told her about Trudy. Wasn't I, she asked, afraid of syphilis? She had a horror of it. Yes, I had been, I replied, but Trudy seemed clean and I had taken a chance and it had been all right. Clarence, she said, had never excited her. She loved me, she added, a great deal and she thought I was a wonderful person, and she'd weigh the matter and let me know. She felt nothing against it, just wanted to think about it. She kissed me goodnight with open lips, and I could feel the tingles run into my abdomen. She'd come again soon, very soon, she promised. I love her. She's a smart girl, and many of the corners that offended me formerly have worn off with the years.

Dr. Pike walked from the garage to the office and nearly caved in. Evelyn has gone to bring him back here and give him lunch. Gosh, I miss him.

February 25   Dr. Pike was brought here for lunch by Evelyn. He came upstairs and felt my back and ribs and directed Billy what to do. Aside from being thin, he looked well. We were pleased to see each other. I told him to charge me for the consultation, as I thought that would help his self-confidence.

February 26   A rocket 250 miles into the air. The daughter of a Hiroshima hen lays square eggs, empty eggs, no-yolk eggs. We progress?

March 5   Strenuous week. First of all, another migraine. On the heels of it, Karlsdorf calling on the telephone, yelling at Evelyn so bad Mrs. Trench could hear him twenty feet away in the kitchen. He wanted it understood, and he wanted no words about it, that there was to be no more coming to see me by his daughter during the middle of the week. She was going to do some real studying from here on out. He was her parent, and he knew best what was good for her. We had no idea whether Eva would or would not be coming.

Karlsdorf has never received anything but pleasantness from us. I recently sent him an album of Viennese operetta records. Evelyn took his wife to the opera. He's a boor, the Prussian petty nobleman's son with service in the cavalry you read about, arrogant, conceited, juvenile where people are concerned, possessed of erratic charm. Most American men would despise him and his authoritarianism and pretensions. While I know that Eva talks too much and refuses to lie to him, her life must be miserable. Were I her, healthy and with a way with people, I'd leave home so fast my going would make smoke. Or I'd recognize I was no scholar and lag on my studies until I flunked out. Not God himself can make a child study. I suppose Eva has taken so wholeheartedly to religion as a refuge from her father. In plain language, he's a bully and a not very smart one.

March 7   Am trembling like an aspen leaf this morning. Drinking beer to calm me down. Had a long discussion with Mrs. Trench. She had gotten all mixed up inside her simple soul about my not wanting her because we might be entering a depression and I couldn't afford her and wished to know if I wanted her to take another job. There was more to it, layers and layers down into her elephant-that-remembers past. I told her that I loved her, needed her, wanted her, was better fixed for a depression which might not come than ever before. Hope I have her straightened out. I'd be lost without Mrs. Trench, and God knows I've told her so until she ought to know it. My idea is to make such an emotional fuss that she won't want to bring up a suggestion that she take another job again. I suspect she's jealous of my getting a new person. Also, she's very money-minded, not stingy, simply aware of money.

March 13 Dr. Pike has evidently fussed and groaned and complained endlessly. Yesterday Evelyn suggested that he let up a bit. He must be better, for he flared up with his quondam independence—"If you don't like coming out here, you know you don't have to come." "Someone had to tell him," Evelyn elucidated, "and you know me, Little Miss Fix-It." She's been wonderful to him. I sent him two queries: Did he appreciate how good Evelyn had been? And how generous I had been with her because we loved him? How I thought he could realize for the first time in his long life just about a quarter of what I had been through all these years. As fine as he has been with me, as sympathetic about pain and injury, he has never had the vaguest conception of weakness nor the imagination to envision it personally. Repeatedly it would be: "Well, Arthur, did you have a walk today?", "Have you been to the movies?", "Say, you ought to drive up to the mountains this week for the foliage." Evelyn delivered my message. To my immeasurable surprise, he wrote me this letter, the second or third he ever sent me, and I thought it commendable and thoughtful and was touched:

Dear Arthur:

At last I seem to be headed right, and barring bad luck will be as good as new very soon.

I just wanted you to know how much I appreciate your kindness in allowing Evelyn to help me so much through this experience. No doubt it has inconvenienced you a lot.

Perhaps we learn through suffering. At any rate I have had enough nausea and downright weakness to make me understand in a small way what you go through more or less constantly.

Please accept my gratitude and kindest regards.

Sincerely,
Dr. Pike

Why I like 'All the King's Men' is because the author dares to express himself with unconventional turns of thought, similes, metaphors, vivid as snakes' tongues or heavy as splashed mud, put down on paper apparently as fast as they fall from the productive hopper of his lively and observant imagination.

March 26 Dr. Pike treated me yesterday. Seemed better. Told him he should try a tonic. What tonic, he asked. Named my Mother's standby. Offered to get it if would give it a try. Replied that he would. All but dropped teeth from surprise. He must feel gloomy indeed to accede to a medical suggestion so meekly. So Evelyn bought the tonic.

Later: Halfway to Place. Crocuses in bloom. A song sparrow singing. A flicker sounding. Ribs hurt and eyes blurred. Afraid I have torn a place inside the rectum from the iron pills constipating me. Always some sort of grit in the ointment.

April 2 It was reassuring to have Eva for two days. She nearly always gives me confidence in myself. We have fun. She's getting to be a large girl, must have grown an inch since last year, weighs 154 lbs. Brown hair, brown eyes, pale skin, small mouth, large nose, large spatulate-fingered hands. No beauty but sweet and composed and gentle. She dresses in too tailored a fashion. Her eyes are large, like Armenian eyes, under heavy eyebrows. She laughs easily and perhaps somewhat too much. She treats me with affection and solicitude. I'm so devoted to her that no doubt one of these days, when she marries, say, I'll get hurt. She's as sexless as a bedpost but not at all unfeminine.

April 4 Evelyn had Juliette and Clarence to dinner last evening. She wanted to know what Juliette would like to eat. I said: "Polish up the silver and put out your best plates, and she'll eat them." Evelyn demurred but acceded. And it was as I said. "I enjoyed the artichoke hearts, Arthur, but the silver goblets and the Coleport china — oh, they were lovely." She's a sort of special article, Juliette, and deserves all kinds of credit for not having allowed herself to become a fat, coarse Jewish mommala. She has the texture of skin the beauty products ads tell you most women have and they haven't. She's clean and well-groomed and clever in her own backhanded way. I really love Juliette. She's like a piece of expensive porcelain. In her intermixed way, brittle and enduring, emotional and intellectual, she loves me; and memories bind us. I do not feel in company with her and with Clarence that odd, deep-seated antipathy I feel for most Jewish people. I possess no more reservations in my attitude toward Juliette and Clarence than I harbor toward almost everyone.

April 12 Here's a start at telling about Janice. Last week, Wednesday I think, I sent Billy to talk to her. She greeted him, he said, with a hug and a kiss. She looks older but is still pretty. She has two children, a boy and a girl. The boy is "rotten spoiled," and the girl is "unbelievably homely." The boy drank Janice's coffee directly after being admonished not to and wasn't even chided, after which he threw his milk on the floor. It was difficult to talk because of him. Billy told her that in his opinion I loved her more than she knew; wouldn't she — etc? No, she would not. She felt bitter toward me because I hadn't accepted her having a child with unselfish pleasure. She was bitter because I had attempted to make her over. No, she would not come to see me. That would only open up everything again. I would be bitter and try to change her. She was happy. It would upset her. No, she would not come. "And," concluded Billy, "it sounded final to me. As far as I can see, she's put you out of her life and what she remembers of you is what she didn't like and what she has forgot is how you helped her. So I left. I brought you a picture of her and her boy and her girl and her husband, Bertram. Here it is."

A Christmas picture, tree, toys, small blond boy, smaller girl, Janice, pretty as ever, dark circles under eyes, porcine-faced husband, unshaven, unsmiling, not, to put it gently, prepossessing at all. I thought: "Anyone who can marry that man and sleep with him and have his mug in front of her every day can't be fastidious."

I thought back. Shoes worn down on heels. Unattractive clothes. No underarm care. No knowledge of how to handle people. Shyness. A lovely voice but few words. Father in love with her and she bewildered psychologically. No opinion of self on which to rely. Ignorance of cooking. Sloppy with desk, with room, with self, unfastidious. Yet with the makings, the ingredients of an attractive person. And with considerable thought and labor I made that attractive person. And either — I have now no idea which — she conformed to my teachings and suggestions from love of me or to shut me up. Of course, I'd like to think the former. At any rate, she learned, and in general what she learned she retained. The male animal always tends to be prideful and fond of what he has altered for the better; whether superficially or otherwise doesn't usually concern him. That Janice warned me repeatedly she wasn't what I thought her, I ignored. I loved perhaps (Billy and Evelyn and Mrs. Trench are sure yes) what I felt Janice was but which she actually wasn't. It seems that she was intrinsically an unfastidious person, else she would not have consented to marry such a repellent man as Davis and thereafter to live and bed with him. I may not be preferable to most people, but, by God, I'm a dozen rungs above that Davis. Even to get a home and children, I can't comprehend how she could make him her mate for life. She could have had other men. That I fail to comprehend.

I'm glad I sent Billy to see her. I'm pleased he brought back the word picture and the snapshot.

I feel that I must give some attention to world and national affairs, not because I still desire to, but because without a general background of current me, myself would be unintelligible. I am at this juncture the center of my world and make no bones about it. I'd rather be without pain than save a million men from pain.

April 21   Dr. Pike treated me yesterday. I talked to him. I said: "I want to talk to you. I've been thinking about you most of the night.

I've told you how much I believe your dislocated pelvis is to blame for how you feel. It puts people, you've told me yourself, in a blue funk. It discourages them. You walk as if you were on eggshells. You try to get your spine fixed instead of the base of the spine, the pelvis. You won't let Dottie treat you. You in effect deny the osteopathic theory. Will you let Dottie treat you?" "Yes," meekly. "And will you eat more?" "I can't. It comes up." "Then let it come up. It will nourish you before it does. Don't eat so damn fast or when you're exhausted. If you'd quit being so scared, you could eat. You can call it by whatever name you please, you're just scared. Of course you can't keep your food down. Eat less and more often. When you quit being so scared and use some judgment about how you eat you can hold it down. Just quit being so scared." "I'm so feeble," he objected. "You're doing as much work right now," I said, "as many men in their twenties. You've got to get your pelvis fixed, trust osteopathy as you've told other people to trust it, eat enough, don't let those medicos with their pernicious anemia scare you, and quit being so scared. You felt sicker to me in January and February than you do now, and I'm psychic about such things. You'll be fine if only you stop being in a panic." He listened.

April 23 Poor Dr. Pike. The hospital boys at the Mass. General have him in process of examination. He's discouraged. He's gotten weak. He won't eat. Doctors in general, medical doctors in particular, when loosed on a patient to discover what ails him, are sufficient to dishearten a gorilla. They are secretive, noncommittal, apt to go off at wrong tangents. Since they are human and conceited as well, they are more than apt to make mistaken diagnoses, and few laymen realize what a guessing game doctors play. The suspense of waiting for conclusions, the boredom of lying in bed in hospital atmosphere, the fear that what may be found out will be the worst all are enough to sicken the soul of a stalwart man. I'm sure that what Dr. Pike is afraid of is cancer. He mumbled something to Evelyn about having to undergo x-ray treatments each week. Maybe they feel he has cancer. Maybe he has it. Maybe he hasn't. But they have him in a panic anyway. And there's no one to stand between him and the loosened reins the doctors hold.

I wish Dottie and her common sense had his case in hand. I still think his dislocated pelvis has more to do with his condition than he knows. I'm worried about him.

April 25 I want to talk with Evelyn about Dr. Pike. She gets angry and turns every conversation into a discussion, every discussion into an argument, when I pop off. God, she's egocentric. You can keep no conversation away from how she feels or what she thinks. Makes conversation with her virtually an impossibility. Of course, she's worried. But she ought to restrain herself long enough once in a while to enable conversation. I've thought of Dr. Pike all night. He won't eat. Why? Maybe the doctors told him he has cancer so he feels he might as well die.

It has for years been my belief that cancer is caused by a virus or germ of some sort. Perhaps it is caused by a solitary virus, not by hosts of them, and the virus only becomes active under propitious circumstances, the virus being capable of lying dormant for years. Dr. Pike could have caught it from Mrs. Pike or from any one of the many patients he has treated throughout the years. If he has not cancer, then it is a matter of the pelvis and fear. Evelyn is to attempt to ascertain about the cancer today, if possible. I instructed her to tell Dr. Pike I wanted to know so he wouldn't blame it on her that she asked. Dr. Pike tells Evelyn he is 74. As nearly as I can calculate, he's a couple of years older than that.

MacArthur, by altering the system of government in Japan, has likely made the Japanese vulnerable to communistic propaganda. He is purported to have asked for additional troops. In my opinion, he should arm the Japanese and permit the old oligarchy to reassume control and the "Thought Police" again to function. It seems to me we of America have only three hopes: that our atomic bombs, long-distance bombers, atomic dust and our newly organized on-the-battle-basis air force will hold back the Russians; that they will choke upon too heavy a diet of conquest; that Stalin will die and the others in power fall to fighting among themselves. We should atomic-bomb Russia suddenly, without warning. It could be done. It should be done. It will not be done.

April 27 Dottie made a special trip to see Dr. Pike yesterday. She told Evelyn that she thought Dr. Pike's days of practicing were over. Though she won't commit herself yet, she says that "on the face of it" it looks bad. Evidently she suspects it is cancer. It looks that way, I fear. It is like having a large force, a buttress, a reinforcement removed from behind me.

I think back upon all the years since 1917 — the tall, self-assured figure came into my darkened room and as if by magic put in place my dislocated collar bone, out of place for two years. Dr. Pike has helped and sustained me and my morale. Save for some few times of misunderstanding, I always felt he would come when I needed him and more often than not remodel me so that I could continue to function. I recall the day in 1917 he made me ride with him up and down Commonwealth Avenue when I wanted to stay in the dark. I recall his stories, the feel of his hands when I was ill with flu, how he fought the surgeon who wished to remove my appendix, how good he has been to Evelyn, how he fell in love with Aunt Helen, how he has worried and fretted and blown his top, how tender he was often, how he came to me in the nights. I've heard so much of his troubles and pleasures that his life seems a piece of my life. We've known each other thirty-two years, and that's a long stretch. I don't want him to suffer. I don't want him to die. I don't want to be without him and his care and his backing. I hope it isn't cancer but dread that it is. If it is, I've been lucky to have had him this long as a friend and as a physician. Evelyn looks tired out this morning. If she's frightened, you wouldn't know it by her words or actions. Is she ever frightened?

While riding down a side street, I noticed a small, oldish woman and a rusty terrier. The woman waved violently at me. She looked a bit oddly dressed and a trifle shabby. It was Alma. She flagged the Baby-Carriage to a stop, opened the door, climbed in and plumped herself down on the back seat. "My dear," she exclaimed, "you have no idea how glad I am to see you. How are you? And the same old car. I want to kiss you." So, while the car was going and many people were on the sidewalk, she got to her feet and planted a kiss on my neck. I was fussed. She directed us to drive her to her house on Clearway Street. "I must see you again. I really must — and soon. You're a sweet man, and I love you no end." And that was Alma, an old friend not often seen, for she refuses to come to talk to me.

April 28 Dottie telephoned about Dr. Pike. The M.G.H. people determined that he has cancer of the bone marrow and that the condition is too far advanced for x-ray treatment to hold in check. Dottie concurs with their diagnosis. The condition is hopeless and Dr. Pike's death is merely a matter of time, months probably. It is the way he has always dreaded dying, after having watched Mrs. Pike die in agony. He has baldly stated that he would kill himself if taken by cancer. And now he has it in one of its most painful forms. He probably suspects the truth. No wonder he has been afraid. In this form cancer causes leukemia. Dr. Pike has jaundice. Because of the anemia caused by the cancer in the marrow, he becomes weaker, and because of the pain he eats less. If I were he, I should wish to be informed of my condition before I became too weak to kill myself. I suspect that such would be his desire.

I pity Dr. Pike from the bottom of my heart. It devastates my equilibrium that this should happen to one of the five people I love most, to one who stood between me and God knows what infringement of providence. I am a man in a forest with his redoubt vanished. I am a ship on the ocean with the home port made inaccessible. I am a military officer with the reserves depleted. I love Dr. Pike from the four corners of my nature. A man who has made himself the servant of his work, whatever his other faults and deviations may have been, is an admirable person above the ordinary rush of people. Salute to him, say I, and may I be pardoned for my emotional, melodramatic feelings — salute to him, and may his ending not be too unbearable. And may his memory be dear to my heart now and forever more to the end of my days.

April 29 My Father is due the 10th and expects to stay an unusually long spell. I asked if Evelyn wished me to write him and tell about Dr. Pike and warn him not to expect too much of her time. She replied no; it would only cause hard feelings. She'll be busy with Dr. Pike for weeks, perhaps months to come. I've fixed everything for her to go to her farm for two weeks in June. She says she doesn't know whether or not she'll go. I replied: "You didn't hesitate to go last summer when I was all but frantic from traffic noises. If you don't go now, I'll draw the conclusion of partiality and that not in my favor." And that is so. I've worked hard to arrange my affairs for her to go. I suppose she doesn't want to desert Dr. Pike. But she didn't hesitate to desert me.

May 1 In my estimation, I am just as bowled over by Dr. Pike's illness and impending death as Evelyn but still have hours of thought to devote to sympathy for her and planning ahead. She might, for decency's sake if nothing else, have tossed me a word of sympathy or understanding. Dr. Pike has mattered to her more than I have; at this juncture, I am of secondary consideration. I am not angry. I am not extraordinarily hurt, it being an old tale. But I am amazed.

Evelyn and I rode in the yards. She wears the red and blue figured silk dress that so becomes her, the black wooden beads I like knotted casually. She's very pretty. I said: "You're an amazing woman, Evelyn." Then I set forth what is written above, the part of it concerned with her apparent lack of sympathy and understanding, at least in words. She cried a little, though I assured her I was neither angry nor hurt.

She declared: "Of course I've thought of you and what Dr. Pike's death will mean to you. But I haven't come to solving that part of the problem yet, and I haven't the mind and the emotions left over from pity for him and for myself to cope with it yet. I would only be submerged in a welter of tears and futility. So you must forgive me if I'm slow on the uptake. And I think you're wrong that I love Dr. Pike more than I do you. It's rather that he makes me esteem myself more than you do, in particular in regard to my relationship with you. He has made me feel I'm useful to you and not an absolute failure in helping you when I get discouraged or you get to work trying to alter my attitude. He's been a tower of strength to me. You don't need him as a reassurance in the way that I do. He's someone who has helped you physically, but you don't rely on him as I do emotionally. Remember how you criticize him?"

"Of course," I replied, "I've criticized him. I criticize everyone, don't I? And if you'll think back, you should remember that I've never criticized him without stating his compensating virtues. I love him perhaps more than you do, and if you don't think I've needed him emotionally and psychologically and are unaware what he has meant to me — more a father than my own Father — you're without proper perspective. I told him a year ago that if he ever died I'd feel like following him into the grave. And that is exactly how I feel. I talk too much in a critical or analytical vein, I guess, and you always recall the drier parts of it and disremember the constructive good parts. And you've read too much of my diaries, where, as you tell me often, the best part of me isn't recorded. Of course I've needed him. Of course I'll be lost without him. Of course you will, too."

"Right now," she said, "I'm devastated by self-pity. I recognize it. But I'll get over that in time. I'm slower to realize things and implications than you are. You'll have to forgive me. I'll come to your problem in time. I can't consider it now and not be dissolved in tears. You do talk too much. I never thought of how your diary had influenced me, but I suppose you're right. I didn't realize that Dr. Pike meant so much to you." "Well, he does. And let me tell you, Evelyn, I'm just as filled with self-pity as you are, so don't feel badly about it." "We'll help each other," she said. I agreed. I said: "Yes, we'll help each other." And I held her hand and patted her and kissed the cheek she held out and uttered the old, old phrases of consolation that can be so pregnant or so empty yet carry, when genuinely and selflessly impelled, as a bridge of feeling, the deepest messages of affection, devotion, assuagement and encouragement.

She is brighter now, and I harbor no antagonism, hurt feelings, anger at being ignored. She's having a difficult experience now, one taxing her fortitude and upsetting her emotional balance. If I have more powers of sympathy and understanding and so can spread them wider, I should do so and not expect as much of her.

I wrote Dr. Pike this, which Evelyn is to take to him later in the day:

Sunday

Dear Dr. Pike —

I'm thinking of you all the time and missing you. During the major portion of my life you have been one of my strongest buttresses against pain and against despair, and your devotion has time and again given me courage and fortitude. I love you probably more than you know and wish I could do more for you right now. Maybe some day soon I can get out to see you. In the meanwhile, consider Evelyn as my ambassador of affection and believe me that you are rarely out of my mind.

It is such a beautiful day. I hope that you have enjoyed the sun and the air that smells of earth and leaves. Evelyn will give this to you when she comes. You have been more like my father than my own Father.

Devotedly,
Arthur

May 6 Dottie worked and heaved and pulled and pushed, and by God she fixed what all the men didn't fix. "What'll I do now to keep it in?" I inquired. "Get drunk," she replied (which I did later, on a tumblerful of Johnny Walker) and added: "I'm going out to Dr. Pike's as soon as I finish with you. I wish I were drunk too before I went. I hate to go. I can't help him." "But you do," I assured her. "You certainly do. He's done a lot for you, sending you patients. This is the least you can do for him, it seems to me. Sure you don't want to in one way. But in another way you should be pleased and glad to be able to help him." "But I have to lie bald-faced." "That won't kill you." "I s'pose not, but I don't like it." "And from here on," I added, "you're the one person I can call on when I'm in a jam. When you're loaded up with business and have to move patients around to come to fix me, I'm perfectly willing you should charge me even more than you do now. What's money for when I have it? If a depression comes and I'm stuck for money, I'm sure you'll be reasonable, as we've never had trouble getting together on that score. But I am counting on you with Dr. Pike no longer practicing, and I hope and expect you'll help me when I need it, and I'm sure you will, for I'm trying hard to be reasonable and not call on you save in an emergency. I wouldn't have gotten in this jam with my neck if I'd called on you earlier, but I didn't. I tried four doctors." She grunted. She hates to come to town. I let the unwilling accent pass. It never does with her to make her commit herself in words. It's better to trust her affection for me when the time comes that I need her. I don't think she'll let me down.

May 8 Evelyn has left for the Place to take a walk and pick lilacs. Yesterday she cried and cried over Dr. Pike. She actually talked sentimentally about him, how he always enjoyed little things like the shape of leaves, the way his setter dog acted, how he laughed, what he enjoyed eating, how like an Indian he looked in the woods. "It's so pitiful that anyone who wants to live so much should die. 'Do you think I'll make the grade, Evelyn?' he asked. He's trying so hard to rest and to be good. For the first time in his life he's striving not to drive himself. And of course it's getting him nowhere. And he can't understand why. And it's the most pitiful thing I ever saw. And he's so filled with poison he falls off into a sort of coma while you're talking to him." And she cried again.

It is amazing to observe Evelyn "take on so," as Namma used to phrase it. I don't remember another such occasion. What I'm wondering is, how will Evelyn treat me, better or worse, after Dr. Pike dies? I have no idea since her reactions are not similar to ordinary reactions. She should value me more, but that's no sign she will. And that I write this with semidetachment does not signify that I am cold about it all or that I do not break a leg to comfort her or that I fail to stay awake nights thinking of Dr. Pike and grieving for how he is and his imminent death and already feeling unprotected and lost without him. I'd swap with him gladly and be dying so that he could live and enjoy life and continue to help those in pain. I would make the change if I could in a moment and feel my life less vain for having done it. I could endure the pain, the process of dying, the bewilderment entailed, were I he, and go on off to the unknown a less futile man.

May 10   Evelyn is wild. The Old Man arrives this afternoon. I don't blame her for being wild.

May 12   The Old Man came day before yesterday. I talked with him for a moment yesterday but felt too badly to chat with him. He looks spry. Damn his heart, why couldn't he have gone instead of Dr. Pike? I'll try not to see him today.

If Evelyn doesn't get hold of herself and control her emotions, much too often bordering on the maudlin, she's likely to be ill. She still pays the troubles I'm having no more attention than one gives to the dog with fleas when the house is falling down. She's never carried on this way about any trouble I ever had or when I tried to kill myself or about her mother when they thought she was dying in Charleston or about any grief of any kind. She loved him, it is evident, more than she did anyone in the world. No wonder she too often shoved me around for his sake.

Women — if I may be dogmatic — seem to care most for those men who are not quite catchable by them, men they know will, if pressed too hard, leave them pronto. Evelyn was too sure of me. I could not or would not make my bluffs effective. When I was sweet, she took it for meekness. Dr. Pike could never be counted upon to remain docile or agreeable, and never could his willful actions be construed as meek. To please him she had to be on her toes constantly. She put infinitely more effort into pleasing him (she denies this) than she did, save occasionally, into pleasing me. He was a wild stallion in effect and I a haltered gelding. It was lucky for me, may I repeat, that he was honorable with me. So she cries and moans and all but keens as the one she loves fades out of this life.

And if I sound resentful about her love for Dr. Pike, I don't mean to. It was my fault, sprung from the most generous motives, that their association ever began in the first place. I paid no attention to Mrs. Banks's warnings. Since it was my fault, I can't fairly harbor resentment. I may think I rate more consideration from Evelyn than I get, but that, too, is a matter of opinion. The next person may feel I get more consideration than I rate. And, also, I may have loved Janice more than I do Evelyn for all I know. Who reads this should know better than I. Of Dr. Pike's attitude and actions I have no criticism. An attractive young woman was all but thrown at him and why shouldn't he take her? He has been, as far as I know or suspect, a model of restraint.

May 16 Several days ago Dr. Pike fell down from weakness when cruising around his rooms at night. Yesterday he consented to a nurse. The doctor told him he didn't have to eat. He told Evelyn yesterday: "Doomed an' know it." He whispers with effort, she says, and cuts sentences down to absolute minimum. "Don't wanna live. Not eat. Go quicker that way." I feel weak in the pit of my stomach recording this. I'm a mariner left on an islet surrounded by inimical islets and foraying perils, standing on the shore while the gunboat that has long forfended his safety, his very existence perhaps, steers away, is so far on the horizon that only a dwindling smoke plume remains, and that will soon have disappeared; he will be alone to meet and counter what impends.

May 17 Dr. C.R. Pike died this morning. The last smoke of the ship has vanished over the horizon. It is best for him and for Evelyn, who was tossing herself yesterday against Virginia's and the nurse's ultimatum that she could no longer see Dr. Pike. She cried all night and drank herself to sleep. She will not let me comfort her, and it scarcely occurs to her to comfort me. She reminds me of a child attempting to act grown-up. I guess I'll never understand her independence. Did she let me comfort her, that would be endearing. Did she comfort me, that would touch me. As it is, she cries by herself and for all the good I do — or so I suspect — I might as well be a stranger.

Billy was giving my pelvis the MacIntosh treatment on the table when the news of Dr. Pike's death came. "A fitting place and circumstance," I thought, "to receive such news." The waiting is over. It has been comparatively sudden as he would have wished it. He was one of the people I loved most in the world, and the person Evelyn loved most. His place, I know, will never be filled. Being a person who lives in the past rather than in the present, I shall remember him until I die. May — and this rather than the above is my epitaph — peace rest his spirit and may many small and lovely natural distractions attend him on his way into the realm of no return.

May 18 Evelyn opened the paper this morning and found an article about Dr. Pike. I turned away, not wishing to be torn emotionally. She read right through. Her lip began to quiver and the tears to wellspring into her eyes. I tried to evidence my solicitude for her. She pushed me away. I left the room. Later, still crying, she followed me. "I didn't mean to push you away," she said. "But you did. You do. You have about as much tact as a meat cleaver." "I'm sorry. I didn't mean it that way. I still have it in my mind that you touch so many women in front of me, what can it mean special to you to touch me." "I'm perfectly willing to stop that. I'd rather touch you if you'd like it." "You don't need to stop." "I know. But suppose I do. Whatever it means to me I'm more than ready to give up if it makes you like to be touched. Suppose I do, Evelyn?" "All right, I'd appreciate it. And I think it would make a real difference." So that I will try.

Once in a while what she really feels comes out. She said last evening: "Why I feel so lost without Dr. Pike is that he helped my soul. He always approved of me. You may love me more than he did, but you don't approve of me. You think I could do better if I really wished to. But he took me as I am and said it was good and didn't try to improve me. He'd say, 'You're so nice, Evelyn,' and when he'd start to fuss at me for something he'd stop himself by saying, 'You don't deserve chiding. You're a fine woman just as you are.' And he made me believe that he believed it. And that reinforced my whole life. The thing I'm most afraid of in my life is of impulsively choosing a stupid course that will be irreparable. He made me have some faith in myself by what he said to me. You make it abundantly evident that you don't approve of me. And that's why I feel lost without him."

I could have punctured her concept full of holes. Dr. Pike wasn't married to her before the law, therefore not subject to that wear and tear, so could afford to take her as she was. He didn't love her as much as I do, for he didn't wish to or at least didn't trouble to work at improving and polishing her. Loving her less, he was more ready to take her as she was. She disremembers all the good things I say to her and recollects the harsh or truthful criticisms I utter. Judging by what he said to me many times about her, he simply gave her the blarney, not his actual thoughts. She took his casualness and his blarney for what they were not, approval. I do not mean to belittle Dr. Pike's devotion for Evelyn, but I do mean to state explicitly that she overestimated him and underestimated and underestimates me.

May 20   Dr. Pike was buried. Evelyn flatly stated she had no intention of attending the services. She cried all day. Wednesday night she was drunk. She drank whiskey steadily yesterday. No such sentimental emotionality was ever exhibited by her before. I did my earnest best to comfort her, but endless laudations of character far from perfect galled on me, though I kept my mouth shut. It surely showed where he stood relative to where I stood. I only hope she doesn't idealize him until he becomes a fetish.

She said: "Are you so bitter over my relations with Dr. Pike that no matter how hard I may try from now on it will do no good? I want to know. It is most important." "Of course not," I emphasized. "Of course not. I'm no idiot not to accept what the gods may offer. Do you think I'm daft?" "Do you feel I'm going to try harder?" "I haven't the vaguest idea. I don't know you. You may and you may not. I'm neutral. I'm waiting to see. I figure I got you involved with Dr. Pike in the first place, so it was primarily my fault. It was foolish, but I did it. The act of generosity which I feel redounded on me has now run its course. Whether you will give me adequate attention or not from here on I can't even guess. I hope so. If you do, I'll be grateful and pleased and try to return my gratitude and pleasure in words and deeds. But I can't guess your course. That's up to you."

And I have no idea what she will be like. Any other person almost, yes; but not her. She has had the upper hand for years. Now, with Dr. Pike dead and Eva loving me and ready, if I am unsatisfied with Evelyn, to marry me, I hold the upper hand. If Dr. Pike's part in our lives is viewed with detachment, aside from professional services, perhaps it is fortunate for me that he died now. I may die of lack of Dr. Pike's services and help but not die of lack of his presence. Without Dr. Pike in the field against me — I speak of the field of affection — I am in better position to get along with Evelyn or so I hope.

May 22   Wow, but I miss Dr. Pike today. I feel he can't be dead, that he must come through the door any moment now. As with Mrs. Serrill and my Mother, as with Jennie and Uncle Joe, he was too vital a force to die when dead. I could put my head on my arms on a table, were I only an Irish woman from the back counties, rock back and forth, and keen my grief with abandon until it wrapped me about and there was nothing else in the world save that great grief.

May 23   Twice I have said to Evelyn: "Now that you have only me, I hope you will pay me more attention." I meant exactly what I said, no more. Yesterday: "Gee I wish you'd sell your farm and get something closer by." She launched into a vituperative, sneering tirade, misquoting me at every point. If I thought I could put the pressure on her now that Dr. Pike was dead, I was very mistaken. In point of fact, now that Dr. Pike wasn't here, there was nothing to tie her down. She thought she had had it out with me last summer. She wasn't going to be pushed around by me, and I might as well realize it. And so on. And so on. Her ugly, nasty voice rising hard and nasal. I tried to point out that I had not said a word about curtailing her time away, for that had been agreed to last summer. By attention I meant attention and nothing else. She brought up the resentment she nurses about my sending Billy to see Father last summer. I wished to curtail her independence. I pointed out that I had watched Grandfather Inman's undue generosity to my Mother and Aunt Nellie all but spoil their marriages. She made further nasty remarks. I asked her what she wanted me to be, a worm, never speaking? Not one woman in a hundred would, I pointed out, take offense at having been asked for more attention. What did she want out of marriage anyway? I was glad I had sent Billy to see my Father. I'd do it again. I lost my temper. I had rarely, I said, known a more selfish and egocentric woman. For three weeks, until I mentioned it, she had never given me a word of solace or sympathy when Dr. Pike was ill. All she had thought about was herself.

She snarled back at me. I cut at her. I am never so angry that I don't bear in mind to be constructive. Out of anger, I do believe, is often derived the most constructive results. It is extremely difficult, however, to retain a proper goal when dealing with Evelyn; it is as if I were talking to someone who spoke a foreign language and understood very little of what I was saying. I cannot communicate with her nor she with me. Therefore we cannot establish smooth contact.

May 31   Eva had a knock-down-and-drag-out fight with her father about coming here for three weeks this summer. By her report, she did well. I'm teaching her never to cause a man to commit himself to a definite "no," for then he feels bound to carry through no matter what. Change the subject or shift the focus of his ire or distract him somehow. And she's standing up to him and talking back without being defensive or losing her temper. I suspect he's jealous of my influence on her. She told him he should be grateful to me, for last winter I prevented her three times from leaving home. She sneaked here yesterday by back ways. This morning she telephoned to tell me everything was all right, which was thoughtful of her. If I can teach her what no one taught me — to lie to suspicious and dictatorial parents — I'll have done her a great service. That is what such parents deserve.

Bought an old Cadillac V-61 for parts, $250, and it was delivered from New Hampshire this morning. Now I can stop worrying about that problem.

June 2 This morning Evelyn was in a nervous fervor to get off to do errands for me. "Golly," I said, "why don't you calm down? I'd rather not get the things done if it's going to upset you." She said: "I must be concentrated to do the job well. And I want to do the things for you. Don't you know that helping you is all I have left to keep me going?" Then she started to cry. I was touched deeply. She left. I said to Billy: "How can I be impatient with her when she says something like that? She keeps my emotions pouring from one shaker into another, as the old-fashioned soda jerkers did their concoctions."

June 3 Evelyn — pardon me for returning to her — stated this morning that she looked forward to the future with hope. Since circumstances had conspired so that I was now her chief interest in life, she was determined to be more malleable and less inflexible. She was not going to demand what she wanted but rely on my generosity and perspicacity to sense when she needed a change and how much time she should have off. My mouth flew wide open. I was flabbergasted. "I figure," she said, "I'm not too old to learn, not too old to take advantage of circumstances, even at this point." "My God," I ejaculated most tactlessly. We discussed further her new professed attitude. I drew out the discussion too long. She flew into a rage, threw the letter she was holding in her hand on the floor, was about to jump up and down on it in a frenzy but restrained herself. "You always take advantage of my willingness to discuss matters I don't like to discuss by continuing to discuss them beyond my point of resistance. I hate it. I hate it. I hate it." Mrs. Trench rushed out of the room. I was momently angry, then, remembering Evelyn was a child, grinned. She recovered her equanimity. It's a hard row my Evelyn has to hoe right now, Dr. Pike lost, thrown back upon a need to readjust to me, myself frantic with pain and worry about doctors and what lies ahead.

June 8 I have $42,000 in savings banks, $6,000 in cash in my brokerage account, $3,000 coming in next month, $2,000 of which I'll add to savings. All this besides the Walton Mills stock, the Bibb

Manufacturing, the Riverside Mills, the Aldona Mills, the Exposition Mills (these are cotton mills in Georgia), the Georgia Power and Light, the Atlantic Company stocks and bonds (coal, ice, beer, refrigerator) and the Coca-Cola. Even if Father leaves me nothing, I should be able to get along, with drastic reductions to be sure. I hope Evelyn's parents leave her nothing.

June 16 I was thinking about Evelyn and Eva last night. If it could be done, which it can't, I would swap this minute. I resent Evelyn's attitude toward me. I heartily detest the endless bickering involved in living with her. I ought to practice deceit constantly. I wonder is she not entirely empty, like a boiler taking water at one end while it runs out simultaneously at the other end? Yes, I would swap her for Eva and, I think, come out the gainer. I am no longer happy with Evelyn at her best. She bores me.

June 20 If I were President of this nation, the first thing I should do would be to select a cabinet and heads of departments among strong and America-loving successful men (and there are plenty) with unbureaucratic views and no bureaucratic past. I should make it clear that I wanted the country run for the country's good and not to fatten and make more powerful bureaucracy and totalitarianism through welfare and bounties. I should make it quite clear that the moment I found an appointee on the upper level being blighted by the bureaucratic blight that is so insidious to most men or putting Government before country or attempting to spend himself into continuance in office, he would be arbitrarily dismissed.

I think that Government could be rejuvenated by a fearless and plain-spoken man surrounding himself by fearless and plain-spoken and honest-acting men. Lincoln had no fear of surrounding himself with influential men (even if some of them were dishonest or cut corners), and he summoned powerful antipathetic forces in his own cabinet. I believe that Americans like and respect plainspokenness and fearlessness and are no more averse to honesty in high places than to dishonesty, as long as it is picturesque and vital and talks in homely and arresting terminology. We are a nation more subject to words than to actions. Will such a man ever be forthcoming? I doubt it. The public is now, thanks to Hoover and Roosevelt and Wallace and Truman, too gimme-gimme-minded, and bureaucracy is too gigantically octopus-like in formation and greediness.

Sooner or later I think we are doomed. Any nation overdominated by its women is.

June 25 I tried out two girls evenings. The Isobel Turner one has too much vital energy for me, though she reads like someone out of a perfect dream. So I decided to take Martha Torrence if she would go to a skin specialist and make sure she hadn't acne. She went and didn't have it. She's cute and small and sweet and dresses prettily. Her smile is wide, though her teeth aren't white or perfect like Evelyn's. Her nose turns up. Her skin is bad and she has freckles, but the effect isn't too noticeable. Her dark hair is cut short. She has green-blue eyes. Her father is an electrician in Waltham. She will be 19 in August, has had a year of art study at the Museum School. She's only five feet two. She looks honest, reliable, affectionate.

Eva leaves today or Tuesday for Stone Hedge, a hotel of about 180 guests on a lake in the Adirondacks. She'll be a salad girl, pay $25 a week and board. I wish I were married to Eva. I've taught her as much in two years as I've taught Evelyn in twenty-seven, and she enjoys learning immensely and trims my advice to suit her nature. She's wonderful to me. She left, on a big pad, in large letters, "Evie loves Artie." Well, Artie loves Eva.

June 26   Martha comes today instead of tomorrow. She's a sweet child, as Billy says, "very, very cute." Her voice isn't too pleasant — a voice without culture. But we all like her. I feel she can learn to help me with the palliative treatments for she's stronger than she looks. She smiles a lot, believing that the act of smiling makes a person liked. Even Evelyn has nothing thus far to say against her. Mrs. Trench, since Martha offers to help her rather than just sits until called on, has taken a yen to her. People should like her as her clothes are well chosen and attractive, her face wreathed in smiles, her words friendly and tactful. Perhaps we are lucky.

July 4   The Fourth without a single firecracker seems not natural. How Sam, Jennie and I used to await the Fourth, save up our nickels for firecrackers, small ones at the insistence of the two families, though Sam of course was allowed larger ones than any my Mother allowed me, a discrimination I resented.

July 30   Evelyn looks haggard. She misses Dr. Pike, but not as much as I do, she being less sentimental and more independent. Still she misses him. She's trying earnestly to be more thoughtful of me. If only she wouldn't scold all the time and instruct everybody except herself how to do everything and all in the most condescending and scornful voice and tactless approach. With Billy she is especially culpable. He says he's so fond of me he'll take it but for no other reason in the world would he. I heard her talking to Martha in the other room, and if I'd been Martha, I'd have walked out. With Fred, casual icemen, truckdrivers, Jews, she's much better.

July 31   We have signed the Atlantic Charter or Agreement, whatever it's called, that gets us pronto into the next European war.

The Communists, having taken Shanghai, are driving south toward Canton. We give the Nationalists no help, which may be the greatest mistake in our history. The recession creeps ahead slowly, but the Stock Market has risen. We dispose of our heritage of wealth to assist and reinforce what remains of what we call "a free world," though the regime in the United Kingdom is very close to Communism and a failure, as all dictatorless socialist states are bound to be.

I'm hot and miserable and wish August were over. It's the least rain for the season, the papers state, for 109 years, and I'm sure the most sunshine since time began. It's been a horrible, horrible summer, with no end in sight. I live on beer and sleeping pills and bromides.

August 7 It sounds to me that in Germany now everything is set for revival. I believe that revival is most often based upon low wages for workers, good earnings for the middle class, high earnings for the rich, plenty of capital and the fewest possible restrictions on trade and commerce. Germany presently should be able to undercut other nations in foreign competition. The exact opposite is occurring in Great Britain—wages for workers are artificially maintained, the middle class is heavily taxed, though not as heavily as in the United States—and witness the falling off of prosperity. Wages of the workers must fall as business falls off. If not, chaos.

I believe that the health and salvation of this country lies in—

1. Less bureaucratic interference in supply and demand and distribution.
2. A return to the gold standard.
3. Helping foreign countries only in return for monetary reforms accomplished, a general lowering of trade barriers between nations, less Socialism, and guarantees on loans.
4. Giving workers stock participation in those companies they have worked for loyally over definite periods, as Sears Roebuck does.
5. Tying in wages and salaries to the Government indices of earnings, business activity, etc., as the agreement between General Motors and the Automotive Union.
6. Reduce Government expenditures by consolidation of bureaus and less Socialism.
7. Transfer all old-age, health, unemployment insurance from the Government—Federal and state—to private insurance companies.
8. Stop or reduce the bonuses to farmers for production.

9. Bribe foreign figures in power and out of power rather than giving unrestricted money to foreign nations. The Byzantines did it for hundreds of years, and it worked.

10. Carry on propaganda campaigns in Communist territory and elsewhere touting private enterprise and Capitalism rather than Democracy and stressing the opportunity under the capitalistic system for the individual to grow wealthy and rise in position and independence. Stress lack of interference by the Government as compared with the regimentation the Communists practice.

August 15 The confusion, the pessimism, the violent complaining, the interest in character and personalities, the searching for eternal theories, the apprehension in regard to the future of these pages must constitute an unpalatable mess, and the occasional sharpness or beauty or emotional content cannot vindicate the bulk. As with Thomas Wolfe, the good jewels of prose and poetry are buried in hundreds of thousands of deletable words.

On the other hand, if one wishes a current-of-thought transcription set down by a failure and a rebel, here it is in this diary. By God, I'm honest if nothing else.

August 17 I invited Dottie to lunch. She arrived. "Where are my eggs? Where is my bacon? And my toast? And my ale?" She settled back in the chair and grinned, her dark-blue eyes under heavy brown eyebrows alert like a free bird's eyes. Billy and Mrs. Trench and I all hastened to wait on her, each according to his talents. "This," she stated flatly, "is the sort of service I recommend. The eggs and bacon, Billy. The toast buttered, Mrs. Trench. The coffee, Artie, no cream. Ah." I watched her put away food with interest. No one eats so lustily — two cans of ale, two eggs, six pieces of bacon, four pieces of toast, two cups of coffee, half a large cantaloupe. "It was lovely, Artie. I wish to compliment Mrs. Trench and Billy." When my friends come to visit me, I want them pleased. I tell them to ask for what they want if I have it or can get it. That makes them happy. That makes me happy.

Dottie must weigh about 180. She has attempted vainly to diet. "I love food. It's one of the delights of living I enjoy most." Her legs are still thin. Her stomach is fat and her rear is wide and her arms are heavy and she is out of proportion everywhere. Her feet are long and very narrow, her head, with its short hair worn the same through every change of fashion, is too small for her body. Her mouth is too small for her face save when she smiles, which is very often. Yet despite the separate parts that fail to match, the incongruities and disproportions of her person, she conveys the impression of being handsome, and always of being a person of presence and authority. When I first knew her, she spoke very little and that in jerks and without color or interest-claiming sequence. Now with a little ale or beer under her wide belt, she can talk for two hours straight, often with amusing viewpoints and blunt turns of speech, even with zest, retelling conversations and happenings. Her children and her patients amuse her. I amuse her. Events amuse her.

As a rule, Dottie, knowing my shut-mouth policy, tells me in detail about her interesting patients. The latest is a woman who said she was unable to relax sufficiently to permit Dottie to examine her vagina. She put her legs together, writhed, wouldn't let herself be touched. Dottie sent her to Robert Ball, the surgeon who operated on Evelyn. All the woman had was a polyp and a tough, unbroken maidenhead. Evidently her husband had never been able to sleep with her. Yet he is devoted to her and she to him. He was so worried, Dottie said, that he all but wept on her shoulder. They're very happy together, Dottie said. "You never know," she concluded, "what marital relations are really like till you get deep into any couple's lives and secrets. Surfaces, in these cases, are deceptive."

Dottie is supremely happy with her husband. They love to play golf together, their scores not being five points apart at the end of a year or three years. Dottie's score is usually between 80 and 90, average about 86. No day is too hot for their golfing. Andy's foot practice is doing well. She sends him patients and he sends her patients. His office is in the Reading business section, hers at home.

Dottie has been particularly good to me since Dr. Pike died. Perhaps he spoke to her about me. She appreciates my not calling on her extra times save when I am out on a limb for fair. I guess I love her next after Evelyn, Billy, Mrs. Trench, more than Eva or Roderic. She's a character in her own right, and I had much to do with her development.

September 3 Gee, I'm frantic. Haven't had bladder in right place since Dr. Pike took sick. Up to bathroom three to eight times a night with it. Have sore throat and intestines not working right. Am wreck. Can't exorcise Dr. Pike from mind and emotions. Wish could have died instead of him. Looking back on events concerned with his death and illness, am sure he felt he had cancer long before others thought so and settled down to starve himself to death rather than suffer prolongedly as Mrs. Pike did. I feel much less a person without him.

September 6 It is now only by remembering about it through long habit that I turn to writing in this book. I'm not sure of the merit of what I wrote with so much diligence, assiduity and high hopes. I have no illusions whatever concerning the worth of what I now write. It is, save for a flare here and there, pure crap— complaints and iterated thoughts and guff—out of the rectum of a rotting shadow and of no possible interest to anyone save a psychologist concentrating upon the disintegration of a person.

Failing to find a replacement for Dr. Pike, whose "strong, long-fingered, intestinal, feeling hands" he sorely missed, Arthur turned to real estate for distraction. He had always blamed his father for sending him to college ("I was never meant to be a poet. I was meant to deal in money"), and now he began to buy old town houses in the once fashionable sections of Beacon Hill and Back Bay (eventually he acquired nine) and convert them into apartments. To assist him in this hard and costly if diverting pastime, he relied on a heating engineer, Dick Bridges, an amiable but not always reliable trouble shooter, to handle remodeling and decoration problems. The "Old Man" had certainly made "an irrecoverable mistake" when he refused to take Arthur into the family business.

Evelyn helped Arthur in these real estate transactions (it was she who mapped out the floor plans of the buildings that Arthur inspected from the outside), but he deemed her faults incurable and fired off more salvos against his "unimaginative, independent, speak-her-mind-if-it-kills-her-and-everyone-else" wife. He reported her "alcoholism" to his father and gossiped about her derelictions to the Garrison Hall girls and mutual friends like Patricia, who with husband Paul paid him a brief visit. Without tender Billy, devoted Rose Trench, affectionate Eva, adoring Martha and Jane ("Did you know how wonderful I think my Artie is?"), he could not have endured his volatile nonwife, "not worth the sauce pan in which she cooks me."

It seemed as if every part of Arthur's body was assaulted in these months—eyes, intestines, testicles, ribs—and so it is little wonder that he gave short shrift to international affairs. He dolefully noted Communist incursions abroad and at home ("Our house is being undercut by termites"), but the impending Armageddon paled in comparison to two private disasters: the crippling of Dottie Bottomley by polio and the decamping of Billy Minor from "his Sadie" and his unsuspecting boss. This last act of treachery threatened Arthur's survival. Lucky for him that Pearl Hollister Leuko, estranged from her Arthur-hating husband, agreed to return to Garrison Hall.

September 7   Reading book about redwoods. Imagine the thrill of the Chinaman who, in 1944 in interior China, came across single specimen of supposedly extinct species of redwood. Later, groves of it were found. Seedling and seeds were brought back to California and are now under study at University of California. As all Oriental trees flourish in the United States, forestry experts dream of new forests of redwoods in places where California trees, most of which will not flourish in the rest of the United States, refuse to grow. I like trees. Would have enjoyed being forestry expert.

September 10   Evelyn, with considerable labor, adding up telephone calls, as she didn't believe I added them correctly. She pays me $10 a month for her calls. Pays $18 for her car at garage. Pays for her gasoline and repair. Pays for her food. Calculates her food costs her $90 a month, though don't see how it does. I have been paying most of her doctors' bills since Dr. Pike died. She is actually tight-fisted about money.

She's really trying at last. She has told me I could resume sexual intercourse. I don't want to by now but am nevertheless grateful for the gesture. She still doesn't understand me nor I her. It seems to me she sleeps and eats her life away and is infinitely lazy. Most duties and obligations and arrangements she procrastinates, like toffee pulled out at long blonde length. I love her despite myself and my every attempt not to.

Note: I am aware of how bitter and disapproving I sound toward my wife. I endeavor not to be. Maybe I perceive her in a warped fashion. Motives mean very little to me and outward manifestations and behavior a great deal. Probably I am unfair. I don't want to be. Just reduce my criticisms by four-fifths if you wish. I have no notion whether or not that is correct.

She makes no new friends, and there must be something at fault in her behavior or it would not be otherwise, for she's well-intentioned and attractive to look at and not seldom pretty. She will do almost anything to help people. She has people to dinner, but they rarely invite her to eat with them in return, and that can't be solely because I'm not on deck. She preaches, and people hate that. She is condescending, and people will not bear that. And her table manners are awful. Life surely would be easier for me if people took to her.

September 12   Have forgotten to mention that Mrs. Karlsdorf spent an hour with me the other evening. She came to pick up some records I had for Mr. Karlsdorf. She's a talker after the fashion of Millicent Barnes. She chatters on and on, frothily, and what she says is not, I suspect, exactly accurate. The edges of truth are skirted for the purpose of effect. But she is likeable, sweet, a bit on the weak side as to character, the result, no doubt, of compromising her Scotch principles in order to get along with her husband all these years. It was bend or break undoubtedly. He has had, Eva told me, various mistresses. His wife once had to threaten to leave him if he did not rid himself of one particular mistress.

September 22 Evelyn continues to apply herself to being helpful and agreeable. She backslides, naturally, but the change in her attitude is apparent. I don't feel she is aware that I care less for her. I hope not. It gives me the advantage indifference gives to any mutual relationship, an advantage hitherto all on her side. I may miss Dr. Pike boundlessly; I may be driven frantic by a neck he could fix in a couple of tries; but his absence has certainly helped me insofar as Evelyn is concerned.

September 23 Evelyn brought horrible woman with harelip for me to talk with, though I've pled not to see freaks — they give me nightmares. Asked afterwards not bring me such side-show specimens. She acted annoyed. I grew angry. She became nasty. Martha said afterwards: "No, Artie dear, you didn't begin so as she should have flown off the handle. I was there. I know." Billy said: "She wasn't warranted in puttin' on a scene. But I guess she'll never learn." Earlier in the day I'd spent half an hour calming Billy down as a result of Evelyn's tongue. She raged and all but foamed at me about the girl, finally apologizing, after being worn down, for going off the deep end. But then she refused to listen to explanations of what she might have done not to incite my anger. She returned to the old "I'd think by this time you'd expect me to be as I am and accept me that way." I really don't get excited the way I used to, and her spells of being agreeable are never long enough to build up optimism too high.

Martha said: "I've been with you three months, Arthur, and I consider you have an unusually sweet disposition and, considering your troubles, a remarkable sense of fairness. You're easy to live with. And if Mrs. Inman tells you Billy and Mrs. Trench and I see you different because we're not married to you, take it from me that's a lot of nonsense. She'd find you easy to live with if she'd let herself realize how exceptionally nice you are. I don't mean to be critical of her; it's just that I enjoy sitting to one side watching people. I feel she doesn't know what a sweet guy she has for a husband or else gives way to tantrums that help nobody and harm herself; just why I don't know. It's a pity, because she can be so sweet often."

September 24 President Truman announces that there has been an atomic explosion in Russia. I wonder what else he wants out of the American taxpayer? Truman is such a liar that this may be just another cock-and-bull yarn the British thought up for him to use. Or it may not be. It is not unreasonable that the Russians and the captured German scientists may have gotten somewhere by now.

September 28 Martha came around. She's cunning and pert. I kissed her. "My, Artie, don't do that. You embarrass me." But she liked it. Billy and I took her riding in the rain in the Pierce. She liked that, too. We all went into Billy's house and visited Sadie. She looks better and happier than ever I've seen her. She and Billy are proud of their house. The stairway is pretty and the house, despite its innumerable gew-gaws, is homelike. Sadie kissed me and made a fuss over me. I don't feel her jealousy or disapproval as formerly. She carries her age well. I like her more than once I did.

September 29 Listened to recording of Verdi's 'Requiem' last evening. Wish could get Gounod's 'Mass.' That Verdi, to my way of thinking, is one of the greatest composers who ever lived, bar none, much greater than Wagner. It is incomprehensible that so much dramatic melody could have poured from a single mind, with most of it superior, not, as say with Puccini, the same dish served again and again with various dressings and garnishes. Even Strauss did not give birth to so much magnificent melody on the top level. Absence of symphonic treatment is, to my mind, refreshing. He walks, Verdi, leaning upon no crutch of symphonic arrangement. Richard Strauss stated that no composer in Europe could do so much with such little basic material. I like Mahler's songs, would have been proud to have written such lovely, sad, minor songs.

If I were Truman, I'd get that saphead internationalist Lilienthal out of control of atomic expansion and put in a forceful and competent man interested in producing bombs and in guarding our secrets. Truman is even less interested in 'America first' than was Roosevelt, a little, incompetent, vain, egotistic man, loyal to all sorts of riffraff, uninstructed in history, economically ignorant, a small man with a waspish temper and open, as was Roosevelt, to flattery and coercible by instruction from the Leftists who have his ear.

October 7 Not since thirty years ago have I run up such osteopathic bills — about $300 a month. Dr. Pike could have fixed what is the matter with the pelvis today. I feel I'd give a small fortune to hear him say, "Well, Arthur, what's the trouble today? Come on, let's get at it." I was lucky, I suppose, that he lived as long as he did.

October 20 My Father comes tonight, and I am deflated by the event. I don't wish to see him. I wish he were out of my life.

October 21 Couldn't sleep last night worrying about Dottie. She works Tuesday with some fever and utter weakness. She becomes weaker. Andy rushed her to Baker Memorial. It sounds like infantile paralysis or virus influenza. I've been waiting for that sadistic old bastard, God, to visit me with his newest affliction. Maybe this will be it. If there is a God — as who am I to know one way or the other? — He or It can be naught but an incompetent devil bent upon some sort of wry amusement, an utter failure as an artisan. Any idiot in his cups could dream up a better, less inefficient, less painful and less violent scheme for human beings — if he favored them — and hardly a crueler scheme for them — if he were bent upon deviltry.

Well, to return to Dottie. I hereby pray that the concatenation of circumstances responsible for her course of existence does not kill or maim her. Without her I would be lost beyond belief. I have been waiting for this next stroke of ill luck. That it won't continue to a direful conclusion is too much for me to conceive. I'll ask Eva to pray to her God.

October 22 It's just what I expected it was, infantile paralysis, polio. She awoke with it Tuesday. As far as we can ascertain second-hand (Andy is staying at the hospital), Dottie's breathing hasn't yet been affected. She has no strength and her neck is stiff. Fred tells me that the crisis should have been passed by now. I hope so but doubt as God will let her off too easily. I asked Eva (her father, by the way, is on the rampage against me again) to pray for Dottie's recovery, since she doubtless had an in with God because of her belief — if there was a God. She claimed I possessed a Catholic viewpoint, using her as my intermediary. I replied yes, but would she pray, for there might just be a God whether I believed so or not? She takes her religion gravely. She would think it over. Christ, I said, was neither admired by me as a character or for what he taught and how taught it, certainly was no part God. It was God, the overall Divinity, I wished her to pray to. It might help Dottie and it might help me. And that is how I feel about it.

October 23 Dottie is in an iron lung six or eight hours a day, chiefly to conserve her strength. She is able to breathe and to move her head and toes. Fred says that the signs are good, but no one can be sure until further period has elapsed, during which she may or may not have a relapse that will cripple or kill her. People know more about how to ease and combat polio than once they did but still have no firm control over it.

Talked to my Father for an hour, myself filled with beer. To hell with feeling in awe of him. I have enough money and houses now to live on if he cut me off entirely. So why pull punches? I didn't agree with him each time I spoke. I stood up for myself. When he began his usual laudation of Evelyn, I replied that yes she was a nice woman, and she had been much more pleasant since Dr. Pike died and had even been better about not getting drunk. He didn't, he said, even know she drank. Of course he didn't, I said. He didn't know a lot of things I'd tried to keep from him. And, I added, it seemed to me that once in a while he might say some complimentary things about me and not always just about Evelyn.

I was drinking beer, two glasses. "If I drank that much of that stuff, I'd be on the floor." "Well, I'm not. I can drink half a bottle of Scotch straight. But it does me no good and this is cheaper and this helps me. It's logical, isn't it, to drink this rather than whiskey? And it helps me tell you a few things you don't know and never would believe anyway and ought to know." He was, for him, meek. He started on Dr. Pike, how he had lived off me. I replied that that was only true for the first years. I didn't blame him for feeling as he did then. But he had never taken into account that when the depression was here, Dr. Pike lowered the price and never lifted it again when other doctors were doing so. And he no doubt failed to realize that Evelyn was in love with Dr. Pike. [He] could have taken her away from me several times but always was cooperative and honorable with me.

He volunteered that he had changed his will and left Evelyn "provided for" only after my death, not on his death. He brags about his successful investments constantly. I inquired were not many of them successful only by luck. Certainly, I observed, if he had foreseen the phenomenal rise in Coca-Cola he would have put more into it than he did? That quieted him.

October 24 Evelyn overheard me telling my Father about how she had been in love with Dr. Pike and he had stood by me. She flew into a fury at me for talking behind her back. I told her I said nothing behind her back I didn't say to her face and only what seemed true to me. I'd say it again, I added. As long as she undervalued me, I'd say what I pleased. I had said much less to fewer people during these last months and would rather stop completely being any way but complimentary if she'd change her attitude toward me.

October 25 Dottie has been out of the iron lung for 12 hours. The mental crisis, when she wished to die, is over, but the physical crisis may not be over for ten days. Until this morning Dr. Rust expected Dottie to die, as he has never seen such a violent case. He will not know for ten days whether Dottie will be crippled or not. I feel lost in the pit of my stomach.

I am not only frightened for her; I am in a panic for myself. It often seems to me that my ill luck spreads outwards to catch in its malefic coils those who are devoted to me. It is as though the curse on me extends by conjunction to those I love and on whom I depend. And not all the argumentation in the world could convince me I do not exist under a special sadistic curse. The pages of history and legend are filled with such cursed people, and my destiny is not an unusual one. I once believed that the good men enjoyed and the bad they suffered balanced each other. I no longer believe that. I believe now that individuals are cursed or blessed, succeed or fail, are well or sick, are prosperous or in poverty, according to their providence, and whether or not they are well-intentioned or rascally, saints or sinners helps or harms their destiny not one whit. They are born what they are. That most people are born in between being cursed and being blessed, enjoy ups and downs that more or less balance in no wise interferes with how I now believe.

I have worried about Dottie until in a funk about her. She can now move her left leg and arm some, turn her head, move three fingers on the right arm and the toes of the right leg. Her spine is unmoveable as yet. I send her flowers every two or three days and telephone constantly for information concerning her state. I miss her tremendously, not as much as I do Dr. Pike, but tremendously and unreservedly. She's out of the contagious ward, but I'll not let any of my family visit her yet awhile, being in mortal fear of the viruses.

November 12   I wrote this letter:

November 10, 1949

Dearest Dottie —

I haven't written you because I was quite ill from a twisted splenic flexure and didn't want to bother you with my troubles or gloom. We tried six doctors, but not one did anything. Billy and I finally fixed it and I am on deck again, and therefore writing you.

I think of you constantly and get my religious friends to pray for you just in case it might help, I personally having no established connections with Divinity. Andy's note was very reassuring. Please thank him for it. He has been what my Mother used to term "a tower of strength," hasn't he? I'm very proud of you and of him, for it takes real spirit and courage to meet a crisis such as yours and keep fighting qualities uppermost.

I'm glad you have enjoyed my flowers. It has been a genuine pleasure sending them. What you have done for me and been to me in the past I'm afraid I can never repay.

My world gets along somehow. I'm planning to take over the Chestnut Street apartment house next week. Then there will be the installation of a gas heater, new bathrooms, painting, fixtures torn out, etc. I try to keep the old mind occupied, in particular from not missing my Dottie too much and being too filled with pity for one with so much courage as to rate admiration rather than pity. You'll show 'em, won't you, Dottie!

Most of the osteopaths have been very good to me, though none is as clever as you. I like personally Buell, from Cambridge. He's a Southerner of the type I went to military school with — a tough hombre. He's trying to fix the cartilage between the 6th and 7th cervicals and the 1st and 2nd dorsals. I know you're interested and won't worry — that's why I'm telling you.

I'll bet you no one misses you as I do. You have been a sort of commonsense governor for my judgments so long that I'm lost without you.

Billy says: "I can't get Dottie off my mind." We all miss you, you see.

With deep and abiding devotion
Your
Arthur

November 19   Eva is a big girl now, weighs about 160. The effect of college on her is anything but beneficial. She was nicer before she went; by the month she becomes more dogmatic and preachy. It was bad enough when she absorbed and interpreted the Bible but even worse now that she is swallowing whole the predigested course in psychology. She already deems herself a master of "digging out and bringing to light exactly the reason why we do things, even if it isn't obvious at first sight." Her scorn for my wrong thinking is not only expressed but sticks out all over her. Which is not at all to say that we don't love each other. We usually avoid religious discussions. This psychology business is, I must admit, downing me. My views are not necessarily those of the current textbooks. I deem adolescence more important in the formation of the mature human than baby-hood or childhood, and inheritance more important generally than environment.

If I were the Karlsdorfs, I'd have her out of that second-rate female institution but fast. She should have gone to no college but if forced to go, then at least a coeducational institution. In all the years I've driven past Lesley, not once have I ever laid eyes on a pretty girl. I love Eva and am grateful beyond measure to her, but I do not approve of what school plus religion is doing to her. She could turn very quickly into a hidebound reformer and self-righteous, didactic fanatic in short order. I can do less for her than formerly, because she's more stubborn and sure she's right. She loves to argue though equipped with a very limited emotional mentality.

December 17   Evelyn hasn't bopped me down for two days, miracle of miracles. Told her I'd quit making belittling remarks about her character (which I indulge in purposely as my one means of defense) if she would quit giving me the works each time I made a statement of any sort — and gladly and willingly so. It won't last, because she'd rather speak her piece than live in peace; but it's been helpful as a sample.

I am reading Stanley Weyman's 'Gentleman of France' on the talking-book and like it very much. It is a relief to have the lower classes villains, as they are and were, and not social heroes thwarted only by inimical conditions.

December 26   I was wondering what new trouble would be next. Here it is, full face. The new John Hancock Life Insurance building has on top of it a beacon supposed to be visible for 65 – 100 miles, and that beacon shines my room up like bright moonlight at night and hurts my eyes. It is a high-power mercury light and the rays are violet rays. Aside from making it difficult to sleep, I am in mortal fear my eyes will be injured. If snow light hurts me, this should also. I'm frightened. And Mrs. Trench and Billy won't be able to leave the shades up to get air this summer. We've been telephoning all morning to find out what is what. Wired Evelyn to come home tonight. My God, who would have thought of this? I can't see anyway — and now this. I wish I were dead and away from noises that impinge and lights that attack and a structure that falls apart and fears that undermine and years without end ahead. It's awful beyond belief.

December 31   All week I have thought about and directed various methods of putting pressure against the John Hancock people about removing or shielding the light. Evelyn has been in one of her rebellious nasty spells and therefore less than the help she might have been. It's a wonder people don't swat her, the contemptuous way she talks to them.

Life insurance assets have doubled during the last ten years. They wield some 58 billions worth of power. They are untaxed in the main yet so restricted by state laws as to what investments they can and cannot make that they bulge with idle cash. Only the savings banks have more billions worth of power. It is nothing to the insurance companies, therefore, what they spend. They put up expensive buildings across the country. A light like this one, however many thousands it may cost, is nothing to them. Wherefore they are difficult to influence. I tried a petition. People wouldn't sign it.

They were (1) afraid of "big business" pressure, (2) pleased to have more light to sleep by, (3) hopeless that anything they thought or felt could influence a big corporation.

Assistance came yesterday from one of the big hotels Billy and Evelyn and Mrs. Trench had canvassed, the Ritz. The manager there said he would arouse the Boston Association of Hotels. So we may be getting somewhere. Mrs. Banks taught me that what a single determined negative individual can accomplish is astonishing. Eva spent all one day telephoning to various authorities, tracking down the authority on mercury vapor lamps to find out how harmful the radiation might be. The answer, for what it is worth, was "no," not at this distance.

1950

January 9 Yesterday morning Billy and I, Evelyn and Dick Bridges, later Patricia and Paul foregathered in Billy's room. Paul and I drank beer. Patricia drank coffee. Dick drank milk. Billy, as usual, was abstemious. It was a pleasant morning. I rather like Paul. He's tall, wide, with a deep voice and slow, courteous manners, a charming smile, not too intelligent, sloping forehead and pinhead on top, capacity for temper. Just the sort of fellow who likes me, given the chance.

He and Patricia are appalled at the prices and the degree of Socialism apparent in the U.S.A. People, they find, are hurried, harried, dirty. The city streets are filthy. Paul, after all taxes and insurance withdrawals, received about $275 a month. They will find difficulty, they are sure, living on that amount. Both of them enjoy army life. Paul is booked to teach for nine months at the base at Augusta, Georgia. He doesn't like teaching. He leaves for Washington Wednesday to put a plea in to be sent either to the West Coast or Japan. Patricia is in love with him and he depends on her as a mother.

Small ride in Pierce with Billy. Clouded up and ripe for snow. Our guests are still sleeping. Yesterday Patricia took her husband the rounds of her numerous relatives. He says he likes being led around for exhibit. How can he? Billy says: "Oh, I've seen hundreds of his type in the Army — vain — you know — good with the ladies — no imagination — a bastard sometimes — pleasant enough mostly — likes the life for the authority it gives him — very vain — a type. I guess he's all right. Not smart and on his toes like Dick Bridges. He'd bore someone like you to death." I suspect that, being directly of German ancestry (he changed his name), he possesses the very traits he decries: rank sentimentality, manners that cover potential cruelty, love of authority, devil with the women, much incidental kindness, pleasure in order, and respect for enforced authority. One feels that most of his expressed views are refurbished secondhand. And that, for my money, is Paul Bowe, ex-motion picture actor, thirty-seven years old, lieutenant in the Military Police, a man exactly fitted for the post and rank he occupies, a proficient officer I imagine. His reports, Patricia states, are minute, precise, faithfully drawn in small handwriting.

January 10 I hope one day soon to find time and energy to write what I think of the Far East mess. It is a shame and a blot and an incipient peril to all Americans and would not have been possible without Communist sympathizers in the State Department, the swallowing whole of Moscow propaganda by Americans, and an incompetent little squirt in the White House. He is a machine-made politician and an ex-necktie salesman who failed in the only business in which he was ever engaged. That's what I think of Truman. Of Dean Acheson and the State Department and of our tragedy in China, more later.

January 18 Never a rest. Out of a clear blue sky yesterday Eva threw an emotional jag at me over reporting payments to her for income tax purposes. She yelled, screamed, stamped, wept for an hour, abandoned logic, insisted on her way no matter at what needless trouble to me. "I intend being honest with the Government no matter what you think or want. I've got to be honest with the Government, and I will be." She expects to report the $10 a week no matter what. The part that bothers me is that such a procedure may call attention to me and bring more examiners like those last spring. I suggested she report if she must but leave my name out. No. I was an ungrateful person who didn't appreciate all she did for me and never made any return. Vituperations. I was, I must confess, shocked and put aback. She didn't even tell me goodbye.

So that's what she is underneath: Germanic, loyalty to an individual as nothing to obedience to a government. And she'll harbor a grudge I'm sure, for people with big noses and very little chins always do that. Hysterical and unreasoning. Well, there'll be considerable recasting in my mind. No more $30 yellow dresses. Less siding with her against her father. More cautious as to words used. She's been too good to me to endanger our relationship by another misunderstanding. I wrote her a note and said I was sorry I was so emotional. I told Martha (they always lunch together Thursdays) to stand up for me if Eva brought up the subject. Eva is too religious. These very religious people always have a 'conscience out' for whatever way they act. I'm sorry this happened. I think Billy is the only person in the world I trust not to turn on me over a misunderstanding.

January 20 At the end of a wild and pain-jammed morning, who should come up the hall but Pearl Hollister Leuko. I was pleased to see her and she seemed pleased to see me. "God, I'm nerved up." And she was. I've read about legs shaking until knees knocked together, though never witnessed it before. She wore a cute dress she had made herself, an awful coat with what Evelyn said was a silver-fox collar (it looked yellow and tawny white, like skunk fur) and an unbecoming black hat. I took off the hat and she took off the coat. "I'm thirty, Artie. Don't I look it? But no fatter. That fools you — huh? Just had to come see how my Artie was. Norman'd wring my neck if he knew. He hates you still. Well, here I am. Yes, I'd love a drink. I need one. See me shake."

To cut down a long tale to the strength of my wrist, Pearl was here almost two hours. She looks older, naturally, and her tongue wags. She talks too loudly. But she's jammed to the thwarts with personality, verve, emotionality — quite a gal. She asked me all about myself with that genuine interest so few friends evince in the affairs of others. She is happy, she said, with Norm. He treats her well. He gives her money each week. He has enlarged his garage and the activities of his Chevrolet agency, is "making money like mad." She uses up her energies making her own clothes. She never dresses until eleven. They have a big Cadillac and a five thousand dollar cruiser on Lake Sunapee and a cabin. They have a new home, small cottage type, in the photograph most attractive. She loves her mother-in-law. She's happy. Janice and Bertram and their children have been to Bradford to visit them. When she left here, she was going to visit Janice. She kissed Billy. She was amiable and amusing. I enjoyed her.

My nights are horrible, pyrotechnically and psychologically. The beacon light hasn't yet been fixed. Thank God for Billy. He's patient with me, and I need patience. Evelyn is tired. Patricia is leaving suddenly to go west to take care of Paul's mother, dying of cancer. She'll leave an empty space behind her, and Evelyn will miss her more than I do. It is very warm, like summer. Never saw a winter like this one. Is the climate of the world gone mad? Here comes Evelyn. I must try to disguise how in a panic I am, for she cannot live without a certain amount of inconsequential small talk. I expect the worst always. Such has been the lesson set by my experience. Sunshine. Blue day. Probably horror of some sort just ahead. No safe avoidance of ambushes.

January 29 It seems all but decided in Washington that we are to build hydrogen bombs, 2,000 of which are said to be powerful enough to depopulate Earth. All our secrets have been given away or stolen by the enterprising Russians so that they are probably already manufacturing atom and hydrogen bombs. We are so infiltrated by spies and fifth columnists in this country and are so lax to guard our own that what we discover or methodize for mass production in short order is no longer ours solely.

Alger Hiss has been declared guilty of lying when he claimed not to have passed Government papers to Russian spies. Of course, that means he was a spy working for Russia, but our double-talk hasn't gotten around to that yet. He was the man at Roosevelt's shoulder at Yalta when we bribed Stalin to come into a war he couldn't have been kept out of by wild horses. Secretary of State Acheson has rushed into print with a statement that he will not turn his back on his good friend Hiss (even if condemned by the court). They seem to be all of a piece in that State Department, Russian-minded at the expense of the United States. Of course Truman should dismiss Acheson. But he won't. The State Department virtually let China go by the board to the Communists.

February 5 You know, I think my Father made an irrevocable mistake when he refused to let me go into his business after graduating from school and forced me to go to college instead. I might never have collapsed even after those five years of school. Generations of Inmans behind me have been businessmen and traders. Perhaps it's in my blood. I like it. I get along with almost any sort of person as a rule. The handling of money intrigues me. I might have learned quickly and become an American somebody rather than a hidden solitary. I might be well and my Father might be proud instead of apologetic.

February 10 Dreamed of Dr. Pike all night. Wish he was here now to care for Evelyn. She must miss him. I was afraid last week, when she was emoting without curb and drinking, that she would deplete herself so that something would happen. I warned her, but of course she paid no attention.

February 11 By the way, the other day Mrs. Trench saw the death notice in the paper of the Reverend Otto Ten Broek. He must have been about eighty. There was another obstructionist tied around my soul for years. Evelyn, Ten Broek, my Father, my Mother.

To deal with people of quick and apt minds, like Dick Bridges, like the new lawyer Clarence recommended, Noah Strong, is a delight to me and instantaneously speeds up my gifts of ingenuity and daring, arouses and fortifies my self-confidence. They admire my qualities, accept my suggestions, say yes and no without argumentation, and at once I am a better man. I enjoy this managing of a property excessively with Dick to help me. It is a something into which the teeth of purpose and imagination can be put. It permits me in a degree to forget myself. It lets me be a man. If Evelyn only pulls back, the heck with her most of the times. Let her buy things and play with her hamster and sleep and eat. Mrs. Trench enjoys helping me, and so does Billy save when he feels I am hardhearted with tenants.

Hell, I don't know them. Out with the ones who won't pay or who make trouble — and not a twinge of conscience. That, I take it, is the way to success in a competing world.

February 13 I'm sick. Evelyn dressed and came upstairs. How can she always manage to be on the scene at the most inopportune time? Wasn't particularly glad to see her; there's too much grief attached to her. I put up my defenses the minute I hear her, being fairly sure the odds are on the side of my being hurt or obstructed. Billy away today. Martha here for couple of hours. Had her busy phoning. She's unusually cute if she wears becoming shoes instead of the bedroom-slipper affairs she affects, keeps her hair washed, has the nicotine cleaned from her teeth, uses a little rouge, shortens her skirts. But she won't. "I'm too tired, Artie." Now I'm in my room, alone.

February 18 I forgot to mention that Uncle Frank Martin Inman died. I recall him teaching his horse to high-step at 552 Peachtree Street, introducing his fiancée to the family, taking me riding in the back of his buggy, the experience at Peachtree Place with the tramp in the hole, his advice to me to ignore my parents and "raise hell, boy," which I wish I had taken. He was not much good, the sort of good fellow men like, fattish, a great spender and a fairly consistent loser because of unregenerate optimism; bullied by Aunt Louise; a man of little wit (though he could tell a good yarn) and less judgment; a person lucky enough always to have someone turn up to care for him in adversity; one who never learned anything; hospitable, generous with his own and others' money, a hunter and fisherman, one who scorned aesthetics of all sorts; religious, a 'joiner,' active in church affairs, with a large male Bible class. He consistently resented my Father's success, talked him down at every opportunity and gave people advice as to how to get the best of "Henry." He died supported by gifts from my Father and owing him some one hundred thousand. I'm sure Uncle Frank cost his brother more than I ever did during the span of his life. I have never fathomed the odd loyalty in my Father which led him to overlook, forgive, support his younger brother without appreciation and even in the face of insult and undercutting.

March 20 This has been a dreadful month, one trouble and affliction piled atop the next, my spine and ribs utterly disarranged. I don't know how to rearrange them. Sometimes three treatments a day. Nose been worse. Last night Mrs. Trench left iron chair where I hit it with knee full tilt. Don't know what is broken or disarranged there. In pain. Worried. No sleep. Lost temper. The weather has been abominable, snow, very cold, snow, very cold, so few rides. Elevator now broken. Evelyn gone to Florida to drive her parents to Aiken, South Carolina. To be gone a week. If I were dying and she had made plans, she wouldn't break them. She's no earthly good. She was woolgathering a couple of weeks ago and got into a severe auto accident and smackup.

Pearl showed up. Her Norman Leuko has kicked her out, and she is after as much money as she can get. She looks tough. She really isn't much good either. So very few women in this world are basically kind, while innumerable men are so. That's all. I'm just writing to eat up time. Billy has been wonderful.

March 21 Billy says Sadie is so violently jealous of Pearl that any use by me of her might endanger his happiness. These female females are out of my range as a rule.

March 22 This real estate venture, while helpful, requires less thought and effort than the Stock Market and a tenth the concentration of writing poetry or keeping a diary for future generations. My concentration now has chiefly to do with these unmanly and uncreative matters: to keep my body somehow lined up enough to lessen great suffering; to keep those who stand between me and the world contented and interested in my welfare; to adjust my emotions and my mind to my disintegration as a man and to enduring, by one subterfuge and another, the prolonged passage of pain-filled time. I no longer possess either the courage or the desperation to venture again through the doorway that possibly escapes time and suffering and consciousness.

April 5 Nothing to do that will pass the time like writing. I bought the Chestnut Street property in order to have something to do and to think about. I wasn't expecting my head to rot on its stalk. The mess of details, the telephone ringing, questions coming at me from all sides to be answered, the bookkeeping that deprives me of Mrs. Trench — all overwhelm me at this point. I wish I had left the money in the bank or put only about ten thousand in stocks. (I've made a considerable profit on speculations since New Year, relative to the small capital used.) I don't fancy this business of not being able to think clearly. Without Billy to help me I'd be swamped. Dottie has been ill almost six months and thus far remains a helpless cripple. Will she ever recover enough to do any constructive treatments on me? If not, will she get so she can diagnose what is wrong?

May 9 Living has been too painful to record. I really think (dare I think?) that the back at last is somewhat improved. I have found a good doctor finally, Dr. Gooch, who lives in Needham and charges $20 a visit, and little I care what he charges. My God, but these last months have been horrible. Dare I hope an end in sight?

My Father comes today, and I don't feel up to talking to him.

May 21 Well, here's God's latest attention to his pet victim. Billy has gone. He was supposed to fix supper for me last evening. He failed to show up. I tried to telephone his house. The phone was off the instrument. I was worried frantic. There was no one here. At 7:20 Sadie called up and asked for Billy. I told her he wasn't here; I was worried something had happened to him. She didn't sound interested. Martha came at 7:30, aired my room with the fans, prepared me some cold supper I couldn't eat. We telephoned Sadie. No Billy. Either, I thought, accident, some cover-up by Sadie, gone with Pearl maybe. Martha phoned the police and the big hospitals. No Billy. I was double frantic, envisioning all sorts of calamities to the man I loved best in the world, on whom I most depended. Evelyn came in at 8:40. She went to Sadie's house. She phoned at 9:30. No Billy. Detectives and a seven-state alarm for his car. I was all but crazy. Nothing more to do. If no accident, then a matter of free will. Told Evelyn to go to bed. Martha couldn't have been sweeter. She left at 10:15. Mrs. Trench returned at 11:00. I told her. She shook all over, as I was doing.

Then, about midnight, Sadie came to talk to Evelyn. She had found Billy's clothes closet empty, the radio I loaned him gone, a note. The note stated he was in love with a young girl, had been for two years; she was going to have a baby. He was leaving. The girl was, Sadie said, named Sandra Booth, "Twinkle" in this diary. Sadie had caught him two years ago and told him to decide between the girl and her. He had promised not to see Sandra any more but had. He had withdrawn all the money from their joint account, taken the car. He didn't have the character, he said, to face her. Sadie left in a taxi to go to the Booth house in Medford. She might not, she said, get Billy back for herself, but by gosh she would do something toward getting him back for me. She would never, so help her God, let him get a divorce. She loved him so much she would take him back any day. That is all I know.

I slept one hour. Mrs. Trench slept three. I don't know what

Evelyn got yet. It was an awful night. It bids fair to be an awful set of days and nights. I don't know how I can live without Billy. What will happen to my morale? What to my pelvis? God, I'm frightened. How can I survive without Billy to put me together continually with considerable skill day or night, to drive my old car, to waken me mornings, to give me gentleness and self-esteem, to falsify, if you will, so skillfully I did not correlate the diverse parts so visible now in retrospect? And what a life he has cut out for himself with that attractive, sexy, unscrupulous girl. It won't last. There'll be woe to it. She'll fuck him dry, sap what manhood and virility he has left, go off with a newer admirer, or I miss my reading of human nature. She has persuaded a weak man to this step, an infatuated man too long married to an older woman.

I still am amazed how, with all his kindness, he could have done this to Sadie and me, I never suspecting. He alertly secretive and giving out a mesh of lies. I'm like Sadie, I'd take him back in a minute. But where has he gone? How find out? Telephone Whitcomb and ascertain where Sadie stands legally, what she can do. I'm bereft, shocked, with the last person in whom I put faith exploded in my face. I could gladly be dead. This completes utterly my course in never cease to be wary and suspicious of everyone, your longest and best friends included. What lies ahead for me I shudder to contemplate. I'll bet poor Sadie had a hell of a night.

Later: Sadie came. She looked dragged through a knothole, said she hadn't slept a wink. She looks much older since the accident Billy had winter before last. She seems more perturbed about what people will think of her than about losing Billy. She didn't see the Booths last night. She is going to see them today. If I were Billy, I'd have left her long ago, as many good qualities as she may have. She says that she put most of the money into the house from her savings — a story divergent from Billy's. He told her he earned only $35 a week here. She thinks him a strong character, which measures the depth of her perceptiveness.

Evelyn thinks Billy will be back Tuesday. Mrs. Trench feels he will be back in two or three weeks. I feel he won't be back at all without effort on my part, if he can be reached. I can write heart-wringing letters, and Mrs. Trench can persuade the shirt off a monkey when she's in form. Mrs. Trench looks washed out. I look blooming, but my eyes won't focus and my temples pound. Where will this end?

May 22 This note from Billy, mailed Saturday morning:

Dear Arthur,
    I hope that you will not be too alarmed as to what I am about to tell you. I am going out of your life forever, which means that we

shall never see one another again. I know that this will be a dreadful blow to you and doing it will grieve me for the rest of my life.

I have been very unhappy for quite some time because I find myself in love with another woman. I also have decided at this time that I must make a complete change because I feel that by staying with you any longer I will find myself suffering the same health that you are now experiencing.

Because of my sympathetic treatments in treating you, by trying to relieve your suffering these past thirteen years, I have done myself great harm and know that I shall experience structural trouble for the remainder of my life. Believe me I am very doubtful that I can make a living feeling the way I have lately.

Arthur, dear, please don't think too badly of me for leaving you this way. You have been very wonderful to me and the best friend I have ever known. I can never forget you and your kindness. I know you love me as I love you.

It will grieve me the remainder of my life for doing this to you. Goodby, good luck, and bless you for every thing you have been and done for me.

Billy

The stuff about his back is three-quarters guff. He hurt his back falling down a couple of years ago. Regarded coldly, the way I have been treated is shameful. Perhaps, as my Mother was, I am too good to those I love, though holding back often with my generous impulses. I believe that Billy has cut out for himself a hard and perhaps losing life. If money gets scarce, the girl will not stick by him, especially does Sadie refuse to give him a divorce. She will then throw him over. I doubt if he can get as much money elsewhere, and not for the reason he gives. He is thirty-eight, of limited capacities. I feel resentful. If he gets a job that will pay him well, he'll have to work hard. If he works hard, he'll have less sex for the girl, and she won't like that either. I think I'll advise Sadie to attempt to get support from him, which would also cripple his style. If people treat me well, there's almost nothing I won't do for them. If they treat me unfairly, I am bitter and not above revenge. I don't want revenge on Billy; I merely want him back, and the sooner he learns Sandra's nature the sooner he may return.

In the meanwhile, I'm to see Pearl at ten-thirty, a few minutes from now. I'm going to offer her the equivalent of seventy dollars a week, and I think it may be an offer difficult for her to turn down, although maybe not.

Later: Am I dead! My temples and testicles throb and ache from the emotional beating of my heart. First, Miss Peabody, the Cumberland Street housekeeper, came to tell us she was through Saturday, moving out; she'd had enough. Eva called to say she'd be a few moments late and I, thinking it was Saturday, told her I didn't care if she was an hour late, which was wrong. Then Sadie came. Then Pearl, who went into a nervous collapse upon seeing her, thinking, as she told me later, something awful about herself and Billy had come up. We all drank beer, and everything took on a more relieved aspect. Pearl was shocked to hear of Billy. He took, Sadie says, two thousand dollars from the savings bank two weeks ago and the rest last week. She's as calm as a cold melon lying in a cool cellar. She says, does Sadie: "I've learned to bear troubles. I can bear this one. I'll have to. I know nothing about the finances of the house, but I guess I can learn. Maybe I'll sell the house. I kind of hate to, though, after all the money I've put into it. I love Billy, and I won't do a thing to get him back. If he comes, I'll take him, but if he don't, he don't, and that's all. I love him better than myself, I guess. If I just don't get a migraine, I'll be all right." Myself, I fail to understand Sadie's reactions, Pearl's seeming more normal.

I'm not able to write very much more. I talked to Pearl. I laid before her my plan, by which she'd get from sixty to seventy dollars a week a year. She's now "thinkin' it over." She seems to desire to come with me. I pay her, if she does, $55 a week, plus $5 extra a week when no extra person like Eva or Martha is working for me by the week, and a bonus of $250 every half-year she is here. She couldn't get that much, I think, anywhere else. She plans to consult her lawyer to find out if taking a job would interfere with getting money from her husband. I hope to God she'll come. She explained that she was emotional and couldn't help it, and I'd have to be patient. I told her she could take any convenient day off and sacrifice pay, or any week. That to get around her feeling of being circumscribed. She is to do what Billy did. She can do everything he did except the treatments and do most of it better, though her personality isn't so soothing.

More talk with Sadie, Mrs. Trench, Pearl, Evelyn. I shall miss a man tremendously. But too many women won't kill me.

If Pearl will come, my great problem will be to find a doctor who can treat the pelvis effectively. I'm exhausted and my temples throb unbearably. Stop.

May 23   Pearl just called up. She will start part-time beginning a week from today. Thank God. I will be as easy on her as possible, because she has been through considerable shock and to start her in with a rush would help no one. I hope her shoulder has improved enough to let her do some work on the pelvis. I *must* keep myself and my emotions under control in order to ease her into steady work.

If Billy could do this to Sadie and me, if he could take joint savings and decamp with them, if he could lie suavely and convincingly and continuously to me who had done him only good, why then probably I'll never lay eyes on him again. His very real charm, his sympathetic nature (if it was actually sympathetic), his gentleness have carried him over many bumps. From here on youth and looks and charm may not be on his side. I wish I could forget him.

May 24   The more I hear about Billy's double-dealing, the more astonished I become and the more I hope that girl eventually two-times him. He certainly has it coming. The lies and the sneaking off arouse my ire and offend my sense of fair play. I was talking to Fred. His round face with the large Armenian eyes and nose, its full mouth and small sheik moustache beamed on me. "Didn't you know Billy was leaving? I did. I've been aware of it for six months." "You've known about it for six months, and you didn't tell me anything?" "Well, you know, professional confidence. A doctor can't tell everything he knows. He's probably knocked her up and beat for California. He sat in the car and asked me about technicalities for half an hour at a time. I told him he was a damn fool — he'd never find another such soft job paying so much. And I reminded him how good his wife had been to him. I told him to forget the girl. I didn't know he'd have the guts." "You should have told me. I feel you have been remiss not to give me a hint at least. I know you. It wouldn't have bothered your conscience, and it might have helped me." "Well, if I'd thought he was going to do this I surely have told you. But I felt he'd never go through with it. I didn't think he'd have the guts. And what could you have done anyway?"

I looked again into the orientally handsome, weak face. I decided neither temper nor argument would be effective. He looked at things one way, I another, racially. "Guts," I said. "It seems to me that to dodge responsibility, to lie to me, to take his wife's money, to beat it without a word connotes cowardice and lack of personal integrity — not guts." "Well —" he said. It was no use. He had, in his way, as much charm and not least a kindred sort of weakness. He was important to me as a doctor. Nothing served by censoring him for what was done. "Tell me," I said, "how a person like Billy can lie so persistently and convincingly. I can't comprehend it." "That's easy, my dear Arthur. You know and I know that he had nothing in the top story. It's that sort of people who can lie the pants off everyone and sound convincing. They are the gangsters and criminals. People with brains can't get away with it. That's easy."

I'm waiting now to find out if Billy forged my name and took the money from our joint account in the South Boston Savings Bank, $5,000. I put nothing past him. "You know," said Roderic last evening, "I never liked the lad much and thought him a pinhead and only esteemed him for the loyalty he appeared to have for you." Everyone else, every single person, is surprised, shocked.

May 31 Poor Pearl was so emotional last night that she slept little. She did very well. She's a smart girl — woman, that is. She no longer resembles a girl. She is thirty-one. Her eyes are small and look as if they hurt. I'd wager she has a high blood pressure. She colors up each time she becomes excited, and the skin of her face is sanguine. She uses that awful pancake make-up. Her expression is somewhat dissolute and hard. She laughs nervously. She speaks too loudly. She talks volubly. Though she may alter, at the moment she is not too attractive. She possesses an exuberant personality which wears her out and, I'm sure, wears out others.

June 4 Pearl, while wild as a colt with burrs under its saddle, has come on the job with a very different attitude from the last time when she was riding high and wide. She's going to have to wear glasses. She looks older than her age. "Boy, I'm the sort who ages fast, Artie. I can't wear girlish dresses any longer. Too damn wide in the hips." She drinks beer upon beer and chain-smokes. She does more work in an hour than Billy was doing in half a day or a day.

"I guess," says Mike, "Billy was just plain fucked out, the way he looked. He said it was his back. I've seen fellows like him before who tried to keep up with a young hot-pants girl."

Sadie, discovering underhand trick after underhand trick Billy did to her, has arrived at the "son of a bitch" stage. While I'm sorry for her, I don't feel drawn toward her, and intuitively I mistrust her even when everyone else comments upon her straightforward honesty. She had a dirty deal, yes, but if I'd been Billy I'd have left her in an honest, aboveboard fashion years ago.

June 16 I'll end this volume with a sketch of the life of William Henry Minor, not much of it, I fear, checkable, as I gathered it from him and now from Pearl and Sadie. He apparently spun around himself a cocoon of secrecy and guile and fabrications overlaid with charm and apparently openfacedness until he must have experienced difficulty at times seeing himself as himself. As children do, he bemused others by natural dissemblement and, it may be, himself.

He is thirty-eight or -nine, maybe somewhat older or younger. His father, who worked in a Springfield company probably as watchman (Billy claimed he managed it), married, deserted his first wife, took up with another woman, whom he didn't marry for years, and by her had five bastard sons. Billy claimed his mother has Sioux Indian blood in her. I always felt she had negro blood in her. Perhaps she had both or neither. Sadie claimed she was a full-blooded Jewess. You can take your choice.

Billy knew he was illegitimate. He went to high school. He played baseball, swam, etc. He worked one or several summers on a large farm. He sold papers or candy on trains. He left home at 18 or 19 and joined the Army. He boxed. He was, he claimed, disgusted with the actions and words of the men. At any rate, he became the pet of the captain. He became a crack shot. He left the Army at the end of three years. He became involved with gangsters (rumrunners he told me, opium smugglers he told Pearl). He came to Boston. He went into the Colonial Laundry, where he worked first in the vats and then on a delivery truck. He boarded with a widow and her two daughters. She was a mother to him (Pearl says she was in love with him). He fell in love with the oldest daughter who proceeded to marry someone else. Sadie, who worked in the laundry, caught him on the rebound. Meanwhile, the widow had persuaded him to become a Catholic. He took on the trappings of a good man.

Sadie claims to have given him money constantly, even before she married him. She claims to have continued to give him money always after their marriage, never to have taken a cent from him. The thousand dollars I gave him toward the purchase of the house she claims he never gave her. He told her he received $50 a week from me, no more. He told Mrs. Trench recently that he had a flush bank account. Sadie claims to have letters from various women with whom he had sexual affairs. Martha tried to get into 311 one night to wash her hands. Billy wouldn't let her in, saying his wife was there. It was Sandra.

His life is a chain of devious lies. He did everything save cheat and two-time by impulse. When his face was in repose, it was all but moronic. In retrospect, I can see how he gypped me and lied to me, as the Irish do, for the pure easiness of it. His charm was unusual. As Pearl puts it, he profited by what I taught him as to how to make use of it. He was gentle with me, often thoughtful, tactful. He must have thought something of me. He was an engaging person, lazy, a gambler, devious. I trusted him, and virtually everyone trusted him. This affair with Sandra, it is now plain, was not the beginning nor will it be the end to his lies and perfidies.

I must be growing up at last, for I have taken his treachery to me and my opinion of him very well. Perhaps I have become a man at last. Never again will I trust fully a living soul, neither in actions nor words, not even in intentions. Perhaps no mature man should trust his fellows. God know I have been prepared for this maturity often enough — Joe, Katinka, my Mother, Janice, Evelyn — to have matured earlier.

Sadie was here the other evening, drunk, foulmouthed, reeking of cheap perfume. She is abhorrent to me. I trust her not at all, and my intuitions as to women are as a rule precisely correct. She is cheap, ignorant, cold, physically and emotionally repellent. It is a little girl's voice she uses. That he could bear up under living with her for these twelve years augurs an utter lack of sensitivity. Perhaps, as Sadie says, he used her for a sucker and a pocketbook. No fortune would repay me for living with her. I trust the veracity of not a word she utters. She's mostly French, and never yet have I met a palatable Frenchman. They lack sensitivity. She was, she says, twice pregnant, and Billy made her have abortions. This may or may not be so. I'm sorry for her, but the less I see of her the better. She'll make a living, never fear.

I'm not at all sure I'd take Billy back if he returned. I'm all but certain Sandra will two-time him. If he looked as worn out in the mornings after his nights here with her, how can he keep up the sexual nightly pace? He's a gambler and a spendthrift, untrained save in laundry work and sharpshooting. His money won't last forever. Then young girl Sandra will turn angry.

Now my problem is if I can live in some sort of balance quite surrounded by women. I really don't know the answer.

Things looked up for Arthur in the spring of 1950. Pearl slipped easily into the Garrison Hall routine and was drinking less. Mr. Karlsdorf touched him for a $200 loan to pay for Eva's college tuition (now the egotistical and irascible old duffer would not dare restrict his daughter's time with Arthur), and cuddly Martha (what a contrast to "impervious" Evelyn) daily became more adorable, even though her mind left something to be desired. Evelyn hardly endeared herself by buying a house in Acton, Massachusetts — an act, as it would turn out, of vast consequence.

Alarmed by American setbacks in the Korean War, Arthur once again harped on the vulnerability of the United States and had savage words for petty, cocksure Truman ("He drinks heavily and has a psychiatric treatment every day") and his Communist-loving advisers. It might take a defeat in Korea to wake up a decadent nation and encourage its leaders to renounce their kid-glove policies. He may have criticized Lincoln in the Diary, but by God, Lincoln had the guts to put topnotch men in control, whether or not they agreed with him, and to "immobilize" dangerous traitors even if it meant revoking habeas corpus and tossing thousands of men into jail.

Billy's defection turned Arthur's thoughts from Korea to Garrison Hall, where his eyes were opened to a more shocking "betrayal." Then his brush-fire skirmishes with Evelyn finally burst into open war.

June 17   Rain, a minor cloudburst, descends slantingly, as in Hokusai and Hiroshige, on the wet red walls of buildings and the bright, feathery green tops of ailanthus trees. Thunder rumbles and growls. I sit in my sixth-story living room in Garrison Hall, facing the two carved chests, the antique English one and the modern one with the 1890 sharp-bow fishing ketch carved on it, sails and waves blown one way, pennon the other, and no one is about save Mrs. Trench in the other room. Evelyn has gone to Concord to have lunch with her mother. The more people who die off, the more attention I receive.

Martha is due at two for the afternoon and to make supper. I become more fond of her, give her council as to how to handle her faultfinding parents, cuddle her and tease her and give her dresses. She's as cute as a little girl could well be, now that her hair is longer and she takes more care with her clothes and shoes. Her hair is brown with reddish lights and naturally curly. Her eyebrows are a lighter brown and her eyelashes brown shading to gold over really lovely, wide, ingenuous blue eyes. Her nose is small and turns up. Her complexion is better than it used to be. She possesses a sweetly petulant mouth and teeth which are engagingly uneven and not white. Her chin is firm and there are two delightful dimples in her cheeks. Her hands and feet are small. She walks with a swirl of skirts. She is not intellectual. She possesses common sense and a droll way of telling a story about herself. She laughs when amused and screws up her face like a baby's when displeased or annoyed. She's always tired. She believes that her perpetual weariness is due to the act she puts on at home in order to sidestep cutting the grass, wheeling the barrow, raking the drive. She's really quite lazy yet has worked so hard in her ceramics course that she has obtained a partial scholarship. She could not very well be sweeter with me. She makes me feel as if she were a doll that could speak and walk, make simple choices, enjoy affection and be affectionate. She'll be twenty in August. She is flirting with her fourth steady boy friend of the year. I should think all the men would tumble over themselves in her direction.

June 23   This has been a hectic week, mostly, for pain in my back and forehead and temples. Yesterday Pearl and Martha used sticks and planks and jabbers and what not to attempt to cause movement between the sixth and seventh ribs. Fred came later with a newly thought-out technique and moved several of the lower ribs. I slept last night, and this morning have been bothering everyone and teasing Pearl to bring some sort of order out of the chaos into which my household affairs had slipped. Now I am dead. But everything is working better. I flatter, deservedly, Mrs. Trench. I tease Pearl. I pet Martha. I am nasty with Evelyn.

June 24 Fred has been here and pumped my stomach. Young son Charlie was with him. Despite the fact that Fred isn't a character boy, I like and enjoy him and am sure he likes and enjoys me. Our imaginations meet easily. He slapped Pearl down with vigor and dispatch a week ago when she was fresh, and she has been a better woman since. She needed it. The company she has been with for five years must have been quite cheap. I'm working hard to get her into some nonblatant clothes and to moderate her voice. She's doing well on her part. Maybe I'll be able to persuade her to cut down on the drinking soon. She lives with her oldest brother and his wife, rents from them a three-room apartment, fifty dollars a month. She receives forty dollars a week from her husband and forty dollars a week thus far from me — ten dollars a day. She's a great help and will continue so I hope.

I've resolved not to become bitter about Billy. He talked against me lately to Pearl, to Fred, but I suppose that was part of the masculine process of justifying himself. Pearl won't tell me some of what he said. I suppose he went all but crazy with desire for Sandra. During the years of our relationship he has been wonderful to me many times, strength to me, self-esteem to me, a buffer and a consolation. Perhaps I should be grateful to him for having driven home the lesson that no person should be absolutely trusted by any other person, however rosy the apparent relations between them.

June 30 Too wild and too exciting a time to write. We are at undeclared war with the Northern Koreans, which is to say, vicariously with the Soviets. This is more of the harvest of Roosevelt's 'hunch' that if he gave Stalin everything he wanted he would end up a good pal. Even though Roosevelt had guaranteed Korea independence, he permitted it to be split up. His ignorance of historical processes was abysmal as is Truman's. Neither man, I feel fairly safe to assert, ever read a dozen histories, and the chances are they read less. It has been evident to an uninformed onlooker like myself that Russia has been building up a military organization in Northern Korea for years. It wasn't to play tiddlywinks with. The Administration has been kept informed of this, in spite of which it withdrew from Southern Korea after setting up a 'democracy' there.

So Southern Korea was invaded, the only bit of non-Communist territory left between Indo-China and the North Pole in far Asia save Macao and Hong Kong. Everyone expected that it would be just another American knuckling down to Moscow. But other things have been happening here in the United States. Several Soviet spies have been tried and convicted, not always of spying to be sure, that being too explicit and too unprovable what with the Administration's withholding of evidence. Also, a Senator named McCarthy has made charges of Communist infiltration and influence in high Government places, has made them so long and so loudly that public opinion, observing the veil of secrecy cast over inquiries and evidence by the Government, has turned to a belief that the charges must be correct. A howl against Secretary of State Acheson has arisen from all quarters — for protecting subversive agents within his department, for handing over China to the Reds, for refusing to aid Chiang in his last stand, Formosa. The military, it is said, has been in constant disagreement with Acheson and Truman.

Praise be that at last the Roosevelt policy of acquiescence to Stalin has been reversed before we are utterly 'sold out on the installment plan' by the State Department boys, spies, Russian sympathizers, 'liberals,' fairies, incompetents and all. Nationalism may look like a fatuous semireligion to some future generation, but right now it is still deeply ingrained in men's spirits and aspirations, and it is well for us and healthy that we openly recognize ourselves as a national structure. It seems to me that the Communists have a religion, an idea, whereas we have not. They have a potent human figurehead whereas we have not. We have a bigger and better arsenal than they and individuals with more initiative. The cards are fairly evenly stacked in the coming great game. Had we armed Japanese and German allies, we might win. We may win anyway if Stalin dies.

July 2   While I do not see how Russia can win World War III in the end, the greater means of manufacture being on our side, I do see how civilians can be all but destroyed. Were I Truman (and make no mistake about it, the President can be imperator at will) I should:

1. Flood all plants with orders for military engines and necessities of all sorts, and whatever the cost it would not total up to the cost of a real and final all-out war.
2. Put conscription into effect immediately.
3. Arm and train the Japanese and the Germans.
4. Reorganize the United Nations without Russia and as a military federation directing and supporting a military force drawn from minor nations.
5. Zone and patrol the ocean some three hundred miles offshore in Canada, the United States, Mexico, in order to examine all

ships for atomic bombs and give adequate radar warning of strange planes and submarines, especially the latter.

6. Put many important plants and armories and arsenals and airfields underground.

7. Educate people as how best to cope with atomic attack and instruct governments, state, county, city, in defense organization.

8. Put great reservoirs of water (as Constantinople in the Middle Ages) underground, and gasoline supplies.

9. Carry on — and this is most important — an expensive and insistent propaganda campaign against Russia within Russia and inside the 'Iron Curtain' nations by radios dropped from wind-carried balloons, by radio, by leaflets circulated by hand and dropped by balloons, by agents organizing inner cells of resistance in Czechoslovakia and China and other countries where it would seem to be profitable and not beyond possibility.

10. Repress Communists in this country with such brutality as to frighten them and their adherents. Brutality, historically speaking, seems necessary in order to obtain strength at home when traitors and deserters are in force and highly organized. Witness Russia itself. And wholesale brutality against an inner sapping power works. Do not believe it does not.

July 4　Fred put rib in place Friday. Tremendous relief, though temples very bad. Rib stayed mobile for three days, jammed yesterday. Terrible night.

July 5　The war appears to be going badly against us. The Reds, rumor has it, may have enveloped our single division. Our jet fighters apparently are incompetent in heavy weather conditions. We have only one aircraft carrier, the Army and Air generals having shouted down the Navy experts who claimed aircraft carriers were of vital importance. The general theory has been that air power could win any war. It is being disproved at a great rate. Churchill, the only historical-minded politician of stature, states that if we are driven out of Korea, that will be the signal for World War III, and the war will be bad for us beyond our present conception. He is probably correct. I doubt if the atomic bomb could be used serviceably in Korea, considering the terrain. Well, for good or ill, it is not unlikely we will receive a good kicking and that by a Soviet minor state. We won't even clamp down laws against the Communists here at home.

I made a long list of what to buy and hoard yesterday. Am getting at it today. I want a deep freeze. I'm selling the Lockheed airplane stock I bought Monday. If we are being defeated, everything will slide to hell on the Market. Better stay quite liquid there. Wish I weren't so sick. Buy rubber goods, clocks, paper things, soaps, meats, etc. Maybe am pessimistic, though doubt it. We should let Japanese flyers have planes and make use of them. We are fools. Thank God we have a fine general at the helm, General Bradley, the man who, historians seem to agree, did most toward the winning of World War II. I have never made up my mind about MacArthur.

July 6 I am aware Martha is lazy, spoiled, petulant sometimes, not too intelligent always, but how she acts and talks with me outweighs by far her deficiencies. I'm not too sure, anyway, that her mental deficiencies are not mostly sprung from reactions against her parents and from lack of know-how. She certainly possesses a comprehending imagination and seems to understand my mental and emotional bogdowns as Billy seemed to understand them.

July 14 Ran into Mrs. Cash this morning. She was dolled up like a new barber's pole. She muttered hello. "Why hello Mrs. Cash," I effused. "How are you?" It was fun. She looked down at the pavement and hurried by as though skirting a rotting skunk cabbage. She didn't answer. She evidently has steam up again. My, but she's a queer one. Most French people seem to be somewhat queer.

July 16 Mike has been working on the steering post of my Cadillac. Pearl keeps company with him, sees him every day, goes off with him nearly every weekend. He wants to marry her, but she won't marry him because he is older than she and a "confirmed Catholic." Whether she is pulling my leg or not I have no notion. She talks of wanting to sleep with him but that he is impotent from long disuse. "Anyway, he gives me affection. You and I, Arthur darling, must have our affection. That's one of our main pleasures in life. Mike gives me that, and it's more important than passion — although I have no objection, you understand, to passion. I'm a different female from the one you used to know, Artie. But no one could be nicer and more considerate than Mike, and he worships the ground I stand on. We get along fine. I've got a nice man. I've got a good job. I've got my car now. I've got a swell apartment. I should be contented and I'm gettin' more so every day. To hell with Norman. He was everything you said he was. I'll never get any money from him, I'll bet. Just try and separate a hunky from his money. He wasn't worth all the care and spoilin' I gave him. He used to hit me and stay out nights and once he broke my nose, but I was willin' to take all that if he'd kept on with me. We had our good times. But I'm not gonna stay with any guy in the world who doesn't want me. I'm done with him for good. I like my new life and bein' with you,

Arthur dear. You're awful good to me and I want to be good to you, and by God, I won't ditch you like Billy did. I never got over leavin' you the other time. But I was young and didn't realize that was no way to commence marriage. I may never marry again."

August 16 In these days propaganda is almost as important an arm of warfare as planes and men and equipment. We are totally without it. Stories come through that our men have no idea why or for what purpose they fight. We have no competent propaganda machine to work upon the enemy. Our spy system everywhere is inefficient and contradictory. The war in Korea is a mirror of conditions here at home, confused, contradictory, unorganized, wasteful. History has shown that a religious war cannot be withstood save by inspired forces.

We let the Russians propound their doctrines within our own borders under cover of the United Nations and lift not a hand to disband and reorganize that institution (set up by Alger Hiss for our discomfort) or to throw out the Russian representative bodily. We even permit convicted Communists out on bail to shout against us. Congress is impotent. We will not go to war with the instigator of all our woes, for we feel it immoral to start a war (already started) or to attack the source of attacks on us.

August 20 This business of Billy has taken the cover off many tucked-away thoughts. I have been reassessing everyone with suspicion. I got to thinking about Dr. Pike and Evelyn, what a trustful dupe I had been. I recalled the dozen or so semimocking inquiries from various sources as to the relations between the two, and how I had defended their relationship, brought about with considerable assiduity by myself. I felt Evelyn was without anyone to take her around, and I had trusted Dr. Pike not to transgress my generosity. I wondered.

I mentioned Evelyn at suppertime Wednesday to Pearl. She said: "I guess she misses Dr. Pike. I don't see how you let that affair go on as it did. I knew about it soon after I came with you but didn't say a word since I knew you knew. God, you used to be able to hear the bed creaking at lunchtime when he was there and what they said as you passed the door. Everyone knew about it. I sometimes thought it was a shame. I guess she's lonesome for him. A woman, you know, loves the man who beds her. I don't mean that Evelyn doesn't love you. I think, though I don't know (nobody ever knows about her), that she loves you. If I was you, Artie darling, I'd not let her get intimate with another man, though that's your business again. You came out the wrong end of the horn before. It would be that way again. You mark my words."

That evening I asked Evelyn: "Did you sleep with Dr. Pike? I'd like a straight answer. It would help me understand you. I know I said you could try it, but I asked you three times directly if you did it and you said no. Now I want to know. Did you sleep with him?" "I don't think I ought to answer that." "Oh yes you should. Did you sleep with him? I want to know. I need to know." "I won't answer." "Yes or no? I must know." "You won't like the answer." "Probably not. But I already know it. I want to hear it from you. Did you?" "Yes I did. You shouldn't have asked me. I shouldn't be telling you. I should be protecting his name."

I gulped inwardly. It was like shivering from sudden immersion in icy water you suspected was icy but could hardly believe was that. "Did you like it?" I asked. "I suppose I did or I wouldn't have done it. But I don't like your questions. They aren't decent. All that is in the past. You told me to sleep with him if I wished." "I told you to try sleeping with him if you wished. How long did you sleep with him?" "Oh," rather pridefully, "I don't remember." "How long?" "Why should you know?" "The only thing you have done," I replied, "in the past several years that I really admired you for was telling your father to reduce your inheritance, and you did it solely, I'm sure, because I asked. I'm asking you to be honest and forthright about this. I must know. I must. How long?" "Well, I began when he was running after Aunt Helen — 1933 or 1934, I forget which (that is probably why he didn't marry her); and it lasted until several years ago." "You mean you slept with him and he slept with you over a period of twelve or so years?" I was set back with a thump of real shock on my heels. "I guess so." "How often a week?" "Oh, often at first, less often later. But this is indecent. I won't listen. I'm going. I should have maintained silence." "You damn well aren't going. And this honesty, if belated, I admire you for. Sit down again."

My head went around and around. My heart thumped. I said: "While naturally, being human and a man, I don't like what you did, I do not consider you are altogether to blame. I know you are weak. You have always lied to me. My attempt to be quite honest with you about Flossie Bert and Hassie was unwise, I now realize. I did urge you to try some man but never urged you to be anyone's mistress. I trusted you not to do that. I should, nevertheless, have taken your natural weakness into account. I was remiss and —" She interrupted, "Unworldly beyond belief." "Yes, and sentimental and trustful. I don't think it is you, Evelyn, who puts me under the guillotine, or your actions. I know you are weak and your code of morals not my code of morals. It is what Dr. Pike did that injures me beyond repair." "He did nothing I did not do." "He was my friend. I liked him and admired him and trusted him and, I think, told him I trusted you with him. Yet he cuckolded me. He deceived me. He betrayed me in my own house. He made free use of my wife and then looked me straight in the eyes. He was all my Mother said he was, weak morally and a two-timer and a betrayer of deep trust." "He did no more than you did with the Bert girl. She had a husband. What's the difference?" "My God, can't you perceive the difference? I didn't know that man. She had a contempt for him. He wasn't my friend of many years. He wasn't trusting me with someone he loved and was in love with as a friend." "Just the same—" "Just the same nothing. I'm no angel. But I've not ever wished to deceive you. You said you wanted me to. I'd never have slept with a girl after Flossie Bert in 1935 if I hadn't felt you cared no more for me sexually and I needed reassurance. I wouldn't have slept with Trudy if you hadn't sicked Whitcomb on me and I wanted revenge and felt your lack of trust in me justified such an act. Yet you lied and Dr. Pike committed adultery in my own home and not just two or three times but over a long, long period. I will never forgive him for it. I wish I had told him to leave you alone the first time I talked with him. I am glad, save where treatments are concerned, he is dead. He betrayed me utterly." "Foolishness," she ejaculated, and added: "It's all over long ago. He didn't deprive you of anything you wanted terribly so what harm did he do you? He was devoted to you."

I was exhausted. I tried to sleep. About two, I wakened Evelyn from a sound sleep and asked her to come upstairs and talk to me. She didn't like it but came. I had been thinking at a frantic pace. By quick intervals my resentment at Dr. Pike had mounted. Evelyn lay on one bed, I on the other. Before I was well started, she was up and half out the door, with "I won't listen to these things about Dr. Pike." "I don't see why not," I replied. "I don't see why not. For twelve or fourteen years he got free tail of my acquiescent wife, and now she won't listen. Is there no justice of any sort within her? Is she absolutely callous as long as she gets her own way? Has she no mind for her cuckolded husband whatever, merely a sentimental regard for a dead lover with whom she was in love? I am a good man and a just man in comparison to other men, and an honest one. And yet you defend a low adulterer, your lover who talked about you callously when fresh out of your bed and who was three times willing to toss you aside, against one who was in love with you and would have stuck to you where he would or not. You stay and listen, please. It is the least you can do."

She returned to the bed. I continued. "I'd like to ask some questions. I want to get this entirely straight in my mind and emotionally. All the time Dr. Pike was getting free tail, he was sending me bills for treating you—" "He had to protect himself against your finding out." "Which signifies he was aware he was doing wrong. And then, when my Father gave you that Bibb, he sent bills to you even while screwing you—if you'll pardon the Anglo-Saxon word, justified in its usage I believe. What sort of cheap two-timer was he anyway? Did he give you the money back outside, if he felt sending bills protected him? Did he?" "No. The arrangement wasn't a financial one. I wasn't a kept woman." "Quite right, not in your mind. In his, perhaps not a kept woman, merely free tail. Any ordinary man would have been generous with you in mere gratitude for what he was receiving." "He paid for my meals and for the gas when we drove to the farm." "You held yourself very cheap, Evelyn." "It wasn't that sort of arrangement." "What sort of arrangement was it then?" "He approved of me. He was the only person in the world who did. I wanted to please him." "If he approved of you, why did he say such belittling things to me about you? You have an idea, and a false one I think, that he meant what he said. I'm sure he didn't as a rule. Couldn't he well afford to give you blarney when he got free tail in return and boundless affection? What else did he give you?" "I don't see where this will get you or get me. What does it matter? It's all over with now. It's a closed book." "For you, maybe. Not for me. I've known one man and one woman. Now I have to know another woman and, even more, another man. What else did he give you?"

Her attitude was that of a female protecting the sweetheart. It rankled me. I had in large part idealized Dr. Pike. I had with complete unworldliness trusted him. I had, worst of all perhaps, admired him. And he had proven to be a betrayer and a cheap enjoyer of my wife's sexual prerogatives and a man very ungenerous with her. That I had been in a degree culpable, especially with her, I was willing to acknowledge and take into account. I had been unworldly, if you will, in trusting him but not, had he been honorable, culpable.

"What else did he give you?" She was unwilling to answer. Finally: "He gave me the rug from his office for the farm and the table there. He gave me one quarter of the price of the farm." "And what else?" "Oh, what does it matter? He gave me a hundred dollars when his farm was sold. He paid for my meals." "Not, at the most, more than two thousand dollars—say twenty-four hundred to be wide and safe. Say twelve years. That is two hundred a year for free tail. Very cheap in him and very I don't know what—perhaps lack of pride—in you! And above the fucking and beyond it, you gave him such affection and devotion and compromise as you never gave me after we were married. I've heard you on the telephone. He had two striding legs and could walk away if you didn't please him. I have no such legs and I have a devotion for you he never felt. You say you didn't (whether you are prevaricating or not) enjoy the bed parties; you liked the blarney. I feel he was a heel and a betrayer. The way he treated his wife should have illuminated me as to that. My fault is that, when I become sentimental about any person, I trust them—Billy, Dr. Pike, Joe Cooper, my Mother. You can defend Dr. Pike (and I am taking into account how much he helped me and was willing to go out of his way to do so) until I am dead, and I shall never regard him as otherwise than a cheap betrayer of trust."

Evelyn's defenses for Dr. Pike ran on and on. She seemed to consider my mental and spiritual torture. "Have you no regrets?" I asked. "None," she replied. "Why should I have? I did it. I did it with my eyes open. It is over now." "Didn't you ever feel cheap and tawdry and double-dealing to get out of the bed with the feeling of his prick still in you and to come up to me and hear my declarations of trust in you and in him? Didn't it?" "Why no. I didn't regard it that way." "Do you love me?" "Why yes. I haven't left you, have I?" "And you still felt no shame?" "None."

That night (I'm not the first husband to be utterly hoodwinked while defending his wife's probity) I slept a single hour and was glad of that.

Later on, I reviewed the conversation. I became determined, if nothing else, to destroy her emotional idealization of Dr. Pike. I'll vilify him in her mind if it takes the remainder of my life. She treasures his memory more than mine though I'm worth six of him ethically, unconventional as I am. I have asked her to remove his picture from her chest of drawers (she never had mine there) and told her I would destroy it if it weren't. I shall never trust a man again—any man. I shall never trust her (not that I did). I wish I were rid of her forever, though haven't the courage to be rid of her, at least not yet. She has been an evil influence in my life. She is all but worthless. Yet she still has a hold over me, like gin over an alcoholic. I will take an extra apparent interest in her Acton property and touch her thereby and conjointly attempt to strip Dr. Pike of his glamour for her and show him to her in his true light, a cheap, parsimonious, sneaking betrayer of a good man's confidence and trust.

I have asked Eva if she still considers marrying me when she is twenty-two or twenty-three. She does, she says. She finds me, even if

I am a heathen, loveable and forthright and just and good and appealing and reliable and honest and always in mind the best interests of those I love. She doesn't mind no children or my lack of youthful sexual powers. I have money and an affectionate nature and a merry disposition, given half a chance, and I am truthful and generous and winning—and that is more than most women can hope for. She loves me devotedly. We agree it is not wise to hurry matters. She sees Evelyn as cold and selfish and self-centered.

August 24   Pearl was very late at suppertime and I lost my temper, the matter of promptness having come up before many times, and she cried and was, I found, drunk. We argued. She answered the telephone poorly about a prospective tenant. She spilled my supper. She had had a fight with Mike and had taken to the wine bottle. I like Pearl all right, but it is no longer love. She said: "I love you, Artie, and I love Mike, and you are my world right now. When I displease either of you, I'm sunk." She says that she must stop drinking so much. I hope so. I doubt so. It was an emotional day underlined by a very bad collarbone.

August 25   Had another long talk with Evelyn, as I wished to get some additional data on matters relative to Dr. Pike and her sexual and moral past and present. I did not expect her to answer at once and to the point but, to my surprise, she did.

Had she enjoyed sleeping with him all those years? She guessed she must have, else she wouldn't have. Was she passionate with him more than with me? It was hard for her to remember since that was all in the past. Sometimes she enjoyed the act. Sometimes she didn't. She enjoyed pleasing him, because he approved of her. Did she enjoy him more than she enjoyed me? She must have. Why? Because, after a due amount of caressing, he went to the point of the matter. He didn't tousle her hair or blow in her ear or rumple her eyebrows or be playful, which annoyed her with me. Did she caress him? She didn't think so. He was so intent upon what he wanted that he was satisfied to caress her. Didn't she have any conscience coming upstairs wet from his attentions to me, her husband? Not that she could recall. Why did she start sleeping with him? Because I suggested it and because she was curious. Couldn't she yet perceive any difference in laying with him several times and keeping it up for twelve or fourteen or fifteen years? No, none. Anyway, it was her private affair, and her conscience in no wise bothered her. And neither could she perceive that in the eyes of almost any average person he had cozened me and betrayed my trust and made free for years on end with my wife in my house, or what corresponded to my house? No she could not. It was a special circumstance. He wasn't depriving me of anything I wanted. Was that for him to judge? Perhaps not. And couldn't she comprehend that to any self-respecting man Dr. Pike had acted the part of a cheapskate, a parsimonious lover, getting everything for less than four dollars a week, not as much as he'd have had to pay a decent tart? No. It wasn't a business affair. And if it wasn't a business affair, was not that all the more reason for his being generous? Had she no pride? Had she put no value upon herself?

What, she queried, was I trying to do, destroy her good memory of Dr. Pike? Yes, I replied, I was. It deserved to be destroyed. He would come from his free tail and his line of flattery and call her selfish and egotistic and a woman who was interested in nothing in the world but what she wanted. The least she could do for me, I thought, would be to exorcize his memory from her mind and sentiment. She owed me that after doing what she had done and countenancing my loss of trust in a man I felt deeply was a secure friend, did she not? She was not, she declared, sentimental about Dr. Pike. He had been an incident. The incident was over. It was all dead as he was, part of the past. To me, I said, it was not all dead, part of the past. It was the immediate present of which the past was integral. Not, she stated flatly, to her. She had taken his picture, as I wished, from her chest of drawers. She had put it away. That was sufficient. She would not tear it up. And that, she concluded, did not prove she still possessed sentiment.

I am to talk with Dr. Sewell [Evelyn's psychiatrist] about her, about Dr. Pike, about myself.

August 27 Last evening Evelyn supplied me suddenly with the key to her entire character. I was saying that I was being more generous about this Dr. Pike business than most men would be and wished she would be generous about regarding him for what he was. She replied nastily: "Perhaps I don't want to be generous." There it is, I exclaimed to myself, the key. It was as if a hundred locked doors down the long bitter corridor of the past snapped open to the touch of the master key. Her coldness, her selfishness, her secretiveness, her adjustable morality, her minimization of my generosity, her lack of willingness to change her will, her inability to comprehend Dr. Pike's parsimony as a sin, her small gifts to people at inopportune moments to cover larger stinginess, her failure to accept and use constructive ideas, even her way of driving a car disregardful of other drivers—all was clear.

August 28 Yesterday I played up to Evelyn. It certainly seems to work. If it works, I certainly can and will change my tactics as the result, not the method, is what matters. She said: "Do you mind if I wear my wedding ring? You never liked it, you will recall. I'd like to wear it." "Of course." I replied, and added: "It's a swell idea. And if you'd like an engagement ring, go buy that. Anything up to a thousand dollars. Would you like that?" "Oh yes, I would. I'd love it. Can I have a sapphire?" I usually eat in my own room, because I don't like the way Evelyn eats. We were alone. "Let's eat together," I suggested. "Pretty soon," she remarked, "I'm going to faint." "Oh, you haven't seen the half of the new Arthur," I said. "Not the half. I've honestly, as I've told you so often and you have as often disbelieved, never before understood you. I would just flounder about and hurt you and hurt myself in my futile efforts to establish contact. Now I understand, all will be different. You'll see. And I'm sure you'll meet me halfway. Symbolically, we'll be engaged and wed anew." "And just about the day when we've adjusted everything, the atomic bomb will fall." "That's exactly it," I agreed.

When we had had luncheon and Evelyn had called my Father at Southwest Harbor to find out had he begun to feel better from his last fainting spell, Evelyn lay on the bed and I began to caress her. Always hitherto she has made a point of keeping her legs together after the modest feminine pattern. It has always provoked me, for she is not an iota modest by nature. This time she dropped her legs apart spontaneously. Where she found the sense to abandon the other procedure I don't know. At any rate, I reacted in masculine fashion. I inquired could I sleep with her. If I wished, but she wasn't sure it was good policy. Neither was I. It was one of the first occasions for years when she hasn't said, "Do we have to do this?" or "How about some other time?" or made gestures of negation or used dissatisfied tones.

I thought of Dr. Pike and of the hundreds upon hundreds of times he had lain with Evelyn, and I was all but stopped. But nature proved the stronger, and anyway I felt it might be good policy. I decided. Evelyn agreed. We were on Mrs. Trench's bed. Evelyn was all for going to my room and my bed. I felt a new setting was advisable for both of us. I locked and beamed the door. We took off our clothes. I am so used to Evelyn's being without a right breast now that I scarcely notice it. The left breast is still pretty and round, like a girl's. She's plumper than formerly. She looked quite handsome spread out there. I was careful to avoid all dalliances such as she had spoken against. Her legs and stomach lying down are especially attractive. She is no firebrand to be with, hardly doing her part actively, not exciting as Trudy was, but I was hellbent upon pleasing her and am able to feel she did not utterly fail to enjoy it. It is the pleasing me she enjoys, she says. She said the same about Dr. Pike. I never wished more fervently to establish amicable and trusting relations with anyone. I thanked and showered her with compliments and affection. I don't see why she cannot, stout castle though she is, be breached. I cannot, try over the years as I may, and God alone knows how I have tried, disburden myself of my love for my wife.

August 30   Yesterday morning Evelyn shopped at the jewelry stores for a ring. She brought six home. Of course, I picked the most expensive, a rectangular Burmese sapphire, dark, in a modern setting of impeccable proportions, price $1,000 flat. "Do you like it, Evelyn?" "Yes, I like it." "Do you want it?" "I think so. What strings are attached to it?" "None. Only that you really want it and will enjoy it and will consider it as my new-era engagement ring to you." "Why do you want to give such a large present to me?" "Because it's evident to me I love you. Because I gave you no ring before or at the time of our marriage and you've always wanted one. Because I want to please you. Because this ring is distingué enough to be appreciated by the knowing and taken for granted by the unknowing. Because it looks so well on your right little finger where you wish to wear it and lets the wedding ring be separate on the other finger where it belongs. About seventy-five percent that; and twenty-five percent because Dr. Pike was such a cheapskate and I feel impulsed to make up for his holding you at such a low evaluation and your unprideful evaluation of yourself. Mostly, I want to please you, I reckon."

Evelyn is what is called slow on the uptake. It was evening before she became femininely impressed by the ring. "I keep it in a drawer. I run to look at it. I put it back. I look at it again. I try it on. It's beautiful, Arthur. It's really beautiful. And it reassures me. And I love it. I'm very, very grateful to you. It's my engagement ring, isn't it?"

While we were riding this morning, I had Evelyn draw up by the bed of honeysuckle across from the Museum. "I have this to say," I began. "I'm in a perfectly good humor but want you to take it seriously, for I've been giving it considerable thought. I wish you to be my wife and my wife alone from here on. I don't want you to go with any other man. I've learned my lesson. If I find you going with any other man, I'll draw up a new will and disinherit you completely (Note: Of course I wouldn't—completely), and if I hear of you going with any man I'll believe the gossip and take steps to find out, and if it is true I'll cut you out of my will. I've learned my lesson. You're my woman only from here on, and I trust you're listening and understand, for it is no bluff. I told you once I'd leave you if you didn't cut down on your time away. That was a bluff. I'll never make another bluff. This is not a bluff. I mean it. Have you listened and have you understood and will you put it deep in your mind and not forget it?" "Yes, I will remember it. I have listened!" "I hope you feel it is just?" "Yes, I feel it is just. I have no intention of ever again becoming involved with another man." "You had no intention of becoming involved with Dr. Pike. It was my mistake in misleading you and in trusting a cad. I won't make the same mistake again. And as for you, see that it doesn't happen again. And that is all. I'm not angry. I merely wish to be plain and to have you understand and remember. It's a lovely, invigorating day, isn't it? Let's finish our drive, honey."

My new policy includes much flattery, more pleasantness, a steady pointing out of what will be my wife's self-interest, less apparent pressure and an instantaneous violent response to specific neglects of my interest. I want to be so generous that she will be ashamed not to meet me a quarter of the way. I don't see why it shouldn't work.

August 31   It's no use. I can't get anywhere with Evelyn. I gave her $1,000 for the damn Acton place as I had promised to do if she sold the goddamn farm. She was nasty even before I gave her the check and more nasty still a couple of hours later.

"If accepting the money for the Acton property is going to place me under obligation to you, I don't want it. Here it is back. And if I'm to feel under obligation for the ring, turn it in.

"If I mean to be a certain way and what I say doesn't sound that way, that's just too bad. I don't care. I'm what I am and you've got to take me that way if you want to take me at all. If you don't, that's okay. I don't care. And you can't high-pressure me into being any more careful of my words and acts than I am. I can't do it — or won't do it, if you like that better. If you get hurt, that's just too bad. You shouldn't be so subject to nuances. You can like what I am and do and say or not, I'm sure I don't care a damn. I've stood for all the pressure I'm going to take. I won't take any more — and if you think I will you're crazy. Why don't we part? You can't do anything with me. I won't do anything more with myself. I can look forward to only a few more years to live, twenty at the most, and I fully intend being and doing as I wish during those years."

September 1   Yesterday Evelyn had a headache and didn't show up until eleven. I was worn out. So was she. We mutually avoided controversial subjects. I said to myself: "Beer to the rescue." Pearl had found an ale with a 20% alcoholic content. We drank that, all of us. Things went better thereafter. Evelyn said no more about not accepting the $1,000 for the Acton property. I doubted if her nature could turn such a sum down. It is my opinion that she has decided sex is one way of ironing out some of our difficulties. She has after twenty-five years of contest given up wearing pants around me. I like that.

I was petting her. "How do you like it best?" I asked, expecting the usually noncommittal response. "This way," she said, taking my hand and fingers and showing me what she liked, "this way." I could see in a trice I had always been too gentle, that she liked her sex with vigor. I acceded. It was exciting. She ended by coming to bed with me, and I must admit we had a good time, though I couldn't rid my private mind of Dr. Pike and of how different matters might have been. It is her symbol, I'm sure, of a new attitude. I must be more careful at my age to confine my activities in sex to once a week. Otherwise, as now, I become sore in bones and muscles. I'm pretty darn good, I suspect, for my age and the limitations of endurance. That helps my spirit, naturally, being a man. "It's the control you exercise," instructed Eddie, years ago, "and how you manage your mind." It is so, as was most of his advice—with reservations.

September 3   I began a month or so ago asking Martha if she would have her virginity cut out and then sleep with me. While lying in bed with me in the afternoon, she said yes she would. I've offered her a hundred bucks, a trip by plane to New York and the doctor's bill there (birth control is illegal here—the Irish Catholics). "You understand, Artie dear Artie, that no amount of money—not a million—would be enough to buy me if I didn't want to?" "I understand." "Well, I just wanted to make sure you understood." "I do, baby, my littlest baby, and I'm very grateful to you indeed." And I am. She very sweet to me. She likes to be touched by me. She lies nicely in the arms. Her body is pleasant to feel. She has considerable sex attraction for me.

I asked Evelyn if she minded if I slept with someone else. She replied that now I knew about her, what objections could she offer. I've learned my lesson at any rate. If I have 'an affair' with Martha, I shall not inform Evelyn you may be sure. I may not anyway, now that Evelyn is acting more like a wife sexually. My powers are limited. Also my interest in sex would become glutted. Martha's a puppchen, though. I enjoy her. She says: "No one in the world has ever been as sweet and understanding with Martha as Artie darling. That's why Martha loves him so very much and wants always—well, almost always—to please him." And she kisses me. And I like it.

Then there is another problem. This one sort of stumps me. Pearl doesn't get sexual satisfaction from Mike. She has an eye on me, and the implications of that eye are plain to read. Last night she returned at 11:30, took a bath, smoothed herself, came in my room in her nightgown. She was ready. "Oh, Artie sweetheart, you are so nice to your Pearl. She loves you an awful lot, honest. She has ideas. She wishes your back didn't hurt." And she nuzzled like a kitten. And she wanted me to feel her stomach, if she were losing weight. And she pressed against me. I thought fast and pleaded the hemorrhoid injection. Otherwise, I said, couldn't we have fun. And there it was, a melon cut open and being presented to me on a silver platter. I'm more than a bit scared of it and her. She talks too much. She is too obvious and potent. I don't want to endanger my new relationship with Evelyn. But here am I, an old codger of fifty-five, invalided, with three agreements to go to bed with three unusually attractive woman in one day. Why wasn't life like this when I was young? Anyway, it is flattering, to say the least.

September 7 Evelyn said: "I've been thinking over about Dr. Pike, what sort of man you feel he was, what sort of man people would have thought him if they had known what you know, what sort of man he was in comparison to you and my feelings toward him. I can tell you that he is no longer in my sentiments. That is what you wanted, isn't it? I tore up the picture of him I liked best."

I thanked her gravely. Was she, I asked, being absolutely honest? It was very important that she be quite honest. Yes, she replied, she was being thoroughly honest; it was important to be honest.

I felt basically relieved. I didn't fully suppose she would concede this so quickly. She must have worked on herself in earnest. I think she means what she says. Her "the past is the past" attitude doubt-less assisted her diligence. It is assumable that the money toward the Acton place helped, and the ring. It is an extraordinarily handsome ring. She seems to love it, and so do I.

Evelyn's entire attitude towards me (hold your hats) appears to have undergone a metamorphosis in the desired direction. She is being less resentful, gentler, not so controversial, sweeter. On Labor Day we got our time mixed and when she didn't return from seeing her mother until two hours after I had expected her and I was, as most men become when worried, wild and faultfinding, she didn't argue or defend herself but came over to the bed where I was lying and put her two bare arms around me and kissed me and told me gently not to worry, she was back and it wouldn't happen again. It was one of the few times she had been wholeheartedly kind to me since our marriage, and I was so touched I wept.

Yesterday Evelyn said: "You asked me ten days or so ago if I'd think it over and let you know whether or not I felt I could ever fall in love with you again as you knew you could with me. I've thought it over. I'm sure I could — darling."

September 25 Some people react to what they abhor by closing off their minds to all thought of the matter. Others — and I am of this class — stare at every line and lineament of what they abhor until they become inured or indurated. I feel that if I ascertain every item of information possible concerning Evelyn's relationship with Dr. Pike, I shall better be able to bear a matter which, I find, has jarred me to my psychological foundations. I discover myself waking at night and being tormented by jealousy for Dr. Pike. Two functioning legs, some Irish blarney and my own decent unworldliness and trust enabled him to take over my wife body and soul and have full use of her for little return. My love, my unremitting efforts in her behalf, my wish for what she gave him went unrewarded and unremunerated. I said to Evelyn: "You should certainly be flattered beyond measure that I feel as violently about what happened as I do and still want you and love you and cherish you. I don't know what sort of a dope I am. I still am busy trying to separate Dr. Pike the doctor and Dr. Pike the rat into two persons so as to be just to the doctor. As for the man, I could cheerfully crucify him and tear off his testicles and jerk out his flattering tongue." "You can't feel that violently," Evelyn protested. "Oh yes I can. Yes I do." "I'm shocked," she said. "Be shocked," I said. "But you should be flattered." Perhaps she is. I don't know. Anyway, here's the somewhat sordid story, as I have it from her bit by bit.

Evelyn went with Dr. Pike in the first place because I thought sleeping with someone else a few times might help her self-confidence, because of her natural curiosity, because several men were making proposals to her simultaneously. She felt herself in a stalemate as far as her marriage was concerned, and if it hadn't been Dr. Pike it would have been someone else. She now admits she was perfectly well aware then that it was to be an experiment, not an affair of long standing, something she has not hitherto admitted. Mrs. Pike had been dead several years. Dr. Pike proposed an affair with Evelyn but refused to tie himself down to a short or long time.

"Where did it happen at first?" I asked. "In his office. In the evening when no one was in the building." "My, my," I said, "just like one of those cheap drugstore romances you buy for a quarter." She bounced to her feet. "All this," she exclaimed, "is indecent enough without your making remarks like that. Are you trying still further to belittle Dr. Pike so as to cure me thoroughly?" "Oh no, not you this time. Myself. You're doing very well exorcising him. I'd be a fool to push you faster. It's myself. I want to look straight at just how cheap he was. Didn't he soon come here and use your bed?" "Fairly soon." "Weren't you ashamed — at first anyway — to come up to me afterwards?" "I didn't like it at first, I guess." "But you kept right on. Why didn't you stop?" "Because he was gentle with me, as you weren't at the time." "How often did he sleep with you?" "Oh, I suppose it averaged once a week." "Did you caress him?" "I imagine not. He didn't need it. He knew what he wanted and was more intent upon getting it without trimmings as you do." "He wanted sex relief primarily?" "This is disgusting. I want to help you, but I don't like it." "Why is it disgusting now when it wasn't then? It happened, didn't it? You liked it then, didn't you?" "Go on. What else do you want to know?" "Did you sleep with him at his house?" "Goodness no. He wouldn't have thought that proper." "When off on your trips?" "We took separate rooms. Sometimes he'd visit me in my room." "Did you use a pessary?" "Certainly." "And you'd come upstairs with it and with his discharge in you and be with me?" "Yes, if occasion warranted." "And that didn't bother you?" "Sometimes." "You know what? You're extremely amoral, really. It shocks me. It shocks me profoundly." "I suppose I am." "And all this being his wife primarily and mine secondarily went on until the latter part of World War II?" "Yes." "Why did he stop?" "He became impotent. That is primarily why, I guess. He used to be terribly ashamed about his impotence." "Didn't it bother you?" "Oh no. I readily got used to not sleeping with him. That, after all, was a secondary matter. He said nice things to me. He was gentle with me. He made me feel as if I were somebody special. I'm sure your intentions were always of the best, Arthur dear, but you must admit your methods weren't always gentle."

"But can't you understand that, for what he was getting, flattery and gentleness were a small price, one he could adhere to because he wasn't married to you?" "He used to say that you had no right to order my life in any way, that no person had such a right over any other person." "He said that after the way he was with Mrs. Pike. The double-tongued bastard. Didn't you know how nasty and stingy he was with Mrs. Pike when she wouldn't give up church activities? He wanted her to be what he wanted her to be, and when she wouldn't he put all the pressure he could on her, and that was plenty. He'd come home drunk and quarrelsome night after night, and I gather from what he said that he beat her. He'd insult her church friends. He raised hell when he couldn't make her after his pattern. He told me so. And you listened to his forked tongue being critical of me? My God, Evelyn, how did you swallow all that? I may not be much of a man, but I'm an honest one and ten times as good and as worthy and as sincere and as commendable as he ever was. How couldn't you see that? I guess we got off to a bad married start. I became frantic because I couldn't teach or instruct you how easily our life might have gone, and because I resorted in desperation to force, and because I thought I was a real important poet and better a unique diarist, and because you read my diary where I'm at my worst, and because I feel so meek inside I blow hard outside. You had your hard time, didn't you, darling? I can see how you miscalculated. But I can't see how you miscalculated so far and how you swallowed what Dr. Pike said. Well, thank you so very much for telling me all this. I know it's been difficult. I think it helps me understand you and hope it helps you understand me. Perhaps, because you had a tough time with me and then I had a tough time with you, the rest of our lives will run easier. You be kind and loving with me and I'll be gentle and self-controlled with you. How about it?"

"Oh yes. And I think everything will be better. I've never tried so hard to see how you look at things. I'm sorry if I was led astray by your own huffing and puffing. I really love you devotedly."

September 26   All night fretted by bitterness toward Dr. Pike. Must stop it. He's dead and my jealousy can do him no ill. But it can do me great ill. I never experienced before what a powerful emotion it can be. One could easily lose all healthy perspective in its dark miasma. That I will not, must not, do.

Dr. Pike pressed Evelyn to leave me and marry him. She refused. Her sense of duty doubtless. Nevertheless she stuck with me. This is the plus side of the ledger. She did stick when very readily she might not have. And she did stick with me during the lean war years.

And at this juncture matters are more my way than since I married. Dr. Pike is dead. The farm is sold and only time will tell what unpalatable mischances are bought with Evelyn's new Acton property — at the moment none. The time Evelyn demands away has been reduced by a week at least. No money is to be left Evelyn by my Father while I live. The Dr. Pike business is out in the open. Evelyn seems to have a different, more appreciative attitude toward me. Her father is dead, and that has made her realize the paucity of real friends and raised my value. Our sex relationship is on a more healthy basis. Alcoholism has been less lately. We have found Dr. Sewell, whom we both like.

October 4–5   I wish to make one matter perfectly plain. However much I am in love with and love Evelyn, however much our relationship may improve, however pleased I may be at her new attitude, I nevertheless hate her and shall, I fear, until I die: hate her for the first time she left me; hate her for her lack of ambition for me; hate her for the time she stole my pistol; hate her for the manner in which her concentration upon her own wishes has lowered my energy and achievements; hate her for being Dr. Pike's mistress without pride and at such trifling cost to him for so many secretive years; hate her for lying to me about that matter; hate her for being alcoholic at Pike's behest; hate her for taking up smoking at his behest, not caring much for it according to her but refusing nonetheless to give it up to please me; hate her for forcing me to belittle myself to Dr. Pike in order to control her movements and preferences; hate her for rewarding my honesty with deceit and untruth; hate her for not sitting up late with me; hate her for her lack of pride in herself and in tasks finished; hate her for buying that farm in Maine when she had given her word not to; hate her for cornering me on this travel business; hate her for sicking Whitcomb on me; hate her for standing upon leaving her money to her nieces and nephew rather than to me; hate her for underestimating my merits consistently; hate her for her perennial absence of kindness; hate her for her contemptuous and supercilious words to me; hate her for her unpleasant cockiness; hate her for her secretiveness; hate her for her resentment at my sensitive nature; hate her because I have not been able to fall out of love with someone for whom I held next to no esteem characterwise; hate her, most of all I think, for her falsehoods and her underestimation of me and her unbroachable egocentricity.

I shall strive to conceal from her (and her lack of intuition does not make it as impossible as might be expected) how I hate the landslide and shale in her character which has all but overwhelmed me repeatedly. At this point I also might as well disguise resentment and lack of admiration and respect, for she is trying for the first time since we married to be sweet and kind and self-controlled and to give me attention and to withhold her various violences against me and to see my side and to assess me with new eyes; and I am appreciative and feel desirous of abstaining from what annoys and bothers her on my part.

October 16 Arguing with Evelyn. Tens of years begged her to call me "darling" without avail. She couldn't "remember to do it." Now she calls everyone "Rose dear" and "Eva dear" and even "Pearl dear" glibly. Angers me to my roots. All my pleas for her to do things, simple things, that will serve to cause me to get along better with her and her with me are ignored until for another reason or even sheer inadvertency, she will do what she has protested doing for years and, like as not, overdo it.

October 20 I am not greatly concerned with Korea. MacArthur's daring amphibious landing was a success. Now the United Nation (United States plus a few British and Australian and many South Korean) forces are pushing into Northern Korea. Meanwhile, Communist forces in Northern Indo-China are pushing back French troops, of which there are about 125,000 garrisoning the country. Truman is flying to Wake Island to consult with MacArthur. The latter is one 'hombre' who fears neither Truman nor his Communist-undermined State Department, the boys who let China go, who wish to let Formosa go, who are willing to recognize Red China in the council of the United Nations. I hope that he will give Bird Brain an instructive dressing down. Somebody should. He's too big for his pants, too purely political-minded, too much under the thumb of the State Department.

Pearl seems ready to be with me whenever I wish, but I am trepidatious as to her powers of dissimulation. Mrs. Trench misses few tricks now where people in front of her are concerned. Should I sleep with Pearl and be apprehended by Evelyn or Mrs. Trench, my name would be mud. No morality involved but some common sense. I'd doubtless best stick to Evelyn now I have taken her over from Pike.

Christ, but that burns me up. I shouldn't have known it would. He was a hypocrite, with talk running cheaply from his mouth in her direction and mine and not the same talk. I can recall vividly how he castigated a man for doing to a wife just what he was doing to my wife. I could twist his pecker into a knot and jerk it there forever. As to Evelyn, of course she should have known better. But there were extenuating circumstances in her case and nature, though not in his. As a matter of fact, I hold that will business against her more than I do the Pike affair. That was crass and selfish and unappreciative and nasty and hurtful, and I'll hate Evelyn for it until I die. I have no inner compunction against hating people for unjustices. Some day I may get even with her. I'll never forget.

October 21 "If growing, as you put it, means that I have to sacrifice any part of myself, my ego, then I'd rather not grow. Perhaps my ego, as you suggest, is the most important thing in life to me. I don't want to hurt anyone purposely, but if they are hurt attempting to alter or guide my ego, well, they'll just have to be hurt. Each person in the world is born equal, and his ego is sacred to himself, not to be impinged upon by anyone else. You want to touch my ego and have it become what you would like it to be. To have anyone seek to touch and influence my ego makes me violently angry and rebellious, and I care not a jot or a tittle whether you are trying to help me or not. That is why it makes me angry when you talk to me at length and say what you call nasty things. If you ever expect me to change and be different in my feelings, you might just as well stop now before you get hurt trying further. I expect to keep what I am intact and as it is if it's the last thing I do. I'm sorry, but that's the way it is, and nothing you can do will make it different. Perhaps I'm not the fine woman you'd like me to turn into. I do possess certain definite good qualities, and I do mean you well. If I talk defeatist to you, that's what I think you want. I don't feel defeatist. Or perhaps it's the easiest way to avoid the pressure of your untiring personality directed at myself. I'll try to cease those expressions if as you say you've told me for twenty-seven years they annoy you. I've appreciated your being gentle with me. But I will not be what you call 'taught' every day by you in words, words, words. I will not stand it. Your intentions probably are of the best and would work on someone else. But not on me. They merely make me frantic and angry. And I assure you they won't get you what you hope for. You'd best stop hoping and enjoy whatever part of me pleases you. That's my advice. I love you, but it could be I'm not fundamentally capable of the sort of unselfish and sacrificing love you wish to fit me with, like an old bathroom with new plumbing. I do have my good points. Enjoy them. I'll try not to say or do the things that bother you. But I will not alter myself for you or for anyone. I am what I am and what I shall remain. You don't like what I am. I'll try to disguise what you dislike when I'm around you, for I wish to please you. But don't expect me to become different fundamentally, because I have no intention, ever, of doing it."

And that is Evelyn from her own mouth. I can never change her. She is correct. She has no desire to change.

October 30 Pearl bound for Chestnut Street to meet Dick Bridges. There's always something amiss in my apartment house, and that I like, for it provides something to think about. All ten apartments are rented at the moment, bringing in $1,025 a month. Pearl assures me I am too good to the tenants. I like to be. I have been under a Jewish landlord, and I don't want to be that way. Also, I'd like to build up a reputation as a desirable landlord. It will pay off sooner or later. And if I make a bit less money being generous, what of it? Next year I should clear after taxes about four to five thousand on what has amounted to a fifty thousand dollar investment. I'm glad I went into the business. Pearl is more help with running it than Billy was. Mrs. Trench enjoys the details and the telephoning, and now and again I call on Evelyn for assistance. She doesn't like it but is no longer rebellious and nasty about helping out. I am gradually prevailing upon Pearl to cut down on her drinking so that her head is becoming clearer and her memory of more assistance.

She goes out with Sadie often. Sadie heard that Billy was in Texas and Mexico City. I'll bet he's spending money like water. I don't feel bitter toward him as I do toward Pike. Anyway, how I feel toward the latter is ambivalent. I miss him as a doctor and am glad he's in the grave as a man. The double feeling makes my emotional stance extremely difficult. I'm getting somewhere though, I think.

November 6 Hold your breath. I think I feel a little better. I cogitated for days on what Dottie or Dr. Pike would do. It seemed to me that the front ends of the right ribs were squeezing down on the intestines. In that case Dottie or Dr. Pike would rotate the spinal vertebrae to the left. I finally got up my nerve and did just that on the bedpost. Crash. Bang. Everything moved. Now the pelvis is sore, but the intestines and gall bladder seem better. Got my jaw in place also for the first time since the operation. Dare I hope?

It is my conviction that any organization (and here I continue to write when I should stop — thoughts flow out — must be better) is only as good over the long run as is its chief executive. We have lost what imagination we ever had. We're ripe to fall from the tree, and there are two more years of this vindictive, petty politician, conceited, misbegotten little fellow, Truman.

November 9 I wrote Janice the following letter this morning, and when I read it to Pearl I became so emotional the tears rolled out of my eyes. "I'm exactly like that, Artie. God knows I am. I can understand just how you feel."

Nov. 9, 1950

Dear Janice —

Pearl told me about visiting you the other evening and how much she enjoyed it. She said that she spoke to you about my Grandmother's garnet necklace that I gave you.

I feel this way about it, Janice. I probably loved you more than anyone in the world save Evelyn, and when I gave the necklace to you I expected at the least to know you the rest of our lives. It has been one of the hardest blows of my life that you have seen fit never to see me, even if, as I have been told, that is due to your husband's not liking me, a restraint I feel you should have stood out against. It is not that I am blaming you for what you are, only that I wish it could have been different. I am a good friend and a loyal one, and if ever you or Bertram were in need of help, you could call on me and it would be a pleasure to assist in any way. I'd love to hear about your home, your children, your pleasures. It does not seem and has never seemed too much to want.

To return to the necklace. If you'd come to see me once in a long while, write me occasionally or telephone, I'd feel reassured and would want one who thought enough of me to make that effort to have what my Grandmother especially treasured, my Grandfather's wedding gift to her. If not, I'd like to have you give or sell me the trinket for Evelyn to have. Believe me, I'm not enjoying writing this, but my conscience is bothering me. If you no longer find your way clear even to keep in contact with me — a very small charity indeed it would seem — then I feel Evelyn should have what was treasured by my ancestors rather than you who have, in a way, disowned me. Oh, I hope you understand. I should rather a thousand times you keep the necklace and reestablish contact with me. Please, I wish you would.

I don't care whether or not Bertram reads this. Maybe he is an older man now and quite sure of you and would understand and be generous.

I'd love to see the daughter. You know what a weakness I have for little girls, and Pearl says she is charming.

Always —
Arthur

November 13   I wrote Evelyn a strong note about how I hated the alternate home in the country business heart and soul and would never like it and would she please not talk about it. Later in the day, she said: "I read your note and I understand and will heed it; and if I say this after consideration, it means much more than if I talk on and on emotionally." So that was that.

We spent a very pleasant day making out a record order, reading 'The Times,' eating lunch, having a bed party, talking, playing records. Perhaps this bed party business is much more important than I had thought it to be. She seems to enjoy it in a mild way, no burning passion or overwhelming enjoyment. She goes at it too hurriedly, it seems to me, to get the most from it, and I'm trying to teach her to work at it less hard. She did better than before. She said I was good. That I already know. It's not exciting and thrilling, as with Trudy, but mildly pleasant. I'm not sure I'd keep it up, with what it is apt to do to my bones in mind, did I not feel it will put her more at ease with me.

She's almost beautiful, lying there with no clothes on. Every time, though, I recollect Dr. Pike and the hundreds of occasions he used her body, and I goddamn well don't like it. Evelyn is doing very little to put jealousy of him out of my mind though she's the only one who can help me. I asked her the other day if she weren't sorry for me, the fix I was in during those years she went with him.

"Of course not," she replied. "Why should I be sorry for you then? Then isn't now anyway. How could I be sorry for you now for what happened then? I haven't ever been sorry for you. You always seem quite able to take care of yourself."

November 14　Martha came in on me yesterday afternoon when I was weeping from anger, sadness, frustration concerning Evelyn. She comforted me. She seems to understand. She says she expects to tell her that it is not her business, but that she loves me and thinks I am good and reasonable and kind and generous, and it hurts her to see how I am disturbed as the result of Evelyn's treatment of me and what she says, and that she, Evelyn, cannot realize how sensitive I am and how she hurts me or she would refrain from doing so. Which, if she does it, may dent Evelyn but probably won't.

November 15　Pearl went to see Janice. Janice told her she has sent back both pieces of jewelry, the garnet necklace my Grandfather Crew had given my Grandmother on their wedding day and the pearl and sapphire cross owned by my Mother. She said that she wished she had never come to work for me, that she had been very unhappy all the years she was here, that she had only stayed because she pitied me, that she had never loved me, that she never wished to hear from me again. Which is, I feel fairly certain, face-saving and falsification stuff she may now believe, women's memory being divided usually into compartments without sequence. But maybe not. Then Bertram arrived. He, as Pearl put it, "blew his top." He never wished to hear of or from that goddamn son of a bitch again. If he did, he would take the matter to a lawyer and bring suit for molesting his wife. He had always hated me. That, I take it, is quite true. "And that, boiled down," concluded Pearl, "is what was said. It was very emotional, all of it. Now you know where you stand."

"In the cellar," I replied. "I'll always rather know the worst, Pearl. Now I can rest easier. And you can add this to the great amount of adverse criticism of me you have heard during your association with me, and hatred. It's lucky you have a mind of your own and your own opinion of me and aren't swayed by what others think. You and I are intense, forthright people, and we are either liked a lot or hated thoroughly. My Lord, the amount of diatribe I have heard against you would fill a book, just as what you have heard against me would. It's lucky neither one of us is swayed by what other people think. And thank you for an uncomfortable errand well done. Now I can be at peace with all the doors closed on the past." And I do feel more comfortable. And I'll bet it tore Janice in half to part with the jewelry. Of all the stingy persons I ever knew she was the most stingy, and probably the cross was the one piece of good jewelry she possessed. But that makes me sad somewhat. I'd rather far have had her friendship than the jewelry. Oh well.

November 18   Evelyn and I went riding in the Pierce in the rain. She hates to drive the Pierce, it is so long and when compared with her Ford unwieldy. I said: "I wish you would tell me you love me." She said: "I can't and drive this leviathan." I said: "I wish you would tell me." She jammed on the brakes, stopped the car dead. "I love you! I love you! I love you!" I looked around to see who was listening. "Somebody'll hear you." "I don't care if they do. I love you! I love you! I love you! Now shall we drive on?" And that is what enchants me, often quite unexpectedly.

November 25   I have sold 100 Coca-Cola, ignoring the promise (as I expected to do, because I don't like him, in which case a promise means nothing to me) to my Father, and have bought American Cyanamid (chemicals, plastics, medicines), Pennsylvania Salt (chemicals) and International Paper in its stead. Coca-Cola has not improved its earning power significantly in more than a dozen years, made less money last year, seems to me to be no longer a gold mine.

December 3   Disaster appears to have overtaken our troops and the handful of other nations' troops in North Korea. It is said that some 300,000 Chinese Red troops have been put into the fight against us so that with some 75,000 North Korean troops, we are outnumbered. No intelligence scouts informed MacArthur that Chinese troops in such force were in North Korea. The South Korean divisions in the center of a 75 mile line were decimated. Many of our troops seemingly are trapped. The Chinese are sweeping southward at a great rate, seeking to encircle the flanks of our retreating divisions. The North Korean capital is being evacuated. Defeat, if not disaster, threatens our forces. And still we do not permit planes to fly into Chinese Manchuria to scout or to loose bombs there, because the United Nations has not yet seen fit to give the word. It is fantastic. Here we are, perhaps losing a war in which we are supplying all the money, virtually all the supplies and weapons, the majority of the fighting men, because we still insist upon heeding the dictates of a body of talkers in which we have only one vote.

Our men are in rout, while Acheson talks and talks. He is the real ruler of this country. I have been listening to him on the radio. It is said that he wears perfume and uses wax for his moustache and affects British airs. His voice is that of a sex pervert. To Truman, he possibly seems a very intelligent and poised and informed man, a diplomat moving in a world steps above Truman's world of small-town thought and boss politics. It is a major calamity that we are saddled with such an ineffective in a position of absolute authority. And he is surrounded by all sorts of advisors in the State Department who, by every hushed-up bit of evidence, are sympathetic to Russia and responsible in large measure for what happened in China.

December 4 We are in a box for fair in Korea. There are said to be some half a million Red troops pocketing and pushing into headlong retreat our some one hundred thousand troops. I think we'll have to get out of Korea and lose face all over the world. To avoid World War III, we'll have to give in to China and Russia. I sent long telegram to the Massachusetts Senators, probably to no effect.

December 6 Evelyn and a house in the country. I really thought she might be considering favorably not having one. But no. She announced yesterday that she had made up her mind. She was sorry, but that was the way it would be. I hit the roof. She had promised, I reminded her, not to decide until spring. She knew, but this was what she had decided. The more I reasoned or objected or pled, the more bitchy she became. She wanted it and to hell with me. It amounted to the fact that she would rather have the house than me if it came to a choice. She doesn't love me deeply. She loves nothing but herself.

December 7 Most of the afternoon I talked at Evelyn. Once she said: "I hope your disapproval doesn't last too long. I miss your touching me." Calculated or not, I weathered that and continued with my spate of words. At moments she would become almost viciously nasty, when I'd back away awhile. "I was walking along the street in Washington one day," she explained, "and I was overwhelmed by such a feeling of desperation that the idea of jumping off a bridge occurred to me. I was frightened. I said to myself: 'I must have a house in the country.' So I must." I told her it seemed to me that, if it came to giving up the house or me, I would be given up. "I didn't say that," she said. "But neither did you or do you say otherwise." She was silent.

Late in the afternoon, Dr. Sewell. A pleasant, agreeable man, disillusioned but not cynical, smart but not a smart aleck, serious, taking pleasure in helping people, not a yes man by any means. He helps Evelyn. He helps me in that he sees her problem as I see it and is able to translate into a language Evelyn can understand my thoughts and theories against which Evelyn has a roadblock in the paths of her mind. As with all February people, she is likelier to hearken to a stranger than to someone close to her. She figures the stranger has no strings to pull.

I explained to him what I felt and thought. I had Pearl waylay him on his way out and tell him a few thoughts apparently on her own. He told her he was very grateful. Evelyn is to go to his office this morning at eleven. I talked at her most of the evening. I have a sore throat and am worn out.

December 9 This Evelyn business is just about wrecking me. Not an inch will she give in, even when I suggest a compromise, approved of as fair and just by Mrs. Trench, by which she would keep the Acton place and would simultaneously be reassured. Get all; give nothing: That is Evelyn's rule for living. Be greedy; never be willing to pay for what others surrender. Be suspicious; trust no one because individuality and the prerogatives thereof might be trespassed upon. Weigh every decision, like a miser counting nine hundred and ninety-nine cents' worth of change in a thousand cents, for fear a single cent be lost.

December 10 Yesterday was a lulu. I used up every power of suasion and dissuasion I owned. Evelyn wouldn't budge. Mrs. Trench declared that my compromise was fair and equable. I was frantic, so weary that "to hell with everything" occurred to me. I solicited Mrs. Trench's assistance. She talked to Evelyn. At 7:30 P.M. Evelyn came into my room. "I've thought it over. I've decided the way I have been acting was no way for a 'new-era baby' to act. I'll agree to your compromise. Now you can relax."

"Why," I asked later, "did you finally decide to my compromise?" "Because," she explained, "I was not acting as a person who is serious about wanting a better future should act. Also, I could see how all but distracted I was making you, and whatever you may think to the contrary, I really do love you more than anyone in the world and don't enjoy causing you to suffer. That's why."

This morning I spent an hour writing out the following:

December 1950

UNDERSTANDING

reached between Arthur and Evelyn Inman

re

the bettering of their lives together.

1. Evelyn agrees to give Arthur power of attorney over her property in Acton, Mass. and to provide, if necessary, a wife's release, so that in case of a condition definitely destructive of his morale or dangerous to her life or health (such as an attachment by her to a man, too many automobile accidents coming and going to Acton, a slow increase in demands by her about time with an unwillingness to stop them) arises and is not rectified by her

within a month after serious attention is called to the matter, then he, Arthur, can sell the Acton property, give to Evelyn the money from the sale (unless the condition objected to by Arthur has not be rectified) for the purpose of buying another place nearer to Boston where the condition objected to does not and will not exist or persist.

This understanding between Evelyn and Arthur will cause him to feel much better about the Acton property and quiet his fears and let him enjoy her enjoyment, and she on her part can feel she has acted wisely and with moderation and psychological acumen.

2. Evelyn and Arthur agree between themselves to put in writing in the future all serious undertakings to their mutual benefit.

3. Evelyn assures Arthur that not ever again will she lie to him or break a promise to him once given, for he wishes mightily to trust her completely, and he admits he has an exaggerated esteem for and dependence on absolute honesty.

4. Evelyn is to make an honest and serious effort not to be away on trips more than two weeks in a year and agrees not to be away on trips for more than three weeks in all unless by Arthur's consent. If that consent is not given, she agrees to harbor no resentment for the refusal, if given.

5. If Arthur can have seven hours of Evelyn's company cheerfully given five days a week, he will be very pleased indeed.

6. Evelyn herewith gives Arthur her solemn assurance not ever again to use his love and her power over him to put an arbitrary "I want" into execution against his judgment, if he is opposed with all the wisdom at his command. This is important not only relative to his confidence and trust in her love and generosity but for the maintenance of his self-esteem, such as it is.

7. Assurance by Evelyn of an even greater effort not to flare up at Arthur or resent simple questions or to be condescending. It would help him.

8. A plea by Arthur to Evelyn not to continue smoking if she can stop it without loss of self-confidence and freedom of choice.

Evelyn Inman
Arthur Inman

"Here," I said to Evelyn, "is the result of an hour's work. Mrs. Trench has read it twice. She says it's fair and just. Don't read it, please. Why not just sign it unread?" To my pure astonishment that is what she did. "Now that," I exclaimed, "is what I like. It shows trust and faith, and it raises my self-esteem and makes me admire you for trusting me."

December 11   I hope that all these words concerning Evelyn will not be, should anyone ever peruse this postscript to my diary, too tedious.

Evelyn's sixteen-year intimacy with Pike has stamped her mind, her emotions, her general outlook, her habits. Before she went with him and loved him, she did not smoke; she did not drink; she was generous with money. She lied less and broke fewer promises.

Evelyn came to think as he thought, to value what he valued, to assume his habits even to his laugh and his mannerisms, to be, in a word, a stubborn and self-willed pale copy of what he was. He could scarcely hold a conversation, for instance, without pulling a poor-mouth about money, and he was incredibly avaricious and tight-fisted. I imagine that purposely or not he belittled me in her eyes in many ways. He understood women very well, and his handling of them was not unsubtle. His practice was mostly among women. No doubt there were many extramarital experiences with them in which he learned their weakness to flattery. A condition was thrown in his lap by me in which he could obtain at petty cost and little effort and no danger to his name a woman who was quickly enslaved by his charms and his blarney into giving him everything for nothing. She was a young and unworldly woman. By degrees she became his mistress in feelings and his lesser shadow. He could have had other women and Evelyn would not have suspected, so completely was she won over. She told me some months back that he stopped sleeping with her because he became impotent. Now she declares emphatically that such was not the case, that probably he found another woman more to his taste.

Yesterday, to exorcise some of the feeling that Evelyn was some sort of impervious monster so bent upon making her own music that she could strip the flesh from my spiritual back to make a drum on which to play her tune, I slept with her. I gave her beer to relax her. While never have I, in my limited experience, held relations with any woman who fitted more perfectly and had all the physical prerequisites I enjoy, being with her is neither very exciting nor too enjoyable. With me at least, she never becomes excited, never reaches a climax, bears with me mostly. Did she, I ask, get excited with Pike? Yes, often though not always. Why did she get excited with him and not with me? I couldn't have done a better job, could I? No, it wasn't that. I was far better than Pike in what I did. It was, she thought, because she wasn't highly sexed anyway, and with me she was perhaps too anxious to please by cooperation whereas with him she just lay there and he was the entire aggressor and did all the work, and she felt therefore that she must please him greatly, and anyway he never failed to tell her she was unique in her appeal for him. He didn't seem to care whether or not she returned his affection. She was flattered by his attitude.

December 12 Last week Mrs. Trench gave vent to what she thought. She said: "To my way of thinking, you're better off with Dr. Pike dead. I never in my life saw a more conceited man." And

Pearl: "I never took a liking to Dr. Pike. He treated everyone as if they were children and not very bright children at that." Pike was a man, I guess, whom people liked and admired very much or belittled and hated. During the long course of these diaries I have, I think, most often dwelled upon his good points. At one time I admired him to the point of worship. I not yet can escape the legacy, the lingering vigor of his personality.

December 18 And here is a letter Evelyn wrote me some three weeks ago in answer to a plea that she state her feelings about Pike before the Acton place week of fighting came up. Maybe she meant it. Maybe she means it. At any rate, it was and is a great solace, the nearest to a love letter she has written me since we were married. [Obviously dictated by Arthur and possibly signed by Evelyn — Ed.]

Dearest Arthur —

Indeed I do wish to reassure you about the Pike matter and to convince you by word and deed that I love you more deeply and enduringly than I have ever loved anyone else in the world. I know this would not be possible had you not shown me by your generosity, kindness and thoughtfulness of me and our life together that you are in every way far more high-minded and reliable than Pike ever was.

How I could have been taken in by that man all those years, how I could have been beguiled by his broad Irish flattery into sacrificing your precious love and devotion, not to mention your interest, for *his* interest, is more than I can now understand.

I hope that you will continue to find it in your heart to think well of me to some extent, in addition to loving me, for without some degree of approbation from you, I find life very dour. I cannot at this moment think of myself with any great approval, and I feel bitter resentment at Pike for his large contribution to the misguidedness of my point of view during all those years. He was older than I, more worldly than I, and being a man, must have been able to imagine your feelings far better than I could have. And he had had a happy prosperous life as a well strong man, so why should he take advantage of you, who had so little health and happiness? It is not fair or decent, or even manly.

So you must not worry about your Evelyn any more, for she has seen the light very clearly on this matter of Pike and is determined to help you to feel more happy about it, so that evil memories will no longer haunt you. Your devotedly loving

Evelyn

December 20   This is a propitious moment, while Evelyn, the subject of this diary, is away and while Eva is sitting beside me sewing on a green pajama bottom, to write about Eva, she who is one of life's comforts to date. She now wears big plastic spectacles, a straw pattern imbedded in them. She stoops forward from the shoulders and neck, as many tall girls do, or girls embarrassed by their breasts. She wears a nylon blouse and a baby blue cardigan sweater buttoned by one button at the very top. She has on no stockings, only short white wool socks and moccasins, very large. I ask her questions, and she answers in a slow voice, words often elided almost out of recognition. She laughs often at the most shallow of jokes. Her smile is sweet and, toward me, motherly.

December 22   I hope, this volume through, I will feel Evelyn is understood, and therefore I can write less concerning her. I love her. She is stupid. She is a weak sister. She possesses certain real virtues. As a rule, I'm not bored with her. She puts up with me and with my limitations and high emotional potential and never has she tried more earnestly to please.

December 31   Up early. After heavy rain, snow. I had hoped it would hold off until eleven or so this morning. A slender chance it may stop but too slender to count upon. Well, we have had an open fall, one enabling me to be out whenever strength or lack of pain permitted. Never in my memory has such a year for riding existed in Boston, and never have I been less able to make use of the cloudiness and lack of snow.

As for the other phases of the year 1950, may I repeat that it has been a nonpareil heller, ranking with 1916, 1918 and the other exceptionally unpleasant years. May I never have another to equal it. Dottie and Dr. Pike; the complete collapse of my back and ribs; the breaking down of my car; the decamping of Billy; the finding out for sure about Pike and Evelyn; the strain of getting accustomed to Pearl; Evelyn's drinking and Pearl's drinking; my long battles with Evelyn over time away on trips and then over the Acton place and her violent nastiness and imperviousness; the pulling of my wisdom tooth; the many migraines and the gall bladder trouble and the weakness now; the trouble with my skull; the not making money in a Stock Market in which any blind fool should be successful; the various small nuisances of real estate; the Korean War. There are doubtless other troubles belonging to 1950, but these are sufficient.

To offset them, there are the evinced love and care of Rose and Eva and Martha; the luck of having Pearl available for Billy's job; the queer sort of defeatistic peace that comes with accepting the knowledge that I love my wife as well as hate her for her stubbornness and willfulness; the dying of Evelyn's father; the coming to hand of Dr. Landon Sewell in an hour of need; the prolonged abstinence at last of Evelyn and her consent to sit up evenings with me; the holding off of the snow.

Which is enough about the year, me, my thoughts, the whole damn mess of 1950.

So far as Arthur could tell, his regimen for cracking Evelyn's allegiance to Dr. Pike seemed to be working, even though she drank too much and looked ten years older. Of more concern for the moment were Mrs. Trench's health (he would be lost without her), his "inflamed intestines," and the general commotion in Garrison Hall caused by a confluence of disturbances: Pearl's injured knee, Eva's emotionalism, Mrs. Trench's grippe, and the physical deterioration of Evelyn's mother, Mrs. Yates. During these troubled weeks, Arthur thought about buying more apartment houses — then gave up the idea. He sent telegrams protesting the dismissal of General MacArthur, the last honest man, and daydreamed about having another wife.

To his utter astonishment and consternation, Evelyn slipped away in the night, leaving a terse message of explanation. The marriage was finished.

1951

January 21 Several weeks have elapsed since the last entry was written in this, the lengthening postscript to my long diary. During the period, further measures have been taken to prepare us for World War III. Our idealistic abasement to the United Nations and the abasement of the United Nations to fear of Russia and the reluctance of Great Britain to give up a profitable trade with Soviet China have pushed us into a shameful obeisance to all the average American disapproves of in his careless, bewildered, optimistic, secret heart. While we are being driven southward in Korea by the reorganized North Koreans backed by the Chinese backed by Russia, we have entertained contemptuous Chinese representatives, have watched the United Nations, abetted by Britain, refuse to brand China as an aggressor, have seen our President and his boss, Acheson, refuse to allow our planes to cross into China, refuse a real blockade of Chinese ports, refuse proffered aid from the Chinese Nationalists in Formosa. We are mired within the quagmire of the United Nations and stripped of our separate independence and pride. That we should get our way or withdraw and make individual treaties with whomever are our friends in the old-fashioned way seems to occur to no one.

The single possibly effective step that has been taken is getting General Eisenhower made supreme commander of the North Atlantic Pact military forces and sending him to Europe. He is not only a soldier but our ranking diplomat. And we have recognized Spain.

Maurice Fremont-Smith (remember him?), now foremost medical intestinal expert in Boston, it is said, due any minute to look me over.

Wish Evelyn were happier. Is any accomplishment she can achieve worth to me her losing her youthful look and her handsomeness? I'm not sure. She's been a bitch for two days. Better now but dejected. Starting work on place in Acton. Angry lately because I warned her not to fall for Dick Bridges who is overseeing the contractor for her. He's lean enough and handsome enough in a weak way to bother me. Said she wasn't interested in him. I replied that she had made the identical statement about Pike. Said I wasn't tactful. Replied I had no intention of being tactful this time; she had made the stew of mistrust and now must drink it. She makes me and makes herself very unhappy chiefly because she is too willful to censor her speech. She laments my contempt for her. I try to explain that the contempt arises not from her mistakes and faults primarily but from her insistence upon justifying and continuing those mistakes and faults and from her rebellion against me. I suppose I get nowhere.

January 22 Dr. Maurice Fremont-Smith came. As charming as I recalled him, tall, thin, slightly stooped, hair white, a bit bald, eyes gray-green, strong, thin calm hands, a cultivated manner and an aristocratic bearing. I have long ago forgotten my anger because he sent me to a psychiatrist who was a dud and dumb, Stanley Cobb. Maurice at once won me. He is smart and imaginative. That he is doubtless a snob in no wise annoys me. If I were he, successful, distinguished, three sons about to enter military service, no doubt social standing and enough earned money, I should be a snob myself. It always amazes me how much simpler it is to establish contact with someone of one's own generation and class than with a person differing from oneself in those respects.

He examined me from throat to testicles. He declared unequivocably that I had no gall bladder trouble or other serious intestinal trouble. He thought my diet perfect but recommended more bulk in the seaweed food and in vegetables. He had taken somewhat of a load off my mind. I am returned thereby to disarranged intestines and ribs and spine.

Evelyn was tight yesterday afternoon.

January 23   Evelyn drank again. As usual, she denied having had anything to drink. She was at Acton with the unpleasant old woman whom she often takes with her in the car. Later in the evening, she came upstairs and admitted to a single drink. Dr. Sewell has, wrongly I feel, told her never to drink to excess but only a single drink at social functions. "If," she asserts, "I feel I can take a single drink and stop there, I won't feel I'm such a weak character that I must stop altogether." Yesterday she stopped at a barbeque place and had a drink while Mrs. Gould had none. "Was that," I asked, "in your mind a social event? In effect, it seems to me, it was a drink by yourself, just what you promised not to do." I think that Sewell's idea is wrong, because it is a mere sophism. To stop altogether requires much more character than to kid oneself that one can stop and then drink when one calls an occasion social. If Evelyn were not made nasty by one drink or could stop there, perhaps it would be another matter. I believe with Alcoholics Anonymous that it is abstaining from the very first drink that counts. But of course Evelyn will not admit she is an alcoholic, which I contend she is, if an alcoholic is one who cannot abstain at will from liquor. She this morning announces that if it pleases me, she will abstain altogether. I hope so.

This business of thinking is making her look old. I must on my side refrain from pushing her too far toward thought, for I neither wish her to get old or ill. "Thinking," she states, half in fun, half seriously, "may end up killing me." I am not disinclined to doubt her assertion. She was designed for laziness and willfulness, not face-to-face self-examination. I must go easy. When Evelyn signed the agreement with me, she stated that being with me very long each day was something she did not think would profit either of us. I am now — she having given it a rather wholehearted trial — inclined to agree with her. I am too high-tensioned and mentally alert a person, too conscious of her defects and virtues, not to drain her vitality. I'll have to cut down on the time I am with her. I told her so. "It's not," she said, "that I don't want to be with you all the time. It's that I don't seem to stand up under such prolonged proximity."

And so — despite my artistic resolve — the pages concerning Evelyn continue to be written and to pile up.

January 24   Evelyn is at the Osteopathic Hospital having further blood analyses made, the blood color having been fine and the blood count normal and she still looking jaundiced and old. It was only about two weeks ago that her cancer doctor went over her. But I'm not satisfied. I never knew her to be so yellow. As Fred says, she has a history of cancer behind her, so you can't be too careful. I couldn't sleep last night. She hasn't been told why she's having the test but doubtless she knows. What is frightening also is that the tests may show nothing and still she may have cancer.

It's my theory that cancer is like the single lug that makes the self-perpetuating oak gall, a single or several germs or viruses. These may lie dormant in the body for years or forever and become active only upon ideal conditions occurring. In Evelyn's case, the history could well go back to Mrs. Pike through Pike. God knows she was intimate enough with him to catch anything he gave her instead of real gifts — the habit of smoking, the habit of drinking, the habit of lying. But of course this time it may not be cancer again. However, I am suspicious. She tires easily. She looks awful.

I told Eva about it. I asked her if Evelyn had cancer by some mischance and should die, would she consider marrying me? Yes, she would. While this may seem the acme of pessimism and rather brutal in assuming what is not yet sure, I feel constrained to plan against the worst contingency possible. It is the only way I can manage to survive. The future looks grim. Some of my doctors may be taken into the armed services, physicians being scarcer than in the other war, if Truman so decides. Some new hospitals are empty because of the dearth of doctors.

February 12 The reports finally came through on Evelyn. They were negative. I was a nervous wreck. Fred gave her some liver medicine. She looks better but is still tired, large circles under her eyes. It was, we have concluded, her engaging in the process of doing some real thinking that wore her out. What then? If, I explain to her, she could only originate enough trust and faith in me to concede that she inherited a nasty disposition, is an alcoholic, then she might achieve by an emotional shortcut what months of deep thinking could gain her. She is "considering the matter." She is nicer with me on the whole. This last month I have striven to let her get to bed early and to rest her generally. Today she has gone to Acton. The work on her house is about three-fourths done. I discuss it with her, and she likes that.

The North Koreans and Chinese are being driven back on themselves in Korea. There appears to be a more competent general in command, now that Walker was killed. I'm glad we stayed there to save our face. It is good for the United States to have such forces. A national debate is in progress between the America-first personages like Hoover and Taft and the internationalists like Acheson and Dewey.

February 25 A difficult week, I fear, on poor Evelyn, with only Eva and Brita [the cleaning woman] to help her at widely separated intervals. Discounting how cross she talks at moments and how violently upset I get now and again at her stupidness, we have come through better than I had hoped. I've tried to get her to bed by nine-thirty and have eaten cold breakfasts prepared the evening before and left in my warm bathroom. My wife is no executive by nature, and prolonged responsibility fuddles her mind. But she has been much less cross than I had expected and at times sweet and disarming to a husband who at his best is demanding.

February 28 Cloudy. Ride. Met Eva by accident. Took her riding. Now am back, feel bloated from gas and ribs cut me. Wish Fred would come. Eva said: "Guess what? Daddy's gone away. I'll spend the afternoon with you." Although her father now makes $150 a week, he has made no move to pay me $200. He does not know that Eva comes here, she keeping it from him. He thinks she spends the afternoons at the library. She becomes increasingly fed up with her parents. They treat her as if she were twelve and aren't aware at all what a good, conscientious girl she is. The other night she threatened to leave home. She told both parents off.

Were I she, I'd leave. I've told her I'd support her through college and that she could live upstairs as long as she didn't come here first, when her father could claim collusion on my part. Evelyn says she would love to have her. Karlsdorf is really both violent and unreasonable with her. She is to him what I was to my parents, an appurtenance. Eva says she no longer feels bound by pity for her mother as she was when her father wasn't making money. Even when her father locks her mother in the closet or insults her or chases after her with a meat cleaver or throws things or hits her, her mother loves him so much that she will stay with him to the end. It is a sex attraction, she feels.

I can't write any more. The ribs are cutting me in half and the gas blowing me up, and it is eleven and no Fred, due an hour ago. Oh, for Dr. Pike or Dottie!

March 20 What would I do without women? I never really swung into the orbit of women until I fell ill in 1916 and then only until 1919 when thereafter for a while women were as scarce as hen's teeth until Alma and Katinka and Evelyn came my way. Since then, an increasing number of women. I don't mind. I'm very grateful to them. Being with them so much doesn't seem to bother my getting along with all sorts of men. I miss Evelyn. These are random thoughts — no more akin to emotions — which flow from the scurrying end of my yellow pencil. Evelyn has trained herself to drive while keeping her eyes front. If she can do that, what with her wavering attention, she can do almost anything. It's a regret that haunts me constantly that she couldn't have seen fit to try to please me sooner in the way and manner which did please me. I still fire up like a boiler with the draught opened each time I think of Dr. Pike and Evelyn and the cheated years they conspired to take from me. I'll never love Evelyn as I did, but she won't know that. She'll think I love her more because I withdraw myself more. Poor Evelyn. She's a child and a devil. Her house in Acton is all but finished. I hope it will help her.

March 23 Scarcely slept because of jammed neck. Dreamed of amorous exploits in queer, forbidden city, of Evelyn and myself disguised as street sweepers, of my inconstancy to her and hers to me, of our final bout together and she crying: "No, not that way. That reminds me of Cyrus." I am up now, shaking with pain and fatigue.

A moment ago, Evelyn, just returned from Washington, called from the hall outside in her unguarded voice, rather harsh-edged, a bit strident and very unrounded. I drew up inside like an untuned stringed instrument touched by an untutored bow.

April 4 I'm bored with a sort of intellectual numbness which, for some obscure reason, permits time to flow past more speedily than formerly. Nothing really interests me save what directly concerns my care and comfort and appeasement from pain. Life has been awful, yet I have somehow persisted. Life will be awful, but doubtless I shall persist. I shall die when it is written on my forehead I shall die and not before. Many irritants which made me frantic when I was deluded that I was a writer of merit I now let slide. I say: What do they matter? I have lived fifty-five years. Those years — and this is a boundless comfort — cannot, at least, be piled upon the years of misery ahead. So the less I fret the quicker the future will be added to the past and the nearer I will come to an ending.

April 9 General MacArthur, while in command of the so-called United Nations Army, is not allowed to command. He cannot use the Chinese Nationalist Army on Formosa. He cannot bomb military centers in Manchuria or China. He cannot blockade Chinese ports. He can only kill men in a front-to-front war, and that constitutes as queer a double-standard war as ever was carried on. MacArthur insists — and I for one feel he is absolutely correct — that he fights while Europe talks and that the best chance of there being no war in Europe lies in his being allowed to use the Nationalist Chinese, the bombers, the blockade to win decisively. Our State Department and the United Nations and Great Britain et al. see otherwise, of course.

April 11 Truman et al. have summarily and in no manly face-to-face manner dismissed General MacArthur from all his military commands. MacArthur has refused in his haughtiness and arrogance to kowtow to the vain Truman by holding in leash his disgust at the Acheson-Marshall policy of containing a death struggle against Communism to Korea and leaving China inviolate. So MacArthur is out, and the President is undoubtedly acting within his powers, and one of the few great figures of our time who devoted his life to America, our greatest outstanding warrior against Communism, the man who believed unwavering that Asia was the place to contend Communism in battle, not Europe, is out. The public is shocked, and Acheson has won his largest victory, and Europe and England are gleeful. Now a Europe-first program is assured, and doubtless concessions will be made to the Chinese Reds to gain peace, and the people of Japan, who all but worshipped MacArthur, will feel betrayed.

I do not like MacArthur personally. I feel that his talents as a general in action have been made too much of — General Ridgeway seems much more capable militarily. But he provided a single-hearted bulwark against Russian encroachment in Asia. He was semidivine to the Japanese. He cannot be replaced. He will have joined Mitchell and Patton in the ranks of the too outspoken patriots. May he come home and win and awaken the American people.

April 22 How miserable can I be? The ride with Mike a month ago dislocated all the bottom bones in the neck, and after weeks of suffering and about $300 worth of doctors, it isn't fixed yet, and all the ribs are tangled up and the balance is wrong. The ear is a mess and the hip pains violently and keeps me awake. Evelyn has been a hellion, nasty, soused to the gills, a poor and unattractive specimen of womanhood. I find myself not in the least in love with her. Fighting with her or with Mrs. Trench makes life sordid and unrewarding.

I heard MacArthur's speech and various welcomes. His popularity has swept the country but will probably tire itself into indifference. Truman has behaved as usual like a petty cad. I suspect — hold your hats — that MacArthur is honest, an honest man. At any rate, he's a great actor, a forthright speaker, a puller of emotional and sentimental stops. Any honest and emotional leader can sweep this country to him, but the politicians are too inured to dishonest double-talk to even perceive honesty and too cautious about reelection and too petty or too dumb to realize what an appeal to disillusioned Americans emotional honesty might have.

I'll go riding now in the Pierce. I dread the long day. I'm bored with Evelyn's shenanigans, momentarily defeated by her unimaginative and imperceptive egotism, wishing I had another wife, grateful for Mrs. Trench and Eva beyond words to convey. It is a long route from birth to death.

April 30 Evelyn left last evening for Washington. She brings her mother back Wednesday. Don't envy her the job. Her mother refuses to wear more than two dresses, ignores stockings with runs, won't fix her hair, insists on old suitcases accompanying her though she scarcely ever unpacks them. The old peoples' home in Brookline on Sewell Street looks and sounds friendly and well-kept. I'm glad Evelyn and I are having this short separation as we're in each other's hair.

May 1 Juliette was here last evening, perfume and few clothes on and flow of words and very evident weakness for me. She's been in a hospital with nervous stomach and nervous heart and worry about her condition and a feeling that life is cheating her. She wants to go to a psychoanalyst. Clarence is set against it. She asked me what I thought her trouble was. She minds "terrifically" being a Jew. The summers at Beverly when she was ostracized seems to have scarred her spirit. She is bored by Clarence's business friends and feels they are critical of her as being "unusual and flighty."

I told her that her chief trouble was the same as mine had been at school — she felt different and instead of accepting the difference as a sign she was more imaginative and more daring and more of an individual than those she thought critical of her, she viewed herself from the outside in with her own eyes. She should learn to feel as I now feel — that if they didn't like her or were critical of her, it was their loss and their lack of imagination. As to people boring her, Clarence's friends, she liked money and what it bought, and being good to Clarence's friends was part of her payment since no one got anything for nothing. As to his friends double-crossing her, that was because she liked to play lady bountiful and usually one could only play lady bountiful to failures. I could tell her everything a psychologist or a psychoanalyst could tell her and for free, if she'd listen, as that sort of stuff was my gift.

She kissed me over and over again. "You know it, Arthur, I love you, I love you, I love you. There's nobody I can talk to as I talk to you. You're wonderful. I feel you regard me as a person, not a Jew. And you're so wise. And even if we don't see each other but seldom, we always take up where we left off, and you love me and I love you." "And you're a high-powered woman sexually and therefore need a high-powered sex life." "And haven't got it." Her torso is as smooth as this page on which I write and warm and firm. I'm very fond of posturing, emotional, self-indulgent Juliette.

May 4 My Father — will he never die? — arrives next Tuesday. My car runs, thank God. I'm not as desperate as last spring, for my ribs aren't so violently painful. My insides aren't perfect but are improved. If I watch my diet, they are bearable, and they no longer weaken me. I am less jealous of Pike. Perhaps the amount of flattery he must have put in on Evelyn merited him the sex outlet he got. Evelyn is too cold sexually for me to enjoy often, and one woman that way soon becomes monotonous. I still resent the other elements of her relationship with him, but the less I love her the less they matter, and that is one indication I do care less. Mrs. Trench is my real irreplaceable treasure. By and large, I do not resent her "spells," for they occur very seldom indeed. Dick is really coming to like me. It's easy to tell. I like him better, too. He's being successful as a real estate salesman and no longer feels he has to toot his own horn so raucously.

May 6 We have had Acheson, British-born, an Anglophile, to lead us; Truman the waspish, ignorant necktie salesman; Roosevelt the reformer, the liar, the ambitious, the America-second personality boy, too subject to flattery and too off-balance with power to know straight up; Hoover with the almost childlike trust in 'the people' and their wisdom; Coolidge the silent, leave-it-alone old-style farmer who always felt "sartin" the weather would change if he but waited; Harding, greatly underrated in my opinion, an affable man devoted to the American supply-and-demand business system; Wilson with his noble yet impracticable ideas and his little understanding of the rogues and personality boys with whom he had to deal. They are, all in all, sorry specimens insofar as America is concerned.

May 9 The Old Man arrived last evening in the midst of one of Evelyn's drunks. It is to be doubted if he noticed, being in most ways no more perceptive or delicately keyed than she. I'll have to talk to him within the hour, and a multitude of squatted-upon memories and associations will wriggle free and throw themselves about beyond control. He, like Haverford School, is horror to me. I wish he'd die and fade into some memory-swallowing limbo. My life long I have been tied to or dependent on people I dislike or fear or distrust or scorn.

Old Man insisted see me. A long hour. Mrs. Trench with me. She now worn out. I worn out. Doubtless Old Man worn out. He looks awful, thin, with skin hanging, barely creeping. Feels terribly. I managed to talk about incidentals. As he was leaving, he said: "What I don't understand is why every time I come there's someone with you. I'm not going to find fault with you. I'm too old and you're too set in your ways. I just want to see and talk to my only son." "The trouble is," I replied, "someone has to be on guard so that I don't speak out of turn. You never have approved of what I said." "It's what you think," he corrected. "Well, of what I think then. You've always hated that." Mrs. Trench poked me in the back. "You have never had any desire to really know me," I insisted. "That's why I have someone with me. But thank you for coming. We had a good talk." Evelyn took him off to Acton. Mrs. Trench slumped on the bed. "I feel as if trucks had run over me. A morning's work is nothing to that." Now I'm drinking beer. Evelyn and Father are gone.

I said to Evelyn earlier: "Are you going to get drunk today? I have Martha coming early in case you do." "Oh no," she said. "You can be at peace." "Well," I said, "I never know, you're such a weakling. The moment anything becomes difficult, you run to alcohol. You don't even recall opening the beer in the icebox, do you?" "Perhaps I should join Alcoholics Anonymous." "Oh no!" I said. "I've thought of that already. Attractive people belong to it, I've heard. In a trice you'd have annexed a man and be screwing him. That's next on the docket anyway, I'm sure. You haven't the principles of a cat in heat or a thirsty dog. Now that you have the love nest at Acton, who knows what man will settle into it? Why the hell don't you do your drinking there?"

May 10 Seen Old Man. To someone else less supercharged emotionally he would seem a courageous and pathetic old fellow, very endearing in some of his gestures, his dependence upon others, his utterances. I helped him down the hall to the elevator. He remarked later to Evelyn that he had fallen low indeed when he had to be assisted by me. He said it whimsically. He is correct, I guess. I did a better job this morning thanks to Rose's prompting. I may never see him again. He takes several heart medicines. Might as well give him a last pleasant memory of me. He has never meant me harm. I do admire him. I feel utterly sad at the moment for what, with a modicum of understanding on his part, might have been.

May 11 Am striving to cheer up Evelyn and flatter her. I am remiss not to do so. She looks pretty today.

May 12 No Evelyn. Martha and Rose went downstairs to look. This note:

Friday night

Dear Arthur: —

After long and careful thought I have decided that our life together holds more disadvantage than advantage for us both. Accordingly, I have moved to my place in Acton. Should you wish to discuss any details of plan or arrangement, you may do so with Judge Boker, who will represent me.

I will of course act in entirely good faith in any of your business arrangements which stand in my name.

Sincerely,
Evelyn

I feel deathly ill. I telephoned Evelyn. She was terse, indifferent, referring me to Judge Boker. Later in the day Rose talked to her. Evelyn replied that she was not supposed to talk. She did say that why she left me was because of nothing recent but was of long standing. She had informed my Father of her determination. Get in touch with Judge Boker.

That was all. How can women turn so indifferent? Rose cried. Martha looked distressed. I waited for Eva at one. Would she marry me? No. She was too young. In two years perhaps. I perforce had to admit her wisdom, so did not urge. She was very sweet to me.

This afternoon I am up in the light writing to Evelyn. Doubtless she will not open the letter, so why include it here? I feel like a felled ox. This, this time, my fault pure and simple. I pressed her too hard, uttered too many bitter words. Still, how could she leave one with whom she has lived for twenty-eight years and who in numberless ways has been very good to her; leave suddenly and on a weekend with no one but Mrs. Trench here? I am frightened as to the future. Without Evelyn, life will be dull. Hate her I may often and often, but love her I will, as I still love Janice, until I die. I am pertinacious in my strong loves.

Arthur Doomed:
The Chronicler Assessed

1951–1963

*B*ook VI *is a radical foreshortening of the unabridged Diary (Volumes 120 to 155). It covers the period that begins with the aftermath of Evelyn's departure and ends with Arthur's death. By now the frequently admonished if yet unmaterialized "Editor," to whom Arthur assigned the responsibility of engineering his translation from obscurity to fame, has become a "character" in his own right.*

The machinery for effecting the Diary's contraction was suggested by an out-of-the-blue letter from Edna Coffin Mercer in the spring of 1981. She had married a Korean after the death of Manuel Pena and had lived for a time in Seoul before she divorced her husband and returned to the United States. Her letter of inquiry about the Inman Project prompted my reply. Then it occurred to me that I might bring Inman's Diary *to a close in the form of a series of letter-essays and use the obliging and perceptive Edna as a sounding board for some concluding speculations about Arthur and his ways.*

ARTHUR TO THE EDITOR

Note: If my diary ever becomes famous, I should thank anyone who wishes to paragraph it in a manner pleasing to the eye and logical. I haven't the time when writing under pressure, nor do I wish to use up so much space on half-empty lines. [1936]

The point is this, should whoever edits my diaries after my death see fit to expunge the indelicate passages (and there are such in the life of each person who lives life at all zestfully), I should, were I a ghost, regard the one who took it upon himself to delete at his judgment as one who had cheated me. Having read Mr. Pepys and come to know him in some sort, I seriously doubt whether his spirit (a mundane one surely) would be grateful to you for your reticence on what he would consider the 'spiciest' moments of his career, though of course not the most important.

It seems to me that in all literature there exists no livelier medium for the recording of the spirit of an age than the day-to-day diary.

And it also seems to me that the very moment an editor, however friendly, commences to choose from any such diary what shall and shall not be published, that moment the diary commences to lose its authentic flavor. I feel very strongly upon this subject. [1938]

I have kept this diary now for twenty-one years. Undoubtedly, should the portions dealing with suffering and dissatisfaction be extracted and gathered together in a single book of lamentations, I would be appalled. Maybe somebody, if the diary is ever published, would see fit to delete these portions. It might be a favor done me; I am not the one to know. Problematical editor, do as you see fit about it. After all, I don't want to write a 'Book of Job.' Yet, on the other hand, how can my viewpoint on men and affairs be evaluated without an adequate presentation of my physical disadvantages and my rebellious spirit. [1939]

What my diary needs most are pruning shears to delete the complaints, in particular so since 1945, for since then it has constituted a personal blowoff valve more than a restrained and observant historical document. [1955]

Editor (if any) delete 19/20ths of all these daily condition reports, going back and back and back — please. They are like a morning laxative, to get me started and in the main nothing more. God knows I'd hate to reread them in full and in sequence. I wouldn't; if I wouldn't, who would? So — I beg of you, Mr. Editor (if ever such), delete. [1957]

A diary is something, a document not — save insofar as meaning is to be made clear — to be tampered with subsequently. Other documents are not, however vivid, in the same category with diaries written on the spot and by the day, for journals are never quite to be trusted not to have adjusted contents to altered habits of social thought, 1850 adjusted to 1870, thus losing period-piece spontaneity. Others may not agree with me. Nor should a diary be edited and deleted and amended, save as the author indicates, and maybe not even then. [1958]

I have been studying paragraphing. Should these diaries ever be issued in print, it is my hope that the sentence structure and punctuation may not be tampered with but that a thorough reconstitution of paragraphing be ruthlessly undertaken, in order to make the body of the text more available to ready scanning, since I am very conscious of the visual inadvisability of such thick, such long, such unbroken paragraphs as, to save paper and space, I generally use. No invitation to the eye lies in my extended, solid paragraphs. [1960]

I have reflected upon this diary as concerns what should be done with it when I die. It is egregious to expect any sane publishing house will consent to printing the whole of it, for much of it is 'filling,' boring, complaining, of no value, and no arrogance or hopefulness (even mine) should expect an undeleted total to be 'taken on.' My prime belief is that I have little personal worth. Why then should what I have written be of prime interest? The question has common sense. So I shall reverse my stand, hoping only that a sensitive and judicious editor may be happened upon. Without the large editing of Thomas Wolfe's works, would he have achieved a place in American letters? You, as a writer, cannot, unless you are widely connected with the contemporaneous literary, hope for a favorable 'cutting.' No normal human mind would wish to follow closely my some ten million words flowed out with sometimes unsieved intensity. I am as likely to be given, postmortem, a 'good' editor as a 'bad' one. Chance has 99 percent to do with fame, it would seem, even with the artistic persistence of effort. [1960]

It is short-sighted of me to cavil over editing, when to reconcile myself to it might, per se, permit publication when not to might preclude opportunity of publication. [1960]

Anita read aloud from Volume 104 [1944], which she's finished. I was thoroughly disappointed in the diary. It is ragged, labored, egocentric and lacks bottom. It hardly compares with the volumes in the series from Volumes 40–56 [1929–33]. It disgruntles me. Perhaps I reached my best performance as a sort of bastard gazetter somewhere between 40–90 [1929–40]. Yes, it would be best for some editor to make selections. [1962]

It could be probable that a stranger, perusing my diary proper, will wish to delete, expurgate, slash the contents. It could be I might owe such an editor great good-fellowship, or, were he a blunderer, despite his efforts and him. It's all a spin of the coin, however it lands — heads, tails. I can do nothing about it, not owning a span of life two centuries long. It's all — how excellent or how dull, how alive or how merely ink and pencil on yellowing paper, whether published or not, whether read or not — a series of gambles. [1962]

EDITOR TO EDNA

Inman Project
Harvard University
20 Garden Street
Cambridge, Massachusetts 02138
(617) 495-3070
July 13, 1981

Ms. Edna Coffin Kim
11A Ponce de Leon Avenue
Fort Lauderdale, Florida 33304
Dear Ms. Kim:

   Your June 30 letter to Arthur Rosenthal reached me today. In answer to your inquiry, the Harvard University Press will publish the Inman Diary. I am the chief editor, and Elizabeth Smith is my assistant. We've been working on the Diary volumes — 155 of them — for the past three years. It is my responsibility to reduce roughly 17 million words to less than one tenth of the total. Hence some one thousand "characters" will be reduced to about forty-five.

   In accordance with Mr. Inman's wishes, only a few of the still-living "characters" will appear under their own names, the ones not concerned with preserving anonymity. You are certainly a main character, much admired (and with good reason) by Arthur Inman and by Evelyn Inman — the heroine of the Diary. Regrettably, because your name for us is somehow bound up with your origins and rich experience, you will have to appear under a pseudonym.

   The Diary entries, whether Arthur realized it or not, show that you had sized him up pretty accurately, but I should be enormously interested now in getting your retrospective judgments on him and his Diary. You have seen only a portion of it — and that long ago. I have studied it exhaustively and consider it a remarkable document. Although clogged with extraneous and turgid sections, it is nevertheless a work of literary and historical importance. Whether or not it will bring him the fame he hungered for remains to be seen.

   I look forward to hearing from you again.

Sincerely,
Daniel Aaron

August 4, 1981

Dear Ms. Kim:

   Elizabeth Smith and I marvel at your ability to recall events and persons so clearly and perceptively after almost a half-century. In most instances, your assessments of Arthur and a number of the "characters" in the Diary seem absolutely on target — and confirmed by other Garri-

son Hall denizens we've questioned. I'm struck, too, by your disagreements with some of Arthur's self-serving allegations. The man you knew so well and whom I have come to know more intimately than I do most of my friends (indeed, his constant admonitions to the "problematical editor" have, in effect, conscripted me as a posthumous "character") still puzzles me. After reading millions of words of the Diary, I ought to be able to tell when he's being honest and when disingenuous, but you knew Arthur: I am here to reconstruct him.

In my last letter I roughly summarized the Diary between the time you quit the household in 1938 and Evelyn's flight from Garrison Hall thirteen years later. Her departure and return, an episode that fills several hundred pages of the Diary, marks the beginning of its long "glissade," to use one of Arthur's favorite words. It must be drastically shortened, along with the remaining thirty-six manuscript volumes, for reasons of space, but here is a compressed version of what happened. It is based upon my shorthand notes.

Arthur crushed. Beseeches Evelyn to come back on any terms she chooses to make. Writes her blaming himself entirely. Confesses that instead of trying to mold her into a compliant wife, he ought to have reformed himself. He is now, he says, undergoing a metamorphosis. No longer jealous of Pike. Admits his selfishness. Feels no resentment for Evelyn, only gratitude, and will strive to do better. Won't she give him another chance? Asks Woody to intervene, and when she refuses he crosses her off his list. But rest of Garrison Hall rallies around him.

Frantic oscillations. Maybe a good thing Evelyn took off. Asks his real estate agent, Miss Laird, if she would consider marrying him. Then sends Evelyn a pedigreed setter dog. She coldly rebuffs his overture. Writes letter to the "Old Man," taking blame for the marital rift. Resolves, if she forgives him, to let Evelyn drink, travel at will, speak to him without restraint. Fearful of divorce. Will kill himself if Evelyn stays away. She is the strong one, he the weaker. Lost utterly.

Evelyn wooed with bad poems and with "moving" letters that would soften the shell of an armadillo. He has been transformed. His changed viewpoint presages a change in character. For example, no longer feels bitter toward his father. Attributing Evelyn's dissatisfaction to his weak sexual performance, he suggests to Roderic that he become her surrogate spouse. Offer declined. All agog after she agrees to come to lunch ("I am a new man, and from now on she is Princess Desirable"). She arrives and talks cold turkey. No, she doesn't love him. She loves her freedom. She doesn't miss him. She wrote him nice letters because he wanted them. Oh God! Now he knows how deeply he has offended her. Yet how cruel she is. Obviously she's getting back at him, wants to wound him. Yes, Fred

Lakian and Martha are right. He's better off without this immoral woman, this liar who deserted him for Pike because of her sexual hunger.

Henry Inman dies (June 12, 1951) at age 82, his death, Arthur thinks, probably hastened by Evelyn's desertion. Not sorry about "Old Man." Now he'll come into his inheritance,[1] and he's glad to be free of his father's "constantly disapproving eye." Continues to bombard Evelyn with letters. Begs her to seek separation, not divorce, if only for tax purposes. Meanwhile behaves in exemplary way, banks his fiery rages, and even calls on Mrs. Yates in her Brookline nursing home. Is Evelyn softening? She hints she might come back but vows to be uncompromising. Plainly, Arthur and the Garrison Hall staff conclude, she isn't "normal." She delivers her terms: separation for the moment; an apartment in the Chestnut Street building; free to go to Reno if nothing works out during next six months. Doesn't want his love letters. (Bitter pill.)

Still, she's growing gentler, Arthur reasons. His strategy seems to be working. She announces plan to sail for France in fall. No demurral from Arthur. (Why does he dote on this cool and unreliable woman?) Helps her plan trip but feels desolate. The unrestricted liberty she craves is only for misanthropes, hermits, and egomaniacs. Apparently she is still under the spell of the treacherous Pike. Evelyn says she may learn to love him but won't be pushed. So Arthur plays the solicitous, understanding husband in the hope that she will in time caress him as lovingly as she does her dog. But he proceeds cautiously, unwilling to give up his girls (though he assures her he has lost his roving eye) unless he's certain she won't abandon him. Hopes her psychiatrist, Landon Sewell, will make her see her coldness and duplicity, but in the privacy of his Diary he discloses to the reader his scheme of dissimulation. He intends to "sneak on padded gumshoes into her mind." Once the "liar" and "cheat" has capitulated and accepts the new Arthur Inman, mild and concessive, he promises to tighten the reins.

The long separation begins. Evelyn wants four months off every year! He weeps and threatens suicide until she tells him not to worry ("You and your mommie will work things out"). His letters and flowers pursue her through Europe as he torments himself with thoughts of "low-brow shithead" Pike "lying on top of my wife and lying to me." Evelyn, damn her, is untouched by his self-pitying messages (she doesn't even take his picture to Europe), yet this "weakling and cheater and liar" is "as necessary to me emotionally as opium to an addict." How can she resist his love letters?

---

[1] According to Arthur, his father's will, except for a few minor bequests, left the income from everything he owned to Arthur. Evelyn was to receive one-fourth of the estate on Arthur's death. In addition, Arthur was to receive $40,000 free and clear. He estimated that his annual income would be somewhere between $30,000 and $36,000.

Pike must still have her in thrall. But then she writes of her return by Christmas. Oh joy!

Arthur has to dissemble his true feelings on eve of their "remarriage" and conceals the Diary bursting with his fulminations. Dreads her coming, yet burns with rage and shame when the "succubus" spends two days in New York instead of rushing to Boston. Feels "rip-roaring bitter" at her and more so at himself for wanting her back. Records with misgiving the chilly reunion, the peck on his cheek. No endearing words, no inquiries about his health. In a long interview enlightens her about the two-timing Pike, wife-beater and womanizer, and lays down his terms. "All I want (and listen close) is just to smooth a bit the outer edges of the rough grindstone that is you, for I am a delicate tool and nick easily."

Next months a strain. The "fascinating and adamantine" Evelyn his despair. She must love him or else she wouldn't have come back, yet he finds her egotistical as ever—grasping, shallow, grudging with her favors. Deplores her drinking and yearns for sexual attention. What would he do without his darling little girls who hug and kiss him, especially when he gives them money and clothes, and whom he freely fondles. But Evelyn is relenting (are his Fabian tactics paying off?). She promises to stop drinking and allows him to watch her bathe.

What has he learned during this dark period? Not to lose his temper, to employ Gandhian passive resistance, and to display a hurt silence to register displeasure. If he feels betrayed and embittered, he must keep it to himself. Alert to pitfalls and dangers and will act accordingly.

That's enough for now, Edna. I'll postpone the course of the troubled marriage for another occasion, but I'd be curious to get your response to the above account of Arthur and Evelyn's shaky reconciliation. He makes a great to-do about his change of character, but the Diary reveals the same dissimulating, panic-ridden, revengeful man ready to crack the whip over the woman he ostensibly loves once she's back in harness. He continues to present himself as the sensitive, forgiving, overgenerous, more sinned-against-than-sinning spouse.

September 2, 1981

Dear Edna:

Your last letter was very illuminating besides being enjoyable. Many thanks again for this and earlier ones. They have corroborated my own hunches about this flawed and sad creature, so gifted and so spoiled, and they include details that have helped Libby and me to reconstruct and refine our conception of him.

I was especially interested in your comment about Arthur's "sadistic treatment" of Evelyn and in your observation that "she might easily have *become a candidate for a mental institution if Arthur hadn't out-foxed himself when he engineered the affair with Dr. Pike." Pike of the Diary is represented as a simple-minded fellow, masterful but almost childlike; you remember him as subtle and intelligent, "with a strong sense of irony" and a "salty turn of phrase." I've been pondering your statement that Arthur's worship of Pike and his animosity toward him "both stemmed from the fact that Dr. Pike was a prime example of what Arthur might have been had his personal development not been arrested," that "to see Dr. Pike and Arthur standing side by side was uncannily like seeing a baked and unbaked figure of the same person."*

Arthur wouldn't have relished the comparison. After 1951 he raged against his former idol and preserver, and try as Evelyn might to forget the whole matter (the past was the past), Arthur kept flinging Pike in her face. He was prompted, so he said, by his "mad passion for truthfulness," but his obsessive references to the Pike affair reflect rather a sadistic, scab-picking mentality. Evelyn told him that without Pike she would have left him ("I wouldn't be what you like today without him") and that for all of Arthur's allegations, Pike was good to her. No matter. In Arthur's eyes he remained the arch-seducer, cad, and cheapskate, the villain responsible for Arthur's unhealable mortification.

That sounds melodramatic, doesn't it. Perhaps it's worth adding that a year before his death, Arthur reviewed (self-defensively as usual but with a certain detachment) the story of the fatal triangle. He had been reading the Diary of 1935 after a span of twenty-seven years and now from a distance watched his wife becoming infatuated with Dr. Pike. He wasn't "so insensitive as to be unaware" of what was going on, he recalled, but how could he have objected to Pike's "chaperonage" when he regarded his own casual affairs of no consequence?

It never occurred to me that a man of Dr. Pike's age could be so stallion-like and she so mare-like. Nor did I dream he would treat one he said was his best friend in such knavish fashion. When I toyed with sex, it was for temporary excitation and experience; I had no notion that to others, passion engaged in was as basic as a river running downhill. Much of what was happening was my own fault, the fault of my ingenuousness. Nor — to be honest — did I dare to tell Dr. Pike off for fear of losing his osteopathic capacity. So I jammed my eyes shut and sat hard on my suspicions and managed most of the time to be blind. I don't think I blamed Evelyn, for it never occurred to me that she could, just because of sex, shift her center of attraction. I was to find out.

But this is to her eternal credit: No matter how often he asked her to leave me, she didn't, until, at any rate, her change of life and my bitterness combined to estrange her. Then, within a few days—though she wouldn't believe it—I had found out that always I had, did, would love her. And so, now, it will always be. What strange cord binds two so normally antagonistic people together? Is devotion really not just habit sinewed by propinquity and self-interest but rather a mysterious and sacred adhesive?

Mind you, Arthur wrote these words at the end of his life. The years immediately following Evelyn's return to Garrison Hall were hardly less tumultuous than the preceding ones. It would take another decade before the mismatched pair would be able (I quote Arthur) "to make themselves, their actions, their spoken words fit a closed daily pattern of existence whereby neither might feel integrity under challenge."

The phantom of Pike stood between them, but so did (at least Arthur believed) their different conceptions of love and sex. He clung to the fancy that his inability to satisfy Evelyn sexually explained her infatuation for Pike of the "tireless cock." He attributed to Freud (whom he never read, always denigrated, and constantly misunderstood) the idea   which he considered possibly valid—that "we all are, fundamentally, screwing, fucking animals with everything else, even survival, subsidiary." But sex for Arthur had nothing to do with "love." He likened it to a good meal, one of "the baser aspects" of love, whereas for Evelyn, he maintained, sex and love were inseparable. And because a "routine" sex relationship injured his body and bored him into the bargain, he generally sought other ways to obtain love and attention.

According to Arthur, Evelyn's compulsive drinking was another source of friction between them—more offensive to him than her cold-cream smells and cigarette breath. He hadn't an inkling of why she should seek an anodyne in alcohol. You might think that his own resort to booze would have suggested some reasons why his wife, too, looked for a route to temporary oblivion, but he ascribed her drinking to weakness of character and took it as personal affront. About Alcoholics Anonymous, which Evelyn had joined a few years before, Arthur observed in 1955:

The chief theory of A.A., as far as I can determine, is the delusory one that overdrinking is an illness, like any other illness, whereas really it is a self-indulgence, mostly a matter of lack of will power and an acquired habit, a dope habit like smoking or taking morphine or sedatives beyond need or eating grossly.

But A.A. gave its members "an out in relieving them of blame" through the ritual of confession. I don't say that Arthur's concern for Evelyn's problem wasn't genuine, but his own personal comfort and peace of mind depended upon an orderly routine in Garrison Hall. When Evelyn or any of the staff were "under the influence," Arthur felt discommoded. (His own drinking was another matter.)

Arthur considered the most grievous of Evelyn's faults her insupportable penchant for travel. He tried every trick in his repertory to keep her tethered, and he punished her in direct and indirect ways when she fled the coop. He sulked and wept and dissembled before and after her European jaunts, itemized the contents of her suitcases, listed her itineraries, and hoped she'd suffer "a couple of harsh or unpleasant psychological experiences" that would discourage further trips. The longer she stayed away, the more he quailed at her return, recalling "the awful, miserable, tactless-on-both-sides homecomings of the past." When she was away, he complained of her short letters and worried about putative lapses. Was she drinking again? Had she picked up a man? Would she be more demanding, more outrageous in her expectations, deflate him? Hating her for deserting him, he hated himself for his hateful thoughts and his groveling dependence upon her.

Nor could he forgive her for her willful reluctance to yield herself to his "long-term ambition"—the completion and eventual publication of his Diary. She helped him, to be sure, but she really didn't give a hoot what happened to him or it. "Whether I die anonymous or illustrious," he noted sadly in 1959,

is of no close importance to her, as if I were a man with an itch, fatuously ambitious and no more, no more, no more. That she acts or believes so puts me flat on the ground. Yet I cannot cause her to regard the matter otherwise. To her, it is evident, I am of no more permanent importance than whether the one day the sun shines and the next day the sky clouds over. Do I amount to anything, I must do so solitarily and not expect psychological support from my wife. Perhaps it should be so—that each man should be masculinely his own responsibility.

Having undervalued Evelyn's services throughout most of the Diary, Arthur had the grace to record her sentiments on their up-and-down marriage after she decided to come back to him. He pictured her then as a hard and willful woman who backed away from his caresses "like a horse from a blowing newspaper." He considered her "selfish and egocentric." But in time he gathered from her how she had compromised more than she had ever intended to do while trying all the while to keep her independence. If she more or less accepted her situation (the rift between them was too "wide and enduring" to bridge), she didn't press what she called her advantages. She admired his "agelessness," his openness to new ideas, his humor. She simply could not play the alternating roles of adoring wife, playful child, and faithful amanuensis. Arthur reports her as saying:

You see, I am not living the sort of existence I was designed for by my nature. I spend, I assure you, much thought and effort being and acting the way which assuages your need. But I am no wonder woman. I get tired or cross or sorry for myself. I labor like a trooper to pull myself back. But it takes time and you become disheartened so quickly. Sometimes you strain to help me when all I need is to be left alone. I don't enjoy being off-center. And I dislike feeling badly. When I feel badly, I can't help you tactfully. But I do try all the time and I do love you, and I do do better than formerly. You know I do. I enjoy much of our work together and I love to read to you, and I take pride in helping you in the ways others can't. But I don't like all the little detail tasks. Doing them makes me feel hemmed in. I wish I could be everything you'd like me to be in as fast rotation as you like, but it is just impossible. You'll have to be satisfied with what I am, I guess, and enjoy me when I suit you. One of my particular virtues, as you must admit, is loyalty. I don't ever mean to scold and nag. I'm just too emotionally conscientious about watching over you and your diaries and your welfare. I do better when I can remove myself emotionally and use my head. It's my head I do best with. And you should — as I think you have come to — always bear in mind that what I do in general pleases you; it is just what I say which upsets you.

Arthur responded to confessional asides of this sort with sympathy even as he acknowledged the profound differences in their aspirations and standards — "our attitudes toward people, friends, work, diversion, life and death." He depended upon Evelyn to "remember with me," but she wanted to expunge those parts of their mutual past still too shocking for her to recur to. Arthur resented her resolution to blot it out, but how could it be otherwise when part of her job was to read his ferocious Diary entries on the subject of the "double-talking and amoral" Pike and selfish, spoiled, spiteful Evelyn? It was, she told him, like "looking down the mouth of a volcano you believed extinct and seeing sulphuric flames." Arthur always came back to his infernal honesty. Why couldn't she see that his disapprobations were far less in number than his expressions of love and affection?

There you have it, Edna. Arthur knew that his Diary was the disruptive agent. How unfortunate, he kept saying, that Evelyn had to see his thoughts in writing. "They are not necessarily abnormal or despicable or even untoward thoughts. They mean no harm. It is simply that they appear in fixed form." This is equivocal, to say the least.

But Arthur did try in the end to put himself in Evelyn's mind (at least he claimed he did) and to register her dislike of his lethal "teasing." She expostulated: "I will stay by you when you are in trouble. I love you very much. I would like it if you could regard me with approbation and gentleness. I am the person you can count on most in the world," and Arthur was touched. He never stopped being amazed by her tolerance for his "little girls" (she even volunteered to buy them contraceptives). And reflecting on the "long, mutually benefiting, harried, never dull, shared and unshared, often frantic, often amusing, unorthodox marriage," he concluded that in spite of the "wear and tear" they had caused each other, they would have been "squashier persons" had their lives run more smoothly.

For all his rationalizations and face-saving dodges, I think Arthur did come to value his faithful partner who sympathized with his wish to die and stayed with him until the end.

September 29, 1981

Dear Edna:

In this letter I shift the focus from Arthur's marital woes (he observed in March 1952 that his Diary had "in some measure turned into a diary of Evelyn") to the historian and political commentator. When you quit Garrison Hall, he still regarded the Diary as a chronicle of his times. After the explosion of the atomic bomb, the Diary changed in content and direction.

Yet Arthur never quite gave up his grand scheme to summarize "current historical happenings." World affairs kept impinging on quotidian ones, and although he devoted less space to politics than during the Depression years when you were with him, he couldn't resist monitoring successive presidencies, sounding alarms about his enfeebled country, and warning of the coming Armageddon between the white and the colored races.

You'll find most of his opinions predictable. I don't have to tell you that his hope of becoming an interpreter and representative of his times was absurd. He was too confined, too prejudiced, too uncritical. I doubt if he ever distinguished his occasional insights (for example, his hunch that Japan might soon supersede the United States as the technical and financial world leader) from his fatuous pronouncements or realized how his biases and want of judgment disqualified him as a reliable social historian.

Arthur's survey of the Eisenhower years is too scurrilous and silly to dwell upon very long, but it's worth a brief summary. During the 1952 presidential campaign, he sided of course with Ike against the "dishonest"-looking Stevenson. Actually he found Nixon more appealing than either, but given the prevailing "Socialist ideology," it really made no

*difference who got in. Ike was a relief after the "petty, vindictive, wasp-
ish" Truman and the Pinko Anglophile Acheson. He may have been a
"dumb, unsure, little boy," but he lacked the imagination to be a crook.
For a few months after the inauguration, Arthur was content. Then the
honeymoon ended, and he returned to his favorite game of savaging
presidents: Eisenhower, it seemed, proved to be soft on communism.*

*Arthur was a perfect specimen of what a historian friend of mine has
called the "paranoid style" of political thinking. He had always been a
great smeller-outer of conspiracy — remember his views about the New
Deal sappers. In the Fifties, the United States, he believed, was particularly vulnerable to Communist espionage. According to his reasoning,
the Soviets had no intention of fighting a war with us. Russian leaders
knew they could achieve their ends through subversion, and one of their
secret weapons was the "Hebraic" minority, "boring from within and
destroying their host nation, swiftly or slowly." From the time of Christ,
the first Jewish termite, to the execution of the Rosenbergs, the conspira-
tors had been at their nefarious work, only this time America was their
target. Poor, simple-minded Ike couldn't deal with them, influenced as
he was by the high-placed Communists who had penetrated the two
previous administrations. Look at the way he botched the Korean War.
The disgraceful armistice was "in effect a Communist victory" and
illustrated "our mania to preserve life in the aggregate" at the expense of
national interests.*

*No wonder Arthur welcomed the advent of Senator Joseph McCarthy,
who awakened the G.O.P. "to the importance and value of anti-Communist propaganda as a vote-getting means." To be sure, Arthur hadn't
changed his opinion of the Irish; they were all "liars and bastards." But
then he had always preferred "scoundrelly rulers" to idealistic ones. The
patriotic and fearless McCarthy might have succeeded in rooting out the
Reds had not Eisenhower stupidly refused to grant McCarthy's investigators access to the files of "suspected executives and Army employees."
The president thereby divided the nation and furthered the Communist
plot to install a fascist-type dictatorship and to accustom the people to
bureaucratic control in preparation for a Communist takeover.*

*Arthur followed the "disgraceful and harmful" McCarthy-Army
hearings with fascinated attention and wept when, three years later in
May 1957, news of his hero's death came over the radio. Coolidge was the
only other public figure whose death had stirred him to tears. I must quote
for you his extraordinary eulogy:*

Certainly McCarthy was ambitious. Certainly he was crude at
times. Certainly at times innocent people suffered. Certainly he
blustered. Certainly he rode a cause for all it was worth. But the

cause was patriotic and one no one else dared ride: the bluster a part of his personality, the suffering of innocent people a part of any cause militantly followed, the roughness of his approach the one weapon Communists understood and feared, the crudeness part of his unpolished upbringing, the ambition no different from that harbored by most men of parts. If he was demagogic, was not Truman, was not Roosevelt, was not Lincoln? I salute a man unafraid and in his way a great patriot. I abhor Eisenhower and his clique who staged the 'Army-McCarthy Hearings,' with all the cards unfairly stacked. I hope now that Mr. Eisenhower is happy. I know that the Communists are, and all the Pinkos and Fellow-Travellers.

Arthur the Patriot suffered with McCarthy; Arthur the Geopolitician, during the hearings and thereafter, anxiously scanned the world arena and scored American setbacks. He saw communism winning in Asia, in the Mideast, eastern Europe, and Central America — and the Eisenhower administration hadn't the wisdom or gumption to check it. I won't try to spell out his mostly simplistic explanations for the Suez crisis, the crushing of the Hungarian revolution, the French defeat in Indo-China. These events and a good many others occurring elsewhere proved to him the impotence of the old colonial powers and the timidity of the United States. History again corrected the popular fallacy that nations wouldn't go to war if they were unprepared or if the chance of victory was slim. Leaders made wars to retain personal power and divert attention from unsolved problems at home.

The Russians, Arthur believed, displayed "a high creative intelligence." They were realistic and patient, but they could be outfaced. Here are my notes on his no-nonsense, get-tough line as expressed in a May 25, 1954, entry:

Will history show that Russian hegemony over half the world is due to "religious fervor" and "Machiavellian diplomacy" or to U.S. "meechy avoidance of force" and failure of "avaricious allies" to back us up? Our propaganda inept, negative. We have failed to deal with Communist penetration in government and key industries, allowed "every Tom, Dick and Harry" nation to "bamboozle us." Now giving China a free hand in Indo-China, permitting the Reds to slip arms into Guatemala ("which has gone Communist without our raising a finger"), and fomenting war in Honduras and Nicaragua, which can only lead to economic deterioration and further Communist inroads. Inman no longer against secret diplomacy. "Daylight diplomacy" much worse with every word and act being flashed the world over and commentators ready to twist and distort to fit their prejudices and convictions and a confused people made jittery and further confused. [It] prevents the sort of hardheaded and factual and often underhanded bargaining around the table which is often necessary in reaching workable terms.

Very alarmed by Russian space triumphs. "Hair-raising to watch and wait."

I detect a pattern in Arthur's fluctuating opinions of American presidents from Wilson to Kennedy. (Lincoln and Teddy Roosevelt are the only two other presidents he wrote very much about.) He welcomes the incumbents but quickly turns against them (save for Coolidge, who could do nothing wrong) and ends by despising them.

Eisenhower is a good example. By the time Ike suffered a heart attack in September 1955, Arthur thought it would be better for the nation if the president died and was replaced by the brainy, charming Nixon — or even better, a "rip-roaring, conservative Southerner," for Ike was not only "dumb," he was a "Big Spender," the worst epithet in Arthur's political lexicon. So was "the millionaire's son, Kennedy," nominated in 1960 as the issue of Communist Cuba heated up. ("Why should any nation in the world respect us," said Arthur, "when we allow a tiny snipe of a country like Cuba to throw us around at will?")

By election day Arthur had lost faith in Nixon, who had needlessly sold out to "Leftist" Rockefeller. With Barry Goldwater out of the picture, the contest was between two "Socialist" parties. Kennedy's victory didn't disturb Arthur very much. True, he was a Roman Catholic and Big Labor's creature. He never had "to dig for a dime" (amusing this coming from Arthur), but he sounded less defensive in his foreign policy than Eisenhower, and who knows, he might be a "whiz." A few months later Arthur pronounced Kennedy a bust — a bigger spender than ever — and doubted if he would stand up to the Russians and Cubans. Hadn't he welshed on his campaign promises to beef up nuclear and space projects? Now Arthur wished Eisenhower was back. Poor JFK, "misinstructed by Leftist Harvard," floundered in a fog of altruism.

I jump to April 1962: Arthur reports six to seven thousand "advisors" in Vietnam "under the hypocritical guise of training yellow soldiers to contest communist advances."

To May: What slush the president dishes out to an audience of United Mine Workers. He fuses with FDR in Arthur's mind, the spoiled, stubborn, willful, impetuous boy president — redeemed only by his forthright speech.

To October 23: The Missile Crisis. Arthur writes, "It must have required great courage on the part of our rulers at this late date, with peril intensified, to make a stand definitely. The cards are dealt, the hands filled, the bets down. Now what?"

To October 30: A postmortem on Cuba. The Russians are celebrating their victory — and properly so. Why? Because the United States has abandoned the Monroe Doctrine, ducked a head-on military confrontation, promised to stay out of Cuba, and guaranteed "the long-term continuation of Soviet education, propaganda and revolutionary headquarters against Central and South America here in the New World."

To November 5, 1963: Arthur can't believe the State Department was smart enough to engineer or connive in the assassination of the Vietnamese dictator Ngo Dinh Diem. Our policy is to sacrifice thousands of lives rather than rub out "a single political rogue sub rosa."

To November 22: Arthur's response to Kennedy's assassination was matter-of-fact but a little curious, too. "It was," he noted, "as if a hex had been lifted, I mean historically speaking, from the country." Yet he wanted to weep for the death of a courageous man. Doubtless the cleverer and less scrupulous brother, Bobby, would be next in line for a presidential nomination. Arthur didn't like the photographs of Lyndon Johnson (a "vainer face it would be hard to find") but changed his opinion when he listened to Johnson's Thanksgiving Day message. Here was "a non-Irish, non-Catholic, noncharming man," experienced and practical, and a relief after "personality overlord" Kennedy. The more he reflected on "St. Kennedy" and his "canonization," with "American eyes thrill-glued to television," the more aloof he became. What would future historians make of the "scuttlebutt" about JFK's amorous affairs? "Of course this side of a man's life is his own business but is, in final analysis, a part of his record as a man, if true."

There's one more theme to take up, Edna, before I end this lengthening letter — what Arthur referred to as the "not improbable war to the death between the white minority and the great colored majority of the world." I know he made no bones about his racial theories to you, but in the last phase of his life he gave increasing space in the Diary to this Impending Struggle. Perhaps skin color lay at the root of racial antagonism, he surmised, but whatever the cause, we had best face the prospect of a world force most likely organized and powered by the resourceful Chinese. Russian indoctrination and arms would fuel the colored crusade, but in the end Russia as well would perforce join the Western camp.

Behind this nightmare of racial war lay an obsession to which his rational side inevitably yielded. Remember how he would occasionally interrupt his diatribes against the Jews, declare himself a sharer of their "spouting vitality," and "wonder seriously" if he should "join the Jewish faith," the only one that made any sense to him? So in September 1960 he publicly relinquished "the bred-in-the-bone idea" that blacks were "naturally inferior in brain power to the whites." He now declared the "higher-type members" of any race or color could become "as intelligent as we are." This revelation, however, did not prevent him from championing South African apartheid or condemning the civil rights agitators in Alabama. Each demonstration, besides giving comfort to the Communists, became "another block in the building of the great racial war towering more menacingly ahead." The prospect haunted him, as the following January 1, 1962, entry suggests.

Nightmares all night about being set down (too much U.N. and all the dozens of petty nations of colored extraction joining it, erasing its usefulness by their preponderance, fostering the color war in due time) in a black republic, of the slights and unkindnesses which befell a Nordic seeking (misplacedly and against racial prejudice on the other foot as it were) haven for himself. Pincushion mountains. Half-roads. Imperturbable blue sky-bowl overhead. Strong odor of black bodies, of musk, acrid.

Until the end Arthur remained faithful to his Anglo-Saxon mystique. The blacks might be psychologically advantaged (he was genuinely grateful to black servants and friends whose tranquil personalities had salved his troubled spirit), but he never ceased regarding "yellow and tan and black peoples" as inferior, and he deplored their elevation at Western expense: "We throw to the yapping international dogs our great heritage of white superiority."

October 20, 1981

Dear Edna:

As a Garrison Hall veteran and one-time intimate of Arthur, you enjoyed and disenjoyed the privilege of watching his world-within-a-world at first hand. This essay-letter will be a reflection on that microcosm and particularly on the feminine component Arthur came more and more to rely upon after Evelyn's flight and return.

He hungered for the leavening company of men (at least he said he did) and devoted pages of the Diary to Garrison Hall elevator operators and janitors; to Jim Cotton, who repaired his radios; to the Baby-Carriage chauffeurs Amos Temple (black) and Reg Helm (white); to lawyers and business associates; to his squadrons of doctors; and to the husbands and boyfriends of his staff. But he depended almost entirely upon women to conduct the around-the-clock operation of his establishment.

The "girls" silently entered his bedroom before daybreak to pull the curtains and blot out the poisonous light before Arthur opened his eyes. They folded his sheets and blankets and aired his quarters according to his precise instructions; cooked his meals and served them at the correct temperature (he often dined in the darkened bathroom); washed his hair and rubbed his head; mended his silk pajamas; took him out on drives; read to him (probably as fast as possible and without expression); kept his books, paid bills, helped him with his income tax and stock market dealings; ran errands; listened to his woes and comforted and flattered him. Many of these assignments had to be carried out in the dark — and for a man angered and upset at any deviation from his routine.

A smooth and harmonious functioning of the G.H. personnel soothed Arthur's spirit. At such times he pictured his little community (you will appreciate this, Edna) as a cooperative family headed by a benign "paterfamilias" who treated his employees as friends — a fact he urged readers to keep "always in mind when reading my chronicle." The service he demanded and got he repaid in affection and concern, not just wages, and by fostering a cheerful work atmosphere, so that Garrison Hall resembled at once "a family, a club, a business management." Domestic tranquillity was not sustained without effort, but the sentiment of "mutuality and shared interest" did much to reduce inevitable tensions and strain.

Yet the Diary shows the heavy psychological price Arthur paid for the "devoted" services of his "family," many of them temperamental persons who quarreled with each other as well as with him and whom he had to coddle and placate. All of this was galling to one who confessed "the untrammeled desires of an Asiatic potentate." His "many-sided helplessness" required him "to strait-jacket and order my behavior, my words, my attitudes" and silently to suffer the "uncalled for moodiness and petulance" of the help. Otherwise they might blackmail him or take to the bottle or develop repulsive habits — or worse, quit without notice. When that happened he panicked, because an unlicensed departure spelled chaos. It took weeks to choose and test a replacement and to restore the old routine. Fearing and hating household change and employing every ruse he could think of to hold his champing females, Arthur sadly came to realize that devotion and affection were ephemeral adhesives, that money was the only trustworthy cement.

Between 1951 and 1963, scores of women entered his employment and left it with his blessings or curses. One remained, the tried-and-true veteran Rose Trench. She first came to Garrison Hall in 1944. Arthur was rather taken with her then. She was gentle and a good cook, if slow and unsure, but most important for Arthur, it was apparent she liked him. Rose soon became the linchpin of the establishment, Arthur's "second wife," a woman to be counted on. It took some time before she reluctantly opened up to him about her father ("a salesman frequently away from home"); her mother ("'a home devil and street angel,' gay, ruthless, loving clothes and men"), who "taught her to fear men"; her trip abroad before World War I with her father; her hatred of her mother—by this time divorced; and her marriage to Mr. Trench. Let Arthur take over.

I think that Rose met Mr. Trench during bond drives or working in his office—at any rate, she met him. He was ten years or so her senior. They were married around 1919 or 1920, or maybe 1918, judging by Wendy's [Rose's daughter] present age. He had a business, or a proper business position, was comparatively well off. One of his brothers is at the present time president of some college or university or other. Mr. Trench (I don't know his first name—Rose never having divulged it) was, during his courting, excruciatingly polite and well-mannered. Rose is susceptible to good manners, often misjudging people by their ownership of them. I feel sure she entered matrimony with no vaguest idea of what sort of man Mr. Trench was, other than that he had good manners and a sufficient income. Rose's mother had never taught her of sex, her sort of woman usually being reticent on the subject and suspicious of informing their children. I don't know—for I doubt if she remembers—how long she was married before she became aware of her husband's foibles and shortcomings. "I knew so little about men that I thought all men were like my husband and all wives had to put up with how their husbands were as cheerfully and agreeably as possible."

It transpired Mr. Trench, whose meticulous way of dressing had so impressed Rose, had a fetish on clothes and cleanliness. He spent more than an hour each morning dressing. He filled her closet with his tailor-made suits. His shirts had to be specially laundered. Each day he brushed the lint from the cuff of his pants and went over his wardrobe. He would not eat supper until he had bathed and changed clothes, even if the meal waited an hour. He chided Rose on scratched furniture, disarranged objects, lack of neatness. Rose, not a neat person, hated his scrutiny of details and his scolding. Then there was mother-in-law trouble from a woman she disliked, especially after the children came. It seemed that Mr. Trench was afraid of empty houses and of the dark. He didn't like to enter an unlit house. He got Rose to meet him at the car line on dark evenings and walk home with him. He believed that all men were brutes and untrustworthy and proceeded to inculcate her with his distrust and fear of them. He was jealous to the point of absurdity, keeping a close watch on her movements and activities. He was, I gather, severe and upright and humorless. He never played with her and rarely if ever joked. He was convinced that the sex act, if indulged in more than once or twice a month, would lead to death through prostate gland trouble. Neither undressed before the other. He didn't caress or pet her.

She tried to meet his whims and to feed him well. She belonged to the Unitarian Church. Her first rebellion was against her mother-in-law. He didn't like it. She scarcely knew anything about birth when she had her first child. I imagine — though Rose doesn't say so — that she devoted herself almost fanatically to her children. At any rate, the husband was jealous of them. They annoyed him also and had to be kept out of the way when he was home. He was severe with them and faultfinding. I'm sure that Rose spoiled them unmercifully. She would stay up into the early hours making dresses for them. "I guess I made a slave of myself for them." She never by word or thought suggests that she may have been difficult to live with, but judging by her temper and her vindictiveness, I'll wager Mr. Trench had no easy time of it in spots.

His jealousy increased beyond the bonds of normality. He was stingy with the money he gave her to spend on Wendy and Josephine. She went into partnership with a Mrs. Needle, mother of a wild son and a daughter who slept with the butcherboy and the bakerboy and anybody and loved it and confided to Rose about it. They made Christmas and Valentine's Day favors, and Rose sold them and did most of the work and liked it. That angered Mr. Trench. Rose played cards and joined the female lodge (her husband was a Mason). She liked that sort of thing. They went to the mountains or the seashore summers. Mr. Trench's jealousy increased. He wouldn't let young men come to the house to call on the girls. He began to stay away nights without warning or explanation. About 1941, she got a divorce and set up her own household. He pled with her not to take the step but would not order his ways, despite promises, to reconcile her. Hardly was she divorced than she had to be operated on for a tumor. She was frightened half out of her mind. It was when she was recovering from the operation that I met her.

From then on, according to Arthur, Rose alternated between ministering angel and Xanthippe; loyal to a fault; self-absorbed while sensitive to any affront, real or fancied; keeper of order among the giddy girls. Arthur deferred to her, bought her jewelry, paid for her vacation trips, buttered her up. All the same, the "marriage" soured, not because Rose grew self-centered about her health but because of her "new and flourishing conceit." She could tell him off with impunity because she was indispensable — and knew it; he had to tailor his wants to her approval. The last volumes of the Diary are filled with savage and comical asides about this nagging chatelaine, her "antennae always out to sense a slight, a preferment of someone else," who put him in the doghouse, misinterpreted his remarks, and yet without whom he would have been hard put to balance his books, pay taxes, handle his investments. "Deal with high-tension women, expect what Rose and Evelyn give me, accept the punishment."

Arthur, as he liked to say, "loved" Rose without being "in love" with her. He also "loved" at one time or another many of the younger women (usually between ages eighteen and twenty-five) he "collected" to be his handmaidens. He was "in love" passionately and obsessively with only a few. The girls of the Fifties resembled their predecessors. That is to say, they came from a variety of backgrounds and measured up to Arthur's exacting criteria of looks, clothes, voices, pronunciation, demonstrativeness. He favored huggers and kissers given to baby-talking and baby-writing ("Artsie-Wartsie, I wuv oo") and not averse to "handling" or "cuddling." Their sexual availability was less important to him than their vitality and vivacity. He preferred tactile intimacy to the sexual act itself. The "bed parties" (loathsome phrase) arranged with girls he nicknamed "Gin-Gin" or "Flo-Flo" or whatever seldom went further than unfatherly embraces and "snugglings."

Lillian Tandy Marston was an exception. With this engaging and uninhibited charmer (she was seventeen when he met her, a recent high-school graduate who possessed "a lovely, cultured enunciation" and a quick intelligence) he had a brief but genuinely exciting erotic experience, which he related in unabashed detail. Lily's adroit lovemaking and "age-old wiles" made up for Evelyn's coolness and gratified his "male ego." Their "parties" went on after Lily married "her Joseph" (she "opined" she was "oversexed"), and the ingenuities she displayed in these encounters contributed to Arthur's sexual education. Women had seemed "princesses" in his romantic youth — "without passion and innately sexless." After Lily, he tended "to regard most of them as secret hotboxes waiting consciously or unconsciously for the brakeman and his long-spouted oil can."

Arthur knew he was taking chances with randy Lily. It was an adventure for them both, he assured himself, and he had no reason to doubt her discretion. Nonetheless, he wasn't entirely easy. He warned her of his "cold, calculating, revengeful, reckless side" lest she ever turn against him. And he warned himself:

Do not become careless. If you're helped psychologically and physically, yet your structure of life is put in jeopardy. The hazard is not light. A slip of watchfulness or of Lily's tongue, and you will be in very serious trouble indeed. So be careful, O my foolish, risk-taking, danger-loving man.

It wasn't until Rose told him of her strange dream, however, that he thrilled to the possibility of blackmail. She dreamt that Lily had a baby and was suing Arthur for $100,000. "Why do you suppose I ever had such an odd dream?" she asked. Arthur needed no further prompting. He didn't stop sleeping with Lily right away, but he sealed up the Diary volume with its dynamite disclosures and substituted another ostensibly covering the same period and filled with spurious entries. "Sound melodramatic? Feel melodramatic and apprehensive and shaky from immersion in the water of Rose's stark warning."

After Lily left for Arizona with jealous Joseph, he missed her wanton attentions, and she figured in his erotic daydreams. All in all, he had kept his head. This could not be said of his off-and-on infatuation with Martha Torrence.

When he first saw her in 1949 ("as cute as a little girl well could be" with "two delightful dimples" and "wide, ingenuous blue eyes"), she enchanted him. In the next three years she grew more precious ("She's my smallest child, my beloved problem girl, my mother-in-a-way, my darling-who-never-scolds-me"). Martha ditched him in 1953 — she was then twenty-one — but came back in 1956 to "her willing slave," and their friendship entered a new and more intense phase.

The violence of his passion was quite extraordinary by the time the affair reached its apogee in 1956. She had married and borne a child during the interim, but she didn't demur when Arthur proposed that she consider herself his secret wife — an intangible role that brought with it tangible benefits. He adored their bed sessions (she dispensed her favors judiciously) and loved to watch her try on the dresses he bought for her. Yet from the start he saw something awry in their arrangement. First, there was the matter of her passion for Buddy, the best friend of her husband, Terry, and Terry's apparent indifference. Second, Martha's sister, Angie, nauseated Arthur with descriptions of Martha's pigpen house (filth, dogs, diapers, mice, unwashed dishes) and told him of Martha's duplicity. Was he being milked? To be on the safe side, he sent away for her horoscope, which revealed the picture of a money-loving, sweet-talking actress. No matter, she fascinated him even though she didn't honor her part of the bargain — to spend so many hours a week with him, to sleep with him when he wanted her. He told himself not to expect too much from this frightened bird, this ruffled spirit, and yet . . .

Arthur remained in the toils of his Circe in spite of her lies and equivocations. He stifled his doubts about Martha's image of herself as abused wife and mother, declared her more of a "natural lady" than "peasant" Evelyn, and doled out gifts and cash. His father-husband relation somewhat inhibited his sexual performance, but his stomach "flip-flopped with delight" when his "gosling" said she couldn't live without "my Artie." Unfortunately, weeks of anxiety followed moments of bliss. Martha found excuses for staying away. He wanted her "body, soul, mind" while realizing he might lose everything if she left her husband. What to do? He was hooked, overboard. Only Evelyn understood how Martha was putting him "through fiery hoops," and Arthur, "appalled" by the depth of his enchantment, told Evelyn that now at last he could appreciate the strength of her attraction to the "charm-dispensing" Pike. Martha might be "a slut in a slum," yet he loved "her trollop ways," needed her words "as a plant needs fertilizer." Evelyn advised him to cleave to his Circe and to stop worrying about it, so he spoke to Martha as follows:

We promised to be honest. Well, I have decided to capitulate. I am apparently unable not to. You may live in a house that, from what I hear and you tell me, stinks, with mice and fleas everywhere. Your dog may shit on the floor and you go trailing it around and dumping out turds, and mice droppings and old garbage may surround you, and your feet may be dirty and your hair unwashed, and for all I know Buddy may be your lover, and much may smack of utter lack of fastidiousness so that I am repelled, but nonetheless and notwithstanding, I love you beyond any capacity of mine to struggle against.

Overcome by her "husband-father's" declaration, Martha swore eternal fidelity, and Arthur experienced raptures "beyond measure." For a time she gave him "top priority." Then suspicions about Martha set him to weeping. He imagined her in bed with Buddy and totaled up the sums he'd spent on her. When she missed her period, he feared she might be pregnant with his child. "My goodness," said tolerant Evelyn after he told her of this possibility, "what picklements you do get yourself in." She gave Martha a sound talking to on the wisdom of having an abortion and the necessity of deciding quickly. Arthur wondered, "Am I not an old alligator seeking solace out of my age class, than which no fool is a bigger fool?" Should he gradually withdraw? Had Buddy turned her against him?

Sick from fear and desire, he decided to drop Martha or risk losing Evelyn and Rose. It was time to stop "juggling with Greek fire" before it consumed him, get off the train before the impending wreck. Fred Lakian concurred, as did Arthur's lawyer, Louise Day Hicks,[2] whose "eyes literally bugged out" as he explained "about Martha and her setup." Once again he sniffed for blackmail. "I'm on a slope that can landslide at a wink of an eye." Yet he felt completely rejected after Martha told him she could see him no more (Terry's orders), and Louise Day Hicks told him not to get in touch with her. "Ah, Martha, he of the melodramatic heart and the pathetic attitudes wishes you not to go out of his life." He blamed himself for pressing her too closely, badgering her with telephone calls, butting into her affairs, and he dispatched Evelyn on an unsuccessful mission to bring her back. (Evelyn's willingness to perform this distasteful assignment was plain proof to Arthur that she didn't love him.)

Gradually Arthur detoxified himself of Martha-love and discovered he could live without her. Lucky for him that he escaped from the affair "untapped financially." As he studied her photographs dispassionately, he saw that she was oversexed even though "she could not be sexy with me because she regarded me paternally." He had been "too generous," "too good," but he resisted the thought that her only motive had been to milk an "easy mark." Some affection was there. Martha never reappeared in the flesh, but in a particularly disturbing nightmare she returned with "hundreds of rhinoseroses" and Irish Catholic vandals.

Arthur was to find peace not with the wayward Marthas of this world but with their younger sisters, the little-girl women between twelve and fifteen he labeled his "jade collection" or "Dresden figurines." For Arthur, "girlness" evaporated by the age of twenty-five, when "the dust and fading of years began to show." He liked the feel of a little girl's skin "as smooth as peeled willow bark" or (to mention some of his other similes) an onion or the chassis of a new car. ("Touch, to me, is like a marvelous binder.") The more liberties he could take with his "pretty fascinators," the more inwardly secure he felt. "They fulfilled," he explained, "the yearnings I had as a boy and young man for the very personalized sort of attention from girls I sentimentally desired." They compensated him for "an otherwise disappointing life." Nothing gave him greater pleasure, not even making money, than the loving, cherishing girls who had not been spoiled by modernity or by the "nauseous influence" of a college education and who acceded to his "masculine advances."

The frequency with which he came back to his "younglings" in the

---

[2] Louise Day Hicks (1923–), Boston lawyer and city official, handled Arthur's legal business between 1952 and his death. In the 1960s she was the acknowledged leader of the antibusing movement in Boston. She served three terms as a member of the Boston School Committee. Hicks put up with Arthur's eccentricities and prejudices and gave him sound professional advice. He, in turn, completely trusted and admired his favorite "Irisher."

Diary and his anticipation of the scorn and disgust his addiction for *nymphets might evoke in unknown readers betray an uneasiness he stoutly denies. Why is an "old codger in his sixties," he will ask, "making snuggles with a wild lass of fifteen — it even sounds lecherous to me." "Rompings" with his precious intimates, he knew perfectly well, were versions of "sex play," although he was uncertain whether the little girls were aware of it. As for himself, he felt no guilt, because he had no designs on his charmers except to touch and be touched by them. The innocent initiation he put them through would not "lead them down the garden path," and the erotic fancies they sometimes aroused in him remained fancies only, "imagination not having gone when virility did." Honesty compelled him not to fudge the record of his secret thoughts. They might strike strait-laced "Mr. Adult" as unconventional and "inapropos," but plenty of men harbored similar ones, and he had no intention of giving up his "hobby" and "pastime," more important to him than fame. When it came to his "jade collection," he was "maudlin, hopeless and beyond hope, so, reader, skip or condemn or go to hell in a basket and be damned to you for lack of understanding and intolerance."*

Arthur's defiance is a little suspect, don't you think? A good many of the "children," after all, came from broken homes. In some cases they were wards of the state living with foster parents who themselves were impressed by Arthur's affability. No wonder the little girls clung to the kind, generous, affectionate surrogate for absent papas and accepted his caresses, presents, and playfulness. (The tape recordings of Arthur ca-vorting with his "kids" positively exude the "charm" and "whimsy" of his personality, which the Diary, he insisted, never managed to catch.) Who else in their lives listened so indulgently to their natterings about boy-friends and parties? What other older man would tell them to call him by his first name ("Oh, Artie, I love you so much!") and advise them about their studies or correct their enunciations? Charmed by his solicitude, they complied with his demands, even to the point of pressuring any member of the junior cohort who for some reason — schoolwork, perhaps, or distaste of his fondlings — stopped coming to see him. I don't say he deliberately preyed upon these guileless and not-so-guileless creatures. I think he genuinely believed he was improving them, that his strictures when they failed to fuss over him were for their own good. But his rationalizations were transparent. The Diary gives him the lie.

As for Evelyn, do you find it strange that she apparently made so little over his affairs with young women? On many occasions, you'll recall, Arthur justified what Diary readers might regard as his excessive atten-tion to women on the grounds that he was living in an age of feminine domination and that one of his purposes was to present women — young, middle-aged, and old — in all their complexity.

But why did she seem to take for granted his awkwardly concealed "parties"? Why indeed did she assist him when his girls flew the coop? Of course she deflected any attempt on his part to tell her the details of his affairs, but the time had long passed when she might have taken umbrage. Besides, Arthur's girls made life more bearable for her by giving her time away. She knew Arthur's terrors and self-revulsion probably better than anyone else, his yearning to blot out his messy life. She may have been bemused by the antics of her eccentric husband and disdainful too, but at bottom she was a loyal wife who guarded his interests. And despite Arthur's conviction that she didn't give a hoot about his Diary, she admired his tenacity and never questioned his aspirations.

November 25, 1981

Dear Edna:

It's time to stop speculating about Arthur in the closing years of his "novel." You have my impressions of his marriage, his politics, and his women. Perhaps this is the moment to let him speak for himself. From time to time — usually when he began a new volume of the Diary or when his birthday rolled around — he would pause to describe his state of mind and circumstances for future readers, just in case his Diary saw the light of day. These orientation vignettes, as you might call them, are too long and too numerous to record in full, but the following excerpts written between 1956 and 1963 fill in the portrait of Arthur Inman I've been sketching.

Here am I, Arthur Crew Inman born, the 'Crew' deleted since my Mother left all her money to the Crews rather than to my Father, from whose side she got it, and me, his copper-haired namesake. I am within weeks of being 61 years of age. My wife, Evelyn Yates Inman, mostly 'Yates,' is in Europe on a long trip taken against my will, and I am being tossed this way and that by the currents of resentment. Rose Trench, about 59 years of age, my best-loved mainstay in life, takes care of me and my monetary affairs. Without her I should, I feel, be let loose to the lions in the arena. [*Arthur lists the people who are most important to him and itemizes the jewelry he has just ordered for his girls.*]

I am a fairly happy person but discontented and resentful and vainly attempting to be philosophical. I'd rather buy clothes and jewelry for the women I love than anything I know else. I'm too generous indeed and have to hold myself down. Buy Evelyn less and less, not requiring gratitude, and others more and more. [1956]

These last several days have been singularly important ones in the personal life of the man named Arthur Inman. He has accomplished a flip-flop in several habits of thinking, so that he is neither intellectually nor emotionally the individual he was a week ago. He has, after serious reflection, concluded he is not necessarily lacking in brain power and intelligence, even perhaps is somewhat gifted in that direction. When his mind fails to function to satisfy him, he has decided, the reason has to do with the vigorous pressures of pain acting upon his spirit and clarity of thought rather than with an endemic averageness of intelligence.

He has acknowledged to himself that few men could have worked harder or accomplished more against the subtle disadvantages of inner division, infelt pain, outward pressures. He has faced squarely that, from here on, he will fall to pieces physically with increased momentum and must, to be the sort of man he admires, handle himself with as much courage as he may well muster. He has acknowledged also that he is singularly lucky in numberless respects, as never hitherto, a somewhat complete man, and the feeling is a ripening and reassuring one. There will be moments of fear, of tidal sweeps of pain, of gloominess, of self-doubt and castigation, perhaps of self-pity even; but on the whole he has torn apart and reassembled a different man. [1956]

Dreamed of Dr. Pike fixing my spine. He was a colorful character. Have some snapshots taken the other day. One of me. Set me aback to see such an old-appearing man with a face so made unexpressionless by pain, the position of the mouth so signifying hurt and weariness. I don't believe I overdraw such a self-portrait, though it does vanish when alertly or with fun I smile back at myself in the mirror. When in repose the balding countenance with the big eyes and drawstring mouth looks old and outworn, no fire signatured or energy, but age taking over with certainty. It is a swift step to turn my thoughts from myself to those on whose care my integrity as a person exists. If I am this much changed, so are they. I don't mind myself being older save as age implies gathering failures of the body and spirit, but I do most surely mind those others aging, losing their potency, their looks, their fire, their capacity to remain young and vigorous while I age. Yet one, of course, portends the other. [1958]

Here am I, 63 years, in the first decade of the atomic-hydrogen era, a rather frightened mortal alert to what transpires next in the two-headed, kill-and-save realm of modern science, living in a relatively small old apartment building in a backwash of an apparently dying city, a backwash which soon will not be so when one of the largest metropolitan developments in these United States will be erected adjacently, a gesture to keep the city longer in function. I will have, if that date be reached, been in residence here 39 years. I rent five small apartments, using one for storage and guests, subletting another. Evelyn, my wife, lives in one; Rose, my secretary and all but my alternate wife, save sexually and by name, in another; and I am in the last. We are, as with most Americans, cluttered with things in profusion — automobiles, air conditioners, electric heaters, radios, record players, furniture, rugs, tape recorders, clothes, shoes, books, vases, electric stovelets, etc., etc., typewriter, adding machines, mirrors, cabinets, towels, dictionaries, phonograph records, chests, blankets, sheets, on and on until it is like a jackdaw's nest. There are telephones and switches and buzzers and bells. I live, being a semi-invalid, a fairly secluded yet not isolated existence. I am what might be called a character, an eccentric if that is more apt. Since I am convinced that any person is only as worthwhile as are his lieutenants and his friends, I set great store by mine and will go to almost any length to retain connections once formed, which is not an American trait.

I own stocks and bonds which bring in a nice income, and there is a larger income from my Father's estate, managed by Douglas Matthews in Atlanta, and to these sources is added a fair income from the only apartment house of four I kept, 96–98 Chestnut Street, near Beacon Hill, 12 apartments. I buy and sell stocks, and in doing so find considerable excitement and have been more successful than otherwise.

I have great labor sleeping nights. I rarely like elderly people. I dislike swing and classic music but like Viennese operetta melodies. I have a talking-book for the blind, play it, like it. My philosophy of life is fairly simple, which prevents an otherwise complicated person flying into more bits than already there are. I want to do and be to those who love and like me as they are to me. I am a sentimentalist by proclivity, a realist when to be one is unavoidable. I possess a vast sense of insecurity and no sense of duty. I find life vastly exciting, yet would rather far not be living it.

To take chances is the breath of existence to me. Without money, I would be nothing. Without my people, I would be nothing. Yet it is possible for me to take large risks in keeping either, when the time for taking risks comes. I am in many respects the product of my past, of my memories, of what happened years ago, and especially is this so at nights, when dreams come. Without considerable ingenuity and a feeling for daring, I would, I suspect, not have weathered life until now. Within myself, I have always been an unconventional thinker and an even more unconventional wisher. People are not bored, however maddened by me, for I have what my dead cousin, Jennie Cooper, had, a vital dynamism based more upon emotional potential than brains. I make new friends fairly easily, like relatively few people. I am honest and generous by nature, have learned to be chary with both, though not learned sufficiently. I have been the recipient in my lifetime of more than my share of devotion, but I work to get and keep it. I do not believe in any god or knowledge-able superior power. And all this has been said over and over again but is recouched now because a new volume begins and the saying establishes environment and atmosphere. [1958]

It is reassuring to some to come across the feeling of defeat in others which one not seldom feels within oneself. Sherman [General William Tecumseh] writes to his wife as of April 15, 1859: "I am doomed to be a vagabond, and shall no longer struggle against my fate. . . . I look on myself as a dead cock in the pit, not worthy of further notice, and will take my chances as they come." [1959]

The man who keeps this record has forty-five minutes alone in which to make a transcript of his thoughts. He wishes to be like one of those engraved crystal pitchers so beautifully made by Steuben Glass, always ready to accept any fluid, anxious to give it particular body and luster as it is contained and poured forth. It [the diary record] is observation colored by taste and stirred with the swizzle stick of imagination. His mind fairly claws at the ineptitudes of style in those old chronicles and must be strained by an overall judgment. He finds himself ashamed at the gaucheries of execution not only in how he writes but in what he writes. He is a late-maturing young man in search of a style and a philosophy of living. His strictures against what his mother induced into his way of thinking and his petty attempts to make himself hard-boiled and his jettisoning of the accepted moralities in a frantic effort to justify himself for his invalidism by making superior a genius he felt he possessed excep-tionally present him as a spoiled and not too attractive individual.

Perhaps he was just that. His vocabulary alternates between the spoken speech of the South, the colloquialisms and slangs of the teenagers of his school and college years, and a rococo overuse of the not seldom out-of-place-sounding words of the highfalutinest English language, and transition from the one to the other lacks not only taste but skill. Yet what is written well increases and what is written loosely decreases. He, the man in the chair entering the year 1960, hopes he learns from past deviations from discrimination. He shall, he promises, not willfully repeat blunders of preference, of choice, of selection. He will spare no effort in this abstract behalf. [1960]

I, Arthur Inman, am of years 65, a semi-invalid. This diary constitutes my major ambition, and keeping it my major work. Being fortunate enough to enjoy what is called an independent income, I am cared for physically by doctors who are also, in varying degrees, my friends, by my immediate family, by the friends who like me. My family at this moment consists of my wife, Evelyn (we were married in 1923), Rose Trench (she came here in 1944), Pearl Hollister Leuko (she has been with me off and on for 14 years), a stopgap secretary named Maggie Bruce. My closest friends are Kathleen Connor (with me two years two or three times a week), Dr. Fred Lakian (who has known me since 1938), Roderic Peters (who has read to me one or two evenings a week since 1928). There are other friends I see more or less often and hear from by letter or visit to Boston irregularly.

I and my immediate family, Evelyn and Rose, live in an old apartment building in a locality on the downtown side in a city on the downslide, very comfortably for our purposes. My hobby and vindication is in endeavoring to make money trading in stocks. I own a lucrative apartment house. I suffer from weak nerves, weak ligaments, weak eyes, a tender digestive system, migraine attacks, too much energy for a fourth-class constitution. My wife owns a house at Harvard, in the outer suburbs, and likes to travel. I lead, for me at any rate, an exciting life, though one I would as soon lose any night in my sleep, which is spasmodic at best. I use Government talking-books, which are recordings of novels and serious works, to help pass the nights.

Mornings I write in here, tend to business and hobbies; afternoons listen a bit to radio and correct what I have written mornings or study financial news; evenings talk to people or listen to Roderic or Evelyn read aloud. I try to ride a very small way several mornings a week in my 1919 open Cadillac, an antique Mike somehow keeps on the road. I try to keep my hours both scheduled and full but needs must rest in bed some 16 hours in 24. I have a curiosity about everything, perhaps an imagination, little or no intellect under command. I strive to keep my fears and annoyances under control. I make a good friend. I believe in nothing, actually, save perhaps time and pain. I rule my actions and thoughts personally by the very clear adumbration of being good to those who are good to me, which, when followed, simplifies social behavior. I enjoy history. I enjoy people. My mind is always, like vibrating antennae, casting about. Being physically and nervously bankrupt gives me a feeling of some animal cornered in a cave, on guard from whatever portends danger. Though I am not happy, yet I am merry betimes. I know that my blessings are many and count them daily. All about and in me is mystery and past making reason. I enjoy helping people until they take advantage of my generosity, then kaput. [1960]

I am in the apartment house (once a third-rate hotel), now second-rate, in a run down neighborhood, but metropolitanly convenient, where I have been since 1919. There are many drawbacks and eye-shuttings to the situation, though, for me, many advantages as to light, quiet, compactness of living quarters. We, Evelyn and I, rent five apartments. One she uses, and it is well-arranged and home-like, sun in it each morning—bedroom, big kitchen, big sitting room, hall and bath. One is the office—a very large room, bath at one end, kitchen at the other. One is my apartment—bedroom, sitting room, bathroom (all small), library and small spare room, little hallway where treating-table is kept—giving a change of light or air. The apartment below mine, rented to secure quiet, is sublet, and an apartment I give free to Kathleen Connor, whom I have in view to adopt eventually if it can be effected.

Over a line of rooftops, the great Prudential Insurance Company of America development has been two years under way, and notice has just been served on the Massachusetts Senate that unless a clarifying decision comes from the Supreme Court, "there will be no Boston Center." Insurance companies and labor unions, be it noted in passing, are the only minorities (save possibly the Jews and the negroes) who are strong enough to issue ultimatums, receive special treatment, unusual preference in this 50-state United States of America land of ours.

I strive, usually with success, to make money on the Stock Market. I have an income from my Father's estate. I own and run an apartment house on Chestnut Street and have a rented rooming house close to here. Evelyn owns a car; I have two. In some ways I am stronger than in the past, in others—such as riding—much weaker. Most of my energies are expended striving to keep those who work for me cheerful and devoted. My employees spend about a third of the time I pay them compiling tax reports for the Federal and state Governments. I believe that unless an unusual ruler comes to this nation of 180 millions we are bound, slow or fast, for the scrapheap, all welfare and union-influenced nations being sooner or later there bound. We live on the lip of nuclear holocaust, and no person of imagination and sensitivity can ignore the odds in favor of it, the chances being founded on human nature.

There are people who do not like to meet new posed problems. After the first shudder of recoil, I do. How else stay alive at sixty-five? It is most important, metal or human, not to rust. May I, is my prayer, retain my sizzling interest in what, on the whole, constitutes a stacked-against-the-dealer poker game. Better, I philosophize, sit in with zest on a rigged deck than give up because you realize it is rigged. And anyway, how do you know, know for sure, there may not be outside circumstances, even slips in luck, which, do you remain alert, will not redound in your final favor? To gamble and give up is not to gamble. [1961]

Here I am, as long as it lasts, at Garrison Hall where I've been since 1919; and here we are, Evelyn and Rose and, we hope, Bob Fisher for evenings, Kathy living in an apartment, one room set aside for storage. Roderic comes Saturday and Monday evenings as a rule to read aloud. Kathy comes Sunday mornings, Sunday and Wednesday evenings to do soft-tissue treatments on my neck and back. Peggy Donaghue comes most Saturday mornings, Mary Ann Bauer Friday, Saturday, Sunday afternoons to read aloud and correct typewritten diaries. Reg Helm, Amos Temple, Lennie Haggerty drive me in my 1919 open Cadillac, the Baby-Carriage. We have no secretary at present. I get along in my semi-invalidism, though sometimes Evelyn and Rose feel pressed not only by the physical care of me but as well by the plethora of my emotional and mental activities, my dynamic restlessness, which as well devours me.

Selma Prince, aged 42 now, mother of four, comes each Friday evening to give a soft-tissue treatment. My doctors are Fred Lakian, Tom Baseheart, Douglas Peyton, Tim Buell, Arthur Garner, Mason Gooch, osteopaths all save Dougie who years ago turned medical and keeps his osteopathic activities quiet. John Hough is my dentist. All these people have been met many times in previous volumes of my diary. I lack people to talk to me evenings.

I trade in stocks. Most of my money, however, is in tax-exempt bonds, and I receive a large payment from my Father's estate in Atlanta and a small one from my Step-grandmother Inman's estate. It costs me to keep alive and in function close to fifty thousand dollars a year, including Federal and state taxes, and my incomes cover that. I still own and run personally, through Freddy Niquette, my part-time janitor, 96 – 98 Chestnut Street. I write in here continually and also correct the old diaries Dorothy Banks and Janice Oliphant copied. The amino acids I take have, I should say, doubled my strength. The present year, thus far at any rate, has witnessed a diminution of the number of migraine attacks. I attempt to ride two or three mornings a week. The talking-books, supplied free by the Federal Government, keep me sane and assist in passing the long nights of limited sleep. I must have read some nine hundred of them by now. Being almost 67½ years of age, tearing down and erecting rife all around me, with what consequences of noise and light I'm unable to predict, it behooves me to 'get on the ball' with my diaries. I would like to find a literary secretary who can read my scrawls and type them. I work against I do not know exactly what deadline — noise and an end to me by me, a natural death, nuclear destruction — take your pick.

I often conclude that my talisman is charm. I exercise it at need. Money and ingenuity and charm. Otherwise, just an ordinary, apprehensive old man, shoved in all likelihood into rest home or oblivion, upon dole. Say what you will critically, few people disregard me: I rate as either intelligent friend or self-indulgent nuthead. It is, I figure, better to be balm or irritant than soothing syrup nobody notices. [1962]

Arthur Inman, at the near age of 68, writing: Me, the author, height 5 feet 10 inches, weight 154 pounds, nature sanguine yet — oppositely — wary, involved. He has no more physical strength than water at a standstill. Yet it is always his hope that in him exists a curious vitality which, in the overall, will convey to those possibly to come a true panorama of this exciting age and time in one of the world's great nations, not by any means always pleasant, at times direful, but always with honesty presented as he sees it. His large view, right or wrong, is that we who constitute America slide, for varied reasons, downhill. That he may prove to have been wrong, in contradiction to his best intuition and knowledge, is not as important as is whether or not he was honest. He is (with the limitations of human nature allowed for) honest, in the large more honest than can be achieved by most chroniclers, for he is possessed of that sense which tells him his only hope for perpetuity is grounded in absolute, unchallengeable honesty, insofar as this diary is concerned. [1963]

These are studied poses, aren't they — Arthur being "honest" with his not-yet-materialized readers — self-portraits for posterity. The writing verges on "Inmanese" (I'll have more to say about that term shortly), the tone confessional but guarded.

Now compare the above with a series of Fifties entries more impulsively composed.

Arthur and Benedict Arnold:

I'm reading the life of Benedict Arnold. In some ways he reminds me of me. He was forever seeking recognition, commendation, wishing for some unassailable position of renown, all to justify himself. After he was crippled, he writhed like a snake. He felt unappreciated. He'd as soon served Washington as Clinton but needed money to justify himself to his wife. He felt unappreciated and insulted by Congress. He didn't want to be a nobody. His very soul was contorted by his strained effort to be successful historically and financially. I hope that all I do is not ruined, as all he did was, by lack of tact. He was an arrogant and unruly man and, what I am not, conceited. But he certainly underwent internal torture. A crippled male is usually a crippled spirit, as was Arnold after his wounding. I cannot but feel sorry for him, however importunate his arrogance and unfortunate his judgment. He was a tortured and maimed soul, not very clever really, though at first lucky. [1955]

Arthur drunk:

I'm drunk now. The left eye is too much for the old man with the whitening eyebrows and the small (they used to be large) brown eyes and the weak, sick-appearing mouth and the big, aggressive nose. I wish I were dead.

I have been studying, in my drunken, truthful state, Evelyn's plans for $33 thousand house. I say: "You had best listen to me in my drunken state, for what I say I mean. In my estimation, you'd best spend money like a drunken sailor to get what you want. I'm a liability, at the best. You're preparing for an old age. Do it! Do it! Spend the money. Make a refuge for yourself. Have it perfect. Do not cut corners. I am, from my knowledge of other men, something special. But what can you foresee will happen? Do it while you have the chance. I love you. I want you contented. Do it! To hell with money. I can support you. I love you. You are my special darling. Do it. To hell with leaving me money — if you by any chance saw matters right — and do it. Fix yourself and your old age. Be selfish about it. I understand." And I do. Poor inside-mixed Evelyn — I love her, love her. I may be a fool emphasized, but I want her happy. She's a unique influence in my life. I love her perhaps more than myself. God help us poor males; the cards are stacked against us. Poor, poor, poor, decastrated, unsworded, hydrogen-bomb-possessed Artie.

Oh, I love Martha, her naked shoulders, her naked legs, her breasts. I'm a fool and a fool and a fool, and I could shed tears that are long and pendant gray rain exuding from the heart of a sentimental idiot. I'm sad. I'm no good. I'm only as good (drunk me) as those who love me—love me for myself. Who is myself? A "pile of shit"—as Pearl says. More than that—I think. I am honesty and no false estimation. Into this world: into and out of it. A shithead with good intentions—me. I want to be good—to be helpful—to be a person devoted to helping others. Am I? Who knows? I am solitary, poopish, frightened Artie. That's me. [1956]

Child of the Civil War:

Want it or not—and perhaps this is a key to my nature without which it is meaningless—I am an offspring, as it were, of the Civil War and of the legend it left behind it. I bear the estamp psychically and physically of the War, of what came after: the Donald Fraser companies standing at salute while a Civil War monument was undraped; the Confederate flag on my Grandfather's coffin; picking up Minié balls where was fought the Battle of Peachtree Creek; Old Lady Marmon in the firelight telling stories of Sherman's march; the little room where people hid in the 'old dormitory' at Donald Fraser; the books, so many of them, absorbed before I was 13, read then, read later, read now; a really deep pride at having sprung from 'Southern' blood. I bear, as well as the antique dream which has only certain jointures with reality as it was, the stigmata of those four dire years of rebellion and failure and what came appallingly to a conquered land during the Reconstruction. [1957]

It was such a hopeless fight the South put up from the beginning, and the breaks usually went against it. Davis was such a stuffed piece of vanity wearing in his self-mirror such a halo of righteousness. There was so much that was epic in the moving struggle; no Greek tragedy ever moved upon a simpler theme. To my way of thinking, the motif of the tragedy was justifiable as Southerners first sang it, and only powers larger than theirs and reservoirs of men and machines greater than theirs made the end either right or certain. Separate states formed a union of states. They entered the union of their own free will; by the very plain terms of the Declaration and the Constitution the right to withdraw was implicit.

This right to withdraw was challenged by Lincoln. He began by deciding to go to war against unconstitutional rebels to maintain the integrity of 'the nation.' When too many people of his own supporting section of what had been the United States of America thought contrariwise, he shifted the casus belli to an ethical premise (which he had earlier denied), the right to freedom of the Southern slaves. This took the war out of mere rebellion and gave it a semireligious turn. It is beside the mark whether slavery was ill-advised (many Southerners thought so) or not. When the war was given an ethical turn by Lincoln, it became in effect a self-righteous crusade. In a crusade, whatever means used soon become justified and justifiable to the crusaders, especially if they are more powerful than those crusaded against. Here was reason and excuse for a war to be waged not only against armies and forts and shot-power but also against civilians.

And Lincoln, however favorably history countenances him, permitted vicious and destructive 'all-out war against civilians.' Witness Sheridan and Pomeroy and Sherman and their ilk, small men in stature usually, who felt inspired to blow themselves up by exhibited destructive ruthlessness. The South became a land to be crusaded against, to be destroyed and subjugated by any means. And Lincoln countenanced it, and Lee did all in his power, when he invaded the North, to discountenance a like ethic. Lincoln is not the godhead modern popular history pictures him. He was the primary spirit instigating the conquest of a people and unchaining the dogs of war and turning his head aside when they destroyed and mangled and tortured. He may not (and I doubt if he did) have liked the sort of civil war Goya pictures: But he did not stop it. His morals — what morals he had, and they were questionable from the beginning, he being a politician primarily — went by the board. The means justified the end.

Nor do I signify that Lincoln wished to resort to subterfuge and double-talk (probably he did not, for in him was considerable nobility and much capacity to grow): He wished chiefly and in the end astigmatically to keep his concept of the old United States and the idea thereof extant at whatever cost. Heroes are made of such constancy to a malicious idea and such personal devotion to a double-barreled cause, once denied, then fostered. Lincoln was an incredible man. But he was also a rogue. It was he who denied the right of habeas corpus to his own people, went against the Supreme Court, inaugurated a civilian concentration camp, went back on his avowed words and theories. He was a larger man than Davis (who was a small, stubborn, unimaginative, courageous person), but the wiser or smarter man in power is more responsible for what happens than the proud pinhead in power.

I imagine it sounds silly to sound off over a civil war which happened almost a century ago. I suppose I am a by-product, an extension, a growth of that war in many respects. It was only forty mere years away when I was born and less than thirty years away for Reconstruction. I am what I am in large measure, I at least realize, due to the extending ripples of that great and violent war. Wherefore, I feel the war, the aftermath, the legend, the propulsive subsequent attitudes. I wish it were not so, but it is. So if I recur in fascinated fashion to the War, treat it as me myself. I shall not avoid it. World War II was but a cynical interlude. World War I, while touching me closer, still is not so intimate as our Civil War, nor so real, nor so pertinent. The Spanish War and the Korean War leave me untouched, they being not personalized. [1958]

Arthur's room:

Still in small spare room and glad to have it: warm and messy, with the beautiful Circassian walnut chest of drawers and the lovely bow-front Sheraton desk in a line on one side of me; the beautiful Persian rug under my feet; the bulking green Army cabinet and the stand with hundreds of records on the other; the cream-colored walls now clouded by grime, patina of the city; the Curimoto in muted yellow and green, actors in a small black frame, on one wall; and over the records atop the desk, all my 78-r.p.m. German and American 10″ operetta pieces, the wildcat skin my parents got in the Yosemite when I was a small boy just turned eight, as soft and fine-furred as it was almost fifty years ago. There are a chair, the locked files in which Rose keeps my private papers, a Gladstone bag of Evelyn's father (marked A.C.Y.) in which are my diaries, an old push-button radio, a discarded phonograph, a small electric radiator, a chest under the window painted in peasant design and odd boxes and books. On a stand at my elbow, a little tray with two crackers and Columnier cheese plus a cup of coffee in a plastic cup (my second regular breakfast), the First National Bank checkbook in its plastic black cover, a pan, a financial advisory report, a yellow pencil. On the floor the morning 'Globe' open to the stock page.

I am writing with another yellow pencil in a ledger of 300 pages, this being the top now of page 102, and the ledger is on the brown laminated tray I've had for so many years it is scarred and worn. The two stylized hunters with no features to their faces, but with black boots and red coats and black caps, still ride together across a land designated only by a plaque of red and amber trees in the background and one section of a fence; one hunter jumps a fence and his horse's legs are in the air, and the two hounds run close, their backs and ears black and their tongues red; neither horse and neither rider and neither hound ever rides out of the picture or off the tray; it is morning, and morning never waxes to day, and you know it is autumn and the air is keen and it will be a calm still morning always, without end. [1954]

Louise Day Hicks:

Louise has been here, and we discussed the will. She's the sort of wife I should have had, calm yet ambitious and energetic, brain smoothly running, nature sweet, a tactful tongue. I'd have been another man with the feeling of a real outgiving person behind me and myself behind a real person. Maybe she's Irish, but by heck perhaps this is the exception. Which, of course, remains to be seen. She's not pretty by any means, but her hair is lovely, dark and soft and naturally curly; her voice is soft and persuasive. She tells me how much she likes my poetry, and I fidget from embarrassment like a small boy rubbing foot behind leg when teacher commends. She's a love. She's a straight shooter and has a yen for me. [1957]

"Nasal recollections":

In thick second-growth spruces I one day found a large stump, deep red-brown in color. Ants had once tunneled it, then abandoned it. I broke off, I remember, a fragment, held it to my nose, sniffed the earthy odor. I can recall returning thereafter to the stump as if drawn to it, that I had thoughts upon life and decay. But it was the color and the odor of it which gave to it almost a sensuous allure.

Perhaps this would be an apropos moment to note the part odors, smells, emanations played in my life before I fell ill.

When I found a woodlot where someone had cut firewood the winter before and dead balsam branches steeped in the sun, I could not get enough of the excitement the resinous odor caused me. I enjoyed hay cut and curing in the sun, split fish salted and drying, the sea odor of shaded wet piles under wharfs, the fresh stimulation of dirt-road smells when showered upon, the undertree perfume of quiet nights, the fragrant, damp ocean tang of fog rolling in and taking over sunlight.

I verily believe I associated each experience I underwent with the smell of it. I can recall the moldy smell of Market Street in Philadelphia when I walked it on a rainy day. I can recall the ozone of electric motors on streetcars. The wet fallen leaf-mat in Pennsylvania woods in winter comes back to me like magic. I remember the sour oil smell of journal boxes on railway trains when men oiled them with long-spouted cans. I recall the wild ginger and the sassafras in Georgia woods. No end to my nasal recollections. The sulphur aroma from the 'paint pot' in the Yellowstone; the zoo smells, fetid and unhuman, in the Central Park Zoo; the paint Tyler had just put on the white Penelope; spilled gasoline; the chemical smell of the carbide waste Father dumped in a pit from the acetylene lighting system at Southwest Harbor; the dining-car heavy food odor of viands and linens on trains; the Crew effluvia at 33 West Harris Street; the Cooper very strong odor of body and breath; how lobsters strongly, muscularly gave forth their sea odor; sun on wooden stained roofs; the acrid scent of sycamore trees along Pennsylvania creeks; lilacs and apple blossoms and violets and ripe grasses along New England roads; steamers with a veritable breathing-forth of old steam and varnish and fuel oil; the repellent fishy stink of young sea gulls and kingfishers; newly washed linens flapping on lines in wind and sun; oil spread heavily on Santa Barbara roads; sweat of horses under me; turpentine on my chest and down my throat when it was sore; the fusty, closed, boiled-fish odor of Maine cottages where the 'natives' lived; hackmatack swamps waterlogged with heavy mud; raspberries in the sun; the earth-like perfume of bluettes in the grass; the odd leftover aroma of wooden churches; the blue smell of morning-glories; the strong sea odor of Maine nights; the wet-wool scent of toboggan parties; the clean, upthrusting, chill, negative smell of ice skated on.

These were olfactory impressions when I was young. No longer now, what with street sand and oil furnace smudge and just getting old, does the nose act as a magic organ to bring me magic impressions. It is a dull old thing, hurting and aching rather than alive and sniffing, though it still seems to absorb what I do not like in smells — perfumes, hand lotions, soaps, powders — all the artificial combinations. [1960]

Literary thoughts:

It's odd, how some authors influence a writer when other authors, some with highest reputations, leave him cold and uninfluenced. Milton, Swift, Dickens, Thackeray, Scott — out the window with them — when Pope and Dunsany and Stevens and Brontë and many modern Britishers, mostly second-raters, have influenced me. One theory, I understand, emphasizes that the writers of other ages who have won fame constitute the norm by which to judge the past and one's own work, while another theory declares that only the secondary writers, insofar as an era is concerned, are indicative. I tend to agree with the second theory. Who makes most clear an age, a decade, are those secondary writers who own genius, and of them I am quite sure Fitzgerald is primary in the 1920–30 decades.

This 'dissolute and despairful' man holds an enchantment over me. If a reader wishes to know me, know Fitzgerald, my reactions to him. It should be illuminating, if inglorious, for I am of his generation, am weak yet curiously, warpedly akin to the young man who must have, outside his writings, been possessed of high charm, unconventionality sometimes scattered centrally yet serviceable when needed. The man, the weakling, the top-call individual fascinates me perhaps to an extent few other authors have. [1963]

Mother — two views:

In thinking over my parents, I find that one side of the impression they made is lacking: their personal habits. My Mother, for instance, since she was ashamed of her crooked, discolored teeth, when she spoke kept her lips in a straight line over the teeth, more often smiled with her eyes or laughed than smiled with her lips. All the years I was growing up she used rice powder on her face, and as her skin was sallow, the powder stood out, especially on her nose. As she grew older, she affected a pair of lorgnettes which hung on a cord about her neck. Her hands were small and surprisingly strong and always feverishly dry, and she wore several rings, diamonds, rubies, sapphires and always a pin at the throat. Her ears were large. She was vain of her unusually small feet, and they were always well-shod from an expensive New York shoe store. Her hazel eyes were superb under eyebrows darker than her hair. Above most else, she hated washing her hair. She would brush it with orris root powder instead. She would, in my estimation, overfrizzle it with curling tongs she kept from my infancy to her later years and heated over gas lights whenever possible or over an electric stove. She never changed her hair style, parted in the middle and held in a low knot on the back of her head.

She cluttered her own room with pictures and photographs of various members of the family. She harbored a real disdain for clothes as concerned herself, while her taste for clothes for others was impeccable. She would, after much fussing from him and against the project, accept clothes from Father, only (after a 'cooling-off period' of nonuse) to give them away. She was as comfortable socially in an old flannel or corduroy bathrobe as in jewels and swanky clothes and had no modesty to speak of in front of trunk movers or waiters in hotels, letting the sides of her robe flare open, the big black triangle of pubic hair made visible through her silk nightgown. Yet she would not, once dressed, take off a stocking in front of me to remove a pebble. As I have noticed with other women, their moral standards when dressed and when in negligee are not the same. She barked orders like a general not only to servants but to those of her peers on a picnic or at a cold supper. Yet she ruined those who worked for her in Maine by her generosity. She loved to organize and improve and change people's directions and aspirations. It was more important to her to be somebody than to have cobwebs brushed out of the corners of her house.

She doted on fancy foods in fancy getups. She ate little herself, picking at her food. Her favorite breakfast consisted of wasted biscuits, oatmeal left on the stove all night served with butter, hot tea; and from it she never varied. She read until one or two at night and didn't want to be disturbed until 9:30 or 10 in the morning, then coming slowly out of her blinded or shaded room, looking perfectly awful and small but with her aristocratic if too-sharp voice going double time, her utterances crammed with phrases and metaphors without end. Give my Mother enough clothes to put a cover around her nakedness; give her her own messianic opinion of herself spiritually; even give her a restricted place to operate in — and she would, as the old Rocky Mountaineers put it, "shine." There might be the smut black corsets on a chair, the rats come brownly out of the hair she wore, the layers of laced and beribboned underwear — but there also was she of the unquenchable spirit. There were white spots on her temple, yellow on her skin, dark circles under her eyes. But she was still, in her own eyes, the unique Bertie Crew Inman who made crosscurrents concur.

My Mother spent an hour or so each summer morning arranging in vases flowers Father had earlier cut in his garden. The creative task delighted her. It was more important to her than having her house thoroughly dusted. She liked to cook occasionally, and what she cooked invariably tasted good, looked well. She gave as few words to her orders to servants as she could, preferring to let household arrangements carry on by their own momentum. She could scotch antipathy at once, crisply and to the point, or ignore it. She gave more thought than was customary for her times to the comfort, physical and mental and spiritual, of those who worked for her; to her they were people to be treasured for their good qualities. Since she liked fancy cookery, she was adamant that things should look tempting and be expertly served, as Sissy or Horace served them. She enjoyed giving parties. She liked picnics. There was no trouble she would not incur in order to be lady bountiful or to help someone "live up to the best in them," perhaps her favorite expression. She both catered to herself and drove herself mercilessly, first one, then the other. She liked being alone for long stretches, read omnivorously (always on her back) detective stories, newspapers, biographies, magazines, histories, two pages at a time, and her eyes never tired. She spent virtually no time repairing her clothes. She liked to write letters, keep notebooks filled with notes and lists, scribble thoughts and poems, all in her hurried writing. She loved to give money, presents, assistance.

And now I come to several items which, as a small boy, annoyed me relative to my Mother's actions. I am of two minds whether to put them down or skip them for her sake. If I am to be exactly honest, I should incontrovertibly put them down. Still I am queazy about it. At any rate, here they are, with doubts. Her corsets, carelessly thrown over chairs, were grimy and black. Granted cleaners were rarer, granted an old corset was more comfortable than a new one, still the other corsets I saw by chance were kept clean. My Mother rarely bathed. But neither do I. But neither did she perspire. What she did, and I do not do, is fail to pull the chain after urinating, so that the water remained yellow from her visit. I hated that as a child and cringed from it, for Father, Aunt Helen, myself, the Serrills were scrupulous about it. It is not that I cannot understand why my Mother neglected cleanliness; it is that living at all was of more importance than living cleanly. I absolve my Mother from culpability completely; yet I blame her and excuse her simultaneously.

She was, whatever else, a live person, and that she was so alive exercised a hundred variant pressures on everyone connected with her. You could no more ignore her than you could ignore the sun in its course. Delicate cards watercolor-painted, beds of pink-and-white flowers done in pastels, vases of flowers avoiding primary colors — that was my Mother also. And yet she could be on occasion as earthy, as forthright, as crude as any unrestrained Gauguin in the South Seas, inartistically so it seemed to her son. Just why she never complained at, never attempted to restrain my Father from hacking and spitting gobs of phlegm on the sooty back of the fireplace so that vague whiteness driveled down in disgusting runlets I do not know, and perhaps nothing exists in memory more indicative of the pair of them than that accepted violence against taste and prudery.

I had, be it taken note of, the misfortune to be born and reared in the era betwixt Victorian odors accepted and the 20th-century mania for cleanliness and deodorants preeminent, so that the one was disliked conscientiously and the other taken for granted, the nose, the eyes pulled two contrary ways. Ten years later, cleanliness and lack of odor expected as a matter of ordinary routine. My Mother crossed over against even the conventions of her time, and I was aware of it. That she was careless purposely about cleanliness bothered me even as my own carelessness in the identical direction, to save strength, bothers me. If I say it again, I'll only repeat. I wish to state with utmost detachment that, historically speaking, cleanliness is a modern worship, not in vogue since the Romans, the Aztecs, the Arabs, and of negligible importance relative to character. [1959]

Note: The following entry is immediately rewritten from what it was, for the reason that it came out a paean of bitterness crosshatched by gobbledegook, mistakes in syntax, obscurities of phraseology which caused me to be startled at the violence I still contain in the neverconscious relative to my Mother. The result shocked me. The sketch, trimmed down, sandpapered, varnished, is this:

Were I strong enough this morning, my Mother's birthday, I'd like to look over old interviews, documents concerning her life, make a summary of them. Pretty she was, and earnest, as is well verified by an oil painting of her at eight or nine as a student of the dance wearing a semiballet frock and a determined expression. Her marriage photographs prove her attractiveness. She grew up in an overstrict Methodist family, no cards, no recreations Sabbaths. She took pianoforte lessons. She played with girls her age. When her mother died in her teens, she took over management of the large house and the servants from her grandmother, Namma, whom the servants disliked. When she was older, Grandfather laid out for her an earthen tennis court, and there she entertained her friends and beaux. "I made a wicked serve," she used to tell me. "In the big parlor," she used to confide, "were so many vases of red American Beauty roses that you could scarcely move about." She had, she said, sixteen proposals before choosing the "catch of the season," as she referred to him, my Father.

Each summer Grandfather would send his family to Monteagle, Tennessee, to a chautauqua there,[3] renting a small house. There were religious talks, lectures, amusements of the Victorian age such as walking and singing. Once a group explored a cave and there a rash young man fired off a revolver and my Mother, so she told me, was frightened that the stalactites would fall. One of my Mother's most prideful tales was of going buggy riding with a young man in love with her. He put his arm over the back of the seat. She said to

---

[3] "Chautauqua" became the generic name for a popular education movement that originated at Lake Chautauqua, New York, and flourished in various parts of the United States in the late nineteenth and early twentieth centuries. Held during the summer months, usually in an outdoor setting, chautauquas featured lectures by well-known figures, concerts, dramatic entertainment, and religious sessions.

him (and I can hear the exact self-righteous tone she must have used): "Sir, take me right home." She felt it was, she told me, an unconventional liberty unwarrantably taken. He took her "right home." She was as naïve as a young miss could well be. Namma explained nothing to her; her mother was dead; the books of the time made life to be lived in a romantic or grubby, unreal seance of morality.

Mother attended *the* select school for girls in Atlanta, Washington Seminary. "I was somewhat of a blue stocking," she much later told me. "I think it was as a graduation present that my father took me to California. I loved the trip, traveling." Someone owning a railway private car invited her to be one of a group of young persons going to "take in" the Chicago World's Fair. "It was a perfect experience, and I loved it." Here was a girl of nineteen or twenty, a Southern belle, unusually pretty, spoiled by attentions, being able to manage her father's big house, more than comparable in appearance to other girls, partaking of the Maffitt quality of heartbreaking charm, intensity, looks, hidebound and narrowed by a strict religious background, father-directed. That she, though not permitted social dancing, though inheriting the Maffitt evangelical background, could yet make herself as popular and as desired by men as she did permits no other conclusion save that she herself must have possessed both personality and charm.

Her predominant proclivities for social climbing subsequent to her marriage are difficult to explain. Perhaps (Grandfather Crew was not rich in comparison with Grandfather Inman) the drive to the uppermost socially in the relatively small, third-rate Southern city where her husband's family status entitled her to top position can only be explained at all by her mother's premature death, her father's habit of frugality at home. At any rate, the social drive persisted to her later days, as did the evangelical prepossession to make people over. Both concentrations were very hard, very unfair on my Father and me. Many times we suffered from virtual oversight while she concentrated upon cousins and friends on the far outer fringe. She felt herself both dedicated and gifted. Rarely did she question either her own sapiency or her own powers, with the result that her earlier warmth waned as she drove herself to drive others. My Father and I, who should have been central, became, in a manner of speaking, taken-for-granted incidentals, save when she wished to reform us or make herself, by our social actions, proud of us socially in a social-climbing way.

Note: This is bitter, I fear, for still, despite my utmost efforts, bitterness crops up, takes over the pity I should feel for a potentially gifted life ruined finally by a misplaced conception of her own Roberta Sutherland Crew Inman importance. [1961]

Catching up with an old "character":

Now and then I resolve to catch up with the lives of people who have once inhabited this diary. For years I have wanted to get in touch with Dorothy Banks. I had no notion what my reception would be, as we had parted (when Janice Oliphant came here) on less friendly terms than my sentimentality had wished it. I telephoned her yesterday. She still lives at the same address. To my surprise, she sounded not only pleased but delighted. If I was set aback at how Beattie's voice had aged, I was almost shocked at how Dorothy's voice had slowed down, lost all vigor and pertness. She is, she told me, almost housebound. Her husband has lost his eyesight and she has to wait on him. He has also lost the use of one leg. She still has a bad leg herself. She finds life dull. She would like to see me but doesn't believe she can make the trip. I volunteered a taxi. I expressed my gratitude for the years she cared for me. I asked was she having a hard time financially. Yes, she was. I told her not to be too proud to call on me in case of necessity. She thanked me and asked about Evelyn and me. I gave her a brief sketch. She thanked me for having called and begged me to call again. The conversation pleased me greatly and refurbished a page from the past for which I remain grateful. This morning I think I'll write her a little note and send her a check for $100. [1960]

Faith healers:

I took a healing treatment. The constant mumbo-jumbo of "O God," "Amen," "We thank you, Father," "May this man be healed," etc. make the healing part — the application, if it is that, of the magnetic or vibratory current — difficult to assess. My mind was open. I do believe that 'faith will move mountains.' The man is tall, six feet three, rugged, with black hairs on his arms and a pleasant voice, gentle, with the hazel eyes of a shrewd businessman. The woman is short and round with upped white hair and the pale-blue eyes of a seeress. She was born, she said, in Atlanta in 1913. Her voice is very pleasant. If power lies in either of these people, it is in the woman. I have no conviction whether I was helped or not. I feel just as wild, just as much in pain today as yesterday. My mind is still open. I did not feel the couple evil. It may be they are dedicated. It may be they turn over most of their fees to some religious (Baptist I think) organization, although I should guess they are financially shrewd and their nest well feathered, which signifies nothing against their gifts or their work. I am so upset from the way my new tooth, cemented in, has thrown my jaw askew that maybe nothing short of a bludgeon well applied could calm me down.

I liked both husband and wife. Her I could like very much, for she has charm, quietness with intensity, ease of manner. It is interesting that these two people entered, as through a side alley out of a busy round, my life. My opinion is that I am by now too split down the center, too pro-and-con, too subdivided by youth vs. age for anyone to heal. I am so greatly incised down the middle that nothing, nobody can ever put me together again functionally. I am, to put it melodramatically, as one lost in the underbrush for the remainder of his allotted mortal days, all paths out overgrown or erased or cul-de-sacs. It is best, I think, to recognize this also, that everything could be infinitely worse and that I have very much to be thankful for, would not swap my dilemma for that of someone imprisoned for life, bed-ridden by arthritis, deaf, insane or penniless. I should, in brief, dwell upon the fortunate aspects of my existence, not the unfortunate ones. Take it from there. Be profoundly grateful for care, friends, money, comforts, privacy, work. Not be sunk by regrets. What is is. No regrets or wishes can make what is what might have been. I am a person of charm and ingenuity. I am able to work, if restrainedly. I can walk in moderation. I can thus far hear and feel and think. The lot of humans by and large is not too benign anyway. My lot could be shudderingly worse. [1960]

Landscape of a nightmare:

The night was pack-jammed with nightmares. On the land where the Jamaica Plain Stable stands, in my dreams is another, bigger Stable faced perpendicularly to the real one. It is huge and damp with many deserted rooms, secret ways, broken places, rats, no lights or furniture. I explore it. I become lost in it. I attempt to live in it. I try to furnish it. I meet people I have never known. It possesses a haunting fascination for me in my dreams and a horror also. It lies there, moribund, its shape never exactly the same from dream to dream, always recognizable, always mysterious as a rotting toadstool in a deep wood is mysterious.

I endeavored to remain awake to circumvent the nightmares. If dreams of Haverford School and of my Mother are counted out, my nightmares classify themselves into dreams of being chased or harried, of being lost and unable to find my way out or back, of being physically weak and people bullying or threatening or deserting me. These are Freudian dreams. All dreams are in intense color, details sharp to the point of minuteness as though eyesight, hearing, smell, touch were stepped-up senses. Very occasionally a dream is comical or gentle or resolves itself happily, but preponderantly they are grim concoctions of the imagination.

As I have noted elsewhere, there exists in the nightmares and afterwards a loose but quite recognizable geography, a continuum partly from real life and partly from pure fancy, with the edges mazily joined and amorphous in outline. What transpires in the dreams can be either whitely moral or blackly immoral or both. Seldom do the dreams foresee the future, but there have been such dreams, traceries fitting later to events with incredible clarity, more often like illusive fragmentations of patterns for a moment fitted tantalizingly into real life later but without totality or significance, so that the mind doubts the verity of the impression and wonders is it not delusion. Often one dream resumes its track where another dream abruptly left off. [1960]

Francis Parkman — soul mate:

Roderic and I are all but finished reading a life of General Sickles, the man who shot his wife's lover, fought during the Civil War, brought Jay Gould to count, a pace-changing personality man of many capacities, enemies, friends. Now we are part way through a life of Francis Parkman, the historian, Boston blue-blood, invalid, aristocrat. Two more fiercely burning men could hardly be further apart in modes of living, aspirations, concentrations, moral standards.

I find in Parkman much about his character which could have been sketched from the same tracing paper as mine. Both have money enough. Both have fairly Catholic minds. Both are semi-invalids. Both have nervous and ocular trouble. Both are long-rangedly set upon producing a major literary and historical work. Both are forever overtaxing their quantum of strength. There are differences, naturally.

In the preface to his biography of Parkman the author states that

the biography of a historian may be as revealing in the insights it affords as that of any statesman, soldier, or other public figure, and a life lived largely in the study may be as adventurous and colorful as a life of action, and in the end far more important in the history of mankind.

In his later life, Parkman wrote, in a sketch of himself left for a friend:

. . . he was vain of enduring them [hardships], cherishing a sovereign scorn for every physical weakness or defect, deceived, moreover, by a rapid development of frame and sinews, which flattered him with the belief that discipline sufficiently unsparing would harden him into an athlete, he slighted the precautions of a more reasonable woodcraft, tired old foresters with long marches, stooped neither for heat nor rain, and slept on the earth without a blanket. Another cause added not a little to the growing evil. It was impossible that conditions of the nervous system abnormal as his had been since infancy should be without their effect on the mind, and some of these were of a nature highly to exasperate him. Unconscious of their character and origin, and ignorant that with time and confirmed health they would have disappeared, he had no other thought than that of crushing them by force, and accordingly applied himself to the work. Hence resulted a state of nervous tension, habitual for several years, and abundantly mischievous in its effects. With a mind overstrained and a body overtasked, he was burning the candle at both ends.

I have read 'The Oregon Trail' three times. During that summer so long ago when Miss Alice Ticknor came to Southwest Harbor to read to me an incredible number of hours each day, I read three, perhaps four volumes of Parkman's history of the French and Indian Wars. In my doubtless unacceptable estimation as a writer of prose, this determined man ranks among the highest lights of his New England era, far superior to Hawthorne and Lowell and many of his contemporaries. [1960]

Greek culture:

I've been studying the Ancient Greek attitude. In essence it's mine. Better never to have been born than born. Ahead, a dim postexistence if any. Live for youth, grace of body. Art rarely mentioned contemporaneously, the honor to Greek art ours. Melancholia, being alive. A bracketed, small space, youth, and that is all to be valued. The gods as fallible as those who project them. Live now. Since no designated or enticing future, philosophy, theories conjectured, concentration upon the dominating present microcosm important. Out of haze; into haze. Therefore, the immediate present paramount. What is earthy, earthly of immediate preeminence. The Greek mind is not at all as it is fatuously presented to us. No mention, or almost none, in ancient writings of architects, sculptors, designers of pottery: only of social and philosophical theoreticians and politicos and conquerors and patriots and heroes and athletes — not, artistically at least, what we moderns value the Greeks for. These Hellos people were a very curious historical germination all but unique. There was a time when I scorned them, so minute was their geographical tenure. It is not so now. Their humanism permitted (forced) an analytical and synthesizing arousement of the inquiring mind that has not, perhaps, been surpassed. It comes to late mind that with the Greek norm before the mental eyesight, perhaps my obligation of scanning the present would have been far easier. I have admired Roman materialism, Roman realism, Roman utilitarian art. Perhaps I made a misjudgment in selecting my ancient standard. There was never, as far as I can find, another culture even approaching the Greek. An American preoccupied with size may very well have overlooked a relatively tiny culture historically dedicated to quality and to the ardently mental, philosophical, theoretical, theocratic, theophysical, destined to influence all Western cultures to follow. [1961]

Thoughts on a space shot:

This morning a second man is supposed, conditions permitting, to be shot into space. Listeners wait at televisions and radios. It is my belief (and no American would admit this) that they wait — at least a large part of their natures do, anxious that the astronaut blow up — major emotional excitation. This is heresy. Yet I feel sure that it is so. We are excitement eaters of the first water. [1961]

Visit from a Jewish plumber:

Just as I was about to put down curtains and rest, it being late, Abe DeCosta, father of Silvia and Hannah, arrived. No previous warning. Rather a handsome fellow, plumber's dirt to the elbows, big glasses, weak mouth, so amusing I'd give dollars to be sufficiently excellent in reporting (he'd probably told the stories twenty times) to place them (with gestures and changes of vocal pace, nuances) here. He was oozing with pride of his three daughters. He spoke often of his nervous psychological difficulties, of not being able properly to breathe. He took to me with a whoop and a holler. He took to Evelyn. He bade her adieu with both hands over hers. I can discern, as Silvia pointed out, what a dear and what an irritation he must be to his wife and children. Nonetheless, I liked him. He haltingly read a letter of appreciation from Hannah to him on Father's Day, wept; and so gracious and appreciative of parenthood the note was I could have Hebraically wept with him, had not some useless Anglo-Saxon governor restrained me from being my one-half Jewish self. Abe DeCosta is in the plumbing business with a partner he hates and would, were he stouter of heart, long hence have been rid of. I should hazard a guess that it was a rewarding visit. Evelyn was as she is with most Jews, fascinating, handsome, on their level apparently, a state she rarely achieves with Anglo-Saxons. I was, as I watched her, proud of her. Hannah returns August 3. [1961]

Memory of the theatre:

I used to like it when the play, preferably the operetta, ended; the curtain rang down on the final chorus; lights came on; the audience filed slowly up the aisles, out the doors, into the foyer; out upon a noisy, disarranged, electric-lighted night world filled with discoordinated noises and movements, cold air striking upon the theatre-bemazed senses, women's perfumes giving place to odors of gasoline and stone exudations, stale tobacco, horse droppings — metropolitan effluvia. It was as if a dream had been sudden dissevered by the impartial knife of reality and a capsuled memory left. [1961]

An apology to Father:

I have an observation to propound about these diaries Anita and I are reading. It is this. My financial convolutions as of then cause my contemporary hair to stand on end. So blithely I tossed money around, using it (the spending, making, speculation) as an excitement to sustain me against boredom and introspection. It was almost as if I were propulsed by a mania. I desired so violently to make money and be independent that risks were taken far beyond caution. I must have given my Father a hard time, save that he was used to Uncle Frank and Uncle Ben Lee, but perhaps it was all the worse because all signposts pointed to my following in their train.

"At this age, Father, I'm really sorry. You were a generous man, not always perceptive, rarely approving, hounded by your wife, under what you felt as your religious and social responsibilities — but unusually generous. There had been ways of braking me, but those were psychological, based upon open explanation and appeal, and that wasn't in you. You mistrusted me, disapproved of me, perhaps were jealous of me. You didn't have a very nice life in many ways, Father, nor were you equipped with a ready and free imagination. Thank you, at this late date, for the generosities beyond any call of even your earnest sense of duty." [1961]

What he's worth:

I have been busy, much to the resistance of Rose, trying to get some order out of the slight chaos of my tax-exempt bonds. The result surprised me. The total amounts to $496,000. The total salable value of my stocks adds up to $390,000, grand total equalling $886,000. Subtract from that brokerage debit balance of $27,000 plus $25,000 mortgage on 96–98 Chestnut plus bank loan of $35,000—or $87,000. To reduce this, tot $30,000 in savings banks, 400 Boeing equalling $21,000, plus value of 43 St. Botolph Street, $10,000, plus a clearance sales value on 96–98 Chestnut of at least $50,000, and the debit balance, on paper, is taken care of. Add two second mortgages, totting $15,000 in all. If my hasty and faulty arithmetic does not err too greatly, my earthly possessions amount to near $900,000. Evelyn's amount to near $300,000. My Father's estate must amount to close to $1,500,000. In a word, Evelyn and I are well-off, not (by today's inflated standards) rich, but comfortably off. Bar disaster, I should no longer fret about financial survival. [1962]

Booze and Lethe:

It must be remembered always that, could I endure it, not lose all my friends, I'd stay continually soused. You come; you push years behind you; you approach an end: Eventually you end. And that's the whole of it. Leave behind your jet trail, and what's that worth save a star-like line across a blue firmament? [1962]

I don't know what you make of these random asides, Edna, but the man who wrote them, if no less self-centered than his former selves, seems to me more receptive to the feelings of others. Perhaps the sadness and frustration of his own life brought a belated recognition of human fallibility and made him a little less critical of, for example, his father, whom he now realized he'd treated scurvily, and his mother, whom he didn't exactly "honor" but whom he no longer utterly rejected.

Deteriorating Arthur looked out upon a downsliding world. Over it hung the Damoclean Bomb. The landscape of his nightmares, peopled by cruel and vengeful assailants, had become as familiar to him as the apartments in Garrison Hall. He accepted his heritage of defeat (Arthur Inman stands for the broken South) self-deprecatingly and urged himself to be patient and to count his blessings, to take comfort in his devoted friends, whether drawn to him by affection or by the magnet of money, and to rest in the pleasant oasis of memory.

Arthur knew, of course, that he was failing physically. His long battle against pain had not and could not be won. Almost every page in the Diary contains some reference to his torments, and although I have omitted most of his daily laments as he instructed me to do, the story of Arthur Inman would be incomplete without some account of his medical history and the osteopathic merry-go-round. I'll save that for my next letter.

December 19, 1981

Dear Edna:
 Whenever I talk to anyone about the Inman Diary, the question usually pops up: were his illnesses real or imaginary? Or if more carefully put, organic or psychological in origin? I think I know what side you'd plump for, but even though I've read and studied Arthur's seventeen-million-word private-public diary-novel, I'm prepared only to pronounce him an arch-complainer who reported his aches, sprains, rips, and tears incessantly and hyperbolically. Many a time I've wanted to say, "Oh, for God's sake, Arthur, shut up!*" and often I've had to laugh at his goings-on about his insides and outsides. But I think his pains were real enough no matter what their source. Some of his doctors didn't take his sufferings very seriously; they looked after him because he paid them well — and promptly, too. But how did Dr. Pike regard him, I wonder?*

 To clarify my own notions as well as yours, I'm going to try now to summarize some facts and theories about Arthur's "case." In doing so, I rely primarily on the reflections of a consultant, Dr. David Musto of the Yale University School of Medicine, and on the testimony of Arthur himself.

 The Diary records almost too fully Arthur's medical history from the time of his first breakdown (when, as he wrote, "My whole nervous system went on strike") to the eve of his death. One wonders how he managed to survive the medications and treatments of his therapists, many of whom, according to Dr. Musto, adhered to the last vestiges of eighteenth-century medical lore. They prescribed ipecac to make him vomit, recommended salt enemas, treated his tonsils and throat with ultraviolet ray, and pumped his stomach. On his own initiative Arthur took excessive amounts of barbiturates and daily spoonfuls of bromides.

 Arthur's seemingly bizarre theories on bacterial infection and his noisome preoccupation with the fecal matter, stomach gas, and "poisons" breeding in his gut can be traced, Dr. Musto believes, to the theory of "autointoxication" current in Arthur's youth. Advanced by Elie Metchikoff, winner of the Nobel Prize for medicine in 1908, it singled out the large intestine as the "reservoir" of fecal waste that poisoned the system. "Delay in emptying the gastrointestinal tract could only increase the amount of poison absorbed by the body." Given this assumption, Arthur's resort to frequent stomach pumpings, laxatives, and emetics becomes understandable.

 Throughout the forty-three years after his initial collapse, Arthur held unwaveringly to the belief that the poisons collecting in various parts of his body (often in the form of "crystals" he inspected following the stomach pumpings) were largely responsible for the attacks of arthritis, influenza, nosebleeds, and migraine headaches — not to mention constipation, chills, cold sweats, diarrhea, hemorrhoids, swollen glands, canker sores, and skin rashes. He experimented with preventive measures (diets, amino acids, bismuth, "Bulgarian bacilli"— yogurt—and the like) but without much success. Gradually he accepted his chronic afflictions — sensitiveness to light, eye and ear trouble, and, above all, slipping bones and loose joints—as constitutional and incurable defects, some of them hereditary, some of them due to parental neglect.

In his early and middle years, however, Arthur had high hopes in osteopathy, for a time the sovereign remedy of his sundry disorders. Osteopathy in Arthur's day (I'm summarizing Dr. Musto) was based on the following principles. The human body functioned normally "unless impeded by some structural deformation" like "a misalignment of bones pressing on nerves, blood vessels, and muscles." This condition affected not only the vertebrae but also other organs in the body. Armed with this key to "the fundamental cause of illness" and skilled in detecting the slightest misalignment of a patient's bones, the trained osteopath manipulated the bones into shape and permitted "the body to work properly."

So here you have Arthur, ordinarily skeptical about most social or scientific systems, unhesitatingly yielding to the "beautiful harmony" of osteopathy. The way to health, he declared in an unpublished essay, lay "in a continuous and unblockaded blood flow," and he cited his own case to show how the master osteopath (not the hacks whom he scathingly dismissed) might prevail after the medical practitioners had given up. "Arthur's frequent requests for treatment," Dr. Musto observes, "made him a meal ticket as well as a therapeutic challenge." I should add that his squadrons of rib-lifters, pelvis-movers, and coccyx-pullers (one a day, he estimated, "to keep the old machine creaking along") gave him something more than physical relief. They also turned into friends, counselors, listeners, and advisees. He was as knowledgeable about their drinking problems and extramarital affairs as he was critical of their respective osteopathic skills and deficiencies. Having plumbed the mysteries of the body, he did not hesitate to tell them precisely what part of his anatomy required attention, and he measured them according to how willingly they complied with his self-diagnoses.

Dr. Musto concedes the possibility that "underlying Arthur's exaggeration of his ailments and the great secondary gain he received from invalidism was some disorder of the connective tissues." A more likely cause for Arthur's "extreme pains, lethargy, headaches, and depression," he thinks, were the daily spoonfuls of bromides he took for years. In short, Arthur may have been suffering from chronic "bromide intoxication," the symptoms of which closely resemble his own descriptions of his physical and emotional disorders: skin rash, spasms of laughing and crying, excitability, seizures of panic, blurring of vision, headaches, interrupted sleep, depression—perhaps even photophobia.

We shall never know for certain, I suppose, but given Arthur's depen-

dence on bromides, Veronal, and sleeping pills and not forgetting his reliance on beer and whiskey after the 1930s, at least part of his real and fancied ills can be plausibly attributed to an unregulated ingestion of alcohol and drugs. But I'll leave that matter to future medical investigators of the 155-volume Diary, if such there be.

In the last few years of his life (perhaps Evelyn's more than casual comments to him about her reading of psychiatric literature had something to do with it), Arthur began to see the Diary as a document "some student of psychology" would peruse. He hoped it might cast a light on the "dubious science," for "few persons have ever transcribed their ailing souls more honestly."

February 2, 1982

Dear Edna:

A short time ago Kathy Connor spent a few hours with us in the Inman Project office. I hardly mentioned her in my account of the Garrison Hall women brigade, because she really belongs to the last five years of the Diary.

Kathy resembled many of the "younglings" who romped with aging Arthur. She was pretty, poor, uneducated, and Irish. He fondled and scolded her as he did the others, but he discovered something special in this ebullient sixteen-year-old when she came to him in the fall of 1958, still in parochial school and working part-time in a bakery concession at Jordan's department store. Kathy's parents had split when she was two, and Arthur despised them for neglecting her. He referred to Mr. Connor, a metal worker, as "one of those scrimey, crummy little feists," a "sentimental man when costing him nothing, untrusting, tricky, self-balancing, selfish, in the true moral sense no good, yet an animal keyed to survival." Mrs. Connor, who cleaned cars for the New York, New Haven Railroad, became in Arthur's prejudiced eyes a rampaging alcoholic and Kathy's chief torment. Yet to his amazement, Kathy survived her "horrid childhood" and turned into a "sweetie." He soon regarded her as his "bewitching daughter," whose unfeigned love overrode his contempt for her religion and Irish origins. "May her silly Catholic God, His Jesus and two-timing Mother, Mary, bless her for how she treats me, talks to me, causes me to feel," he exclaims in a 1960 entry, and he seriously considered adopting her.

I go into these details about Kathy (who, by the way, is a very nice person) because she was a part of the household when Arthur's "bark," to use his own metaphor, "capsized." You're all too familiar with his gripe about the girls who ditched him for marriage or college or a career after he had taught them how to speak and dress and handle boyfriends. At times he feared his slum-child Galatea would also "betray" her Pygmalion. She grew cocky on occasion after she left her mother's place for Garrison

Hall (where she occupied an apartment) and rebelled at the rules he imposed: to check in after she returned from a date, to be prompt in her appointments with him, to wear the dresses he paid for only *in Garrison Hall. He in turn rebuked "Miss Know-It-All" for her untidiness. Her room, he complained, looked like a rabbit hutch. (Kathy informs me that the disarray of clothes camouflaged a forbidden TV set.) He deplored her ignorance and her low-class gaucheries and gave her his "silent treatment" when she displeased him.*

But their sometimes strained relationship never snapped, because Kathy genuinely loved her surrogate papa, and Arthur remained devoted to his little "Irisher." If he monitored her social life, partly because he wanted to keep her in harness and liked to play God, I think in her case he took his parental responsibilities seriously. (Today Kathy feels indebted to him for his efforts to make her think well of herself.) His "daughter," thanks to the Inman imprimatur, was ipso facto a lady. He commanded her to enter Newbury Clothiers — where she was a saleswoman for a time — by the front door, not by the employees' entrance, when he drove her to work in the Baby-Carriage. Even more, she was his beloved comforter and entertainer. Her escapades and her stories about the Connors, some sordid, some hilarious, proved excellent "diary-fodder." She brought into his lightless room a whiff of Boston. Endearing Kathy — "daughter," "special playmate," "wife" ("minus big sex, you understand") — was still buoying up her doleful "daddy" in his last hours.

I can't even begin to spell out here the decline and fall of Arthur Inman. Long before he met Kathy, he had predicted that "noise" would kill him (it had already triggered one suicide attempt), and in 1956 he suddenly faced "a new and appalling" situation, the announcement in the press of tentative plans for a freeway into the city connecting with the South Shore "speedway." Arthur was convinced that one of its exits close to Garrison Hall would become "an inferno of motion and sound." A second blow came six months later, the proposed construction of a building complex in the Boston and Albany Railroad yards, his long-time refuge. He didn't feel the full shock of the enormity until he learned the ghastly details: the fifty-two floor Prudential Tower sheathed in aluminum; the huge auditorium and big hotel; the shopping center, garage, and toll road; and the demolition of Mechanics Hall. This impending desecration, which he was powerless to avert, signaled his own doom. The slow but irresistible progress of the Prudential Center sounds in the Diary like the ticking of a time bomb.

May 20, 1959:

Good grief, what a racket! It made me frantic yesterday, there now being three drivers all in action, and has my hair raised on end today. The racket began at 8:30 this morning. The earplugs can't cut it out, only down.

The curtain wall is being driven in right along Huntington Avenue, as close to here as possible. At least half the enclosing walls between the railroad tracks, Huntington Avenue, West Newton Street are in, I should say. When that is completed, the earthdiggers get to work, 24 feet down for the 52-story structure, 12 feet down for the smaller buildings. Then the pile-driving proper. How long will the latter take, and how loud will it be? All this, mind you, constitutes only about two-thirds of a one-third slice in the middle of the railroad yards, though it will probably be, as I am situated, the noisiest part for me. The auditorium and hotel will be away over near the fire and police stations by Boylston Street. The section near the Lenox Hotel is supposed to house six twenty-story apartment houses. The railroad tracks and traffic throughway to the South Station area are supposed to run underground. A new bridge will be built at Huntington Avenue and Exeter Street. The project will take from six to eight years to complete. May the work never get behind so that extra shifts have to be used. Then I'd be in genuine psychological trouble. My ears are so shallow and sensitive that the plugs, worn a long time (over an hour) cause them to ache and throb.

September 7, 1960:

The Massachusetts Senate yesterday signed the bill to make the Prudential Center possible, some sort of meeting of minds between the grafting politicos, the wish-to-avoid-taxes company and the Supreme Court having been achieved, making the Center come under some sort of Public Authority arrangement. Noise has started at once this morning, for the Governor will sign the bill. Well, I've had a peaceful summer at any rate.

December 8, 1960:

These mornings are long in passing. It's as if they are the tide going out on a shallow beach. And the years, to one who does not wish them, creep like the tortoise. I suppose that, does one hoard and count the years, the mornings, they pass like driven spume. It is nineteen years since I tried to kill myself, and even then it was as if I had persisted a thousand years. Yet here I am, a thousand cycles added, still in function, however piddling. Nineteen years more, I'll only be eighty-four. Not a prepossessing projection. Interests will no doubt come and go, days and years be slowly put behind me, but slower and more slowly marches time. I surely shall give way somewhere under the duress of the myriad pressures afflicting age. My nightmares, let alone my pains and limitations, suffice to put a quietus on hopes of most sorts. I put foot in front of foot like a tired marathon runner until the repetition blurs the goal, and the goal becomes both sterile and futile.

February 28, 1960:

Never is the worry and dread of the Prudential Center and the proposed six-lane, toll-road expressway off my mind. Of late, this is especially so, for it would seem plans are coming to a head. Designs in the papers show the huge road passing under Huntington Avenue into large turnarounds and debouching backwards into Huntington Avenue, Irvington Street and the Copley Square area. The big Irvington Chambers, a rooming-house hotel for men which stands at the end of the alley behind my sitting room window (this concerns me), will be torn down, some of the garages at the end of St. Botolph Street, perhaps the houses on this side of Irvington Street, so that I will be open to the voice of the ninety thousand cars each way each day calculated as the turnpike load. A veritable host of cars will be let loose upon an already tangled traffic situation.

The Prudential people plus the so-called czar of Massachusetts — he who has so much power he has but to shake his whip and businessmen, the legislature, politicians bow, scrape, accede, one William Callahan by name[4]— are behind what is afoot. Virtually no one has risen to oppose Callahan and the Prudential, not business groups, not citizen committees, not newspapers; and the Governor, when he did so, was with celerity brought to heel.

Some years ago Radio Station W.N.E.X., a small one, inaugurated a new program. One Jerry Williams was imported to direct a three-hour forum, discussion and call-answering service six nights a week from ten to one in the morning. A fairly cheap, often illiterate complex of people call in, though many with ideas and some not illiterate at all. Williams is far to the left in his ideas and as a rule rudely talks down or shuts off those persons disagreeing with him so

---

[4] William F. Callahan (1891–1964), known as the "Maharajah of the Macadam" and as "probably the most controversial political figure in the Commonwealth since James Michael Curley," was at one time commissioner of the state Public Works Department and chairman of the Massachusetts Turnpike Authority. Under his aegis Route 128, the Massachusetts Turnpike, and the Sumner Tunnel under Boston Harbor were started and completed. While Callahan was changing Boston's urban landscape, he skirmished with the legislative, executive, and judicial branches of the state government and was tarred by his many critics who denounced him as "a master of manipulation." His part in enabling the Prudential Insurance Company to launch its $150,000,000 center in the Back Bay made him Arthur's arch-enemy.

that his program is much less interesting than did he act the fair moderator. At times, however, it does claim the attention. A man, an ex-Massachusetts Senator, the other evening spoke against the projected toll road. Evidently many listeners called in, for last evening Williams had speak a panel of those antagonistic both to the toll road and the Prudential nexus as a monstrous collective grab by the state's most powerful politician and the huge insurance company to be engineered to the calamity of the city and the expense of the taxpayers.

All this of course is called progress and has been tirelessly propagandized. To be forthright, I care not a jot what happens to Boston the city, but what happens to my immediate surroundings concerns me vitally, and I would be willing and ready to put five, ten thousand into stopping the project if I were sure it would do it, which of course I cannot be — a couple of thousand anyway. I've been telephoning on the subject like mad. Everyone contacted is most gloomy. A fairly young crusader, personable, with drive and pertinacity, is needed. Innumerable dwelt-in buildings, if the toll road goes through will be commandeered and torn down, the residents disposed of. This will lead to a large reduction in collectable taxes, raise the tax rate even higher. As I drove with Amos this morning, an enormous warehouse, a large hotel, many minor properties were in process of being razed. Parking properties with low taxes are visible, like gums naked from teeth drawn, everywhere. This graft-ridden city shrinks yearly in population. The jackdaws pluck out its eyes, their greed unprincipled, unsheathed, insatiable.

March 8, 1961:

Five-sixths of the morning have been spent telephoning to people about contesting the projected six- or eight-lane highway which will necessitate the tearing down of most of the buildings in this vicinity to make space for cloverleaf entries and exits, the demolition of all the edifices between me and Huntington Avenue — in fine, the opening up wide to my ears of all the noise in the world. The public, one soon learns, feels utterly helpless to contest anything against Callahan and the Prudential, a case of 'what the hell's the use.'

March 16, 1961:

My bathroom provides a cubbyhole in which I can withdraw. It is very small, roughly five by six. The lower part of the walls is tiled, and the floor is tiled. The window is high, and it is blocked by celotex, and on the deep sill are an extra medicine cabinet and assorted medicines. A glass holder is beside it and holds one of the pretty red-pink antique tumblers Evelyn gave me years ago. The low bathtub runs across the room under the window and in it are a small electric heater and assorted medicines and cracker cans. A board is set across one end of the tub, and on it are medicines, crackers, bottles, cut-glass tumblers and my favorite plastic glass, one of my pistols, various gourds for pushing my back. A roll of cotton sits atop the handles to the tub. On the shower rod hang assorted towels. Pass, the old Mach plumber, put in the small toilet and the small washbowl from when the bathrooms were remodeled in 1934, as they gave me more room. A chair on gliders sits in front of the washbowl. The old Coward aluminum tray fits firmly under the faucets of the washbowl, and on it my food is brought at breakfast and supper, and from it, sitting in my chair, I eat. A set-in medicine case is over the washbowl. A switch outside the door turns the heat on and off and another inside can control the light. Steampipes go up and down behind my chair, and there is a rod to hold to.

The little room has thick walls and shuts out most noises. Many times a day I go there to sit and be calm, to wash, to munch crackers, to find solace and solitude, to escape noise and people. I like it very much for it encloses me as in a snug cocoon with always a hatch by which to come and go. On the back of the wooden door hang a red and white short bathrobe, a towel, toilet paper. The water is always too hot. Since fairly recently less chloride is in the water; it tastes refreshing. There are three varieties of crackers and casava wafers. Everything is arranged so I can put my hands on it in the dark, from the bag-covered old enema can to the stomach-pumping tubes, the alcohol and sulpha drugs to the amino acids and sleeping and pain-killing pills in varied bottles to the big bromide bottle and cream of bismuth.

March 17, 1961:

I am man. I am animal. I am no more, no less, despite my mind, than animal. If I am no more than animal, then as animal dies and amounts only to manure for other forms of life, so do I. If such is the case, what difference I die a natural death or perish by my own desperate hand?

March 25, 1961:

Fear (at least with me) is like waves on an incoming tide: Each wave rises, lunges forward, sucks back, to be followed by another wave, and another, each advancing up the beach as the tide rises. My fear (and it is fear, not just worry, just nervousness, just apprehension) is like a head of water behind a frail dam when freshets flow. It is fear of what's ahead, how I shall or can meet it. It is fear of decisions to make. It is, as Roosevelt once called it, fear of fear. Steinbeck (as he portrays the Okies about to leave their taken-over farms, their familiar landmarks and belongings, what they have grown up with, is a real part of them) limns how I feel, and that is a part of fear, as is worry, nervousness, apprehension a part, not the whole, of fear. My mind tires of assessing this against that, weighing probabilities, peering at possibilities. I am too old, too tired, too used up to wish, if this building is preempted, to move. I know no haven to move to where noise is not too great, inconveniences not too unbearable, not too much sunlight, too much light, an elevator, a garage somewhere near and all the rest. My beds alone wouldn't stand up under moving. Nor would I, to be realistic. Nor would Evelyn and Rose perhaps. I think (I do not know) that I'd rather die than be uprooted and set down somewhere else, my roots torn and broken and strained. Perhaps (this also I think but do not know) I may find what's ahead so unbearable as to make the final course a matter of hara-kiri courage.

December 21, 1961:

Of first importance, the Massachusetts Supreme Court has "given the go-ahead signal," as the radio newsmen phrase it, to the Prudential Center. It starts the building program with its fifty-story erection in March. I cringe in my imagination at the noise, the lights, at what is destined to take place, at what is in schedule, alas. Lucky I've been that this so long has been delayed. Will it rejuvenate Callahan and his attempt at a toll road? Here we go 'round the mulberry bush, oh-ho!

January 23, 1962:

Three of the largest nationwide brokerage and bond houses have bought the Massachusetts Toll Road bonds. This is no trial, no consignment for sale. It is done. The toll road will go through, be built, decimate this district. Houses will be demolished. Cloverleafs will be pushed through. If this building is not torn down, all around it will be, and we will become an island in a sea of surging traffic. Meanwhile the Prudential with noise and lights will be under construction.

The issue of bonds, it turns out, are bought by the brokerage companies, by them, win or lose, will be marketed. Callahan, indefatigable, probably sly, because of a throat cancer operation, determined at seventy to put himself and his project over, now has a pocketful of kale, millions to stick to his gluey fingers in passing, to put over on Boston what Bostonians are too indifferent or too defeated to reject one way or another. It constitutes a documentary case against the inbuilt evils of the balloting system, i.e., Democracy, as it now stands. It is also evidence to exurbia, leaving the cities of America to the wolves, the Irish, the Italian, the Jewish (mostly the Irish) wolves.

I am striving with all the inner-directed force I possess to keep my spirits up, be busy, joke with those around me. My world, because of the toll-road activities, not to mention the Prudential ones, may be destined to fall to pieces in comparatively short order. Why, my common sense admonishes me, let the future make life (due to my maunderings) gray for those around me? That would be the epitome of selfishness. Keep up the semblance of spirits. In particular is that applicable with Rose who is devastated by the contemplation that her building will most certainly be torn down. I may tell myself that all this furor of change may lead me to suicide, but it should be no part of mine to moan and groan and make the days miserable for those around me. If the worst is as I contemplate, I can exit surely. At least that!

January 24, 1962:

This is my plan. Noises, lights, ruckus generally may at any time put pressure on me making it worthwhile to end my life. Before that, in the weeks, the months left, I shall use all forces at my command to conclude the completion of all volumes of my diary possible, have them microfilmed, deposit them in several bombproof or out-of-the-way shelters. I must proceed as if a definite time limit were in force upon me and my activities. Expecting a termination, until it arrives, be of artificial cheer astutely denied.

February 18, 1962:

I become more nervous at this noise in the jaw with each day that passes, and each day that passes makes the jaw creak or crepitate or catch so loudly it can be heard across the room. The more nervous I become, the worse the noise becomes and the more conscious of it I become. I go into a very trance of telling myself I will have to live with it and therefore reconcile myself to it, which makes me all the more nervous. It didn't do it sitting up but now does it in all positions, though worse in bed, not at all when eating or sleeping — yet. This can drive me frantic beyond my handling of it. I carry around with me, as close to the ear as can be, my own private, nonceasing noise. Here's a dilemma I perceive no way out of.

I don't, writing this, mean to be melodramatic, though God

knows I feel so. I think I'll get my pistol out of the bathroom where it is kept, wrap it in plastic, put it under the bed in a cubby there where, too desperate, I can grasp and use it. Life becomes less propitious by the week with the next japes of fate closer, and what I write in here constantly more personal and less worthwhile, the former intensity of curiosity no longer uncontainable and artisanship flagging, myself terribly tired, my allotted historical task all but completed.

April 16, 1962:

Since water was allowed to collect to protect the underpinnings of the Prudential Tower, a lake has been formed. On it a bateau-like boat is moored. Sea gulls float as they do in picture postcards. Sometimes there are little waves. Blue skies are reflected. Lately, big pumps have been put to work emptying the body of water. Now the level had dropped two or three feet. In the relatively short period of the lake, a beach of sorts has been formed, sloping, with small rocks and pebbles of varied size strewing it. Very soon now the ordered bustle and noise of erection will be in progress. The little short-lived lake will have vanished. The sea gulls will go elsewhere. Who knows about the boat? Maybe workmen on a cold day will break it up for firewood to make a temporary fire. Then no one will recall the lake and what a pleasant park might have been made, just as in due time no one will recollect the old railroad yards.

I remember an afternoon in the early twenties when I used to sit on the roof of this building, and daylight was ending, and in the yards and through the yards steam locomotives passed, blowing white steam and dark smoke upward, and track joints clicked under steel wheels and brass engine bells rang, and sunset flared crimsonly above Mechanics Hall roof, and pigeons flew against it, and in the far distance was Corey Hill, and down the center track moved a long night express departing for some western city, and it was all very beautiful and melancholy, like an animated painting.

July 22, 1962:

My mind turned backward to the first years I lived here at Garrison Hall and how different prevalent noises were then. Very rarely now is the ear aware of trains, never of locomotives, for rail traffic has diminished to a trickle. Late at night then there was no roar of motor traffic. This hotel stood midway between two railway systems. Steam locomotives were unchallenged. Hardly an hour of the day or night but was heard steam escaping, bells ringing, wheels clicking on joints, the long roll-along of heavy freights and passenger expresses, the lighter sound of locals, whistles now and again. I enjoyed the railway sounds. On restless nights dreams could be woven of comings and goings, of distances, of shining tracks, switch lights, semaphores, and the burnt-oil odor of trains now and again drifted in the open window. There was a specially bulky freight which rolled out of the city each morning about five. You could see the 'limited' trains arriving from the west, porters at doors, panaches of steam arising — hear the sussuration of air brakes. Very early in the morning as I lay in bed, I could hear a parade of horsedrawn wagons going to market downtown. On Huntington Avenue, there ran in the center a two-trolley-wide reservation for streetcars, and not several moments would pass without rumble of wheels and clang of bells. There would be varied noises in the alley — the scissors-grinder man, the rag man, the fruit-and-vegetable man, the umbrella man, the clack of horses' hoofs, the clang of iron wheels.

September 19, 1962:

We gaze (I stare) out of the window and watch the eight- or ten-story-high, apparently as-frail-as-a-spider-web crane swing back and forth as if human and direct the two- or four- or six-ton ball against the Lenox Garage, a building constructed of reinforced concrete to last forever. I feel the pit of my stomach reel. It is obscene to fix eyes upon the easy ruination of a decently built structure while thinking that this is for Callahan, an Irish prima donna of destruction and construction. So ineluctably goes the process, so ruthlessly, so uninterruptibly, that the process has the force of a slow landslide down a mountain where sturdy evergreens grew to splendor, by right of primogeniture unassailable. Rose: "I don't like it, but here it is." Evelyn's "It's as exciting as a storm." Myself: "Curse this movement. Napoleon I, when he slashed the avenues through Paris, began it all." None of which causes to hesitate the heavy-balled destruction of what once someone hopefully built against time.

The workers back after an hour's pause on the tearing down of the Lenox Garage. Lewdly the high control crane, its heavy ball dependent, sways, moves purposefully, bangs into concrete reinforced by steel. Dust arises. Windows no one cares to save splintered. I feel nausea and a topping contempt for our civilization as blind to sentiment as if we were possessed of stones for eyes. I won't look. I am ill. My Baby-Carriage lived there. Mike held forth on the third floor. My memories are nil of course, like chaff dispersed, to the makers of the 1960's. I am ready to pewk. All the nineteenth century goes blank with the swinging of the weighted ball. However silly I am, big tears roll down my far-too-seeing eyes. Here goes America and its confidence and its pride, and here comes America and its abdication to credit and its purblind destruction of its shaped past. However critical of my assumption you may be — this is where one of my generation should die, be dead. From here on the sanctity of the individual, as Cleveland saw it, goes by the board. I would be better off not here.

October 9, 1962:

Top construction men on Prudential Tower, mostly American Indians, receive incredible remunerations. Probably also do the crane operators who are making such a conglomerate racket outside my window down the street. My familiar skyline is gone. Soon the trees will all be down and the lone jaybird who visits every autumn will have no place to come. Evelyn and I saw a sparrow hawk coursing the studios to be torn down. On what is left of the Armory roof no sea gulls perch now, scold, scream, as for so many years they have done. A sign on the cab of the bang-bang machine reads: "Look how handsome the operator is!"

October 26, 1962:

The Prudential Tower is 28 stories into the sky, soon will be goosing God.

November 17, 1962:

The Prudential Tower keeps creeping up to the sky. The wrecking of buildings continues. I feel nervous constantly as to how loud and disturbing traffic will be with all the protecting structures between my bedroom and Huntington Avenue razed. Will this, I wonder, be an end of my resistance, hence of life? I still have no intention of moving. I'd rather kill myself than undergo moving and resettlement. I've lived much too long anyway. I recall the fall of 1941. Also, everyone might be better off shed of me. And these thoughts I put down in calmness and no particular agitation of the moment. As a matter of fact, I deem living on as I do, when extinction would be preferable, as cowardly, myself therefore, to any degree you like, a coward as to that penultimate matter. The Romans, the Japanese faced my state of mind and age with more practical valor.

November 21, 1962:

The Prudential Tower is up to 34 or 35 stories, can now be seen from everywhere. The City Auditorium is well under way. Nearly all houses on this block have been vacated and all the St. Botolph Street studios. Reg and I rode out through Brookline yesterday. The demolition from the Cottage Farm Bridge inward is appalling, must be an eighth of a mile wide. Catercornered from my bedroom window, men with shouts and zest have been stripping a doomed house of sinks, radiators, fire escapes, stoves, refrigerators, tossing most of the fittings out the windows to crash onto a waiting truck. It strikes me as close to obscene the intensity, the callousness with which Americans tear down, discard, throw away. It was not much more than a century or so ago when parents handed down as treasures long-worn broadcloth suits, iron cooking pots, feather beds, oxbows, rifles, articles hard come by and to be treasured. Our wasteful lavishness has far outstripped Roman lavishness which, in the main, had to do with the wealthy classes. Our lavishness has percolated down to the lower classes. Abundance, I sometimes think, has filmed our perspective perilously. Yet, some economists state categorically, how else live healthily with overproduction? Economically what they hold may be correct. But insofar as moral character is in question, in all probability the opposite.

November 27, 1962:

The Prudential Tower is in the last quarter of its erection. Most of the lower steelwork has already been concreted. A sample sheet of whatever metal sheathing is to be used stands on one of the floors. It seems to be sky-blue. Since the Tower will dominate what light comes into my library, my reaction to the color of sheathing is to me a matter of importance. Light-blue reflections are not easy to take, I fear. This hideout, Garrison Hall, has given me a long refuge. I should be grateful for that. I am grateful. But no man enjoys having his refuge encroached upon. I shall meet what lies ahead with what fortitude I may muster—in the meanwhile teeter on the precipitous footing of the brink of the future.

December 10, 1962:

The Armory is mostly down. No longer does the huge arched slate roof hunch itself between my sitting room windows and the multitudinous city lights so that on all walls reflect, if I wish to have air at night, an assortment of electric brilliances, making the room as bright as bright twilight, bruising my eyes. As the Tower rises, additional lights strung along the soaring wall of the building facing my bedroom make my bedroom brighter. When the buildings on Huntington Avenue are removed, there will be many new lights assaulting (this is how I think of it) my bedroom window at night. When snow falls, the refulgency will worsen. It is more heartbreaking to have an identity vulnerable to light and sound than to be weak, perhaps than to be blind or deaf, though not both at once.

For the present, the triangle between Huntington and Dartmouth and Stuart Streets is being demolished so that soon the restaurant, Lander's, where Flood used to buy roast pork for me Sundays, the Copley Theatre where Katinka played, the haberdashery where I traded, the rest of the stores familiar for long will soon physically be no more.

December 24, 1962:

The Tower has only seven or eight stories to go. Vertical metal rods are affixed to some of the lower floors. Soon the blue aluminum integument will be attached there. The hotel and the garage are in process of erection near Boylston Street and on this side the foundations for the small low-lying stores. The Prudential Tower, simply a straight up-and-down edifice, already dominates the Boston skyline, visible for miles, very homely no matter what they sheathe it with or the color.

I recall the Boston skyline as seen from the Cambridge side when first I came here — church spires and the gold dome of the State House very beautiful in a romantic manner as the sun glinted on bright points through the haze of a windless morning across the basin. Well, that is gone, and many of the famous historical buildings continue to be demolished to be replaced by high, rectangular, straight-line superstructures. A few of the people of Boston have objected to the wholesale destruction of many of the historical old sites, but no one has listened, and the Irish and Jews and Italians who reap the harvest of wealth from the monstrous reconstruction operations keep blithely, busily on their dollar-gaining way, and the old Yankees move from the city to exurbia. The remaining residents of Boston (and they diminish in number by the year as buildings are sacrificed in favor of throughways) are indifferent or declare that "this is progress."

It was good to have known Boston before the full flux of the motor-car era, before the skyline was tossed heavenward, while horseback riders still trotted and cantered along the bridlepaths in the well-kept parks and people of quality still sauntered along the Commonwealth Avenue Mall and taxes were moderate and people of consequence dwelt in houses of their own on Commonwealth Avenue, Marlboro and Beacon, Chestnut and Mt. Vernon Streets.

January 8, 1963:

Callahan's home was broken into and he was slugged on the head with a sawed-off shotgun. No real harm was done him. "I wish," I exclaimed to Rose, "he'd been killed. Anyone who's put as many sick and ill people out of their homes deserves nothing better. I wish he'd been killed." "Oh no," she exclaimed even more vehemently, "you couldn't wish that." "I do," I said. "If it angers you, I'll shut up. But I'll darned well wish it still. He deserves nothing better." "Well I'm sure . . ." she began. I walked away. "Killing's too good for the likes of him," as the saying aptly puts it.

February 1, 1963:

Crane, power saw, trucks, men leisurely work at demolishment of trees and building on the St. Botolph Street side of the alley. An end to my aural safety draws closer steadily. Evelyn watches at the window in Rose's room to be sure that the tall ailanthus trees in #41 are not sawed heedlessly down. What happens to my urban surroundings touches me as closely as does anything at the present. I could write about it and its implications by the hour, which is why, is it not, I should spare the pen and the reader as often as possible and turn elsewhere?

February 7, 1963:

Before writing about anything else, let me describe the Hokusai scene in the back alley. Gray day. Great piles of debris as from a natural disaster. A bright vermilion, short crane in its clawed teeth grabbed mouthfuls of shattered material, swinging them with ease into a huge high-sided truck. The tall thin shanks of the other cranes moving slowly against the neutral sky. On opposite buildings, workers in white or red hard hats shooting electric flame into fire escapes, other men pulling on long ropes to lower the cut ironwork to another truck. Long streamers of vermilion sparks flying, where flame touches metal, into still air. Dust in billowing clouds blowing. What the great Japanese artist could hardly have included in his prints: the tumble of displaced walls, the clatter of old wood, the shouts of men, the thud of fire escapes falling, the angry yet indifferent whir of motors operating cranes, the frantic beating of my heart as it reacts to the destruction of its sheltering cocoon.

March 11, 1963:

At a quarter to seven the racket began. The building here on the other side away from it, in the small spare room, rocks and shivers, now and then thuds. Think what it must have been like in the siege by the Turks of St. Elmo on Malta with cannon thundering all day, and balls thudding against walls, and limestone dust choking breathing, and harquebuses firing, and Janissaries and fanatics primed by hashish attacking, and corpses by the hundreds rotting in the hot sun, and Greek fire burning on armor, and food not good, and everywhere noise and shouting. And this day after day, and wounds festering, and the Knights upheld by the Crusades spirit, and the Turks and their allies pushed on by a Jihad, and all Europe and the Ottoman Empire watching.

March 26, 1963:

Jumping out of my skin with nervousness from the nearer and nearer demolition, motors racing, walls falling (the ball is being used), the building shaking and creaking. Three-fifths of the long row of buildings along Huntington Avenue must be down now, and the pace is being quickened. By the end of this week, the building opposite my bedroom window will be under attack. With every building demolished, new electric lights and signs are let free to shine in my sitting room where it is so bright I have to shield my eyes with something to raise the window opened at night. As soon as the buildings opposite my bedroom are down, God knows what shafts of light will shine in on my walls past the curtain I tie out at night to get air. I feel a Medieval baron in his besieged keep, forces and weapons constricting ever tighter around his security. It may be I'll survive this, but again I may not. I shall try, now that D-Day is here, to survive within the limits of my disposable defenses. My trustiest weapons are designed by ingenuity. They are indeed my final weapons. Until tested, who can know their temper?

Arthur's "final weapons" failed after the "muting walls" of neighboring buildings went down and the investment of his bastion, the crashing sounds of pile-drivers, and the floods of unwelcome light became intolerable. He took "about 15" sleeping pills and woke up in the Massachusetts General Hospital, not uncheerful, and noted the improvement of the cuisine since his last suicide attempt. Hospital noises were soothing, "not like the angry noise of trucks going up hill near where I was," and he relished the "assuaging quietness."

The only sour note was Rose Trench. She took his suicide try as a "direct slight" against her. "It seems beyond her conception," Arthur observed, "that I have, after all, a separate life from hers, one to keep or discard at my will, not at her will." To calm her down, he confessed himself a "worm," but she refused to forgive him for his treachery after her seven-

teen years of devotion and vowed never to work for him at night again. He might at least have waited for Evelyn to come home before he swallowed the pills.

Evelyn and Kathy, on the other hand, were wonderfully supportive, along with the friends who visited him during his eleven-day stint in the hospital. But soon the zest at "meeting adversity" vanished, and he felt nakedly alone. His old despair returned as he contemplated the days ahead. "I am a turtle which has lost his carapace," he complained, for he dared not go back to beleaguered Garrison Hall. He was a nuisance, "a dear nuisance" to some perhaps, "but still a nuisance."

From the hospital Arthur moved to Pelham Hall, an apartment hotel in Brookline that tireless Evelyn had secured, and began the business "of reorganizing myself, my environment, my properties, my activities." He tried to adjust to his new surroundings, but the transplanting did not take. Noise, "the most violent or persistent pain," assaulted him to the point where he felt "half-demented." The sound of banging pipes denied him sleep, and although a house he impulsively bought on Marlboro Street seemed to promise escape, it might take weeks before he could move in. Meanwhile the Pelham Hall noises — bathroom pipes, cawing crows, elevators, cars, slamming doors — were unendurable. "How kind it would have been for Rose Trench to have permitted me to die." Six months in the Brookline quarters only fed his death wish. "There's a big Colt pistol in my shirt drawer," he wrote in October. "Use it or not use it, there it is, thanks to the phenomenal understanding of my wife."

Then migraine attacks ("Elephants have trod on me") began to synchronize with what he now for the first time called "my phobia against noises," and with them nightmares, daymares.

This, neglected to relate until now, after midday, a dream, a scarifying nightmare. Was underneath huge city. Had with me unaccountable score of people, tremblingly old, dependently young. No way up to surface. My responsibility. Miles upon miles of reasonable-appearing yet delusive tunnels, not lit by any specific lights, rather by bright, disconcerting effulgence. Down steps. Up steps. Through drains. In arched-over back alleys. Up, pulled by cables, flumes of crowded air. Down chutes. Never, ever arriving anywhere. On and on, weariness, disappointment, disgruntlement, an iterated theme never resolving, the very endlessness of the action stultifying to heart, spirit, esprit. Where, the mind asked, will this ever end? People left behind. Stone walls. Hard inimical surfaces. But always, always effulgence of light, stark clear. And no terminus anywhere. Wake up at last, wringing wet with fear, with being thwarted. Walk around apartment, shrugging off articulateness of nightmare. Back to bed and dream of bloody vivisection of men, crimson down tubes, on hands, in face, on face. Awake again; say to self: "Rather perish than sleep, dream again." [October 25]

Full of pain, bored, irritable, nothing could distract him for long: not sex or reading or cuddling little girls. "I feel a harried ninety years old," he wrote, "with gathering pressures closing in about. I have lived too long. I have written too much." Early in December 1963 he promised not to fool around with pills again and took comfort in the pistol stowed under his bed. He confessed himself a failure and doubted that his work would survive — it would have been better for himself and everyone connected with him if he had died in 1941.

"I feel like the tag end of a rough time," reads a December 3 entry. On December 4 he reported: "This has truly been, is a session in hell. Eight migraines yesterday, and one more at six this morning, with violent headaches and nausea." On December 5 he scrawled a message that is virtually indecipherable. I make it out:

This is being horrible beyond the credible. Twelve divisions of migraines. Idetic images until I am harried and frightened into desperation. Can't see more than is adequate to get around. Everything overgrown with hands and the imaginary element of substance visible.

But I can't be sure.

Thirty-five years before, Arthur had written:

Some day it is my hope that this record will suddenly and brusquely break off. By that token you will know that I have come into the courage necessary to make an end of the magnificent jest. Meanwhile I scribble on.

The end came on Thursday, December 5, the same day President Kennedy's assassin was shot in a Dallas jail. Earlier in the previous evening, Kathy Connor stepped into Arthur's room and found him agitated to the extreme. He told her of horrid shapes with deformed hands stretching out to seize him, creatures with tongues protruding from their ears, eyes glaring out of foreheads, bursts of intensely colored fire. When she touched him he screamed with pain and asked her to leave. She did so reluctantly. The next day she spent at the school where she was studying to become an occupational therapist. Late in the afternoon she called Evelyn and learned from her that Arthur had shot himself.

A small number of friends and two Georgia cousins came to the funeral on Saturday, a gloomy dank day. In her account of the ceremony,

Kathy recalls the curious eulogy by a minister who offered veiled excuses for the deceased he had never known. The body lay in an open casket, and before the funeral began, Kathy had an hour alone with Arthur. She had seen lots of corpses at wakes, but she wasn't prepared, she says, for the sight of Arthur. "Joseph, Mary and Jesus," she says she said, "what have they done to you?" The Arthur who loathed perfume and powder and who more than once had ordered his girls to scrub the paint off their faces was gussied up with cosmetics. It made her laugh and cry. She told him he looked terrible. She reminded him of her promise not to abandon him — and straightened his tie. As she got ready to leave, she spied a bit of blood in his ear and removed it with a moistened corner of her dress.

A Medical Report on Arthur Inman

Index

A Medical Report on Arthur Inman

by David F. Musto, M.D.

Arthur Inman's behavior is so unusual that a reader of his diary has the immediate reflex to label him severely neurotic. To examine his complaints further seems an admission that one has been taken in by his bizarre act. Nevertheless, his complaints are worth examination. Some may have been caused by the excessive and often harmful drugs he took on his own or through prescriptions. It is also possible that he did have physical defects that underlay some of his complaints, but that these defects were unnoted by medical examination or were beyond the suspicion or knowledge of the medical profession in Arthur's lifetime. For example, there are regrettable instances of persons categorized as neurotic invalids who were eventually found to be suffering from hypothyroidism or some other hormonal imbalance. Shuttled from one physician to the next, these alleged cranks, malingerers, or hysterics were later, thanks to the advance of medical knowledge, discovered to have actual physical problems. Some patients, of course, were more psychologically than physically affected, but we owe anyone with a medical history like Arthur Inman's the consideration of taking his complaints seriously and reflecting on what might have been the physical causes of his symptoms.

THEORETICAL BACKGROUND OF ARTHUR'S THERAPY

Before entering Arthur's sickroom, I think it useful to discuss the assumptions that underlay his thinking and that of his therapists. In many ways, his medical world represented the last vestige of eighteenth-century medicine in its theories, ministrations, and medications. As late as 1915, he was taking calomel (mercurous chloride) — an old standby prescribed since the seventeenth century — for a run-down feeling and joint pains. (In fact his experiences with medical treatment spanned the transition from the old ways to modern medicine — in 1950 he was taking the "miracle drug" penicillin for a flu-like illness.) In addition to mercury compounds, he was given large doses of bromides for relaxation, ipecac to stimulate vomiting, ultraviolet ray treatment of tonsils and throat, repeated stomach-pumping, and excessive doses of barbiturates. But the medications are not the most unfamiliar feature of Arthur's medical career; the typical way of explaining illness in the early twentieth century and the esoteric theories of osteopathy make even more difficult our understanding of Arthur's and his therapists' approach to disease.

Practitioners in the early part of this century explained almost all illness by a few basic ideas. These included the concepts of acid/alkaline, antibodies/antigens, poisons and toxins produced by intestinal bacteria, physical distortions of organs, poor absorption of nutrients, defective diet, and allergy. Part of Arthur's treatment was based on combinations of these ideas. One widely used explanation for disease was "auto-intoxication": the theory that bacteria in the intestinal tract produced poisons affecting the whole body. Auto-intoxication was the major diagnosis during Arthur's breakdown in the spring of 1916. Its chief advocate was Dr. Elie Metchnikoff, who was awarded the Nobel Prize for Medicine in 1908. In 1903 Metchnikoff published *La Nature Humaine,* a broad view of human life and obstacles to longevity resting on the inutility of the large intestine and the dire effects of poisons produced by intestinal bacteria. In a happy future Dr. Metchnikoff foresaw the early excision of the large intestine as a public health measure. In the meantime, one could counteract potential disaster from the bacteria by eating yogurt, a concoction of life-lengthening lactic acid bacilli. A quotation from Metchnikoff's influential book will illustrate the weight given "poisons" by advanced physicians in the first three decades of this century:

> The large intestine must be regarded as one of the organs possessed by man and yet harmful to his health and his life. The large intestine is the reservoir of the waste of the digestive processes, and this waste stagnates long enough to putrefy. The products of putrefaction are harmful. When fecal matter is allowed to remain in the intestine, as in cases of constipation, a common complaint, certain products are absorbed by the organism and produce poisoning, often of a serious nature . . . In fine, the presence of a large intestine in the human body is the cause of a series of misfortunes.[1]

[1] Elie Metchnikoff, *The Nature of Man,* trans. P. Chalmers Mitchell (New York: Putnam, 1903), p. 73.

This language is not far different from that of Arthur and his therapists. They also believed poisons could arise from infections on the skin, in the mouth, or elsewhere. Poisons in the gut, however, were the most serious and insidious. Delay in emptying the gastrointestinal tract could only increase the amount of poison absorbed by the body; consequently it justified stomach-pumping, laxatives, enemas, and emetics such as ipecac.

The ideology of osteopathy does not appear any more strange than this key assumption of the "regular" physicians. Osteopathic theory can be simply summarized: All the body's functions progress normally unless impeded by some structural deformation, a misalignment of bones pressing on nerves, blood vessels, or muscles. But a misalignment does more than cause low back pain or a sore knee; it also affects organs in the path of the nerves and blood vessels. The stomach and intestines, lungs and heart, can all be adversely affected by ribs out of place. Misaligned vertebrae in the neck can cause colds, earaches, headaches, and nasal allergies. Even the skull, whose bones other than the jawbone we think of as firmly joined together, can be moved and realigned. Commonly, only the osteopath is able to detect the small misalignments, perhaps as little as a sixteenth of an inch, to which he attributes illness.

Knowledge of the fundamental cause of illness allowed osteopaths to manipulate the patient's bones back into place and permit the body to work properly. Otherwise, osteopaths, like regular physicians, prescribed medications and advised on diet. This branch of the medical profession has gradually evolved from its separate origin in the 1890s to a group nearly indistinguishable from regular physicians today. In Arthur's lifetime, however, especially in the period immediately after World War I, osteopathy held closely to its unique core belief. As a result, a beautiful harmony existed between Arthur's concern over his loose joints and a phalanx of osteopaths who would assure him that loose joints could account for any ailment he suffered. The members of the young, expanding osteopathic profession were not inclined to deny anyone's complaints and felt confident that osteopathy could prevail where the regulars had confessed defeat. Arthur's frequent requests for treatment and his generous, prompt payments made him a meal ticket as well as a therapeutic challenge.

I don't know whether Arthur ever accepted Dr. Bottomley's[2] explanation for his ailments, that "overexpanded veins" (1946)

---

[2] As in the Diary, all names except those of public figures have been changed.

were the root of the troubles. This hypothesis can be traced back to the eighteenth-century theorists and from them to Asclepiades (second century B.C.), who attributed disease to a constricted or relaxed *(strictum et laxum)* condition of the solid parts of the body—as opposed to Hippocrates, who found disease in an imbalance of the humors.

ANCESTRY

Arthur Crew Inman's ancestry would have given a nineteenth-century alienist or neurologist little reason to pause before categorizing him as a hereditary neurasthenic. His grandfather's brother, John Inman, spent two years in an asylum after financial reverses. His aunt, Nellie Inman Cooper, led a life of invalidism with symptoms similar to Arthur's: lethargy, painful eyes, and difficulty in walking due to some ankle problem. Another member of the extended family was in a mental hospital as of 1960. Arthur's maternal grandmother had a "complete two years' nervous breakdown" (1922) when a young woman.

Arthur was born on May 11, 1895, in Atlanta, Georgia, the only child of Henry Arthur Inman (1869–1951) and Roberta Crew Inman (1873–1933). Late in his life he recalled a family account that his mother "refused to eat during pregnancy" and that she "had a hard time bearing me." He was said to have been very weak at birth and within a few days to have developed jaundice.

Henry A. Inman was a businessman who approached life in a practical, uncomplicated manner. Apparently he had little sympathy for his son's interest in poetry, nor does he seem to have given much credence to an organic basis for Arthur's invalidism. Arthur perceived him as distant, disappointed, and rejecting. Henry's health was generally good, and he died suddenly of a heart attack in his early eighties. Henry's father, Samuel Inman, died of a heart attack in 1915. Samuel Inman's chief interest to this study is his collarbone or clavicle, which would often, it is said, slip out of place. Arthur also claimed this disability, although in his case it was not confined to the collarbone. Henry, like Arthur, had weak eyes that often pained him and required many visits to eye doctors, but the exact nature of his weakness is not clear. Henry's "bilious attacks" (1908) appear to have been migraine.

Roberta Crew Inman habitually retired to her room when life

became difficult. According to Arthur (1954), "she took to her bed at every chance," both from weariness and in order to get away from her husband. Her health was otherwise generally good until a minor stroke in 1927 left her with some impairment of speech and gait. After a further stroke, she died at the age of 60 in 1933. Unlike her husband, she favored Arthur's literary interests, helped him publish his poems, and foresaw him as a substantial American poet. She did not, however, express her affection in any physical way, by touching, holding or kissing, and this deficit in his upbringing left Arthur with a sense of loss and unlovableness. Besides denying him the open affection he craved, his mother accused him of overdramatizing his illnesses. In retrospect, he concluded that he would have been "better off if my mother had viewed my minor sicknesses with some sympathy" (1954). Still, she exhausted herself caring for him during his "breakdown" in 1916 when, according to her husband, she was "as ill as Arthur himself" (1916).

Many of the chief complaints Arthur suffered for most of his adult life — slipping bones, migraine headaches, eye trouble, invalidism, and tiring easily — could be found in the medical history of his ancestors. He eventually decided that his loose joints were a constitutional or hereditary and uncorrectable defect. He found little in his childhood illnesses to account for his adult condition. The only serious one was whooping cough, from which he believed he had nearly died. He also had had mumps "on one side." Otherwise he did not recall significant illnesses. In his early years, however, there began a tendency toward headaches brought on by bright lights. His first migraine is said to have come on in 1907 on a visit to New Orleans. According to Arthur's account, his meals in childhood were dull, lacked meat, and included too much polished rice. He would later wonder whether these dietary deficiencies had prevented his growing strong. In June 1902 he had a "sunstroke" in Philadelphia, which seems to have left him even more sensitive to bright lights and the sun. The exact nature of the sunstroke is unclear, but it may have been prostration from a very hot day in which his mother dragged him around the city buying new clothes. Here again she is portrayed as energetically pursuing what she thought was in his best interests while, in reality, injuring him.

Before reviewing a long list of Arthur's medical complaints, I would like to look at three major elements in his medical history that are related to most of the other problems: the "breakdown" of spring 1916; his affliction with "loose joints"; and his chronic bromide intoxication, or bromism.

ARTHUR'S COLLAPSE OF 1916

Elements of Arthur's invalidism existed before 1916 in his life and in the lives of his closest relatives, but in a few months between February and August these features were crystallized into a fairly stable pattern of illness that would persist until his suicide in 1963. The year 1916 began with pains in his shoulders, knees, and ribs ("intercostal neuralgia"), for which he received osteopathic treatment in Haverford from a Dr. Blutcher. During Christmas vacation of 1915 his father had taken him to a regular physician in Atlanta who had pumped his stomach and prescribed calomel. Back in Haverford, Dr. Blutcher, the first osteopath that we know Arthur visited, also treated him for a "bilious attack." Joint pains waxed and waned; he was able to pass a "physical training examination" late in January. On the evening of January 14 he went in an open car to perform with a musical group at a mental hospital. Although he dates his breakdown from this event, he does not give the trip such importance in the line-a-day diary he kept at the time. By February 1 he felt "much better" and apparently was in good spirits after receiving passing grades for the semester. Within a few days, however, he began to decline in health. He lost his appetite, had pains in his abdomen, complained of eye pain and headaches, and lost weight. As usual, he felt his parents did not realize the seriousness of the illness until too late. On February 29 he was admitted to Hahnemann Hospital in Philadelphia, where he spent four weeks at bed rest and received a high-calorie diet. Physicians diagnosed "autotoxic poisoning" and stomach ulcers. During his illness he reported several nosebleeds. He gained sixteen pounds, weighing 120 by discharge on March 29. When discharged he was still weak and could walk only with difficulty.

"Auto-intoxication" I have already discussed. The diagnosis of stomach ulcers is a bit difficult to evaluate. He did have stomach pain, but there is no mention of blood in his feces or of x-ray confirmation. After discharge, his mother took him to Atlantic City, where he continued an invalid's regimen. Then and later at Southwest Harbor, he complained of exhaustion, headaches, "constant stomach gas," ribs out of place, nosebleeds, "nervous chills," nausea, and a fear that his collarbone might "fly out of place."

Looking at his medical record up until his summer trip to Southwest Harbor, we notice Arthur's increasing emphasis on his bone structure as the basic flaw in his health. Perhaps there was an underlying hereditary defect in connective tissue, and consequently he did have "loose joints," but, unless we accept the osteopathic ideology, this was not the chief complaint that brought Arthur to Hahnemann Hospital. I think some infectious disease a likely cause for the collapse, perhaps a viral infection such as mononucleosis.

Regardless of whatever balance existed between organic and psychic causes of his disability, it is clear that the illness allowed him to achieve some deep wishes to be alone but cared for. On January 22, 1914, he had hoped for the day when he would have money to build himself a house "in the forest or in the mountains, away off from any human being," where he could live "with nature who is not criticizing." On February 18, during a spell of blues or a "grouch," he reported an "overwhelming desire to get away from everybody —and read sensible books." On April 1, describing himself as "the most selfish, self-centered person I know," he noted that he had kept secret his wish "to get away from all people and live alone with nature and a dog for company." A month or so before the beginnings of the discomfort that would usher in his breakdown, he listed some more desiderata for the future, including this prescient passage: "[In an isolated house] I would have someone to do all the hard work and to cook me good meals. I would have a small house made for him . . . I would have a pretty, interesting girl to come and read to me when I wanted" (1915).

Returning to his summer of illness, Arthur became progressively more restricted in activity. He stayed in bed most of the day, and complained that he ached all over and suffered from extreme lethargy. Mentions of nosebleeds became less frequent. I cannot determine just what he meant by "nervous chills." If these were periods of shaking without fever, I suppose they could have been caused by tension.

Because Arthur demanded an osteopath to reset his ribs, Dr. Ida Frome came to Southwest Harbor from her home in Seal Harbor on June 20, 1916. This day would be memorable for Arthur as the day he began to be saved from death or insanity—but not, unfortunately, from lifelong invalidism. "Doccie" took Arthur into her arms and into her home; she devoted most of her time to him from the first of July until mid-October. She vowed in her letters to her "dear, dear boy" that if her "life or time" were her own, "it should be absolutely for" him (1916).

Dr. Frome soothed Arthur with affection and osteopathic massage and provided him with the most fully supportive environment he had ever experienced. Osteopathic treatment and the freedom wrung from his parents to arrange an environment to his stringent requirements I believe had satisfactory secondary benefits. Thereafter, Arthur established an isolated living space, hired aides to cook and work for him, paid interesting women to read to him, arranged for osteopathic treatments whenever he felt the need, sometimes several treatments in one day, and pursued literary endeavors. Could he have achieved this degree of personal freedom as a businessman?

During his breakdown and in the forty-three years following, Arthur never dropped the notion that poisons collected in his body. As I have pointed out, this was not an unusual way to explain illness. The permutations of this belief are impressive. In February 1929 he ascribed a migraine attack to poisons from an infected throat. He had tried to purify his blood in 1932 after accepting the judgment of Dr. Pike that he had been poisoned with carbon dioxide during a flu bout. In 1938 he looked back to the breakdown and summed it up: "I was full of poisons." That same year he felt the need to "purify his blood" to cure his arthritis. I suspect that his belief in stomach crystals, for which he vomited with ipecac and had his stomach pumped, derived from the tradition that poisons collect somewhere in the body, usually in the gastrointestinal tract, and have a systemic effect. Attempts to rid himself of poison were second only to his efforts to strengthen and adjust his loose joints.

LOOSE JOINTS

At the core of Arthur's complaints, if not his illness, was a looseness of all his joints. "The ligaments . . . fail to hold the joints adequately together," he wrote in 1943. "When the arrangement of the bony structure becomes too disturbed, the nerves are pushed, the blood supply impeded, the function of the organs put out of kilter . . . There remains no alternative save to call in one who is capable, by training, of realigning bones and thus relieving tension and restoring normal blood, nerve, organic and muscular conditions." Such statements illustrate how well osteopathic theory was blended with what he thought was an underlying, probably "inherited weakness." His firm belief in osteopathy prompted him to search his past, the years before the breakdown, for any damage to bones or joints. According to osteopathy, years might pass after an injury before the systemic effect surfaced. Consequently, he deduced that "The many falls and tumbles I had experienced [at Haverford School] had put my spinal structure out of whack. The several summers of swinging at Southwest had twisted the structure further" (1938). The spinal column had a crucial role in causing disease, according to osteopathic theory, and Arthur put special emphasis on the coccyx, the vestigial vertebrae at the end of the column. In many people these small bones are broken at some time from a fall or some other cause, but in Arthur's case x-ray evidence of a dislocation or an old break had serious import: it "was an ill day when, about 14 or 15, I broke my coccyx — smashed it the x-rays show" (1954). Even as late as 1962, he cited the bad effects of slight changes in the coccyx as an excuse for drinking whiskey. Drinking, he maintained, was a way to alleviate the powerful effects of "the light rays on snowy days" which (so he believed) pulled his "coccyx sideways" (1962).

In retrospect, Arthur reckoned that he "must have spent a fourth of my time at school and college with one wrist or the other in splints, painful to the point of unendurability, or so it seemed" (1956). Reviewing his line-a-day diary for the school and college years, I do not get the impression of such severe disability, although there are occasional references to wrist, shoulder, and knee pains. These references are the most frequent in the year or so before the breakdown, when, he records in his diary, his sadistic classmates deliberately twisted his wrists to cause him pain. College ended that form of maltreatment, and he began to ascribe the pain to athletic accidents. Although a quantum leap in the frequency of joint complaints occurs after the breakdown, there is a pattern of trouble with joints in school and college.

Could Arthur have had looseness of joints? The reports of examinations by many regular physicians in the Diary never point to looseness of joints as one of his problems. In fact, "thirty-four eminent doctors . . . in the main blamed my malady on imagination" (1925). We don't have any of these evaluations, but I doubt if Arthur would have omitted any mention of loose joints by his doctors. Those who did agree with Arthur were the osteopaths, and the record of their opinions and treatments in the Diary does not inspire confidence.

The evidence for joint looseness rests on some scattered references. In the spring of 1963 Arthur was examined on admission to Massachusetts General Hospital while comatose from a suicide attempt. The examination noted "a peculiar flexibility of ribs." In 1943 Arthur recorded that "x-rays show that a three-eighths to one-half inch gap occurs between the surfaces of the spread bones" when he bent his wrist sideways (1943). So far, however, we have not been able to locate anyone who recalls that Arthur was "double-jointed," and his wife denies that she ever saw a "dislocation." Yet I think it possible that underlying Arthur's exaggeration of his ailments and the great secondary gain he received from invalidism was some disorder of connective tissues and that, like his grandfather, he had some looseness of joints. I am less persuaded that this looseness caused pain and disability. Having relaxed ligaments is not too unusual. Arthur's condition cannot be attributed to either of the two major hereditary disorders, Ehlers-Danlos Syndrome and Marfan Syndrome, that are often associated with loose joints; these syndromes usually have other characteristics as well that are not evident in Arthur's history.

If we assume that his connective tissue disorder was mild — not of the india-rubber-man category — there is no need to seek extraordinary dislocations in childhood or before the breakdown. Mildly lax joints are not routinely detected on physical examination, nor should they cause any particular pain. I incline to the possibility, then, that there was some basis for Arthur's complaints about his joints, an anatomical anomaly, which provided the nidus for a life of invalidism. I do not know that this possibility can be established. The extreme pains, lethargy, headaches, and depression that Arthur may have attributed to loose joints are much more likely to have been linked to regular and excessive ingestion of bromides.

BROMISM

How much bromide Arthur ingested in an average week or month cannot be determined from the information we have so far uncovered, but undoubtedly he took excessive doses for decades. In 1925 he had been taking 10 spoonfuls of bromide daily while noting "fits of dry sobbing." In 1927 he recorded that he was taking "as much bromide as I can cram down," but still he was "going crazy." In 1946 he was taking 25 spoonfuls daily in order to relax. In July 1948 he recorded 30 spoonfuls; in May 1951, 25 spoonfuls; in November of that year "almost a full glass of bromide"; and in October 1952 "more bromides every hour" or so. Bromides, sleeping pills (usually the long-acting barbiturate Veronal), and alcohol became standbys for relief.

Bromides are excreted slowly by the kidneys; only half a dose is excreted in about two weeks. Clearly, regular doses would lead to high blood levels of bromide. During most of Arthur's life, bromides were so easily available and widely prescribed in the United States that chronic and acute bromide intoxication were widespread. In the 1930s the dangers of bromide poisoning became well documented. The accumulation of overwhelming evidence of the dangers of bromide eventually led to severe reduction in prescribing of bromide and has almost eliminated bromide from over-the-counter medications. Warnings of the drug's dangers, if he was ever aware of them, do not seem to have reduced Arthur's ingestion of bromide.

Studies of bromide intoxication in the 1930s revealed that as high as 7 percent of patients admitted to state mental hospitals suffered solely from chronic bromide intoxication and returned to normal upon cessation of the drug. The reaction of individuals to bromide intoxication is variable, but the range of reactions and relative frequency read like pages from Arthur's Diary. A report published in 1950 based on twenty-seven cases in Boston found the most common symptom to be weakness, at times weakness of only one side of the body. Pains, local and generalized, were common; one patient had visited many physicians and had had many x-rays taken to determine the cause of back pain. Emotional lability —easy laughing or crying—was frequent, and often there was a skin rash. Further findings include excitability and fear reactions. Drowsiness, stupor, and even coma could be late stages in bromide intoxication. Perhaps one reason why the Diary records only a few such collapses is Arthur's practice of frequent salt enemas, for sodium chloride helps to flush bromide from the body.[3]

One pioneer study on bromide intoxication, by E. B. Craven, describes cases similar to those above but reports additional characteristics of interest to anyone reading the Diary: blurring of vision, interrupted and disordered sleep, headache, double vision, and poor convergence of the eyes for near objects.[4] Craven's results were confirmed later by F. M. Hanes and A. Yates, who analyzed four hundred cases. These authors were interested in the effects of chronic intoxication in the early stages. They found that such patients complain of "dull morning headache, constipation, indigestion, fatigue, irritability, sleeplessness, difficulty in concentrating and poor memory . . . The picture is one of mild neurosis, and the usual therapy is bromide sedation . . . Bromide alleviates temporarily the symptoms which it produces, and it should be regarded by physicians as a habit-forming drug." A rash was noted in about a fourth of the patients, usually "acne of the face and upper trunk, though now and then papular, or papulopustular in type." The

---

[3] H. A. Perkins, "Bromide Intoxication: Analysis of Cases from a General Hospital," *Archives of Internal Medicine* 85 (1950):783–794.

[4] E. B. Craven, Jr., "The Clinical Picture of Bromide Poisoning," *American Journal of Medical Science* 186 (1933):525–532.

authors conclude that "chronic bromide intoxication should be considered in all psychoneurotic patients."[5]

To my mind there can be no question that Arthur suffered from bromide intoxication. Which of his many complaints are due solely to bromides, which partly, and which have other causes are difficult questions. I believe his symptoms most likely attributable to bromides are blurred and double vision, sleep disorders, skin rashes, weakness, depression, unusual visual patterns, headache, and emotional lability. Even what Arthur termed "nystagmus," involuntary movement of the eyes, may have some basis in bromide intoxication, for there is at least one report of "ocular bobbing" associated with overdosage of the drug.[6] His acute photophobia may also have been accentuated by bromism. Further, I suspect that many of the skipped days in the Diary are related to bromism, which might easily have interrupted even Arthur's unenergetic routine. Part of his description of himself at 49 indicates how closely bromism, I believe, reduced him to incapacity: "I tired all too readily. I cannot sleep long nor much. Nightmares afflict my sleep with uneasiness and what amounts to dread" (1944). A higher level of intoxication might well account for a period of complete collapse.

It is worth mentioning here his longterm use of Veronal, a long-acting, slowly excreted barbiturate, which could only have increased his lethargy and confusion and might have caused nystagmus, skin rash, and folic acid deficiency. The last would be implicated in Arthur's soreness and sores of the mouth and tongue, and would be another cause for skin rash. There may be some significance to his statement that folic acid pills improved his health (1948).

SPECIFIC COMPLAINTS

Headache

I am confident that Arthur suffered from migraine. His father also had "bilious attacks," which Arthur interprets as an earlier term for migraine. The existence of a family history, the onset of the attacks at about the age of ten, and the persistence of attacks with characteristic prodromal symptoms, pain, and other side-effects, including some one-sided paralysis and strange visual patterns, fur-

---

[5] F. M. Hanes and A. Yates, "An Analysis of Four Hundred Instances of Chronic Bromide Intoxication," *Southern Medical Journal* 31 (1938):667–671 (quotations pp. 669–670).

[6] D. W. Paty and H. Sherr, "Ocular Bobbing in Bromism: A Case Report," *Neurology* 22 (1972):526–527.

ther support the diagnosis. Photophobia is a common complaint of migraine patients, causing them to seek a dark room. Other headaches, however, I would associate with bromism. Perhaps the bromism would trigger some of the migraines.

Photophobia

I have no specific explanation for Arthur's persistent photophobia. Excluding the photophobia of migraine attacks, Arthur had no disease that I can detect which would explain a life of photophobia. The common causes of this complaint are early stage of viral infection, infection of the iris or conjunctiva, acute glaucoma, and intraocular inflammation. Idiopathic photophobia can be present without other abnormality, but the physiology of photophobia is not sufficiently understood to explain such a lifelong sensitivity to light.

Arthur was not unique in his elaborate precautions against sunlight or bright artificial light. The originator of Outward Bound, Kurt Hahn, had sunstroke early in life and thereafter avoided direct sunlight, even to the extent of wearing a specially made, lead-lined hat. Arthur's father had a long and painful history of eye trouble and habitually shielded his eyes from direct sunlight, at least when his eyes were bothering him. Arthur's photophobia was exacerbated, of course, by his staying almost always in a dark environment, but that would not have been the original cause.

Blurred Vision, Spots, Myopia

Arthur's myopia increased from about -1.5 to -2.0 diopters in 1930 to about -3.0 diopters in 1947 (letter of Dr. Furman, February 8, 1979) and appears to have returned to about the former level in 1959 and 1963 (letter of Dr. Brant, December 15, 1978). This would indicate no serious or progressive eye disorder. He resisted light examination of his eyes.

"Spots" before the eyes is a common complaint, particularly in myopic, older persons. The cause, if the spots are not serious and progressive, is specks of substance in the vitreous humor of the eye (the clear substance that fills the eye).

Blurred vision, a recurrent complaint, I would attribute to medications Arthur took so frequently, especially bromides.

Constipation, Diarrhea, Abdominal Distention

So many factors impinge on Arthur's gastrointestinal tract that I do not know how they can be disentangled. He favored enemas, particularly saline enemas. Repeated enemas would interfere with the normal rate of progression of digested food through the body and (since the diagnosis of constipation or diarrhea is his subjective judgment in the Diary) confuse bowel changes that might have had other causes.

His diet was usually bland with a lot of cream added. The lack of roughage and exercise would contribute to his constipation. So would alcohol. But large amounts of whiskey could lead to loose bowels or diarrhea.

Abdominal distention may often be due to aerophagia, or air-swallowing, a not uncommon problem and a habit not usually noticed by the sufferer. Another possibility is difficulty in digesting lactose. Arthur mentions that "cow's milk" was given him by his mother in childhood and that it disagreed with him (1954). In April 1952 he also attributed intestinal trouble to milk, which he detested. What Arthur did not know is that lactose occurs in many foods, including cream and other dairy products. If he did have lactose intolerance, these could have been another cause of diarrhea and gas production in the intestine.

Hemorrhoids

That Arthur had hemorrhoids is certain. He reported several treatments with a corrosive substance being injected into the hemorrhoids, a simple procedure that did not require hospitalization. The cause is uncertain and probably, like varicose veins, is mostly hereditary.

Prostatitis, Testicular Pain, Bladder Infections

In the Diary these complaints are not easy to separate. Arthur's self-diagnosis often depends on where he feels the pain, but locating pain in these areas, which are so close together and subject to referred pain, is difficult. Physicians at times diagnosed bladder infection and treated him with a urinary antiseptic. Prostatic and testicular pain was first mentioned in the late 1930s, with recurrence in 1946 and 1949. I do not know of any specific diagnosis for these discomforts. He does not appear to have had a venereal disease. In about 1945 he complained of a rash about the anus which he thought was fungal but which examinations indicated was not. The rash may have been related to medications, but more likely to heat and poor ventilation in a bedridden, inactive person.

Sore Throat, Mouth, Tongue

I have mentioned some ways in which medication could cause these sores. He was also maltreated for a sore throat in 1924 and 1928 by a Dr. Cass, who used ultraviolet rays. The resulting "blisters and scabs all over the throat and mouth" (1929) healed slowly and may have recurred under other, relatively mild irritation to the mucous membranes of the region. The "canker sores" he mentions may have been caused by a common herpes virus or medication or been vitamin deficiency lesions.

Allergies

Arthur complained of "rose cold" in spring and "hay fever" in the summer. He probably had nasal allergies, as these descriptions imply. In 1922 Dr. Cass of ultraviolet infamy, tested him for various substances by placing bits of possible allergens beneath the skin. Arthur found he reacted to some and not others. The significance of these tests is uncertain, and I mention them merely to indicate the interest in allergies; not much confidence can be placed in them. The test for allergies may mislead. A major skin reaction may occur to a substance which otherwise causes no problems for the patient; a negative skin test may occur for a troublesome allergen.

Depression

What Arthur referred to as "grouches" were periods of depression, lasting two to three days, when he felt miserable, wanted to be away from everyone, and thought himself inferior. These moods date back at least to his Haverford School days. How much these depressive fits were caused by medications, chiefly bromides and barbiturates, it is hard to say.

Meniere's Disease

I think it possible that Arthur did at least once suffer from Meniere's disease, a viral infection of the ear's inner structure that establishes our sense of balance (1944). Bromide intoxication, however, can also cause dizziness and uncertainty of stance and should be considered as a possible cause of the complaints.

Gall Bladder Disease

Although Arthur believed he had gall bladder disease in the early 1950s, x-rays revealed no significant disorder (1951, 1953). I suspect the cause to be some of the other factors, already noted, affecting his gastrointestinal system.

Skin Cancer

Arthur casually mentions in 1953 that he has skin cancer on his shoulder. I do not find any follow-up to this statement, and there is no evidence that he had cancer of the skin.

Alcoholism

Arthur began drinking to relieve tension in the late 1930s. He states he was "blotto" for the first time in March 1942, after drinking three-quarters of a glass of whiskey. Later he drank a lot of beer and took to Scotch whiskey, especially Johnny Walker. There are frequent references to Scotch whiskey between 1945 and 1952, as well as several comments in the vein of "living on bromides, sleeping pills and beer" (1949). How much he drank is not easy to determine, but like the amount of bromides and sleeping pills, the amount seems to have been large and regular.

The most likely results of this drinking combined with other drugs would be to deepen depression, disturb sleep, and create hangover symptoms and perhaps vitamin deficiencies. I do not find any evidence of liver cirrhosis, although the "gall bladder attacks" may have been liver disorders resulting from his long ingestion of alcohol and drugs.

CONCLUSION

A review of Arthur Inman's medical history from the start of his invalidism leaves little doubt that his life — leaving out his singular personality — was cruelly complicated by medical maltreatment and by excessive, chronic ingestion of bromides, alcohol, and other powerful chemicals. These attempts to cure had almost without exception a destructive effect on his emotional stability, judgment, and physical health. And yet, his illness had a positive aspect. Prior to the crisis of 1916 Arthur felt insufficiently loved by his parents and unprepared to face the demands of a business life after college. His illness in late adolescence allowed him to create a secure environment in which he was able to be productive along the lines he chose. Whether his initial illness could have ended without a life of invalidism is difficult to say. The secondary gain was so great and solved so many of his emotional problems that he had little incentive to change his style of life. He persisted in his goal to write a response to the times in which he lived, and he succeeded. Under the envelope of illness Arthur Inman had an indomitable will; it is in this interplay between sickness and creativity that his fascination lies.

Index

Ford, Henry, 774
Foreign policy: AI's views on, 342, 679,
1268, 1542–1543, 1544. *See also*
Imperialism; individual countries
Forrest, Beatrice (Beattie), 23, 24–25,
29–30, 31, 132
Forrest, Mrs. (Beattie's mother), 29–30,
75
Fortinus, Sextus Julius, 1288
Fortune, 413, 757
Four Freedoms, 990
France, 149, 437, 445, 482, 520,
536–537, 689, 791; and Germany,
438, 677, 862, 983; and racial
supremacy, 501, 664n; and Nazis,
525, 953, 971, 975, 979, 998, 1034;
and Italy, 586, 656, 668, 930; AI's
opinion of, 677, 807, 920, 969, 972,
1287, 1482, 1487; and approaching
war, 803, 828, 896, 911; and Spain,
898, 910; in World War II, 931, 972,
976, 992, 1007, 1026, 1070, 1221;
defeat of, in Indo-China, 1542
Franco, Francisco, 727, 896, 1385
Frank, Leo, 617
Frankfurter, Felix, 681, 744, 850
Frazer, Claire Noel (Molly), 408, 410,
415, 423, 430–431, 462, 473, 477,
510, 890, 1216, 1229; and Sam
Mercer, 435–436, 437–438, 446,
451, 455, 464, 465, 474, 478, 483,
492, 509–510, 516, 539, 548, 558,
635, 704, 1091, 1230, 1269; and
Edna, 485, 492, 502, 509–510, 516,
663, 704; and Fred Wickes,
486–487; and Evelyn, 487–488,
559, 735, 1105; and baby, 601, 635;
and Diary, 728, 811; visits to AI,
1057, 1079, 1105–1106; departure,
1115–1116
Frazier-Lemnke Farm Mortgage
Moratorium Act (1935), 623, 751
Freda (rowboat), 81, 112–113
Frederick the Great, 1152–1154
The Freeman, 212
Freeman's Bureau, 98
Fremont-Smith, Dr. Maurice, 111, 1517
Freud, Sigmund, 1259, 1537
Friendship, AI on, 803–804
Friml, Rudolph, 452–453, 462, 943
Froissart, Jean, 471, 623, 961
From a Russian Diary, 192–193
Frome, Dr. Ida (Doccie), 132,

135–140, 141, 152, 198, 211–212,
296, 1354, 1359; death, 623,
637–638
Frost, Robert, 329, 919, 967, 978
Frost Fire (AI), 186, 188, 190, 941;
reviews of, 175, 330
Fuller, Alvin T., 547
Fuller, Horace, 42, 56, 63, 65, 111,
112, 139, 142, 143, 148, 152, 1003

Gallatin, Albert, 921
Gallup poll, 934, 1005
Galsworthy, John, 122
Gandhi, Mohandas Karamchand, 445,
1380
Gannett, Lewis, 934
Garbo, Greta, 472, 509
Garner, John Nance, 767
Garrison, Mr. and Mrs., 212, 216, 671
Garrison, William Lloyd, 212, 216
Garrison Hall, 2, 6, 9, 10, 12, 13, 216,
359–360, 517, 583, 623, 754, 757,
842; move to, 133, 153, 157, 163;
return to, 175, 180, 223, 228, 243;
ménage, 242, 393, 455, 643,
756–757, 791, 860, 896, 990, 1160,
1242; "talkers," 258, 275, 474, 503,
532, 583; AI's attachment to, 338,
400; rents, 343, 393, 614, 798;
gossip about AI in, 349, 359–360,
383–384; descriptions of, 755–756,
990, 1109, 1556, 1558, 1559; daily
routines, 756, 903, 1110–1111,
1226, 1537, 1558, 1560; use of elevator, 981, 990, 1325; as cooperative
family, 1546; AI's room, 1565–
1566; as refuge, 1593
Garsoyan, Johnny, 396, 412–413, 414,
417, 455, 539, 559, 640, 802, 1008;
divorce from Hassie, 1121–1122
Gatsby, Jay, 12
General Motors strike, 743, 754, 774
Genghis Khan, 7, 12, 226, 848, 872, 953
George, Henry: *Poverty and Progress,* 575
George V, death of, 669
Georgia, 617n, 632, 785n, 877, 1391
Georgia Institute of Technology,
35–36, 105
Germany, 7, 129, 149, 197, 263, 463,
482, 536, 982; toys from, 40–41;
and reparations, 395, 425, 438;
literature of, 433–434, 467, 890;

Osteopathy (*Continued*)
doctors, 132, 135, 142, 152, 299, 368, 369, 470, 1432, 1443, 1467, 1560, 1579; AI on, 665, 1055, 1108; AI's rage against, 753; and Diary, 958. *See also* Doctors
O'Sullivan, Maurice: *Twenty Years A-Growing*, 547
Othello, 1105
Otto, Emperor, 428
Oxford Group, 711, 712

Pacific, war in, 1053, 1054, 1086, 1121, 1136, 1159, 1283
Pacifism, 527, 532, 546
Paine, Thomas, 921
Palestine, 1301, 1349, 1394, 1398, 1436
Paradise Lost (Milton), 45
Parker, H. Byron, 121–123
Parkman, Francis, 177–178, 226, 859, 921, 1575–1576; *The Oregon Trail*, 892, 1576
Parrish, Maxfield, 455
Pascal, Blaise, 860
Pass (plumber), 561, 626, 677, 852–853
Passion, 172, 234, 237, 288, 418, 495, 522, 536, 585; and love, 218, 219, 220–221; simulation of, 237; and jealousy, 295, 499; and petting, 427–428; and mind, 601; and AI's young girls, 1392–1393; and affection, 1487. *See also* Love; Sex
The Passion of Yang Kwei-fei (George Soulié De Morant), 424
The Paston Letters, 490
Patriotism, 514, 1542; AI's, 803, 1060, 1061, 1067, 1101, 1104, 1136. *See also* World War II, hoarding in
Patton, Gen. George, S., 1181–1197, 1522
Paz, Roberto, 82, 101, 102, 104, 433
Pearl, Dr. Joseph, 1149, 1163, 1166, 1198–1199, 1206
Pearl Harbor, 1023, 1048–1049, 1053, 1054, 1290
Pecora, Ferdinand, 553; *Wall Street under Oath*, 553
Peel, Sir Robert, 689
Peeples, Edwin A.: *Swing Low*, 1336
Pegan Hill, 327, 389, 399, 400, 407, 414
Peggy (Impie), 518–519, 922–924, 1029, 1039, 1282

Pelvis, 4, 165, 296, 347, 473, 626, 1140, 1155, 1159, 1443; treatments, 152, 153, 434, 950, 1164, 1348, 1450, 1463, 1476, 1478, 1479, 1506, 1581; dislocations, 157, 159, 167, 174, 333, 897, 927, 1131, 1150, 1344, 1346
Pena, Manuel John, 517, 521, 548, 549–550, 645–646, 647, 663, 731, 735, 839, 840, 863, 1529; personal history, 560–561; AI and, 568, 569; driving AI, 606–607; AI's dependence on, 623, 626, 627, 804; Midwest tour, 643, 650, 652; AI's backing, 644, 682; and Billy Minor, 685, 687; arrest, 742–743; and Edna, 756, 830, 835, 937; and World War II, 1100
Pepys, Samuel, 417, 874, 1529
A Pepys of Mogul India, 1635–1708, 868n
Percy, William Alexander: *Lanterns on the Levee*, 1087
Perkins, Frances, 534
Pershing, Gen. John Joseph, 979, 1058
Pétain, Marshal Henri Philippe, 976n, 1286, 1287
Peterkin, Julia, 455
Peters, Roderic, 371, 426, 491, 516, 583, 684, 791, 809, 864, 1480, 1533; reading to AI, 375, 376–377, 382, 390, 667, 691, 694, 710, 734–735, 747, 756, 775, 782, 787, 860, 918, 968, 991, 1060, 1110, 1139, 1200, 1210, 1326, 1343, 1404, 1433, 1558, 1575; descriptions of, 377, 688; AI's criticism of, 379–380, 808; AI's feeling about, 481, 930, 1171; and Diary, 528, 575, 671; AI's dependence on, 623, 1079, 1116, 1155, 1273, 1432; and wife, 722–723, 725; pride, 813–814; and World War II, 913, 1061, 1067, 1079, 1096, 1117–1118, 1145–1146; and draft, 1182, 1215, 1216; return to civilian life, 1291, 1303–1304, 1349, 1351
The Petrified Forest (play), 610
Philadelphia, 22, 25, 33, 82, 88, 90, 104, 105, 118, 120, 121, 127; Coopers in, 51, 86, 95, 96, 125–126, 219; Chestnut Street Opera House, 96; doctors in, 117, 130